To The Brookdale Community College Student:

Welcome to your Cultural Anthropology course.

Your instructors have created this custom textbook just for you.

Please note that some of the chapters are not included. The chapters that were removed, you will not be covering in this course. Removing this content has decreased the price of your textbook significantly.

There are also additional outside Readings and questions included in this custom textbook.

Good Luck.

PEARSON
ALWAYS LEARNING

Cultural Anthropology
with Additional Readings for Brookdale Community College

Second Custom Edition
2015

Taken from:
Anthropology, Fourteenth Edition
by Carol R. Ember, Melvin Ember, Peter N. Peregrine

Cover Art: Courtesy of Barbara Jones

Taken from:

Anthropology, Fourteenth Edition
by Carol R. Ember, Melvin Ember, Peter N. Peregrine

New York, New York 10013

Pearson Learning Solutions, 330 Hudson Street, New York, New York 10013
A Pearson Education Company
www.pearsoned.com

Printed in the United States of America

5 17

000200010271968934

ML/AP

PEARSON

ISBN 10: 1-323-16802-8
ISBN 13: 978-1-323-16802-8

For Mel—

Always the optimist, who believed that there were laws governing human behavior that could be found if you thought hard enough, worked hard enough, and tested ideas against the anthropological record.

1933–2009

Brief Contents

Contents

Chapter 16 Economic Systems 337

Chapter 18 Sex and Gender 392

Chapter 19 Marriage and the Family 416

Chapter 20 Marital Residence and Kinship 445

Chapter 22 Political Life: Social Order and Disorder 489

Chapter 23 Religion and Magic 515

Chapter 24 The Arts 539

Part V Using Anthropology

Chapter 25 Practicing and Applying Anthropology 557

Chapter 26 Health and Illness 573

Chapter 27 Global Problems 591

Readings

Boxes

Applied Anthropology

Current Research and Issues

Migrants and Immigrants

Perspectives on Gender

maps

Preface

This fourteenth edition of *Anthropology* reflects both a new approach to the publication of the book and a thorough re-examination of the text itself. We retain our emphasis on the holistic four-field approach that we consider central to the discipline of anthropology and the important role of applied anthropology (called by some the fifth field of anthropology).

We have responded to reviewers' desire to have more pedagogical material included in the text. In response we have added learning objectives to each chapter and have completely revised the end-of-chapter summary materials so that they give both a clear overview of the important material covered in the chapter and link that material back to the learning objectives. We also include more review and thought questions.

We have always tried to go beyond descriptions to explain not only *what* humans are and were like but also *why* they got to be that way, in all their variety. This edition is no different. An important part of updating the text is finding new explanations, and we try to communicate the necessity to evaluate these new explanations logically as well as on the basis of the available evidence. Throughout the book, we try to communicate that no idea, including ideas put forward in textbooks, should be accepted even tentatively without supporting tests that could have gone the other way.

What's New to This Edition

Engaging Pedagogically-Driven Design

NEW! Learning Objectives have been added to each chapter helping readers to focus on the material ahead. Chapter-ending summary materials have been completely revised to link back to the Learning Objectives presenting a more clear overview of the important material covered in the chapter.

A Clear Understanding of Humans

NEW! Application of major topics. *Applied Anthropology* Boxes provide students a better understanding of the vast range of issues to which anthropological knowledge can be usefully applied. These boxes offer an additional way to show how anthropology helps people lead better lives. Significant expansion of practicing anthropology with an expanded chapter and separation of medical anthropology into its own chapter.

Focus on Contemporary issues

NEW! Environmental issues. An expanded focus on environmental issues is presented.

Chapter-by-Chapter Changes

Part I: Introduction

Chapter 1: What Is Anthropology? Two new boxes on individual anthropologists–an ethnographer and a physical anthropologist–and their work.

Chapter 2: Research Methods in Anthropology In a new section we provide a brief introduction to some of the major ideas that have guided this history of anthropology in the United States. The new applied box describes work that forensic anthropologists conducted to identify the remains of Philip II of Macedon.

Part IV: Cultural Variation

Chapter 12: Culture and Culture Change This chapter has been revised considerably to make it more engaging. New examples on food preferences and taboos are used to illustrate that culture is learned. The section on controversies about the concept of culture has been rewritten. A new section and figure on baby names in the United States illustrates random copying of neutral traits. A broader and more historical view of globalization is introduced. The revolution section now contains a discussion of the Arab Spring and the difficulties of bringing about change by revolution. The second box has been updated and discusses an applied anthropologist's attempts to accommodate Bedouin needs in designed change programs with the Oman government.

Chapter 15: Getting Food We have expanded our discussion of complex foragers for this edition. To put food-getting in better historical perspective, we have significantly expanded our discussion of the origin of food production in prehistory—when it occurred and the theories about why it occurred.

Chapter 16: Economic Systems We have introduced a body of experimental and observational research providing evidence that sharing and cooperation may be universally associated with pleasure.

Chapter 18: Sex, Gender, and Culture This chapter has been extensively rewritten to be more engaging and easier to read with more subheadings for clarity. The box on women in combat has been updated to reflect recent changes in policy.

Chapter 19: Marriage and the Family The third updated box discusses why one-parent families are on the increase in countries like ours. The fourth box, on the changing family and social security in Japan has been completely rewritten and updated.

Chapter 20: Marital Residence and Kinship To make this chapter more engaging, this chapter now opens with a new introduction with a piece of poetry from Robert Frost that we hope raises awareness of what it means to be kin.

Chapter 22: Political Life: Social Order and Disorder We have added a new section that discusses the concepts of nation-states, nationalism and political identity, pointing out that people living in states may not identify with the state they live in nor have their notion of nationhood correspond to political boundaries. In the warfare section we also discuss the controversy about whether violence has increased or decreased in human history.

Chapter 23: Religion and Magic We have added a new theoretical discussion on the need for human cooperation and the recent research that supports that theory. Also added is new research on the relationships between religiosity and stress and anxiety as well as a new discussion on how most religions began as minority sects or cults. The first box, which is updated, raises the question of whether and to what degree religion promotes moral behavior, cooperation, and harmony.

Chapter 24: The Arts In a new section we discuss the problematic and fuzzy distinctions made in labeling some art negatively as "tourist" art versus more positively as "fine" art.

Part V: Using Anthropology

Chapter 25: Practicing and Applying Anthropology This chapter used to include medical anthropology, but to enable us to expand other areas of applied anthropology, we have moved medical anthropology into its own chapter. The introductory section now explicitly discusses specializations in practicing and applied anthropology such as development anthropology, environmental anthropology, business or organizational anthropology, museum anthropology, cultural resource management, and forensic anthropology. We have updated the ethics section with an extended discussion of displacement projects, their risks, and whose lives are actually improved. We have also greatly expanded and updated the section on anthropologists as advocates and collaborators forensics section with detail about estimating time of death. The sections on environmental anthropology and business and organizational anthropology are completely new. The first box is new to this chapter and is about how to get development programs to include more women. The second box is new and is about anthropological work to help a car company improve its business culture.

Chapter 26: Health and Illness This is now its own chapter, broken out from the previous edition where it was combined with applied anthropology. Much of the research has been updated.

Chapter 27: Global Problems We have extensively updated the research in this chapter. In revising the section on natural disasters and the famines that frequently result from them, we give increasing attention to the inequalities that contribute to them. New research on relationships to gender equality is included in the family violence section. In the section on war, we discuss changes over the long course of history, the complex relationship between disasters and war, and the increasing attention to how the vulnerability of populations to disasters can be reduced. The first box has been extensively reworked and updated and now emphasizes climate change and ways anthropologists can contribute to understanding solutions.

Organization of the Text

Part I: Introduction

We see anthropology as a unified discipline that combines the insights of ethnographers, linguists, archaeologists, and physical anthropologists to create a holistic understanding of humans. In this section, we introduce the discipline of anthropology, outline its history and its major theoretical perspectives, and give an overview of the methods employed by anthropologists.

Chapter 1: What Is Anthropology? Chapter 1 introduces the student to anthropology. We discuss what we think is distinctive about anthropology in general, and about each of its subfields in particular. We outline how each of the subfields is related to other disciplines such as biology, psychology, and sociology. We direct attention to the increasing importance of applied anthropology and the importance of understanding others in today's more globalized world. To emphasize the excitement of research we include three boxes on individual researchers (an ethnographer, an archaeologist, and a physical anthropologist).

Chapter 2: Research Methods in Anthropology In this chapter, we begin by discussing what it means to explain and what kinds of evidence are needed to evaluate an explanation. We provide a brief introduction to some of the major ideas that have guided the history of anthropology in the United States. We then turn to the major types of study in anthropology—ethnography, within-culture comparisons, regional comparisons, worldwide cross-cultural comparisons, and historical research. We follow this with a brief introduction to the unique methods that archaeologists and biological anthropologists use and end with a discussion of ethics in anthropological research. There are two boxes: the first box evaluates alternative theories and the second explores changes in gender roles during the Shell Mound Archaic period in the southeastern United States.

Part IV: Cultural Variation

In the chapters that follow, we try to convey the range of cultural variation with ethnographic examples from all over the world. Wherever we can, we discuss possible explanations of why societies may be similar or different in regard to some aspect of culture. If anthropologists have no explanation as yet for the variation, we say so. If we are to train students to go beyond what we know now, we have to tell them what we do not know, as well as what we think we know.

Chapter 12: Culture and Culture Change After introducing the concept of culture and some of the controversies surrounding the concept, we emphasize that culture is always changing. Throughout the chapter we discuss individual variation and how such variation may be the beginning of new cultural patterns. We also discuss attitudes that hinder the study of culture, cultural relativism and the issue of human rights, patterning of culture, culture and adaptation, and mechanisms of culture change, before getting to the emergence of new cultures and the impact of globalization.

The first box is on culture change and persistence in China. The second box discusses an applied anthropologist's attempts to accommodate Bedouin needs in designed change programs with the Oman government. The third box discusses the increasing cultural diversity within countries of the world as a result of immigration and migration.

Chapter 15: Getting Food This chapter discusses how societies vary in getting their food, how they have changed over time, and how the variation seems to affect other kinds of cultural variation. Our first box explores where particular foods came from and how different foods and cuisines spread around the world as people migrated. Our second box deals with the negative effects in preindustrial times of irrigation, animal grazing, and overhunting. To put food-getting in better historical perspective, we discuss the origin of food production in prehistory—when it occurred and the theories about why it occurred.

Chapter 16: Economic Systems Not only does this chapter describe variation in traditional economic systems and how much of it has been linked to ways of getting food, but there is also integrated discussion of change brought about by local and global political and economic forces. This chapter begins with a discussion of how societies vary in the ways they allocate resources, convert or transform resources through labor into usable goods, and distribute and perhaps exchange goods and services. The first box addresses the controversy over whether communal ownership leads to economic disaster. The second box discusses the impact of working abroad and sending money home. The third illustrates the impact of the world system on local economies, with special reference to the deforestation of the Amazon.

Chapter 18: Sex and Gender This chapter opens with a section on culturally varying gender concepts, including diversity in what genders are recognized. After discussing universals and differences in gender roles in subsistence and leadership, we turn to theories about why men dominate political leadership and what may explain variation in relative status of women and men. In the second part of the chapter we discuss variation in attitudes and practices regarding heterosexual and homosexual sexuality. In the first box, we examine cross-cultural research about why some societies allow women to participate in combat. A second box discusses research on why women's political participation may be increasing in some Coast Salish communities of western Washington State and British Columbia now that they have elected councils. The last is a box that examines the impact of economic development on women's status.

Chapter 19: Marriage and the Family After discussing various theories and evidence about why marriage might be universal, we move on to discuss variation in how one marries, restrictions on marriage, whom one should marry, and how many one should marry. We close with a discussion of variation in family form and customs of adoption. We now discuss the phenomenon of couples choosing to live together, and to better prepare students for understanding kinship charts in the chapter that follows, we have a diagram explaining different types of family structures. Our first box discusses arranged marriage and how it has changed among South Asian immigrants in England and the United States. The second box discusses variation in love, intimacy, and sexual jealousy. The third box discusses why one-parent families are on the increase in countries like ours. The fourth box is on the changes in family structure in Japan and how it has affected "social security.

Chapter 20: Marital Residence and Kinship Rather than jumping right into principles of kinship, we broadly discuss the different functions of kinship, the consequences of different kinship systems, and how the importance of kin changes with economic fortunes. In addition to describing the variation that exists in marital residence, kinship structure, and kinship terminology, this chapter discusses theory and research that try to explain that variation. The first box, "Blood is Thicker than Water," discusses the role that Chinese lineages play in supporting migration and making a living in the diaspora. The second box explores how variation in residence and kinship affects the lives of women. The third box discusses how cross-cultural research on the floor area of residences in matrilocal versus patrilocal societies can be used to help archaeologists make inferences about the past. The last box discusses the possible relationship between neolocality and adolescent rebellion.

Chapter 22: Political Life: Social Order and Disorder We look at how societies have varied in their levels of political organization, the various ways people become leaders, the degree to which they participate in the political process, and the peaceful and violent methods of resolving conflict. We emphasize change, including what may explain shifts from one type of organization to another, such as colonialization and other outside forces have transformed legal systems and ways of making decisions. We then discuss the concepts of nation-states, nationalism, and political identity. The first box is on the role of migrants in the growth of cities. The second box deals with the cross-national and cross-cultural relationship between economic development and democracy. The third box deals with how new local courts among the Abelam of New Guinea are allowing women to address sexual grievances.

Chapter 23: Religion and Magic The chapter opens with a discussion of how the concepts of the supernatural and natural have varied over time and space and then turn to theories about why religion is universal. We go on to discuss variation in the types, nature, and structure of gods, spirits, and forces; human/god interactions, concepts of life after death; ways to interact with the supernatural; and the number and types of religious practitioners. A major portion of the chapter deals with religious change, religious conversion and revitalization, and fundamentalist movements. The first box, raises the question of whether and to what degree religion promotes moral behavior, cooperation, and harmony. The second discusses the role of colonialism in religious change.

Chapter 24: The Arts After discussing how art might be defined and the appearance of the earliest art, we discuss variation in the visual arts, music, and folklore, and review how some of those variations might be explained. In regard to how the arts change over time, we discuss the myth that the art of "simpler" peoples is timeless, as well as how arts have changed as a result of European contact. We address the role of ethnocentrism in studies of art in a section on how Western museums and art critics look at the visual art of less complex cultures. Similarly in a new section we discuss the problematic and fuzzy distinctions made in labeling some art negatively as "tourist" art versus more positively as "fine" art. The first box explores ancient and more recent rock art and the methods that can be used to help preserve it. The second box discusses the global spread of popular music. The last box deals with universal symbolism in art, particularly research on the emotions displayed in masks.

Part V: Using Anthropology

Anthropology is not a discipline that focuses on pure research; rather, most anthropologists believe their work is truly valuable only if it can be used to improve the lives of others. In this section we examine how anthropological knowledge is used in a variety of settings and towards a variety of ends.

Chapter 25: Practicing and Applying Anthropology An introductory section discusses specializations in practicing and applied anthropology. We move on to an expanded section on ethics, evaluating the effects of planned change, and difficulties in bringing about change. Since most of the examples in the first part of the chapter have to do with development, the remainder of the chapter gives an introduction to a number of other specialties; environmental anthropology, business and organizational anthropology, museum anthropology, cultural resource management, and forensic anthropology.

Chapter 26: Health and Illness This chapter concerns itself with cultural understandings of health and illness, the treatment of illness (particularly from a biocultural rather than just a biomedical point of view), varying medical practitioners, and political and economic influences on health. To give a better understanding of what medical anthropologists do, we focus on AIDS, mental and emotional disorders (particularly susto and depression), and undernutrition. The first box discusses an anthropologist's attempt to evaluate why an applied medical project didn't work, and the second updated box explores eating disorders, biology, and the cultural construction of beauty.

Chapter 27: Global Problems We begin this chapter with a discussion of the relationship between basic and applied research, and how research may suggest possible solutions to various global social problems, including natural disasters and famines, homelessness, crime, family violence, war, and terrorism. There are three boxes. The first now emphasizes climate change and ways anthropologists can contribute to understanding solutions. The second box is on how the problem of refugees has become a global problem. The last box describes ethnic conflicts and whether or not they are inevitable.

Features

Applied Anthropology Boxes. Anthropology is not a discipline focused on pure research. Most anthropologists want their work to be actively used to help others. And in our increasingly interconnected world, it would seem that anthropological knowledge would become increasingly valuable for understanding others. For these reasons, in the last few editions we have emphasized applied anthropology. Twenty-two of the 27 chapters have an applied anthropology box in each chapter. We hope this will provide students a better understanding of the vast range of issues to which anthropological knowledge can be usefully applied.

Current Research and Issues Boxes. These boxes deal with current research, topics students may have heard about in the news, and research controversies in anthropology. Examples include molecular anthropology, variation in love, intimacy, and sexual jealousy in the husband-wife relationship; increasing global inequality; and whether ethnic conflicts are ancient hatreds.

Migrants and Immigrants Boxes. These boxes deal with humans on the move, and how migration and immigration have impacted recent and contemporary social life. Examples include why some immigrant groups retained their "mother tongues" longer than others, the spread of foods in recent times, arranging marriages in the diaspora, and the problem of refugees.

Perspectives on Gender Boxes. These boxes involve issues pertaining to sex and gender, both in anthropology and everyday life. Examples are sexism in language, separate women's associations and women's status and power, and mother–infant communication and the origin of language.

Dorling Kindersley Maps To emphasize important themes, we have adapted maps originally produced by Dorling Kindersley, a leading publisher of educational maps.

Student-Friendly Pedagogy

Readability. We derive a lot of pleasure from trying to describe research findings, especially complicated ones, in ways that introductory students can understand. Thus, we try to minimize technical jargon, using only those terms students must know to appreciate the achievements of anthropology and to take advanced courses. We think readability is important not only because it may enhance the reader's understanding of what we write but also because it should make learning about anthropology more enjoyable! When new terms are introduced, which of course must happen sometimes, they are set off in boldface type and defined in the text, set off in the margins for emphasis, and of course also appear in the glossary at the end of the book.

Learning Objectives. Learning objectives are new to this edition. Each chapter begins with learning objectives that indicate what students should know after reading the material. The learning objectives are reinforced with specific questions at the end of each chapter that unite the topics, help students gauge their comprehension, and signal what topics they might have to reread.

Key Terms and Glossary. Important terms and concepts appearing in boldface type within the text are defined in the margins where they first appear. All key terms and their definitions are repeated in the Glossary at the end of the book.

Summaries. In addition to the learning objectives provided at the beginning of each chapter, each chapter has a detailed summary organized in terms of the learning objectives that will help students review the major concepts and findings discussed, along with review questions to reinforce and to complement the summary.

End of Book Notes. Because we believe in the importance of documentation, we think it essential to tell our readers, both professionals and students, what our conclusions are based on. Usually the basis is published research. The abbreviated notes in this edition provide information to find the complete citation in the bibliography at the end of the book.

Supplements

This textbook is part of a complete teaching and learning package that has been carefully created to enhance the topics discussed in the text.

Instructor's Resource Manual with Tests: For each chapter in the text, this valuable resource provides a detailed outline, list of objectives, discussion questions, and classroom activities. In addition, test questions in multiple-choice and short-answer formats are available for each chapter; the answers to all questions are page-referenced to the text.

MyTest: This computerized software allows instructors to create their own personalized exams, to edit any or all of the existing test questions and to add new questions. Other special features of this program include random generation of test questions, creation of alternate versions of the same test, scrambling question sequence, and test preview before printing.

PowerPoint™ Presentation Slides: These PowerPoint slides combine text and graphics for each chapter to help instructors convey anthropological principles in a clear and engaging way.

Strategies in Teaching Anthropology, Sixth Edition (0-205-71123-5): Unique in focus and content, this book focuses on the "how" of teaching anthropology across all four fields and provides a wide array of associated learning outcomes and student activities. It is a valuable single-source compendium of strategies and teaching "tricks of the trade" from a group of seasoned teaching anthropologists, working in a variety of teaching settings, who share their pedagogical techniques, knowledge, and observations.

The Dorling Kindersley/Prentice Hall Atlas of Anthropology (0-13-191879-6): Beautifully illustrated by Dorling Kindersley, with narrative by leading archaeological author Brian M. Fagan, this striking atlas features 30 full-color maps, timelines, and illustrations to offer a highly visual but explanatory geographical overview of topics from all four fields of anthropology. Please contact your Prentice Hall representative for ordering information.

Acknowledgments

Over the years we have had many editors, but we especially want to thank Nancy Roberts for her long and steadfast stewardship over many editions, her insightful suggestions, and especially her passionate interest in the educational enterprise. We also want to thank Nicole Conforti and Jenna Vittorioso for seeing the manuscript through the production process. Carol Ember especially wants to thank Tulin Duda for her extensive research help and her thoughtful and inquisitive editing to make the book more accessible to students.

We want to thank the following people for reviewing our chapters and offering suggestions for the fourteenth edition: Richard Blanton, *Purdue University*; Kristrina Shuler, *Auburn University*; Wanda Clark, *South Plains College*; Jim Mielke, *University of Kansas*; Heidi Luchsinger, *East Carolina University*; and Andrew Buckser, *Purdue University*.

We continue to appreciate reviewers from previous editions: Alice Baldwin-Jones, *City College of New York*; Richard E. Blanton, *Purdue University*; James L. Boone, *University of New Mexico*; Beau Bowers, *Central Piedmont Community College*; Gregory Campbell, *University of Montana*; Garrett Cook, *Baylor University*; Daniel R. Maher, *University of Arkansas-Fort Smith*; Sheperd Jenks, *Albuquerque TVI Community College*; Max E. White, *Piedmont College*; Jean M. Wynn, *Manchester Community College*

Thank you all, named and unnamed, who gave us advice.

Carol R. Ember, Melvin Ember, and Peter N. Peregrine

About the Authors

CAROL R. EMBER started at Antioch College as a chemistry major. She began taking social science courses because some were required, but she soon found herself intrigued. There were lots of questions without answers, and she became excited about the possibility of a research career in social science. She spent a year in graduate school at Cornell studying sociology before continuing on to Harvard, where she studied anthropology, primarily with John and Beatrice Whiting.

For her PhD dissertation, she worked among the Luo of Kenya. While there, she noticed that many boys were assigned "girls' work," such as babysitting and household chores, because their mothers (who did most of the agriculture) did not have enough girls to help out. She decided to study the possible effects of task assignment on the social behavior of boys. Using systematic behavior observations, she compared girls, boys who did a great deal of girls' work, and boys who did little such work. She found that boys assigned girls' work were intermediate in many social behaviors compared with the other boys and girls. Later, she did cross-cultural research on variation in marriage, family, descent groups, and war and peace, mainly in collaboration with Melvin Ember, whom she married in 1970. All of these cross-cultural studies tested theories on data for worldwide samples of societies.

From 1970 to 1996, she taught at Hunter College of the City University of New York. She has served as president of the Society of Cross-Cultural Research and was one of the directors of the Summer Institutes in Comparative Anthropological Research, which were funded by the National Science Foundation. She has recently served as President of the Society for Anthropological Sciences and is currently the Past President. Since 1996, she has been at the Human Relations Area Files, Inc., a nonprofit research agency at Yale University, first serving as Executive Director, then as Acting President, and is currently President of that organization.

MELVIN EMBER majored in anthropology at Columbia College and went to Yale University for his PhD. His mentor at Yale was George Peter Murdock, an anthropologist who was instrumental in promoting cross-cultural research and building a full-text database on the cultures of the world to facilitate cross-cultural hypothesis testing. This database came to be known as the Human Relations Area Files (HRAF) because it was originally sponsored by the Institute of Human Relations at Yale. Growing in annual installments and now distributed in electronic format, the HRAF database currently covers more than 385 cultures, past and present, all over the world.

Melvin Ember did fieldwork for his dissertation in American Samoa, where he conducted a comparison of three villages to study the effects of commercialization on political life. In addition, he did research on descent groups and how they changed with the increase of buying and selling. His cross-cultural studies focused originally on variation in marital residence and descent groups. He has also done cross-cultural research on the relationship between economic and political development, the origin and extension of the incest taboo, the causes of polygyny, and how archaeological correlates of social customs can help us draw inferences about the past.

After four years of research at the National Institute of Mental Health, he taught at Antioch College and then Hunter College of the City University of New York. He served as president of the Society for Cross-Cultural Research. From 1987 until his death in September, 2009, he was president of the Human Relations Area Files, Inc., a nonprofit research agency at Yale University.

PETER N. PEREGRINE came to anthropology after completing an undergraduate degree in English. He found anthropology's social scientific approach to understanding humans more appealing than the humanistic approach he had learned as an English major. He undertook an ethnohistorical study of the relationship between Jesuit missionaries and Native American peoples for his master's degree and realized that he needed to study archaeology to understand the cultural interactions experienced by Native Americans before their contact with the Jesuits.

While working on his PhD at Purdue University, Peter Peregrine did research on the prehistoric Mississippian cultures of the eastern United States. He found that interactions between groups were common and had been shaping Native American cultures for centuries. Native Americans approached contact with the Jesuits simply as another in a long string of intercultural exchanges. He also found that relatively little research had been done on Native American interactions and decided that comparative research was a good place to begin examining the topic. In 1990, he participated in the Summer Institute in Comparative Anthropological Research, where he met Carol R. Ember and Melvin Ember.

Peter Peregrine is professor of anthropology at Lawrence University in Appleton, Wisconsin and external professor at the Santa Fe Institute in Santa Fe, New Mexico. He also serves as research associate for the Human Relations Area Files. He continues to do archaeological research, and to teach anthropology and archaeology to undergraduate students.

CHAPTER 1

What Is Anthropology?

LEARNING OBJECTIVES

Explain the general definition and purpose of anthropology.	1.1
Describe the scope of anthropology.	1.2
Explain the holistic approach.	1.3
Explain anthropology's distinctive curiosity.	1.4
Differentiate among the five major fields of anthropology.	1.5
Explain the ways in which anthropologists specialize within their fields of study.	1.6
Communicate the relevance of anthropology.	1.7

1.1 Explain the general definition and purpose of anthropology.

Anthropology A discipline that studies humans, focusing on the study of differences and similarities, both biological and cultural, in human populations. Anthropology is concerned with typical biological and cultural characteristics of human populations in all periods and in all parts of the world.

What Is Anthropology?

Anthropology, by definition, is a discipline of infinite curiosity about human beings. The term comes from the Greek *anthropos* for "man, human" and *logos* for "study." Anthropologists seek answers to an enormous variety of questions about humans. They are interested in both universals and differences in human populations. They want to discover when, where, and why humans appeared on the earth, how and why they have changed, and how and why the biological and cultural features of modern human populations vary. Anthropology has a practical side too. Applied and practicing anthropologists put anthropological methods, information, and results to use in efforts to solve practical problems.

The study of human beings is not an adequate definition of anthropology, however, since it would appear to incorporate a whole catalog of disciplines: sociology, psychology, political science, economics, history, human biology, and perhaps even the humanistic disciplines of philosophy and literature. Most of the disciplines concerned with human beings have existed longer than anthropology, and each has its distinctive focus. There must, then, be something unique about anthropology—a reason for its having developed and grown as a separate discipline for over a century.

•••

1.2 Describe the scope of anthropology.

Listen to the Audio: The Traits that Make Us Human

The Scope of Anthropology

Anthropologists are generally thought of as individuals who travel to little-known corners of the world to study exotic peoples or dig deep into the earth to uncover the fossil remains, tools, and pots of people who lived long ago. Though stereotypical, this view does suggest how anthropology differs from other disciplines concerned with humans. Anthropology is broader in scope, both geographically and historically. Anthropology is concerned explicitly and directly with all varieties of people throughout the world, not just those close at hand or within a limited area. Anthropologists are also interested in people of all periods. Beginning with the immediate ancestors of humans, who lived a few million years ago, anthropology traces the development of humans until the present. Every part of the world that has ever contained a human population is of interest to anthropologists.

Anthropologists have not always been as global and comprehensive in their concerns as they are today. Traditionally, they concentrated on non-Western cultures and left the study of Western civilization and similarly complex societies, with their recorded histories, to other disciplines. In recent years, however, this division of labor among the disciplines has begun to disappear. Now anthropologists work in their own and other complex societies.

What induces anthropologists to choose so broad a subject for study? In part, they are motivated by the belief that any suggested generalization about human beings, any possible explanation of some characteristic of human culture or biology, should be shown to apply to many times and places of human existence. If a generalization or explanation does not prove to apply widely, anthropologists are entitled or even obliged to be skeptical about it. The skeptical attitude, in the absence of persuasive evidence, is our best protection against accepting invalid ideas about humans.

Because anthropologists are acquainted with human life in an enormous variety of geographic and historical settings, they are also often able to correct mistaken beliefs about different groups of people.

For example, when American educators discovered in the 1960s that African American schoolchildren rarely drank milk, they assumed that lack of money or education was the cause. But evidence from anthropology suggested a different explanation. Anthropologists had known for years that people do not drink fresh milk in many parts of the world where milking animals are kept; rather, they sour it before they drink it, or they make it into cheese. Why they do so is now clear. Many people lack the enzyme lactase that is necessary for breaking down lactose, the sugar in milk. When such people drink regular milk, it actually interferes with digestion. Not only is the lactose in milk not digested, but other nutrients are less likely to be digested as well. In many cases, drinking milk will cause cramps, stomach gas, diarrhea, and nausea. Studies indicate that milk intolerance is found in many parts of the world.[1] The condition is common in adulthood among Asians, southern Europeans, Arabs and Jews, West Africans, Inuit (Eskimos), and North and South American native peoples, as well as African Americans.

The Holistic Approach

1.3 Explain the holistic approach.

Holistic Refers to an approach that studies many aspects of a multifaceted system.

In addition to its worldwide and historical scope, anthropology has the distinguishing feature of having a **holistic** approach to the study of human beings. Anthropologists study the many aspects of human experience as an integrated whole. For example, an anthropologist's description of a group of people is likely to encompass their physical environment, a history of the area, how their family life is organized, general features of their language, their settlement patterns, their political and economic systems, their religion, and their styles of art and dress. The goal is not only to understand these aspects of physical and social life separately but to glean connections among them. Throughout this book, you will see that these seemingly separate factors in a culture regularly co-occur; that is, they form patterns of traits. Anthropologists want not only to identify those patterns but to explain them.

Anthropological Curiosity

1.4 Explain anthropology's distinctive curiosity.

Thus far, we have described anthropology as being broader in scope, both historically and geographically, and more holistic in approach than other disciplines concerned with human beings. But this statement again implies that anthropology is the all-inclusive human science. How, then, is anthropology really different from the other disciplines? We suggest that anthropology's distinctiveness lies principally in the kind of curiosity it arouses.

Anthropologists tend to focus on the *typical* characteristics of the human populations they study rather than on individual variation or variation in small groups. Why do some populations have lighter skin than others? Why do some societies practice polygamy whereas others prohibit it? Where and when did people first start to farm rather than collecting and hunting wild resources? Anthropologists want to know why the characteristics that others might take for granted exist. Whereas economists take a monetary system for granted and study how it operates, anthropologists ask how frequently monetary systems occur, why they vary, and why only some societies have had them during the last few thousand years. It is not that anthropologists do not concern themselves with individuals. For instance, in studying political systems, anthropologists might want to know why certain people tend to be leaders. But when they study individual traits of leaders in order to answer the question, it may be because they want to better understand the political process in a larger social group, such as a society. Or, anthropologists might ask an even broader question, such as whether certain qualities of leaders are universally preferred.

Because anthropologists view human groups holistically, their curiosity may lead them to find patterns of relationships between seemingly unrelated characteristics. So, for example, the presence of the ability to digest lactose (a physical trait) in a population seems to be found in societies that depend heavily on dairying. In recent times, as more anthropologists work in larger and more complex societies, the focus of inquiry has shifted from looking at a whole society to smaller entities such as neighborhoods, communities, organizations, or social networks. But the focus on the whole entity is still strong.

Fields of Anthropology

1.5 Differentiate among the five major fields of anthropology.

In the past, an anthropologist covered as many subjects as possible. Today, as in many other disciplines, so much information has accumulated that anthropologists tend to specialize in one topic or area (see Figure 1.1). Some are concerned primarily with the *biological* or *physical characteristics* of human populations; others are interested principally in what we call *cultural characteristics*. Hence, there are two broad classifications of subject

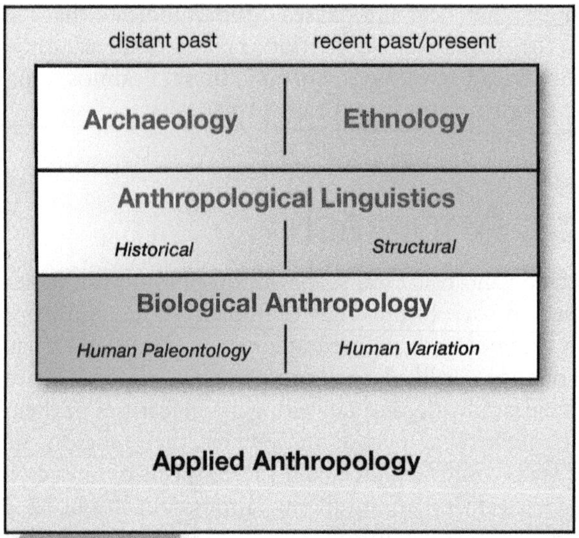

FIGURE 1.1 **The Four Fields of Anthropology**

The subdisciplines of anthropology (In bold letters) may be classified according to the period with which each is concerned (distant past or recent past and present) or by subject matter. Traditionally, the three fields shown in Blue are classified as Cultural Anthropology, as distinct from Biological (or Physical) Anthropology, shown in green. Found in all four fields is a fifth subfield Applied Anthropology.

Biological (physical) anthropology The study of humans as biological organisms, dealing with the emergence and evolution of humans and with contemporary biological variations among human populations.

Cultural anthropology The study of cultural variation and universals in the past and present.

Applied (practicing) anthropology The branch of anthropology that concerns itself with applying anthropological knowledge to achieve practical goals.

matter in anthropology: **biological (physical) anthropology** and **cultural anthropology**. While biological anthropology is one major field of anthropology, cultural anthropology is divided into three subfields—archaeology, linguistics, and ethnology. Ethnology, the study of recent cultures, is now usually referred to by the parent name cultural anthropology. Crosscutting these four fields is a fifth, **applied** or **practicing anthropology**.

Biological Anthropology

Human paleontology The study of the emergence of humans and their later physical evolution. Also called **paleoanthropology**.

Human variation The study of how and why contemporary human populations vary biologically.

Fossils The hardened remains or impressions of plants and animals that lived in the past.

Primate A member of the mammalian order Primates, divided into the two suborders of prosimians and anthropoids.

Primatologists People who study primates.

Biological (physical) anthropology seeks to answer two distinct sets of questions. **Human paleontology** or **paleoanthropology** poses questions about the emergence of humans and their later evolution. A focus on **human variation** includes questions about how and why contemporary human populations vary biologically.

To reconstruct evolution, human paleontologists search for and study the buried, hardened remains or impressions—known as **fossils**—of humans, prehumans, and related animals. Paleontologists working in East Africa, for instance, have excavated the fossil remains of humanlike beings that lived more than 4 million years ago. These findings have suggested the approximate dates when our ancestors began to develop two-legged walking, very flexible hands, and a larger brain.

In attempting to clarify evolutionary relationships, human paleontologists may use not only the fossil record but also geological information on the succession of climates, environments, and plant and animal populations. Moreover, when reconstructing the past of humans, paleontologists are interested in the behavior and evolution of our closest relatives among the mammals—the prosimians, monkeys, and apes—which, like ourselves, are members of the order of **Primates**. Anthropologists, psychologists, and biologists who specialize in the study of primates are called **primatologists**. The various species of primates are observed in the wild and in the laboratory. One especially popular subject of study is the chimpanzee, which bears a close resemblance to humans in behavior and physical appearance, has a similar blood chemistry, and is susceptible to many of the same diseases. It now appears that chimpanzees share 99 percent of their genes with humans.[2]

From primate studies, biological anthropologists try to discover characteristics that are distinctly human, as opposed to those that might be part of the primate heritage. With this information, they may be able to infer what our prehistoric ancestors were like.

Birute Galdikas works with two orangutans in Borneo.

The inferences from primate studies are checked against the fossil record. The evidence from the earth, collected in bits and pieces, is correlated with scientific observations of our closest living relatives. In short, biological anthropologists piece together bits of information obtained from different sources. They construct theories that explain the changes observed in the fossil record and then attempt to evaluate their theories by checking one kind of evidence against another. Human paleontology thus overlaps such disciplines as geology, general vertebrate (particularly primate) paleontology, comparative anatomy, and the study of comparative primate behavior.

Watch the Animation: The Subfields of Biological Anthropology

The second major focus of biological anthropology, the study of human variation, investigates how and why contemporary human populations differ in biological or physical characteristics. All living people belong to one species, ***Homo sapiens***. Yet much varies among human populations. Investigators of human variation ask such questions as: Why are some peoples generally taller than others? How have human populations adapted physically to their environmental conditions? Are some peoples, such as Inuit (Eskimos), better equipped than other peoples to endure cold? Does darker skin pigmentation offer special protection against the tropical sun?

Homo sapiens All living people belong to one biological species, *Homo sapiens*, which means that all human populations on earth can successfully interbreed. The first *Homo sapiens* may have emerged about 200,000 years ago.

To understand better the biological variations among contemporary human populations, biological anthropologists use the principles, concepts, and techniques of at least three other disciplines: human genetics (the study of inherited human traits); population biology (the study of environmental effects on, and interaction with, population characteristics); and epidemiology (the study of how and why diseases affect different populations in different ways). Although research on human variation overlaps research in other fields, biological anthropologists remain primarily concerned with human populations and how they vary biologically.

Cultural Anthropology

Cultural anthropology is the study of how and why cultures in the past and present vary or are similar. But what is *culture?* The concept of culture is so central to anthropology that we will devote an entire chapter it. Briefly, the term *culture* refers to the customary ways that a particular population or society thinks and behaves. The culture of a social group includes many things—from the language that people speak, childrearing, and the roles assigned to males and females to religious beliefs and practices and preferences in music. Anthropologists are interested in all of these and other learned behaviors and ideas that have come to be widely shared or customary in the group.

Current Research and Issues

Researcher at Work: Alyssa Crittenden

When an anthropologist's best-laid plans meet the "facts on the ground," the results can be unexpected. For Alyssa Crittenden, an anthropology professor at the University of Nevada, fieldwork also brought some delightful revelations.

In 2004, Crittenden began working with the Hadza, a hunter-gatherer people in Tanzania. (Because hunter-gatherers subsist by foraging for their food, they represent the basic economy and way of life that has characterized most of human history. Therefore, such few remaining peoples are valued subjects for anthropological study.) As a biological anthropologist, Crittenden was especially interested in what Hadza culture might reveal about the evolution of the human diet. She chose the diets of women for study and measured the relationship between their reproductive capacity and the amount and nutritional value of the food they foraged. Yet that data told only part of the previously untold story of Hadza women.

Alyssa Crittenden interacting with Hadza children.

"I quickly realized," Crittenden says, "that I could not study the women's diet in isolation. These women belonged to a community of people, a support system of kin and neighbors. To understand women's contributions to the Hadza economy, I had to be an ethnographer, as well as a biological anthropologist." Thus, after 10 years of fieldwork among the Hadza, Crittenden characterizes herself as a biocultural anthropologist.

One surprising discovery Crittenden made was that Hadza children were hunters and gatherers in their own right. They were helping their mothers indirectly by providing their own food and thus contributing to their economy. This evidence contradicted what was known about the children of other hunter-gatherer groups, such as the San of the Kalahari Desert, whose children were observed to help process mongongo nuts but otherwise do little else but play. The difference may partly be due to the environment. The Kalahari has less variable terrain, less water, and more predators than southwestern Tanzania.

For Hadza children, foraging for their own food becomes an extension of play. Children who are 5 years old and younger can contribute up to 50 percent of their caloric needs by foraging for their own food. By the time they turn 6, children can contribute up to 75 percent of their own food. While girls collect water and plant foods, boys also hunt, using a bow and arrow like their elders. Indeed, at age 3, Hadza boys receive their own child-sized bow and arrow and begin to hunt for the birds, rodents, bush babies, and lizards that make up their meat diet. Moreover, children learn to process and cook their own food. Crittenden observed children as young as 4 years old building their own miniature fires with embers from camp to cook their foraged meals.

Hadza children spend their days together in groups, seemingly unsupervised, though there is usually an older child nearby keeping an eye on them. Toddlers join a group of children as soon as they are weaned—that is, when their mothers can no longer carry them, usually between 1 1/2 and 3 years of age.

"Observing Hadza children, you can't help but wonder how the long, dependent childhood most of us experience evolved," says Crittenden.

Source: Crittenden 2013.

Archaeology **Archaeology** is the study of past cultures, primarily through their material remains. Archaeologists seek not only to reconstruct the daily life and customs of peoples who lived in the past but also to trace cultural changes and to offer possible explanations for those changes. While their subject matter is similar to that of historians, archaeologists reach much farther back in time. Historians deal only with societies that left written records, which limits their scope to the last 5,000 years of human history and to the small proportion of societies that developed writing. Human societies have existed for more than a million years, however, and archaeologists serve as historians for all those past societies that lacked a written record. With scant or no written records to study, archaeologists must try to reconstruct history from the remains of human cultures. Some of these remains are as grand as the Mayan temples discovered at Chichén Itzá in Yucatán, Mexico. More often, what remains is as ordinary as bits of broken pottery, stone tools, and garbage heaps.

Most archaeologists deal with **prehistory**, the time before written records. But a specialty within archaeology, called **historical archaeology**, studies the remains of recent peoples who left written records. This specialty, as its name implies, employs the methods of both archaeologists and historians to study recent societies.

To understand how and why ways of life have changed through time in different parts of the world, archaeologists collect materials from sites of human occupation. Usually, these sites must be unearthed. On the basis of materials they have excavated and otherwise collected, they then ask a variety of questions: Where, when, and why did the distinctive human characteristic of toolmaking first emerge? Where, when, and why did agriculture first develop? Where, when, and why did people first begin to live in cities?

To collect the data they need to suggest answers to these and other questions, archaeologists use techniques and findings borrowed from other disciplines, as well as what they can infer from anthropological studies of recent and contemporary cultures. For example, to guess where to dig for evidence of early toolmaking, archaeologists rely on geology to tell them where sites of early human occupation are likely to be found, because of erosion and uplifting, near the surface of the earth. More recently, archaeologists have employed aerial photography and even radar imaging via satellite (a technique developed

Archaeology The branch of anthropology that seeks to reconstruct the daily life and customs of peoples who lived in the past and to trace and explain cultural changes. Often lacking written records for study, archaeologists must try to reconstruct history from the material remains of human cultures. See also **Historical archaeology**.

Prehistory The time before written records.

Historical archaeology A specialty within archaeology that studies the material remains of recent peoples who left written records.

Archaeologists try to reconstruct the cultures of past societies like those who created this "Cliff Palace" in what is today Mesa Verde National Park.

Perspectives on Gender

Researcher at Work: Elizabeth M. Brumfiel

Elizabeth M. Brumfiel (1945–2012) became interested in the origins of social inequality when she was an undergraduate. Archaeologists had known for some time that substantial wealth differences between families developed only recently—that is, only since about 6,000 years ago. Some archaeological indicators of inequality are clear: elaborate burials with valuable goods for some families and large differences in houses and possessions. When Brumfiel was in graduate school at the University of Michigan, she did not accept the then-current explanation that inequality provided benefits to the society—for example, that the standard of living of most people improved as the leaders got richer. Consequently, when Brumfiel undertook her PhD research in central Mexico, she began to test the "benefit" explanation in an area that had been independent politically and then became part of the Aztec Empire. She studied the surface material remains in the area and historical documents written by Europeans and Aztec nobility. Her findings contradicted the benefit explanation of social inequality; she found little improvement in the standard of living of the local people after the Aztec Empire had absorbed them.

Brumfiel also focused on how everyday women lived and how the expansion of the Aztec Empire had affected them. She found that women's workload increased under the Aztecs. Brumfiel studied Aztec artwork for evidence of differences in status based on gender. In art from the Aztec capital of Tenochtitlán, images of militarism and masculinity became increasingly important with the growth of the empire, thus elevating the position of men. Sculptures of women, on the other hand, showed them in positions of work (kneeling). Yet the images of women in the area of Brumfiel's fieldwork did not change. Unlike their rulers, these commoners usually depicted women as standing, not kneeling.

Aztec artwork showing daily activities of women.

Just as Brumfiel challenged conventional wisdom, she recognized that others too will challenge her work. As she said, she was quite comfortable with knowing that someone will think that she has "gotten it wrong, and will set out on a lifetime of archaeological research to find her own answers."

Sources: Brumfiel 2008, 2009.

by NASA) to pinpoint sites. To infer when agriculture first developed, archaeologists date the relevant excavated materials by a process originally developed by chemical scientists. Information from the present and recent past can also help illuminate the distant past. For example, to try to understand why cities first emerged, archaeologists may use information from historians, geographers, and political scientists about how recent and contemporary cities are related economically and politically to their hinterlands. By discovering what recent and contemporary cities have in common, archaeologists can speculate about why cities developed originally.

Anthropological Linguistics **Anthropological linguistics** is the anthropological study of language. Linguistics, or the study of languages, is an older discipline than anthropology, but the early linguists concentrated on the study of languages that had been written for a long time—languages such as English, which existed in written form for nearly a thousand years. Anthropological linguists began to do fieldwork in places where the language was not yet written. This meant that anthropologists could not consult a dictionary or grammar to help them learn the language. Instead, they first had to construct a dictionary and grammar. Then they could study the structure and history of the language.

Anthropological linguistics The anthropological study of languages.

Like biological anthropologists, linguists study changes that have taken place over time as well as contemporary variation. **Historical linguistics** is the study of how languages change over time and how they may be related. **Descriptive** or **structural linguistics** is the study of how contemporary languages differ, especially in their construction. **Sociolinguistics** examines how language is used in social contexts.

Historical linguistics The study of how languages change over time.

Descriptive (structural) linguistics The study of how languages are constructed.

Sociolinguistics The study of cultural and subcultural patterns of speaking in different social contexts.

In contrast with human paleontologists and archaeologists, who have physical remains to help them reconstruct change over time, historical linguists deal only with languages—and usually unwritten ones at that. (Remember that writing is only about 5,000 years old, and only a few languages have been written.) Because unwritten languages are transmitted orally, the historical evidence dies with the speakers. Linguists interested in reconstructing the history of unwritten languages must begin in the present, with comparisons of contemporary languages. On the basis of these comparisons, they draw inferences about the kinds of change in language that may have occurred in the past and that may account for similarities and differences observed in the present. Historical linguists might typically ask, for example, whether two or more contemporary languages diverged from a common ancestral language. And if so, how far back in time they began to differ?

Unlike historical linguists, descriptive (structural) linguists are concerned with discovering and recording the principles that determine how sounds and words are put together in speech. For example, a structural description of a particular language might tell us that the sounds *t* and *k* are interchangeable in a word without causing a difference in meaning. In American Samoa, one could say *Tutuila* or *Kukuila* to name the largest island, and everyone, except perhaps newly arrived anthropologists who knew little about the Samoan language, would understand that the same island was meant.

Sociolinguists are interested in the social aspects of language, including what people speak about, how they interact conversationally, their attitudes toward speakers of other dialects or languages, and how they speak differently in different contexts. In English, for example, we do not address everyone we meet in the same way. "Hi, Sandy" may be the customary way a person greets a friend. But we would probably feel uncomfortable addressing a doctor by her or his first name; instead, we would probably say, "Good morning, Dr. Brown." Such variations in language use, which are determined by the social status of the people being addressed, are significant for sociolinguists.

Ethnology (Cultural Anthropology) The subfield of **ethnology**, now commonly called *cultural anthropology*, seeks to understand how and why peoples today and in the recent past differ or are similar in their customary ways of thinking and acting. They ask how and why cultures develop and change and how one aspect of culture affects others. Cultural anthropologists seek answers to a variety of questions, such as: Why is the custom of marriage nearly universal in all cultures? Why do families live with or near their kin in some societies but not in others? What changes result from the introduction of money to a previously nonmonetary economy? How are relationships impacted when family members move far away to work? What happens to a society that suffers severe stress because

Ethnology The study of how and why recent cultures differ and are similar.

Current Research and Issues

Researcher at Work: Timothy G. Bromage

When Timothy Bromage was young, his parents took him to hear a lecture by the legendary paleoanthropologist Louis Leakey. He was not sure why they had driven so far and paid so much to hear the lecture nor why they had dragged him along, but he knows that visit started him on the way to becoming a paleoanthropologist himself. Decades later, Bromage's lectures have undoubtedly inspired other young people to study the life histories of our ancient ancestors. He hopes future paleoanthropologists will also think outside the box of their discipline when they begin their research. That approach has led Bromage to major breakthroughs in his study of ancient teeth and facial bones.

In graduate school, Bromage was struck by the fact that fossils were treated as static, as if age did not make a difference. Yet humans—ancient and modern—change physically during their lives. Working with new methods and a scanning electron microscope at the University College London, Bromage found that it is possible to determine how ancient faces change as an organism matures. Different individuals die at different ages, but, in examining fossils, Bromage and his colleagues saw distinctive patterns of bone tissue forming and dissolving across the period of development. Working with specimens that were about 2 million years old, Bromage found that the hominins commonly referred to as australopithecines grew to adulthood in an apelike manner. The front parts of the skull built up tissue that grew into forward-jutting faces and jaws. Bromage found that a later group ahominin, the paranthropoids, had a pattern of facial growth that resulted in a flatter face, more like the face of a modern human than that of the australopithecines.

Bromage has also looked at patterns of enamel deposition in ancient fossil teeth using similar techniques. Early hominin teeth are important specimens in paleoanthropology because they tend to survive well-preserved, which means they can be analyzed in much the same way as the teeth of recent humans. It has been known for some time that when children grow, tooth enamel is put down daily, but every 8 or 9 days there are substantial changes in tooth enamel formation. Why this happens was not well understood. But Bromage and his colleagues have discovered that these rhythmic cycles may be a kind of systemic growth spurt. Bone and tissue (muscle and organs) grow at the same time, and heart and respiration rates increase, suggesting that our bodies have a metabolic clock that makes sure that cells divide and bones grow in time to accommodate growing organs. Smaller animals have shorter cycles. Comparisons with other primates have enabled Bromage to infer some life history differences in fossil forms. Such research shows the promise of the integrative approach Bromage favors. Working across disciplines and collaboratively adds to our knowledge of human evolution as well as to health research today.

Sources: Bromage 2009; Lacruz, Rossi, and Bromage 2005, 2006.

Ethnographer A person who spends some time living with, interviewing, and observing a group of people to describe their customs.

Ethnography A description of a society's customary behaviors and ideas.

of natural disasters or violent conflicts? Although the aim of ethnologists is largely the same as that of archaeologists, ethnologists generally use data collected through observation and interviews of living peoples.

One type of ethnologist, the **ethnographer**, usually spends a year or so living with, interviewing, and observing the people whose customs are being studied. This fieldwork provides the data for a detailed description (**ethnography**) of customary behavior and thought. Earlier ethnographers tended to strive for holistic coverage of a people's way of life. In part because those earlier ethnographies already exist for many cultures, recent ethnographers have tended to specialize or focus on narrower realms such as ritual healing or curing, interaction with the environment, effects of modernization or globalization, or gender issues. Ethnographies often go beyond description; they may address current anthropological issues or try to explain some aspect of culture.

Because many cultures have undergone extensive change in the recent past, an accurate view of them may depend on understanding what their life was like before the changes came about. **Ethnohistorians** study how the way of life of a culture has changed over time. They examine such written documents as missionary accounts, reports by traders and explorers, and government records to identify the cultural changes that have occurred. Unlike ethnographers, who rely mostly on their own observations and interviewing, ethnohistorians rely on the reports of others. They often must piece together and make sense of widely scattered, and even apparently contradictory, information.

Ethnohistorian An ethnologist who uses historical documents to study how a particular culture has changed over time.

Ethnographic and ethnohistorical research are both very time-consuming, and it is rare for one person to study more than a few cultures. It is the role of the **cross-cultural researcher** (who may be a cultural anthropologist or some other kind of social scientist) to discover general patterns across cultures—that is, what characteristics are universal, which traits vary and why, and what the consequences of the variability might be. They may ask such questions as: Why is there more gender inequality in some societies than in others? Is family violence related to aggression in other areas of life? What are the effects of living in a very unpredictable environment? In testing possible answers to such questions, cross-cultural researchers use data from samples of cultures (usually described initially by ethnographers) to try to arrive at explanations or relationships that hold across cultures. Archaeologists may find the results of cross-cultural research useful for making inferences about the past, particularly if they can discover material indicators of cultural variation.

Cross-cultural researcher An ethnologist who uses ethnographic data about many societies to test possible explanations of cultural variation to discover general patterns about cultural traits—what is universal, what is variable, why traits vary, and what the consequences of the variability might be.

Because ethnologists may be interested in many aspects of customary behavior and thought—from economic behavior to political behavior to styles of art, music, and religion—ethnology overlaps with disciplines that concentrate on some particular aspect of human existence, such as sociology, psychology, economics, political science, art, music, and comparative religion. But the distinctive feature of cultural anthropology is its interest in how all these aspects of human existence vary from society to society, in all historical periods, and in all parts of the world.

Applied (Practicing) Anthropology

All knowledge may turn out to be useful. In the physical and biological sciences, it is well understood that technological breakthroughs like DNA splicing, spacecraft docking in outer space, and the development of miniscule computer chips could not have taken place without an enormous amount of basic research to uncover the laws of nature in the physical and biological worlds. If we did not understand fundamental principles, the technological achievements we are so proud of would not be possible. Researchers are often driven simply by curiosity, with no thought to where the research might lead, which is why such research is sometimes called *basic research*. The same is true of the social sciences. If a researcher finds out that societies with combative sports tend to have more wars, it may lead to other inquiries about the relationships between one kind of aggression and another. The knowledge acquired may ultimately lead to discovering ways to correct social problems, such as family violence and war.

For most of anthropology's history as a profession, anthropologists generally worked in academic institutions. But more and more, anthropologists are increasingly working outside academia—today there are probably more anthropologists who work outside academia than in it.[3] Applied or practicing anthropology is explicitly intended to making anthropological knowledge useful.[4] Practicing anthropologists, as practitioners of the subdiscipline increasingly call themselves, may be trained in any or all of the fields of anthropology. In contrast to basic researchers, who are almost always employed in colleges, universities, and museums, applied anthropologists are commonly employed in settings outside traditional academia, including government agencies, international development agencies, private consulting firms, businesses, public health organizations, medical schools, law offices, community development agencies, and charitable foundations.

A large number of emigrants from the former Soviet Union, particularly from Black Sea cities and towns such as Odessa, live in the Brighton Beach neighborhood of Brooklyn. Migrant and immigrant communities, such as "Little Odessa," are an increasing focus of anthropological study.

Biological anthropologists may be called upon to give forensic evidence in court, or they may work in public health or design clothes and equipment to fit human anatomy. Archaeologists may be involved in preserving and exhibiting artifacts for museums and in doing contract work to find and preserve cultural sites that might be damaged by construction or excavation. Linguists may work in bilingual educational training programs or may work on ways to improve communication. Ethnologists may work in a wide variety of applied projects ranging from community development, urban planning, health care, and agricultural improvement to personnel and organizational management and assessment of the impact of change programs on people's lives.[5]

In the past two decades, the speed of globalization has created great changes in applied or practicing anthropology. Whereas the field used largely to be the province of Western—and often colonizing—nations, it has since grown into a vital localized discipline all over the world. In a number of countries, among them Russia, China, Mexico, Egypt, Ecuador, and Brazil, applied or practicing anthropology focused on solving practical social problems dominates over the research-driven four fields.[6]

1.6 Explain the ways in which anthropologists specialize within their fields of study.

Specialization

As disciplines grow, they tend to develop more and more specialties. This trend is probably inevitable since, as knowledge accumulates and methods become more advanced, there is a limit to what any one person can reasonably master. Thus, in addition to the general divisions we have outlined already, particular anthropologists tend to identify themselves with a variety of specializations. Anthropologists commonly have a geographic specialty, which may be as broad as Old World or New World or as narrow as the southwestern United States. Those who study the past (archaeologists or human paleontologists) may specialize in specific time periods. Ethnologists often specialize in specific subject matters in addition to one or two cultural areas. Just as most of the chapters in this book refer to broad subject specialties, so do some ethnologists identify themselves as ***economic anthropologists***, ***political anthropologists***, or ***psychological anthropologists***. Others may identify themselves by theoretical orientations, such as ***cultural ecologists***, anthropologists who are concerned with the relationship between culture and the physical and social environments. These specialties are not mutually exclusive, however. A cultural ecologist, for example, might be interested in the effects of the environment on economic behavior, political behavior, or childrearing.

Does specialization isolate an anthropologist from other kinds of research? Not necessarily. Some specialties have to draw on information from several fields, inside and outside anthropology. For example, *medical anthropologists* study the cultural and biological contexts of human health and illness. Therefore, they need to understand the economy, diet, and patterns of social interaction as well as attitudes and beliefs regarding illness and health. They may also need to draw on research in human genetics, public health, and medicine.

The Relevance of Anthropology

1.7 Communicate the relevance of anthropology.

Anthropology is a comparatively young discipline. Anthropologists only began to go to live with people in faraway places in the late 1800s. Compared to our knowledge of the physical laws of nature, we know much less about people, about how and why they behave as they do. That anthropology and other sciences dealing with humans began to develop only relatively recently is not in itself a sufficient reason for our knowing less than in the physical sciences. Why, in our quest for knowledge of all kinds, did we wait so long to study ourselves? Leslie White has suggested that those phenomena most remote from us and least significant as determinants of human behavior were the first to be studied. The reason, he surmises, is that humans like to think of themselves as citadels of free will, subject to no laws of nature. Hence, White concludes, there is no need to see ourselves as objects to be explained.[7]

The idea that it is impossible to account for human behavior scientifically, either because our actions and beliefs are too individualistic and complex or because human beings are understandable only in otherworldly terms, is a self-fulfilling notion. We cannot discover principles explaining human behavior if we neither believe such principles exist nor bother to look for them. The result is ensured from the beginning; disbelief in principles of human behavior will be reinforced by the failure to find them. If we are to increase our understanding of human beings, we first have to believe it is possible to do so.

If we aim to understand humans, it is essential that we study humans in all times and places. We must study ancient humans and modern humans. We must study their cultures and their biology. How else can we understand what is true of humans generally or how they are capable of varying? If we study just our own society, we may come up only with explanations that are culture-bound, not general or applicable to most or all humans. Anthropology is useful, then, to the degree that it contributes to our understanding of human beings everywhere.

Watch **the** Video: Cooperation and Conflict: Caucasus and C. Asia

In addition, anthropology is relevant because it helps us avoid misunderstandings between peoples. If we can understand why other groups are different from ourselves, we might have less reason to condemn them for behavior that appears strange to us. We may then come to realize that many differences between peoples are products of physical and cultural adaptations to different environments. For example, someone who first finds out about the !Kung as they lived in the Kalahari Desert of southern Africa in the 1950s might assume that the !Kung were "backward." (The exclamation point in the name !Kung signifies one of the clicking sounds made with the tongue by speakers of the !Kung language.) The !Kung wore little clothing, had few possessions, lived in meager shelters, and enjoyed none of our technological niceties, such as radio and computers.

But let us reflect on how a typical North American community might react if it awoke to find itself in an environment similar to that in which the !Kung lived. People would find that the arid land makes both agriculture and animal husbandry impossible, and they might have to think about adopting a nomadic existence. They might then discard many of their material possessions so that they could travel easily to take advantage of changing water and food supplies. Because of the extreme heat and the lack of extra water for laundry, they might find it more practical to be almost naked than to wear clothes. They would undoubtedly find it impossible to build elaborate homes. For social security, they might start to share the food brought into the group. Thus, if they survived at all, they might end up looking and acting far more like the !Kung than like typical North Americans.

Physical differences, too, may be seen as results of adaptations to the environment. For example, in our society, we admire people who are tall and slim. If these same individuals were forced to live above the Arctic Circle, however, they might wish they could trade their tall, slim bodies for short, compact ones because stocky physiques conserve body heat more effectively and may therefore be more adaptive in cold climates.

Exposure to anthropology might also help to alleviate misunderstandings that arise between people of different cultural groups from subtle causes operating below the level of consciousness. For example, different cultures have different conceptions of the gestures and interpersonal distances that are appropriate under various circumstances. For example, different cultures have different conceptions of eye contact during conversation. Whereas some people—North Americans, most Europeans, and Arabs, among them—expect to maintain eye contact during conversation, in Japanese culture the gaze is averted when interacting with a superior or venerated older person. North Americans may feel suspicious when someone does not look them in the eye when speaking. But in another culture that same direct gaze may be experienced as brazen. If our intolerance for others results in part from a lack of understanding of why peoples vary, then the knowledge that anthropologists accumulate may lessen that intolerance.[8]

As the world becomes increasingly interconnected or globalized, the importance of understanding and trying to respect cultural and physical differences becomes more and more important. Minor misunderstandings can escalate quickly into more serious problems. Even when powerful countries think they are being helpful, they may convey that other countries are inferior. They may also unknowingly promote behaviors that are not in the best interest of the people they are trying to help. At the extreme, misunderstandings can lead to violent confrontations. In today's world, going to war with modern weapons of mass destruction can kill more people than ever before.

Is understanding and respecting cultural and biological differences enough? Although education is undoubtedly useful, many anthropologists believe that more direct action is needed to solve real-world problems at both the global and local levels. At the global level, we have to deal with many types of violent conflict, the degradation of the environment, the growing inequality between rich and poor countries, and major threats to health. At the local level, we have to grapple with whether particular development plans are advantageous and how to improve nutrition and health of particular societies. One solution does not necessarily fit all—what is good for some may not be good for others in different circumstances. To find out if some change will be advantageous requires careful study. Many ethical issues arise. Is it ethical to try to interfere with other people's lives? Is it ethical not to, if they are suffering or ask for help?

Knowledge of our past may bring both a feeling of humility and a sense of accomplishment. If we are to attempt to deal with the problems of our world, we must be aware of our vulnerability so that we do not think that problems will solve themselves. But we also have to think enough of our accomplishments to believe that we can find solutions to problems. Much of the trouble we get into may be a result of feelings of self-importance and invulnerability—in short, our lack of humility. Knowing something about our evolutionary past may help us to understand and accept our place in the biological world. Just as for any other form of life, there is no guarantee that any particular human population, or even the entire human species, will perpetuate itself indefinitely. The earth changes, the environment changes, and humanity itself changes. What survives and flourishes in the present might not do so in the future.

Yet our vulnerability should not make us feel powerless. We have many reasons to feel confident about the future. Consider what we have accomplished so far. By means of tools and weapons fashioned from sticks and stones, we were able to hunt animals larger and more powerful than ourselves. We discovered how to make fire, and we learned to use it to keep ourselves warm and to cook our food. As we domesticated plants and animals, we gained greater control over our food supply and were able to establish more permanent settlements. We mined and smelted ores to fashion more durable tools. We built cities and irrigation systems, monuments and ships. We made it possible to travel from one continent to another in a single day. We conquered some illnesses and prolonged human life.

In short, human beings and their cultures have changed considerably over the course of history. Human populations have often been able to adapt to changing circumstances. Let us hope that humans continue to adapt to the challenges of the present and future.

Summary and Review

What Is Anthropology?

1.1 Explain the general definition and purpose of anthropology.

- Anthropology is a discipline of curiosity about human beings that seeks to understand both universals and differences in human populations.
- Anthropology seeks answers to biological and cultural questions about humans for both academic and practical purposes.
- Anthropology is distinct from other disciplines concerned with human beings in its scope, its holistic approach, and its distinctive curiosity.

? What are the academic and practical purposes of anthropology?

The Scope of Anthropology

1.2 Describe the scope of anthropology.

- The field of anthropology has a broad scope, both geographically and historically.
- Anthropologists are interested in all varieties of people in every part of the world.
- Anthropologists are interested in people of all periods, from millions of years ago to the present.
- The broad scope of anthropology is required to confirm that any suggested generalization about human beings, any explanation of some characteristic of human culture or biology, is applicable to many times and places of human existence, not just a limited group.

? What are the global goals of anthropological study?

The Holistic Approach

1.3 Explain the holistic approach.

- Anthropologists study the many aspects of human experience as an integrated whole.
- Anthropologists look for patterns of traits and attempt to explain them.

? What elements of the human experience might be considered in a holistic approach in anthropology?

Anthropological Curiosity

1.4 Explain anthropology's distinctive curiosity.

- Anthropology's distinctiveness lies principally in the kind of curiosity it arouses.
- Anthropologists tend to focus on *typic*al characteristics of the human populations they study rather than on individual variation or variation in small groups.
- Because anthropologists view human groups holistically, their curiosity may lead them to find patterns of relationships between seemingly unrelated characteristics.

? What typifies anthropological curiosity?

Fields of Anthropology

1.5 Differentiate among the five major fields of anthropology.

- Anthropology comprises two broad classifications of subject matter: biological (physical) anthropology and cultural anthropology.
- Biological anthropology poses questions about the emergence of humans and their later evolution (paleontology) and about how and why contemporary human populations vary biologically (human variation).
- Cultural anthropology is the study of how and why cultures in the past and present vary or are similar in terms of the ways that a particular population or society thinks and behaves.

- Cultural anthropology includes three subfields: archaeology, linguistics, and ethnology (often called *cultural anthropology*).
- A fifth subfield, applied or practicing anthropology, cuts across all four subfields.
- The purpose of applied (or practicing) anthropology is explicitly to make anthropological knowledge useful. Practicing anthropologists may be trained in any or all of the fields of anthropology.

> ? How are the five major fields of anthropology different? What are some examples of applied anthropology?

Specialization

1.6 Explain ways in which anthropologists specialize within their fields of study.

- Anthropologists specialize by focusing on a geographic area; a period of time; particular subject matter such as economics, politics, or psychology; or particular theoretical orientations.
- Anthropologists might have more than one specialization.

> ? What are some examples of anthropological specializations and their purposes?

The Relevance of Anthropology

1.7 Communicate the relevance of anthropology.

- Anthropology is a young discipline, beginning in the late 1800s. Initially, especially among Westerners, there was resistance to the idea of accounting for human behavior scientifically.
- Anthropology considers both culture and biology of humans in all times and places. Anthropology is useful to the degree that it contributes to our understanding of human beings everywhere.
- In addition, anthropology is relevant because it helps to avoid misunderstandings between peoples. If those in one culture can understand why other groups are different from them, they might have less reason to condemn others for behavior that appears strange.
- As the world becomes increasingly interconnected or globalized, the importance of understanding and trying to respect cultural and physical differences becomes more and more important.

> ? How is anthropology relevant to society?

Think on it

1. Why study **anthropology**? What are its goals, and how is it useful?
2. How does anthropology differ from other **fields** you have encountered that deal with humans? (Compare with psychology, sociology, political science, history, or biology, among others.)
3. Compare the three anthropologists featured in this chapter. What do their **stories** have in common?
4. How might the **knowledge** gained from anthropology be both humbling and empowering?

CHAPTER 2

Research Methods in Anthropology

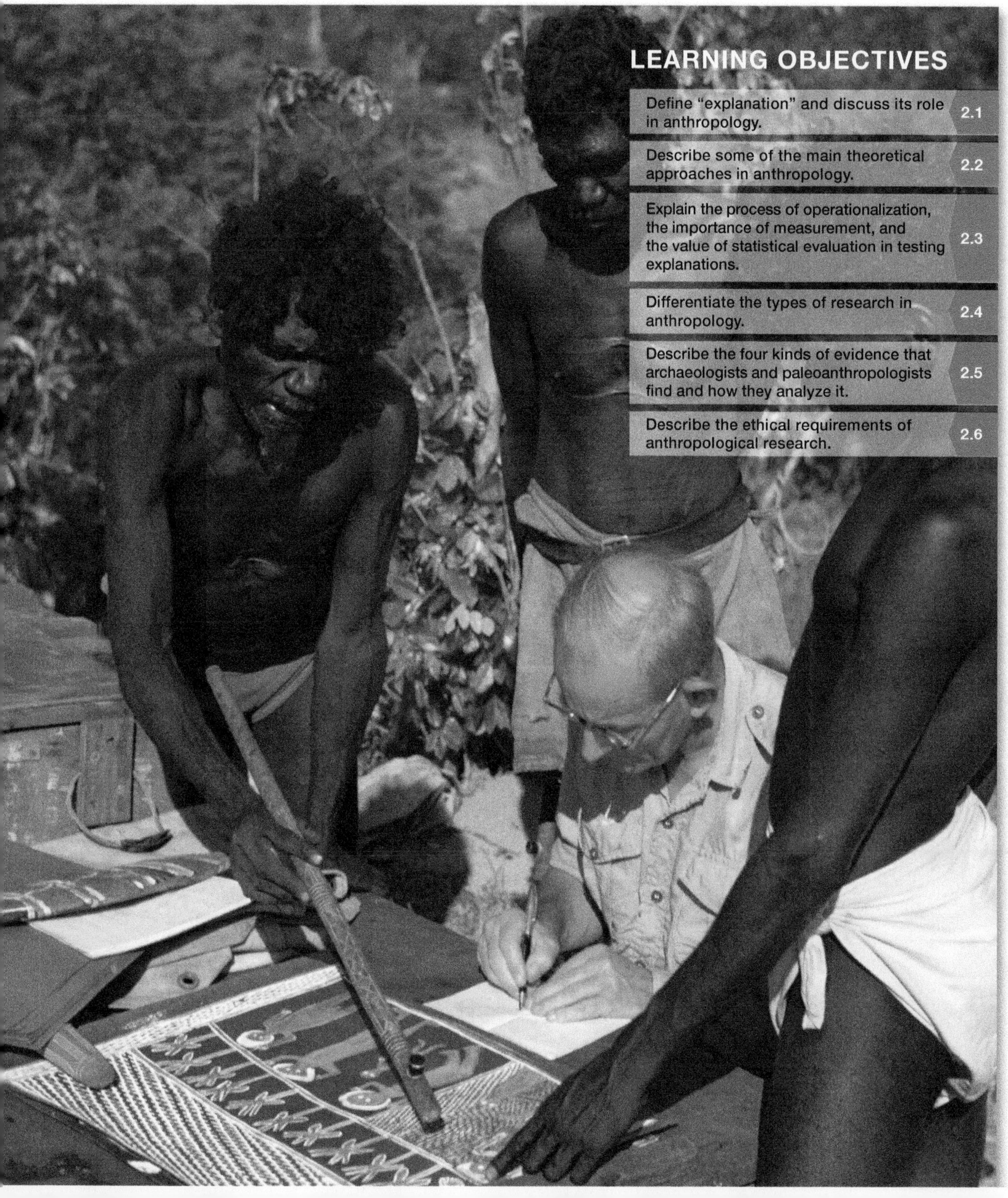

LEARNING OBJECTIVES

- **2.1** Define "explanation" and discuss its role in anthropology.
- **2.2** Describe some of the main theoretical approaches in anthropology.
- **2.3** Explain the process of operationalization, the importance of measurement, and the value of statistical evaluation in testing explanations.
- **2.4** Differentiate the types of research in anthropology.
- **2.5** Describe the four kinds of evidence that archaeologists and paleoanthropologists find and how they analyze it.
- **2.6** Describe the ethical requirements of anthropological research.

The intellectuals who developed science in the mid-17th century understood very well that human knowledge of the world could be biased and incomplete. Rather than rejecting the possibility of objective understanding, the founders of science created a way of generating understanding based on the rigorous testing of ideas. As anthropologist Philip Salzman explains:

> *The scientific method, the heart of science, was invented because it was understood that human error, wish-fulfillment, duplicity, dishonesty, and weakness would commonly distort research findings. The scientific requirements that the procedures of all studies must be specified in detail so that others could repeat them, and the actual replication of findings by other scientists in other venues, were established to minimize the distorting effects of human subjectivity and moral weakness in the quest for knowledge.*[1]

Although one goal of anthropology is to understand what it means to be a human in a different cultural context, a goal for which science and its pursuit of explanations may not be appropriate, most anthropologists believe that objective knowledge about other cultures is possible through science.

2.1 Define "explanation" and discuss its role in anthropology.

Explanation An answer to a *why* question. In science, there are two kinds of explanation that researchers try to achieve: associations and theories.

Variable A thing or quantity that varies.

Laws (scientific) Associations or relationships that almost all scientists accept.

Explanations

An **explanation** is an answer to a *why* question. There are many types of explanations, some more satisfying than others. For example, suppose we ask why a society has a long postpartum sex taboo. We could guess that the people in that society want to abstain from sex for a year or so after the birth of a baby. Is this an explanation? Yes, because it does suggest that people have a purpose in practicing the custom; it therefore partly answers the *why* question. But such an explanation would not be very satisfying because it does not specify what the purpose of the custom might be. How about the idea that people have a long postpartum sex taboo because it is their tradition? That too is an explanation, but it is not satisfactory for a different reason. It is a *tautology;* that is, the thing to be explained (the taboo) is being explained by itself, by its prior existence. To explain something in terms of tradition is to say that people do it because they already do it, which is not informative. What kinds of explanations are more satisfactory, then? In science, investigators try to achieve two kinds of explanations: *associations* and *theories.*

The statement that water becomes ice at 32°F (0°C) defines an association between two variables: water and temperature. A theory explains why an association exists.

Associations or Relationships

One way of explaining something (an observation, an action, a custom) is to say how it conforms to a general principle or relationship. So to explain why the water left outside in the basin froze, we say that it was cold last night and that water freezes at 32°F (0°C). The statement that water solidifies (becomes ice) at 32°F is a statement of a relationship or association between two **variables**—things or quantities that vary. In this case, variation in the state of water (liquid vs. solid) is related to variation in the temperature of the air (above vs. below 32°F). The truth of the relationship is suggested by repeated observations. In the physical sciences, such relationships are called **laws** when almost all scientists accept them. We find such explanations satisfactory because they allow us to predict what will happen in the future or to understand something that has happened regularly in the past.

In the social sciences, associations are usually stated *probabilistically;* that is, we say that two or more variables tend to be related in a predictable way, which means that there are usually some exceptions. For example, to explain why a society has a long postpartum sex taboo, we can point to the association (or correlation) that John Whiting found in a worldwide sample of societies: Societies with apparently low-protein diets tend to have long postpartum sex taboos.[2] We call the relationship between low-protein diets and the sex taboo a **statistical association**, which means that the observed relationship is unlikely to be due to chance.

Statistical association A relationship or correlation between two or more variables that is unlikely to be due to chance.

Theories

Even though laws and statistical associations explain by relating what is to be explained to other things, we want to know more: why those laws or associations exist. Why does water freeze at 32°F? Why do societies with low-protein diets tend to have long postpartum sex taboos? Therefore, scientists try to formulate theories that will explain the observed relationships (laws and statistical associations).[3]

Theories Explanations of associations or laws.

Theories—explanations of laws and statistical associations—are more complicated than the observed relationships they are intended to explain. It is difficult to be precise about what a theory is. By way of example, let us return to the question of why some societies have long postpartum sex taboos. We have already seen that a known statistical association can be used to help explain it. If a society has a low-protein diet, it will generally have a long postpartum sex taboo. But most people would ask additional questions: Why does a low-protein diet explain the taboo? What is the mechanism by which a society with such a diet develops the custom of a long postpartum sex taboo? A theory is intended to answer such questions.

John Whiting theorized that a long postpartum sex taboo may be an adaptation to certain conditions. Particularly in tropical areas, where the major food staples are low in protein, babies are vulnerable to the protein-deficiency disease called *kwashiorkor*. But if a baby could continue to nurse for a long time, it might have more of a chance to survive. The postpartum sex taboo might be adaptive, Whiting's theory suggests, because it increases the likelihood of a baby's survival. That is, if a mother puts off having another baby for a while, the first baby might have a better chance to survive because it can be fed mother's milk for a longer time. Whiting suggests that parents may be aware, whether unconsciously or consciously, that having another baby too soon might jeopardize the survival of the first baby, and so they might decide that abstaining from intercourse for more than a year after the birth of the first baby would be a good idea.

As this example of a theory illustrates, there are differences between a theory and an association. A theory is usually more complicated, containing a series of statements. An association usually states quite simply that there is a relationship between two or more measured variables. Another difference is that although a theory may mention some things that are observable, such as the presence of a long postpartum sex taboo, it contains other concepts or statements that could not be observed. For example, with regard to Whiting's theory, it would be difficult to find out if the people who adopted the custom of a long postpartum sex taboo had some awareness that babies would thereby have a better chance to survive. Then, too, the concept of adaptation—that some characteristic promotes greater reproductive success—is difficult to verify because of the challenge of finding out whether different individuals or groups have different rates of reproduction because they do or do not practice the supposedly adaptive custom. Thus, some concepts or implications in a theory are unobservable (at least at the present time), and only some aspects may be observable. In contrast, statistical associations or laws are based entirely on observations.[4]

Why Theories Cannot Be Proved

Many people think that the theories they learned in physics or chemistry courses have been proved. Unfortunately, many students get that impression because their teachers present lessons in an authoritative manner. Scientists and philosophers of science now generally agree that no theory can be said to be proved or unquestionably true, although some theories may have considerable evidence supporting them. This is because many of the concepts and ideas in theories are not directly observable and therefore not directly verifiable. For example, scientists may try to explain how light behaves by postulating

Theoretical construct Something that cannot be observed or verified directly.

that it consists of particles called photons, but photons cannot be observed, even with the most powerful microscope. So, exactly what a photon looks like and exactly how it works remain in the realm of the unprovable. The photon is a **theoretical construct**, something that cannot be observed or verified directly. Because all theories contain such constructs, theories cannot be proved entirely or with absolute certainty.[5]

Why should we bother with theories, then, if we cannot prove that they are true? Perhaps the main advantage of a theory as a kind of explanation is that it may lead to new understanding or knowledge. A theory can suggest new relationships or imply new predictions that might be supported or confirmed by new research. For example, Whiting's theory about long postpartum sex taboos has implications that researchers could investigate. Because the theory discusses how a long postpartum sex taboo might be adaptive, we would expect that certain changes would result in the taboo's disappearance. For example, suppose people adopted either mechanical birth-control devices or began to give supplementary high-protein foods to babies. With birth control, a family could space births without abstaining from sex, so we would expect the custom of postpartum abstinence to disappear. Additionally, we would expect it to disappear with protein supplements for babies because *kwashiorkor* would then be less likely to afflict the babies. Whiting's ideas might also prompt investigators to try to find out whether parents are consciously or unconsciously aware of the problem of close birth spacing in areas with low supplies of protein.

Falsification Showing that a theory seems to be wrong by finding that implications or predictions derivable from it are not consistent with objectively collected data.

Hypotheses Predictions, which may be derived from theories, about how variables are related.

Although theories cannot be proved, they are rejectable. The method of **falsification**, which shows that a theory seems to be wrong, is the main way that theories are judged.[6] Scientists derive implications or predictions that should be true if the theory is correct. So, for example, Whiting predicted that societies with long postpartum sex taboos would be found more often in the tropics than in temperate regions and that they would be likely to have low-protein food supplies. Such predictions of what might be found are called **hypotheses**. If the predictions turn out not to be correct, the researcher is obliged to conclude that something may be wrong with the theory or something wrong with the test of the theory. Theories that are not falsified are accepted for the time being because the available evidence seems to be consistent with them. But remember that no matter how much the available evidence seems to support a theory, we can never be certain it is true. There is always the possibility that some implication of it, some hypothesis derivable from it, will not be confirmed in the future.

2.2 Describe some of the main theoretical approaches in anthropology.

A Brief History of Anthropological Theory

Theoretical orientation A general attitude about how phenomena are to be explained.

John Whiting's theory explaining why a long postpartum sex taboo might be adaptive is only one of many theories that anthropologists employ in their research. The history of anthropology reflects broad themes the types of theories anthropologists have used. Whiting's theory, for example, can be placed within the body of ecological theories. Let's take a look at some of the variety of **theoretical orientations** that have been important to anthropologists.

Early Evolutionism

The theory of evolution had a strong impact on anthropology in the 19th century. The prevailing view was that culture generally develops (or evolves) in a uniform and progressive manner, just as Darwin argued species did. It was thought that most societies pass through the same series of stages, to arrive ultimately at a common end. Two 19th-century anthropologists whose writings exemplified the theory that culture generally evolves uniformly and progressively were Edward B. Tylor (1832–1917) and Lewis Henry Morgan (1818–1881). Both maintained that culture evolved from the simple to the complex and that all societies passed through three basic stages of development: from savagery through barbarism to civilization.[7] "Progress" was therefore possible for all. To account for cultural variation, Tylor and Morgan postulated that different contemporary societies were at different stages of evolution. According to this view, the "simpler" peoples of the day had not yet reached "higher" stages. Though important at the beginning of anthropology, the evolutionism of Tylor and Morgan is largely rejected today.

"Race" Theory

Evolutionism also influenced another branch of early anthropological theory, one that posited that the reason human cultures differed in their behaviors was because they represented separate subspecies of humans, or "races." This idea was also influenced by the fact that, by the 19th century at least, it became clear that few cultures were being "civilized" in the way Europeans expected. Rather than attribute this to the strength of cultural tradition, some attributed it to the innate capabilities of the people—in other words, to their "race." Members of "uncivilized races" were, by their very nature, incapable of being "civilized." Such ideas were widely held during the late 19th and early 20th centuries, and American anthropology played a large role in showing that "race" theory was unsupported in a variety of contexts. Unfortunately, "race" theory persists in some disciplines.[8]

Boasian Anthropology

The beginning of the 20th century brought the end of evolutionism's reign in American anthropology. Its leading opponent was Franz Boas (1858–1942), whose main disagreement with the evolutionists involved their assumption that universal laws governed all human culture. Boas pointed out that these 19th-century "armchair anthropologists" lacked sufficient data to formulate many useful generalizations. Boas also strongly opposed "race" theory, and made significant contributions to the study of human variation that demonstrated how supposedly "racial" characteristics actually varied depending on where a person grew up.[9]

Boas stressed the idea that single cultural traits had to be studied in the context of the society in which they appeared. According to the method he advocated, the essence of science is to mistrust all expectations and to rely only on facts. But, as we argue in this chapter, collecting data without some preliminary theorizing, without ideas about what to expect, is problematic, for the facts that are most important may be ignored whereas irrelevant ones may be recorded. Boas's concern with innumerable local details did not encourage a belief that it might be possible to explain the major variations in culture, and by the 1950s many anthropologists felt that the Boasian focus on describing cultures rather than explaining how and why cultures varied limited the scope of anthropology. Two major approaches to anthropology emerged from this movement away from description: ecological and interpretive.

Ecological Approaches

Julian Steward (1902–1972) was one of the first to advocate the study of **cultural ecology**—the analysis of the relationship between a culture and its environment. Steward felt that the explanation for some aspects of cultural variation could be found in the adaptation of societies to their particular environments.[10] Cultural ecologists assume that cultural adaptation involves the mechanism of *natural selection*—the more frequent survival and reproduction of the better adapted. Environment, including the physical and social environments, affects the development of culture traits in that "individuals or populations behaving in certain different ways have different degrees of success in survival and reproduction and, consequently, in the transmission of their ways of behaving from generation to generation."[11]

Cultural ecology The analysis of the relationship between a culture and its environment.

Today anthropologists who refer to themselves as evolutionary or behavioral ecologists (as opposed to cultural ecologists) explore how particular characteristics may be adaptive for an individual in a given environment (cultural ecologists tend to focus on the group or culture more than the individual).[12] *Adaptive* means the ability of individuals to get their genes into future generations. This viewpoint implies that behavior is transmitted in some way (by genes or learning) to people who share your genes (usually offspring).[13] If a certain behavior is adaptive for individuals in a particular environment (or a particular historical context in which these individuals are able to reproduce more than others), it should become more widespread in future generations as the individuals with those traits increase in number. One important contemporary idea, dual-inheritance theory, gives much more weight to culture as part of the evolutionary process. Dual inheritance refers to both genes and culture playing different but nonetheless important and interactive roles in transmitting traits to future generations.[14]

Current Research and Issues

Evaluating Alternative Theories

In working among the Abelam of New Guinea, Richard Scaglion was puzzled why they invest so much energy in growing giant ceremonial yams, sometimes more than 10 feet long. Also, why do they abstain from sex for six months while they grow them? Of course, to try to understand, we need to know much more about the Abelam way of life. Scaglion had read about them, lived among them, and talked to them, but, as many ethnographers have discovered, answers to why questions don't just leap out at you. Answers, at least tentative ones, often come from theoretical orientations that suggest how or where to look for answers. Scaglion considers several possibilities. As Donald Tuzin had suggested for a nearby group, the Plains Arapesh, yams may be symbols of, or stand for, shared cultural understandings. (Looking for the meanings of symbols is a kind of interpretative approach to ethnographic data.) The Abelam think of yams as having souls that appreciate tranquility. Yams also have family lines; at marriage, the joining of family lines is symbolized by planting different yam lines in the same garden. During the yam-growing cycle (remember that yams appreciate tranquility), lethal warfare and conflict become channeled mostly into competitive but nonlethal yam-growing contests. So yam growing may be functional in the sense that it helps to foster harmony.

Then again, ceremonial yam growing may have adaptive ecological consequences. Just as the Tsembaga pig feasts seemed to keep human population in line with resources, Scaglion thinks that ceremonial yam growing did too. Growing pig populations damage gardens and create conflicts, but pigs are also given away during competitive yam ceremonies, so the pig population declines. Wild animals that are hunted also have a chance to replenish themselves because hunting is frowned upon during the yam-growing cycle.

As Scaglion's discussion illustrates, theoretical orientations help researchers derive explanations. They do not have to be "rival" explanations, in the sense that one has to be right and others wrong; more than one theory may help explain some phenomenon. But we can't assume that a theory is correct and helps us to understand just because it sounds good. The important point is that we need something more to evaluate theory.

The Abelam create elaborate ceremonial masks to adorn their largest yams during the harvest festival.

We have to find ways to test a theory against evidence. Until we do that, we really don't know how many, or if indeed any, of the theories available are helpful.

Source: Scaglion 2009a.

The ecological approaches have led to an active program of research in anthropology. However, these approaches have aroused considerable controversy, particularly from those cultural anthropologists who do not believe that biological considerations or cultural adaptations have much to do with understanding culture.

Interpretive Approaches

Since the 1960s, writers in the field of literary criticism have influenced the development of a variety of "interpretive" approaches in cultural anthropology, particularly with respect to ethnography.[15] Clifford Geertz (1926–2006) popularized the idea that a culture is like a literary text that can be analyzed for meaning. According to Geertz, ethnographers choose to interpret the meaning of things in the cultures they study that are of interest to themselves. Then they try to convey their interpretations of cultural meaning to people of their own culture. Thus, according to Geertz, ethnographers are a kind of selective intercultural translator.[16]

For many interpretive anthropologists, the goal of anthropology is to understand what it means to be a person living in a particular culture, rather than to explain why cultures vary. The task of understanding meaning, these scholars claim, cannot be achieved scientifically, but can only be approached through forms of literary analysis.

Many of these anthropologists think that interpretation is the only achievable goal in cultural anthropology because they do not believe it is possible to describe or measure cultural phenomena in objective or unbiased ways. Scientific anthropologists do not agree. To be sure, interpretive ethnographies provide insights into other cultures. But we do not have to believe what an interpretation suggests, no matter how eloquently it is stated. (We are rarely given objective evidence to support the interpretation.) As we discuss below, scientific researchers have developed many techniques for minimizing bias and increasing the objectivity of measurement. Thus, interpretative anthropologists who deny the possibility of scientific understanding of human behavior and thinking may not know how much has been achieved so far by scientific studies of cultural phenomena. Let's take a look at how scientific anthropologists test explanations of cultural phenomenon.

Evidence: Testing Explanations

2.3 Explain the process of operationalization, the importance of measurement, and the value of statistical evaluation in testing explanations.

In any field of investigation, theories are generally the most plentiful commodity, apparently because of the human predisposition to try to make sense of the world. It is necessary, then, for us to have procedures that enable us to select from among the many available theories those that are more likely to be correct. As Peter Caws pointed out, "Just as mutations arise naturally but are not all beneficial, so hypotheses [theories] emerge naturally but are not all correct. If progress is to occur, therefore, we require a superfluity of hypotheses and also a mechanism of selection."[17] In other words, generating a theory or interpretation is not enough. We need some reliable method of testing whether or not that theory is likely to be correct. If a theory is not correct, it may detract from our efforts to achieve understanding by misleading us into thinking the problem is already solved.

The strategy in all kinds of testing in science is to predict what one would expect to find if a particular theory were correct, and then to conduct an investigation to see if the prediction is generally consistent with the data. If the prediction is not supported, the investigator is obliged to accept the possibility that the theory is wrong. If, however, the prediction holds true, then the investigator is entitled to say that evidence supports the theory. Thus, conducting research designed to test expectations derived from theory allows researchers to eliminate some theories and to accept others, at least tentatively.

Operationalization and Measurement

We test predictions derived from a theory to see if the theory may be correct—to see if it is consistent with observable events or conditions in the real world. A theory and the predictions derived from it are not useful if there is no way to measure the events or conditions mentioned in the predictions. If there is no way of relating the theory to observable events, it does not matter how good the theory sounds; it is still not a useful scientific theory.[18] To transform theoretical predictions into statements that might be verified, a researcher provides an **operational definition** of each of the concepts or variables mentioned in the prediction. An operational definition is a description of the procedure that is followed to measure the variable.[19]

Operational definition A description of the procedure that is followed in measuring a variable.

Whiting predicted that societies with a low-protein diet would have a long postpartum sex taboo. Amount of protein in the diet is a variable; some societies have more, others have less. Length of the postpartum sex taboo is a variable; a society may have a short taboo or a long taboo. Whiting operationally defined the first variable, *amount of protein,* in terms of staple foods.[20] For example, if a society depended mostly on root and tree crops (such as cassava and bananas), Whiting rated the society as having low protein. If the society depended mostly on cereal crops (such as wheat, barley, corn, oats), he rated it as having moderate protein because cereal crops have more protein by weight than root and tree crops. If the society depended mostly on hunting, fishing, or herding for food, he rated it as having high protein. The other variable in Whiting's prediction, *length of postpartum sex taboo,* was operationalized as follows: A society was rated as having a long taboo if couples customarily abstained from sex for more than a year after the birth of a baby; abstention for a year or less was considered a short taboo.

Specifying an operational definition for each variable is extremely important because it allows other investigators to check a researcher's results.[21] Science depends on *replication,* the repetition of results. Only when many researchers observe a particular association can we call that association or relationship a law. Providing operational definitions is also

Yanomamö Indians of Brazil depend on plantains (shown here) and cassava root crops and have a relatively low-protein diet.

extremely important because it allows others to evaluate whether a measure is appropriate. Only when we are told exactly how something was measured can we judge whether the measure reflects what it is supposed to reflect. Specifying measures publicly is so important in science that we are obliged to be skeptical of any conclusions offered by a researcher who fails to say how variables were measured.

Measure To describe how something compares with other things on some scale of variation.

To **measure** something is to say how it compares with other things on some scale of variation. People often assume that a measuring device is always a physical instrument, such as a scale or a ruler, but physical devices are not the only way to measure something. *Classification* is also a form of measurement. When we classify people as male or female or employed versus unemployed, we are dividing them into *types*. Deciding which type they belong to is a kind of measurement because doing so allows us to compare them. We can also measure things by deciding which cases or examples have more or less of something (e.g., more or less protein in the diet). The measures employed in physical science are usually based on scales that allow us to assign numbers to each case; we measure height in meters and weight in grams, for example. However we measure our variables, the fact that we can measure them means that we can test our hypotheses to see if the predicted relationships actually exist, at least most of the time.

Sampling

After deciding how to measure the variables in some predicted relationship, investigators must decide how to select which cases to study to see if the predicted relationship holds. If the prediction is about the behavior of people, the sampling decision involves which people to observe. If the prediction is about an association between societal customs, the sampling decision involves which societies to study. Investigators must decide not only which cases to choose but also how many to choose. No researcher can investigate all the possible cases, and so choices must be made. Some choices are better than others. The best sample is almost always some kind of random sample. A **random sample** is one in which all cases selected have an equal chance of being included in the sample. Almost all statistical tests used to evaluate the results of research require random sampling because only results based on a random sample can be assumed to be probably true for some larger set or universe of cases.

Random sample A sample in which all cases selected have had an equal chance to be included.

Sampling universe The list of cases to be sampled from.

Before researchers can sample randomly, they must specify the **sampling universe**, that is, the list of cases to be sampled from. Suppose an anthropologist is doing fieldwork in a society. Unless the society is very small, it is usually not practical to use the whole society as the sampling universe. Because most fieldworkers want to remain in a community for a considerable

The Inuit of Nunavut depend largely on sea mammals and fish and have a relatively high-protein diet.

length of time, the community usually becomes the sampling universe. If a cross-cultural researcher wants to test an explanation, it is necessary to sample the world's societies. But we do not have descriptions of all the societies—past and present—that have existed in the world. Thus, samples are usually drawn from published lists of described societies that have been classified or coded according to standard cultural variables,[22] or they are drawn from the Human Relations Area Files *eHRAF World Cultures,* a finely-indexed, online, and annually growing collection of ethnographies on more than 285 societies—past and present—around the world.[23] There is also a collection of archaeological traditions—*eHRAF Archaeology.*

Random sampling is not often employed in anthropology, but a nonrandom sample might still be fairly representative if the investigator has not personally chosen the cases for study. We should be particularly suspicious of any sample that may reflect the investigator's own biases or interests. For example, if investigators pick only the people with whom they are friendly, the sample is suspicious. If researchers select sample cases (i.e., societies and traditions) because books on them happen to be on their own bookshelves, such samples are also suspicious. A sampling procedure should be designed to get a fair, unbiased representation of the sampling universe. If we want to increase our chances of getting a representative sample, we have to use a random sampling procedure. To do so, we conventionally number the cases in the statistical universe and then use a table of random numbers to draw our sample cases.

Statistical Evaluation

When researchers have measured the variables of interest for all the sample cases, they are ready to see if the predicted relationship actually exists in the data. Remember, the results may not turn out to be what the theory predicts. Sometimes researchers construct a *contingency table,* like that shown in Table 2.1, to see if the variables are associated as predicted. In Whiting's sample of 172 societies, each case is assigned to a box, or cell, in the table, depending on how the society is measured on the two variables of interest. For example, a society that has a long postpartum sex taboo and a low-protein diet is placed in the third row of the Long Duration column. (In Whiting's sample [see Table 2.1], there are 27 such societies.) A society that has a short postpartum sex taboo and a low-protein diet is placed in the third row in the Short Duration column. (There are 20 such societies in the sample.) The statistical question is: Does the way the cases are distributed in the six central cells of the table generally support Whiting's prediction? If we looked just at the table, we might not know what to answer. Many cases appear to be in the expected places. For example, most of the high-protein cases

TABLE 2.1 Association Between Availability of Protein and Duration of Postpartum Sex Taboo

AVAILABILITY OF PROTEIN	DURATION OF POSTPARTUM SEX TABOO Short (0–1 Year)	Long (More Than One Year)	Total
High	47	15	62
Medium	38	25	63
Low	20	27	47
Total	105	67	172

Source: Based on Whiting 1964, 520.

(47 of 62) have short taboos, and most of the low-protein cases (27 of 47) have long taboos. But there are also many exceptions (e.g., 20 cases have low protein and a short taboo). So, although many cases appear to be in the expected places, there are also many exceptions. Do the exceptions invalidate the prediction? How many exceptions would compel us to reject the hypothesis? Here is where we resort to *statistical tests of significance.*

Probability value (*p-value*) The likelihood that an observed result could have occurred by chance.

Statistically significant Refers to a result that would occur very rarely by chance. The result (and stronger ones) would occur fewer than 5 times out of 100 by chance.

Statisticians have devised various tests that tell us how "perfect" a result must be to convince us to believe that there is probably an association between the variables of interest, and that one variable generally predicts the other. Essentially, every statistical result is evaluated in the same objective way. We ask: What is the chance that this result is purely accidental, that there is no association at all between the two variables? Although some of the mathematical ways of answering this question are complicated, the answer always involves a **probability value** (or ***p*-value**)—the likelihood that the observed result or a stronger one could have occurred by chance. The statistical test used by Whiting gives a *p*-value of less than .01 ($p < .01$) for the observed result. In other words, there is less than 1 chance out of 100 that the relationship observed is purely accidental. A *p*-value of less than .01 is a fairly low probability; most social scientists conventionally agree to call any result with a *p*-value of .05 or less (5 or fewer chances out of 100) a **statistically significant**, or probably true, result. When we describe relationships or associations in the rest of this book, we are almost always referring to results that have been found to be statistically significant.

But why should a probably true relationship have any exceptions? If a theory is really correct, shouldn't *all* the cases fit? There are many reasons why we can never expect a perfect result. First, even if a theory is correct (e.g., if a low-protein diet really does favor the adoption of a long postpartum sex taboo), there may still be other causes that we have not investigated. Some of the societies could have a long taboo even though they have high protein. For example, societies that depend mostly on hunting for their food, and would therefore be classified as having a high-protein diet, may have a problem carrying infants from one campsite to another and may practice a long postpartum sex taboo so that two infants will not have to be carried at the same time.

Exceptions to the predicted relationship might also occur because of *cultural lag.*[24] Cultural lag occurs when change in one aspect of culture takes time to produce change in another aspect. Suppose that a society recently changed crops and is now no longer a low-protein society but still practices the taboo. This society would be an exception to the predicted relationship, but it might fit the theory if it stopped practicing the taboo in a few years. Measurement inaccuracy is another source of exception. Whiting's measure of protein, which is based on the major sources of food, is not a very precise measure of protein in the diet. It does not take into account the possibility that a "tree crop" society might get a lot of protein from fishing or raising pigs. Some supposedly low-protein societies might therefore have been misclassified, which could be one reason why there are 20 cases in the lowest cell in the left-hand column of Table 2.1. Measurement error usually produces exceptions.

Significant statistical associations that are predictable from a theory offer tentative support for the theory. But much more is needed before we can be fairly confident about the theory. Replication is needed to confirm whether other researchers can reproduce the predictions using other samples. Other predictions should be derived from the theory to see if they too are supported. The theory should be pitted against alternative explanations to see which theory works better. We may have to combine theories if the alternative explanations also predict the relationship in question. The research process in science thus requires time and patience. Perhaps most important, it requires that researchers be humble. No matter how wonderful one's own theory seems, it is important to acknowledge that it may be wrong. If we do not acknowledge that possibility, we cannot be motivated to test our theories. If we don't test our theories, we can never tell the difference between a better or worse theory, and we will be saddled forever with our present ignorance. In science, knowledge or understanding is explained variation. Thus, if we want to understand more, we have to keep testing our beliefs against sets of objective evidence that could contradict our beliefs.

Types of Research in Anthropology

2.4 Differentiate the types of research in anthropology.

Anthropologists use several methods to conduct research. Each has certain advantages and disadvantages in generating and testing explanations. The types of research in anthropology can be classified according to two criteria. One is the spatial scope of the study (e.g., the analysis of a single society, analysis of societies in a region, or analysis of a worldwide sample of societies). The other criterion is the temporal scope of the study—historical versus nonhistorical. Combinations of these criteria are shown in Table 2.2.

In this section, we mostly discuss research strategies in cultural anthropology. However, most of these have parallels in archaeology and biological anthropology, as Table 2.2 makes clear. Archaeology and biological anthropology have special methods, and we devote the last section of the chapter to some of those methods.

Ethnography

Around the beginning of the 20th century, anthropologists realized that, if they were to produce anything of scientific value, they would have to study their subject in depth. To describe cultures more accurately, they started to live among the people they were studying. They observed, and even took part in, the important events of those societies and carefully questioned the people about their native customs. This method is known as **participant-observation**. Participant-observation always involves **fieldwork**, which is firsthand experience with the people being studied, but fieldwork may also involve other methods, such as conducting a census or a survey.[25]

Participant-observation Living among the people being studied—observing, questioning, and (when possible) taking part in the important events of the group. Writing or otherwise recording notes on observations, questions asked and answered, and things to check out later are parts of participant-observation.

Fieldwork, the cornerstone of modern anthropology, is the means by which most anthropological information is obtained. Regardless of other methods that anthropologists may use, participant-observation conducted usually for a year or more is regarded as

Fieldwork Firsthand experience with the people being studied and the usual means by which anthropological information is obtained. Regardless of other methods that anthropologists may use (e.g., censuses, surveys), fieldwork usually involves participant-observation for an extended period of time, often a year or more. See **Participant-observation.**

TABLE 2.2 Types of Research in Anthropology

Scope	Nonhistorical	Historical
Single case	Ethnography/fieldwork*	Ethnohistory*
	Archaeological site excavation*	Culture history*
	Single species study/fieldwork*	Evolutionary history of a species*
	Language study/fieldwork*	Language history
Region	Controlled comparison	Controlled comparison
	Regional comparison of archaeological or other sites	Regional comparison of archaeological or other sites
	Cross-species comparison	Cross-species comparison
	Language family comparison	Language family comparison
Worldwide sample	Cross-cultural research	Cross-historical research
	Cross-archaeological research	Cross-archaeological research
	Cross-species comparison	Cross-species comparison
	Cross-linguistic comparison	Comparative historical linguistics

*All of these can also involve comparisons within the research setting—of different individuals, social groups, populations, or sites.

fundamental. In contrast to the casual descriptions of travelers and adventurers, anthropologists' descriptions record, describe, analyze, and eventually formulate a picture of the culture, or at least part of it.[26] After doing fieldwork, an anthropologist may prepare an *ethnography,* a description and analysis of a single society.

How an anthropologist goes about doing long-term participant-observation in another culture—and, more important, doing it well—is not so straightforward. Much of it depends on the person, the culture, and the interaction between the two. Without a doubt, the experience is physically and psychologically demanding, comparable often to a rite of passage. Although it helps enormously to learn the local language before going, often it is not possible to do so, and so most anthropologists find themselves struggling to communicate in addition to trying to figure out how to behave properly. Participant-observation carries its own dilemma. Participation implies living like the people who are being studied, trying to understand subjectively what they think and feel by doing what they do, whereas observation implies a certain amount of objectivity and detachment.[27] Because participant-observation is such a personal experience, it is not surprising that anthropologists have begun to realize that *reflecting* on their experiences and their personal interaction with the people they live with is an important part of understanding the enterprise.

An essential part of the participant-observation process is finding some knowledgeable people who are willing to work with you (anthropologists call them *informants*) to help you interpret what you observe and tell you about aspects of the culture that you may not have a chance to see or may not be entitled to see. For example, it is not likely that you will see many weddings in a village of 200 people in a year or two of fieldwork. So how can you know who will be a good informant? It is obviously important to find people who are easy to talk to and who understand what information you need. But how do you know who is knowledgeable? You can't just assume that the people you get along with have the most knowledge. (Besides, knowledge is often specialized; one person may know much more about some subjects than others.) At a minimum, you have to try out a few different people to compare what they tell you about a subject. What if they disagree? How do you know who is more trustworthy or accurate? Fortunately, formal methods have been developed to help anthropologists select the most knowledgeable informants. One method, called the cultural consensus model, relies on the principle that those things that most informants

Anthropologist Nadine Peacock doing fieldwork among the Efe in the Ituri Forest, Zaire.

agree on are probably cultural. After you establish which things appear to be cultural by asking a sample of informants the same questions about a particular cultural domain, it will be easy to discover which informants are very likely to give answers that closely match the cultural consensus. These individuals are your best bets to be the most knowledgeable in that domain.[28] It may seem paradoxical, but the most knowledgeable and helpful individuals are not necessarily "typical" individuals. Many anthropologists have pointed out that key informants are likely to feel somewhat marginal in their culture. After all, why would they want to spend so much time with the visiting anthropologist?[29]

Participant-observation is valuable for understanding some aspects of culture, particularly the things that are the most public, readily talked about, and most widely agreed upon. But more systematic methods are important too: mapping, house-to-house censuses, behavior observations (e.g., to determine how people spend their time), as well as focused interviews with a sample of informants.

Ethnographies and ethnographic articles on particular topics provide much of the essential data for all kinds of studies in cultural anthropology. To make a comparison of societies in a given region or worldwide, anthropologists would require ethnographic data on many societies. With regard to the goal of generating theory, ethnography—with its in-depth, firsthand, long-term observation—provides investigators with a wealth of descriptive material covering a wide range of phenomena. Thus, it may stimulate interpretations about the way different aspects of the culture are related to each other and to features of the environment. Ethnographers in the field have the opportunity to get to know the context of a society's customs by directly asking the people about those customs and by observing the phenomena that appear to be associated with those practices. In addition, ethnographers who develop a possible explanation for some custom can test that hunch by collecting new information related to it. In this sense, ethnographers are similar to physicians who are trying to understand why a patient has certain symptoms of illness.

Although ethnography is extremely useful for generating explanations, a field study of a single site does not generally provide sufficient data to test a hypothesis. For example, an ethnographer may think that a particular society practices *polygyny* (one man married to two or more women simultaneously) because it has more women than men. But the ethnographer could not be reasonably sure that this explanation was correct unless the results of a comparative study of a sample of societies showed that most polygynous societies have more women than men. After all, the fact that one society has both these conditions could be a historical accident rather than a result of some necessary connection between the two conditions.

Ethnography as Source Material

Ethnography is a valuable source of information for anthropologists in all the subfields of the discipline. Data from ethnographies is particularly useful in cross-cultural research and remains the single best source of information on the many aspects of culture that anthropologists seek to understand. Because undertaking ethnographic research is time-consuming and challenging, however, the available data on a particular culture may be several decades old. How, then, do we know whether the data are still valid? The answer lies in how the concept of time is treated by anthropologists. Changes in fundamental cultural beliefs, customs, and traits have occurred slowly in most cultures—a fact that explains why anthropologists use the present tense, or the so-called ethnographic present, in their written observations. It can safely be assumed that general observations will probably hold true whether the ethnography was written 20 years or 10 years ago. However, anthropologists are also aware that dramatic cultural change occurs. When using ethnographic data from several cultures, anthropologists make sure that all of the information was gathered in the same time period. That way, the data are considered valid for each of the cultures at the same point in time and a comparison can be made reliably.

Within-Culture Comparisons

Ethnographers could test a theory within one society if they decide to compare individuals, families, households, communities, or districts. The natural variability that exists can be used to create a comparison. Suppose we want to verify Whiting's assumption that longer postpartum taboos enhance the survival of babies in a society with a low-protein diet. Although almost all couples might practice a long postpartum sex taboo because it is customary, some couples might not adhere to the taboo consistently, and some couples might not conceive quickly after the taboo is lifted. So we would expect some variation in spacing between births. If we collected information on the births of each mother and the survival outcome of each birth, we would be able to compare the survival rates of children born a short time after the mother's last pregnancy with those of children born after longer intervals. A significantly higher survival rate for the births after longer intervals would support Whiting's theory. What if some communities within the society had access to more protein than others? If Whiting's theory is correct, those communities with more protein should also have a higher survival rate for babies. If there were variation in the length of the postpartum sex taboo, the communities with more protein should have shorter taboos.

Whether or not we can design intracultural tests of hypotheses depends on whether we have sufficient variability in the variables of the hypotheses. We do more often than not, and we can make use of that variation to test hypotheses within a culture.

Regional Controlled Comparisons

In a regional controlled comparison, anthropologists compare ethnographic information obtained from societies found in a particular region—societies that presumably have similar histories and occupy similar environments. Anthropologists who conduct a regional comparison are apt to be familiar with the complex of cultural features associated with that region. These features may provide a good understanding of the context of the phenomenon that is to be explained. An anthropologist's knowledge of the region under study, however, is probably not as great as the ethnographer's knowledge of a single society. Still, the anthropologist's understanding of local details is greater in a regional comparison than in a worldwide comparison. The worldwide comparison is necessarily so broad that the investigator is unlikely to know a great deal about any of the societies being compared.

The regional controlled comparison is useful not only for generating explanations but also for testing them. Because some of the societies being compared will have the characteristic that is to be explained and some will not, anthropologists can determine whether the conditions hypothesized to be related are in fact related, at least in that region. We must remember, however, that two or more conditions may be related in one region for reasons peculiar to that region. Therefore, an explanation supported in one region may not fit others.

Cross-Cultural Research

Read **the** Document: On Cross-Cultural Research

Anthropologists can generate interpretations on the basis of worldwide comparisons by looking for differences between those societies having and those lacking a particular characteristic. But the most common use of worldwide comparisons has been to test explanations. An example is Whiting's test of his theory about the adaptive functions of a long postpartum sex taboo. Recall that Whiting hypothesized that, if his theory were correct, variation in protein supplies in the adult diet should predict variation in the duration of the postpartum sex taboo. Cross-cultural researchers first identify conditions that should generally be associated if a particular theory is correct. Then they look at a worldwide sample of societies to see if the expected association generally holds true. Although it is possible for cross-cultural researchers to choose any set of societies upon which to test theories and hypotheses, it is preferable to avoid personal bias in the selection of the sample societies. One of the worst possible samples would be to choose the ethnographies from your own bookshelf (you are unlikely to have collected them in a random way). As we indicated in the sampling section, most cross-culturalists choose a published sample of societies that was not constructed for any specific hypothesis test. Two of the most widely used samples are the Standard Cross-Cultural Sample (SCCS) of 186 societies and the annually growing *eHRAF World Cultures.* Because HRAF actually contains ethnographies that are subject-indexed by paragraph, researchers can quickly find information to code a new variable across a large number of societies. In contrast, the SCCS sample contains pointers to ethnography, not ethnographies themselves. However, thousands of variables have now been coded by other researchers for this sample, so researchers who want to use data coded by others tend to use this sample[30] or the overlap between the SCCS sample and eHRAF.[31]

The advantage of cross-cultural research is that the conclusion drawn from it is probably applicable to most societies, if the sample used for testing has been more or less randomly selected and therefore is representative of the world. In other words, the results of a cross-cultural study are probably applicable to most societies and most regions, in contrast with the results of a regional comparison, which may or may not be applicable to other regions.

As we have noted, the greater the number of societies examined in a study, the less likely investigators will have detailed knowledge of the societies involved. So, if a cross-cultural test does not support a particular explanation, the investigators may not know enough about the sample societies to know how to modify the interpretation or come up with a new one. In this situation, the anthropologists may reexamine the details of one or more particular societies to stimulate fresh thinking on the subject. Another limitation of cross-cultural research, as a means of both generating and testing explanations, is that only those explanations for which the required information is generally available in ethnographies can be tested. Investigators interested in explaining something that has not been generally described must resort to some other research strategy to collect data.

Historical Research

Ethnohistory consists of studies based on descriptive materials about a single society at more than one point in time. It provides the essential data for historical studies of all types, just as ethnography provides the essential data for all nonhistorical types of research. Ethnohistorical data may consist of sources other than the ethnographic reports prepared by anthropologists—accounts by explorers, missionaries, traders, and government officials. Ethnohistorians, like historians, cannot simply assume that all the documents they find are simply descriptions of fact; they were written by very different kinds of people with very different goals and purposes. So they need to separate carefully what may be fact from what may be speculative interpretation. To reconstruct how a culture changed over hundreds of years, where the natives left few or no written accounts, anthropologists have to seek out travelers' accounts and other historical documents that were written by non-natives. Mary Helms had to do this when she decided to do fieldwork among the Miskito of Nicaragua, to reconstruct how their life had changed under the conditions of European colonialism. She was particularly interested in discovering why the Miskito were able to preserve a lot of political independence.[32]

Ethnohistorians need to analyze pieces of information from a variety of sources such as the accounts of European explorers. Pictured here is a group of Roanoke Native Americans fishing in the late 1500s. It provides ethnohistorians with good information on how these people harvested fish.

Source: John White/Copyright The British Museum.

In terms of generating and testing hypotheses, studies of single societies over time tend to be subject to the same limitations as studies of single societies confined to a single period. Like their nonhistorical counterparts, studies that concentrate on a single society observed through time are likely to generate more than one hypothesis, but they do not generally provide the opportunity to establish with reasonable certainty which of those hypotheses is correct. Cross-cultural historical studies (of which we have only a few examples thus far) suffer from the opposite limitation. They provide ample means of testing hypotheses through comparison, but, because of the necessity of working with secondhand data, they are severely constrained in their ability to generate hypotheses derived from the available data.

There is, however, one advantage to historical studies of any type. The goal of theory in cultural anthropology is to explain variation in cultural patterns, that is, to specify what conditions will favor one cultural pattern rather than another. Such specification requires us to assume that the supposed causal, or favoring, conditions antedated the pattern to be explained. Theories or explanations, then, imply a sequence of changes over time, which are the stuff of history. Therefore, if we want to come closer to an understanding of the reasons for the cultural variations we are investigating, we should examine historical sequences. They will help us determine whether the conditions we think caused various phenomena truly antedated those phenomena and thus might more reliably be said to have caused them. If we can examine historical sequences, we may be able to make sure that we do not put the cart before the horse.

The major impediment to historical research is that collecting and analyzing historical data—particularly when they come from the scattered accounts of explorers, missionaries, and traders—tends to be very time consuming. It may be more efficient to test explanations nonhistorically first to eliminate some interpretations. Only when an interpretation survives a nonhistorical test should we look to historical data to test the presumed sequence. Archaeological evidence is one answer to this problem; many archaeological sites contain evidence from several cultures that lived in that location over time. Even when sites contain evidence for only one period of time, sites dating from different times can be compared to examine historical trends.

2.5 Describe the four kinds of evidence that archaeologists and paleoanthropologists find and how they analyze it.

Studying the Distant Past

Culture history A history of the cultures that lived in a given area over time. Until the 1950s, building such culture histories was a primary goal of archaeological research.

One goal of archaeological research is the description or reconstruction of what happened in the past. Archaeologists attempt to determine how people lived in a particular place at a particular time, and when and how their lifestyles changed. Also of interest, of course, is whether new populations carrying new cultures arrived, or whether people with a particular culture moved out of a given area. Creating histories of cultures and their changes over time is called, simply enough, **culture history**. Doing culture history was the primary goal of archaeology until the 1950s.[33]

A second major goal of archaeological research, and one that has become the primary goal since the 1950s, is testing specific explanations about human evolution and behavior. In part, this change in focus results from our increased knowledge about the past—the culture history of many areas is well known today. But this change is also due to changes going on in anthropology as a whole. Historical particularism was dominant in American anthropology until the 1950s. It suggested that variation in human cultures was best explained by considering the specific historical developments of particular cultures. Like the purpose of historical particularism, the purpose of culture history was to trace historical developments. After the 1950s, a variety of new approaches arose in anthropology, most of them sharing the idea that the environment and how humans use it actively shapes cultures and mostly explains cultural variability. Archaeology became a key tool for anthropologists attempting to understand how changes in the ways humans used the environment explained variation in human cultures. One of the results of this focus on hypothesis testing and human use of the environment was research on agricultural origins. Another was a concern with the rise of cities and states, which radically transformed human use of the environment. In addition to testing explanations, archaeology has a primary role within anthropology in its attempt to identify and understand general trends and patterns in human biological and cultural evolution. As we discussed earlier, cross-cultural research (comparative ethnography) has this goal as well. But only archaeology is able to look through long stretches of time and directly examine evolutionary trends. A major emphasis in paleoanthropology is demonstrating long-term trends and patterns in the biological evolution of humans. These trends and patterns help us understand how and why we have come to be the way we are.

Watch **the** Video: Pathways to Archaeology

Archaeologists and paleoanthropologists rely on four kinds of evidence to learn about the past: *artifacts, ecofacts, fossils,* and *features.*

Artifacts

Artifact Any object made by a human.

Anything made or modified by humans is an **artifact**. The book you are reading now, the chair you are sitting in, the pen you are taking notes with are all artifacts. In fact, we are surrounded by artifacts, most of which we will lose or throw away. That is exactly how things enter what we call the "archaeological record." Think about it: How much garbage do you produce in a day? What kinds of things do you throw away? Mostly paper, probably, but also wood (from the ice cream bar you ate at lunch), plastic (like the pen that ran out of ink last night), and even metal (the dull blade on your razor). Into the garbage they go and out to the dump or landfill. Under the right conditions, many of those items will survive for future archaeologists to find. Most of the artifacts that make up the archaeological record are just this kind of mundane waste—the accumulated garbage of daily life that archaeologists may recover and examine to reconstruct what daily life was like long ago. By far the most common artifacts from the past are stone tools, which archaeologists call **lithics**. Indeed, lithics are the only kind of artifact available for 99 percent of human history.

Lithics The technical name for tools made from stone.

Ecofacts

Ecofacts are natural objects that humans have used or affected. A good example is the bone from animals that people have eaten. These bones are somewhat like artifacts, but they haven't been made or modified by humans, just used and discarded by them. Another example is pollen found at archaeological sites. Because humans bring plants back to their houses to use, pollens from many plants are commonly found. These pollens may not have come from the same location. The only reason they are together is that they have been brought together by human use. Other examples are the remains of insect and animal pests that associate with humans, such as cockroaches and mice. Their remains are found in sites because they associate with humans and survive by taking advantage of the conditions that humans create. Their presence is in part caused by human presence, and thus they are also considered ecofacts.

Ecofacts Natural items that humans have used; things such as the remains of animals eaten by humans or plant pollens found on archaeological sites are examples of ecofacts.

Fossils

Fossils, although rare, are particularly informative about human biological evolution. **Fossils** may be impressions of an insect or leaf on a muddy surface that now is stone. A fossil may also consist of the actual hardened remains of an animal's skeletal structure. When an animal dies, the organic matter that made up its body begins to deteriorate. The teeth and skeletal structure are composed largely of inorganic mineral salts, and soon they are all that remains. Under most conditions, these parts eventually deteriorate too. But once in a great while, conditions are favorable for preservation—for instance, when volcanic ash, limestone, or highly mineralized groundwater is present to form a high-mineral environment. If the remains are buried under such circumstances, the minerals in the ground may become bound into the structure of the teeth or bone, hardening the remains and thus making them less likely to deteriorate.

Fossils The hardened remains or impressions of plants and animals that lived in the past.

But we don't have fossil remains of everything that lived in the past, and sometimes we only have fragments from one or a few individuals. So the fossil record is very incomplete. For example, Robert Martin estimates that the earth has probably seen 6,000 primate species; remains of only 3 percent of those species have been found. It is hardly surprising that primate paleontologists cannot identify most of the evolutionary connections between early and later forms. The task is particularly difficult with small mammals, such as the early primates, which are less likely than large animals to be preserved in the fossil record.[34]

Features

Features are kinds of artifacts, but archaeologists distinguish them from other artifacts because they cannot be easily removed from an archaeological site. Hearths are good examples. When humans build a fire on bare ground, the soil becomes heated and is changed—all the water is driven out of it and its crystalline structure is broken down and reformed. When archaeologists find a hearth, what exactly is found? An area of hard, reddish, even slightly magnetic soil, often surrounded by charcoal and ash. Here, then, is an artifact—an object of human manufacture. But it would be very hard, if not impossible, for archaeologists to take the hearth back to the lab for study like a lithic or ceramic. A hearth is really an intrinsic feature of a site—hence the name *feature*.

Features Artifacts of human manufacture that cannot be removed from an archaeological site. Hearths, storage pits, and buildings are examples of features.

Hearths are common features, but the most common features by far are called *pits*. Pits are simply holes dug by humans that are later filled with garbage or eroded soil. They are usually fairly easy to distinguish because the garbage or soil they are filled with is often different in color and texture from the soil the pit was dug into. *Living floors* are another

Vietnamese archaeologists expose the remains of the ancient citadel of Hanoi, preserved below the modern city.

common type of feature. These are the places where humans lived and worked. The soils in these locations are often compacted through human activity and are full of minute pieces of garbage—seeds, small stone flakes, beads, and the like—that became embedded in the floor. A large or very deep area of such debris is called a *midden*. Middens are often the remains of garbage dumps or areas repeatedly used over long periods of time, such as caves. Finally, *buildings* are common features on archaeological sites. These can range from the remains of stone rings that once held down the sides of tents to palaces built of stones that had been shaped and fitted together. Even the remains of wooden houses (or parts of them) have been preserved under some conditions. Features can be a diverse array of things that provide lots of information about the past.

Finding the Evidence of the Past

Sites Locations where the material remains of human activity have been preserved in a way that archaeologists or paleoanthropologists can recover them.

Evidence of the past is all around us, but finding it is not always easy or productive. Archaeologists and paleoanthropologists usually restrict their searches to what are called *sites*. **Sites** are known or suspected locations of past human activity that contain a record of that activity. Sites can be small, such as places where humans camped for perhaps only one night, or as large as ancient cities.

Sites are created when the remnants of human activity are covered or buried by some natural process. The most dramatic process is volcanic activity. The most impressive example of this must be Pompeii, an entire city that was buried in the eruption of Mount Vesuvius in A.D. 79. Today, archaeologists are digging out the city and finding the remains of ancient life just as it was left in the moments before the eruption.[35] Less dramatic processes are the natural processes of dirt accumulation and erosion. Wind- or water-borne soil and debris can cover a site either quickly (as in a flood) or over a long period of time, preserving intact the artifacts, ecofacts, fossils, and features left by humans. Finally, the processes through which soils are built up can also bury artifacts, ecofacts, fossils, and features in a way that allows archaeologists to uncover them later. In forests, for example, falling leaves cover the locations where humans camped. Over time, the leaves decay and build up soil, covering the remains of the human encampment slowly but completely over many years.

Because humans often reuse good locations to live and work in, many sites contain the remains of numerous human occupations. The most valuable sites to archaeologists and paleoanthropologists are those in which the burial processes worked quickly enough that each use of the site is clearly separated from the previous one. Such sites are called **stratified**; each layer, or *stratum,* of human occupation is separate, like a layer in a layer cake. Not only do stratified sites allow archaeologists or paleoanthropologists to distinguish the sequence of site occupations, but the strata themselves provide a way to know the relative ages of the occupations—earlier occupations will always be below later ones.

Stratified An archaeological deposit that contains successive layers or strata.

There is no single method of finding sites, and indeed many sites are found by happenstance. But when archaeologists and paleoanthropologists want to go out and find sites, they typically employ one of two basic methods: pedestrian survey and remote sensing. *Pedestrian survey* is what the name suggests—walking around and looking for sites. But archaeologists and paleoanthropologists can use sampling and systematic surveying methods to reduce the area to be covered on foot. *Remote sensing* techniques allow archaeologists and paleoanthropologists to find archaeological deposits from a remote location, usually the current surface of the ground beneath which the archaeological deposits are buried. Most remote sensing techniques are borrowed from exploration geology and are the same ones geologists use to find mineral or oil deposits. They typically involve the measurement of minute variations in phenomena like the earth's magnetic or gravitational field, or changes in an electric current or pulse of energy directed into the ground. When these subtle changes, called *anomalies,* are located, more detailed exploration can be done to map the extent and depth of the buried archaeological deposits.

Watch **the** Video: Being an Archaeologist

Whether they are identified by pedestrian survey or remote sensing, there is only one way to recover archaeological deposits once they are found them—by *excavation.* **Excavation** itself is a complex process with two goals: (1) to find every scrap of evidence (or a statistically representative sample) about the past that a given site holds and (2) to record the horizontal and vertical location of that evidence with precision. Archaeologists and paleoanthropologists have developed many excavation strategies and techniques to accomplish these goals, but all of them involve the careful removal of the archaeological deposits; the recovery of artifacts, ecofacts, fossils, and features from the soil in which those deposits have been buried; and the detailed recording of where each artifact, ecofact, fossil, and feature was located on the site.

Excavation The careful removal of the archaeological deposits; the recovery of artifacts, ecofacts, fossils, and features from the soil in which those deposits have been buried.

To date, no one has figured out a way to recover artifacts, ecofacts, fossils, and features from a site without destroying the site in the process, and this is one of the strange ironies of archaeological research. As we discuss shortly, the relationships between and among artifacts, ecofacts, fossils, and features are of most interest to archaeologists, and precisely these relationships are destroyed when archaeologists remove them from a site. For this reason, most excavation by professional archaeologists today is done only when a site is threatened with destruction, and then only by highly trained personnel using rigorous techniques. Archaeologists and paleoanthropologists collect data in basically the same ways, with one important difference. Archaeologists are most concerned with recovering intact features, whereas paleoanthropologists are most concerned with recovering intact fossils. This leads to some differences in approaches to collecting data, particularly where to look. So archaeologists tend to seek out undisturbed sites where intact features can be found. In contrast, disturbances are a plus for paleoanthropologists, because disturbed sites may make finding fossils easier—they may be eroding out of the surface of the ground and be easily visible without digging. This doesn't mean archaeologists never excavate disturbed sites, because they do. And paleoanthropologists have sometimes made important discoveries by excavating undisturbed sites.[36]

Putting It All in Context

You might have gained the impression from our discussion that archaeologists and paleoanthropologists analyze artifacts, ecofacts, fossils, and features as individual objects,

Perspectives on Gender

Women in the Shell Mound Archaic

How we can learn about and understand gender roles in prehistoric cultures? How is gender preserved in the archaeological record? Information about gender roles can be recovered if one is aware of how particular kinds of material culture are associated ethnographically with particular gender roles and with changes in them over time. Archaeologists argue that such an awareness leads not only to a better understanding of gender in prehistory but can also lead to a fuller understanding of prehistoric cultures overall.

An example is Cheryl Claassen's work on the Shell Mound Archaic culture of the Tennessee River Valley. The Shell Mound Archaic peoples were hunter and gatherers who lived between about 5,500 and 3,000 years ago. The most distinctive feature of the Shell Mound Archaic is the large mounds of mollusk shells they constructed for burying their dead. Tens of thousands of shells were piled together to create these mounds. Yet, around 3,000 years ago, shellfishing and thus the creation of shell burial mounds stopped abruptly. Claassen wondered why.

Artist's interpretation of a Shell Mound Archaic camp.

Suggested explanations include climate change, overexploitation of shellfish, and the migration of shellfishing peoples from the area. None has proven wholly satisfactory. In contemporary cultures, women and children typically do the shellfishing, and Claassen decided to approach the problem through the perspective of women's workloads. The end of shellfishing would have meant that women would have had a lot of free time—free time that could have been put to use in some other way. Did some other activities become more important, so that women's labor was needed more for those other tasks?

Women's labor might have been redirected toward domesticated crops. There is archaeological evidence that about 3,000 years ago several productive crops that required intensive labor came into wide use. Women were likely the ones burdened with such work. They not only would have harvested these crops but also would have been the ones to process and prepare meals from them. Thus, the emergence of agricultural economies would have required women to undertake new labor in food production and processing that may well have forced them to stop engaging in other tasks, like shellfishing, especially if the new tasks produced a larger food supply.

The development of agricultural activities might also have brought about changes in ritual and ceremonialism. The shell burial mounds were clearly central to Shell Mound Archaic death ceremonies. Later societies in the region buried their dead in earthen mounds. Could this be a reflection of the new importance dirt had in an emerging agricultural economy? If so, what role did women play in ceremonies of death and burial? If they were no longer the providers of the raw materials needed for burial, does that mean their status in society as a whole changed?

We may never know exactly why the Shell Mound Archaic disappeared or how women's work and women's roles in society changed. But as Claassen points out, taking a gender perspective provides new avenues along which to pursue answers to these questions as well as interesting new questions to pursue.

Sources: Claassen 1991, 2009.

Context The relationships between and among artifacts, ecofacts, fossils, and features.

separate from one another. Nothing could be farther from the truth. In fact, putting these materials in context with one another is really what archaeology and paleoanthropology are all about. **Context** is how and why the artifacts and other materials are related. Artifacts, ecofacts, fossils, and features in isolation may be beautiful or interesting by themselves, but only when they are placed in context with the other materials found on a site are we able to "read" and tell the story of the past.

To illustrate this point, let's consider a set of letters that were found separately: A E G I M N N. They are arranged here in alphabetical order, the way a set of beautiful artifacts might be arranged in a museum display in order of size. Do these arrangements tell us anything? No. What if we knew something about the relationships between and among these letters—their context? What if, for example, we knew that the *M* was the first letter found, and that the *A* and *E* were found next to the *M*, but in reverse order, that one *N* was found between the *E* and *I*, and that the other *N* was found between the *I* and the *G*? Knowing in what context the letters were found would tell us that the letters should be arranged like this: *M E A N I N G*. And meaning is exactly what context gives to artifacts, ecofacts, fossils, and features.

Dating the Evidence from the Past

An important, indeed vital, part of putting artifacts and other materials into context is putting them in chronological order. To reconstruct the evolutionary history of the primates, for example, one must know how old primate fossils are. For some time, relative dating methods were the only methods available. The last half century has seen important advances in absolute dating, including techniques that allow the dating of the earliest phases of primate evolution. **Relative dating** is used to determine the age of a specimen or deposit relative to another specimen or deposit. **Absolute dating**, or **chronometric dating**, is used to measure how old a specimen or deposit is in years.

Relative Dating Methods The earliest, and still the most commonly used, method of relative dating is based on **stratigraphy**, the study of how different rock or soil formations are laid down in successive layers or strata (see Figure 2.1). Older layers are generally deeper or lower than more recent layers. Indicator artifacts or ecofacts are used to establish a stratigraphic sequence for the relative dating of new finds. These **indicator artifacts or ecofacts** are items of human manufacture or remains from animals and plants that spread widely over short periods of time, or that disappeared or changed fairly rapidly. Different artifacts and ecofacts are used as indicators of relative age in different areas of the world. In Africa, elephants, pigs, and horses have been particularly important in establishing stratigraphic sequences. Figure 2.1 shows the stratigraphy of Olduvai Gorge, an important site where early human fossils have been found. The stratigraphy here was established in part on the basis of fossil pigs.[37] The various species of pig in the successive strata are different, allowing archaeologists or paleoanthropologists to differentiate the strata based on the species found within them. Once the stratigraphy of an area is established, the relative ages of two different fossils, or features, in the same or different sites are indicated by the associated indicator artifacts or ecofacts. Major transitions in indicator artifacts or ecofacts define the epochs and larger units of geologic time. The dates of the boundaries between such units are estimated by absolute dating, described in the next section.

If a site has been disturbed, stratigraphy will not be a satisfactory way to determine relative age. As noted earlier, remains from different periods may be washed or blown together by water or wind. Or a landslide may superimpose an earlier layer on a later layer. Still, it may be possible using absolute, or chronometric, dating methods to estimate the relative age of the different fossils found together in a disturbed site.

Absolute, or Chronometric, Dating Methods Many of the absolute dating methods are based on the decay of a radioactive isotope. Because the rate of decay is known, the age of the specimen can be estimated, within a range of possible error. **Radiocarbon**, or **carbon-14 (^{14}C), dating** is perhaps the most popularly known method of determining the absolute age of a specimen. It is based on the principle that all living matter possesses a certain amount of a radioactive form of carbon (carbon-14, or ^{14}C). Radioactive carbon, produced when nitrogen-14 is bombarded by cosmic rays, is absorbed from the air by plants and then ingested by animals that

Relative dating A method of dating fossils that determines the age of a specimen or deposit relative to a known specimen or deposit.

Absolute dating A method of dating fossils in which the actual age of a deposit or specimen is measured. Also known as **chronometric dating**.

Chronometric dating See **Absolute dating**.

Stratigraphy The study of how different rock formations and fossils are laid down in successive layers or strata. Older layers are generally deeper or lower than more recent layers.

Indicator artifacts and ecofacts Items that changed relatively rapidly and which, thus, can be used to indicate the relative age of associated items.

Radiocarbon (or carbon-14, ^{14}C) dating A dating method uses the decay of carbon-14 to date organic remains. It is reliable for dating once-living matter up to 50,000 years old.

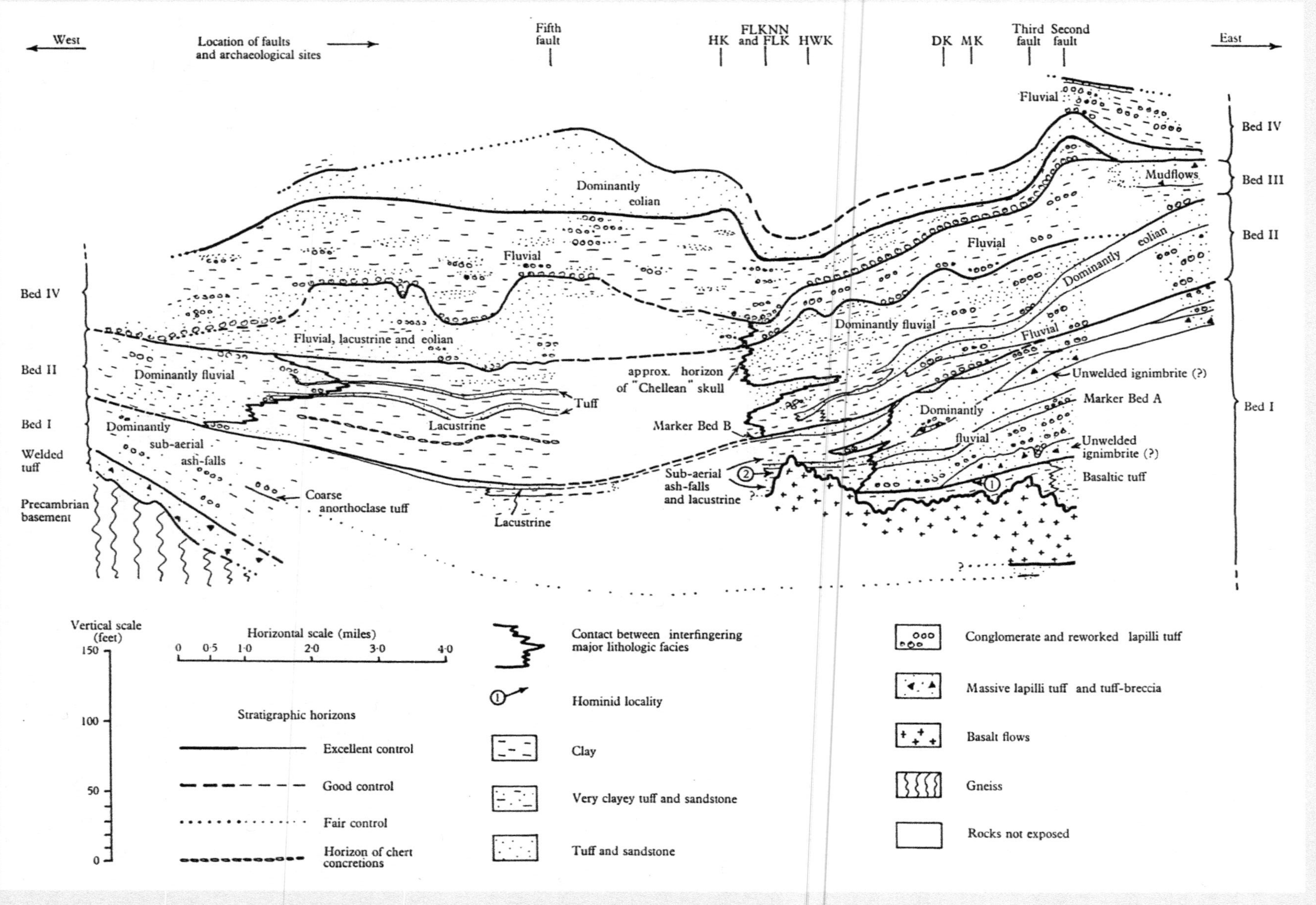

FIGURE 2.1 **Stratigraphy of Beds I-IV along Olduvai Main Gorge**

Notice how complex the four stratigraphic layers are—each has numerous layers of soil and rock within them. Index fossils, particularly pigs, along with a series of potassium-argon dates, allowed the researchers to identify the four major strata of the site, which correspond to four major periods of human occupation. Reprinted by permission of Cambridge University Press. Copyright © 1965.

Source: Leakey 1965.

eat the plants (see Figure 2.2). After an organism dies, it no longer takes in any of the radioactive carbon. Carbon-14 decays at a slow but steady pace and reverts to nitrogen-14. (By *decays,* we mean that the ^{14}C gives off a certain number of beta radiations per minute.) The rate at which the carbon decays—its **half-life**—is known: ^{14}C has a half-life of 5,730 years. In other words, half of the original amount of ^{14}C in organic matter will have disintegrated 5,730 years after the organism's death; half of the remaining ^{14}C will have disintegrated after another 5,730 years; and so on. After about 50,000 years, the amount of ^{14}C remaining in the organic matter is too small to permit reliable dating.

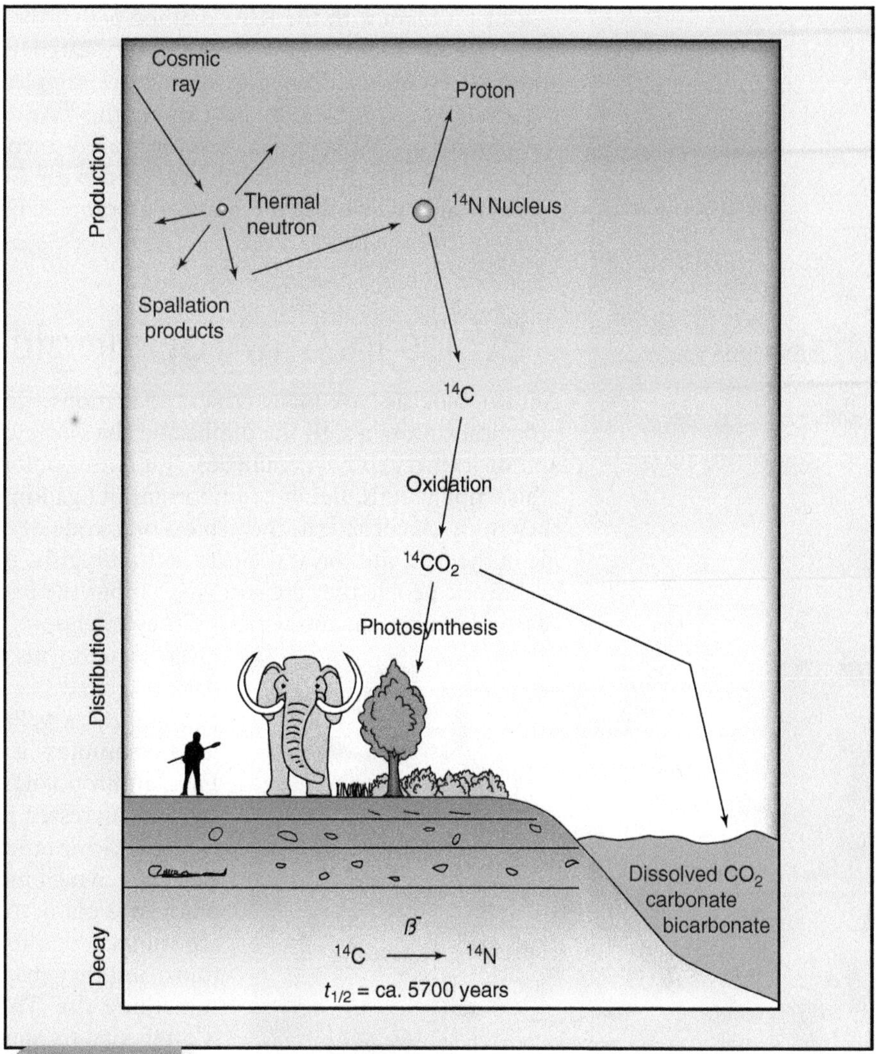

FIGURE 2.2 The Carbon-14 Cycle

Source: Taylor and Aitken 1997.

To discover how long an organism has been dead—that is, to determine how much ^{14}C is left in the organism and therefore how old it is—we either count the number of beta radiations given off per minute per gram of material or use a particle accelerator to measure the actual amount of ^{14}C in a sample. Modern ^{14}C emits about 15 beta radiations per minute per gram of material, but ^{14}C that is 5,730 years old emits only half that amount (the half-life of ^{14}C) per minute per gram. So, if a sample of some organism gives off 7.5 radiations a minute per gram, which is only half the amount given off by modern ^{14}C, the organism must be 5,730 years old. Similarly, because the amount of ^{14}C in a sample slowly declines over time, the atoms in a sample can be sent through a particle accelerator to separate them by weight (the lighter ^{12}C accelerates faster than the heavier ^{14}C) and measure the actual amount of each. This method, called accelerator mass spectrometry (AMS), is more accurate than the beta radiation method, requires only a very small sample of material, and provides a way to date specimens that are up to 80,000 years old.[38]

Half-life The time it takes for half of the atoms of a radioactive substance to decay into atoms of a different substance.

Another very common absolute dating technique based on radioactive decay uses potassium-40 (^{40}K), a radioactive form of potassium that decays at an established rate and forms argon-40 (^{40}Ar). The half-life of ^{40}K is a known quantity, so the age of a material containing potassium can be measured by the amount of ^{40}K compared with the amount of ^{40}Ar it contains.[39] Radioactive potassium's (^{40}K's) half-life is very long—1,330 million years. This means that **potassium-argon (K-Ar) dating** may be used to date samples from 5,000 years up to 3 billion years old.

Potassium-argon (K-Ar) dating A chronometric dating method that uses the rate of decay of a radioactive form of potassium (^{40}K) into argon (^{40}Ar) to date samples from 5,000 years to 3 billion years old. The K-Ar method dates the minerals and rocks in a deposit, not the fossils themselves.

The K-Ar method is used to date potassium-rich minerals in rock, not the fossils that may be found in the rock. A very high temperature, such as occurs in a volcanic event, drives off any original argon in the material. The amount of argon that accumulates afterward from the decay of radioactive potassium is directly related to the amount of time since the volcanic event. This type of dating has been extremely useful in East Africa, where volcanic events have occurred frequently since the Miocene, which began 24 million years ago. If the material to be dated is not rich in potassium, or the area did not experience any high-temperature events, other methods of absolute dating are required.

One problem with the K-Ar method is that the amounts of potassium and argon must be measured on different rock samples; researchers must assume that the potassium and argon are evenly distributed in all the rock samples from a particular stratum. Researchers got around this problem by developing the **^{40}Ar-^{39}Ar dating** method. After measuring the amount of ^{40}Ar, a nuclear reactor is used to convert another kind of argon, ^{39}Ar, to potassium so that the potassium-argon ratio can be measured from the same sample.[40]

There are many other methods of absolute dating; indeed, new methods are being developed all the time.

2.6 Describe the ethical requirements of anthropological research.

Ethics in Anthropological Research

Anthropologists have many ethical obligations—to the people they study, to their anthropological colleagues, to the public and the world community, and even to their employers and their own and host countries. But anthropologists agree that, should a conflict arise in ethical obligations, the most important obligation is to protect the interests of the people they study. According to the profession's code of ethics, anthropologists should tell people in the field site (or, if they are archaeologists, people who are direct descendants of the prehistoric people they are studying) about the research, and they should respect the right of people to remain anonymous if they so choose.[41] For this reason, informants are often given pseudonyms, or fake names; many anthropologists have extended this principle to using a fake name for the community as well. But the decision to create a fake name for a community is questionable in many circumstances.[42] First, anthropologists "stick out," and it is not hard for anyone interested to figure out where they lived and worked. Governments may have to be asked for research clearance, which means that they know where the anthropologist is going to do the fieldwork. Second, people who are studied are often proud of their place and their customs, and they may be insulted if their community is called something else. Third, important geographic information is often vital to understanding the community. You have to reveal if it is located at the confluence of two major rivers or if it is the trading center of the region. Lastly, it may be difficult for future anthropologists to conduct follow-up studies if the community is disguised. Of course, if a community were truly in danger, there would be no question that an anthropologist has an obligation to try to protect it.

Archaeologists must be aware of the effects of their work on descendant communities. Many people, for example, find the excavation of ancestor's remains to be offensive.

Honest, objective reporting is also an obligation to the anthropological profession, to the public at large, and to the observed community. But suppose a custom or trait that the community views as reasonable is considered objectionable by outsiders? Such customs could range from acts that outsiders consider criminal, such as infanticide, to those that are considered repugnant, such as eating dogs. Archaeologists have caused outrage by presenting evidence of cannibalism in ancient populations.[43] An anthropologist may believe that publication of the information could bring harm to the population. Kim Hill and Magdalena Hurtado faced this situation when they realized that infanticide rates were high in the group they studied in South America. They did not want to play up their findings, nor did they want to dissimulate. After they met with community leaders to discuss the situation, they agreed not to publish their findings in Spanish to minimize the possibility that the local media or neighboring groups might learn of their findings.[44]

Everyday decisions like how to compensate people for their time are not easy either. Nowadays, many if not most informants expect to be paid or receive gifts. But in the early days of anthropology, in places where money was not an important part of the native economy, the decision to pay people was not a clear ethical choice. If money is rare, paying people increases the importance of money in that economy. Even nonmonetary gifts can increase inequalities or create jealousies. On the other hand, doing nothing by way of compensation doesn't seem right either. As an alternative, some anthropologists try to find some community project that they can help with—that way, everyone benefits. This is not to say that the anthropologists are necessarily a burden on the community. People often like to talk about their customs, and they may want others to appreciate their way of life. And anthropologists are often amusing. They may ask "funny" questions, and when they try to say or do customary things, they often do them all wrong. Probably every anthropologist has been laughed at sometimes in the field.

Archaeologists must always be concerned with the ethics of their work when undertaking or reporting the results of their research. Archaeology does not simply describe past cultures; it can also have a profound effect on living peoples. For example, many people find the idea of archaeologists excavating, cleaning, and preserving the remains of ancestors to be offensive. Therefore, archaeologists must be sensitive to the desires and beliefs of the populations that descend from the ones they are researching. In addition, artifacts from some ancient cultures are in great demand by art and antiquities collectors, and archaeological finds can lead to uncontrolled looting if archaeologists are not careful about how and to whom they report their discoveries. Wholesale ransacking of ancient cemeteries in some parts of China, for example, started because new archaeological discoveries led Chinese antiquities to become increasingly popular among collectors and hence increasingly valuable to those able to discover them.[45]

Although it is the ethical responsibility of archaeologists to consult with descendant populations and to be careful about how archaeological finds are reported, it is also an ethical responsibility of archaeologists to present the results of their work to the general public. Publishing archaeological results increases public awareness about the past and the importance of historic preservation. If people know how much can be learned from the archaeological record, they may be less likely to destroy it or to support those who destroy it for personal gain. Of course, when archaeologists excavate sites, they also destroy some of the context of the artifacts, ecofacts, fossils, and features found in the sites. But if they leave some of the sites unexcavated, they are preserving them (at least partially) for future investigation. To offset their partial destruction, archaeologists are ethically obligated to publish the results of their work. Reporting the results of archaeological research, therefore, plays a central role in both archaeological research and archaeological ethics.

^{40}Ar-^{39}Ar dating Used in conjunction with potassium-argon dating, this method gets around the problem of needing different rock samples to estimate potassium and argon. A nuclear reactor is used to convert the ^{39}Ar to ^{39}K, on the basis of which the amount of ^{40}K can be estimated. In this way, both argon and potassium can be estimated from the same rock sample.

Read **the** Document: Preserving Iraq's Battered Heritage

Summary and Review

Explanations

2.1 Define "explanation" and discuss its role in anthropology.

- Scientists try to achieve two kinds of explanations—associations (observed relationships between two or more variables) and theories (explanations of associations).
- A theory is more complicated than an association. Some concepts or implications in a theory are unobservable; an association is based entirely on observations.
- Theories can never be proved with absolute certainty. There is always the possibility that some implication, some derivable hypothesis, will not be confirmed by future research.

- A theory may be rejectable through the method of falsification. Scientists derive predictions that should be true if the theory is correct. If the predictions turn out to be incorrect, scientists are obliged to conclude that something may be wrong with the theory.

> ? How do associations and theory differ as explanations?

Brief History of Theoretical Approaches

2.2 Describe some of the main theoretical approaches in anthropology.

- The prevailing evolutionary theory during the 19th century was based on a belief that culture generally evolves in a uniform and progressive manner.
- During the early 20th century, the leading opponent of early evolutionism was Franz Boas, whose historical particularism rejected the idea that universal laws governed all human culture. Boas championed collecting as much data as possible, from which laws would supposedly emerge.
- Later in the 20th century, the idea of cultural ecology, the analysis of interactions between a culture and its environment, began a debate about whether biological ecology should be separated from cultural ecology. Cultural ecologists ask how a particular culture trait may be adaptive in its environment.
- Today anthropologists who refer to themselves as evolutionary or behavioral ecologists explore how particular characteristics may be adaptive for an individual in a given environment (cultural ecologists tend to focus on the group or culture more than the individual). However, dual-inheritance theory, gives much more weight to culture as part of the evolutionary process. Dual inheritance refers to both genes and culture playing different but nonetheless important and interactive roles in transmitting traits to future generations.
- Influenced by literary criticism, a variety of "interpretive" approaches developed beginning in the 1960s. For many interpretive anthropologists, the goal of anthropology is to understand what it means to be a person living in a particular culture, rather than to explain why cultures vary. The task of understanding meaning, these scholars claim, cannot be achieved scientifically.
- Scientific anthropologists do not agree that explanation is not achievable and have developed many techniques for minimizing bias and increasing the objectivity of measurement.

> ? What are some examples of different theoretical approaches in anthropology?

Evidence: Testing Explanations

2.3 Explain the process of operationalization, the importance of measurement, and the value of statistical evaluation in testing explanations.

- A theory needs to be tested to determine whether it is likely to be correct. A general strategy is to predict what one would expect to find if a particular theory were correct and then to conduct an investigation to see whether the prediction is generally consistent with the data.
- A satisfactory test specifies operationally how to measure the variables involved in the relationships that are expected to exist so other researchers can try to replicate, or repeat, the results.
- Tests of predictions should use samples that are unbiased and representative of the whole. The most objective way to obtain a representative sample is to select the sample cases randomly, but sometimes anthropologists must depend on a sample that is not random.
- The results of tests are evaluated by statistical methods that assign probability values to the results. These values make it possible to distinguish between probably true and probably accidental results.

> ? What are the main steps in testing explanations?

Types of Research in Anthropology

2.4 Differentiate the types of research in anthropology.

- The types of research in anthropology can be classified according to two criteria: (1) the spatial scope of the study and (2) the temporal scope of the study.
- In cultural anthropology, the basic research methods within the two main criteria are (a) ethnographic fieldwork and ethnohistory, (b) historical and nonhistorical regional controlled comparisons, and (c) historical and nonhistorical cross-cultural research.

> ? What are the main types of research in anthropology?

Studying the Distant Past

2.5 Describe the four types of evidence that archaeologists and paleoanthropologists find and how they analyze it.

- Three goals of archaeology are (1) to understand a culture's history, (2) to test specific explanations about human evolution and behavior, and (3) to identify and understand general trends and patterns in human biological and cultural evolution.
- Archaeologists and paleoanthropologists collect four basic types of evidence about the past: artifacts, ecofacts, fossils, and features. Artifacts are any objects made by humans. Ecofacts are natural objects that humans use or modify. Fossils are the preserved remains of ancient plants and animals. Features are artifacts that cannot be removed from archaeological sites.
- Archaeological sites are locations where the evidence of the past has been preserved. Sites are found through pedestrian survey or remote sensing, and artifacts, ecofacts, fossils, and features are recovered from sites through excavation.
- A key part of any archaeological survey or excavation is the preservation of context—the relationships between and among artifacts, ecofacts, fossils, and features.
- Accurate techniques for dating archaeological material contribute significantly to determining context. Relative dating techniques determine the age of archaeological materials relative to other materials of known ages. Absolute dating techniques determine the age of the archaeological deposits or materials themselves.

What are examples of each kind of evidence that might be found at an archaeological site?

Ethics in Anthropological Research

2.6 Describe the ethical requirements of anthropological research.

- Anthropologists must inform the people they are studying (or the descendants of those people) about their work and its purpose.
- Anthropologists must ensure that their work does no harm and that the confidentiality of people they study is protected. They must be particularly careful to identify appropriate and nondisruptive ways to compensate groups who participate in studies.
- Archaeologists must present the results of their work to the general public. Publishing archaeological results increases public awareness about the past and the importance of historic preservation.

Give an example of unethical behavior for an anthropologist and then a different example of ethical behavior. Explain why each is either unethical or ethical.

Think on it

1. Why are **theories** important?
2. Can a **unique event** be explained?
3. How does measurement go beyond **observation**?
4. Why is **scientific understanding** always uncertain?

CHAPTER 12

Culture and Culture Change

LEARNING OBJECTIVES

- 12.1 Discuss the concept of culture as used in anthropology, its salient properties, and controversies surrounding the concept of culture.
- 12.2 Describe direct and indirect cultural constraints and how they relate to norms.
- 12.3 Identify attitudes that hinder the study of cultures.
- 12.4 Critically assess the concept of cultural relativism.
- 12.5 Describe the methods by which anthropologists describe cultures.
- 12.6 Explain why culture is integrated or patterned.
- 12.7 Describe and give examples of how cultures change through discovery and invention, diffusion, and acculturation.
- 12.8 Relate culture change to the process of adaptation to a changing environment.
- 12.9 Evaluate the problems and opportunities posed by globalization.
- 12.10 Describe and give examples of ethnogenesis, or the emergence of new cultures.
- 12.11 Characterize what anthropologists predict about future cultural diversity.

Perhaps all of us consider ourselves to be unique, with a set of opinions, preferences, habits, and quirks distinct from anyone else's. Indeed, all individuals are unique, and yet most people also share a set of preferences, beliefs, and habits that characterize the society in which they live. People who live in North America, for example, are likely to feel that eating dog meat is wrong, believe that bacteria or viruses cause illness, and habitually sleep on a bed that consists of a mattress supported on some kind of base. Such shared ideas and behaviors are part of what anthropologists mean when they refer to culture. Most people rarely question their shared assumptions and traits until they encounter others who have quite different beliefs and customs. Thus, North Americans may never consider the possibility of eating dog meat until they learn that it is commonly eaten in some societies. (Likewise, people in some other societies may be equally repelled or consider taboo some kinds of meat that North Americans eat). North Americans may realize that their belief in germs is cultural once they see that people in some societies believe that witchcraft or evil spirits cause illness. They may understand that sleeping on a bed is a custom when they learn that people in many societies sleep on the floor or on the ground and, indeed, cook and converse sitting on the floor or ground. When people start to compare and contrast other cultures with their own to learn how they are different, they are beginning to think anthropologically. In fact, anthropology began as a profession when Europeans began to explore and move to faraway places, and they were confronted with the striking facts of cultural variation.

Anthropologists also want to understand how and why cultures change. Most of us are aware that "times have changed," especially when we compare our lives with those of our parents. Some of the most dramatic changes have occurred in women's roles and in attitudes about sex and marriage. Advances in technology have also led to cultural changes that could not have been foreseen. Culture change is not unusual; throughout history, humans have replaced or altered customary behaviors and attitudes as their needs changed. Just as no individual is immortal, no particular cultural pattern is impervious to change. Culture change may be gradual or rapid. Within the last 600 years or so, the pace of change has accelerated, largely because of contact between different societies. Exploration, colonization, trade, and more recently multinational business, the Internet, and social media have led to an economic and cultural interconnectedness among the world's cultures that we call globalization. Anthropologists want to assess not only the impact of these changes on cultures but what they mean for the future of cultural diversity.

Defining Culture

12.1 Discuss the concept of culture as used in anthropology, its salient properties, and controversies surrounding the concept of culture.

In everyday usage, the word *culture* had long referred to a desirable quality we can acquire by attending a sufficient number of plays and concerts and visiting art museums and galleries. But today the anthropological meaning of the term may be more common. People now routinely refer to a particular society's culture, such as American culture, a subgroup's culture, such as Chinese-American, or a transcultural phenomenon, such as "youth culture" and "online culture." In each case, *culture* refers, as Ralph Linton explained, "to the total way of life," from the most mundane activities, such as washing dishes, to the more profound aspects of life. From the point of view of the social scientist, then, "every human being is cultured, in the sense of participating in some culture or other."[1]

Linton emphasized common habits and behaviors in what he considered culture, but the totality of life also includes not just what people do but also how they commonly think and feel. As we define it here, **culture** is the set of learned behaviors and ideas (including beliefs, attitudes, values, and ideals) that are characteristic of a particular society or other social group. Behaviors can also produce products or *material culture*—things such as houses, musical instruments, and tools that are the products of customary behavior. In anthropology, all aspects of culture are important.

Culture The set of learned behaviors and ideas (including beliefs, attitudes, values, and ideals) that are characteristic of a particular society or other social group.

Society A group of people who occupy a particular territory and speak a common language not generally understood by neighboring peoples. By this definition, societies do not necessarily correspond to countries.

Although groups from families to societies share cultural traits, anthropologists have traditionally been concerned with the cultural characteristics of *societies*. Many anthropologists define a **society** as a group of people who occupy a particular territory and speak a common language not generally understood by neighboring peoples. By this definition, societies may or may not correspond to countries. There are many countries—particularly newer ones—that have within their boundaries different peoples speaking mutually unintelligible languages. By our definition of society, such countries are composed of many different societies and therefore many cultures. Also, by our definition of society, some societies may include more than one country. For example, we would have to say that Canada and the United States form a single society because the two groups generally speak English, live next to each other, and share many common ideas and behaviors. That is why we refer to "North American culture." The terms *society* and *culture* are not synonymous. Society refers to a group of people; culture refers to the learned and shared behaviors, ideas, and characteristic of those people. As we will discuss shortly, we also have to be careful to describe culture as of particular time period; what is characteristic of one time may not be characteristic of another.

Culture Is Commonly Shared

If only one person thinks or does a certain thing, that thought or action represents a personal habit, not a pattern of culture. For a thought or action to be considered cultural, some social group must commonly share it. We usually share many behaviors and ideas with our families and friends. We commonly share cultural characteristics with those whose ethnic or regional origins, religious affiliations, and occupations are the same as or similar to our own. We share certain practices and ideas with most people in our society. We also share some cultural traits with people beyond our society who have similar interests (such as rules for international sporting events) or similar roots (as do the various English-speaking nations).

When we talk about the commonly shared customs of *a* society, which constitute the traditional and central concern of cultural anthropology, we are referring to *a* culture. When we talk about the commonly shared customs of a group within a society, which are a central concern of sociologists and increasingly of concern to anthropologists, we are referring to a **subculture**. When we study the commonly shared customs of some group that includes different societies, we usually qualify the term; for example, we may call or refer to the cultural characteristics of societies in or derived from Europe as Western culture, or the presumed cultural characteristics of poor people the world over as the *culture of poverty*.

Subculture The shared customs of a subgroup within a society.

Even when anthropologists refer to something as cultural, there is always individual variation, and not everyone in a society shares a particular cultural characteristic of that society. It is cultural in North American society, for example, for adults to live apart from their parents. But not all adults in the society do so, nor do all adults wish to do so. The custom is considered cultural because most adults practice it. In every society studied by anthropologists—in the simplest as well as the most complex—individuals do not all think and act the same.[2] Indeed, individual variation is a major source of new culture.[3]

Culture Is Learned

Not all things shared generally by a group are cultural. Typical hair color is not cultural, nor is the act of eating. For something to be considered cultural, it must be learned as well as shared. A typical hair color (unless dyed) is not cultural because it is genetically determined. Humans eat because they must; but what and when and how they eat are learned and vary from culture to culture. That food preferences are cultural is especially apparent in which meats a society believes are acceptable to eat. In 2013, the discovery in Europe that ground meat sold as beef also contained horsemeat was greeted with horror. The British, perhaps because they have a high regard for the horse and view horses as pets—that is, with particular familiarity—were especially horrified.[4] Yet horsemeat is considered a delicacy in some parts of Europe and Central Asia. North Americans may be slightly less repelled by the idea of horsemeat, but they generally react with the same horror to eating dog meat.

Guinea pigs, another American household pet, are a common meat in the Andes dating back to the Incas and have recently been introduced in a few Peruvian restaurants in the United States.[5] Is there less aversion to eating guinea pigs than dogs? It appears that there may be, perhaps because dogs have been domesticated for a very long time and are often "part of the family." There is some culture somewhere that avoids every kind of meat North Americans commonly eat. Muslim, Jewish, and Hindu cultures reject pork meat because of religious laws, although why their religions have a pork taboo is still a matter of debate. Many Cushitic-speaking pastoral groups in northeastern Africa reject fish and disapprove of neighboring groups that eat seafood. Meanwhile, some sub-Saharan pastoralists and some cultures in Southeast Asia and the Pacific Islands keep cocks to wake them in the morning and raise chickens for spiritual rites, such as sacrifice and divination, but will not eat the fowl or its eggs. Hindus are generally vegetarian but are especially repelled by the idea of eating beef, for they view the cow as sacred.[6] What accounts for these food preferences and aversions? We know some of the reasons given: religious taboos, age-old superstitions or myths, unfamiliarity, or too much familiarity. And scholars debate their historical and psychological roots. We only know for sure that they are cultural and therefore learned behaviors.

To some extent, all animals exhibit learned behaviors, some of which most individuals in a population may share and may therefore be considered cultural. But different animal species vary in the degree to which their shared behaviors are learned or instinctive. The sociable ants, for instance, despite all their patterned social behavior, do not appear to have much, if any, culture. They divide their labor, construct their nests, form their raiding columns, and carry off their dead—all without having been taught to do so and without imitating the behavior of other ants. Our closest biological relatives, the monkeys and the apes, not only learn a wide variety of behaviors on their own, they also learn from each other. Some of their learned responses are as basic as those involved in maternal care; others are as frivolous as the taste for candy. Frans de Waal reviewed seven long-term studies of chimpanzees and identified at least 39 behaviors that were clearly learned from others.[7] If shared and socially learned, these behaviors could be described as cultural.

The proportion of an animal's life span occupied by childhood roughly reflects the degree to which the animal depends on learned behavior for survival. Monkeys and apes have relatively long childhoods compared to other animals. Humans have by far the longest childhood of any animal, reflecting our great dependence on learned behavior. Although humans may acquire much learned behavior by trial and error and imitation, as do monkeys and apes, most human ideas and behaviors are learned from others. Much of it is probably acquired with the aid of spoken, symbolic language. Using language, a human parent can describe a snake and tell a child that a snake is dangerous and should be avoided. If symbolic language did not exist, the parent would have to wait until the child actually saw a snake and then, through example, show the child that such a creature is to be avoided. Without language, we probably could not transmit or receive information so efficiently and rapidly, and thus would not be heir to so rich and varied a culture.

To sum up, we may say that something is cultural if it is a learned behavior or idea (belief, attitude, value, ideal) that the members of a society or other social group generally share.

Controversies About the Concept of Culture

Not all anthropologists define culture as we do here. We have included learned and shared behaviors as well as ideas. Cognitive anthropologists are most likely to say that culture refers not to behaviors but to the rules and ideas behind them, and that culture therefore resides in people's heads.[8] Although every individual will have slightly different constructs that are based in part on their own unique experiences, many people in a society share many of the same experiences, and therefore they will share many ideas. It is those shared ideas that cognitive anthropologists describe as culture. Whether or not you include behavior as part of culture, both views of culture assume that there will be individual variation, and it is up to the anthropologist to discern the shared nature of culture. Individual variation is the source of new culture.

Another view of culture is that it is an entity, a force, that profoundly affects the individuals who live within its influence. The most extreme version of this view, one that was more acceptable in the past, holds that culture has a "life" of its own that could be studied without much regard for individuals at all.[9] People are born blank slates, it is argued, and culture puts its stamp on in each generation. There are a number of problems with viewing culture as having a life of its own. First, where does it reside exactly? Second, if individuals do not matter, what are the mechanisms of culture change?

People sometimes behave differently when they are in social groups rather than alone. Violent mob behavior is an extreme but telling example. People who would never dream of behaving badly sometimes find themselves doing so to go along with a group. Taking part in a collective ritual that gives a person a feeling of "oneness" is another example of how group behavior can be transformative. If people do or feel things in groups that they would not do alone, we need to look at behavior, as well as the rules or ideas in people's heads, in describing a culture. Therefore, in contrast to many cognitive anthropologists, we define culture as including both behavior and the products of behavior.

Cultural Constraints

12.2 Describe direct and indirect cultural constraints and how they relate to norms.

Norms Standards or rules about what is acceptable behavior.

The noted French sociologist Émile Durkheim stressed that culture is something *outside* us that exerts a strong coercive power on us and constrains our actions and beliefs. Because we generally conform to our culture, we are not always aware of being constrained by its standards and rules for acceptable behavior.[10] Social scientists refer to these standards or rules as **norms**. Some recent research suggests that people may in fact be biased toward normative information. When a group of undergraduates were asked to read texts about Tikopians, whose culture they knew little about, they were more likely to remember a fact if it was presented as "traditional," "practiced by everyone," or a "custom."[11] The importance of a norm usually can be judged by how members of a society respond when it is violated.

Cultural constraints are of two basic types, *direct* and *indirect*. Naturally, the direct constraints are the more obvious. For example, if you have a loud argument in a restaurant, you are likely to attract disapproval, an indirect constraint, but if the argument turns into a physical fight, you may be arrested for disturbing the peace, which is a direct constraint.

Although indirect forms of cultural constraint are less obvious than direct ones, they are usually no less effective. Durkheim illustrated this point when he wrote, "I am not obliged to speak French with my fellow-countrymen, nor to use the legal currency, but I cannot possibly do otherwise. If I tried to escape this necessity, my attempt would fail miserably."[12] In other words, if Durkheim had decided he would rather speak Icelandic than French, nobody would have tried to stop him. But hardly anyone would have understood him either. And although he would not have been put into prison for trying to buy groceries with Icelandic money, he would have had difficulty convincing the local merchants to sell him food.

In a series of classic experiments on conformity, Solomon Asch revealed how strong social pressure can be. Asch coached the majority of a group of college students to give deliberately incorrect answers to questions involving visual stimuli. A "critical subject," the one student in the room who was not so coached, had no idea that the other participants would purposely misinterpret the evidence presented to them. Asch found that, in one-third of the experiments, the critical subjects consistently gave incorrect answers, seemingly allowing their own correct perceptions to be distorted by the obviously incorrect statements of the others. In another 40 percent of the experiments, the critical subject yielded to the opinion of the group some of the time.[13] These studies have been replicated in the United States and elsewhere. Although the degree of conformity appears to vary in different societies, most studies still show conformity effects.[14] Many individuals still do not give in to the wishes of the majority, but a recent study using MRIs has shown that perceptions can actually be altered if participants consciously alter their answers to conform to others.[15]

Attitudes That Hinder the Study of Cultures

12.3 Identify attitudes that hinder the study of cultures.

Many of the Europeans who first traveled to faraway places were shocked and offended by customs they observed, which is not surprising. People commonly feel that their own behaviors and attitudes are the correct ones and that people who do not share those patterns are immoral or inferior.[16] For example, most North Americans would react negatively to child betrothal, a kind of arranged marriage, but not question their own practice of dating a series of potential partners before selecting one. When we judge other cultures solely in terms of our own culture we are being **ethnocentric**—that is, we hold an attitude called **ethnocentrism**.

Ethnocentric Refers to judgment of other cultures solely in terms of one's own culture.

Ethnocentrism The attitude that other societies' customs and ideas can be judged in the context of one's own culture.

Our own customs and ideas may appear bizarre or barbaric to an observer from another society. Hindus in India, for example, would consider our custom of eating beef disgusting. In their culture, the cow is a sacred animal and may not be slaughtered for food. In many societies, a baby is almost constantly carried by someone, in someone's lap, or asleep next to others.[17] People in such societies may think it is cruel of us to leave babies alone for long periods of time, often in devices that resemble cages (cribs and playpens). Even our most ordinary customs—the daily rituals we take for granted—might seem thoroughly absurd when viewed from an outside perspective. An observer of our society might justifiably take notes on certain strange behaviors that seem quite ordinary to us, as the following description shows:

> *The daily body ritual performed by everyone includes a mouth-rite. Despite the fact that these people are so punctilious about the care of the mouth, this rite involves a practice which strikes the uninitiated stranger as revolting. It was reported to me that the ritual consists of inserting a small bundle of hog hairs into the mouth, along with certain magical powders, and then moving the bundle in a highly formalized series of gestures. In addition to the private mouth-rite, the people seek out a holy-mouth man once or twice a year. These practitioners have an impressive set of paraphernalia, consisting of a variety of augers, awls, probes, and prods. The use of these objects in the exorcism of the evils of the mouth involves almost unbelievable ritual torture of the client. The holy-mouth man opens the client's mouth and, using the above-mentioned tools, enlarges any holes which decay may have created in teeth. Magical materials are put into these holes. If there are no naturally occurring holes in the teeth, large sections of one or more teeth are gouged out so that the supernatural substance can be applied. In the client's view, the purpose of these ministrations is to arrest decay and to draw friends. The extremely sacred and traditional character of the rite is evident in the fact that the natives return to the holy-mouth man year after year, despite the fact that their teeth continue to decay.*[18]

Societies vary in their acceptance of an elderly person living apart from family. In the United States and in the UK it is fairly common for an elderly person to live alone or in a facility with non-family members. But in societies where the elderly, such as this great grandmother in central Poland, regularly live with family, having the elderly live alone may be viewed quite negatively.

We are likely to protest that to understand the behaviors of a particular society—in this case, our own—the observer must try to find out what the people in that society say about why they do things. For example, the observer might find out that periodic visits to the "holy-mouth man" are for medical, not magical, purposes. Indeed, the observer, after some questioning, might discover that the "mouth-rite" has no sacred or religious connotations whatsoever. Actually, Horace Miner, the author of the passage on the "daily rite ritual," was not a foreigner. An American, he described the "ritual" the way he did to show how the behaviors involved might be interpreted by an outside observer.

Ethnocentrism hinders our understanding of the customs of other people and, at the same time, keeps us from understanding our own customs. If we think that everything we do is best, we are not likely to ask why we do what we do or why "they" do what "they" do.

We may not always glorify our own culture. Other ways of life may sometimes seem more appealing. Whenever we are weary of the complexities of civilization, we may long for a way of life that is "closer to nature" or "simpler" than our own. For instance, a young North American whose parent is holding two or three jobs just to provide the family with bare necessities might briefly be attracted to the lifestyle of the !Kung of the Kalahari Desert in the 1950s. The !Kung shared their food and therefore were often free to engage in leisure activities during the greater part of the day. They obtained all their food by men hunting animals and women gathering wild plants. Because they had no facilities for refrigeration, sharing a large freshly killed animal was clearly more sensible than hoarding meat that would soon rot. Moreover, the sharing provided a kind of social security system for the !Kung. If a hunter was unable to catch an animal on a certain day, he could obtain food for himself and his family from someone else in his band. Then, at some later date, the game he caught would provide food for the family of another, unsuccessful hunter. This system of sharing also ensured that people too young or too old to help with collecting food would still be fed.

Could we learn from the !Kung? Perhaps we could in some respects, but we must not glorify their way of life either or think that their way of life might be easily imported into our own society. Other aspects of !Kung life would not appeal to many North Americans. For example, when the nomadic !Kung decided to move their camps, they had to carry all the family possessions, substantial amounts of food and water, and all young children below age 4 or 5. This is a sizable burden to carry for any distance. The nomadic !Kung traveled about 1,500 miles in a single year and, understandably, families had few possessions.[19]

Both ethnocentrism and its opposite, the glorification of other cultures, hinder effective anthropological study.

12.4 Critically assess the concept of cultural relativism.

Cultural Relativism

Early thinkers on human evolution tended to think of Western cultures as being at the highest or most progressive stage of evolution. Not only were these ideas based on poor evidence of the details of world ethnography, they also seemed to be ethnocentric glorifications of Western culture. The influential anthropologist Franz Boas and many of his students—such as Ruth Benedict, Melville Herskovits, and Margaret Mead—rejected the view that cultures progressed through stages of civilization.[20] They stressed that the early evolutionists did not sufficiently understand the details of the cultures they theorized about, nor the context in which these customs appeared. Challenging the attitude that Western cultures were obviously superior, the Boasians insisted that a society's customs and ideas should be described objectively and understood in the context of that society's problems and opportunities. This approach is known as **cultural relativism**. Does cultural relativism mean that the actions of another society, or of our own, should not be judged? Does our insistence on objectivity mean that anthropologists should not make moral judgments about the cultural phenomena they observe and try to explain? Does it mean that anthropologists should not try to bring about change? Not necessarily.

Cultural relativism The attitude that a society's customs and ideas should be viewed within the context of that society's problems and opportunities.

Although the concept of cultural relativism remains an important anthropological tenet, today many anthropologists make a distinction between keeping an open mind when studying other cultures and being morally relativistic—that is, suspending all judgment about behaviors they believe to be wrong. What if, for example, a culture practices slavery, violence against women, torture, or genocide? If the strong doctrine of relativism is adhered to, then these cultural practices are not to be judged, and we should not try to eliminate them. A more measured form of cultural relativism asserts that anthropologists should strive for objectivity in describing a people and should be wary of superficial or quick judgment in their attempts to understand the reasons for cultural behavior. Tolerance should be the basic mode unless there is strong reason to behave otherwise.[21] As Michael Brown concludes, cultural relativism is less a comprehensive theory than a useful rule of thumb that keeps anthropologists alert to perspectives in other cultures that might challenge their own cultural beliefs about what is true.[22]

Human Rights and Relativism

Watch the Video: Relativity

The news increasingly reports behaviors that Western countries consider to be violations of human rights. Examples range from jailing people for expressing certain political ideas to ethnic massacre. But faced with criticism from the West, people in other parts of the world are saying that the West should not dictate its ideas about human rights to other countries. Indeed, many countries say that they have different codes of ethics. Are the Western countries being ethnocentric by taking their own cultural ideas and applying them to the rest of the world? Should we instead rely on the strong version of the concept of cultural relativism, considering each culture on its own terms? If we do that, it may not be possible to create a universal standard of human rights.

What we do know is that all cultures have ethical standards, but they do not emphasize the same things. For example, some cultures emphasize individual political rights; others emphasize political order. Some cultures emphasize protection of individual property; others emphasize the sharing or equitable distribution of resources. People in the United States may have freedom to dissent, but they can be deprived of health insurance or of food if they lack the money to buy them. Cultures also vary markedly in the degree to which they have equal rights for minorities and women. In some societies, women are killed when a husband dies or when they disobey a father or brother.

Some anthropologists argue strongly against cultural relativism. For example, Elizabeth Zechenter says that cultural relativists claim there are no universal principles of morality but insist on tolerance for all cultures. If tolerance is one universal principle, why shouldn't there be others? In addition, she points out that the concept of cultural relativism is often used to justify traditions desired by the dominant and powerful in a society. She points to a case in 1996, in Algeria, where two teenage girls were raped and murdered because they violated the fundamentalist edict against attending school. Are those girls any less a part of the culture than the fundamentalists? Would it make any difference if most Algerian women supported the murders? Would that make it right? Zechenter does not believe that international treaties, such as the Universal Declaration of Human Rights, impose uniformity among diverse cultures. Rather, they seek to create a floor below which no society is supposed to fall.[23]

Can the concept of cultural relativism be reconciled with the concept of an international code of human rights? Probably not completely. Paul Rosenblatt recognizes the dilemma but nonetheless thinks that something has to be done to stop torture and "ethnic cleansing," among other practices. He makes the case that "to the extent that it is easier to persuade people whose viewpoints and values one understands, relativism can be a tool for change . . . a relativist's awareness of the values and understanding of the elite makes it easier to know what arguments would be persuasive. For example, in a society in which the group rather than the individual has great primacy, it might be persuasive to show how respect for individual rights benefits the group."[24]

12.5 Describe the methods by which anthropologists describe cultures.

Describing a Culture

If all individuals are unique and all cultures have some internal variation, how do anthropologists discover what may be cultural? Understanding what is cultural involves two parts—separating what is shared from what is individually variable, and understanding whether common behaviors and ideas are learned.

To understand better how an anthropologist might make sense of diverse behaviors, let us examine the diversity at a professional football game in the United States. When people attend a football game, various members of the crowd behave differently while "The Star-Spangled Banner" is being played. As they stand and listen, some people remove their hats; a child munches popcorn; a veteran of the armed forces stands at attention; a teenager searches the crowd for a friend; and the coaches take a final opportunity to intone secret chants and spells designed to sap the strength of the opposing team. Yet, despite these individual variations, most of the people at the game respond in a basically similar manner: Nearly everyone stands silently, facing the flag. Moreover, if you go to several football games, you will observe that many aspects of the event are notably similar. Although the plays will vary from game to game, the rules of the game are never different, and although the colors of the uniforms differ by teams, the players never appear on the field dressed in swimsuits.

If an anthropologist observes dancing in mainstream North American culture, she or he will note that most dancing involves a pair, usually a male and female, but sometimes there are group dances such as the rave as shown here. Yet usually individuals or couples will not simply imitate those around them but will create different patterns of movements and steps.

Although the variations in individual reactions to a given stimulus are theoretically limitless, in fact they tend to fall within easily recognizable limits. A child listening to the anthem may continue to eat popcorn but will probably not do a rain dance. Similarly, the coaches are unlikely to react to that same stimulus by running onto the field and embracing the singer. Variations in behavior, then, are confined within socially acceptable limits, and part of the anthropologists' goals is to find out what those limits are. They may note, for example, that some limitations on behavior have a practical purpose: A spectator who disrupts the game by wandering onto the field would be required to leave. Other limitations are purely traditional. In our society, it is considered proper for a man to remove his overcoat if he becomes overheated, but others would undoubtedly frown upon his removing his trousers even if the weather were quite warm. Using observation and interviewing, anthropologists discover the customs and the ranges of acceptable behavior that characterize the society under study.

Watch the Video: Africa: Polygamist Wives

Similarly, anthropologists interested in describing courtship and marriage in our society would encounter a variety of behaviors. Dating couples vary in where they go (coffee shops, movies, restaurants, bowling alleys), what behaviors they engage in on dates, and how long they date before they split up or move on to more serious relationships. If they decide to marry, ceremonies may be simple or elaborate and involve either religious or secular rituals. Despite this variability, the anthropologists would begin to detect certain regularities in courting practices. Although couples may do many different things on their first and subsequent dates, they nearly always arrange the dates by themselves; they try to avoid their parents when on dates; they often manage to find themselves alone at the end of a date; they put their lips together frequently; and so forth. After a series of more and more closely spaced encounters, a man and woman may decide to declare themselves publicly as a couple, either by announcing that they are engaged or by revealing that they are living together or intend to do so. Finally, if the two of them decide to marry, they must in some way have their union recorded by the civil authorities.

In our society, a person who wishes to marry cannot completely disregard the customary patterns of courtship. If a man saw a woman on the street and decided he wanted to marry her, he could conceivably choose a quicker and more direct form of action than the usual dating procedure. He could get on a horse, ride to the woman's home, snatch her up in his arms, and gallop away with her. In Sicily, until the last few decades, such a couple would have been considered legally married, even if the woman had never met the man before or had no intention of marrying. But in North American society, any man who acted in such a fashion would be arrested and jailed for kidnapping and would probably have his sanity challenged. Although individual behaviors may vary, most social behavior falls within culturally acceptable limits.

In the course of observing and interviewing, anthropologists also try to distinguish actual behavior from the ideas about how people in particular situations ought to feel and behave. In everyday terms, we speak of these ideas as *ideals*; in anthropology, we refer to them as *ideal cultural traits.* Ideal cultural traits may differ from actual behavior because the ideal is based on the way society used to be. (Consider the ideal of "free enterprise," that industry should be totally free of governmental regulation.) Other ideals may never have been actual patterns and may represent merely what people would like to see as correct behavior. Consider the idealized belief, long cherished in North America, that everybody is "equal before the law," that everybody should be treated in the same way by the police and courts. Of course, we know that this is not always true. The rich, for example, may receive less jail time and be sent to nicer prisons. Nevertheless, the ideal is still part of our culture; most of us continue to believe that the law should be applied equally to all.

When dealing with customs that are overt or highly visible within a society—for example, the custom of sending children to school—an investigator can determine the existence of such practices by direct observation and by interviewing a few knowledgeable people. But when dealing with a domain of behavior that may include many individual variations, or when the people studied are unaware of their pattern of behavior and cannot answer questions about it, the anthropologist may need to collect information from

Distance between people conversing varies cross-culturally. The faces of the Rajput Indian men on the left are much closer than the faces of the American women on the right.

a larger sample of individuals to establish what the cultural trait is.

One example of a cultural trait that most people in a society are not aware of is how far apart people stand when they are having a conversation. Yet there is considerable reason to believe that unconscious cultural rules govern such behavior. These rules become obvious when we interact with people who have different rules. We may experience considerable discomfort when another person stands too close (indicating too much intimacy) or too far (indicating unfriendliness). Often we interpret that behavior as individual behavior without realizing that the person is actually following his or her cultural rules. Within Europe, for example, there seems to be a gradient from north to south. Northern Europeans tend to stand further apart, and southern Europeans stand closer.[25]

If we wanted to arrive at the cultural rule for conversational distance between casual acquaintances, we could study a sample of individuals from a society and determine the ***modal response,*** or ***mode.*** The mode is a statistical term that refers to the most frequently encountered response in a given series of responses. So, for the North American pattern of casual conversational distance, we would plot the actual distance for many observed pairs of people. Some pairs may be 2 feet apart, some 2.5, and some 4 feet apart. If we count the number of times every particular distance is observed, these counts provide what we call a ***frequency distribution.*** The distance with the highest frequency is the ***modal pattern.*** Very often the frequency distribution takes the form of a ***bell-shaped curve,*** as shown in Figure 12.1. There, the characteristic being measured is plotted on the horizontal axis (in this case, the distance between conversational pairs), and the number of times each distance is observed (its frequency) is plotted on the vertical axis. If we were to plot how a sample of North American casual conversational pairs is distributed, we would probably get a bell-shaped curve that peaks at around 3 feet.[26] Is it any wonder, then, that we sometimes speak of keeping others "at arm's length"?

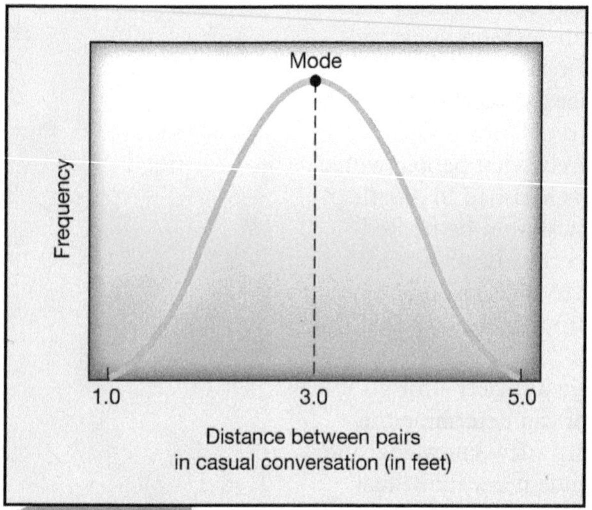

FIGURE 12.1 Frequency Distribution Curve

Although we may be able to discover by interviews and observation that a behavior, thought, or feeling is widely shared within a society, how do we establish that something commonly shared is learned, and therefore cultural? Establishing that something is or is not learned may be difficult. Because children are not reared apart from adult caretakers, the behaviors they exhibit as part of their genetic inheritance are not clearly separated from those they learn from others around them. We suspect that particular behaviors and ideas are largely learned if they vary from society to society. We also suspect genetic influences when particular behaviors or ideas are found in all societies. For example, children the world over seem to acquire language at about the same age and progress through similar stages. These facts suggest that human children have certain genetic capacities for language acquisition. However, the particular languages spoken by people in different societies show considerable variability. This variability suggests that particular languages have to be learned. Similarly, if the courtship patterns of one society differ markedly from those of another, we can be fairly certain that those courtship patterns are learned and therefore cultural.

Culture Is Patterned

12.6 Explain why culture is integrated or patterned.

Anthropologists have always known that culture is not a hodgepodge of unrelated behaviors and ideas—that a culture is mostly integrated. In saying that a culture is mostly *integrated,* we mean that the elements or traits that make up that culture are not just a random assortment of customs but are mostly adjusted to or consistent with one another.

Watch the Animation: Characteristics of Culture

A culture may also tend to be integrated for psychological reasons. The ideas of a culture are stored in the brains of individuals. Research in social psychology has suggested that people tend to modify beliefs or behaviors that are not cognitively or conceptually consistent with other information.[27] We do not expect cultures to be completely integrated, just as we do not expect individuals to be completely consistent. But if a tendency toward cognitive consistency is found in humans, we might expect that at least some aspects of a culture would tend to be integrated for that reason alone. How this pressure for consistency works is not hard to imagine. Children, for example, seem to be very good at remembering *all* the things their parents say. If they ask for something and the parents say no, they may say, "But you said I could yesterday." Such pressure to be consistent may even make parents change their minds! Of course, not everything one wants to do is consistent with the rest of one's desires, but there surely is pressure from within and without to make it so.

Humans are also capable of rational decision making; they can usually figure out that certain things are not easy to do because of other things they do. For example, if a society has a long postpartum sex taboo (a custom in which couples abstain from sex for a year or more after the birth of a baby), we might expect that most people in the society could figure out that it would be easier to observe the taboo if husband and wife did not sleep in the same bed. Or, if people drive on the left side of the road, as in England, it is easier and less dangerous to drive a car with a steering wheel on the right because that placement allows you to judge more accurately how close you are to cars coming at you from the opposite direction.

Consistency or integration of culture traits may also be produced by less conscious psychological processes. People may generalize (transfer) their experiences from one area of life to another. For example, where children are taught that it is wrong to express anger toward family and friends, it turns out that folktales parallel the childrearing; anger and aggression in the folktales tend to be directed only toward strangers, not toward family and friends. It seems as if the expression of anger is too frightening to be expressed close to home, even in folktales.

Adaptation to the environment is another major reason for traits to be patterned. Customs that diminish the survival chances of a society are not likely to persist. Either the people clinging to those customs will become extinct, taking the customs with them, or the customs will be replaced, thereby possibly helping the people to survive. By either process, **maladaptive customs**—those that diminish the chances of survival and reproduction—are likely to disappear. The customs of a society that enhance survival and reproductive success are **adaptive customs** and are likely to persist. Hence, we assume that if a society has survived long enough to be described in the annals of anthropology (the "ethnographic record"), much, if not most, of its cultural repertoire is adaptive, or was at one time.

Maladaptive customs Cultural traits that diminish the chances of survival and reproduction in a particular environment.

Adaptive customs Cultural traits that enhance survival and reproductive success in a particular environment.

When we say that a custom is adaptive, however, we mean it is adaptive only with respect to a specific physical and social environment. What may be adaptive in one environment may not be adaptive in another. Therefore, when we ask why a society may have a particular custom, we really are asking if that custom makes sense as an adaptation to that society's particular environmental conditions. If certain customs are more adaptive in particular settings, then those "bundles" of traits will generally be found together under similar conditions. For example, the !Kung, as we have mentioned, subsisted by hunting wild animals and gathering wild plants. Because wild game is mobile and different plants mature at different times, a nomadic way of life may be an adaptive strategy. Because this food-getting strategy cannot support that many people in one area, small social groups make more sense than large communities. Since people move frequently, it is also probably more adaptive to have few material possessions. These cultural traits usually occur together when people depend on hunting and gathering for their food.

Culture Is Imperfectly Patterned

Not all aspects of culture are consistent, nor is a society forced to adapt its culture to changing environmental circumstances. Even in the face of changed circumstances, people may choose not to change their customs. The Tapirapé of central Brazil, for example, did not alter their custom of limiting the number of births even though they had suffered severe population losses after contact with Europeans and their diseases. The Tapirapé population fell to fewer than 100 people from over 1,000. They were on the way to extinction, yet they continued to value small families. Not only did they believe that a woman should have no more than three children, but they took specific steps to achieve this limitation. They practiced infanticide if twins were born, if the third child was of the same sex as the first two children, and if the possible fathers broke certain taboos during pregnancy or in the child's infancy.[28]

Of course, it is also possible that a people will behave maladaptively, even if they try to alter their behavior. After all, although people may alter their behavior according to what they perceive will be helpful to them, what they perceive to be helpful may not prove to be adaptive. The tendency for a culture to be integrated or patterned, then, may be cognitively and emotionally, as well as adaptively, induced.

12.7 Describe and give examples of how cultures change through discovery and invention, diffusion, and acculturation.

How and Why Cultures Change

When you examine the history of a society, it is obvious that its culture has changed over time. Some of the shared behaviors and ideas that were common at one time are modified or replaced at another time. That is why, in describing a culture, it is important to understand that a description pertains to a particular time period. (Moreover, in many large societies, the description may only be appropriate for a particular subgroup.) For example, the !Kung of the 1950s were mostly dependent on the collection of wild plants and animals and moved their campsites frequently, but later they became more sedentary to engage in wage labor. Whether we focus on some aspect of past behavior or on contemporary behavior depends on what question we want to answer. If we want to maximize our understanding of cultural variation, such as variation in religious belief and practice, it may be important to focus on the earliest descriptions of a group before they were converted to a major world religion. On the other hand, if we want to understand why a people adopted a new religion or how they altered their religion or resisted change in the face of pressure, we need to examine the changes that occurred over time.

In the remainder of this chapter, we will discuss how and why cultures change and briefly review some of the widespread changes that have occurred in recent times. In general, the impetus for change may come from within the society or from without. From within, the unconscious or conscious pressure for consistency will produce culture change if enough people adjust old behavior and thinking to new. And change can also occur if people try to invent better ways of doing things. Michael Chibnik suggests that people who confront a new problem conduct mental or small "experiments" to decide how to behave. These experiments may give rise to new cultural traits.[29] A good deal of culture change may be stimulated by changes in the external environment. For example, if people move into an arid area, they will either have to give up farming or develop a system of irrigation. In the modern world, changes in the social environment are probably more frequent stimuli for culture change than changes in the physical environment. Many North Americans, for example, started to think seriously about conserving energy and about using sources of energy other than oil only after oil supplies from the Middle East were curtailed in 1973 and 1974. A significant amount of the radical and rapid culture change that has occurred in the last few hundred years has been due to the imperial expansion of Western societies into other areas of the world. Native Americans, for instance, were forced to alter their lifestyles drastically when they were driven off their lands and confined to reservations.

Discovery and Invention Discoveries and inventions, which may originate inside or outside a society, are ultimately the sources of all culture change. But they do not necessarily lead to change. If an invention or discovery is ignored, no change in culture results. Only when society accepts an invention or discovery and uses it regularly can we begin to speak of culture change.

The new thing discovered or invented, the innovation, may be an object—the wheel, the plow, the computer—or it may involve behavior and ideas—buying and selling, democracy, monogamy. According to Ralph Linton, a discovery is any addition to knowledge, and an invention is a new application of knowledge.[30] Thus, a person might discover that children can be persuaded to eat nourishing food if the food is associated with an imaginary character that appeals to them. Someone else might then exploit that discovery by inventing a cartoon character named Popeye who acquires miraculous strength by devouring cans of spinach.

Unconscious Invention Societies have various types of inventions. One type is the consequence of setting a specific goal, such as eliminating tuberculosis or placing a person on the moon. Another type emerges less intentionally. This second process of invention is often referred to as *accidental juxtaposition* or *unconscious invention*. Linton suggested that some inventions, especially those of prehistoric days, were probably the consequences of literally dozens of tiny initiatives by "unconscious" inventors. These inventors made their small contributions, perhaps over many hundreds of years, without being aware of the part they were playing in bringing one invention, such as the wheel or a better form of hand ax, to completion.[31] Consider the example of children playing on a fallen log, which rolls as they walk and balance on it, coupled with the need at a given moment to move a slab of granite from a cave face. The children's play could have suggested the use of logs as rollers and thereby set in motion a series of developments that culminated in the wheel.

In reconstructing the process of invention in prehistoric times, however, we should be careful not to look back on our ancestors with a smugness generated by our more highly developed technology. We have become accustomed to turning to the science sections of our magazines and newspapers and finding, almost daily, reports of miraculous new discoveries and inventions. From our point of view, it is difficult to imagine such a simple invention as the wheel taking so many centuries to come into being. We are tempted to surmise that early humans were less intelligent than we are. But the capacity of the human brain has been the same for perhaps 100,000 years; there is no evidence that the inventors of the wheel were any less intelligent than we are.

Intentional Innovation Some discoveries and inventions arise out of deliberate attempts to produce a new idea or object. It may seem that such innovations are obvious responses to perceived needs. For example, during the Industrial Revolution, there was a great demand for inventions that would increase productivity. James Hargreaves, in 18th-century England, is an example of an inventor who responded to an existing demand. Textile manufacturers were clamoring for such large quantities of spun yarn that cottage laborers, working with foot-operated spinning wheels, could not meet the demand. Hargreaves, realizing that prestige and financial rewards would come to the person who invented a method of spinning large quantities of yarn in a short time, set about the task and developed the spinning jenny.

Current Research and Issues

Culture Change and Persistence in China

Governments can change a culture by force, as communist China has tried to do since its inception in 1949. Among the government's revolutionary policies was the push for intensive agriculture and a one-child-per-family rule. Yet a study by Burton Pasternak, a U.S. anthropologist, and colleagues from Canada and China suggests that, despite strong pressures from the government, what change persists in a culture mainly reflects what is possible ecologically and economically. The researchers studied four communities of Han who had moved outside the Great Wall to colonize the Inner Mongolian frontier (Inner Mongolia is part of China).

Han farmers who crossed the Great Wall were searching for a better life. Though many found the climate and soil conditions too difficult and returned home, others adjusted to the grasslands and remained. Some Han continued to depend on farming on the fringes of the grasslands. Others farther out on the grasslands became herders. The Han who switched to herding are now in many respects more like the native Mongol herders than like Han or Mongol farmers. The gender division of labor among the Han pastoralists became much sharper than among the Han farmers because men are often far away with the herds. Pastoralist children, not that useful in herding because mistakes can be very costly, are more likely than farm children to stay in school for a long time. Perhaps because of the greater usefulness of children on the farm, Han farm families have more children than Han pastoralists. But both groups have more than the prescribed one child per family. Herdsmen are less likely than farmers to need cooperative labor, so Han pastoralists are more likely to live as an independent family apart from kin than as an extended family, which was traditional.

Although an increasing number of Han have become more like Mongols in their pastoral adaptations, many Mongols have adopted an urban way of life and moved away from their pastoral life. The Chinese government was initially responsible for encouraging non-Mongols to move into Inner Mongolia, particularly into its new capital, Hohhot. At the same time, many Mongols moved from the grasslands and into the capital city. Chinese policy was intended to make each non-Han ethnic group a minority in its traditional land, but the government paradoxically also tried to encourage minority ethnic pride in their traditional culture. The city of Hohhot, therefore, is filled with images of the traditional herding culture in its buildings and monuments.

As described by anthropologist William Jankowiak, who studied the Mongols in the capital city of Hohhot, the results were not what the Chinese government intended. In many ways, to be sure, the urban Mongols had abandoned their traditional culture and assimilated to the dominant Han culture. But we see the force of ecology more than the hand of tradition in the outcome. Many Mongols in the city no longer speak the Mongol language. Parents find it difficult to get children to speak Mongol when they live among Han. The scarcity of housing makes it difficult for the Mongols to form an ethnic enclave or even live near kin as they did in the past. In contrast to life in the rural areas, which revolves around kinship, city life requires interacting with strangers as well as relatives. Indeed, nonkin are often more important to you than kin. As one person said to Jankowiak, "We hide from our cousins but not our friends."

Sources: Davis and Harrell 1993; Pasternak 2009; Jankowiak 2004.

But perceived needs and the economic rewards that may be given to the innovator do not explain why only some people innovate. We know relatively little about why some people are more innovative than others. The ability to innovate may depend in part on such individual characteristics as high intelligence and creativity, and creativity may be influenced by social conditions.

A study of innovation among Ashanti artist carvers in Ghana suggests that creativity is more likely in some socioeconomic groups than in others.[32] Some carvers produced only traditional designs; others departed from tradition and produced "new" styles of carving. Two groups were found to innovate the most—the wealthiest and the poorest carvers. These two groups of carvers may tolerate risk more than the middle socioeconomic group. Innovative carving entails some risk because it may take more time and it may not sell. Wealthy carvers can afford the risk, and they may gain some prestige as well as income if their innovation is appreciated. The poor are not doing well anyway, and they have little to lose by trying something new.

Some societies encourage innovativeness more than others, and this can vary substantially over time. Patricia Greenfield and her colleagues describe the changes in weaving in a Mayan community in the Zinacantán region of Chiapas, Mexico.[33] In 1969 and 1970, innovation was not valued. Rather, tradition was; there was the old "true way" to do everything, including how one dressed. There were only four simple weaving patterns, and virtually all males wore ponchos with the same pattern. By 1991, virtually no poncho was the same and the villagers had developed elaborate brocaded and embroidered designs. In a period of 20 years, innovation had increased dramatically. Two other things had also changed. The economy was more commercialized; textiles as well as other items were now bought and sold. Weaving was taught in a less directed way. Whereas mothers used to give their daughters highly structured instruction, often with "four hands" on the loom, they were later allowed to learn more by themselves, by trial and error. The result was more abstract and varied designs.

Who Adopts Innovations? Once someone discovers or invents something, there is still the question of whether others will adopt the innovation. Many researchers have studied the characteristics of "early adopters." Such individuals tend to be educated, high in social status, upwardly mobile, and, if they are property owners, have large farms and businesses. The individuals who most need technological improvements—those who are less well off—are generally the last to adopt innovations. The theory is that only the wealthy can afford to take the substantial risks associated with new ways of doing things. In periods of rapid technological change, therefore, the gap between rich and poor is likely to widen because the rich adopt innovations sooner, and benefit more from them, than the poor.[34]

Does this imply that the likelihood of adopting innovations is a simple function of how much wealth a possible adopter possesses? Not necessarily. Frank Cancian reviewed several studies and found that upper-middle-class individuals show more conservatism than lower-middle-class individuals. Cancian suggested that, when the risks are unknown, lower-middle-class individuals are more receptive to innovation because they have less to lose. Later on, when the risks are better known—that is, as more people adopt the innovation—the upper-middle class catches up to the lower-middle class.[35] In general, people are more likely to adopt a behavior as it becomes more common.[36]

The speed with which an innovation is adopted may depend partly on how new behaviors and ideas are typically transmitted—or taught—in a society. If children learn most of what they know from their parents or from a relatively small number of elders, then innovation will be slow to spread throughout the society, and culture change is likely to be slow. Innovations may catch on more rapidly if individuals are exposed to various teachers and other "leaders" who can influence many in a relatively short time, and the more peers we have, the more we might learn from them.[37] Perhaps this is why the pace of change appears to be so fast today. In societies like North America, and increasingly in the industrializing world, it is likely that people learn in schools from teachers, from leaders in their specialties, and from peers.

Costs and Benefits An innovation that is technologically superior is not necessarily going to be adopted since it comes with costs as well as benefits for both individuals and large-scale industries. Take the computer keyboard. The keyboard used most often on computers today is called the QWERTY keyboard (named after the first letters that appear on the left side of keyboard). This curious ordering of the letters was actually invented to slow typing speed down! Early typewriters had mechanical keys that jammed if the typist went too fast.[38] Since computer keyboards do not have that problem, keys arranged for faster typing would probably be better and have, indeed, been invented. Yet they have not caught on, perhaps because people are reluctant to take the time or make the effort to change.

In large-scale industries, technological innovations may be very costly to implement. A new product or process may require a manufacturing or service facility to be revamped and workers to be retrained. Before a change is made, the costs of doing so are weighed against the potential benefits. If the market is expected to be large for a new product, the product is more likely to be produced. If the market is judged small, the benefits may not be sufficient inducement to change. Companies may also judge the value of an innovation by whether competitors could copy it. If the new innovation can easily be copied, the inventing company may not find the investment worthwhile. Although the market may be large, the inventing company may not be able to hold onto market share if other companies could produce the product quickly without having to invest in research and development.[39]

Diffusion

Diffusion The process by which cultural elements are borrowed from another society and incorporated into the culture of the recipient group.

The source of new cultural elements in a society may also be another society. The process by which cultural elements are borrowed from another society and incorporated into the culture of the recipient group is called **diffusion**. Borrowing sometimes enables a group to bypass stages or mistakes in the development of a process or institution. For example, Germany was able to accelerate its program of industrialization in the 19th century through technological borrowing because it could avoid some of the errors its English and Belgian competitors had made. Japan's industrialization followed the same pattern. Indeed, in recent years, some of the earliest industrialized countries have fallen behind their imitators in certain areas of production, such as automobiles, televisions, cameras, and computers.

Diffusion has far-reaching effects. In a well-known passage, Linton conveyed how integral diffusion is to our lives, even while we are largely ignorant about it. Considering the first few hours in the day of an American man in the 1930s, Linton tells us he

> *. . . awakens in a bed built on a pattern which originated in the Near East but which was modified in northern Europe before it was transmitted to America. He throws back covers made from cotton, domesticated in India, or linen, domesticated in the Near East, or silk, the use of which was discovered in China. All of these materials have been spun and woven by processes invented in the Near East. . . . He takes off his pajamas, a garment invented in India, and washes with soap invented by the ancient Gauls. He then shaves, a masochistic rite which seems to have derived from either Sumer or ancient Egypt.*
>
> *Before going out for breakfast he glances through the window, made of glass invented in Egypt, and if it is raining puts on overshoes made of rubber discovered by the Central American Indians and takes an umbrella, invented in southeastern Asia. . .*
>
> *On his way to breakfast he stops to buy a paper paying for it with coins, an ancient Lydian invention. . . . His plate is made of a form of pottery invented in China. His knife is of steel, an alloy first made in southern India, his fork a medieval Italian invention, and his spoon a derivative of a Roman original. . . . After his fruit (African watermelon) and first coffee (an Abyssinian plant), . . . he may have the egg of a species of bird domesticated in Indo-China, or thin strips of the flesh of an animal domesticated in eastern Asia which have been salted and smoked by a process developed in northern Europe. . . .*
>
> *While smoking (an American Indian habit), he reads the news of the day, imprinted in characters invented by the ancient Semites upon a material invented in China by a process invented in Germany. As he absorbs the accounts of foreign troubles he will, if he is a good conservative citizen, thank a Hebrew deity in an Indo-European language that he is 100 percent American.*[40]

Patterns of Diffusion The three basic patterns of diffusion are direct contact, intermediate contact, and stimulus diffusion.

1. *Direct contact.* Elements of a society's culture may first be taken up by neighboring societies and then gradually spread farther and farther afield. The spread of the use of paper (a sheet of interlaced fibers) is a good example of extensive diffusion by direct contact. The invention of paper is attributed to the Chinese Ts'ai Lun in A.D. 105. Within 50 years, paper was being made in many places in central China. Although the art of papermaking was kept secret for about 500 years, it was distributed as a commodity to much of the Arab world through the markets at Samarkand. But when Samarkand was attacked by the Chinese in A.D. 751, a Chinese prisoner of war was forced to set up a paper mill. Paper manufacture soon spread to the rest of the Arab world; it was first manufactured in Baghdad in A.D. 793, Egypt about A.D. 900, and Morocco about A.D. 1100. Papermaking was introduced as a commodity in Europe by Arab trade through Italian ports in the 12th century. The Moors built the first European paper mill in Spain about 1150. The technical knowledge then spread throughout Europe, with mills being built in Italy in 1276, France in 1348, Germany in 1390, and England in 1494.[41] In general, the pattern of accepting the borrowed invention was the same in all cases: Paper was first imported as a luxury, then in ever-expanding quantities as a staple product. Finally, and usually within one to three centuries, local manufacture began.
2. *Intermediate contact.* Diffusion by intermediate contact occurs through the agency of third parties. Frequently, traders carry a cultural trait from the society that originated it to another group. For example, Phoenician traders introduced the ancient Greeks to the first alphabet, which the Phoenicians had themselves received from the Ugarit, another Semitic culture. At times, soldiers serve as intermediaries in spreading a culture trait. European crusaders, such as the Knights Templar and the Knights of St. John, acted as intermediaries in two ways: They carried Christian culture to Muslim societies of North Africa and brought Arab culture back to Europe. In the 19th century, Western missionaries in all parts of the world encouraged natives to wear Western clothing. Hence, in Africa, the Pacific Islands, and elsewhere, native peoples can be found wearing shorts, suit jackets, shirts, ties, and other typically Western articles of clothing.
3. *Stimulus diffusion.* In stimulus diffusion, knowledge of a trait belonging to another culture stimulates the invention or development of a local equivalent. A classic example of stimulus diffusion is the Cherokee syllabic writing system created by a Native American named Sequoya so that his people could write down their language. Sequoya got the idea from his contact with Europeans. Yet he did not adopt the English writing system; indeed, he did not even learn to write English. What he did was utilize some English alphabetic symbols, alter others, and invent new ones. All the symbols he used represented Cherokee syllables and in no way echoed English alphabetic usage. In other words, Sequoya took English alphabetic ideas and gave them a new Cherokee form. The stimulus originated with Europeans; the result was singularly Cherokee.

The Selective Nature of Diffusion It is tempting to think that the dynamics of diffusion are like a stone sending concentric ripples over still water, but that would oversimplify the way diffusion actually occurs. Not all cultural traits are borrowed as readily as the ones we have mentioned, nor do they usually expand in neat, ever-widening circles. Rather, diffusion is a selective process. The Japanese, for instance, accepted much from Chinese culture, but they also rejected many traits. Rhymed tonal poetry, civil service examinations, and foot binding, which the Chinese favored, were never adopted in Japan. The poetry form was unsuited to the structure of the Japanese language; the examinations were unnecessary in view of the entrenched power of the Japanese aristocracy; and foot binding was repugnant to a people who abhorred body mutilation of any sort.

A Masai man in Kenya can call home or around the world from the plains of Kenya.

Not only would we expect societies to reject items from other societies that they find repellent, we would also expect them to reject ideas and technology that do not satisfy some psychological, social, or cultural need. After all, people are not sponges; they do not automatically soak up the things around them. If they did, the amount of cultural variation in the world would be extremely small, which is clearly not the case. Diffusion is also selective because the extent to which cultural traits can be communicated differs. Elements of material culture, such as mechanical processes and techniques, and overt practices, such as physical sports, are relatively easy to demonstrate. Consequently, they are accepted or rejected on their merits. When we move beyond the material world, however, we encounter real difficulties, which Linton (again) aptly described:

> *Although it is quite possible to describe such an element of culture as the ideal pattern for marriage . . . it is much less complete than a description of basketmaking. . . . The most thorough verbalization has difficulty in conveying the series of associations and conditioned emotional responses which are attached to this pattern [marriage] and which gave it meaning and vitality within our own society. . . . This is even more true of those concepts which . . . find no direct expression in behavior aside from verbalization. There is a story of an educated Japanese who after a long discussion on the nature of the Trinity with a European friend . . . burst out with: "Oh, I see now, it is a committee."*[42]

Finally, diffusion is selective because the overt form of a particular trait, rather than its function or meaning, frequently seems to determine how the trait will be received. For example, an enthusiasm for women to have bobbed hair (short haircuts) swept through much of North America in the 1920s but never caught on among the Native Americans of northwestern California. To many women of European ancestry, short hair was a symbolic statement of freedom. To Native American women, who traditionally cut their hair short when in mourning, it was a reminder of death.[43]

In the process of diffusion, then, we can identify a number of different patterns. We know that cultural borrowing is selective rather than automatic, and we can describe how a particular borrowed trait has been modified by the recipient culture. But our current knowledge does not allow us to specify when one or another of these outcomes will occur, under what conditions diffusion will occur, and why it occurs the way it does.

Acculturation

Acculturation The process of extensive borrowing of aspects of culture in the context of superordinate-subordinate relations between societies; usually occurs as the result of external pressure.

On the surface, the process of change called **acculturation** seems to include much of what we have discussed under the label of diffusion because acculturation refers to the changes that occur when different cultural groups come into intensive contact. As in diffusion, the source of new cultural items is the other society. But more often than not, anthropologists use the term *acculturation* to describe a situation in which one of the societies in contact is much more powerful than the other. Thus, acculturation can be seen as a process of extensive cultural borrowing in the context of superordinate-subordinate relations between societies.[44] There is probably always some borrowing both ways, but generally the subordinate or less powerful society borrows the most.

External pressure for culture change can take various forms. In its most direct form—conquest or colonialization—the dominant group uses force or the threat of force to try to bring about culture change in the other group. In the Spanish conquest of Mexico, for example, the conquerors forced many of the native groups to accept Catholicism. Although such direct force is not always exerted in conquest situations, dominated peoples often have little choice but to change. Examples of such indirectly forced change abound in the history of Native Americans in the United States. Although the federal government made few direct attempts to force people to adopt American culture, it did drive many native groups from their lands, thereby obliging them to give up many aspects of their traditional ways of life. To survive, they had no choice but to adopt many of the dominant society's traits. When Native American children were required to go to schools, which taught the dominant society's values, the process was accelerated.

A subordinate society may acculturate to a dominant society even in the absence of direct or indirect force. Perceiving that members of the dominant society enjoy more secure living conditions, the dominated people may identify with the dominant culture in the hope that they will be able to share some of its benefits by doing so. Or they may elect to adopt cultural elements from the dominant society because they perceive that the new element has advantages. For example, in Arctic areas, many Inuit and Saami groups seemed eager to replace dog sleds with snowmobiles without any coercion.[45] There is evidence that the Inuit weighed the advantages and disadvantages of the snowmobile versus the dog sled and that its adoption was gradual. Similarly, rifles were seen as a major technological improvement, increasing the success rate in hunting, but the Inuit did not completely abandon their former ways of hunting. More recently, the Inuit are trying out GPS devices for navigating.[46]

Acculturation processes vary considerably depending upon the wishes of the more powerful society, the attitudes of the less powerful, and whether there is any choice. More powerful societies do not always want individuals from another culture to assimilate or "melt into" the dominant culture completely; instead, they may prefer and even actively promote a *multicultural* society. Multiculturalism can be voluntary or may arise out of deliberate segregation. Then, too, even though the less powerful group may be pressured to acquire some of the dominant group's cultural traits, they may resist or even reject those cultural elements, at least for a considerable length of time.

Many millions of people, however, never had a chance to acculturate after contact with Europeans. They simply died, sometimes directly at the hands of the conquerors, but probably more often as a result of the new diseases the Europeans inadvertently brought with them. Depopulation because of measles, smallpox, and tuberculosis was particularly common in North and South America and on the islands of the Pacific. Those areas had previously been isolated from contact with Europeans and from the diseases of that continuous landmass we call the Old World—Europe, Asia, and Africa.[47] The story of Ishi, the last surviving member of a group of Native Americans in California called the Yahi, is a moving testimonial to the frequently tragic effect of contact with Europeans. In the space of 22 years, the Yahi population was reduced from several hundred to near zero. The historical record on this episode of depopulation suggests that European Americans murdered 30 to 50 Yahi for every European American murdered, but perhaps 60 percent of the Yahi died in the 10 years following their initial exposure to European diseases.[48]

Applied Anthropology

Development Programs and Culture Change: A Bedouin Case Study

Most governments of the world today want to "develop" their countries. They want to increase their crop yields and their exports, build major roads and irrigation projects, and industrialize. However, many development schemes have failed in part because they do not adequately consider the cultures of the people whose lives they affect. Governments, as well as international agencies that lend money, increasingly turn for advice to anthropologists to help plan and evaluate projects. While governments may not fully appreciate traditional ways of life, anthropologists understand that people are unlikely to accept a change if it does not integrate well with other aspects of their culture.

In many countries of the Middle East, governments have pressured nomadic Bedouin peoples to settle down. Yet government settlement schemes, by force or with enticements, have also often failed. The Bedouin way of life is essentially at odds with nation states, in which land is increasingly privately owned or converted for industrial uses (such as oil production) and resources are regulated. But Bedouin require vast stretches of grassland and a water source for their herds, resources that were traditionally available to them as members of kinship-based groups that maintained grazing rights over large territories.

Although there are many Bedouin groups in the Middle East and North Africa, they share key cultural traits. They are, as anthropologist Dawn Chatty points out, at once tribal, nomadic, and pastoral. And these three traits are a large part of a Bedouin's identity. When government-built settlements have been created to replace the Bedouin tent, the tribe has often continued its pastoral life near the settlement until overgrazing left a human-made desert or the water supply ran out. The nomadic Bedouin would then abandon such settlements to seek other grazable land and water, and they would again pitch their familiar tents.

Even an enlightened state may find that culture change cannot be imposed on the Bedouin. In the 1980s, Dawn

The Bedouin still often erect tents in fixed housing settlements as in this Israeli Negev settlement.

Chatty was asked by the government of the Middle Eastern country of Oman to help design a project to extend basic social services to the Bedouin without coercing them to alter their way of life. It isn't often that governments fund in-depth studies to try to understand the needs of the people being affected, but Chatty was able to persuade the Oman government that such a study was necessary as a first step. With United Nations funding, she evaluated the needs of the Harasiis pastoralists, a Bedouin group in Oman. Because the government wanted some action right away, the project soon incorporated a mobile health unit that could begin a program of primary care as well as immunization against measles, whooping cough, and polio. After a period of evaluation, the project team also recommended an annual distribution of tents, the establishment of dormitories so that children could live at schools, a new system of water delivery, and veterinary and marketing assistance.

The government was receptive to the recommendations of Chatty's group. Soon a "tribal" complex was built for the Harasiis. It included offices for their government representative, a medical clinic, a school, a mosque, a "reverse osmosis" water plant, a police station, and villas for government employees. But the complex was never occupied. It appears that the Harasiis would continue to pursue their nomadic way of life.

Yet the Bedouin are not reluctant to change in all respects. As Chatty chronicles, many readily gave up relying on camels for transport in favor of trucks. Trucks are a modern adaptation, yet they still allow mobility. Now the Bedouin are able to get water from wells and transport water to their animals by truck. The adoption of trucks led to other changes. Since small animals can be more readily transported to new pastures by truck, many Bedouin have given up their dependence on camels and shifted to sheep and goat herding. Because money is required to buy trucks and pay for gasoline and repairs, Bedouin spend more time working for wages in temporary jobs. Aside from such adaptations from within, though, they have resisted enforced change. As for Chatty, she views her experience philosophically. She, like other applied anthropologists, has learned a great deal about the environmental and political conditions that impact the world's more marginalized cultures. And she continues to believe that it is her job to push for what Michael Cernea called "putting people first."

Sources: Chatty 1996, 2006; Cernea 1991, 7; Strachan 2011.

Nowadays, many powerful nations—and not just Western ones—may seem to be acting in more humanitarian ways to improve the life of previously subjugated as well as other "developing" peoples. For better or worse, these programs, however, are still forms of external pressure. The tactic used may be persuasion rather than force, but most of the programs are nonetheless designed to bring about acculturation in the direction of the dominant societies' cultures. For example, the introduction of formal schooling cannot help but instill new values that may contradict traditional cultural patterns. Even health care programs may alter traditional ways of life by undermining the authority of shamans and other leaders and by increasing population beyond the number that can be supported in traditional ways. Confinement to reservations or other kinds of direct force are not the only ways a dominant society can bring about acculturation.

The process of acculturation also applies to immigrants, most of whom, at least nowadays, choose to leave one country for another. Immigrants are almost always a minority in the new country and therefore are in a subordinate position. If the immigrant's culture changes, it is almost always in the direction of the dominant culture. Immigrant groups vary considerably in the degree and speed with which they adopt the new culture and the social roles of the new society in which they live. An important area of research is explaining the variation in acculturation and assimilation. (*Assimilation* is a concept very similar to acculturation, but *assimilation* is a term more often used by sociologists to describe the process by which individuals acquire the social roles and culture of the dominant group.)

Listen to the Audio: Children of Immigrants: Adapting to Life in NYC

Revolution

Certainly the most drastic and rapid way a culture can change is as a result of **revolution**—replacement, usually violent, of a country's rulers. Historical records, as well as our daily newspapers, indicate that people frequently rebel against established authority. Rebellions, if they occur, almost always occur in state societies where there is a distinct ruling elite. They take the form of struggles between rulers and ruled, between conquerors and conquered, or between representatives of an external colonial power and segments of the native society. Rebels do not always succeed in overthrowing their rulers, so rebellions do not always result in revolutions. And even successful rebellions do not always result in culture change; the individual rulers may change, but customs or institutions may not. The sources of revolution may be mostly internal, as in the French Revolution, or partly external, as in the Russian-supported 1948 revolution in Czechoslovakia and the United States-supported 1973 revolution against President Allende in Chile.

Revolution A usually violent replacement of a society's rulers.

The American War of Independence was a colonial rebellion against the greatest imperial power of the 18th century, Great Britain. The 13 colonies owed at least a part of their success in the war to aid from France, which had been waging its own "Seven Years' War" against the British, and more indirectly from Spain, which would also declare war on the greater imperial power. Actually, the American war was closely following what we would now call a world war. In the 19th century and continuing into the middle and later years of the 20th century, there would be many other wars of independence against imperial powers in Latin America, Europe, Asia, and Africa. We don't always remember that the American rebellion was the first anti-imperialist wars in modern times and the model for many that followed. Just like many of the most recent liberation movements, the American rebellion was also part of a larger worldwide war involving people from many rival nations. A total of 30,000 German-speaking soldiers fought, for pay, on the British side; an army and navy from France fought on the American side. There were volunteers from other European countries, including Denmark, Holland, Poland, and Russia.

As in many revolutions, those who were urging revolution were considered "radicals." At a now-famous debate in Virginia in 1775, delegates from each colony met at a Continental Congress. Patrick Henry put forward a resolution to prepare for defense against the British armed forces. The motion barely passed, by a vote of 65 to 60. Henry's speech is now a part of American folklore. He rose to declare that it was insane not to oppose the British and that he was not afraid to test the strength of the colonies against Great Britain. Others might hesitate, he said, but he would have "liberty or death." The radicals who supported Henry's resolution included many aristocratic landowners, two of whom,

George Washington and Thomas Jefferson, became the first and third occupants of the highest political office in what became the United States of America.[54]

Not all peoples who are suppressed, conquered, or colonialized eventually rebel against established authority. Why this is so, and why rebellions and revolts are not always successful in bringing about culture change, are still open questions. But some possible answers have been investigated. The historian Crane Brinton examined the classic revolutions of the past, including the American, French, and Russian revolutions, and suggested a set of conditions that may give rise to rebellion and revolution:

1. *Loss of prestige of established authority*, often as a result of the failure of foreign policy, financial difficulties, dismissals of popular ministers, or alteration of popular policies. France in the 18th century lost three major international conflicts, with disastrous results for its diplomatic standing and internal finances. Russian society was close to military and economic collapse in 1917, after 3 years of World War I.
2. *Threat to recent economic improvement.* In France, as in Russia, those sections of the population (professional classes and urban workers) whose economic fortunes had only shortly before taken an upward swing were "radicalized" by unexpected setbacks, such as steeply rising food prices and unemployment. The same may be said for the American colonies on the brink of their rebellion against Great Britain.
3. *Indecisiveness of government*, as exemplified by lack of consistent policy, which gives the impression of being controlled by, rather than in control of, events. The frivolous arrogance of Louis XVI's regime and the bungling of George III's prime minister, Lord North, with respect to the problems of the American colonies are examples.
4. *Loss of support of the intellectual class.* Such a loss deprived the prerevolutionary governments of France and Russia of any avowed philosophical support and led to their unpopularity with the literate public.[55]

The classic revolutions of the past occurred in countries that were industrialized only incipiently at best. For the most part, the same is true of the rebellions and revolutions in recent years; they have occurred mostly in countries we call "developing." The evidence from a worldwide survey of developing countries suggests that rebellions have tended to occur where the ruling classes depended mostly on the produce or income from land and therefore were resistant to demands for reform from the rural classes that worked the land. In such agricultural economies, the rulers are not likely to yield political power or give greater economic returns to the workers because to do so would eliminate the basis (landownership) of the rulers' wealth and power.[56]

Some political scientists have a broader definition of revolution and argue that not all great revolutions occur on the battlefield, nor are they all inspired by public rebellions. Some, like the culture revolution Ataturk brought to Turkey in 1919, for example, are largely the work of charismatic leaders.[57] Ataturk's government was responsible for molding a formerly imperial Muslim nation into a democracy and separating church (or mosque) and state. In retrospect, it was a monumental achievement since the role of clerics in government and the definition of democracy have remained ambiguous in much of the Middle East.

Since the winter of 2010, the world has witnessed a remarkable series of popular uprisings known collectively as the Arab Spring that have affected nearly every Muslim nation. It all began in the winter of 2010, when a street vendor in Tunisia set himself on fire after the police confiscated his fruit and vegetable cart. He had been an educated man, as more and more young Tunisians have been in the last few decades, but was unable to find other work in a country that had a 30 percent unemployment rate. His story was met with widespread and persistent protests, and, with the world watching and listening through social media, Tunisia's president fled to Saudi Arabia less than 2 months later, and the Tunisian people were promised a free and democratic election. Within months, similar public protests toppled the leaders of Egypt, Libya, and Yemen. The leaders of nearly every Muslim nation have been affected by the uprising, and many of those who are still in power have promised reforms, reorganized their governments, or promised to leave when their current terms of office end.[58] But in many of the countries, turmoil and bloodshed is still on-going. It is too soon to know whether these uprisings will lead to the cultural change many Arab citizens want. But we can glean some characteristics these modern revolutions all seem to share. Their success depends on foreign support and intervention, in part because the citizens of authoritarian regimes have not been allowed to organize competing political parties. Social media has played a role in the speed with which change has occurred, in part because many leaders are less likely to use force when the world is watching.[59] The goal in each nation appears to be a democratically elected government and the end of oppressive regimes.

Finally, a particularly interesting question is why revolutions sometimes, perhaps even usually, fail to measure up to the high hopes of those who initiate them. When rebellions succeed in replacing the ruling elite, the result is often the institution of a military dictatorship even more restrictive and repressive than the government that existed before. The new ruling establishment may merely substitute one set of repressions for another rather than bring any real change to the nation. On the other hand, some revolutions have resulted in fairly drastic overhauls of societies.

The idea of revolution has been one of the central myths and inspirations of many groups both in the past and in the present. The colonial empire building of countries, such as England and France, created a worldwide situation in which rebellion became nearly inevitable. In numerous technologically underdeveloped lands, which have been exploited by more powerful countries for their natural resources and cheap labor, a deep resentment has often developed against the foreign ruling classes or their local clients. Where the ruling classes, native or foreign, refuse to be responsive to those feelings, rebellion becomes the only alternative. In many areas, it has become a way of life.

Anti-government protesters during a 2011 rally in Morocco that became part of what is known as the Arab Spring movement.

Culture Change and Adaptation

12.8 Relate culture change to the process of adaptation to a changing environment.

We have discussed the fact that culture is patterned, and that adaptation to the environment is one reason why certain culture traits are clustered, because more than one trait is likely to be *adaptive* in a particular environment. We make the assumption that most of the customary behaviors of a culture are probably *adaptive*, or at least not maladaptive, in that environment. Even though customs are learned and not genetically inherited, cultural adaptation may resemble biological adaptation in one major respect. The frequency of certain genetic alternatives is likely to increase over time if those genetic traits increase their carriers' chances of survival and reproduction. Similarly, the frequency of a new learned behavior will increase over time and become customary in a population if the people with that behavior are most likely to survive and reproduce.

One of the most important differences between cultural evolution and genetic evolution is that individuals often can decide whether or not to accept and follow the way their parents behave or think, whereas they cannot decide whether or not to inherit certain genes. When enough individuals change their behavior and beliefs, we say that the culture has changed. Therefore, it is possible for culture change to occur much more rapidly than genetic change.

A dramatic example of intentional cultural change was the adoption and later elimination of the custom of *sepaade* among the Rendille, a pastoral population that herds camels, goats, and sheep in the desert in northern Kenya. According to the *sepaade* tradition, some women had to wait to marry until all their brothers were married. These women could well have been over 40 by the time they married. The Rendille say that this tradition was a result of intense warfare between the Rendille and the Borana during the mid-19th century. Attacked by Borana on horseback, the male warriors had to leave their camels unattended, and the frightened camels fled. The daughters of one male age-set were appointed to look after the camels, and the *sepaade* tradition developed. In 1998, long after warfare with the Borana ceased, the elders decided to free the *sepaade* from their obligation to postpone their own marriages. Interviews with the Rendille in the 1990s revealed that many individuals were fully aware of the reason for the tradition in the first place. Now, they said, there was peace, so there was no longer any reason for the *sepaade* tradition to continue.[49]

The adoption of the *sepaade* is an example of culture change in a changing environment. But what if the environment is stable? Is culture change more or less likely? Robert Boyd and Peter Richerson have shown mathematically that, when the environment is relatively stable and individual mistakes are costly, staying with customary modes of behavior (usually transmitted by parents) is probably more adaptive than changing.[50] But what happens when the environment, particularly the social environment, is changing? There are plenty of examples in the modern world of circumstances that force a change: People have to migrate to new places for work; medical care leads to increased population so that land is scarcer; people have had land taken away from them and are forced to make do with less land; and so on.

It is particularly when circumstances change that individuals are likely to try ideas or behaviors that are different from those of their parents. Most people would want to adopt behaviors that are more suited to their present circumstances, but how do they know which behaviors are better? There are various ways to find out. One way is by experimenting, trying out various new behaviors. Another way is to evaluate the experiments of others. If a person who tries a new technique seems successful, we would expect that person to be imitated, just as we would expect people to stick with new behaviors they have personally tried and found successful. Finally, one might choose to do what most people in the new situation decide to do.[51]

Why one choice rather than another? In part, the choice may be a function of the cost or risk of the innovation. It is relatively easy, for example, to find out how long it takes to cut down a tree with an introduced steel ax as compared with a stone ax. Not surprisingly, innovations such as a steel ax catch on relatively quickly because comparison is easy and the results clear-cut. But what if the risk is very great? Suppose the innovation involves adopting a whole new way of farming that you have never practiced before. You can try it, but you might not have any food if you fail. As we discussed earlier, risky innovations are likely to be tried only by those individuals who can afford the risk. Other people may then evaluate their success and adopt the new strategy if it looks promising. Similarly, if you migrate to a new area, say, from a high-rainfall area to a drier one, it may pay to look around to see what most people in the new place do; after all, the people in the drier area probably have customs that are adaptive for that environment.

We can expect, then, that the choices individuals make may often be adaptive ones. But it is important to note that adopting an innovation from someone in one's own society or borrowing an innovation from another society is not always or necessarily beneficial, either in the short or the long run. First, people may make mistakes in judgment, especially when some new behavior seems to satisfy a physical need. Why, for example, have smoking and drug use diffused so widely even though they are likely to reduce a person's chances of survival? Second, even if people are correct in their short-term judgment of benefit, they may be wrong in their judgment about long-run benefit. A new crop may yield more than the old crop for five consecutive years, but the new crop may fail miserably in the sixth year because of lower-than-normal rainfall or because the new crop depleted soil nutrients. Third, people may be forced by the more powerful to change with few if any benefits for themselves.

Whatever motivates humans to change their behavior, the theory of natural selection suggests that a new behavior is not likely to become cultural or remain cultural over generations if it has harmful reproductive consequences, just as a genetic mutation with harmful consequences is not likely to become frequent in a population.[52] Still, we know of many examples of culture change that seem maladaptive—the switch to bottle-feeding rather than nursing infants, which may spread infection because contaminated water is used, or the adoption of alcoholic beverages, which may lead to alcoholism and early death.

Baby Girl Names	1970's	1980's	1990's	2000's
Amanda	#17	#3	#6	#63
Amy	#2	#15	#64	#115
Ashley	#140	#4	#2	#10
Emily	#66	#25	#3	#1
Emma			#56	#3
Hannah		#91	#11	#5
Jennifer	#1	#2	#1	#39
Jessica	#11	#1	#16	#23
Kimberly	#5	#17	#36	#56
Madison			#29	#2
Michelle	#4	#12	#32	#72
Olivia		#195	#38	#4
Samantha	#109	#26	#5	#8
Sarah	#19	#5	#4	#12

FIGURE 12.2

The names shown here were in the top 5 baby names for at least one decade from the 1970s to the 2000s. The number shown is the rank for the decade. If a row is blank it means that the name was not in the top 200. Note that although there is some overlap between adjacent decades in popular names, there is, with the exception of Jennifer, no overlap every other decade. Baby names are widely thought to be a type of culture change that results from random copying, but has no adaptive consequences.

Source: http://www.socialsecurity.gov/OACT/babynames/decades/index.htm

Copying others doing something different is an important part of culture change, but sometimes there is no apparent adaptive consequence. Extrapolating from genetic research that shows that biological change can sometimes occur nonselectively—that is, by pure chance—cultural anthropologists have identified coincidences in popular culture change that they explain as examples of neutral or random copying. Random copying appears to occur with enough frequency that it creates patterns and repetitions that are especially apparent in popular culture. For example, random copying may explain why a large proportion of the public chooses the same favorite song or the same names for their babies (see Figure 12.2).[53]

Globalization: Problems and Opportunities

12.9 Evaluate the problems and opportunities posed by globalization.

Investment capital, people, and ideas are moving around the world at an ever faster rate.[60] Transportation now allows people and goods to circle the globe in days; telecommunications and the Internet make it possible to send a message around the world in seconds and minutes. Economic exchange is enormously more global and transnational. The word **globalization** is often used nowadays to refer to "the massive flow of goods, people, information, and capital across huge areas of the earth's surface."[61] The process of globalization has resulted in the worldwide spread of cultural features, particularly in the domain of economics and international trade. We buy from the same companies (that have factories all over the world), and we sell our products and services for prices that are set by world market forces. We can eat pizza, hamburgers, curry, or sushi in most urban centers.

Globalization The ongoing spread of goods, people, information, and capital around the world.

In some ways, cultures are changing in similar directions. They have become more commercial, more urban, and more international. The job has become more important, and kinship less important, as people travel to and work in other countries and return just periodically to their original homes. Ideas about democracy, the rights of the individual, and alternative medical practices and religions have become more widespread; people in many countries of the world watch the same TV shows, wear similar fashions, and listen to the same or similar music. In short, people are increasingly sharing behaviors and beliefs with people in other cultures, and as Paul Durrenberger says, the cultures of the world are less and less things "with edges."[62]

Globalization as we know it began in earnest about A.D. 1500 with exploration by and expansion of Western societies.[63] We tend to think of globalization from a Western perspective. But a form of continental diffusion between Asia, Africa, and Europe had been occurring since at least the beginning of written history, in large part because of the scope and power of empires. The great ancient empires, ruled by Assyrian, Chinese, and Egyptian dynasties, transformed the cultures of the peoples they conquered but were also themselves changed by their encounters. The Roman Empire extended its reach to western Asia in the time of Christ. Arab caliphates ruled parts of medieval Europe and revived long dormant scientific and mathematical traditions. The Mongol Empire swept across Central Asia and into the Baltics in the 13th century. All of these contacts had already transformed parts of the world. Nevertheless, it is safe to say that globalization is occurring today at an unprecedented pace and scale. Very few places in the world have not been affected by globalization.[64] Most of the recent external pressures have come from Western societies, but not all. Far Eastern societies, such as Japan and China, have also stimulated culture change.

But diffusion of a culture trait does not mean that it is incorporated in exactly the same way, and the spread of certain products and activities through globalization does not mean that change happens in the same way everywhere. For example, the spread of multinational fast-food restaurants, such as McDonald's or Kentucky Fried Chicken, has come to symbolize globalization. But the behavior of the Japanese in such restaurants is quite different from that of Americans. Perhaps the most surprising difference is that the Japanese who visit a McDonald's actually engage in more familial intimacy and sharing than they do in their traditional restaurants. We imagine that establishments like McDonald's

Worldwide communication and the spread of ideas is facilitated by technology such as satellite TV and the internet. Balconies are used to dry clothes and to hang satellite dishes in this city in Algeria.

promote fast eating. But Japan has long had fast food—noodle shops at train stations, street vendors, and boxed lunches. Sushi, which is usually ordered in the United States at a sit-down restaurant, is often served in Japan at a bar with a conveyor belt—individuals only need to pluck off the wanted dish as it goes by. Observations at McDonald's in Japan suggest that mothers typically order food for the family while the father spends time with the children at a table, a rare event since fathers often work long hours and cannot get home for dinner often. The French fries are typically shared by the family. Even burgers and drinks are passed around, with many people taking a bite or a sip. Japan has historically borrowed food, such as the Chinese noodle soup now called ramen. Indeed, in a survey, ramen was listed as the most representative Japanese food. The burger was the second most-often listed. McDonald's has become Japanese—the younger generation does not even know that McDonald's is a foreign company—they think it is Japanese.[65]

Enormous amounts of international investment fuel world trade. Shifts in the world marketplace may drastically affect a country's well-being more than ever before. There are many negative effects of colonialism, imperialism, and globalization. For example, 60 percent of Pakistan's industrial employment is in textile and apparel manufacturing, but serious unemployment resulted when that manufacturing was crippled by restrictive American import policies and fears about war between India and Afghanistan.[66] Native peoples in many places have lost their land and been forced to work for inadequate wages in mines, plantations, and factories owned by foreign capitalists. Undernutrition, if not starvation, is a common problem. Also, global travel has hastened the spread of such diseases as HIV and severe acute respiratory syndrome (more widely known by its abbreviation SARS), and increasing deforestation has led to a spread of malaria.[67]

Are there any positive consequences of globalization? The "human development indicators" collected by the United Nations suggest many improvements, including increases in life expectancy and literacy in most countries. The increased life expectancy is undoubtedly largely due to the spread of medicines developed in the advanced economies of the West. There is generally less warfare as colonial powers enforced pacification within the colonies that later became independent states. Most important, perhaps, has been the worldwide growth of middle classes whose livelihoods depend on globalizing commerce. The middle classes in many countries have also become agents of social change; empowered by their strength in numbers, they have pressured governments to reduce social injustice and enact democratic reforms.

World trade is the primary engine of economic development. With it, per capita income is increasing. Forty years ago, the countries of Asia were among the poorest countries in the world in terms of per capita income. Since then, because of their involvement in world trade, their incomes have risen enormously. In 1960, South Korea was as poor as India. Now its per capita income is 20 times higher than India's. Singapore is an even more dramatic example. In the late 1960s, its economy was failing. Today, its per capita income is higher than Britain's.[68] Mexico used to be a place where North Americans built factories to produce garments for the North American market. Now its labor is no longer so cheap. But because Mexico has easy access to the North American market and because its large labor force is acquiring the necessary skills, it is developing high-tech manufacturing with decent salaries.[69]

Not every country has a large labor force, a fact that has promoted a world trade in people. Many countries now export labor to other countries, with their government's blessing. Mexico has done so for a long time. Millions of people from Bangladesh are overseas on government-sponsored work contracts. Virtually every family in a Bangladeshi village depends on someone who works overseas and sends money home. Without those remittances, many would face starvation.[70]

Does the higher per capita income that can come with globalization mean that life has improved generally in a country? Not necessarily. Inequality within countries can increase with technological improvements, since the rich often benefit the most. In addition, economic wealth is increasingly concentrated in a relatively small number of countries. Although most countries may be doing better on average, there is also more income and class inequality, and poverty is more widespread.

Although many of the changes associated with globalization seem to be driven by the economic and political power of the richer countries, the movement of ideas, art, music, and food is more reciprocal, in large part because people who migrate bring their culture with them. Thanks to migration, North Americans regularly eat tortilla chips and salsa, sushi, and curries; listen to reggae music; dance to Latin American rhythms; live with African carvings; and wear beaded necklaces.

In counterreaction to globalization, there has also been increased interest recently in gaining knowledge about the indigenous plants, healing traditions, and shamanistic practices within countries. As indigenous knowledge comes to be viewed as potentially valuable, shamans have been able to speak out on national and international issues. In Brazil, for example, shamans have organized to speak out against "biopiracy"—the perceived unethical appropriation of biological knowledge for commercial purposes. In a more globalized world, such indigenous activists can be heard by more people than ever before: In spite of the fact that indigenous people constitute less than 1 percent of the Brazilian population, some activist groups have been able to keep in touch with international environmentalists, using tape recorders and video cameras to convey information about their local situation.[71]

It is probably not possible to go back to a time when societies were not so dependent on each other, not so interconnected through world trade, and not so dependent on commercial exchange. Even those who are most upset with globalization find it difficult to imagine that it is possible to return to a less connected world. For better or worse, the world is interconnected and will remain so. The question now is whether the average economic improvements in countries will eventually translate into economic improvements for most individuals.

Ethnogenesis Creation of a new culture.

12.10 Describe and give examples of ethnogenesis, or the emergence of new cultures.

Ethnogenesis: The Emergence of New Cultures

Many of the processes that we have discussed—expansion and domination by the West and other powerful nations, peoples' reduced ability to earn their livelihoods by traditional means, the imposition of schools or other methods to force acculturation, attempts to convert people to other religions, and globalization—have led to profound changes in culture. But if culture change in the modern world has made cultures more alike in some ways, it has not eliminated cultural differences. Indeed, many cultures still vary considerably. Moreover, the aftermath of violent events, such as depopulation, relocation, enslavement, and genocide, can lead to **ethnogenesis**, a process whereby a group creates a new culture.[72]

Osceola, a Seminole chief, was born of a British father and a Creek mother. He led his people against the settlers in the Seminole Wars but was captured and died in confinement at Fort Moultrie, South Carolina.

Some of the most dramatic examples of ethnogenesis occur in areas where escaped slaves (called Maroons) have settled. Maroon societies emerged in the past few hundred years in a variety of New World locations, from the United States to the West Indies and northern parts of South America. One such new culture in South America, now known as Aluku, emerged when slaves fled from coastal plantations in Suriname to the swampy interior country along the Cottica River. After a war with the Dutch colonists, this particular group moved to French Guiana. The escaped slaves, originating from widely varying cultures in Africa or born on Suriname plantations, organized themselves into autonomous communities with military headmen.[73] Although Aluku settlements shifted location as a way of evading enemies, co-residence in a community and collective ownership of land became important parts of their emerging identities. Communities took on the names of the specific plantations from which their leaders had escaped. Principles of inheritance through the female line began to develop, and full-fledged

Migrants and Immigrants

Increasing Cultural Diversity Within the Countries of the World

The modern world is culturally diverse in two ways. There are native cultures in every part of the world, and today most countries have people from different cultures who have arrived relatively recently. Recent arrivals may be migrants coming for temporary work, or they may be refugees, forced by persecution or genocide to migrate, or they may be immigrants who voluntarily come into a new country. Parts of populations have moved away from their native places since the dawn of humanity. The first modern-looking humans moved out of Africa only in the last 100,000 years, and people have been moving ever since. The people we call Native Americans were actually the first to come to the New World; most anthropologists think they came from northeast Asia.

The large Chinese community in Rome, Italy, celebrates the Chinese New Year in one of the town's main squares.

In the last 200 years, the United States and Canada have experienced extensive influxes of people. Native Americans are vastly outnumbered by descendants of earlier immigrants and by newcomers from Europe, Africa, Asia, Latin America, and elsewhere. North America not only has native and regional subcultures but also ethnic, religious, and occupational subcultures, each with its own distinctive set of culture traits. Thus, North American culture is partly a "melting pot" and partly a mosaic of cultural diversity. Many of us (aside from anthropologists) like the variety such diversity brings to our lives.

Many of the population movements in the world today, as in the past, are responses to persecution and war. The word *diaspora* is often used nowadays to refer to these major dispersions. Most were and are involuntary; people are fleeing danger and death. But this is not always the case. Scholars distinguish between different types of diasporas, including "victim," "labor," "trade," and "imperial." The Africans who were sold into slavery; the Armenians who fled genocide in the early 20th century; the Jews who fled persecution and genocide in various places over the centuries; the Palestinians who fled to the West Bank, Gaza, Jordan, and Lebanon in the mid-20th century; and the Rwandans who fled genocide toward the end of the 20th century may have mostly been victims. But the Chinese, Italians, and Poles may have mostly moved to take advantage of job opportunities, the Lebanese to trade, and the British to extend and service their empire.

Often categories of diaspora overlap; population movements can and have occurred for more than one reason. As economics and politics are more globalized, diasporas are becoming more "transnational"; and the ease of global communications allows people to maintain social, economical, and political ties to their homelands. Some diasporic communities play an active role in the politics of their homelands, and some nation-states have begun to recognize their far-flung emigrants as important constituencies.

Cultural anthropologists are increasingly studying migrant, refugee, and immigrant groups and focusing on how the groups have adapted their cultures to new surroundings, what they have retained, how they relate to the homeland, how they have developed an ethnic consciousness, and how they relate to other minority groups and the majority culture.

Sources: M. Ember et al. 2005; Levinson and M. Ember 1997.

matriclans became the core of each village. They practiced slash-and-burn cultivation, with women doing most of the work. Aluku also established spiritual practices. Each village had its own shrine, the *faaka tiki,* where residents invoked the clan ancestors, as well as a special house where the deceased were brought and honored before being taken to the forest for burial. And Aluku clans inherited avenging spirits with whom they could communicate through mediums.

The Aluku are a clear example of ethnogenesis because the culture did not exist 350 years ago. It emerged and was created by people trying to adapt to circumstances not of their own making. In common with other cases of emerging ethnic identity, the Aluku came not only to share new patterns of behavior but also to see themselves as having a common origin (a common ancestor), a shared history, and a common religion.[74]

The emergence of the Seminole in Florida is another example of ethnogenesis. The early settlers who moved to what is now Florida and later became known as Seminole largely derived from the Lower Creek Kawita chiefdom. The Kawita chiefdom, like other southeastern Muskogean chiefdoms, was a large, complex, and multiethnic paramount chiefdom. Its ruler, Kawita, relied on allegiance and tribute from outlying districts on which he imposed ritual and linguistic hegemony.[75]

A combination of internal divisions among the Lower Creek, vacant land in northern Florida, and weak Spanish control over northern Florida apparently prompted dissidents to move away and settle in three different areas in Florida. Three new chiefdoms were established, essentially similar to those the settlers left and still under the supposed control of Kawita.[76] But the three chiefdoms began to act together under the leadership of Tonapi, the Talahassi chief. After 1780, over a period of 40 or so years, the three Seminole chiefdoms formally broke with Kawita. Not only was geographic separation a factor, but the political and economic interests of the Creek Confederacy and of the Seminole had diverged. For example, the Creek supported neutrality in the American Revolution, but the Seminole took the side of the British. During this time, the British encouraged slaves to escape by promising freedom in Florida. These Maroon communities allied themselves with the emerging Seminole. The composition of the Seminole population again changed dramatically after the War of 1812 and the Creek War of 1814.[77] First, a large number of Creek refugees, mostly Upper Creek Talapusa (who spoke a different Muskogean language), became Seminole. Second, the Seminole ranks were also expanded by a large number of escaped slaves and Maroons who fled when the Americans destroyed a British fort in 1816. Larger scale political events continued to influence Seminole history. When the Americans conquered Florida, they insisted on dealing with one unified Seminole council, they removed the Seminole to a reserve in Florida, and later, after the second Seminole war, removed most of them to Oklahoma.[78] It would seem from this and other cases that cultural identities can be shaped and reshaped by political and economic processes.

12.11 Characterize what anthropologists predict about future cultural diversity.

Cultural Diversity in the Future

Measured in terms of travel time, the world today is much smaller than it has ever been. It is possible now to fly halfway around the globe in the time it took people less than a century ago to travel to the next state. In the realm of communication, the world is even smaller. We can talk to someone on the other side of the globe in a matter of minutes, we can send that person a message (by cell phone or the Internet) in seconds, and through television we can see live coverage of events in that person's country. More and more people are drawn into the world market economy, buying and selling similar things and, as a consequence, altering the patterns of their lives in sometimes similar ways. Still, although modern transportation and communication facilitate the rapid spread of some cultural characteristics to all parts of the globe, it is highly unlikely that all parts of the world will end up the same culturally. Cultures are bound to retain some of their original characteristics or develop distinctive new adaptations. Even though television has diffused around the world, local people continue to prefer local programs when they are available. And even when people all over the world watch the same program, they may interpret it in very different ways. People are not just absorbing the messages they get, they often resist or revise them.[79]

Until recently, researchers studying culture change generally assumed that the differences between people of different cultures would become minimal. But in the last 30 years or so, it has become increasingly apparent that, although many differences disappear, many people are affirming ethnic identities in a process that often involves deliberately introducing cultural difference.[80] Eugeen Roosens describes the situation of the Huron of Quebec, who in the late 1960s seemed to have disappeared as a distinct culture. The Huron language had disappeared and the lives of the Huron were not obviously distinguishable from those of the French Canadians around them. The Huron then developed a new identity as they actively worked to promote the rights of indigenous peoples like themselves. That their new defining cultural symbols bore no resemblance to the past Huron culture is beside the point.

One fascinating possibility is that ethnic diversity and ethnogenesis may be a result of broader processes. Elizabeth Cashdan found that the degree of ethnic diversity appears to be related to environmental unpredictability, which is associated with greater distance from the equator.[81] More predictability seems to be associated with greater ethnic diversity. There are many more cultural groups nearer to the equator than in very northern and southern latitudes. Perhaps, Cashdan suggests, environmental unpredictability in the north and south necessitates wider ties between social groups to allow cooperation in case local resources fail. This may minimize the likelihood of cultural divergence, that is, ethnogenesis. Hence, there will be fewer cultures further from the equator.

Future research on culture change should increase our understanding of how and why various types of change are occurring. If we can increase our understanding of culture change in the present, we should be better able to understand similar processes in the past. We may be guided in our efforts to understand culture change by the large number of cross-cultural correlations that have been discovered between a particular cultural variation and its presumed causes.[82] All cultures have changed over time; variation is the product of differential change. Thus, the variations we see are the products of change processes, and the discovered predictors of those variations may suggest how and why the changes occurred.

Summary and Review

Defining Culture

12.1 Discuss the concept of culture as used in anthropology, its salient properties, and controversies surrounding the concept of culture.

- Culture is the set of learned behaviors and ideas (including beliefs, attitudes, values, and ideals) that are characteristic of a particular society or other social group.
- Behaviors can also produce products or material culture, including houses, musical instruments, and tools that are the products of customary behavior.
- Anthropologists have traditionally been concerned with the cultural characteristics of societies. Societies may or may not correspond to countries; many countries, particularly newer ones, contain many societies.
- The terms *society* and *culture* are not synonymous. Society refers to a group of people; culture refers to the learned and shared behaviors, ideas, and characteristic of those people.
- Even when anthropologists refer to something as cultural, there is always individual variation, and not everyone in a society shares a particular cultural characteristic of that society.
- For something to be considered cultural, it must be not only shared but also learned.
- Cognitive anthropologists are most likely to say that culture refers not to behaviors but to the rules and ideas behind them, and that culture therefore resides in people's heads.
- Another view is that culture is an entity, a force, that profoundly affects the individuals who live within its influence.

? What are the salient properties of culture?

Cultural Constraints

12.2 Describe direct and indirect cultural constraints, and how they relate to norms.

- Because members of a culture generally conform to that culture, they are not always aware of being constrained by its standards and rules for acceptable behavior, which social scientists refer to as norms.
- Cultural constraints can be direct or indirect.

> ? What is an example of a direct cultural constraint and an indirect cultural constraint?

Attitudes That Hinder the Study of Cultures

12.3 Identify attitudes that hinder the study of cultures.

- Ethnocentrism—a view of one's cultural behaviors and attitudes as correct and those of other cultures as immoral or inferior—can bias objectively observing another culture.
- Ethnocentrism also keeps a person from understanding his or her own customs.
- Glorification of one's own culture or that of another also hinders effective anthropological study.

> ? What are some examples of ethnocentrism?

Cultural Relativism

12.4 Critically assess the concept of cultural relativism.

- The idea of cultural relativism rejects the notion that Western cultures are at the highest or most progressive stage of evolution.
- Cultural relativism attempts to objectively describe and understand a society's customs and ideas in the context of that society's problems and opportunities.
- Following the idea of cultural relativism helps anthropologists be alert to perspectives in other cultures that might challenge their own cultural beliefs about what is true and that might lead them to make moral judgments.
- Approaches using cultural relativism pose conflicts with efforts to create universal standards of human rights. However, universal human rights advocates might increase their persuasiveness if they are aware of the viewpoints and values within a particular culture.

> ? What are some of the controversies surrounding the concept of cultural relativism?

Describing a Culture

12.5 Describe the methods by which anthropologists describe cultures.

- Understanding what is cultural involves (a) separating what is shared from what is individually variable and (b) understanding whether common behaviors and ideas are learned.
- Variations in behavior are typically confined within socially acceptable limits.
- Anthropologists try to distinguish actual behavior from ideal cultural traits—the ideas about how people in particular situations ought to feel and behave. Ideal cultural traits may differ from actual behavior because the ideal is based on the way society used to be.
- When a domain of behavior includes many individual variations or when the people studied are unaware of their pattern of behavior, the anthropologist may need to collect information from a larger sample of individuals to establish what the cultural trait is.
- Anthropologists suspect that something is largely learned if it varies from society to society and is genetically influenced when it is found in all societies.

> ? How do anthropologists distinguish between what is cultural or individually variable?

Culture Is Patterned

12.6 Explain why culture is integrated or patterned.

- A culture that is mostly integrated is one in which elements or traits are mostly adjusted to or consistent with one another.
- Integration may be influenced by psychological processes and by people transferring experiences from one area of life to another.
- Cultural traits may become patterned through adaptation. Customs that diminish the survival chances of a society are not likely to persist. However, what may be adaptive in one environment may not be adaptive in another.

> ? What are some examples of cultural patterning or integration?

How and Why Cultures Change

12.7 Describe and give examples of how cultures change through discovery and invention, diffusion, and acculturation.

- Examining the history of a society will reveal that its culture has changed over time. Consequently, in describing a culture, it is important to understand that a description pertains to a particular time period.
- A good deal of culture change may be stimulated by changes in the external environment.
- Inventions and discoveries (including behavior and ideas), when accepted and regularly used by a society, will change the culture. These inventions and discoveries might be unintentional or intentional.
- Relatively little is known about why some people are more innovative than others. The ability to innovate may depend in part on such individual characteristics as high intelligence and creativity. Creativity may be influenced by social conditions.
- In general, people are more likely to adopt a behavior or innovation as it becomes more common. The speed with which an innovation is adopted may depend partly on how new behaviors and ideas are typically transmitted—or taught—in a society.
- New cultural elements in one society may come from another society. Innovation occurring in this way is called diffusion. The three basic patterns of diffusion are direct contact, intermediate contact, and stimulus diffusion.
- Diffusion is a selective process. New traits and elements will be rejected or accepted depending on complex variables.
- Acculturation is another type of change that occurs when different cultural groups come into intensive contact. Acculturation occurs primarily when one of the two societies in contact is more powerful than the other.
- One of the most drastic and rapid way a culture can change is as a result of revolution—replacement, usually violent, of a country's rulers.
- The sources of revolution may be mostly internal, or partly external. Revolutions are not always successful in their goals, nor necessarily in bringing about culture change.
- Not all people who are suppressed, conquered, or colonialized eventually rebel against established authority. Revolutions are more likely in countries that are just becoming industrialized.

? How do cultures change through discovery and invention, diffusion, and acculturation?

Culture Change and Adaptation

12.8 Relate culture change to the process of adaptation to a changing environment.

- The frequency of a new learned behavior will increase over time and become customary in a population if the people exhibiting that behavior are most likely to survive and reproduce. It is possible for culture change to occur much more rapidly than genetic change.
- When circumstances change, individuals are particularly likely to try ideas or behaviors that are different from those of their parents.

? What is an example of how adaptation can lead to culture change?

Globalization: Problems and Opportunities

12.9 Evaluate the problems and opportunities posed by globalization.

- The process of globalization has resulted in the worldwide spread of cultural features, particularly in the domain of economics and international trade.
- In some ways, cultures are changing in similar directions. They have become more commercial, more urban, and more international.
- A form of continental diffusion between Asia, Africa, and Europe had been occurring since at least the beginning of written history, in large part because of the scope and power of empires.
- Worldwide diffusion of a culture trait does not mean that it is incorporated in exactly the same way among societies, and the spread of certain products and activities through globalization does not mean that change happens in the same way everywhere.
- Negative effects of globalization include unemployment, native peoples' loss of land, increasing class inequality, undernutrition and starvation, and spread of disease.
- Positive effects of globalization include increases in life expectancy and literacy, less warfare, and growth of middle classes, which have become agents of social change.

- Movement of ideas, art, music, and food among cultures tends to be reciprocal.

> **?** Using some examples, what are some examples of positive and negative effects of globailization?

Ethnogenesis: The Emergence of New Cultures

12.10 Describe and give examples of ethnogenesis, or the emergence of new cultures.

- Despite the trend of globalization, many cultures still vary considerably, and new cultures have been created—a process called ethnogenesis.
- In particular, cases of violent events such as depopulation, relocation, enslavement, and genocide can lead to ethnogenesis.

> **?** What is ethnogenesis? Under what conditions is it more likely?

Cultural Diversity in the Future

12.11 Characterize what anthropologists predict about future cultural diversity.

- Although modern transportation and communication facilitate the rapid spread of some cultural characteristics to all parts of the globe, it is highly unlikely that all parts of the world will end up the same culturally.
- Many people are affirming ethnic identities in a process that often involves deliberately introducing cultural difference.
- One study suggests that there are many more cultural groups nearer to the equator than in very northern and southern latitudes, possibly associated with levels of greater environmental predictability.

> **?** Why will globalization processes likely not result in the development of a homogenous worldwide culture?

Think on it

1. Would it be adaptive for a **society** to have everyone adhere to the cultural norms? Explain your answer.
2. Not all people faced with **external pressure** to change do so or do so at the same rate. What factors might explain why some societies rapidly change their culture?
3. Does the concept of **cultural relativism** promote international understanding, or does it hinder attempts to have international agreement on acceptable behavior, such as human rights?

CHAPTER

15 Getting Food

LEARNING OBJECTIVES

15.1	Describe foraging and complex foraging, and identify the general societal features associated with food collecting.
15.2	Describe the various forms of food production (horticulture, intensive agriculture, and pastoralism), and identify the general societal features associated with each.
15.3	Identify environmental restraints on food-getting.
15.4	Discuss the origin of food production.
15.5	Describe and critically discuss the spread and intensification of food production.

The way we get our food has changed dramatically over the course of human history. Today almost half of the world's people live in cities, and food is obtained by buying it. Where and when we buy food may be culturally determined; Europeans and Asians, for example, are more likely to prefer going to a market daily to buy fresh food. North Americans have accustomed themselves to going to a supermarket, where they get a stockpile of food for the week. Those of us who buy our food from a supermarket can buy a week's worth of food within an hour, refrigerate it, and move on to other activities. Seasons don't daunt us. Week after week, we know food will be there. But we do not think of what would happen if the food were not delivered to the supermarket. We wouldn't be able to eat, and without eating for a while, we would die. Despite the old adage "Man [or woman] does not live by bread alone," we could not live at all without bread or the equivalent. Food-getting activities, then, take precedence over other activities important to survival. Reproduction, social control (the maintenance of peace and order within a group), defense against external threat, and the transmission of knowledge and skills to future generations—none could take place without energy derived from food. But it is not merely energy that is required for survival and long-term reproduction. Food-getting strategies need to provide the appropriate combination of nutrients throughout varying seasons and changing environmental conditions. Food-getting activities are also important because the way a society gets its food strongly predicts other aspects of a culture, from community size and permanence of settlement to the type of economy and its degree of inequality, the type of political system, and even art styles and religious beliefs and practices.

In contrast with our own and similar societies, there are still many societies in which almost all able-bodied adults are directly engaged in getting food for themselves and their families. Such economies are described as **subsistence economies**. For millions of years, humans obtained their food by gathering wild plants, hunting or scavenging wild animals, and fishing; agriculture was unknown. Agriculture is a relatively recent phenomenon, dating back only about 10,000 years. And industrial or mechanized agriculture is hardly more than a century old. Harvesting machines have been used a little bit longer, but self-propelled machines had to wait for the internal combustion engine and the rise of the oil industry.

Subsistence economies Economies in which almost all able-bodied adults are largely engaged in getting food for themselves and their families.

In this chapter, we look at the ways different societies get food and discuss some of the features associated with the different patterns. We ask why societies vary in their food-getting strategies. We shall see that the physical environment by itself has only a limited or restraining effect on how a society gets most of its food. To explain the variation more fully, we discuss at the end of the chapter why societies in the prehistoric past switched from collecting wild food resources to cultivating plants and raising animals.

Foraging May be generally defined as a food-getting strategy that obtains wild plant and animal resources through gathering, hunting, scavenging, or fishing; also known as food collection.

Foraging

15.1 Describe foraging and complex foraging, and identify the general societal features associated with food collecting.

Foraging or *food collection* may generally be defined as a strategy whereby humans gather, hunt, scavenge, or fish to obtain their food from plants and animals found in the wild. Although foraging was the way humans got their food for most of human history, foragers—also commonly referred to as **hunter-gatherers**—are not very numerous in the world today. Most foraging societies currently live in what have been called the *marginal areas* of the earth—deserts, the Arctic, and dense tropical forests—habitats that do not allow easy exploitation by modern agricultural technologies. In the last few hundred years, only about 5 million people have been foragers.[1]

Hunter-gatherers People who collect food from naturally occurring resources, that is, wild plants, animals, and fish. The term *hunter-gatherers* minimizes sometimes heavy dependence on fishing. Also referred to as **foragers** or *food collectors*.

Yet the relatively few foraging societies still available for observation have been the focus of intense anthropological study. Of course, our knowledge of human culture depends on an understanding of all its variations, from foragers to intensive agriculturalists to post-industrial cultures. But why is there so much focus on hunter-gatherers when there are so few societies left and foraging as a way of life for the world's humanity is mostly in the past? The main reason has been a belief in the significance of the hunter-gatherer way of life in the evolution of human culture. Anthropologists have argued that if we want to understand

Like the Ngatatjara, the Aborigine of Australia's Northern Territory are also foragers. This woman is digging for a major source of protein for her family, witchetty grubs, the large moth larvae that are found under the so-called witchetty bush.

many aspects of culture, we cannot disregard cultures whose primary subsistence strategy characterized most of human history. Some even surmise that much of human behavior is shaped by that long stretch of history when humans were foragers. We must nevertheless be cautious in drawing inferences about the past from our observations of recent and contemporary foragers. First, early foragers lived in almost all types of environments, including some bountiful ones. Therefore, what we observe of recent and contemporary foragers, who generally live in deserts, the Arctic, and tropical forests, may not be comparable to what the forager way of life might have been in more favorable past environments.[2] Second, contemporary foragers are not relics of the past. Like all contemporary societies, they have evolved and are still evolving. Indeed, recent research reveals considerable variation in economic behavior, as well as in social structure, among foraging groups that share common ancestry, which suggests that recent foragers have responded to differences in local environmental conditions.[3] Third, recent and contemporary foragers have been interacting with kinds of societies that did not exist until after 10,000 years ago—agriculturalists, pastoralists, and intrusive, powerful state societies.[4] Evidence from South Asia and Southeast Asia, for example, suggests that trade with agriculturalists was probably an important component of foragers' economic strategies for millennia.[5] And, in the recent past, foraging people have increasingly depended not only on trade but also on agriculture and commercial activities as additional means of subsistence.

Long before the English began to colonize Australia in 1788 (by sending shiploads of convicts to establish settlements), that vast continent was home to several hundred ancient societies that spoke many languages and lived in a variety of environments but had in common the foraging way of life. One of these aboriginal societies, the Ngatatjara, still lived by gathering wild plants and hunting wild animals in the Gibson Desert of western Australia as late as 1967, when Richard Gould's 15-month visit among them was coming to an end. The description of daily life among the Ngatatjara that follows is based on Gould's observations.[6] (Because it is customary in ethnographic writing, we adopt the present tense in the narrative, but readers should remember that we are referring to the society's life in the 1960s.)

The desert environment of the Ngatatjara averages less than 8 inches of rain per year, and the temperature in summer may rise to 118°F. The few permanent water holes are separated by hundreds of square miles of sand, scrub, and rock. Even before Europeans arrived in Australia, the area was sparsely populated, with less than one person per 35 to 40 square miles. Now there are even fewer people because the aboriginal population was decimated by introduced diseases and colonial mistreatment.

The Ngatatjara, like most Australian aborigines, are traditionally nomadic and move their campsites often in search of food. Each campsite is isolated and inhabited by only a small number of people, or by clusters of groups including as many as 80 people. Camp is never set up right next to a watering spot, which is the natural destination of the game the men hope to capture. If the camp is too close, the noise might frighten away the animals. The Ngatatjara are also careful not to encroach on the needs of neighboring bands (some of which may be in-laws) by seeming to take over the scarce watering spots.

On a typical day, the camp begins to stir just before sunrise, while it is still dark. Children are sent to fetch water, and the people breakfast on water and food left over from the night before. In the cool of early morning, the adults talk and make plans for the day. Where should they go for food—to places they have been recently or a new place? Sometimes there are other considerations. One woman, for instance, may want to look for plants that have the kind of bark she uses to make new sandals. The conversation can go on for a while, since the group prefers that everyone is in agreement about what to do.

Once the women decide which plants they want to gather and where they think those plants are most likely to be found, they take up their digging sticks and set out with large wooden bowls of drinking water balanced on their heads. Their children ride on their hips or walk alongside them. Meanwhile, the men may have decided to hunt emus, 6-foot-tall ostrichlike birds that do not fly. The men go to a creek bed where they will wait to ambush any game that may come along. They lie patiently behind a screen of brush they have set up, hoping for a chance to throw a spear at an emu or even a kangaroo. They can throw only once because the game will run away if they miss.

By noon, all have returned to camp, the women each with their wooden bowls filled with up to 15 pounds of fruit or other plant foods and perhaps some lizards, the men more often than not with only some small game, such as rabbits. Because the men often return from the hunt empty-handed, the daily cooked meal is likely to be mostly plant food. The women will prepare the meal, and it will be eaten toward evening, after the group has spent an afternoon resting, gossiping, and making or repairing tools.

Life has changed dramatically for Australian aborigines since the late 1960s. Today, many live in small, settled villages. Anthropologist Victoria Burbank describes one such village in the Northern Territory of Australia where she did fieldwork in the 1980s. The once-nomadic aborigines live in a village that Burbank calls "Mangrove." The village, founded around a Protestant mission in the 1950s, is home to a population of 600 who live in houses with stoves, refrigerators, toilets, washing machines, and even television sets. Their children attend school full-time, and there is a health clinic for their medical needs. They still forage occasionally, but most of their food comes from the store. Some earn wages; many more subsist on government welfare checks.[7]

The Inupiaq of the North American Arctic

The diet of the Australian aborigines has been mainly wild plant foods. The foraging Inupiaq peoples, on the other hand, live year-round in the North American Arctic, where plants are too scarce to be an important part of the diet. From Greenland and Labrador in the east to Alaska in the west, the indigenous Arctic peoples have depended almost entirely on sea and land mammals and fish. (The term *Eskimo* is used widely in the West, but it is not a word in any of the native languages in that area. Many of the native Arctic groups, particularly those now living in Canada, prefer to be named Inuit.) We focus here on the traditional life of the north Alaskan Inupiaq in the beginning of the 19th century, as reconstructed by Ernest Burch (the "ethnographic present" in the following discussion).[8] Northern Alaska is relatively "warm" for its latitude but not for most of us farther south; little sun and below-zero temperatures for a month or so in the winter are hardly warm. Rivers and lakes freeze in October and do not thaw until May. Even the ocean freezes for part of the winter.

What the Inupiaq get for food depends mostly on the season, but the critical resources are sea mammals (ranging in size from whales to seals), fish, and caribou or wild reindeer. The usual technique for hunting sea mammals is to hurl a toggle harpoon into the animal from a kayak. Because it is very difficult to kill a moving sea mammal, hunters attach a line to the animal with the harpoon; on the other end of the line is a sealskin float that indicates where the harpooned sea mammal can be located. The sea mammal gets more and more tired pulling the float until the hunter is able to kill it with a lance. One man alone can manage to hunt smaller sea mammals, but groups of men are needed to hunt whales. In the winter, when the sea ice is frozen, hunters use a different hunting technique. Hunters must locate a breathing hole and then wait, immobile and attentive, for hours or sometimes days until a seal comes up for air. The instant a seal surfaces, the hunters must aim perfectly with the harpoon.

The women butcher the animal, prepare it for eating or storage, and process the skin. Women sew all of the skin clothing. They also hunt small animals, such as hares, and do much of the fishing. Various techniques are used for fishing—hook and line, spearing, and ambushing with nets and dams. Women make the fishing nets, and it takes the better part of a year to make one. Although there are not many plants to gather, the women do that too.

Related families usually live together and move camp by boat or sled to be in the best place to intercept the migratory animals and fish. For instance, caribou migrate, so the Inupiaq try to catch them by building a corral in a place through which they are expected to pass. A network of interrelated families lives and moves in a territory of thousands of square miles, moving outside it only when they have made arrangements with other groups to do so.

Much has changed since the time just described. Now the Inupiaq live in villages or towns with many modern conveniences. In the village of Kivalina, there are permanent houses with electricity, telephones, and television sets. Dog teams have been replaced by all-terrain vehicles and snowmobiles. There are powerful outboard motors rather than skin boats. Many men and women have full-time, wage-paying jobs. But even though the people may buy most of their food, there is still a preference for traditional foods, so the Inupiaq still hunt and fish on the weekends.

General Features of Foragers

Despite the differences in terrain and climate under which they live and the different food-collecting technologies they use, Australian aborigines, indigenous Arctic peoples, and most other recent foragers have certain characteristic cultural patterns (see Table 15.1). Most live in small communities in sparsely populated territories and follow a nomadic lifestyle, forming no permanent settlements. As a rule, they do not recognize individuals' land rights. Their communities generally do not have different classes of people and tend to have no specialized or full-time political officials.[9] Division of labor in foraging societies is based largely on age and gender: Men exclusively hunt large marine and land animals and usually do most of the fishing, and women usually gather wild plant foods.[10] Foragers must decide what plants or animals to target. Optimal foraging theory, which we discuss in the next chapter, helps explain some of the decisions foragers make.

Is there a typical pattern of food-getting among foragers? Many anthropologists have assumed that foragers typically get their food more from gathering than from hunting, and that women contribute more than men to subsistence because women generally do the gathering.[11] Although gathering is the most important food-getting activity for some foragers (e.g., the Ngatatjara aborigines and the !Kung of southern Africa), this is not true for most food-collecting societies known to us. A survey of foraging societies indicates that there is a lot of variation with regard to which food-getting activity is most important to the society. However, gathering and hunting each typically contribute about 26–35 percent; but fishing is typically more important.[12] That is why we prefer the term *foragers* rather than

TABLE 15.1 Variation in Food-Getting and Associated Features

	FOOD COLLECTORS	FOOD PRODUCERS		
	Foragers	Horticulturalists	Pastoralists	Intensive Agriculturalists
Population density	Lowest	Low to moderate	Low	Highest
Maximum community size	Small	Small to moderate	Small	Large (towns and cities)
Nomadism/permanence of settlements	Generally nomadic or seminomadic	More sedentary: communities may move after several years	Generally nomadic or seminomadic	Permanent communities
Food shortages	Infrequent	Infrequent	Frequent	Frequent
Trade	Minimal	Minimal	Very important	Very important
Full-time craft specialists	None	None or few	Some	Many (high degree of craft specialization)
Individual differences in wealth	Generally none	Generally minimal	Moderate	Considerable
Political leadership	Informal	Some part-time political officials	Part- and full-time political officials	Many full-time political officials

the often-used *hunter-gatherers*; the term *foragers* allows us to recognize the importance of fishing. In any case, because men generally do the fishing as well as the hunting, the men usually contribute more to food-getting than do the women among recent foragers.[13]

Read **the** Document: Kalahari San: Sometime Hunter-Gatherers

Because foragers move their camps often and walk great distances, it may seem that the food-collecting way of life is difficult. Although we do not have enough quantitative studies to tell us what is typical of most foragers, studies of two Australian aborigine groups[14] and of one !Kung group[15] indicate that those foragers do not spend many hours getting food. For example, !Kung adults spend an average of about 17 hours per week collecting food. Even when you add the time spent making tools (about 6 hours a week) and doing housework (about 19 hours a week), the !Kung seem to have more leisure time than many agriculturalists, as we discuss later.

Complex Foragers

When we say that foragers tend to have certain traits, this does not mean that all of them have those traits. There is considerable variability among societies that depend on foraging. Foraging societies that depend heavily on fishing (such as on the Pacific Coast of the northwestern United States and Canada or on the south coast of New Guinea) are more likely to have bigger and more permanent communities and more social inequality than foraging societies elsewhere that depend mostly on game and plants.[16] The Pacific Coast and New Guinea coastal people also tend to have higher population densities, food storage,[17] occupational specialization, resource ownership, slavery, and competitiveness.[18] Two foraging groups that have depended heavily on annual salmon runs, the Tlingit of southeastern Alaska and the Nimpkish of British Columbia, have had a three-tiered status system of high status, commoners, and slaves. The high-status individuals were obliged to stage elaborate, competitive feasts and ritually distribute valuables.[19] The social inequality and competitiveness in these cultures differs greatly from what we find in typical foragers, who generally show little social differentiation. In a worldwide study of foragers, there also tended to be more intercommunity fighting in those societies that were more dependent on fishing. Perhaps conflict arose because some fishing sites were more predictable than others, leading people to fight to defend them.[20]

Food production The form of subsistence technology in which food-getting is dependent on the cultivation and domestication of plants and animals.

In New Guinea, about 40 societies depend almost exclusively on foraging. Wild sago provides most of the carbohydrates for these foragers, but they vary considerably on how they obtain animal protein. Paul Roscoe has found that the amount of dependence upon fishing is strongly associated with density of population and settlement size. For example, societies with more than 75 percent dependence upon fishing have average community sizes of about 350 people, as compared with community size of about 50 for those with less than 25 percent dependence upon fishing. Some villages were much larger. One Asmat village had over 1,400 people, and a Waropen village over 1,700.

Horticulture Plant cultivation carried out with relatively simple tools and methods; nature is allowed to replace nutrients in the soil, in the absence of permanently cultivated fields.

Food Production

15.2 Describe the various forms of food production (horticulture, intensive agriculture, and pastoralism), and identify the general societal features associated with each.

Beginning about 10,000 years ago, certain peoples in widely separated geographic locations made the revolutionary changeover to **food production**. That is, they began to domesticate plants and animals. (Domesticated plants and animals are different from the ancestral wild forms.) With the domestication of these food sources, people acquired control over certain natural processes, such as animal breeding and plant seeding. Today, most peoples in the world depend for their food on some combination of domesticated plants and animals.

Anthropologists generally distinguish three major types of food production systems—*horticulture*, *intensive agriculture*, and *pastoralism*.

Horticulture

The word **horticulture** may conjure up visions of people with "green thumbs" growing orchids and other flowers in greenhouses. But to anthropologists, the word means the growing of crops of all kinds with relatively simple tools and methods, in the absence of permanently cultivated fields. The tools are usually hand tools, such as the digging stick or hoe, not plows or other equipment pulled by animals or tractors. And the methods used do not include fertilization, irrigation, or other ways to restore soil fertility after a growing season.

There are two kinds of horticulture. The more common one involves a dependence on **extensive (shifting) cultivation**. The land is worked for short periods and then left idle for some years. During the years when the land is not cultivated, wild plants and brush grow; when the fields are later cleared by *slash-and-burn techniques,* nutrients are returned to the soil. The other kind of horticulture involves a dependence on long-growing tree crops. The two kinds of horticulture may be practiced in the same society, but in neither case is there permanent cultivation of field crops.

Extensive (shifting) cultivation A type of horticulture in which the land is worked for short periods and then left to regenerate for some years before being used again. Also called **shifting cultivation.**

Slash-and-burn A form of shifting cultivation in which the natural vegetation is cut down and burned off. The cleared ground is used for a short time and then left to regenerate.

Most horticultural societies do not rely on crops alone for food. Many also hunt or fish; a few are nomadic for part of the year. For example, the Kayapo of the Brazilian Amazon leave their villages for as long as three months at a time to trek through the forest in search of game. The entire village participates in a trek, carrying large quantities of garden produce and moving their camp every day.[21] Other horticulturalists raise domestic animals, but these are usually not large animals, such as cattle and camels.[22] More often than not, horticulturalists raise smaller animals, such as pigs, chickens, goats, and sheep.

Let us look now at two horticultural societies, the Yanomamö of the Brazilian-Venezuelan Amazon and the Samoans of the South Pacific.

The Yanomamö Dense tropical forest covers most of Yanomamö territory. From the air, the typical village is located in a forest clearing and looks like a single, large, circular lean-to with its inner side open to the central plaza. Each individual family has its own portion of the lean-to under the common roof. Each family's portion of the lean-to has a back wall (part of the closed back wall around the circular village structure), but the portions are open on the sides to each other as well as onto the central plaza of the village. The Yanomamö get most of their calories from garden produce, but according to Raymond Hames, the Yanomamö actually spend most of their time foraging.[23]

A Yanomamö woman prepares a cassava meal.

Before the people can plant, the forest must be cleared of trees and brush. Like most shifting cultivators, the Yanomamö use a combination of techniques: slashing the undergrowth, felling trees, and using controlled burning to clear a garden spot—in other words, **slash-and-burn** horticulture. Before the 1950s, the Yanomamö had only stone axes, so felling trees was quite difficult. Now they have steel machetes and axes given or traded to them by missionaries.

Because of the work involved in clearing a garden, the Yanomamö prefer to make use of forest patches that have little thorny brush and not too many large trees.[24] After the ground is cleared, the Yanomamö plant plantains, manioc, sweet potatoes, taro, and a variety of plants for medicine, condiments, and craft materials. Men do the heavy clearing work to prepare a garden, and they as well as women plant the crops. Women usually go to the gardens daily to weed and harvest. After two or three years, the yields diminish and the forest starts growing back, making continued cultivation less desirable and more difficult, so they abandon the garden and clear a new one. If they can, they clear adjacent forest, but if gardens are far from the village, they will move the village to a new location. Villages are moved about every five years because of gardening needs and warfare. There is a great deal of intervillage raiding, so villages are often forced to flee to another location.

Extensive cultivation requires a lot of territory because new gardens are not cleared until the forest grows back. What is often misunderstood is why it is so important to shift gardens. Not only is a burned field easier to plant, but the organic matter that is burned provides necessary nutrients for a good yield. If horticulturalists come back too quickly to a spot with little plant cover, a garden made there will not produce a satisfactory yield.

The Yanomamö crops do not provide much protein, so hunting and fishing are important to their diet. Men hunt birds, peccaries, monkeys, and tapir with bows and arrows. Women, men, and children enjoy fishing. They catch fish by hand, with small bows and arrows, and by stream poisoning. Everybody gathers honey, hearts of palm, Brazil nuts, and cashews, although the men usually climb trees to shake down the nuts. Much of the foraging is done from the village base, but the Yanomamö, like the Kayapo, may go on treks to forage from time to time.

The Samoans The Samoans numbered about 56,000 people in 1839, soon after European missionaries arrived.[25] The islands of Samoa, which are about 2,300 miles south of the Hawaiian Islands, are volcanic in origin, with central ridges and peaks as high as 6,000 feet. Though the land is generally steep, the islands have a lush plant cover watered by up to 200 inches of rain a year (about five times the amount of rain that falls on New York City in a year). All that rain does not interfere much with outdoor activity because the torrential showers do not last long and the water disappears quickly into the porous volcanic soil. The temperature is relatively constant, rarely falling below 70°F or rising above 88°F. Strong cooling trade winds blow most of the year, generally from the east or southeast, and on the coasts one hears a continuous low rumble from the huge Pacific swells that break upon the fringing coral reefs offshore.

Samoan horticulture involves mostly three tree crops requiring little work except in harvesting. Once planted, and with hardly more than a few years of waiting, the breadfruit tree continues to produce about two crops a year for up to a half century. Coconut trees may continue to produce for a hundred years. And banana trees make new stalks of fruit, each weighing more than 50 pounds, for many years; merely cutting down one stalk induces the plant to grow another. Young men do most of the harvesting of tree crops. Women do the occasional weeding.

The Samoans also practice some shifting cultivation; men periodically clear small patches of land for taro, a root crop that is a staple food. The taro patches can produce a few crops before they must be allowed to revert to bush so that soil fertility can be restored. But even taro cultivation does not require much work; planting requires nothing more than slightly burying the top sliced off a root just harvested. Young men do most of the planting and harvesting. The taro patches are weeded infrequently, mostly by women. This kind of casual farming behavior prompted Captain Bligh, of *Mutiny on the Bounty* fame, to describe the Tahitians as lazy.[26] Captain Bligh's attitude was ethnocentric. South Pacific islanders such as the Samoans and Tahitians cannot weed as often as European farmers without risking the erosion of their soil because, in contrast with European farmlands, which are generally flat or only slightly sloping, the land of Samoa and Tahiti is mostly steep. The Samoan and Tahitian practice of not weeding crops and growing them in glorious and messy confusion minimizes soil erosion; the deep and shallow root structures of the various plants growing together prevent the loose volcanic soil from being washed away by the torrential showers.

The Samoans keep chickens and pigs, which they eat only occasionally. The major source of animal protein in the Samoan diet is fish, caught inside and outside the reef. Younger men may swim in the deep sea outside the reef and use a sling to spear fish; older men are more likely to stand on the reef and throw a four-pointed spear at fish swimming inside the reef. For many years, people in the villages of Samoa have sold copra, the sun-dried meat of the ripe coconut, to the world market for coconut oil. Men generally cut the copra from the shells after the ripe coconuts fall by themselves to the ground. With the cash earned from the sale of copra, people buy imported items such as machetes, kerosene, and flour. People in most villages still produce most of the foods they eat, but many have migrated to towns on the bigger islands and to cities in Hawaii and on the U.S. mainland to find wage-paying jobs.

General Features of Horticulturalists In most horticultural societies, simple farming techniques have tended to yield more food from a given area than is generally available to foragers. Consequently, horticulture is able to support larger, more densely populated communities. The way of life of horticulturalists is more sedentary than that of foragers, although communities may move after some years to farm a new series of plots. (Some horticulturalists have permanent villages because they depend mostly on food from trees that keep producing for a long time.) In contrast with most recent food-collecting groups, horticultural societies exhibit the beginnings of social differentiation. For example, some individuals may be part-time craftworkers or part-time political officials, and certain members of a kin group may have more status than other individuals in the society.

Intensive Agriculture

Intensive agriculture Food production characterized by the permanent cultivation of fields and made possible by the use of the plow, draft animals or machines, fertilizers, irrigation, water-storage techniques, and other complex agricultural techniques.

People engaged in **intensive agriculture** use techniques that enable them to cultivate fields permanently. Essential nutrients may be put back in the soil through the use of fertilizers, which may be organic material (most commonly dung from humans or other animals) or inorganic (chemical) fertilizers. But there are other ways to restore nutrients. The Luo of western Kenya plant beans around corn plants. Bacteria growing around the roots of the bean plant replace lost nitrogen, and the corn plant conveniently provides a pole for the bean plant to wind around as it grows. Some intensive agriculturalists use irrigation from streams and rivers to ensure an adequate supply of waterborne nutrients. Crop rotation and plant stubble that has been plowed under also restore nutrients to the soil.

In general, the technology of intensive agriculturalists is more complex than that of horticulturalists. Plows rather than digging sticks are generally employed. But there is enormous variation in the degree to which intensive agriculturalists rely on mechanization rather than hand labor. In some societies, the most complex machine is an animal-drawn plow; in the corn and wheat belts of the United States, huge tractors till, seed, and fertilize 12 rows at a time.[27]

Let's look at two groups of intensive agriculturalists, those of rural Greece and those of the Mekong Delta in Vietnam.

Rural Greece The village of Vasilika is situated at the foot of Mount Parnassus on the Boeotian plain. As described by Ernestine Friedl in the 1950s, its population was about 220 inhabitants.[28] Grapevines and wheat are cultivated for domestic use. The agricultural year begins in March with pruning of the vines and hoeing of the fields, tasks regarded as men's work. Winemaking begins in September, after the grain harvest, and involves the whole family. Men, women, and children talk and joke as they pick the grapes and put them into large baskets. After they remove the leaves and stems, the men trample the fruit, and the newly pressed grape juice, or *must*, is transferred to barrels. After adding whatever sugar and alcohol are needed, farmers also add resin to give the wine its characteristic flavor.

The villagers use horses to plow their wheat fields in October, and in November they sow the seed by hand. The wheat crop is harvested the following summer, usually by machine. Wheat constitutes the staple village food and is eaten as bread, as a cereal (called *trakhana*), or as noodles. It is also commonly bartered for other food items, such as fish, olive oil, and coffee.

Cash crops A cultivated commodity raised for sale rather than for personal consumption by the cultivator.

Cotton and tobacco are the main **cash crops**—that is, crops raised for sale. In this dry plains country, the success of the cotton crop depends on irrigation, and the villagers use efficient diesel pumps to distribute water. The real work in the cotton fields begins after the spring plowing and seeding have been completed. Then the young plants must be hoed and mulched, a task done mostly by women. The season of cotton cultivation is especially hard on women, who must do all the cooking and household chores in addition to working in the cotton fields. Irrigation, which begins in July, is men's work. It is usually done three times a season and involves the clearing of shallow ditches, the mounting of pumps, and the channeling of water. Cotton picking, which starts in October, is considered women's work. For picking, as well as hoeing and harvesting, a farmer owning more than five acres usually hires women from the same village or neighboring villages and sometimes even from distant towns. The cotton ginning is carried out by centrally located contractors, who are paid on the spot with 6 percent of each farmer's crop. Most of the seed reclaimed in the ginning is used for the next year's planting. The remainder is pressed into cakes to serve as supplementary food for ewes at lambing time. Tobacco yields a larger cash income than cotton, and the tobacco crop fits well into what would otherwise be slack periods in cultivation.

Raising animals plays a relatively minor role in the villagers' economic life. Each farmer has a horse or two for heavy draft work, a mule or donkey, about two dozen sheep, and some fowl.

Farmers at Vasilika are responsive to modern developments; they are prepared to experiment to a certain extent, especially with mechanization. Where the amount of acreage under cultivation warrants the expense, tractors are hired for plowing. Specialists are regularly called in to handle harvesting, cotton ginning, and similar tasks. Indeed, the Greek farmer is content to be a farmer and to rely on the skills of others to repair his roof, maintain his water pump, and provide the mechanical know-how for crop production.

Rural Vietnam: The Mekong Delta The village of Khanh Hau, situated along the flat Mekong Delta, comprised about 600 families when Gerald Hickey described it in the late 1950s, before the Vietnam War.[29] The delta area has a tropical climate, with a rainy season that lasts from May to November. As a whole, the area has been made habitable only through extensive drainage.

Wet rice cultivation is the principal agricultural activity of Khanh Hau. It is part of a complex, specialized arrangement that involves three interacting components: (1) a complex system of irrigation and water control; (2) a variety of specialized equipment, including plows, waterwheels, threshing sledges, and winnowing machines; and (3) a clearly defined set of socioeconomic roles—from those of landlord, tenant, and laborer to those of rice miller and rice merchant.

In the dry season, the farmer decides what sort of rice crop to plant, whether of long (120 days) or short (90 days) maturation. The choice depends on the capital at his disposal, the current cost of fertilizer, and the anticipated demand for rice. The seedbeds are prepared as soon as the rains have softened the ground in May. The soil is turned over (plowed) and broken up (harrowed) as many as six separate times, with two-day intervals for "airing" between operations. During this time, the rice seeds are soaked in water for at least two days to stimulate sprouting. Before the seedlings are planted, the paddy is plowed once more and harrowed twice in two directions at right angles.

Planting is a delicate, specialized operation that must be done quickly and is performed most often by hired male laborers. But efficient planting is not enough to guarantee a good crop. Proper fertilization and irrigation are equally important. In the irrigating, steps must be taken to ensure that the water level remains at exactly the proper depth over the entire paddy. Water is distributed by means of scoops, wheels, and mechanical pumps. Successive crops of rice ripen from late September to May; all members of the family may be called upon to help with the harvest. After each crop is harvested, it is threshed, winnowed, and dried. Normally, the rice is sorted into three portions: one is set aside for use by the household in the following year; one is for payment of hired labor and other services (such as loans from agricultural banks); and one is for cash sale on the market. Aside from the harvesting, women do little work in the fields, spending most of their time on household chores. In families with little land, however, young daughters help in the fields and older daughters may hire themselves out to other farmers.

The villagers also cultivate vegetables, raise pigs, chickens, and the like, and frequently engage in fishing. The village economy usually supports three or four implement makers and a much larger number of carpenters.

Vietnamese farmers in the Mekong Delta working in a flooded rice paddy. Much of the delta was originally tropical forest.

General Features of Intensive Agricultural Societies Societies with intensive agriculture are more likely than horticulturalists to have towns and cities, a high degree of craft specialization, complex political organization, and large differences in wealth and power. Studies suggest that intensive agriculturalists work longer hours than horticulturalists.[30] For example, men engaged in intensive agriculture average 9 hours of work a day, 7 days a week; women average almost 11 hours of work per day. Most of the work for women in intensive agricultural societies involves food processing and work in and around the home, but they also spend a lot of time working in the fields. We discuss some of the implications of the work patterns for women in the chapter on sex and gender.

Intensive agricultural societies are more likely than horticultural societies to face famines and food shortages, even though intensive agriculture is generally more productive than horticulture.[31] Why, if more food can be produced per acre, is there more risk of shortage among intensive agriculturalists? Intensive agriculturalists may be more likely to face food shortages because they are often producing crops for a market. Producing for a market pushes farmers to cultivate plants that give them the highest yield rather than cultivating plants that are drought-resistant or that require fewer nutrients. Farmers producing for a market also tend to concentrate on one crop. Crop diversity is often a protection against total crop failure because fluctuations in weather, plant diseases, or insect pests are not likely to affect all the crops. There are also fluctuations in market demand. If the market demand drops and the price falls for a particular crop, farmers may not have enough cash to buy the other food they need.

The Commercialization and Mechanization of Agriculture Some intensive agriculturalists produce very little for sale; most of what they produce is for their own use. But there is a worldwide trend for intensive agriculturalists to produce more and more for a market. This trend is called **commercialization**, which may occur in any area of life and which involves increasing dependence on buying and selling, usually with money as the medium of exchange. Some of the push toward commercialization comes from external pressures, from governments that impose taxes that must be paid by money. But some of the shift occurs when subsistence farmers choose to plant a cash crop to earn money for various reasons. For example, the Malaiyali farmers of India grow a cash crop, tapioca (cassava), as a way of responding to unpredictable rainfall. Tapioca is fairly drought-tolerant, grows in poor soils, and can be planted later in the year when the rainfall has become more predictable.[32]

Commercialization The increasing dependence on buying and selling, with money usually as the medium of exchange.

The increasing commercialization of agriculture is associated with several other trends. One is that farm work is becoming more mechanized as hand labor becomes scarce because of migration to industrial and service jobs in towns and cities, or because hired hand labor has become too expensive. A second trend is the emergence and spread of *agribusiness*, large corporation-owned farms that may be operated by multinational companies and worked entirely by hired, as opposed to family, labor. For example, consider how cotton farming has changed in the southeastern United States. In the 1930s, tractors replaced mules and horses used in plowing. This change allowed some landowners to evict their sharecroppers and expand their holdings. After World War II, mechanical cotton pickers replaced most of the harvest laborers. But a farmer had to have a good deal of money to acquire those machines, each of which cost many tens of thousands of dollars.[33] So the mechanization of cotton farming sent many rural farm laborers

Watering a field in Hula Valley, Israel with robotic irrigation.

off to the cities of the North in search of employment, and the agricultural sector increasingly became big business. A third trend associated with the commercialization of agriculture, including animal raising, is a reduction in the proportion of the population engaged in food production. In the United States today, for example, less than 1 percent of the total population work on farms.[34] A fourth trend is that much of what people produce for sale nowadays is shipped to or received from markets in other countries. For example, in the summer months, fruits and vegetables are often shipped to markets where consumers have little local fresh produce. The spread of different kinds of food is not new (see the box "Food on the Move") but is accelerating in today's world. In the next chapter on economics, we discuss more fully some of the apparent consequences of the worldwide changeover to commercial or market economies.

"Market Foraging" in Industrial Societies Food in countries such as the United States and Canada comes largely from intensive agriculture and animal husbandry practiced by a small proportion of the population. Those food specialists make their living by selling animal and plant products to marketers, distributors, and food processors. Indeed, most people know very little about how to grow crops or raise animals. Food appears in markets or supermarkets already processed by other specialists. It comes in paper or plastic packages, looking far different from how it originally looked in the field or on the feedlot. Thus, most of us are "market foragers," collecting our food from stores. In some ways, we behave very much like foragers of wild plants and animals. But there are also enormous differences between our kind of foraging and the original kind. If our society did not have very productive intensive agriculture and animal husbandry, we would not have towns and cities, thousands of different full-time occupations (hardly any of which are involved in food-getting), a centralized government, or many of our other characteristics.

Pastoralism

Most agriculturalists keep and breed some animals (practice animal husbandry), but a small number of societies depend mostly for their living on domesticated herds of animals that feed on natural pasture.[35] We call such a system **pastoralism**. We might assume that pastoralists breed animals to eat their meat, but most do not. Pastoralists more often get their animal protein from live animals in the form of milk, and some pastoralists regularly take blood, which is rich in protein, from their animals to mix with other foods. The herds often indirectly provide food because many pastoralists trade animal products for plant foods and other necessities. In fact, a large proportion of their food may actually come from trade with agricultural groups.[36] For example, some pastoral groups in the Middle East derive much of their livelihood from the sale of what we call oriental rugs, which are made from the wool of their sheep on hand looms. Two pastoral societies we shall examine are the Basseri of southern Iran and the Saami of Scandinavia.

Pastoralism A form of subsistence technology in which food-getting is based directly or indirectly on the maintenance of domesticated animals.

Read **the** Document: Ariaal Pastoralists of Kenya: Studying Pastoralism, Drought, and Development in Africa's Arid Lands

The Basseri The Basseri, described by Fredrik Barth as of the 1960s, are a tribe of about 16,000 tent-dwelling nomads.[37] Their herds consist principally of sheep and goats, though donkeys and camels are raised for pulling or carrying, and the wealthier men have horses for riding. Theirs is a dry, arid habitat, with rainfall averaging no more than 10 inches a year. The Basseri's pastoral way of life is based on a regular, migratory exploitation of the grazing lands within their territory, which measures about 15,000 square miles in all. In winter, when the mountains to the north are covered with snow, the plains and foothills to the south offer extensive pasturage. During the spring, grazing is excellent on a plateau near the center of the territory. By summer, when most of the lower-lying pastures have dried up, sufficient food for the herds can be found in the mountains at an altitude of nearly 6,000 feet.

Annual migrations are so important to the economies of the Basseri and other pastoralist societies of that region that they have developed the concept of *il-rah*, or "tribal road." A major pastoral tribe such as the Basseri has a traditional route and schedule. The route, consisting of the localities in the order in which each is visited,

Migrants and Immigrants

Food on the Move

People in North America get most of their food from stores. Most people do not know where the food comes from originally—where it was first grown or raised. This is partly because relatively few are directly involved in food-getting (less than 1 percent of the workers in the United States). Even when you count all the activities related to food-getting, such as marketing and transportation, only 14 percent of U.S. workers have anything to do with the production and distribution of food. But nowadays, many of the foods we buy in markets—tacos, salsa, bagels, pasta, pizza, sausage, soy sauce, and teriyaki—have become mainstream "North American" food. Where did these foods come from? Originally, they were eaten only by ethnic and immigrant minorities who came to the United States and Canada. Some, but not all, of their foods caught on and became widely consumed. They became, in short, as "American" as apple pie.

Outdoor market in Venice, Italy showing that the potatoes are from America.

The ingredients in many of these food items resulted from previous movements of people even further back in time. Consider the ingredients in pizza, a favorite food now for many of us. The dough is made from wheat flour, which was first grown in the Middle East, perhaps as much as 10,000 years ago. How do anthropologists know that? Archaeologists have discovered wheat kernels that old in Middle Eastern sites, and they have found flat stones and stone rolling pins from that time that we know were used to grind kernels into flour (we can tell from microscopic analysis of the residue on the stone). What about other ingredients that may be found in pizza? Cheese was first made in the Middle East too, at least 5,000 years ago (we have writings from that time that mention cheese). Tomatoes were first grown in South America, probably several thousand years ago. They got to Italy, the birthplace of the tomato pie (which became transformed into pizza), less than 200 years ago. Just 100 years ago, tomatoes (the key ingredient in pizza for some) were so new in eastern Europe that people were afraid to eat them because their leaves are poisonous to humans and some other animals. Another food we associate with Italian cuisine, spaghetti-type noodles, came to Italy (from China) less than 500 years ago. So the major ingredients of pizza, just like round-noodle pasta, are all not native to Italy.

The amazing thing about foods is that they so often travel far and wide, generally carried by the people who like to eat them. And some of our foods, when alive, also travel widely. For example, the bluefin tuna (which can weigh more than a thousand pounds) swims thousands of miles from feeding to breeding grounds in the North Atlantic, Mediterranean, and Caribbean. This largest of all existing fishes is being hunted into extinction because its meat is so prized for what the Japanese call *sushi*, a kind of food that has spread from Japan throughout the world.

Sources: Diament 2005, A32–34; Revkin 2005, F1, F4.

follows existing passes and lines of communication. The schedule, which regulates the length of time each location will be occupied, depends on the maturation of different pastures and the movements of other tribes. The *il-rah* is regarded, in effect, as the property of the tribe. Local populations and authorities recognize the tribe's right to pass along roads and cultivated lands, to draw water from the public wells, and to pasture flocks on public land.

The Basseri herd sheep and goats together, with one shepherd (a boy or unmarried man) responsible for a flock of 300 to 400 animals. Children of both sexes are usually responsible for herding the baby animals (lambs and kids). Milk and its by-products are the most important commodities, but wool, hides, and meat are also important to the economy of the Basseri. Both wool and hides are traded, but they are even more useful within the tribe. The Basseri, especially the women, are skilled spinners and weavers, and much of their time is spent at these activities. Saddlebags and pack bags are woven on horizontal looms from homespun wool and hair, as are carpets, sleeping rugs, and the characteristic black tents made of panels of woven goat hair. Woven goat hair provides an exceptionally versatile cloth. For winter use, it retains heat and repels water; in the summer, it insulates against heat and permits free circulation of air. Lambskin hides also serve many purposes. When plucked and turned inside out, they are made into storage bags to hold water, buttermilk, sour milk, and other liquids.

Most of the Basseri must trade for the necessities and luxury items they do not produce within the community. The staple items they sell are butter, wool, lambskins, rope, and occasionally livestock.

The Saami The Saami (Lapps) practice reindeer herding in northwestern Scandinavia where Finland, Sweden, and Norway share common frontiers. It is a typical Arctic habitat: cold and windswept, with long, dark days for half the year. Considerable change has occurred recently, so we first discuss the food-getting strategy in the 1950s, as described by Ian Whitaker and T. I. Itkonen.[38]

The Saami herd their reindeer either intensively or, more often, extensively. In the *intensive system,* the herd is constantly under observation within a fenced area for the whole year. Intensively herded reindeer and other animals are accustomed to human contact. Hence, the summer corralling of the females for milking and the breaking in of the ox-reindeer for use as work animals are not difficult tasks. The *extensive system* involves allowing the animals to migrate over a large area. It requires little surveillance and encompasses large herds. Under this system, the reindeer are allowed to move through their seasonal feeding cycles watched by only one or two scouts. The other Saami stay with the herd only when it has settled in its summer or winter habitat. But milking, breaking in, and corralling are harder in the extensive than in the intensive system because the animals are less accustomed to humans.

A Saami reindeer herder feeds two of her animals in the snow.

Even under the extensive system, which theoretically permits Saami to engage in subsidiary economic activities such as hunting and fishing, the reindeer herd is the essential, if not the only, source of income. A family might possess as many as 1,000 reindeer, but usually the figure is half that number. Studies show 200 to be the minimum number of reindeer needed to provide for a family of four or five adults. Women may have shared the herding chores in the past under the intensive system, but now, under the extensive system, men do the herding. Women still do the milking. The Saami eat the meat of the bull reindeer; the female reindeer are kept for breeding purposes. Bulls are slaughtered in the fall, after the mating season. Meat and hides are frequently sold or bartered for other food and necessities.

Reindeer are still herded nowadays, but snowmobiles, all-terrain vehicles, and even helicopters have replaced sleds for herding. Ferries move reindeer to and from different pastures, and the herders communicate by field telephones. With faster transportation, many Saami now live in permanent homes and can still get to their herds in hours. Saami children spend much of their time in school and, consequently, do not learn much of the herding ways. The Norwegian government now regulates pastoralism, licensing pastoralists and trying to limit the number of reindeer they can herd.[39] And many Saami no longer have reindeer.

Applied Anthropology

The Effect of Food-Getting on the Environment

Many people are now aware of industrial pollution—the dumping of industrial wastes in the ground or into rivers, the spewing of chemicals into the air through smokestacks—but we don't often realize how much humans have altered the environment by the ways they collect and produce food. Consider irrigation. Irrigation has made agriculture productive in arid or unpredictable rainfall environments. Water can be channeled from rivers; rainwater can be caught in terraces carved out of hillsides; ancient water can be pumped up from vast underground reservoirs called aquifers. Plants absorb water and leave behind the salts, so over time the land may get saltier. But much of the water use is wasteful and evaporates into the air before even reaching the plants, leading to higher concentration of minerals and salts. If drainage is poor and if the water table rises, the salt concentrations are not washed away. Eventually, the soil becomes too salty to grow crops effectively and crops have to be grown elsewhere.

Some archaeologists have suggested that the accumulation of toxic salts in the soil at least partly explains the doom or decline of various groups in the past. For example, salinization probably contributed to the decline of Sumer, an early empire in Mesopotamia, and other early states in what is now southern Iraq and southwestern Iran. Today, much of the soil is still too salty for cultivation. Irrigation schemes during Saddam Hussein's regime also seriously degraded the downstream Iraqi marshes, putting over 60 bird species at risk. The loss of the marshlands reduced the ability of the marshland to filter the water before it reached the Persian Gulf, which led to declines in productivity of the coastal fisheries.

The lessons of history have not been learned yet. The San Joaquin Valley of California, perhaps the most productive agricultural area in the world, now has a serious salinization problem. One solution in many of the areas of the Great American Desert is to pump water up from underground. Indeed, in many places there is a great deal of water underground. For example, the Ogallala aquifer, which underlies parts of Nebraska, Kansas, Texas, Oklahoma, Colorado, and New Mexico, contains water left from the ice ages. But the pumping solution, if it is a solution, is only a short-term fix, for the huge Ogallala aquifer is also the fastest-disappearing aquifer. The only question is how long it will take to disappear totally.

Too many people raising too many animals can also have serious effects on the environment. The European-American settlers raised cattle and sheep on the Great American Desert, but many parts of it were overgrazed. It took the swirling dust storms of the 1930s to make people realize that overgrazing as well as poor farming practices could be disastrous. The problems are not just recent ones. The Norse colonized Greenland and Iceland around A.D. 800; but overgrazing of pasture undoubtedly contributed to soil erosion and the disappearance or decline of the colonies by A.D. 1500.

Are environmental problems associated only with food production? Although food producers may be the worst offenders, there is reason to think that foragers may also have sometimes overfished, overgathered, or overhunted. For example, some scholars suspect that the movement of humans into the New World was mainly responsible for the disappearance of the mammoth. Unfortunately, there is little evidence that humans have been good conservers in the past. That does not mean that humans cannot do better in the future—but they have to want to.

Sources: Los Angeles Times 1994; Reisner 1993; Hillel 2000; Curtis et al. 2005; Dirks 2009.

General Features of Pastoralism In recent times, pastoralism has been practiced mainly in grassland and other semiarid habitats that are not especially suitable for cultivation without some significant technological input such as irrigation. Most pastoralists are nomadic, moving camp fairly frequently to find water and new pasture for their herds. But other pastoralists have somewhat more sedentary lives. They may move from one settlement to another in different seasons, or they may send some people out to travel with the herds in different seasons. Pastoral communities are usually small, consisting of a group of related families.[40] Individuals or families may own their own animals, but the community makes decisions about when and where to move the herds.

As we have noted, there is a great deal of interdependence between pastoral and agricultural groups. That is, trade is usually necessary for pastoral groups to survive. Like agriculturalists, pastoralists are more vulnerable than foragers and horticulturalists to famine and food shortages. Pastoralists usually inhabit drought-prone regions, but recent pastoralists have had their access to grazing lands reduced, and political pressures have pushed them to decrease their movement over large areas. Mobility kept the risk of overgrazing to a minimum, but overgrazing in small territories has increased the risk of desertification.[41]

Environmental Restraints on Food-Getting

15.3 Identify environmental restraints on food-getting.

Of great interest to anthropologists is why different societies have different methods of getting food. Archaeological evidence suggests that major changes in food-getting, such as the domestication of plants and animals, have been independently invented in at least several areas of the world. Yet, despite these comparable inventions and their subsequent spread by diffusion and migration, there is still wide diversity in the means by which people obtain food.

Listen to the Audio: A Fragile Balance: Population and Environment in Early State Societies

How much does the physical environment affect food-getting? Anthropologists have concluded that the physical environment by itself has a restraining, rather than a determining, effect on the major types of subsistence. Because they have very short growing seasons, cold regions of the earth are not particularly conducive to growing plants. No society we know of has practiced agriculture in the Arctic; instead, people who live there rely primarily on animals for food. But both foraging (as among the Inuit) and food production (as among the Saami) can be practiced in cold areas. Indeed, cross-cultural evidence indicates that neither foraging nor food production is significantly associated with any particular type of habitat.[42]

We know that foraging has been practiced at one time or another in almost all areas of the earth. The physical environment does seem to have some effect on what kind of foraging is practiced, that is, on the extent to which foragers will depend on plants, animals, or fish. Farther away from the equator, foragers depend much less on plants for food and much more on animals and fish.[43] Lewis Binford argues that fishing becomes increasingly important in cold climates because foragers need nonportable housing in severe winters to protect themselves from the cold. Therefore, they cannot rely on large animals, which usually have to feed themselves by moving over considerable distances in the winter. Fishing is more localized than hunting, and therefore foragers who rely on fishing can stay in their nonportable houses in winter.[44]

There is one habitat that may have precluded foraging until recent times. If it were not for the nearness of food producers, particularly agriculturalists, recent foragers, such as the Mbuti of central Africa, could probably not have supported themselves in the tropical forest habitats where they now live.[45] Tropical forests are lush in plants, but they do not provide much in the way of reachable fruits, seeds, and flowers that humans can eat. Animals are available in tropical forests, but typically they are lean and do not provide humans with sufficient carbohydrates or fat. Like the Mbuti groups who hunt and gather in the forest, many tropical foragers trade for agricultural products; other collectors cultivate some crops in addition to hunting and gathering. It would seem, then, that foragers could not survive in tropical forests were it not for the carbohydrates they obtain from agriculturalists.

Aerial view of irrigated fields, major canal and arid desert in Imperial Valley, California. In the past, this environment only supported foragers.

When we contrast horticulture and intensive agriculture, the physical environment appears to explain some of the variation. Approximately 80 percent of all societies that practice horticulture or simple agriculture are in the tropics, whereas 75 percent of all societies that practice intensive agriculture are not in tropical forest environments.[46] Tropical forests have abundant rainfall. But despite the attractiveness of lush vegetation and brilliant coloring, tropical forestlands do not usually offer favorable environments for intensive agriculture. Perhaps the heavy rainfall quickly washes away certain minerals from cleared land. Also, the difficulty of controlling insect pests and weeds, which abound in tropical forests,[47] may make intensive agriculture less productive.

But difficulty is not impossibility. Today, there are some areas, for instance the Mekong Delta in Vietnam, whose tropical forests have been cleared and prevented from growing again by the intensive cultivation of rice in paddies. And, although cultivation is not normally possible in dry lands, because of insufficient natural rainfall to sustain crops, agriculture can be practiced where there are oases—small, naturally watered areas where crops can be grown with a simple technology—or rivers that can be tapped by irrigation, one of the techniques used with intensive agriculture.

The animals that pastoralists raise depend primarily on grass for food, so it is not surprising that pastoralism is typically practiced in grassland regions of the earth. These regions may be **steppes** (dry, low grass cover), **prairies** (taller, better-watered grass), or **savannas** (tropical grasslands). The grassland habitat favors large game and hence supports both hunting and pastoral technologies, except where machine technology makes intensive agriculture possible, as in parts of the United States, Canada, and Ukraine.

Steppe Grassland with a dry, low grass cover.

Prairie Grassland with a high grass cover.

Savanna Tropical grassland.

Very different strategies of food-getting have been practiced in the same environment over time. A dramatic illustration is the history of the Imperial Valley in California. The complex systems of irrigation now used in that dry-land area have made it a very productive region. Yet about 400 years ago, this same valley supported only hunting and gathering groups who subsisted on wild plants and animals.

It is evident from the Imperial Valley example and many others like it that the physical environment does not by itself account for the system of food-getting in an area. Even a polar environment could have agriculture with heated greenhouses, though it would be too expensive. Technological advances as well as enormous capital investment in irrigation, labor, and equipment have made intensive agriculture possible in the Imperial Valley. But the agriculture there is precarious, depending on sources of water and power from elsewhere. In a prolonged drought, it may be difficult or too expensive to obtain the needed water. And should the prices for vegetables fall, the farming businesses in the Imperial Valley could find themselves unable to finance the investment and borrowing of capital that they need to continue. So technological, social, and political factors rather than environmental factors mostly determine what kind of food-getting can be practiced in a given environment.

15.4 Discuss the origin of food production.

The Origin of Food Production

From about 40,000 to about 15,000 years ago, which we know best archaeologically for Europe, people seem to have gotten most of their food from hunting the available migratory herds of large animals, such as wild cattle, antelope, bison, and mammoths. These hunter-gatherers were probably highly mobile to follow the migrations of the animals.

Beginning about 14,000 years ago, people in some regions began to depend less on big game hunting and more on relatively stationary food resources, such as fish, shellfish, small game, and wild plants. Saltwater and freshwater food supplies may have become more abundant in many areas after the glaciers withdrew. As the ice melted, the level of the oceans rose and formed inlets and bays where crabs, clams, and sea mammals could be found. In some areas, particularly Europe and the Near East, the exploitation of local and relatively permanent resources may have supported an increasingly settled way of life.

We see the first evidence of a changeover to food production—the cultivation and domestication of plants and animals—in the Near East about 8000 B.C. This shift occurred, probably independently, in other areas as well. There is evidence of cultivation around 6000 B.C. in China, Southeast Asia (what is now Malaysia, Thailand, Cambodia, and Vietnam), and Africa. In the New World, there appear to have been several places of original cultivation and domestication. The highlands of Mexico (about 7000 B.C.) and the central Andes around Peru (by about 6000 B.C.) were probably the most important in terms of food plants used today.

Most peoples today are food producers rather than foragers. But why did people start to produce their food? We know that an economic transformation occurred in widely separate areas of the world beginning about 10,000 years ago, as people began to domesticate plants and animals. But why did domestication occur? And why did it occur independently in different places within a period of a few thousand years? (Considering that people depended only on wild plants and animals for millions of years, the differences in exactly when domestication first occurred in different parts of the world seem small.)

There are many theories of why food production developed; most have tried to explain the origin of domestication in the Near East. Lewis Binford and Kent Flannery suggested that some change in external circumstances, not necessarily environmental, must have induced or favored the changeover to food production.[48] As Flannery pointed out, there is no evidence of a great economic incentive for hunter-gatherers to become food producers. In fact, as we have seen, some contemporary hunter-gatherers may actually obtain adequate nutrition with far less work than many agriculturalists.

Binford and Flannery thought that the incentive to domesticate animals and plants may have been a desire to reproduce what was wildly abundant in the most bountiful or optimum hunting and gathering areas. Because of population growth in the optimum areas, people might have moved to surrounding areas containing fewer wild resources. In those marginal areas, people would have turned to food production to reproduce what they used to have.

The Binford-Flannery model seems to fit the archaeological record in the Levant, the southwestern part of the Fertile Crescent, where population increase did precede the first signs of domestication.[49] But as Flannery admitted, in some regions, such as southwestern Iran, the optimum hunting and gathering areas do not show population increase before the emergence of domestication.[50]

The Binford-Flannery model focuses on population pressure in a small area as the incentive to turn to food production. Mark Cohen theorized that population pressure on a global scale explains why so many of the world's peoples adopted agriculture within the span of a few thousand years.[51] He argued that hunter-gatherers all over the world gradually increased in population, so that the world was more or less filled with foragers by about 10,000 years ago. Thus, people could no longer relieve population pressure by moving to uninhabited areas. To support their increasing populations, they would have had to exploit a broader range of less desirable wild foods; that is, they would have had to switch to broad-spectrum collecting, or they would have had to increase the yields of the most desirable wild plants by weeding, protecting them from animal pests, and perhaps deliberately planting the most productive among them. Cohen suggested that people might have tried a variety of these strategies to support themselves but would generally have ended up depending on cultivation because that would have been the most efficient way to allow more people to live in one place.

Recently, some archaeologists have returned to the idea that climatic change played a role in the emergence of agriculture. It seems clear from the evidence now available that the climate of the Near East about 13,000 to 12,000 years ago became more seasonal; the summers got hotter and drier, and the winters became colder. These climatic changes may have favored the emergence of annual species of grain that archaeologically we see proliferating in many areas of the Near East.[52] Some foragers intensively exploited the seasonal grains, developing an elaborate technology for storing and processing the grains and giving up their previous nomadic existence to do so. The transition to agriculture may have occurred when sedentary foraging no longer provided sufficient resources for the population. This change could have happened for a number of reasons. First, sedentarization itself may have led to shortages of resources, either because population increased with sedentarization[53] or because people in permanent villages depleted the local wild resources nearby.[54] Second, climate change may have reduced the available stands of wild grain. In at least one area of the Near East, the onset of drier and cooler weather may have led foragers to try to cultivate their food supplies.[55] Change to a more seasonal climate might also have led to a shortage of certain nutrients for foragers. In the dry seasons, certain nutrients would have been less available. For example, grazing animals become lean when grasses are not plentiful, and so meat from hunting would have been in short supply in the dry seasons. Although it may seem surprising, some recent hunter-gatherers have starved when they had to rely on lean meat. If they could have somehow increased their carbohydrate or fat intake, they might have been more likely to get through the periods of lean game.[56] So it is possible that some foragers in the past thought of planting crops to get them through the dry seasons when hunting, fishing, and gathering did not provide enough carbohydrates and fat for them to avoid starvation.

15.5 Describe and critically discuss the spread and intensification of food production.

The Spread and Intensification of Food Production

Whatever the reasons for the switch to food production, we still need to explain why it supplanted foraging as the primary mode of subsistence. We cannot assume that hunters and gatherers simply adopted production as a superior way of life once they understood the process of domestication. After all, as we have noted, domestication may entail more work and provide less security than the food-collecting way of life.

The spread of agriculture may be linked to the need for territorial expansion. As a sedentary, food-producing population grew, it may have been forced to expand into new territory. Some of this territory may have been vacant, but foragers probably already occupied much of it. Although food production is not necessarily easier than collection, it is generally more productive per unit of land. Greater productivity enables more people to be supported in a given territory. In the competition for land between the faster-expanding food producers and the foragers, the food producers may have had a significant advantage: They had more people in a given area. Thus, the foraging groups may have been more likely to lose out in the competition for land. Some groups may have adopted cultivation, abandoning the foraging way of life to survive. Other groups, continuing as foragers, may have been forced to retreat into areas not desired by the cultivators. Today, as we have seen, the small number of remaining foragers inhabit areas not particularly suitable for cultivation—dry lands, dense tropical forests, and polar regions.

Just as prior population growth might account for the origins of domestication, further population growth and ensuing pressure on resources at later periods might also at least partly explain the transformation of horticultural systems into intensive agricultural systems. Ester Boserup suggested that intensification of agriculture, with a consequent increase in yield per acre, is not likely to develop naturally out of horticulture because intensification requires much more work.[57] She argued that people will be willing to intensify their labor only if they have to. Where emigration is not feasible, the prime mover behind intensification may be prior population growth. The need to pay taxes or tribute to a political authority may also have stimulated intensification.

Boserup's argument about intensification is widely accepted. However, her assumption that more work is required with intensive agriculture has recently been questioned. Comparing horticultural (swidden or shifting) rice production with rice produced on permanent fields using irrigation, Robert Hunt found that *less*, not more, labor is required with irrigation.[58] Still, population increase may generally provide the impetus to intensify production to increase yields to support the additional people.

Intensive agriculture has not yet spread to every part of the world. Horticulture continues to be practiced in certain tropical regions, and there are still some pastoralists and foragers. Some environments may make it somewhat more difficult to adopt certain subsistence practices. For example, intensive agriculture cannot supplant horticulture in some tropical environments without tremendous investments in chemical fertilizers and pesticides, not to mention the additional labor required.[59] And enormous amounts of water may be required to make agriculturalists out of foragers and pastoralists who now exploit semiarid environments. However, difficulty is not impossibility. Anna Roosevelt points out that although horticulture was a common food-getting strategy in Amazonia in recent times, archaeological evidence indicates that there were complex societies practicing intensive agriculture on raised, drained fields in the past.[60] The physical environment does not completely control what can be done with it.

Summary and Review

Foraging

15.1 Describe foraging and complex foraging, and identify the general societal features associated with food collecting.

- Foraging—hunting, gathering, and fishing—depends on wild plants and animals and is the oldest human food-getting technology.
- People in most foraging societies live in small communities that are nomadic or seminomadic. Division of labor is usually only along age and gender lines, personal possessions and land rights are limited, people are usually not differentiated by class, and political leadership is informal.
- Complex foraging societies have bigger and more permanent communities as well as more social inequality; they tend to depend heavily on fishing. These societies tend to have higher population densities, food storage, occupational specialization, resource ownership, slavery, and competitiveness.

? Explain the difference between foraging and complex foraging.

Food Production

15.2 Describe the various forms of food production (horticulture, intensive agriculture, and pastoralism) and identify the general societal features associated with each.

- Horticultural societies grow crops of all kinds with relatively simple tools and methods and do not permanently cultivate fields. Many also hunt or fish; a few are nomadic for part of the year. Horticultural societies tend to be larger, more sedentary, and more densely populated than foragers, and they tend to exhibit the beginnings of social differentiation.
- Intensive agricultural societies use techniques that enable them to cultivate fields permanently, including fertilization, crop rotation, irrigation, and plowing under stubble. Societies using intensive agriculture are more likely than horticulturalists to have towns and cities, a high degree of craft specialization, complex political organization, and large differences in wealth and power.
- Societies using pastoralism depend mostly on domesticated herds of animals that feed on natural pasture. They tend to be found in drought-prone regions. People in pastoral societies mostly live in small communities that are typically nomadic or seminomadic. Pastoral people typically do not eat their animals but use their milk and blood; they get other foods from trade with agricultural groups.

? What are the similarities and differences among the three main types of food production?

Environmental Restraints on Food-Getting

15.3 Identify environmental restraints on food-getting.

- Cross-cultural evidence indicates that neither foraging nor food production is significantly associated with any particular type of habitat.

- Foragers farther from the equator depend much more on animals and fish; those closer to the equator depend more on plants. It is thought that foragers in tropical forests could not survive without the carbohydrates they obtain from agriculturalists.
- Approximately 80 percent of all societies that practice horticulture or simple agriculture are in the tropics, whereas 75 percent of all societies that practice intensive agriculture are not in tropical forest environments; an exception is tropical rice paddies. Pastoralism is typically practiced in grassland regions.
- The physical environment does not by itself account for the system of food-getting in an area; technological, social, and political factors rather than environmental factors mostly determine food-getting practices in a given environment.

> ? What are some environmental restraints on food-getting?

The Origins of Food Production

15.4 Discuss the origin of food production.

- From about 40,000 to about 15,000 years ago, people seem to have gotten most of their food from hunting migratory herds of large animals.
- Beginning about 14,000 years ago, some populations began to depend more on relatively stationary food resources such as fish, shellfish, small game, and wild plants, which may have supported an increasingly settled way of life.
- The first evidence of a changeover to food production—the cultivation and domestication of plants and animals—is found in the Near East about 8000 B.C., a shift that occurred, probably independently, also in other areas.
- Possible factors influencing food production: (a) As growing populations expanded further from bountiful wild resources, they domesticated animals and plants in an effort to reproduce former abundance; (b) global population growth may have filled most of the world's habitable regions, forcing people to domesticate plants and animals; and (c) climate change may have favored settling near seasonal stands of wild grain, and growing populations in such areas may have led to domestication of plants and animals.

> ? What evidence and theories explain the origin of food production?

The Spread and Intensification of Food Production

15.5 Describe and critically discuss the spread and intensification of food production.

- Food production is generally more productive per unit of land than food collection, although it can be more difficult and time consuming.
- Greater food productivity appears to lead to population growth, which may partially explain competition for land, which gives food producers an advantage over foragers.
- When emigration is not feasible, greater population growth may lead to intensive agricultural systems, and the need to pay taxes or tribute to a political authority may also stimulate continued intensification.

> ? Why did food production dominate over foraging in many parts of the world?

Think on it

1. Why might meat be valued more than **plant foods** in many societies?
2. Why might foragers be less likely than intensive **agriculturalists** to suffer from food shortages?
3. Why do certain foods in a **society** come to be preferred?

Economic Systems

CHAPTER 16

LEARNING OBJECTIVES

Compare and contrast the allocation of resources among foragers, horticulturalists, intensive agriculturalists, and pastoralists, and discuss how colonialism and the state have affected that allocation.	16.1
Explain the different types of economic production and economic exchange and their effect on labor.	16.2
Explain the three general types of systems for distributing goods and services (reciprocity, redistribution, and market or commercial exchange).	16.3
Discuss the worldwide trend toward commercialization and its social effects.	16.4

When we think of economics, we think of things and activities involving money. We think of the costs of goods and services, such as food, rent, haircuts, and movie tickets. We may also think of factories, farms, and other enterprises that produce the goods and services we need, or think we need. Inevitably, we think about the economy as a system that employs people to produce goods and services in exchange for wages. Workers in industrial societies may stand before a moving belt for eight hours, tightening identical bolts that glide by. In a post-industrial society, workers more likely provide a knowledge-based service, such as computer programming. In either case, people receive money, a symbol of the value placed on a commodity or a service, in exchange for the tasks they perform. The bits of colored paper and coins we call cash—or, as is more often the case today, the value on the checks or plastic cards that stand in for the colored paper—may be exchanged for food, shelter, and other goods and services.

Yet many societies—indeed, most cultures known to anthropology—did not have money or the equivalent of the factory worker until relatively recently. Still, all societies have economic systems, whether or not they involve money. All societies have customs specifying how people gain access to natural resources; customary ways of transforming or converting those resources, through labor, into necessities and other desired goods and services; and customs for distributing and perhaps exchanging goods and services. Many aspects of a culture, including family and kinship groups, the political system, and the presence or absence of inequality based on social class or gender, affect the form its economy takes. However, the major factor in variations among economic systems is the way in which each society gets its food. In this chapter, we shall look at traditional economic systems according to their food-getting strategies before turning to recent local and global changes.

In the earlier days of anthropology, it was easier to study the economic system of a people in relative isolation from other societies. But today, nearly every society on earth has felt the impact of global political and economic forces. Because of the influence of colonialism, imperialism, and capitalism, most people have had no choice but to become part of the world market system, even though the degree to which societies have accepted or resisted outside influences has varied considerably. Moreover, no society is immune to change. Even people who have resisted external economic forces to live in traditional economic systems have undergone change over the last few centuries.

16.1 Compare and contrast the allocation of resources among foragers, horticulturalists, intensive agriculturalists, and pastoralists, and discuss how colonialism and the state has affected that allocation.

The Allocation of Resources

Every society has access to natural resources—land, water, plants, animals, minerals—and every society has cultural rules for determining who has access to particular resources and what can be done with them. In societies like the United States, which have private property systems, people buy and sell land and many other things. Land is divided into precisely measurable units, the borders of which may be recorded in a municipal land register. Individuals usually own relatively small plots of land and the resources that exist on them. Generally, large plots of land are collective property. The owner may be a family, a corporation, or a government agency, such as the National Park Service, which owns so-called public land on behalf of the entire population. In the United States, property ownership entails the exclusive right to use land or other resources in whatever legal ways the owner wishes, including the right to withhold or prevent use by others. In many societies, including the United States, property owners also have the right to "alienate" property—that is, to sell, give away, bequeath, or destroy the resources owned.

Societies specify what they consider property and the rights and duties associated with that property.[1] Because conceptions of property are social in nature, they may change over time. For example, the French government retroactively made all of the country's beaches public, thereby declaring that the ocean shore is not a resource that an individual can own. As a result, all the hotel owners and individuals who had fenced-off portions of the best beaches for their exclusive use had to remove the barriers. Even in countries like the United States, which has a strong private property system, people cannot do anything they want with their property. Like many other governments around the world, the U.S. government has the right of *eminent domain:* It may take land for use in the construction of a highway or another purpose that serves "the greater public good." The state compensates owners, but individuals cannot prevent confiscation. The notion that the individual property owner has obligations to the greater good of the society is behind other laws. For example, it has long been illegal in the United States to burn down your house or to use it as a brothel or a munitions arsenal. More recently, federal, state, and local governments have adopted legislation that prevents property owners from undertaking activities that pollute the air and the water supply.

Natural Resources: Land

Societies differ in their rules for access to land. Anthropologists have found that the differences generally relate to a society's food-getting method. Let us now examine how foragers, horticulturalists, pastoralists, and intensive agriculturalists structure rights to land in different ways. We look at traditional patterns first. As we shall see later, state societies that have colonized native societies in the New World, Africa, and Asia have had a considerable impact on traditional rights to land.

Read the Document: Defending the Land: Sovereignty and Forest Life in the James Bay Cree Society

Foragers Individuals in food-collecting societies generally do not own land. Nor do they buy or sell land, probably because what is valued in foraging is the game and wild plant life on the land, not the land itself. The foraging Hadza of Tanzania, for example, believe that they do not have exclusive rights over the land on which they hunt. Members of the group can hunt, gather, or draw water wherever they like.[2] Nor do the Hadza defend the territories they use from outsiders—that is, members of other language groups. But the Hadza are somewhat unusual. Collective ownership by groups of related people (kinship groups) or by territorial groups (bands or villages) is common among foragers. If game migrates away and the supply of plant foods dwindles, the land is of no use to a forager. Where the wild food supply is likely to fluctuate, communal ownership of a large tract of land is more desirable than individually owned small parcels of land.

This is not to say that private ownership of land does not exist among foragers. Among foragers heavily dependent on fishing in rivers, individual or family ownership is more common,[3] perhaps because fishing in rivers is more predictable than other kinds of foraging. And, in some foraging societies, individuals and families have private rights to trees.[4] Although foragers generally do not have private ownership of important land resources, there is considerable variation in the extent of communal ownership. It is more common in food-collecting societies for a group of individuals, usually kin, to "own" land. To be sure, such ownership is not usually exclusive; typically, some degree of access is provided to members of neighboring bands.[5]

At the other extreme, local groups try to maintain exclusive rights to particular territories. Why have some foragers been more territorial than others? One suggestion is that, when the plants and animals collected are predictably located and abundant, groups are more likely to be sedentary and to try to maintain exclusive control over territories. In contrast, when plant and animal resources are unpredictable in location or amount, territoriality will tend to be minimal.[6] Territorial foragers appear to have predictably located resources *and* live in more permanent villages, so it is hard to know which factor is more important in determining whether territory will be defended.

Horticulturalists Like foragers, most horticulturalist individuals and families do not own land. Their lack of interest in laying claim to the land may be explained by the dynamics of subsistence farming. Using simple tools and no fertilizers other than the ash they create when they slash and burn vegetation to clear a field, most horticulturalists must periodically move on to other farmable land because they have depleted the soil in one area of its nutrients. Individuals or families have little incentive to claim permanent access to land that, given the technology available to them, they cannot use permanently. Nevertheless, horticulturalist societies are more likely than foraging societies to assign the use of particular plots of land to individuals or families.

The Kamayura of the Xingu region of the Amazon practice slash-and-burn horticulture. The rain forest is in the background.

For example, among the Mundurucú of Brazil, the village controls the rights to use land. People in the community can hunt and fish where they like, and they have the right to clear a garden plot wherever communal land is not being used. Gardens may be cultivated for only two years before the soil is exhausted; then the land reverts to the community. The Mundurucú distinguish between the land and the produce on the land; the produce belongs to the person who cultivates it. Similarly, the person who kills an animal or catches a fish owns it, no matter where it was obtained, even if he or she will later be expected to share the bounty.

Individual rights to land arose among the Mundurucú when they moved beyond subsistence to marketable products: the men began to tap rubber trees and sell the natural latex they harvested. Rights to a particular forest path of tapped trees could be inherited by a son or a son-in-law, but they could not be bought and sold.[7]

Pastoralists The territory of pastoral nomads usually far exceeds that of most horticultural societies. Because their wealth ultimately depends on mobile herds, uncultivated pasture for grazing, and water for drinking, pastoralists often combine the adaptive habits of both foragers and horticulturalists. Like foragers, they generally need to know the potential of a large area of land. The pastoral Basseri of Iran, for example, moved over an area of 15,000 square miles to obtain supplies of grass and water. Like horticulturalists, pastoralists must move on when they have exhausted a resource. In their case, the resource is grass, which must renew itself after extensive grazing.

Because land is only good if there is sufficient pasture and water, there would be considerable risk to individuals or families to own land that did not predictably have grass and water. Therefore, like most foragers and horticulturalists, members of pastoralist communities generally have free access to pasture land.[8] While they tend to hold grazing land communally, pastoralists customarily own their herds individually.[9] Fredrik Barth argued that, if animals were not privately owned, the entire group might be in trouble because the members might be tempted to eat up their productive capital—their animals—in bad times. On the other hand, when a family owns its herd and the herd drops below the minimum number of animals necessary for survival, the family can drop out of nomadic life, at least temporarily, and work for wages in sedentary agricultural communities. In so doing, one family does not jeopardize other pastoral families. On the other hand, if the fortunate were to share their herds with the unfortunate, all might approach bankruptcy. Thus, Barth argued, individual ownership is adaptive for a pastoral way of life.[10]

John Dowling questioned whether private ownership is an inducement to save for future production. As he pointed out, pastoral nomads are not the only ones who have to save some of their "crop" for future production. Horticulturalist societies also must save some of their crop, in the form of seeds or tubers, for future planting, and manage to do so even though they generally lack private ownership of productive resources. Dowling suggested that private ownership develops only in pastoral societies that depend on selling their products to non-pastoralists.[11] Thus, it may be the opportunity to sell their products, as well as their labor, that explains both the possibility of dropping out of nomadic life and the private ownership of animals among most pastoralists.

Current Research and Issues

Does Communal Ownership Lead to Economic Disaster?

In a controversial paper called "The Tragedy of the Commons," ecologist Garrett Hardin suggested that herders make an economically rational decision by grazing more animals than a pasture can sustain when they use common land—he would later explain that he meant *unregulated* common land. Economic logic dictates, according to Hardin, that herders have more to gain from owning more livestock than they have to lose by overgrazing land they do not own, since they are not accountable for the land. The tragedy Hardin saw results when overgrazing degrades pastureland to the point where herders can no longer sustain their herds. In the trade-off between self-interest and environmental destruction, Hardin also included water supplies, the air, and the oceans. He believed that a fisher is likely to take as many fish as possible from the ocean, a kind of commons, and not worry about the consequences. On the other hand, Harden argued, individuals might try to conserve natural resources if they own them, because they make an equally rational economic calculation that degrading those resources will cost them over the long term by decreasing their yields. The theory, then, is that private owners will find it rational to conserve their resources to minimize costs and maximize yields.

Does the evidence support Hardin's theory? Does communal ownership tend to result in overexploitation of resources and lower yields, and private ownership tend to result in conservation of resources and higher yields? This question is an active area of research in economic anthropology. We do know about instances in which communal grazing lands have been more productive than private grazing lands in comparable climates. For example, the Borana of Ethiopia, who have communal grazing, produce more animal protein per acre at lower cost than Australian cattle-ranchers, even though their climates are similar. And there are instances, such as the overgrazing in the Great American Desert, where private ownership did lead to degradation of the environment.

Fishing people often have communal rights to places to fish as in this area of Zaire.

Commercialization may be more important than private versus communal ownership in explaining overgrazing or overfishing, at least initially. In the Micronesian islands of Palau, which had traditional conservation practices, serious overfishing became a problem apparently only when people started to sell fish to Japanese colonists for imported trade goods. Some of those goods (nets and motors) helped to make fishing easier. Eventually, overfishing resulted in reduced catches and increased costs of fishing, and the Palauans had to buy much of their fish in imported cans.

It may also be that sustainability requires some regulation by political authorities. Before 1995, the halibut fishery in Alaska was facing collapse. Competing fishers rushed to fill their holds, no matter how dangerous the weather. Because the fishers often overshot the industry quota, regulators shortened the fishing season to just a few days. And when the boats returned after a few days with a year's worth of fish, the market was flooded and prices fell. In 1995, business became better and safer after a system of "catch shares" was adopted. The fishers were each allocated a transferable quota that they could use to catch fish or sell to others. The quotas are a percentage of the total allowable catch, which regulators set each year. Consequently, captains could plan when to fish without worrying about weather or being beaten to the schools of fish by other fishers, regulators could extend the fishing season, and prices for halibut climbed. The new regulatory system was a success. The halibut fishery was sustained and the fishers were better off. But regulation does not always work, judging by the "groundfishing" (fishing for fish, like cod, that feed off the ocean bottom) industry off the New England coast. In contrast to lobster fishermen who have accepted regulation, groundfishers have not. Perhaps this is because the groundfishing industry did not play a role in creating the regulations, nor does it have a cohesive community that can police itself.

Is there a lesson here for sustaining and even enhancing resources in general? If so, which is more likely to lead to conservation, communal ownership or private ownership? We cannot say yet with any confidence. We need more comparisons of cases to tell us. It may be that conservation can be fostered in either type of system, if the people involved are so motivated.

Sources: Hardin 1968; Johannes 1981; Dirks 2009; Stokstad 2008; Acheson 2006.

Like hunter-gatherers, pastoralist groups vary in the degree of ownership rights they possess to territories through which they move their animals. The Basseri have rights to pass through certain areas, including agricultural areas and even cities, but they do not own the entire territory upon which they depend. On the other hand, the Baluch, another pastoralist group in the border region between Iran, Pakistan, and Afghanistan, claim a "tribal" territory, which they defend by force, if necessary.[12]

Intensive Agriculturalists Individual ownership of land resources—including the right to use the resources and the right to sell or otherwise dispose of them—is common among intensive agriculturalists. The development of sole ownership is partly the result of the potential to use land season after season, which gives it lasting value. The concept of individual ownership is also partly a political (and social policy) matter. The U.S. Congress, for example, transformed government-owned frontier land west of the Mississippi River into privately owned land shortly before the Civil War, when the South had seceded from the Union. Under the Homestead Act of 1862, if a person cleared a 160-acre piece of land and farmed it for five years, the federal government would consider that person the owner of the land. Aside from being a populist social policy, the act served other political goals: It preempted the westward spread of the large-scale Southern plantation farming that relied on slave labor and created a larger voting population, since only property owners could vote at the time. The Homestead Act is similar to the custom in some societies by which a kin group, a chief, or a community is obligated to assign a parcel of land to anyone who wishes to farm it. Unlike the farmer of such a parcel, once American homesteaders became landowners, the laws of the country gave them the right to dispose of it at will by selling or giving it away. Moreover, property owners could use their economic and hence political power to pass laws that favored themselves.

Intensive agriculture is not always associated with private ownership. Nor does it always occur in complex political systems that have differences in wealth and power. Some communist and socialist nations—politically complex systems that seek to diminish differences in wealth and power—undertook intensive agriculture by forming state-run agricultural collectives. For example, after World War II, the small farm holdings in Zamfirovo, a village in Bulgaria, were incorporated into a cooperative. Most of the villagers worked as laborers on the new cooperative, but the cooperative also allocated to every household a small plot on which to grow its own grain, vegetables, and grapes. Such plots were fairly productive, and Westerners have often attributed their productivity to private enterprise. But the cooperative in Zamfirovo, at least, provided much of the labor needed to plant and plow these plots, so their productivity could hardly have been the result of private enterprise alone. In 1989, after the overthrow of the communist regime, the cooperative was dissolved, and the land was divided and sold to private owners.[13]

Colonialism, the State, and Land Rights Almost universally around the world, colonial conquerors and settlers have taken land away from the natives or aborigines. Even if the natives were given other land in exchange, as in Brazil and the United States, these so-called reservations were often, if not always, poorer in potential than the original land. (If the reservation land had not been poorer in quality, the settlers might have taken possession of it for themselves.) In addition, the new centralized governments often tried to change how the natives owned the land, almost always in the direction of individual or private ownership. If kin groups or larger social entities owned the land, it would be more difficult for the new settlers to get the natives to give it up, either by sale or threat. Individual owners could be dispossessed more easily.[14]

The newcomers who benefited from these forced changes were not always people of European background, but they were commonly people from expanding state societies. Beginning in the late 15th century, the expanding groups came mostly from Western Europe. But in recent times, as well as in the millennia before and after the time of Christ, conquerors and settlers have come from India, China, Japan, Arabia, Scandinavia, Russia, and other countries. This is not to say that native peoples in Africa, Asia, and the New World were never guilty of conquering and exploiting others on their continents or elsewhere. They were. The Aztecs in Mexico and Central America, the native kingdoms in West Africa after about 800 years ago, and the Arabs after the rise of Islam were just some of the expanding state societies of the past. Imperialism and colonialism have existed wherever there have been "civilized" (urban) societies. In North America, the British recognized the principle that lands not ceded to the crown would be native hunting grounds, but such recognition of rights by the British and then by the United States remained in force only as long as the various native groups remained numerous enough to constitute a threat to the settlers. President Andrew Jackson, for example, called for removal of all eastern Native American groups to "permanent" settlements west of the Mississippi. Some 90,000 people were removed. But, as settlers moved west, the reservations were often reduced in size.[15]

In much of colonial Africa, governments ceded land to European-owned companies for development. Reserves were established for large native populations, who then were invariably forced to work as laborers on European-owned plantations and in European-owned mines.[16] For example, in the 19th century, the land of the pastoral Masai stretched from the Lake Turkana area of northern Kenya down to northern Tanzania. The British pushed the Masai onto a reserve in the southern part of Kenya, south of the Mombasa-Uganda railway, and gave some of their prime grazing lands and water resources near Nairobi, as well as near the Naivasha and Nakuru lakes, to Europeans for farming and ranching. (Nairobi, which was then the administrative center of the British protectorate, is now the capital of Kenya.) The Masai grazing land was reduced by about 60 percent, and the Masai were also forbidden to graze in the areas where game parks were established by the British for tourism.[17] Europeans, who constituted less than 1 percent of the population in Kenya, acquired access to or control of 20 percent of the land, mostly in the highlands, where there was the greatest potential for commercial production of tea and coffee.[18]

The taking of land by state authorities does not happen with colonialism and imperialism alone. Indigenous revolutionary movements have collectivized land, as in Russia, or broken up large private landholdings, as in Mexico. Typically, state authorities do not like communal land-use systems, and they particularly view mobile pastoralists unfavorably, because their mobility makes them difficult to control. Governments usually try to settle pastoralists or break up communally held pasture into small units.[19] In Kenya, for example, after independence from the British, the pastoral Masai continued to lose grazing territory. The post-colonial national government, which strongly promotes tourism, not only needed land for the game parks it considered vital but also undertook the construction of massive greenhouses to grow flowers for the European market. Whereas the flower industry has flourished—flowers are Kenya's major horticultural export today—Lake Naivasha, where many greenhouses are located, has been polluted and overused. The pastoral Masai have also suffered. With the advice of international development agencies, the Kenyan government pushed for privatization of grazing land. But grazing on individually owned plots requires capital to grow or buy food for cattle, pay for medicines, and get cattle to market.[20]

Technology

Every society has a *technology*, a set of practical tools and skills with which it converts resources into food and other goods. Technologies include tools (such as digging sticks and harpoons), constructions (such as nets and traps), and learned skills (such as how and where to set up a fish trap). The technologies used and the ways in which access to them is allotted vary considerably among societies. Foragers and pastoralists, for example, typically employ relatively small tool kits. They must limit their number of tools, and their material possessions in general, to what they can comfortably carry with them. Access to technology is generally available to all members of forager and horticultural societies.

In industrial or post-industrial societies, on the other hand, the opportunity to acquire or use a particular technology (which may be enormously expensive, as well as complex) is hardly available to all. Most of us may be able to buy a drill or a hammer, but only a few of us have acquired the skill to make such tools. Even fewer of us could buy the factory—the system of technologies—needed to make the tools. Likewise, some of us can bake delicious breads, but few of us have the access to technology or the skill needed to mill grains into the flour we need. Nor do we have the same need to learn such technologies, for we can exchange the products of our specialized skills for products from other specialists.

While forager and pastoralist societies generally lack specialized labor, most individuals in such societies learn the skills they need to convert resources into food and other goods. The tools foragers most need are weapons for the hunt, digging sticks, and receptacles for gathering and carrying. Of all foragers, the Inuit probably had the most sophisticated weapons, including harpoons, compound bows, and ivory fishhooks. Yet the Inuit also had relatively fixed settlements with available storage space and dog teams and sleds for transportation.[21]

Foragers consider tools to belong to the person who made them. There is no way of gaining superiority over others through the possession of tools, because whatever resources for toolmaking are available to one are available to all. In addition, the custom of sharing applies to tools as well as to food. Elizabeth Thomas, speaking of the !Kung, said, "The few possessions that Bushmen have are constantly circulating among the members of their groups."[22]

Pastoralists, like foragers, are somewhat limited in their possessions, for they too are nomadic. But pastoralists can use their animals to carry some possessions. Each family owns its own tools, clothes, and perhaps a tent, as well as its own livestock. The livestock are the sources of other needed articles, for the pastoralists often trade their herd products for the products of the townspeople. Horticulturalists, on the other hand, are more self-sufficient than pastoralists. Their principal farming tools are the knife for slashing and the hoe or stick for digging. What a person makes is considered his or her own, yet everyone is often obligated to lend tools to others. In Chuuk society, the owner of a canoe has first use of it; the same is true for farming implements. Yet if a close relative needs the canoe and finds it unused, the canoe may be taken without permission. A distant relative or neighbor must ask permission to borrow any tools, but the owner may not refuse. If owners were to refuse, they would risk being scorned and refused if they were to need tools later.

Societies with intensive agriculture and industrialized societies are likely to have tools that are made by specialists and that must, therefore, be acquired by trade or purchase. Probably because complex tools cost a considerable amount of money, they are less likely than simple tools to be shared, except by those who contributed to the purchase price. A diesel-powered combine, for example, requires a large amount of capital for its purchase and upkeep. The person who has supplied the capital is likely to regard the machine as individual private property and to regulate its use and disposal. The owner must then use the machine to produce enough surplus to pay for its cost and upkeep, as well as for its replacement. The owner may rent the machine to neighboring farmers during slack periods to obtain a maximum return on the investment.

Expensive equipment, however, is not always individually owned in societies with intensive agriculture or industrialized economies. Even in capitalist countries, there may be collective ownership of machines by cooperatives or co-ownership with neighbors.[23] Governments often own very expensive equipment or facilities, such as airports, highways, and dams, on behalf of the entire society. Rights of use depend on the facility. Anyone can use a highway, but only contributing municipalities can draw upon the water in a dam. Other productive resources in industrial societies, such as factories or service companies, may be owned jointly by shareholders, who purchase a portion of a corporation's assets in return for a proportionate share of its earnings. The proportion of technology and facilities owned by various levels of government also reflects the type of political-economic system—socialist and communist countries have more public ownership than do capitalist countries.

16.2 Explain the different types of economic production and economic exchange and their effect on labor.

The Conversion of Resources

All societies transform or convert resources through labor into food, tools, and other goods. This conversion of resources constitutes what economists call *production*. In this section, after briefly reviewing different types of production, we examine what motivates people to work, how societies divide up the work to be done, and how they organize work. Some aspects of the conversion of natural resources are culturally universal, but there is also an enormous amount of cultural variation.

Types of Economic Production

Domestic When they were first described, most of the societies known to anthropology had a *domestic*—family or kinship—mode of production. Labor consisted of people getting food and producing shelter and implements for themselves and their kin. Families usually had the right to exploit productive resources and control the products of their labor. Even part-time specialists, such as potters, could support themselves without their craftwork if they needed to.

Industrial At the other extreme, *industrial* societies rely largely on mechanized production, in agriculture as well as in factories. Because machines and materials are costly, only some individuals (capitalists), corporations, or governments can afford the expenses of production. Therefore, most people in industrial societies labor for others as wage earners. Although wages can buy food, people out of work lose their ability to support themselves unless they are protected by welfare payments or unemployment insurance.

In postindustrial economies, computers and robots rather than people do much of the work in factories.

Tributary Found in nonindustrial societies, a third system is the *tributary* type of production, wherein most people still produce their own food but an elite or aristocracy controls a portion of production, including the products of specialized crafts. As the name implies, people pay a tribute of labor or produce to the elite landowner or ruler who grants them access to land. The feudal societies of medieval Western Europe were examples of tributary production, as was czarist Russia when it practiced serfdom.[24]

Post-industrial It is often suggested that the U.S. economy and other developed economies are now moving from *industrialism* to *post-industrialism*. In many areas of commerce, computers have radically transformed the workplace. Because computers can "drive" machines and robots, much of the manual work required in industry is disappearing. Businesses are now more knowledge and service oriented. Information has become so easily accessible through telecommunication that *telecommuting* has entered the English vocabulary to describe how people can now work for wages at home. This economic transformation has important implications for both home life and the workplace. With inexpensive home computers and speedy data transmission by telephone and other means, more people are able to work at home. In addition, when information and knowledge become more important than capital equipment, more people can own and have access to the productive resources of society.[25] If "who owns what" partly determines who has political and other influence, the wider ownership of resources that is possible in post-industrial society may eventually translate into new, more democratic political forms and processes.

Incentives for Labor

Why do people work? Probably all of us have asked ourselves this question. Our concern may not be why other people are working, but why we have to work. Clearly, part of the answer is that work is necessary for survival. Although there are always some able-bodied adults who do not work as much as they should and rely on the labor of others, no society would survive if most able-bodied adults were idle. In fact, most societies probably succeed in motivating most people to want to do (and even enjoy) what they have to do. But are the incentives for labor the same in all societies? Anthropologists believe the answer is both yes and no. One reason people work is because they must. But why do people in some societies apparently work *more* than they must?

Read the Document: Variation in Economy

The Profit Motive? We can be fairly certain that a particular and often-cited motive—the profit motive, or the desire to exchange something for more than it costs—is not universal or always the dominant motive. There can be no profit motive among people who produce food and other goods primarily for their own consumption, as do most foragers, most horticulturalists, and even some intensive agriculturalists. Such societies have what we call a *subsistence economy*, not a money or commercial economy. Anthropologists have noticed that people in subsistence economies (with a domestic mode of production) often work less than people in commercial economies (with tributary or industrial modes of production). Indeed, foragers appear to have a considerable amount of leisure time, as do many horticulturalists. It has been estimated, for example, that the men of the horticultural Kuikuru tribe in central Brazil spent about three and a half hours a day on subsistence. It appears that the Kuikuru could have produced a substantial surplus of manioc, their staple food, by working 30 minutes more a day.[26] Yet they and many other peoples do not produce more than they need. Why should they? They cannot store a surplus for long because it would rot; they cannot sell it because there is no market nearby; and they do not have a political authority that might collect it for some purpose. Although we often think "more is better," a food-getting strategy with such a goal might even be disastrous, especially for foragers. The killing of more animals than a group could eat might seriously jeopardize the food supply in the future, because overhunting could reduce reproduction among the hunted animals.[27] Horticulturalists might do well to plant a little extra, just in case part of the crop failed, but a great deal extra would be a tremendous waste of time and effort.

Chayanov's Rule It has been suggested that, when resources are converted primarily for household consumption, people will work harder if they have more consumers in the household. That is, when there are few able-bodied workers and a proportionately large number of consumers (perhaps because there are many young children and elderly people), the workers have to work harder. But when there are proportionately more workers, they can work less. This idea is called *Chayanov's rule*.[28] Alexander Chayanov found this relationship in data on rural Russians before the Russian Revolution.[29] But it appears to work in other places, too. Paul Durrenberger and Nicola Tannenbaum collected data in several villages in Thailand and found general support for Chayanov's rule,[30] and Michael Chibnik found support for Chayanov's rule when he compared data from 12 communities in five areas of the world. The communities ranged in complexity from New Guinea horticulturalists to Swiss commercial farmers. Although Chayanov restricted his theory to farmers who produced food mostly for their own consumption and did not hire labor, Chibnik's analysis suggests that Chayanov's rule applies even to hired labor.[31] On the other hand, Durrenberger and Tannenbaum found that political and social factors explained some of the variability in household production. In villages that lacked social classes, for example, families with a high ratio of workers to consumers produced less, apparently to avoid doing much better than other families. In contrast, in the villages that had social classes, households with a high ratio of workers to consumers produced more and gained prestige from their efforts.[32]

Social Rewards of Sharing There appear to be many societies in which some people work harder than they would need to in order to support their own families. What motivates them to work harder? They often share and transfer food and goods well beyond their own households, at times extending their reach to the whole community or even groups of communities. In such societies, social rewards come to those who are generous, who give things away. Thus, people who work harder than they have to for subsistence may be motivated to do so in order to gain respect or esteem.[33] Also, in many societies extra food and goods may be needed at times for special purposes and occasions; goods and services may be needed to arrange and celebrate marriages, to form alliances, and to perform rituals and ceremonies (including what we would call sporting events). Thus, how the culture defines what one works for and what is required may go beyond what is necessary.

Achievement In commercial economies such as the United States—where food, other goods, and services are sold and bought—people seem to be motivated to keep any extra income for themselves and their families. Extra income is converted into bigger dwellings, more expensive furnishings and food, and other elements of a "higher" standard of living. But the desire to improve one's standard of living is probably not their only motive. Some people may work partly to satisfy a need for achievement[34] or because they find their work enjoyable. In addition, just as in precommercial societies, some people may work partly to gain respect or influence by giving some of their income away. Not only are philanthropists and movie stars respected for giving to charities, but society encourages such giving by making it an allowable tax deduction. Still, commercial societies emphasize giving less than subsistence economies. People consider charity by the religious or rich appropriate and even admirable but would find giving away so much as to become poverty-stricken foolish.

A child in Bangladesh smashes bricks to earn a little salary.

Forced and Required Labor

Thus far, we have mostly discussed *voluntary labor*—voluntary in the sense that no formal organization within the society compels people to work and punishes them for not working. Social training and social pressure are powerful enough to persuade an individual to perform some useful task. In both food-collecting and horticultural societies, individuals who can stand being the butt of jokes about laziness will still be fed. At most, the other members of the group will ignore them. There is no reason to punish them and no way to coerce them to do the work expected of them.

Taxation More complex societies have ways of forcing people to work for the authorities, whether those authorities are kings or presidents. An indirect form of forced labor is taxation. The average tax in the United States (local, state, and federal) is about 33 percent of income, which means that the average person works four months out of the year for the various levels of government. If a person decides not to pay the tax, the money will be taken forcibly, or the person may be put in prison.

Corvée Money is the customary form of tax payment in a commercial society. In a politically complex but nonmonetary society, people may pay their taxes in other ways—by performing a certain number of hours of labor or by giving up a certain percentage of what they produce. The **corvée**, a system of required labor, existed in the Inca Empire in the central Andes before the Spanish conquest. Each male commoner was assigned three plots of land to work: a temple plot, a state plot, and his own plot. The enormous stores of food that went into state warehouses were used to supply the nobles, the army, the artisans, and all other state employees. If labor became overabundant, the people were still kept occupied; it is said that one ruler had a hill moved to keep some laborers busy. In addition to subsistence work for the state, Inca commoners were subject to military service, to duty as personal servants for the nobility, and to other "public" service.[35] Elderly villagers in the Chiang Mai area of Thailand describe corvée this way: "Villagers had to work one *rai* [*rai myong* or 0.1 acre] per person for them [the rulers] for nothing. *And* one had to do it properly. The lord's underlings would take a banana tree trunk and stick it upright in the field after it was plowed. If it fell over, that meant it was well plowed. Otherwise, one would have to keep on plowing until the ground was soft."[36]

Corvée A system of required labor.

Conscription or the draft, or compulsory military service, is also a form of corvée, in that a certain period of service is required, and failure to serve can be punished by a prison term or involuntary exile. Emperors of China had soldiers drafted to defend their territory and to build the Great Wall along the northern borders of the empire. The wall extends over 1,500 miles, and thousands were drafted to work on it.

Slavery is the most extreme form of forced work, in that slaves have little control over their labor. The practice of enslaving people has existed in almost every part of the world at one time or another, in simpler as well as in more complex societies. Slaves are often obtained from other cultures directly; they are kidnapped, captured in war, or given as tribute. Or they may be obtained indirectly through barter or trade. Slaves have sometimes come from the same culture; people have become slaves to repay a debt, as punishment for a crime, or even because it was an alternative to poverty. The degree to which slaves can gain their freedom varies among slave societies.

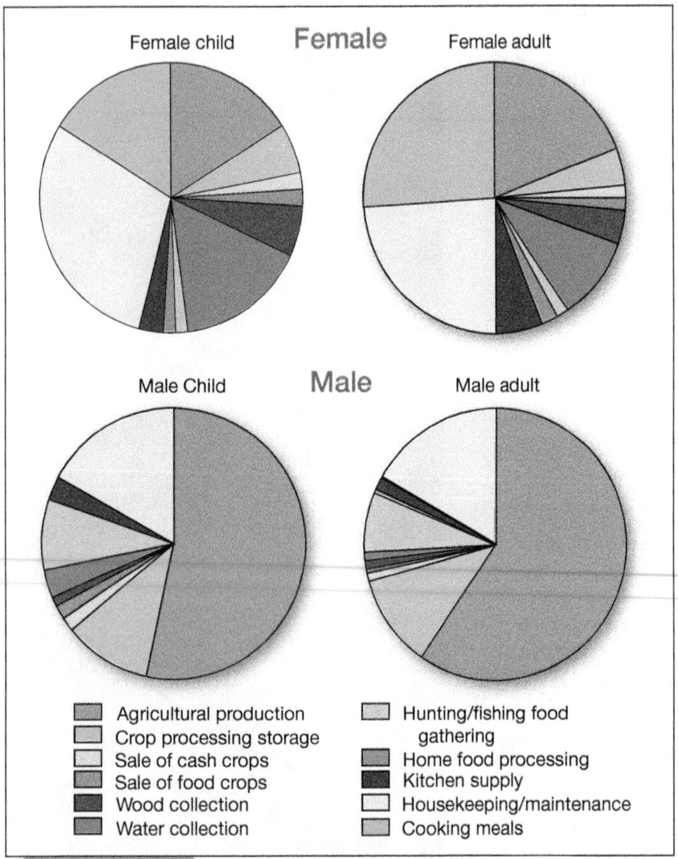

FIGURE 16.1 A Comparison of the Proportion of Work Tasks Done by Adults and Children in the Cote D'lvoire

Source: From J. Levine et al. 2002.

Division of Labor

All societies have some division of labor, some customary assignment of different kinds of work to different kinds of people. Universally, males and females, and adults and children, do not do the same kinds of work. In a sense, then, division of labor by gender and age is a kind of universal specialization of labor. Many societies known to anthropology divide labor only by gender and age; other societies have more complex specialization.

By Gender and Age All societies make use of gender differences to some extent in their customary assignment of labor. In the chapter on sex and gender, we discuss the division of labor by gender in detail.

Age is also a universal basis for division of labor. Clearly, children cannot do work that requires a great deal of strength. But, in many societies, girls and boys contribute much more in labor than do children in our own society. For example, they help in animal tending, weeding, and harvesting and do a variety of domestic chores such as child care, fetching water and firewood, and cooking and cleaning.
In agricultural communities in the Ivory Coast, children's tasks mirror the tasks of same-sex adults (see Figure 16.1). In some societies, a child who is 6 years old is considered old enough to be responsible for a younger sibling for a good part of the day.[37] Animal tending is often important work for children. Children in some societies spend more time at this task than adults.[38]

Why do children do so much work in some societies? If adults, particularly mothers, have heavy workloads, and children are physically and mentally able to do the work, a good part of the work is likely to be assigned to children.[39] As we have seen, food producers probably have more work than foragers, so we would expect that children would be likely to work more where there is herding and farming. Consistent with this expectation, Patricia Draper and Elizabeth Cashdan found differences in children's work between nomadic and settled !Kung. Even though recently settled !Kung have not switched completely from foraging to food production, children's as well as adults' activities have changed considerably. The children living in nomadic camps had virtually no work at all; adults did all the gathering and hunting. But the settled children were given lots of chores, ranging from helping with animals to helping with the harvest and food processing.[40]

What we have said about the !Kung should not imply that children in foraging societies always do little work. For example, among the Hadza of Tanzania, children between the ages of 5 and 10 are able to get one-third to one-half of their calories as they forage with their mothers. The Hadza also have more children than the !Kung.[41] Is there a relationship between children's work and fertility? When children in a society do a great deal of work, parents may value them more and may consciously want to have more children.[42] This may be one of the reasons why birth rates are especially high in intensive agricultural societies where workloads are very high.[43]

Beyond Gender and Age In societies with relatively simple technologies, there is little specialization of labor beyond that of gender and age. But as a society's technology becomes more complex and it is able to produce large quantities of food, more of its people are freed from subsistence work to become specialists in some other tasks.

In contrast with foragers, horticultural societies may have some part-time specialists. Some people may devote special effort to perfecting a particular skill or craft—pottery making, weaving, house building, doctoring—and in return for their products or services be given food or other gifts. Among some horticultural groups, the entire village may specialize part-time in making a particular product, which can then be traded to neighboring people.

With the development of intensive agriculture, full-time specialists—potters, weavers, blacksmiths—begin to appear. The trend toward greater specialization reaches its peak in industrialized societies, where workers develop skills in one small area of the economic system. Full-time specialization makes people dependent on the necessity to sell their labor or products to make a living. In societies with full-time occupational specialization, different jobs are usually associated with differences in prestige, wealth, and power, as we shall see in the chapter on social stratification.

The Organization of Labor

The degree to which labor has to be organized reaches its peak in industrial societies, which have great occupational specialization and complex political organization. The coordination required to produce an automobile on an assembly line is obvious; so is the coordination required to collect taxes from every wage earner.

In many food-collecting and horticultural societies, there is little formal organization of work. Work groups tend to be organized only when productive work requires it and to dissolve when they are no longer needed. Furthermore, the groups so organized often have changing composition and leadership; participation tends to be individualistic and voluntary.[44] Perhaps this flexibility is possible because, when virtually everyone has the same work to do, little instruction is needed, and almost anyone can assume leadership. Still, some types of work require more organization than others. Hunting big game usually requires coordinated efforts by a large number of hunters; so might catching fish in large nets. For example, on Moala, a Fijian island in the Pacific, net fishing is a group affair. A party of 20 to 30 women wades out on the reef and makes a semicircle of nets. At a signal from an experienced woman, usually the chief's wife, the women move together at the ends, forming a circle. After the fish are caught in the nets, the women bite them on the backs of their heads to kill them and put them in baskets that they carry ashore. Around Christmas, the village, or several villages, undertakes a larger fish drive. The day before, more than 100 people make a "sweep," some 1,600 yards long, from coconut fronds. The next day, the men, women, and children all participate in the surround, catching thousands of fish.[45]

Kinship ties are an important basis for work organization, particularly in nonindustrial societies. For example, among the horticultural Kapauku of western New Guinea, the male members of a village are a kin group, and all work together to build drainage ditches, large fences, and bridges.[46] With increasing technological complexity, the basis of work organization begins to shift to more formally organized groups.[47] In modern industrial societies, the predominant basis of organization is the *contract*—the agreement between employers and employees whereby the latter perform a specified amount of work for a specified amount of wages. Although the arrangement may be entered into voluntarily, laws and the power of the state enforce the obligation of the parties to abide by the contract.

Making Decisions About Work

Foragers ignore many of the plant and animal species in their environment, choosing to go after only some. Why? The people may say that some animals are taboo whereas others are delicious. But where do such customary beliefs come from? Are they adaptive? And if there are no customary preferences for certain plants and animals, how can we explain why a food collector will go after certain foods and ignore others on a particular day? Food producers also make choices constantly. For example, a farmer has to decide when to plant, what to plant, how much to plant, when to harvest, how much to store, and how much to give away or sell. Researchers have tried to explain why certain economic decisions become customary and why individuals make certain economic choices in their everyday lives.

A !Kung woman roasting nuts. Nuts yield fewer calories than hunted meat for every hour of work, but nuts are more dependable.

A frequent source of ideas about choices is **optimal foraging theory**, which was developed originally by students of animal behavior and which has been applied to decision making by foragers. Optimal foraging theory assumes that individuals seek to maximize the returns, in calories and nutrients, on their labor in deciding which animals and plants to hunt or collect. Natural selection should favor optimal foraging because "good" decisions would increase the chances of survival and reproduction. Research in different food-collecting societies supports the optimal foraging model.[48] For example, the Aché of eastern Paraguay consistently prefer to hunt peccaries (wild pig-like mammals) rather than armadillos. Although peccaries take much longer to find and are harder to kill than armadillos, a day spent hunting peccaries yields more than 4,600 calories per hour of work, whereas hunting armadillos yields only about 1,800 calories an hour.[49] Other factors in addition to calorie yield, such as predictability of resources, may also influence which foods are collected. For example, the !Kung of the Kalahari Desert depend largely on mongongo nuts, even though these nuts yield fewer calories per hour of work than does meat. But mongongo nuts in season are more dependable than game is. Once a group of !Kung hikes to a grove of ripe mongongo nuts, they know they can obtain food there until the supply is exhausted; they are not as certain of getting game when they seek it.[50] Similarly on Ifaluk, an atoll in the Federated States of Micronesia, where fishing is the main source of animal protein, men most often choose to fish in the place where there is the highest return on average. But they do not always fish there; if the return on a previous day was lower than average, they tend to choose other spots.[51]

How does a farmer decide whether to plant a particular crop and how much land and labor to devote to it? Christina Gladwin and others suggested that farmers make decisions in steps, with each choice point involving a yes or no answer. For example, in the high-altitude region of Guatemala, farmers could choose to plant about eight crops, or combinations of them, such as corn and beans, which grow together well. A farmer will quickly exclude some choices because of the answers to certain questions: Can I afford the seed and fertilizer? Can this crop be watered adequately? Is the altitude appropriate? And so on. If any of the answers is no, the crop is not planted. By a further series of yes-or-no decisions, farmers presumably decide which of the remaining possibilities will be planted.[52]

Optimal foraging theory The theory that individuals seek to maximize the returns (in calories and nutrients) on their labor in deciding which animals and plants they will go after.

Individuals may not always be able to state clearly their rules for making decisions, nor do they always have complete knowledge about the various possibilities, particularly when some of the possibilities are new. That does not mean, however, that researchers cannot predict or explain economic choices. For example, Michael Chibnik found that men in two villages in Belize and in Central America were not able to say why they devoted more or less time to working for wages versus growing crops. But their behavior was still predictable. Older men grew crops because wage labor was more physically demanding; and in the village with a higher cost of living, men were more likely to work for wages.[53]

The Distribution of Goods and Services

16.3 Explain the three general types of systems for distributing goods and services (reciprocity, redistribution, and market or commercial exchange).

Goods and services are distributed in all societies by systems that, however varied, can be classified under three general types: reciprocity, redistribution, and market or commercial exchange.[54] The three systems often coexist in a society, but one system usually predominates. The predominant system seems to be associated with the society's food-getting technology and, more specifically, its level of economic development.

Reciprocity

Reciprocity Giving and taking (not politically arranged) without the use of money.

Reciprocity consists of giving and taking without the use of money; it mainly takes the form of gift giving or generalized reciprocity. There may also be exchanges of equal value (barter or nonmonetary trade) or balanced reciprocity without the use of money.[55]

Generalized Reciprocity When goods or services are given to another, without any apparent expectation of a return gift, we call it **generalized reciprocity**. Generalized reciprocity sustains the family in all societies. Parents give food, clothing, and labor to children because they want to or perhaps feel obliged to, but they do not usually calculate exactly how their children will reciprocate years later. These gifts are one-way transfers. In this sense, all societies have some kind of generalized reciprocity. But some societies depend on it almost entirely to distribute goods and services.

Lorna Marshall recounted how the !Kung divided an eland brought to a site where five bands and several visitors were camping—more than 100 people in all. The owner of the arrow that had first penetrated the eland was, by custom, the owner of the meat. He first distributed the forequarters to the two hunters who had aided him in the kill. After that, the distribution depended on kinship: Each hunter shared with his wives' parents, wives, children, parents, and siblings, and they in turn shared with their kin. Sixty-three gifts of raw meat were recorded, after which further sharing of raw and cooked meat was begun. The !Kung distribution of large game—clearly, generalized reciprocity—is common among foragers. But giving away is not limited to game. For example, when Marshall left the band that had sponsored her in 1951, she gave each woman in the band a present of enough cowrie shells to make a necklace—one large shell and 20 small ones. When she returned in 1952, she found no cowrie shell necklaces and hardly a single shell among the people in the band. Instead, the shells appeared by ones and twos in the ornaments of the people of neighboring bands.[56]

Zebu meat is divided for villagers as part of a festival in Mananjary, Madagascar

Although generalized reciprocity may seem altruistic or unselfish, researchers have suggested that giving may in fact benefit the givers in various ways. For example, parents who help their children may not only perpetuate their genes (the ultimate biological benefit) but may also be likely to receive care and affection from their grown-up children when the parents are old. And giving parents may be happier and enjoy life more than nongiving parents. So, in the shorter as well as the longer run, givers may derive economic and psychological benefits, in addition to reproductive benefits.

Generalized reciprocity Gift giving without any immediate or planned return.

Parent-child giving may seem easy to understand, but why do some societies rely more on generalized reciprocity than others, particularly beyond the family? Sharing may be most likely when resources are unpredictable. A !Kung band may share its water with other bands because they may have water now but not in the future. A related group in the Kalahari, the G//ana,[57] has been observed to share less than other groups. It turns out that the resources available to the G//ana are more predictable because the G//ana supplement their hunting and gathering with plant cultivation and goat herding. Cultivated melons (which store water) appear to buffer the G//ana against water shortages, and goats buffer them against shortages of game. Thus, whereas the !Kung distribute the meat right after a kill, the G//ana dry it and then store it in their houses.[58]

The idea that unpredictability favors sharing may also explain why some foods are more often shared than others. Wild game, for example, is usually unpredictable; when hunters go out to hunt, they cannot be sure that they will come back with meat. Wild plants, on the other hand, are more predictable; gatherers can be sure when they go out that they will come back with at least some plant foods. In any case, it does appear that foragers tend to share game much more than wild plant foods.[59] Even among people who depend largely on horticulture, such as the Yanomamö of Venezuela and Brazil, food items that are less predictably obtained (hunted game and fish) are shared more often than the more predictably obtained garden produce.[60] But although meat is shared more than plant food, horticulturalists often share foraged or cultivated plants. Why? Sharing plant food may be advantageous to horticulturalists who are some distance from their gardens because they may not have to go as often. And sharing may solidify a social relationship so that other families will help in times of need, such as sickness or accident, when it may be hard to work.[61] Does food sharing increase the food supply for an individual? Calculations for the Aché of eastern Paraguay, who get most of their food from hunting when they go on food-collecting trips, suggest that the average individual gets more food when food is shared. Even the males who actually do the hunting get more, although the benefits are greater for the females and children on the trip.[62] Mathematically, the risk that an individual food collector will not find enough food on a particular day will be appreciably reduced if at least six to eight adult collectors share the food they collect. Food-collecting bands may often contain only 25 to 30 people, which is about the size that is needed to ensure that there are six to eight adult collectors.[63]

Although giving things to others may be expected in some societies, this does not necessarily mean that everyone does so willingly or without some social pressure. For example, the !Kung call "far-hearted" anyone who does not give gifts, and they express their disapproval openly.

Day-to-day unpredictability is one thing; more prolonged scarcity is another. What happens to a system of generalized reciprocity when resources are scarce because of a drought or other disaster? Does the ethic of giving break down? Evidence from a few societies suggests that the degree of sharing may actually *increase* during the period of food shortage.[64] For example, in describing the Netsilik Inuit, Asen Balikci said, "Whenever game was abundant, sharing among non-relatives was avoided, since every family was supposedly capable of obtaining the necessary catch. In situations of scarcity, however, caribou meat was more evenly distributed throughout camp."[65] Sharing may increase during mild scarcity because people can minimize their deprivation, but generalized reciprocity may be strained by extreme scarcity such as famine.[66]

Researchers generally find it difficult to explain the concept of sharing because they assume that, other things being equal, individuals will tend to be selfish. Most theories about sharing point out that sharing gives individuals advantages in certain circumstances. And it is in those circumstances that societies have found ways to make sharing a moral issue or to otherwise make non-sharers extremely uncomfortable. But increasingly a variety of evidence—experimental and observational—suggests that altruism, or selfless behavior, may be more common than we think. Even some nonhuman primates, such as chimpanzees, share with another chimp when they are given an experimental choice to do so.[67] Experimental evidence suggests that sharing in humans is likely even among people who do not know each other or who have no expectation of any return in the future from that person. Experimenters set up "games" in which they can control for or eliminate certain responses. For example, in one two-person game a player receives an amount of money and must decide what share of it to offer to the second player. The second player can accept or reject the offer; but, if he or she rejects the offered amount, neither player gets any money. If the second player accepts the offered amount, both players receive the proposed division. If selfishness were normal, one would expect that the proposer of the division would try to give away as little as possible and the second player should always accept whatever is offered because otherwise nothing is gained. Surprisingly, equal divisions are commonly proposed and low offers are commonly rejected because they are viewed as unfair. If a person views the offer as unfair and forfeits any money, he or she seems willing to "punish" the greedy individual. While such experiments were mostly done at first in Western societies, we now have results from over 15 other societies that largely confirm the earlier results.[68] And there is now evidence suggesting that cooperation may even evoke pleasure. Researchers studying brain activity in women, who are playing a game allowing either cooperative or greedy strategies, found to their surprise that cooperation made certain areas of the brain light up. These areas are normally associated with pleasure, such as when eating desserts. And friends spontaneously smile more when they share.[69] So cooperation may be more "natural" than some people think.[70]

But what does "more natural" mean? Do humans have a genetic propensity to share? And if they do, altruism presents a genetic puzzle, because there are costs to altruistic actions such as helping a person in danger or giving away some of your food or money. And these costs should lead to a genetic disadvantage. To try to address the paradox, evolutionary anthropologists postulate that if altruism were mostly kin-based, and kin share many of your genes, then helping your relatives could increase altruism. Or, if you reciprocate with a partner (they help you and you help them), both individuals may do better. The problem for these theories is that in many societies, particularly foraging societies, sharing has been shown to be widespread, particularly when it involves large game. Neither kin-selection altruism or reciprocal altruism seem to explain such sharing. As we discussed earlier, a group of male hunters and their families may do better if they share large game. The ethic of cooperation and generosity is widespread among foragers, so perhaps altruists benefitted in another way. Suppose early human societies unconsciously rewarded people who were generous and punished people who were not. These cultural behaviors and values could, over the long stretch of time that humans were foragers, have favored some altruistic propensities if benefits, such as prestige and getting better mates, outweighed the costs.[71] If this scenario were correct, we would have an interaction between cultural and genetic evolution that promoted altruism. Some researchers believe that altruism is at least partly genetic, since even 14- to 18-month-old children will offer help when they perceive that is needed; confronted with someone who has dropped an object and not picked it up, they will pick it up.[72] But regardless of whether humans have some biological propensity to altruism, some cultures value altruism more than others. It is that variation that we need to explain.

Balanced Reciprocity **Balanced reciprocity** is explicit and short term in its expectations of return. In contrast to generalized reciprocity or a one-way transfer, which has no expectation of a return, balanced reciprocity involves either an immediate exchange of goods or services or an agreed-upon exchange over a limited period of time. *Barter* is the term used most often for this type of nonmonetary exchange of goods and services. The !Kung, for instance, trade with the Tswana Bantu: a gemsbok hide for a pile of tobacco, five strings of beads made from ostrich eggshells for a spear, or three small skins for a good-sized knife.[73] In the 1600s, the Iroquois of the North American Northeast traded deerskin to Europeans for brass kettles, iron hinges, steel axes, woven textiles, and guns.[74] The !Kung and Iroquois acquired trade goods by balanced reciprocity, but such exchanges were not crucial to their economies.

Balanced reciprocity Giving with the expectation of a straightforward immediate or limited-time trade.

In contrast, some societies depend much more heavily on balanced reciprocity. For example, the Efe, who hunt and gather in the Ituri forest of central Africa, get most of their calories from manioc, peanuts, rice, and plaintains grown by another group—the agricultural Lese. Efe men and women provide labor to the Lese and in exchange receive a portion of the harvest as well as goods such as metal pots and spears.[75] Pastoralists, too, are rarely self-sufficient, as we mentioned in the preceding chapter. They have to trade their pastoral products to agriculturalists to get the grain and other things they need.

Balanced reciprocity may mostly involve labor. Cooperative work parties usually exchange or balance gifts of labor. A cooperative work party, or *kuu*, among the Kpelle of Liberia may number from 6 to 40 people, all of whom are generally relatives or friends. In addition to promising return work on a particular date, each farmer rewards the work party's hard day's labor by providing a feast and sometimes rhythmic music to work by.[76] When we say that an exchange is balanced, we do not mean to imply that the things exchanged are exactly equivalent in value or that the exchange is purely economic. In the absence of a money economy, where there is no explicit standard by which value can be judged, there is no way to assess value objectively. The point is that the parties in balanced reciprocity are freely giving each other the respective goods and services they each want; they are not coerced into doing so, so presumably they are not conceiving of the exchange as unbalanced.[77] And when something is valued, it may be valued for other than economic reasons. The exchange itself may also be fun, adventuresome, or aesthetically pleasing, or it may enhance social relationships.

Because exchanges can have different motivations, they can have different meanings. Consequently, some economic anthropologists now want to distinguish between gift and commodity exchanges. *Gift exchanges* are personal and involve the creation or perpetuation of some kind of enduring relationship between people and groups. In our society, the exchange of dinner invitations or Christmas gifts is motivated by social considerations;

Men perform the kula dance at an inter-island exchange celebration in the Trobriand Islands.

we are not interested only in the actual food or objects received. In contrast, *commodity exchanges*, which can occur even in the absence of money, focus on the objects or services received—the transaction itself is the motive. When the transaction is completed, the relationship between the parties involved usually ends.[78]

The *Kula* Ring The horticultural Trobriand Islanders, who live off the eastern coast of New Guinea, worked out an elaborate scheme for trading ornaments, food, and other necessities with the people of neighboring islands. The exchange of goods between far-flung islands is essential, for some of the islands are small and rocky and cannot produce enough food to sustain their inhabitants, who specialize instead in canoe building, pottery making, and other crafts. Other islanders produce far more yams, taro, and pigs than they need. However, the practical side of the trade is hidden beneath a complex ceremonial exchange, called the ***kula* ring**, an exchange of valued shell ornaments across a set of far-flung islands.[79]

Two kinds of ornaments are involved in the ceremonial exchanges—white shell armbands (*mwali*), which are given only in a counterclockwise direction, and red shell necklaces (*soulava*), which are given only in a clockwise direction. The possession of one or more of these ornaments allows a man to organize an expedition to the home of one of his trading partners on another island. The high point of an expedition is the ceremonial giving of the valued *kula* ornaments. During the two- to three-day visit, the trading of necessities goes on. Some of the exchange takes the form of gift giving between trading partners. By the time the visitors leave, they have accomplished a year's trading without seeming to do so.

But the practical advantages of the *kula* ring are not the only gains. There may be purely social ones, for goods are traded with ease and enjoyment. A trading expedition takes on the flavor of adventure rather than of business. Many of the traditions of the islands are kept alive: Myth, romance, ritual, and history are linked to the circulating ornaments, especially the larger, finer pieces, which are well known and recognized as heirlooms. A man is able to possess many valued things within his lifetime, each for a year or so. Each object, when it is received, arouses enthusiasm in a way that one lifelong possession could not.[80] The *kula* ring continued to be an important institution after Papua New Guinea became an independent country. For example, active participation in the *kula* ring helped candidates in the 1960s and the 1970s to be elected to the national parliament.[81]

The *kula* is not the only form of exchange in Trobriand life. For example, on the two days following a burial, the kin of the deceased give yams, taro, and valuables to those who helped care for the deceased before death, to those who participated in the burial ceremonies, and to those who came to mourn the deceased. After these initial exchanges, the hamlet settles into mourning. Women from other hamlets bring food to the people in mourning, and the mourning women prepare bundles of banana leaves and weave skirts of banana fiber for later distribution. Husbands help their wives accumulate valuables to "buy" extra bundles of banana leaves. Then the women's mortuary ceremony is held. It is very competitive—each of the mourning women tries to distribute the most bundles and skirts. As many as 5,000 bundles and 30 skirts might be distributed by one mourning woman in a single day. Each of these giveaways completes a balanced reciprocity: The giver is reciprocating for gifts of goods and services received in the past. A woman's brothers gave her yams and taro during the year. She gives her brothers' wives bundles or skirts, which are also given to those who helped make the special mourning skirts and to those who brought or cooked food during the mourning period.[82]

Sometimes the line between generalized and balanced reciprocity is not so clear. Consider our gift giving at Christmas. Although such gift giving may appear to be generalized reciprocity, and it often is in the case of gift giving from parents to children, there may be strong expectations of balance. Two friends or relatives may try to exchange presents of fairly equal value, based on calculations of what last year's gift cost. If a person receives a $5 present when he or she gave a $25 present, that person may be hurt and perhaps angry. On the other hand, a person who receives a $500 present when he or she gave a $25 present may well also be dismayed. But Christmas giving, like the Trobriand *kula* ring, also illustrates that exchanges are not simply economic but serve many other purposes, including fun.

Kinship Distance and Type of Reciprocity Most food-collecting and horticultural societies depend on some form of reciprocity for the distribution of goods and labor. Marshall Sahlins suggested that the form of the reciprocity depends largely on the kinship distance between people. Generalized reciprocity may be the rule for family members and close kinsmen. Balanced reciprocity may be practiced among equals who are not closely related. People who would consider it inappropriate to trade with their own families will trade with neighboring groups.[83] In general, the importance of reciprocity declines with economic development.[84] In societies with intensive agriculture, and even more so in industrialized societies, reciprocity distributes only a small proportion of goods and services.

Reciprocity as a Leveling Device Reciprocal gift giving may do more than equalize the distribution of goods within a community, as in the sharing that takes place among the !Kung. It may also tend to equalize the distribution of goods between communities.

Many Melanesian societies in and near New Guinea have the custom of holding pig feasts in which 50, 100, or even 2,000 pigs are slaughtered. Andrew Vayda, Anthony Leeds, and David Smith have suggested that these enormous feasts, though apparently wasteful, are just one of the outcomes of a complex of cultural practices that are highly advantageous to a community. The people of these societies cannot accurately predict how much food they will produce during the year. Some years they will have bumper crops and other years very poor crops because of fluctuations in the weather. Overplanting can be a hedge against such fluctuations, but it can also result in overproduction when the weather supports an average or exceptionally good yield. What can a community do with this extra food? Because root plants such as yams and taro, which are the main crops cultivated by Melanesian societies, do not keep well over long periods, the surplus is fed to pigs. In effect, pigs serve as food repositories and food processors, since the same plump, yam-fed pigs become a food source during lean times. However, if there are several years of crop surplus, the resulting increase in pigs can become too much of a good thing. Pigs wanting food can destroy yam and taro patches. What does a village do when the pig population grows to a menacing proportion? It invites other villages to a gigantic pig roast. Over the years, the pig feasts serve to equalize the food consumption, and especially the protein consumption, of all the villages that participate in the feasts.[85] Thus, the custom of pig feasts may be a way for villages to "bank" surplus food by storing up "social credit" with other villages, which will return that credit in subsequent feasts.

Potlatch A feast among Pacific Northwest Native Americans at which great quantities of food and goods are given to the guests in order to gain prestige for the host(s).

In some Melanesian societies, the pig feasts foster an element of competition among the men who give them. "Big men" may try to bolster their status and prestige by the size of their feasts. A reputation is enhanced not by keeping wealth but by giving it away. A similar situation existed among many Native American groups of the Pacific Northwest, where a chief might attempt to enhance his status by holding a **potlatch**. At a potlatch, a chief and his group would give away blankets, pieces of copper, canoes, large quantities of food, and other items to their guests. The host chief and his group would later be invited to other potlatches.

The competitive element in the potlatch appears to have intensified after contact with Europeans. Because of the fur trade, the number of trade goods increased, and so more items could be given away. Possibly more important was the population decline among the Indians, caused by diseases such as smallpox that European traders introduced. Distant relatives of chiefs who had no direct heirs might compete for the right to the title, each attempting to give away more than the others.[86] Chiefs may also have attempted to attract men to their half-empty villages by spectacular giveaways.[87] Decimated groups might have coalesced to maintain the potlatching. For example, when the Tlingit population declined to a low in the 1910s, kin groups coalesced to assemble enough resources for a potlatch.[88] Although the potlatch system seems wasteful in that goods were often destroyed in the competition, the system probably also served to equalize the distribution of goods among competing groups.

On one level of analysis, the Melanesian pig feasts and the Pacific Northwest potlatches were all reciprocal exchanges between communities or villages. But these exchanges were not just intercommunity versions of reciprocal gift giving between individuals. Because these feasts were organized by people who collected goods, they also involved another mode of distribution, which anthropologists call *redistribution*.

Redistribution

Redistribution The accumulation of goods (or labor) by a particular person or in a particular place and their subsequent distribution.

Redistribution is the accumulation of goods or labor by a particular person or agency, or in a particular place, for the purpose of subsequent distribution. Although redistribution is found in all societies, it becomes an important mechanism only in societies that have political hierarchies—that is, chiefs or other specialized officials and agencies. In all societies, there is some redistribution, at least within the family. Members of the family pool their labor, products, or income for the common good. But in many societies, there is little or no redistribution beyond the family. It seems that redistribution on a territorial basis emerges when there is a political apparatus to coordinate centralized collection and distribution of goods or to mobilize labor for some public purpose.

In the African state of Bunyoro, in western Uganda, for example, the king (called the *mukama*) retained much of the wealth for himself and his close kin. The *mukama* had the authority to grant the use of land and all other natural resources to his subordinate chiefs, and they in turn granted it to the common people. In return, everyone was required to give the *mukama* large quantities of food, crafts, and even labor services. The *mukama* then redistributed these goods and services, in theory at least, to all the people. The *mukama* was praised with names that emphasized his generosity: *Agutamba* ("he who relieves distress") and *Mwebingwa* ("he to whom the people run for help"). But it is clear that much of what the king redistributed did not find its way back to the common people, who produced the bulk of the goods. Instead, the wealth was distributed largely according to rank within the state.[89]

Other redistribution systems are more equal. For example, among the Buin of Melanesia, "the chief is housed, dressed, and fed exactly like his bondsman."[90] Even though the chief owns most of the pigs, everyone shares equally in the consumption of the wealth. In general, however, where redistribution is important, as in societies with higher levels of productivity, the wealthy are more likely than the poor to benefit from the redistributions.[91]

Why do redistribution systems develop? Elman Service suggested that they develop in agricultural societies that contain subregions suited to different kinds of crops or natural resources. Foragers can take advantage of environmental variation by moving to different areas. With agriculture, the task is more difficult; it might be easier to move different products across different regions.[92] If the demand for different resources or products becomes too great, reciprocity between individuals might become awkward. So it might be more efficient to have someone—a chief, perhaps—coordinate the exchanges.

Marvin Harris agreed that redistribution becomes more likely with agriculture, but for a somewhat different reason. He argued that competitive feasting, as in New Guinea, is adaptive because it encourages people to work harder to produce somewhat more than they need. Why would this feature be adaptive? Harris argued that, with agriculture, people really have to produce more than they need so that they can protect themselves against crises such as crop failure. The groups that make feasts may be indirectly ensuring themselves against crises by storing up social credit with other villages, who will reciprocate by making feasts for them in the future. On the other hand, inducements to collect more than they need may not be advantageous to food-collecting groups, who might lose in the long run by overcollecting.[93]

Market or Commercial Exchange

When we think of markets, we usually think of bustling, colorful places where goods are bought and sold. The exchanges usually involve money. In our own society, we have supermarkets and the stock market and other places for buying and selling that we call shops, stores, and malls. In referring to **market** or **commercial exchange,** economists and economic anthropologists are referring to exchanges or transactions in which the "prices" are subject to supply and demand, whether or not the transactions actually occur in a marketplace.[94] Market exchange involves not only the exchange (buying and selling) of goods but also transactions of labor, land, rentals, and credit.

Market (or commercial) exchange Transactions in which the "prices" are subject to supply and demand, whether or not the transactions occur in a marketplace.

On the surface, many market exchanges resemble balanced reciprocity. One person gives something and receives something in return. How, then, does market exchange differ from balanced reciprocity? It is easy to distinguish market exchange from balanced reciprocity when money is directly involved, because reciprocity is defined as not involving money. But market exchange need not always involve money directly.[95] For example, a landowner grants a tenant farmer the right to use the land in exchange for a portion of the crop. So, to call a transaction market exchange, we have to ask whether supply and demand determine the price. If a tenant farmer gave only a token gift to the landowner, we would not call it market exchange, just as a Christmas gift to a teacher is not payment for teaching. If tenants, however, are charged a large portion of their crops when the supply of land is short, or if landowners lower their demands when few people want to tenant-farm, then we would call the transactions market or commercial exchange. The forces of supply and demand create considerable risk for those dependent on monetary exchange for life's necessities. A wage earner who loses a job may not be able to afford food or shelter; a farmer relying on a cash crop may not get a price sufficient to support the family. Societies with monetary exchange usually have considerable inequities in wealth and power.

Kinds of Money Although market exchange need not involve money, most commercial transactions, particularly nowadays, do involve what we call money. Some anthropologists define money according to the functions and characteristics of the **general-purpose money** used in our own and other complex societies, for which nearly all goods, resources, and services can be exchanged. According to this definition, money performs the basic functions of serving as an accepted medium of exchange, a standard of value, and a store of wealth. As a medium of exchange, it allows all goods and services to be valued in the same objective way; we say that an object or service is worth so much money. Also, money is nonperishable and therefore savable or storable, and it is almost always transportable and divisible, so transactions can involve the buying and selling of goods and services that differ in value.

General-purpose money A universally accepted medium of exchange.

Although money can technically be anything, the first money systems used rare metals such as gold and silver. These metals are relatively soft and therefore can be melted and shaped into standard sizes and weights. The earliest standardized coins we know of are said to have been made by the Lydians in Asia Minor and the Chinese in the 7th century A.D. It is important to realize that money has little or no intrinsic value; rather, it is society that determines its value. In the United States today, paper bills, bank checks, and credit and debit cards are fully accepted as money, and money is increasingly transferred electronically.

General-purpose money is used both for commercial transactions (buying and selling) and for noncommercial transactions (payment of taxes or fines, personal gifts, contributions to religious and other charities). General-purpose money provides a way of condensing wealth: Gold dust or nuggets are easier to carry around than bushels of wheat; paper bills, a checkbook, and plastic cards are handier than a herd of sheep or goats.

In many societies, money is not an all-purpose medium of exchange. Many peoples whose food production per capita is not sufficient to support a large population of non-producers of food have **special-purpose money**. This consists of objects of value for which only some goods and services can be exchanged on the spot or through balanced reciprocity. In some parts of Melanesia, pigs are assigned value in terms of shell money—lengths of shells strung together in units each roughly as long as the distance covered by a man's outstretched arms. According to its size, a pig will be assigned a value in tens of such units up to 100.[96] But shell money cannot be exchanged for all the goods or services a person might need. Similarly, a Pacific Northwest native could exchange food, but not most other goods and services, for a "gift of wealth," such as blankets. The gift was a "receipt" that entitled the person to receive an equal amount of food, but little else, later.

Special-purpose money
Objects of value for which only some goods and services can be exchanged.

Degrees of Commercialization Most societies were not commercialized at all, or only barely so, when first described in the ethnographic record by explorers, missionaries, and anthropologists. That is, most societies as first described did not rely on market or commercial exchange to distribute goods and services. But commercial exchange has become the dominant form of distribution in the modern world. Most societies of the ethnographic past are now incorporated into larger nation-states; for example, the Trobriand Islanders and other societies in Melanesia are now districts in the nation of Papua New Guinea. Selling today goes far beyond the nation-state. The world is now a multinational market.[97]

But there is considerable variation in the degree to which societies today depend on market or commercial exchange. Many societies still allocate land without purchase and distribute food and other goods primarily by reciprocity and redistribution, participating only peripherally in market exchange. These are societies in transition; their traditional subsistence economies are becoming commercialized. Among the Luo of western Kenya, for example, most rural families still have land that their kin groups allocated to them. The food they eat they mostly produce themselves. But many men also work for wages—some nearby, others far away in towns and cities, where they spend a year or two. These wages are used to pay government taxes, to pay for children's schooling, and to

Trade and the sale of farm products takes place in a multicultural market in the Lower Omo Valley, Ethiopia.

buy commercially produced items, such as clothes, kerosene lamps, radios, fish from Lake Nyanza, tea, sugar, and coffee. Occasionally, families sell agricultural surpluses or craft items such as reed mats. Economies such as that of the rural Luo are not fully commercialized, but they may become so in the future.

What anthropologists call *peasant economies* are somewhat more commercialized than transitional subsistence economies, such as that of the Luo. Although **peasants** also produce food largely for their own consumption, they regularly sell part of their surplus (food, other goods, or labor) to others, and land is one of the commodities they buy, rent, and sell. But although their production is somewhat commercialized, peasants are still not like the fully commercialized farmers in industrialized societies, who rely on the market to exchange all or almost all of their crops for all or almost all of the goods and services they need.

Peasants Rural people who produce food for their own subsistence but who must also contribute or sell their surpluses to others (in towns and cities) who do not produce their own food.

In fully commercialized societies such as our own, market or commercial exchange dominates the economy; prices and wages are regulated, or at least significantly affected, by the forces of supply and demand. A modern industrial or post-industrial economy may involve international as well as national markets in which everything—natural resources, labor, goods, services, prestige items, religious and ceremonial items—has a price, stated in the same money terms. Reciprocity is reserved for family members and friends or remains behind the scenes in business transactions. Redistribution, however, is an important mechanism. It is practiced in the form of taxation and the use of public revenue for transfer payments and other benefits to low-income families—welfare, Social Security, health care, and so on. But commercial exchange is the major way goods and services are distributed.

Why Do Money and Market Exchange Develop? Most economists think that money is invented in a society, or copied from another society, when trade increases and barter becomes increasingly inefficient. The more important or frequent trade is, the more difficult it is to find a person who can give something you want and wants something you have to give. Money makes it easy to trade. It is a valuable that may be exchanged for *anything,* and so it is an efficient medium of exchange when trade becomes important. In contrast, many anthropologists do not link the origins of money or market exchange to the necessities of trade. Instead, they link the origins of money to various noncommercial "payments," such as the *kula* valuables and the taxes that have to be paid to a political authority. All of the available explanations of money suggest that money will be found mostly in societies at higher levels of economic development; and indeed it is. When simpler societies have money, dominant and more complex societies have usually introduced it.[98] In the next major section, we discuss more fully the impact of colonialism and global markets on societies that were not so long ago subsistence economies.

Most theories about the development of money and market exchange assume that producers have regular surpluses they want to exchange. But why do people produce surpluses in the first place? Perhaps they are motivated to produce extra only when they want to obtain goods from a distance and the suppliers of such goods are not well known to them, making reciprocity less likely as a way to obtain those goods. So some theorists suggest that market exchange begins with external, or intersocietal, trade; kin would not likely be involved, so transactions would involve bargaining and therefore are market exchange, by definition. Finally, some argue that as societies become more complex and more densely populated, social bonds between individuals become less kinlike and friendly, and therefore reciprocity becomes less likely.[99] Perhaps this is why traders in developing areas are often foreigners or recent immigrants.[100]

In any case, Frederic Pryor's cross-cultural research supports the notion that all types of market exchange—goods, labor, land, and credit—are more likely with higher levels of economic productivity. Pryor also found that market exchange of goods appears at lower levels of economic development than market exchange of labor and credit; market exchange of land, probably because it is associated with private property (individual ownership), appears mostly at the highest levels of productivity. Perhaps surprisingly, smaller societies tend to have more market exchange or trade with other societies. Larger societies can presumably get more of what they need from inside the society; for example, until recently, China had relatively little foreign trade throughout much of its history.[101]

Fiesta sponsors spend a great deal of money for food and drink as well as for musicians and dancers. Shown is the annual religious fiesta of the Zapotec Indian village of Teotitlan del Valle, Oaxaca, Mexico.

Possible Leveling Devices in Commercial Economies In societies that depend substantially on market or commercial exchange, some people tend to have more wealth than others have. Nevertheless, societies also have practices that may lessen the inequality and at least partially act as leveling devices. Some anthropologists have suggested that the fiesta tradition in highland Indian communities of Latin America may be a practice that tends to equalize income.[102] In these peasant villages, annual fiestas are held to celebrate the Christian saints the villagers most revere. A remarkable feature of the fiesta system is the extraordinary amount of money and labor a sponsoring family must contribute. Sponsors must hire ritual specialists; pay for church services, musicians, and costumes for dancers; and cover the total cost of food and drink for the entire community. The costs incurred can very easily amount to a year's wages.[103]

Still other anthropologists argue that fiestas do not really level wealth at all. First, true economic leveling would entail the redistribution of important productive resources such as land or animals; the fiesta only temporarily increases the general level of consumption. Second, the resources the sponsors expend are usually extra resources that have been accumulated specifically for the fiesta, which is why the sponsors are always appointed in advance. Third, and perhaps most important, the fiestas do not seem to have reduced long-term wealth distinctions within the villages.[104]

In nations such as ours, can the income tax and the social-assistance programs it pays for, such as welfare and disaster relief, be thought of as leveling devices? Theoretically, our tax system is supposed to work that way, by taxing higher incomes at higher rates. But we know that, in fact, it doesn't. Those in higher income brackets can often deduct an appreciable amount from their taxable incomes and therefore pay taxes at a relatively low rate. Our tax system may help some to escape extreme poverty, but, like the fiesta system, it has not eliminated marked distinctions in wealth.

16.4 Discuss the worldwide trend toward commercialization and its social effects.

The Worldwide Trend Toward Commercialization

One of the most important changes resulting from the expansion of Western societies and the capitalist system is the increasingly worldwide dependence on commercial exchange. The borrowed customs of buying and selling may at first be supplementary to traditional means of distributing goods in a society. As new commercial customs take hold, however, the economic base of the receiving society alters. Inevitably, social, political, and even biological and psychological changes accompany such a change.

When examining contemporary examples of change resulting from commercialization, it is important to remember that the phenomenon has ancient roots. Some early state societies, including the Chinese, Persians, Greeks, Romans, Arabs, Phoenicians, and Hindus, practiced commercial exchange, and their influence was felt well beyond their own territories. We may cast some light on how and why earlier cultures changed when we consider several questions: How, and why, does a contemporary society change from a subsistence to a commercial economic base? What are the resultant cultural changes? Why do they occur?

In general, the limited evidence available suggests that a previously noncommercial people may begin to sell and buy things simply to live, not just because they may be attracted by goods they can obtain only by commercial exchange. If the resources available to a group have been significantly reduced per person—because the group has been forced to resettle on a small "reservation" or because population has increased—the group may be likely to take advantage of any commercial opportunities that become available, even if such opportunities require considerably more work, time, and effort.[105]

Many anthropologists have noted that with the introduction of money, customs of sharing seem to change dramatically. Money, perhaps because it is nonperishable and largely hideable, tends to invoke feelings of not wanting to share. The plight of a man from the central highlands of New Guinea is typical. He agrees that it is not good manners to refuse a request from a relative or village friend; nonetheless, to keep his income from being "eaten," he tries to conceal some of his income. Some of the strategies include opening a savings account into which his pay is deposited, purchasing a semipermanent house, or joining a revolving credit association.[106] A recent series of experiments in the United States, where money has always been fundamental to the economic system, suggests that even the mere reminder of money causes people to behave more independently and to be less helpful to others.[107]

Migratory Labor

One way commercialization can occur is for some members of a community to move to a place that offers the possibility of working for wages. This happened in Tikopia, an island near the Solomon Islands in the South Pacific. In 1929, when Raymond Firth first studied the island, its economy was still essentially noncommercial—simple, self-sufficient, and largely self-contained.[108] Some Western goods were available but, with the exception of iron and steel in limited quantities, not sought after. Their possession and use were associated solely with Europeans. This situation changed dramatically with World War II. During the war, military forces occupied neighboring islands, and people from Tikopia migrated to those islands to find employment. In the period following the war, several large commercial interests extended their activities in the Solomons, thus creating a continued demand for labor. As a result, when Firth revisited Tikopia in 1952, he found the economic situation already significantly altered. More than 100 Tikopians had left the

A Nigerian woman weaves a straw mat for sale.

island to work for varying periods. The migrants wanted to earn money because they aspired to standards of living previously regarded as appropriate only to Europeans. Already, living conditions on Tikopia were changing. Western cooking and water-carrying utensils, mosquito nets, kerosene storm lamps, and so forth had come to be regarded as normal items in a Tikopia household.

The introduction of money into the economy of Tikopia not only altered the economic system but also affected other areas of life. Compared with the situation in 1929, land was under more intensive cultivation in 1952, with introduced manioc and sweet potatoes supplementing the old principal crop, taro. Pressures on the food supply resulting from improved living standards and an increased population seem to have weakened the ties of extended kinship. For example, the nuclear families constituting the extended family (the landholding and land-using unit in 1929) were not cooperating as much in 1952. In many cases, in fact, the land had actually been split up among the constituent nuclear families; land rights had become more individualized. People were no longer as willing to share with members of their extended family, particularly with respect to the money and goods acquired by working in the Solomons.

In many areas of the world, the money sent back home has become a major factor in the economy (see the box "Working Abroad to Send Money Home"). Often remittances are not sent through the formal banking system but rather through an informal network of brokers. In the Middle East and South Asia, the system is called *hawala* and is based on an honor system. For instance, the Hazara, the third largest ethnic group in Afghanistan, have migrated throughout the 20th century to cities in Afghanistan as well as to Pakistan and Iran. The banks in Afghanistan are not functioning, and the Hazara often do not have official identification papers, so they use *hawala* brokers to transfer money back home.[109] The money from remittances often far exceeds the money spent by development efforts.[110] But unlike development efforts, usually supported by wealthier countries, money received by remittances can be channeled where families want. Migration becomes part of a family's economic strategy. Of course, not all families can employ that strategy—the poorest families cannot afford the costs of long-distance migration.[111]

Nonagricultural Commercial Production

Commercialization can also occur when a self-sufficient society comes to depend more and more on trading for its livelihood. Such a change is exemplified by the Mundurucú of the Amazon Basin, who largely abandoned general horticulture for commercial rubber production. A similar change may also be seen in the Montagnais of northeastern Canada, who came to depend increasingly on commercial fur trapping, rather than hunting, for subsistence. Robert Murphy and Julian Steward found that when modern goods from industrialized areas became available through trade, both the Mundurucú and the Montagnais devoted their energies to producing specialized cash crops or other trade items. They did this to obtain other industrially made objects.[112] The primary socioeconomic change that occurred among the Mundurucú and the Montagnais was a shift from cooperative labor and community autonomy to individualized economic activity and a dependence on an external market.

Among the Mundurucú, for example, before close trading links were established, the native population and the Europeans had been in contact for some 80 years without the Mundurucú way of life being noticeably altered. The men did give up their independent military activities to perform as mercenaries for the Brazilians, but they continued to maintain their horticultural economy. Some trading took place with Brazilians, with the chief acting as agent for the village. Barter was the method of exchange. Traders first distributed their wares, ranging from cheap cottons to iron hatchets, trinkets, and so on; they returned about three months later to collect manioc, India rubber, and beans from the Mundurucú. At this time (1860), however, rubber was only a secondary item of commerce.

The rapidly growing demand for rubber from the 1860s onward increased the importance of Mundurucú-trader relationships. Traders now openly began to appoint agents, called *capitoes,* whose job it was to encourage greater rubber production. *Capitoes* were given economic privileges and hence power, both of which began to undercut the

Migrants and Immigrants

Working Abroad to Send Money Home

Filipino and Chinese domestic workers gather on their day off on a Hong Kong street.

Throughout recorded history, people have been going to other places to make a living. They do it not only to support themselves but also to support their families back home. Indeed, the people left behind might suffer terribly, or even starve, without these *remittances*, the term economists use when referring to the money people send back home. People who went to another country to work generated more than $440 billion in remittances in 2010.

In the 19th century, men from China were recruited to come to North America to build the transcontinental railroads, and Italians were recruited to work on building the railroads in New York State, New Jersey, Connecticut, and Massachusetts. In the years after World War II, when West German businesses were short of labor because so many people had been killed in the war, men from Turkey were recruited to come to Germany to fill the available jobs. Now, 30 to 40 years later, they make up a sizeable proportion of the population. Most if not all of the labor-short countries in western Europe (including England and France, the Netherlands, Sweden, Norway, Italy, and Spain) have attracted considerable numbers of immigrants in recent years. Indeed, much like the United States before them, the countries of western Europe are now becoming quite diverse culturally.

We may think that many if not most immigrants want to stay in the countries they have moved to. But this was not always true in the past, and it is not always true today. Many in the past just wanted to stay a few years. They wanted to earn money to help relatives back home, and maybe (if they were lucky) they could earn enough money to return home themselves and buy a farm or other small business. They often didn't become citizens in the new country because they didn't intend to stay. But until recently, most immigrants never went home again, and by the second or third generation, they had lost their native languages. In the last few decades, people who move to other countries to work often go home again—and again and again. They have become "transnationals," fluent in at least two languages and comfortable living in different countries alternately. They may even retain two (or more) citizenships. Consider how different this is from many past immigrants who were highly motivated to "pass." It is not clear yet what explains why some people are more comfortable now with not passing. Could it be that some places are less ethnocentric than in the past? If so, why is that?

Not all moves to another country turn out well for the migrants. Consider the poor young women from Sri Lanka who are recruited to work as housemaids in other countries. They may be burned or beaten if their work is deemed unacceptable, and they may return home with no money saved from their work time abroad. One in every 19 citizens of Sri Lanka now works abroad, most of them as housemaids. For a country like Sri Lanka, migration has become a safety valve for the economy. The Sri Lankan economy may be advantaged by the remittances received, but not without suffering for some of the migrants.

Sources: M. Ember et al. 2005; Waldman 2005.

position of the traditional chief. In addition, the process of rubber collection itself began to alter Mundurucú social patterns by moving people away from their jungle-based communities.

Wild rubber trees are found only along rivers, which are often a considerable distance from the jungle habitat of the Mundurucú and can be exploited only during the dry season (late May to December). So the Mundurucú man who elected to gather rubber had to separate himself from his family for about half the year. Furthermore, rubber collecting is a solitary activity. Each tapper must daily work his territory, consisting of about 150 trees, and he must live close to his trees because the work lasts all day. Therefore, the tapper usually lives alone or in a small group except during the rainy season, when he returns to his village.

At this stage in the commercialization process, the Mundurucú became increasingly dependent on goods the trader supplied. Firearms were useless without regular quantities of gun powder and lead or shot; clothing required needles and thread for repairs. But these items could be earned only through increased rubber production, which in turn led to greater dependency on the outside world. Inevitably, the ability to work with traditional materials and the desire to maintain traditional crafts disappeared. Metal pots took the place of clay ones, and manufactured hammocks replaced homemade ones. Gradually, the village agricultural cycle ceased to be followed by all in the community so that rubber production would not suffer. The authority of the traditional chiefs was weakened as that of the *capitoes* was enhanced.

The point of no return was reached when significant numbers of Mundurucú abandoned the villages for permanent settlements near their individual territories of trees. These new settlements lacked the unity, the sense of community, of former village life. Nuclear families held and carefully maintained property in the interest of productivity.

With the discovery of gold, many Mundurucú young men have turned to panning for gold in rivers. The required equipment is simple, and gold is easier to transport and trade than rubber. Because gold can be sold for cash, which is then used for purchases, trading relationships are no longer so important. Cash is now used to buy transistor radios, tape recorders, watches, bicycles, and new kinds of clothing, in addition to firearms, metal pots, and tools. With money as a medium of exchange, the traditional emphasis on reciprocity has declined. Even food may now be sold to fellow Mundurucú, a practice that would have been unthinkable in the 1950s.[113]

Supplementary Cash Crops

Read **the** Document: Nandi: From Cattle-Keepers to Cash-Crop Farmers

A third way commercialization occurs is when people cultivating the soil produce a surplus above their subsistence requirements, which is then sold for cash. In many cases, this cash income must be used to pay rent or taxes. Under these circumstances, commercialization may be said to be associated with the formation of a peasantry.

Peasants first appeared with the emergence of state and urban civilizations about 5,000 years to 6,000 years ago, and they have been associated with civilization ever since.[114] To say that peasants are associated with urban societies perhaps needs some qualification. The contemporary, highly industrialized urban society has little need of peasants. Their scale of production is small and their use of land "uneconomic." A highly industrialized society with a large population of nonfood producers requires mechanized agriculture. As a result, the peasant has passed, or is passing, out of all but the most peripheral existence in industrial countries.

What changes does the development of a peasantry entail? In some respects, there is little disturbance of the cultivator's (now peasant's) former way of life. The peasant still has to produce enough food to meet family needs, to replace what has been consumed, and to cover a few ceremonial obligations (e.g., the marriage of a child, village festivals, and funerals). But in other respects, the peasant's situation is radically altered. For, in addition to the traditional obligations—indeed, often in conflict with them—the peasant now has to produce extra crops to meet the requirements of a group of outsiders—landlords or officials of the state. These outsiders expect to be paid rent or taxes in produce or currency, and they are able to enforce their expectations because they control the military and the police.

Introduction of Commercial and Industrial Agriculture

Commercialization can come about through the introduction of commercial agriculture, cultivation for sale rather than personal consumption. The system of agriculture may come to be industrialized. In other words, some of the production processes, such as plowing,

Applied Anthropology

Impact of the World System—Deforestation of the Amazon

The great rain forest drained by the Amazon River and its tributaries covers more than a billion acres. The Amazon forest is not only the home to many largely self-sufficient indigenous cultures; it also supports about 20 percent of all the earth's plant and animal species. The vast forests absorb CO_2, which helps to reduce global warming. The forest also puts needed moisture into the atmosphere through evaporation—about 8 trillion tons of water a year. Global warming will lead to reduced rainfall, putting stress on the ability of the forest to grow or the existing trees to survive.

The Amazon forest and other tropical forests have been disappearing at an alarming rate because of the accelerated clearing of forest by humans, primarily for ranching and farming. About 15 percent of the Amazon forests have already been cleared. Some have suggested that the world demand for wood, hamburger, and crops for biofuels is largely responsible for the diminution of the Amazon forest. Like many tropical forests, the Amazon has large numbers of desirable hardwood trees. Forests in Africa and Asia are already largely depleted, so the demand for wood from the Amazon has grown considerably. In addition, the Amazon Development Agency in Brazil has offered incentives to clear forest for cattle ranching, which can provide hamburger to fast-food restaurants. Clearing land for crops has increased because of the need for food for cattle and for production of crops suitable for biofuels.

The indigenous people often find themselves in a land squeeze, with loggers, cattle ranchers, and miners trying to encroach on their territory. With less land, food-getting and traditional economic practices are in jeopardy. But it is naive to assume that the indigenous people are interested only in maintaining their traditional economies. They often accept the dilemma of economic development: They might lose some land, but selling rights to loggers and miners brings in money, which they can use to buy things they need and want. And indigenous people themselves, although they contribute relatively little to the direct deforestation that is occurring, are increasingly involved in the world market economy. Researchers studying the Tsimane of the Bolivian lowlands, mainly foragers who also farm, have found that those who grow a cash crop are most likely to clear more forest.

Development experts and applied anthropologists are searching for ways to achieve development without destroying or degrading the environment. For example, indigenous groups are encouraged to gather Brazil nuts, a wild but renewable resource, for sale. Others are encouraged to harvest latex (natural rubber) and hearts of palm. Medicinal plants have economic value to multinational pharmaceutical and biotechnical companies, which have discovered that the conservation of biodiversity may be economically advantageous to themselves as well as to the local people and to scientists who want to study the diversity. The countries with large portions of Amazon forest have played an important role in encouraging development but have worked to reduce deforestation with international pressure. For example, in Brazil, the annual rate of forest clearing declined between 2005 and 2010 because of the intervention of the Brazilian government. The international community is also working on a plan that would encourage countries to reduce deforestation, perhaps in exchange for monetary credits.

Can development be sustainable? Whether we like it or not, economic development and the desire for it are not going to go away. But we need to do more than applaud or bemoan economic development. In particular, we need more research that reveals what impact particular changes will have on people, other animals, plants, and the environment. Most of all, for the sake of human rights, we need to listen to the people whose lives will be most affected, to understand their needs as well as those of the developers.

Sources: Holloway 1993; Moran 1993; Winterbottom 1995, 60–70; Betts et al. 2008; Nepstad et al. 2008; Vadez et al. 2008; Nolte et al. 2013.

weeding, irrigation, and harvesting, can be done by machine. Commercial agriculture is, in fact, often as mechanized as any manufacturing industry. Land is worked for the maximum return it will yield, and labor is hired and fired just as impersonally as in other industries.

E. J. Hobsbawm noted some of the developments that accompanied the introduction of commercial agriculture in 18th-century England and in continental Europe somewhat later.[115] The close, near-familial relationship between farmer and farm laborer disappeared, as did the once-personal connection between landlord and tenant. Land came to be regarded as a source of profit rather than a way of life. Fields were merged into single units and enclosed, and local grazing and similar privileges were reduced. Labor was hired at market rates and paid in wages. Eventually, as the emphasis on large-scale production for a mass market increased, machines began to replace farmers.

The introduction of commercial agriculture brings several important social consequences. Gradually, a class polarization develops. Farmers and landlords become increasingly separated from laborers and tenants, just as the employer in town becomes socially separated from the employees. Gradually, too, manufactured items of all sorts are introduced into rural areas. Laborers migrate to urban centers in search of employment, often meeting even less sympathetic conditions there than exist in the country.

The changeover to commercial agriculture may result in an improved standard of living in the short and long run. But sometimes the switch is followed by a decline in the standard of living if the market price for the commercial crop declines. For example, the changeover of the farmer-herders of the arid *sertão* region of northeastern Brazil after 1940 to the production of sisal (a plant whose fibers can be made into twine and rope) seemed to be a move that could provide a more secure living in their arid environment. But when the world price for sisal dropped and the wages of sisal workers declined, many workers were forced to curtail the caloric intake of their children. The poorer people were obliged to save their now more limited food supplies for the money earners, at the expense of the children.[116]

Commercialization can start in various ways: People can begin to sell and buy because they begin to work near home or away for wages, or because they begin to sell nonagricultural products, surplus food, or cash crops (crops grown deliberately for sale). One type of commercialization does not exclude another; all types can occur in any society. However commercialization begins, it seems to have predictable effects on traditional economics. The ethic of generalized reciprocity declines, particularly with respect to giving away money. (Perhaps because it is nonperishable and hideable, money seems more likely than other goods to be kept for one's immediate family rather than shared with others.) Property rights become individualized rather than collective when people begin to buy and sell. Even in societies that were previously egalitarian, commercialization usually results in more unequal access to resources and hence a greater degree of social stratification.

Summary and Review

The Allocation of Resources

16.1 Compare and contrast the allocation of resources among foragers, horticulturalists, intensive agriculturalists, and pastoralists and discuss how colonialism and the state have affected that allocation.

- Every society has access to natural resources—land, water, plants, animals, minerals—and cultural rules for determining who has access to particular resources. Societies differ in their rules for land access, but the differences generally relate to a society's food-getting method.
- In food-collecting societies individual or family ownership of land is generally lacking. If there is ownership, it is tends to be by collective groups such as kinship groups or through communities. Territoriality is stronger when the plants and animals collected are predictably located and abundant.
- Horticulturalist societies also tend to lack individual or family ownership, probably because their technologies do not enable them to effectively use the same land permanently, but they are more likely to assign individuals or families use of a particular plot of land.
- Pastoralists often combine the adaptive habits of both foragers and horticulturalists because they need large territories for grazing herds. While they tend to hold grazing land communally, pastoralists customarily own their herds individually.
- Individual ownership of land resources is common among intensive agriculturalists. However, some communist and socialist nations undertake intensive agriculture by forming state-run agricultural collectives.
- Almost universally worldwide, colonial conquerors and settlers from expanding state societies have taken land from the native people. Typically, state authorities do not like communal land-use systems and see mobile pastoralists as difficult to control.

- Every society has a technology, a set of tools, constructions, and skills with which it converts resources into food and other goods. Technological access varies, generally being widespread among forager and horticultural societies, but not among industrial or postindustrial societies.

? How has the worldwide phenomenon of colonialism and the effects of statehood affected land rights?

The Conversion of Resources

16.2 Explain the different types of economic production and economic exchange and their effect on labor.

- Production is the conversion of resources through labor into food, tools, and other goods.
- In domestic production, the family controls conversion of resources. In tributary production, people pay a tribute of labor or goods to an authority for access to land. In industrial production, people labor as wage earners. In post-industrial production, information and services are the main products.
- People in subsistence economies with a domestic mode of production often work less than people in commercial economies with tributary or industrial modes of production and tend not to produce more than they need.
- People may be motivated to work harder than they have to for subsistence to gain social respect or esteem or to satisfy a need for achievement, especially in commercial economies.
- Forms of forced labor are found in more complex societies and can be indirect (taxation and corvée) or direct (slavery).
- Many societies divide labor only by gender and age; other societies have more complex specialization. Horticultural societies may have some part-time specialists. Societies with intensive agriculture have some full-time specialists, and industrialized societies have many.
- In many food-collecting and horticultural societies, there is little formal organization of work. The need to coordinate labor is highest in industrialized societies.
- Optimal foraging theory assumes that individuals seek to maximize the returns, in calories and nutrients, on their labor by deciding which animals and plants to hunt or collect.

? What are the different types of economic production? Looking at different aspects of labor, how do they vary with type of society?

The Distribution of Goods and Services

16.3 Explain the three general types of systems for distributing goods and services (reciprocity, redistribution, and market or commercial exchange).

- Goods and services are distributed in all societies under three general types of systems: reciprocity, redistribution, and market or commercial exchange, each of which is associated with a society's food-getting technology and level of economic development.
- Reciprocity systems do not involve money. Sharing may (a) create social relationships that ensure help when needed, (b) equalize distribution of goods within and between communities, and (c) be most likely when resources are unpredictable.
- In redistribution systems, one person or agency accumulates goods or labor for the purpose of later distribution. Redistribution is found in all societies but is an important mechanism only in societies that have political hierarchies.
- Market or commercial exchange involves the buying and selling of goods and transactions of labor, land, rentals, and credit. General-purpose money provides an objective value for all goods and services. Special-purpose money can be used for only some goods and services.
- Societies may begin to use money when trade and barter increases or when political authorities demand noncommercial fees such as taxes. Social bonds between individuals may become less kinlike in more complex and populated societies, making reciprocity less likely.

? What are the major ways of distributing goods and services, and how do they relate to a society's food-getting technology?

The Worldwide Trend Toward Commercialization

16.4 Discuss the worldwide trend toward commercialization and explain its social effects.

- The expansion of Western societies and the capitalist system has led to an increasingly worldwide dependence on commercial exchange. Inevitably, social, political, and even biological and psychological changes accompany such a change.

- Many anthropologists have noted that with the introduction of money, customs of sharing seem to change dramatically.
- Commercialization can occur when some society members move to places that offer possible work for wages, when a self-sufficient society increasingly depends on trading, and when people cultivating crops produce a surplus sell it for cash.
- Commercial systems of agriculture may become industrialized. The introduction of commercial agriculture brings several important social consequences, including class polarization.

> ? What are examples of social, political, biological, and psychological changes that might occur as a result of dependence on commercial exchange?

Think on it

1. What conditions might enable us to achieve a world of **sustainable resources**?
2. What are the possible effects of a **post-industrial economy** in which a large proportion of the population has inexpensive access to computers and information?
3. Do you expect the amount of **privately owned resources** to change appreciably in the future? State your reasons.
4. What might be the beneficial consequences of the worldwide trend toward **commercialization**?
5. Why might an increasing understanding of **cultural variation** also provide an increasing understanding of **cultural change**?

CHAPTER 18 Sex and Gender

LEARNING OBJECTIVES

- **18.1** Describe variation in gender concepts.
- **18.2** Identify differences in physique and physiology between males and females.
- **18.3** Explain differences in gender roles.
- **18.4** Analyze relative gender differences in term of contributions to work.
- **18.5** Discuss gender differences in terms of political leadership and warfare cross-culturally.
- **18.6** Analyze relative status among women cross-culturally.
- **18.7** Discuss gender differences in personality.
- **18.8** Explain variability in sexual behavior and attitudes between different cultures.

In North America, it is common for parents and others to remark on how different their little girls or boys are. Even newborn boys and girls are commonly described as having different personalities. And yet trained observers watching infants wrapped in neutral-colored blankets, instead of pink for girls and blue for boys, cannot detect much difference at all. The underlying belief is that boys and girls are born with different natures. This is captured in an old nursery rhyme:

> *What are little boys made of?*
> *"Snips and snails, and puppy dogs' tails*
> *That's what little boys are made of!"*
> *What are little girls made of?*
> *Sugar and spice and all things nice*
> *That's what little girls are made of!"*[1]

Different characterizations are not unique to North American culture; boys and girls are, it appears, perceived differently the world over. Moreover, societies usually have fairly clear ideas about the roles that females and males should have during different life stages. Along with different gender roles at every stage of life comes another mystifying fact: Women nearly everywhere have fewer social advantages than men. Why? Is there a fundamental difference between the sexes, other than the observable physical differences, that explains both gender roles and the relative status of the genders? Or are gender differences created by society to serve the interests of the community—or of men?

It was the beginning of the women's movement in the 1960s that prompted scholars to seriously consider the part society plays in creating gender differences in behavior and the type of roles females and males are assigned. Although it may seem that the debate is about nature *or* nurture, most social scientists recognize that it is nearly impossible to disentangle the two when parents and others do not treat females and males exactly the same way.

One way anthropologists begin to try to understand what might be cultural is to examine similarities and variations in a phenomenon cross-culturally. In the following pages, we will look at how concepts about gender vary across many cultures. We will also review what is known about how and why females and males may differ physically, in gender roles, and in personality. Finally, we will discuss another topic of infinite curiosity: How and why sexual behavior and attitudes about sex vary from culture to culture.

•••

Humans are born either female or male, with very rare exceptions. And each individual possesses different reproductive organs, a fact of life that humans share with most animal species. But having different organs of reproduction does not explain why males and females may also differ in other physical ways. Unlike some other animal species, such as pigeons, gulls, and chipmunks, in which the two sexes differ little in appearance, human males and females typically also differ physically.[2] In other words, the fact that we are a species with two sexes does not explain why human females and males came to look different, nor does it explain why human males and females should differ in behavior or be treated differently by society. Indeed, as we mentioned earlier, females usually have fewer advantages than males, which is why we were careful in the preceding chapter to say that egalitarian societies have no *social groups* with unequal access to resources, power, and prestige. In fact, within social groups, such as families, even egalitarian societies usually give males greater access to some rewards. Some **gender stratification**, or unequal access by different genders to prestige, authority, power, rights and economic resources, appears to be a cultural universal. However, societies differ in the degree and type of gender stratification.

Gender stratification The degree of unequal access by the different genders to prestige, authority, power, rights, and economic resources.

Gender differences Differences between females and males that reflect cultural expectations and experiences.

Sex differences The typical differences between females and males that are most likely due to biological differences.

Because many of the differences between females and males appear to reflect cultural expectations and experiences, researchers now usually prefer to speak of **gender differences**, reserving the term **sex differences** for purely biological differences.[3] Unfortunately, because biological and cultural influences are not always clearly separable, it is sometimes difficult to know which term to use. As we discuss differences and similarities between females and males, keep in mind that not all cultures conceive of gender as including just two categories. Sometimes "maleness" and "femaleness" are thought of as opposite ends of a continuum, or there might be three or more categories of gender, such as "female," "male," and "other."[4]

18.1 Describe variation in gender concepts.

Gender Concepts

Read the Document: Condemning Our Kids to Life on Venus or Mars

In the United States and many Western societies, there are only two genders—female and male. Your gender is assigned at birth based on external biological attributes. However, not all individuals feel comfortable with their gender assignment. The term *transgender* is now used to describe people who do not feel that their assigned gender fits them well.

The division into just two genders—male/female—is very common cross-culturally. But a strict dichotomy is far from universal. Some societies, like the Cheyenne Native Americans of the Great Plains, recognized male, female, and a third gender, referred to by the Cheyenne as "two-spirits." (Europeans referred to this third gender type generally as a *berdache*.[5]) "Two-spirit" people were usually biological males. The gender status of "two-spirit" was often recognized after a boy returned from his vision quest, a preadolescent rite of passage of several days that he spent in isolation in the wilderness. The boy's "vision," or epiphany, would lead him to become a two-spirit person. He would wear women's dress and take on many of the activities of women. A two-spirit might even be taken as a second wife by a man, but whether the man and the two-spirit person engaged in sex is not known. The role of a "two-spirit" person was not equivalent to that of a woman. Indeed, two-spirits played unique gender roles at weddings and childbirth. Accounts of "two-spirit" biological females who take on the role of men are less common, but they do occur in a number of native North American societies, such as the Kaska of Yukon Territory, the Klamath of southern Oregon, and the Mohave of the Colorado River area in the southwestern United States. These biological female "two-spirits" could marry women, and such relationships were lesbian relationships.[6]

In Oman, there is a third gender role called *xanith*. Anatomically male, *xaniths* speak of themselves as "women." However, *xaniths* have their own distinctive dress; they wear clothes that are neither male nor female but somewhere in between. Men in Oman typically wear white clothes and women bright patterns, whereas *xaniths* wear unpatterned pastels. Men have short hair, women long, and *xaniths* keep theirs medium-length. Omani women are generally secluded in their houses and can go out only with permission from their husbands, but a *xanith* is free to come and go and to work as a servant and/or a homosexual prostitute. Unlike a "two-spirit," who is likely to maintain a third gender role for life, a *xanith* may change gender role. If a *xanith* decides to marry and is able to have intercourse with his bride, he becomes a "man." An older *xanith* who is no longer attractive may decide to become an "old man."[7]

18.2 Identify differences in physique and physiology between males and females.

Physique and Physiology

Sexually dimorphic A marked difference in size and appearance between males and females of a species.

As we have noted, males and females cannot readily be distinguished in some animal species. Although they differ in chromosome makeup and in their external and internal organs of reproduction, they do not differ otherwise. In contrast, humans are **sexually dimorphic**—that is, the two sexes of our species are generally different in size and appearance. Females have proportionately wider pelvises. Males typically are taller and have heavier skeletons. Females have a larger proportion of their body weight in fat; males have a larger proportion of body weight in muscle. Males typically have greater grip strength, proportionately larger hearts and lungs, and greater aerobic capacity (greater intake of oxygen during strenuous activity).

North American culture tends to view "taller" and "more muscled" as better, which may reflect a bias toward males. But how did these differences come about? Natural selection may have favored these traits in males but selected against them in females. Females achieve their ultimate height shortly after puberty, but boys continue to grow for years after puberty. Because females bear children, selection may have favored earlier cessation of growth, and therefore less ultimate height so that the nutritional needs of a fetus would not compete with a growing mother's needs.[8] Similarly, there is some evidence that females are less affected than males by nutritional shortages, presumably because they tend to be shorter and have proportionately more fat.[9] Natural selection may also have favored more proportionate "fatness" in females because it resulted in greater reproductive success.

Athletes can build up their muscle strength and increase their aerobic work capacity through training. Given that fact, cultural factors, such as how much a society expects and allows males and females to engage in muscular activity, could influence the degree to which females and males differ muscularly and in aerobic capacity. Similar training may account for the recent trend toward decreasing differences between females and males in certain athletic events, such as marathons and swim meets, even when we account for the hormonal differences that enable males to develop greater muscle mass. When it comes to female and male physique and physiology, what we see may be the result of both culture and genes.[10]

Gender Roles

Who Does What Work?

18.3 Explain differences in gender roles.

In the chapter on economic systems, we noted that all societies assign or divide labor somewhat differently between females and males. Because role assignments have a clear cultural component, we speak of them as **gender roles**. What is of particular interest about the gender division of labor is not so much that every society has different work for males and females but, rather, that so many societies divide up work in similar ways. The question, then, is: Why are there universal or near-universal patterns in such assignments?

Gender roles Roles that are culturally assigned to genders.

The world of work has changed for much of the world and continues to change. We know a considerable amount about division of labor by gender in societies that make or made their living by collecting or producing their own food. We know less as yet about cross-cultural patterns in industrial and post-industrial societies. Table 18.1 summarizes which activities are performed by which gender in all or almost all societies, which activities are usually performed by one gender, and which activities are commonly assigned to either gender or both. If every culture assigned work arbitrarily to the genders, the table would reveal no patterns. Although many tasks are assigned to both genders (the middle column), clearly some patterns are worldwide. One of the most striking is in primary subsistence activities; males almost always hunt and trap animals, and females usually gather wild plants. Do this and the other distributions of activities in the table suggest why females and males generally do different things? Scholars have suggested four explanations or theories that we label *strength theory, compatibility-with-child-care theory, economy-of-effort theory,* and *expendability theory.*

Read the Document: Universal and Variable Patterns of Gender Difference

Strength Theory The idea that males generally possess greater strength and a superior capacity to mobilize their strength in quick bursts of energy (because of greater aerobic work capacity) is called the strength theory. Males may best perform activities that require lifting heavy objects (hunting large animals, butchering, clearing land, or working with stone, metal, or lumber), throwing weapons, and running with great speed (as in hunting). And none of the activities females usually perform, with the possible exception of collecting firewood, seem to require the same degree of physical strength or quick bursts of energy. But the strength theory is not completely convincing, if only because it cannot readily explain all the observed patterns. It is not clear, for example, that the male activities of trapping small animals, collecting wild honey, or making musical instruments require physical strength. Moreover, as we will see shortly, women do hunt in some societies, suggesting that differences in strength cannot play a very important role.

Compatibility-with-Child-Care Theory Males are capable of caring for infants, of course, but for obvious biological reasons, they cannot breast-feed. In most societies, women breast-feed their children, on average, for two years, so the compatibility-with-child-care theory suggests that for much of human history it would have been maladaptive to have women take on roles that interfere with their ability to feed their child regularly or put their child in danger while taking care of them. The tasks women perform may also need to be ones that can be stopped and resumed if an infant needs care.[11]

TABLE 18.1 Worldwide Patterns in the Division of Labor by Gender

	Primary Subsistence Activities	Secondary Subsistence and Household Activities	Other Activities
Nearly always males	Hunt and trap animals, large and small		Lumber Make boats Mine and quarry Make musical instruments Make bone, horn, and shell objects Engage in combat
Usually males	Fish Herd large animals Collect wild honey Clear land and prepare soil for planting	Butcher animals	Build houses Make nets and rope Exercise political leadership
Either gender or both	Collect shellfish Care for small animals Plant and tend crops Harvest crops Milk animals	Preserve meat and fish	Prepare skins Make leather products, baskets, mats, clothing, and pottery
Usually females	Gather wild plants	Care for children Cook Prepare vegetable foods, drinks, and dairy products Launder Fetch water Collect fuel Spin yarn	
Nearly always females		Care for infants	

Sources: Murdock and Provost 1973, 203–25; Whyte 1978a, 217 (political leadership and warfare); Weisner and Gallimore 1977, 169–80 (child care).

The compatibility theory may explain why *only* infant care is listed in Table 18.1 as almost always woman's work. Nursing and caring for their infants and other children may have so consumed women's lives that, until recently, there may have been practically no other universal or near-universal women-only activities. This theory may also explain why men usually perform such tasks as hunting, trapping, fishing, collecting honey, lumbering, and mining. Those tasks are dangerous for infants to be around and, in any case, would be difficult to coordinate with infant care. A group may also make fine distinctions in the division of labor that are consistent with the compatibility theory: Among the Aché hunter-gatherers of Paraguay, for example, women collect the type of honey produced by stingless bees, while men collect other honey.[12]

Finally, the compatibility theory may explain why men seem to take over certain crafts in societies that have full-time specialization. Although the distinction is not shown in Table 18.1, crafts such as basket, mat, and pottery making tend to be women's activities in noncommercial societies but men's activities in societies with full-time craft specialists.[13] Similarly, weaving is typically a female activity unless it is produced for trade.[14] Full-time specialization and production for trade may be less compatible with child care. Cooking is a good example in our own society. Many women are excellent cooks and traditionally did most of the cooking at home, but chefs and bakers tend to be men. In order to work as chefs, women would require caretakers for their babies and young children, and shorter hours than chefs and bakers typically work.

The compatibility theory does not explain, however, why men usually prepare soil for planting, make objects out of wood, or work bone, horn, and shell. All of those tasks could probably be stopped to tend to a child, and none of them is any more dangerous to children nearby than is cooking.

Economy-of-Effort Theory Why do males tend to perform tasks such as woodcarving that could be done by women who also tend children? The economy-of-effort theory may help explain task patterns that the strength and compatibility theories do not readily address. For example, it may be advantageous for men to make wooden musical instruments because they generally lumber.[15] Lumbering may give men more knowledge about the physical properties of various woods and make it more likely that they know how to work with different woods. The economy-of-effort interpretation also suggests that it would be advantageous for one gender to perform tasks that are located near each other. That is, if women have to be near home to nurse and take care of young children, it would be economical for them to perform other chores in or near the home.

Females usually care for young children, but sometimes males do more as this father in Shanghai, China.

Expendability Theory The idea that men, rather than women, will tend to do the dangerous work in a society because the loss of men is not as great a disadvantage reproductively as the loss of women is called the expendability theory. If some men lose their lives in hunting, deep-water fishing, mining, quarrying, lumbering, and the like, reproduction need not suffer as long as most fertile women have sexual access to men—for example, if the society permits two or more women to be married to the same man.[16] If an activity is dangerous, why would anybody, male or female, be willing to do it? Perhaps it is because societies glorify and reward some such acts.

Theoretical Weaknesses The productive and domestic tasks that societies everywhere have carried out are a well-established body of knowledge. We also have data on whether men, women, or both perform each task. The theories that we discussed are all, to some extent, based on these data. And singly or in combination, each theory seems to explain much of the division of labor by gender; yet each theory has weaknesses. Critics of the strength theory have pointed out that women in some societies do engage in very heavy labor.[17] They argue that if women in some societies can develop the strength to do such work, then perhaps strength is more a function of training than has been believed.

The compatibility theory's central idea that labor is divided to conform to the requirements of child care is also debatable. In fact, the reverse can be true: Child care can conform to the demands of other work. Women who spend a good deal of time in agricultural work outside the home, for example, often ask others to watch and feed their infants while they are unavailable to nurse.[18] For example, agricultural work in the mountainous areas of Nepal would seem to be especially incompatible with child care. Heavy loads must be carried up and down steep slopes, the fields are far apart, and labor takes up most of the day. Yet women perform this work anyway and leave their infants with others for long stretches of time.[19]

In some societies, women hunt—one of the activities considered most incompatible with child care and generally done only by men. Many Agta women of the Philippines seem able to manage both tasks. They regularly hunt wild pig and deer; and women alone or in groups kill almost 30 percent of the large game in the Agta diet.[20] The compatibility theory, like the other proposed explanations for the division of labor by gender, assumes that women do not perform work that may jeopardize their reproductive ability. Yet Agta women who hunt and even take their nursing babies on hunting trips do not have lower reproductive rates than the women who choose not to hunt. To be fair, the circumstances under which these women hunt may be more compatible with child care: The hunting grounds are only about a half hour from camp; dogs accompany them to assist in the hunting and protect them and their babies; and because they tend to hunt in groups, others can help carry their babies, as well as the carcasses. However, these factors, too, suggest that women can effectively accommodate the differing needs of two competing tasks.

Hunting by women is also fairly common among the Aka, forest foragers in the Central African Republic. Aka women participate in and sometimes lead cooperative net-hunting, in which an area is circled and animals are flushed out and caught in nets. The women spend approximately 18 percent of their time net-hunting, which is more time than Aka men devote to the task.[21] In the Canadian subarctic, teams of Chipewyan women would hunt small animals, such as muskrats or rabbits, and would commonly join their husbands to hunt large animals, such as moose. Some Chipewyan precautions suggest that the compatibility between hunting and child care was a consideration, however. Women would avoid hunting moose after their fourth or fifth month of pregnancy. They usually joined hunting teams as newlyweds and after their childbearing years. Women also did not participate in long-distance hunts.[22]

As these examples of women who hunt and who work in agriculture suggest, we would be in a better position to evaluate the various theories and, perhaps, to propose one if we knew more precisely what each activity humans perform requires. Without a systematic study of how much strength is required for each task, how dangerous each task is, or which tasks can be interrupted for child care and later resumed, theories about the way societies divide up their work can be little more than guesses.

Changing Labor and Gender Roles As fewer societies remain isolated and more adopt technologies to help them perform certain tasks, both the tasks and who performs them are bound to change. As we know from our own and other industrial societies, when machines replace human strength, when women have fewer children, and when child care can be delegated, the division of labor changes, as do the tasks that need to be performed. Yet, remarkably, labor appears to divide by gender even in a post-industrial world.

18.4 Analyze relative gender differences in term of contributions to work.

Relative Contributions to Work: Who Works More?

Most contemporary societies typically equate "work" with earning money. Until relatively recently, "homemaker" did not count as an occupation in the United States, for example. Yet, as we discussed in the chapters on food-getting and economics, we humans lived in subsistence economies for most of our history, and the invention of money is relatively recent. Most societies known to anthropology, whether they were foragers or food producers, focused primarily on the basic necessities.

Primary subsistence activities The food-getting activities: gathering, hunting, fishing, herding, and agriculture.

Secondary subsistence activities Activities that involve the preparation and processing of food either to make it edible or to store it.

When anthropologists research the division of labor by gender, they usually focus on **primary subsistence activities**—gathering, hunting, fishing, herding, and farming. As if there were a predisposed bias against household work, less attention has been paid to gender contributions toward **secondary subsistence activities**, such as food preparation for eating or storing. Yet, with a few exceptions, food can never be consumed without some preparation. For example, hunting cannot contribute much to the diet unless the meat is brought home (cut up or carried whole), skinned, cleaned, prepared for cooking, and then cooked. If the animal is large, the meat must be prepared for distribution and/or storage. And as skins and other parts are often used for clothing or tools, someone has to prepare those. As Hetty Jo Brumbach and Robert Jarvenpa point out, the Western model of hunting focuses on the "kill" (perhaps derived from the notion of sport-hunting) and ignores the complexity of processes associated with it. This view may hide women's role in "hunting" and emphasize the male's role as "hunter."[23]

Overall Work

We can also ask whether males or females generally do more work. We do not yet have that many studies of how females and males spend their time, but studies of horticultural and intensive agricultural societies so far suggest that, if we count all the kinds of economic activities shown in Table 18.1, women typically work more total hours per day than men.[24] We do not know if this is a truly cross-cultural universal. However, we do know that in many societies where women earn wages, they are still responsible for the bulk of the household work as well as the child care at home.

Subsistence Work

Primary subsistence activities are by nature generally located farther from the family's dwelling, and female and male contributions of this kind of work vary across cultures. Because the length of time spent on primary subsistence activities is generally not available, we estimate how much each gender contributes to the diet in terms of caloric intake from primary subsistence activities.

In some societies, women have traditionally contributed more to the economy than men both in terms of time spent and caloric intake. For example, among the Tchambuli of New Guinea in the 1930s, the women did all of the fishing—going out early in the morning by canoe to their fish traps and returning when the sun was hot. Some of the catch was traded for sago (a starch) and sugarcane, and it was the women who went on the long canoe trips to do the trading.[25]

In contrast, men did almost all of the primary subsistence work among the Toda of India. As they were described early in the 20th century, they depended for subsistence almost entirely on the dairy products of their water buffalo, either by using the products directly or by selling them for grain. Only men tended the buffalo and also prepared the dairy products, which women were not permitted to do. Women performed mostly housework, preparing the purchased grain for cooking, cleaning house, and decorating clothing.[26]

In many farming societies, women can do some agriculture and take care of their young children at the same time, as this mother in Zambia demonstrates.

A survey of a wide variety of societies has revealed that these extremes are not common. Usually both women and men contribute a good deal toward primary food-getting activities, but men usually contribute more in most societies.[27] Because women are almost always occupied with infant- and child-care responsibilities, it is not surprising that men usually perform most of the primary subsistence work, which generally has to be done away from the home.

Why do women in some societies do as much or more than men in primary subsistence work? Some of the variation is explained by the society's types of food-getting activity. In societies that depend on hunting, fishing, and herding—generally male activities—for most of their calories, men usually contribute more than women.[28] For example, among the Inuit, who traditionally depended mostly on hunting and fishing, as well as among the Toda, who depended mostly on herding, men did most of the primary subsistence work. In societies that depend on gathering, primarily women's work, women tend to do most of the food-getting.[29] The !Kung are an example. But the predominant type of food-getting is not always predictive. For example, among the Tchambuli, who depended mostly on fishing, women did most of the work. Most societies depend upon some form of food production rather than foraging. With the exception of clearing land, preparing the soil, and herding large animals, which are usually men's tasks, men, women, or both do the work of planting, crop tending (weeding, irrigating), and harvesting (see Table 18.1). We need some explanation, then, of why women do most of the farming work in some societies but men do it in others. Different patterns predominate in different areas of the world. In Africa, south of the Sahara, women generally do most of the farming. In much of Asia and Europe and the areas around the Mediterranean, men do more.[30]

The type of agriculture may help explain some of the variation. Men's contribution to primary subsistence tends to be much higher than women's in intensive agricultural societies, particularly with plow agriculture. In contrast, women's contribution is relatively high compared with men's and sometimes higher in horticultural societies. According to Ester Boserup, when population increases and there is pressure to make more intensive use of the land, cultivators begin to use the plow and irrigation, and males start to do more.[31] But it is not clear why.

Why should women not contribute a lot to farming just because plows are used? In trying to answer this question, most researchers shift to considering how much time males and females spend in various farming tasks rather than estimating the total caloric contribution of females versus males. The reason for this shift is that gender contribution to farming varies substantially over the various phases of the production sequence, as well as from one crop to another. Thus, the total amount of time females versus males work at farming tasks is easier to estimate than how much each gender contributes to the diet in terms of calories. How would caloric contribution be judged, for example, if men clear the land and plow, women plant and weed, and both harvest the crop?

Plow agriculture could increase male contribution to subsistence because plowing takes longer and minimizes weeding time. Cross-culturally, men usually clear land. (This does not mean that women are not able to plow, for there are examples of women plowing when necessary.[32]) It has been estimated that, in one district in Nigeria, 100 days of work are required to clear one acre of virgin land for plowing by tractor; only 20 days are required to prepare the land for shifting cultivation. Weeding is a task that probably can be combined with child care, and perhaps women may have mostly performed it previously for that reason.[33] But the fact that men do the plowing, which may take a lot of time, does not explain why women do relatively fewer farming tasks, including weeding, in societies that have the plow.[34]

Another explanation for the apparent decrease in women's contribution in intensive agriculture is that they have less time to spend in the fields. Intensive agriculturalists rely heavily on such grain crops as corn, wheat, and oats, which require a great deal of preparation and processing, tasks commonly performed by women. Grains are usually dried before storing. To be edible, dried grains must either be cooked in water for a long time or be preprocessed to cook faster. Cooking requires collecting water and firewood, neither of which is usually close by, and both of which are women's tasks. In addition, there is more cleaning of pots and utensils to be done. Soaking, grinding, or pounding can reduce cooking time for hard grains, but the process that speeds up cooking the most—grinding—is itself very time-consuming unless done by machine.[35] Then there is also child care and the additional housework that children entail.

Household work may also increase substantially with intensive agriculture because women in such societies have *more* children than women in horticultural societies.[36] If we add child care and the housework that children entail to the intensive food processing and cooking the women undertake, it is easy to understand why women cannot contribute more time than men, or as much time as men, to intensive agriculture. Yet women's contribution, though less than men's in the fields, is nonetheless substantial. In addition to working at home, women in such societies may labor outside the home four and a half hours a day, seven days a week, on average.[37]

Unlike intensive agricultural societies, those that subsist on horticulture rely a great deal on women's contributions. Why? Women in horticultural societies may not have as much household work as intensive agricultural women, but neither do the men. Why, then, don't men do relatively more in horticulture also? In fact, men in horticultural societies are often drawn away from cultivation into other types of activities. One of the most common is warfare, in which all able-bodied men are expected to participate.

There is evidence that, if males are engaged in warfare when primary subsistence work has to be done, then the women will do work.[38] Men may also be removed from primary subsistence work if they have to work in distant towns and cities for wages or if they periodically go on long-distance trading trips.[39]

When women contribute a lot to primary food-getting activities, we might expect effects on their childrearing. Several cross-cultural studies suggest that, indeed, this expectation is correct. In contrast to societies with a low female contribution to primary subsistence (in terms of contributing calories), highly contributing females feed their infants solid foods earlier, enabling others besides the mothers to feed them.[40] Also girls in such societies are likely to be trained to be industrious, probably to help their mothers, and female babies are more valued.[41]

Political Leadership and Warfare

18.5 Discuss gender differences in terms of political leadership and warfare cross-culturally.

In almost every known society, men rather than women tend to lead in the political arena. One cross-cultural survey found that only men were leaders in about 88 percent of the surveyed societies. Among the 10 percent of societies that had women in leadership positions, they were either outnumbered by or less powerful than the male leaders.[42] In the remaining 2 percent, leadership was fairly evenly distributed between men and women. If we look at sovereign nations, not cultures, the mean average of women in national parliaments and legislative bodies is 19 percent.[43]

Whether or not we consider warfare to be part of the political sphere of life, we find an almost universal dominance of males in that arena. In 87 percent of the world's societies in the anthropological record, women never participate actively in war.[44] Among modern nation-states, as of 2013, only 12 countries allow military women in combat.[45] The United States only recently changed its policy to allow such participation. (See the box "Why Do Some Societies Allow Women to Participate in Combat?" for a discussion of women in combat in the remaining 13 percent of societies.)

Even in *matrilineal* societies, in which the descent of a kin group is passed down through the mother and the female ancestors, formal political positions are usually held by men. Among the matrilineal Iroquois of what is now New York State, women controlled the resources and had considerable informal influence on political affairs. They could nominate, elect, and impeach their male representatives. Women could decide between life and death for prisoners of war, forbid the men of their households to go to war, and intervene to bring about peace. Nonetheless, the highest political body among the League of the Iroquois, which comprised five tribal groups, was a council of 50 male chiefs.[46]

Why have men (at least so far) almost always dominated the political sphere of life? Some scholars suggest that men's role in warfare gives them the edge in political leadership, particularly because they control weapons, an important resource.[47] Evidence suggests, however, that force is rarely used to obtain leadership positions;[48] superior strength is not the deciding factor. Rather, warfare may be related to political leadership for another reason. War affects survival, and it occurs regularly in most societies. Therefore, decisions about war may be among the most important kinds of political actions that occur in most societies. It stands to reason that the people who know the most about warfare make these decisions.

Two other factors may be involved in male predominance in politics. One is the generally greater height of men. Why height should be a factor in leadership is unclear, but studies suggest that taller people are more likely to be leaders.[49] Finally, there is the possibility that men dominate politics because they spend more time in the outside world than do women. Men's activities typically take them farther from home, whereas women tend to work more around the home. If societies choose leaders at least in part because of what they know about the larger world, then men will have some advantage. In support of this reasoning, Patricia Draper found that in settled !Kung groups, women no longer engaged in long-distance gathering, and they seemed to have lost much of their former influence in decision-making.[50] Involvement in child care may also detract from influence. In a

Perspectives on Gender

Why Do Some Societies Allow Women to Participate in Combat?

There have been some female warriors throughout history. In the 18th and 19th centuries, women made up one wing of the standing army in the West African Kingdom of Dahomey, for example, and constituted one-third of the armed forces at one point. Yet most societies and most countries have excluded women from combat, and some have excluded women from all military activities or planning.

Why, then, do some societies allow women to be warriors? Psychologist David Adams compared about 70 societies studied by anthropologists to try to answer that question. He found that women are active warriors at least occasionally in 13 percent of the sample societies. In native North America, the Comanche, Crow, Delaware, Fox, Gros Ventre, and Navajo had women warriors. In the Pacific, there were active warrior women among the Maori of New Zealand, on Majuro Atoll in the Marshall Islands, and among the Orokaiva of New Guinea. In none of these societies were the warriors usually women, but women were allowed to engage in combat if they wanted to.

How are societies with women warriors different from those that exclude women from combat? They differ in one of two ways. Either they conduct purely external wars, fighting only against people in other societies, or they marry within their own community in a society. Adams argues that either of these two conditions, which are not particularly common, will preclude conflicts of interest between wives and husbands. In purely external war, couples who come from the same society (though not necessarily the same community) will share the same loyalties. If war occurs internally, between communities and larger groups within a society, there will be no conflict of interest between husband and wife as long as they grew up in the same community. In short, wives who do not have allegiances in the "enemy" camp can, by implication, be trusted to fight alongside their husbands.

In most societies, internal war takes place at least occasionally, but wives also usually come from other communities. If women in such societies engaged in combat, they might have to fight against their fathers, paternal uncles, and brothers. Wouldn't we expect a person in such a situation to have torn loyalties and try to warn her kin of planned attacks against them? The potential for disloyalty would explain why women in such societies are forbidden to make or handle weapons or go near meetings in which war plans are discussed.

Many countries today engage in purely external war. Other things being equal, we might extrapolate from Adams's findings and expect barriers against woman warriors to disappear completely in such societies. In 2011 Australia and in 2013 the United States joined 10 other countries in allowing women in combat. It may be a trend, but most countries disallow such participation, and woman warriors are rare. Even in Adams's study, not all societies with purely external war or intra-community marriage had woman warriors. Other conditions may have to be present before women and men participate equally in combat. We may have to consider the degree to which the society seeks to maximize reproduction (and therefore protect women from danger) and the degree to which the society depends on women for subsistence during wartime.

Inevitably, one inquiry about women and society leads to other compelling questions. Does greater participation in the military increase women's presence in politics? In wartime, do women participate more or less in politics? Does the nature of war change when women play an active role in politics or in the military?

Source: From D. B. Adams 1983; J. S. Goldstein 2001; 2004; Mutrine 2013; Siegel 2011.

study of village leadership among the Kayapo of Brazil, Dennis Werner found that women with heavy child-care burdens were less influential than women not as involved in child care; he suggests that they had fewer friends and missed many details of what was going on in the village.[51]

These various explanations suggest why men generally dominate politics, but we still need to explain why women participate in politics more in some societies than in others. Marc Ross investigated this question in a cross-cultural survey of 90 societies.[52] In that sample, the degree of female participation in politics varied considerably. For example, among the Mende of Sierra Leone, women regularly held high office, but among the Azande of Zaire, women took no part in public life. One factor that predicts the exclusion of women from politics is the organization of communities around male kin. As we will see later, when they marry, women usually have to leave their communities and move to their husband's household. If women are outsiders joining a community with many related males, the males will have political advantages because of their inside knowledge of their community's members and its past events.

The Relative Status of Women

18.6 Analyze relative status among women cross-culturally.

In the small Iraqi town of Daghara, women and men live very separate lives.[53] In many respects, women appear to have very little status. Like women in some other parts of the Islamic world, women in Daghara live mostly in seclusion, staying in their houses and interior courtyards. If they must go out, they can do so only with male approval and must shroud their faces and bodies in long black cloaks. These cloaks must be worn in mixed company, even at home. Women are essentially excluded from political activities. Legally, they are considered to be under the authority of their fathers and husbands. Even the sexuality of women is controlled; there is strict emphasis on virginity before marriage. Because women are not permitted even casual conversations with strange men, the possibilities of extramarital or even premarital relationships are very slight. In contrast, hardly any sexual restrictions are imposed on men.

But some societies, such as the Mbuti of Zaire, seem to approach equal status for males and females. Like most food collectors, the Mbuti have no formal political organization to make decisions or to settle disputes. When public disputes occur, both women and men take part in the uproar. Not only do women make their positions known, but their opinions are often heeded. Even in domestic quarrels involving physical violence between husband and wife, others usually intervene to stop them, regardless of who hit whom first.[54] Women control the use of dwellings; they usually have equal say over the disposal of resources they or the men collect, over the upbringing of their children, and about whom their children should marry. One of the few signs of inequality is that women are somewhat more restricted than men with respect to extramarital sex.[55]

Read **the** Document: The Status of Women

But many social scientists have asked why the *status* of women appears to vary from one society to another. There are many theories about why women have relatively high or low status. One of the most common theories is that women's status will be high when they contribute substantially to primary subsistence activities. This theory would predict that women should have very little status when food-getting depends largely on hunting, herding, or intensive agriculture. A second theory suggests that men will be more valued and esteemed than women where warfare is particularly important. A third theory suggests that men will have higher status where there are centralized political hierarchies, since men usually play the dominant role in politics. The fourth theory predicts that women will have higher status where kin groups and couples' places of residence after marriage are organized around women.

One of the problems in evaluating these theories is that decisions have to be made about the meaning of *status*. There are probably as many definitions of status as there are researchers interested in the topic. To some, the relative status of the sexes means how much value society confers on females versus males. To others, it means how much power and authority men and women have relative to each other. To still others, it means what kinds of rights women and men possess to do what they want to do.

Many of the terms, such as value, power, authority, and rights, mean something slightly different. And we have to access what domain we are talking about—for example, with respect to authority, do we mean authority in the home, in the public arena, in the kin group, or in religious life? Do all these aspects of status vary together? Cross-cultural research by Martin Whyte suggests that they do not. For each sample society in his study, Whyte rated 52 items that might be used to define the relative status of the sexes. These items included such things as which sex can inherit property, whose authority is final in disciplining unmarried children, and whether the gods in the society are male, female, or both. The results of the study indicate that very few of these items are related. Therefore, Whyte concluded, we cannot talk about status as a single concept. Rather, it seems more appropriate to talk about the relative status of women in different spheres of life.[56]

Even though Whyte found no necessary connection between one aspect of status and another, he decided to ask whether some of the theories correctly predict why some societies have many, as opposed to few, areas in which the status of women is high. Or, why is there less or more gender stratification? Let us turn first to the ideas *not* supported by the available cross-cultural evidence. Contrary to popular belief, the idea that generally high status stems from a greater caloric contribution to primary subsistence activities is not supported.[57] For example, women seem to have higher status the more a society depends upon hunting, but women do little of the primary subsistence work in hunting societies. And it is commonly thought that warfare should bolster male status, but there is no consistent evidence that a high frequency of warfare generally lowers women's status in different spheres of life.[58]

Perspectives on Gender

Women's Electoral Success on the Northwest Coast

Political life has changed dramatically since first contact with Europeans for most Native American groups, including the Coast Salish of western Washington State and British Columbia. With impetus from the U.S. and Canadian governments, each of the recognized Coast Salish communities now has an elected council. But who is getting elected? Even though women did not have much of a role in traditional politics, now the Coast Salish groups are electing a lot of women. From the 1960s to the 1980s, women held over 40 percent of the council seats in the 12 Washington State groups, and in the 1990s, women held 28 percent of the seats in the 50 British Columbian groups. The proportion of women on the councils varies from 6 percent among the Tulalip to 62 percent among the Stillaguamish. What accounts for the women's electoral success? And why does that success vary from one group to another, even though the groups are closely related culturally?

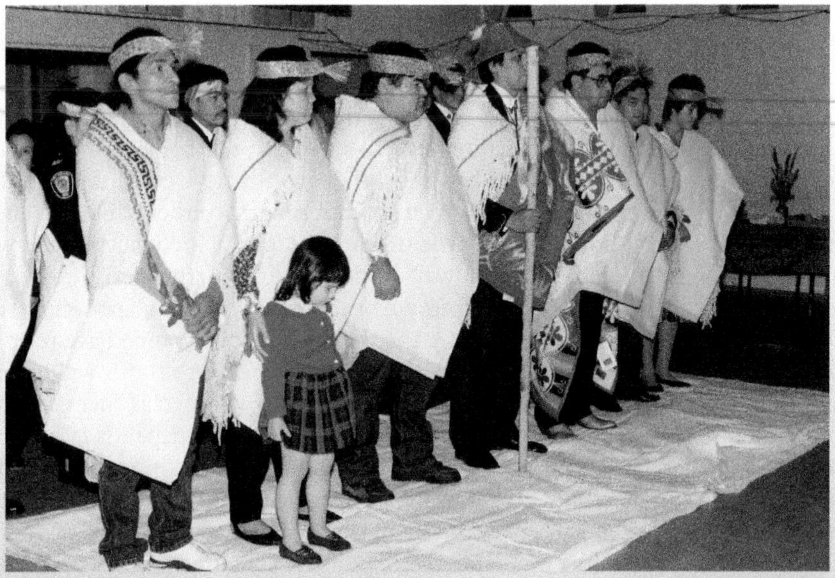

Women as well as men serve on political councils in many Coast Salish communities. Here, we see a swearing-in ceremony for the Special Chiefs' Council in Sardis, British Columbia.

According to Bruce Miller, who did a comparative study of women's electoral success in Coast Salish communities, women may generally have more of a political role now because new economic opportunities in the service and technical sectors allow them to contribute more to the household economy. But why do women win proportionately more council seats in some communities than in others? Miller found that women win proportionately more seats in communities with less income, the least income derived from fishing, and the smallest populations. Why should lower household income predict more electoral success for women? Miller suggests that it is not so much the amount of income but rather the degree to which women (compared with men) contribute to household income. In groups with economic difficulties, the jobs women are able to get play a vital role in the household. Federally funded programs such as the War on Poverty helped women to acquire technical skills and jobs. Simultaneously, many men in some communities lost their jobs in logging and agriculture.

But a high dependence on fishing income seems to favor men politically. Families that operate vessels with a large drawstring net to catch fish at sea can make hundreds of thousands of dollars a year. Men predominantly do such fishing, and where there is such lucrative fishing, the successful men dominate the councils. Even though women may have jobs too, their income is not as great as the successful fisherman's.

Why should women be more successful politically in smaller communities? Miller suggests that women have a better chance to be known personally when the community is small, even though working outside the home in technical or service jobs cuts down on the time women can devote to tribal ceremonials and other public events.

Does female income relative to male and community size help explain the relative political success of women elsewhere? We do not know yet, but subsequent research may help us find out.

Source: B. G. Miller 1992, 1994.

What does predict higher status for women in many areas of life? Although the results are not strong, there is some support in Whyte's study for the theory that women have somewhat higher status where kin groups and marital residence are organized around women. (We discuss these features of society more fully in the chapter on marital residence and kinship.) The Iroquois are a good example. Even though Iroquois women could not hold formal political office, they had considerable authority within and beyond the household. Related women lived together in longhouses with husbands who belonged to other kin groups. In the longhouse, the women's authority was clear, and they could ask objectionable men to leave. The women controlled the allocation of the food they produced. Allocation could influence the timing of war parties, because men could not undertake a raid without provisions. Women were involved in the selection of religious leaders, half of whom were women. Even in politics, although women could not speak or serve on the council, they largely controlled the selection of councilmen and could institute impeachment proceedings against those to whom they objected.[59]

In pre-industrial societies, women have generally lower status in societies with more political hierarchy.[60] Lower status for women is also associated with other indicators of cultural complexity—social stratification, plow-and-irrigation agriculture, large settlements, private property, and craft specialization. Only women's informal influence increases with cultural complexity. But informal influence may simply reflect a lack of *real* influence.[61] Why cultural complexity is associated with women having less authority in the home, less control over property, and more restricted sexual lives in pre-industrial societies is not yet understood. However, the relationship between cultural complexity and gender equality appears to be reversed in industrial and post-industrial societies. Judging by a comparative study of gender attitudes in 61 countries, it seems that countries that rely on agriculture, such as Nigeria and Peru, have the least favorable attitudes toward gender equality; industrial societies, such as Russia and Taiwan, have moderately favorable attitudes; and post-industrial societies, such as Sweden and the United States, have the most favorable attitudes toward gender equality.[62] One critical difference that may explain this reversal is the role that formal education plays in industrial and post-industrial societies. Education almost always increases status, and the more girls and young women are educated, the greater the likelihood that their status will increase. Furthermore, although the mechanisms are not well understood, education usually results in lowered fertility, which perhaps frees women to pursue other interests. As we discussed earlier, one study among the Kayapo found that women with more children are considered less influential.[63]

Western colonialism appears to have been generally detrimental to women's status. Although the relative status of men and women may not have been equal before the Europeans arrived, colonial influences seem generally to have undermined the position of women. There are many examples of Europeans restructuring landownership around men and teaching men modern farming techniques, even in places where women were usually the farmers. In addition, men more often than women could earn cash through wage labor or through sales of goods (such as furs) to Europeans.[64] From these historical lessons and from recent developments, we are beginning to understand some of the conditions that enhance or decrease women's status. If we can understand which of these conditions are most important, societies that want to may be able to reduce gender inequality.[65]

Personality Differences

18.7 Discuss gender differences in personality.

Much of the research on gender differences in personality has taken place in the United States and other Western countries where psychology is a major field of study. Although such studies are informative, they do not tell us whether the observed differences hold true in cultures very different from our own. Fortunately, we now have systematic observational studies for various non-Western societies. These studies recorded the minute details of behavior of substantial numbers of males and females. Most of the studies have observed children in different cultural settings. Any conclusions about female-male differences in aggressiveness, for example, are based on actual counts of the number of times a particular individual tried to hurt or injure another person during a given amount of observation time. Almost all of these differences are a matter of degree, not a matter of a behavior being present or absent in females or males.

Applied Anthropology

Economic Development and Women's Status

Based on the writings of Ester Boserup and subsequent scholarship on women in development, the prevailing opinion was that development usually made things worse for women. Development agents commonly targeted men for learning new technology and how to produce crops for sale. Today, women in developing countries are still largely left out and women still face difficulties, but recent research has documented how women often find creative ways to participate in commercial enterprises.

Microfinance programs for small business have helped women in developing countries to build status and independence.

Some of the creative strategies women use in Kenya to get around their structural disadvantages include buying or renting land with their proceeds, "pooling" small pieces of land to meet minimum requirements for commercial growers, joining women's rotating credit associations, and looking to the private sector for training and materials for contract agriculture.

Women's scale of production can range from raising a few extra pigs for sale in southwestern China to more complex activities, such as contract farming for crop exports in Kenya, or market trading in Ghana.

In contrast to men nearly every where in developing countries, women use the money from their commercial enterprises to purchase food and household goods and to educate their children. If their incomes or savings grow, they may pay for large appliances, furniture, and farm machinery and vehicles. Most of the recent studies suggest that bringing money into the household translates into lasting changes in the status of women, including increased educational opportunities, greater say in household decisions, and higher social status in the community.

Some opportunities for women also open up when men move into other domains. For example, among the Ashanti of Ghana, many men moved out of market trading to take advantage of more lucrative cocoa production. Women had long been traders along with men, but with the departure of men, women took over many of men's former market niches and began to engage in longer-distance trade. In Kenya, male migration has increased the number of women who manage the farm and head households.

Such examples of economic empowerment among women in agricultural societies are encouraging, even though farming keeps them close to home and away from other, more public opportunities. How do women fare in industrial societies, where only a small proportion of people engage in farming? According to a survey of 61 countries, gender equality is more favored in industrializing countries than in agricultural societies. With industrialization, infant and child mortality decline, lessening the pressure on women to reproduce. Perhaps this frees them to pursue education and work outside the home. Post-industrial countries, with even lower fertility rates, are even more accepting of gender equality. As women learn more and get out in the world more, gender inequality appears to decline.

Sources: Anita Spring 2000a; 2000b; 2000c; Bossen 2000; G. Clark 2000; Doyle 2005.

Aggression Which differences in personality are suggested by these systematic studies? The most consistent difference is in the area of aggression. Boys try to hurt others more frequently than girls do. In the Six Cultures project, an extensive comparative study of children's behavior, this difference was statistically significant as early as 3 to 6 years of age.[66] Six different research teams observed children's behavior in Kenya (among the Gusii), Mexico, India, the Philippines, Okinawa, and the United States. A more recent cross-cultural comparison of four other cultures (the Logoli of Kenya, Nepal, Belize, and American Samoa) supports the finding that boys are generally more aggressive.[67] Studies in

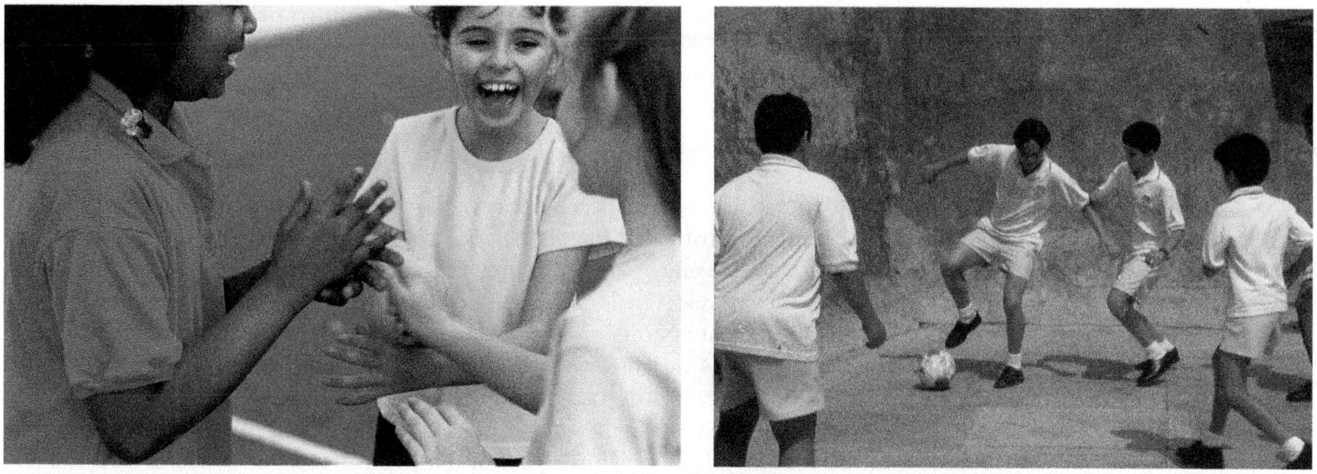

Cross-culturally, girls more often play in small, intimate groups, boys in larger groups with more interpersonal distance.

the United States are consistent with the cross-cultural findings as well: In a large number of observational and experimental studies, boys exhibited more aggression than girls.[68]

Other female-male differences have turned up with considerable consistency, but we have to be cautious in accepting them, either because they have not been documented as well or because there are more exceptions. There seems to be a tendency for girls to exhibit more responsible behavior, including nurturance (trying to help others). Girls seem more likely to conform to adult wishes and commands. Boys try more often to exert dominance over others to get their own way. In play, boys and girls show a preference for their own gender. Boys seem to play in large groups, girls in small ones. And boys seem to maintain more personal distance between each other than girls do.[69]

If we assume that these differences are consistent across cultures, how can we explain them? Many writers and researchers believe that because certain female-male differences are so consistent, they are probably rooted in the biological differences between the two sexes. Aggression is one of the traits most often attributed to biology, particularly because gender difference in this behavior appears so early in life.[70] But an alternative argument is that societies bring up boys and girls differently because they almost universally require adult males and females to perform different types of roles. If most societies expect adult males to be warriors or to be prepared to be warriors, shouldn't we expect most societies to encourage or idealize aggression in males? And if females are almost always the caretakers of infants, shouldn't we also expect societies generally to encourage nurturing behaviors in females?

Researchers tend to adopt either the biological or the socialization view, but it is possible that both kinds of causes are important in the development of gender differences. For example, parents might turn a slight biological difference into a large gender difference by maximizing that difference in the way they socialize boys versus girls.

It is difficult for researchers to distinguish the influence of genes and other biological conditions from the influence of socialization. As we discussed in the beginning of this chapter, we have research indicating that parents treat boy and girl infants differently as early as birth.[71] In spite of the fact that objective observers can see no major "personality" differences between girl and boy infants, parents often claim to.[72] But parents may unconsciously want to see differences and may therefore produce them in socialization. Even early differences could be learned, therefore, rather than resulting from biological differences. Remember, too, that researchers cannot do experiments with people; for example, parents' behavior cannot be manipulated to find out what would happen if boys and girls were treated in exactly the same ways.

However, there is considerable experimental research on aggression in nonhuman animals. These experiments suggest that the hormone androgen is partly responsible for higher levels of aggression. For example, in some experiments, females injected with androgen at about the time the sexual organs develop (before or shortly after birth) behave more aggressively when they are older than do females without the hormone.

These results may or may not apply to humans, of course, but some researchers have investigated human females who were "androgenized" in the womb because of drugs given to their mothers to prevent miscarriage. By and large, the results of these studies are similar to the experimental studies—androgenized human females show similar patterns of higher aggression.[73] Some scholars take these results to indicate that biological differences between males and females are responsible for the male-female difference in aggression;[74] others suggest that even these results are not conclusive because females who get more androgen show generally disturbed metabolic systems, and general metabolic disturbance may itself increase aggressiveness. Furthermore, androgen-injected females may look more like males because they develop male-like genitals; therefore, they may be treated like males.[75] Even the degree of aggression in males that can be attributed to androgens—and specifically, testosterone—is variable, it seems. Studies in endocrinology suggest that high testosterone levels in themselves do not cause men to be more aggressive. Rather, it appears that aggression results when testosterone surges in response to a distress signal of a sort sent by the amygdala, which is a part of the brain that communicates with the emotional center of the brain, the hypothalamus. In other words, if a male is otherwise in a mellow mood, a surge of testosterone is not likely to incite him to violence.[76]

Is there any cross-cultural evidence that socialization differences may account for differences in aggression? Although a survey of ethnographers' reports on 101 societies does show that more societies encourage aggression in boys than in girls, most societies show no difference in aggression training.[77] The few societies that do show differences in aggression training can hardly account for the widespread sex differences in actual aggressiveness. But the survey does not necessarily mean that there are no consistent differences in aggression training for boys and girls. All it shows is that there are no *obvious* differences. For all we know, the learning of aggression and other "masculine" traits by boys could be produced by subtle types of socialization.

Hadza boy with his first bow and arrow. In most hunting-gathering societies, boys learn hunting skill quite early.

One possible type of subtle socialization that could create gender differences in behavior is the chores children are assigned. It is possible that little boys and girls learn to behave differently because their parents ask them to do different kinds of work. Beatrice and John Whiting reported from the Six Cultures project that in societies where children were asked to do a great deal of work, they generally showed more responsible and nurturant behavior. Girls, who are almost always asked to do more work than boys, may be more responsible and nurturant for this reason alone.[78] If this reasoning is correct, we should find that boys asked to do girls' work would behave more like girls.

A study of Luo children in Kenya by Carol Ember supports this view.[79] Girls were usually asked to babysit, cook, clean house, and fetch water and firewood. Boys were usually asked to do very little because boys' traditional work was herding cattle, and most families in the community studied had few cattle. But for some reason, more boys than girls had been born, and many mothers without girls at home asked their sons to do girls' chores. Systematic behavior observations showed that much of the behavior of the boys who did girls' work was intermediary between the behavior of other boys and the behavior of girls. The boys who did girls' work were more like girls in that they were less aggressive, less domineering, and more responsible than other boys, even when they weren't working. So it is possible that task assignment has an important influence on how boys and girls learn to behave.

Research in behavioral biology lends support to another kind of social effect. It seems that social conditioning may be as important as—if not more important than— testosterone in predicting aggression in males. A male who is deprived of testosterone but had been conditioned previously to be aggressive will continue to be so. On the other hand, a formerly nonviolent male who is given extra testosterone is not likely to be more aggressive in the face of frustration.[80]

As we noted, an observed difference in aggression does not mean that males are aggressive and females are not. Perhaps because males are generally more aggressive, female aggression has been studied less often. For that reason, Victoria Burbank focused on female aggression in an Australian aborigine community she calls Mangrove. During her 18 months there, Burbank observed some act of aggression almost every other day. Consistent with the cross-cultural evidence, men initiated aggression more often than women, but women were initiators about 43 percent of the time. The women of Mangrove engaged in almost all the same kinds of aggression as men did, including fighting, except that their aggression tended not to be as lethal as male violence. Men most often used lethal weapons; when women fought with weapons, they mostly used sticks, not spears, guns, or knives. Burbank points out that, in contrast to Western cultures, female aggression is not viewed as unnatural or deviant but, rather, as a natural expression of anger.[81]

Dependence One common mistaken belief is that girls are more dependent than boys. The results obtained by the Six Cultures project cast doubt on this notion.[82] First, girls are no more likely to show "dependent" behavior than boys if we think of dependency as seeking help or emotional reassurance from others. To be sure, the results do indicate that boys and girls have somewhat different styles of dependency. Girls more often seek help and contact, whereas boys more often seek attention and approval.

Sociability and Passivity The Six Cultures results showed no reliable differences in sociability, or seeking and offering friendship, between the sexes. Of course, boys and girls may be sociable in different ways, because boys generally play in larger groups than girls. As for the supposed passivity of girls, the evidence is also not particularly convincing. Girls in the Six Cultures project did not consistently withdraw from aggressive attacks or comply with unreasonable demands. The only thing that emerged as a female-male difference was that older girls were less likely than boys to respond to aggression with aggression. But this finding may not reflect passivity as much as the fact that girls are less aggressive than boys, which we already knew.

Sexuality

18.8 Explain variability in sexual behavior and attitudes between different cultures.

In view of the way the human species reproduces, it is not surprising that sexuality is part of our nature. But no society we know of leaves sexuality to nature; all have at least some rules governing "proper" conduct. There is much variation from one society to another in the degree of sexual activity permitted or encouraged before marriage, outside marriage, and even within marriage. And societies vary markedly in their tolerance of nonheterosexual sexuality.

Cultural Regulations of Sexuality: Permissiveness Versus Restrictiveness

Read the Document: Variations in Sexual Attitudes, Norms, and Practices

All societies seek to regulate sexual activity to some degree, and there is a lot of variation cross-culturally. Some societies allow premarital sex; others forbid it. The same is true for extramarital sex. In addition, a society's degree of restrictiveness is not always consistent throughout the life span or for all aspects of sex. For example, a number of societies ease sexual restrictions during adolescence but impose more restrictions for adults.[83] Then, too, societies change over time. The United States has traditionally been restrictive, but until recently—before the emergence of the AIDS epidemic—more permissive attitudes had been gaining acceptance.

Premarital Sex The degree to which sex before marriage is approved or disapproved of varies greatly from society to society. The Trobriand Islanders, for example, approved of and encouraged premarital sex, seeing it as an important preparation for marriage. Both girls and boys were given complete instruction in all forms of sexual expression at the onset of puberty and were allowed plenty of premarital opportunity for intimacy. Some societies not only allow premarital sex on a casual basis but specifically encourage trial marriages between adolescents. Among the Ila-speaking peoples of central Africa, at harvest time, girls were given houses of their own and could play at being wife with the boys of their choice.[84]

Premarital sex was discouraged in many other societies. For example, among the Tepoztlan Indians of Mexico, a girl's life became "crabbed, cribbed, confined" from the time of her first menstruation. She was not to speak to or encourage boys in the least way. To do so would be to court disgrace, to show herself to be crazy. The responsibility of guarding the chastity and reputation of one or more daughters of marriageable age was often a burden for the mother. One mother said she wished that her 15-year-old daughter would marry soon because it was inconvenient to "spy" on her all the time.[85] In many Arabic societies, a girl's premarital chastity was tested after her marriage. After the wedding night, blood-stained sheets were displayed as proof of the bride's virginity.

Cultures do not remain the same, however; attitudes and practices can change markedly over time, as they have in the United States and in many European countries. In the past, sex was generally delayed until after marriage in Western societies; in the 1990s, most Americans, like their counterparts in Europe, accepted or even approved of premarital sex.[86]

Sex in Marriage Not surprisingly, there are many common features in the sexual relations of married couples, but there is also considerable cross-cultural variation. In most societies, some form of face-to-face sexual intercourse or coitus is the usual pattern, most preferring the woman on her back and the man on top. Couples in most cultures prefer privacy, which is easier in societies with single-family dwellings or separate rooms. But privacy is difficult to attain in societies that have unpartitioned and multifamily dwellings. The Siriono of Bolivia, for example, slept in hammocks 10 feet apart, and a house could contain as many as 50 hammocks. Not surprisingly, couples in such societies have preferred to have sex outdoors in a secluded location.[87]

Night is often preferred for sex, but some cultures have opted specifically for day. For example, the Chenchu of India believed that a child conceived at night might be born blind. In some societies, couples engage in sex quickly with little or no foreplay; in others, foreplay may take hours.[88] Attitudes toward marital sex and the frequency of it vary widely from culture to culture. In one cross-cultural survey, frequent marital sex is generally viewed as a good thing, but in 9 percent of the societies studied, frequent sex is viewed as undesirable and a cause of weakness, illness, and sometimes death.[89] People in most societies abstain from intercourse during menstruation, during at least part of pregnancy, and for a period after childbirth. Some societies prohibit sexual relations before certain activities, such as hunting, fighting, planting, brewing, and iron smelting. Our own society is among the most lenient regarding restrictions on intercourse within marriage, imposing only rather loose (if any) restraints during mourning, menstruation, and pregnancy.[90]

Extramarital Sex Extramarital sex is not uncommon in many societies. In about 69 percent of the world's societies, men have extramarital sex more than occasionally, as do women in about 57 percent of societies. The frequency of such sexual activity is higher than we might expect, given that only a slight majority of societies admit that they allow extramarital sex for men, and only 11 percent of societies acknowledge allowing it for women.[91]

There is quite a difference, then, between the restrictive code and actual practice of many societies. The Navajo of the 1940s were said to forbid adultery, but young married men under the age of 30 had about a quarter of their heterosexual contacts with women other than their wives.[92] And although people in the United States in the 1970s almost overwhelmingly rejected extramarital sex, 41 percent of married men and about 18 percent of married women had had extramarital sex. In the 1990s, with the onset of the AIDS epidemic, proportionately more men and women reported that they had been faithful to their spouses.[93] Cross-culturally, most societies also have a double standard with regard to men and women, with restrictions on women being considerably greater.[94] A substantial number of societies openly accept extramarital relationships. The Chukchee of Siberia, who often traveled long distances, allowed a married man to engage in sex with his host's wife, with the understanding that he would offer the same hospitality when the host visited him.[95]

Although a society may allow extramarital sex, a recent cross-cultural study of individual reactions to extramarital sex finds that men and women try a variety of strategies to curtail such sex. Men are much more likely than women to resort to physical violence against their wives; women are more likely to distance themselves from their husbands. Gossip may be employed to shame the relationship, and a higher authority may be asked to intervene in more complex societies. Researchers conclude that married women and men universally consider extramarital sex inappropriate, even in societies that occasionally permit it.[96]

Homosexuality When most people, including most researchers, discuss homosexuality, they usually refer to sex between males or sex between females. The biological male-female dichotomy corresponds to the gender male-female dichotomy in Western societies, but as we have seen earlier in this chapter, some other societies do not have the same gender concepts. The meaning of homosexuality, therefore, may differ according to the society. The Navajo of the American Southwest, for example, traditionally recognized four genders. Only relationships between people of the same gender would be considered homosexual, and they considered such relationships inappropriate.[97] Biologically speaking, such cross-gender relationships would be considered homosexual in the Western view, and most of the research to date has adopted this view, labeling sexual relations between biologically males or females as homosexuality.

The range in the world's societies of permissiveness or restrictiveness toward homosexual relations is as great as that for any other kind of sexual activity. Among the Lepcha of the Himalayas, a man was believed to become homosexual if he ate the flesh of an uncastrated pig. At the same time, the Lepcha denied that homosexual behavior existed among them, and they viewed it with disgust.[98] Perhaps because many societies deny that homosexuality exists, little is known about homosexual practices in the restrictive societies. Among the permissive ones, there is variation in the type and pervasiveness of homosexuality. In some societies, homosexuality is accepted but limited to certain times and certain individuals. For example, among the Papago of the southwestern United States, there were "nights of saturnalia" in which homosexual tendencies could be expressed. The Papago also had many male transvestites who wore women's clothing, did women's chores, and, if not married, could be visited by men.[99] A woman did not have the same freedom of expression. She could participate in the saturnalia feasts, but only with her husband's permission, and female transvestites were nonexistent.

Backstage beauty preparations for hijra and gay people in Chennai, India

Homosexuality occurs even more widely in other societies. The Berber-speaking Siwans of North Africa expected all males to engage in homosexual relations. In fact, fathers made arrangements for their unmarried sons to be given to an older man in a homosexual arrangement. Siwan custom limited a man to one boy. Such arrangements were made openly until 1909, when fear of the Egyptian government made them a secret matter. Almost all Siwan men were reported to have engaged in a homosexual relationship as boys; later, when they were between 16 and 20, they married girls.[100] Such prescribed homosexual relationships between people of different ages are a common form of homosexuality.[101] Among the most extremely pro-homosexual societies, the Etoro of New Guinea preferred homosexuality to heterosexuality. Heterosexuality was prohibited as many as 260 days a year and was forbidden in or near the house and gardens. Male homosexuality, on the other hand, was not prohibited at any time and was believed to make crops flourish and boys become strong.[102] Even among the Etoro, however, men were expected to marry women after a certain age.[103]

Only recently have researchers paid much attention to erotic relationships between females. Although early studies found relatively few societies with female-female sexual relationships, Evelyn Blackwood located reports of 95 societies with such practices, suggesting that it is more common than previously thought.[104] As with male homosexuality, some societies institutionalize same-sex sexual relationships—the Kaguru of Tanzania have female homosexual relationships between older and younger women as part of their initiation ceremonies, reminiscent of the male-male "mentor" relationships in ancient Greece.

Cross-culturally, it is extremely unusual to find "gays" or exclusive male or female homosexuals. In most societies, males and females are expected to marry, and homosexuality, if tolerated or approved, either occurs as a phase in one's life or occurs along with heterosexuality.[105]

Reasons for Sexual Restrictiveness

Read **the** Document: Legal License, Race, Sex, and Forbidden Unions

Before we deal with the question of why some societies are more restrictive than others, we must first ask whether all forms of restrictiveness go together. The research to date suggests that societies that are restrictive with regard to one aspect of heterosexual sex tend to be restrictive with regard to other aspects. Thus, societies that frown on sexual expression by young children also punish premarital and extramarital sex.[106] Furthermore, such societies tend to insist on modesty in clothing and are constrained in their talk about sex.[107] But societies that are generally restrictive about heterosexuality are not necessarily restrictive about homosexuality. For instance, societies restrictive about premarital sex are neither more nor less likely to restrict homosexuality. The situation is somewhat different regarding extramarital sex. Societies in which male homosexuality is prevalent tend to disapprove of males having extramarital heterosexual relationships.[108] If we are going to explain restrictiveness, then, it appears we have to consider heterosexual and homosexual restrictiveness separately.

Let us consider homosexual restrictiveness first. One study finds that societies that forbid abortion and infanticide for married women (most societies permit these practices for illegitimate births) are likely to be intolerant of male homosexuality.[109] This and other findings are consistent with the point of view that homosexuality is less tolerated in societies that would like to increase their population. Such societies may be intolerant of all kinds of behaviors that minimize population growth. Homosexuality would have this effect if we assume that a higher frequency of homosexual relations is associated with a lower frequency of heterosexual relations. The less frequently heterosexual relations occur, the lower the number of conceptions there might be. Another indication that intolerance may be related to a desire for population growth is that societies with famines and severe food shortages are more likely to allow homosexuality. Famines and food shortages suggest population pressure on resources; under these conditions, homosexuality and other practices that minimize population growth may be tolerated or even encouraged.[110]

Population pressure may also explain why our own society has become somewhat more tolerant of homosexuality recently. Of course, population pressure does not explain why certain individuals become homosexual or why most individuals in some societies engage in such behavior, but it might explain why some societies view such behavior more or less permissively.

Let us now turn to heterosexual behavior. What kinds of societies are more permissive than others? Although we do not yet understand the reasons, we do know that greater restrictiveness toward premarital sex tends to occur in more complex societies—societies that have hierarchies of political officials, part-time or full-time craft specialists, cities and towns, and class stratification.[111] It may be that, as social inequality increases, parents become more concerned with preventing their children from marrying "beneath them." Permissiveness toward premarital sexual relationships might lead a person to become attached to someone not considered a desirable marriage partner. Even worse, from the family's point of view, an "unsuitable" sexual liaison might result in a pregnancy that could make it impossible for a girl to marry "well." Controlling mating, then, may be a way of trying to control property. Consistent with this view is the finding that virginity is emphasized in rank and stratified societies, in which families are likely to exchange goods and money in the course of arranging marriages.[112]

The biological fact that humans depend on sexual reproduction does not by itself help explain why females and males differ in so many ways across cultures or why societies vary in the way they handle male and female roles. We are only beginning to investigate these questions. When we eventually understand more about how and why females and males differ in gender roles, personality, and sexuality, we may be better able to decide how much we want the biology of sex to shape our lives.

Summary and Review

Gender Concepts

18.1 Describe variation in gender concepts

- The division into just two genders—male/female—is very common cross-culturally, but a strict dichotomy is far from universal.
- Some cultures have additional gender designations besides male and female.

> ? What are some examples of varying gender concepts?

Physique and Physiology

18.2 Identify differences in physique and physiology between males and females.

- Humans are sexually dimorphic: Females have proportionately wider pelvises and a larger proportion of fat; males typically are taller and have heavier skeletons, a larger proportion of muscle, greater grip strength, proportionately larger hearts and lungs, and more aerobic capacity.
- Females achieve their ultimate height shortly after puberty, but boys continue to grow for years after puberty. Natural selection may have favored earlier cessation of female growth so the nutritional needs of a fetus would not compete with a growing mother's needs.
- Gender differences may be the result of both culture and genes.

> ? How might gender differences result from both culture and genes?

Gender Roles

18.3 Explain differences in gender roles.

- Many societies divide up work in similar ways. Four theories—strength theory, compatibility-with-child-care theory, economy-of-effort theory, and expendability theory—try to explain why females and males generally do different work, but each has theoretical weaknesses.
- Strength theory says that males generally possess greater strength and a superior capacity to mobilize their strength in quick bursts of energy; however, not all male activities require strength, and women do hunt in some societies.
- The compatibility-with-child-care theory suggests that women make child care a priority and fit in other tasks but does not explain why men usually prepare soil for planting and make wood, bone,

horn, and shell objects, tasks that can probably be stopped to tend to a child and no more dangerous than cooking.

- The economy-of-effort interpretation suggests that it would be advantageous for one gender to perform tasks that are related in terms of knowledge and training and tasks that are physically located near each other.
- The expendability theory is the idea that men will tend to do the dangerous work in a society because the loss of men is not as great a disadvantage reproductively as the loss of women. However, it does not explain why men would put themselves in danger.
- As societies change, gender roles tend to change but still remain divided in some way.

? What are some of the near-universals and differences in gender roles cross-culturally? Discuss domestic, productive, and political roles.

Relative Contributions to Work: Who Works More?

18.4 Analyze relative gender differences in term of contributions to work.

- Most contemporary societies typically equate "work" with earning money, but that view is relatively recent to human history.
- Anthropologists may skew research about division of labor by focusing more on gathering, hunting, fishing, herding, and farming than on food preparation and storage and, in so doing, distort the importance of each gender's contributions.
- In horticultural and intensive agricultural societies, studies so far suggest that women typically work more total hours per day than men.
- Usually both women and men contribute a good deal toward primary food-getting activities, but men usually contribute more in most societies. The type of agriculture may help explain some of the variation.
- Cross-cultural studies suggest that, when women contribute a lot to primary food-getting activities, infants are fed solid foods earlier, enabling others to feed them; girls are likely to be industrious, probably to help their mothers; and female babies are more valued.

? What might explain why men and women do relatively more work?

Political Leadership and Warfare

18.5 Discuss gender differences in terms of political leadership and warfare cross-culturally.

- In almost every known society, men tend to lead in political arenas, possibly because men's role in warfare may give them the edge in political leadership and because men spend more time in the outside world than do women.
- Males almost universally dominate in warfare, perhaps because warfare requires strength and quick bursts of energy, combat is not compatible with child care, and women's fertility is more important to a population than their usefulness as warriors.

? What theories might support the findings about gender differences in political leadership and warfare?

The Relative Status of Women

18.6 Analyze relative status among women cross-culturally.

- Theories suggest that women will have higher status when: (1) women contribute substantially to primary subsistence activities; (2) where residence is organized around women; (3) where warfare is unimportant; and (4) where political hierarchies are less centralized.
- The idea that generally high status for women stems from greater caloric contribution to primary subsistence activities is not supported by research evidence. Nor is generally higher status for men associated with more warfare.
- The idea of status has multiple dimensions that are not always linked. Thus, research needs to look at women's status in various spheres of life, why some societies have many areas in which women's status is high and others have few, or why there is less or more gender stratification.
- Education almost always increases status, and the more girls and young women are educated, the greater the likelihood that their status will increase.

? How might the relative status of women and men be measured? What are some of the findings on cross-cultural variations in status by gender?

Personality Differences

18.7 Discuss gender differences in personality.

- Observed differences between male and female personalities in Western and non-Western countries are a matter of degree, not a matter of a behavior being present or absent.
- Aggression is the most consistent personality difference: Boys try to hurt others more often than girls do. This difference appears early, so it may have biological causes, possibly hormonal. But societies may also raise boys and girls differently from very early ages, so nature and nurture are hard to separate.
- Cross-culturally, girls are no more likely to show "dependent" behavior than boys if dependency is seen as seeking help or emotional reassurance from others; however, studies show that boys and girls have somewhat different styles of dependency.
- Cross-culturally, studies show no reliable differences in levels of sociability between the sexes, although male and female styles of sociability may differ.
- Cross-culturally, studies do not confirm that girls are more passive than boys, but they do show that older girls were less likely than boys to respond to aggression with aggression.

? What are some of the cross-cultural findings about gender differences in personality?

Sexuality

18.8 Explain variability in sexual behavior and attitudes between different cultures.

- All societies have rules governing "proper" sexual conduct, but they vary. In addition, a society's degree of restrictiveness is not always consistent throughout the life span or for all aspects of sex. Approval or disapproval of premarital sex varies greatly cross-culturally.
- Sexual attitudes and practices can change markedly over time in societies.
- Attitudes toward marital sex and its frequency and location vary widely cross-culturally. The restrictive codes for extramarital sex in many societies vary greatly from actual practice.
- Cross-culturally, the meaning of homosexuality may differ, and acceptance or limitations vary greatly. In most societies, males and females are expected to marry, and homosexuality, if tolerated or approved, occurs either as a phase in one's life or along with heterosexuality.
- Current research suggests that societies that are restrictive with regard to heterosexual sex may not be restrictive about homosexuality. Homosexuality may be tolerated or encouraged in societies that minimize population growth.
- Greater restrictiveness toward premarital sex tends to occur in more complex societies—societies that have hierarchies of political officials, part-time or full-time craft specialists, cities and towns, and class stratification.

? What may explain variability in sexual behavior and attitudes between different cultures?

Think on it

1. Would you expect female-male differences in personality to disappear in a society with complete **gender equality** in the workplace?
2. Under what circumstances would you expect male-female differences in **athletic performance** to disappear?
3. What conditions may make the **election** of a female head of state most likely?

CHAPTER

19 Marriage and the Family

LEARNING OBJECTIVES

- **19.1** Define marriage in anthropological terms.
- **19.2** Explain the near-universality of marriage across cultures.
- **19.3** Identify the various ways that marriage is marked out in different societies and the economic exchanges that accompany it.
- **19.4** Critically assess different explanations for the universality of the incest taboo.
- **19.5** Discuss the types of restrictions on whom one can marry.
- **19.6** Describe the three different rules regarding how many persons one can marry, and explain social or economic reasons for each.
- **19.7** Describe and explain variation in family form.
- **19.8** Explain reasons for extended-family households.

Marriage is customary in every society known to anthropologists, with only one or two exceptions. When a cultural institution is as common as marriage but apparently not absolutely essential to human survival—people can reproduce and have families without marriage—anthropologists ask *why*. One popular answer today might be that people marry for love. Many of us can recognize the adoration mixed with desire that compelled High Horse, a young Dakotan of North America, to want to marry Good Plume, a "beautiful" Cheyenne girl he had gotten to know:

> . . . *I want her so much that I cannot eat and I cannot sleep, and if I do not get her, maybe I shall just starve to death.*

But mere passion has in much of the world been frowned upon as the basis for as important a social contract as marriage. High Horse's friend, for example, was alarmed by his friend's lovesick delirium and determined to cure him.[1]

We have no certain way of knowing how far back in time humans began to have more or less permanent male-female bonding or customary marriages, but physical anthropologists surmise that such bonds were possibly in place over a million years ago when early humans relied more heavily on hunting. Written records, which exist for only 5,000 years or so of human history, describe marriages—and divorces—in the early kingdoms of West Asia.[2] We do know that the fundamental concept of marriage is nearly universal, and in this chapter we will look at it in all its forms, for how one marries, whom one marries, and even how many people a person can be married to simultaneously vary from society to society. Indeed, although each marriage usually involves one pair at a time, most societies have allowed a man to be married to more than one woman at a time, and a few have allowed a woman more than one husband. And we will explore the debate over why humans marry.

Families are unequivocally universal, for all societies have parent-child groups. The form and size of the family, however, can also vary from society to society. Extended families with two or more related parent-child groups are the norm in a majority of societies, whereas others have smaller, independent families. Marriage is not necessarily the basis for family life. One-parent families are increasingly common in our own and other societies today. Although marriage has not disappeared in these places—it is still customary to marry—more individuals are choosing to have children without being married. Yet the majority of people continue to think that marriage and family belong together.

•••

Marriage

19.1 Define marriage in anthropological terms.

Marriage is customary in nearly every known society. The fact that it exists nearly everywhere does not mean **marriage** takes the same form or is recognized in similar ways. Marriage is a socially approved sexual and economic union, usually between a woman and a man. It is presumed, by both the couple and others, to be more or less permanent, and it subsumes reciprocal rights and obligations between the two spouses and between spouses and their future children.[3]

Marriage A socially approved sexual and economic union, usually between a man and a woman, that is presumed, both by the couple and by others, to be more or less permanent, and that subsumes reciprocal rights and obligations between the two spouses and their future children.

Marriage is a socially approved sexual union in that the couple's sexual relationship is implicitly understood and legitimated. A woman might say, "I want you to meet my husband," but she could not say, "I want you to meet my lover" without embarrassment in most societies. Although the union may one day end in divorce, couples in all societies enter into marriage expecting a long-term commitment. Implicit too in marriage are reciprocal rights and obligations regarding property, finances, and childrearing. As George Peter Murdock noted, "Sexual relations can occur without economic cooperation, and there can be a division of labor between men and women without sex. But marriage unites the economic and the sexual."[4]

Read **the** Document: Varieties of Marital Relationships

As we will see, societies have had a variety of marriage practices. Customs marking the onset of the union—the nuptials or wedding ceremony—may have been elaborate and lasted for several days or have hardly existed. A Ho-Chunk (or Winnebago) bride, for example, experienced no formal wedding ceremony. If the marriage was arranged by

The bride's relatives arrive at the groom's home bearing gifts and Piki bread from the bride's family at a traditional Hopi engagement ceremony in Arizona.

the couple's parents, as was customary, the families would exchange presents when the engagement was made, and then the groom would move in with the bride's family, where he might stay for two years as a dutiful son-in-law before returning to his own home with his wife. If the couple eloped, the marriage might be even less ceremonious. One man, Crashing Thunder, recalled eloping with a young woman at his grandfather's instructions:

I told her of my intention and asked her to go home with me. . . . After a while she came back all dressed up and ready. She had on a waist covered with silver buckles and a beautifully colored hair ornament and she wore many strings of beads around her neck, and bracelets around her wrists. Her fingers were covered with rings and she wore a pair of ornamental leggings. She wore a wide-flap ornamented moccasin and in each ear she had about half a dozen ear holes and they were full of small silver pieces made into ear ornaments. She was painted also. She had painted her cheeks red and the parting of her hair red.

Crashing Thunder takes his resplendent bride home on horseback but stops along the way for a singing engagement with his band. Because they have eloped "and that is the custom," he has his bride hide under "a small oak bush" for the night. It rains all night, and she is "soaked through and through" when Crashing Thunder returns the next day to retrieve her. When they arrive at his grandfather's house, the bride takes off her finery and gives it to her in-laws, who give her "other clothing to wear." And that is that.[5]

The Na and Nayar Exceptions

We say that marriage is customary in almost all societies, but there are some interesting exceptions. Two are the Na of China and, in the 19th century, the Nayar subcaste of India.

The Na of Yunnan in southwest China, with a population of about 40,000, have customarily not married or lived with their sexual partners. Rather, men and women lived their entire lives in residential groups made up of their respective maternal kin (grandmother, great-uncles, brothers, sisters, and their children). The maternal household cooperated economically and raised the children. The Na practice *sese,* the consensual sexual union of an unmarried couple.[6] When a couple agrees to see each other, the man visits the woman discreetly in the evening and returns to his own residence the next morning. No other tie exists between the lovers, nor is there any expectation that the relationship be longstanding or monogamous. The offspring of such relationships normally take the woman's family name and are raised by her family.

However, the Chinese government has tried off and on since 1959 to impose marriage among the Na and even to fine them for illegitimate births, but without much success. Traditionally, only a few women and men, usually of the aristocratic class, chose to live together. While the government has become more flexible about Na customs, some Na are now choosing to marry, especially when they work in the Chinese government or work away from their community. Young people's attitudes are also changing, largely because of their education in Chinese schools, where they become self-conscious when asked their fathers' names.[7]

In the nineteenth century, the Nayar, a subcaste in India, also lacked the custom of marriage.[8] The Na and the Nayar may both have had frequently absent men. Nayar men hired themselves out to fight for princes in various parts of India. In the Na case, between the 1920s and the 1950s, the Na raised horses and mules for caravans they organized to transport merchandise throughout the western part of Yunnan. Of course, the relative absence of men cannot be the only reason for the absence of marriage in these groups; long-distance travel by men occurs in some other ethnic groups along with marriage.

Same-Sex Marriages

In addition to male-female marriages, some societies recognize same-sex marriages. Although they are far from common in any known society, same-sex marriages may be socially approved unions and entail reciprocal rights and obligations similar to those between heterosexual women and men. In some cultures, a biological female or male is expected to take on the opposite gender role and become the wife or husband in the union. Cheyenne Indians allowed a married man to take as a second wife a biological man who belonged to the third-gender "two-spirits."

It is not clear that Cheyenne male-male marriages involved homosexual relationships, but temporary homosexual marriages are known to have occurred among the Azande of Africa. Before the British took control over what is now Sudan, Azande warriors who could not afford wives often married "boy-wives." The boy-wives had sexual relations with their husbands and also performed many of the chores traditionally delegated to female wives. As in normal marriages, gifts (although less substantial) were given by the "husband" to the parents of his boy-wife. The husband performed services for the boy's parents and could sue any other lover of the boy in court for adultery.[9]

Female-female marriages are reported to have occurred in many African societies, but there is no evidence of sexual relationships between the partners. It seems, rather, that female-female marriages were a socially approved way for a woman to take on the legal and social roles of father and husband.[10] Such marriages have existed, for example, among the Nandi, a pastoral and agricultural society of Kenya, as a way to resolve the failure to produce a male heir to property through a regular marriage. A woman, even if her husband is still alive, will become "husband" to a younger female and "father" the younger woman's future children. The female husband provides the marriage payments required for obtaining a wife, renounces female work, and takes on the obligations of husband. No sexual relations are permitted between the female husband and the new wife (or between the female husband and her own husband). Rather, the female husband arranges for her new wife to have a male consort in order to have children and subsequently becomes the socially designated father. If asked who their father is, children of such a marriage will name the female husband.[11]

Why Is Marriage Nearly Universal?

19.2 Explain the near-universality of marriage across cultures.

We said earlier that humans can survive and reproduce without marriage, but saying that does not mean that marriage isn't advantageous. In fact, because virtually all societies practice female-male marriage as we have defined it, we can assume that the custom is adaptive. But saying that does not specify exactly how it may be adaptive. Several interpretations have traditionally been offered to explain why all human societies have the custom of marriage. Each suggests that marriage solves problems found in all societies—how to share the products of a gender division of labor; how to care for infants, who are dependent for a long time; and how to minimize sexual competition. To evaluate the plausibility of these interpretations, we must ask whether marriage provides the best or the only reasonable solution to each problem. After all, we are trying to explain a custom that is virtually universal. The comparative study of other animals, some of which have something like marriage, may help us to evaluate these explanations.

Gender Division of Labor

Females and males in every society known to anthropology perform different economic activities. This gender division of labor has often been cited as a reason for marriage.[12] As long as there is a division of labor by gender, society has to structure a way for women and men to share the products of their labor. Marriage would be one way to solve that problem. But it seems unlikely that marriage is the only possible solution. The hunter-gatherer rule of sharing could be extended to include all the products brought in by both women and men. Or a small group of men and women, such as brothers and sisters, might be pledged to cooperate economically. Thus, although marriage may solve the problem of sharing the fruits of a division of labor, it clearly is not the only possible solution.

Prolonged Infant Dependency

Humans exhibit the longest period of infant dependency of any primate. The child's prolonged dependence places the greatest burden on the mother, who is the main child caregiver in most societies. The burden of prolonged child care by human females may limit the kinds of work they can do. They may need the help of a man to do certain types of work, such as hunting, that are incompatible with child care. Because of this prolonged dependency, it has been suggested, marriage is necessary.[13] But here the argument becomes essentially the same as the division-of-labor argument, and it has the same logical weakness. It is not clear why a group of women and men, such as a hunter-gatherer band, could not cooperate in providing for dependent children without marriage.

Sexual Competition

Unlike most other female primates, the human female may engage in intercourse at any time throughout the year. Some scholars have suggested that more or less continuous female sexuality may have created a serious problem: considerable sexual competition between males for females. It is argued that society had to prevent such competition to survive, that it had to develop some way of minimizing the rivalry among males for females to reduce the chance of lethal and destructive conflict.[14]

There are several problems with this argument. First, why should continuous female sexuality make for more sexual competition in the first place? One might argue the other way around. More availability should make for less competition. When there is only a brief breeding season, competition should be greater. Second, males of many animal species, even some in which females are frequently sexually receptive (such as many of our close primate relatives), do not show much aggression over females. Third, why couldn't sexual competition, even if it existed, be regulated by cultural rules other than marriage? For instance, society might have adopted a rule whereby men and women circulated among all the opposite-sex members of the group, each person staying a specified length of time with each partner. Such a system presumably would solve the problem of sexual competition. On the other hand, such a system might not work particularly well if individuals came to prefer certain other individuals. Jealousies attending those attachments might give rise to even more competition.

A Look at Other Mammals and Birds

None of the theories we have discussed explains convincingly why marriage is the only or the best solution to a particular problem. In addition, some comparative evidence on mammals and birds casts doubt on those theories.[15] How can evidence from other animals help us evaluate theories about human marriage? If we look at animals that, like humans, exhibit some stable female-male mating, as opposed to those that are completely promiscuous, we can perhaps see what factors may predict male-female bonding in the warm-blooded animal species. Female-male bonding occurs in most species of birds and some mammals, such as wolves and beavers. Among 40 mammal and bird species, neither division of labor, nor prolonged infant dependency, nor greater female sexuality correlates with male-female bonding in the direction predicted by the theories discussed earlier. The birds and mammals studied have nothing comparable to a humanlike division of labor, but they exhibit female-male unions nevertheless. The two other suggested factors—prolonged infant dependency and female sexuality—relate to male-female bonding in the opposite direction to what was expected. Mammal and bird species that have longer infant dependency periods or more female sexuality are less likely to have male-female bonding.

A black-browed albatross on the Falkland Islands. Most bird species have male-female bonding.

Does any factor predict male-female bonding among other mammals and birds and thereby also help explain human marriage? It appears that animal species in which females are able to simultaneously feed themselves and their babies after birth (*postpartum*) tend not to mate stably. On the other hand, species in which postpartum mothers cannot feed themselves and their babies at the same time do typically form male-female bonds. Among the typical bird species, a mother would have difficulty feeding herself and her babies simultaneously. Because her young cannot fly for some time, the mother risks losing them to predators if she leaves the nest untended to search for food. If a male has bonded with her, as males in most bird species do, he can bring food or take his turn watching the nest. Among animal species that have no postpartum feeding problem, babies are able to travel with the mother almost immediately after birth as she moves about to eat (as do such grazers as horses), or the mother can transport the babies as she moves about to eat (as do baboons and kangaroos). We believe the human female has a postpartum feeding problem. When humans lost most of their body hair, babies could not readily travel with the mother by clinging to her fur. And when humans began to depend on certain kinds of food-getting that could be dangerous, such as hunting, mothers could not safely engage in such work with their infants along.[16]

Research by Frank Marlowe on the Hadza foragers of Tanzania appears to support our view of female-male bonding. Hadza women and men both forage for food, with the women providing more berries and other plant foods while the men provide more meat and honey. Generally, it appears that Hadza women could support themselves and their children without a mate. Married women forage more regularly and contribute more food (in terms of calories) to the family diet, *except* when they have a nursing infant. Marlowe found that the father of an infant made up for the mother's lower food contribution while she was nursing. In fact, Hazda fathers with nursing children contributed significantly more food to the household than fathers with older children.[17]

Even if we assume that human mothers have a postpartum feeding problem, we must ask if marriage is the most likely solution to the problem. It may well be, because other conceivable solutions probably would not work as well. If a mother took turns babysitting with another mother, for example, neither might be able to collect enough food for both mothers and the two sets of children dependent on them. A mother and father share the same set of children, making it easier for them to feed themselves and their children adequately. Another possible solution is males and females living in a promiscuous group. We believe that a particular mother in that kind of arrangement would probably not be able to count on any male, if he didn't think he was the father, to watch her baby when she had to go out for food or to bring her food when she had to watch her baby. The need to solve the postpartum feeding problem by itself helps to explain why some animals, including humans, have relatively stable male-female bonds.[18] Can research of this kind with other animals be applied to human beings? We believe it can, though not everybody will agree.

How Does One Marry?

19.3 Identify the various ways that marriage is marked out in different societies and the economic exchanges that accompany it.

When we say that marriage is a socially approved sexual and economic union, we mean that all societies have some way of marking the onset of a marriage, but the ways of doing so vary considerably. For reasons that we don't fully understand, some cultures mark marriages by elaborate rites and celebrations; others mark marriages in much more informal ways. And most societies have economic transactions before, during, or even after the onset of the marriages.

Marking the Onset of Marriage

Read the Document: Rotuma: Interpreting a Wedding

Many societies mark the beginning of a marriage with a ceremony. Others, such as the Taramiut Inuit of the Arctic, the Trobriand Islanders, and the Kwoma of New Guinea, use different social signals to indicate that a marriage has taken place.

Among the Taramiut Inuit, an engaged couple's success at producing offspring marks the onset of marriage. The betrothal, or engagement, is considered extremely important and is arranged between the parents at or before the time their children reach puberty. Later, when the young man is ready, he moves in with his betrothed's family for a trial period. If all goes well—that is, if the young woman gives birth to a baby within a year or so—the couple is considered married and the wife goes with her husband to his camp. If the couple does not conceive, the young man returns to his family without a wife.[19]

In keeping with the general openness of their society's attitudes toward sexual matters, a Trobriand couple advertises its desire to marry "by sleeping together regularly, by showing themselves together in public, and by remaining with each other for long periods at a time."[20] When a girl accepts a small gift from a boy, she demonstrates that her parents favor the match. Before long, she moves to the boy's house, takes her meals there, and accompanies her husband all day. Then the word goes around that the two are married.[21]

The Kwoma practice a trial marriage followed by a ceremony that makes the couple husband and wife. The girl lives for a while in the boy's home. When the boy's mother is satisfied with the match and knows that her son is too, she waits for a day when he is away from the house. Until that time, the girl has been cooking only for herself, and the boy's food has been prepared by his womenfolk. Now the mother has the girl prepare his meal. The young man returns and begins to eat his soup. When the first bowl is nearly finished, his mother tells him that his betrothed cooked the meal, and his eating it means that he is now married. At this news, the boy customarily rushes out of the house, spits out the soup, and shouts, "Faugh! It tastes bad! It is cooked terribly!" A ceremony then makes the marriage official.[22]

Just in the last three decades, "living together" has become more of an option in the United States and other Western countries. For most, living together is a prelude to marriage or kind of a trial marriage. For some, living together has become an alternative to marriage. Statistics in the United States suggest that by 1995 more than half of married women under the age of 45 had lived with a man without being married for at least some time period.[23]

Among those societies that have ceremonies marking the onset of marriage, feasting is a common public expression of the unification of the two families by marriage. A feast opens and ends the ceremony among the Reindeer Tungus of Siberia, for example. A wedding date is set after protracted negotiations between the two families and their larger kin groups. Go-betweens assume most of the responsibility for the negotiating. The wedding day opens with the two kin groups, probably numbering as many as 150 people, pitching their lodges in separate areas and offering a great feast. After the groom's gifts have been presented, the bride's dowry is loaded onto reindeer and carried to the groom's lodge. There, the climax of the ceremony takes place. The bride takes the wife's place—that is, at the right side of the entrance of the lodge—and members of both families sit in a circle. The groom enters and follows the bride around the circle, greeting each guest, while the guests, in their turn, kiss the bride on the mouth and hands. Finally, the go-betweens spit three times on the bride's hands, and the couple is formally husband and wife. More feasting and revelry bring the day to a close.[24]

In many cultures, marriage includes ceremonial expressions of hostility between the couples' families. Mock fights are staged or, in many societies, taunting and teasing take place. On occasion, such mock fights can have genuinely aggressive overtones, as among the Gusii of Kenya:

> *Five young clansmen of the groom come to take the bride and two immediately find the girl and post themselves at her side to prevent her escape, while the others receive the final permission of her parents. When it has been granted the bride holds onto the house posts and must be dragged outside by the young men. Finally she goes along with them, crying and with her hands on her head.*[25]

But the battle is not yet over. Mutual antagonism continues right onto the marriage bed, even up to and beyond coitus. The groom is determined to display his virility; the bride is equally determined to test it. "Brides," Robert and Barbara LeVine remarked, "are said to take pride in the length of time they can hold off their mates." Men can also win acclaim. If the bride is unable to walk the following day, the groom is considered a "real man."[26] Such expressions of hostility usually occur in societies in which the two sets of kin are actual or potential rivals or enemies. In many societies, it is common to marry women from "enemy" villages.

As the Gusii example suggests, marriage ceremonies often symbolize important elements of the culture. Whereas some ceremonies may symbolize hostility between the two families, others may promote harmony between the families. On the Polynesian island of Rotuma, for example, a female clown is an important part of the ceremony. She is responsible for creating an enjoyable, joking atmosphere that facilitates interaction between the two sides.[27]

Economic Aspects of Marriage

"It's not man that marries maid, but field marries field, vineyard marries vineyard, cattle marry cattle," goes a German peasant saying. In its down-to-earth way, the expression states a reality in many societies: Marriage involves economic considerations. In our culture, economic considerations may or may not be explicit. However, in about 75 percent of the societies known to anthropology,[28] one or more explicit economic transactions take place before or after the marriage. The economic transaction may include any of several forms: bride price, bride service, exchange of females, gift exchange, dowry, or indirect dowry. The distribution of those forms among societies that have economic marriage transactions is shown in Figure 19.1.

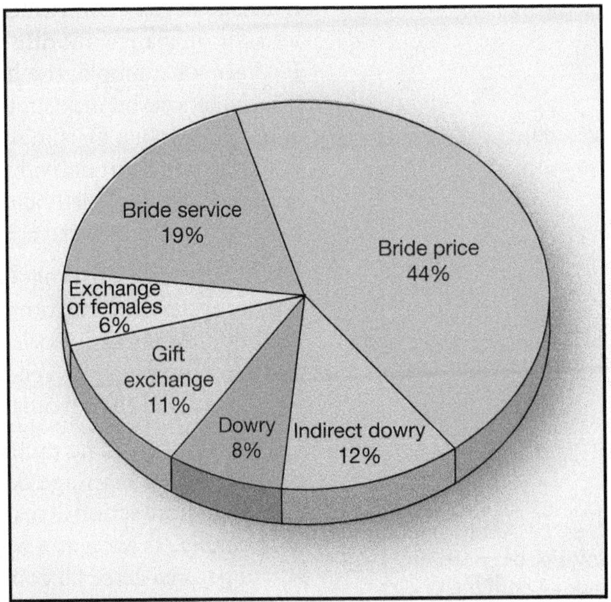

FIGURE 19.1 Distribution of Economic Marriage Transactions Among Societies That Have Them

Note that there are societies in the ethnographic record (25 percent) that lack any substantial economic transactions at marriage.

Source: Based on data from Schlegel and Eloul 1988, 291–309.

Bride Price A gift of money or goods from the groom or his kin to the bride's kin is known as **bride price** or **bride wealth**. The gift usually grants the groom the right to marry the bride and the right to her children. Of all the forms of economic transaction involved in marriage, bride price is the most common. In one cross-cultural sample, 44 percent of societies that had economic transactions at marriage practiced bride price; in almost all of those societies, the bride price was substantial.[29] Bride price is practiced all over the world, but it is especially common in Africa and Oceania. Payment may be made in different currencies; livestock and food are two of the more common. With the increased importance of commercial exchange, money has increasingly become part of bride price payments. Among the Nandi, the bride price consists of five to seven cattle, one or two sheep and goats, cowrie shells, and money equivalent to the value of one cow. Even in unusual female-female marriages, the female "husband" must pay a bride price to arrange the marriage and be considered the "father."[30]

Bride price A substantial gift of goods or money given to the bride's kin by the groom or his kin at or before the marriage. Also called **bride wealth**.

The Subanun of the Philippines exact a high bride price—several times the annual income of the groom plus three to five years of bride service (described in the next section).[31] Among the Manus of the Admiralty Islands of New Guinea, a groom requires an economic backer, usually an older brother or an uncle, if he is to marry, but it will be years before he can pay off his debts. Depending on the final bride price, payments may be concluded at the time of the marriage, or they may continue for years afterward.[32]

Despite the connotations that bride price may have, the practice does not reduce a woman to the position of slave. It is, nevertheless, associated with societies in which women have relatively low status. The bride price may be important to the woman and her family. Indeed, the fee they receive can serve as a security. If the marriage fails through no fault of hers and the wife returns to her kin, the family might not return the bride price to the groom. On the other hand, the wife's kin may pressure her to remain with her husband, even though she does not wish to, because they do not want to return the bride price or are unable to do so. A larger bride price is associated with more difficulty in obtaining a divorce.[33]

What kinds of societies are likely to have the custom of bride price? Cross-culturally, societies with bride price are likely to practice horticulture and lack social stratification. Bride price is also likely where women contribute a great deal to primary subsistence activities[34] and where they contribute more than men to all kinds of economic activities.[35] Although these findings might suggest that women are highly valued in such societies, recall that the status of women relative to men is not higher in societies in which women contribute a lot to primary subsistence activities. Indeed, bride price is likely to occur in societies in which men make most of the decisions in the household,[36] and decision making by men is one indicator of lower status for women.

Bride service Work performed by the groom for his bride's family for a variable length of time either before or after the marriage.

Bride Service The next most common type of economic transaction at marriage—occurring in about 19 percent of the societies with economic transactions—requires the groom to provide **bride service**, or work for the bride's family, sometimes before the marriage begins, sometimes after. Bride service varies in duration. In some societies, it lasts for only a few months; in others, as long as several years. Among the North Alaskan Eskimo, for example, the boy works for his in-laws after the marriage is arranged. To fulfill his obligation, he may simply catch a seal for them. The marriage may be consummated at any time while he is in service.[37] In some societies, bride service sometimes substitutes for bride price. An individual might give bride service to reduce the amount of bride price required. Native North and South American societies were likely to practice bride service, particularly if they were egalitarian food collectors.[38]

Exchange of Females Of the societies that have economic transactions at marriage, 6 percent have the custom whereby a sister or female relative of the groom is exchanged for the bride. Among the societies that practice exchange of females are the Tiv of West Africa and the Yanomamö of Venezuela and Brazil. These societies tend to be horticultural and egalitarian, and their women make a relatively high contribution to primary subsistence.[39]

Gift Exchange The exchange of gifts of about equal value by the two kin groups about to be linked by marriage occurs somewhat more often (about 11 percent of those with economic transactions) than the exchange of females.[40] Among the Andaman Islanders, for example, as soon as a boy and girl indicate their intention to marry, their respective sets of parents cease all communication and begin sending gifts of food and other objects to each other through a third party. The gift exchange continues until the marriage is completed and the two kin groups are united.[41]

Dowry A substantial transfer of goods or money from the bride's family to the bride.

In one Sudanese society the amount of bride price varies by height. A tall girl may bring 150 cows, a short girl just 30.

Dowry A substantial transfer of goods or money from the bride's family to the bride, the groom, or the couple is known as a **dowry**.[42] Unlike the types of transactions we have discussed so far, the dowry, which is given in about 8 percent of societies with economic transactions, is usually not a transaction between the kin of the bride and the kin of the groom. A family has to have wealth to give a dowry, but because the goods go to the new household, no wealth comes back to the family that gave the dowry. Payment of dowries was common in medieval and Renaissance Europe, where the size of the dowry often

determined the desirability of the daughter. The custom is still practiced in parts of eastern Europe and in sections of southern Italy and France, where land is often the major item the bride's family provides. Parts of India also practice the dowry.

In contrast to societies with bride price, societies with dowry tend to be those in which women contribute relatively little to primary subsistence activities, there is a high degree of social stratification, and a man is not allowed to be married to more than one woman simultaneously.[43] Why does dowry tend to occur in these types of societies? One theory suggests that the dowry is intended to guarantee future support for a woman and her children, even though she will not do much primary subsistence work. Another theory is that the dowry is intended to attract the best bridegroom for a daughter in monogamous societies with a high degree of social inequality. The dowry strategy is presumed to increase the likelihood that the daughter and her children will do well reproductively. Both theories are supported by recent cross-cultural research, with the second predicting dowry better.[44] But many stratified societies in which women and men have only one spouse at a time (including our own) do not practice dowry. Why this is so still needs to be explained.

Indirect Dowry The dowry is provided by the bride's family to the bride, the groom, or the couple. But sometimes the payments to the bride originate from the groom's family. Because the goods are sometimes first given to the bride's father, who passes most if not all of them to her, this kind of transaction is called **indirect dowry.**[45] Indirect dowry occurs in about 12 percent of the societies in which marriage involves an economic transaction. For example, among the Basseri of southern Iran, the groom's father assumes the expense of setting up the couple's new household. He gives cash to the bride's father, who uses at least some of the money to buy his daughter household utensils, blankets, and rugs.[46]

Indirect dowry Goods given by the groom's kin to the bride (or her father, who passes most of them to her) at or before her marriage.

Restrictions on Marriage: The Universal Incest Taboo

19.4 Critically assess different explanations for the universality of the incest taboo.

Romantic literature and Hollywood notwithstanding, marriage is seldom based solely on mutual love, independently discovered and expressed by the two life-partners-to-be. Nor is it based on sex or wealth alone. Even when love, sex, and economics are contributing factors, regulations specify whom one may or may not marry. Perhaps the most rigid regulation, found in *all* cultures, is the **incest taboo**, which prohibits sexual intercourse or marriage between some categories of kin.

Incest taboo Prohibition of sexual intercourse or marriage between mother and son, father and daughter, and brother and sister; often extends to other relatives.

The most universal aspect of the incest taboo is the prohibition of sexual intercourse or marriage between mother and son, father and daughter, and brother and sister. No society in recent times has permitted either sexual intercourse or marriage between those pairs. A few societies in the past, however, did permit incest, mostly within the royal and aristocratic families, though generally it was forbidden to the rest of the population. For example, the Incan and Hawaiian royal families allowed marriage within the family. Probably the best-known example of allowed incest involved Cleopatra of Egypt.

It seems clear that the Egyptian aristocracy and royalty indulged in father-daughter and brother-sister marriages. Cleopatra was married to two of her younger brothers at different times.[47] The reasons seem to have been partly religious—a member of the family of the pharaoh, who was considered a god, could not marry any "ordinary" human—and partly economic, for marriage within the family kept the royal property undivided. Between 30 B.C. and A.D. 324, incest was allowed in ancient Egypt not only among the royal family but among commoners; an estimated 8 percent of commoner marriages were brother-sister marriages.[48]

In spite of such exceptions, no culture we know of today permits or accepts incest within the nuclear family. Why is the familial incest taboo universal? Several explanations have been suggested.

Childhood-Familiarity Theory

The childhood-familiarity theory, suggested by Edward Westermarck, was given a wide hearing in the early 1920s. Westermarck argued that people who have been closely associated with each other since earliest childhood, such as siblings, are not sexually attracted to each

Children in an Israeli kibbutz.

other and would therefore avoid marriage with each other.[49] This theory was rejected upon the subsequent discovery that some children were sexually interested in their parents and siblings. More recent studies have suggested, however, that there might be something to Westermarck's theory.

Yonina Talmon investigated marriage patterns among the second generation of three well-established collective communities (*kibbutzim*) in Israel. In these collectives, children live with many members of their peer group in quarters separate from their families. They are in constant interaction with their peers from birth to maturity. The study among 125 couples revealed that, despite parental encouragement of marriage within the peer group, there was "not one instance in which both mates were reared from birth in the same peer group."[50] Children reared in common not only avoided marriage, they also avoided any sexual relations among themselves.

Talmon reported that the people reared together firmly believed that overfamiliarity breeds sexual disinterest. As one of them told her, "We are like an open book to each other. We have read the story in the book over and over again and know all about it."[51] Talmon's evidence reveals not only the onset of disinterest and even sexual antipathy among children reared together but a correspondingly heightened fascination with newcomers or outsiders, particularly for their "mystery."

Arthur Wolf's study of the Chinese in northern Taiwan also supports the idea that something about being reared together produces sexual disinterest. Wolf focused on a community still practicing the Chinese custom of *t'ung-yang-hsi,* or "daughter-in-law raised from childhood":

> *When a girl is born in a poor family . . . she is often given away or sold when but a few weeks or months old, or one or two years old, to be the future wife of a son in the family of a friend or relative which has a little son not betrothed in marriage. . . . The girl is called a "little bride" and taken home and brought up in the family together with her future husband.*[52]

Wolf's evidence indicates that this arrangement is associated with sexual difficulties when the childhood "couple" later marry. Informants implied that familiarity caused the couple to be disinterested and to fail to be stimulated by one another. Such couples produce fewer offspring than spouses who are not raised together, are more likely to seek extramarital sexual relationships, and are more likely to get divorced.[53]

The Talmon and Wolf findings are consistent with Westermarck's belief that the incest taboo may indicate avoidance more than it does a prohibition of certain matings. Another study, undertaken by Hilda and Seymour Parker, that may be consistent with

Westermarck's explanation of the incest taboo compared two groups of fathers: those who had allegedly sexually abused their daughters and those who had not.[54] To maximize the similarities among the men in their test group, the Parkers selected the fathers from the same prisons and psychiatric facilities. The Parkers found that the fathers who had committed incest with their daughters were much more likely to have had little involvement with bringing up their daughters; they were not at home or rarely at home during the daughters' first three years of life. The fathers who avoided incest had been more closely involved with their daughters' early childhood.

Although Westermarck's theory suggests that sexual aversion develops during early childhood, some researchers have asked whether the childhood familiarity theory could explain the extension of incest taboos to first cousins. The familiarity argument would imply that first-cousin marriage should be prohibited in societies where first cousins grow up in the same community. However, such societies are not more likely to prohibit first-cousin marriage.[55]

Even if it is likely that familiarity in childhood normally leads to sexual disinterest,[56] we must ask why societies need to prohibit marriages that would voluntarily be avoided because of disinterest. And if familiarity breeds disinterest, what are we to make of couples who remain actively interested in each other sexually after years of marriage?

Freud's Psychoanalytic Theory

Sigmund Freud proposed that the incest taboo is a reaction against unconscious, unacceptable desires.[57] He suggested that the son is attracted to his mother (as the daughter is to her father) and as a result feels jealousy and hostility toward his father. But the son knows that these feelings cannot continue, for they might lead the father to retaliate against him; therefore, they must be renounced or repressed. Usually the unacceptable feelings are repressed and retreat into the unconscious. But the desire to possess the mother continues to exist in the unconscious, and, according to Freud, horror at the thought of incest is a reaction to, or a defense against, the forbidden unconscious impulse.

Freud's theory may account for the aversion felt toward incest, or at least the aversion toward parent-child incest, but it, too, does not explain why society needs an explicit taboo, particularly on brother-sister incest. Nor does it account for the findings that support Westermarck's hypothesis that familiarity breeds sexual disinterest.

Family-Disruption Theory

The family-disruption theory, often associated with Bronislaw Malinowski,[58] can best be summed up as follows: Sexual competition among family members would create so much rivalry and tension that the family could not function as an effective unit. Because the family must function effectively for society to survive, society has to curtail competition within the family. The familial incest taboo is thus imposed to keep the family intact.

But while this theory might explain why father-daughter and mother-son incest would need to be prohibited, why couldn't societies have a rule that brothers and sisters could marry when they were adults? Hypothetically, brother-sister incest would not disrupt the authority of the parents if the children were allowed to marry when mature. And brother-sister marriages did exist in ancient Egypt. The family-disruption theory, then, does not explain the origin of the incest taboo.

Cooperation Theory

The cooperation theory was proposed by the early anthropologist Edward B. Tylor and further elaborated by Leslie A. White and Claude Lévi-Strauss. It emphasizes the value of the incest taboo in promoting cooperation among family groups and thus helping communities to survive. As Tylor saw it, certain operations necessary for the welfare of the community can be accomplished only by large numbers of people working together. To break down suspicion and hostility between family groups and make such cooperation possible, early humans developed the incest taboo to ensure that individuals would marry members of other families. The ties created by intermarriage would serve to hold the community together. Thus, Tylor explained the incest taboo as an answer to the choice "between marrying out and being killed out."[59]

The idea that marriage with other groups promotes cooperation sounds plausible, but is there evidence to support it? There are, of course, societies such as the Gusii in which marriage is often between hostile groups. But is that society an exception? And does marriage itself promote cooperation? Because people in all recent societies marry outside the family, we cannot test the idea that such marriages promote cooperation more than marriages within the family. We can ask whether other kinds of out-marriage, such as marriage with other communities, promote cooperation with those communities. The evidence suggests not. There is no greater peacefulness between communities when marriages are forbidden within the community and arranged with other communities than when they are not.[60]

Even if marriage outside the family promoted cooperation with other groups, why would it be necessary to prohibit all marriages within the family? Couldn't families have required some of their members to marry outside the family if they thought it necessary for survival, but permitted incestuous marriages when such alliances were not needed? Although the incest taboo might enhance cooperation between families, other customs can also promote alliances. The need for cooperation does not adequately explain why the incest taboo exists in all societies. In particular, the cooperation theory does not explain the sexual aspect of the incest taboo. Premarital and extramarital sex is common and tolerated in many societies. Incestuous sex could likewise theoretically be allowed, as long as children were required to marry outside the family.

Inbreeding Theory

One of the oldest explanations for the incest taboo is inbreeding theory. It focuses on the potentially damaging consequences of inbreeding or marrying within the family. People within the same family are likely to carry the same harmful recessive genes. Inbreeding, then, will tend to produce offspring who are more likely to die early of genetic disorders than are the offspring of unrelated spouses. Recent evidence suggests that inbreeding also tends to increase the likelihood of diseases that affect people later in life, such as heart disease and diabetes.[61] For many years, inbreeding theory was rejected because of what is known from dog-breeding, in which, for example, a half-brother and half-sister might be bred (line breeding) or brothers and sisters might be bred (inbreeding). The inbreeding practiced to produce prize-winning dogs, however, is not a good guide to whether inbreeding is harmful; dog breeders have not counted the runts they cull at the expense of producing one superficially show-worthy dog. Nor have they needed to worry about the genetic ailments a dog may eventually display. Indeed, dog-breeders as well as mating humans now have a good deal of evidence that the closer the degree of inbreeding, the more harmful the genetic effects.[62]

Genetic mutations occur frequently. Although many pose no harm to the individuals who carry a single recessive gene, matings between two people who carry the same gene often produce offspring with a harmful or lethal condition. Close blood relatives are much more likely than unrelated individuals to carry the same harmful recessive gene. If close relatives mate, their offspring have a higher probability than the offspring of nonrelatives of inheriting the harmful trait.

One study compared children produced by familial incest with children of the same mothers produced by nonincestuous unions. About 40 percent of the incestuously produced children had serious abnormalities, compared with about 5 percent of the other children.[63] Matings between less closely related kin also show harmful, though not as harmful, effects of inbreeding. The likelihood that a child will inherit a double dose of a harmful recessive gene is lower the more distantly the child's parents are related. Also consistent with inbreeding theory is the fact that rates of abnormality are consistently higher in the offspring of uncle-niece marriages (which are allowed in some societies) than in the offspring of cousin marriages; for the offspring of uncle-niece marriages, the likelihood of inheriting a double dose of a harmful recessive is twice that for the offspring of first cousins.[64]

Although most scholars acknowledge the harmful effects of inbreeding, some question whether people in former days would deliberately have invented or borrowed the incest taboo because they knew that inbreeding was biologically harmful. William Durham's cross-cultural survey suggests that they did. Ethnographers do not always report the perceived consequences of incest, but Durham found that biological harm to offspring was mentioned in 50 percent of ethnographic reports.[65] For example, Raymond Firth reporting on the Tikopia, who live on an island in the South Pacific, wrote:

> *The idea is firmly held that unions of close kin bear with them their own doom, their* mara. . . . *The idea* [mara] *essentially concerns barrenness. . . . The peculiar barrenness of an incestuous union consists not in the absence of children, but in their illness or death, or some other mishap. . . . The idea that the offspring of a marriage between near kin are weakly and likely to die young is stoutly held by these natives and examples are adduced to prove it.*[66]

Durham concluded that if the harm of inbreeding was widely recognized, people may have deliberately invented or borrowed the incest taboo.[67] But whether or not people actually recognized the harmfulness of inbreeding, the demographic consequences of the incest taboo would account for its universality: Reproductive and hence competitive advantages probably accrued to groups practicing the taboo. Thus, even though cultural solutions other than the incest taboo might provide the desired effects assumed by the family-disruption theory and the cooperation theory, the incest taboo is the only possible solution to the problem of inbreeding.

As is discussed toward the end of the next section, a society may or may not extend the incest taboo to first cousins. That variation is also predictable from inbreeding theory, a fact that lends additional support to the idea that the incest taboo was invented or borrowed to avoid the harmful consequences of inbreeding.

Whom Should One Marry?

19.5 Discuss the types of restrictions on whom one can marry.

Probably every child in our society knows the story of Cinderella—the poor, downtrodden, but lovely girl who accidentally meets, falls in love with, and marries a prince. It is a charming tale, but it is misleading as a guide to mate choice. The majority of marriages simply do not occur in so free and coincidental a way in any society. In addition to the familial incest taboo, societies often have other rules regarding the mate, such as whether they may or not be cousins, whether they should or should not come from the same community, and even whether the couple has choice in the matter.

Even in a post-industrial, urbanized society such as ours, where mate choice is theoretically free, people tend to marry within their own class and geographic area. Studies in the United States consistently indicate that a person is likely to marry someone who lives close by.[68] Because we tend to live in neighborhoods with people from similar class backgrounds, it is unlikely that many of these alliances are Cinderella stories. Moreover, it is worth remembering that even Cinderella's story stretches convention only so far. She was, after all, a well-born girl who just happened to be oppressed by her evil stepmother and stepsisters—until, that is, the prince discovers that only Cinderella's *aristocratically* dainty foot will fit in the glass slipper. Parental preferences are not just found in complex societies. Even in societies with subsistence economies, parents prefer their children marry someone of a "good family background."[69]

Arranged Marriages

Listen to the Audio: Matched by Mom: Arranged Marriage in America

Parents invariably play a role in who their offspring marry. In many societies, parents or other family members determine who their sons and daughters will marry, with the respective families or go-betweens handling the negotiations. Sometimes betrothals are completed while the future partners are still children, as was formerly the custom in much of Hindu India, China, Japan, and eastern and southern Europe. Implicit in the arranged marriage is the conviction that the joining together of two different kin groups to form new social and economic ties is too important to be left to free choice and romantic love.

In some societies, arranged marriages were more likely to take place among the elite or royal families; commoners or poorer people could make their own choices. King Solomon, according to biblical texts, married the daughter of the Egyptian pharaoh, his old enemy. In order to protect his growing empire, Alexander the Great married the daughter of the Persian king Darius III. Beginning with the 12th-century rule of the first

English king, Henry I, until the late-20th-century marriage of Prince Charles and Lady Diana, the British monarchy arranged the unions of heirs to the throne.

Even in modern Western societies, where people assume that they choose their mates freely, parents' choices were shown to influence who their sons and daughters married well into the mid-20th century.[70] Given the freedom to choose, do people today pick someone very different from the spouse their parents might have selected for them? Perhaps not. One experiment showed that, whether selecting a husband or wife for their offspring or for themselves, people placed three key traits at the top of a list of 18: emotional stability, a dependable character, and a pleasing disposition. It seems that secondary traits, such as good looks, mattered more if someone were choosing a mate for him or herself.[71]

Good looks appear to matter less when an arranged marriage is also a class alliance, as among the Kwakiutl of British Columbia.

> *When I was old enough to get a wife—I was about 25—my brothers looked for a girl in the same position that I and my brothers had. Without my consent, they picked a wife for me—Lagius'[s] daughter. The one I wanted was prettier than the one they chose for me, but she was in a lower position than me, so they wouldn't let me marry her.*[72]

Arranged marriages are becoming less common in many places, and couples are beginning to have more a voice in selecting their marriage partners. Marriages were still arranged, for example, on the Pacific island of Rotuma in 1960, and the bride and groom would sometimes not meet until the wedding day. A Rotuma wedding ceremony may be much the same today as it was then, but couples are now allowed to "go out" and have a say about whom they wish to marry.[73] In a small Moroccan town, arranged marriages are still the norm, although a young man may ask his mother to make a marriage offer to a particular girl's parents, who may then ask her whether she wants to accept the marriage offer. But dating is still not acceptable, so getting acquainted is hard to arrange.[74]

Exogamy and Endogamy

Exogamy The rule specifying marriage to a person from outside one's own group (kin or community).

A widespread marriage practice is the regulation of whether a partner comes from outside or inside one's own kin group or community. The rule of **exogamy** requires that the marriage partner come from outside one's own kin group or community. Exogamy can take many forms. It may mean marrying outside a particular group of kin or outside a particular village or group of villages. Often, then, spouses come from a distance. For example, in Rani Khera, a village in India, 266 married women originally came from some 200 different villages that were, on average, between 12 and 24 miles away. Meanwhile, 220 local women had gone to 200 other villages to marry. As a result of these exogamous marriages, Rani Khera, a village of 150 households, was linked to 400 other nearby villages.[75] When there are rules of exogamy, violations are often believed to cause harm. On the islands of Yap in Micronesia, people who are related through women are referred to as "people of one belly." The elders say that if two people from the same kinship group married, they would not have any female children and the group would die out.[76]

People in exogamous societies with very low population densities often have to travel considerable distances to meet mates. A study of foragers and horticulturalists found a clear relationship between population density and the distance between the communities of the husband and wife—the lower the density, the greater the marriage distance. Because forager societies generally have lower population densities than horticulturalists, they generally have further to go to find mates. Among the !Kung, for instance, the average husband and wife had lived 40 miles (65 kilometers) from each other before they were married.[77]

Endogamy The rule specifying marriage to a person within one's own group (kin, caste, community).

The opposite rule, **endogamy**, obliges a person to marry within a particular group. The caste groups of India traditionally have been endogamous. The higher castes believed that marriage with lower castes would "pollute" them, and such unions were forbidden. Caste endogamy is also found in some parts of Africa. In East Africa, a Masai warrior would never stoop to marry the daughter of an ironworker, nor would a former ruling-caste Tutsi in Rwanda, in central Africa, think of marrying a person from the hunting caste Twa.

Migrants and Immigrants

Arranging Marriages in the Diaspora

What happens when people move from a place with arranged marriage to a place where marriage is based on free choice and romantic love? Many people around the world or their parents are from places that reject love marriage because it could fizzle out. Love was not considered a sufficient basis for marriage. So parents and other kin, or hired go-betweens, would select your marriage partner, preferably someone from the same socioeconomic background. For example, in many parts of South Asia, one was supposed to marry someone from the same caste and class until recently. Many immigrant parents still insist that their children's marriages be arranged. But this is changing. Consider how some young South Asians in England are "arranging" their own marriages.

These young South Asian Hindus in Great Britain are "speed dating." They talk with potential spouses for three minutes each. Traditionally, parents arrange marriages.

Go-betweens are replaced by Web sites, chat rooms, and personal advertisements on the Internet. A couple who "meet" first electronically might arrange a face-to-face meeting, in what's called "South Asian speed dating"; they agree to meet and talk—for just three minutes—at a restaurant or bar, and then they move on. The participants, who are in their 20s and middle class, consider themselves hip. They are quite comfortable blending behaviors from West and East. Is the same true for South Asians in the United States?

Rakhi is a lawyer in New York City. She is the daughter of Sikh immigrants from Punjab, India. (The Sikhs are a religious group.) As a young girl, Rakhi had built a shrine to an American movie star in her bedroom. But at the age of 27, she decided to marry someone like herself. Because she was focused on her career and didn't have time to date, her mother enlisted the help of a Sikh matchmaker who had been instructed by the mother of a man named Ranjeet to find a wife for him. Ranjeet also had thought he would marry for love. "But seeing how different cultures treated their families, I realized the importance of making the right match," he said. When the matchmaker organized a party to which she invited Rakhi and Ranjeet (and their mothers), Rakhi's mother whispered: "I think he's the one." After the two young people dated secretly for two months, the matchmaker was once again summoned, this time to negotiate the marital arrangements. Some time later, Rakhi and Ranjeet were married in a Sikh temple in a New York suburb.

Sources: Alvarez 2003, Section 1, p. 3; Henderson 2002, Section 9, p. 2.

Cousin Marriages

When referring to their cousins, people in the United States generally do not differentiate between types of cousins. In some other societies, such distinctions can be important, particularly with regard to first cousins. The terms for the different kinds of first cousins may indicate which cousins are suitable marriage partners (sometimes even preferred mates) and which are not. Although most societies prohibit marriage with all types of first cousins,[78] some societies allow and even prefer particular kinds of cousin marriage.

When first-cousin marriage is allowed or preferred, it is usually with some kind of cross-cousin. **Cross-cousins** are children of siblings of the opposite sex; that is, a person's cross-cousins are the father's sisters' children and the mother's brothers' children. The Chippewa Indians used to practice cross-cousin marriage, as well as cross-cousin joking. With his female cross-cousins, a Chippewa man was expected to exchange broad, risqué jokes, but he would not do so with his parallel cousins, with whom severe propriety was the rule.

Cross-cousins Children of siblings of the opposite sex. One's cross-cousins are the father's sisters' children and mother's brothers' children.

Parallel cousins Children of siblings of the same sex. One's parallel cousins are the father's brothers' children and the mother's sisters' children.

Parallel cousins are children of siblings of the same sex; a person's parallel cousins, then, are the father's brothers' children and the mother's sisters' children. In general, in any society that allows cross-cousin but not parallel-cousin marriage, a joking relationship exists between a man and his female cross-cousins. In marked contrast, the man will maintain a formal and respectful relationship with female parallel cousins. The joking relationship apparently signifies the possibility of marriage, whereas the respectful relationship extends the incest taboo to parallel cousins.

Parallel-cousin marriage is fairly rare, but some Muslim societies have historically preferred such marriages and allowed other cousin marriages as well. The Kurds, who are mostly Sunni Muslims, preferred that a young man marry his father's brother's daughter (for her part, the young woman would be marrying her father's brother's son). The woman will stay close to home in such a marriage, since her father and his brother usually live near each other. Because the bride and groom are also in the same kin group, marriage in this case also entails kin group endogamy.[79]

Levirate A custom whereby a man is obliged to marry his deceased brother's wife.

Sororate A custom whereby a woman is obliged to marry her deceased sister's husband.

What kinds of societies allow or prefer first-cousin marriage? There is evidence from cross-cultural research that cousin marriages are most likely to be permitted in relatively large and densely populated societies. Perhaps this is because such marriages, and thus the risks of inbreeding, are less likely in large populations. However, a number of small, sparsely populated societies also permit or even prefer cousin marriage. How can these cases be explained? It appears that most of the small societies that permit cousin marriage have lost a lot of people to epidemics. For example, many societies around the world, particularly in the Pacific and in North and South America, suffered severe depopulation in the first generation or two after contact with Europeans, who introduced diseases (including measles, pneumonia, and smallpox) to which the native populations had little or no resistance. Such societies may have permitted cousin marriage to provide enough mating possibilities within a reduced population of eligible mates.[80]

Monogamy Marriage between only one man and only one woman at a time.

Polygamy Plural marriage; one individual is married to more than one spouse simultaneously. **Polygyny** and **polyandry** are types of polygamy.

Levirate and Sororate

Cultural rules that oblige individuals to marry the spouse of a deceased relative are exceedingly common and have been an obligatory form of second marriage in a majority of the societies known to anthropology.[81] **Levirate** is a custom whereby a man is obliged to marry his deceased brother's wife. **Sororate** obliges a woman to marry her deceased sister's husband.

Polygyny The marriage of one man to more than one woman at a time.

Polyandry The marriage of one woman to more than one man at a time.

Among the Chukchee of Siberia, levirate obliges the next oldest brother to become the successor husband to his brother's widow. He cares for her and the children, assumes the sexual privileges of the husband, and unites the deceased's reindeer herd with his own, though he keeps ownership of the herd in the name of his brother's children. If there are no brothers, the widow is married to a cousin of her first husband. The custom is regarded more as a duty than a right.[82]

19.6 Describe the three different rules regarding how many persons one can marry, and explain social or economic reasons for each.

How Many Does One Marry?

Today, in most Western societies, **monogamy**, not only is the form of marriage in which one has only one spouse at a time (usually one man and one woman) customary, but plural marriage is illegal. However, cross-culturally, most societies known to anthropology have allowed some form of **polygamy**, or plural spouse marriage. There are two types of polygamy. **Polygyny**, the form of marriage that allows a man to be married to more than one woman at the same time, is very common. The mirror image of polygyny, the marriage of one woman to more than one man at the same time, is called **polyandry**. It is practiced in just a few societies. However, societies with polygamy cannot practice it exclusively because few, if any, societies have twice as many of one gender than the other. So in a polygynous society, for example, most men will be married monogamously at any given time. *Group marriage*, in which more than one man is married to more than one woman at the same time, sometimes occurs but is not customary in any known society.

Polygyny

Although polygyny is now illegal in most Western societies, it was very much a part of Judeo-Christian history and appeared to be a privilege of rulers and elites. The Old Testament includes many references to men with multiple wives. King David and his son, King Solomon, are both said to have had hundreds of wives and concubines, though such extravagant numbers are likely to be exaggerated. In early Medieval Europe, rulers practiced polygyny to ensure that they would have a male heir. And rulers took more than one wife as a way to build alliances with or annex neighboring kingdoms. Polygyny continues to be a mark of great wealth or high status in many societies, but in those societies only the very wealthy are expected to (or can) support more than one wife. Some Muslim societies, especially Arabic-speaking ones, still view polygyny in this light. But a man does not always have to be wealthy to be polygynous; indeed, in some societies in which women are important contributors to the economy, it seems that men try to have more than one wife to become wealthier.

Among the Siwai, a society in the South Pacific, status is achieved through feast giving. Pork is the main dish at these feasts, so the Siwai associate raising pigs with prestige. The great interest in pigs also sparks an interest in wives, because in Siwai society women raise the food needed to feed pigs. Thus, although having many wives does not in itself confer status among the Siwai, the increase in pig herds—and prestige—that can result offers men a strong incentive to be polygynous.[83] Polygynously married Siwai men do seem to have greater prestige, but they also complain that a household with multiple wives is difficult. Sinu, a Siwai, described his plight:

> *There is never peace for a long time in a polygynous family. If the husband sleeps in the house of one wife, the other one sulks all the next day. If the man is so stupid as to sleep two consecutive nights in the house of one wife, the other one will refuse to cook for him, saying, "So-and-so is your wife; go to her for food. Since I am not good enough for you to sleep with, then my food is not good enough for you to eat." Frequently the co-wives will quarrel and fight. My uncle formerly had five wives at one time and the youngest one was always raging and fighting the others. Once she knocked an older wife senseless and then ran away and had to be forcibly returned.*[84]

Sororal and Nonsoral Polygyny Jealousy and conflict between co-wives seem not to be present in a minority of polygynous societies. Margaret Mead reported that married life among the Arapesh of New Guinea, even in polygynous marriages, was "so even and contented that there is nothing to relate of it at all."[85] What might explain such harmony? One possible explanation is that the co-wives are sisters. **Sororal polygyny**, a man's marriage to two or more sisters, seems to work because siblings, having grown up together, are more likely to get along and cooperate than co-wives who practice **nonsororal polygyny**—that is, who are not related. Indeed, a recent cross-cultural study confirms that persistent conflict and resentment were all-too-common in societies with nonsororal polygyny. The most commonly reported complaint was insufficient access to the husband for sex and emotional support.[86]

Sororal polygyny The marriage of a man to two or more sisters at the same time.

Nonsororal polygyny Marriage of a man to two or more women who are not sisters.

Perhaps because conflict is so common among co-wives, particularly with nonsororal polygyny, polygynous societies appear to have invented similar customs to try to lessen conflict and jealousy in co-wives:

1. Whereas sororal co-wives nearly always live under the same roof, co-wives who are not sisters tend to have separate living quarters. Among the African Plateau Tonga, who practice nonsororal polygyny, co-wives live in separate dwellings and the husband shares his personal goods and his favors among his wives according to principles of strict equality. The Crow of the northern plains of North America, on the other hand, practiced sororal polygyny; their co-wives usually shared a tepee.
2. Co-wives have clearly defined equal rights in matters of sex, economics, and personal possessions. For example, the Tanala of Madagascar require the husband to spend a day with each co-wife in succession. Failure to do so constitutes adultery and entitles the slighted wife to sue for divorce and alimony of up to one-third of the husband's

property. Furthermore, the land is shared equally among all the women, who expect the husband to help with its cultivation when he visits them.

3. Senior wives often have special prestige. The Tonga of Polynesia, for example, bestow the status of "chief wife" upon the first wife. Her house stands to the right of her husband's and is named the "house of the father." The other wives are called "small wives," and their houses are to the left of the husband's. The chief wife has the right to be consulted first, before the small wives, and her husband is expected to sleep under her roof before and after a journey. Because later wives are often favored because they tend to be younger and therefore more attractive, practices that elevate the first wife's status may serve as compensation for her loss of physical attractiveness by increased prestige.[87]

Why Is Polygyny a Common Practice? Although jealousy and conflict are noted as common problems in polygynous marriage, the practice may also offer social benefits. Married females as well as males in Kenya believed that polygyny provided economic and political advantages, according to a study conducted by Philip and Janet Kilbride. Because they tend to be large, polygynous families provide plenty of farm labor and extra food that can be marketed. They also tend to be influential in their communities and are likely to produce individuals who become government officials.[88] And in South Africa, Connie Anderson found that women choose to be married to a man with other wives because the other wives could help with child care and household work, provide companionship, and allow more freedom to come and go. Some women said they chose polygynous marriages because there was a shortage of marriageable males.[89]

How can we account for the fact that polygyny is allowed and often preferred in most of the societies known to anthropology? Ralph Linton suggested that polygyny derives from a general male primate urge to collect females.[90] But if that were so, then why wouldn't all societies allow polygyny? Other explanations of polygyny have been suggested. We restrict our discussion here to those that statistically and strongly predict polygyny in worldwide samples of societies.

Postpartum sex taboo Prohibition of sexual intercourse between a couple for a period of time after the birth of their child.

One theory is that polygyny will be permitted in societies that have a long **postpartum sex taboo**.[91] In these societies, a couple must abstain from intercourse until their child is at least a year old. John Whiting suggested that couples abstain from sexual intercourse for a long time after their child is born for health reasons. A Hausa woman reported:

> *A mother should not go to her husband while she has a child she is suckling. If she does, the child gets thin; he dries up, he won't be strong, he won't be healthy. If she goes after two years it is nothing, he is already strong before that, it does not matter if she conceives again after two years.*[92]

The symptoms the woman described seem to be those of *kwashiorkor*. Common in tropical areas, kwashiorkor is a protein-deficiency disease that occurs particularly in children suffering from intestinal parasites or diarrhea. If a child gets protein from mother's milk during its first few years, the likelihood of contracting kwashiorkor may be greatly reduced. By observing a long postpartum sex taboo, and thereby ensuring that her children are widely spaced, a woman can nurse each child longer. Consistent with Whiting's interpretation, societies whose principal foods are low-protein staples, such as taro, sweet potatoes, bananas, breadfruit, and other root and tree crops, tend to have a long postpartum sex taboo. Societies with long postpartum sex taboos also tend to be polygynous. Perhaps, then, a man's having more than one wife is a cultural adjustment to the taboo. As a Yoruba woman said,

> *When we abstain from having sexual intercourse with our husband for the two years we nurse our babies, we know he will seek some other woman. We would rather have her under our control as a co-wife so he is not spending money outside the family.*[93]

Even if we agree that men will seek other sexual relationships during the period of a long postpartum sex taboo, it is not clear why polygyny is the only possible solution to the problem. After all, it is conceivable that all of a man's wives might be subject to the postpartum sex taboo at the same time. Furthermore, there may be sexual outlets outside marriage.

Current Research and Issues

Love, Intimacy, and Sexual Jealousy in Marriage

A nomadic Fulani woman in Ghana grooming her husband.

Americans believe that love should be a basis of marriage. Does this ideal characterize most societies? We know the answer to that question: No. In fact, in many places, romantic love is believed to be a poor basis for marriage and is strongly discouraged. However, even though romantic love may not be a basis for marriage everywhere, it does occur almost everywhere. A cross-cultural survey suggests that about 89 percent of the world's societies show signs of romantic love—accounts of personal longing, love songs or love depicted in folklore, elopement because of affection, and passionate love that is described by informants and quoted in ethnographies. If love is nearly universal, then why is it often discouraged as a basis for marriage?

Three conditions appear to predict that a society will discourage romantic love in marriage. One is that the husband and wife live in an extended family. In this situation, the family seems more concerned with how the in-marrying person gets along with others and less concerned with whether the husband and wife love each other. A second condition predicting the discouragement of romantic love as a basis for marriage is that one of the spouses does most of the primary subsistence work or earns most of the couple's income. Third, romantic love is unlikely when men have more sexual freedom than women. In general, then, romantic love is discouraged as a basis for marriage under conditions of inequality—if one of the spouses is highly dependent on the other or the other's kin or the woman has fewer sexual rights than the man.

Intimacy is different from romantic love. It refers to how close the married couple are to each other—eating together, sleeping in the same bed, spending their leisure time together, as well as having frequent sex. In some societies, couples are together a lot; in others, they spend very little time together. Foraging societies seem on average to have more marital intimacy than more complex herding and agricultural societies, but the reasons are not entirely clear. Also, a high involvement in war seems to detract from intimacy.

When it comes to sexual jealousy, men are far more likely to be violent than women. Infidelity is, incidentally, the most frequently reported reason for a husband to divorce a wife. According to anthropologists with a biological orientation, fathers always have some uncertainty about whether their children are theirs; for that reason alone males are more likely to try to guard against rival males.

But how can we account for the considerable variation in jealousy from one society to another? It does seem that the more a society emphasizes the importance of getting married, the more it limits sex to the marriage relationship, the more it also emphasizes property, the more its males appear to exhibit sexual jealousy.

Does romantic love as a basis for marriage increase or decrease sexual jealousy? Does romantic love predict intimacy, or is romantic love more likely with less frequent contact between the spouses? We are still far from understanding how the different aspects of marriage are related. All we know is that an emphasis on love and intimacy does not preclude marital violence or marital dissolution.

Sources: Hendrix 2009; Betzig 1989; Jankowiak and Fischer 1992; de Munck and Korotayev 1999.

Another explanation of polygyny is that it is a response to an excess of women over men. Such an imbalanced sex ratio may occur because of the prevalence of warfare in a society. Because men and not women are generally the warriors, warfare almost always takes a greater toll of men's lives. Given that almost all adults in noncommercial societies are married, polygyny may be a way of providing spouses for surplus women. Indeed, there is evidence that societies with imbalanced sex ratios in favor of women tend to have both polygyny and high male mortality in warfare. Conversely, societies with balanced sex ratios tend to have both monogamy and low male mortality in warfare.[94]

Even though illegal, many in the state of Utah still practice polygyny. The husband in the top row of this picture has five wives and 35 children.

A third explanation is that a society will allow polygyny when men marry at an older age than women. The argument is similar to the sex-ratio interpretation. Delaying the age when men marry would create an artificial, though not an actual, excess of marriageable women. Why marriage for men is delayed is not clear, but the delay does predict polygyny.[95]

Is one of these explanations better than the others, or are all three factors—long post-partum sex taboo, imbalanced sex ratio in favor of women, and delayed age of marriage for men—important in explaining polygyny? One way of trying to decide among alternative explanations is to do what is called a *statistical-control analysis,* which allows us to see if a particular factor still predicts when the effects of other possible factors are removed. In this case, when the possible effect of sex ratio is removed, a long postpartum sex taboo no longer predicts polygyny and hence is probably not a cause of polygyny.[96] But both an actual excess of women and a late age of marriage for men seem to be strong predictors of polygyny. Added together, these two factors predict polygyny even more strongly.[97]

Behavioral ecologists have also suggested ecological reasons why both men and women might prefer polygynous marriages. If there are enough resources, men might prefer polygyny because they can have more children if they have more than one wife. If resources are highly variable and men control resources, women might find it advantageous to marry a man with many resources even if she is a second wife. A recent study of foragers suggests that foraging societies in which men control hunting or fishing territories are more likely to be polygynous. This finding is consistent with the theory, but the authors were surprised that control of gathering sites by men did not predict polygyny.[98] The main problem with the theory of variable resources and their marital consequences is that many societies, particularly in the "modern" world, have great variability in wealth but little polygyny. Behavioral ecologists have had to argue, therefore, that polygyny is lacking because of socially imposed constraints. But why are those constraints imposed?

The sex-ratio interpretation can explain the absence of polygyny in most commercialized modern societies. Very complex societies have standing armies, and in such societies male mortality in warfare is rarely as high *proportionately* as in simpler societies. Also, with commercialization, there are more possibilities for individuals to support themselves in commercialized societies without being married. The degree of disease in the environment may also be a factor.

Bobbi Low has suggested that a high incidence of disease may reduce the prevalence of "healthy" men. In such cases, it may be to a woman's advantage to marry a healthy man even if he is already married, and it may be to a man's advantage to marry several unrelated women to maximize genetic variation (and disease resistance) among his children. Indeed, societies with many pathogens are more likely to have polygyny.[99] A recent cross-cultural study compared the degree of disease as an explanation of polygyny with the imbalanced sex-ratio explanation. Both were supported. The number of pathogens predicted particularly well in more densely populated complex societies, where pathogen load is presumably greater. The sex-ratio explanation predicted polygyny particularly well in sparser, nonstate societies.[100] Nigel Barber used data from modern nations to test these ideas. He found that sex-ratio and pathogen stress predicted polygyny in modern nations as well.[101]

Polyandry

George Peter Murdock's "World Ethnographic Sample" included only four societies (less than 1 percent of the total) in which polyandry, or the marriage of several men to one woman, was practiced.[102] When the husbands are brothers we call it **fraternal polyandry**; if they are not brothers, it is **nonfraternal polyandry**. Some Tibetans, the Toda of India, and the Sinhalese of Sri Lanka have practiced fraternal polyandry. Among some Tibetans who practice fraternal polyandry, biological paternity seems to be of no particular concern; there is no attempt to link children biologically to a particular brother, and all children are treated the same.[103]

Fraternal polyandry The marriage of a woman to two or more brothers at the same time.

Nonfraternal polyandry Marriage of a woman to two or more men who are not brothers.

One possible explanation for the practice of polyandry is a shortage of women. The Toda practiced female infanticide;[104] the Sinhalese had a shortage of women but denied the practice of female infanticide.[105] A correlation between shortage of women and polyandry would account for why polyandry is so rare in the ethnographic record; an excess of men is rare cross-culturally.

Another possible explanation is that polyandry is an adaptive response to severely limited resources. Melvyn Goldstein studied Tibetans who live in the northwestern corner of Nepal, above 12,000 feet in elevation. Cultivable land is extremely scarce there, with most families having less than an acre. The people say they practice fraternal polyandry to prevent the division of a family's farm and animals. Instead of dividing up their land among them and each taking a wife, brothers preserve the family farm by sharing a wife. Although not recognized by the Tibetans, their practice of polyandry minimizes population growth. There are as many women as men of marriageable age. But about 30 percent of the women do not marry, and although these women do have some children, they have far fewer than married women. Thus, the practice of polyandry minimizes the number of mouths to feed and therefore maximizes the standard of living of the polyandrous family. In contrast, if the Tibetans practiced monogamy and almost all women married, the birth rate would be much higher and there would be more mouths to feed with the severely limited resources.[106]

Polyandry is still customary in some Tibetan communities, although monogamous marriages actually outnumber polyandrous marriages. This is because a set of brothers may start off being married to one woman, but younger brothers may later opt to marry separately and form their own households. Also, some households have only one son or daughter and polyandrous marriages are not possible. Family wealth increases the likelihood of a young brother leaving, but this mostly happens when the polyandrous household lacks agricultural fields, herds, and opportunities for trade.[107] In polygynous societies, monogamous marriages also outnumber polygynous marriages at any given time. But the reasons are different. Most polygynous societies practice nonsororal marriages, and when a man first marries, he is married monogamously. Because significant resources are needed to marry again (a bride price is common), subsequent marriages occur later in life.

Family A social and economic unit consisting minimally of a parent and a child.

The Family

19.7 Describe and explain variation in family form.

Family form varies from one society to another and even within societies, but all societies have families. A **family** is a social and economic unit consisting minimally of one or more parents (or parent substitutes) and their children. Members of a family have certain reciprocal rights and obligations, particularly economic ones. Family members usually live in one household, but common residence is not a defining feature of families. In our society,

A Naro hunter-gatherer family in the Central Kalahari desert of Botswana.

children may live away while they go to college. Some members of a family may deliberately set up separate households to manage multiple business enterprises while maintaining economic unity.[108] In simpler societies, the family and the household tend to be indistinguishable; only in more complex societies, and in societies that become dependent on commercial exchange, may some members of a family live elsewhere.[109]

Adoption

In many societies, the family does not have enough kin in the nuclear or extended family. They need to add new members to perform all of the necessary chores or to inherit access to family property. There may be a shortage of family members because of infertility or deaths (particularly of young children) from introduced diseases or natural disasters, such as hurricanes or because the adults do not get along and cooperate in the traditional ways. Many societies adopt children to deal with one or another of these problems, or families adopt one or more related children to relieve the pressure on resources in the family that adopts the child "out."

The family Melvin Ember lived with at the beginning of his fieldwork in the Pacific islands of American Samoa had six children. The oldest, Tavita, was 11 at the time and in school most of the day, as were three of the other children. Tavita had been adopted informally. His natural mother, who lived in the same village, was a sister of Tavita's adoptive mother. By adopting Tavita "out," his natural family, which already had nine children, was relieved of the responsibility of feeding and caring for him. In addition to depopulation and hurricanes, reducing the number of mouths to feed was a common reason for adoption in Samoan villages then, as it was elsewhere in the far Pacific islands.[110] A number of factors generated unusual population growth, particularly the availability of more jobs and improved medical care (there was a medical dispensary in every village and a hospital on the main island).[111]

Of course, adoption occurs in industrial societies as well. As of the 1990s (the latest figures available), there have been more than 100,000 legally recognized adoptions in the United States per year. About 50 percent of the adoptions are of children who are relatives, and usually close relatives; a large number of these adoptions may be solutions to resource problems for the natural mothers. More than 10,000 children from abroad who are not usually relatives are adopted each year. Most of the known adoptions, foreign and domestic, are arranged by middle-class or wealthier people, since a sizeable amount of money may have been spent, particularly for foreign adoptions. Most of the adopted children, domestic and foreign, apparently turn out as well adjusted as natural children.[112]

Nuclear family A family consisting of a married couple and their young children.

Independent family A family unit consisting of one monogamous (nuclear) family, or one polygynous or one polyandrous family.

Extended family A family consisting of two or more single-parent, monogamous, polygynous, or polyandrous families linked by a blood tie.

Variation in Family Form

The minimal family has one parent (or parent substitute). Single-parent families, usually headed by the mother, are common in some societies, but most societies typically have larger families. These larger family units usually include at least one **nuclear family** (a married couple and their children), but there is often polygamy, so there may be more than one spouse with more than one set of children. If a single-parent family, nuclear family, polygynous, or polyandrous family lives alone, each is an **independent family**. However, the **extended family** is the prevailing form of family in more than half the societies known to anthropology.[113] It may consist of two or more single-parent, monogamous, polygynous, or polyandrous families linked by a blood tie. Most commonly, the extended family consists of a married couple and one or more of the married children, all living in the same house or household. The constituent nuclear families are normally linked through the parent-child tie. An extended family, however, is

Current Research and Issues

One-Parent Families: Why the Recent Increase?

In most societies known to anthropology one-parent families are relatively uncommon. However, although some parents are clearly choosing to stay single, many might prefer to marry if they could find an appropriate spouse. In some countries, and among some ethnic groups within some countries, there are many fewer males than females, and sometimes a high proportion of the males have poor economic prospects. In the former Soviet Union, males are more likely to have died from war, alcoholism, and accidents. The United States does not have such a skewed sex ratio, but in some neighborhoods, particularly poor neighborhoods, there are very high mortality rates for young males, and many males in such neighborhoods do not have work. In a study by Daniel Lichter and his colleagues, an estimated 80 African American men were available for every 100 African American women between the ages of 21 and 28. Counting only the men who are employed full- or part-time, the number of available men per 100 women dropped below 50. A recent comparison of 85 countries finds that single parenthood is much more likely when there is higher male unemployment and there are also fewer men than women of a comparable age. There may be considerable merit to the argument that one-parent families, usually headed by women, will be likely when a spouse (particularly an employed one) is hard to find.

Another popular explanation for the rise in number of one-parent families is that, in contrast to the past, women can manage without husbands because of support from the state. This scenario seems to fit Sweden, where unmarried and divorced mothers receive many social supports and allowances for maternity and educational leave. But Iceland has few social supports from the government and yet has the highest rate of out-of-wedlock births of all the Scandinavian countries. In the United States, the welfare argument fails to predict changes over time. The program called Aid to Families with Dependent Children provided aid largely to single mothers. If the theory about government help was correct, increases in such aid would generally predict increases in the percentage of mother-headed households. Yet the percentage of families receiving aid and the value of aid decreased during the 1970s, whereas the percentage of mother-headed households increased. In the 1980s, it was more difficult to go "on welfare," but the percentage of mother-headed households increased anyway.

Women might be more able to manage alone if they have high-paying employment, and therefore we might expect more one-parent families by choice as more women enter the job market. Work equity may explain the choices of some women, but recent research finds that employed women generally are *more* rather than less likely to marry.

There is, nevertheless, a general association between commercial economies and the possibility of one-parent families. Is there something about subsistence economies that promotes marriage and something about commercial economies that detracts from it? Although marriage is not universally based on love or companionship, it entails a great deal of economic and other kinds of interdependence, particularly in not-so-commercial economies. Market economies allow individuals other possibilities; goods and services can be bought and sold, and governments may take over functions that kin and family normally handle. Either by choice or necessity, the one-parent family is likely to remain an option for some people.

Sources: Burns and Scott 1994; Lichter et al. 1992; Whitehead and Popenoe 2005; Barber 2003.

sometimes composed of families linked through a sibling tie. Such a family might consist of two married brothers, their wives, and their children. Extended families may be very large, containing many relatives and including three or four generations. For a diagram of these different types of family, see Figure 19.2.

Extended-Family Households

In a society composed of extended-family households, marriage does not bring as pronounced a change in lifestyle as it does in our culture, where the couple typically moves to a new residence and forms an independent family unit. Newlyweds in extended families are assimilated into an existing family unit. Margaret Mead described such a situation in Samoa:

> *In most marriages there is no sense of setting up a new and separate establishment. The change is felt in the change of residence for either husband or wife and in the reciprocal relations which spring up between the two families. But the young couple live in the main household, simply receiving a bamboo pillow, a mosquito net and a pile of mats for their bed. . . . The wife works with all the women of the household and waits on all the men. The husband shares the enterprises of the other men and boys. Neither in personal service given or received are the two marked off as a unit.*[114]

A young couple in Samoa, as in other societies with extended families, generally has little decision-making power over the governing of the household. Often the responsibility

Applied Anthropology

The Changing Family and "Social Security": A Look at Japan

Much of the world has seen major changes in demography and family structure. People are living longer and having fewer children. Women are more often working for wages, and fewer generations are living together. These changes make it much more difficult for family to provide "social security" for the older generation as they have done in the past. In the course of this transition, governments have been pushed to step in and provide some programs for retirees, for those unable to work, and for the elderly who lack family support.

Anthropologists and other social scientists can play a significant role in helping governments to craft or change their policies. They can share their knowledge of the cultural practices, beliefs, and attitudes that must be considered when social policy is crafted for a particular group. They can identify how cultural models and expectations have changed over time. They can help uncover the stresses and ambivalences that suggest how cultures are changing or even what kinds of public programs people may be ready to accept. As an example of the insights anthropologists can share, let us look at Japan, which happens to have the most aging population in the world combined with one of the lowest birth rates.

Prior to World War II, the ideal and typical Japanese family was a small extended family of three generations—in the first generation was a married couple, in the second generation, the eldest son and his wife, and in the third generation, the unmarried children. If there were only daughters, it was common to adopt a daughter's husband as a son. The head of the household was the oldest male, who passed on the role to his eldest son. Although the eldest son was technically responsible for the care of his parents, it was his wife who did most of the work of caring for her in-laws. This cultural model, called "filial piety," worked less well after World War II. The Allied occupation of Japan made the legal family the nuclear family and declared that inheritance should be equal across siblings, including daughters. Also, in the last quarter of the 20th century, Japanese women's attitudes toward their family roles changed and the expression "Never marry the eldest son" was coined. Increasingly, newly married women negotiated living quarters separate from their in-laws. Is the cultural model of filial piety gone in Japan? Changes in the country's social structure would indicate that it is; after all, three-generation families constituted only 9 percent of Japanese families in 2008.

Given such broad social changes, we would expect the public to embrace the new programs Japan began providing for the elderly and frail in the 1990s, including some residential facilities, home care services, bath services, and day care. In 2000, the Japanese government established a mandatory long-term-care insurance program whereby everyone over 65 who needs care gets services and equipment, though what is received is decided by the elderly person in conjunction with family members. Day care has come to be commonly used at least a few days a week, particularly because of the large public baths at the centers. Bathing was particularly difficult to manage at home, and it was a service tailored to the needs of both caregivers and recipients.

But the extended family still exists as a "moral" entity: Parents continue to be viewed as important guides in the decisions of their adult children, and half of Japanese over 65 still live with their children. The Japanese still have the strong sense that the best caretaker is an adult child. Nursing homes are viewed as dumping grounds resorted to by unfilial children.

At the same time, the form filial piety is taking may be changing. Interviews with women suggest that there is considerable ambivalence regarding the tradition of caring for a mother-in-law. The young women who said "Never marry the eldest son" and chose to live in a nuclear household in the late 20th century are now voicing their opinions about who they prefer to embrace in their filial piety. They would rather take care of their own aging mothers, not their mothers-in-law.

Researchers do not pretend to have the answers for what works or how care for the elderly is paid for, but they can provide insights into what people consider important, what they are ambivalent about, and, therefore, what might work. As is clear from a look at Japan's "social security" problem, cultures are a nuanced and complicated audience for policy makers.

Sources: de la Puente et al. 2012; Lee 2010; Long et al. 2009; Traphagan 2006, 2009; Saito 1998.

of running the household rests with the senior male. Nor can the new family accumulate its own property and become independent; it is a part of the larger corporate structure:

> *So the young people bide their time. Eventually, when the old man dies or retires, they will own the homestead, they will run things. When their son grows up and marries, he will create a new subsidiary family to live with them, work for the greater glory of their extended family homestead, and wait for them to die.*[115]

The extended family is more likely than the independent nuclear family to perpetuate itself as a social unit. In contrast with the independent nuclear family, which by definition disintegrates with the death of its senior members (the parents), the extended family is always adding junior families (monogamous, polygamous, or both), whose members become the senior members when their elders die.

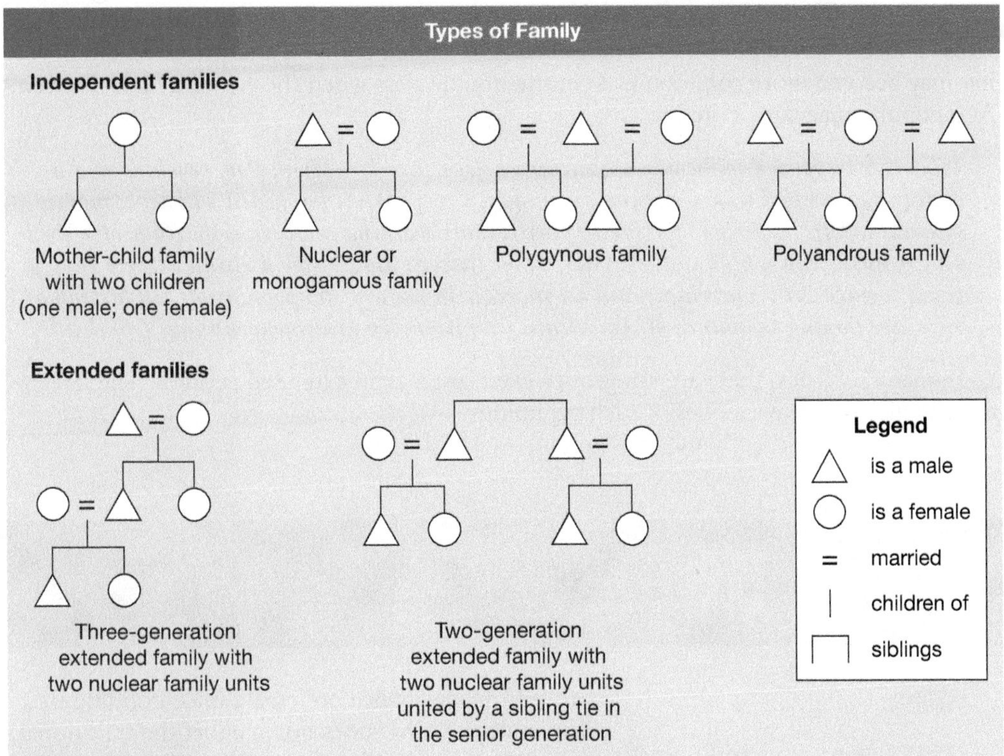

FIGURE 19.2 Anthropologists commonly use diagrams to represent family structures.

At the top are four types of independent family assuming only two children (one male, one female) and only two spouses where multiple spouses are allowed. At the bottom are two types of extended family. These diagrams show only small extended families, but extended families can have many constituent family units if there are many children as well as plural marriages.

Possible Reasons for Extended-Family Households

19.8 Explain reasons for extended-family households.

Why do most societies known to anthropology have extended-family households? Such households usually occur in sedentary, agricultural societies, suggesting that the type of economy could be a determining factor. Agricultural life, as opposed to a hunter-gatherer life, may favor extended families. The extended family may be a social mechanism that prevents the economically ruinous division of family property in societies in which property such as cultivated land is important. Conversely, the need for mobility in hunter-gatherer societies may make it difficult to maintain extended-family households. During certain seasons, the hunter-gatherers may be obliged to divide into nuclear families that scatter into other areas.[116]

But agriculture is only a weak predictor of extended-family households. Many agriculturalists lack them, and many nonagricultural societies have them. A different theory is that extended-family households come to prevail in societies that have incompatible activity requirements—that is, requirements that cannot be met by a mother or a father in a one-family household. In other words, extended-family households are generally favored when the work a mother has to do outside the home (cultivating fields or gathering foods far away) makes it difficult for her to also care for her children and do other household tasks. Similarly, extended families may be favored when the required outside activities of a father (warfare, trading trips, or wage labor far away) make it difficult for him to do the subsistence work required of males. There is cross-cultural evidence that societies with such incompatible activity requirements are more likely to have extended-family households than societies with compatible activity requirements, regardless of whether or not the society is agricultural. Even though they have incompatible activity requirements, however, societies with commercial or monetary exchange may not have extended-family households. In commercial societies, a family may be able to obtain the necessary help by "buying" the required services.[117]

Of course, even in societies with money economies, not everyone can buy required services. Those who are poor may need to live in extended families, and extended-family living may become more common even in the middle class when the economy is depressed. As a popular magazine noted,

> *Whatever happened to the all-American nuclear family—Mom, Pop, two kids and a cuddly dog, nestled under one cozy, mortgaged roof? What happened was an economic squeeze: layoffs, fewer jobs for young people, more working mothers, a shortage of affordable housing and a high cost of living. Those factors, along with a rising divorce rate, a trend toward later marriages and an increase in the over-65 population, all hitting at once, are forcing thousands of Americans into living in multigenerational families.*[118]

In many societies, there are kin groups even larger than extended families. The next chapter discusses the varieties of such groupings.

Summary and Review

Marriage

19.1 Define marriage in anthropological terms.

- Marriage is customary in nearly every known society, even though humans can survive and reproduce without marriage.
- Although its form varies, marriage everywhere is understood to be a socially approved sexual and economic union, usually between a woman and a man.
- Marriage is presumed, by both the couple and others, to be more or less permanent, and it subsumes reciprocal rights and obligations between the two spouses and between spouses and their future children.

? What are some of the exceptions to the universality of marriage?

Why Is Marriage Nearly Universal?

19.2 Explain the near-universality of marriage across cultures.

- Various traditional explanations for marriage suggest that marriage solves problems found in all societies—how to share the products of a gender division of labor; how to care for infants, who are dependent for a long time; and how to minimize sexual competition.
- Marriage is not the only way to share the products of their labor, to support the prolonged dependency of infants, or to minimize sexual competition, so those explanations cannot explain near universality of marriage.
- Comparative evidence on female-male bonding in mammals and birds does not support the traditional theories explaining near universality of marriage.
- Bird and mammal species in which mothers cannot feed themselves and their babies at the same time *do* typically form male-female bonds, which may be true also for humans and may support a reason for marriage.

? What are four major explanations about why marriage exists? What are the pros and cons of each?

How Does One Marry?

19.3 Identify the various ways that marriage is marked out in different societies and the economic exchanges that accompany it.

- How one marries varies considerably across cultures.
- Marking the onset of marriage seems to be important, whether or not an actual ceremony takes place. Marriage ceremonies may symbolize hostility between the two families or promote harmony between them.
- Marriage involves economic factors, explicit or not, in about 75 percent of the societies known to anthropology. Bride price is the most common form; bride service is second most common. Other forms include exchange of females, gift exchange, and forms of the dowry.

? What are some of the ways marriages vary? What kinds of economic transactions are associated with marriage?

Restrictions on Marriage: The Universal Incest Taboo

19.4 Critically assess different explanations for the universality of the incest taboo.

- The incest taboo, found in *all* cultures, may be the most rigid regulation. The incest taboo prohibits sexual intercourse or marriage between some categories of kin, most universally, between mother and son, father and daughter, and brother and sister.
- Childhood-familiarity theory says that people who have been closely associated with each other since earliest childhood are not sexually attracted to each other and would avoid marriage with each other, but it does not explain incest taboos for first-cousin marriage.
- Freud's psychoanalytic theory proposed that the incest taboo is a reaction against unconscious, unacceptable desires, but it does not explain why society needs an explicit taboo nor does it account for some evidence of childhood aversion.
- Family-disruption theory proposes that the familial incest taboo curtails sexual competition among family members to keep the family intact, but it does not adequately account for why independent adult brothers and sisters could not interact sexually.
- Cooperation theory suggests that the incest taboo promotes cooperation among family groups by supporting interfamily marriage, thus helping communities to survive, but the evidence does not seem to support it.
- Inbreeding theory focuses on the damaging biological consequences of the practice. Evidence supports that societies are aware of these dangers. Adaptive reproductive and hence competitive advantages probably accrued to groups practicing the taboo.

? How might the universality of the familial incest taboo be explained? Critically assess the logic of the theories and the evidence.

Whom Should One Marry?

19.5 Discuss the types of restrictions on whom one can marry.

- In addition to the familial incest taboo, societies often have other rules regarding the mate such as whether they may be cousins, whether they should come from the same community, and even whether the couple has choice in the matter.
- Parents invariably play a role, directly or indirectly, in who their offspring marry, including negotiating arranged marriages, which tend to increase economic benefits. Arranged marriages are becoming less common, and couples have stronger voices in selecting partners.
- Exogamy requires that the marriage partner come from outside one's own kin group or community. Endogamy obliges a person to marry within a particular group. The caste groups of India traditionally have been endogamous.
- When first-cousin marriage is allowed, it is usually between cross-cousins (children of siblings of the opposite sex). Marriage among parallel cousins (children of siblings of the same sex) is rare, but some Muslim societies have preferred such marriages.
- Large and densely populated societies may permit cousin marriages more often because such marriage are less likely in large populations. Small societies that have lost many people to epidemics may permit cousin marriage to provide enough mating possibilities.
- Cultural rules that oblige individuals to marry the spouse of a deceased relative are exceedingly common. The levirate custom obliges a man to marry his brother's widow; the sororate custom obliges a woman to marry her deceased sister's husband.

? What are some of the ways cultures restrict or express preferences for whom one marries?

How Many Does One Marry?

19.6 Describe the three different rules regarding how many persons one can marry, and explain social or economic reasons for each.

- Most Western societies allow only monogamy (one spouse at a time) and prohibit polygamy (plural spouse marriage). However, most societies known to anthropology have allowed some form of polygamy—polygyny, or more rarely polyandry or group marriage.
- Polygyny, the form of marriage that allows a man to be married to more than one woman at the same time, has been and is very common, especially among those with high status. Evidence seems to show that polygyny provides economic and political advantages.
- The theory that polygyny is permitted in societies that have a long postpartum sex taboo predicts it less strongly than explanations that it is a response to an excess of women over men and that a society will allow polygyny when men marry at an older age than women.
- Polyandry, the marriage of one woman to more than one man at the same time, is practiced in just a few societies. Polyandry may be practiced when there are a shortage of women or as an adaptive response to severely limited resources.

- Group marriage, in which more than one man is married to more than one woman at the same time, sometimes occurs but is not customary in any known society.

> How are monogamy, polygyny, and polyandry defined, and what may explain why each form is preferred in societies that practice that form?

The Family

19.7 Describe and explain variation in family form.

- All societies have families, but family forms vary considerably. A family is a social and economic unit consisting minimally of one or more parents (or parent substitute) and their children. Family members have reciprocal rights and obligations, particularly economic ones.
- Adoption occurs when a family does not have enough kin to perform chores or to inherit or when one family needs to relieve pressure on resources.
- The extended family is the prevailing form of family in more than half the societies known to anthropology and may consist of two or more single-parent, monogamous, polygynous, or polyandrous families linked by a blood tie.
- In most societies known to anthropology, one-parent families are relatively uncommon. However, in many Western countries there has been a dramatic increase recently in the percentage of one-parent families, most of which are female-headed.
- Single parenthood occurs more with higher male unemployment and lower ratios of men to women of comparable age and in commercial economies. Evidence does not support the idea that single-parenthood increases because the state supports women to manage independently.
- Marriage in an extended family does not bring as pronounced a change in lifestyle as it does when marriage forms an independent unit. The extended family is more likely than the independent nuclear family to perpetuate itself as a social unit.

> What defines the concept of family?

Possible Reasons for Extended-Family Households

19.8 Explain reasons for extended-family households.

- Extended-family households usually occur in sedentary, agricultural societies and may be a social mechanism that prevents economically damaging division of family property. But agriculture is only a weak predictor of extended-family households.
- Another theory is that extended-family households are generally favored when a mother's work outside the home makes it difficult to also care for her children and do household tasks or when the required outside activities of a father interfere with subsistence tasks.
- Cross-cultural evidence supports the above theory, regardless of whether or not the society is agricultural. However, in commercial societies, a family may be able to obtain the necessary help by "buying" the required services.
- In the United States, layoffs, fewer jobs, more working mothers, affordable housing shortages, high costs, a rising divorce rate, increasingly later marriages, and increases in the over-65 population are leading to increases in the number of extended families.

> How would you describe and explain variation in family form?

Think on it

1. Will it remain customary in our society to **marry**? Why do you think it will or will not?
2. Do you think **extended-family** households will become more common in our society? Why?
3. Why is **polyandry** so much less common than **polygyny**?

Marital Residence and Kinship

CHAPTER 20

LEARNING OBJECTIVES

- 20.1 Describe the various patterns of marital residence.
- 20.2 Discuss the structure of kinship and distinguish among the various types of affiliation.
- 20.3 Discuss variation in unilineal descent systems.
- 20.4 Describe the functions of unilineal descent systems.
- 20.5 Describe ambilineal systems.
- 20.6 Discuss how residence can vary.
- 20.7 Explain the emergence of unilineal descent systems.
- 20.8 Explain how ambilineal and bilateral systems might emerge.
- 20.9 Explain the various systems of kinship terminology.

In a well-known prose poem published in 1915, Robert Frost tells the story of Mary and Warren, a married couple who own a subsistence farm in the United States. One day the couple's old hired hand, Silas, returns to them after having quit the farm in search of paying work. He is ill and dying. Mary takes him in, but when she tells her husband that Silas has returned "home," Warren, who is less sympathetic, corrects her, saying, Home is where, when you have to go there, they have to take you in.

"We," he adds, are not Silas's "kin." Mary, who badly wants to help the old man, is quick to appease her husband by agreeing: "I should have called it something you somehow haven't to deserve."[1]

In a few words, Frost captures what all societies known to anthropology believe about kinship: Kin are the people who are obligated to help you (and you they), whether the help is deserved or not. But societies differ in whom a society defines as "kin," which kin you affiliate with, which kin you live near, how much beyond the immediate family kin matter, and *what* rights and obligations apply to *which* kin. Thus the meaning and the structure of kinship varies.

Before societies formed governments, courts, police departments, armies, and other services, they often depended on their kinship groups to maintain social order, divide up property and goods, and protect the community from harm. Indeed, kinship often determined the destiny of the individual. So fundamental have the rules of kinship been to human culture that they remain central to many people's belief systems even when their economic and social well-being no longer depend upon it.

Why, then, is kinship beyond and even within families less important in North America and other similar societies? Part of the answer lies in an economy where goods and labor are bought and sold, which compels adult men and women to go where the work is. They usually move away and establish a new place of residence apart from their parents or other relatives when they marry, if they have not already moved away before. *Neolocal* (new place) residence profoundly weakens the strength of kinship ties and kinship groups. Living with or near kin, in contrast, makes the formation of strong kin groups more likely. And living with or near kin is the prevailing pattern in most of the world's societies.

Because the rules of kinship are culturally determined, we might expect to find as many kinds of kinship structures as there are societies. Yet, remarkably, scholars have found that there are only a limited number of patterns of kinship structures observed the world over. Moreover, the different aspects of kinship are related to each other. Rules about where couples live after they marry predict the structure of kinship groups, and these in turn predict what types of kin terms they use to refer to their relatives. In North American society, for instance, newlyweds usually set up a separate household. An anthropologist who happens to come from a different kind of society can hazard a pretty good guess about the importance of the nuclear family from the fact that the North American terms for *mother* and *father* are not commonly used to refer to anyone outside the nuclear family, whereas in most societies these terms refer to other people as well; *father* may be the term for the biological father and the father's brother.

As we explore the kinship systems and marital residence patterns of the world, we will see that in most societies the nuclear family is embedded in an important extended family or other larger kin group. Many societies have kin groups that include several or many families and hundreds or even thousands of people, and kinship plays a powerful role in many aspects of an individual's life. But even in societies where kinship is not so important, kin become more important in certain conditions. We may recall, for example, that during the recession in the United States between 2007 and 2009, 1.3 million men and women between the ages of 24 and 34 moved in with their parents. Many elderly people moved in with their relatives as well.[2] Kin, it seems, still existed, and they still had to "take you in."

Patterns of Marital Residence

20.1 Describe the various patterns of marital residence.

In many industrial and postindustrial societies, a young man and woman establish **neolocal residence** residence when they marry, setting up a new household apart from their parents and other relatives. In the United States and Canada, some upper-income families begin earlier than others to train their children to live away from home by sending them to boarding schools at age 13 or 14, as well as sleep-away summer camps even earlier. Young adults of all income levels learn to live away from home most of the year if they join the army or attend an out-of-town college. So familiar is neolocal residence to us that we tend to assume that all societies must follow the same practice.

On the contrary, of the 565 societies in Murdock's "World Ethnographic Sample," only about 5 percent have had the practice of setting up separate households for newlyweds.[3] In the vast majority of societies, then, a new couple lives within, or very close to, the household of either the groom's or the bride's parents or other close relatives. It stands to reason that when a newly married couple lives near kin, relatives will play important roles in their lives and those of their offspring. As we will see, the practice of living with and near kin has meant that the kin group has been the basis of social organization in many cultures.

The smallest building block of a society's social structure is the family, usually comprised of at least one married couple and their eventual offspring. With few exceptions, couples in almost all societies live together after they are married. As we noted above, married couples in most societies customarily live with or near kin. Therefore, some young people must leave home when they marry. But which married offspring remain at or near home and which reside elsewhere? We pay particular attention to where these new family units take root and grow because it can predict *which* relatives and other allied groups are likely to be important in a society. Although societies vary in the way they deal with this question, the prevailing pattern of marital residence is likely to be one of the following:

Neolocal residence A pattern of residence whereby a married couple lives separately, and usually at some distance, from the kin of both spouses.

Patrilocal residence A pattern of residence in which a married couple lives with or near the husband's parents.

Matrilocal residence A pattern of residence in which a married couple lives with or near the wife's parents.

Bilocal residence A pattern of residence in which a married couple lives with or near either the husband's parents or the wife's parents

Avunculocal residence A pattern of residence in which a married couple settles with or near the husband's mother's brother.

1. **Patrilocal residence**. Sons stay and daughters leave, so that a married couple lives with or near the husband's parents (67 percent of all societies).
2. **Matrilocal residence**. Daughters stay and sons leave, so that a married couple lives with or near the wife's parents (15 percent of all societies).
3. **Bilocal (or ambilocal) residence.** Either the son or the daughter may leave, so that the married couple lives with or near either the wife's or the husband's parents (7 percent of all societies).
4. **Avunculocal residence**. Both the son and daughter normally leave, but the son and his wife settle with or near his mother's brother (4 percent of all societies).[4]
5. **Neolocal residence.** Both sons and daughters leave; married couples live apart from the relatives of both spouses (5 percent of all societies).

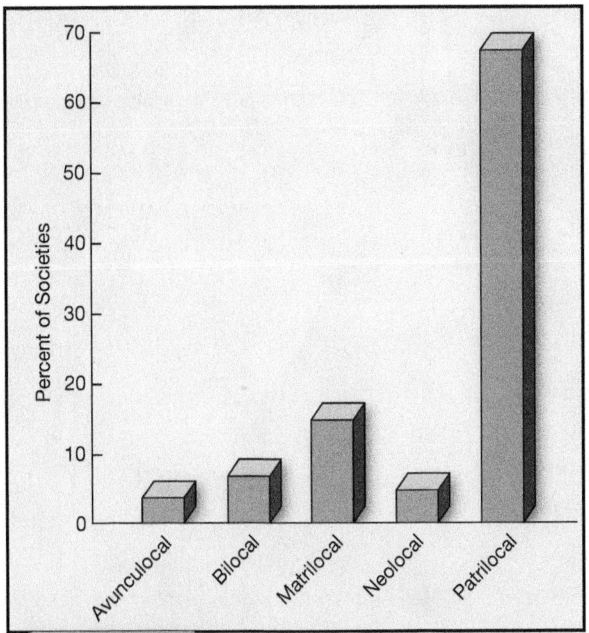

FIGURE 20.1 **Percentage of Societies in the Ethnographic Record with Various Marital Residence Patterns**

Source: Calculated from Allan D. Coult and Robert W. Habenstein 1965.

In these definitions, we use the phrase "the married couple lives *with or near*" a particular set of relatives. When couples live with or near the kin of one spouse, the couple may live in the same household with those kin, creating an *extended-family* household, or they may live separately in an *independent-family* household, but nearby. (Also, in contrast to bilocal residence, matrilocal, patrilocal, and avunculocal residence each specify only one pattern and are often called nonoptional or **unilocal residence**.)

unilocal residence A pattern of residence (patrilocal, matrilocal, or avunculocal) that specifies just one set of relatives that the married couple lives with or near.

How does place of residence affect the social life of the couple? Of course, it largely determines which people the couple interacts with and depends upon. The group the couple joins is also likely to be more influential in the lives of their offspring. Whether the couple lives in or near the husband's or the wife's parent's place can also be expected to have important consequences for their status. If married couples live patrilocally, as occurs in most societies, the wife may be far from her own kin. The feeling of being an outsider may be particularly strong if the wife has moved into a patrilocal extended-family household. She will be an outsider among a group of male relatives who have grown up together.

Among the Tiv of central Nigeria,[5] the patrilocal extended family consists of the "great father," who is the head of the household; his younger brothers; his sons; and his younger brothers' sons; followed by all the in-marrying wives and all unmarried children. The sisters and daughters of the head of household who have married will have gone to live where their husbands live. Authority is strongly vested in the male line and particularly in the oldest male of the household. The "great father" determines bride price, settles disputes, administers punishment, and plans for new buildings.

If, on the other hand, the husband comes to live with or near his wife's parents, the wife and her kin take on greater importance, and the husband is the outsider. As we shall see, however, matrilocal marital residence does not endow women with the same power that patrilocal residence confers on men.

Three Iroquois women sing in an Iroquois longhouse in Ontario. The core of a traditional longhouse were matrilineally related women.

The Structure of Kinship

20.2 Discuss the structure of kinship and distinguish among the various types of affiliation.

Anthropologists often speak of the web of kinship as providing the main structure of social action in noncommercial societies. Kinship connections can structure many areas of social life—from the access an individual has to productive resources to the kinds of political alliances formed between communities and larger territorial groups. In some societies, kinship connections have an important bearing on matters of life and death.

Recall the society Shakespeare described in *Romeo and Juliet*. The deadly feud between the kin groups of Romeo, who belonged to the house (or *lineage*) of Montague, and Juliet, who was of the house of Capulet, would lead to their own famously tragic fate. Although Verona in the late medieval period, when the play takes place, was a thriving city-state and a center of commerce, its daily life and political system were dominated by several competing—and at times feuding—kin groups. Sets of kin of common descent—that is, descended from the same ancestor—lived together, and allegiance to kin was a serious matter. If a commercial (though preindustrial) society that was ruled by princes and councils of lords could be so structured by kinship, we can imagine how much more essential kinship connections and kin groups are for establishing social order and keeping the peace in noncommercial societies.

If kinship is important, there is still the question of which set of kin a person affiliates with and depends on. After all, if every single relative were regarded as equally important, there would be an unmanageably large number of people depending on each other and, perhaps, competing for the group's limited resources. Consequently, most societies in which kinship connections are important have rules that assign each person to a particular and definable set of kin.

rules of descent Rules that connect individuals with particular sets of kin because of known or presumed common ancestry.

unilineal descent Affiliation with a group of kin through descent links of one sex only.

Patrilineal descent The rule of descent that affiliates individuals with kin of both sexes related to them through men only.

Types of Affiliation with Kin

Societies observe three main types of affiliation with kin: *unilineal descent*, *ambilineal descent*, and *bilateral kinship*. The first two types, unilineal and ambilineal descent, are based on **rules of descent**, which are rules that connect individuals with particular sets of kin because of known or presumed common ancestry. By the particular rule of descent operating in their society, individuals can know more or less immediately which set of kin to turn to for support and help. As we shall see, the interconnections of bilateral kinship, which is not based on rules of descent or ancestry, are more ambiguous.

Unilineal Descent When a person is affiliated with a group of kin through descent links of one sex only—either males only or females only—the kin group is said to follow **unilineal descent**. Unilineal descent can be either patrilineal or matrilineal.

1. **Patrilineal descent** affiliates individuals with kin of both sexes related to them *through men only*. Just as patrilocal residence is much more common than matrilocal residence, patrilineal descent is more common than matrilineal descent. As Figure 20.2 illustrates, children in patrilineal systems in each generation belong to the kin group of their father; their father, in turn, belongs to the group of his father; and so on. Although a man's sons and daughters are all members of the same descent group, affiliation with that group is transmitted only by the sons to their children.

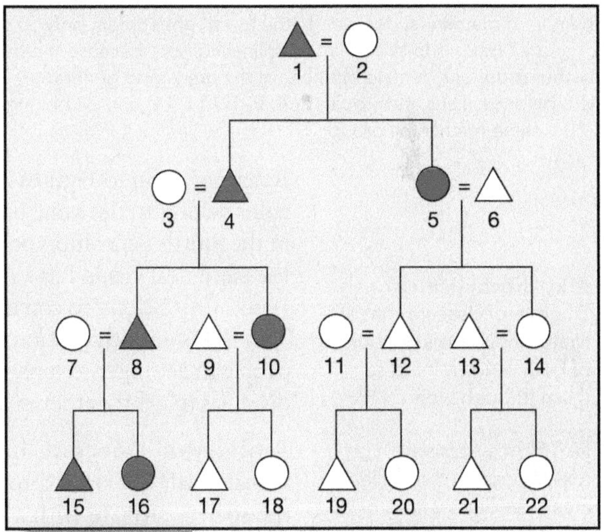

FIGURE 20.2 Patrilineal Descent

Individuals 4 and 5, who are the children of 1 and 2, affiliate with their father's patrilineal kin group, represented by the color red. In the next generation, the children of 3 and 4 also belong to the red kin group, because they take their descent from their father, who is a member of that group. However, the children of 5 and 6 do not belong to this patrilineal group, because they take their descent from their father, who is a member of a different group. That is, although the mother of 12 and 14 belongs to the red patrilineal group, she cannot pass on her descent affiliation to her children, and because her husband (6) does not belong to her patrilineage, her children (12 and 14) belong to their father's group. In the fourth generation, only 15 and 16 belong to the red patrilineal group, because their father is the only male member of the preceding generation who belongs to the red patrilineal group. In this diagram, then, 1, 4, 5, 8, 10, 15, and 16 are affiliated by patrilineal descent; all the other individuals belong to other patrilineal groups.

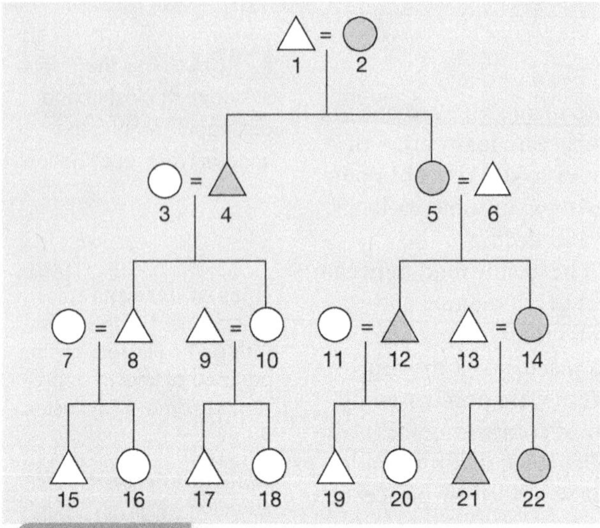

FIGURE 20.3 Matrilineal Descent

Individuals 4 and 5, who are the children of 1 and 2, affiliate with their mother's kin group, represented by the color green. In the next generation, the children of 5 and 6 also belong to the green kin group, because they take their descent from their mother, who is a member of that group. However, the children of 3 and 4 do not belong to this matrilineal group, because they take their descent from their mother, who is a member of a different group; their father, although a member of the green matrilineal group, cannot pass his affiliation on to them under the rule of matrilineal descent. In the fourth generation, only 21 and 22 belong to the green matrilineal group, because their mother is the only female member of the preceding generation who belongs. Thus, individuals 2, 4, 5, 12, 14, 21, and 22 belong to the same matrilineal group.

2. **Matrilineal descent** affiliates individuals with kin of both sexes related to them *through women only*. In each generation, then, children belong to the kin group of their mother. As Figure 20.3 illustrates, a woman's sons and daughters are all members of the same descent group, but only her daughters can pass on their descent affiliation to their children.

Unilineal rules of descent affiliate an individual with a line of kin extending back in time and into the future. By virtue of this line of descent, whether it extends through males or females, some very close relatives are excluded. For example, in a patrilineal system, your mother and your mother's parents do not belong to your patrilineal group, but your father and his father (and their sisters) do. In your own generation in a matrilineal or patrilineal system, some cousins are excluded, and in your children's generation, some of your nieces and nephews are excluded.

However, although unilineal rules of descent exclude certain relatives from membership in one's kin group, the excluded relatives are not necessarily ignored or forgotten, just as practical considerations restrict the effective size of kinship networks in our own society. Indeed, in many unilineal societies, excluded kin may be entrusted with important responsibilities. For example, when a person dies in a patrilineal society, members of the mother's patrilineal descent group may customarily be accorded the right to perform certain rituals at the funeral.

Unilineal rules of descent can form clear-cut, and hence unambiguous, kinship groups. These groups can, and often do, act as separate units even after the death of individual members. Referring again to Figures 20.2 and 20.3, we can see that the individuals in the highlighted color belong to the same patrilineal or matrilineal descent group without ambiguity; individuals in the fourth generation belong to the group just as much as those in the first generation. Say the patrilineal group has a name, the Hawks. Individuals know whether or not they are Hawks. If not, they belong to some other group, for each person belongs to only one line of descent. This fact is important if kin groups are to act as separate, nonoverlapping units. It is difficult for people to act together unless they know exactly who should get together. And it is easier for individuals to act together as a group if each one belongs to only one such group or line.

Matrilineal descent The rule of descent that affiliates individuals with kin of both sexes related to them through women only.

ambilineal descent The rule of descent that affiliates individuals with groups of kin related to them through men or women.

double descent or double unilineal descent A system that affiliates individuals with a group of matrilineal kin for some purposes and with a group of patrilineal kin for other purposes.

Ambilineal Descent In contrast to unilineal descent, **ambilineal descent** affiliates individuals with kin related to them through men *or* women. In other words, some people in the society affiliate with a group of kin through their fathers; others affiliate through their mothers. Consequently, the descent groups show both female and male genealogical links, as illustrated in Figure 20.4.

The three rules of descent—patrilineal, matrilineal, and ambilineal—are usually, but not always, mutually exclusive. Most societies can be characterized as having only one rule of descent, but two principles are sometimes used to affiliate individuals with different sets of kin for different purposes. Some societies have what is called **double descent or double unilineal descent**, whereby individuals affiliate for some purposes with a group of matrilineal kin and for other purposes with a group of patrilineal kin. Thus, two rules of descent, each traced through links of one sex only, are operative at the same time. For example, if there is a patrilineal system and a matrilineal one, individuals would belong to two groups at birth: the matrilineal group of the mother and the patrilineal group of the father. Imagine combining Figures 20.2 and 20.3. Individuals 4 and 5 would belong to both the patrilineal group (red in Figure 20.2) to which their father belongs and the matrilineal group (green in Figure 20.3) to which their mother belongs.

The way a society assigns names does not necessarily convey information about a rule of descent. Many societies, even with rules of descent, do not give individuals the name of their kin group or of their father or mother. For example, among the patrilineal Luo of Kenya, babies were traditionally given names that described the circumstances of their birth (such as "born-in-the-morning"); their names did not include their father's or kin group's name. Only after the British established a colony in Kenya, and continuing after independence, did children get their father's personal name as a surname. (The British themselves did not acquire surnames until the Middle Ages.)

It is customary in North American society for children to have a last, or "family," name—usually their father's last name. All the people with the same last name do not conceive of themselves as descended from the same common ancestor; all Smiths do not consider themselves related. Nor do such people act together for any particular purpose. Many societies, including our own, do not have lineal (matrilineal, patrilineal, or ambilineal) descent groups—sets of kin who believe they descend from a common ancestor. These are societies with **bilateral kinship**. *Bilateral* means "two-sided," and in this case it refers to the fact that one's relatives on both the mother's and father's sides are equal in importance or, more usually, in unimportance. Kinship reckoning in bilateral societies does not refer to common descent but rather is horizontal, moving outward from close to more distant relatives rather than upward to common ancestors (see Figure 20.5).

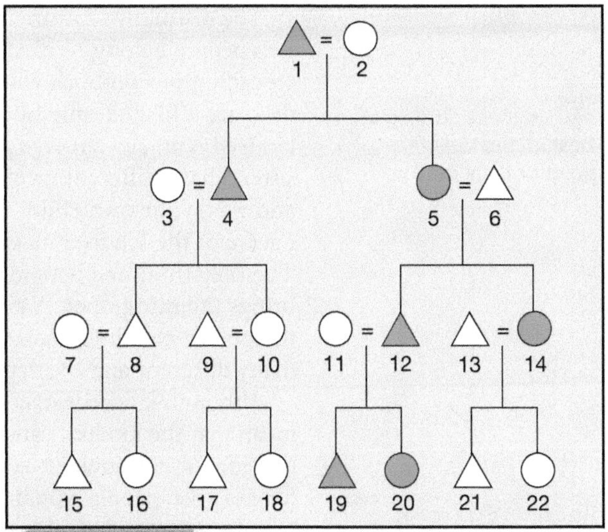

FIGURE 20.4 Ambilineal Descent

A hypothetical ambilineal group of kin is indicated by the color blue. Members 4 and 5 belong to this group because of a male link, their father (1); members 12 and 14 belong because of a female link, their mother (5); and members 19 and 20 belong because of a male link, their father (12). This is a hypothetical example because any combination of lineal links is possible in an ambilineal descent group.

The term **kindred** describes a person's bilateral set of relatives who may be called upon for some purpose. Most bilateral societies have kindreds that overlap in membership. In North America, we think of the kindred as including the people we might invite to weddings, funerals, or some other ceremonial occasion; a kindred, however, is not usually a definite group. As anyone who has been involved in creating a wedding invitation list knows, a great deal of time may be spent deciding which relatives ought to be invited and which ones can legitimately be excluded. Societies with bilateral kinship differ in precisely how distant relatives have to be before they are lost track of or before they are not included in ceremonial activities. In societies such as our own, in which kinship is relatively unimportant, fewer relatives are included in the kindred. In other bilateral societies, however, where kinship connections are somewhat more important, more would be included.

bilateral kinship The type of kinship system in which individuals affiliate more or less equally with their mother's and father's relatives.

kindred A bilateral set of close relatives who may be called upon for some purpose.

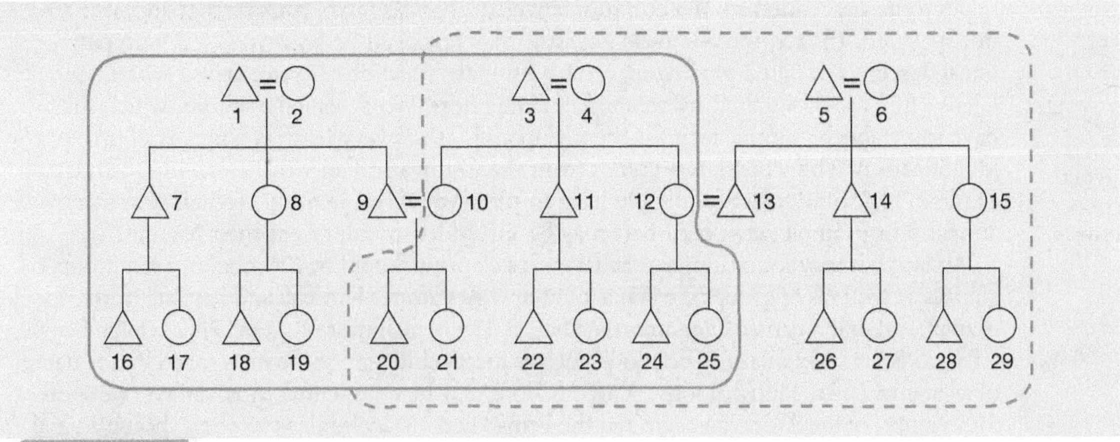

FIGURE 20.5 Bilateral Kinship

In a bilateral system, the kindred is ego-centered; hence, it varies with different points of reference (except for brothers and sisters). In any bilateral society, the kindred minimally includes parents, grandparents, aunts, uncles, and first cousins. So, if we look at the close kindred of the brother and sister 20 and 21 (enclosed by the solid line), it would include their parents (9 and 10), their aunts and uncles (7, 8, 11, 12), their grandparents (1, 2, 3, 4), and their first cousins (16–19, 22–25). But the kindred of the brother and sister 24 and 25 (shown by the dashed line) includes only some of the same people (3, 4, 10–12, 20–23); in addition, the kindred of 24 and 25 includes people not in the kindred of 20 and 21 (5, 6, 13–15, 26–29).

ego In the reckoning of kinship, the reference point or focal person.

The distinctive feature of bilateral kinship is that, aside from brothers and sisters, no two people belong to exactly the same kin group. Your kindred contains close relatives spreading out on both your mother's and father's sides, but the members of your kindred are affiliated only by way of their connection to you (**ego**, or the focus). Thus, the kindred is an *ego-centered* group of kin. Because different people (except for brothers and sisters) have different mothers and fathers, your first cousins will have different kindreds, and even your own children will have different kindred from yours. The ego-centered nature of the kindred makes it difficult for it to serve as a permanent or persistent group. The only thing the people in a kindred have in common is the ego or focal person who brings them together. A kindred usually has no name, no common purpose, and only temporary meetings centered around the ego.[6] Furthermore, because everyone belongs to many different and overlapping kindreds, the society is not divided into clear-cut groups.

Although kindreds may not form clear-cut groups as in a unilineal society, this does not mean that the kindred cannot be turned to for help. In a bilateral society, the kindred may provide social insurance against adversity. Among the Chipewyan of subarctic Canada, for example, people would borrow a fishing net from a kindred member, or ask a kindred member to provide child care for a young person whose parent was ill. But recently, with the national and provincial governments providing resources such as housing and medical assistance, and with the increase in opportunities for wage labor, the kindred has ceased to be the main source of help for people in need. Aid from the state is making kinship less useful.[7]

lineage A set of kin whose members trace descent from a common ancestor through known links.

20.3 Discuss variation in unilineal descent systems.

Variation in Unilineal Descent Systems

In a society with unilineal descent, people usually refer to themselves as belonging to a particular unilineal group or set of groups because they believe they share common descent in either the male (patrilineal) or female (matrilineal) line. Anthropologists distinguish several types of unilineal descent groups: lineages, clans, phratries, and moieties.

Lineages A **lineage** is a set of kin whose members trace descent from a common ancestor through known links. There may be *patrilineages* or *matrilineages*, depending on whether the links are traced through males only or through females only. Lineages are often designated by the name of the common male or female ancestor. In some societies, people belong to a hierarchy of lineages. That is, they first trace their descent back to the ancestor of a minor lineage, then to the ancestor of a larger and more inclusive major lineage, and so on.

clan A set of kin whose members believe themselves to be descended from a common ancestor or ancestress but cannot specify the links back to that founder; often designated by a totem. Also called a **sib**.

sib See Clan.

totem A plant or animal associated with a clan (sib) as a means of group identification; may have other special significance for the group.

Clans A **clan** (also sometimes called a **sib**) is a set of kin whose members believe themselves to be descended from a common ancestor, but the links back to that ancestor are not specified. In fact, the common ancestor may not even be known. Clans with patrilineal descent are called *patriclans;* clans with matrilineal descent are called *matriclans.* Clans often are designated by an animal name (Bear, Wolf), called a **totem**, which may have some special significance for the group and, at the very least, is a means of group identification. The word *totem* comes from the Ojibwa Indian word *ototeman*, "a relative of mine." In some societies, people have to observe taboos relating to their clan totem animal. For example, clan members may be forbidden to kill or eat their totem.

Although it may seem strange that an animal or plant should be a symbol of a kin group, animals as symbols of groups are familiar in our own culture. Football and baseball teams, for example, are often named after animals (Detroit Tigers, Baltimore Ravens, Philadelphia Eagles, Chicago Bears). Voluntary associations, such as men's clubs, are sometimes called by the name of an animal (Elks, Moose, Lions). Entire nations may be represented by an animal; we speak, for instance, of the American eagle and the British lion.[8] Why humans so often choose animal names to represent groups is an intriguing question for which we have no tested answer as yet.

phratry A unilineal descent group composed of a number of supposedly related clans (sibs).

moiety A unilineal descent group in a society that is divided into two such maximal groups; there may be smaller unilineal descent groups as well.

Phratries A **phratry** is a unilineal descent group composed of supposedly related clans or sibs. As with clans, the descent links in phratries are unspecified.

Moieties When a whole society is divided into two unilineal descent groups, we call each group a **moiety**. (The word *moiety* comes from a French word meaning "half.") The people in each moiety believe themselves to be descended from a common ancestor, although

Migrants and Immigrants

Blood Is Thicker Than Water

With the spread of money economies, many societies no longer have important functioning kin groups. Yet the customary functions of such large kin groups as lineages, clans, phratries, and moieties are far from disappearing in the modern world. Lineages continue to be important for many Chinese, as well as for people in various parts of Africa and on islands in the Pacific. In some societies, lineages and clans still control the cultivable land and other valuable property. And, where they no longer serve a direct economic purpose, kinship groups can nonetheless provide social order, a sense of identity, and a belief system.

The duties and rights societies associate with kinship may be particularly useful when it comes time to migrate to other countries. When that time comes, and it comes for millions of people every year, "blood is thicker than water," as the old saying goes. Migrants generally look to settle near or with relatives at first. The relatives may be genealogically close (siblings, uncles, aunts). Or they may be more distantly related members of one's lineage or clan. Indeed, if you come from a region that has lineages, the first person you might look up (even before you leave home) might be a lineage mate.

This is often what happens when Chinese from the Hong Kong area go abroad to seek their fortune. Consider the lineage known as the "Man," one of the five major lineages that dominated political life until the 1960s in the Hong Kong New Territories. Anthropologist James L. Watson has studied this group for more than 35 years, in the area around Hong Kong and in other parts of the world to which they have migrated. The Man had survived for nearly six centuries on a kind of rice grown in the salty paddies along the Shenzhen River, which became the border between British Hong Kong and China in 1898.

San Tin's farmers had faced a crisis in the early 1950s. The markets for their rice were located on the Chinese side of the river, which was no longer regularly accessible. Unlike other lineages in the area, the Man could not convert to growing vegetables or white rice, which could not be grown in their salty paddies. They had two choices: go to Hong Kong to work in its booming factories or migrate to England to work in Chinese restaurants. Just before the British authorities banned migration to England in 1962, 85 to 90 percent of San Tin's able-bodied men left for Britain, lineage mates following lineage mates, to work in factories and hotels as well as restaurants.

The migrants had little money and few assets. Yet, by the mid-1970s, the diaspora of San Tin had managed to establish a chain of Chinese restaurants in England and other parts of Europe. Today, most of the grandchildren of the original migrants are wealthy professionals, and some are multimillionaires. Many in the current generation cannot speak or read Cantonese, the Chinese language of their ancestors. They now speak English, Dutch, or German.

People who consider themselves members of the Man lineage trace their descent from Man Sai-go, the ancestor who settled near San Tin in the 14th century. Today, about 4,000 people living in more than 20 countries claim descent from Man Sai-go. The village of San Tin became a remittance economy, with wives, children, and elders left behind, supported by the money sent home by the migrants who returned to San Tin for a visit every few years and then went back to Europe to work. Many of the migrants, when they retired, decided to join their children's families in the diaspora and never again returned to San Tin.

The history of San Tin and its people illustrates how a supposedly premodern form of kinship, the Chinese lineage, is still very much alive in the modern world.

Sources: Brettell 1996, 793–97; McKeown 2005, 65–76; J. L. Watson 2004, 893–910.

they cannot specify how. Societies with moiety systems usually have relatively small populations (fewer than 9,000 people). Societies with phratries and clans tend to be larger.[9]

Combinations Although we have distinguished several different types of unilineal descent groups, we do not wish to imply that all unilineal societies have only one type of descent group. Many societies have two or more types in various combinations. For example, some societies have lineages and clans; others may have clans and phratries but no lineages; and still others may have clans and moieties but neither phratries nor lineages. Aside from the fact that a society that has phratries must also have clans (because phratries are combinations of clans), all combinations of descent groups are possible. Even if societies have more than one type of unilineal kin group—for example, lineages and clans—there is no ambiguity about membership. Small groups are simply subsets of larger units; the larger units include people who say they are unilineally related further back in time.

Patrilineal Organization

Patrilineal organization is the most frequent type of descent system. The Kapauku Papuans, a people living in the central highlands of western New Guinea, are an example of a patrilineal society with various types of descent groups.[10] The hierarchy of groups to

Watch the Animation: Patrilineal Descent

which the Kapauku are affiliated by virtue of the patrilineal descent system plays an extremely important part in their lives. All Kapauku belong to a patrilineage, to a patriclan that includes their lineage, and to a patriphratry that includes their clan.

The male members of a patrilineage—all the living males who can trace their actual relationship through males to a common ancestor—constitute the male population of a single village or, more likely, a series of adjoining villages. In other words, the lineage is a *territorial unit.* The male members of the lineage live together by virtue of a patrilocal rule of residence and a fairly stable settlement pattern. A son stays near his parents and brings his wife to live in or near his father's house; the daughters leave home and go to live with their husbands. If the group lives in one place over a long period, the male descendants of one man will live in the same territory. If the lineage is large, it may be divided into sublineages composed of people who trace their descent from one of the sons of the lineage ancestor. The male members of a sublineage live in a contiguous block within the larger lineage territory.

The members of the same patrilineage address each other affectionately, and within this group, a headman maintains law and order. Killing within the lineage is considered a serious offense, and any fighting that takes place is done with sticks rather than lethal weapons such as spears. The sublineage headman tries to settle grievances within the sublineage as quickly and as peacefully as possible. If a sublineage mate commits a crime against outsiders, all members of the sublineage may be considered responsible and their property seized, or a member of the sublineage may be killed in revenge by the victim's kin.

The Kapauku also belong to larger and more inclusive patrilineal descent groups—clans and phratries. All the people of the same clan believe they are related to each other in the father's line, but they are unable to say how they are related. If a member of the patriclan eats the clan's plant or animal totem, it is believed that the person will become deaf. Kapauku are also forbidden to marry anyone from their clan. In other words, the clan is exogamous.

Unlike the members of the patrilineage, the male members of the patriclan do not all live together. Thus, the lineage is the largest group of patrilineal kinsmen that is localized. The lineage is also the largest group of kinsmen that acts together politically. Among clan members, there is no mechanism for resolving disputes, and members of the same patriclan (who belong to different lineages) may even go to war with one another.

The most inclusive patrilineal descent group among the Kapauku is the phratry, each of which is composed of two or more clans. The Kapauku believe that the phratry was originally one clan, but that, in a conflict between brothers of the founding family, the younger brother was expelled, and he formed a new clan. The two resulting clans are viewed as patrilineally related because their founders are said to have been brothers. The members of a phratry observe all the totemic taboos of the clans that belong to that phratry. Intermarriage of members of the same clan is forbidden, but members of the same phratry, if they belong to different clans, may marry.

The Kapauku, then, have lineages with demonstrated kinship links and two kinds of descent groups with unknown descent links (clans and phratries).

Matrilineal Organization

Watch the Animation: Matrilineal Descent

Although societies with matrilineal descent seem in many respects like mirror images of their patrilineal counterparts, they differ in one important way. That difference has to do with who exercises authority. In patrilineal systems, descent affiliation is transmitted through males, and it is also the males who exercise authority. Consequently, in the patrilineal system, lines of descent and of authority converge. In a matrilineal system, however, although the line of descent passes through females, females rarely exercise authority in their kin groups. Usually males do. Thus, the lines of authority and descent do not converge.[11] Anthropologists do not completely understand why this is so, but it is an ethnographic fact. In any case, because males exercise authority in the kin group, an individual's mother's brother becomes an important authority figure because he is the individual's closest male matrilineal relative in the parental generation. The individual's father does not belong to the individual's own matrilineal kin group and thus has no say in kin group matters.

The divergence of authority and descent in a matrilineal system has some effect on community organization and marriage. Most matrilineal societies practice matrilocal residence. Daughters stay at home after marriage and bring their husbands to live with them; sons leave home to join their wives. But the sons who are required to leave will be the ones who eventually exercise authority in their kin groups. This situation presents a

Perspectives on Gender

Variation in Residence and Kinship: What Difference Does It Make to Women?

Ethnographic evidence suggests that it is hard for a woman in a patrilocal society to move at marriage into another village where her husband has plenty of relatives and she has few. For example, Leigh Minturn gives us the text of a letter that one new Rajput bride sent to her mother shortly after she married into her husband's village. The letter was written when the bride had been gone six weeks, but she repeatedly asked if her mother, her father, and her aunts had forgotten her. She begged to be called home and said her bags were packed. She described herself as "a parrot in a cage" and complained about her in-laws. Seven years later the mother reported the daughter to be happy. Still, a few other brides did have more serious symptoms: ghost possession, 24- to 36-hour comas, serious depression, or suicide. What research has not told us is whether these serious symptoms are present more often in patrilocal, patrilineal societies than in other societies. Conversely, do men have some symptoms in matrilocal, matrilineal societies that they do not have in patrilocal societies? We do not know.

What about the status of women? Some research suggests that matrilocality and matrilineality enhance some aspects of women's status, but perhaps not as much as we might think. Even in matrilineal societies, men are usually the political leaders.[12] The main effect of matrilocality and matrilineality appears to be that women control property, but they also tend to have more domestic authority in the home, more equal sexual restrictions, and more value placed on their lives. Alice Schlegel pointed out that women's status only tends to be relatively high in matrilineal societies when neither the husband nor the brother dominates. Matrilocality and matrilineality might not enhance women's status because of the dominance of male matrilineal kin, but patrilocality and patrilineality are very likely to detract from women's status. Residence and descent also predict societal attempts to control reproduction. According to Suzanne Frayser, patrilineal societies are more likely than other societies to prohibit premarital and extramarital sex for women, and they are more likely to make it very difficult for a woman to divorce her husband.

Of course, we have to remember that there is considerable variation within patrilocal/patrilineal societies and matrilocal/matrilineal societies. In the patrilineal society that Audrey Smedley studied—the Birom of the Jos Plateau in Nigeria—women were formally barred from owning property, from holding political offices, and from major decision making. Yet, they had considerable autonomy in their personal lives in everyday life, including the legal right to take on lovers. Indeed, they had considerable indirect influence on decision making and were strong supporters of the patrilineal system. Smedley speculates that women support patrilineality in some environmental circumstances because it serves their interests and those of their children too. For example, male crops are highly valued, but such crops are grown on the more dangerous plains where men risked death at the hands of raiders from other groups. Food was scarce, so it may have been adaptive for everyone, including women, to give special status to men for growing crops in dangerous places.

Sources: Minturn 1993, 54–71; M. K. Whyte 1978b, 132–34; Schlegel 2009; N. Diamond 1975; Smedley 2004; Frayser 1985, 338–47.

problem. The solution that seems to have been realized in most matrilineal societies is that, although the males move away to live with their wives, they usually do not move too far away; indeed, they often marry women who live in the same village. Thus, matrilineal societies tend not to be locally exogamous—that is, members often marry people from inside the village—whereas patrilineal societies are often locally exogamous.[13]

The matrilineal organization on Chuuk, a group of small islands in the Pacific, illustrates the general pattern of authority in matrilineal systems.[14] The Chuukese have both matrilineages and matriclans. The matrilineage is a property-owning group whose members trace descent from a known common ancestor in the female line. The female lineage members and their husbands occupy a cluster of houses on the matrilineage's land. The property of the lineage group is administered by the oldest brother of the group, who allocates the productive property of his matrilineage and directs the work of the members. He also represents the group in dealings with the district chief and all outsiders, and he must be consulted on any matter that affects the group. There is also a senior woman of the lineage who exercises some authority, but only insofar as the activities of the women are concerned. She may supervise the women's cooperative work (they usually work separately from the men) and manage the household.

Within the nuclear family, the father and mother have the primary responsibility for raising and disciplining their children. When a child reaches puberty, however, the father's right to discipline or exercise authority over the child ceases. The mother continues to exercise her right of discipline, but her brother may interfere. A woman's brother rarely interferes with his sister's child before puberty, but he may exercise some authority after puberty, especially because he is an elder in the child's own matrilineage. On Chuuk, men rarely move far from their birthplace. As Ward Goodenough pointed out, "Since matrilocal residence takes the men away from their home lineages, most of them marry women whose lineage houses are within a few minutes' walk of their own."[15]

Although there are some differences between patrilineal and matrilineal systems, there are many similarities. In both types of systems there may be lineages, clans, phratries, and moieties, alone or in any combination. These kin groups, in either matrilineal or patrilineal societies, may perform any number of functions. They may regulate marriage, they may come to each other's aid economically or politically, and they may perform rituals together.

20.4 Describe the functions of unilineal descent systems.

Functions of Unilineal Descent Groups

Unilineal descent groups exist in societies at all levels of cultural complexity.[16] Apparently, however, they are most common in noncommercial food-producing, as opposed to food-collecting, societies.[17] Unilineal descent groups often have important functions in the social, economic, political, and religious realms of life.

Regulating Marriage

In unilineal societies, individuals are not usually permitted to marry within their own unilineal descent groups. In some, however, marriage may be permitted within more inclusive kin groups but prohibited within smaller kin groups. In a few societies, marriage within the kin group is actually preferred.

But, in general, the incest taboo in unilineal societies is extended to all presumed unilineal relatives. For example, on Chuuk, which has matriclans and matrilineages, people are forbidden to marry anyone from their matriclan by the rule of descent group exogamy. The matrilineage is included within the matriclan, so the rule of descent group exogamy also applies to the matrilineage. Among the Kapauku, who have patriphratries, patriclans, and patrilineages, the largest descent group that is exogamous is the patriclan. The phratry may once have been exogamous, but the exogamy rule no longer applies to it. Some anthropologists have suggested that rules of exogamy for descent groups may have developed because the alliances between descent groups generated by such rules may be selectively favored under the conditions of life most unilineal societies face.

Economic Functions

Members of a person's lineage or clan are often required to side with that person in any quarrel or lawsuit, to help him or her get established economically, to contribute to a bride price or fine, and to support the person in life crises. Mutual aid often extends to economic cooperation on a regular basis. The unilineal descent group may act as a corporate unit in landownership. For example, among the Chuukese and the Kapauku, a lineage owns house sites and farmland. Descent group members may also support one another in such enterprises as clearing virgin bush or forest for farmland and providing food and other items for feasts, potlatches, curing rites, and ceremonial occasions, such as births, initiations, marriages, and funerals.

The descent group sometimes views money earned—either by harvesting a cash crop or by leaving the community for a time to work for cash wages—as belonging to all. In recent times, however, young people in some places have shown an unwillingness to part with their money, viewing it as different from other kinds of economic assistance.

Political Functions

The word *political*, as used by members of an industrialized society, generally does not apply to the vague powers that may be entrusted to a headman or the elders of a lineage or clan. But these people may have the right to assign land for use by a lineage member or a clan member. Headmen or elders may also have the right to settle disputes between two members within a lineage, although they generally lack power to force a settlement. And they may act as intermediaries in disputes between a member of their own clan and a member of an opposing kin group.

Certainly one of the most important political functions of unilineal descent groups is their role in warfare—the attempt to resolve disputes within and outside the society by violent action. In societies without towns or cities, the organization of such fighting is often in the hands of descent groups. The Tiv of central Nigeria, for instance, know very well at any given moment which lineages they will fight against, which lineages they will join as allies in case of a fight, which they will fight against using only sticks, and which must be attacked using bows and arrows.

Religious Functions

A clan or lineage may have its own religious beliefs and practices, worshiping its own gods or goddesses and ancestral spirits. The Tallensi of West Africa revere and try to pacify their ancestors. They view life as we know it as only a part of human existence; for them, life existed before birth and will continue after death. The Tallensi believe that the ancestors of their descent groups have changed their form but have retained their interest in what goes on within their society. They can show their displeasure by bringing sudden disaster or minor mishap and their pleasure by bringing unexpected good fortune. But

Among the Bhil of India, graveyards have ancestral memorials in the fields.

people can never tell what will please them; ancestral spirits are, above all, unpredictable. Thus, the Tallensi try to account for unexplainable happenings by attributing them to the ever-watchful ancestors. Belief in the presence of ancestors also provides security; if their ancestors have survived death, so will they. The Tallensi religion is thus a religion of that descent group. The Tallensi are not concerned with other people's ancestors; they believe only one's own ancestors can plague or protect one.[18]

20.5 Describe ambilineal systems.

Ambilineal Systems

Societies with ambilineal descent groups are far less numerous than unilineal or even bilateral societies. Ambilineal societies, however, resemble unilineal ones in many ways. For instance, the members of an ambilineal descent group believe that they are descended from a common ancestor, although frequently they cannot specify all the genealogical links. The descent group is commonly named and may have an identifying emblem or even a totem; the descent group may own land and other productive resources; and myths and religious practices are often associated with the group. Marriage is often regulated by group membership, just as in unilineal systems, although kin group exogamy is not nearly as common as in unilineal systems. Moreover, ambilineal societies resemble unilineal ones in having various levels or types of descent groups. They may have lineages and higher orders of descent groups, distinguished (as in unilineal systems) by whether or not all the genealogical links to the supposed common ancestors are specified.[19]

The Samoans of the South Pacific are an example of an ambilineal society.[20] Samoa has two types of ambilineal descent groups, corresponding to what would be called clans and subclans in a unilineal society. Both groups are exogamous. Associated with each ambilineal clan are one or more chiefs. A group takes its name from the senior chief; subclans, of which there are always at least two, may take their names from junior chiefs.

The distinctiveness of the Samoan ambilineal system, compared with unilineal systems, is that individuals could belong to a number of ambilineal groups because people may be affiliated with an ambilineal group through their father or mother (and the parents, in turn, could be affiliated with any of their parents' groups). Affiliation with a Samoan descent group is optional, and people may theoretically affiliate with any or all of the ambilineal groups to which they are related. In practice, however, people are primarily associated with one group—the ambilineal group whose land they actually live on and cultivate—although they may participate in the activities (e.g., house building) of several groups. Because a person may belong to more than one ambilineal group, the society is not divided into separate kin groups, in contrast with unilineal societies. Consequently, the core members of each ambilineal group cannot all live together, as they could in unilineal societies, because each person belongs to more than one group and cannot live in several places at once.

Not all ambilineal societies have the multiple descent group membership that occurs in Samoa. In some ambilineal societies, a person may belong to only one group at any one time. In such cases, the society can be divided into separate, nonoverlapping groups of kin.

20.6 Discuss how residence can vary.

Explaining Variation in Residence

Questions can be raised as to why different societies have different patterns of residence. If married couples in most societies live with or near kin, as in patrilocal, matrilocal, bilocal, and avunculocal patterns of residence, then why do couples in some societies, such as our own, typically live apart from kin? And, among the societies in which couples live with or near kin, why do most choose the husband's side (patrilocal residence), but some the wife's side (matrilocal residence)? Why do some non-neolocal societies allow a married couple to go to either the wife's or the husband's kin (bilocal residence), whereas most others do not allow a choice?

Neolocal Residence

Many anthropologists have suggested that neolocal residence is related to the presence of a money or commercial economy. They argue that when people can sell their labor or their products for money, they can buy what they need to live without having to depend on kin. Because money is not perishable, unlike crops and other foods in a world largely lacking refrigeration, it can be stored for exchange at a later time. Thus, a money-earning family can resort to its own savings during periods of unemployment or disability, or it might be able to rely on monetary aid from the government, as in our own society. This strategy is impossible in nonmonetary economies, where people must depend on relatives for food and other necessities if they cannot provide their own for some reason.

There is cross-cultural evidence to support this interpretation. Neolocal residence tends to occur in societies with monetary or commercial exchange, whereas societies without money tend to have patterns of residence that locate a couple near or with kin.[21] The presence of money, then, partially accounts for neolocal residence: Money seems to allow couples to live on their own. Still, this fact does not quite explain why they choose to do so.

One reason may be that couples in commercial societies do better on their own because the jobs available require physical or social mobility. Or perhaps couples prefer to live apart from kin because they want to avoid some of the interpersonal tensions and demands that may be generated by living with or near kin. But why couples, when given money, should *prefer* to live on their own is not completely understood.

Matrilocal Versus Patrilocal Residence

It is traditionally assumed that in societies in which married children live near or with kin, the pattern of residence will tend to be patrilocal if males contribute more to the economy and matrilocal if women contribute more. However plausible that assumption may seem, the cross-cultural evidence does not support it. Where men do most of the primary subsistence work, residence is patrilocal no more often than would be expected by chance. Conversely, where women do an equal amount or more of the subsistence work, residence is no more likely to be matrilocal than patrilocal.[22] And if we counted all work inside and outside the home, most societies should be matrilocal because women usually do more. But that is not true either; most societies are not matrilocal.

We can predict whether residence will be matrilocal or patrilocal, however, from the type of warfare practiced in the society. In most societies known to anthropology, neighboring communities or districts are enemies. The type of warfare that breaks out periodically between such groups is called *internal*, because the fighting occurs between groups that speak the same language. In other societies, the warfare is never within the same society but only with other language groups. This pattern of warfare is referred to as purely *external*. Cross-cultural evidence suggests that in societies where warfare is at least sometimes internal, residence is almost always patrilocal rather than matrilocal. In contrast, residence is usually matrilocal when warfare is purely external.[23]

How can we explain this relationship between type of warfare and matrilocal versus patrilocal residence? One theory is that patrilocal residence tends to occur with internal warfare because there may be concern over keeping sons close to home to help with defense. Because women do not usually constitute the fighting force in any society, having sons reside at home after marriage might be favored as a means of maintaining a loyal and quickly mobilized fighting force in case of surprise attack from nearby. If warfare is purely external, however, people may not be so concerned about keeping their sons at home because families need not fear attack from neighboring communities or districts.

With purely external warfare, then, the pattern of residence may be determined by other considerations, especially economic ones. If the women do most of the primary subsistence work in societies with purely external warfare, families might want their daughters to remain at home after marriage, so the pattern of residence might become matrilocal. If warfare is purely external but men still do more of the primary subsistence work, residence should still be patrilocal. Thus, the need to keep sons at home after marriage when there

Applied Anthropology

From Cross-Cultural Research to Archaeology: Reconstructing Marital Residence in the Prehistoric U.S. Southwest

Applied anthropology uses anthropological knowledge to solve problems. Usually, the problem is a practical problem outside anthropology. For example, forensic anthropology applies biological anthropology to help solve murders and other crimes. But sometimes the application is from one subfield of anthropology to another.

Cross-cultural studies using ethnographic data indicate that sisters are very likely to live in the same household if marital residence is matrilocal. The family unit is therefore likely to be larger with matrilocal residence, and the living (nonstorage) floor area of the house is also likely to be larger. In contrast to patrilocal societies, where the average living floor area is about 29 square meters (generally ranging from 14 to 43 square meters), the living floor area in matrilocal societies averages 175 square meters (generally ranging from 79 to 271 square meters). Apparently, sisters have less trouble living together than nonsisters, perhaps because they have grown up together.

Pueblo Bonito in Chaco Canyon, New Mexico.

Most anthropologists would assume that a relationship derived from comparative ethnography on preindustrial societies would apply also to human behavior in the prehistoric past. If that is true, and there is no good reason to doubt it, archaeological sites with living floor areas totaling more than 79 square meters are likely to have had matrilocal marital residence. This prediction has been applied to the transition from pit houses to great houses in the U.S. Southwest. The pit houses between A.D. 500 and A.D. 700 averaged 15 square meters in floor area, in contrast to the multiroom households from A.D. 900 to A.D. 1100 (as in Pueblo Bonito in New Mexico's Chaco Canyon) that ranged in size from 70 square meters to 300 square meters). The latter households were probably matrilocal. Archaeologists know that the households had multiple rooms because there are double walls between adjacent households.

Years ago, some archaeologists suggested that a descent line of matrilineally related women, who would have occupied a site over time if couples lived matrilocally, should exhibit distinctive pottery design elements when compared with the pottery from other sites. After all, mothers would have taught daughters who would have taught their daughters. Perhaps because their calculations and measures were not simple counts such as number of potsherds found, the work by these pioneering archaeologists was ignored if not rejected. The study of kinship in archaeology, following the findings of cross-cultural research, is still wide open, particularly to investigators who are trained in statistical methods.

Sources: Peregrine 2001b; M. Ember 1973; Divale 1977; Hill 1970; Longacre 1970.

is internal warfare may take precedence over any considerations based on division of labor. Perhaps only when internal warfare is nonexistent may a female-dominant division of labor give rise to matrilocal residence.[24]

The frequent absence of men because of long-distance trade or wage labor in distant places may also provide an impetus for matrilocal residence even after warfare ceases. For example, among the Miskito of eastern Central America, matrilocality allowed domestic and village life to continue without interruption when men were away from home for long periods of time, working as lumberers, miners, and river transporters. More recently, men have worked away from home as deep-sea divers for lobster, for which there is a lot of demand in the international economy. These jobs were not always available, but when they were, the men went away to work at them to earn money. Even though some men would always be away from home, the Miskito continued to get food in their traditional ways, from farming (done mostly by the women) and from hunting and fishing (which was mostly men's work).[25]

Bilocal Residence

In societies that practice bilocal residence, a married couple goes to live with or near either the husband's or the wife's parents. Although this pattern seems to involve a choice for the married couple, theory and research suggest that bilocal residence may occur out of necessity instead. Elman Service suggested that bilocal residence is likely to occur in societies that have recently suffered a severe and drastic loss of population because of the introduction of new infectious diseases.[26] Over the last 400 years, contact with Europeans in many parts of the world has resulted in severe population losses among non-European societies that lacked resistance to the Europeans' diseases. If couples need to live with some set of kin to make a living in noncommercial societies, it seems likely that couples in depopulated, noncommercial societies might have to live with whichever spouse's parents and other relatives are still alive. This interpretation is supported by the cross-cultural evidence. Recently depopulated societies tend to have bilocal residence or frequent departures from unilocality, whereas societies that are not recently depopulated tend to have one pattern or another of unilocal residence.[27]

In hunter-gatherer societies, a few other circumstances may also favor bilocal residence. Bilocality tends to be found among those hunter-gatherers who have very small bands or unpredictable and low rainfall. Residential "choice" in these cases may be a question of adjusting marital residence to where the couple will have the best chance to survive or to find close relatives with whom to live and work.[28] Figure 20.6 illustrates the main predictors of the various marital residence patterns.

Avunculocal Residence

Now that we have learned about matrilineal systems, the avunculocal pattern of residence, whereby married couples live with or near the husband's mother's brother, may become clearer. Although avunculocal residence is relatively rare, just about all

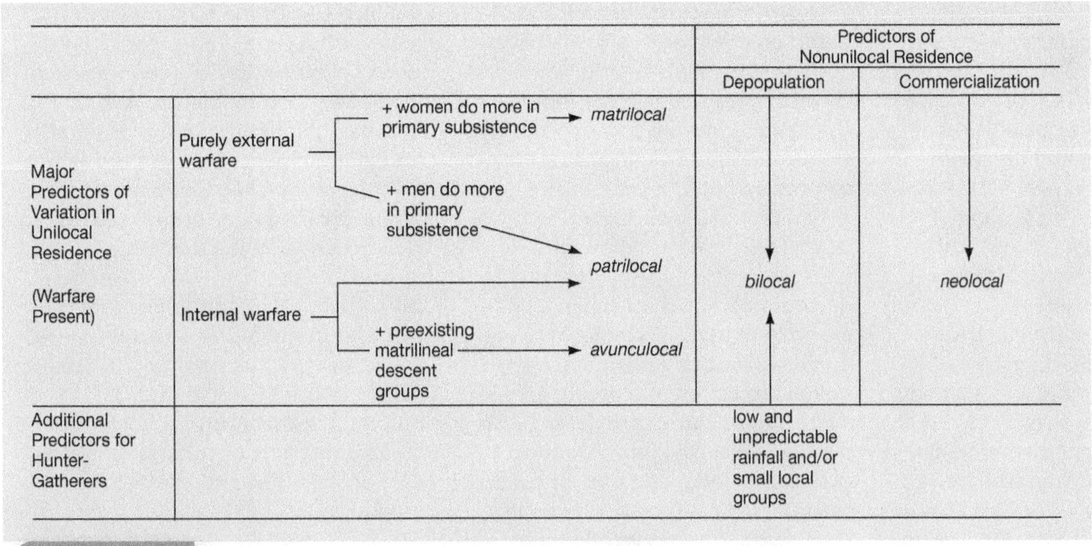

FIGURE 20.6 The Main Predictors of Marital Residence Patterns

An arrow indicates the suggested causal direction.

Source: Adapted from M. Ember and C. R. Ember 1983.

Current Research and Issues

Do Neolocality and Rebellious Teenagers Go Together?

In the United States, it is nearly taken for granted that adolescence brings turmoil and parent-child conflict. Teenagers, parents, and educators worry about how to reduce the conflict. But why does the conflict occur in the first place? Is it "natural" for adolescents to be rebellious? Are they rebellious in all cultures? If not, why not?

Margaret Mead first raised this issue in her bestselling ethnography, *Coming of Age in Samoa*, in which she observed that adolescence caused little conflict among the Samoans she lived with during the 1920s. Some researchers criticized her analysis, but many field and comparative studies by anthropologists have since found that, indeed, adolescence is not experienced in the same way in all societies. In a systematic cross-cultural study of adolescence, Alice Schlegel and Herbert Barry concluded that relations between adolescents and their families were generally harmonious around the world. They suggested that when family members depend upon each other throughout their lives, independence, as expressed in adolescent rebelliousness, would be foolhardy. Indeed, Schlegel and Barry found that adolescents are likely to be rebellious only in societies, like our own, that have neolocal residence and considerable job and geographic mobility. Why should this be? We can speculate that adolescent rebellion in a mobile society is an elaborate psychodrama that both parents and children play out to prepare themselves for separation. Adolescents know that they must leave their parents soon, a prospect that may arouse anxiety.

What if our social structure were different? What if children, as well as their parents, knew that some among them were going to spend the rest of their lives with or near their parents? And even those children who moved away knew, as they would in societies practicing matrilocal, patrilocal, avunculocal, or bilocal residence, that they were going to spend the rest of their lives with or near another kin group, their in-laws. Could teenagers in non-neolocal societies afford to have serious conflicts with their parents? Could parents afford serious conflicts with teenagers who would not be leaving when they matured and married? We think not. We suggest that adolescent conflict would be too disruptive of the social order in a non-neolocal society; it would, therefore, have to be minimized or suppressed.

There is another reason why rebellious teenagers may be associated with neolocal family structure. Neolocal households commonly occur in societies whose economies are based on commerce, a kind of livelihood that presents people with more choices, particularly in the rapidly changing modern world. If children must know and do things that their parents do not know about, is a generation gap inevitable?

Not necessarily. Other conditions are probably also necessary to generate parent-child conflict, if the example of a Moroccan town is any guide. As part of a comparative research project on adolescence, Susan and Douglas Davis interviewed young people in a small Moroccan town that had experienced a lot of cultural change. Parents mostly worked in agricultural jobs; their children aspired to urban, white-collar jobs. Grandparents had rarely seen a car; teenagers took trains to the capital. Only a few parents had gone to school; most teenagers were schooled. Yet little serious parent–child conflict occurred. In fact, 40 percent of the teenagers said that they had never disagreed with their mothers.

What conditions other than rapid social change might account for the difference between Moroccan and North American teenagers? Morocco has an authoritarian political structure with a monarchy and a clear hierarchy of offices. Moroccan society rewards allegiance to the group, and adults in the Moroccan town avoided open conflict. Can teenagers rebel in a society that discourages conflict and personal autonomy? Further research is needed to untangle the web of cause and effect that predicts rebellion in teenagers. We need to study samples of cultures that have different combinations of neolocality, rapid change, cultural emphasis on individual autonomy, and an authoritarian political system. Whatever we discover in the future about its cause, we know now that adolescent rebelliousness is neither inevitable nor natural, but that it is probably linked to other aspects of cultural variation—as Margaret Mead suggested many years ago.

Sources: Mead 1961/1928; Schlegel and Barry 1991; M. Ember 1967; S. S. Davis 1993; 2009.

avunculocal societies are matrilineal. As we have seen, the mother's brother plays an important role in decision making in most matrilineal societies. Aside from his brothers, who is a boy's closest male matrilineal relative? It is his mother's brother. Going to live with the mother's brother, then, provides a way of localizing male *matrilineal* relatives. But why should some matrilineal societies practice that form of residence? The answer may involve the prevailing type of warfare.

Avunculocal societies, in contrast with matrilocal societies, fight internally. Like patrilocality, avunculocality may be a way of keeping related—in this case, matrilineally related—married men together to mount a quick defense against surprise attacks from nearby. When faced with fighting close to home, societies with strong, functioning matrilineal descent groups may choose to switch initially to avunculocality rather than patrilocality. Such a transition would make sense when the close warfare results in high male mortality, which could make patrilineal descent more difficult to trace in such societies than matrilineal descent.[29]

The Emergence of Unilineal Systems

20.7 Explain the emergence of unilineal descent systems.

Unilineal kin groups play an essential role in the organization of many societies. But not all societies have such groups. In societies that have complex systems of political organization, officials and agencies take over many of the functions that kin groups might perform, such as organizing work and warfare and allocating land. But not all societies that lack complex political organization have unilineal descent systems. Why, then, do some societies have unilineal descent systems, but others do not?

It is generally assumed that unilocal residence, patrilocal or matrilocal, is necessary for the development of unilineal descent. Patrilocal residence, if practiced for some time in a society, will generate a set of patrilineally related males who live in the same territory. Matrilocal residence over time will similarly generate a localized set of matrilineally related females. It is no wonder, then, that matrilocal and patrilocal residence patterns are cross-culturally associated with matrilineal and patrilineal descent, respectively.[30]

Athough unilocal residence might be necessary for the formation of unilineal descent groups, it apparently is not the only condition required. For one thing, many societies with unilocal residence lack unilineal descent groups. For another, even though related males or related females live together by virtue of a patrilocal or matrilocal rule of residence, it does not necessarily follow that the related people will actually view themselves as a descent group and function as such. What other conditions are needed, then, to impel the formation of unilineal descent groups?

There is evidence that unilocal societies that engage in warfare are more apt to have unilineal descent groups than those without warfare.[31] The presence of warfare may provide societies that lack complex political organization with an impetus to form an unambiguous, single line of descent. After all, the unity of the group is more certain when no other clan, phratry, or moiety vies for their loyalty.[32] A unilineal descent group can function as a discrete unit—and do so mostly, perhaps, in warfare.

Explaining Ambilineal and Bilateral Systems

20.8 Explain how ambilineal and bilateral systems might emerge.

Why do some societies have ambilineal descent groups? Although the evidence is not clear-cut, it may be that societies with unilineal descent groups are transformed into ambilineal ones under special conditions, particularly depopulation. We have noted that depopulation may transform a previously unilocal society into a bilocal society. If a previously unilocal society also had unilineal descent groups, the descent groups may become transformed into ambilineal groups. If a society used to be patrilocal and patrilineal, for example, but some couples began to live matrilocally, their children would be associated through their mother with a previously patrilineal descent group on whose land they may be living. Once this situation happens regularly, the unilineal principle may become transformed into an ambilineal principle.[33] Thus, ambilineal descent systems may be a recent development resulting from depopulation caused by the introduction of European diseases.

The conditions that favor bilateral systems are in large part opposite to those that favor unilineal descent. As we discussed, unlineal descent seems to develop in a nonstate society with unilocal residence that has warfare. If one needs an unambigious set of allies, bilateral systems are unlikely to provide them. Recall that bilateral systems are ego-centered; and every person, other than siblings, has a slightly different set of kin to rely on. Consequently, in bilateral societies, it is often not clear to whom one can turn and which person has responsibility for aiding another. Such ambiguity, however, might not be a liability in societies without warfare. In complex political systems that organize fighting on behalf of large populations, a standing army usually provides the fighting force, and mobilization of kin is not so important. Perhaps because warfare is somewhat less likely in foraging societies,[34] bilateral systems may often develop in foraging societies, just like bilaterality is likely in more complex societies because they don't need to rely on descent groups for war. Neolocal residence, which becomes more common with commercialization and market exchange, also works against unilineal descent and therefore also makes a bilateral system more likely.

Kinship Terminology

20.9 Explain the various systems of kinship terminology.

classificatory terms Kinship terms that merge or equate relatives who are genealogically distinct from one another; the same term is used for a number of different kin.

consanguineal kin One's biological relatives; relatives by birth.

affinal kin One's relatives by marriage.

Our society, like all others, has **classificatory terms** for kinds of kin. Most of us probably never stop to think about why we name relatives the way we do. For example, we call our mother's brother and father's brother (and often mother's sister's husband and father's sister's husband) by the same term—*uncle*. It is not that we are unable to distinguish between our mother's or father's brother or that we do not know the difference between **consanguineal kin** (blood kin) and **affinal kin** (kin by marriage, or what we call *in-laws*). Instead, it seems that we do not usually find it necessary to distinguish between various types of uncles in our society.

However natural our system of classification may seem to us, numerous anthropological field studies have revealed that societies differ markedly in how they group or distinguish relatives. The kinship terminology used in a society may reflect its prevailing kind of family, its rule of residence, its rule of descent, and other aspects of its social organization. Kin terms may also give clues to prior features of the society's social system, if, as many anthropologists believe,[35] the kin terms of a society are very resistant to change. The major systems of kinship terminology are the Inuit (Eskimo) system, the Omaha system, the Crow system, the Iroquois system, the Sudanese system, and the Hawaiian system.

Because it is the most familiar to us, let us first consider the kinship terminology system employed in our own and many other commercial societies. But it is by no means confined to commercial societies. In fact, this system is found in many Inuit societies.

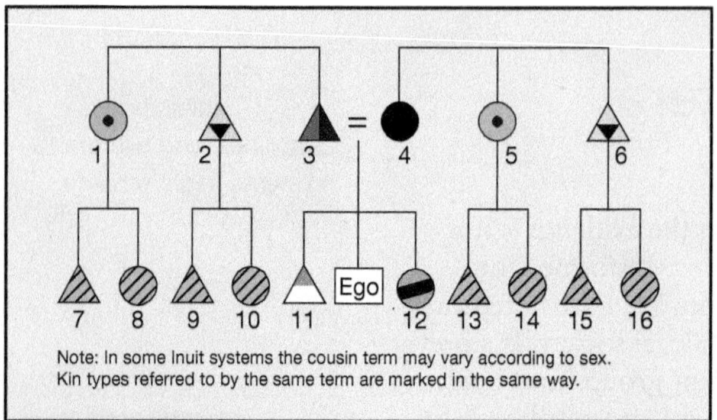

FIGURE 20.7 Inuit (Eskimo) Terminology System

Inuit, or Eskimo System

The distinguishing features of the Inuit, or Eskimo system (see Figure 20.7) are that all cousins are lumped together under the same term but are distinguished from brothers and sisters; all aunts are lumped under the same term and distinguished from the mother; and all uncles are lumped under the same term and distinguished from the father. In Figure 20.7 and in subsequent figures, the kin types that are referred to by the same term are colored and marked in the same way; for example, in the Inuit system, kin types 2 (father's brother) and 6 (mother's brother) are referred to by the same term (*uncle* in English). Note that in this system—in contrast to the others we will examine—no other relatives are generally referred to by the same terms used for members of the nuclear family—mother, father, brother, and sister.

The Inuit type of kinship terminology is not generally found where there are unilineal or ambilineal descent groups; the only kin group that appears to be present is the bilateral kindred.[36] Remember that the kindred in a bilateral kinship system is an ego-centered group. Although relatives on both my mother's and my father's sides are equally important, my most important relatives are generally those closest to me. This is particularly true in our society, where the nuclear family generally lives alone, separated from and not particularly involved with other relatives except on ceremonial occasions. Because the nuclear family is most important, we would expect to find that the terminology for kin types in the nuclear family is different from the terminology for all other relatives. And the mother's and father's sides are equally important (or unimportant), so it makes sense that we use the same terms (*aunt, uncle*, and *cousin*) for both sides of the family.

Omaha System

The Omaha system of kin terminology is named after the Omaha of North America, but the system is found in many societies around the world, usually those with patrilineal descent.[37] Referring to Figure 20.8, we can see immediately which types of kin are lumped together in an Omaha system. First, father and father's brother (numbers 2 and 3) are both referred to by the same term. This way of classifying relatives contrasts markedly with ours, in which no term that applies to a member of the nuclear family (father, mother, brother, sister) is applied to any other relative. What could account for the Omaha system of lumping? One interpretation is that the father and father's brother are lumped in this system because most societies in which this system is found have patrilineal kin groups. Both father and father's brother are in the parental generation of my patrilineal kin group and may behave toward me similarly. My father's brother also probably lived near me as a child because patrilineal societies usually have patrilocal residence. The term for father and father's brother, then, might be translated "male member of my patrilineal kin group in my father's generation."

A second lumping, which at first glance appears similar to the lumping of father and father's brother, is that of mother and mother's sister (4 and 5), both of whom are called by the same term. But more surprisingly, mother's brother's daughter (16) is also referred to by this term. Why? If we think of the term as meaning "female member of my mother's patrilineage of *any* generation," then the term makes sense. Consistent with this view, all the male members of my mother's patrilineage of any generation (mother's brother, 6; mother's brother's son, 15) are also referred to by one term.

It is apparent, then, that relatives on the father's and the mother's sides are grouped differently in this system. For members of my mother's patrilineal kin group, I lump all male members together and all female members together regardless of their generation. Yet for members of my father's patrilineal kin group, I have different terms for the male and female members of different generations. George Peter Murdock suggested that a society lumps kin types when there are more similarities than differences among them.[38]

Using this principle, and recognizing that societies with an Omaha system usually are patrilineal, I realize that my father's patrilineal kin group is the one to which I belong and in which I have a great many rights and obligations. Consequently, people of my father's generation are likely to behave quite differently toward me than are people of my own generation. Members of my patrilineal group in my father's generation are likely to exercise authority over me, and I am required to show them respect. Members of my patrilineal group in my own generation are those I am likely to play with as a child and to be friends with. Thus, in a patrilineal system, people on my father's side belonging to different generations are likely to be distinguished.

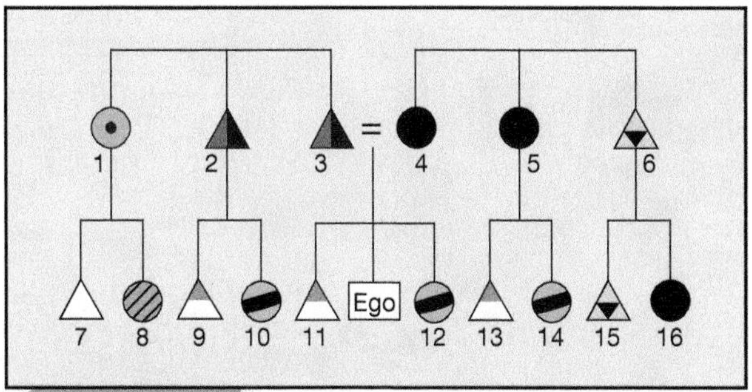

FIGURE 20.8 **Omaha Kinship Terminology System**

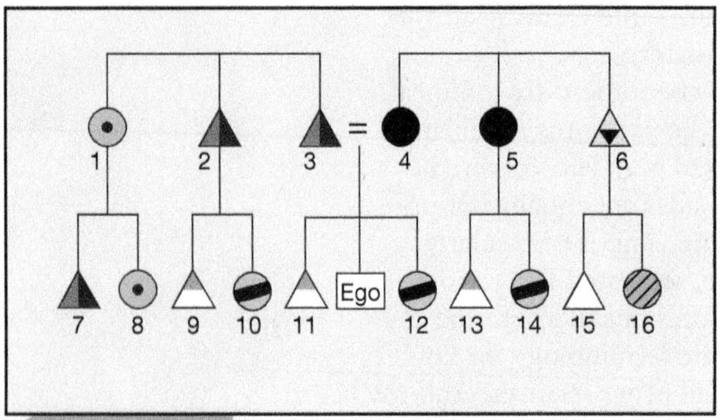

FIGURE 20.9 **Crow Terminology System**

On the other hand, my mother's patrilineage is relatively unimportant to me (because I take my descent from my father). And because my residence is probably patrilocal, my mother's relatives will probably not even live near me. Thus, inasmuch as my mother's patrilineal relatives are comparatively unimportant in such a system, they become similar enough to be lumped together.

Finally, in the Omaha system, I refer to my male parallel cousins (my father's brother's son, 9; and my mother's sister's son, 13) in the same way I refer to my brother (12). I refer to my female parallel cousins (my father's brother's daughter, 10, and my mother's sister's daughter, 14) in the same way I refer to my sister (12). Considering that my father's brother and mother's sister are referred to by the same terms I use for my father and mother, this lumping of parallel cousins with **siblings** (brothers and sisters) is not surprising. If I call my own mother's and father's children (other than myself) "brother" and "sister," then the children of anyone whom I also call "mother" and "father" ought to be called "brother" and "sister" as well.

siblings A person's brothers and sisters.

Crow System

The Crow system, named after another North American culture, has been called the mirror image of the Omaha system. The same principles of lumping kin types are employed, except that the Crow system is associated with matrilineal descent,[39] so the individuals in my mother's matrilineal group (which is my own) are not lumped across generations, whereas the individuals in my father's matrilineal group are. Comparing Figure 20.9 with Figure 20.8, we find that the lumping and separating of kin types are much the same in both, except that the lumping across generations in the Crow system appears on the father's side rather than on the mother's side. In other words, I call both my mother and my mother's sister by the same term (because both are female members of my matrilineal descent group in my mother's generation). I call my father, my father's brother, and my father's sister's son by the same term (all male members of my father's matrilineal group in any generation). I call my father's sister and my father's sister's daughter by the same term (both female members of my father's matrilineal group). And I refer to my parallel cousins in the same way I refer to my brother and sister.

Iroquois System

The Iroquois system (see Figure 20.10), named after the Iroquois of North America, is like the Omaha and Crow systems in that I refer to my father and my father's brother (2 and 3) by the same term, and my mother and my mother's sister (4 and 5) by the same term. However, unlike the Omaha and Crow systems, the Iroquois system treats cousins of my own generation differently. In the Omaha and Crow systems, one set of cross-cousins is lumped in the kinship terminology with the generation above. In the Iroquois system, both sets of cross-cousins (mother's brother's children, 15 and 16; and father's sister's children, 7 and 8) are referred to by the same terms, distinguished by sex. That is, mother's brother's daughter and father's sister's daughter are both referred to by the same term. Also, mother's brother's son and father's sister's son are referred to by the same term. Parallel cousins always have terms different from those for cross-cousins and are sometimes, but not always, referred to by the same terms as one's brother and sister.

The Iroquois longhouses could house over 80 people. The female members of a matrilineage with their in-marrying husbands traditionally lived in one longhouse.

Like the Omaha and Crow systems, the Iroquois system has different terms for relatives on the father's and the mother's sides. Such differentiation tends to be associated with unilineal descent, which is not surprising because unilineal descent involves affiliation with either mother's or father's kin. Why Iroquois, rather than Omaha or Crow, terminology occurs in a unilineal society requires explanation. One possible explanation is that Omaha or Crow is likely to occur in a developed, as opposed to a developing or decaying, unilineal system.[40] Another possibility is that Iroquois terminology emerges in societies that prefer marriage with both cross-cousins,[41] who are differentiated from other relatives in an Iroquois system.

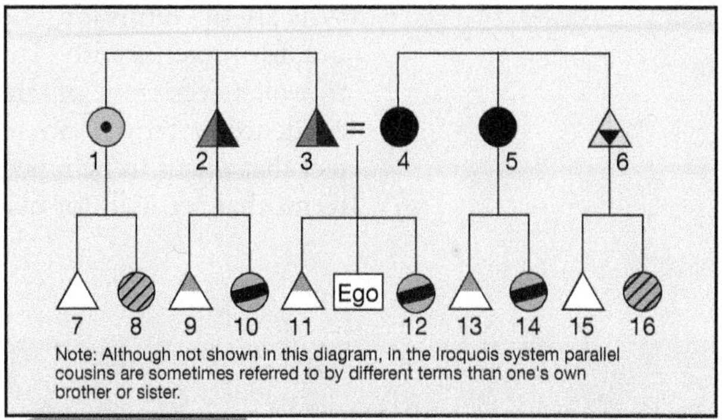

FIGURE 20.10 **Iroquois Kinship Terminology System**

Sudanese System

Unlike the Omaha, Crow, and Iroquois systems, the Sudanese system usually does not lump any relatives in the parents' and ego's generations. That is, the Sudanese system is usually a *descriptive system*, in which a different **descriptive term** is used for *each* of the relatives, as shown in Figure 20.11. What kinds of societies are likely to have such a system? Although societies with Sudanese terminology are likely to be patrilineal, they probably are different from most patrilineal societies that have Omaha or Iroquois terms. Sudanese terminology is associated with relatively great political complexity, class stratification, and occupational specialization. It has been suggested that under such conditions, a kinship system may reflect the need to make fine distinctions among members of descent groups who have different opportunities and privileges in the occupational or class system.[42]

descriptive term A unique term used for a distinct relative.

The Omaha, Crow, Iroquois, and Sudanese systems, although different from one another and associated with somewhat different predictors, share one important feature: The terms used for the mother's and father's side of the family are not the same. If you imagine folding the kinship terminology diagrams in half, the two sides would not be the same. As we have seen in the Inuit system, however, the terms on the mother's and father's side of the family are *exactly* the same. This feature suggests that the two sides of the family are equally important or equally unimportant. The Hawaiian system discussed next also has the same terms on both sides, but kinship outside the nuclear family is more important.

Hawaiian System

The Hawaiian system of kinship terminology is the least complex in that it uses the smallest number of terms. In this system, all relatives of the same sex in the same generation are referred to by the same term (see Figure 20.12). Thus, all my female cousins are referred to by the same term as my sister; all male cousins are referred to by the same term as my brother. Everyone known to be related to me in my parents' generation is referred to by one term if female (including my mother) and by another term if male (including my father).

The fact that societies with Hawaiian kin terminology tend not to have unilineal descent groups[43] helps explain why kinship terms are the same on both sides of the family.

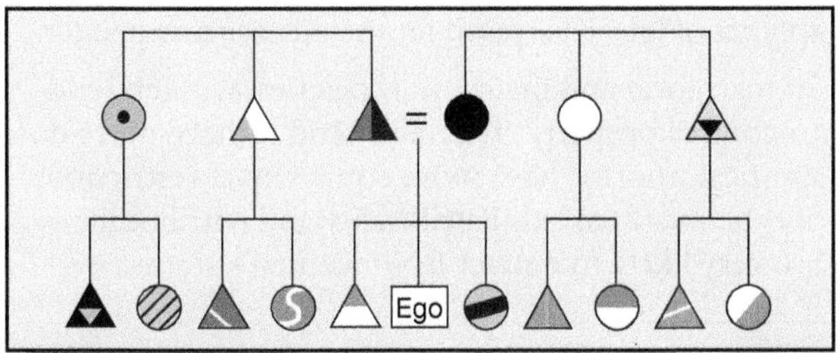

FIGURE 20.11 **Sudanese Kinship Terminology System**

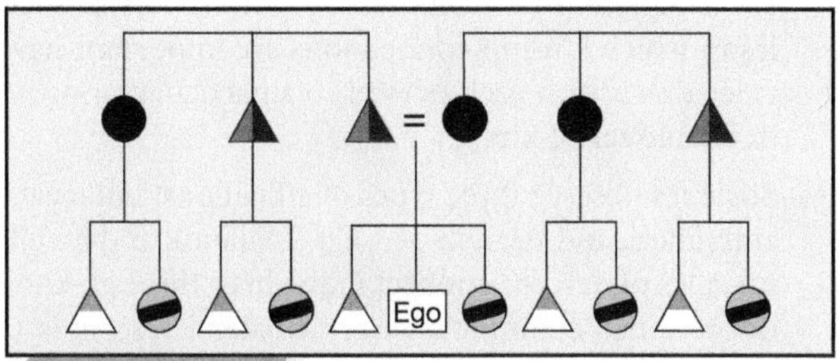

FIGURE 20.12 **Hawaiian Kinship Terminology System**

Why are the terms for mother, father, sister, and brother used for other relatives? Perhaps because societies with Hawaiian terminology are likely to have large extended families[44] to which every type of relative in Figure 20.12 may belong because of alternative (bilocal) residence patterns.[45] So, in contrast to our own society, many kin are very important, a fact that seems to be reflected in the practice of referring to other relatives with the same terms that are used for nuclear family members.

Summary and Review

Patterns of Marital Residence

20.1 Describe the various patterns of marital residence.

- In many industrial and postindustrial societies, a young man and woman establish neolocal residence when they marry, setting up a new household apart from their parents and other relatives. Worldwide, that practice is much less common.
- The more common practice of living with and near kin has meant that kin have been an important basis of social organization in many cultures.
- Patterns of marital residence include patrilocal, matrilocal, bilocal, avunculocal, and neolocal. Place of residence largely determines which people the couple and their offspring interact with and depend on and can affect what status a wife or husband has.

? How does the custom of patrilocal and matrilocal marital residence affect males and females?

The Structure of Kinship

20.2 Discuss the structure of kinship and distinguish among the various types of affiliation.

- The web of kinship provides the main structure of social action in noncommercial societies. Most societies in which kinship connections are important have rules that assign each person to a particular and definable set of kin.
- Societies observe three types of affiliations: unilineal, ambilineal, and bilateral kinship. Unilineal and ambilineal rules of descent connect individuals through known or presumed common ancestry. Bilateral descent is not based on a line of descent but moves outward to relatives on both sides of one's family.
- Unilineal descent forms clear and unambiguous groups of kin. This may also be true of ambilineal descent.
- *Kindred* describes one's bilateral relatives but it is usually not a clearly defined group. In bilateral kinship, aside from brothers and sisters, no two people belong to exactly the same kin group. People in a kindred have in common only the focal person who brings them together.

? What is the difference between unilineal, ambilineal and bilateral affiliations?

Variation in Unilineal Descent Systems

20.3 Discuss variation in unilineal descent systems.

- Unilineal descent groups comprise four types: lineages (kin of definite descent from an ancestor), clans (kin of believed descent from an ancestor), phratries (unilineal groups of supposedly related clans), and moieties (either of a society's two unilineal groups).
- Many unilineal societies have two or more types of descent groups in various combinations.
- In patrilineal systems, descent affiliation is through males, and males also tend to exercise authority; in matrilineal systems descent affiliation is through females, but females do not usually exercise authority in many spheres of life. The reason for the difference is unclear.
- In matrilocal and matrilineal societies, women tend to control property. They also tend to have more domestic authority, have more equal sexual restrictions, and be more valued. Patrilocality and patrilineality are very likely to detract from women's status.

? How do patrilineal and matrilineal systems affect women's status?

Functions of Unilineal Descent Groups

20.4 Describe the functions of unilineal descent systems.

- Unilineal descent groups exist in societies at all levels of cultural complexity but are most common in noncommercial food-producing societies. Unilineal descent groups often have important functions in the social, economic, political, and religious realms of life.
- Specific functions of descent groups include regulating marriage, economic aid, assistance with work enterprises, contributions to social occasions, assigning land rights, defense, and settling of disputes within and outside the society.

? Give an example for each of four functions (social, economic, political, and religious) of unilineal descent groups.

Ambilineal Systems

20.5 Describe ambilineal systems.

- Societies with ambilineal descent groups are far less numerous than unilineal or even bilateral societies.
- Ideas in ambilineal societies about descent from a common ancestor, identifying names or emblems, and regulation of land use and marriage resemble those of unilineal societies.

? What distinguishes ambilineal systems from other types of descent systems?

Explaining Variation in Residence

20.6 Discuss how residence can vary.

- Cross-cultural evidence shows that neolocal residence is related to the presence of a commercial economy. Perhaps this is because when people can sell their labor or their products, they can buy what they need to live without depending on kin.
- Cross-cultural evidence does not support the idea that, in societies in which married children live near or with kin, the pattern of residence will tend to be patrilocal if males contribute more to the economy and matrilocal if women contribute more.
- Where warfare is at least sometimes internal, residence is usually patrilocal, probably because people may want to keep their sons at home to ward off attack from neighboring communities. Residence is usually matrilocal when warfare is purely external, particularly if women contribute substantially to subsistence.
- The frequent absence of men because of long-distance trade or wage labor in distant places may also provide an impetus for matrilocal residence.
- Theory and research suggest that bilocal residence may occur out of necessity in societies that have recently suffered a severe and drastic loss of population resulting from the introduction of new infectious diseases and in small hunter-gatherer societies with unpredictable rainfall.
- Avunculocal residence, which puts matrilineally-related males together, may be favored by internal warfare when the society is matrilineal.

? What factors influence development of neolocal, matrilocal, patrilocal, and avunculocal societies?

The Emergence of Unilineal Systems

20.7 Explain the emergence of unilineal descent systems.

- Unilocal residence, whether patrilocal or matrilocal, is probably necessary for the development of unilineal descent but does not by itself predict unilineal societies.
- There is evidence that unilocal societies that engage in warfare are more apt to have unilineal descent groups than those without warfare.

? How do issues of warfare affect the development of unilineal systems?

Explaining Ambilineal and Bilateral Systems

20.8 Explain how ambilineal and bilateral systems might emerge.

- Societies with unilineal descent groups may be transformed into ambilineal ones under special conditions, particularly depopulation, and may be a recent development resulting from depopulation caused by the introduction of European diseases.

- The conditions that favor bilateral systems are generally opposite to those that favor unilineal descent.
- In complex political systems, standing armies provide the fighting force, so mobilization of kin is less important. Neolocal residence, more common with commercialization, also works against unilineal descent and makes a bilateral system more likely.

> What factors favor the likelihood of bilateral systems, and what factors favor the likelihood of ambilineal systems?

Kinship Terminology

20.9 Explain the various systems of kinship terminology.

- Anthropological field studies show that societies differ markedly in how they group or distinguish relatives. The kinship terminology used in a society may reflect its prevailing kind of family, rule of residence, rule of descent, and other aspects of its social organization.
- The major systems of kinship terminology are the Inuit (Eskimo) system, the Omaha system, the Crow system, the Iroquois system, the Sudanese system, and the Hawaiian system.
- The Inuit type of kinship terminology is not generally found where there are unilineal or ambilineal descent groups; the only kin group that appears to be present is the bilateral kindred, so the same terms are used for both sides of the family.
- The Omaha and Crow systems of kin terminology are associated with unilineal descent (patrilineal and matrilineal, respectively). The terms differ on each side of the family and are lumped across generations on the less important side of the family.
- The Iroquois system is like the Omaha and Crow systems in having terms for "mother" and "father" extend beyond the nuclear family, but the Iroquois system does not have lumping across generations. No cousins have the same terms as in the parental generation.
- The Sudanese system uses a different term for *each* relative. The system is associated with relatively great political complexity, class stratification, and occupational specialization and may reflect the need to make fine distinctions among members of descent groups.
- The Omaha, Crow, Iroquois, and Sudanese systems, although different from one another, share one important feature: The terms used for the mother's and father's side of the family are not the same.
- The Hawaiian system of kinship terminology, the least complex, uses the smallest number of terms. All relatives of the same sex in the same generation are referred to by the same term.

> In what ways do kinship terminology systems reflect social organization?

Think on it

1. What other things about our society would change if we practiced other than **neolocal residence**?
2. Why does **kinship** provide the main structure of social action in many noncommercial societies?
3. Why might it be important for **unilineal descent groups** to not overlap in membership?

Political Life: Social Order and Disorder

22 CHAPTER

LEARNING OBJECTIVES

- Discuss the cross-cultural variation in the types of political organization. 22.1
- Explain the spread of state societies. 22.2
- Describe and explain the variation in political structure in various societies. 22.3
- Critically examine the methods used for resolving conflict, including warfare, in different societies. 22.4

For people in the United States, the phrase *political life* has many connotations. It may call to mind the various branches of government: the executive branch, from the president on the national level to governors on the state level to mayors on the local level; legislative institutions, from Congress to state legislatures to city councils; and administrative bureaus, from federal government departments to local agencies.

Political life may also evoke thoughts of political parties, interest groups, lobbying, campaigning, and voting. In other words, when people living in the United States think of political life, they may think first of "politics," the activities (not always apparent) that influence who is elected or appointed to political office, what public policies are established, how they get established, and who benefits from those policies.

But in the United States and in many other countries, *political life* involves even more than government and politics. Political life also involves ways of preventing or resolving troubles and disputes both within and outside the society. Internally, a complex society such as ours may employ mediation or arbitration to resolve industrial disputes, a police force to prevent crimes or track down criminals, and courts and a penal system to deal with lawbreakers as well as with social conflict in general. Externally, such a society may establish embassies in other nations and develop and utilize its armed forces both to maintain security and to support domestic and foreign interests.

By means of all these informal and formal political mechanisms, complex societies establish social order and minimize, or at least deal with, social disorder.

Formal governments have become more widespread around the world over the last 100 years, as powerful colonizing countries have imposed political systems upon others or as people less formally organized realized that they needed governmental mechanisms to deal with the larger world. But many societies known to anthropology did not have political officials, political parties, courts, or armies. Indeed, the band or village was the largest autonomous political unit in 50 percent of the societies in the ethnographic record, as of the times they were first described. And those units were only informally organized; that is, they did not have individuals or agencies formally authorized to make and implement policy or resolve disputes. Does this mean they did not have political life? If we mean political life as we know it in our own society, then the answer has to be that they did not. But if we look beyond our formal institutions and mechanisms—if we ask what functions these institutions and mechanisms perform—we find that all societies have had political activities and beliefs to create and maintain social order and cope with social disorder.

Many of the kinds of groups we discussed in the three previous chapters, on families, descent groups, and associations, have political functions. But when anthropologists talk about *political organization* or *political life,* they are particularly focusing on activities and beliefs pertaining to *territorial groups.* Territorial groups, on whose behalf political activities may be organized, range from small communities, such as bands and villages, to large communities, such as towns and cities, to multilocal groups, such as districts or regions, entire nations, or even groups of nations.

As we shall see, the different types of political organizations, as well as how people participate in politics and how they cope with conflict, are often strongly linked to variation in food-getting, economy, and social stratification.

Variation in Types of Political Organization

22.1 Discuss the cross-cultural variation in the types of political organization.

Societies in the ethnographic record vary in *level of political integration*—that is, the largest territorial group on whose behalf political activities are organized—and in the degree to which political authority is centralized or concentrated in the integrated group. When we describe the political integration of particular societies, we focus on their traditional political systems. In many societies known to anthropology, the small community (band or village) was traditionally the largest territorial group on whose behalf political activities were organized. The authority structure in such societies did not involve any centralization; there was no political authority whose jurisdiction included more than one community. In other societies, political activities were traditionally organized sometimes on behalf of a multilocal group, but there was no permanent authority at the top. And in still other societies, political activities were often traditionally organized on behalf of multilocal territorial groups, and there was a centralized or supreme political authority at the top. In the modern world, however, every society has been incorporated into some larger, centralized political system.

Elman Service suggested that most societies can be classified into four principal types of political organization ranging from less to more centralized—bands, tribes, chiefdoms, and states.[1] Although no classification system fits all cases, Service's classification is a useful way to show how societies vary in trying to create and maintain social order.[2] We often use the present tense in our discussion because that is the convention in ethnographic writing, but readers should remember that most societies that used to be organized at the band, tribe, or chiefdom level are now incorporated into larger political entities. With a handful of exceptions, there are no politically autonomous bands or tribes or chiefdoms in the world anymore.

Watch the Animation: Trends in Political Organization

Band Organization

Some societies were composed of fairly small and usually nomadic groups of people. Each of these groups is conventionally called a **band** and is politically autonomous. That is, in **band organization**, the local group (sometimes as small as a family) or community is the largest group that acts as a political unit. Because most recent foragers had band organization, some anthropologists contend that this type of political organization characterized nearly all societies before the development of agriculture, or until about 10,000 years ago. But we have to remember that almost all of the described food-collecting societies are or were located in marginal environments, and almost all were affected by more dominant societies nearby.[3] So it is possible that what we call "band organization" may not have been typical of foragers in the distant or prehistoric past.

Band A fairly small, usually nomadic local group that is politically autonomous.

Band organization The kind of political organization where the local group or band is the largest territorial group in the society that acts as a unit. The local group in band societies is politically autonomous.

Bands are typically small, with less than 100 people usually, often considerably less. Each small band occupies a large territory, so population density is low. Band size often varies by season, with the band breaking up or recombining according to the food resources available at a given time and place. Inuit bands, for example, are smaller in the winter, when food is hard to find, and larger in the summer, when there is sufficient food to feed a larger group.

Political decision making within the band is generally informal. The "modest informal authority"[4] that does exist can be seen in the way decisions affecting the group are made. Because the formal, permanent office of a leader typically does not exist, decisions such as when a camp has to be moved or how a hunt is to be arranged are either agreed upon by the community as a whole or made by the best qualified member. Leadership, when an individual exercises it, is not the consequence of bossing or throwing one's weight about. Each band may have its informal **headman**, or its most proficient hunter, or a person most accomplished in rituals. There may be one person with all these qualities, or several people, but such a person or people will have gained status through the community's recognition of skill, good sense, and humility. Leadership, in other words, stems not from power but from influence, not from office but from admired personal qualities.

Headman A person who holds a powerless but symbolically unifying position in a community within an egalitarian society; may exercise influence but has no power to impose sanctions.

In Inuit bands, each settlement may have its headman, who acquires his influence because the other members of the community recognize his good judgment and superior skills. The headman's advice concerning the movement of the band and other community matters is generally heeded, but he possesses no permanent authority and has no power to impose sanctions of any kind. Inuit leaders are male, but men often consult their wives in private, and women who hunt seem to have more influence than those who do not.[5] In any case, leadership exists only in a very restricted sense, as among the Iglulik Inuit, for example:

> *Within each settlement ... there is as a rule an older man who enjoys the respect of the others and who decides when a move is to be made to another hunting center, when a hunt is to be started, how the spoils are to be divided, when the dogs are to be fed.... He is called* isumaitoq, *"he who thinks." It is not always the oldest man, but as a rule an elderly man who is a clever hunter or, as head of a large family, exercises great authority. He cannot be called a chief; there is no obligation to follow his counsel, but they do so in most cases, partly because they rely on his experience, partly because it pays to be on good terms with this man.*[6]

A Masai elder blesses a warrior by smearing the fat of a ceremonial ox on his face during an Eunoto ceremony when the warriors become junior elders and thenceforth are permitted to marry.

A summary of the general features of band organization can be found in Table 22.1. Note, however, that there are exceptions to these generalizations. For example, not all known foragers are organized at the band level or have all the features of a band type of society. Classic exceptions are the Native American societies of the Northwest Pacific coast, who had enormous resources of salmon and other fish, relatively large and permanent villages, and political organization beyond the level of the typical band societies in the ethnographic record.

Tribal Organization

When local communities mostly act autonomously but there are kinship groups (such as clans or lineages) or associations (such as age-sets) that can potentially integrate several local groups into a larger unit (**tribe**), we say that the society has **tribal organization**. Unfortunately, the term *tribe* is sometimes used to refer to an entire society; that is, an entire language group may be called a tribe. But a tribal type of political system does not usually permit the entire society to act as a unit; all the communities in a tribal society may be linked only occasionally for some political (usually military) purpose. Thus, what distinguishes tribal from band political organization is the presence in the former of some multilocal, but not usually societywide, integration. The multilocal integration, however, is *not permanent,* and it is *informal* in the sense that political officials do not head it. Frequently, the integration is called into play only when an outside threat arises; when the threat disappears, the local groups revert to self-sufficiency.[7] Tribal organization may seem fragile—and, of course, it usually is—but the fact that there are social ways to integrate local groups into larger political entities means that societies with tribal organization are militarily a good deal more formidable than societies with band organization.

Tribe A territorial population in which there are kin or nonkin groups with representatives in a number of local groups.

Societies with tribal political organization are similar to band societies in their tendency to be egalitarian (see Table 22.1). At the local level, informal leadership is also

TABLE 22.1 Suggested Trends in Political Organization and Other Social Characteristics

Type of Organization	Highest Level of Political Integration	Specialization of Political Officials	Predominant Mode of Subsistence	Community Size and Population Density	Social Differentiation	Major Form of Distribution
Band	Local group or band	Little or none; informal leadership	Foraging or food collecting	Very small communities; very low density	Egalitarian	Mostly reciprocity
Tribe	Sometimes multilocal group	Little or none; informal leadership	Extensive (shifting) agriculture and/or herding	Small communities; low density	Egalitarian	Mostly reciprocity
Chiefdom	Multilocal group	Some	Extensive or intensive agriculture and/or herding	Large communities; medium density	Rank	Reciprocity and redistribution
State	Multilocal group; often entire language group	Much	Intensive agriculture and herding	Cities and towns; high density	Class and caste	Mostly market exchange

characteristic. In those tribal societies where kinship provides the basic framework of social organization, the elders of the local kin groups tend to have considerable influence; where age-sets are important, a particular age-set is looked to for leadership. But, in contrast to band societies, societies with tribal organization generally are food producers. And because cultivation and animal husbandry are generally more productive than hunting and gathering, the population density of tribal societies is generally higher, local groups are larger, and the way of life is more sedentary than in hunter-gatherer bands.[8]

Tribal organization The kind of political organization in which local communities mostly act autonomously but there are kin groups (such as clans) or associations (such as age-sets) that can temporarily integrate a number of local groups into a larger unit.

Kinship Bonds Frequently communities are linked to each other by virtue of belonging to the same kin group, usually a unilineal group such as a lineage or clan. A **segmentary lineage system** is one type of tribal integration based on kinship. A society with such a system is composed of segments, or parts, each similar to the others in structure and function. Every local segment belongs to a hierarchy of lineages stretching farther and farther back genealogically. The hierarchy of lineages, then, unites the segments into larger and larger genealogical groups. The closer two groups are genealogically, the greater their general closeness. In the event of a dispute among members of different segments, people related more closely to one contestant than to another take the side of their nearest kinsman. The well-known Arab saying "I against my brothers; my brothers and I against our cousins; my brothers and cousins and I against the world" well expresses the contingency of relationships in conflict settings.[9]

Segmentary lineage system A hierarchy of more inclusive lineages; usually functions only in conflict situations.

Complementary opposition The occasional uniting of various segments of a segmentary lineage system in opposition to similar segments.

The Tiv of Northern Nigeria offer a classic example of a segmentary lineage system, one that happens to link all the Tiv into a single genealogical structure or tribe. The Tiv are a large society, numbering more than 800,000. Figure 22.1 is a representation of the Tiv lineage structure as described by Paul Bohannan. In the figure, there are four levels of lineages. Each of the smallest lineages, symbolized by *a* through *h*, is in turn embedded in more inclusive lineages. So minimal lineages *a* and *b* are together in lineage *1*. Lineages *1* and *2* are embedded in lineage *A*. Territorial organization follows lineage hierarchy. As shown in the bottom of the figure, the most closely related lineages have territories near each other. Minimal lineages *a* and *b* live next to each other; their combined territory is the territory of their higher-order lineage, *1*. Lineage *A* in turn has a territory that is differentiated from lineage *B*. All of Tivland is said to descend from one ancestor, represented by *I*.[10]

Tiv lineage organization is the foundation of Tiv political organization. A look at Figure 22.1 helps to explain how a dispute between lineages (and territories) *a* and *b* remains minor because no more than "brother" segments are involved. But a dispute between *a* and *c* involves lineages *1* and *2* as well, with the requirement that *b* assists *a* and *d* supports *c*. This process of mutual support, called **complementary opposition,** means that segments will unite only in a confrontation with some other group. Groups that will fight with each other in a minor dispute might coalesce at some later time against a larger group.

The segmentary lineage system was presumably very effective in allowing the Tiv to intrude into new territory and take land from other tribal societies with smaller descent groups. Individual Tiv lineage segments could call on support from related lineages when faced with border troubles. Conflicts within the society—that is, between segments—especially in border areas, were often turned outward, "releasing internal pressure in an explosive blast against other peoples."[11]

Segmentary lineage systems may have military advantages even when they do not unite the entire society. A classic example is the Nuer of the Upper Nile region, who had tribal,

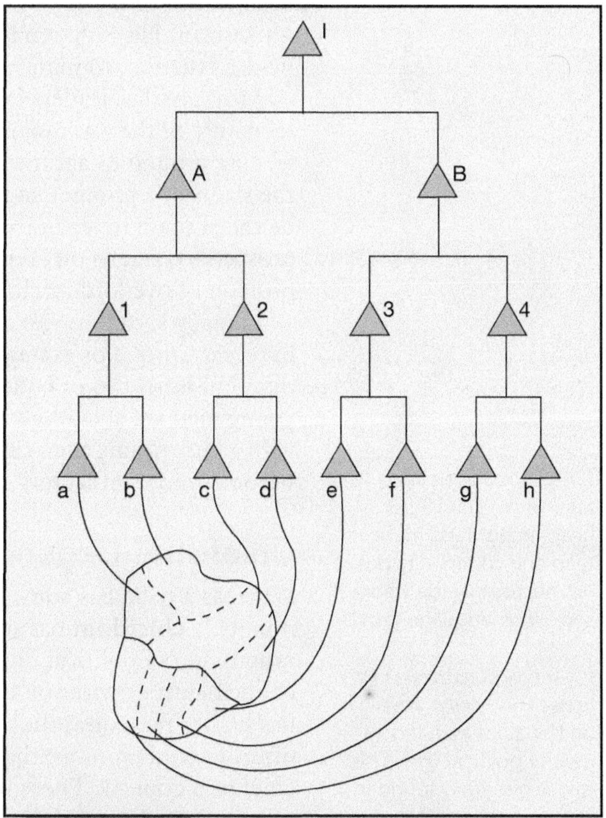

FIGURE 22.1 **Tiv Lineage Segments and Their Territories**

Source: Adapted from P. Bohannan 1954.

but not societywide, organization because of their segmentary lineages. In the early 1800s, the Nuer had a territory of about 8,700 square miles, and the neighboring Dinka had ten times that much. But by 1890, the Nuer had cut a 100-mile swath through Dinka territory, increasing Nuer territory to 35,000 square miles. Even though the Nuer and Dinka were culturally very similar, the segmentary lineage organization of the Nuer seems to have given them a significant military advantage in their incursions into Dinka territory.[12]

A segmentary lineage system may generate a formidable military force, but the combinations of manpower it produces are temporary, forming and dissolving as the occasion demands.[13] Tribal political organization does not make for a political system that more or less permanently integrates a number of communities.

Age-Set Systems Societies with age-sets have a group of people of the same sex and similar age who move through some or all of their life stages together. Usually entry into an age-set begins at or before puberty in a group initiation ceremony held regularly over the years. Often the age-sets encompass a number of communities, so that a sense of solidarity is formed. Age-sets can function as the basis of a tribal type of political organization, as among the Karimojong of northeastern Uganda.[14]

The Karimojong age-set system has an important bearing on day-to-day tribal life. As herders, Karimojong adults are often separated from their usual settlements. Herders will meet, mingle for a while, then go their separate ways, but each may call upon other members of his age-set wherever he goes. The age-set system is important among the Karimojong because it immediately allocates to each individual a place in the system and thereby establishes for him an appropriate pattern of response. A quarrel in camp will be settled by the representatives of the senior age-set who are present, regardless of which section of the tribe they may belong to.

Among the Karimojong, political leaders are not elected from among the elders of a particular age-set, nor are they appointed; they acquire their positions informally. Usually a man's background, and the ability he has demonstrated in public debates over a period of time, will result in his being considered by the men of his neighborhood to be their spokesman. His function is to announce what course of action seems required in a particular situation, to initiate that action, and then to coordinate it after it has begun.

Most political leaders exercise their authority within the local sphere because the pastoral nature of the Karimojong economy, with its dispersed groups and movement from one feeding ground to another, offers no alternative. From time to time, an elder may acquire the status of a prophet and be awarded respect and obedience on a tribal scale. He will be called upon to lead sacrifices (to avert misfortune), to undertake rainmaking (to bring prosperity), and so on. Yet even a prophet's prestige and authority do not warrant him a position of overlord or chief.[15]

In many societies with age-set systems, the authority of the elders has been weakened in recent times. For example, among the Karimojong, the council of elders could mete out punishment to offenders and watch them to make sure they behave. Nowadays, young men are able to get guns during raids, and elders find it risky to punish someone with a gun. Young men can also more readily move away, and social control by the elders becomes more difficult.[16]

Chiefdom Organization

Whereas a tribe has some informal mechanism that can integrate more than one community, a **chiefdom** has some *formal* structure that integrates more than one community into a political unit, such as a district. The formal structure could consist of a council with or without a chief, but most commonly there is a person—the **chief**—who has higher rank or authority than others. Most societies at the chiefdom level of organization contain more than one political unit or chiefdom, each headed by a district chief or a council. There may also be more than one level of chief beyond the community, such as district chiefs and higher-level chiefs. Some chiefdom societies integrate the whole society, with a paramount chief at the top. Others are not as centralized. Compared with tribal societies, societies with chiefdoms are more densely populated

Chiefdom A political unit, with a chief at its head, integrating more than one community but not necessarily the whole society or language group.

Chief A person who exercises authority, usually on behalf of a multicommunity political unit. This role is generally found in rank societies and is usually permanent and often hereditary.

and their communities are more permanent, partly as a consequence of their generally greater economic productivity[17] (see Table 22.1).

The position of chief, which is sometimes hereditary and generally permanent, bestows high status on its holder. Most chiefdoms have social ranking and accord the chief and his family greater access to prestige. The chief may redistribute goods, plan and direct the use of public labor, supervise religious ceremonies, and direct military activities on behalf of the chiefdom.[18] In South Pacific chiefdoms, the chiefs carried out most of these duties. In Fijian chiefdoms, for example, the chief was responsible for the redistribution of goods and the coordination of labor:

> *[The chief] could summon the community's labor on his own behalf, or on behalf of someone else who requested it, or for general purposes.... Besides his right to summon labor, he accumulated the greater proportion of the first fruits of the yam crop ... and he benefited from other forms of food presentation, or by the acquisition of special shares in ordinary village distribution.... Thus, the paramount [chief] would collect a significant part of the surplus production of the community and redistribute it in the general welfare.*[19]

A chief from Moorea in French Polynesia.

In contrast to leaders in tribal societies, who generally have to earn their privileges by their personal qualities, hereditary chiefs are said to have those qualities in their "blood." A high-ranking chief in Polynesia, a huge triangular area of islands in the South Pacific, inherited special religious power called *mana*. *Mana* sanctified his rule and protected him.[20] Chiefs in Polynesia had so much religious power that missionaries could convert people to Christianity only after their chiefs had been converted.[21]

In most chiefdoms, the chiefs did not have the power to compel people to obey them; people would act in accordance with the chief's wishes because the chief was respected and often had religious authority. But in the most complex paramount chiefdoms, such as those of Hawaii and Tahiti, the chiefs seemed to have more compelling sanctions than the "power" of respect or *mana*. Substantial amounts of goods and services collected by the chiefs were used to support subordinates, including specialists such as high priests, political envoys, and warriors who could be sent to quell rebellious factions.[22] When redistributions do not go to everybody—when chiefs are allowed to keep items for their own purposes—and when a chief begins to use armed force, the political system is on the way to becoming what we call a state.

State An autonomous political unit with centralized decision making over many communities with power to govern by force (e.g., to collect taxes, draft people for work and war, and make and enforce laws). Most states have cities with public buildings; full-time craft and religious specialists; an "official" art style; a hierarchical social structure topped by an elite class; and a governmental monopoly on the legitimate use of force to implement policies.

State Organization

A **state**, according to one more or less standard definition, is "an autonomous political unit, encompassing many communities within its territory and having a centralized government with the power to collect taxes, draft men for work or war, and decree and enforce laws."[23] States, then, have a complex, centralized political structure that includes a wide range of permanent institutions with legislative, executive, and judicial functions and a large bureaucracy. Central to this definition is the concept of legitimate force used to implement policies both internally and externally. In states, the government tries to maintain a monopoly on the use of physical force.[24] This monopoly can be seen in the development of formal and specialized instruments of social control: a police force, a militia, or a standing army.

Just as a particular society may contain more than one band, tribe, or chiefdom, so may it contain more than one state. The contiguously distributed population speaking a single language may or may not be politically unified in a single state. Ancient Greece was composed of many city-states; so, too, was Italy until the 1870s. German speakers are also not politically unified; Austria and Germany are separate states, and Germany itself was not politically unified until the 1870s. We say that a society has **state organization** when it is composed of one or more political units that are states.

State organization A society is described as having state organization when it includes one or more states.

A state may include more than one society. Multisociety states are often the result of conquest or colonial control when the dominant political authority, itself a state, imposes a centralized government over a territory with many different societies and cultures, as the British did in Nigeria and Kenya.

Colonialism is a common feature of state societies. But not all colonialisms are alike. Archaeology and history tell us about various kinds of colonialism. The expanding state society may send people to build a new imperial settlement in some other place to trade or protect trade routes, like the British, Spanish, and others did. Or the colonial power may displace and move parts of the original population, as the Inka empire did.[25] Most of the expanding state societies we know about are usually called *empires.* They incorporated other societies and states. The extension of U.S. power in modern times, for example, by persuading other countries to let the United States build military bases, has led some commentators to refer to an American empire, even though the United States did not always establish colonies where they had economic and political control.[26]

Nearly all of the multisociety states that emerged after World War II were the results of successful independence movements against colonial powers.[27] Most have retained their political unity despite the fact that they still contain many different societies. For example, Nigeria remains unified despite a civil war; the eastern section called Biafra (mostly populated by people of Ibo culture) tried unsuccessfully 30 years ago to secede, and subsequently there has been serious conflict among some of the constituent societies.

Migrants and Immigrants

The Growth of Cities

Nearly half of the world's human population now lives in cities, which are usually defined as communities where few are directly involved in food-getting. An even larger proportion of humanity will be urban dwellers in the future.

The explosive growth of cities over the past century is largely the result of migration from rural areas of the country and from rural areas in other countries. Recall the exodus of the Irish to Britain and the United States because of the "potato famine," the massive migrations from the villages of Germany, Italy, and Greece in the 19th and 20th centuries, and the huge migrations particularly in the last 50 years from rural Mexico and China. Poverty is one "push" factor. Flight from persecution is another. Many parts of the world are not safe, particularly for poor people. True, in the modern world, it is possible for some people to go "home" for a visit, even halfway around the world. But, for many migrants now and in the recent past, the move was one way. Because you may have run away from poverty, persecution, and war, you couldn't (or wouldn't) go home again.

Cities everywhere have problems, even in the most developed countries. Providing water, power, sanitation, and other services to perhaps millions of city dwellers is difficult and expensive. Yet in every country, people are leaving rural areas and going to cities. Some are political refugees, like the Hmong from Laos who now live in St. Paul, Minnesota. Then there are the people from Congo and Sudan, from Kosovo and Northern Ireland, who have fled civil wars. There are other reasons to leave too. Technological improvements may have reduced the need for rural labor, which happened in the U.S. South after the 1930s. Or the rural opportunities cannot support the increased number of mouths to be fed. Usually people do not go to other rural areas but rather to cities, often in other countries, where jobs are available. In the more urbanized countries, the cities have acquired "suburbs," where many of the people in a metropolitan area may actually live. But hardly anyone is left on the farm—only just a few percent of the population in the more developed countries.

In the last half of the 20th century, with the building of suburbs, there seems to have been a turning away from cities in many countries. Cities lost population as people moved to the suburbs to have more living space, a garden, "better" schools for their children, or to escape from the threat of violence. But recently, the flow has started to reverse in North America and elsewhere. The suburbanites are coming back to the cities, perhaps because people are getting tired of commuting longer distances to jobs and recreation. This is particularly so with wealthier people whose children have grown up and moved away, and with more people living until older ages, many want to move closer to the places where they mostly spend their time. Despite the social inequality and violence, cities have always been the places to go for jobs and other activities. Concerts, theaters, restaurants, museums, amusement parks, hospitals, and professional sports stadiums have always been located in cities or nearby.

The "push" out of the rural areas and the "pull" of the cities are hard to resist, despite the enormous political problems of urban living. As the old song laments, "Howya goin' keep 'em down on the farm after they've seen Paree?"

Source: M. Ember and Ember 2002.

Multisociety or multiethnic states may also form voluntarily, in reaction to external threat. Switzerland comprises cantons, each of which speaks mainly French, German, Italian, or Romansch; the various cantons confederated originally to shake off control by the Holy Roman Empire. But some states have lost their unity recently, including the former Union of Soviet Socialist Republics (USSR) and much of Yugoslavia.

In addition to their strictly political features, intensive agriculture generally supports state-organized societies. The high productivity of the agriculture allows for the emergence of cities, a high degree of economic and other kinds of specialization, and market or commercial exchange. In addition, state societies usually have class stratification (see Table 22.1). Cities have grown tremendously in the last 100 years, largely as a result of migration and immigration. (See the Migrants and Immigrants box on "The Growth of Cities.")

When states come into existence, people's access to scarce resources is radically altered. So, too, is their ability not to listen to leaders: You usually cannot refuse to pay taxes or avoid labor or military conscription and go unpunished. Of course, the rulers of a state do not maintain the social order by force alone. The people must believe, at least to some extent, that those in power have a legitimate right to govern. If the people think otherwise, history suggests that those in power may eventually lose their ability to control. Witness the recent downfall of Communist parties throughout most of eastern Europe and the former Soviet Union.

So force and the threat of force are not enough to explain the legitimacy of power and the inequities that occur commonly in state societies. But then what does? There are various theories. The rulers of early states often claimed divine descent to buttress their legitimacy, but this claim is rare nowadays. Another theory is that, if parents teach their children to accept all authority, such lessons may generalize to the acceptance of political authority. Some analysts think that people accept state authority for no good reason; the rulers are just able to fool them. Finally, some theorists think that states must provide people with real or rational advantages; otherwise, people would not think that the rulers deserve to exercise authority. Legitimacy is not an all-or-none phenomenon; it varies in degree.[28]

A state society can retain its legitimacy, or at least its power, for a long time. For example, the Roman Empire was a complex state society that dominated the Mediterranean and Near East for hundreds of years. It began as a city-state that waged war to acquire additional

Popular demonstrations can have major effects on states. These protests in the Ukraine in 2004 disputed election results and subsequently the courts voided the election.

territory. At its height, the Roman Empire embraced more than 55 million people;[29] the capital city of Rome had a population of well over a million.[30] The empire included parts of what are now Great Britain, France, Spain, Portugal, Germany, Rumania, Turkey, Greece, Armenia, Egypt, Israel, and Syria.

Another example of a state society was the kingdom of Nupe in West Africa, now part of the nation-state of Nigeria. Nupe society was rigidly stratified. At the top of the social system was the king, or *etsu*. Beneath the king, members of the royal family formed the highest aristocratic class. Next in order were two other classes of nobility: the local chiefs and the military leaders. At the bottom were the commoners, who had neither prestige nor power and no share in political authority.

The Nupe king possessed ultimate authority in many judicial matters. Local village councils handled minor disputes and civil cases, but serious criminal cases were the prerogative of the king. Such cases, referred to as "crimes for the king," were brought before the royal court by the king's local representatives. The king and his counselors judged the cases and determined suitable punishments.

The most powerful influence of the state over the Nupe people was in the area of taxation. The king was given the power to impose taxes and collect them from every household. Payment was made either in money (cowrie shells originally and, later, British currency) or certain gifts, such as cloth, mats, and slaves. The king kept much of the revenue collected, and his local representatives and lords shared the remainder. In return for the taxes they paid, the people received security—protection against invasion and domestic disorder.[31]

Although all state societies employ coercion or the threat of it, some states are more autocratic than others. This is not just today, or in the recent past, but also in the distant past. The less autocratic states are characterized by more "collective action." They produce more public goods, such as transportation systems and redistribution systems, in times of need. The rulers do not aggrandize themselves as much or live that luxuriously. And, the rulers must rule within limits and must respond to grievances. They are accountable. The Lozi state of central southern Africa had more collective action than the Nupe state described. The Lozi built an extensive system of drainage canals that also facilitated transportation. In hungry times, royal herds and the "state" gardens were used to feed distressed villages. And rulers were not that much more elevated in standard of living. In contrast, the Nupe state financed very little in the way of public works, had little redistribution, and the rulers lived in elaborate palaces.[32] Collective action is a continuum; states at the higher end of that continuum have not been limited to a few world regions or particular time periods. Collection action theorists suggest that, when the state relies more heavily on resources from taxpayers, the rulers must give the public more in return or else face noncompliance and rebellion. Richard Blanton and Lane Fargher's comparative study of premodern states supports collection action theory.[33]

Nation-State, Nationalism, and Political Identity

States are political entities; people within them do not necessarily share much beyond a bureaucracy, a set of laws, and being subject to similar social controls. People within them may not have a sense of identity with the state they live in. A sense of identity is more likely if a state is composed of a dominant culture or ethnic group, but most states, certainly almost all empires, have commonly been multicultural or multiethnic entities.[34] In order to increase a sense of identity, some states have deliberately tried to incorporate and assimilate other cultural groups by promoting a common language and religion; other states have tolerated and sometimes even promoted multiculturalism. Multiculturalism does not preclude identification with the state as well as one's own ethnicity—after all, toleration of divergent ethnic identities may forge a sense of pride in state government. Scholars often use the term **nation** to refer to the idea that a set of people share a common territory, history, and identity.[35] We may call it a state or a **nation-state** when the concepts of nation and state co-occur; that is when the people in a state share a sense of nationhood. If there is a strong sense of identity with the nation, willingness to fight and die for it, **nationalism** is a term often used as an expression of that loyalty. Arjun Appadurai notes that the concept of nationalism includes "full attachment," which goes well beyond the concept of legitimacy. In his view, full attachment includes strong emotions such as excitement at national parades, tears at hearing the national anthem, and intense anger when a nation is thought

Nation A set of people sharing a common territory, history, and a sense of identity.

Nation-state The co-occurrence of a political state and a nation

Nationalism The strong sense of loyalty, attachment, and devotion to a nation (see nation).

Applied Anthropology

Democracy and Economic Development

As people increasingly produce goods and services for a market and as the pace of economic development quickens, economies are increasingly integrated into the world system. What effect, if any, does economic development have on political participation? Can we speculate about the future on the basis of comparative research?

Most of the comparative research on the relationship between economic development and political participation has been cross-national, comparing data on different countries. Some countries are more democratic than others, with characteristics such as contested elections, an elected head of state, an elected powerful legislature, and the protection of civil liberties. In capitalist countries, more democracy is generally associated with higher levels of economic development, as measured by indicators such as per capita output; in countries that are not very industrialized, there is little democracy at the national level. Why should more democracy be associated with more economic development? The prevailing opinion is that economic development increases the degree of social equality in the country; and the more equality among interest groups, the more they demand participation in the political process, and hence the more democracy.

Lech Walesa played an important role in the relatively peaceful transition in Poland from communism to democracy.

What about the societies usually studied by anthropologists, the ones in what we call the cross-cultural or ethnographic record? We know that some of the highest levels of political participation occur in foraging societies. Many adults in such societies have a say in decisions, and leadership is informal; leaders can retain their roles only if people voluntarily go along with them. Concentrated power and less political participation are more likely in chiefdoms and states than in band and tribal societies. The more hierarchical chiefdoms and states usually depend on agriculture, particularly intensive agriculture, which can produce more goods and services per capita than foraging economies can. So the relationship between economic development and political participation in the ethnographic record is *opposite* to what we find cross-nationally. That is, the more economic development, the less political participation in the societies studied by anthropologists. Why should this be so? It seems that social equality *decreases* as economic development increases in the ethnographic record (which does not include many industrialized societies). In that record, an economically developed society is likely to have features such as plowing, fertilizers, and irrigation, which make permanent cultivation of the fields and permanent communities possible. Such intensive agricultural activity is more conducive to concentrated wealth than is hunter-gatherer subsistence or shifting cultivation (horticulture). Thus, in the ethnographic record, the more economically developed societies have more social inequality and therefore less democracy.

The two sets of findings, the cross-national and the cross-cultural, are not that hard to reconcile. Social and economic inequality appears to work against democracy and extensive political participation. Social inequality increases with the switch from foraging to agriculture. But social inequality decreases with the switch from preindustrial agriculture to high (industrial) levels of economic development. Political participation decreases with the first switch and increases with the second, because social inequality first increases and then decreases.

So what does comparative research suggest about the future? If the middle and working classes feel they are not getting a fair return on their labor, their demands should increase. The elite may be willing to satisfy those increased demands; if they do, their power will be reduced. In either case, unless the elite try to retain their power at any cost, there should be more political participation and more democracy, at least in the long run.

Sources: Bollen 1993; Muller 1997; M. Ember, Ember, and Russett 1997; Ross 2009b.

to be insulted.[36] But the concepts of nation and nationalism are not necessarily associated with states. There are groups living within state boundaries that comprise separate nations (some describe French and English Canada as two nations within one) or who strive for separate nationhood for themselves. There are also groups that cross country borders, like the Kurds of Iraq, Iran, Turkey, and Syria who feel a sense of nationhood as Kurds and their homeland "Kurdistan."[37] Nationalism can even transcend big distances. Even when people are widely scattered in other countries, sometimes even are citizens of other countries, they may have a strong sense of nationalism about their ancestral home. They may demonstrate their nationalism by lobbying, demonstrating, setting up Web sites, sending contributions, and even giving their lives for the cause of creating a separate nation.[38]

Factors Associated with Variation in Political Organization

The kinds of political organization we call band, tribal, chiefdom, and state are points on a continuum of levels of political integration or unification, from small-scale local autonomy to large-scale regional unification. There also is variation in political authority, from a few temporary and informal political leaders to large numbers of permanent, specialized political officials, from the absence of coercive political power to the monopoly of public force by a central authority. These aspects of variation in political organization are generally associated with shifts from foraging to more intensive food production, from small to large communities, from low to high population densities, from an emphasis on reciprocity to redistribution to market exchange, and from egalitarian to rank to fully stratified class societies.

The associations just outlined, which seem to be confirmed by the available cross-cultural evidence, are summarized in Table 22.1. With regard to the relation between level of subsistence technology and political complexity, one cross-cultural study employing a small random sample of societies found that the greater the importance of agriculture in a society, the larger the population that is politically unified and the greater the number and types of political officials.[39] A massive cross-cultural survey reported a similar trend: The more intensive the agriculture, the greater the likelihood of state organization; conversely, societies with no more than local political institutions are likely to depend on hunting, gathering, and fishing.[40]

Community size appears to be an especially sensitive predictor of political complexity—larger communities strongly predict not only a wider range of political officials in a society, but also more administrative levels of decision making.[41] In particular, societies with state organization tend to have cities and towns, whereas those with only local political organization are more likely to have communities with an average population of fewer than 200 people.[42] Cross-cultural research also tends to confirm that societies with higher levels of political integration are more likely to exhibit social differentiation, especially in the form of class distinctions.[43]

Does this evidence provide us with an explanation for why political organization varies? Clearly, the data indicate that several factors are associated with political development, but exactly why changes in organization occur is not yet understood. Although economic development may be a necessary condition for political development,[44] that relation does not fully explain why political organization should become more complex just because the economy can support it. Some theorists have suggested that competition among groups may be a more important reason for political consolidation. For example, Elman Service suggested competition as a reason why a society might change from a band level of political organization to a tribal level. Band societies are generally hunter-gatherers. With a changeover to agriculture, population density and competition among groups may increase. Service believed that such competition would foster the development of some informal organization beyond the community—namely, tribal organization—for offense and defense.[45] Indeed, both unilineal kinship groups and age-set systems seem to be associated with warfare.

Among agriculturalists, defensive needs might also be the main reason for switching from informal multivillage political organization to more formal chiefdom organization. Formally organized districts are probably more likely to defeat autonomous villages or even segmentary lineage systems.[46] If warfare were very frequent and intense, it is possible that war leaders, with the help of loyal warriors, could enhance their positions and become more permanent political leaders.[47] In addition, there may be economic reasons for political development. With regard to chiefdoms, Service suggested that chiefdoms will emerge when redistribution among communities becomes important or when large-scale coordinated work groups are required. The more important these activities are, the more important—and hence more "chiefly"—the organizer and his family presumably become.[48] But redistribution is far from a universal activity of chiefs.[49]

Theory and research on the anthropology of political development have focused mostly on the high end of the scale of political complexity, and particularly on the origins of the first state societies. Those earliest states apparently rose independently of one another, after about 3500 B.C., in what are now southern Iraq, Egypt, northwestern India, northern China, and central Mexico. There are several theories of why states arose. The irrigation theory suggests that the administrative needs of maintaining extensive irrigation systems may have been the impetus for state formation.[50] The circumscription theory suggests that states emerge when competition and warfare in physically or socially circumscribed areas lead to the subordination of defeated groups, which are obliged to submit to the control of the most powerful group.[51] Theories involving trade suggest that the organizational requirements of producing exportable items, redistributing imported items, and defending trading parties would foster state formation.[52] The state, by definition, implies the power to organize large populations for collective purposes. But at this point, most anthropologists believe that no one theory is able to explain the formation of every state. Perhaps different organizational requirements in different areas all favored centralized government.[53]

The Spread of State Societies

22.2 Explain the spread of state societies.

The state level of political development has come to dominate the world. Societies with states have larger communities and higher population densities than do band, tribal, and chiefdom societies. They also have armies that are ready to fight at almost any time. State systems that have waged war against chiefdoms and tribes have almost always won, and the result has usually been the political incorporation of the losers. For example, the British and, later, the U.S. colonization of much of North America led to the defeat and incorporation of many Native American societies.

The defeat and incorporation of the Native Americans was at least partly due to the catastrophic depopulations they suffered because of epidemic diseases, such as smallpox and measles, that European colonists introduced. Catastrophic depopulation was commonly the outcome of the first contacts between European Americans and the natives of North and South America, as well as the natives of the far islands in the Pacific. People in the New World and the Pacific had not been exposed, and therefore were not resistant to the diseases the European Americans carried with them when they began to colonize the world. Before the expansion of Europeans, the people of the New World and the Pacific had been separated for a long time from the people and diseases on the geographically continuous landmass we separate into Europe, Africa, and Asia. Smallpox, measles, and the other former scourges of Europe had largely become childhood diseases that most individuals of European ancestry survived.[54]

Whether by depopulation, conquest, or intimidation, the number of independent political units in the world has decreased strikingly in the last 3,000 years, and especially in the last 200 years. Robert Carneiro estimated that in 1000 B.C., there may have been between 100,000 and 1 million separate political units in the world; today, there are fewer than 200.[55] In the ethnographic record, about 50 percent of the 2,000 or so societies described within the last 150 years had only local political integration. That is, the highest level of political integration in one out of two recent societies was the local community.[56] Thus, most of the decrease in the number of independent political units has occurred fairly recently.

But the recent secessions from the former Soviet Union and Yugoslavia and other separatist movements around the world suggest that ethnic rivalries may make for departures from the trend toward larger and larger political units. Ethnic groups that have been dominated by others in multinational states may opt for political autonomy, at least for a while. On the other hand, the separate nations of western Europe are becoming more unified every day, both politically and economically. So the trend toward larger political units may be continuing, even if there are departures from it now and then.

Extrapolating from past history, a number of investigators have suggested that the entire world will eventually come to be politically integrated, perhaps as soon as the 23rd century and no later than A.D. 4850.[57] Only the future will tell if this prediction will come true and if further political integration in the world will occur peacefully—with all parties agreeing—or by force or the threat of force, as has happened so often in the past.

22.3 Describe and explain the variation in political structure in various societies.

Variation in Political Process

Anthropologists are increasingly interested in the politics, or political processes, of the societies they study: who acquires influence or power, how they acquire it, and how political decisions are made. But even though we have descriptive accounts of politics in many societies, there is still little comparative or cross-cultural research on what may explain variation in politics.[58]

Getting to Be a Leader

In those societies that have hereditary leadership, which is common in rank societies and in state societies with monarchies, rules of succession usually establish how leadership is inherited. Such leaders are often identifiable in some obviously visible ways; they may be permanently marked or tattooed, as in chiefdoms in Polynesia, or they may wear elaborate dress and insignia, as in class-stratified societies. But for societies whose leaders are *chosen*, either as informal leaders or as political officials, we need a lot more research to understand why some kinds of people are chosen over others.

A few studies have investigated the personal qualities of leaders in tribal societies. One study, conducted among the Mekranoti-Kayapo of central Brazil, found that leaders, in contrast to followers, tend to be rated by their peers as higher in intelligence, generosity, knowledgeability, ambitiousness, and aggressiveness. Leaders also tend to be older. And despite the egalitarian nature of Mekranoti society (at least with respect to sharing resources), sons of leaders are more likely than others to become leaders.[59] The Mekranoti leaders also tend to be taller, consistent with research in the United States.

Research in another Brazilian society, the Kagwahiv of the Amazon region, suggests another personal quality of leaders: They seem to have positive feelings about their fathers and mothers.[60] In many respects, studies of leaders in the United States show them to be not that different from their counterparts in Brazil. But there is one major difference: Mekranoti and Kagwahiv leaders are not wealthier than others; in fact, they give their wealth away. U.S. leaders are generally wealthier than others.[61]

"Big Men" In some egalitarian tribal societies, the quest for leadership seems quite competitive. In parts of New Guinea and South America, "big men" compete with other ambitious men to attract followers. Men who want to compete must show that they have magical powers, success in gardening, and bravery in war. But, most important, they have to collect enough goods to throw big parties at which the goods are given away. Big men have to work very hard to attract and keep their followings, for dissatisfied followers can always join other aspiring men.[62] The wives of big men are often leaders too. Among the Kagwahiv, for example, a headman's wife is usually the leader of the women in the community; she is responsible for much of the planning for feasts and often distributes the meat at them.[63]

Although the phenomenon of big men leaders is common throughout New Guinea, researchers are beginning to see variation in the type and extent of "bigmanship" in different areas of New Guinea. For example, in the southern Highlands, groups of men (not just big men) may engage in large-scale giveaways, so big men are not so different from ordinary men. In the northwestern Highlands, on the other hand, big men stand out from other men in striking ways. They make policy for groups of people and organize collective events, they have substantial access to pigs or to valuables acquired in exchanges, and they have control over a substantial amount of labor (more than one wife and fellow kin).[64]

We know that some big men are "bigger" than others, but how does a man get to be a big man? Among the Kumdi-Engamoi, a central Highlands group, a man who wants to be considered a *wua nium* (literally, a "great-important-wealthy man") needs to have many wives and daughters, because the amount of land controlled by a man and how much can be produced on that land depend on the number of women in his family. The more wives he has, the more land he is given to cultivate. He must also be a good speaker. Everyone has the right to speak and give speeches, but to get to be known as a big man requires speaking well and forcefully and knowing when to sum up a consensus. It usually takes a man until his thirties or forties to acquire more than one wife and to make his name through exchanges. When a man wants to inaugurate an exchange, he needs to get shells and pigs from his family and relatives. Once he has achieved a reputation as a *wua nium,* he can keep it only if he continues to perform well—that is, if he continues to distribute fairly, make wise decisions, speak well, and conduct exchanges.[65]

"Big Women" In contrast to most of mainland New Guinea, the islands off the southeastern coast are characterized by matrilineal descent. But, like the rest of New Guinea, the islands also have a shifting system of leadership in which people compete for "big" status. Here, though, the people competing are women as well as men, and so there are "big women" as well as "big men." On the island of Vanatinai, for example, women and men compete with each other to exchange valuables. Women lead canoe expeditions to distant islands to visit male as well as female exchange partners, women mobilize relatives and exchange partners to mount large feasts, and the women get to keep the ceremonial valuables exchanged, at least for a while.[66]

The prominence of women on Vanatinai may be linked to the disappearance of warfare—the colonial powers imposed peace; we call this "pacification." Interisland exchanges became frequent when war became rarer in the early 20th century, giving women and men more freedom to travel. For men, but not women, war provided a path to leadership; champion warriors would acquire great renown and influence. It is not that women did not participate in war; they did, which is unusual cross-culturally, but a woman could not become a war leader. Now, in the absence of war, women have an opportunity through exchanges to become leaders, or "big women."

In one respect, however, women have less of an opportunity to acquire influence now. There are local government councils now, but all the councillors are male. Why? Some women were nominated for the posts, but they withdrew in embarrassment because they could not speak English. Big men or big women do not automatically have a path to these new positions; mostly young males who know English become the councillors. But this situation may change. With the opening of a government primary school in 1984, both girls and boys are learning English, so women in the future may be more likely to achieve leadership by becoming councillors.

Researchers continue to explore other features that may enhance a person's ability to become leaders where leadership is not hereditary. One fascinating new finding is that in the United States, after controlling for age and perceived attractiveness, individuals who are judged prior to the election to be more "competent" from photographs of their faces are more likely to win in congressional elections.[67] What makes a face look more "competent"? Generally, it has fewer "babyish" features—it is less round, has a bigger chin, smaller eyes, and a smaller forehead.[68] However, in wartime, more masculine facial qualities appear to be preferred in a leader; in peacetime, more

In many egalitarian societies, leadership shifts informally from one person to another. In much of New Guinea, there is more competition for achieving "big" status. On Vanatinai, the women compete as well as the men, so there are "big women" as well as "big men." Here a "big woman" paints the face of her cousin's widow for a feast honoring the dead man.

feminine qualities.[69] Whether these facial features also predict leadership cross-culturally is not yet known.

Political Participation

Read the Document: Political Participation

Political scientist Marc Ross conducted cross-cultural research on variation in degree of political participation. Ross phrased the research question: "Why is it that in some polities there are relatively large numbers of persons involved in political life, while in others, political action is the province of very few?"[70]

Political participation in preindustrial societies ranges from widespread to low or nonexistent. In 16 percent of the societies examined, there is widespread participation; decision-making forums are open to all adults. The forums may be formal (councils and other governing bodies) or informal. Next in degree of political participation are societies (37 percent) that have widespread participation by some but not all adults (men but not women, certain classes but not others). Next are societies (29 percent) that have some but not much input by the community. Finally, 18 percent of the societies have low or nonexistent participation, which means that leaders make most decisions, and involvement of the average person is very limited.

Degree of political participation seems to be high in small-scale societies, as well as in modern democratic nation-states, but not in between (feudal states and preindustrial empires). Why? In small-scale societies, leaders do not have the power to force people to act; thus, a high degree of political participation may be the only way to get people to go along with decisions. In modern democracies, which have many powerful groups outside the government—corporations, unions, and other associations are examples—the central authorities may only theoretically have the power to force people to go along; in reality, they rely mostly on voluntary compliance. For example, the U.S. government failed when it tried with force (Prohibition, 1920–1933) to stop the manufacture, transport, and sale of alcoholic beverages.

Another factor may be early family experiences. Some scholars recently have suggested that the type of family people are raised in predicts the degree of political participation in a society. A large extended family with multiple generations tends to be hierarchical, with the older generations having more authority. Children may learn that they have to obey and subordinate their wishes to their elders. Societies with polygyny also seem to have less political participation. The ways of interacting in the family may carry over to the political sphere.[71]

A high degree of political participation seems to have an important consequence. In the modern world, democratically governed states rarely go to war with each other.[72] So, for example, the United States invaded three countries—Grenada, Panama, and Iraq—between 1980 and 1993, but no democracies. Similarly, it appears that more participatory, that is, more "democratic," political units in the ethnographic record fight with each other significantly less often than do less participatory political units, just as seems to be the case among modern nation-states.[73] Does this mean that democracies are more peaceful in general? Here there is more controversy. Judging by the frequency of war, modern democratic states do not look very different from autocratic states in their tendency to go to war. However, if you look at the severity of war as measured by casualty rates, democratic societies do look less warlike.[74] Exactly why more participation or more democracy is likely to lead to peace remains to be established.

Resolution of Conflict

22.4 Critically examine the methods used for resolving conflict, including warfare, in different societies.

The resolution of conflict may be accomplished peacefully by avoidance, community action, mediation or the negotiation of compromises, apology, appeal to supernatural forces, or adjudication by a third party. As we shall see, the procedures used usually vary with degree of social complexity; decisions by third parties are more likely in hierarchical societies.[75] But peaceful solutions are not always possible, and disputes may erupt into violent conflict. When violence occurs within a political unit in which disputes are usually settled peacefully, we call such violence *crime,* particularly when committed by an individual. When the violence occurs among groups of people from separate political units—groups among which there is no procedure for settling disputes—we usually call such violence *warfare*. When violence occurs among subunits of a population that had been politically unified, we call it *civil war*. Although we talk about conflict resolution as either peaceful or violent in the sections below, it is important to understand that even when violent resolution methods occur, peace-making efforts often follow, including reconciliation, intervention by third parties, or by avoidance.[76]

Peaceful Resolution of Conflict

Most modern industrialized states have formal institutions and offices, such as police, district attorneys, courts, and penal systems, to deal with minor disputes and more serious conflicts that may arise in society. All these institutions generally operate according to **codified laws**—that is, a set of explicit, usually written rules stipulating what is permissible and what is not. Transgression of the law by individuals gives the state the right to take action against them. The state has a monopoly on the legitimate use of force in the society, for it alone has the right to coerce subjects into agreement with regulations, customs, political edicts, and procedures.

Codified laws Formal principles for resolving disputes in heterogeneous and stratified societies.

Many societies lack such specialized offices and institutions for dealing with conflict. Yet, because all societies have peaceful, regularized ways of handling at least certain disputes, some anthropologists speak of the *universality of law*. E. Adamson Hoebel, for example, stated the principle as follows:

> *Each people has its system of social control. And all but a few of the poorest of them have as a part of the control system a complex of behavior patterns and institutional mechanisms that we may properly treat as law. For, "anthropologically considered, law is merely one aspect of our culture—the aspect that employs the force of organized society to regulate individual and group conduct and to prevent redress or punish deviations from prescribed social norms."*[77]

So how do you know what the laws are in societies without codified law? In Hoebel's view, the laws of a society become evident when you observe authorities threatening or using force when individuals or groups violate the rules. But others suggest that Hoebel's view of law is too narrow because nonviolent mechanisms such as shunning, gossip, and public opinion can be quite effective in the absence of force.[78]

Read the Document: Law and Society

Law, then, whether informal as in simpler societies, or formal as in more complex societies, provides a means of dealing peacefully with whatever conflicts develop. That does not mean that conflicts are always resolved peacefully. But that also does not mean that people cannot learn to resolve their conflicts peacefully. The fact that there are societies with little or no violent conflict means that it may be possible to learn from them; it may be possible to discover how to avoid violent outcomes of conflicts. How come South Africa could move relatively peacefully from a society dominated by people from Europe to one with government and civil rights shared by all groups? On the other hand, Bosnia had very violent conflict among ethnic groups and needed intervention by outside parties to keep the warring sides apart.[79]

Avoidance Violence can often be avoided if the parties to a dispute voluntarily avoid each other or are separated until emotions cool down. Anthropologists have frequently remarked that foragers are particularly likely to make use of this technique. People may move to other bands or move their dwellings to opposite ends of camp. Shifting horticulturalists may also split up when conflicts get too intense. Avoidance is obviously easier in societies, such as band societies, that are nomadic or seminomadic and in which people have temporary dwellings. And avoidance is more feasible when people live independently and self-sufficiently (e.g., in cities and suburbs).[80] But even if conditions in such societies may make avoidance easier, we still need to know why some societies use avoidance more than confrontation as a way of resolving conflict.

Community Action Societies have found various ways of resolving disputes peacefully. One such way involves action by a group or the community as a whole; collective action is common in simpler societies that lack powerful authoritarian leaders.[81] Many Inuit societies, for example, frequently resolve disputes through community action. An individual's failure to heed a taboo or to follow the suggestions of a shaman leads to expulsion from the group, because the community cannot accept a risk to its livelihood. People who fail

Although mediation is commonly used in relatively egalitarian societies, it is also used in societies with courts and other formal adjudication procedures for minor conflicts. A teacher in the United States tries to mediate a dispute between two boys.

to share goods voluntarily will find them confiscated and distributed to the community, and they may be executed in the process. A single case of murder, as an act of vengeance (usually because of the abduction of a wife or as part of a blood feud), does not concern the community, but repeated murders do. Franz Boas gave a typical example:

There was a native of Padli by the name Padlu. He had induced the wife of a native of Cumberland Sound to desert her husband and follow him. The deserted husband, meditating revenge ... visited his friends in Padli, but before he could accomplish his intention of killing Padlu, the latter shot him. ... A brother of the murdered man went to Padli to avenge the death ... but he also was killed by Padlu. A third native of Cumberland Sound, who wished to avenge the death of his relatives, was also murdered by him.

On account of these outrages, the natives wanted to get rid of Padlu, but yet they did not dare to attack him. When the pimain *(headman) of the Akudmurmuit learned of these events he started southward and* asked every man in Padli whether Padlu should be killed. All agreed; *so he went with the latter deer hunting ... and ... shot Padlu in the back.*[82]

The killing of an individual is the most extreme action a community can take—we call it *capital punishment*. The community as a whole or a political official or a court may decide to administer such punishment, but capital punishment seems to exist in nearly all societies, from the simplest to the most complex.[83] It is often assumed that capital punishment deters crime. If it did, we would expect the abolition of capital punishment to be followed by an increase in homicide rates. But that does not seem to happen. A cross-national study indicates that the abolition of capital punishment tends to be followed by a decrease in homicide rates.[84]

Negotiation The process by which the parties to a dispute try to resolve it themselves.

Mediation The process by which a third party tries to bring about a settlement in the absence of formal authority to force a settlement.

Negotiation and Mediation In many conflicts, the parties to a dispute may come to a settlement themselves by **negotiation**. There aren't necessarily any rules for how they will do so, but any solution is "good" if it restores peace.[85] Sometimes an outside or third party is used to help bring about a settlement among the disputants. We call it **mediation** when the outside party tries to help bring about a settlement, but that third party does not have the formal authority to force a settlement. Both negotiation and mediation are likely when the society is relatively egalitarian and it is important for people to get along.[86]

Among the Nuer of East Africa, a pastoral and horticultural people, disputes within the community can be settled with the help of an informal mediator called the "leopard-skin chief." His position is hereditary and makes its holder responsible for the social well-being of the district. Matters such as cattle stealing rarely come to the attention of the leopard-skin chief. But if, for example, a murder has been committed, the culprit will go at once to the house of the leopard-skin chief. Immediately the chief cuts the culprit's arm so that blood flows; until the cut has been made, the murderer may not eat or drink. If the murderer is afraid of vengeance by the slain man's family, he will remain at the house of the leopard-skin chief, which is considered sanctuary. Then, within the next few months, the chief attempts to mediate among the parties to the crime. He tries to arrange compensation by the slayer's kin to avoid a feud, and he persuades the dead man's kin that they ought to accept the compensation, usually in the form of cattle. The chief then collects the cattle—40 to 50—and takes them to the dead man's home, where he performs various sacrifices of cleansing and atonement.[87] Throughout the process, the chief acts as a go-between. He has no authority to force either party to negotiate, and he has no power to enforce a solution once it has been arrived at. However, he is able to take advantage of the fact that both disputants are anxious to avoid a blood feud.

Ritual Reconciliation—Apology The desire to restore a harmonious relationship may also explain ceremonial apologies. An apology is based on deference—the guilty party shows obeisance and asks for forgiveness. Such ceremonies tend to occur in recent chiefdoms.[88] For example, among the Fijians of the South Pacific, when a person offends someone of higher status, the offended person and other villagers begin to avoid, and gossip about, the offender. If offenders are sensitive to village opinion, they will perform a ceremony of apology called *i soro*. One of the meanings of *soro* is "surrender." In the ceremony, the offender bows the head and remains silent while an intermediary speaks, presents a token gift, and asks the offended person for forgiveness. The apology is rarely rejected.[89]

Oaths and Ordeals Still another way of peacefully resolving disputes is through oaths and ordeals, both of which involve appeals to supernatural power. An **oath** is the act of calling upon a deity to bear witness to the truth of what one says. An **ordeal** is a means used to determine guilt or innocence by submitting the accused to dangerous or painful tests believed to be under supernatural control.[90]

Oath The act of calling upon a deity to bear witness to the truth of what one says.

Ordeal A means of determining guilt or innocence by submitting the accused to dangerous or painful tests believed to be under supernatural control.

A common kind of ordeal, found in almost every part of the world, is scalding. Among the Tanala of Madagascar, the accused person, having first had his hand carefully examined for protective covering, has to reach his hand into a cauldron of boiling water and grasp, from underneath, a rock suspended there. He then plunges his hand into cold water, has it bandaged, and is led off to spend the night under guard. In the morning, his hand is unbandaged and examined. If there are blisters, he is guilty.

How could an innocent person really hope to be vindicated in an ordeal? Lawrence Rosen points out that there may have been a high probability that the person subject to an ordeal was actually guilty since human, not supernatural, judgment would be involved in identifying the suspect in the first place. Especially in small communities, people would have previous knowledge of that person, so there may have been probable cause of guilt.[91]

Oaths and ordeals have also been practiced in Western societies. Both were common in medieval Europe.[92] Even today, in our own society, vestiges of oaths can be found. Children can be heard to say "Cross my heart and hope to die," and witnesses in courts of law are obliged to swear to tell the truth.

Why do some societies use oaths and ordeals? John Roberts suggested that their use tends to be found in fairly complex societies in which political officials lack sufficient power to make and enforce judicial decisions or would make themselves unnecessarily vulnerable were they to attempt to do so. So the officials may use oaths and ordeals to let the gods decide guilt or innocence.[93] In contrast, smaller and less complex societies probably have no need for elaborate mechanisms such as courts, oaths, and ordeals to ascertain guilt. In such societies, everyone is aware of what crimes have been committed and who the guilty parties probably are.

Adjudication, Courts, and Codified Law We call it **adjudication** when a third party acting as judge makes a decision that the disputing parties have to accept. Judgment may be rendered by one person (a judge), a panel of judges, a jury, or a political agent or agency (a chief, a royal personage, a council). Judges and courts may rely on codified law and stipulated punishments, but codified law is not necessary for decisions to be made. Codified laws and courts are not limited to Western societies. From the late 17th century to the early 20th century, for example, the Ashanti of West Africa had a complex political system with elaborate legal arrangements. The Ashanti state was a military-based empire possessing legal codes that resembled those of many ancient civilizations.[94] Ashanti law was based on a concept of natural law, a belief that there is an order of the universe whose principles lawmakers should follow in the decisions they make and in the regulations they design. In Ashanti court procedure, elders examined and cross-examined witnesses as well as parties to the dispute. There were also quasi-professional advocates, and appeals against a verdict could be made directly to a chief. Particularly noteworthy was the emphasis on intent when assessing guilt. Drunkenness constituted a valid defense for all crimes except murder and cursing a chief, and a plea of insanity, if proved, was upheld for all offenses. Ashanti punishments could be severe. Physical mutilation, such as slicing off the nose or an ear—even castration in sexual offenses—was often employed. Fines were more frequent, however, and death sentences could often be commuted to banishment and confiscation of goods.

adjudication The process by which a third party acting as judge makes a decision that the parties to a dispute have to accept.

Perspectives on Gender

New Courts Allow Women to Address Grievances in Papua New Guinea

Women in a village in the Karawari River area of East Sepik Province.

In most societies in New Guinea, women did not traditionally participate in the resolution of disputes. And they could not bring actions against men. But when village courts were introduced, women began to go to court to redress offenses against them.

In colonial times, the introduced Western-style courts followed Western law, primarily Australian and British common law, not native customary law. After Papua New Guinea became an independent country, those courts remained in place. The lowest of the courts, called local courts, were located in town centers, often far from villages, so villagers rarely brought cases to them. But, in 1973, a new kind of court was created. Called village courts, they were designed to settle local disputes in the villages, using a blend of customary law (relying on compromise) and Western law. In contrast to the local courts, magistrates in the village courts were not outsiders but were selected from the pool of traditional and local leaders who knew the local people.

When Richard Scaglion studied changes in village courts among the Abelam from 1977 to 1987, he noticed a shift toward the increased use of these courts by women. In 1977, most of the complainants were male, but most of them were female by 1987. In a wider study of court cases over many regions of Papua New Guinea, Scaglion and Rose Whittingham found that most of the cases in which women were the plaintiffs were attempts to redress sex-related offenses (sexual jealousy, rape, incest, domestic disputes) committed by males. Most disputes in New Guinea villages are settled informally by self-help or by appeal to a "big man"; the courts are appealed to only as a last resort. Serious sex-related cases are unlikely to be settled informally but, rather, in the village court. Apparently women do not believe that they can get satisfaction informally. So they go to the village court, where they win some sort of punishment for the defendant in about 60 percent of the cases, just about the same rate that men achieve when they bring a case seeking punishment. Even in village courts near big cities, women appear largely successful in breaking their grievances, usually against men.

Culture change introduced from the outside often works against native peoples. But Papuan New Guinea women have benefited from the new village court system, particularly in redressing grievances against males. The traditional system for resolving disputes was largely male-dominated (women could not be plaintiffs), and so the possibility of taking disputes to the new courts has given women some measure of legal equality with men.

Sources: Scaglion 1990; Scaglion and Whittingham 1985. Goddard 2004.

Why do some societies have codified systems and others do not? One explanation, advanced by E. Adamson Hoebel, A. R. Radcliffe-Brown, and others, is that there is little need for formal legal guidelines in small, closely knit communities because competing interests are minimal. Hence, simple societies need little codified law. There are relatively few matters to quarrel about, and the general will of the group is sufficiently well known and demonstrated frequently enough to deter transgressors.

This point of view is echoed in Richard Schwartz's study of two Israeli settlements. In one communal kibbutz, a young man aroused a good deal of community resentment because he had accepted an electric teakettle as a gift. The general opinion was that he had overstepped the code about not having personal possessions, and he was so informed. Accordingly, he gave the kettle to the communal infirmary. Schwartz observed that "no organized enforcement of the decision was threatened, but had he disregarded the expressed will of the community, his life ... would have been made intolerable by the antagonism of public opinion."[95]

In this community, where people worked and ate together, not only did everyone know about transgressions, but a wrongdoer could not escape public censure. Thus, public opinion was an effective sanction. In another Israeli community, however, where individuals lived in widely separated houses and worked and ate separately, public opinion did not work as well. Not only were community members less aware of problems, but they had no quick way of making their feelings known. As a result, they established a judicial body to handle trouble cases.

Larger, more heterogeneous and stratified societies are likely to have more frequent disputes, which at the same time are less visible to the public. Individuals in stratified societies are generally not so dependent on community members for their well-being and hence are less likely to know of, or care about, others' opinions. In such societies, codified laws and formal authorities for resolving disputes develop—in order, perhaps, that disputes may be settled impersonally enough so that the parties can accept the decision and social order can be restored.

A good example of how more formal systems of law develop is the experience of towns in the American West during the gold rush period. These communities were literally swamped by total strangers. The townsfolk, having no control (authority) over these intruders because the strangers had no local ties, looked for ways to deal with the trouble cases that were continually flaring up. A first attempt at a solution was to hire gunslingers, who were also strangers, to act as peace officers or sheriffs, but this strategy usually failed. Eventually, towns succeeded in having federal authorities send in marshals backed by federal power.

Is there some evidence to support the theory that codified law is necessary only in larger, more complex societies? Data from a large, worldwide sample of societies suggest that codified law is associated with political integration beyond the local level. Murder cases, for example, are dealt with informally in societies that have only local political organization. In societies with multilocal political units, specialized political authorities tend to judge or adjudicate murder cases.[96] There is also some cross-cultural evidence that violence within a society tends to be less frequent when there are formal authorities (chiefs, courts) who have the power to punish murderers.[97] In general, adjudication or enforced decisions by outside authorities tend to occur in hierarchical societies with social classes and centralized power.[98]

Violent Resolution of Conflict

Controversy exists over whether violence has increased or decreased over the course of human history. Recently studied foragers have appeared to be fairly peaceful, fostering the view that warfare has increased over time. However, many of those foraging societies had considerable fighting in the past, suggesting that it is problematic to extrapolate to prehistory from recent societies.[99] What does prehistoric data tell us? Archaeologists were not always looking for signs of warfare and violence, but recent research suggests much more violence than previously believed. Some scholars have concluded, looking at both archaeological data and data from recent societies, that overall violence has declined markedly over the course of history.[100]

But regardless of the trends over time, the fact remains that there is enormous variation from society to society. In some societies, people often resort to violence when regular, effective alternative means of resolving a conflict are not available. If we can understand that variation, we may be better able to understand the changes over time.

Violence among individuals that is not considered legitimate is generally called **crime**. What is considered legitimate varies considerably from society to society. When socially organized violence occurs among territorial entities such as communities, districts, or nations, we call it **warfare**. The type of warfare varies in scope and complexity from society to society. Sometimes a distinction is made among feuding, raiding, and large-scale confrontations.[101]

Crime Violence not considered legitimate that occurs within a political unit.

Warfare Socially organized violence between political entities such as communities, districts, or nations.

Some scholars talk about a cultural pattern of violence. More often than not, societies with one type of violence have others. Societies with more war tend to have warlike sports, malevolent magic, severe punishment for crimes, high murder rates, feuding, and family violence.[102]

There are more peaceful societies. These societies are not conflict-free, but they try more to resolve conflict nonviolently. And like the Semai, they discourage aggression in their children without providing an aggressive model. What explains these more peaceful cultural patterns? Cross-cultural evidence supports the view that frequent warfare is the key to understanding all kinds of violence. Not only is war correlated with other kinds of aggression, but societies that are forced to stop fighting by more powerful societies appear to encourage aggression in their children less. It seems that, if war is frequent, the society encourages boys to be aggressive, so that they will grow up to be effective warriors. But socializing for aggression can spill over into other areas of life; high rates of crime and other violence may be inadvertent or unintended consequences of the encouragement of aggressiveness.[103] And societies with a lot of war commonly bestow high status on their warriors. Warriors are generally proud of their accomplishments, considering it an honor to be a brave and fierce warrior.[104]

Individual Violence Although it may seem paradoxical at first, violent behavior itself is often used to try to control behavior. In some societies, it is considered necessary for parents to beat children who misbehave. They don't consider this criminal behavior or child abuse; they consider it punishment. Similar views may attach to interpersonal behavior among adults. If a person trespasses on your property or hurts someone in your family, some societies consider it appropriate or justified to kill or maim the trespasser. Is this social control, or is it just lack of control?

Systems of individual self-help are characteristic of egalitarian societies.[105] How is this different from "community action," which earlier we classified under peaceful resolution of conflict? Because community action is explicitly based on obtaining a consensus, it is likely to lead to the ending of a particular dispute. Individual action, or self-help, particularly if it involves violence, is not.

Feuding A state of recurring hostility between families or groups of kin, usually motivated by a desire to avenge an offense against a member of the group.

Feuding Feuding is an example of how individual self-help may not lead to a peaceful resolution of conflict. **Feuding** is a state of recurring hostilities between families or groups of kin, usually motivated by a desire to avenge an offense—whether insult, injury, deprivation, or death—against a member of the group. The most common characteristic of the feud is that all members of the kin group carry the responsibility to avenge. The killing of any member of the offender's group is considered appropriate revenge, because the kin group as a whole is regarded as responsible. Nicholas Gubser told of a feud within a Nunamiut Inuit community, caused by a husband killing his wife's lover, that lasted for decades. The Nunamiut take feuds seriously, as do many societies, especially when murder has been committed. Closely related members of the murdered man recruit as many relatives as they can and try to kill the murderer or one of his close kin. Then the members of the murderer's kindred are brought into the feud. The two kindreds may snipe at each other for years.[106]

Feuds are by no means limited to small-scale societies; they occur as frequently in societies with high levels of political organization.[107]

Raiding A short-term use of force, generally planned and organized, to realize a limited objective.

Raiding **Raiding** is a short-term use of force, planned and organized, to realize a limited objective. This objective is usually the acquisition of goods, animals, or other forms of wealth belonging to another, often neighboring community.

Raiding is especially prevalent in pastoral societies, in which cattle, horses, camels, or other animals are prized and an individual's own herd can be augmented by theft. Raids are often organized by temporary leaders or coordinators whose authority may not last beyond the planning and execution of the venture. Raiding may also be organized for the purpose of capturing people. Sometimes people are taken to marry—the capture of women to be wives or concubines is fairly common[108]—or to be slaves. Slavery has been practiced in about 33 percent of the world's known societies, and war has been one way of obtaining slaves either to keep or to trade for other goods.[109] Raiding, like feuding, is often self-perpetuating: The victim of a raid today becomes the raider tomorrow.[110]

Large-Scale Confrontations Individual episodes of feuds and raids usually involve relatively small numbers of people and almost always an element of surprise. Because they are generally attacked without warning, the victims are often unable to muster an immediate defense. Large-scale confrontations, in contrast, involve a large number of people and planning of strategies of attack and defense by both sides. Large-scale warfare is usually practiced among societies with intensive agriculture or industrialization. Only these societies possess a technology sufficiently advanced to support specialized armies, military leaders, strategists, and so on. But large-scale confrontations are not limited to state societies; they occur, for example, among the horticultural Dugum Dani of central New Guinea.

Large-scale confrontations occur in societies with armies, but they also occur in nonstate societies. The Masai of Kenya (shown here) battled with Kalenjin (not shown) over a land dispute following the 2008 disputed election.

The military history of the Dani, with its shifting alliances and confederations, is reminiscent of that of Europe, although Dani battles involve far fewer fighters and less sophisticated weaponry. Among the Dani, long periods of ritual warfare are characterized by formal battles announced through a challenge sent by one side to the opposing side. If the challenge is accepted, the protagonists meet at the agreed-upon battle site to set up their lines. Fighting with spears, sticks, and bows and arrows begins at midmorning and continues either until nightfall or until rain intervenes. There may also be a rest period during the midday heat during which the two sides shout insults at each other or talk and rest among themselves.

The front line of battle is composed of about a dozen active warriors and a few leaders. Behind them is a second line, still within arrow range, composed of those who have just left the forward line or are preparing to join it. The third line, outside arrow range, is composed of noncombatants—males too old or too young to participate and those recovering from wounds. This third line merely watches the battle taking place on the grassy plain. On the hillsides far back from the front line, some of the old men help to direct ancestral ghosts to the battle by gouging a line in the ground that points in the direction of the battlefield.[111]

Yet, as total as large-scale confrontations may be, even such warfare has cultural rules. Among the Dani, for instance, no fighting occurs at night, and weapons are limited to simple spears and bows and arrows. Similarly, in state societies, governments will sign "self-denying" pacts restricting the use of poison gas, germ warfare, and so forth. Unofficially, private arrangements are common. One has only to glance through the memoirs of national leaders of the two world wars to become aware of locally arranged truces, visits to one another's front positions, exchanges of prisoners of war, and so on.

Explaining Warfare

Most societies in the anthropological record have had warfare between communities or larger territorial groups. The vast majority of societies had at least occasional wars when they were first described, unless they had been pacified or incorporated by more dominant societies.[112] Yet, relatively little research has been done on the possible causes of war and why it varies in type and frequency. For instance, why have some people fought a great deal, and others only infrequently? Why in some societies does warfare occur internally, within the society or language group?

We have answers, based on cross-cultural studies, to some of those questions. There is evidence that people in preindustrial societies go to war mostly out of fear, particularly a fear of expectable but unpredictable natural disasters that will destroy food resources (e.g., droughts, floods, locust infestations). People may think they can protect themselves against such disasters ahead of time by taking things from defeated enemies. In any case, preindustrial societies with higher frequencies of war are very likely to have had a history of expectable but unpredictable disasters.[113] The fact that chronic (annually recurring and therefore predictable) food shortages do not predict higher frequencies of war suggests that people go to war in an attempt to cushion the impact of the disasters they expect to occur in the future but cannot predict. Consistent with this tentative conclusion is the fact that the victors in war almost always take land or other resources from the defeated. And this is true for simpler as well as more complex preindustrial societies.[114] Might similar motives affect decisions about war and peace in the modern world?

We know that complex or politically centralized societies are likely to have professional armies, hierarchies of military authority, and sophisticated weapons.[115] But surprisingly, the frequency of warfare seems to be not much greater in complex societies than in simple band or tribal societies.[116] We have some evidence that warfare is unlikely to occur internally (within a society or territory) if it is small in population (21,000 or fewer people); in a larger society, there is a high likelihood of warfare within the society, among communities or larger territorial divisions.[117] In fact, complex societies, even if they are politically unified, are not less likely than simpler societies to have internal warfare.[118]

What about the idea that men in band and tribal societies may mostly go to war over women?[119] If this were true, those band and tribal societies with the most frequent wars should have shortages of women, and those with little or no war—less often than once in 10 years—should have more equal numbers of women and men. But the cross-cultural evidence clearly contradicts this theory. Band and tribal societies with more wars do not have fewer women.[120]

What, if anything, do we know about recent warfare among nation-states? Although many people think that military alliances lessen the chance of war, it turns out that nations formally allied with other nations do not necessarily go to war less often than nations lacking formal alliances. Countries that are allies are, of course, less likely to go to war with each other; however, alliances can drag dependent allies into wars they don't want.[121] Countries that are economically interdependent, that trade with each other for necessities, are less likely to go to war with each other.[122] Finally, military equality among nations, particularly when preceded by a rapid military buildup, seems to increase rather than lessen the chance of war among those nations.[123]

Clearly, these findings contradict some traditional beliefs about how to prevent war. Military buildups do not make war less likely, but trade does. What else may? We have already noted that participatory ("democratic") political systems are less likely to go to war with each other than are authoritarian political systems. Although war may be common in the world, it is not inevitable. Societies change over time. The Vikings were extremely militaristic, but Norway today is now a peaceful society. A comparative study of Polynesian societies shows that, although all derive from a common cultural heritage, the size of the islands people settled on strongly influenced their patterns of interpersonal violence and warfare. The smallest islands had the lowest levels of violence and the least warfare. It appears that cooperation and harmony were more likely than violence in small "face-to-face" societies.[124]

Political and Social Change

In addition to commercialization and religious change brought about by the expansion of Western and other countries, political changes have often occurred when a foreign system of government has been imposed. But, as recent events in the former Soviet Union and South Africa indicate, dramatic changes in a political system can also occur more or less voluntarily. Perhaps the most striking type of political change in recent years is the spread of participatory forms of government—"democracy."

To political scientists, democracy is usually defined in terms of voting by a substantial proportion of the citizenry, governments brought to power by periodic contested elections, a chief executive either popularly elected or responsible to an elected legislature, and often also civil liberties such as free speech. Depending on which criteria are used, only 12 to 15 countries qualified as democracies as of the beginning of the 20th century. The number decreased after World War I, as emerging dictatorships in Russia, Italy, Germany, central Europe, Japan, and elsewhere replaced democratic institutions. After World War II, despite all the rhetoric associated with the founding of the United Nations, the picture was not much different. Some members of the new North Atlantic Treaty Organization (NATO) were not democracies, and neither were many members of the wider Western alliance system, in Latin America, the Middle East, and Asia.

Not until the 1970s and 1980s did people, not just political scientists, start noticing that democracy was becoming more common in the world. By the early 1990s, President George H. W. Bush and then-candidate Bill Clinton were talking about the spread of the "democratic peace." As of 1992, about half of the countries in the world had more or less democratic governments, and others were in transition to democracy.[125] Social scientists do not yet understand why this change is happening. But it is possible that the global communication of ideas has a lot to do with it. Authoritarian governments can censor their own newspapers and prevent group meetings, and sophisticated technology can block Internet use and cell phone connections, but ultimately authoritarian governments really cannot stop the movement of ideas. The movement of ideas, of course, does not explain the acceptance of those ideas. Why democracy has recently diffused to more countries than ever before still requires explanation, as does why some countries do not find it appealing.

Summary and Review

Variation in Types of Political Organization

22.1 Discuss the cross-cultural variation in the types of political organization.

- Over the last century, countries have either imposed political systems on others or have developed governmental structures to deal with the larger world. Before colonization, the band or village was the largest autonomous political unit in 50 percent of recorded societies.
- Societies range on a continuum from less to more centralized types of political organization: bands, tribes, chiefdoms, and states.
- Studies support collection action theory: When the state relies more heavily on resources from taxpayers, the rulers must give the public more in return or else face noncompliance and rebellion.
- *Nation* refers to the idea that a people share a common territory, history, and identity. Nations can be associated with states (nation-states), but not necessarily always.
- The more intensive the agriculture, the greater the likelihood of state organization. Larger communities predict a wider range of political officials and more levels of decision making. Societies with higher levels of political integration tend to exhibit social differentiation.
- Anthropologists do not clearly understand why changes in political organization occur, although competition among groups, need for defense, economic and technological variables, and trade may be strong factors.

? What are some factors that may explain change in political organization?

The Spread of State Societies

22.2 Explain the spread of state societies.

- State societies have larger communities and higher population densities than do band, tribal, and chiefdom societies. They also have armies ready to fight. State systems waging war against chiefdoms and tribes have almost always won and politically incorporated the losers.
- Depopulation, conquest, or intimidation has decreased the number of independent political units

worldwide, particularly in the last 200 years. It is estimated that, in 1000 B.C., between 100,000 and 1 million separate political units existed in the world; today, fewer than 200.

> **?** How might the spread of state societies be explained?

Variation in Political Process

22.3 Describe and explain the variation in political structure in various societies.

- In some tribal societies where becoming a leader has been studied, leadership appears to depend upon individual characteristics such as intelligence, generosity, and height. In some societies, leadership is more competitive and leaders are described as "big men" or "big women."
- Adult political participation varies considerably in preindustrial societies. Small-scale societies are likely to have high participation, whereas more complex societies less. But with industrialization, the trend reverses somewhat and political participation increases.
- More "democratic," political units in the ethnographic record fight have fought with each other significantly less often or with less severity than have less participatory political units, which also seems to be the case among modern nation-states.

> **?** What are some examples of different political processes? What may explain the differences?

Resolution of Conflict

22.4 Critically examine the methods used for resolving conflict, including warfare, in different societies.

- Resolution of conflict may be accomplished peacefully by avoidance, community action, mediation, apology, appeal to supernatural forces, or adjudication by a third party. The procedures used usually vary according to the degree of social complexity.
- Crime is violence within a political unit that usually settles disputes peacefully. Warfare is socially organized violence among groups of people from different territorial units. Civil war is violence among subunits of a population that had been politically unified.
- Law, whether informal as in simpler societies or formal as in more complex societies, is a means of dealing peacefully with conflict. Data from a large, worldwide sample of societies suggest that codified law is associated with political integration beyond the local level.
- More often than not, societies with one type of violence have other types. Societies with more war tend to have warlike sports, malevolent magic, severe punishment for crimes, high murder rates, feuding, and family violence.
- Systems of individual self-help, characteristic of egalitarian societies, tend toward violence and away from consensus. Systems of community action are explicitly based on obtaining a consensus and likely lead to the ending of particular disputes.
- Societal complexity does not explain warfare frequency, but unpredictable disasters may play a role. Countries that are both democratic are less likely to fight each other. Military buildups do not make war less likely, but trade does.
- Political changes typically occur when a foreign system of government is imposed, but changes in a political system can also occur voluntarily. A striking type of political change in recent years is the spread of participatory forms of government—"democracy."

> **?** What are some of the different types of mechanisms for resolving conflict peacefully and violently? Provide examples.

Think on it

1. When, if ever, do you think the world will be **politically unified**? Why do you think so?
2. Why don't informal methods of **social control** work well in societies like our own? Why don't formal methods work better than they currently do?
3. What does research on **war and violence** suggest about how to reduce their likelihood?

Religion and Magic

CHAPTER 23

LEARNING OBJECTIVES

- 23.1 Characterize the universality of religion and discuss various explanations for that universality.
- 23.2 Discuss the range of variability in religious beliefs.
- 23.3 Describe the variability in religious practices and practitioners cross-culturally.
- 23.4 Discuss religion in terms of adaptation.
- 23.5 Explain and give examples of various forms of religious change, such as conversion and revitalization movements.

Religion Any set of attitudes, beliefs, and practices pertaining to supernatural power, whether that power rests in forces, gods, spirits, ghosts, or demons.

Supernatural Powers believed to be not human or not subject to the laws of nature.

As far as we know, all societies have possessed beliefs that can be grouped under the term *religion*. These beliefs vary from culture to culture and from time to time. Yet, despite their variety, we shall define **religion** as any set of attitudes, beliefs, and practices pertaining to *supernatural power*, whether that power be forces, gods, spirits, ghosts, or demons.

In our society, we divide phenomena into the natural and the supernatural, but not all languages or cultures make such a neat distinction. Moreover, what is considered **supernatural**—powers believed to be not human or not subject to the laws of nature—varies from society to society. Some of the variation is determined by what a society regards as natural. For example, some illnesses commonly found in our society are believed to result from the natural action of bacteria and viruses. In other societies, and even among some people in our own society, illness is thought to result from supernatural forces, and thus it forms a part of religious belief.

Beliefs about what is, or is not, a supernatural occurrence also vary within a society at a given time or over time. In Judeo-Christian traditions, for example, floods, earthquakes, volcanic eruptions, comets, and epidemics were once considered evidence of supernatural powers intervening in human affairs. It is now generally agreed that they are simply natural occurrences—even though many still believe that supernatural forces may be involved. Thus, the line between the natural and the supernatural varies in a society according to what people believe about the causes of things and events in the observable world. Similarly, what is considered sacred in one society may not be so considered in another.

In many cultures, what we would consider religious is embedded in other aspects of everyday life. That is, it is often difficult to separate the religious, economic, or political from other aspects of the culture. Such cultures have little or no specialization of any kind; there are no full-time priests, no purely religious activities. So the various aspects of culture we distinguish (e.g., in the chapter titles of this book) are not separate and easily recognized in many societies, as they are in complex societies such as our own. However, it is sometimes difficult even for us to agree whether or not a particular custom of ours is religious. After all, the categorizing of beliefs as religious, political, or social is a relatively new custom. The ancient Greeks, for instance, did not have a word for religion, but they did have many concepts concerning the behavior of their gods and their own expected duties to the gods.

When people's duties to their gods are linked with duty to their princes, it is difficult to separate religious from political ideas. As an example of our own difficulty in labeling a particular class of actions or beliefs as religious or social, consider our attitudes about wearing clothes. Is our belief that it is necessary to wear clothing, at least in the company of nonlovers, a religious principle, or is it something else? Recall that in Genesis, the wearing of clothes or fig leaves is distinctly associated with the loss of innocence: Adam and Eve, after eating the apple, covered their nakedness. Accordingly, when Christian missionaries first visited islands in the Pacific in the 19th century, they forced the native women to wear more clothes, particularly to cover their sexual parts. Were the missionaries' ideas about sex religious or social, or perhaps both?

23.1 Characterize the universality of religion and discuss various explanations for that universality.

The Universality of Religion

Religious beliefs and practices are found in all known contemporary societies, and archaeologists think they have found signs of religious belief associated with *Homo sapiens* who lived at least 60,000 years ago. People then deliberately buried their dead, and many graves contain the remains of food, tools, and other objects that were probably thought to be needed in an afterlife. Some of the artistic productions of modern humans after about 30,000 years ago may have been used for religious purposes. For example, sculptures of females with ample secondary sex characteristics may have been fertility charms.

Cave paintings in which the predominant images are animals of the hunt may reflect a belief that the image had some power over events. Perhaps early humans thought that their hunting would be more successful if they drew images depicting good fortune in hunting. The details of religions practiced in the distant past cannot be recovered. Yet evidence of ritual treatment of the dead suggests that early people believed in the existence of supernatural spirits and tried to communicate with, and perhaps influence, them.

Animatism A belief in supernatural forces.

Animism A belief in a dual existence for all things—a physical, visible body, and a psychic, invisible soul.

We may reasonably assume the existence of prehistoric religion, and we have evidence of the universality of religion in historic times, so we can understand why the subject of religion has been the focus of much speculation, research, and theorizing. As long ago as the 5th century B.C., Herodotus made fairly objective comparisons among the religions of the 50 or so societies he traveled to from his home in Greece. He noted many similarities among their gods and pointed out evidence of diffusion of religious worship. Since Herodotus's time some 2,500 years ago, scholars, theologians, historians, and philosophers have speculated about religion. Some have claimed superiority for their own forms of religion, others have derided the naive simplicity of others' beliefs, and some have expressed skepticism concerning all beliefs.

Speculation about which religion is superior is not an anthropological concern. What is of interest to anthropologists is why religion is found in all societies and how and why it varies from society to society. Many social scientists—particularly anthropologists, sociologists, and psychologists—have offered theories to account for the universality of religion. Most think that religions are created by humans in response to certain universal needs or conditions. We consider five such needs or conditions here: (1) a need for intellectual understanding, (2) reversion to childhood feelings, (3) anxiety and uncertainty, (4) a need for community, and (5) a need for cooperation.

Read the Document: Universals and Variation in Religious Belief and Practice

The Need to Understand

One of the earliest social scientists to propose a major theory of the origin of religion was Edward Tylor. In Tylor's view, religion originated in people's speculation about dreams, trances, and death. The dead, the distant, those in the next house, animals—all seem real in dreams and trances. Tylor thought that the lifelike appearances of these imagined people and animals suggest a dual existence for all things—a physical, visible body and a psychic, invisible soul. In sleep, the soul can leave the body and appear to other people; at death, the soul permanently leaves the body. Because the dead appear in dreams, people come to believe that the souls of the dead are still around.[1]

Tylor thought that the belief in souls was the earliest form of religion; **animism** is the term he used to refer to belief in souls.[2] But many scholars criticized Tylor's theory for being too intellectual and not dealing with the emotional component of religion. One of Tylor's students, R. R. Marett, felt that Tylor's animism was too sophisticated an idea to be the origin of religion. Marett suggested that **animatism**—a belief in impersonal supernatural forces (e.g., the power of a rabbit's foot)—preceded the creation of spirits.[3] A similar idea is that when people believe in gods, they are *anthropomorphizing*—attributing human characteristics and motivations to nonhuman, particularly supernatural, events.[4] Anthropomorphizing may be an attempt to understand what is otherwise incomprehensible and disturbing.

This stone carved pillar from Gobekli Tepe (southeastern Anatolia) in the garden of Sanliurfa Museum, Sanliurfa, Turkey, dates to over 11,000 years ago. Gobekli Tepe is believed to the oldest known place of worship. The mountaintop site had more than 200 stone pillars arranged in circles.

Reversion to Childhood Feelings

Sigmund Freud believed that early humans lived in groups, each of which was dominated by a tyrannical man who kept all the women for himself.[5] Freud postulated that, on maturing, the sons were driven out of the group. Later, they joined together to kill and eat the hated father. But then the sons felt enormous guilt and remorse, which they expressed (projected) by prohibiting the killing of a totem animal (the father substitute). Subsequently, on ritual occasions, the cannibalistic scene was repeated in the form of a totem meal. Freud believed that these early practices gradually became transformed into the worship of deities or gods modeled after the father.

Most social scientists today do not accept Freud's interpretation of the origin of religion. But there is widespread agreement with his idea that events in infancy can have long-lasting and powerful effects on beliefs and practices in adult life. Helpless and dependent on parents for many years, infants and children inevitably and unconsciously view their parents as all-knowing and all-powerful. When adults feel out of control or in need, they may unconsciously revert to their infantile and childhood feelings. They may then look to gods or magic to do what they cannot do for themselves, just as they looked to their parents to take care of their needs. As we shall see, there is evidence that feelings about the supernatural world parallel feelings in everyday life.

Anxiety and Uncertainty

Freud thought that humans would turn to religion during times of uncertainty, but he did not view religion positively, believing that humans would eventually outgrow the need for religion. Others viewed religion more positively. Bronislaw Malinowski noted that people in all societies are faced with anxiety and uncertainty. They may have skills and knowledge to take care of many of their needs, but knowledge is not sufficient to prevent illness, accidents, and natural disasters. The most frightening prospect is death itself. Consequently, there is an intense desire for immortality. As Malinowski saw it, religion is born from the universal need to find comfort in inevitable times of stress. Through religious belief, people affirm their convictions that death is neither real nor final, that people are endowed with a personality that persists even after death. In religious ceremony, humans can commemorate and communicate with those who have died and achieve some measure of comfort in these ways.[6]

Theorists such as William James, Carl Jung, Erich Fromm, and Abraham Maslow have viewed religion even more positively: Religion is not just a way of relieving anxiety; it is thought to be therapeutic. James suggested that religion provides a feeling of union with something larger than oneself,[7] and Jung suggested that it helps people resolve their inner conflicts and attain maturity.[8] Fromm proposed that religion gives people a framework of values,[9] and Maslow argued that it provides a transcendental understanding of the world.[10]

A considerable amount of research supports the idea that religion generally relieves stress, anxiety, and uncertainty.[11] Engaging in religious rituals appears to lower individuals' blood pressure; elevated blood pressure is often caused by stress. Regular church-goers have lower incidence of depression than non church-goers. Fisherman who go out on longer deep-sea trips are more likely to believe in magical avoidances. People faced with terrorism close to home are more likely to engage in prayer or psalm recitation.[12] If religion is good for health by reducing anxiety, why has the number of religious believers declined recently in so many countries? A comparison of countries suggests that the number of nonbelievers in a country is related to fewer stresses in the environment. So, greater economic development, less inequality, higher life expectancy, more peacefulness, and lower disease loads are all associated with a higher number of nonbelievers. These relationships support the idea that when uncertainty is lessened, the need for religion is lessened.[13]

The Need for Community

All those theories of religion agree on one thing: Whatever the beliefs or rituals, religion may satisfy psychological needs common to all people. But some social scientists believe that religion springs from society and serves social, rather than psychological, needs. Émile Durkheim, a French sociologist, pointed out that living in society makes humans feel pushed and pulled by powerful forces. These forces direct their behavior, pushing them to resist what is considered wrong, pulling them to do what is considered right. These are the forces of public opinion, custom, and law. Because they are largely invisible and unexplained, people would feel them as mysterious forces and therefore come to

Fishermen working on a boat deck in choppy seas. The more danger involved in fishing, the more taboos fisherman seem to have.

believe in gods and spirits. Durkheim suggested that religion arises out of the experience of living in social groups; religious belief and practice affirm a person's place in society, enhance feelings of community, and give people confidence. He proposed that society is really the object of worship in religion.

Consider how Durkheim explained totemism, so often discussed by early religious theorists. He thought that nothing inherent in a lizard, rat, or frog—animal totems for some Australian aboriginal groups—would be sufficient to make them *sacred.* The totem animal therefore must be a symbol. But a symbol of what? Durkheim noted that there are things that are always unknown about others, particularly their inner states. It is from these unknowns that the mystical aspects of religion arise. But the form religion takes has a lot to do with how societies are structured. Durkheim noted that in societies organized into clans, each clan has its own totem animal; the totem distinguishes one clan from another. So the totem is the focus of the clan's religious rituals and symbolizes both the clan and the clan's spirits. It is the clan that is affirmed in ritual.[14]

Guy Swanson accepted Durkheim's belief that certain aspects or conditions of society generate the responses we call religious, but he thought that Durkheim was too vague about exactly what in society would generate the belief in spirits or gods. So what might? Swanson suggested that the belief in spirits derives from the existence of *sovereign groups* in a society. These are the groups that have independent jurisdiction (decision-making powers) over some sphere of life—the family, the clan, the village, the state. Such groups are not mortal; they persist beyond the lifetimes of their individual members. According to Swanson, then, the spirits or gods that people invent personify or represent the powerful decision-making groups in their society. Just like sovereign groups in a society, the spirits or gods are immortal and have purposes and goals that supersede those of individuals.[15]

Need for Cooperation

While Durkheim stressed the solidarity that religion created in groups, more recently, evolutionary theorists have focused on a specific aspect of solidarity—human cooperation. Evolutionary theorists have to deal with a paradox—human groups are quite cooperative, but how did cooperation arise when helping others has a cost to an individual? If a village needs to be defended, it is advantageous for an individual to run away and let others risk their lives, but if everyone cooperates, the group is more likely to ward off the attackers. What keeps people together and prevents individuals from letting others bear all the costs? Religion, some theorists argue, particularly the kind where supreme beings are concerned with morality, provides a strong mechanism to promote cooperation.[16] First, participating in rituals and ceremonies promotes communal feelings. Second, supernatural beings can "police" better—they cannot only "see all," but they can invoke powerful punishments such as sickness or death.[17] Presumably then people will be more likely watch their behavior. But what if an individual just pretends to participate in religious behavior to gain benefits from others? Here is where another mechanism is suggested. If religions require considerable participation and sacrifices (such as fasting, curtailment of activities, specialized dress), religious participation will be hard to fake for an individual who wants to deceive.

23.2 Discuss the range of variability in religious beliefs.

Variation in Religious Beliefs

There is no general agreement among scholars as to why people need religion, or how spirits, gods, and other supernatural beings and forces come into existence. (Any or all of the needs we have discussed, psychological or social, may give rise to religious belief and practice.) Yet there is general recognition of the enormous variation in the details of religious beliefs and practices. Societies differ in the kinds of supernatural beings or forces they believe in and the character of those beings. They also differ in the structure or hierarchy of those beings, in what the beings actually do, and in what happens to people after death. Variation exists also in the ways in which the supernatural is believed to interact with humans.

Types of Supernatural Forces and Beings

Supernatural Forces Some supernatural forces have no personlike character. As we discussed earlier, Marett referred to such religious beliefs as animatism. For example, a supernatural, impersonal force called **mana**, after its Malayo-Polynesian name, is thought to inhabit some objects but not others, some people but not others. A farmer in Polynesia places stones around a field; the crops are bountiful; the stones have mana. During a subsequent year, the stones may lose their mana and the crops will be poor. People may also possess mana, as, for example, the chiefs in Polynesia were said to do. However, such power is not necessarily possessed permanently; chiefs who were unsuccessful in war or other activities were said to have lost their mana.

Mana A supernatural, impersonal force that inhabits certain objects or people and is believed to confer success and/or strength.

The word *mana* may be Malayo-Polynesian, but a similar concept is also found in our own society. We can compare mana to the power that golfers may attribute to some, but unhappily not all, of their clubs. A ballplayer might think a certain sweatshirt or pair of pants has supernatural power or force and that more runs or points will be scored when they are worn. A four-leaf clover has mana; a three-leaf clover does not.

Objects, people, or places can be considered **taboo**. Anthony Wallace distinguished mana from taboo by pointing out that things containing mana are to be touched, whereas taboo things are not to be touched, for their power can cause harm.[18] Thus, those who touch them may themselves become taboo. Taboos surround food not to be eaten, places not to be entered, animals not to be killed, people not to be touched sexually, people not to be touched at all, and so on. An Australian aborigine could not normally kill and eat the animal that was his totem; Hebrew tribesmen were forbidden to touch a woman during menstruation or for seven days afterward.

Taboo A prohibition that, if violated, is believed to bring supernatural punishment.

Supernatural Beings Supernatural beings fall within two broad categories: those of nonhuman origin, such as gods and spirits, and those of human origin, such as ghosts and ancestral spirits. Chief among the beings of nonhuman origin, **gods** are named personalities. They are often *anthropomorphic*—that is, conceived in the image of a person—although they are sometimes given the shapes of other animals or of celestial bodies, such as the sun or moon. Essentially, the gods are believed to have created

Gods Supernatural beings of nonhuman origin who are named personalities; often anthropomorphic.

themselves, but some of them then created, or gave birth to, other gods. Although some are seen as creator gods, not all peoples include the creation of the world as one of the acts of gods.

After their efforts at creation, many creator gods retire. Having set the world in motion, they are not interested in its day-to-day operation. Other creator gods remain interested in the ordinary affairs of human beings, especially the affairs of one small, chosen segment of humanity. Whether or not a society has a creator god, the job of running the creation is often left to lesser gods. The Maori of New Zealand, for example, recognize three important gods: a god of the sea, a god of the forest, and a god of agriculture. They call upon each in turn for help and try to get all three to share their knowledge of how the universe runs. The gods of the ancient Romans, on the other hand, specialized to a high degree. There were three gods of the plow, one god to help with the sowing, one for weeding, one for reaping, one for storing grain, one for manuring, and so on.[19]

Beneath the gods in prestige, and often closer to people, are multitudes of unnamed **spirits**. Some may be guardian spirits for people. Some, who become known for particularly efficacious work, may be promoted to the rank of named gods. Some spirits who are known to the people but are never invoked by them are of the hobgoblin type. Hobgoblins delight in mischief and can be blamed for any number of small mishaps; still other spirits take pleasure in deliberately working evil on behalf of people.

Spirits Unnamed supernatural beings of nonhuman origin who are beneath the gods in prestige and often closer to the people; may be helpful, mischievous, or evil.

Many Native American groups believed in guardian spirits that had to be sought out, usually in childhood. For example, among the Sanpoil of northeastern Washington, boys and sometimes girls would be sent out on overnight vigils to acquire their guardians.

On the Day of the Dead, Mexican families adorn their loved ones' tombs and provide offerings of some the deceased's favorite things. It is believed that the spirits of the dead will return for a visit.

Most commonly the spirits were animals, but they could also be uniquely shaped rocks, lakes, mountains, whirlwinds, or clouds. The vigil was not always successful. When it was, the guardian spirit appeared in a vision or dream, and always at first in human form. Conversation with the spirit would reveal its true identity.[20]

Ghosts Supernatural beings who were once human; the souls of dead people.

Ancestor spirits Supernatural beings who are the ghosts of dead relatives.

Ghosts are supernatural beings who were once human, and **ancestor spirits** are ghosts of dead relatives. The belief that ghosts or their actions can be perceived by the living is almost universal.[21] The near-universality of the belief in ghosts may not be difficult to explain. There are many cues in everyday experience that are associated with a loved one, and even after the death, those cues might arouse the feeling that the dead person is still somehow present. The opening of a door or the smell of tobacco or perfume in a room may evoke the idea that the person is still present, if only for a moment. Then, too, loved ones live on in dreams. Small wonder, then, that most societies believe in ghosts. If the idea of ghosts is generated by these familiar associations, we might expect that ghosts in most societies would be close relatives and friends, not strangers—and they are.[22]

Although the belief in ghosts is nearly universal, the spirits of the dead do not play a very active role in the life of the living in all societies. In his cross-cultural study of 50 societies, Swanson found that people are likely to believe in active ancestral spirits where descent groups are important decision-making units. The descent group is an entity that exists over time, back into the past as well as forward into the future, despite the deaths of individual members.[23] The dead feel concern for the fortunes, the prestige, and the continuity of their descent group as strongly as the living. As a Lugbara elder (in northern Uganda in Africa) put it, "Are our ancestors not people of our lineage? They are our fathers and we are their children whom they have begotten. Those that have died stay near us in our homes and we feed and respect them. Does not a man help his father when he is old?"[24]

The Character of Supernatural Beings

Whatever type they may be, the gods or spirits venerated in a given culture tend to have certain personality or character traits. They may be unpredictable or predictable, aloof from or interested in human affairs, helpful or punishing. Why do the gods and spirits in a particular culture exhibit certain character traits rather than others?

We have some evidence from cross-cultural studies that the character of supernatural beings may be related to the nature of child training. Melford Spiro and Roy D'Andrade suggested that the god–human relationship is a projection of the parent–child relationship, in which case child-training practices might well be relived in dealings with the supernatural.[25] For example, if a child was nurtured immediately by her parents when she cried or waved her arms about or kicked, she might grow up expecting to be nurtured by the gods when she attracted their attention by performing a ritual. On the other hand, if her parents often punished her, she would grow up expecting the gods to punish her if she disobeyed them. William Lambert, Leigh Minturn Triandis, and Margery Wolf, in another cross-cultural study, found that societies with hurtful or punitive child-training practices are likely to believe that their gods are aggressive and malevolent; societies with less punitive child training are more likely to believe that the gods are benevolent.[26] These results are consistent with the Freudian notion that the supernatural world should parallel the natural. It is worth noting in this context that some peoples refer to the god as their father and to themselves as his children.

Structure or Hierarchy of Supernatural Beings

The range of social structures in human societies from egalitarian to highly stratified has its counterpart in the supernatural world. Some societies have gods or spirits that are not ranked; one god has about as much power as another. Other societies have gods or spirits that are ranked in prestige and power. For example, on the Pacific islands of Palau, which was a rank society, gods were ranked as people were. Each clan worshiped a god and a goddess that had names or titles similar to clan titles. Although a clan god was generally important only to the members of that clan, the gods of the various clans in a village were believed to be ranked in the same order that the clans were. Thus, the god of the highest-ranking clan was respected by all the clans of the village. Its shrine was given the place of honor in the center of the village and was larger and more elaborately decorated than other shrines.[27]

Although the Palauans did not believe in a high god or supreme being who outranked all the other gods, some societies do. Consider Judaism, Christianity, and Islam, which we call **monotheistic** religions. Although *monotheism* means "one god," most monotheistic religions actually include more than one supernatural being (e.g., demons, angels, the Devil). But the supreme being or high god, as the creator of the universe or the director of events (or both), is believed to be ultimately responsible for all events.[28] A **polytheistic** religion recognizes many important gods, no one of which is supreme.

Monotheistic Believing that there is only one high god and that all other supernatural beings are subordinate to, or are alternative manifestations of, this supreme being.

Polytheistic Recognizing many gods, none of whom is believed to be superordinate.

Why do some societies have a belief in a high god and others do not? Recall Swanson's suggestion that people invent gods who personify the important decision-making groups in their society. He therefore hypothesized that societies with hierarchical political systems should be more likely to believe in a high god. In his cross-cultural study of 50 societies (none of which practiced any of the major world religions), he found that belief in a high god is strongly associated with three or more levels of "sovereign" (decision-making) groups. Of the 20 sample societies that had a hierarchy of three or more sovereign groups—for instance, family, clan, and chiefdom—17 possessed the idea of a high god. Of the 19 societies that had fewer than three levels of decision-making groups, only two had a high god.[29] Consistent with Swanson's findings, societies dependent on food production, particularly plow agriculture, are more likely to have a belief in a high god than are food-collecting societies.[30] These results strongly suggest, then, that the realm of the gods parallels and may reflect the everyday social and political worlds. In the past, many state societies had state religions in which the political officials were also the officials of the temples (e.g., the pharaohs in Egypt). In recent times, most state societies have separated church and state, as in the United States and Canada.

Intervention of the Gods in Human Affairs

According to Clifford Geertz, when people face ignorance, pain, and the unjustness of life, they explain the events by the intervention of the gods.[31] Thus, in Greek religion, the direct intervention of Poseidon as ruler of the seas prevented Odysseus from getting home for 10 years. In the Old Testament, the direct intervention of Yahweh caused the great flood that killed most of the people in the time of Noah. In other societies, people may search their memories for a violated taboo that has brought punishment through supernatural intervention.

In addition to unasked-for divine interference, there are numerous examples of requests for divine intervention, either for good for oneself and friends or for evil for others. Gods are asked to intervene in the weather and to make the crops grow, to send fish to the fisherman and game to the hunter, to find lost things, and to accompany travelers and prevent accidents. They are asked to stop the flow of lava down the side of a volcano, to stop a war, or to cure an illness.

The gods do not intervene in all societies. In some, they intervene in human affairs; in others, they are not the slightest bit interested; and in still others, they interfere only occasionally. We have little research on why gods are believed to interfere in some societies and not in others. We do, however, have some evidence suggesting when the gods will take an interest in the morality or immorality of human behavior. Swanson's study suggests that the gods are likely to punish people for immoral behavior when there are considerable differences in wealth in the society.[32] His interpretation is that supernatural support of moral behavior is particularly useful where inequalities tax the ability of the political system to maintain social order and minimize social disorder. Envy of others' privileges may motivate some people to behave immorally; the belief that the gods will punish such behavior might deter it. More generally, the concern of gods with moral behavior is more likely in large, complex societies (see the box "Religion: A Force for Cooperation and Harmony?").

Applied Anthropology

Religion: A Force for Cooperation and Harmony?

Most social science theories about religion suggest that religious beliefs and rituals promote social cohesion and cooperation within the group that shares them. Some religions, including the major religions in the modern world (Buddhism, Christianity, Islam, Hinduism, Judaism), are more explicit than others in their direct concern with moral behavior. Moralizing religions believe that the gods will reward moral behavior and punish immoral behavior, and are generally found in large and complex societies. Such societies are likely to have towns or cities and neighbors may not know each other well, and although there may be codified law and courts, these mechanisms may not be sufficient to promote social order. Complex societies are likely to have considerable social inequality, increasing the likelihood of property-related crime. The cross-cultural evidence is consistent with the theory that morality-based religions and collective rituals minimize antisocial behavior in groups of unrelated individuals. And within countries, individuals who believe in God or the concepts of heaven or hell are more likely to say that transgressions, such as cheating on taxes or having an affair, are never justified.

The Shaker community in New Lebanon, New York was an example of a strong religious commune. In this 1870s drawing, Shaker members dance and worship.

Perhaps to promote solidarity, religions in complex societies often extend kin terms to members of the religious communities, calling each other "brothers" and "sisters" or sometimes "God's children." Experimental evidence suggests individuals are more generous toward strangers if their religious feelings have been aroused. Religious communes are also four times as likely to survive compared with secular communes.

These studies raise important questions about exactly why and when moralizing religions came into existence and whether the spread of these religions had to do with their adaptive consequences. But there are also questions raised about mechanisms. For example, religious communes, as compared with secular communes, usually impose more requirements from members, such as food taboos, fasts, constraints on sex and possessions, and so on. A comparative study of communes suggests that the religious elements are more important than the commitments themselves. However, in experimental research, there are some hints that nonreligious conditions could also make people more cooperative. Experimental reminders of secular morality had as much effect as reminders of God. Also, there are examples of modern societies, especially in northern Europe, that are very cooperative but not very religious.

But, even if religious belief and ritual promote greater in-group trust and cooperation, there is a dark side to strongly held religious belief—the potential for greater out-group conflict. History is replete with examples of people hurting others in the name of religion. Christianity and Islam are the two largest religions, possibly because of their zeal to convert others. Some of the biggest conflicts have occurred where the two largest religions meet. The Christian Crusades of the 11th century through 13th century were attempts to "liberate" sites in the Holy Land controlled by Muslims. Osama bin Laden cited the establishment of U.S. bases in Saudi Arabia, which "defiled" sacred lands in his view, as justification for the September 11, 2001, attacks on the United States. Religions, or, more precisely, religious groups, do not necessarily promote violence. After all, some of the founders of various religions preached nonviolence and harmony. Exactly what persuades a religious group to commit violence is not well understood. There are five warning signs. One is when leaders act as if only they know the truth. A second is a call to blind obedience to a religious leader. A third is when the people believe it is possible to establish an "ideal world." A fourth is acting as if "the end justifies the means." Lastly, and perhaps the clearest, is a call for a "holy war."

In the globalized world today, there is more admixture of all types. Whether the major religions will adapt peacefully to create a new morality for the new global circumstances remains to be seen. We can hope that simply learning more about other individuals and groups—their hopes, dreams, and expectations, how they have adapted to their environments—may enhance tolerance.

Sources: Winkelman and Baker 2010, 259–265, 314–318; Norenzayan and Shariff 2008; Sosis and Bressler 2003; Stark 2001; Roes and Raymond 2003; Atkinson and Bourrat 2011.

Life After Death

In many societies, ideas about an afterlife are vague and seemingly unimportant, but many other peoples have very definite and elaborate ideas of what happens after death. The Lugbara of Uganda see the dead as joining the ancestors of the living and staying near the family homesite. They retain an interest in the behavior of the living, both rewarding and punishing them. The Zuni of the southwestern United States think the dead join the past dead, known as the *katcinas,* in a katcina village at the bottom of a nearby lake. There they lead a life of singing and dancing and bring rain to the living Zuni. Just as they are swift to punish the priest who fails in his duty, they also punish the people in masks who ineffectively impersonate the katcinas during the dance ceremonies.[33]

The Chamulas have merged the ancient Mayan worship of the sun and moon with the Spanish conquerors' Jesus and Mary. Their vision of life after death contains a blending of the two cultures. All souls go to the underworld, where they live a humanlike life except that they are incapable of sexual intercourse. After the sun travels over the world, it travels under the underworld, so that the dead have sunlight. Only murderers and suicides are punished, being burned by the Christ-sun on their journey.[34]

Many Christians believe that the dead are divided into two groups: The unsaved are sent to everlasting punishment and the saved to everlasting reward. Accounts differ, but hell is often associated with torture by fire, heaven with mansions. Several societies see the dead as returning to earth to be reborn. The Hindus use this pattern of reincarnation to justify one's caste in this life and to promise eventual release from the pain of life through the attainment of *nirvana,* or inclusion into the One.

A recent cross-cultural study asks why some societies judge where you will go after death and others do not. Support was found for the idea that judgmental beliefs parallel the society's economic practices. Some societies have considerable delay between labor inputs and return of food. For example, intensive agriculturalists need considerable labor input to plow, fertilize, or create irrigation systems, and many months go by until crops can be harvested. Not planning ahead has dire long-term consequences. In contrast, mistakes by hunter-gatherers are realized more quickly and can be corrected more quickly. Religions that foster the idea that actions in the present will be judged after death reinforce the need for long-term planning. Consistent with this idea, societies with intensive agriculture are the most likely to believe that their actions in life affect where their souls will go after death.[35] This finding is consistent with Swanson's conclusion discussed previously that the gods are generally likely to punish people for immoral behavior when there are considerable differences in wealth in the society. Intensive agricultural societies tend to have considerable differences in wealth.

In many respects, the afterworld in many religions may resemble the everyday world, but we still have only a few comparative studies that show exactly how.

Variation in Religious Practices

23.3 Describe the variability in religious practices and practitioners cross-culturally.

Beliefs are not the only elements of religion that vary from society to society. Societies vary in the kinds of religious practitioners they have. There is also variation in how people interact with the supernatural. The manner of approach to the supernatural varies from supplication— requests, prayers, and so on—to manipulation. Many of these interactions are highly *ritualized.* **Rituals** are repetitive sets of behaviors that occur in essentially the same patterns every time they occur. In a certain sense, a good deal of culture is ritualized—from the way we greet people to the way we eat a meal.[36] But usually when we refer to ritual, particularly religious rituals, we mean much more than that. They tend to be elaborated, formal, indicative of something special, and, in the case of religious rituals, involve the supernatural in some way—as audience, as a recipient of a request, as a force to be manipulated, and so on.[37] Religious rituals are generally collective and are thought to strengthen faith.[38]

Rituals Repetitive sets of behaviors that occur in essentially the same patterns every time they occur. Religious rituals involve the supernatural in some way.

Ways to Interact with the Supernatural

How to get in touch with the supernatural has proved to be a universal problem. Wallace identified a number of ways people the world over use—though not necessarily all together—including, but not limited to, prayer (asking for supernatural help), physiological experience (doing things to the body and mind), simulation (manipulating imitations of things), feasts, and sacrifices.[39] Prayer can be spontaneous or memorized, private or public, silent or spoken. The Lugbara do not say the words of a prayer aloud, for doing so would be too powerful; they simply think about the things that are bothering them. The gods know all languages.

Doing things to the body or mind may involve drugs (hallucinogenics such as peyote or opiates) or alcohol; social isolation or sensory deprivation; dancing or running until exhausted; being deprived of food, water, and sleep; and listening to repetitive sounds such as drumming. Such behaviors may induce trances or altered states of consciousness.[40] Erika Bourguignon found that achieving these altered states, which she generally referred to as *trances,* is part of religious practice in 90 percent of the world's societies.[41] In some societies, trances are thought to involve the presence of a spirit or power inside a person that changes or displaces that person's personality or soul. These types are referred to as possession trances. Other types of trances may involve the journey of a person's soul, experiencing visions, or transmitting messages from spirits. Possession trances are especially likely in societies that depend on agriculture and have social stratification, slavery, and more complex political hierarchies. Nonpossession trances are most likely to occur in food-collecting societies. Societies with moderate levels of social complexity have both possession and nonpossession trances.[42]

One puzzle is why there is a preponderance of women thought to be possessed. Alice Kehoe and Dody Giletti suggested that women are more likely than men to suffer from nutritional deficiencies because of pregnancy, lactation, and men's priority in gaining access to food. Calcium deficiency in particular can cause muscular spasms, convulsive seizures, and disorientation, all of which may foster the belief that an individual is possessed.[43] Douglas Raybeck and his colleagues suggest that women's physiology makes them more susceptible to calcium deficiency even with an equivalent diet. In addition, women are subject to more stress because they are usually less able to control their lives. Higher levels of stress, they suggest, lower the body's reserves of calcium.[44] Erika Bourguignon suggests a more psychological explanation of women's preponderance in possession trances. In many societies, women are brought up to be submissive. But when possessed, women are taken over by spirits and are not responsible for what they do or say—therefore, they can unconsciously do what they are not able to do consciously.[45] Although intriguing, these suggestions need to be tested on individuals in field situations.

Voodoo employs simulation, or the imitation of things. Dolls are made in the likeness of an enemy and then are maltreated in hopes that the original enemy will experience pain and even death.

Divination Getting the supernatural to provide guidance.

Divination seeks practical answers from the supernatural about anything that is troublesome—decisions to be made, interpersonal problems, or illness. Diviners are believed to have the ability to read the intent of the spirits. Diviners use a variety of methods, including altered states of consciousness and simulation through the use of objects such as Ouija boards or tarot cards.[46]

Omar Moore suggested that among the Naskapi hunters of Labrador, divination is an adaptive strategy for successful hunting. The Naskapi consult the diviner every three or four days when they have no luck in hunting. The diviner holds a caribou bone over the fire, as if the bone were a map, and the burns and cracks that appear in it indicate where the group should hunt. Moore, unlike the Naskapi, did not believe that the diviner really can find out where the animals will be; the cracks in the bones merely provide a way of randomly choosing where to hunt. Because humans are likely to develop customary patterns of action, they might be likely to look for game according to some plan. But game might learn to avoid hunters who operate according to a plan. Thus, any method of ensuring against patterning or predictable plans—any random strategy—may be advantageous. Divination by "reading" the bones would seem to be a random strategy. It also relieves any individual of the responsibility of deciding where to hunt, a decision that might arouse anger if the hunt failed.[47]

The eating of a sacred meal is found in many religions. For instance, Holy Communion is a simulation of the Last Supper. Australian aborigines, normally forbidden to eat their totem animal, have one totem feast a year at which they eat the totem. Feasts are often part of marriage and funeral ceremonies, as well as a fringe benefit of the sacrifice of food to the gods.

Some societies make sacrifices to a god in order to influence the god's action, either to divert anger or to attract goodwill. Characteristic of all sacrifices is that something of value is given up to the gods, whether it be food, drink, sex, household goods, or the life of an animal or person. Some societies feel that the god is obligated to act on their behalf if they make the appropriate sacrifice. Others use the sacrifice in an attempt to persuade the god, realizing there is no guarantee that the attempt will be successful.

Of all types of sacrifice, we probably think that the taking of human life is the ultimate. Nevertheless, human sacrifice is not rare in the ethnographic and historical records. Why have some societies practiced it? One cross-cultural study found that, among preindustrial societies, those with full-time craft specialists, slavery, and the corvée are most likely to practice human sacrifice. The suggested explanation is that the sacrifice mirrors what is socially important: Societies that depend mainly on human labor for energy (rather than animals or machines) may think of a human life as an appropriate offering to the gods when people want something very important.[48] Later studies found that societies with human sacrifice were at a mid-range level of political complexity, having alliances and confederacies with other polities but only weak political integration. Such societies also seemed to be subject to population pressure and frequently carried out warfare for land and other resources. Human sacrifice, with humans from the outside groups, may have been an attempt to terrorize people from the other polities.[49]

Magic

All these modes of interacting with the supernatural can be categorized in various ways. One dimension of variation is how much people in society rely on pleading, asking, or trying to persuade the supernatural to act on their behalf, as opposed to whether they believe they can compel the supernatural to help by performing certain acts. For example, prayer is asking; performing voodoo is presumably compelling. When people believe their action can compel the supernatural to act in some particular and intended way, anthropologists often refer to the belief and related practice as **magic**.

Magic The performance of certain rituals that are believed to compel the supernatural powers to act in particular ways.

Magic may involve manipulation of the supernatural for good or for evil. Many societies have magical rituals designed to ensure good crops, the replenishment of game, the fertility of domestic animals, and the avoidance and cure of illness in humans. We tend to associate the belief in magic with societies simpler than our own, but some people in complex societies take magic seriously, and many follow some magical practices.

People who engage in risky activities may try to ensure their safety by carrying or wearing lucky charms. They believe the charms protect them by invoking the help of supernatural beings or forces. We might also believe we can protect ourselves by not doing some things. For example, baseball players on a hitting streak may choose not to change their socks or sweatshirt for the next game (to continue their luck). Why magic appeals to some individuals but not others in our own society may help us explain why magic is an important part of religious behavior in many societies.

As we will see, the witch doctor and the shaman often employ magic to effect a cure. But the use of magic to bring about harm has evoked perhaps the most interest.

Listen to the Audio: Shamanism Endures in an Evolving Mongolia

Sorcery and Witchcraft

Sorcery and witchcraft are attempts to invoke the spirits to work harm against people. Although the words *sorcery* and *witchcraft* are often used interchangeably, they are also often distinguished. **Sorcery** may include the use of materials, objects, and medicines to invoke supernatural malevolence. **Witchcraft** may be said to accomplish the same ills by means of thought and emotion alone. Evidence of witchcraft can never be found. This lack of visible evidence makes an accusation of witchcraft both harder to prove and harder to disprove.

Sorcery The use of certain materials to invoke supernatural powers to harm people.

Witchcraft The practice of attempting to harm people by supernatural means, but through emotions and thought alone, not through the use of tangible objects.

To the Azande of Zaire, in central Africa, witchcraft was part of everyday living. It was not used to explain events for which the cause was known, such as carelessness or violation of a taboo, but to explain the otherwise unexplainable. A man is gored by an elephant. He must have been bewitched because he had not been gored on other elephant hunts. A man goes to his beer hut at night, lights some straw, and holds it aloft to look at his beer. The thatch catches fire and the hut burns down. The man has been bewitched, for huts did not catch fire on hundreds of other nights when he and others did the same thing. Some of the pots of a skilled potter break; some of the bowls of a skilled carver crack—witchcraft. Other pots and bowls treated exactly the same have not broken.[50]

The witch craze in Europe during the 16th and 17th centuries and the witch trials in 1692 in Salem, Massachusetts, remind us that the fear of others, which the belief in witchcraft presumably represents, can increase and decrease in a society within a relatively short period of time. Many scholars have tried to explain these witch hunts. One factor often suggested is political turmoil, which may give rise to widespread distrust and a search for scapegoats. In the case of Europe during the 16th and 17th centuries, small regional political units were being incorporated into national states, and political allegiances were in flux. In addition, as Swanson noted, the commercial revolution and related changes were producing a new social class, the middle class, and "were promoting the growth of Protestantism and other heresies from Roman Catholicism."[51] In the case of Salem, the government of Massachusetts colony was unstable, and there was much internal dissension. In 1692, the year of the witchcraft hysteria, Massachusetts was left without an English governor, and judicial practices broke down. These extraordinary conditions saw the accusation of a single person for witchcraft become the accusation of hundreds and the execution of 20 people. Swanson suggested that the undermining of legitimate political procedures may have generated the widespread fear of witches.[52]

It is also possible that epidemics of witchcraft accusation, like that in Salem as well as other New England and European communities, may be the result of real epidemics—epidemics of disease. The disease implicated in Salem and elsewhere is the fungus disease called ergot, which can grow on rye plants. (The rye flour that went into the bread that the Salem people ate may have been contaminated by ergot.) It is now known that people who eat grain products contaminated by ergot suffer from convulsions, hallucinations, and other symptoms, such as crawling sensations in the skin. We also now know that ergot contains LSD, the drug that produces hallucinations and other delusions that resemble those occurring in severe mental disorders.

The presumed victims of bewitchment in Salem and other places had symptoms similar to those of victims of ergot poisoning today. They suffered from convulsions and the sensations of being pricked, pinched, or bitten. They had visions and felt as if they were flying through the air. We cannot know for sure that ergot poisoning occurred during those times when witchcraft accusations flourished. There is no direct evidence, of course, because the "bewitched" were not medically tested. But we do have some evidence that seems to be consistent with the ergot theory. Ergot is known to flourish on rye plants under certain climatic conditions—particularly a very cold winter followed by a cool, moist spring and summer. Tree-ring growth indicates that the early 1690s were particularly cold in eastern New England, and the outbreaks of witchcraft accusation in Europe seem to have peaked with colder winter temperatures.[53] Interestingly, too, when witchcraft hysteria was greatest in Europe, Europeans were using an ointment containing a skin-penetrating substance that we now know produces hallucinations and a vivid sensation of flying.[54] It may not be cause for wonder, then, that our popular image of witches is of people flying through the air on broomsticks.

But whether or not epidemics of witchcraft hysteria are due to epidemics of ergot poisoning or episodes of political turmoil or both, we still have to understand why so many societies in the ethnographic record believe in witchcraft and sorcery in the first place. Why do so many societies believe that there are ways to invoke the spirits to work harm against people? One possible explanation, suggested by Beatrice Whiting, is that sorcery or witchcraft will be found in societies that lack procedures or judicial authorities to deal with crime and other offenses. Her theory is that all societies need some form of social control—some way of deterring most would-be offenders and of dealing with actual offenders. In the absence of judicial officials who, if present, might deter and deal with antisocial behavior, sorcery may be a very effective mechanism for social control. If you misbehave, the person you mistreated might cause you to become ill or even die. The cross-cultural evidence seems to support this theory. Sorcery is more important in societies that lack judicial authorities than in those that have them.[55]

Types of Practitioners

Individuals may believe that they can directly contact the supernatural, but almost all societies also have part-time or full-time religious or magical practitioners. Research suggests there are four major types of practitioners: shamans, sorcerers or witches, mediums, and priests. As we shall see, the number of types of practitioners in a society seems to vary with degree of cultural complexity.[56]

The Shaman The word *shaman* may come from a language that was spoken in eastern Siberia. The **shaman** is usually a part-time male specialist who has fairly high status in his community and is often involved in healing.[57] More generally, the shaman deals with the spirits to try to get their help or to keep them from causing harm.[58] Here we focus on the methods shamans use to help others.

Shaman A religious intermediary, usually part-time, whose primary function is to cure people through sacred songs, pantomime, and other means; sometimes called witch doctor by Westerners.

The shaman enters into a trance, or some other altered state of consciousness, and then journeys to other worlds to get help from guardians or other spirits. Dreams may be used to provide insight or as a way for shamans to commune with spirits. People may seek help for practical matters, such as where to get food resources or whether to relocate, but solving a health problem is most often the goal of the shaman.[59] Shamans may also bring news from spirits, such as a warning about an impending disaster.[60]

Someone may receive a "call" to the role of shaman in recovering from an illness, through a vision quest, or in a dream. Shamans-in-training may enhance the vividness of their imagery by using hallucinogens, sleep or food deprivation, or engaging in extensive physical activity such as dancing. An important part of the process of being a shaman is learning to control the imagery and the spirit powers. Shamanistic training can take several years under the guidance of a master shaman.[61]

Sorcerers and Witches In contrast with shamans, who have fairly high status, sorcerers and witches of both sexes tend to have very low social and economic status in their societies.[62] Suspected sorcerers and witches are usually feared because they are thought to know how to invoke the supernatural to cause illness, injury, and death. Because sorcerers use materials for their magic, evidence of sorcery can be found, and suspected sorcerers are often killed for their malevolent activities. Because witchcraft supposedly is accomplished by thought and emotion alone, it may be harder to prove that someone is a witch, but the difficulty of proving witchcraft has not prevented people from accusing and killing others for being witches.

Shamans are usually male. Here, female shamans in Korea perform a healing ritual.

Mediums Part-time religious practitioners who are asked to heal and divine while in a trance.

Priests Generally full-time specialists, with very high status, who are thought to be able to relate to superior or high gods beyond the ordinary person's access or control.

Mediums **Mediums** tend to be females. These part-time practitioners are asked to heal and divine while in possession trances—that is, when they are thought to be possessed by spirits. Mediums are described as having tremors, convulsions, seizures, and temporary amnesia.[63]

Priests **Priests** are generally full-time male specialists who officiate at public events. They have very high status and are thought to be able to relate to superior or high gods who are beyond the ordinary person's control. In most societies with priests, the people who get to be priests obtain their offices through inheritance or political appointment.[64] Priests are sometimes distinguished from other people by special clothing or a different hairstyle. The training of a priest can be vigorous and long, including fasting, praying, and physical labor, as well as learning the dogma and the ritual of his religion. Priests in the United States complete four years of theological school and sometimes serve first as apprentices under established priests. Priests do not receive a fee for their services but are supported by donations from parishioners or followers. Priests often have some political power as a result of their office—the chief priest is sometimes also the head of state or is a close adviser to the chief of state—and their material well-being is a direct reflection of their position in the priestly hierarchy.

The dependence on memorized ritual both marks and protects the priest. If a shaman repeatedly fails to effect a cure, he will probably lose his following, for he has obviously lost the support of the spirits. But if a priest performs his ritual perfectly and the gods choose not to respond, the priest will usually retain his position and the ritual will preserve its assumed effectiveness. The nonresponse of the gods will be explained in terms of the people's unworthiness of supernatural favor.

Practitioners and Social Complexity More complex societies tend to have more types of religious or magical practitioners. If a society has only one type of practitioner, it is almost always a shaman; such societies tend to be nomadic or seminomadic food collectors. Societies with two types of practitioners (usually shaman healers and priests) have agriculture. Those with three types of practitioners are agriculturalists or pastoralists with political integration beyond the community (the additional practitioner type tends to be either a sorcerer or witch or a medium). Finally, societies with all four types of practitioners have agriculture, political integration beyond the community, and social classes.[65]

23.4 Discuss religion in terms of adaptation.

Religion and Adaptation

As we have seen in this chapter, many anthropologists take the view that religions are adaptive. Some theorists argue that religion helps individuals reduce anxiety and uncertainty. Others stress societal needs of solidarity and cooperation. These are general needs, and it is easy to imagine why reducing anxiety or increasing cooperation would be important. But some particular customary aspects of religious belief, at least on the surface, do not appear to be adaptive. For example, the Hindu belief in the sacred cow has seemed to many to be the very opposite of a useful or adaptive custom. Their religion does not permit Hindus to slaughter cows. Why do the Hindus retain such a belief? Why do they allow all those cows to wander around freely, defecating all over the place, and not slaughter any of them? The contrast with our own use of cows could hardly be greater.

Marvin Harris suggested that the Hindu use of cows may have beneficial consequences that some other use of cows would not have. Harris pointed out that there may be a sound economic reason for not slaughtering cattle in India. The cows, and the males they produce, provide resources that could not easily be gotten otherwise. At the same time, their wandering around to forage is no strain on the food-producing economy.

The resources provided by the cows are varied. First, a team of oxen and a plow are essential for the many small farms in India. The Indians could produce oxen with fewer cows, but to do so they would have to devote some of their food production to feeding those cows. In the present system, they do not feed the cows, and even though poor nutrition makes the cows relatively infertile, males, which are castrated to make oxen, are still produced at no cost to the economy. Second, cow dung is essential as a cooking fuel and fertilizer. The National Council of Applied Economic Research estimated that an amount of dung equivalent to 45 million tons of coal is burned annually. Moreover, it is delivered practically to the door each day at no cost. Alternative sources of fuel, such as wood, are scarce or costly. In addition, about 340 million tons of dung are used as manure—essential in a country obliged to derive three harvests a year from its intensively cultivated land. Third, although Hindus do not eat beef, cattle that die naturally or are butchered by non-Hindus are eaten by the lower castes, who, without the upper-caste taboo against eating beef, might not get this needed protein. Fourth, the hides and horns of the cattle that die are used in India's enormous leather industry. Therefore, because the cows do not themselves consume resources needed by people and it would be impossible to provide traction, fuel, and fertilizer as cheaply by other means, the taboo against slaughtering cattle may be very adaptive.[66]

Religious Change

23.5 Explain and give examples of various forms of religious change, such as conversion and revitalization movements.

In any society, religious beliefs and practices change over time, but some types of change are quite dramatic. Perhaps the most dramatic is religious conversion, particularly when large numbers of people switch to a completely new religion presented by missionaries or other proselytizers. Changing religion so drastically is perplexing to many scholars of religion who believe that religious beliefs are deeply connected to one's sense of identity, one's family, one's community, and ideas about the world.[67] Within the last few centuries, conversion has sometimes followed Western expansion and exploration. Contact with Westerners and other outsiders has also produced religious change in more indirect ways. In some native societies, contact has led to a breakdown of social structure and the growth of feelings of helplessness and spiritual demoralization. *Revitalization movements* have arisen as apparent attempts to restore such societies to their former confidence and prosperity. In recent times, religious *fundamentalist* movements have flourished. Some scholars have argued that such movements are also responses to the stress of rapid social change.

As we will see, religious change, particularly of the dramatic kind, usually does not occur in a vacuum but is often associated with other dramatic changes—economic, political, and demographic.

Religious Conversion

The two world religions with the greatest interest now in obtaining converts have been Christianity and Islam. Christian missionaries, supported by their churches back home, have been some of the earliest Western settlers in interior regions and out-of-the-way places. Traders have been the main proselytizers of Islam. Conversion to one of the world religions has often been associated with colonization and the expansion of state societies (see the box "Colonialism and Religious Affiliation"). The presence of people from other religions does not necessarily mean that people convert to the new religion. For example, missionaries have not met with equal success in all parts of the world. In some places, large portions of the native population have converted to the new religion with great zeal. In others, missionaries have been ignored, forced to flee, or even killed. We do not fully understand why missionaries have been successful in some societies and not in others.

We now examine the process of conversion on the island of Tikopia as an example of religious change brought about by direct contact with missionaries.

Christianity on Tikopia Tikopia was one of the few Polynesian societies to retain its traditional religious system into the first decades of the 20th century. An Anglican mission was first established on the island in 1911. With it came a deacon and the founding of two schools for about 200 pupils. By 1929, approximately half the population had converted, and in the early 1960s, almost all of Tikopia gave at least nominal allegiance to Christianity.[68]

Traditional Tikopian belief embraced a great number of gods and spirits of various ranks who inhabited the sky, the water, and the land. One god in particular—the original creator and shaper of the culture—was given a place of special importance, but he was in no way comparable to the all-powerful God of Christianity. Unlike Christianity, Tikopian religion made no claim to universality. The Tikopian gods did not rule over all creation, only over Tikopia. It was thought that if one left Tikopia, one left the gods behind.

The people of Tikopia interacted with their gods and spirits primarily through religious leaders who were also the heads of descent groups. Clan chiefs presided over rituals associated with the everyday aspects of island life, such as house construction, fishing, planting,

Migrants and Immigrants

Colonialism and Religious Affiliation

Many of us might like to think that we belong to a particular religious group because we prefer its beliefs and practices. And that may be true for people who have chosen to switch their religious affiliation. But many religious people affiliate with the religion they grew up with, or one very much like it.

Clearly, religious affiliation is a complex issue. But one thing stands out. You are not likely to choose an affiliation you have never been exposed to. This goes for people who believe in religion and also for people who don't. Most North Americans say they are Christians. But how come?

Would so many in North America be Christians if Europeans (mostly Christian) hadn't established colonies here and elsewhere in the last 500 years? Would there be Muslims in Indonesia, the Philippines, and North Africa if Arab kingdoms hadn't established colonies in those places after the 7th century? Would there have been Hindus in Sumatra if South Asians hadn't migrated and established the Srivijayan kingdom in Sumatra before the time of Christ? Would there have been Jews in Yemen (until their emigration to Israel 50 years ago) if King Solomon's state had not colonized in the land of the Queen of Sheba more than 2,000 years ago? An expanding state society can directly or indirectly force a change in people's religious affiliation. It is not coincidental that the new religious affiliation usually matches the dominant society's.

Church on Rangiroa, French Polynesia.

Religion in some form may be a cultural universal. People may worship the supernatural, pray to it for help and guidance, and even try to control it (with "lucky charms" and other magic). But religion is not the same everywhere, as is evident in this chapter. Why people convert to a major religion carried by an expanding state society is still not completely understood. Sometimes the people do not convert, or do not convert right away. Anthropologist Elizabeth Brusco has written that one primary motivation for conversion, long recognized by scholars, is the desire to maximize advantages. In recent times, missionaries have offered new beliefs and practices that may be appealing, but they have also offered what Brusco calls "protection, access to food and other desirable goods, medical care, literacy, technology, status, and, at times, political power." Was the same true, at least somewhat, in the past? Was adopting the new religion the best way to survive colonialism and its consequences?

Even if people adopt a religion, they often change important parts of it. For example, the Lahu of southwest China became Buddhist, but the Buddha became a male-female couple rather than just a male. The Lahu were a stateless society (prior to the expansion of the Han Chinese) with a strong emphasis on gender equality. By identifying Buddha with their indigenous god, Xeul Sha, the image of the Buddha was changed. According to Lahu origin myths, Xeul Sha is a male-female pair of twins. They marry and propagate humanity. The identification of Xeul Sha with Buddha means that Buddha is considered a pair of male-female gods by most Lahu Buddhist villagers.

Sources: Brusco 1996; Stevens 1996; Du 2003.

and harvesting. The chief was expected to intercede with the gods on the people's behalf, to persuade them to bring happiness and prosperity to the group. Indeed, when conditions were good, it was assumed that the chief was doing his job well. When disaster struck, the prestige of the chief often fell in proportion. Why did the Tikopia convert to Christianity? Firth suggested several contributing factors.

First, the mission offered the people the prospect of acquiring new tools and consumer goods. Although conversion alone did not provide such benefits, attachment to the mission made them more attainable. Later, it became apparent that education, particularly in reading and writing English, was helpful in getting ahead in the outside world. Mission schooling became valued and provided a further incentive for adopting Christianity.

Second, conversion may have been facilitated by the ability of chiefs, as religious and political leaders, to bring over entire descent groups to Christianity. Should a chief decide to transfer his allegiance to Christianity, the members of his kin group usually followed him. In 1923, when Tafua, chief of the Faea district of Tikopia, converted to the new religion, he brought with him his entire group—nearly half the population of the island. The ability of the chiefs to influence their kin groups, however, was both an asset and a hindrance to missionary efforts because some chiefs steadfastly resisted conversion.

A final blow to traditional Tikopian religion came in 1955, when a severe epidemic killed at least 200 people in a population of about 1,700. According to Firth, "the epidemic was largely interpreted as a sign of divine discrimination" because three of the outstanding non-Christian religious leaders died.[69] Subsequently, the remaining non-Christian chiefs voluntarily converted to Christianity, and so did their followers. By 1966, all Tikopia, with the exception of one old woman, had converted to the new faith.

Although many Tikopians feel their conversion to Christianity has been a unifying, revitalizing force, the changeover from one religion to another has not been without problems. Christian missionaries on Tikopia have succeeded in eliminating the traditional Tikopian population-control devices of abortion, infanticide, and male celibacy. It is very possible that the absence of these controls will continue to intensify population pressure. The island, with its limited capacity to support life, can ill afford this outcome. Firth summed up the situation Tikopian society faced:

> *In the history of Tikopia complete conversion of the people to Christianity was formerly regarded as a solution to their problems; it is now coming to be realized that the adoption and practice of Christianity itself represents another set of problems. As the Tikopia themselves are beginning to see, to be Christian Polynesians in the modern technologically and industrially dominated world, even in the Solomon Islands, poses as many questions as it supplies answers.*[70]

Unfortunately, not all native peoples have made the transition to Christianity as painlessly as the Tikopia. In fact, the record is dismal in most cases. All too frequently, missionary activity tends to destroy a society's culture and self-respect. It offers nothing in return but an alien, repressive system of values ill suited to the people's real needs and aspirations. Phillip Mason, a critic of European evangelists in Africa, pointed out some of the psychological damage inflicted by missionary activity.[71] The missionaries repeatedly stressed sin and guilt; they used the color black to represent evil and the color white to signify good; and they showed hostility toward pagan culture. Most damaging of all was their promise that Africans, provided they adopted the European's ways, would gain access both to the Europeans' heaven and to European society. But no matter how diligently Africans attempted to follow missionary precepts or climb the socioeconomic ladder, they were soon blocked from entry into European homes, clubs, and even churches and seminaries.

Explaining Conversion Anthropologists have just begun to try to understand religious conversion. As the box on colonialism and religious affiliation and the Tikopia case suggest, some of the motivation for switching to a new religion may have to do with economic and political advantages associated with converting to the new religion. With regard to the recent spread of Islam in Africa, Jean Ensminger suggests that Islam provided opportunities for those who wanted to engage in trade— "Islam brought a common language of trade (Arabic), a monetary system, an accounting system, and a legal code to adjudicate financial contracts and disputes."[72] These institutions were shared across ethnic groups, making it possible to engage in long-distance trade. But what increased the attractiveness of Islamic trade? Ensminger's study of the Orma, a pastoralist group in Kenya, is instructive, for despite the presence of Islam for 300 years, it did not appear to be of interest to them. The Orma chiefs did trade, but the Orma were mostly self-sufficient, and the need for trade appeared to be relatively low. However, the Orma were in serious trouble after successful attacks by the Masai and Somali in the late 1800s, which almost decimated them and depleted their cattle. After 1920, as they began to recover their population somewhat and their cattle began to be replenished, there was rapid conversion to Islam, mostly led by the young, who perhaps were attracted by the economic opportunities.[73]

Loss of population and the demoralization that it brings may also have played a significant role in conversion. Daniel Reff, comparing widespread conversion to Christianity in the Roman Empire after A.D. 150 and in northern Mexico after A.D. 1593, notes the parallels in both. In both situations, there were ravaging epidemics along with the presence of Christian personnel ready to help heal the sick. In Europe, about 8 percent of the population died before smallpox epidemics subsided in A.D. 190, and population continued to decline into the Middle Ages, perhaps to half of what it was. Population losses might have been more extreme in Mexico. In northern Mexico, an estimated 75 percent of the native populations died from disease. In Europe, Christians provided charity, food, and shelter for the ill, without regard to their status. The Jesuit missions in Mexico did not have that many personnel, but they did what they could to provide food, water, and "medicine."[74] Do epidemics play a role in other places? An exploratory cross-cultural study suggests that rapid population loss, usually from introduced diseases, predicts religious conversion, particularly when people believe that their traditional gods could help them.[75] If gods could have helped but didn't and people are dying in unusual numbers, people may think that the "gods have failed." In such circumstances, it is not surprising that people would be receptive to a new religion, particularly if it is preached by missionaries who are not dying.

Revitalization

Revitalization movements New religious movements intended to save a culture by infusing it with a new purpose and life.

The long history of religion includes periods of strong resistance to change as well as periods of radical change. Anthropologists have been especially interested in the founding of new religions or sects. The appearance of new religions is one of the things that may happen when cultures are disrupted by contact with dominant societies. Various terms have been suggested for these religious movements—cargo cults, nativistic movements, messianic movements, millenarian cults. Wallace suggested that they are all examples of **revitalization movements**, efforts to save a culture by infusing it with a new purpose and new life.[76] We turn to examples of such movements from North America and Melanesia.

A revitalization movement that became known as the Ghost Dance spread eastward from the Northwest from the 1870s to the 1890s. It was generally believed that, if people did the dance correctly, ghosts would come to life with sufficient resources to allow the people to return to their old ways, and, as a result of some cataclysm, the whites would disappear.

Source: Ogallala Sioux performing the Ghost Dance at the Pine Ridge Indian Agency, South Dakota. Illustration by Frederic Remington, 1890.

The Seneca and the Religion of Handsome Lake The Seneca reservation of the Iroquois on the Allegheny River in New York State was a place of "poverty and humiliation" by 1799.[77] Demoralized by whiskey and dispossessed from their traditional lands, unable to compete with the new technology because of illiteracy and lack of training, the Seneca were at an impasse. In this setting, Handsome Lake, the 50-year-old brother of a chief, had the first of a number of visions. In them, he met with emissaries of the Creator who showed him heaven and hell and commissioned him to revitalize Seneca religion and society. This he set out to do for the next decade and a half. As his principal text, he used the *Gaiwiio,* or "Good Word," a gospel that contains statements about the nature of religion and eternity and a code of conduct for the righteous. The *Gaiwiio* is interesting both for the influence of Quaker Christianity it clearly reveals[78] and for the way the new material was merged with traditional Iroquois religious concepts.

The first part of the "Good Word" has three main themes, one of which is the concept of an apocalypse. Handsome Lake offered many signs by which the faithful could recognize impending cosmic doom. Great drops of fire would rain from the skies and a veil would be cast over the earth. False prophets would appear, witch women would openly cast spells, and poisonous creatures from the underworld would seize and kill those who had rejected the *Gaiwiio.* Second, the *Gaiwiio* emphasized sin. The great sins were disbelief in the "good way," drunkenness, witchcraft, and abortion. Sins had to be confessed and repented. Finally, the *Gaiwiio* offered salvation. Salvation could be won by following a code of conduct, attending certain important traditional rites, and performing public confession.

The second part of the *Gaiwiio* sets out the code of conduct. This code seems to orient the Seneca toward advantageous European American practices without separating them from their culture. The code has five main sections:

1. *Temperance.* All Seneca leaders were fully aware of the social disorders arising out of abuse of liquor. Handsome Lake went to great lengths to illustrate and explain the harmfulness of alcohol.
2. *Peace and social unity.* Seneca leaders were to cease their futile bickering, and all were to be united in their approach to the larger society.
3. *Preservation of tribal lands.* Handsome Lake, fearing the piecemeal alienation of Seneca lands, was far ahead of his contemporaries in demanding a halt in land sales to non-Seneca.
4. *Proacculturation (favoring external culture traits).* Though individual property and trading for profit were prohibited, the acquisition of literacy in English was encouraged so that people would be able to read and understand treaties and to avoid being cheated.
5. *Domestic morality.* Sons were to obey their fathers, mothers should avoid interfering with daughters' marriages, and husbands and wives should respect the sanctity of their marriage vows.

Handsome Lake's teaching seems to have led to a renaissance among the Seneca. Temperance was widely accepted, as were schooling and new farming methods. By 1801, corn yields had been increased tenfold, new crops (oats, potatoes, flax) had been introduced, and public health and hygiene had improved considerably. Handsome Lake himself acquired great power among his people. He spent the remainder of his life fulfilling administrative duties, acting as a representative of the Iroquois in Washington, and preaching his gospel to neighboring tribes. By the time of Handsome Lake's death in 1815, the Seneca clearly had undergone a dramatic rebirth, attributable at least in part to the new religion. Later in the century, some of Handsome Lake's disciples founded a church in his name that, despite occasional setbacks and political disputes, survives to this day.

Although many scholars believe cultural stress gives rise to these new religious movements, it is still important to understand exactly what the stresses are and how strong they have to become before a new movement emerges. Do different kinds of stresses produce different kinds of movements? And does the nature of the movement depend on the cultural elements already present? Let us consider some theory and research on the causes of the millenarian cargo cults that began to appear in Melanesia from about 1885 on.

Cargo Cults The *cargo cults* can be thought of as religious movements "in which there is an expectation of, and preparation for, the coming of a period of supernatural bliss."[79] Thus, an explicit belief of the cargo cults was the notion that some liberating power would bring all the Western goods (cargo in pidgin English) the people might want. For example, around 1932, on Buka in the Solomon Islands, the leaders of a cult prophesied that a tidal wave would sweep away the villages and a ship would arrive with iron, axes, food, tobacco, cars, and arms. Work in the gardens ceased, and wharves and docks were built for the expected cargo.[80]

What may explain such cults? Peter Worsley suggested that an important factor in the rise of cargo cults and millenarian movements in general is the existence of oppression—in the case of Melanesia, colonial oppression. He suggested that the reactions in Melanesia took religious rather than political forms because they were a way of pulling together people who previously had no political unity and who lived in small, isolated social groups.[81] Other scholars, such as David Aberle, suggested that *relative deprivation* is more important than oppression in explaining the origins of cults; when people feel that they could have more, and they have less than what they used to have or less than others, they may be attracted to new cults.[82] Consistent with Aberle's general interpretation, Bruce Knauft's comparative study of cargo cults found that such cults were more important in Melanesian societies that had had decreasing cultural contact with the West, and presumably *decreasing* contact with valued goods, within the year prior to the cult's emergence.[83]

Fundamentalism For some scholars, one of the main attributes of fundamentalism is the literal interpretation of a sacred scripture. But recent scholars have suggested that fundamentalist movements need to be understood more broadly as religious or political movements that appear in response to the rapidly changing environment of the modern world. In this broader view, fundamentalism occurs in many religions, including those of Christians, Jews, Islamics, Sikhs, Buddhists, and Hindus. Although each movement is different in content, Richard Antoun suggests that fundamentalist movements have the following elements in common: the selective use of scripture to inspire and assert proof of particular certainties; the quest for purity and traditional values in what is viewed as an impure world; active opposition to what is viewed as a permissive secular society and a nation-state that separates religion from the state; and an incorporation of selected modern elements such as television to promote the movements' aims.[84]

Fundamentalist religious movements do appear to be linked to the anxieties and uncertainties associated with culture change in general and globalization in particular. Many people in many countries are repelled by new behaviors and attitudes, and react in a way that celebrates the old. As Judith Nagata puts it, fundamentalism is a "quest for certainty in an uncertain world."[85] Protestant fundamentalism flourished at the end of the 19th century in the United States as immigrant groups came into the country in great numbers and the country became industrialized and increasingly urbanized. The fundamentalists denounced foreign influences, the decline of the Bible as a guide to moral behavior, and the teaching of evolution, and they succeeded in getting the country to prohibit the sale of alcoholic beverages. Recent Islamic fundamentalist movements seem to be responses to a different kind of challenge to the social order—increasing Westernization. Westernization may have first arrived in conjunction with colonial rule. Later, it may have been promoted by Western-educated native elites.[86] Antoun suggests that fundamentalist movements deliberately push certain practices because the leaders know they will outrage the secular opposition. Examples in recent Islamic fundamentalist movements are the extreme punishment of cutting off a hand for theft and requiring women to be covered by veils or head-to-toe covering in public.[87] Unfortunately, in present-day discourse, fundamentalism tends to be equated by Westerners with Islam itself. But, in historical perspective, all major religions have had fundamentalist movements in times of rapid culture change.

Few of us realize that nearly all of the major churches or religions in the world began as minority sects or cults. Indeed, some of the most established and prestigious Protestant churches were considered radical social movements at first. For example, what we now know as the United Church of Christ, which includes the Congregational Church, was founded by radicals in England who wanted church governance to be in the hands of the local congregation. Many of these radicals became the people we call Pilgrims, who had to flee to the New World. But they were very fundamentalist in their beliefs; for example, as late as the 1820s, Congregationalist-dominated towns in Connecticut prohibited celebrations of Christmas outside of church because such celebrations were not mentioned in the Bible. Nowadays, Congregationalists are among the most liberal Protestants.[88]

We should not be surprised to learn that most of the various Protestant churches today, including some considered very conservative, began as militant sects that set out to achieve a better world. After all, that's why we call them "Protestant." At first, the rebellion was against Rome and the Catholic Church. Later, sects developed in opposition to church and government hierarchies. And remember that Christianity itself began as a radical group in the hinterland of the Roman Empire. So new sects or cults were probably always political and social, as well as religious, movements. Recall that the word *millennium,* as used in discussions of religious movements, refers to a wished-for or expected future time when human life and society will be perfect and free of troubles; the world will then be prosperous, happy, and peaceful. Nowadays, the wish for a better world may or may not be religiously inspired. Some people who seek a more perfect world believe that humans alone must achieve it.

Ideas about the millennium, and the origins of new cults and religions, might best be viewed then as human hopes: Which ones do people have? Do they vary from culture to culture, and why? Are some hopes universal? And how might they be achieved?

If the recent as well as distant past is any guide, we expect religious belief and practice to be revitalized periodically, particularly during times of stress. And even though the spread of world religions minimizes some variation, globalization has also increased the worldwide interest in shamanism and other features of religion that are different from the dominant religions. Thus, we can expect the world to continue to have religious variation.

Summary and Review

The Universality of Religion

23.1 Characterize the universality of religion and discuss various explanations for that universality.

- Religion is any set of attitudes, beliefs, and practices pertaining to supernatural power, whether that power be forces, gods, spirits, ghosts, or demons.
- Religious beliefs and practices are found in all known contemporary societies, and archaeologists think they have found signs of religious belief associated with *Homo sapiens* who lived at least 60,000 years ago.
- Theories about the universality of religion suggest that humans create religions in response to universal needs or conditions, including a need for intellectual understanding, reversion to childhood feelings, anxiety and uncertainty, and a need for community and/or cooperation.

? How might the universality of religion be explained? Critically discuss various theories.

Variation in Religious Beliefs

23.2 Discuss the range of variability in religious beliefs.

- Although scholars generally do not agree as to why people need religion or how supernatural beings and forces come into existence, they recognize the enormous variation in the details of religious beliefs.
- Variation in religious belief are reflected in the kinds and characters of supernatural beings or forces, the structure or hierarchy of those beings, what the beings actually do, and what happens to people after death.
- Across all cultures, objects, people, or places can embody good forces or harmful forces, and supernatural beings can have either nonhuman or human origins as well as varying character traits; specifics vary from culture to culture.
- Religious belief can promote in-group trust/cooperation or out-group conflict. Warning signs of conflict are leaders claiming only they know the truth, a call to blindly obey, a belief that no ideal world is possible, actions using the end to justify the means, and calls for a holy war.

- Among societies, concepts of life after death can include heaven, hell, and reincarnation. Support was found for the idea that judgmental beliefs parallel the society's economic practices.

> ? What are some important variations in beliefs about a supernatural beings or forces across societies?

Variation in Religious Practices

23.3 Describe the variability in religious practices and practitioners cross-culturally.

- Religious practices can vary in terms of kinds of religious practitioners and how people interact with the supernatural. Many practices involve rituals, repeated behaviors and patterns, which are generally collective and thought to strengthen faith.
- People's interactions with the supernatural vary widely and include prayer, divination, physiological experience, simulation, feasts, and sacrifices. Achieving altered states, referred to as trances, is part of religious practice in 90 percent of the world's societies.
- Interacting with the supernatural can be categorized as pleading, asking, or persuading the supernatural to act a certain way or as compelling the supernatural through magic, which can be used for good or harm. Sorcery is important in societies that lack judicial authorities.
- Almost all societies have part-time or full-time religious or magical practitioners that can fall into four major types: shamans, sorcerers or witches, mediums, and priests. The number of types of practitioners in a society seems to increase with degree of cultural complexity.

> ? What are some of the important variations in religious practices? What different types of religious practitioners are found across cultures?

Religion and Adaptation

23.4 Discuss religion in terms of adaptation.

- Some theorists argue that religion is adaptive because it helps individuals reduce anxiety and uncertainty as well as develop solidarity and cooperation.
- Some particular customary aspects of religious belief such as the Hindu taboo against slaughtering cows may not appear to be adaptive but probably are.

> ? What is an example of an adaptive religious belief?

Religious Change

23.5 Explain and give examples of various forms of religious change, such as conversion and revitalization movements.

- Perhaps the most dramatic is religious conversion, particularly when large numbers of people switch to a completely new religion presented by missionaries or other proselytizers.
- Religious change also happens in more indirect ways, including revitalization and fundamentalist movements, which appear to be responses to the stress of rapid social change. All major religions have had fundamentalist movements in times of rapid culture change.
- Dramatic economic, political, and demographic change is associated with religious change, particularly of the dramatic kind.
- Nearly all of the major churches or religions in the world began as minority sects or cults, which were probably always political and social, as well as religious, movements.

> ? What are examples of various types of religious change?

Think on it

1. How does your conception of **God** compare with beliefs about supernatural beings in other religious systems?
2. What do you think is the future of **religion**? Explain your answer.
3. Could any of the religious practices you know about be classified as **magic**? Are they associated with anxiety-arousing situations?

24 CHAPTER

The Arts

LEARNING OBJECTIVES

- Analyze the purposes of body decoration and adornment. 24.1
- Explain variation in the arts in relationship to other societal features. 24.2
- Identify ethnocentric attitudes and practices toward non-Western art by Westerners. 24.3
- Assess the relationship of culture contact and artistic change. 24.4

Most societies do not have a word for art.[1] Perhaps that is because art, particularly in societies with relatively little specialization, is often an integral part of religious, social, and political life. Indeed, most of the aspects of culture we have already discussed—economics, kinship, politics, religion—are not easily separated from the rest of social life.[2]

The oldest art found so far comes from caves in South Africa. Pieces of red ochre were engraved there more than 77,000 years ago. In Australia, people painted on walls of rock shelters and on cliff faces between 70,000 and 60,000 years ago. And in southern Africa, Spain, and France, people painted slabs of rock 28,000 years ago (see the box "Rock Art: Preserving a Window into the Past"). Art is clearly an old feature of human cultures. We say that those earliest paintings are art, but what do we mean by "art"? A stone spear point and a bone fishhook obviously require skill and creativity to make. But we do not call them art. Why do we feel that some things are art and others are not?

Some definitions of art emphasize its evocative quality. From the viewpoint of the person who creates it, art expresses feelings and ideas; from the viewpoint of the observer or participant, it evokes feelings and ideas. The feelings and ideas on each side may or may not be exactly the same. And they may be expressed in a variety of ways—drawing, painting, carving, weaving, body decoration, music, dance, or story. An artistic work or performance is intended to excite the senses, to stir the emotions of the beholder or participant. It may produce feelings of pleasure, awe, repulsion, or fear, but usually not indifference.[3]

But emphasizing the evocative quality of art may make it difficult to compare the art of different cultures because what is evocative in one culture may not be evocative in another. For example, a humorous story in one culture may not be funny in another. Thus, most anthropologists agree that art is more than an attempt by an individual to express or communicate feelings and ideas. There is also some cultural patterning or meaning; societies vary in their characteristic kinds and styles of art.[4] The anthropological study of art places particular emphasis on the cultural context in which art is produced.[5]

Artistic activities are always cultural in part, involving shared and learned patterns of behavior, belief, and feeling. What are some of the ideas about art in our own culture? We tend to think that anything useful is not art.[6] If a basket has a design that is not necessary to its function, we may possibly consider it art, especially if we keep it on a shelf; but the basket with bread on the table would probably not be considered art. The fact that such a distinction is not made in other societies strongly suggests that our ideas about art are cultural. Among Native Americans in the Pacific Northwest, elaborately carved totem poles not only displayed the crests of the lineages of their occupants, they also supported the house.[7] The fact that artistic activities are partly cultural is evident when we compare how people in different societies treat the outsides of their houses. Most North Americans share the value of decorating the interiors of their homes with pictures—paintings, prints, or photographs hung on the walls. But they do not share the value of painting pictures on the outside walls of their houses, as Native Americans did in the Pacific Northwest.

In our society, we also insist that a work must be unique to be considered art. This aspect is clearly consistent with our emphasis on the individual. However, even though we require that artists be unique and innovative, the art they produce must still fall within some range of acceptable variation. Artists must communicate to us in a way we can relate to, or at least learn to relate to. Often, they must follow certain current styles of expression that other artists or critics have set if they hope to have the public accept their art. The idea that an artist should be original is a cultural idea; in some societies, the ability to replicate a traditional pattern is more valued than originality.

So art seems to have several qualities: It expresses as well as communicates. It stimulates the senses, affects emotions, and evokes ideas. It is produced in culturally patterned ways and styles. It has cultural meaning. In addition, some people are thought to be better at it than others.[8] Art does not require some people to be full-time artistic specialists; many societies in the ethnographic record had no full-time specialists of any kind. But although everyone in some societies may participate in some arts (dancing, singing, body decoration), it is usually thought that certain individuals have superior artistic skill.[9]

To illustrate the cross-cultural variation that exists in artistic expression, we will consider first the art of body decoration and adornment.

Body Decoration and Adornment

24.1 Analyze the purposes of body decoration and adornment.

In all societies, people decorate or adorn their bodies. The decorations may be permanent—scars, tattoos, or changes in the shape of a body part. Or they may be temporary, in the form of paint or objects such as feathers, jewelry, skins, and clothing that are not strictly utilitarian. Much of this decoration seems to be motivated by aesthetic considerations, which, of course, vary from culture to culture. The actual form of the decoration depends on cultural traditions. Body ornamentation includes the pierced noses of some women in India, the elongated necks of the Mangebetu of central Africa, the tattooing of North American males and females, the body painting of the Caduveo of South America, and the variety of ornaments found in almost every culture.

Applied Anthropology

Rock Art: Preserving a Window into the Past

If the art of an ancient or earlier culture reflects the preoccupations and ideas of the culture, and if we are interested in understanding what the creators of the art thought, the art of the past and its surroundings must be preserved as much as possible. One type of ancient art frequently found is what anthropologists call "rock art," drawings and paintings on cliff faces and the walls of caves. Some of the most famous are the cave paintings of Europe, dating from about 30,000 years ago, but a large number of other rock art sites are in danger and in need of preserving.

Unlike a painting or a decorated object, rock art is part of its environment, and the environmental area as well as the rock art needs to be preserved. Excavation of the area may provide information that not only allows us to date the drawings and paintings, it may also tell us what the people did to produce the art and why they produced it. For example, in one French cave, analysis of charcoal indicates that the artists made fires to produce the charcoal they would use in their drawings. In another cave in Montana, pollen found below the paintings came from a number of plants. Many of the plants have known medicinal properties, and the pollens may indicate what shamans had in their medicine bags. Talking to the descendants of the creators of the rock art is also essential. Sometimes anthropologists learn things that surprise them. For instance, near Alice Springs, Australia, some branches were knocking against some rock art and the preservers considered cutting some of the branches. The aboriginal elders were horrified at the idea because the trees were believed to harbor the souls of the deceased, and it would have been a crime to cut them.

Although there are natural threats to rock art, the greatest threats come from humans. Religious change with European contact often lessened the interest of indigenous populations in their earlier sacred sites, making for less protest when development projects are proposed. Tours to previously isolated sites often lead to more destruction from graffiti or unauthorized attempts to reproduce or photograph the art. Ironically, though, making the rock art the center of a park helps protect it.

Raising awareness of rock art is one of the most important ways of protecting it in its environment. Although nothing beats seeing rock art in its natural setting, modern methods (holograms, laser recording, 3D imagery) and computer-assisted enhancement have made it possible to have life-size replicas, allowing the public to see more than they can in some mostly inaccessible caves. These replicas and images also give anthropologists and other scientists materials for appreciation and study. The greater the number of displays in public facilities (museums, parks) that expose tourists to rock art, the more valuable it may become. Anthropologists or not, we all seem to be fascinated by the ancient graphics. We try to imagine what motivated the original artists. If we could reconstruct those motives, they might suggest why we choose subjects and techniques in our own art, as well as in our graffiti.

The archaeological context of rock art can help us understand the rock art. Teaching people how to preserve rock art is applied anthropology that will help to preserve a priceless heritage and a source of knowledge about humans in the past.

Source: Clottes 2008.

A Wodaabe Fulani man from Niger attending a ceremony.

However, in addition to satisfying aesthetic needs, body decoration or adornment may be used to delineate social position, rank, sex, occupation, local and ethnic identity, or religion within a society. Along with social stratification come visual means of declaring status. The symbolic halo (the crown) on the king's head, the scarlet hunting jacket of the English gentleman, the eagle feathers of the Native American chief's bonnet, the gold-embroidered jacket of the Indian rajah—each mark of high status is recognized in its own society. Jewelry in the shape of a cross or the Star of David indicates Christian or Jewish inclinations. Clothes may set apart the priest, nun, or member of a sect such as the Amish.

The erotic significance of some body decoration is also apparent. Women draw attention to erogenous zones of the body by painting, as on the lips, and by attaching some object—an earring, a flower behind the ear, a necklace, bracelet, brooch, anklet, or belt. Men draw attention, too, by beards, tattoos, and penis sheaths (in some otherwise naked societies) that point upward. We have only to follow the fashion trends for women of Europe and North America during the past 300 years, with their history of pinched waists, ballooned hips, bustled rumps, exaggerated breasts, painted faces, and exposed bosoms, to realize the significance of body adornment for sexual provocation. Why some societies emphasize the erotic adornment of women and others emphasize it in men is not yet understood.

Type of body adornment may reflect politics. Polynesians decorate their bodies with tattoos, which are permanent. In Samoa, for example, tattoos distinguished the chiefly class from commoners. Bands and stripes were restricted to people of high status; low-status people could have tattoos only of solid black and only from waist to knees. Within the ruling class, the number of tattooed triangles down a man's leg indicated his relative rank. Because tattooing is permanent, it is a form of body decoration well suited to a society with inherited social stratification. On the other hand, in Melanesia, as is typical with the "big men" type of leadership that is somewhat fluid, Melanesians paint their bodies, and the painting is ephemeral. It disappears within a short time or after the first wash.[10]

A need to decorate the human body seems universal. We have noted some of the various methods people have used to adorn themselves in different societies. We are also aware of body-decoration practices that raise questions to which we have no ready answers. What explains adornment of the body by permanent marking such as scarification, bound feet, elongated ears and necks, shaped heads, pierced ears and septums, and filed teeth? Why do different societies adorn, paint, or otherwise decorate different parts of the body for sexual or other reasons? And what leads some members of our society to transfer body decoration to their animals? Why the shaped hair of the poodle, the braided manes of some horses, and the diamond collars, painted toenails, coats, hats, and even boots for some pets?

24.2 Explain variation in the arts in relationship to other societal features.

Explaining Variation in the Arts

In our society, we stress the freedom of the artist, so it may seem to us that art is completely free to vary. But our emphasis on uniqueness obscures the fact that different cultures not only use or emphasize different materials and have different ideas of beauty, but they also may have characteristic styles and themes. It is easy to see styles when we look at art that is different from our own; it is harder to see similarity when we look at the art of our own culture. If we look at dance styles, for example, we may think that the dance style of the 1940s is completely different from the dance style of today. It might take an outsider to notice that, in our culture, we still generally see couples dancing as a pair rather than in a group line or circle, as in dances we call "folk dances." And, in our culture, females and males dance together rather than separately. Furthermore, our popular music still has a beat or combination of beats and is made by many of the same kinds of instruments as in the past.

But where do these similarities in form and style come from? Much of the recent research on variation in the arts supports the idea that form and style in visual art, music, dance, and folklore are very much influenced by other aspects of culture. Some psychological anthropologists would go even further, suggesting that art, like religion, expresses the typical feelings, anxieties, and experiences of people in a culture. And the typical feelings and anxieties in turn are influenced by basic institutions such as childrearing, economy, social organization, and politics.

Consider how the physical form of art a society prefers may reflect its way of life. For example, Richard Anderson pointed out that the art of traditionally nomadic people such as the !Kung, Inuit, and Australian aborigines is mostly carryable.[11] Song, dance, and oral literature are very important in those societies and are as portable as they can be. Those societies decorate useful objects that they carry with them—harpoons for the Inuit, boomerangs for the Australian aborigines, ostrich egg "canteens" for the !Kung. But they don't have bulky things such as sculpture or elaborate costumes. And what about the presence of artists or art critics? Although some people in small-scale societies are more artistic than others, specialized artists, as well as critics or theoreticians of art, tend to be found only in societies with a complex, specialized division of labor.

Visual Art

Perhaps the most obvious way artistic creations reflect how we live is by mirroring the environment—the materials and technologies available to a culture. Stone, wood, bones, tree bark, clay, sand, charcoal, berries for staining, and a few mineral-derived ochres are generally available materials. In addition, depending on the locality, other resources are accessible: shells, horns, tusks, gold, copper, and silver. The different uses to which societies put these materials are of interest to anthropologists, who may ask, for example, why a people chooses to use clay and not copper when both items are available. Although we have no conclusive answers as yet, such questions have important ramifications. The way in which a society views its environment is sometimes apparent in its choice and use of artistic materials. Certain metals, for example, may be reserved for ceremonial objects of special importance. Or the belief in the supernatural powers of a stone or tree may cause a sculptor to be sensitive to that particular material.[12]

The traditional political systems of Africa ranged from centralized kingdoms (on the complex end of the continuum) to village-based or segmentary lineage systems in which leadership was ephemeral or secret (tied to secret societies). Masks that conceal identity are often used in the uncentralized systems; crowns or other headdresses indicating high status are frequent in the kingdoms. Among the uncentralized Ibo of eastern Nigeria, masks are often worn by the young men of a village when they criticize the behavior of the village elders. In the kingdom of Ngoyo, in western Zaire, the king's status is indicated by his special cap as well as by his special three-legged stool.

What is particularly meaningful to anthropologists is the realization that although the materials available to a society may to some extent limit or influence what it can do artistically, the materials by no means determine what is done. Why does the artist in Japanese society rake sand into patterns, the artist in Navajo society paint sand, and the artist in Roman society melt sand to form glass? Moreover, even when the same material is used in the same way in different societies, the form or style of the work varies enormously from culture to culture.

A society may choose to represent objects or phenomena that are especially important to the people or elite. An examination of the art of the Middle Ages tells us something about the medieval preoccupation with theological doctrine. In addition to revealing the primary concerns of a society, the content of that society's art may also reflect the culture's social stratification. Authority figures may be represented in obvious ways. In the art of ancient Sumerian society, the sovereign was portrayed

The same materials may be used artistically in different ways. In Japan (on the left), sand is raked into patterns. In the Northern Territory of Australia (on the right), the Yuendumu paint the sand.

as being much larger than his followers, and the most prestigious gods were given oversized eyes. Also, differences in clothing and jewelry styles within a society usually reflect social stratification.

Art historians have always recognized certain possible relationships between the art of a society and other aspects of its culture. Much of this attention has been concentrated on the content of art because European art has been representational for such a long time. But the style of the art may reflect other aspects of culture. John Fischer, for example, examined the stylistic features of art with the aim of discovering "some sort of regular connection between some artistic feature and some social situation."[13] He argued that the artist expresses a form of social fantasy. In other words, in a stable society, artists will respond to those conditions in the society that bring security or pleasure to them and the society.

Assuming that "pictorial elements in design are, on one psychological level, abstract, mainly unconscious representations of persons in the society,"[14] Fischer reasoned that egalitarian societies would tend to have different stylistic elements in their art as compared with stratified societies. Egalitarian societies are generally composed of small, self-sufficient communities that are structurally similar and have little differentiation between people. Stratified societies, on the other hand, generally have larger, more interdependent, and more dissimilar communities and great differences among people in prestige, power, and access to economic resources. Fischer hypothesized, and found in a cross-cultural study, that certain elements of design were strongly related to the presence of social hierarchy. His findings are summarized in Table 24.1.

Repetition of a simple element, for example, tends to be found in the art of egalitarian societies, which have little political organization and few authority positions. If each element unconsciously represents individuals within the society, the relative sameness of people seems to be reflected in the repetitiveness of design elements. Conversely, the combinations of different design elements in complex patterns that tend to be found in the art of stratified societies seem to reflect the high degree of social differentiation that exists in such societies.[15]

According to Fischer, the egalitarian society's empty space in a design represents the society's relative isolation. Because egalitarian societies are usually small and self-sufficient, they tend to shy away from outsiders, preferring to find security within their own group. In contrast, the art of stratified societies is generally crowded. The hierarchical society does not seek to isolate individuals or communities within the group because they must be interdependent, each social level ideally furnishing services for those above it and help for those beneath it. As Fischer suggested, we can, in general, discern a lack of empty space in the designs of societies in which security is not sought by avoiding strangers but rather "security is produced

TABLE 24.1 Stylistic Differences by Type of Society

Stratified Society	Egalitarian Society
Integrated unlike elements	Repetition of simple motifs
Little empty space	Ample unused or empty space
Asymmetrical design	Symmetrical design
Framed figures	Unframed figures

Source: Based on Fischer 1961.

by incorporating strangers into the hierarchy, through dominance or submission as the relative power indicates."[16]

Symmetry, the third stylistic feature related to type of society, is similar to the first. Symmetry may suggest likeness or an egalitarian society; asymmetry suggests difference and perhaps stratification. The fourth feature of interest here, the presence or absence of enclosures or boundaries—"frames" in our art—may indicate the presence or absence of hierarchically imposed rules circumscribing individual behavior. An unenclosed design may reflect free access to most property; in egalitarian societies, the fencing off of a piece of property for the use of only one person is unknown. In the art of stratified societies, boundaries or enclosures may reflect the idea of private property. Or they may symbolically represent the real differences in dress, occupation, type of food allowed, and manners that separate the different classes of people.

Studies such as Fischer's offer anthropologists new tools with which to evaluate ancient societies that are known only by a few pieces of pottery or a few tools or paintings. If art reflects certain aspects of a culture, then the study of whatever art of a people has been preserved may provide a means of testing the accuracy of the guesses we make about their culture on the basis of more ordinary archaeological materials. For example, even if we did not know from classical Greek writings that Athens became much more socially stratified between 750 B.C. and 600 B.C., we might guess that such a transformation had occurred because of the changes we can see over time

Read the Document: Learning About the Past through Archaeological ceramics

Changes in Greek vases show how increasing stratification is associated with integration of unlike elements as well as more crowded design. The one on the left dates from around 1000 B.C. when there was less stratification. The vase on the right dates from the time period between 750 B.C. and 600 B.C., when stratification was at its maximum.

in the way the Athenians decorated vases. Consistent with Fischer's cross-cultural findings, as Athens became more stratified, its vase painting became more complex, more crowded, and more enclosed.[17]

Music

When we hear the music of another culture, we often don't know what to make of it. We may say it does not "mean" anything to us, not realizing that the "meaning" of music has been programmed into us by our culture. In music as well as in art, our culture largely determines what we consider acceptable variation, what we say has "meaning" to us. Even

Migrants and Immigrants

The Spread of Popular Music

Music is a very visceral art. You feel it in your gut. Hearing a piece of music can make your belly vibrate and give you goosebumps. You don't forget that experience. The ideas expressed in a song can get to you, but you're mostly moved by the sound. You feel it. Music can lift you up or make you sad.

In the past, we wouldn't have known about lots of music if not for migration. Would there be "country music" radio stations in the United States if lots of people hadn't moved out of the South in the 20th century? Country music itself was an amalgam of Appalachian folk music heavily influenced by music from the British Isles and also by African music. The banjo, adapted by country musicians, was created by African Americans who modeled it on the African stringed musical instrument called a banjar. Though the fiddle, an important instrument in country music, was European in origin, many of the fiddlers in the South were African American, and country music incorporated African rhythmic styles and improvisation. There were other influences also—the guitar came from Spain, and yodeling from the Swiss. African American music also influenced much of popular American music—ragtime, the blues, jazz, rhythm and blues, rock and roll, disco, and rap, to name just a few. African influences also came to the United States via the Caribbean and South America where people from different cultures created a creolized music. Would we have liked "salsa" dancing, a form of Afro-Cuban music, or reggae and hip-hop from

Korean rapper Psy performs in Rockefeller Plaza in New York City.

Jamaica, if there were no immigration? The answer is probably not.

Of course, now there are other ways of hearing music besides migration. Satellite television and Internet sites like YouTube now make popular culture from other places internationally accessible. Such accessibility can help create fusion of different cultural styles such as the music and dance of the South Korean pop star Psy.

The movement of popular music is not guaranteed. For example, although there are many immigrants and migrants of Chinese or South Asian descent in the United States and Canada, Chinese or South Asian music has not become popular. Why the music of some immigrants and migrants is adopted or incorporated whereas other music is not is not yet understood. Some technologies like cell phones are perceived as very useful and spread widely as people earn more and can afford to buy them. Music is not something that is or is not useful—the ideas and feelings communicated answer our needs. Although young people, the most frequent consumers of popular music, are often looking for something "new," the latest style is probably not that different in some respects from the last style. Cultures have musical preferences, and musical styles that are very different are not readily accepted. However, with all the migration, immigration, and communication in the modern world, it is likely that the market demand for new popular music will continue to expand.

Sources: Nicholls 1998; D. R. Hill 2005, 363–73.

a trained musicologist, listening for the first time to music of a different culture, will not be able to hear the subtleties of tone and rhythm that members of the culture hear with ease. This predicament is similar to that of the linguist who, exposed to a foreign language, cannot at first distinguish phonemes, morphemes, and other regular patterns of speech.

Not only do instruments vary, but music itself varies widely in style from society to society. For example, in some societies, people prefer music with a regularly recurring beat; in others, they prefer changes in rhythm. There are also variations in singing styles. In some places, it is customary to have different vocal lines for different people; in other places, people all sing together in the same way.

Is variation in music, as in the other arts, related to other aspects of culture? On the basis of a cross-cultural study of more than 3,500 folk songs from a sample of the world's societies, Alan Lomax and his co-researchers found that song style seems to vary with cultural complexity. Now many of these folk songs are available as part of an online Global Jukebox.[18] As we will see, these findings about variation in song style are similar to Fischer's findings about variation in art.

Lomax and his co-researchers found some features of song style to be correlated with cultural complexity. (The societies classified as more complex tend to have higher levels of food-production technology, social stratification, and higher levels of political integration.) For example, wordiness and clearness of enunciation were found to be associated with cultural complexity. The association is a reasonable one: The more a society depends on verbal information, as in giving complex instructions for a job or explaining different points of law, the more strongly will clear enunciation in transmitting information be a mark of its culture. Thus, hunter-gatherer bands, in which people know their productive role and perform it without ever being given complex directions, are more likely than we are to base much of their singing on lines of nonwords, such as our refrain line "tra-la-la-la-la." Their songs are characterized by lack of explicit information, by sounds that give pleasure in themselves, by much repetition, and by relaxed, slurred enunciation.[19]

Examples of the progression from repetition or nonwords to wordy information are found within our society. The most obvious, and universal, example of a song made entirely of repetition is the relaxed lullaby of a mother repeating a comforting syllable to her baby while improvising her own tune. But this type of song is not characteristic of our society. Although our songs sometimes have single lines of nonwords, it is rare for an entire song to be made of them. Usually, the nonwords act as respites from information:

Deck the halls with boughs of holly,
Fa la la la la,
La la la la.[20]

In associating variation in music with cultural complexity, Lomax found that elaboration of song parts also corresponds to the complexity of a society. Societies in which leadership is informal and temporary seem to symbolize their social equality by an *interlocked* style of singing. Each person sings independently but within the group, and no one singer is differentiated from the others. Rank societies, in which there is a leader with prestige but no real power, are characterized by a song style in which one "leader" may begin the song but the others soon drown out his or her voice. In stratified societies, where leaders have the power of force, choral singing is generally marked by a clear-cut role for the leader and a secondary "answering" role for the others. Societies marked by elaborate stratification show singing parts that are differentiated and in which the soloist is deferred to by the other singers.

Lomax also found a relationship between **polyphony**, where two or more melodies are sung simultaneously, and a high degree of female participation in food-getting. In societies in which women's work is responsible for at least half of the food, songs are likely to contain more than one simultaneous melody, with the higher tunes usually sung by women. Moreover:

Polyphony Two or more melodies sung simultaneously.

> *Counterpoint was once believed to be the invention of European high culture. In our sample it turns out to be most frequent among simple producers, especially gatherers, where women supply the bulk of the food. Counterpoint and perhaps even polyphony may then be very old feminine inventions. . . . Subsistence complementarity is at its maximum among*

gatherers, early gardeners, and horticulturalists. It is in such societies that we find the highest occurrence of polyphonic singing.[21]

In societies in which women do not contribute much to food production, the songs are more likely to have a single melody and to be sung by males.[22]

In some societies, survival and social welfare are based on a unified group effort; in those cultures, singing tends to be marked by cohesiveness. That is, cohesive work parties, teams of gatherers or harvesters, and kin groups, who work voluntarily for the good of the family or community, seem to express their interconnectedness in song by blending both tone and rhythm.

Some variations in music may be explained as a consequence of variation in childrearing practices. For example, researchers are beginning to explore childrearing as a way to explain why some societies respond to, and produce, regular rhythm in their music, whereas others enjoy free rhythm that has no regular beat. One hypothesis is that a regular beat in music is a simulation of the regular beat of the heart. For nine months in the womb, the fetus feels the mother's regular 80 or so heartbeats a minute. Moreover, mothers generally employ rhythmic tactics in quieting crying infants—patting their backs or rocking them. But the fact that children respond positively to an even tempo does not mean that the regular heartbeat is completely responsible for their sensitivity to rhythm. In fact, if the months in the womb were sufficient to establish a preference for rhythm, then every child would be affected in exactly the same manner by a regular beat, and all societies would have the same rhythm in their music.

Barbara Ayres suggested that the importance of regular rhythm in the music of a culture is related to the rhythm's *acquired reward value*—that is, its associations with feelings of security or relaxation. In a cross-cultural study of this possibility, Ayres found a strong correlation between a society's method of carrying infants and the type of musical rhythm the society produced. In some societies, the mother or an older sister carries the child, sometimes for two or three years, in a sling, pouch, or shawl, so that the child is in bodily contact with her for much of the day and experiences the motion of her rhythmic walking. Ayres discovered that such societies tend to have a regularly recurring beat in their songs. Societies in which the child is put into a cradle or is strapped to a cradleboard tend to have music based either on irregular rhythm or on free rhythm.[23]

The question of why some societies have great tonal ranges in music whereas others do not was also studied by Ayres, who suggested that this difference might also be explained by certain childrearing practices. Ayres theorized that painful stimulation of infants before weaning might result in bolder, more exploratory behavior in adulthood, which would be apparent in the musical patterns of the culture. This hypothesis was suggested to her by laboratory experiments with animals. Contrary to expectations, those animals given electric shocks or handled before weaning showed greater-than-usual physical growth and more exploratory behavior when placed in new situations as adults. Ayres equated the range of musical notes (from low to high) with the exploratory range of animals and forcefulness of accent in music with boldness in animals.

The kinds of stress Ayres looked for in ethnographic reports were those that would be applied to all children or to all of one sex—for example, scarification; piercing of the nose, lips, or ears; binding, shaping, or stretching of feet, head, ears, or any limb; inoculation; circumcision; or cauterization. The results showed that in societies in which infants are stressed before the age of 2, music is marked by a wider tonal range than in societies in which children are not stressed or are stressed only at a later age. Also, a firm accent or beat is characteristic of music more often in societies that subject children to stress than in societies that do not.[24]

Cultural emphasis on obedience or independence in children is another variable that may explain some aspects of musical performance. In societies in which children are generally trained for compliance, cohesive singing predominates; where children are encouraged to be assertive, singing is mostly individualized. Moreover, assertive training of children is associated with a raspy voice or harsh singing. A raspy voice seems to be an indication of assertiveness and is most often a male voice quality. Interestingly enough, in societies in which women's work predominates in subsistence production, the women sing with harsher voices.

Current Research and Issues

Do Masks Show Emotion in Universal Ways?

Face masks are commonly used in rituals and performances. They not only hide the real face of the mask wearer but often evoke powerful emotions in the audience—anger, fear, sadness, joy. You might think, because so many things vary cross-culturally, that the ways in which emotion is displayed and recognized in masks vary too. But apparently they do not vary that much.

Research on the universality of emotion evoked by masks builds on work done by Paul Ekman and Carroll Izard. Ekman and Izard showed photographs to members of different cultural groups and asked them to identify the emotions displayed in the photographs. A particular emotion was identified correctly by most viewers, whatever the viewer's native culture. Coding schemes were developed to enable researchers to compare the detailed facial positions of individual portions of the face (eyebrows, mouth, etc.) for different emotions. What exactly do we do when we scowl? We contract the eyebrows and lower the corners of the mouth; in geometric terms, we make angles and diagonals on our faces. When we smile, we raise the corners of the mouth; we make it curved.

Psychologist Joel Aronoff and his colleagues compared two types of wooden face masks from many different societies—masks described as threatening (e.g., designed to frighten off evil spirits) versus masks associated with nonthreatening functions (a courtship dance). As

Maori wood carving in the Auckland War Memorial Museum, Auckland, New Zealand.

suspected, the two sets of masks had significantly different proportions of certain facial elements. The threatening masks had eyebrows and eyes facing inward and downward and a downward-facing mouth. The threatening masks also were more likely to have pointed heads, chins, beards, and ears, as well as projections from the face such as horns. In more abstract or geometrical terms, threatening features generally tend to be angular or diagonal, and nonthreatening features tend to be curved or rounded.

But is it the facial features themselves that convey threat, or is it the design elements of angularity and diagonality that convey threat? To help answer this question, students in the United States were asked to associate adjectives with drawings of abstract pairs of design features (e.g., a V shape and a U shape). Even with abstract shapes, the angular patterns were thought of as less "good," more "powerful," and "stronger" than the curved shapes. In subsequent studies, students recognized the V shape more quickly than other shapes, and this shape triggered more response in the brain in areas associated with threat.

We should not be surprised to discover that humans all over the world use their faces, and masks, to show emotions in the same ways. Aren't we all members of the same species? That's why a movie made in Hollywood or Beijing may evoke the same feelings wherever people see it. The universality of human emotion as expressed in the face becomes obvious only when we see faces (and masks) from elsewhere, showing emotions in ways that are unmistakable to us.

Thus, we become aware of universality (in masks as well as other cultural things) in the same way we become aware of variation—by exposure through reading and direct experience with the ways cultures do and do not vary.

Sources: Aronoff et al. 1988; Aronoff et al. 1992; Larson et al. 2007; Larson et al. 2009.

Other voice characteristics may also be associated with elements of culture. For example, sexual restrictions in a society seem to be associated with voice restrictions, especially with a nasalized or narrow, squeezed tone. These voice qualities are associated with anxiety and are especially noticeable in sounds of pain, deprivation, or sorrow. Restrictive sexual practices may be a source of pain and anxiety, and the nasal tone in song may reflect such emotions.[25]

The cross-cultural results about music should be able to explain change over time as well as variation within a society. Future research in a variety of societies may help test the theories of Lomax and Ayres.[26]

Folklore

Folklore is a broad category comprising all the myths, legends, folktales, ballads, riddles, proverbs, and superstitions of a cultural group.[27] In general, folklore is transmitted orally, but it may also be written. Games are also sometimes considered folklore, although they may be learned by imitation as well as transmitted orally. All societies have a repertoire of stories that they tell to entertain each other and teach children. Examples of our folklore include fairy

Folklore Includes all the myths, legends, folktales, ballads, riddles, proverbs, and superstitions of a cultural group. Generally, folklore is transmitted orally, but it may also be written.

Just as in art and song, dance style seems to reflect societal complexity. In less complex societies, everyone participates in dances in much the same way, as among the Huli of New Guinea.

tales and the legends we tell about our folk heroes, such as George Washington's confessing that he chopped down the cherry tree. Folklore is not always clearly separable from the other arts, particularly music and dance; stories often are conveyed in those contexts.

Although some folklore scholars emphasize the traditional aspects of folklore and the continuity between the present and the past, more recently attention has been paid to the innovative and emergent aspects of folklore. In this view, folklore is constantly created by any social group that has shared experiences. So, for example, computer programmers may have their jokes and their own proverbs (e.g., "Garbage in, garbage out!").[28] Jan Brunvand compiled a set of ***urban legends***. One such legend is "The Hook." The story, which has many versions, is basically about a young couple parked on Lover's Lane with the radio on. There is an announcement that a killer with an artificial hand is loose, so the girl suggests that they leave. The boy starts the car and drives her home. When he walks around the car to open her door, he finds a bloody hook attached to the door handle.[29] There are even legends on college campuses. What is the answer to the question of how long students should wait for a tardy professor? Students have an answer, ranging from 10 to 20 minutes. Is this a rule, or only a legend? Brunvand reported that he never found a regulation about how long to wait for the professor on any campus that tells this story![30]

Some folklore scholars are interested in universal or recurrent themes. Clyde Kluckhohn suggested that five themes occur in the myths and folktales of all societies: catastrophe, generally through flood; the slaying of monsters; incest; sibling rivalry, generally between brothers; and castration, sometimes actual but more commonly symbolic.[31] Edward Tylor, who proposed that religion is born from the human need to explain dreams and death, suggested that hero myths follow a similar pattern the world over—the central character is exposed at birth, is subsequently saved by others (humans or animals), and grows up to become a hero.[32] Joseph Campbell argued that hero myths resemble initiations—the hero is separated from the ordinary world, ventures forth into a new world (in this case, the supernatural world) to triumph over powerful forces, and then returns to the ordinary world with special powers to help others.[33]

In more complex societies, such as Japan, there tend to be leading roles and minor roles as in a Geisha show.

Myths may indeed have universal themes, but few scholars have looked at a representative sample of the world's societies, and therefore we cannot be sure that current conclusions about universality are correct. Indeed, most folklore researchers have not been interested in universal themes but in the particular folktales told in specific societies or regions. For example, some scholars have focused on the "Star Husband Tale," a common Native American story. Stith Thompson presented 84 versions of this tale; his goal was to reconstruct the original version and pinpoint its place of origin. By identifying the most common elements, Thompson suggested that the basic story (and probably the original) is the following:

> *Two girls sleeping out of doors wish that stars would be their husbands. In their sleep the girls are taken to the sky where they find themselves married to stars, one of which is a young man and the other an old man. The women are warned not to dig, but they disregard the warning and accidentally open up a hole in the sky. Unaided they descend on a rope and arrive home safely.*[34]

The tale, Thompson suggested, probably originated in the Plains and then spread to other regions of North America.

Alan Dundes has concentrated on the structure of folktales; he thinks that Native American folktales, including the "Star Husband Tale," have characteristic structures. One is a movement away from disequilibrium. Equilibrium is the desirable state; having too much or too little of anything is a condition that should be rectified as soon as possible. Disequilibrium, which Dundes calls *lack*, is indicated by the girls in the "Star Husband Tale" who do not have husbands. The lack is then corrected, in this case by marriage with the stars. This tale has another common Native American structure, says Dundes—a sequence of prohibition, interdiction, violation, and consequence. The women are warned not to dig, but they do—and as a consequence, they escape for home.[35] It should be noted that the consequences in folktales are not always good. Recall the Garden of Eden tale. The couple are warned not to eat the fruit of a tree; they eat the fruit; they are cast out of their paradise. Similarly, Icarus in the Greek tale is warned not to fly too high or low. He flies too high; the sun melts the wax that holds his feathered wings, and he falls and drowns.

As useful as it might be to identify where certain tales originated, or what their common structures might be, many questions remain. What do the tales mean? Why did they arise in the first place? Why are certain structures common in Native American tales? We are still a long way from answering many of these questions, and trying to answer them is difficult. How does one try to understand the meaning of a tale?

It is easy for people to read different meanings into the same myth. For example, consider the myth the Hebrews told of a paradise in which only a man was present until Eve, the first woman, arrived and ate the forbidden fruit of knowledge. One might conclude that men in that society had some grudge against women. If the interpreter were a psychoanalyst, he, or especially she, might assume that the myth reflected the male's deeply hidden fears of female sexuality. A historian might believe that the myth reflected actual historical events and that men were living in blissful ignorance until women invented agriculture—the effect of Eve's "knowledge" led to a life of digging rather than gathering.

It is clearly not enough to suggest an interpretation. Why should we believe it? We should give it serious consideration only if some systematic test seems to support it. For example, Michael Carroll suggested a Freudian interpretation of the "Star Husband Tale"—that the story represents repressed sentiments in the society. Specifically, he suggested that incestuous intercourse is the underlying concern of this myth, particularly the desire of a daughter to have intercourse with her father. He assumed that the stars symbolize fathers. Fathers, like stars, are high above, in children's eyes. Carroll predicted that, if the "Star Husband Tale" originated on the Plains, and if it symbolizes intercourse, then the Plains groups should be more likely than other societies to have intercourse imagery in their versions of the tale. That seems to be the case. Analyzing 84 versions of the tale, Carroll found that Plains societies are the Native American groups most likely to have imagery suggesting intercourse, including the lowering of a rope or ladder—symbolizing the penis—through a sky hole—symbolizing the vagina.[36]

Few studies have investigated why there is cross-cultural variation in the frequency of certain features in folktales. One feature of folktale variation that has been investigated cross-culturally is aggression. George Wright found that variation in childrearing patterns predicted some aspects of how aggression is exhibited in folktales. Where children are severely punished for aggression, more intense aggression appears in the folktales. And in such societies, strangers are more likely than the hero or friends of the hero to be the aggressors in the folktales. It seems that where children may be afraid to exhibit aggression toward their parents or those close to them because of fear of punishment, the hero or close friends in folktales are also not likely to be aggressive.[37]

Other kinds of fears may be reflected in folktales. A cross-cultural study by Alex Cohen found that unprovoked aggression is likely in folktales of societies that are subject to unpredictable food shortages. Why? One possibility is that the folktales reflect reality; after all, a serious drought may seem capricious, not possibly provoked by any human activity, brought on by the gods or nature "out of the blue." Curiously, however, societies with a history of unpredictable food shortages hardly mention natural disasters in their folktales, perhaps because disasters are too frightening. In any case, the capriciousness of unpredictable disasters seems to be transformed into the capricious aggression of characters in the folktales.[38]

Folklore, just like other aspects of art, may at least partly reflect the feelings, needs, and conflicts that people acquire as a result of growing up in their culture.

Viewing the Art of Other Cultures

24.3 Identify ethnocentric attitudes and practices toward non-Western art by Westerners.

Sally Price raised some critical questions about how Western museums and art critics look at the visual art of less complex cultures. Why is it that when artworks from Western or Oriental civilizations are displayed in a museum here, they carry the artist's name? In contrast, art from less complex cultures, often labeled "primitive art," tends to be displayed without the name of the artist; instead, it is often accompanied by a description of where it came from, how it was constructed, and what it may be used for. More words of explanation seem to accompany displays of unfamiliar art. Price suggested that the art pieces that we consider the most worthy require the least labeling, subtly conveying that the viewer needs no help to judge a real work of art.[39] In addition, art acquired from less complex cultures tends to be labeled by the name of the Westerner who acquired it. It is almost as if the fame of the collector, not the art itself, sets the value of such art.[40]

Just as the art from less complex cultures tends to be nameless, it also tends to be treated as timeless. We recognize that Western art and the art from classical civilizations change over time, which is why it must be dated, but the art from other places seems to be viewed as representing a timeless cultural tradition.[41] Do we know that the art of peoples with simpler technology changes less, or is this assumption a kind of ethnocentrism? Price, who has studied the art of the Saramakas of Suriname, points out that although Westerners think of Saramakan art as still representing its African ancestry, Saramakans themselves can identify shifts in their art styles over time. For example, they describe how calabashes used to be decorated on the outside, then the style changed to decorating the inside. With respect to textile arts, Saramakans articulate four transitions beginning from free-form embroidery to elaborate cross-stitch embroidery. They can also recognize the artist who made particular carved calabashes as well as identify those who were innovators of designs and techniques.[42]

Although it seems that individual artists can usually be recognized in any community, some societies do appear to be more "communal" than others in their art style. For example, let us compare the Puebloan peoples of the Southwest with native peoples of the Great Plains. Traditionally, women Puebloan potters did not sign their pots, and they largely followed their pueblo's characteristic style. In contrast, each Plains warrior stressed his individual accomplishments by painting representations of those accomplishments on animal hides. Either the warrior would do it himself or he would ask someone else to do it for him. These hides were worn by the warrior or displayed outside his tipi.[43]

Artistic Change, Culture Contact, and Global Trade

24.4 Assess the relationship of culture contact and artistic change.

It is unquestionably true that contact with the West did alter some aspects of the art of other cultures, but that does not imply that their art was changeless before. What kinds of things changed with contact? In some places, artists began to represent European contact itself. For example, in Australia, numerous rock paintings by aborigines portray sailing ships, men on horseback carrying pistols, and even cattle brands. With encouragement from Europeans, indigenous artists also began drawing on tree bark, canvas, and fiberboard to sell to Europeans. Interestingly, the art for sale mostly emphasizes themes displayed before contact and does not include representations of ships and guns.[44] As aboriginal populations were decimated by European contact, a lot of their traditional art forms disappeared, particularly legends and rock paintings that were associated with the sacred sites of each clan. The legends described the creation of the sacred places, and art motifs with painted human or animal heroes marked the sites.[45]

In North America, contact between native groups produced changes in art even before the Europeans came. Copper, sharks' teeth, and marine shells were traded extensively in precontact times and were used in the artwork of people who did not have access to those materials locally. Ceremonies were borrowed among groups, and with the new ceremonies came changes in artistic traditions. Borrowing from other native groups continued after European contact. The Navajo, who are well known today for their rug weaving, were not weavers in the 17th century. They probably obtained their weaving technology from the Hopi and then began to weave wool and herd sheep. European contact also produced material changes in art; new materials, including beads, wool cloth, and silver, were introduced. Metal tools such as needles and scissors could now be used to make more tailored and more decorated skin clothing. In the Northwest, the greater availability of metal tools made it possible to make larger totem poles and house posts.[46]

"Tourist" Art and "Fine" Art

When Westerners do notice changes over time in the art of less complex societies, it seems to be because they are concerned about whether the art represents traditional, "authentic" forms or is "tourist art." As we have seen, the concept of "traditional" art is problematic because it suggests that the art of less complex societies does not change. Tourist art is often evaluated negatively, perhaps because of its association with just being produced for money. But famous Western artists often also worked for fees or were supported by elite patrons, and yet the fact that they were paid does not seem to interfere with our evaluation of their art.[47]

Watch the Video: Silversmith on a Navajo Reservation Speaks About His Craft

After they were placed on reservations, virtually all Native Americans had to change their ways of making a living. Selling arts and crafts earned some of them supplementary income. Most of these crafts used traditional techniques and traditional designs, altered somewhat to suit European expectations. Outsiders played important roles in encouraging changes in arts and crafts. Some storekeepers became patrons to particular artists who were then able to devote themselves full time to their craft. Traders would often encourage changes, such as new objects—for example, ashtrays and cups made of pottery. Scholars have played a role too. Some have helped artisans learn about styles of the past that had disappeared. For example, with the encouragement of anthropologists and others in the Santa Fe area, Maria and Julian Martinez of San Ildefonso Pueblo brought back a polished black-on-black pottery style originally produced by nearby ancient peoples.[48]

Modern Navajo weavings at the Hubbell Trading Post National Historic Site, Arizona. Navajo weaving generally became more complex over time.

Until about 50 years ago the Pintupi of the western Australian desert were foragers. They were not involved in commercial activities until they were settled on reserves by the government. The Pintupi still maintain a rich ceremonial life reenacting the mystery of events that gives the world its shape and social meaning. These rituals involve song, myths, body decoration, and the production of objects. In 1971, after encouragement from an "outsider," some Pintupi began to turn their designs into acrylic paintings on canvas or wood and put them up for sale. Are these designs "authentic" or just made up for others, such as tourists and art dealers? Painters insist that the designs are not "made up" but rather represent the Dreaming, or stories of the ancestral beings. These paintings are now sold in major Australian cities and have made their way to cities all over the world. Some are now considered "fine art" and are accompanied by documentation of stories of the ancestral beings' travel across the landscape. Thus, the acrylic paintings acquire value in the outside world by invoking tradition.[49]

One characteristic of what is labeled "fine art" appears to be its exclusivity.[50] If it is prepared for tourists, the presumption is that it is turned out in quantity and is therefore lacking in the innovativeness and skill of "fine art." The presumption is that is bought by people, not very knowledgeable, as souvenirs rather than art. However, the fuzzy line between the two is illustrated by the creation of the New Guinea Sculpture Garden at Stanford University.[51] A group of Iatmul and Kwoma men from the Sepik River region of New Guinea called "master-carvers" were brought to Stanford to create sculptures in a forest-like space on the campus meant to "evoke" the Sepik River environment. They were treated as "artists" and they had titles for their art and their name indicated on the work, but despite being encouraged to avoid traditional forms and to express their individual artistry and innovation in this new space, they created variations of their work back home. Yet back home, where supposedly art was just for money and tourists, carvers actually strived for creating unique objects. They also procured new materials and experimented with new aesthetic styles, as we believe artists do. So, were the carvers brought to Stanford doing more "fine art" because they were more creative, or were the carvers back home labeled doing "tourist art" more creative?

Some of the artistic changes that have occurred after contact with the West are partly predictable from the results of cross-cultural research on artistic variation. Remember that Fischer found that egalitarian societies typically had less complex designs and more symmetry than did stratified societies. With the loss of traditional ways of making a living and with the increase in wage labor and commercial enterprises, many Native American groups have become more socially stratified. Extrapolating from Fischer's results, we would predict that designs on visual art should become more complex and asymmetrical as social stratification increases. Indeed, if early reservation art (1870–1901) among the Shoshone-Bannock of southeastern Idaho is compared with their recent art (1973–1983), it is clear that the art has become more complex as social stratification has increased.[52] It could also be true that the art changed because the artists came to realize that more asymmetry and complexity would sell better to people who collect art.

Summary and Review

Body Decoration and Adornment

24.1 Analyze the purposes of body decoration and adornment.

- People in all societies decorate or adorn their bodies for aesthetic considerations; to delineate social position, rank, sex, occupation, local and ethnic identity, or religion within a society; and for sexual provocation.
- The level of permanence of body decoration and adornment can reflect important characteristics of a culture.

? Body decoration is universal; what are some of the ways it varies among cultures?

Explaining Variation in the Arts

24.2 Explain variation in the arts in relationship to other societal features.

- Societies vary in terms of an emphasis on uniqueness, materials, ideas of beauty, and characteristic styles and themes. Form and style in visual art, music, dance, and folklore are very much influenced by other aspects of culture.
- Art may express the typical feelings, anxieties, and experiences of people in a culture. The form of art a society prefers may reflect its way of life; choice and use of artistic materials often reflects how a society views its environment.
- Repetition of elements, use of space, symmetry, and presence or absence of enclosed figures are stylistic features that vary strongly depending on the degree of stratification.
- Making sense of another culture's music is similar to making sense of a foreign language. Cultural differences in music reflect widely varying rhythms, singing styles, and tonal ranges. Some features of song style can be correlated with cultural complexity.
- Folklore is not always clearly separable from the other arts, particularly music and dance.

> ? How do some aspects of art (visual art and music) vary with differences in social and political systems?

Viewing the Art of Other Cultures

24.3 Identify ethnocentric attitudes and practices toward non-Western art by Westerners.

- Westerners tend to classify art from less complex societies as "primitive art" and display it differently from Western and Oriental art.
- To Westerners, non-Western art is considered unchanging in style, but studies indicate that members of the non-Western cultures are aware of nuanced changes in their art.
- Although it seems that individual artists can usually be recognized in any community, some societies do appear to be more communal than others in their art style.

> ? What are some of the specific differences in how Westerners view their own art and art of non-Western societies?

Artistic Change, Culture Contact, and Global Trade

24.4 Assess the relationship of culture contact and artistic change.

- As cultures come into contact, the art within those cultures tends to change, partly to reflect the contact itself and partly because new materials and techniques are introduced.
- As societies change and become more complex after cultural contact and global trade, changes such as social stratification may well affect the art of those societies.

> ? What are some examples of changes in art?

Think on it

1. How **innovative** or original can a successful artist be? Explain your answer.
2. What kind of **art** do you prefer, and why?
3. Do you think art made for **tourists** is inferior? Whatever you think, why do you think so?

Practicing and Applying Anthropology

CHAPTER 25

LEARNING OBJECTIVES

- 25.1 Discuss the ethical code of applied anthropology and discuss the ethical issues faced by practicing anthropologists.
- 25.2 Discuss the need to evaluate the effects of planned change.
- 25.3 Identify and give examples of some difficulties in implementing planned change.
- 25.4 Describe the field of environmental anthropology.
- 25.5 Describe the field of business and organizational anthropology.
- 25.6 Describe the field of cultural resource management.
- 25.7 Describe the field of museum anthropology.
- 25.8 Describe the field of forensic anthropology.

Anthropology is no longer a merely academic subject. A large number of anthropologists in the United States are applied and practicing anthropologists, employed outside of colleges and universities.[1] The fact that so many organizations hire anthropologists suggests an increasing realization that anthropology, what it has discovered and can discover about humans, is useful. Anthropologists who call themselves practicing or applied anthropologists work for a large variety of organizations, government agencies, international development agencies, private consulting firms, public health organizations, medical schools, public-interest law firms, community development agencies, charitable foundations, and profit-seeking corporations.

Practicing or applied anthropology The branch of anthropology that concerns itself with applying anthropological knowledge to achieve practical goals, usually in the service of an agency outside the traditional academic setting

Practicing or applied anthropology as a profession is explicitly concerned with making anthropological knowledge useful. Applied or practicing anthropologists may be involved in one or more phases of a project: assembling relevant knowledge and collecting data, developing plans and policies, assessing the likely social and environmental impacts, implementation, and evaluating the project and its effects.[2] Anthropologists are most often involved in gathering information rather than constructing policy or initiating action.[3] The organizations that hire the applied anthropologists usually set policy and have staff to execute projects. However, anthropologists are increasingly finding themselves involved in policy making and action. The field of applied or practicing anthropology is very diverse. In this chapter, we first focus on issues affecting applied anthropology generally: ethics; evaluating the effects of planned change; and the difficulties of implementing change. In these first sections, we mainly use examples from *development anthropology*, one of the oldest applied fields. **Development anthropology** is one of the main subfields of applied or practicing anthropology, aimed at improving people's lives, particularly decreasing poverty and hunger.[4] We then turn to some other applied specialties such as *environmental anthropology, business or organizational anthropology, museum anthropology, cultural resource management*, and *forensic anthropology*. Medical anthropology, which has both basic and applied aspects, is discussed in its own chapter. These fields by no means exhaust the wide-ranging applications in which anthropologists participate.

Development anthropology One of the main subfields of applied or practicing anthropology, aimed at improving people's lives, particularly decreasing poverty and hunger.

25.1 Discuss the ethical code of applied anthropology and discuss the ethical issues faced by practicing anthropologists.

Ethics of Applied Anthropology

Anthropologists have usually studied people who are disadvantaged—by imperialism, colonialism, and other forms of exploitation—and so it is no wonder that we care about the people's lives we have shared. But caring is not enough to improve others' lives. We may need basic research that allows us to understand how a condition might be successfully treated. A particular proposed "improvement" might actually not be an improvement; well-meaning efforts have sometimes produced harmful consequences. And even if we know that a change would be an improvement, there is still the problem of how to make that change happen. The people to be affected may not want to change. Is it ethical to try to persuade them? And, conversely, is it ethical *not* to try? Applied anthropologists must take all of these matters into consideration in determining whether and how to act in response to a perceived need.

Anthropology as a profession has adopted certain principles of responsibility. Above all, an anthropologist's first responsibility is to those who are being studied; everything should be done to ensure that their welfare and dignity will be protected. Anthropologists also have a responsibility to those who will read about their research; research findings should be reported openly and truthfully.[5] But because applied anthropology often deals with planning and implementing changes in some population, ethical responsibilities can become complicated. Perhaps the most important ethical question is: Will the change truly benefit the potentially affected population?

Watch the Video: What is Applied Anthropology?

In May 1946, the Society for Applied Anthropology established a committee to draw up a specific code of ethics for professional applied anthropologists. After many meetings and revisions, a statement on ethical responsibilities was finally adopted in 1948 and revised subsequently.[6] According to the code, the targeted community should be included as much as possible in the formulation of policy, so that people in the community may know in advance how the program will affect them. Perhaps the most important aspect of the code is the pledge not to recommend or take any action that is harmful to the interests of the community. The National Association for the Practice of Anthropology goes further: If the work the employer expects of the employee violates the ethical principles of the profession, the practicing anthropologist has the obligation to try to change those practices or, if change cannot be brought about, to withdraw from the work.[7]

Ethical issues are often complicated. Thayer Scudder described the situation of Gwembe Tonga villagers who were relocated after a large dam was built in the Zambezi Valley of central Africa. Economic conditions improved during the 1960s and early 1970s as the people increasingly produced goods and services for sale. But then conditions deteriorated. By 1980, the villagers were in a miserable state; rates of mortality, alcoholism, theft, assault, and murder were up. Why? One reason was that they had cut back on producing their own food in favor of producing for the world market. Such a strategy works well when world market prices are high; however, when prices fall, so does the standard of living.[8] The situation described by Scudder illustrates the ethical dilemma for many applied anthropologists. As he said: "So how is it that I can still justify working for the agencies that fund such projects?" He points out that large-scale projects are almost impossible to stop. The anthropologist can choose to stand on the sidelines and complain or try to influence the project to benefit the affected population as much as possible.[9] Along these lines, Michael Cernea has modeled eight risks of displacement due to water projects, which include landlessness, joblessness, homelessness, marginalization, food insecurity, increased morbidity, loss of access to common property resources, and community disarticulation.[10] He asserts that all these risks make it important to avoid resettlement, but if it is undertaken there needs to be serious political commitment by governments to provide adequate resources and legal protections.

Many development projects, particularly large-scale projects such as building dams or urban renewal projects, inevitably involve the large-scale displacement of people. About 10 million people a year are displaced by such projects. Whose lives are improved? The ethical difficulty is that some lives may be improved and others worsened. While a development project may claim to increase economic growth for a region or country as a whole, it usually results in much worse conditions for the people displaced by it. It is almost always the case that the people immediately affected do not wish to relocate. And the people forced to move are invariably less powerful because they are poor or have minority status.

Some of the problems result from the fact that anthropologists are not often involved until after a decision is made to go ahead with a change program. This situation has begun to change as applied anthropologists are increasingly asked to participate in earlier stages of the planning process. Anthropologists are also increasingly asked to help in projects initiated by the affected party. Such requests may range from help in solving problems in corporate organizations to helping Native Americans with land claims. Because the project is consistent with the wishes of the affected population, the results are not likely to put the anthropologist into an ethical dilemma.

When physical anthropologists and archaeologists work with skeletal and even fossil materials, the ethical complications can become extremely complex. Consider the case of "Kennewick Man," a 9,200-year-old skeleton found in July 1996 along the Columbia River in Washington State. Before anthropologists could study the skeleton, the U.S. Army Corps of Engineers decided to turn the remains over to the Umatilla Indians, as the remains were found on Corps land within their reservation. The physical anthropologists and archaeologists who wanted to study this very old skeleton faced an ethical quandary: A group claiming to be related to the individual did not want the study to be undertaken, but, without the study, the group's claim of relationship could not be firmly established.[11] The physical anthropologists and archaeologists filed a lawsuit under the Native American Graves Protection and Repatriation Act of 1900, which provides absolute protection to Native American graves on federal land and which makes it a felony to collect, possess, or transfer human remains of known affinity to an existing Native American culture, except if approved by the members of that culture.[12]

Applied Anthropology

Getting Development Programs to Include Women Farmers

When Anita Spring first did fieldwork in Zambia in the 1970s, she was not particularly interested in agriculture. Rather, medical anthropology was her interest. Her work focused on customary healing practices, particularly involving women and children. She was surprised at the end of the year when a delegation of women came to tell her that she did not understand what it meant to be a woman. "To be a woman is to be a farmer," they said. She admits that it took her a while to pay attention to women as farmers, but then she began to participate in efforts to provide technical assistance to them. Spring realized that all too often development agents downplay women's contributions to agriculture.

How does one bring about change in male-centered attitudes and practices? One way is to document how much women actually contribute to agriculture. Beginning with the influential writing of Ester Boserup in *Woman's Role in Economic Development* (1970), scholars began to report that in Africa south of the Sahara, in the Caribbean, and in parts of Southeast Asia, women were the principal farmers or agricultural laborers. Moreover, as agriculture became more complex, it required more work time in the fields, so the women's contribution to agriculture increased. In addition, because men increasingly went away to work, women had to do much of what used to be men's work on the farms.

In the 1980s, Spring designed and directed the Women in Agricultural Development Project in Malawi, funded by the Office of Women in the U.S. Agency for International Development. Rather than focusing just on women, the project aimed to collect data on both female and male agriculturalists and how development agents treated them. The project did more than collect information; mini-projects were set up and evaluated, and successful training techniques were shared with development agents in other regions. Spring points out that the success of the program was due not just to the design of the project but to Malawi's willingness to change. It also helped that the United Nations and other donor organizations increasingly focused attention on women. It takes the efforts of many to bring about change. Increasingly, applied anthropologists like Anita Spring are involved in these efforts from beginning to end, from the design stage to implementation and evaluation.

Source: Spring 1995; 2000b.

At the core of the legal case was this question: To whom does this skeleton belong? If this is an individual who is related to contemporary Native Americans, then do the Umatilla get to speak for all Native American groups, even though 9,000 years separate them? Or should other Native American groups, who may also be descended from this individual or his group, also have a say in what happens? If this is an individual who appears not to be related to contemporary Native Americans, then should the U.S. government decide what happens to his remains? Underlying these questions was a deeper struggle between anthropologists and Native Americans over historic preservation and whose wishes and ideas carry the most weight. Archaeologists and physical anthropologists feel ethical responsibilities that can be in conflict when dealing with human remains. As part of the archaeological record, archaeologists and physical anthropologists have an ethical responsibility to protect and preserve human remains. As anthropologists, they have the ethical responsibility to consult with and follow the wishes of local groups with whom they are working. The Kennewick Man case highlights this ethical conflict, for which there seems no easy answer.

Evaluating the Effects of Planned Change

25.2 Discuss the need to evaluate the effects of planned change.

The decision as to whether a proposed change would benefit the affected population is not always easy to make. In certain cases, as when improved medical care is involved, the benefits offered to the target group would seem to be unquestionable—we all feel sure that health is better than illness. However, what about the long-term effects? Consider a public health innovation such as inoculation against disease. Once the inoculation program was begun, the number of children surviving would probably increase. But will there be enough food for the additional population? Given the level of technology, capital, and land resources possessed by the population, there might not be enough resources to feed more people. Thus, the death rate, because of starvation, might rise to its previous level and perhaps even exceed it. Without additional changes to increase the food supply, the inoculation program in the long term might merely change the causes of death. This example shows that even if a program of planned change has beneficial consequences in the short run, a great deal of thought and investigation has to be given to its long-term effects.

Debra Picchi raised questions about the long-term effects on the Bakairí Indians of a program by the Brazilian National Indian Foundation (FUNAI) to produce rice with machine technology.[13] The Bakairí of the Mato Grosso region largely practice slash-and-burn horticulture in gallery forests along rivers, with supplementary cattle raising, fishing, and hunting. In the early part of the 20th century, their population had declined to 150 people, and they were given a relatively small reserve, much of it parched and infertile (*cerrado*). When the Bakairí population began to increase, FUNAI introduced a scheme to plant rice on formerly unused *cerrado* land, using machinery, insecticides, and fertilizer. FUNAI paid the costs for the first year and expected that the scheme would be self-supporting by the third year. The project did not go so well because FUNAI did not deliver all the equipment needed and did not provide adequate advice. Only half the expected rice was produced. Still, it was more food than the Bakairí had previously, so the program should have been beneficial to them.

But there were unanticipated negative side effects. Using *cerrado* land for agriculture reduced the area on which cattle could be grazed; cattle are an important source of high-quality protein. Mechanization also makes the Bakairí more dependent on cash for fuel, insecticides, fertilizer, and repairs. But cash is hard to come by. Only some individuals can be hired—usually men with outside experience who have the required knowledge of machinery. So the cash earned in the now-mechanized agriculture goes mainly to a relatively small number of people, creating new inequalities of income.

The benefits of programs or applied efforts are sometimes obvious. For example, Haiti has experienced serious deforestation. The process began in colonial times when the Spanish exported wood and the French cleared forests to grow sugarcane, coffee, and indigo. After Haiti's independence, foreign lumber companies continued to cut and sell hardwood. Wood is needed by the local population for fuel and for construction, but rapid population increases have increased the demand for fuel and wood, and the trees were rapidly diminishing. The loss of tree cover also speeds up erosion of topsoil. Forestry experts, environmentalists, and anthropologists all agree about the need to stop this trend. How to bring about the appropriate change is not so easy. The poorer people become, the more likely they are to cut down trees to sell.[14]

These failures were not the fault of anthropologists—indeed, most instances of planned change by governments and other agencies usually have begun without the input of anthropologists at all. Applied anthropologists have played an important role in pointing out the problems with programs like these that fail to evaluate long-term consequences. Such evaluations are an important part of convincing governments and other agencies to ask for anthropological help in the first place. Ironically, failure experiences are learning experiences: Applied anthropologists who study previous examples of planned change can often learn a great deal about what is likely or not likely to be beneficial in the long run.

25.3 Identify and give examples of some difficulties in implementing planned change.

Difficulties in Instituting Planned Change

After numerous reforestation projects failed in Haiti, an anthropologist, Gerald Murray, was asked to help design a program that would work.[15] Understanding why previous projects failed was the first step in helping Murray design an effective project. One problem seems to have been that previous projects were run through the government's Ministry of Agriculture. The seedling trees that were given away were referred to as "the state's trees." So when project workers told farmers not to cut the new trees down so as to protect the environment, farmers took this statement to mean that the land on which the trees were planted might be considered government land, which the farmers could not care less about. In the project proposed by Murray, private voluntary organizations rather than the Haitian government were used to distribute trees and the farmers were told that they were the tree owners. Ownership included the right to cut the trees and sell the wood, just as they could sell crops. In previous projects, farmers were given heavy, hard-to-transport seedlings that took a long time to mature. They were told to plant in a large communal woodlot, an idea inconsistent with the more individualistic Haitian land tenure arrangements. In the new plan, the tree seedlings given away were fast-growing species that matured in as little as four years. In addition, the new seedlings were very small and could be planted quickly. Perhaps most important of all, the new trees could be planted in borders or interspersed with other crops, interfering little with traditional crop patterns. To Murray's great surprise, by the end of two years, 2,500 Haitian households had planted 3 million seedlings. Over 20 years, the estimate is that over a 100 million trees were planted and over 350,000 farm families were involved in the project, more than 40 percent of rural households.[16] Also, farmers were not rushing to cut down trees. Because growing trees do not spoil, farmers were postponing their cutting and sale until they needed cash. So even though farmers were told that it was all right to cut down trees, a statement contrary to the message of previous reforestation projects, the landscape was filling up with trees.

Murray's lengthy participant observation and interviewing had helped him predict what might overcome the previous implementation difficulties and fit in with the Haitian farmers' needs. The idea that wood could be an important marketable cash crop was much more consistent with farmers' existing behavior—they already sold crops for cash when they needed it. The difference now was that, instead of cutting down naturally grown wood, they were raising wood just as they raised other crops.

Whether a program of planned change can be successfully implemented depends largely on whether the people want the proposed change and like the proposed program. Before an attempt can be made at cultural innovation, the innovators must determine whether the population is aware of the benefits of the proposed change. Lack of awareness can be a temporary barrier to solving the problem at hand. For example, health workers have often had difficulty convincing people that they were becoming ill because something was wrong with their water supply. Many people do not believe that disease can be transmitted by water. At other times, the population is perfectly aware of the problem. A case in point involved Taiwanese women who were introduced to family-planning methods beginning in the 1960s. The women knew they were having more children than they wanted or could easily afford, and they wanted to control their birth rate. They offered no resistance—they merely had to be given the proper devices and instructions, and the birth rate quickly fell to a more desirable, and more manageable, level.[17]

Anthropologists as Advocates and Collaborators

Development anthropologists have played an important role researching and documenting the mostly negative effects on populations that have been relocated. Occasionally, a few projects have had better outcomes, and researchers try to understand what factors appear to ameliorate the situation. Two factors critical to success appear to be collecting good data in affected communities prior to the project and consulting with the community.

In the past, anthropologists mostly played a role in researching change projects. There were some notable exceptions however. For example, in the 1950s Sol Tax advocated "action anthropology, which emphasized the role of the anthropologist in helping communities make choices and decide how they want to change."[18] One famous action-oriented project (the Vicos Project) led by Cornell anthropologists actually took over a hacienda in Peru with the aim of transforming the serf-like system into one where the indigenous population controlled the resources and ran the community.[19] For a long time those projects were exceptions. However, in the 1990s anthropologists have increasingly become advocates for affected communities, working with NGOs to resist resettlement or to lobby for better conditions. Advocates see themselves as providing a voice that is not otherwise heard. Critics are concerned that the advocate is only representing one point of view.

Even if the programs are well intentioned and even if the appropriate evaluations are made to ensure that the population will not be seriously harmed, the population targeted for the change is usually not involved in the decision making. Some anthropologists think that collaborative research is more ethical because it involves the people affected in all phases of the project, from participating in the research design to execution and publishing.[20] Wayne Warry decided to be more collaborative when he was asked by a Native Canadian elder whether he (Warry) would tolerate his own methods and interpretations if he were the native.[21] This question prompted him to involve himself in a project with Native Canadian collaborators, directed by the Mamaweswen Tribal Council. The project assesses health care needs and develops plans to improve local community health care. Funding is provided by the Canadian government as part of a program to transfer health care to the First Nations. Native researchers are conducting the surveys and workshops to keep the community informed about the project. The tribal council also reviews any publications and shares in any profits resulting from those publications.

Applied anthropologists are also increasingly asked to work on behalf of indigenous grassroots organizations which have proliferated recently in the developing world. In some cases, these small groups and networks of such groups are starting to hire their own technical assistance.[22] When such organizations do the hiring, they control the decision making. There is increasing evidence that grassroots organizations are the key to effective development. For example, Kenyan farmers who belong to grassroots organizations produce higher farm yields than those farmers who do not belong, even though the latter group is exposed to more agricultural extension agents.[23] Grassroots organizations can succeed where government or outside projects fail. We have plenty of instances of people effectively resisting projects. Their willingness to change, and their participation in crucial decision making, may be mostly responsible for the success of a change project.

Large development projects planned by powerful governments or agencies rarely are stoppable, but even they can be resisted successfully. The Kayapo of the Xingu River region of Brazil were able to cancel a plan by the Brazilian government to build dams along the river for hydroelectric power. The Kayapo gained international attention when some of their leaders appeared on North American and European television and then successfully organized a protest, in 1989, by members of several tribal groups. Their success seemed to come in part from their ability to present themselves to the international community as guardians of the rain forest—an image that resonated with international environmental organizations that supported their cause. Although to outsiders it might seem that the Kayapo want their way of life to remain as it was, the Kayapo are not opposed to all change. In fact, they want greater access to medical care, other government services, and manufactured goods from outside.[24]

Native South Americans from different groups gather to show their unity as they protest against the construction of the Belo Montedam. They are demanding that the Brazilian government hold prior consultations with indigenous peoples before building dams that affect their lands and livelihoods.

There is another kind of collaboration that is becoming increasingly important. Many projects require team efforts, working with people from other disciplines. Anthropologists increasingly have to be conversant with the theory and methods in other fields to understand and negotiate with other members of their team. Earlier anthropologists might have been more likely to work alone. Now that is less likely.[25]

25.4 Describe the field of environmental anthropology.

environmental anthropology It focuses on issues relating to the interaction of humans with their environments, at the local, regional, and global levels, particularly on how to understand and alleviate the degradation of the environment.

Environmental Anthropology

Given the looming environmental challenges that humans face, it is not surprising that *environmental anthropology* has become a rapidly growing field. The field of **environmental anthropology** focuses on issues relating to the interaction of humans with their environments, at the local, regional and global levels, particularly focusing on how to understand and alleviate the degradation of the environment.[26] Researchers ask questions such as: How do local people view the environment? What are the effects of those views? How can needed resources be sustained? Does participation by communities in change programs lead to better outcomes? What kinds of programs can help to improve the lives of those living in the worst environments?

There is increasing recognition that imposition of environmental policies from the top down does not work very well and that efforts are more likely to succeed if the affected communities participate in the planning of programs. Erin Dean describes a pilot program in Tanzania to manage forest resources that attempts to be participatory.[27] Tanzania has about 2 million hectares of land under some participatory management program. There are two kinds of forestry management programs. In one, the government retains ownership of the forestland and trees, but responsibilities and benefits are shared with communities. In the second one, communities register for full ownership of the forestland and trees as well as full responsibility. The Meru-Usa plantation, on the upper slopes of Mount Meru, has its roots in colonial times when the Germans seized land for European settlement and at the same time created a forest reserve. Because of land seizures, the agricultural Masai living in this area had to intensify their agriculture. But this did not solve the Masai's need for timber because agricultural intensification deprived the Masai of timber that would formerly grow in fields that lay fallow. Consequently, the forest reserve became contested. And, to make matters worse, the trees that were planted in the reserve used more water than native trees. To deal with the increased tension, the manager of the Meru-Usa plantation decided to try to get village cooperation, and the Tanzanian government decided to make it a pilot program. Masai farmers help weed in areas where young trees are growing and in exchange are allowed to collect fallen limbs and plant some crops until the trees grow tall enough and make too much shade. The pilot project also included school environmental programs and lessons in some revenue-generating projects, such as bee-keeping. While progress has occurred, Dean reports that co-management was a goal but was not yet achieved.

Much of the work that environmental anthropologists do is at the local level where they can employ detailed ethnographic methods. But when the environmental issue involves a large region, this strategy does not work well because a single community or even a few communities will not provide representative information. Researchers make use of methods such as remote sensing from satellites combined with geographic information systems (GISs) for a large region. Satellite data, which can be geo-referenced using GIS, can be analyzed for changes in vegetation.[28] But these technological advances alone are not sufficient, for without research on the ground, scientists cannot be sure how the land is used now and in the past. For instance, they would want to know whether land was previously burned, or when the land was last logged, what species of tree have been cut, how many people live in a household, or how households allocate labor. In other words, "ground-truthing" is needed. This is where anthropology comes in. Working with interdisciplinary teams, smaller units of land can be sampled, and fieldworkers can talk to people in those areas to find out how land was actually used and who lives on the land.

A promising technology in arid areas is drip irrigation where water is applied in droplets near the plant's root zone through small tubes. A Masai group living near the Kenya-Tanzanian border are observing.

The example just given indicates how anthropologists need to interface with other methods and people from other disciplines to tackle more than local problems. But that does not mean that local knowledge is irrelevant. Climate change is a worldwide phenomenon, yet environmental anthropologists believe that understanding the resilience of local communities and their resourcefulness is necessary. As described by Jennifer Hirsch and colleagues, the Field Museum in Chicago is undertaking research in 10 Chicago neighborhoods designed to facilitate the involvement of different communities in reducing carbon emissions.[29] If successful, community leaders will participate in long-term planning for their communities and the larger area. The research team consists of anthropologists, Chicago Department of Environment staff, and community leaders. The anthropologists employed mixed methods, including about 4 months of ethnographic research in each community, to assess concerns about climate change and steps people were taking to conserve energy. They found awareness, but the anthropologists also identified some barriers. For example, in one middle class neighborhood some people objected to putting clothes out to dry as it was seen as a marker of low status. In a lower income neighborhood, people were afraid that building "green" housing would ultimately lead to increases in housing prices and ultimately force them to move. Also, there was significant distrust of the city, including distrust of the climate action plan. The researchers suggested that the city build on existing concerns of the communities (such as interest in weatherization and retrofitting houses to make them more energy efficient). They also suggested that local organizations could become role models and demonstration sites. The good news is that the city government has implemented some of the suggestions.

Business and Organizational Anthropology

25.5 Describe the field of business and organizational anthropology.

More and more businesses and organizations have come to realize that anthropologists have useful knowledge to contribute. Anthropologists bring to the table grounding in thinking holistically—looking at the larger culture in which organizations are situated, the culture and subcultures of the organization, and the perspectives of different groups. And anthropologists understand the need to observe and listen first in an unstructured way. Doing ethnographic research is not just for understanding the businesses themselves and their *organizational cultures* but also to enable businesses to assess the needs of potential customers and users. Understanding cultures becomes even more important as trade becomes more global, international investments and joint ventures increase, and the multinational corporations spread their reach.

Business anthropologists often do not have the luxury of a year or more of study. Often they may only have a few days or weeks and have to make a "rapid assessment." To address this problem, teams of researchers often work together using observation, videos, interviewing, and analyses of social networks and documents (such as e-mails) to see if different types of data collected by different people lead to the same conclusion.[30]

Differences between people from different cultures can have profound effects on how people work together. Anthropologists know that communication is much more than the formal understanding of another language. People in some countries, such as the United States, expect explicit, straightforward verbal messages, but people in other countries are more indirect in their verbal messages.[31] In Japan and China, for example, negative messages are less likely than messages expressing politeness and harmony. Many Eastern cultures have ways of saying no without saying the word. People in the United States emphasize the future, youth, informality, and competitiveness, but the emphases in other societies are often the opposite. In any business arrangement, perhaps no difference is as salient as the value a culture places on time. As we say, "Time is money."[32] If a meeting is arranged and the other person is late, say, 45 minutes, people from the United States consider it rude, but such a delay is well within the range of acceptable behavior in many South American countries.

Read **the** Document: A Shaman to Organizations

Businesses usually will ask for help in understanding their organizational culture when they perceive a problem. The culture of a business may interfere with the acceptance of new kinds of workers, mergers with other companies, or changing to meet new business needs. If the culture needs to be changed, it is first necessary to understand that culture and how and why it developed the way it did. Even something as seemingly minor as observing a parking lot and surrounding grounds is revealing. If there are many reserved spaces for executives and few amenities for workers, this may suggest a rigid hierarchy and less concern for employees.[33] Of course, an anthropologist would need to verify this

Applied Anthropology

General Motors: Creating a Better Business Culture

After World War II, General Motors (GM) was the largest corporation in the United States. But beginning in the 1960s imported cars from Germany and Japan began to seriously challenge GM's dominance. In addition, tastes were changing as consumers began opting for better fuel economy, cleaner emissions, and greater safety.

GM realized that it needed to change and in the 1980s began to explore new partnerships. They also hired an anthropologist, Elizabeth Briody, to conduct organizational research. In the mid-2000s, Briody led an expanded research team of six. In both time periods, the aim was the same. The researchers realized that in order to change, you first have to "see" what is going on. So, using ethnographic methods, the researchers undertook to understand the culture of the organization, including how work was organized, how people related to each other, and how people thought about their work and work conditions. They also asked how people of all statuses at GM how they wanted it to be—in other words, their ideal workplace culture.

Applied anthropologists Elizabeth Briody and Robert Trotter, part of the research team studying the culture at GM.

Briody's observations of the mid-1980s suggested that the GM culture emphasized efficiency and meeting quotas. The emphasis was on the productivity of an individual, and rewards and blame were assigned to individuals. Departments tried to optimize their own productivity. Leadership was authoritarian. In short, there was little cooperation or collaboration, and there was more emphasis on quantity rather than quality. Interviews, though, revealed that almost everyone, from top management on down, wanted a culture of collaboration, where everyone could contribute ideas, where teams took responsibility for solving problems, and where people were respectful of each other. Although most of the people interviewed wanted a different culture, the research team knew that culture change in organizations, just as in the broader society, is not easy to accomplish. So the researchers set out to design 10 "tools" designed to help individuals appreciate and learn collaboration techniques. Many of the exercises required small-group discussion, itself a collaborative enterprise. They even invented a video game to learn about the impact of different types of decision making to solve a problem (one that actually occurred).

Did GM change? By many objective measures, GM improved substantially since the 1980s. Measures of quality increased, injuries and illnesses are down, and even productivity is 54 percent higher. The manufacturing culture has shifted to more sharing and team responsibilities. Jobs are now rotated so work injuries decline and people have more understanding of the wider process. With more responsibilities, workers are more empowered. All cultures change, but the process of change is aided by the will to do so and the willingness to undertake steps to learn how to make the process easier.

Source: Briody, Trotter, and Meerwarth 2010.

inference with information from other sources. (For a long-term project design to change a business culture, see the box "General Motors: Creating a Better Business Culture.")

Anthropologist Jill Kleinberg's research provides a case study on the challenges of having people from very different cultures work together successfully. Kleinberg studied six Japanese-owned firms in the United States.[34] All six firms employed both Japanese and Americans, although the Japanese dominated the managerial positions. The main goal of the study was to discover why there was considerable tension in the six firms. Kleinberg's first order of business was to interview people about their views of work and their jobs. She found clear differences between the Japanese and the American employees that seemed to reflect broader cultural differences. Americans wanted a clear definition of the job and its attached responsibilities, and they also wanted their job titles, authority, rights, and pay to match closely. The Japanese, on the other hand, emphasized the need to be flexible in their responsibilities as well as their tasks. They also felt that part of their responsibility was to help their co-workers. Americans were uncomfortable because the Japanese managers did not indicate exactly what the workers were supposed to do; even if there was a job description, the manager did not appear to pay attention to it. Americans were given little information, were left out of decision making, and were frustrated by the lack of opportunity to advance. The Japanese thought that the Americans were too hard to manage, too concerned with money and authority, and too concerned with their own interests.

Kleinberg recommended giving all employees more information about the company as well as conducting training sessions about cross-cultural differences in business cultures. She also recommended making the Japanese philosophy of management more explicit during the hiring process so that the company would be able to find Americans who were comfortable with their philosophy. But she also suggested that the managerial structure be somewhat "Americanized" so that American employees could feel at ease. Finally, she recommended that Americans be given more managerial positions and contact with their Japanese counterparts overseas. These suggestions might not eliminate all problems, but they would increase mutual understanding and trust.

Businesses and organizations also need help in developing and marketing products that people may want, and many have found that anthropologists are quite good at finding out because they go out and watch and ask questions. For example, Susan Squires watched families with young kids at breakfast to help a breakfast food company develop products. Parents tried to get kids to eat nutritious breakfasts, but kids typically didn't want to eat at 6:30 or 7 or only wanted a heavily sugared cereal. Some kids skipped breakfast and got hungry later in the morning and ended up eating their lunch early. Squires' observations led the company to develop a portable yoghurt in a tube called Go-Gurt.[35]

Cultural Resource Management

25.6 Describe the field of cultural resource management.

Large-scale programs of planned change like those discussed earlier in this chapter have an impact not only on living people. They can also have an impact on the archaeological record left by the ancestors of living people. Recovering and preserving the archaeological record before programs of planned change disturb or destroy it is called **cultural resource management (CRM)**. CRM work is carried out by archaeologists who are often called contract archaeologists because they typically work under contract to a government agency, a private developer, or a native group.

cultural resource management (CRM) The branch of applied anthropology that seeks to recover and preserve the archaeological record before programs of planned change disturb or destroy it.

What kinds of impact can programs of planned change have on the archaeological record? In the 1960s, a large number of hydroelectric dam projects were initiated to provide flood control and to bring a stable source of electrical power to developing nations. In Egypt, a dam was built on the Nile River at a site called Aswan. Archaeologists realized that once the dam was in place a huge lake would form behind it, submerging thousands of archaeological sites, including the massive temple of Rameses II. Something needed to be done; the archaeological record had to be salvaged or protected. In the language of CRM, there needed to be a *mitigation plan* put into action. And there was. As the Aswan dam was being built, archaeologists went to work excavating sites that would be flooded. Archaeologists and engineers designed a way to take apart the temple of Rameses II and rebuild it, piece by piece, on higher ground where it would not be flooded. By the time the dam was completed in 1965, hundreds of sites had been investigated and two entire temple complexes moved.

Commuters look at 4th century ruins uncovered as part of a large scale CRM project associated with construction of the Athens metro system.

Large-scale development projects are not the only projects that involve CRM archaeologists. In many nations, including the United States and Canada, historic preservation laws require any project receiving federal funds to ensure that archaeological resources are protected or their damage mitigated. Highway construction projects in the United States are common places to find CRM archaeologists at work. Virtually all highway projects rely on federal funding, and before a highway can be built, a complete archaeological survey of the proposed right-of-way has to be made. If archaeological sites are found, potential damage to them must be mitigated. A CRM archaeologist will work with the construction company, the state archaeologist, and perhaps a federal archaeologist to decide on the best course of action. In some cases, the archaeological site will be excavated. In others, the right-of-way may be moved. In still others, the decision is to allow the archaeological site to be destroyed because it would be too costly to excavate or the site may not be significant enough to warrant excavation. Regardless of the decision, the CRM archaeologist plays a crucial role in assessing and protecting the archaeological record.

CRM archaeologists do not work only for state or federal agencies. In many nations today, CRM archaeologists are also working with native peoples to protect, preserve, and manage archaeological materials for them. Indeed, archaeologist John Ravesloot recently stated that "the future of American archaeology is with Indian communities functioning as active, not passive, participants in the interpretation, management, and preservation of their rich cultural heritage."[36] One example of such a working relationship is the Zuni Heritage and Historic Preservation Office. During the 1970s, the Pueblo of Zuni decided it needed to train tribal members in archaeology to ensure that Zuni cultural resources and properties were managed properly. It hired three professional archaeologists and, with additional assistance from the National Park Service and the Arizona State Museum, initiated a program to train and employ tribal members in cultural resource management. Working with these non-Zuni archaeologists, the Pueblo of Zuni were able to establish their own historic preservation office that today manages and coordinates all historic preservation on the Zuni reservation, a task that the federal government managed until 1992. The Pueblo also established the Zuni Cultural Resource Enterprise, a Zuni-owned CRM business that employs both Zuni and non-Zuni archaeologists and carries out contract archaeology projects both on and off the Zuni reservation.[37]

In addition to working with native peoples, CRM archaeologists are also working with the public through was has come to be known as public archaeology. One of the basic ideas behind public archaeology is that because most CRM archaeology is done with public money, it is important for the public to benefit from the results of archaeological research. Unfortunately, that is not always the case, and today popular media is far more likely to discuss archaeology in the context of ancient alien contact or Biblical fundamentalism than the context of mainstream anthropology. Working directly with the public, for example by having "open houses" at archaeological sites or hosting artifact identification days, is one way that CRM archaeologists can help to overcome popular misconceptions of the past as well as learn more about the past.[38]

Equally important is for archaeologists to undertake work that is meaningful to local communities, and this too is part of public archaeology. For example, CRM archaeologists in Hawaii are starting to work directly with Native Hawaiian communities to provide information on ancestral practices, and in turn Native Hawaiian communities are helping CRM archaeologists to identify and preserve important archaeological sites. As explained by Hawaiian archaeologists Sean Nāleimaile and Lokelani Brant, by incorporating Native Hawaiian "cultural practices and resource management systems into existing frameworks of CRM, we will reestablish successful strategies to maintain our resources. More importantly, these foundations work to reestablish these cultural practices in the now."[39] Public archaeologists believe that engaging the interests and needs of local communities, as is happening in Hawaii, serves to improve both the CRM work and the local community.

Cultural resource management accounts for the majority of archaeology jobs in the United States.[40] As development and construction projects continue to affect the archaeological record, the need for well-trained CRM archaeologists is likely to persist.

25.7 Describe the field of museum anthropology.

Museum Anthropology

Museums have been an important part of anthropology since the very beginnings of the field. As early anthropologists returned from archaeological excavations and ethnographic explorations, they brought with them artifacts from the peoples and cultures they encountered. These materials were collected in museums—often natural history museums since, at the time (the mid to late 19th century), non-Western artifacts were not considered art, nor were the cultures of non-Western peoples considered part of history. Thus the objects non-Western peoples produced and the information about their cultures were deposited with similar items from other forms of animal life. Today we recognize this as an ethnocentric, perhaps even racist, view of non-Western people, but many anthropological and archaeological collections are still deposited and maintained in natural history museums. Many other museums exist today as well, from cultural museums to historic site museums to museums showcasing traditional works of art, and anthropologists work in all of these.

Anthropologists typically hold one of three positions in museums: curators, collection managers, or educators. Curators are responsible for the overall content and use of collections. They oversee the museum collections with an eye to their value for research and their importance to the history of their field. In some cases curators acquire (or accession) materials in order to fill areas that are inadequately represented in their collections; in other cases they have to make difficult decisions about discarding (or de-accessioning) materials that are no longer of use. Curators also lead teams that evaluate and develop the museum's exhibits. Collection managers work to ensure that the museum's collections are preserved. They make sure that storage facilities and records are properly maintained, and they regularly check the collections to make sure they are not deteriorating. When deterioration is found, collections managers work with conservators to repair damage and determine ways to keep further damage from occurring. Finally, museum educators work with the public to teach them about the peoples and cultures represented in the museum's collections.[41]

Regardless of their position, public education is a central role for all museum anthropologists. A good example can be seen in recent work involving a traditional native New Zealand Maori meeting house, or *marae,* on display at the Field Museum in Chicago. A *marae* is used in Maori culture as a place where individuals are allowed to air grievances and settle disputes in an atmosphere of respect and open-mindedness. Field Museum curator of Pacific anthropology John Terrell wished that Chicago had such a space and then realized that the *marae* itself might be used as one; in other words, that the Maori *marae* might become a Chicago *marae.* Terrell worked with a group of Maori and a group of teachers from Chicago public schools to explore this idea, and today the *marae* is used by groups seeking to discuss difficult issues in a context of mutual respect.[42] In this way Terrell was able to not only display an important cultural object but also, with the assistance of the collections manager and museum education staff, develop a way for the object to be used by the Chicago community in a manner similar to its use within Maori culture.

A Maori meeting house in New Zealand.

25.8 Describe the field of forensic anthropology.

Forensic Anthropology

Forensic anthropology The application of anthropology, usually physical anthropology, to help identify human remains and assist in solving crimes.

Many of us are fascinated by detective stories. We are interested in crimes and why they occur, and we like to read about them, fictional or not. **Forensic anthropology** is the specialty in anthropology that is devoted to helping solve crimes and identifying human remains, usually by applying knowledge of physical anthropology.[43] It is attracting increasing attention by the public and an increasing number of practitioners. One forensic anthropologist says she is called "the bone lady" by law enforcement personnel.[44] Like others in her line of work, she is asked to dig up or examine human bones to help solve crimes. Narrowing down identification is one of the first priorities, but it is not as simple as on television shows. Are these the bones of a man or woman? How old was the person? How well the forensic anthropologist can answer these seemingly simple questions depends upon whether the remains include most bones of the skeleton. Identification of an adult's sex from remains is easier if the pelvis is present, but establishing sex in nonadult remains is not reliable from skeletal remains.[45] With regard to estimating age, only a wide age range can be estimated for adults, but a much narrower range can be estimated for nonadult remains. Forensic anthropologists are often asked for "race" as well. As we discussed in earlier chapters, "race" is not a useful biological category when applied to humans, but it is a significant social category. Forensic anthropologists can estimate with fairly high accuracy whether a person's ancestors came from Asia, Europe, or Africa, but they cannot detect skin color.[46] The police files may suggest that an adult male with Asian ancestry disappeared five years ago. The forensic anthropologist could say with a high probability that the remains were of an Asian male adult. Dental, surgical, or hospital records from that individual might lead to unique features that could be matched for more precise identification. Sometimes the forensic anthropologist can suggest the cause of death when the law enforcement people are stumped.

Listen to the Audio: Group Works to Identify Remains in Guatemela

Another important piece of evidence that is often provided by forensic anthropologists is the time of death. Establishing when a victim died can be essential to solving a crime. Forensic anthropologists use changes in the body as it decays to estimate how long an individual has been dead. In the short term, one to three days after death, the body decays primarily through the action of digestive enzymes and bacteria already in the body. Forensic anthropologists use indicators such as body temperature (which decreases about one degree an hour after death), skin discoloration, or the build-up of lactic acid in the muscles (which causes them to progressively stiffen over the 12 hours after death) to determine time of death. Over the longer term, three days to a month after death, the action of factors outside the body contribute significantly to decay. The most important of these factors is the activity of insects. Blow flies, for example, deposit eggs on dead tissue during specific periods after death. The eggs then hatch into maggots, again during a specific period of time, and the maggots slowly grow into adults. By carefully examining the presence and maturity of the eggs and maggots of various species of flies, the forensic anthropologist can provide a good estimate of the time of death.[47]

A forensic anthropologist digs out a body, apparently a victim of state-sponsored violence in Argentina between 1976 and 1983.

Some cultural anthropologists have also done forensic work, often in connection with legal cases involving Native Americans. For example, in 1978, Barbara Joans was asked to advise the defense in a trial of six older Bannock-Shoshoni women from the Fort Hall reservation who were accused of fraud. They had received "supplemental security income (SSI)," which the social service agency claimed they had no right to receive because they had not reported receiving rent money on land that they owned. Joans presented evidence that the women, although they spoke some English, did not have enough proficiency to understand the nuances of what the SSI people told them. The judge agreed with the defense and ruled that the SSI would have to use a Bannock-Shoshoni interpreter in the future when they went to the reservation to describe the requirements of the program.[48]

In recent years, Clyde Snow and other forensic anthropologists have been called on to confirm horrendous abuses of human rights. Governments have been responsible for the systematic killing of their citizens, and forensic anthropologists have helped to bring the perpetrators to justice. For example, Snow and other forensic anthropologists helped to confirm that the military dictatorship in Argentina in the 1980s was responsible for the deaths of many Argentine civilians who had "disappeared." The forensic anthropologists were also able to determine the location of mass graves and the identity of victims of state-organized brutality in Guatemala. In addition to bringing the perpetrators to justice, confirming the massacres and identifying the victims help the families of the "disappeared" put their anguish behind them. A special session (called "Uncovering the 'Disappeared': Clyde Snow and Forensic Anthropologists Work for Justice"[49]) at the annual meeting of the American Anthropological Association in November 2000 honored Snow and other forensic anthropologists.

Summary and Review

Ethics of Applied Anthropology

25.1 Discuss the ethical code of applied anthropology and discuss the ethical issues faced by practicing anthropologists.

- Applied anthropology researches how a condition might be treated, whether or not it would actually be an improvement, and whether it is actually a change that is wanted by the people affected.
- Anthropology as a profession has adopted ethical codes of responsibility, above all a responsibility to ensure the welfare and dignity of those who are being studied and a responsibility to report openly and truthfully to those who will read about their research.
- Even with a code of ethics, complicated ethical issues arise for anthropologists in connection with development projects as well as for physical anthropologists and archaeologists.

? What are some examples of ethical issues and dilemmas facing those practicing applied anthropology?

Evaluating the Effects of Planned Change

25.2 Discuss the need to evaluate the effects of planned change.

- Even if a program of planned change has beneficial consequences in the short run, a great deal of thought and investigation has to be given to its long-term effects, which could eventually produce negative results.
- Applied anthropologists have played an important role in pointing out the problems with development programs that fail to evaluate long-term consequences. Governments and other agencies are beginning to ask for anthropological help in the planning stages of projects.

? What factors may be important in bringing about successful change?

Difficulties in Instituting Planned Change

25.3 Identify and give examples of some difficulties in implementing planned change.

- Whether a program of planned change can be successfully implemented depends largely on whether the people want the proposed change and like the proposed program. Lack of awareness can be a temporary barrier to solving the problem at hand.
- A growing trend is for anthropologists to become advocates for affected communities, involving the people affected in all phases of the project, from participating in the research design to execution and publishing.
- Applied anthropologists are increasingly asked to work on behalf of indigenous grassroots organizations. Grassroots organizations can succeed with development projects where government or outside projects fail.
- Anthropologists are also collaborating more with people from other disciplines.

? In what way are anthropologists mediators between affected communities and those initiating change? Give an example.

Environmental Anthropology

25.4 Describe the field of environmental anthropology.

- Environmental anthropology focuses on issues relating to the interaction of humans with their environments at the local, regional, and global levels, particularly focusing on how to understand and alleviate the degradation of the environment.

- There is increasing recognition that imposing environmental policies from the top down does not work very well and that efforts are more likely to succeed if the affected communities participate in the planning of programs.

> What kinds of questions do environmental anthropologists ask?

Business and Organizational Anthropology

25.5 Describe the field of business and organizational anthropology.

- Anthropologists can help businesses understand other cultures, which is becoming an even more important aspect as trade becomes more global, international investments and joint ventures increase, and the multinational corporations spread their reach.
- Within a business, anthropologists can help business members understand their own organizational culture, especially when it may interfere with the acceptance of new kinds of workers, mergers with other companies, or changing to meet new business needs.
- Businesses and organizations also need help in developing and marketing products that people may want, and anthropologists are quite good at finding out because they observe and ask questions.

> What issues related to globalization affect the work of business and organizational anthropologists?

Cultural Resource Management

25.6 Describe the field of cultural resource management.

- Cultural resource management involves recovering and preserving the archaeological record before programs of planned change disturb or destroy it.
- Another focus of cultural resource management is public archaeology, educating the public about the past.

> Why is it important for cultural resource management anthropologists to educate the public?

Museum Anthropology

25.7 Describe the field of museum anthropology.

- An early practice, which still occurs, was to archive artifacts from non-Western societies in museums of natural history. More and more today, other types of museums are providing less biased views of non-Western cultures.
- Public education is a central role for all museum anthropologists.

> How have practices in museum anthropology changed in the past several decades? Give an example.

Forensic Anthropology

25.8 Describe the field of forensic anthropology.

- Forensic anthropology is devoted to helping solve crimes and identifying human remains, usually by applying knowledge of physical anthropology.
- A relatively new area of forensic anthropology is work to confirm abuses of human rights, especially in terms of systematic killings of citizens.

> What kinds of challenges do forensic anthropologists face? Give examples.

Think on it

1. What particular **advantages** do anthropologists have in trying to solve practical problems?
2. What disadvantages do anthropologists have in trying to solve **practical problems**?
3. Is it **ethical** to try to influence people's lives when they have not asked for help or if they don't want the change? Explain your answer.

Health and Illness

CHAPTER 26

LEARNING OBJECTIVES

- Discuss cultural understandings of health and illness. 26.1
- Discuss various approaches to studying treatment of illness. 26.2
- Describe political and economic influences on health. 26.3
- Discuss a sampling of health conditions and diseases studied by medical anthropologists. 26.4

Illness and death are significant events for people everywhere. No one is spared. So it should not be surprising that how people understand the causes of illness and death, how they behave, and what resources they marshal to cope with these events are extremely important parts of culture. Some argue that we will never completely understand how to treat illness effectively until we understand the cultural behaviors, attitudes, values, and larger social and political milieu in which people live. Others argue that society and culture have little to do with the outcome of illness—the reason that people die needlessly is that they do not get the appropriate medical treatment.

medical anthropology The anthropological study of health and illness and associated beliefs and practices.

But anthropologists, particularly those in **medical anthropology**, who are actively engaged in studying health and illness and associated beliefs and practices, are increasingly realizing that biological and social factors need to be considered if we are to reduce human suffering. For instance, some populations have an appalling incidence of infant deaths due to diarrhea. The origin of this situation is mostly biological in the sense that the deaths are caused by bacterial infection. But why are so many infants exposed to those bacteria? Usually, the main reason is social. The affected infants are likely to be poor. Because they are poor, they are likely to live with infected drinking water. Similarly, malnutrition may be the biological result of a diet that is poor in protein, but such a diet is usually also a cultural phenomenon, reflecting a society with classes of people with very unequal access to the necessities of life. In many ways, therefore, medical anthropology is developing in the direction of a "biocultural synthesis."[1]

The growth of jobs in medical anthropology is one of the more striking developments in contemporary anthropology. Medical anthropology has developed into a very popular specialty, and the Society for Medical Anthropology is now among the largest units in the American Anthropological Association.[2]

The medical profession's ways of treating illness may be able to treat some conditions well, but by itself the medical profession cannot tell us why some groups are more affected than others or why the effectiveness of treatment varies from group to group. This section discusses cultural variation in conceptions of health and illness, cultural universals and variables in how illness is treated, the political and social forces that affect health, and contributions of medical anthropology to the study and treatment of some diseases and health conditions.

26.1 Discuss cultural understandings of health and illness.

Cultural Understandings of Health and Illness

Medical researchers and medical practitioners in the United States and other Western societies do not exist in a social vacuum. Many of their ideas and practices are influenced by the culture in which they live. We may think of medicine as purely based on "fact," but it is clear on reflection that many ideas stem from the culture in which the researchers reside. Consider the recent shift in attitudes toward birth. Not so long ago in the United States, fathers were excluded from the birth, hospitals whisked the baby away from the mother and only brought the baby to her infrequently, and visitors (but not attending nurses and doctors) had to wear masks when holding the baby. Rationalizations were given for those practices, but looking back at them, they do not appear to be based on scientific evidence. Many medical anthropologists now argue that the *biomedical paradigm* (the system in which physicians are trained) itself needs to be understood as part of the culture.[3]

ethnomedicine The health-related beliefs, knowledge, and practices of a cultural group.

Discovering the health-related beliefs, knowledge, and practices of a cultural group—its **ethnomedicine**—is one of the goals of medical anthropology. How do cultures view health and illness? What are their theories about the causes of illness? Do those theories impact how illnesses are treated? What is the therapeutic process? Are there specialized medical practitioners, and how do they heal? Are there special medicines, and how are they administered? These are just some of the questions asked by the anthropological study of ethnomedicine.

Concepts of Balance or Equilibrium

Many cultures have the view that the body should be kept in equilibrium or balance. The balance may be between hot and cold, or wet and dry, as in many cultures of Latin America and the Caribbean.[4] The notion of balance is not limited to opposites. For example, the ancient Greek system of medicine, stemming from Hippocrates, assumed that there were four "humors"—blood, phlegm, yellow bile, and black bile—that must be kept in balance. These humors have hot and cold as well as wet and dry properties. The Greek medical system was widely diffused in Europe and spread to parts of the Islamic world. In Europe, the humoral medical system was dominant until the germ theory replaced it in the 1900s.[5] In the Ayurvedic system, whose practice dates back 4,000 years in North India, Pakistan, Bangladesh, Sri Lanka, and the Arab world, there are three humors (phlegm, bile, and flatulence), and a balance between hot and cold is also important.[6] The Chinese medical system, which dates back about 3,500 years, initially stressed the balance between the contrasting forces of *yin* and *yang* and later added the concept of humors, which were six in number in Chinese medicine.[7]

The concepts of hot and cold and *yin* and *yang* are illustrated in Emily Ahern's ethnographic description of the medical system of the Taiwanese Hokkien.[8] The body requires both hot and cold substances; when the body is out of balance, a lack of one substance can be restored by eating or drinking the missing substance. So, for example, when Ahern was faint with heat, she was told to drink some bamboo shoot soup because it was "cold." In the winter, you need more hot substances; in the summer, you want fewer. Some people can tolerate more imbalance than others; people who are older, for instance, can tolerate less imbalance than those who are young. A loss of blood means a loss of heat. So, for a month after childbirth, women eat mostly a soup made of chicken, wine, and sesame oil—all "hot" ingredients. Hot things to eat are generally oily, sticky, or come from animals; cold things tend to be soupy, watery, or made from plants.

The body also has *yin* and *yang* parts. The *yang* part is visible to the living. The *yin* part exists in the underworld in the shape of a house and tree. The roof of the house corresponds to a person's head, the walls to the skin, a woman's reproductive organs correspond to the flowers on the woman's tree, the roots of the tree to the legs, and so on. A shaman can enable villagers to go into a trance to look around in the underworld where the dead live. If a person has a health problem, a traveler may be sent to the underworld to see what is wrong with the person's *yin* house or tree. Fixing the *yin* house or tree should restore health to the *yang* part

Morning tai chi exercise in Shanghai, China.

of the body. The *yin* world is also where ghosts reside; they sometimes may cause illness. In that case, people may ask for help from powerful gods who reside in the *yang* world.

Supernatural Forces

The Taiwanese Hokkien believe that most illnesses have natural or physiological causes, but around the world, it is more common to believe that illnesses are caused by supernatural forces. In fact, in a cross-cultural study of 139 societies, George P. Murdock found that only two societies did not have the belief that gods or spirits could cause illness, making such a belief a near universal. And 56 percent of those sample societies thought that gods or spirits were the major causes of illness.[9] As we discussed in the chapter on religion and magic, sorcery and witchcraft are common in the world's societies. Although humans practice both sorcery and witchcraft for good or evil, making people ill is one of their major uses. Illness can also be thought of as caused by the loss of one's soul, fate, retribution for violation of a taboo, or contact with a polluting or taboo substance or object. Sorcery is believed to be a cause of illness by most societies on all continents; retribution because of violation of a taboo is also very frequent in all but one region of the world. The belief that soul loss can cause illness is absent in the area around the Mediterranean, uncommon in Africa, infrequent in the New World and the Pacific, and has its highest frequency in Eurasia.[10]

On Chuuk (Truk), an atoll in the central Pacific, serious illnesses and death are mainly believed to be the work of spirits. Occasionally, the spirits of relatives are to blame, although they usually do not cause serious damage. More often, illness is caused by the spirit of a particular locality or a ghost on a path at night.[11] Nowadays, one of two therapeutic options or their combination is often chosen—hospital medicine or Chuuk medicine. Chuuk medical treatment requires a careful evaluation of symptoms by the patient and the patient's relatives because different spirits inflict different symptoms. If the symptom match is clear, the patient may choose an appropriate Chuuk medical formula to cure the illness. The patient may also ask whether he or she has done something wrong, and if so, what might point to the appropriate spirit and countervailing formula. For example, there is a taboo on having sexual relations before going to sea. If a person who violated this prohibition becomes ill, the reef spirits will be suspected. The Chuuk medical formula is supposed to cure illness quickly and dramatically. For this reason, Chuuk patients ask for a discharge from a hospital if their condition does not improve quickly. If treatment fails, the Chuukese believe that they need to reevaluate the diagnosis, sometimes with the aid of a diviner.[12] In contrasting their theories of illness to the American germ theory, the people of Chuuk point out that although they have seen ghosts, they have never seen the germs that Americans talk about. Using both methods, some people recover and some do not, so the ultimate cause is a matter of faith.[13]

Among the Ojibwa, the most serious illnesses, the ones resistant to ordinary treatment, are thought to be due to retribution for doing wrong to another person, an animal, or a spirit. To cure such an illness, in yourself or in your children, you must reflect on your own conduct to see what you did wrong. Bad conduct cannot be withheld from the doctor or from the other people in the *wigwam*. On the contrary, only after confessing can medicine help.[14] The Hopi similarly believed that patients were responsible for their own illness, but the cause might be not just improper actions but also bad thoughts and anxiety. Witches could also cause illness, but the action of witches was most effective against people who were depressed or worried, so good thoughts ward off illness.[15]

The Biomedical Paradigm

In most societies, people simply think that their ideas about health and illness are true. Often people are not aware that there may be another way of viewing things until they confront another medical system. Western medical practice has spread widely. People with other medical systems have had to recognize that Western practitioners may consider their ideas about health and illness to be deficient, so they often need to decide which course (Western or non-Western) to follow in dealing with illness. Change, however, is not entirely one way. For example, for a long time, the Western medical profession disparaged the Chinese practice of acupuncture, but now more medical practitioners are recognizing that acupuncture may provide effective treatment of certain conditions.

Most medical anthropologists use the term **biomedicine** to refer to the dominant medical paradigm in Western cultures today, with the *bio* part of the word emphasizing the biological emphasis of this medical system. Biomedicine appears to focus on specific diseases and cures for those diseases. Health is not the focus, as it is thought to be the *absence* of disease. Diseases are considered to be largely from physical (e.g., trauma, accidents) or biological (e.g., bacteria, viruses, infection) causes, and there is relatively little interest in psychological factors affecting the person or the larger social and cultural systems in which they are embedded. Metaphorically, the body seems to be viewed as a "machine," and it is believed that technological advances can transcend our biological limitations. Doctors generally do not treat the whole body but tend to specialize, with the human body partitioned into zones that belong to different specialties. Death is seen as a failure, and biomedical practitioners do everything they can to prolong life, regardless of the circumstances under which the patient would live life.[16]

biomedicine The dominant medical paradigm in Western societies today

Applied Anthropology

Exploring Why an Applied Project Didn't Work

When applied projects do not succeed, it is important for researchers to try to figure out why. Part of the problem may be that the intended recipients' ideas about how things work may be very different from the researchers' ideas. Consider the following example.

In Guatemala, village health care workers were not only testing people for malaria but were also offering free antimalarial drugs. Yet only 20 percent of people with malaria symptoms took advantage of the free treatment. More surprisingly, most people with symptoms spent the equivalent of a day's wages to buy an injection that was not effective! Why?

Finding the answer was not easy. First, researchers designed interviews to elicit folk concepts about illness—kinds of illnesses, their symptoms, their causes, and how they are treated. They conducted interviews with a random sample of households to find out what illnesses people reported and what they did about them. Then they asked people to consider different hypothetical scenarios (vignettes) to find out what treatment they would choose. All of these methods were well thought out, but the answers still did not predict what people actually did when they thought they had malaria. Finally, the researchers devised precise comparisons of the kinds of pills the health care workers passed out and the pills and ampoules for injections that the drugstore sold. They compared them two at a time, varying dosages and brands. People did think that more pills were more effective, as indeed they were. But they thought that the colorfully wrapped store-bought pill was more effective than the equivalent white unwrapped free pill, even though it was not. They also thought that one store-bought ampoule used for injections, for which they would pay a day's wages, was more effective than four pills of any kind! In fact, one ampoule was equivalent to only one pill.

Applied researchers often use such trial-and-error methods to find out how to get the information they need. Methods that work in one field setting don't always work in others. Researchers must sometimes let the subjects structure their own answers. At other times, as in this case, they may have to make very specific comparisons to get predictive answers. The people in the Guatemala study didn't believe that the free pills were strong enough to work, so they didn't use them. More research would be needed to uncover why they did not believe the free pills were effective. Was it because they were free? Was it because the store-bought drugs were attractively packaged? Or was there a belief that injections work better than pills? That's what the research process is like; it always leads to new questions. Even if researchers think they understand what was happening in one area of Guatemala, comparative research would be needed to find out if these beliefs are found throughout Guatemala or other areas of Central and South America. Do they apply to other medicines as well?

Although we don't yet have answers to these more extensive questions, anthropologists have developed efficient methods for assessing variation in beliefs within and among cultures. We now know that if we ask one or two informants, we cannot assume that the answer is cultural. But that doesn't mean that we need to ask hundreds of people. If a belief is cultural and therefore commonly held, asking 10 to 20 individuals the same question is sufficient to provide the researcher with a high probability that an answer is correct. (The agreement among respondents is called cultural consensus.) So, for example, Guatemalan respondents mostly agreed about which illnesses were contagious. But they disagreed a lot about whether a particular disease should be treated with a "hot" or a "cold" remedy. Using cultural consensus methods, researchers can compare rural and urban residents, and they can also compare informants in different cultures. When we have more of these systematic comparisons, medical anthropologists and health practitioners may have a better understanding of how to implement medical care.

Sources: Romney et al. 1986; Weller 2009.

One of the most important discoveries that profoundly changed the course of Western medicine was Louis Pasteur's isolation of the organisms responsible for some major infectious diseases. Pasteur's discoveries stimulated the search for other disease-causing germs using scientific methods. But the *germ theory* of disease, although powerful, may have led researchers to pay less attention to the patient and the patient's social and cultural milieu.[17] For an example of how anthropologists try to redress the balance, see the box "Exploring Why an Applied Project Didn't Work."

Treatment of Illness

26.2 Discuss various approaches to studying treatment of illness.

Anthropologists who study diseases in this and other cultures can be roughly classified into two camps. First, there are those (the more relativistic) who think that the culture so influences disease symptoms, incidence, and treatment that there are few if any cultural universals about any illness. If each culture is unique, we should expect its conception and treatment of an illness to be unique too, not like beliefs and practices in other cultures. Second, there are those (the more universalistic) who see cross-cultural similarities in the conception and treatment of illness, despite the unique qualities (particularly in the belief system) of each culture. For example, native remedies may contain chemicals that are the same as, or similar in effect to, chemicals used in remedies by Western biomedicine.[18] Readers should note that our classification here of medical anthropologists is a crude one; many medical anthropologists do not fall unambiguously into one or the other group. And the reality might be that a given culture is very much like other cultures in some respects but unique in other respects.

In their extensive research on Maya ethnomedicine, Elois Ann Berlin and Brent Berlin make a strong case that, although studies of the Maya have emphasized beliefs about illness that are based on supernatural causes, a good deal of Maya ethnomedicine is about natural conditions, their signs and symptoms, and the remedies used to deal with those conditions. In regard to gastrointestinal diseases, the Berlins found that the Maya have a wide-ranging and accurate understanding of anatomy, physiology, and symptoms. Furthermore, the remedies they use, including recommendations for food, drink, and herbal medicines, have properties that are not that different from those of the biomedical profession.[19]

Carole Browner also suggests that the emphasis on "hot-cold" theories of illness in Latin America has been overemphasized to the neglect of other factors that influence choices about reproductive health and female health problems. In a study of the medical system in a highland Oaxacan community, Browner finds that certain plants are used to expel substances from the uterus—to facilitate labor at full term, to produce an abortion, or to induce menstrual flow. Other plants are used to retain things in the uterus—to prevent excess blood loss during menstruation, to help healing after delivery, and to prevent miscarriage. Most of these plant remedies appear to work.[20]

The biomedical establishment has become increasingly aware of the value of studying the "traditional" medicinal remedies discovered or invented by people around the world. In studying the indigenous medicines of the Hausa of Nigeria, Nina Etkin and Paul Ross asked individuals to describe the physical attributes of more than 600 plants and their possible medicinal uses, more than 800 diseases and symptoms, and more than 5,000 prepared medicines. Although many medicines were used for treating sorcery, spirit aggression, or witchcraft, most medicines were used for illnesses regarded by the Hausa as having natural causes. Malaria is a serious endemic medical problem in the Hausa region, as in many areas of Africa. The Hausa use approximately 72 plant remedies for conditions connected with malaria—among them anemia, intermittent fever, and jaundice. Experimental treatment of malaria in laboratory animals supports the efficacy of many of the Hausa remedies. But perhaps the most important part of the Etkin and Ross findings is the role of diet. Although most medical research does not consider the possible medical efficacy of the *foods* that people eat in combating illness, food is, of course, consumed in much larger quantities and more often than medicine. It is noteworthy, therefore, that the Hausa eat many plants with antimalarial properties; in fact, dietary consumption of these plants appears to be greatest during the time of year when the risk of malarial infection is

Listen to the Audio: The Benefits of Blueberries and the Bitterness of Broccoli

at its highest. Recent research has also discovered that foods and spices like garlic, onions, cinnamon, ginger, and pepper have antiviral or antibacterial properties.[21]

Medical Practitioners

In our society, we may be so used to consulting a full-time medical specialist (if we do not feel better quickly) that we tend to assume that biomedical treatment is the only effective medical treatment. If we are given a medicine, we expect it to have the appropriate medical effect and make us feel better. So, many in the biomedical system, practitioners and patients alike, are perplexed by the seeming effectiveness of other medical systems that are based in part on symbolic or ritual healing. As we noted earlier, many native plants have been shown to be medically effective, but their use is often accompanied by singing, dancing, noise making, or rituals. Our difficulty in understanding the healing in such practices probably stems from the assumption in biomedicine that the mind is fundamentally different from the body. Yet there is increasing evidence that the *form* of treatment may be just as important as the *content* of treatment.[22]

The practitioners who deal with more than the body are sometimes referred to as *personalistic* practitioners. In a personalistic view, illness may be viewed as being due to something in one's social life being out of order. The cause could be retribution by gods or spirits for one's own bad behavior or thoughts, or the work of an angry individual practicing sorcery or witchcraft. A bad social situation or a bad relationship may be thought of as provoking physical symptoms because of anxiety or stress. In societies with occupational specialization, priests, who are formally trained full-time religious practitioners, may be asked to convey messages or requests for healing to higher powers.[23] Societies with beliefs in sorcery and witchcraft as causes of illness typically have practitioners who are believed to be able to use magic in reverse—that is, to undo the harm invoked by sorcerers and witches. Sometimes sorcerers or witches themselves may be asked to reverse illnesses caused by others. However, they may not be sought out because they are often feared and have relatively low status.[24] Shamans are charismatic leaders who perform many functions in societies lacking political hierarchies, but perhaps one of their most important functions is their role as medical practitioner.[25] Shamans, mediums, sorcerers, and priests are usually acting as personalistic healers. A more naturalistic view of illness, common to most physicians as well as chemists and herbalists, is that certain substances or treatments will fix the problem.[26]

The Shaman The *shaman*, usually a male part-time specialist, is often involved in healing.[27] Westerners often call shamans "witch doctors" because they don't believe that shamans can effectively cure people. Do shamans effectively cure people? Actually, Westerners are not the only skeptics. A Native American named Quesalid from the Kwakiutl of the Pacific Northwest didn't believe that shamanism was effective either. So he began to associate with the shamans to spy on them and was taken into their group. In his first lessons, he learned

> *a curious mixture of pantomime, prestidigitation, and empirical knowledge, including the art of simulating fainting and nervous fits, . . . sacred song, the technique for inducing vomiting, rather precise notions of auscultation or listening to sounds within the body to detect disorders and obstetrics, and the use of "dreamers," that is, spies who listen to private conversations and secretly convey to the shaman bits of information concerning the origins and symptoms of the ills suffered by different people. Above all, he learned the ars magna. . . . The shaman hides a little tuft of down in the corner of his mouth, and he throws it up, covered with blood at the proper moment—after having bitten his tongue or made his gums bleed—and solemnly presents it to his patient and the onlookers as the pathological foreign body extracted as a result of his sucking and manipulations.*[28]

A Mongolian shaman kisses niece during healing.

His suspicions were confirmed, but his first curing was a success. The patient had heard that Quesalid had joined the shamans and believed that only he could heal him. Quesalid remained with the shamans for the four-year apprenticeship, during which he could take no fee, and he became increasingly aware that his methods worked. He visited other villages, competed with other shamans in curing hopeless cases and won, and finally seemed convinced that his curing system was more valid than those of other shamans. Instead of denouncing the trickery of shamans, he continued to practice as a renowned shaman.[29]

After working with shamans in Africa, E. Fuller Torrey, a psychiatrist and anthropologist, concluded that they use the same mechanisms and techniques to cure patients as psychiatrists and achieve about the same results. He isolated four categories used by healers the world over:

1. *The naming process.* If a disease has a name—"neurasthenia" or "phobia" or "possession by an ancestral spirit" will do—then it is curable; the patient realizes that the doctor understands his case.
2. *The personality of the doctor.* Those who demonstrate some empathy, nonpossessive warmth, and genuine interest in the patient get results.
3. *The patient's expectations.* One way of raising the patient's expectations of being cured is the trip to the doctor; the longer the trip—to the Mayo Clinic, Menninger Clinic, Delphi, or Lourdes—the easier the cure. An impressive setting (the medical center) and impressive paraphernalia (the stethoscope, the couch, attendants in uniform, the rattle, the whistle, the drum, the mask) also raise the patient's expectations. The healer's training is important. And high fees also help to raise a patient's expectations. (The Paiute doctors always collect their fees before starting a cure; if they don't, it is believed that they will fall ill.)
4. *Curing techniques.* Drugs, shock treatment, conditioning techniques, and so on have long been used in many different parts of the world.[30]

Biomedical research is not unaware of the effect of the mind on healing. In fact, considerable evidence has accumulated that psychological factors can be very important in illness. Patients who believe that medicine will help them often recover quickly even if the medicine is only a sugar pill or a medicine not particularly relevant to their condition. Such effects are called *placebo* effects.[31] Placebos do not just have psychological effects. Although the mechanisms are not well understood, they may also alter body chemistry and bolster the immune system.[32]

Shamans may coexist with medical doctors. Don Antonio, a respected Otomi Indian shaman in central Mexico, has many patients, perhaps not as many as before modern medicine, but still plenty. In his view, when he was born, God gave him his powers to cure, but his powers are reserved for removing "evil" illnesses (those caused by sorcerers). "Good" illnesses can be cured by herbs and medicine, and he refers patients with those illnesses to medical doctors; he believes that doctors are more effective than he could be in those cases. The doctors, however, do not seem to refer any patients to Don Antonio or other shamans.[33]

Physicians The most important full-time medical practitioner in the biomedical system is the physician, and the patient-physician relationship is central. In the ideal scheme of things, the physician is viewed as having the ability, with some limits, of being able to treat illness, alleviate suffering, and prolong the life of the patient, as well as offering promises of patient confidentiality and privacy. The patient relies on the physician's knowledge, skill, and ethics. Consistent with the biomedical paradigm, doctors tend to treat patients as having "conditions" rather than as complete people. Physicians presumably rely on science for authoritative knowledge, but they place a good deal of importance on the value of their own clinical experience. Often, physicians consider their own observations of the patient to be more valuable than the reports by the patient. Because patients commonly go to physicians to solve a particular condition or sickness, physicians tend to try to do something about it even in the face of uncertainty. Physicians tend to rely on technology for diagnoses and treatment and place relatively low value on talking with patients. In fact, physicians tend to give patients relatively little information, and they may not listen very well.[34]

Despite the importance of physicians in biomedicine, patients do not always seek physician care. In fact, one-third of the population of the United States regularly consults with alternative practitioners, such as acupuncturists or chiropractors, often unbeknownst to the physician. Somewhat surprisingly, individuals with more education are more likely to seek alternative care.[35]

Political and Economic Influences on Health

26.3 Describe political and economic influences on health.

People with more social, economic, and political power in a society are generally healthier.[36] Inequality in health in socially stratified societies is not surprising. The poor usually have more exposure to disease because they live in more crowded conditions, and the poor are more likely to lack the resources to get quality care. For many diseases, health problems, and death rates, incidence or relative frequency varies directly with social class. In the United Kingdom, for example, people in the higher social classes are less likely to have headaches, bronchitis, pneumonia, heart disease, arthritis, injuries, and mental disorders, to name just a few of the differences.[37] Ethnic differences also predict health inequities. In the United States recently, the differences between African Americans and European Americans in health have narrowed somewhat in some respects, but those favoring European Americans are still substantial. As of 1987, the difference in life expectancy was seven years, As of 2009, the difference in life expectancy was about four years. Infant mortality has not shown improvement. In 1987, African American infant mortality was about twice the rate for European American infants; in 2007, the ratio was 2.4.[38] Robert Hahn has estimated that poverty accounted for about 19 percent of the overall mortality in the United States.[39]

Inequities, because of class and ethnicity, are not limited to within-society differences. Power and economic differentials *among* societies also have profound health consequences. Over the course of European exploration and expansion, indigenous peoples died in enormous numbers from introduced diseases, wars, and conquests; they had their lands expropriated and diminished in size and quality. When incorporated into colonial territories or into countries, indigenous people usually become minorities, and they are almost always very poor. These conditions of life not only affect the incidence of disease, they also tend to lead to greater substance abuse, violence, depression, and other mental pathologies.[40]

Health Conditions and Diseases

26.4 Discuss a sampling of health conditions and diseases studied by medical anthropologists.

Medical anthropologists have studied an enormous variety of conditions. What follows is only a small sampling.

AIDS

Epidemics of infectious disease have killed millions of people within short periods of time throughout recorded history. The Black Death—bubonic plague—killed between 25 percent and 50 percent of the population of Europe, perhaps 75 million people, during the 14th century; an epidemic during the 6th century killed an estimated 100 million people in the Middle East, Asia, and Europe. Less noted in our history books, but also devastating, was the enormous depopulation that accompanied the expansion of Europeans into the New World and the Pacific from the 1500s on. Not only were people killed directly by European conquerors, millions also died from introduced diseases to which the natives

Millions of children in sub-Saharan Africa are orphaned because of AIDS. These orphaned children in Uganda look on during a visit by Britain's Queen Elizabeth to their center.

had little or no resistance, diseases such as smallpox and measles that the Europeans brought with them but were no longer dying from.

The current state of medical science and technology may lull us into thinking that epidemics are a thing of the past. But the sudden emergence of the disease we call **AIDS (acquired immune deficiency syndrome)** reminds us that new diseases, or new varieties of old diseases, can appear at any time. Like all other organisms, disease-causing organisms also evolve. The human immunodeficiency virus (HIV) that causes AIDS emerged only relatively recently. Viruses and bacteria are always mutating, and new strains emerge that are initially a plague on our genetic resistance and on medical efforts to contain them.

Millions of people around the world now have the symptoms of AIDS, and millions more are infected with HIV but do not know they are infected. As of 2011, 34 million adults and children in the world were living with HIV/AIDS.[41] There are a few signs of improvement since the beginning of the epidemic. The percentage of people newly infected globally is now stable. Some countries and regions have improved in countering AIDS deaths with prevention efforts—notable examples are in the Caribbean, where deaths declined 48 percent from 2005 to 2011, and in sub-Saharan Africa, where they declined by nearly 33 percent in the same period. In addition, the number of new cases worldwide each year has gone down, and also fewer people are dying from AIDS. However, some regions of the world such as Eastern Europe, Central Asia, the Middle East, and North Africa have gotten worse. And despite improvements in sub-Saharan Africa, the region still has the majority of HIV cases in the world.

AIDS (acquired immune deficiency syndrome) A disease caused by the HIV virus

AIDS is a frightening epidemic not only because of its death toll, but also because it takes a long time (on average four years) after exposure for symptoms to appear. This means that many people who have been infected by HIV but do not know they are infected may continue, unknowingly, to transmit the virus to others.[42]

Transmission occurs mostly via sexual encounters, through semen and blood. Drug users may also transmit HIV by way of contaminated needles. Transmission by blood transfusion has been virtually eliminated in this and other societies by medical screening of blood supplies. In some countries, however, there is still no routine screening of blood prior to transfusions. HIV may be passed from a pregnant woman to her offspring through the placenta and after birth through her breast milk. The rate of transmission between a mother and her baby is from 20 percent to 40 percent. Children are also at great risk because they are likely to be orphaned by a parent's death from AIDS. At the turn of the 21st century, approximately 14 million children were parentless because of AIDS.[43]

Many people think of AIDS as only a medical problem that requires only a medical solution, without realizing that behavioral, cultural, and political issues need to be addressed as well. It is true that developing a vaccine or a drug to prevent people from getting AIDS and finding a permanent cure for those who have it will ultimately solve the problem. But, for a variety of reasons, we can expect that the medical solution alone will not be sufficient, at least not for a while. First, to be effective worldwide, or even within a country, a vaccine has to be inexpensive and relatively easy to produce in large quantities; the same is true of any medical treatment. Second, governments around the world have to be willing and able to spend the money and hire the personnel necessary to manage an effective program.[44] Third, future vaccination and treatment will require the people at risk to be willing to get vaccinated and treated, which is not always the case. Witness the fact that a considerable number of parents in the United States refuse to have their children vaccinated against some childhood diseases. Researchers who have studied the reasons for parental refusal find that the refusers are likely to believe that vaccines are not necessary to protect their child or that vaccines are not safe. Although it may seem counterintuitive, vaccine refusers are more likely to be of higher status and education.[45]

A significant barrier to HIV/AIDS treatment has been the expense of the needed drugs. Fortunately, the Clinton Health Access Initiative negotiated a much-reduced cost for 70 poorer countries.[46] The reduced cost of less than $200 per year is still not cheap for people with little money, but the lower cost makes it possible for aid organizations to foot the bills.

Listen to the Audio: Bolivia's Traditions, Diversity Impede AIDS Fight

In the meantime, the risk of HIV infection can be reduced only by changes in social, particularly sexual, behavior. But to persuade people to change their sexual behavior, it is necessary to find out exactly what they do sexually, why they do what they do, and to evaluate the efficacy of intervention programs.

Research so far suggests that different sexual patterns are responsible for HIV transmission in different parts of the world. In the United States, England, northern Europe, Australia, and Latin America, the recipients of anal intercourse, particularly men, are the most likely individuals to acquire HIV infection; vaginal intercourse can also transmit the infection, usually from the man to the woman. Needle sharing can transmit the infection, too. In Africa, the most common mode of transmission is vaginal intercourse, and so women get infected more commonly in Africa than elsewhere.[47] In fact, in Africa there are slightly more cases of HIV in women as compared with men.[48]

It is important to recognize these differences because prevention outcomes that work for some epidemics may not work for others. HIV epidemics can be divided into those that are concentrated in some populations such as sex workers, drug users, and men having sex with other men, or more generalized. Promotion of condom use has been effective in some cases in some specialized epidemics, such as in Thailand and Cambodia where condom use became required in brothels. But generalized epidemics of AIDS such as those in Africa occur among the majority populations, most of whom are heterosexual married people.[49] Prevention programs have largely stressed condom use, testing for HIV, and treatment for sexually transmitted infections. In some places such programs have been successful. Perhaps for this reason, such programs have been the predominant form of intervention. However, some recent critics have argued that the predominant programs are not effective where the epidemic is generalized, and it is time to try new methods.[50] Some research even shows negative effects. For example, while people testing positive are more likely to use condoms, there is some evidence that people who test negative (the majority of those tested) are more likely to engage in risky behavior. Edward Green points out that AIDS-prevention community has failed to consider the importance of trying to change sexual behavior, either because they believe it won't work or because they do not believe in curtailing sexual freedom. But the main successes have come from countries that have employed low-cost education programs stressing abstinence and avoidance of multiple sexual partners. Uganda showed remarkable change. In just 10 years from 1992 to 2002 prevalence of HIV declined from 18 percent to 6 percent. This corresponded with a dramatic reduction in premarital sex and a decline in extramarital sex.[51] There is also increasing recognition that prevention groups need to work with local leaders, including traditional healers, to figure out the best ways to proceed.

Some researchers are arguing that although the immediate cause of HIV infection may be mostly related to sexual practice, larger political and social issues, such as poverty and gender inequality, increase the likelihood of such infection. For example, sexually transmitted diseases increase the risk of HIV infection three to five times, but those who are poor are less likely to get adequate treatment. Gender inequality is likely to increase the likelihood that women have to submit to unsafe sex, and women are even less likely than men to have access to adequate medical care.[52]

As of now, there are only two known ways to reduce the likelihood of sexual HIV transmission. One way is to abstain from sexual intercourse; the other is to use condoms. Male circumcision now appears to decrease the risk of HIV infection, but studies have not yet evaluated long-term effects.[53] Educational programs that teach how AIDS spreads and what one can do about it may reduce the spread somewhat, but such programs may fail where people have incompatible beliefs and attitudes about sexuality. For example, people in some central African societies believe that deposits of semen after conception are necessary for a successful pregnancy and generally enhance a woman's health and ability to reproduce. It might be expected then that people who have these beliefs about semen would choose not to use condoms; after all, condoms in their view are a threat to public health.[54] Educational programs may also emphasize the wrong message. Promiscuity may increase the risk of HIV transmission, so hardly anyone would question the wisdom of advertising to reduce the number of sexual partners. And, at least in the homosexual community in the United States, individuals report fewer sexual partners than in the past. What was not anticipated, however, was that individuals in monogamous relationships, who may feel safe, are less likely to use condoms or to avoid the riskiest sexual practices. Needless to say, sex with a regular partner who is infected is not safe![55] In what may seem like something of a paradox, the United Nations observed that, for most women in the world today, the major risk factor for being infected with HIV is being married.[56] It is not marriage *per se* that heightens the risk of HIV infection; rather, the proximate cause may be the lower likelihood of condom use or less abstinence by a married couple.

The stigmas associated with AIDS also hinder efforts to reduce its spread. In some societies, there is the widespread belief that homosexual men are particularly likely to get infected.[57] In other societies, AIDS may be thought to be due to promiscuity. If a woman asks a man to use a condom, she may be assumed to be a prostitute. In addition, many people mistakenly fear even proximity to AIDS victims, as if any kind of contact could result in infection.

To solve the problem of AIDS, we may hope that medical science will develop an effective and inexpensive vaccination or treatment that all can afford. There is a vaccine that seems to reduce HIV infection in monkeys to hardly detectable levels.[58] Perhaps soon there will be a similar vaccine for humans. In the meantime, we can try to understand why people engage in certain risky sexual practices. Such understanding may allow us to design educational and other programs that would help inhibit the spread of AIDS.

Mental and Emotional Disorders

Diagnosing mental or emotional disorders in one culture is difficult enough; diagnosing them in others poses much greater difficulty. Many researchers start with Western categories of mental illness and try to apply them elsewhere without first trying to understand native conceptions of mental disorder. In addition, "mental" and "physical" disorders are rarely separate. For example, a host of illnesses can produce a loss of energy that some may see as depression, and fear or anger can produce physical symptoms such as a heart attack.[59]

When Western anthropologists first started describing mental illness in non-Western societies, there seemed to be unique illnesses in different cultures. These are referred to as *culture-bound syndromes*. For example, a mental disorder called *pibloktoq* occurred among some Eskimo adults of Greenland, usually women, who became oblivious to their surroundings and acted in agitated, eccentric ways. They might strip themselves naked and wander across the ice and over hills until they collapsed of exhaustion. Another disorder, *amok*, occurred in Malaya, Indonesia, and New Guinea, usually among males. John Honigmann characterized it as a "destructive maddened excitement ... beginning with depression and followed by a period of brooding and withdrawal [culminating in] the final mobilization of tremendous energy during which the 'wild man' runs destructively berserk."[60] *Anorexia nervosa*, the disorder involving aversion to food, may be unique to the relatively few societies that idealize slimness.[61] (See the box "Eating Disorders, Biology, and the Cultural Construction of Beauty.")

Some scholars think that each society's views of personality and concepts of mental illness have to be understood in their own terms. Western understandings and concepts cannot be applied to other cultures. For example, Catherine Lutz suggested that the Western concept of depression cannot be applied to the Pacific island of Ifaluk. The people there have many words for thinking or feeling about "loss and helplessness," but all their words are related to a specific need for someone, such as when someone dies or leaves the island. Such thoughts and feelings of loss are considered perfectly normal, and there is no word in their language for general hopelessness or "depression."[62] Therefore, Lutz questioned the applicability of the Western concept of depression as well as other Western psychiatric categories.

Other researchers are not so quick to dismiss the possible universality of psychiatric categories. Some think they have found a considerable degree of cross-cultural uniformity in conceptions of mental illness. Jane Murphy studied descriptions by the Inuit and the Yoruba,

Applied Anthropology

Eating Disorders, Biology, and the Cultural Construction of Beauty

Cultures differ about what they consider beautiful. In many cultures, fat people are considered more beautiful than thin people. Melvin Ember did fieldwork years ago on the islands of American Samoa. When he returned to the main island after three months on a distant island, a prominent chief said: "You look good. You gained weight." In reality, he had lost 30 pounds! The chief clearly thought that fat was better than thin and was trying to say something nice. Among the Azawagh Arabs of Niger, fatness was not merely valued and considered beautiful; great care was taken to ensure that young girls became fat by insisting and sometimes forcing them to drink large quantities of milk-based porridge.

Around the world, fatness is generally considered more desirable than thinness not only because it is considered more beautiful but also because it is thought to be a marker of health and fertility. This view is in strong contrast to the ideal in the United States and many other Western societies, where fatness is thought to be unattractive and to reflect poor health. Thinness, particularly in the upper classes, is considered beautiful. How can we explain these differences in what is considered beautiful?

A common assumption is that fatness will be valued in societies subject to food scarcity. However, cross-cultural research suggests that the picture is more complicated. It appears that many societies with unpredictable resources actually value thinness, particularly in societies that have little or no technological means of storing food. At first glance, this seems puzzling. Shouldn't an individual who stores calories on the body be better off than an individual who is thin when facing starvation? Perhaps. But 10 thin individuals will generally consume less than 10 heavier people, so perhaps there is a group advantage to being thin. Indeed, many societies with frequent episodes of famine encourage fasting or eating very light meals, as among the Gurage of Ethiopia.

Cultures vary in their ideals of beauty, and ideals change over time. In the United States in the 1950s, "somewhat plump" was idealized. Beginning in the 1960s, thinness became idealized.

The strongest cross-cultural predictor of valuing fatness in women is what is often referred to as "machismo." Societies with a strong emphasis on male aggression and sexuality are the most likely to value fatness in women; those with little machismo value thinness. Why? One theory is that machismo actually reflects male insecurity and fear of women. Such men may not be looking for closeness or intimacy with their wives, but they may want to show how potent they are by having lots of children. If fatness suggests fertility, men may look for wives who are fatter. Consistent with this idea, the ideal of thinness in women became more common in North America with the rise of women's movements in the 1920s and late 1960s. Consider that Marilyn Monroe epitomized beauty in the 1950s; she was well-rounded, not thin. Thin became more popular only when women began to question early marriage and having many children. Behaviors associated with machismo became less acceptable at those times.

Cultural beliefs about what is considered a beautiful body impose enormous pressures on females to achieve the ideal body type—whether it be fat or thin. In the United States and other Western countries, the effort to be thin can be carried to an extreme, resulting in the eating disorders anorexia and bulimia. The irony of "thinness" being idealized in the United States and other Western countries is that obesity is becoming more common in those societies. As of 2010, the incidence of obesity in adults increased in the United States to 36 percent, and medical researchers worried about the increase in heart disease and diabetes resulting from obesity. Whether or not obesity is a result of an eating disorder (in the psychological sense) is more debatable. Researchers are finding biological causes of obesity, such as resistance to the hormone leptin, which regulates appetite, suggesting that much of the obesity "epidemic" has biological causes. Still, fast food, increasing sedentariness, and extremely large portion sizes are probably contributing factors also.

Sources: P. J. Brown and Sweeney 2009; Loustaunau and Sobo 1997, 85; N. Wolf 1991; R. Popenoe 2004; C. R. Ember et al. 2005; J. M. Friedman 2003; Ogden et al. 2012.

in Nigeria, of severely disturbed people. She found that their descriptions not only were similar to each other but also corresponded to North American descriptions of schizophrenia. The Inuit word for "crazy" is ***nuthkavihak***. They use this word when something inside a person seems to be out of order. ***Nuthkavihak*** people are described as talking to themselves, believing themselves to be animals, making strange faces, becoming violent, and so on. The Yoruba have a word, ***were***, for people who are "insane." People described as ***were*** sometimes hear voices, laugh when there is nothing to laugh at, and take up weapons and suddenly hit people.[63] More recently, a careful study of symptoms of schizophrenia in the Republic of Palau, which has one of the highest incidences of schizophrenia in the world, finds that principal symptoms and their relationships are comparable to patterns found in New York.[64]

Robert Edgerton found similarities in conceptions of mental illness in four East African societies. He noted not only that the four groups essentially agreed on the symptoms of psychosis but also that the symptoms they described were the same ones that are considered psychotic here.[65] Edgerton believed that the lack of exact translation in different cultures, such as the one pointed out by Lutz regarding Ifaluk, does not make comparison impossible. If researchers can come to understand another culture's views of personality and if the researchers can manage to communicate these views to people of other cultures, we can compare the described cases and try to discover what may be universal and what may be found only in some cultures.[66]

Some mental illnesses, such as schizophrenia and depression, seem so widespread that many researchers think they are probably universal. Consistent with this idea is the fact that schizophrenic individuals in different cultures seem to share the same patterns of distinctive eye movements.[67] Still, cultural factors may influence the risk of developing such diseases, the specific symptoms that are expressed, and the effectiveness of different kinds of treatment.[68] There may be some truly culture-bound (nearly unique) syndromes, but others thought at one time to be unique may be culturally varying expressions of conditions that occur widely. *Pibloktoq,* for example, may be a kind of hysteria.[69]

Biological, but not necessarily genetic, factors may be very important in the etiology of some of the widespread disorders such as schizophrenia.[70] With regard to hysteria, Anthony Wallace theorized that nutritional factors such as calcium deficiency may cause hysteria and that dietary improvement may account for the decline of this illness in the Western world since the 19th century.[71] By the early 20th century, the discovery of the value of good nutrition, coupled with changes in social conditions, had led many people to drink milk, eat vitamin-rich foods, and spend time in the sun (although spending a lot of time in the sun is no longer recommended because of the risk of skin cancer). These changes in diet and activity increased the intake of vitamin D and helped people to maintain a proper calcium level. Consequently, the number of cases of hysteria declined.

Regarding *pibloktoq,* Wallace suggested that a complex set of related variables may cause the disease. The Inuit live in an environment that supplies only a minimum amount of calcium. A diet low in calcium could result in two different conditions. One condition, rickets, would produce physical deformities potentially fatal in the Inuit hunting economy. People whose genetic makeup made them prone to rickets would be eliminated from the population through natural selection. A low level of calcium in the blood could also cause muscular spasms known as tetany. Tetany, in turn, may cause emotional and mental disorientation similar to the symptoms of *pibloktoq.* Such attacks last for only a relatively short time and are not fatal, so people who developed *pibloktoq* would have a far greater chance of surviving in the Arctic environment with a calcium-deficient diet than would people who had rickets.

Although researchers disagree about the comparability of mental illnesses among cultures, most agree that effective treatment requires understanding a culture's ideas about a mental illness—why people think it occurs, what treatments are believed to be effective, and how families and others respond to those afflicted.[72]

Susto *Susto* is often described as a "folk illness" or a culture-bound syndrome because there doesn't seem to be any direct counterpart in biomedical terms. In many areas of Latin America, it is believed that a person suffers susto, or becomes *astudado,* when a nonmaterial essence from the body becomes detached during sleep or after suffering a fright. This essence is either held captive by supernatural forces or wanders freely outside the body.[73] Susto patients are described as restless during sleep, and listless, depressed, debilitated, and indifferent to food and hygiene during the day. Some researchers have suggested that people labeled as suffering from susto may in fact be suffering from mental illness. Believing that such conclusions were incomplete or premature, Arthur Rubel, Carl O'Nell, and Rolando Collado-Ardón designed a three-culture comparative study to evaluate whether susto victims were suffering from social, psychological, or organic problems. They compared individuals suffering from susto to other individuals matched by culture, age, and sex who defined themselves as "sick" when they came to health clinics (but who did not claim susto as their illness). The three cultures were Chichimec, Zapotec, and a Spanish-speaking mestizo community.[74]

From previous study of susto victims, Rubel and his colleagues hypothesized that susto was likely to strike people in socially stressful situations where they may think they are inadequate in required roles. For example, two cases of susto occurred among women who desperately wanted more children, but each had had a number of miscarriages (one had seven, the other two). In addition to measuring social stress, the researchers also had physicians evaluate organic problems with reference to the World Health Organization's *International Classification of Diseases.* Degree of psychiatric impairment was judged in an interview based on questions other researchers had previously developed. And seven years after the study, the researchers found out which, if any, of the studied individuals had died.

The research results supported the social stress hypothesis: Susto victims were significantly more likely to feel inadequate about social roles. The researchers did not expect to find evidence that susto victims had more psychiatric impairment or more organic disease. However, to their surprise, susto victims were also more likely to have had serious physical health problems. In fact, susto victims were more likely to have died in the seven years after the study. It is hard to say whether the susto victims had more disease because they were debilitated by susto or were more prone to susto because they were physically sicker. The researchers guess that because many of the conditions that created social role impairment were of long duration (such as many miscarriages), it seemed likely that susto itself put its victims at risk for biological diseases.[75]

Depression It is estimated that hundreds of millions of people suffer from depression. Depressive symptoms include feelings of hopelessness and sadness, often with thoughts of death. There are often other symptoms as well—weight loss, fatigue, and disrupted sleep.[76] Cultures appear to vary in how depression is expressed; in many societies the somatic symptoms are more often presenting symptoms.[77] Just as one kind of stress seems to be involved in the folk illness susto, researchers have considered the role of other kinds of stress in producing various other forms of mental illness, such as depression. One of the most important stressors may be economic deprivation. Many studies have found that the lower classes in socially stratified societies have much higher proportions of all kinds of mental illness. Acute stressors like death of a loved one, divorce, loss of a job, or a natural disaster predict higher rates of mental illness for all social classes; however, these events take more of a toll in lower-class families.[78]

In a study designed to evaluate the effect of these and other stressors on the prevalence of depression in an African American community in a southern city, William Dressler combined fieldwork methods and hypothesis testing to try to better understand depression.[79] Although many studies rely on treatment or hospitalization rates, Dressler decided that such rates drastically underestimate the incidence of depression, inasmuch as many people do not seek treatment. He decided to rely on a symptom checklist, which asked such questions as how often in the last week a person felt like crying, felt lonely, or felt hopeless about the future. Although such checklists do not provide clear divisions for characterizing someone as mildly depressed or seriously depressed, they do allow researchers to compare people along a continuum.

Dressler measured a variety of different possible stressors, including life crises, economic worries, perceived racial inequality, and problems in social roles, and found that some of the objective stressors, like life crises and unemployment, predict depression in the expected direction only in the lower classes. That is, for lower-class African Americans, unemployment and other life crises predicted more depression, but that result was not found among middle- and upper-class individuals. These results are consistent with previous findings that many stressors take more of a toll among poorer individuals. On the other hand, more subjective economic stressors, such as feeling you are not making enough money, predict depression across all class lines. So does "social role" stress, such as thinking you are missing promotions because you are African American or thinking that your spouse expects too much.[80]

Undernutrition

What people eat is intrinsically connected to their survival and the ability of a population to reproduce itself, so we would expect that the ways people obtain, distribute, and consume food have been generally adaptive.[81] For example, the human body cannot synthesize eight

Read the Document: Were Early Agriculturalists Less Healthy than Food Collectors?

A Malawian child collecting food at a distribution center.

amino acids. Meat can provide all of these amino acids, and combinations of particular plants can also provide them for a complete complement of protein. The combination of maize and beans in many traditional Native American diets, or *tortillas* and *frijoles* in Mexico, can provide all the needed amino acids. In places where wheat (often made into bread) is the staple, dairy products combined with wheat also provide complete protein.[82] Even the way that people have prepared for scarcity, such as breaking up into mobile bands, cultivating crops that can better withstand drought, and preserving food in case of famine, are probably adaptive practices in unpredictable environments. Geneticists have proposed that populations in famine-prone areas may have had genetic selection for "thrifty genes"—genes that allow individuals to need a minimum of food and store the extra in fatty tissue to get them past serious scarcity.[83] Customary diets and genetic changes may have been selected over a long stretch of time, but many serious nutritional problems observed today are due to rapid culture change. For instance, although "thrifty genes" may be adaptive during famine, they may become maladaptive when food is readily available. The high prevalence of diabetes and obesity in many populations today may be linked to such genes.

Often the switch to commercial or cash crops has harmful effects in another direction—creating undernutrition. For example, when the farmer-herders of the arid region in northeastern Brazil started growing sisal, a drought-resistant plant used for making twine and rope, many of them abandoned subsistence agriculture. The small landholders used most of their land for sisal growing and, when the price of sisal fell, they had to work as laborers for others to try to make ends meet. Food then had to be mostly bought, but if a laborer or sisal grower didn't earn enough, there was not enough food for the whole family.

Analysis of allocation of food in some households by Daniel Gross and Barbara Underwood suggests that the laborer and his wife received adequate nutrition, but the children often received much less than required. Lack of adequate nutrition usually results in retarded weight and height in children. As is commonly the case when there is substantial social inequality, the children from lower-income groups weigh substantially less than those from higher-income groups. But even though there were some economic differences before sisal production, the effects on nutrition appeared negligible before, judging from the fact that there was little or no difference in weight among adults from higher and lower socioeconomic positions who grew up prior to sisal production. But after sisal production, 45 percent of the children from lower economic groups were undernourished as compared with 23 percent of those children from the higher economic groups.[84]

People who now depend on buying food for their subsistence are subject to global economic changes as well. In 2008, not only was there a global economic recession, but there were serious increases in the cost of food. There were riots and demonstrations in over 50 countries, and it was estimated that 40 million more people became undernourished in 2008 on top of the already existing 923 million people.[85] As of 2010–2012, there was slight improvement, but 12 percent of the world's population was estimated to be undernourished.[86]

This is not to say that commercialization is always deleterious to adequate nutrition. For example, in the Highlands of New Guinea, there is evidence that the nutrition of children improved when families started growing coffee for sale. However, in this case, the families still had land to grow some crops for consumption. The extra money earned from coffee enabled them to buy canned fish and rice, which provided children with higher amounts of protein than the usual staple of sweet potatoes.[87]

Nutritional imbalances for females have a far-reaching impact on reproduction and the health of the infants they bear. In some cultures, the lower status of women has a direct bearing on their access to food. Although the custom of feeding males first is well known, it is less often realized that females end up with less nutrient-dense food such as meat. Deprivation of food sometimes starts in infancy where girl babies, as in India, are weaned earlier than boy babies.[88] Parents may be unaware that their differential weaning practice has the effect of reducing the amount of high-quality protein that girl infants receive. Indeed, in Ecuador, Lauris McKee found that parents thought that earlier weaning of girls was helpful to them. They believed that mothers' milk transmitted sexuality and aggression, both ideal male traits, to their infants and so it was important that girl babies be weaned early. Mothers weaned their girls at about 11 months and their boys at about 20 months, a 9-month difference. McKee found that girl infants had a significantly higher mortality than boy infants in their second year of life, suggesting that the earlier weaning time for girls and their probable undernutrition may have been responsible.[89]

Often minimized in the discussion of undernutrition is the powerful relationship between conflict and hunger. Not only does hunger sometimes lead to unrest and conflict, but food deprivation is often used as "weapon" during war. Examples are stealing or destroying food resources, destroying economic infrastructure, and diversion of food aid to the military. Indirectly, food production is hurt by terrorizing the population, disrupting migration routes and health care services, recruiting people for military service, or outright killing.[90]

Summary and Review

Cultural Understandings of Health and Illness

26.1 Discuss cultural understandings of health and illness.

- Anthropologists, particularly those in medical anthropology, who are actively engaged in studying health and illness and associated beliefs and practices are increasingly realizing that biological *and* social factors need to be considered to reduce human suffering.
- Western medical researchers and medical practitioners may think of medicine as purely based on "fact," but it is clear on reflection that many ideas stem from the culture in which the researchers reside.
- Many cultures have the view that the body should be kept in equilibrium or balance, although the balance may entail varying elements and varying means to maintain equilibrium.
- Research shows that a majority of cultures believe that gods or spirits could cause illness to some degree. Illness can also be thought of as caused by the loss of one's soul, fate, retribution for violation of a taboo, or contact with a polluting or taboo substance or object.
- In most societies, people simply think that their ideas about health and illness are true. Often people are not aware that there may be another way of viewing things until they confront another medical system.
- Biomedicine is the dominant Western medical paradigm today, focusing on diseases and cures. Health is seen as the *absence* of disease; death, as a failure. Medical interest tends not to consider psychological factors, social/cultural influences, or links within the human body.

? When medical anthropologists are looking to understand ethnomedical systems, what kinds of questions do they ask?

Treatment of Illness

26.2 Discuss various approaches to studying treatment of illness.

- Two competing mindsets influence medical anthropology: Some anthropologists who study diseases within cultures think there are few cultural universals about any illness, and some think there are cross-cultural similarities in the conception and treatment of illness.
- The kinds of food eaten in a culture and when they are eaten may significantly combat illness in various societies.
- Increasing evidence indicates that the *form* of treatment may be just as important as the *content* of treatment.
- Personalistic practitioners deal with more than the body when someone is ill. Shamans, mediums, sorcerers, and priests usually act as personalistic healers. Physicians, chemists, and herbalists take a more naturalistic view that certain substances or treatments will cure.

- Four categories important to healers worldwide are the naming process, the personality of the doctor, the patient's expectations, and curing techniques.

> ? What is common to treatment of illness in different cultures? What kinds of things are different?

Political and Economic Influences on Health

26.3 Describe political and economic influences on health.

- The incidence or relative frequency for many diseases, health problems, and death rates varies directly with social class and ethnicity.
- Power and economic differentials *among* societies also have profound health consequences.

> ? In what ways do political and economic forces affect health?

Health Conditions and Diseases

26.4 Discuss a sampling of health conditions and diseases studied by medical anthropologists.

- Medical anthropologists have studied an enormous variety of conditions, including epidemics of infectious disease such as AIDS as well as conditions related to mental and emotional disorders and undernutrition.
- Epidemics of infectious disease, including AIDS, have killed millions of people within short periods of time throughout recorded history. Epidemics like AIDS are more than a medical problem and need to be addressed through behavioral, cultural, and political measures.
- Although researchers disagree about the comparability of mental illnesses among cultures, most agree that effective treatment requires understanding a culture's ideas about a mental illness.
- Biological but not necessarily genetic factors may be very important in the etiology of some of the widespread mental disorders. Nutritional factors may play a large role.
- The ways people obtain, distribute, and consume food have been generally adaptive; many serious nutritional problems observed today are due to rapid culture change.

> ? What are some of the approaches medical anthropologists have used to research the AIDS epidemic?

Think on it

1. Using one example discussed in the chapter, explain what is meant by a **"biocultural synthesis."**
2. Drawing on your own experiences with the health system (biomedical or another system), explain what ideas about **medicine** may be cultural.
3. Why do native remedies often contain chemicals that are the same as, or similar in effect to, **chemicals** used in Western biomedicine remedies?
4. Politics, some argue, affects **health.** Explain some of the ways it does so.

Global Problems

CHAPTER 27

LEARNING OBJECTIVES

27.1 Explain how cultural, economic, and social factors can cause or exacerbate natural events and cause disasters and famine.

27.2 Describe the factors that lead to inadequate housing and homelessness.

27.3 Discuss the magnitude, causes, and consequences of family violence.

27.4 Explain how cultural and societal features relate to crime, especially in regard to homicide.

27.5 Discuss warfare in terms of cultural, social, and ecological factors, and describe the reasons societies go to war.

27.6 Describe the difficulty of defining terrorism and discuss what is known about the factors associated with it.

27.7 Discuss some lessons learned from anthropology that could make the world a better place.

Almost every day, the news makes us aware that terrible social problems threaten people around the world. War, crime, family violence, natural disasters, poverty, famine—all these and more are the lot of millions of people in many places. And now there is an increasing threat of terrorism. Can anthropological and other research help us solve these global social problems? Many anthropologists and other social scientists think so.

High-tech communications have increased our awareness of problems all over the world, and we seem to be increasingly more aware of, and bothered by, problems in our own society. For these two reasons, and perhaps also because we know much more than we used to about human behavior, we may be more motivated now to try to solve those problems. We call them "social problems" not just because a lot of people worry about them but also because they have social causes and consequences, and treating or solving them requires changes in social behavior.

The idea that we can solve social problems, even the enormous ones such as war and family violence, is based on two assumptions. First, we have to assume that it is possible to discover the causes of a problem. And second, we have to assume that we may be able to do something about the causes, once they are discovered, and thereby eliminate or reduce the problem. Not everyone would agree with these assumptions. Some would say that our understanding of a social problem cannot ever be sufficient to suggest a solution guaranteed to work. To be sure, no understanding in science is perfect or certain; there is always some probability that even a well-supported explanation is wrong or incomplete. But the uncertainty of knowledge does not rule out the possibility of application. With regard to social problems, the possible payoff from even incomplete understanding could be a better and safer world. This possibility is what motivates many researchers who investigate social problems. After all, the history of the various sciences strongly supports the belief that scientific understanding can often allow humans to control nature, not just predict and explain it. Why should human behavior be any different?

So what do we know about some of the global social problems, and what policies or solutions are suggested by what we know?

27.1 Explain how cultural, economic, and social factors can cause or exacerbate natural events and cause disasters and famine.

Natural Events, Disasters, and Famine

Natural events such as floods, droughts, earthquakes, and insect infestations are usually but not always beyond human control, but their effects are not.[1] We call such events accidents or emergencies when only a few people are affected, but we call them disasters when large numbers of people or large areas are affected. The harm caused is not just a function of the magnitude of the natural event. Between 1980 and 2002, the United States had slightly more earthquakes than India. Yet over 32,000 people died in those earthquakes compared to about 140 people in the United States. More broadly, richer countries have lower death tolls even though there is no significant differences in exposure to natural shocks or their magnitude between rich and poor countries.[2] The vast majority of deaths occurred in lower income countries.[3] These comparative figures demonstrate that climatic and other events in the physical environment become worse disasters because of events or conditions in the social environment.

If people live in houses that are designed to withstand earthquakes—if governing bodies require such construction and the economy is developed enough so that people can afford such construction—the effects of an earthquake will be minimized. If poor people are forced to live in deforested floodplains to be able to find land to farm (as in coastal Bangladesh), if the poor are forced to live in shanties built on precarious hillsides (like those of Rio de Janeiro), the floods and landslides that follow severe hurricanes and rainstorms can kill thousands and even hundreds of thousands.

Thus, because natural events can have greater or lesser effects on human life, depending on social conditions, they are also social problems, problems that have social causes and possible social solutions. Legislating safe construction of a house is a social solution. The 1976 earthquake in Tangsham, China, killed 250,000 people, mostly because they lived in top-heavy adobe houses that could not withstand severe shaking, whereas the 1989 Loma Prieta earthquake in California, which was of comparable intensity, killed 65 people.

A family in Sichuan gathers for a meal outside their home after a 2013 earthquake. Tens of thousands of homeless survivors of China's devastating quake are living in makeshift tents or on the streets, facing shortages of food and supplies as well as an uncertain future.

One might think that floods, of all disasters, are the least influenced by social factors. After all, without a huge runoff from heavy rains or snow melt, there cannot be a flood. But consider why so many people have died from Hwang River floods in China. (One such flood, in 1931, killed nearly 4 million people, making it the deadliest single disaster in history.) The floods in the Hwang River basin have occurred mostly because the clearing of nearby forests for fuel and farmland has allowed enormous quantities of silt to wash into the river, raising the riverbed and increasing the risk of floods that burst the dams that normally would contain them. The risk of disastrous flooding would be greatly reduced if different social conditions prevailed—if people were not so dependent on firewood for fuel, if they did not have to farm close to the river, or if the dams were higher and more numerous.

Famines, episodes of severe starvation and resultant death, often appear to be triggered by physical events such as a severe drought or a hurricane that kills or knocks down food trees and plants. But famines do not inevitably follow such an event. Social conditions can prevent a famine or increase the likelihood of one. Consider what is likely to happen in Samoa after a hurricane.[4] Whole villages that have lost their coconut and breadfruit trees, as well as their taro patches, pick up and move for a period of time to other villages where they have relatives and friends. The visitors stay and are fed until some of their cultivated trees and plants start to bear food again, at which point they return home. This kind of intervillage reciprocity probably could occur only in a society that has relatively little inequality in wealth. Nowadays, the central government or international agencies may also help out by providing food and other supplies.

Researchers point out that famine rarely results from just one bad food production season. During one bad season, people can usually cope by getting help from relatives, friends, and neighbors or by switching to less desirable foods. The 1974 famine in the African Sahel occurred after eight years of bad weather; a combination of drought, floods, and a civil war in 1983 to 1984 contributed to the subsequent famine in the Sahel, Ethiopia, and Sudan.[5] Famine almost always has some social causes. Who has rights to the available food, and do those who have more food distribute it to those who have less? Cross-cultural research suggests that societies with individual property rights rather than shared rights are more likely to suffer famine.[6] Nonetheless, government assistance can lessen the risk of famine in societies with individual property.

Relief provided by government may not always get to those who need it the most. In fact, famine can occur in countries that have adequate food but that fail to distribute it to populations with severe food stress.[7] Or, if food is distributed, it may not be equitable. In India, for example, the central government provides help in time of drought to minimize the risk of famine. But the food and other supplies provided to a village may end up being unequally distributed, following the rules of social and gender stratification. Members of the local elite arrange to function as distributors and find ways to manipulate the relief efforts to their advantage. Lower-class and lower-caste families still suffer the most. Within the family, biases against females, particularly young girls and elderly women, translate into their getting less food. It is no wonder, then, that in times of food shortage and famine, the poor and other socially disadvantaged people are especially likely to die.[8]

Read **the** Document: Hunger and Famine

Considerable progress has been made in eliminating famine. There have been no famines in Europe since the 1940s and none in Asia since the 1970s. Contemporary famines are now confined to sub-Saharan Africa. Why do they persist? Since a majority of Africans produce their own food, failures of production are partially to blame. But for a famine to occur, there also must be exchange failures (inability to barter or purchase food). In addition, a famine will only result if social support networks, governments, or the international community provide inadequate help. The famine of 1999–2000 in Ethiopia in the pastoral Somali region followed a multi-year drought in 1997 and 1998. Both drought and disease killed many livestock. The Somali relied heavily on sales of livestock to the Middle East, and the loss of cash meant that they could not buy sufficient food. Ethiopia had an "early warning system" in place, but it focused on the highland areas, not the lowlands where the pastoralists lived. Some NGOs sounded warnings, but they were ignored until the BBC started broadcasting information. By the time information got out, the response by the international community could not avert much of the loss of life.[9]

Thus, the people of a society may not all be equally at risk in case of disaster. In socially stratified societies, the poor particularly suffer. They are likely to be forced to overcultivate, overgraze, and deforest their land, making it more susceptible to degradation. A society most helps those it values the most.

People in the past, and even recently in some places, viewed extreme natural events as divine retribution for human immorality. For example, the great flood described in the Old Testament was understood to be God's doing. But scientific research increasingly allows us to understand the natural causes of disasters, and particularly the social conditions that magnify or minimize their effects. To reduce the impact of disasters, then, we need to reduce the social conditions that magnify the effects of disasters. If humans are responsible for those social conditions, humans can change them. If earthquakes destroy houses that are too flimsy, we can build stronger houses. If floods caused by overcultivation and overgrazing kill people directly (or indirectly by stripping their soils), we can grow new forest cover and provide new job opportunities to floodplain farmers. If prolonged climate-related disasters or wars threaten famine, social distribution systems can lessen the risk. In short, we may not be able to do much about the weather or other physical causes of disasters, but we can do a lot—if we want to—about the social factors that make disasters disastrous. The challenge is—how do you make people want to?

27.2 Describe the factors that lead to inadequate housing and homelessness.

Inadequate Housing and Homelessness

The world's urban population, particularly in developing countries, is growing rapidly. In 2010, a slight majority of the people in the world lived in urban areas, and it is projected to be about 70 percent by 2050.[10] But rapid growth is occurring in places with inadequate ability to provide decent infrastructure. And so, in most nations, those who are poor typically live in inadequate housing, in areas we call *slums*. In many of the developing nations, where cities are growing very rapidly, squatter settlements emerge as people build dwellings (often makeshift) that are typically declared illegal, either because the land is illegally occupied or because the dwellings violate building codes. Squatter settlements are often located in degraded environments that are subject to flooding and mudslides or have inadequate or polluted water.[11] The magnitude of the problem is made clear in some statistics. As of 2012, it was estimated that 1 billion people or about 33 percent of urban dwellers lived in slums. In some world regions, the slum problem is much worse. In Africa,

62 percent of urban dwellers live in slums.[12] Four in ten of the nonpermanent houses in slums were in high-risk environments such as flood zones or landslide-prone areas.[13]

But contrary to what some people have assumed, not all dwellers in illegal settlements are poor; all but the upper-income elite may be found in such settlements.[14] Moreover, although squatter settlements have problems, they are not chaotic and unorganized places that are full of crime. Most of the dwellers are employed, aspire to get ahead, live in intact nuclear families, and help each other.[15] People live in such settlements because they cannot find affordable housing, and they house themselves as best they can. Many researchers think that such self-help tendencies should be assisted to improve housing because governments in developing countries can seldom afford costly public housing projects. But they could invest somewhat in infrastructure—sewers, water supplies, roads—and provide construction materials to those who are willing to do the work required to improve their dwellings.[16] In some countries, the urban slum and shack dwellers have organized into more formal local collective action groups that have even joined into international alliances with the support of some NGOs. Local federations have pushed for co-production, which means that the local collective action group becomes actively engaged in design, implementation, and management of improvements to their communities.[17] Thailand is one of the countries that supports these collective efforts to upgrade slums by offering subsidies and soft loans. But the communities must first form community savings groups before they can get government assistance. They then need to negotiate for land to lease or buy collectively. The cooperative can then make plans and loans to individuals. The importance of collective ownership is not only that it fosters working together for a collective good, but it also prevents individuals from selling out as soon as their house is upgraded.[18]

Housing in slum areas or shantytowns does provide shelter, minimal though it may be. But many people in many areas of the world have no homes at all. Even in countries such as the United States, which is affluent by world standards, large numbers of people are homeless. They sleep in parks, over steam vents, in doorways, subways, and cardboard boxes. Homelessness is difficult to measure. In 1987, more than 1 million people were estimated to be homeless in the United States.[19] About 3.5 million people experienced homelessness in 2000, almost 40 percent of them children. Most researchers agree that homelessness has increased in the last few decades; the United States Conference of Mayors reported increases after the recession in 2007.[20]

Who are the homeless, and how did they get to be homeless? We have relatively little research on these questions, but what we do have suggests differences in the causes of homelessness in different parts of the world. In the United States, unemployment and the shortage of decent low-cost housing appear to be at least partly responsible for the large number of homeless people.[21] But there is also another factor: the deliberate policy to reduce the number of people hospitalized for mental illness and other disabilities. For example, from the mid-1960s to the mid-1990s, New York State released thousands of patients from mental hospitals. Many of these ex-patients had to live in cheap hotels or poorly monitored facilities with virtually no support network. With very little income, they found it especially hard to cope with their circumstances. Ellen Baxter and Kim Hopper, who studied the homeless in New York City, suggest that one event is rarely sufficient to render a person homeless. Rather, poverty and disability (mental or physical) seem to lead to one calamity after another and, finally, homelessness.[22]

Read **the** Document: Homelessness

Many people cannot understand why homeless individuals do not want to go to municipal shelters, but observations and interviews with the homeless individuals suggest that violence pervades the municipal shelters, particularly the men's shelters. Many feel safer on the streets. Some private charities provide safe shelters and a caring environment. These shelters are filled, but the number of homeless people they can accommodate is small.[23] Even single-room-occupancy hotels are hardly better. Many of them are infested with vermin, the common bathrooms are filthy, and they, like the shelters, are often dangerous.[24]

Some poor individuals may be socially isolated, with few or no friends and relatives and little or no social contact. But a society with many such individuals does not necessarily have much homelessness. Socially isolated individuals, even mentally ill individuals, could still have housing, or so the experience of Melbourne, Australia, suggests. Universal health insurance there pays for health care as well as medical practitioners' visits to isolated and ill individuals, wherever they live. Disabled individuals receive a pension or sickness benefits sufficient to allow them to live in a room or apartment. And there is still a considerable supply of cheap

Applied Anthropology

Climate Change: What Can Anthropologists Contribute to Research and Policy?

Climate change is a global concern. Scientists are about 90 percent certain that human activities, such as the burning of coal and fossil fuels, over the past 250 years have led to the world heating up. And they are worried about the worsening consequences. There is already increased melting of polar ice and the more the temperature rises, the more the higher sea level will flood low-lying coastal areas, including many world cities. Storms, floods, and droughts will continue to intensify. The weather will become even more erratic. Places at high latitudes are likely to see increased rainfall and snow; places at low latitudes are likely to have less rainfall and more drought. The earth normally traps heat in the atmosphere by gases such as carbon dioxide, water vapor, and methane. These are called "greenhouse gases." And while some warmth is essential for life, the amounts of these gases have dramatically increased. Scientists have told us that the need to reduce greenhouse gases and prepare for more extreme conditions is *now.* But bringing about change is not easy.

Many environmental anthropologists use ethnographic methods to study how communities perceive changes in the weather and landscapes around them as well as the measures they take to try to adapt. So, for example, Sakka horse and cattle breeders living in Siberia live in land with extreme temperature fluctuations from −76 degrees to 104 degrees Fahrenheit. Their cattle are in barns for nine months a year and live on hay gathered in the summer. But almost everyone notes that the climate has changed; winter and spring both come later, the weather is erratic, and there is so much rain in the summer that hay doesn't grow well and doesn't dry out. But the Sakka do not frame climate change the way we do. Some attribute the changes to the building of hydroelectric dams, others to rockets "mixing up" the sky. The Sakka adapted before around the year 1200 when they moved from more southerly climates to Siberia. But it is not clear that they can adapt now. The melting permafrost may turn their land into swampland unfit for animal husbandry.

Susan Crate points out that "global climate change—its causes, effects, and amelioration—is intimately and ultimately about culture (p. 570)," but it is the industrialized and post-industrial world that has largely caused global warming—therefore dramatic change will be needed in the cultural behavior of that world. Therefore, many argue that cultural anthropologists need to broaden their horizons and become more engaged in understanding how policy is formulated by climate scientists and governments, and they need to work with interdisciplinary teams. They also need to show how the effects of climate change are related to the broader social, political, and economic context of the people they study, and finally, they need to engage more—both by making the situation known of the people they study and engaging in projects that plan and pursue how to cope with climate change.

Understanding how societies have responded to climate change in the past is an important component. Archaeologists have studied livelihoods, the interaction of groups, and changes in local environments in the past. In some places, decades-long or century-long droughts have led to extreme changes—abandonment of sites, regional collapses, and movements to other places; smaller environmental changes, such as the Little Ice Age in Europe; and decreased agricultural productivity.

Sources: Oerlemans 2005; Baer and Singer 2009; IPPC 2007; Crate 2008; Roncoli, Crane and Orlove 2009.

housing in Melbourne. Research in Melbourne suggests that a severe mental disorder often precedes living in marginal accommodations—city shelters, commercial shelters, and cheap single rooms. About 50 percent of the people living in such places were diagnosed as previously having some form of mental illness; this percentage is similar to what seems to be the case for homeless people and people living in marginal accommodations in the United States.

The contrast between the United States and Australia makes it clear that social and political policies cause homelessness. Individuals with similar characteristics live in both Australia and the United States, but a larger percentage of them are homeless in the United States.[25] As Kim Hopper noted, perhaps the important question is not what makes some people homeless but rather why the rest of the people in a society tolerate homelessness.[26]

Because homelessness cannot occur if everybody can afford housing, some people would say that homelessness can happen only in a society with great extremes in income. Statistics on income distribution in the United States clearly show that, since the 1970s, the rich have gotten much richer and the poor have gotten much poorer.[27] The United States now has more income inequality than any country in Western Europe and more than most high-income countries. In fact, the profile of inequality in the United States more closely resembles that of developing countries, such as Cambodia and Morocco[28] (see the discussion in the chapter on social stratification).

In the United States and many other countries, most homeless people are adults. Whereas adults are "allowed" to be homeless, public sensibilities in the United States appear to be outraged by the sight of children living in the streets; when authorities discover homeless children, they try to find shelters or foster homes for them. But many countries have "street children." In the late 1980s, 80 million of the world's children lived in the streets: 40 million in Latin America, 20 million in Asia, 10 million in Africa and the Middle East, and 10 million elsewhere.[29] In the 2000s, the estimated number grew to about 150 million worldwide.[30]

Lewis Aptekar, who studied street children in Cali, Colombia, reported some surprises.[31] Whereas many of the homeless in the United States and Australia are mentally disabled, the street children in Cali, ranging in age from 7 to 16, are mostly free of mental problems; by and large, they also test normally on intelligence tests. In addition, even though many street children come from abusive homes or never had homes, they usually seem happy and enjoy the support and friendship of other street children. They cleverly and creatively look for ways to get money, frequently through entertaining passersby.

Although observers might think that the street children must have been abandoned by their families, most of them in actuality have at least one parent they keep in touch with. Street life begins slowly, not abruptly; children usually do not stay on the streets full time until they are about 13 years old. Though street children in Cali seem to be in better physical and mental shape than their siblings who stay at home, they often are viewed as a "plague." The street children come from poor families and cope with their lives as best they can, so why are they not viewed with pity and compassion? Aptekar suggests that well-off families see the street children as a threat because a life independent of family may appeal to children, even those from well-off families, who wish to be free of parental constraint and authority.

Whether people become homeless and whether they have shantytowns seem to depend on a society's willingness to share wealth and help those in need. The street children of Cali may remind us that children as well as adults need companionship and care. Addressing physical needs without responding to emotional needs may get people off the streets, but it won't get them a "home."

A homeless boy in Calcutta, India with his belongings.

Migrants and Immigrants

Refugees Are a Global Social Problem

The continuing turmoil in many countries throughout the world has created a flow of refugees that is much larger than ever before in world history. An estimated 140 million people became refugees in the 20th century. In 2012 alone, over 45 million people were displaced; the highest number since 1994. More than half of the refugees in 2012 came from five countries—Afghanistan, Somalia, Iraq, Syria, and Sudan. In the past, thousands of people might have had to flee persecution and war. Now that refugees number in the many millions per year, the problems of how to minimize suffering and find long-term solutions are more complex. Refugees flee to other parts of the country (internally displaced persons), to neighboring countries, and some to countries on the other side of the world. The refugees from the civil wars in Somalia are not unusual; 10 percent of the Somali population is now living outside of Somalia, perhaps a million people altogether. Much of the burden of sheltering refugees falls to nearby countries. For example, over 640,000 have sought refuge from the Syrian conflict in Iraq, Turkey, Lebanon, Jordan, and Egypt. Often people are channeled into refugee camps where the United Nations and other international agencies try to find "durable" solutions. Voluntary repatriation is considered the ideal solution, but it requires that the conflict be over and that the home country is willing to protect and reintegrate those who have fled. The process, however, can be a long one, especially if conflict is protracted. Resettlement in other countries is another option, but not that many countries are willing to take a large number of people. For example, in 2012, half a million refugees were repatriated, but only about 89,000 people were resettled in other countries (the United States received about 66,000 people).

Kachin women gather as children play at a camp for internally displaced people in northern Kachin state, Myanmar.

What is often not realized about refugees is that often families strategize about who stays and who goes. Persecution is real, but it takes resources to flee. That is, those who are better off in the first place have the best chance to flee the furthest. Those family members who do get out may be able to channel money to other family members back home to help them leave as well.

Almost all people seeking refuge are fleeing conflict. Therefore the ultimate answer to the problem of refugees has to be to prevent those conflicts in the first place or to minimize their escalation.

Some researchers are predicting that a whole new type of refugee problem will soon emerge—"climate change refugees." With changes in climate, millions of people will be forced to leave their homes because of flooding or worsening drought. The crisis is likely to be worse in developing countries that haven't been able to commit resources to adapt to climate changes. Migration may be the only choice for some nations like Tuvalu, which consists of low-lying islands in the Pacific. One estimate is that by 2050 there will be over 200 million climate refugees. The world has not only been slow to acknowledge climate change, but little has been done to plan for it. If there will be so many climate refugees, there will need to be some analogous mechanisms for coping with and resettling these refugees, just like some have developed for refugees fleeing persecution.

Sources: Van Hear 2004, 2006; UNHCR 2013; Biermann and Boas 2010.

27.3 Discuss the magnitude, causes, and consequences of family violence.

Family Violence and Abuse

In U.S. society, we hear regularly about the abuse of spouses and children, which makes us think that such abuse is increasing—but is it? This seems to be a simple question, but it is not so simple to answer. We have to decide what we mean by *abuse*.

Is physical punishment of a child who does something wrong child abuse? Not so long ago, teachers in public schools in the United States were allowed to discipline children by hitting them with rulers or paddles, and many parents used switches or belts. Many would consider these practices to be child abuse, but were they abusive when they were generally accepted? Some would argue that abuse is going beyond what a culture considers appropriate behavior. Others would disagree and would focus on the violence and severity of parents' or teachers' behavior, not the cultural judgment of appropriateness. And abuse need not involve physical violence. It could be argued that verbal aggression and neglect may be just as harmful as physical aggression. Neglect presents its own problems of definition. People from other cultures might argue that we act abusively when we put an infant or child alone in a room to sleep.[32] Few would disagree about severe injuries that kill a child or spouse or require medical treatment, but other disciplinary behaviors are more difficult to judge.

To avoid having to decide what is or is not abuse, many researchers focus their studies on variation in the frequencies of specific behaviors. For example, one can ask which societies have physical punishment of children without calling physical punishment abusive.

According to four national interview surveys of married or cohabiting couples in the United States conducted from 1975 onwards, physical violence against older children appears to have decreased in frequency over time, as did serious assaults by husbands against wives. But serious assaults by wives on husbands did not decrease.[33] In fact, to many people's surprise, in over 200 studies of partner violence carried out mostly in the United States, husbands and wives commit about an equal number of attacks on their partners.[34] Perhaps the perception that males commit more violence toward their wives stems from the fact that wives are more often injured. The United States remains a society with a lot of physical violence in families. By far the most violence is directed to children by parents. Ninety-four percent of parents report hitting a 3- to 5-year-old child during the year. (Parents often do not consider slapping or spanking violence.) Next most violent group are siblings to other siblings, then toddlers hitting parents. While parents being violent to each other is the rarest type of family violence in the family, it is far from rare. About 16 percent of men and women report experiencing violence from a partner.[35] If we focus on crimes reported to the police, family violence accounted for 33 percent of all crimes, and nearly a quarter of murders were against a family member. And in terms of crime, females are more likely than males to be victims of family violence crimes, but males are more likely to experience violent crime from strangers and acquaintances.[36] Just as women face more risk from those close to them, so do children. When a child is the target of violence, it usually comes from the birth mother.[37]

Cross-culturally, if one form of family violence occurs, others are also likely. So, for example, wife beating, husband beating, child punishment, and fighting among siblings are all significantly associated with each other. But the relationships among these types of family violence are not that strong, which means that they cannot be considered as different facets of the same phenomenon. Indeed, somewhat different factors seem to explain different forms of family violence.[38] We focus here on two forms of violence that are most prevalent cross-culturally: violence against children and violence against wives.

Violence Against Children

Cross-culturally, many societies practice and allow infanticide. Frequent reasons for infanticide include illegitimacy, deformity of the infant, twins, too many children, or that the infant is unwanted. Infanticide is usually performed by the mother, but this does not mean that she is uncaring; it may mean that she cannot adequately feed or care for the infant or that it has a poor chance to survive. The reasons for infanticide are similar to those given for abortion. Therefore, it seems that infanticide may be performed when abortion does not work or when unexpected qualities of the infant (e.g., deformity) force the mother to reevaluate her ability to raise the child.[39]

Much of the violence directed at children is believed to be morally correct—a necessary way of teaching children to behave. The old proverb warns: "Spare the rod and spoil the child." In recent years in the United States and elsewhere, there has been some turning away from corporal or bodily punishment, and more people in this country and elsewhere would like parents to stop spanking their children. They point to evidence that spanking and other corporal punishment is associated with a child later hitting others in kindergarten or elsewhere. Later in life, children who are corporally punished are more likely to physically assault their dating partners or spouses, be convicted of a crime, and have bouts of depression.[40] So it is possible that corporal punishment is a cradle of violence.

So if we want to reduce family violence, one thing we could do is reduce the conditions that predict corporal punishment of children. The frequency of corporal punishment does not vary that much from one country to another, and most approve of the practice. There is more variation in the cross-cultural record, and we can use that record to predict the variation.

Physical punishment of children occurs at least sometimes in over 70 percent of the world's societies.[41] And physical punishment is frequent or typical in 40 percent of the world's societies.

The main predictors of corporal punishment in the ethnographic or cross-cultural record are two conditions that are practically universal in the nation-states of the world, namely, a money economy and a stratified social system. If parents want children to do well when they grow up in a world with power inequality, might parents practice corporal punishment to convey that some people (particularly employers) are much more powerful than others? To a child, parents are clearly powerful. Not only are they taller and physically stronger, they also control and dispense important resources (food, love). So, perhaps, parents may consciously or unconsciously think that, if children fear those who are more powerful, they may be less likely to get into trouble and more likely to be able to get and keep a job.[42] Research in the United States is consistent with the cross-cultural finding: Those at the bottom of the socioeconomic hierarchy are more likely than those at the top to practice corporal punishment of children.[43] Unfortunately, parents probably do not realize that physical punishment may produce more violent behavior in their children, an outcome they probably do not want or intend. Donna Goldstein poignantly describes the plight of a woman in a shantytown near Rio de Janeiro who supports more than 10 children in a one-room shack. Her discipline is harsh, but she is trying, as Goldstein points out, to ensure that the kids "have the skills, as well as the attitudes of obedience, humility, and subservience, necessary for a poor black person to survive in urban Brazil."[44]

Do these results suggest how corporal punishment of children could decrease? At one level, it is difficult to see how. Societies that use money and have social classes are not likely to become egalitarian. But societies could move in the direction of de-emphasizing economic and power inequality. When parents hit their children, it is generally not because they want their children to be violent; they want them to behave properly. If they understood the connection between parental violence and child violence, they might begin to change their practices.

Some countries already have not-so-high rates of corporal punishment. These are the more democratic countries—with contested elections that allow people to replace leaders peacefully, and laws that protect civil rights such as the right to express dissent. (The agreement to disagree, and protecting civil rights, means that you don't have to worry so much about losing your job if you disagree with your employer's beliefs.) Sweden and the other Scandinavian countries have lower rates of approval of corporal punishment. Is this because Scandinavia is more democratic, allowing people (even workers in factories) to participate more in decision making in the workplace and not just in elections? We think so. But only time will tell if increasing democracy, and less need for workers to act subservient, will translate into less violent ways of socializing children.

Violence Against Wives

Cross-culturally, wife beating is a common form of family violence; it occurs at least occasionally in about 85 percent of the world's societies. In about half the societies, wife beating is sometimes serious enough to cause permanent injury or death.[45] It is often assumed that wife beating is common in societies in which males control economic and political resources. In a cross-cultural test of this assumption, David Levinson found that not all indicators of male dominance predict wife beating, but many do. Specifically, wife beating is most common when men control the products of family labor, when men have the final say in decision making in the home, when divorce is difficult for women, when remarriage for a widow is controlled by the husband's kin, or when women do not have any female work groups.[46] Similarly, in the United States, the more one spouse in the family makes the decisions and has the power, the more physical violence occurs in the family. Wife beating is even more likely when the husband controls the household and is out of work.[47]

When we compare countries, although wife beating is widespread, there is very wide variability in prevalence. For example, in Japan, 13 percent of women report ever experiencing violence from their male partner, but it is reported as high as 61 percent in rural Peru.[48]

In some places, such as the United States and other Western countries, women are about as equally likely to be violent toward their husbands as their husbands are to them. So wife beating seems unlikely to be caused by gender inequality. As it turns out, degree of gender empowerment, or the relative emancipation of women, does predict the variability among nations. The United States and many other Western countries do not have gender equality, but they have more equality than countries like India, Korea, and Jordan. And it is in the countries with more equality that male and female partners are about equal in their propensity to hit each other; it is in the more male-dominated countries that males are much more likely to hit their spouses than the other way around. It is also the case that in such countries, wife beating tends to be approved of.[49]

Wife beating appears to be related to broader patterns of violence. Societies that have violent methods of conflict resolution within communities, physical punishment of criminals, high frequency of warfare, and cruelty toward enemies generally have more wife beating.[50]

Reducing the Risk

What can be done to minimize family violence? First, we have to recognize that probably nothing can be done as long as people in a society do not acknowledge that a problem exists. If severe child punishment and wife beating are perfectly acceptable to almost everyone in a society, they are unlikely to be considered social problems that need solutions. In our own society, many programs are designed to take abused children or wives out of the family situation or to punish the abuser. (Of course, in these situations, the violence has already occurred and was serious enough to have been noticed.) Cross-culturally, at least with respect to wife beating, intervention by others seems to be successful only if the intervention occurs before violence gets serious. As one would expect, however, those societies most prone to a high rate of wife beating are the least likely to practice immediate intervention. More helpful perhaps, but admittedly harder to arrange, is the promotion of conditions of life that are associated with low family violence. Research so far suggests that promoting the equality of men and women and the sharing of childrearing responsibilities may go a long way toward lessening incidents of family violence.[51] And reducing the risk of corporal punishment of children may reduce the risk of violence when they have families.

Crime

27.4 Explain how cultural and societal features relate to crime, especially in regard to homicide.

What is a crime in one society is not necessarily a crime in another. Just as it is difficult to decide what constitutes abuse, it is difficult to define *crime*. In one society, it may be a crime to walk over someone's land without permission; in another, there might not be any concept of personal ownership and therefore no concept of trespassing. In seeking to understand variation in crime, many researchers have not surprisingly preferred to compare those behaviors that are more or less universally considered crimes and that are reliably reported. For example, in a large-scale comparison of crime in 110 nations over a span of 70 years, Dane Archer and Rosemary Gartner concentrated on homicide rates. They argued that homicide is harder for the public to hide and for officials to ignore than other crimes. A comparison of interviews about crime with police records suggests that homicide is the most reliably reported crime in official records.[52]

Nations not only have very different crime rates when we compare them at a given point in time, the rates also vary over time within a nation. In the last 600 years, homicide rates have generally declined in Western societies. In England, where homicide rates have been well documented for centuries, the chance of murder during the 13th and 14th centuries was 10 times higher than in England today. Around 2010, some of the lowest homicide rates were found in Norway, Austria, Hong Kong, Japan, Bahrain, and Oman. Some of the highest homicide rates were in Jamaica, El Salvador, and Venezuala. The United States has a higher homicide rate than almost any of the countries in Europe.[53]

One of the clearest findings to emerge from comparative studies of crime is that war is associated with higher rates of homicide. Archer and Gartner compared changes in homicide rates of nations before and after major wars. Whether a nation is defeated or victorious, homicide rates tend to increase after a war. This result is consistent with the idea that a society or nation legitimizes violence during wartime. That is, during wartime, societies approve of killing the enemy; afterward, homicide rates may go up because inhibitions against killing have been relaxed.[54] Ted Gurr suggested that the long-term downtrend in crime in Western societies seems to be consistent with an increasing emphasis on humanistic values and nonviolent achievement of goals. But such goals may be temporarily suspended during wartime. In the United States, for example, surges in violent crime rates occurred during the 1860s and 1870s (during and after the Civil War), after World War I, after World War II, and during the Vietnam War.[55] But recently the homicide rate in the United States has declined.[56]

In the types of societies that anthropologists have typically studied, homicide statistics are not often available. However, where statistics are available the variation appears to be much greater than among modern nations. Nations vary from about .5 homicides per 100,000 people to about 52 per 100,000. Using statistics calculated by anthropologists, the range is from about 1 to 683.[57] Thus, some of the highest homicide rates described are more than 10 times the rate of any known country today. Cross-cultural studies of homicide usually measure homicide rates by comparing and rank-ordering ethnographers' statements about the frequency of homicide. For example, the statement that murder is "practically unheard of" is taken to mean that the murder rate is lower than where it is reported that "homicide is not uncommon." Despite the fact that the data on cultural homicide rates are not quantitative, the cross-cultural results are consistent with the cross-national results; more war is usually associated with more homicide and assault, as well as with socially approved aggressive behaviors (as in aggressive games) and severe physical punishment for wrongdoing.[58] A cross-cultural study suggests that the more war a society has, the more the society socializes or trains boys in aggression, and such socialization strongly predicts higher rates of homicide and assault.[59]

Read **the** Document: Crime: Variations across Cultures and Nations

Capital punishment—execution of criminals—is severe physical punishment for wrongdoing. It is commonly thought that the prospect of capital punishment deters would-be murderers. Yet, cross-national research suggests otherwise. More countries show murder rates going down rather than up after capital punishment was abolished.[60] Capital punishment may legitimize violence rather than deter it.

Research conducted in the United States suggests that juvenile delinquents (usually boys) are likely to come from broken homes, with the father absent for much of the time the boy is growing up. The conclusion often drawn is that father absence somehow increases the likelihood of delinquency and adult forms of physical violence. But other conditions that may cause delinquency are also associated with broken homes, conditions such as the stigma of not having a "regular" family and the generally low standard of living of such families. It is therefore important to conduct research in other societies, in which father absence does not occur in concert with these other factors, to see if father absence by itself is related to physical violence.

For example, in many polygynous societies, children grow up in a mother-child household; the father lives separately and is seldom around the child. Does the father absence explanation of delinquency and violence fit such societies? The answer is apparently yes: Societies in which children are reared in mother-child households, where fathers sleep at a distance, or the father spends little time caring for the child tend to have more physical violence by males than do societies in which fathers spend time with children.[61] The rate of violent crime is also more frequent in nations that have more women than men, which is consistent with the theory that father absence increases violence.[62]

More research is needed to discover exactly what accounts for these relationships. It is possible, as some suggest, that boys growing up without fathers are apt to act "supermasculine" to show how "male" they are. But it is also possible that mothers who rear children alone have more frustration and more anger, and therefore are likely to provide an aggressive role model for the child. In addition, high male mortality in war and an excess of women predicts polygyny; therefore, boys in polygynous societies are likely to be exposed to a warrior tradition.[63]

Trying to act supermasculine, however, may be likely to involve violence only if aggression is an important component of the male gender role in society. If men were expected by society to be sensitive, caring, and nonviolent, boys who grew up without fathers might try to be supersensitive and supercaring. So society's expectations for males probably shape how growing up in a mother-child household affects behavior in adolescence and later.[64] The media may also influence the expectations for males. Numerous studies in the United States show that, even controlling for other factors like parental neglect, family income, and mental illness, more television watching in childhood and adolescence predicts

Evidence indicates that violence on TV encourages violence in real life.

more overt aggression later. Estimates show that an hour of prime-time television depicts 3–5 violent acts, and an hour of children's television depicts 20–25 violent acts.[65]

One widely held idea is that poor economic conditions increase the likelihood of crime, but the relationship does not appear to be strong. Also, the findings are somewhat different for different types of crime. For example, hundreds of studies in this and other countries do not show a clear relationship between changes in economic well-being as measured by unemployment rates and changes in violent crime as measured by homicide. The rate of homicide does not appear to increase in bad times. Property crimes, however, do increase with increases in unemployment. There are some stressful conditions though that do predict more homicide. A high disease load is one such condition.[66] Homicide is usually highest in nations or societies with high poverty and income inequality.[67] Why income inequality predicts homicide but downturns in the economy do not is something of a puzzle.[68]

The fact that property crime is linked to unemployment is consistent with the cross-cultural finding that theft (but not violent crime) tends to occur less often in egalitarian societies than in stratified ones. Societies with equal access to resources usually have distribution mechanisms that offset any differences in wealth. Hence, theft should be less of a temptation and therefore less likely in an egalitarian society. Theft rates are higher in socially stratified societies despite the fact that they are more likely than egalitarian societies to have police and courts to punish crime. Societies may try to deter property and other crimes when the rates of such are high, but we do not know that these efforts actually reduce the rates.

So what does the available research suggest about how we might be able to reduce crime? The results so far indicate that homicide rates are highest in societies that socialize their boys for aggression. Such socialization is linked to war and other forms of socially approved violence—capital punishment, television and movie violence by heroes, violence in sports. The statistical evidence suggests that war encourages socialization for aggression, which in turn results unintentionally in high rates of violence. The policy implication of these results is that, if we can reduce socialization for aggression by reducing the risk of war and therefore the necessity to produce effective warriors, and if we can reduce other forms of socially approved violence, we may thereby reduce the rates of violent crime. The reduction of inequalities in wealth may also help to reduce crime, particularly theft. And although it is not yet clear why, it appears that raising boys with a male role model around may reduce the likelihood of male violence in adulthood.

27.5 Discuss warfare in terms of cultural, social, and ecological factors, and describe the reasons societies go to war.

War

There are two important points to note about war. First, war is an unfortunate fact of life in most societies known to anthropology. Almost every society had at least occasional wars when it was first described, unless it had been pacified (usually by Western colonial powers).[69] However, this does not imply that war is inevitable or "natural" since some societies were peaceful. Second, it is now fairly clear that warfare has declined over the long stretch of history.[70] That being so, the presumption is that if warfare has already declined, it can continue to decline further.

Since the Civil War, the United States has not had any wars within its territory, but it is unusual in that respect. Before pacification, most societies in the ethnographic record had frequent armed combat among communities or larger units that spoke the same language. That is, most warfare was internal to the society or language group. Even some wars in modern times involved speakers of the same language; recall the wars among Italian states before the unification of Italy and many of the "civil" wars of the last two centuries. Although people in some societies might fight against people in other societies, such "external" wars were usually not organized on behalf of the entire society or even a major section of it.[71] That is, warfare in the ethnographic record did not usually involve politically unified societies. The absolute numbers of people killed may have been small, but this does not mean that warfare in nonindustrial societies was a trivial matter. Indeed, it appears that nonindustrial warfare may have been even more lethal *proportionately* than modern warfare, judging by the fact that wars killed from 25 percent to 30 percent of the males in some nonindustrial societies.[72]

In nonindustrial societies, warfare appears to be more likely when there are unpredictable climate-related disasters (droughts, floods, hurricanes, among others) that destroy food supplies.[73] Since warfare is not predicted by chronic food shortages, it seems that people may be motivated to fight mostly by fear of future loss. If so, we would expect them to take resources when they win. And they do. The victors in war almost always take resources (land, animals, other things) from the defeated, even when the victors have no current resource problems.[74] The relationship between climate change and war has been analyzed over centuries in both China and Korea. Armed conflict appears to be greater in periods of worsening climate and more frequent disasters.[75] Another factor apparently making for more war is teaching children to mistrust others. People who grow up to be mistrustful of others may be more likely to go to war than to negotiate or seek conciliation with "enemies." Mistrust or fear of others seems to be partly caused by threat or fear of disasters.[76]

Is warfare in and between modern state societies explainable in much the same way that nonindustrial warfare seems to be explainable? Here the evidence is less clear. First, the relationship between natural disasters and war seems to be opposite in state societies. Perhaps because states usually have standing armies that need to be supplied, states appear less likely to fight when there are food-related disasters. Second, the realities of industrialized societies probably require an expanded conception of disasters. In the modern world, with its complex economic and political dependencies among nations, possible curtailments of other resources, such as oil, may be more important factors. However, interstate wars today are uncommon, and it is internal wars and civil wars that constitute most of the present armed conflict. While disasters might not clearly be related to war in state societies, recent research suggests that civil wars are predicted by the per capita income of the country—all of the wars today are in poorer regions. Conversely, in rich nations, prosperity appears to make war unattractive.[77]

Threat of disasters and poverty both indicate that people face risks to their livelihoods. War is one way to try to obtain resources, but the costs are enormous. But we may be coming to realize (since the end of the Cold War) that war is not the only way to ensure access to resources. There may be a better way in the modern world, a way that is more cost-effective as well as more preserving of human life. The international community, governments and NGOs, has already shown commitment to intervening in the face of disasters. Assurance of disaster relief worldwide might reduce the fear of disasters. But far more important than responding to disasters that have already occurred is to reduce the vulnerability of populations to disasters in the first place by reducing poverty. With respect to poverty, the United Nations has declared a commitment to reducing world poverty by half by 2015 in its Millenium Development Goals statement. If poverty is also a condition making civil war more likely, reduction in such wars should also be more likely. The certainty of international cooperation could compensate for the uncertainty of resources.

Consider how Germany and Japan have fared in the years since their "unconditional surrender" in World War II. They were forbidden to participate in the international arms race and could rely on others, particularly the United States, to protect them. Without a huge burden

Current Research and Issues

Ethnic Conflicts: Ancient Hatreds or Not?

In the period after World War II, ethnic conflicts appeared to rise dramatically and reached a peak in the early 1990s. Violent conflicts erupted between ethnic groups in the former Yugoslavia, Russia, and Spain (in Europe), in Rwanda, Sierra Leone, and the Sudan (in Africa), and in Sri Lanka and Indonesia (in Asia)—to name just a few of the many instances. Such conflicts are often thought to be intractable and inevitable because they are supposedly based on ancient hatreds. But is that true?

An Iraqi policeman of Kurdish descent walks between coffins draped with Kurdish flags. More than 700 Kurds were honored in a ceremony in northern Iraq in 2012. Estimates are that up to 180,000 people were killed when Saddam Hussein's troops began a military campaign against Iraq's minority Kurds in 1988.

Social scientists are a long way from understanding the conditions that predict ethnic conflicts, but they do know that ethnic conflicts are not necessarily ancient or inevitable. For example, anthropologists who did fieldwork in the former Yugoslavia in the 1980s described villages where different ethnic groups had lived side by side for a long time without apparent difficulty. The differences between them were hardly emphasized. Mary Kay Gilliland worked in a midsize town (Slavonski Brod) in the Slavonian region of Croatia, which was part of Yugoslavia. The people in the town identified themselves as from Slavonia rather than as Croats, Serbs, Hungarians, Czechs, Muslims (from Bosnia or from Albania), or Roma (Gypsies). Mixed marriages were not uncommon, and people discussed differences in background without anger. But in 1991, when Gilliland returned to Croatia, people complained about Serb domination of the Yugoslav government and there was talk of Croatia seceding. Symbols of Croat nationalism had appeared—new place names, a new flag—and Croats were now said to speak Croatian rather than the language they shared with the Serbs (Serbo-Croatian or Croato-Serbian). Later in 1991, violence broke out between Serbs and Croats, and atrocities were committed on both sides. Ethnicity became a matter of life or death, and Croatia seceded from Yugoslavia. At the same time, Tone Bringa, a Norwegian anthropologist who worked in Bosnia (which was then still a region of Yugoslavia), reported that the people there also paid little attention to ethnicity. A few years later, however, ethnic violence erupted among Bosnian Serbs, Muslims, and Croats, and only the intervention of the United Nations established a precarious peace.

Ethnic differences do not always lead to violence. Most of the time, even when ethnic groups have faced discrimination, people of different ethnic backgrounds live in peace with each other. So the basic question is why do some places with ethnic differences erupt in violence, but not all? Why do different ethnic groups get along in some places?

We need more research to answer this question. With all of the forced and voluntary immigration in the world, many countries are becoming more multiethnic or multicultural. The possibility of ethnic violence has become a global social problem. Gilliland suggests, among other things, that discontent over economic and political power (inequitable access to resources and opportunities) drove the Croatians to violence and secession. Does this predict ethnic violence more generally? Some cross-national studies have tested this and other theories, but so far there are no clear answers. A lot more is known about what doesn't predict ethnic violence than what does. For example, the degree of political repression does not predict ethnic conflict generally, nor does degree of intergroup hatred, income inequality, or colonial history. If we knew which factors generally give rise to ethnic violence, we might be able to think of ways to reduce or eliminate the causal conditions.

Sources: Gilliland 1995; Bringa 1995; M. H. Ross 2009a; J. Goldstein 2011.

of armaments, Germany and Japan thrived. But countries that competed militarily, particularly the United States and the Soviet Union at the height of the Cold War, experienced economic difficulties. Doesn't that scenario at least suggest the wisdom of international cooperation, particularly the need for international agreements to ensure worldwide disaster relief? Compared with going to war and its enormous costs, going to peace would be a bargain!

Recent research in political science and anthropology suggests an additional way to reduce the risk of war. Among the societies known to anthropology, studies indicate that people in more participatory—that is, more "democratic"—political systems rarely go to war with each other.[78] Thus, if authoritarian governments were to disappear from the world because the powerful nations of the world stopped supporting them militarily and otherwise, the world could be more peaceful for this reason too.

Although democratically governed states rarely go to war with each other, it used to be thought that they are not necessarily more peaceful in general, that they are as likely to go to war as are other kinds of political systems, but not so much with each other. For example, the United States has gone to war with Grenada, Panama, and Iraq—all authoritarian states—but not with democratic Canada, with which the United States has also had disputes. But now a consensus is emerging among political scientists that democracies are not only unlikely to go to war with each other, they are also less warlike in general.[79] The theory suggested by the cross-national and cross-cultural results is that democratic conflict resolution within a political system generalizes to democratic conflict resolution between political systems, particularly if the systems are both democratic. If our participatory institutions and perceptions allow us to resolve our disputes peacefully, internally and externally, we may think that similarly governed people would also be disposed to settle things peacefully. Therefore, disputes between participatory political systems should be unlikely to result in war.

The understanding that participatory systems rarely fight each other, and knowing why they do not, would have important consequences for policy in the contemporary world. The kinds of military preparations believed necessary and the costs people would be willing to pay for them might be affected. On the one hand, understanding the relationship between democracy and peace might encourage war making against authoritarian regimes to overturn them—with enormous costs in human life and otherwise. On the other hand, understanding the consequences of democracy might encourage us to assist the emergence and consolidation of more participatory systems of government in the countries of Eastern Europe, the former Soviet Union, and elsewhere. In any case, the relationship between democracy and peace strongly suggests that it is counterproductive to support any undemocratic regimes, even if they happen to be enemies of our enemies, if we want to minimize the risk of war in the world. The latest cross-national evidence suggests that extending democracy around the world will in the long run minimize the risk of war. However, change in political systems is not easy or simple. In fact, societies transitioning to democracy are more prone to ethnic conflict and civil war. It is between stable or mature democracies that you find the lowest likelihood of war.[80] Encouraging nations to be more interdependent economically, and encouraging the spread of international nongovernmental organizations (like professional societies and trade associations) to provide informal ways to resolve conflicts, would also minimize the risk of war, judging by results of recent research by political scientists.[81]

Terrorism

27.6 Describe the difficulty of defining terrorism and discuss what is known about the factors associated with it.

Ever since September 11, 2001, when terrorists crashed airliners into the World Trade Center towers in New York City and into the Pentagon in Arlington, Virginia, people all over the world realize that terrorism has become a social problem globally. It is now painfully clear that organized groups of terrorists can train their people to kill themselves and thousands of others half a world away, not only by hijacking airliners and flying them into skyscrapers but also by using easily transported explosives and biological weapons. Social scientists are now actively trying to understand terrorism, in the hope that research may lead to ways to minimize the likelihood of future attacks. But there are lots of questions to answer. What is *terrorism*, and how shall it be defined? How long has terrorist activity been around? What are the causes of terrorism? What kinds of people are likely to become terrorists? And what are the consequences of terrorism?

Answering these questions is not so simple. Most people can point to instances that hardly anyone would have trouble calling terrorism—spraying nerve gas in a Japanese subway, Palestinian suicide bombers targeting Israeli civilians, Ku Klux Klan members lynching African Americans.[82] It is harder to identify the boundaries among terrorism, crime, political repression, and warfare.[83] Most researchers agree that terrorism involves the threat or use of violence against civilians. Terrorism is usually also politically or socially organized, in contrast to most crimes, which are usually perpetrated by individuals acting on their own. (To be sure, crime can be socially organized too, as, for example, in what we call "organized crime.") One marker of the difference between most crime and terrorism is that criminals rarely take public credit for their activities because they want to avoid being caught. In terrorism, the perpetrators usually proclaim their responsibility. In terrorism also, the violence is directed mostly at unarmed people, including women and children. It is intended to frighten the "enemy," to *terrorize* them, to scare them into doing something that the terrorists want to see happen. Generally, then, **terrorism** may be defined as the use or threat of violence to create terror in others, usually for political purposes.[84] Some define terrorism as perpetrated by groups that are not formal political entities. However, this criterion presents some difficulty. What are we to call it when governments support death squads and genocide against their own civilians? Some scholars call this "state terror."[85] And what are we to call the activities of some governments that support secret operations against other countries (often referred to as "state-sponsored terrorism")? Finally, although some nations conducting war explicitly try to avoid civilian casualties and focus primarily on combatants (armed soldiers), their weapons, and resources or "assets" such as factories, air strips, and fuel depots, many attacks in wartime throughout history have purposefully targeted civilians (e.g., the United States dropped atomic bombs on Hiroshima and Nagasaki to persuade the Japanese to end World War II).

Terrorism The use or threat of violence to create terror in others, usually for political purposes.

One thing is certain about terrorism: It is not a new development. Some of the words we use for terrorists—for example, "zealots" and "assassins"—derive from terrorist movements in the past. The Zealots, Jewish nationalists who revolted against the Romans occupying Judea in the first century, would hide in crowds and stab officials and priests as well as soldiers. In the 11th and 12th centuries in southwest Asia, the Fedayeen (a group of Muslim Isma'ili Shi'ites) undertook to assassinate Sunni rulers despite the almost certainty of their own capture or death. The rulers said that the Fedayeen were under the influence of hashish and called them "Hashshashin," which is the root of the later term *assassin*.[86] In the late 18th and early 19th centuries, the "reign of terror" occurred during and after the French Revolution.

A woman cries during a candlelight interfaith service at Arlington Street Church April 16, 2013 in Boston, Massachusetts, in the aftermath of two explosions that struck near the finish line of the Boston Marathon April 15.

In the early and middle 20th century, the dictator Joseph Stalin ordered the execution of many millions of people who were considered enemies of the Soviet state. Six million Jews and millions of other innocents were exterminated by the German Third Reich in the 1930s and 1940s.[87] And many Latin American regimes, such as that in Argentina, terrorized and killed dissidents in the 1970s and 1980s.[88] Now there is a heightened fear of terrorists who may have access to weapons of mass destruction. In a world made smaller by global transportation, cell phones, and the Internet, terrorism is a greater threat than ever before.

We still lack much systematic research that explains why terrorism occurs and why people are motivated to become terrorists. But there is a good deal of research about state terrorism. Political scientist R. J. Rummel estimates that governments have killed nearly 262 million people in the 20th century (he calls this kind of terrorism "democide"). State terrorism has been responsible for four times more deaths than all the wars, civil and international, that occurred in the 20th century. Regimes in the Soviet Union (1917–1987), China (1923–1987), and Germany (1933–1945) were responsible for killing more than a total of 190 million civilians. Proportionately, the Khmer Rouge regime in Cambodia topped them all, killing over 30 percent of its population from 1975 to 1978.[89] What predicts state terrorism against one's own people? Rummel finds one clear predictor—totalitarian governments. By far, they have the highest frequencies of domestic state terrorism, controlling for factors such as economic wealth, type of religion, and population size. As Rummel puts it, "power kills; absolute power kills absolutely."[90] Democratic countries are less likely to practice state terrorism, but when they do, it occurs during or after a rebellion or a war.[91] If state terrorism is more likely to occur in totalitarian regimes, terrorists and terrorist groups may be more likely to occur in such societies. If so, the spread of democracy may be our best hope of minimizing the risk of terrorism in the world, just as the spread of democracy seems to minimize the likelihood of war between countries.

We know relatively little so far about what predicts who will become a terrorist. We do know that terrorists often come from higher social statuses and generally have more education than the average person.[92] But while terrorists are not commonly poor, it is important to ask whether the societies in which terrorism thrives are deprived in some way. A suggestive piece of evidence is that if we focus on the most deadly terrorist organizations, they do tend to occur in countries that are lower in measures of human development, that have poor records of political rights and civil liberties, and that have higher concentrations of young people.[93]

27.7 Discuss some lessons learned from anthropology that could make the world a better place.

Making the World Better

Many social problems afflict our world, not just the ones discussed in this chapter and elsewhere in this book.[94] But we have tried in this chapter to encourage positive thinking about global social problems; we have suggested how the results of past and future scientific research could be applied to solving some of those problems.

We may know enough now that we can do something about our problems, and we will discover more through future research. Social problems are mostly of human making and are, therefore, susceptible to human unmaking. There may be obstacles on the road to solutions, but we can overcome them if we want to. So let's go for it!

Summary and Review

Natural Disasters and Famine

27.1 Explain how cultural, economic, and social factors can cause or exacerbate natural events and cause disasters and famine.

- Climatic and other events in the physical environment become worse disasters because of events or conditions in the social environment. Therefore, disasters are also social problems, which have social causes and possible social solutions.
- Famine almost always has some social causes and is determined by who has rights to the available food

and whether those who have more food distribute it to those who have less.

- Cross-cultural research suggests that societies with individual rather than shared property rights are more likely to suffer famine.

> What are some examples of how cultural, economic, and social factors cause or exacerbate natural disasters? What might be some solutions?

Inadequate Housing and Homelessness

27.2 Describe the factors that lead to inadequate housing and homelessness.

- In 2010, half of the people in the world lived in urban areas, and it is projected to be about 70 percent by 2050.
- As of 2012, approximately 1 billion people or about 33 percent of urban dwellers lived in slums. Four in ten of nonpermanent houses in slums were in high-risk areas such as flood zones or areas prone to landslides.
- All but the upper-income elite may be found in illegal settlements. Squatter settlements are not chaotic, unorganized, or full of crime. Most dwellers cannot find affordable housing, but they are employed, aspire to get ahead, live in intact nuclear families, and help each other.
- Research suggests differences in the causes of homelessness in different parts of the world. Social and political policies cause homelessness.
- Many countries have "street children." In the late 1980s, 80 million of the world's children lived in the streets. In the 2000s, the estimated number grew to about 150 million worldwide.

> What factors lead to inadequate housing and homelessness and what may help minimize these conditions?

Family Violence and Abuse

27.3 Discuss the magnitude, causes, and consequences of family violence.

- To avoid having to decide what is or is not abuse, many researchers focus their studies on variation in the frequencies of specific behaviors, for example, which societies have physical punishment of children.
- Much of the violence directed at children is believed to be morally correct by the people practicing it.
- Children who are corporally punished are more likely to later physically assault their dating partners or spouses, be convicted of a crime, and have depression. Corporal punishment is possibly a cradle of violence.
- Two main predictors of corporal punishment in the cross-cultural record that are practically universal in the nation-states of the world are a money economy and a stratified social system.
- Wife beating occurs in 85 percent of the world's societies; it is most common when men control family labor and have the final say in the home, when divorce is difficult for women, when a husband's kin control remarriage for a widow, or when women have no female work groups.

> What are some of the causes and consequences of family violence? What might be done to minimize it?

Crime

27.4 Explain how cultural and societal features relate to crime, especially in regard to homicide.

- What is a crime in one society is not necessarily a crime in another. Researchers tend to look at homicide rates to assess variability among societies in terms of crime.
- Whether a nation is defeated or victorious, homicide rates tend to increase after a war.
- More countries show murder rates going down rather than up after capital punishment was abolished.
- Homicide is usually highest in nations or societies with high poverty and income inequality.

> What are some of the conditions that increase the likelihood of crime? What might decrease it?

War

27.5 Discuss warfare in terms of cultural, social, and ecological factors, and describe the reasons societies go to war.

- Armed conflict appears to be greater in periods of worsening climate and more frequent climate-related natural events associated with disasters.
- Teaching children to mistrust others may be another factor predicting war. People who grow up to be

mistrustful may be more likely to go to war than to negotiate or seek conciliation. Mistrust or fear of others seems to be partly caused by threat or fear of disasters.

- Interstate wars today are uncommon; internal wars and civil wars constitute most of the present armed conflict. Recent research suggests that civil wars are predicted by the per capita income of the country—all of the wars today are in poorer regions.

> ? What are some of the predictors of more warfare? What might minimize warfare?

Terrorism

27.6 Describe the difficulty of defining terrorism and discuss what is known about the factors associated with it.

- One marker of the difference between most crime and terrorism is that criminals rarely take public credit for their activities because they do not want to be caught. Terrorist perpetrators usually proclaim their responsibility.
- Terrorist violence is directed mostly at unarmed people, including women and children. It is intended to frighten the "enemy," to scare them into doing something that the terrorists want to see happen.
- Terrorism is not a new development and goes back to at least the first century. Today, there is a heightened fear of terrorists who may have access to weapons of mass destruction.
- More research has been done on state terrorism than on terrorism. State terrorism has resulted in four times more deaths than all the wars, civil and international, that occurred in the 20th century. A clear predictor of state terrorism is the presence of a totalitarian government.
- Terrorists generally come from higher statuses and have higher levels of education. Terrorist organizations tend to arise in countries that have lower measures of human development, poor records of political rights and civil liberties, and higher concentrations of young people.

> ? What are the difficulties in defining terrorism? What may explain state terrorism?

Making the World Better

27.7 Discuss some lessons learned from anthropology that could make the world a better place.

- Social problems such as disasters, famine, inadequate housing, homelessness, family violence, crime, war, and terrorism can be studied, and the research findings can be applied to improve or resolve those problems.
- Factors that create social problems are not always obvious, so it is important to look carefully at beliefs and practices within and among cultures to better understand the dynamics of these problems.

> ? For each of the global problems discussed, what may lessen the problems?

Think on it

1. What particular advantages do anthropologists have in trying to solve **practical** problems?
2. Select one of the **social** problems discussed in this chapter and suggest what you think could be done to reduce or eliminate it.
3. Do **global** problems require solutions by global agencies? If so, which?

Glossary

Absolute dating A method of dating fossils in which the actual age of a deposit or specimen is measured. Also known as **chronometric dating.**

Accent Differences in pronunciation characteristic of a group.

Acclimatization Impermanent physiological changes that people make when they encounter a new environment.

Acculturation The process of extensive borrowing of aspects of culture in the context of superordinate–subordinate relations between societies; usually occurs as the result of external pressure.

Acheulian A stone toolmaking tradition dating from 1.5 million years ago. Compared with the Oldowan tradition, Acheulian assemblages have more large tools created according to standardized designs or shapes. One of the most characteristic and prevalent tools in the Acheulian tool kit is the so-called hand axe, which is a teardrop-shaped bifacially flaked tool with a thinned sharp tip. Other large tools might have been cleavers and picks.

Achieved qualities Those qualities people acquire during their lifetime.

Adapid A type of prosimian with many lemurlike features; appeared in the Early Eocene.

Adaptation Refers to genetic changes that allow an organism to survive and reproduce in a specific environment.

Adaptive customs Cultural traits that enhance survival and reproductive success in a particular environment.

Adjudication The process by which a third party acting as judge makes a decision that the parties to a dispute have to accept.

Aegyptopithecus An Oligocene anthropoid and probably the best-known propliopithecid.

Affinal kin One's relatives by marriage.

Age-grade A category of people who happen to fall within a particular, culturally distinguished age range.

Age-set A group of people of similar age and the same sex who move together through some or all of life's stages.

Agriculture The practice of raising domesticated crops.

AIDS (Acquired Immune Deficiency Syndrome) A disease caused by the HIV virus.

Allele One member of a pair of genes.

Allen's rule The rule that protruding body parts (particularly arms and legs) are relatively shorter in the cooler areas of a species' range than in the warmer areas.

Ambilineal descent The rule of descent that affiliates individuals with groups of kin related to them through men or women.

Ancestor spirits Supernatural beings who are the ghosts of dead relatives.

Animatism A belief in supernatural forces.

Animism A belief in a dual existence for all things—a physical, visible body, and a psychic, invisible soul.

Anthropoids One of the two suborders of primates; includes monkeys, apes, and humans.

Anthropological linguistics The anthropological study of languages.

Anthropology A discipline that studies humans, focusing on the study of differences and similarities, both biological and cultural, in human populations. Anthropology is concerned with typical biological and cultural characteristics of human populations in all periods and in all parts of the world.

Applied (practicing) anthropology The branch of anthropology that concerns itself with applying anthropological knowledge to achieve practical goals.

^{40}Ar–^{39}Ar dating Used in conjunction with potassium-argon dating, this method gets around the problem of needing different rock samples to estimate potassium and argon. A nuclear reactor is used to convert the ^{39}Ar to ^{39}K, on the basis of which the amount of ^{40}K can be estimated. In this way, both argon and potassium can be estimated from the same rock sample.

Arboreal Adapted to living in trees.

Archaeology The branch of anthropology that seeks to reconstruct the daily life and customs of peoples who lived in the past and to trace and explain cultural changes. Often lacking written records for study, archaeologists must try to reconstruct history from the material remains of human cultures. See also **Historical archaeology.**

Archaic Time period in the New World during which food production first developed.

Ardipithecus ramidus Perhaps the first hominin, dating to about 4.5 million years ago. Its dentition combines apelike and australopithecine-like features, and its skeleton suggests it was bipedal.

Artifact Any object made by a human.

Ascribed qualities Those qualities that are determined for people at birth.

Association An organized group not based exclusively on kinship or territory.

Atlatl A spear propelled off a grooved board; named for the Aztec word for "spear-thrower."

Australopithecines Members of the genus *Australopithecus*

Australopithecus Genus of Pliocene and Pleistocene hominins.

Australopithecus afarensis A species of *Australopithecus* that lived 4 million to 3 million years ago in East Africa and was definitely bipedal.

Australopithecus africanus A species of *Australopithecus* that lived between about 3 million and 2 million years ago.

Australopithecus anamensis A species of *Australopithecus* that lived perhaps 4.2 million years ago.

Australopithecus bahrelghazali An early australopithecine, dating to about 3 million years ago, and currently represented by only a single jaw. It is an interesting species because it is found in western Chad, distant from the East African Rift Valley where all other early australopithecines have been found.

Australopithecus garhi An australopithecine, dating to about 2.5 million years ago.

Australopithecus sediba An australopithecine from South Africa that dates to around 2 million years ago and has some *Homo*-like features.

Avunculocal residence A pattern of residence in which a married couple settles with or near the husband's mother's brother.

Balanced reciprocity Giving with the expectation of a straightforward immediate or limited-time trade.

Balancing selection A type of selection that occurs when a heterozygous combination of alleles is positively favored even though a homozygous combination is disfavored.

Band A fairly small, usually nomadic local group that is politically autonomous.

Band organization The kind of political organization where the local group or band is the largest territorial group in the society that acts as a unit. The local group in band societies is politically autonomous.

Behavioral ecology Typically tries to understand contemporary human behavior using evolutionary principles. In addition to the principle of individual selection, behavioral ecologists point to the importance of analyzing economic tradeoffs because individuals have limited time and resources.

Bergmann's rule The rule that smaller-sized subpopulations of a species inhabit the warmer parts of its geographic range and larger-sized subpopulations the cooler areas.

Bifacial tool A tool worked or flaked on two sides.

Bilateral kinship The type of kinship system in which individuals affiliate more or less equally with their mother's and father's relatives.

Bilocal residence A pattern of residence in which a married couple lives with or near either the husband's parents or the wife's parents.

Bilophodont Having four cusps on the molars that form two parallel ridges. This is the common molar pattern of Old World monkeys.

Biological (physical) anthropology The study of humans as biological organisms, dealing with the emergence and evolution of humans and with contemporary biological variations among human populations.

Biomedicine The dominant medical paradigm in Western societies today.

Bipedalism Locomotion in which an animal walks on its two hind legs.

Blade A thin flake whose length is usually more than twice its width. In the blade technique of toolmaking, a core is prepared by shaping a piece of flint with hammerstones into a pyramidal or cylindrical form. Blades are then struck off until the core is used up.

Brachiators Animals that move through the trees by swinging hand over hand from branch to branch. They usually have long arms and fingers.

Bride price A substantial gift of goods or money given to the bride's kin by the groom or his kin at or before the marriage. Also called **bride wealth.**

Bride service Work performed by the groom for his bride's family for a variable length of time either before or after the marriage.

Burin A chisel-like stone tool used for carving and for making such artifacts as bone and antler needles, awls, and projectile points.

Canines The cone-shaped teeth immediately behind the incisors; used by most primates to seize food and in fighting and display.

Carpolestes A mouse-sized arboreal creature living about 56 million years ago; a strong candidate for the common primate ancestor.

Cash crop A cultivated commodity raised for sale rather than for personal consumption by the cultivator.

Caste A ranked group, often associated with a certain occupation, in which membership is determined at birth and marriage is restricted to members of one's own caste.

Catarrhines The group of anthropoids with narrow noses and nostrils that face downward. Catarrhines include monkeys of the Old World (Africa, Asia, and Europe), as well as apes and humans.

Cercopithecoids Old World monkeys.

Cerebral cortex The "gray matter" of the brain; the center of speech and other higher mental activities.

Chief A person who exercises authority, usually on behalf of a multicommunity political unit. This role is generally found in rank societies and is usually permanent and often hereditary.

Chiefdom A political unit, with a chief at its head, integrating more than one community but not necessarily the whole society or language group.

Chromosomes Paired rod-shaped structures within a cell nucleus containing the genes that transmit traits from one generation to the next.

Chronometric dating See **Absolute dating.**

Civilization Urban society, from the Latin word for "city-state."

Clan A set of kin whose members believe themselves to be descended from a common ancestor but cannot specify the links back to that founder; often designated by a totem. Also called a **sib.**

Class A category of people who have about the same opportunity to obtain economic resources, power, and prestige.

Classificatory terms Kinship terms that merge or equate relatives who are genealogically distinct from one another; the same term is used for a number of different kin.

Class societies Societies containing social groups that have unequal access to economic resources, power, and prestige.

Cline The gradually increasing (or decreasing) frequency of a gene from one end of a region to another.

Code-switching Using more than one language in the course of conversing.

Codified laws Formal principles for resolving disputes in heterogeneous and stratified societies.

Cognates Words or morphs that belong to different languages but have similar sounds and meanings.

Commercial exchange See **Market (or commercial) exchange.**

Commercialization The increasing dependence on buying and selling, with money usually as the medium of exchange.

Complementary opposition The occasional uniting of various segments of a segmentary lineage system in opposition to similar segments.

Consanguineal kin One's biological relatives; relatives by birth.
Context The relationships between and among artifacts, ecofacts, fossils, and features.
Continental drift The movement of the continents over the past 135 million years. In the early Cretaceous (circa 135 million years ago), there were two "supercontinents": *Laurasia*, which included North America and Eurasia; and *Gondwanaland*, which included Africa, South America, India, Australia, and Antarctica. By the beginning of the Paleocene (circa 65 million years ago), Gondwanaland had broken apart, with South America drifting west away from Africa, India drifting east, and Australia and Antarctica drifting south.
Core vocabulary Nonspecialist vocabulary.
Corvée A system of required labor.
Cretaceous Geological epoch 135 million to 65 million years ago, during which dinosaurs and other reptiles ceased to be the dominant land vertebrates, and mammals and birds began to become important.
Crime Violence not considered legitimate that occurs within a political unit.
Cro-Magnons Humans who lived in western Europe about 35,000 years ago, they were once thought to be the earliest specimens of modern-looking humans, or ***Homo sapiens***. But it is now known that modern-looking humans appeared earlier outside of Europe; the earliest so far found lived in Africa.
Cross-cousins Children of siblings of the opposite sex. One's cross-cousins are the father's sisters' children and mother's brothers' children.
Cross-cultural researcher An ethnologist who uses ethnographic data about many societies to test possible explanations of cultural variation to discover general patterns about cultural traits—what is universal, what is variable, why traits vary, and what the consequences of the variability might be.
Crossing-over Exchanges of sections of chromosomes from one chromosome to another.
Cultural anthropology The study of cultural variation and universals in the past and present.
Cultural ecology The analysis of the relationship between a culture and its environment.
Cultural relativism The attitude that a society's customs and ideas should be viewed within the context of that society's problems and opportunities.
Cultural resource management (CRM) The branch of applied anthropology that seeks to recover and preserve the archaeological record before programs of planned change disturb or destroy it.
Culture The set of learned behaviors, beliefs, attitudes, values, and ideals that are characteristic of a particular society or other social group.
Culture history A history of the cultures that lived in a given area over time. Until the 1950s, building such culture histories was a primary goal of archaeological research.
Cuneiform Wedge-shaped writing invented by the Sumerians around 3000 B.C.
Descriptive term A unique term used for a distinct relative.
Descriptive (structural) linguistics The study of how languages are constructed.
Development anthropology One of the main subfields of applied or practicing anthropology, aimed at improving people's lives, particularly decreasing poverty and hunger.
Dialect A variety of a language spoken in a particular area or by a particular social group.
Diastema A gap between the canine and first premolar found in apes.
Diffusion The borrowing by one society of a cultural trait belonging to another society as the result of contact between the two societies.
Directional selection A type of natural selection that increases the frequency of a trait (the trait is said to be positively favored, or adaptive).
Diurnal Active during the day.
Divination Getting the supernatural to provide guidance.
DNA Deoxyribonucleic acid; a long, two-stranded molecule in the genes that directs the makeup of an organism according to the instructions in its genetic code.
Domestication Modification or adaptation of plants and animals for use by humans. When people plant crops, we refer to the process as cultivation. It is only when the crops cultivated and the animals raised have been modified—are different from wild varieties—that we speak of plant and animal domestication.
Dominant The allele of a gene pair that is always phenotypically expressed in the heterozygous form.
Double descent or double unilineal descent A system that affiliates individuals with a group of matrilineal kin for some purposes and with a group of patrilineal kin for other purposes.
Dowry A substantial transfer of goods or money from the bride's family to the bride.
Dryopithecus Genus of ape from the later Miocene found primarily in Europe. It had thin tooth enamel and pointed molar cusps very similar to those of the fruit-eating chimpanzees of today.
Dual-inheritance theory In contrast to other evolutionary ecological perspectives, this theory gives much more importance to culture as part of the evolutionary process. Dual inheritance refers to both genes and culture playing different, but nonetheless important and interactive roles in transmitting traits to future generations.
Ecofacts Natural items that humans have used; things such as the remains of animals eaten by humans or plant pollens found on archaeological sites are examples of ecofacts.
Economic resources Things that have value in a culture, including land, tools and other technology, goods, and money.
Egalitarian societies Societies in which all people of a given age-sex category have equal access to economic resources, power, and prestige.
Ego In the reckoning of kinship, the reference point or focal person.
Enculturation See **Socialization.**
Endogamy The rule specifying marriage to a person within one's own group (kin, caste, community).
Environmental anthropology Focuses on issues relating to the interaction of humans with their environments, at the local, regional, and global levels, particularly focusing on how to understand and alleviate the degradation of the environment.
Eocene A geological epoch 55 million to 34 million years ago during which the first definite primates appeared.
Epipaleolithic Time period during which food production first developed in the Near East.
Ethnicity The process of defining ethnicity usually involves a group of people emphasizing common origins and language, shared history, and selected aspects of cultural difference such as a difference in religion. Because different groups are doing the perceiving, ethnic identities often vary with whether one is inside or outside the group.
Ethnocentric Refers to judgment of other cultures solely in terms of one's own culture.
Ethnocentrism The attitude that other societies' customs and ideas can be judged in the context of one's own culture.
Ethnogenesis Creation of a new culture.
Ethnographer A person who spends some time living with, interviewing, and observing a group of people to describe their customs.
Ethnographic analogy Method of comparative cultural study that extrapolates to the past from recent or current societies.
Ethnography A description of a society's customary behaviors and ideas.
Ethnohistorian An ethnologist who uses historical documents to study how a particular culture has changed over time.
Ethnology The study of how and why recent cultures differ and are similar.
Ethnomedicine The health-related beliefs, knowledge, and practices of a cultural group.
Evolutionary psychology A type of evolutionary ecological approach that is particularly interested in universal human psychology. It is argued that human psychology was primarily adapted to the environment that characterized most of human history—the hunting-gathering way of life.
Excavation The careful removal of archaeological deposits; the recovery of artifacts, ecofacts, fossils, and features from the soil in which those deposits have been buried.
Exogamy The rule specifying marriage to a person from outside one's own group (kin or community).
Explanation An answer to a *why* question. In science, there are two kinds of explanation that researchers try to achieve: associations and theories.
Extended family A family consisting of two or more single-parent, monogamous, polygynous, or polyandrous families linked by a blood tie.
Extensive cultivation A type of horticulture in which the land is worked for short periods and then left to regenerate for some years before being used again. Also called **shifting cultivation.**
Falsification Showing that a theory seems to be wrong by finding that implications or predictions derivable from it are not consistent with objectively collected data.
Family A social and economic unit consisting minimally of a parent and a child.
Features Artifacts of human manufacture that cannot be removed from an archaeological site. Hearths, storage pits, and buildings are examples of features.
Feuding A state of recurring hostility between families or groups of kin, usually motivated by a desire to avenge an offense against a member of the group.
Fieldwork Firsthand experience with the people being studied and the usual means by which anthropological information is obtained. Regardless of other methods that anthropologists may use (e.g., censuses, surveys), fieldwork usually involves participant-observation for an extended period of time, often a year or more. See **Participant-observation.**
Folklore Includes all the myths, legends, folktales, ballads, riddles, proverbs, and superstitions of a cultural group. Generally, folklore is transmitted orally, but it may also be written.
Food production The form of subsistence technology in which food-getting is dependent on the cultivation and domestication of plants and animals
Foragers People who subsist on the collection of naturally occurring plants and animals. Also referred to as **hunter-gatherers** or *food collectors.*
Foraging May be generally defined as a food-getting strategy that obtains wild plant and animal resources through gathering, hunting, scavenging, or fishing; also known as food collection.
Foramen magnum Opening in the base of the skull through which the spinal cord passes en route to the brain.
Forensic anthropology The application of anthropology, usually physical anthropology, to help identify human remains and assist in solving crimes.
Fossils The hardened remains or impressions of plants and animals that lived in the past.
Fraternal polyandry The marriage of a woman to two or more brothers at the same time.
Gender differences Differences between females and males that reflect cultural expectations and experiences.
Gender roles Roles that are culturally assigned to genders.
Gender stratification The degree of unequal access by the different genders to prestige, authority, power, rights, and economic resources.
Gene Chemical unit of heredity.
Gene flow The process by which genes pass from the gene pool of one population to that of another through mating and reproduction.
Generalized reciprocity Gift giving without any immediate or planned return.
General-purpose money A universally accepted medium of exchange.
Genetic drift The various random processes that affect gene frequencies in small, relatively isolated populations.
Genotype The total complement of inherited traits or genes of an organism.
Genus A group of related species; pl., genera.
Ghosts Supernatural beings who were once human; the souls of dead people.
Globalization The ongoing spread of goods, people, information, and capital around the world.
Gloger's rule The rule that populations of birds and mammals living in warm, humid climates have more melanin (and therefore darker skin, fur, or feathers) than populations of the same species living in cooler, drier areas.
Gods Supernatural beings of nonhuman origin who are named personalities; often anthropomorphic.
Group marriage Marriage in which more than one man is married to more than one woman at the same time; not customary in any known human society.
Half-life The time it takes for half of the atoms of a radioactive substance to decay into atoms of a different substance.
Hand axe A teardrop-shaped stone tool characteristic of Acheulian assemblages.
Hard hammer A technique of stone tool manufacture where one stone is used to knock flakes from another stone. Flakes produced through hard hammer percussion are usually large and crude.

Headman A person who holds a powerless but symbolically unifying position in a community within an egalitarian society; may exercise influence but has no power to impose sanctions.
Hermeneutics The study of meaning.
Heterozygous Possessing differing genes or alleles in corresponding locations on a pair of chromosomes.
Hieroglyphics "Picture writing," as in ancient Egypt and in Mayan sites in Mesoamerica (Mexico and Central America).
Historical archaeology A specialty within archaeology that studies the material remains of recent peoples who left written records.
Historical linguistics The study of how languages change over time.
Holistic Refers to an approach that studies many aspects of a multifaceted system.
Hominins The group of hominoids consisting of humans and their direct ancestors.
Hominoids The group of catarrhines that includes both apes and humans.
Homo Genus to which modern humans and their ancestors belong.
Homo antecessor Refers to a group of hominin fossils found in the Atapuerca region of Spain that appear to be transitional between Neandertals and modern humans. They are closely related to *Homo heidelbergensis*, and many scholars believe they are the same species.
Homo erectus The first hominin species to be widely distributed in the Old World. The earliest finds are possibly 1.8 million years old. The brain (averaging 895–1,040 cc) was larger than that found in any of the australopithecines or *H. habilis* but smaller than the average brain of a modern human.
Homo ergaster A species closely related to *Homo erectus* but found only in East Africa. Some scholars do not see enough difference between *Homo erectus* and *Homo ergaster* to count them as different species.
Homo floresiensis A dwarf species of hominin that lived on the Indonesian island of Flores until about 12,000 years ago and probably descended from an isolated *Homo erectus* population.
Homo habilis Dating from about 2 million years ago, an early species belonging to our genus, *Homo*, with cranial capacities averaging about 630–640 cc, about 50 percent of the brain capacity of modern humans.
Homo heidelbergensis A transitional species between *Homo erectus* and *Homo sapiens*.
Homo neandertalensis The technical name for the Neandertals, a group of robust and otherwise anatomically distinct hominins that are close relatives of modern humans— so close that some believe they should be classified as *Homo sapiens neandertalensis*.
Homo rudolfensis Early species belonging to our genus, *Homo*. Similar enough to *Homo habilis* that some paleoanthropologists make no distinction between the two.
Homo sapiens All living people belong to one biological species, *Homo sapiens*, which means that all human populations on earth can successfully interbreed. The first *Homo sapiens* may have emerged about 200,000 years ago.
Homozygous Possessing two identical genes or alleles in corresponding locations on a pair of chromosomes.
Horticulture Plant cultivation carried out with relatively simple tools and methods; nature is allowed to replace nutrients in the soil, in the absence of permanently cultivated fields.
Human paleontology The study of the emergence of humans and their later physical evolution. Also called **paleoanthropology.**
Human variation The study of how and why contemporary human populations vary biologically.
Hunter-gatherers People who collect food from naturally occurring resources, that is, wild plants, animals, and fish. The term *hunter-gatherers* minimizes sometimes heavy dependence on fishing. Also referred to as **foragers** or *food collectors*.
Hybridization The creation of a viable offspring from the mating of two different species.
Hylobates The family of hominoids that includes gibbons and siamangs; often referred to as the lesser apes (as compared with the great apes such as gorillas and chimpanzees).
Hypotheses Predictions, which may be derived from theories, about how variables are related.
Hypoxia A condition of oxygen deficiency that often occurs at high altitudes. The percentage of oxygen in the air is the same as at lower altitudes, but because the barometric pressure is lower, less oxygen is taken in with each breath. Often, breathing becomes more rapid, the heart beats faster, and activity is more difficult.
Incest taboo Prohibition of sexual intercourse or marriage between mother and son, father and daughter, and brother and sister; often extends to other relatives.
Independent family A family unit consisting of one monogamous (nuclear) family, or one polygynous or one polyandrous family.
Indirect dowry Goods given by the groom's kin to the bride (or her father, who passes most of them to her) at or before her marriage.
Indicator artifacts and ecofacts Items that changed relatively rapidly and which, thus, can be used to indicate the relative age of associated items.
Indirect percussion A toolmaking technique common in the Upper Paleolithic. After shaping a core into a pyramidal or cylindrical form, the toolmaker can put a punch of antler or wood or another hard material into position and strike it with a hammer. Using a hammer-struck punch enabled toolmakers to strike off consistently shaped blades.
Insectivore The order or major grouping of mammals, including modern shrews and moles, that is adapted to feeding on insects.
Intensive agriculture Food production characterized by the permanent cultivation of fields and made possible by the use of the plow, draft animals or machines, fertilizers, irrigation, water-storage techniques, and other complex agricultural techniques.
Kenyanthropus platyops A nearly complete 3.5 million year old skull found in western Kenya. It is thought by some scholars to be a species of australopithecine (and hence should not be regarded as a separate genus).
Kenyapithecus An apelike primate from the Middle Miocene found in East Africa. It had very thickly enameled teeth and robust jaws, suggesting a diet of hard, tough foods. Probably somewhat terrestrial.
Kindred A bilateral set of close relatives who may be called upon for some purpose.
Kinesics The study of communication by nonvocal means, including posture, mannerisms, body movement, facial expressions, and signs and gestures.
Knuckle walking A locomotor pattern of primates such as the chimpanzee and gorilla in which the weight of the upper part of the body is supported on the thickly padded knuckles of the hands.
Laws (scientific) Associations or relationships that almost all scientists accept.
Levalloisian method A method that allowed flake tools of a predetermined size to be produced from a shaped core. The toolmakers first shaped the core and prepared a "striking platform" at one end. Flakes of predetermined and standard sizes could then be knocked off. Although some Levallois flakes date from as far back as 400,000 years ago, they are found more frequently in Mousterian tool kits.
Levirate A custom whereby a man is obliged to marry his deceased brother's wife.
Lexical content Vocabulary or lexicon.
Lexicon The words and morphs, and their meanings, of a language; approximated by a dictionary.
Lineage A set of kin whose members trace descent from a common ancestor through known links.
Lithics The technical name for tools made from stone.
Lower Paleolithic The period of the Oldowan and Acheulian stone tool traditions.
Magic The performance of certain rituals that are believed to compel the supernatural powers to act in particular ways.
Maladaptive customs Cultural traits that diminish the chances of survival and reproduction in a particular environment.
Mana A supernatural, impersonal force that inhabits certain objects or people and is believed to confer success and/or strength.
Manumission The granting of freedom to a slave.
Market (or commercial) exchange Transactions in which the "prices" are subject to supply and demand, whether or not the transactions occur in a marketplace.
Marriage A socially approved sexual and economic union, usually between a man and a woman, that is presumed, both by the couple and by others, to be more or less permanent, and that subsumes reciprocal rights and obligations between the two spouses and their future children.
Matrilineal descent The rule of descent that affiliates individuals with kin of both sexes related to them through women only.
Matrilocal residence A pattern of residence in which a married couple lives with or near the wife's parents.
Measure To describe how something compares with other things on some scale of variation.
Mediation The process by which a third party tries to bring about a settlement in the absence of formal authority to force a settlement.
Medical anthropology The anthropological study of health and illness and associated beliefs and practices.
Mediums Part-time religious practitioners who are asked to heal and divine while in a trance.
Meiosis The process by which reproductive cells are formed. In this process of division, the number of chromosomes in the newly formed cells is reduced by half, so that when fertilization occurs the resulting organism has the normal number of chromosomes appropriate to its species, rather than double that number.
Mesolithic The archaeological period in the Old World beginning about 12,000 B.C. Humans were starting to settle down in semipermanent camps and villages, as people began to depend less on big game (which they used to have to follow over long distances) and more on relatively stationary food resources such as fish, shellfish, small game, and wild plants rich in carbohydrates, proteins, and oils.
Messenger RNA A type of ribonucleic acid that is used in the cell to copy the DNA code for use in protein synthesis.
Microlith A small, razorlike blade fragment that was probably attached in a series to a wooden or bone handle to form a cutting edge.
Middle Paleolithic The time period of the Mousterian stone tool tradition.
Miocene The geological epoch from 24 million to 5.2 million years ago.
Mitosis Cellular reproduction or growth involving the duplication of chromosome pairs.
Moiety A unilineal descent group in a society that is divided into two such maximal groups; there may be smaller unilineal descent groups as well.
Molars The large teeth behind the premolars at the back of the jaw; used for chewing and grinding food.
Monogamy Marriage between only one man and only one woman at a time.
Monotheistic Believing that there is only one high god and that all other supernatural beings are subordinate to, or are alternative manifestations of, this supreme being.
Morph The smallest unit of a language that has a meaning.
Morpheme One or more morphs with the same meaning.
Morphology The study of how sound sequences convey meaning.
Mousterian tool assemblage Named after the tool assemblage found in a rock shelter at Le Moustier in the Dordogne region of southwestern France. Compared with an Acheulian assemblage, the Middle Paleolithic (40,000–300,000 years ago) Mousterian has a smaller proportion of large core tools such as hand axes and cleavers and a bigger proportion of small flake tools such as scrapers. Flakes were often altered or "retouched" by striking small flakes or chips from one or more edges.
Mutation A change in the DNA sequence, producing an altered gene.
Nation A set of people sharing a common territory, history, and a sense of identity.
Nation-state The co-occurrence of a political state and a nation.
Nationalism The strong sense of loyalty, attachment, and devotion to a nation (see nation).
Natural selection The outcome of processes that affect the frequencies of traits in a particular environment. Traits that enhance survival and reproductive success increase in frequency over time.
Neandertal The common name for the species *Homo neandertalensis*.
Negotiation The process by which the parties to a dispute try to resolve it themselves.
Neolithic Originally meaning "the new stone age," now meaning the presence of domesticated plants and animals. The earliest evidence of domestication comes from the Near East about 8000 B.C.

Neolocal residence A pattern of residence whereby a married couple lives separately, and usually at some distance, from the kin of both spouses.

Nocturnal Active during the night.

Nonfraternal polyandry Marriage of a woman to two or more men who are not brothers.

Nonsororal polygyny Marriage of a man to two or more women who are not sisters.

Normalizing selection The type of natural selection that removes harmful genes that arose by mutation.

Norms Standards or rules about what is acceptable behavior.

Nuclear family A family consisting of a married couple and their young children.

Oath The act of calling upon a deity to bear witness to the truth of what one says.

Obsidian A volcanic glass that can be used to make mirrors or sharp-edged tools.

Occipital torus A ridge of bone running horizontally across the back of the skull in apes and some hominins.

Oldowan The earliest stone toolmaking tradition, named after the tools found in Bed I at Olduvai Gorge, Tanzania, from about 2.5 million years ago. The stone artifacts include core tools and sharp-edged flakes made by striking one stone against another. Flake tools predominate. Among the core tools, so-called choppers are common.

Oligocene The geological epoch 34 million to 24 million years ago during which definite anthropoids emerged.

Omnivorous Eating both meat and vegetation.

Omomyid A type of prosimian with many tarsierlike features that appeared in the early Eocene.

Operational definition A description of the procedure that is followed in measuring a variable.

Opposable thumb A thumb that can touch the tips of all the other fingers.

Optimal foraging theory The theory that individuals seek to maximize the returns (in calories and nutrients) on their labor in deciding which animals and plants they will go after.

Ordeal A means of determining guilt or innocence by submitting the accused to dangerous or painful tests believed to be under supernatural control.

Orrorin tugenensis An apparently bipedal primate dating to between 5.8 and 6 million years, making it possibly the earliest known hominin.

Paleoanthropology See **Human paleontology.**

Paleocene The geological epoch 65 million to 55 million years ago.

Paralanguage Refers to all the optional vocal features or silences apart from the language itself that communicate meaning.

Parallel cousins Children of siblings of the same sex. One's parallel cousins are the father's brothers' children and the mother's sisters' children.

Paranthropoid Members of the genus *Paranthropus.*

Paranthropus A genus of early hominins that had very large teeth and jaws. Once thought to be part of the *Australopithecus* genus, but now considered a separate genus.

Paranthropus aethiopicus An early paranthropoid.

Paranthropus boisei An East African paranthropoid species dating from 2.2 million to 1.3 million years ago with somewhat larger cranial capacity than *A. africanus.* No longer thought to be larger than australopithecines, it is robust primarily in the skull and jaw, most strikingly in the teeth. Compared with *P. robustus, P. boisei* has even more features that reflect a huge chewing apparatus.

Paranthropus robustus A paranthropoid species found in South African caves dating from about 1.8 million to 1 million years ago. Not as large in the teeth and jaws as *P. boisei.*

Parapithecids Small monkeylike Oligocene primates found in the Fayum area of Egypt.

Participant-observation Living among the people being studied—observing, questioning, and (when possible) taking part in the important events of the group. Writing or otherwise recording notes on observations, questions asked and answered, and things to check out later are parts of participant-observation.

Pastoralism A form of subsistence technology in which food-getting is based directly or indirectly on the maintenance of domesticated animals.

Patrilineal descent The rule of descent that affiliates individuals with kin of both sexes related to them through men only.

Patrilocal residence A pattern of residence in which a married couple lives with or near the husband's parents.

Peasants Rural people who produce food for their own subsistence but who must also contribute or sell their surpluses to others (in towns and cities) who do not produce their own food.

Percussion flaking A toolmaking technique in which one stone is struck with another to remove a flake.

Personality integration of culture The theory that personality or psychological processes may account for connections between certain aspects of culture.

Pierolapithecus A Middle Miocene ape that has wrists and vertebrae that would have made it capable of brachiation, but also has relatively short fingers like modern monkeys.

Phenotype The observable physical appearance of an organism, which may or may not reflect its genotype or total genetic constitution.

Phone A speech sound in a language.

Phoneme A sound or set of sounds that makes a difference in meaning to the speakers of the language.

Phonology The study of the sounds in a language and how they are used.

Phratry A unilineal descent group composed of a number of supposedly related clans (sibs).

Physical (biological) anthropology See **Biological (physical) anthropology.**

Platyrrhines The group of anthropoids that have broad, flat-bridged noses, with nostrils facing outward; these monkeys are currently found only in the New World (Central and South America).

Pleistocene A geological epoch that started 1.6 million years ago and, according to some, continues into the present. During this period, glaciers have often covered much of the earth's surface and humans became the dominant life form.

Plesiadipis The most well known of the plesiadipiforms, possibly an archaic primate.

Pliocene The geological epoch 5.2 million to 1.6 million years ago during which the earliest definite hominins appeared.

Political economy The study of how external forces, particularly powerful state societies, explain the way a society changes and adapts.

Polyandry The marriage of one woman to more than one man at a time.

Polygamy Plural marriage; one individual is married to more than one spouse simultaneously. **Polygyny** and **polyandry** are types of polygamy.

Polygyny The marriage of one man to more than one woman at a time.

Polyphony Two or more melodies sung simultaneously.

Polytheistic Recognizing many gods, none of whom is believed to be superordinate.

Pongids Hominoids whose members include both the living and extinct apes.

Potassium-argon (K-Ar) dating A chronometric dating method that uses the rate of decay of a radioactive form of potassium (^{40}K) into argon (^{40}Ar) to date samples from 5,000 years to 3 billion years old. The K-Ar method dates the minerals and rocks in a deposit, not the fossils themselves.

Postpartum sex taboo Prohibition of sexual intercourse between a couple for a period of time after the birth of their child.

Potlatch A feast among Pacific Northwest Native Americans at which great quantities of food and goods are given to the guests in order to gain prestige for the host(s).

Power The ability to make others do what they do not want to do or influence based on the threat of force.

Practicing anthropology The branch of anthropology that concerns itself with applying anthropological knowledge to achieve practical goals, usually in the service of an agency outside the traditional academic setting.

Prairie Grassland with a high grass cover.

Prehensile Adapted for grasping objects.

Prehistory The time before written records.

Pressure flaking Toolmaking technique whereby small flakes are struck off by pressing against the core with a bone, antler, or wooden tool.

Prestige Being accorded particular respect or honor.

Priests Generally full-time specialists, with very high status, who are thought to be able to relate to superior or high gods beyond the ordinary person's access or control.

Primary subsistence activities The food-getting activities: gathering, hunting, fishing, herding, and agriculture.

Primate A member of the mammalian order Primates, divided into the two suborders of prosimians and anthropoids.

Primatologists People who study primates.

Probability value (p-value) The likelihood that an observed result could have occurred by chance.

Proconsul The best-known genus of proto-apes from the Early Miocene.

Prognathic A physical feature that is sticking out or pushed forward, such as the faces in apes and some hominid species.

Propliopithecids Apelike anthropoids dating from the Early Oligocene, found in the Fayum area of Egypt.

Prosimians Literally "pre-monkeys," one of the two suborders of primates; includes lemurs, lorises, and tarsiers.

Protolanguage A hypothesized ancestral language from which two or more languages seem to have derived.

Quadrupeds Animals that walk on all fours.

Race In biology, race refers to a subpopulation or variety of a species that differs somewhat in gene frequencies from other varieties of the species. Many anthropologists do not think that the concept of race is usefully applied to humans because humans do not fall into geographic populations that can be easily distinguished in terms of different sets of biological or physical traits. Thus, "race" in humans is largely a culturally assigned category.

Rachis The seed-bearing part of a plant. In the wild variety of grain, the rachis shatters easily, releasing the seeds. Domesticated grains have a tough rachis, which does not shatter easily.

Racism The belief, without scientific basis, that some "races" are inferior to others.

Radiocarbon (or carbon-14, 14C) dating A dating method uses the decay of carbon-14 to date organic remains. It is reliable for dating once-living matter up to 50,000 years old.

Raiding A short-term use of force, generally planned and organized, to realize a limited objective.

Random sample A sample in which all cases selected have had an equal chance to be included.

Rank societies Societies that do not have any unequal access to economic resources or power, but with social groups that have unequal access to status positions and prestige.

Recessive An allele phenotypically suppressed in the heterozygous form and expressed only in the homozygous form.

Reciprocity Giving and taking (not politically arranged) without the use of money.

Redistribution The accumulation of goods (or labor) by a particular person or in a particular place and their subsequent distribution.

Relative dating A method of dating fossils that determines the age of a specimen or deposit relative to a known specimen or deposit.

Religion Any set of attitudes, beliefs, and practices pertaining to supernatural power, whether that power rests in forces, gods, spirits, ghosts, or demons.

Revitalization movements New religious movements intended to save a culture by infusing it with a new purpose and life.

Revolution A usually violent replacement of a society's rulers.

Ribosome A structure in the cell used in making proteins.

Rituals Repetitive sets of behaviors that occur in essentially the same patterns every time they occur. Religious rituals involve the supernatural in some way.

Rules of descent Rules that connect individuals with particular sets of kin because of known or presumed common ancestry.

Sagittal crest A ridge of bone running along the top of the skull in apes and early hominins.

Sagittal keel An inverted V-shaped ridge running along the top of the skull in *Homo erectus.*

Sahelanthropus tchadensis A hominoid found in Chad dating to around 7 million years ago.

Sampling universe The list of cases to be sampled from.

Savanna Tropical grassland.

Secondary institutions Aspects of culture, such as religion, music, art, folklore, and games, which presumably reflect or are projections of the basic, or typical, personality in a society.

Secondary subsistence activities Activities that involve the preparation and processing of food either to make it edible or to store it.
Sedentarism Settled life.
Segmentary lineage system A hierarchy of more inclusive lineages; usually functions only in conflict situations.
Segregation The random sorting of chromosomes in meiosis.
Sex differences The typical differences between females and males that are most likely due to biological differences.
Sexually dimorphic A marked difference in size and appearance between males and females of a species.
Sexual dimorphism See **Sexually dimorphic.**
Shaman A religious intermediary, usually part-time, whose primary function is to cure people through sacred songs, pantomime, and other means; sometimes called witch doctor by Westerners.
Shifting cultivation See **Extensive cultivation.**
Sib See **Clan.**
Siblings A person's brothers and sisters.
Sickle-cell anemia (sicklemia) A condition in which red blood cells assume a crescent (sickle) shape when deprived of oxygen, instead of the normal (disk) shape. The sickle-shaped red blood cells do not move through the body as readily as normal cells, and thus cause damage to the heart, lungs, brain, and other vital organs.
Sites Locations where the material remains of human activity have been preserved in a way that archaeologists or paleoanthropologists can recover them.
Sivapithecus A genus of ape from the later Miocene known for its thickly enameled teeth, suggesting a diet of hard, tough, or gritty items. Found primarily in western and southern Asia and now thought to be ancestral to orangutans.
Slash-and-burn A form of shifting cultivation in which the natural vegetation is cut down and burned off. The cleared ground is used for a short time and then left to regenerate.
Slaves A class of people who do not own their own labor or the products thereof.
Socialization A term anthropologists and psychologists use to describe the development, through the direct and indirect influence of parents and others, of children's patterns of behavior (and attitudes and values) that conform to cultural expectations. Also called **enculturation.**
Society A group of people who occupy a particular territory and speak a common language not generally understood by neighboring peoples. By this definition, societies do not necessarily correspond to nations.
Sociobiology Systematic study of the biological causes of human behavior. Compare with **behavioral ecology, evolutionary psychology**, and **dual-inheritance theory.**
Sociolinguistics The study of cultural and subcultural patterns of speaking in different social contexts.
Soft hammer A technique of stone tool manufacture in which a bone or wood hammer is used to strike flakes from a stone.
Sorcery The use of certain materials to invoke supernatural powers to harm people.
Sororal polygyny The marriage of a man to two or more sisters at the same time.
Sororate A custom whereby a woman is obliged to marry her deceased sister's husband.
Special-purpose money Objects of value for which only some goods and services can be exchanged.
Speciation The development of a new species.
Species A population that consists of organisms able to interbreed and produce viable and fertile offspring.
Spirits Unnamed supernatural beings of nonhuman origin who are beneath the gods in prestige and often closer to the people; may be helpful, mischievous, or evil.
State An autonomous political unit with centralized decision making over many communities with power to govern by force (e.g., to collect taxes, draft people for work and war, and make and enforce laws). Most states have cities with public buildings; full-time craft and religious specialists; an "official" art style; a hierarchical social structure topped by an elite class; and a governmental monopoly on the legitimate use of force to implement policies.
State organization A society is described as having state organization when it includes one or more states.
Statistical association A relationship or correlation between two or more variables that is unlikely to be due to chance.
Statistically significant Refers to a result that would occur very rarely by chance. The result (and stronger ones) would occur fewer than 5 times out of 100 by chance.
Steppe Grassland with a dry, low grass cover.
Stratified An archaeological deposit that contains successive layers or strata.
Stratigraphy The study of how different rock formations and fossils are laid down in successive layers or strata. Older layers are generally deeper or lower than more recent layers.
Structural linguistics See **Descriptive (structural) linguistics.**
Subculture The shared customs of a subgroup within a society.
Subsistence economies Economies in which almost all able-bodied adults are largely engaged in getting food for themselves and their families.
Supernatural Believed to be not human or not subject to the laws of nature.
Symbolic communication An arbitrary (not obviously meaningful) gesture, call, word, or sentence that has meaning even when its *referent* is not present.
Syntax The ways in which words are arranged to form phrases and sentences.
Taboo A prohibition that, if violated, is believed to bring supernatural punishment.
Taurodontism Having teeth with an enlarged pulp cavity.
Terrestrial Adapted to living on the ground.
Terrorism The use or threat of violence to create terror in others, usually for political purposes.
Theoretical construct Something that cannot be observed or verified directly.
Theoretical orientation A general attitude about how phenomena are to be explained.
Theories Explanations of associations or laws.
Totem A plant or animal associated with a clan (sib) as a means of group identification; may have other special significance for the group.
Tribal organization The kind of political organization in which local communities mostly act autonomously but there are kin groups (such as clans) or associations (such as age-sets) that can temporarily integrate a number of local groups into a larger unit.
Tribe A territorial population in which there are kin or nonkin groups with representatives in a number of local groups. There is no formal integration of the local groups.
Unifacial tool A tool worked or flaked on one side only.
Unilineal descent Affiliation with a group of kin through descent links of one sex only.
Unilocal residence A pattern of residence (patrilocal, matrilocal, or avunculocal) that specifies just one set of relatives that the married couple lives with or near.
Unisex association An association that restricts its membership to one sex, usually male.
Universally ascribed qualities Those ascribed qualities (age, sex) that are found in all societies.
Upper Paleolithic The time period associated with the emergence of modern humans and their spread around the world.
Variable A thing or quantity that varies.
Variably ascribed qualities Those ascribed qualities (such as ethnic, religious, or social class differences) that are found only in some societies.
Vertical clinging and leaping A locomotor pattern characteristic of several primates, including tarsiers and galagos. The animal normally rests by clinging to a branch in a vertical position and uses its hind limbs alone to push off from one vertical position to another.
Warfare Socially organized violence between political entities such as communities, districts, or nations.
Witchcraft The practice of attempting to harm people by supernatural means, but through emotions and thought alone, not through the use of tangible objects

Notes

Chapter 1

1. Harrison 1975; Durham 1991, 228–37; Ingram et al. 2009.
2. Chimpanzee Sequencing and Analysis Consortium 2005.
3. Nolan 2003, 2.
4. Van Willigen 2002, 7.
5. Kedia and van Willigen 2005; Miracle 2009.
6. Hill and Baba 2006.
7. White 1968.
8. Baba and Hill 2006; Moran and Harris 2007, 64, 84–87.

Chapter 2

1. Salzman 2001, 135.
2. J. Whiting 1964.
3. Nagel 1961, 88–89.
4. Ibid., 83–90.
5. Ibid., 85. See also McCain and Segal 1988, 75–79.
6. McCain and Segal 1988, 62–64.
7. Tylor 1971/1958.
8. Ceci and Williams 2009.
9. Langness 1974, 50.
10. Steward 1955a, 30–42.
11. Vayda and Rappaport 1968, 493.
12. Irons 1979, 10–12.
13. Low 2009.
14. Boyd and Richerson 2005, 103–04.
15. Clifford 1986, 3.
16. Geertz 1973c, 3–30, 412–53; see also Marcus and Fischer 1986, 26–29.
17. Caws 1969, 1378.
18. McCain and Segal 1988, 114.
19. Ibid., 56–57, 131–32.
20. Whiting 1964, 519–20.
21. McCain and Segal 1988, 67–69.
22. For examples, see Murdock 1967 and Murdock and White 1969, 329–69.
23. See the HRAF Web site: www.yale.edu/hraf.
24. Ogburn 1922, 200–80.
25. Bernard 2011, 257–58.
26. Peacock 1986, 54.
27. Bernard 2011, 278–80.
28. Romney et al. 1986; Bernard 2011, 371–78.
29. Bernard 2011, 151–52.
30. See Murdock and White 1969 for a description of the SCCS sample; *eHRAF World Cultures* is described at www.yale.edu/hraf; for a description of many different cross-cultural samples, see C. R. Ember and M. Ember 2009.
31. C. R. Ember 2007.
32. Helms 2009.
33. Trigger 1989.
34. Martin 1990, 42.
35. Etienne 1992.
36. Isaac 1997.
37. Leakey 1965, 73–78.
38. R. E. Taylor 1998.
39. R. C. Walter 1998.
40. F. H. Brown 2000, 225.
41. American Anthropological Association (http://www.aaanet.org/coe/Code_of_Ethics.pdf).
42. Szklut and Reed 1991.
43. Lambert et al. 2000, 405.
44. Hill and Hurtado 2004.
45. Waldbaum 2005.

Chapter 12

1. Linton 1945, 30.
2. Sapir 1938, cited by Pelto and Pelto 1975, 1.
3. Pelto and Pelto 1975, 14–15.
4. Castle 2013.
5. Bland 2013.
6. Simoons 1994, 65–71, 101, 109–11, 261–65.
7. de Waal 2001, 269.
8. DeMunck 2000, 22.
9. Ibid., 2000, 8.
10. Durkheim 1938/1895
11. O'Gorman, Wilson, and Miller 2008.
12. Durkheim 1938/1895, 3.
13. Asch 1956.
14. Bond and Smith 1996.
15. Berns et al. 2005.
16. M. F. Brown 2008, 372.
17. Hewlett 2004.
18. Miner 1956, 504–505, reproduced by permission of the American Anthropological Association.
19. Lee 1972.
20. M. F. Brown 2008, 364.
21. Hatch 1997.
22. M. F. Brown. 2008, 363.
23. Zechenter 1997.
24. Rosenblatt 2004.
25. E. T. Hall and Hall 1990, 11–12.
26. Hall 1966, 159–60.
27. R. Brown 1965, 549–609.
28. Wagley 1974.
29. Chibnik 1981, 256–68.
30. Linton 1936, 306.
31. Ibid., 310–11.
32. Silver 1981.
33. Greenfield et al. 2000.
34. Rogers 1983, 263–69.
35. Cancian 1980.
36. Efferson et al. 2008.
37. Hewlett and Cavalli-Sforza 1986; Cavalli-Sforza and Feldman 1981.
38. Valente 1995, 21.
39. W. Cohen 1995.
40. Linton 1936, 326–27.
41. *Britannica Online* 1998; *Academic American Encyclopedia* 1980.
42. Linton 1936, 338–39.
43. G. M. Foster 1962, 26.
44. Bodley 1990, 7.
45. Pelto and Müller-Wille 1987, 207–43.
46. Aporta and Higgs 2005.
47. Bodley 1990, 38–41.
48. T. Kroeber 1967, 45–47.
49. Roth 2001.
50. Boyd and Richerson 1996/1985, 106.
51. Ibid., 135.
52. D. T. Campbell 1965. See also Boyd and Richerson 1996/1985 and Durham 1991.
53. Bentley et al. 2007; Mesoudi and Lycett 2009.
54. The historical information we refer to comes from a book by Nevins 1927. For how radical the American Revolution was, see G. Wood 1992.
55. Brinton 1938.
56. Paige 1975.
57. Tanter and Midlarsky 1967
58. Blight, Pulham, and Torpey 2012
59. Howard, Duffy, and Freelon et al. 2011
60. Bestor 2001, 76.
61. Trouillot 2001, 128.
62. Durrenberger 2001a; see also Hannerz 1996.
63. McNeill 1967, 283–87; Guest and Jones 2005, 4.
64. Guest and Jones 2005, 4.
65. Traphagan and Brown 2002.
66. Bradsher 2002, 3.
67. Guest and Jones 2005.
68. Yergin 2002, A29.
69. G. Thompson 2002, A3.
70. Sengupta 2002, A3.
71. Conklin 2002.
72. J. D. Hill 1996, 1.
73. Bilby 1996, 127–28, referring to Hoogbergen 1990, 23.
74. Bilby 1996, 128–37.
75. Sattler 1996, 42.
76. Ibid., 50–51.
77. Ibid., 54.
78. Ibid., 58–59.
79. Kottak 1996, 136; 153.
80. Roosens 1989, 9.
81. Cashdan 2001.
82. C. R. Ember and Levinson 1991.

Chapter 15

1. Hitchcock and Beisele 2000, 5.
2. C. R. Ember 1978b.
3. Kent 1996.
4. Schrire 1984a; Myers 1988.
5. Morrison and Junker 2002.
6. The discussion of the Australian aborigines is based on R. A. Gould 1969.
7. Burbank 1994, 23; Burbank 2009b.
8. Burch 2009; 1988.
9. Data from Textor 1967 and Service 1979.
10. Murdock and Provost 1973, 207.
11. R. B. Lee 1968; DeVore and Konner 1974.
12. C. R. Ember 1978b; Cordain et al. 2000.
13. C. R. Ember 1978b.
14. McCarthy and McArthur 1960.
15. R. B. Lee 1979, 256–58, 278–80.
16. Palsson 1988; Roscoe 2002.
17. Keeley 1991.
18. R. L. Kelly 1995, 293–315.
19. Mitchell 2009; Tollefson 2009.
20. C. Ember 1975.
21. D. Werner 1978.
22. Textor 1967.
23. This section is largely based on Hames 2009.
24. Chagnon 1983, 60.
25. This section is based mostly on Melvin Ember's fieldwork on the islands of American Samoa in 1955 to 1956.
26. Oliver 1974, 252–53.
27. S. S. King 1979.
28. Friedl 1962.
29. Hickey 1964, 135–65.
30. C. R. Ember 1983, 289.
31. Textor 1967; Dirks 2009; Messer 1996, 244.
32. Finnis 2006.
33. Barlett 1989, 253–91.
34. U.S. Environmental Protection Agency 2014.
35. Salzman 1996.
36. Lees and Bates 1974; A. L. Johnson 2002.
37. Barth 1965.
38. Whitaker 1955; Itkonen 1951.
39. Paine 1994.
40. Textor 1967.
41. Dirks 2009.
42. Data from Textor 1967.
43. L. R. Binford 1990; see also Low 1990a, 242–43.
44. The few foragers in cold areas relying primarily on hunting have animals (dogs, horses, reindeer) that can carry transportable housing; see L. R. Binford 1990.
45. Bailey et al. 1989.
46. Data from Textor 1967.
47. Janzen 1973. For an argument supporting the "weeding" explanation, see Carneiro 1968.
48. L. R. Binford 1971; Flannery 1971.
49. G. A. Wright 1971, 470.
50. Flannery 1986, 10–11.
51. M. N. Cohen 1977b, 138–41; see also M. N. Cohen 1977a, 279.
52. Byrne 1987, 21–34, referred to in Blumler and Byrne 1991; D. O. Henry 1989; McCorriston and Hole 1991.
53. Henry 1989, 41.
54. McCorriston and Hole 1991.
55. Weiss and Bradley 2001.
56. Speth and Spielmann 1983.
57. Boserup 1993/1965.
58. R. C. Hunt 2000.
59. Janzen 1973.
60. Roosevelt 1992.

Chapter 16

1. Hoebel 1968/1954, 46–63.
2. Woodburn 1968.
3. Pryor 2005, 36.
4. Ibid.
5. Leacock and Lee 1982, 8; Pryor 2005, 36.
6. R. Dyson-Hudson and Smith 1978, 121–41; E. Andrews 1994.
7. R. Murphy 1960, 69, 142–43.
8. Salzman 1996.
9. Not all pastoralists have individual ownership. For example, the Tungus of northern Siberia have kin group ownership of reindeer. See Dowling 1975, 422.
10. Barth 1965, 124.
11. Dowling 1975.
12. Salzman 2002.
13. Creed 2009.
14. Bodley 2008, 77–93; Wilmsen 1989, 1–14.
15. Bodley 2008, 95-98.
16. Ibid., 106–8.
17. Fratkin 2008.
18. Ibid., 86–9.
19. Salzman 1996, 904–5.
20. Salzman 2002; Lawrence 2011.
21. Service 1979, 10.
22. E. M. Thomas 1959, 22.
23. Gröger 1981.
24. Plattner 1989, 379–96.
25. Hage and Powers 1992.
26. Carneiro 1968, cited in Sahlins 1972, 68.
27. M. Harris 1975, 127–28.
28. Sahlins (1972, 87) introduced North American anthropology to Alexander Chayanov and coined the phrase *Chayanov's rule*. See discussion in Durrenberger and Tannenbaum 2002.
29. Chayanov 1966, 78; for a discussion of Chayanov's analysis, see Durrenberger 1980.
30. Durrenberger and Tannenbaum 2002.
31. Chibnik 1987.
32. Durrenberger and Tannenbaum 2002.
33. Sahlins 1972, 101–48.
34. McClelland 1961.
35. Steward and Faron 1959, 122–25.
36. Bowie 2006, 251.
37. B. B. Whiting and Edwards 1988, 164.
38. Nag et al. 1978, 295–96.

39. B. B. Whiting and Edwards 1988, 97–107.
40. Draper and Cashdan 1988, 348.
41. N. B. Jones et al. 1996, 166–69.
42. Nag et al. 1978, 293; see also Bradley 1984–1985, 160–64.
43. C. R. Ember 1983, 291–97.
44. Udy 1970: 35–37.
45. Sahlins 1962, 50–52.
46. Pospisil 1963, 43.
47. Udy 1970, 35–39.
48. E. A. Smith 1983, 626.
49. K. Hill et al. 1987, 17–18.
50. Sih and Milton 1985.
51. Sosis 2002.
52. Gladwin 1980, 45–85.
53. Chibnik 1980.
54. Polanyi 1957.
55. Sahlins 1972, 188–96.
56. L. Marshall 1961, 239–41.
57. The "//" sign in the name for the G//ana people symbolizes a click sound not unlike the sound we make when we want a horse to move faster.
58. Cashdan 1980, 116–20.
59. H. Kaplan and Hill 1985; H. Kaplan et al. 1990; Gurven et al. 2002, 114.
60. Hames 1990.
61. Gurven et al. 2002, 114.
62. H. Kaplan et al. 1990.
63. Winterhalder 1990.
64. Mooney 1978.
65. Balikci 1970 quoted in Mooney 1978, 392.
66. Mooney 1978, 392.
67. E.M. Johnson 2011.
68. Fehr and Fischbacher 2003, Ensminger 2002a; Henrich et al. 2005.
69. Mehu, Grammer, and Dunbar, 2007.
70. Angier 2002: F1, F8.
71. Boehm 2008.
72. Warneken and Tomasello 2009.
73. Marshall 1961, 242.
74. Abler 2009.
75. N. Peacock and Bailey 2009.
76. Gibbs 1965, 223.
77. Humphrey and Hugh-Jones 1992.
78. Blanton 2009; Gregory 1982.
79. Uberoi 1962.
80. Malinowski 1920; Uberoi 1962.
81. J. Leach 1983, 12, 16
82. Weiner 1976, 77–117.
83. Sahlins 1972, 196–204.
84. Pryor 1977, 204, 276.
85. Vayda et al. 1962.
86. Drucker 1967.
87. M. Harris 1975, 120.
88. Tollefson 2009.
89. Beattie 1960.
90. Thurnwald 1934, 125.
91. Pryor 1977, 284–86.
92. Service 1962, 145–46.
93. M. Harris 1975, 118–21.
94. Plattner 1985, viii.
95. Pryor 1977, 31–33.
96. Thurnwald 1934, 122.
97. Plattner 1985, xii.
98. Pryor 1977, 153–83; Stodder (1995, 205) finds that monetary trade is more likely with capital-intensive agriculture.
99. Pryor 1977, 109–11.
100. B. Foster 1974.
101. Pryor 1977, 125–48.
102. E. Wolf 1955, 452–71; Carrasco 1961.
103. W. R. Smith 1977; M. Harris 1964.
104. Ibid.
105. See, e.g., Gross et al. 1979.
106. Pollier 2000.
107. Vohs et al. 2006.
108. The description of Tikopia is based on Firth 1959, Chapters 5, 6, 7, and 9, passim.
109. Monsutti 2004.
110. Ibid., Eversole 2005.
111. Eversole 2005.
112. Most of this discussion is based on R. F. Murphy and Steward 1956.
113. Burkhalter and Murphy 1989.
114. E. Wolf 1966, 3–4.
115. Hobsbawm 1970.
116. Gross and Underwood 1971.

Chapter 18

1. Attributed to English poet Robert Southey (1774–1843) in Opie and Opie, 100–01.
2. Leibowitz 1978, 43–44.
3. Schlegel 1989, 266; Epstein 1988, 5–6; Chafetz 1990, 28.
4. Jacobs and Roberts 1989.
5. Segal 2004; Segal also cites the work of W. Williams 1992.
6. Lang 1999, 93–94; Blackwood 1984b.
7. Wikan 1982, 168–86.
8. Stini 1971.
9. Frayer and Wolpoff 1985, 431–32.
10. For reviews of theories and research on sexual dimorphism and possible genetic and cultural determinants of variation in degree of dimorphism over time and place, see Frayer and Wolpoff 1985 and Gray 1985, 201–209, 217–25.
11. J. K. Brown 1970b, 1074.
12. See Hurtado et al. 1985, 23.
13. Murdock and Provost 1973, 213; Byrne 1994.
14. R. O'Brian 1999.
15. D. R. White et al. 1977, 1–24.
16. Mukhopadhyay and Higgins 1988, 473.
17. J. K. Brown 1970b, 1073–78; and D. R. White et al. 1977.
18. Nerlove 1974.
19. N. E. Levine 1988.
20. M. J. Goodman et al. 1985.
21. Noss and Hewlett 2001.
22. Brumbach and Jarvenpa 2006a; Jarvenpa and Brumbach 2006.
23. Brumbach and Jarvenpa 2006b.
24. C. R. Ember 1983, 288–89.
25. Mead 1950 [originally published 1935], 180–84.
26. Rivers 1967 [originally published 1906], 567.
27. M. Ember and Ember 1971, 573, table 1.
28. Schlegel and Barry 1986.
29. Wood and Eagly 2002, 706, drawing on data from H. Kaplan et al. 2000.
30. Boserup 1970, 22–25; see also Schlegel and Barry 1986, 144–45.
31. Boserup 1970, 22–25.
32. Bossen 2000.
33. Ibid., 31–34.
34. C. R. Ember 1983, 286–87; data from Murdock and Provost 1973, 212; Bradley 1995.
35. C. R. Ember 1983.
36. Ibid.
37. Ibid., 287–93.
38. M. Ember and Ember 1971, 579–80.
39. Ibid., 581; see also Sanday 1973, 1684.
40. Nerlove 1974.
41. Schlegel and Barry 1986.
42. Whyte 1978a, 217.
43. World Bank 2011, 386–87.
44. Whyte 1978a; D. B. Adams 1983.
45. Mutrine 2013.
46. J. K. Brown 1970a.
47. Sanday 1974; Divale and Harris 1976.
48. Quinn 1977, 189–90.
49. D. Werner 1982; Stogdill 1974, cited in ibid.; see also Handwerker and Crosbie 1982.
50. Draper 1975, 103.
51. D. Werner 1984.
52. M. H. Ross 1986.
53. This description is based on the fieldwork of Elizabeth and Robert Fearnea (1956–1958), as reported in M. K. Martin and Voorhies 1975, 304–31.
54. Begler 1978.
55. Ibid. See also Whyte 1978a, 229–32.
56. Whyte 1978b, 95–120; see also Quinn 1977.
57. Whyte 1978b, 124–29, 145; see also Sanday 1973.
58. Whyte 1978b, 129–30.
59. J. K. Brown 1970a.
60. Whyte 1978b, 135–36.
61. Ibid., 135.
62. Doyle 2005.
63. D. Werner 1984.
64. Quinn 1977, 85; see also Etienne and Leacock 1980, 19–20.
65. Chafetz 1990, 11–19.
66. B. B. Whiting and Edwards 1973.
67. R. L. Munroe et al. 2000, 8–9.
68. Maccoby and Jacklin 1974.
69. For a more extensive discussion of behavior differences and possible explanations of them, see C. R. Ember 1981.
70. B. B. Whiting and Edwards 1973.
71. For references to this research, see C. R. Ember 1981, 559.
72. Rubin et al. 1974.
73. For a discussion of this evidence, see Ellis 1986, 525–27; C. R. Ember 1981.
74. For example, Ellis (1986) considers the evidence for the biological view of aggression "beyond reasonable dispute."
75. For a discussion of other possibilities, see C. R. Ember 1981.
76. R. M. Sapolsky 1997, 23–26.
77. Rohner 1976.
78. B. B. Whiting and Whiting 1975; see also B. B. Whiting and Edwards, 1988, 273.
79. C. R. Ember 1973, 424–39.
80. R. M. Sapolsky 1997, 25–26.
81. Burbank 1994.
82. B. B. Whiting and Edwards 1973, 175–79; see also Maccoby and Jacklin 1974.
83. Heise 1967.
84. C. S. Ford and Beach 1951, 191.
85. O. Lewis 1951, 397.
86. Farley 1996, 60.
87. C. S. Ford and Beach 1951, 23–25, 68–71.
88. Ibid., 40–41, 73.
89. Broude 2009.
90. C. S. Ford and Beach 1951, 82–83.
91. Broude and Greene 1976.
92. Kluckhohn 1948, 101.
93. M. Hunt 1974, 254–57; Lewin 1994.
94. Broude 1980, 184.
95. C. S. Ford and Beach 1951, 114.
96. Jankowiak et al. 2002.
97. Lang 1999, 97, citing Thomas 1993.
98. J. Morris 1938, 191.
99. Underhill 1938, 117, 186.
100. 'Abd Allah 1917, 7, 20.
101. Cardoso and Werner 2004.
102. R. C. Kelly 1974.
103. Cardoso and Werner 2004.
104. Blackwood and Wieringa 1999, 49; Blackwood 1984a.
105. Cardoso and Werner 2004, 207.
106. Data from Textor 1967.
107. W. N. Stephens 1972, 1–28.
108. Broude 1976, 243.
109. D. Werner 1979; D. Werner 1975.
110. D. Werner 1979, 345–62; see also D. Werner 1975, 36.
111. Data from Textor 1967.
112. Schlegel 1991.

Chapter 19

1. Neihardt 1951.
2. Coontz 2005.
3. W. N. Stephens 1963, 5.
4. Murdock 1949, 8.
5. Stephens 1963, 170–71; Radin 1923.
6. Hua 2001.
7. Ibid.
8. Gough 1959; Unnithan 2009.
9. Evans-Pritchard 1970, 1428–34.
10. D. O'Brien 1977; Oboler 1980.
11. Oboler 2009.
12. Murdock 1949, 7–8.
13. Ibid., 9–10.
14. See, for example, Linton 1936, 135–36.
15. M. Ember and C. R. Ember 1979.
16. Ibid.
17. Marlowe 2003, 221–23.
18. M. Ember and C. R. Ember 1979.
19. Graburn 1969, 188–200.
20. Malinowski 1932, 77.
21. Ibid., 88.
22. J. W. M. Whiting 1941, 125.
23. Doyle 2004; Bumpass and Lu 2000.
24. Service 1978.
25. LeVine and LeVine 1963, 65.
26. Ibid.
27. For an extensive discussion of the symbolism of Rotuman weddings, see A. Howard and Rensel 2009.
28. Schlegel and Eloul 1987. Huber, Danaher and Breedlove (2011) point out that most societies have more than one type of transaction.
29. Schlegel and Eloul 1988, 295, Table 1. We used the data to calculate the frequency of various types of economic transaction in a worldwide sample of 186 societies.
30. Oboler 2009.
31. Frake 1960.
32. Mead 1931, 206–208.
33. Borgerhoff Mulder et al. 2001.
34. Schlegel and Eloul 1988, 298–99.
35. Pryor 1977, 363–64.
36. Ibid.
37. Spencer 1968, 136.
38. Schlegel and Eloul 1988, 296–97.
39. Ibid.
40. Ibid.
41. Radcliffe-Brown 1922, 73.
42. Murdock 1967; Goody 1973, 17–21.
43. Pryor 1977, 363–65; Schlegel and Eloul 1988, 296–99.
44. Research is reported in Gaulin and Boster 1990, 994–1005. The first theory discussed herein is associated with Boserup 1970. The second is put forward by Gaulin and Boster.
45. Schlegel and Eloul 1988, following Goody 1973, 20.
46. Barth 1965, 18–19; as reported in (and coded as indirect dowry by) Schlegel and Eloul 1987, 131.
47. Middleton 1962, 606.
48. Durham 1991, 293–94, citing research by Hopkins 1980.
49. Westermarck 1894.
50. Talmon 1964, 492.
51. Ibid., 504.
52. A. Wolf 1968, 864.
53. A. Wolf and Chieh-shan Huang 1980, 159, 170, 185.
54. H. Parker and S. Parker 1986.
55. M. Ember 1975; Durham 1991, 341–57.
56. For a discussion of mechanisms that might lead to sexual aversion, see S. Parker 1976; 1984.
57. Freud 1943.
58. Malinowski 1927.
59. Quoted in L. A. White 1949, 313.
60. Kang 1979, 85–99.
61. Rudan and Campbell 2004.
62. Stern 1973, 494–95, as cited in M. Ember 1975, 256. For a review of the theory and evidence, see Durham 1991.
63. Seemanova 1971, 108–28, as cited in Durham 1991, 305–09.

64. Durham 1991, 305–09.
65. Ibid., 346–52.
66. Firth 1957, 287–88, cited (somewhat differently) in Durham 1991, 349–50.
67. A mathematical model of early mating systems suggests that people may have noticed the harmful effects of inbreeding once populations began to expand as a result of agriculture; people therefore may have deliberately adopted the incest taboo to solve the problem of inbreeding. See M. Ember 1975. For a similar subsequent suggestion, see Durham 1991, 331–39.
68. Goode 1982, 61–62.
69. Apostolou 2010.
70. Sussman 1953.
71. Apostolou 2011.
72. C. S. Ford 1941, 149.
73. A. Howard and Rensel 2004.
74. S. S. Davis 2009.
75. Goode 1970, 210.
76. Lingenfelter 2009.
77. MacDonald and Hewlett 1999, 504–506.
78. M. Ember 1975, 262, Table 3.
79. Busby 2009.
80. M. Ember 1975, 260–69; see also Durham 1991, 341–57.
81. Murdock 1949, 29.
82. Bogoras 1909, cited in W. Stephens 1963, 195.
83. Oliver 1955, 352–53.
84. Ibid., 223–24, quoted in W. Stephens 1963, 58.
85. Mead 1950, 101.
86. Jankowiak et al. 2005.
87. The discussion of these customs is based on W. Stephens 1963, 63–67.
88. Kilbride and Kilbride 1990, 202–206.
89. C. Anderson 2000, 102–103.
90. Linton 1936, 183.
91. J. W. M. Whiting 1964.
92. Ibid., 518.
93. Ibid., 516–17.
94. M. Ember 1974b.
95. M. Ember 1984–1985. The statistical relationship between late age of marriage for men and polygyny was first reported by Witkowski 1975.
96. M. Ember 1974b, 202–05.
97. M. Ember 1984–1985. For other predictors of polygyny, see D. R. White and Burton 1988.
98. Sellen and Hruschka 2004.
99. Low 1990b.
100. M. Ember et al. 2007.
101. Barber 2008.
102. Coult and Habenstein 1965; Murdock 1957.
103. M. C. Goldstein 1987, 39.
104. Stephens 1963, 45.
105. Hiatt 1980.
106. M. Goldstein 1987. Formerly, in feudal Tibet, a class of serfs who owned small parcels of land also practiced polyandry. Goldstein suggests that a shortage of land would explain their polyandry too. See M. C. Goldstein 1971.
107. Haddix 2001.
108. For example, see M. L. Cohen 1976.
109. Pasternak 1976, 96.
110. Silk 1980; Damas 1983.
111. Melvin Ember, pers. comm.
112. K. Gibson 2009.
113. Coult and Habenstein 1965.
114. Mead 1961/1928, quoted in Stephens 1963, 134–35.
115. Ibid., 135.
116. Nimkoff and Middleton 1960.
117. Pasternak et al. 1976, 109–23.
118. Block 1983.

Chapter 20

1. Frost 1914, 14
2. Taylor et al. 2010, 7
3. Coult and Habenstein 1965; Murdock 1957.
4. Percentages calculated from Coult and Habenstein 1965.
5. L. Bohannan and P. Bohannan 1953.
6. J. D. Freeman 1961.
7. Jarvenp. 2004.
8. Murdock 1949, 49–50.
9. C. R. Ember et al. 1974, 84–89.
10. Pospisil 1963.
11. Schneider 1961a.
12. Lockett, 1933, 6, 9-12.
13. M. Ember and Ember 1971, 581.
14. Schneider 1961b.
15. Goodenough 1951, 145.
16. Coult and Habenstein 1965.
17. Data from Textor 1967.
18. Fortes 1949.
19. Davenport 1959.
20. The description of the Samoan descent system is based on M. Ember's 1955 to 1956 fieldwork. See also M. Ember 1959, 573–77; and Davenport 1959.
21. M. Ember 1967.
22. M. Ember and C. R. Ember 1971. See also Divale 1974.
23. M. Ember and Ember 1971, 583–85; Divale 1974.
24. M. Ember and Ember 1971. For a different theory—that matrilocal residence precedes, rather than follows, the development of purely external warfare—see Divale 1974.
25. Helms 2009; Herlihy 2007; see also M. Ember and Ember 1971.
26. Service 1962, 137.
27. C. R. Ember and M. Ember 1972.
28. C. R. Ember 1975.
29. M. Ember 1974a.
30. Data from Textor 1967.
31. C. R. Ember et al. 1974.
32. The importance of warfare and competition as factors in the formation of unilineal descent groups is also suggested by Service 1962 and Sahlins 1961, 332–45.
33. C. R. Ember and Ember 1972.
34. C. R. Ember and Ember 1997.
35. See, for example, Murdock 1949, 199–222.
36. Reported in Textor 1967.
37. Ibid.
38. Murdock 1949, 125.
39. Textor 1967.
40. L. A. White 1939.
41. Goody 1970.
42. Pasternak 1976, 142.
43. Textor 1967.
44. Ibid.
45. This conjecture is based on unpublished cross-cultural research by the Embers.

Chapter 22

1. Service 1962; Lewellen 2003, 17-18.
2. See A. Johnson and Earle 2000 for a different classification scheme.
3. Schrire 1984b; see also Leacock and Lee 1982, 8.
4. Service 1962, 109.
5. Briggs 1974.
6. Mathiassen 1928, 213.
7. Service 1962, 114–15; Lewellen 2003: 26-27.
8. Lewellen 2003,27.
9. Salzman 2008, 68.
10. Bohannan 1954, 3.
11. Sahlins 1961, 342.
12. R. C. Kelly 1985, 1.
13. Sahlins 1961, 345.
14. N. Dyson-Hudson 1966, Chapters 5 and 6.
15. Ibid.
16. Chapman and Kagaha 2009; see also Skoggard and Abate 2010.
17. Lewellen 2003, 31.
18. Ibid., 31-34.
19. Sahlins 1962, 293–94.
20. Sahlins 1963, 295.
21. Sahlins 1983, 519.
22. Sahlins 1963, 297.
23. Carneiro 1970, 733.
24. Weber 1947, 154.
25. Lightfoot 2005.
26. Ferguson 2004.
27. Wiberg 1983.
28. For an extensive review of the various theories about legitimacy, see R. Cohen 1988, 1–3.
29. Finley 1983.
30. Carcopino 1940, 18–20.
31. Our discussion of Nupe is based on S. F. Nadel 1935, 257–303.
32. Blanton and Fargher 2008.
33. Ibid.
34. Goldmann, Hannerz, and Westin 2000; Appadurai 2000.
35. Glick-Schiller 2004.
36. Appadurai 2000, 130.
37. Hassanpour and Mojab 2004.
38. Glick Schiller 2004,
39. M. Ember 1963.
40. Textor 1967.
41. M. Ember 1963; Feinman 2011.
42. Textor 1967.
43. Naroll 1961. See also Ross 1981.
44. M. Ember 1963, 244–46.
45. Service 1962; see also Braun and Plog 1982; Haas 1990.
46. A. Johnson and Earle 1987, 158; Carneiro 1990.
47. Carneiro 2012, 17-18.
48. Service 1962, 112, 145.
49. Feinman and Nietzel 1984.
50. Wittfogel 1957; see also discussion in Carneiro 2012, 8-9.
51. Carneiro 1970; Carneiro 2012.
52. Polanyi et al. 1957, 257–62; Sanders 1968; Wright and Johnson 1975; Chang 1986, 234–94.
53. For a more detailed description and evaluation of the available theories, see Chapter 11 in C. Ember et al. 2014.
54. McNeill 1976.
55. Carneiro 1978, 215.
56. Textor 1967.
57. Carneiro 1978; Hart 1948; Naroll 1967; Marano 1973, 35–40 (cf. Peregrine, Ember, and Ember 2004 and other articles in Graber 2004).
58. For a review of the descriptive literature until the late 1970s, see Vincent 1978.
59. D. Werner 1982.
60. Kracke 1979, 232.
61. D. Werner 1982.
62. Sahlins 1963.
63. Kracke 1979, 41.
64. Lederman 1990.
65. Brandewie 1991.
66. Lepowsky 1990.
67. Todorov et al. 2005.
68. Zebrowitz and Montepare 2005.
69. A. C. Little et. al. 2007; Todorov et al. 2005.
70. Ross 1988, 73. The discussion in this section draws mostly from Zebrowitz and Montepare 2005, 73–89, and from Ross 2009b.
71. Bondarenko and Korotayev 2000; Korotayev and Bondarenko 2000.
72. For studies of international relations that support these conclusions, see footnotes 2 and 3 in C. R. Ember, Ember, and Russett 1992; see also Chapter 3 in Russett and Oneal 2001.
73. C. R. Ember, Ember, and Russett 1992.
74. Rummel 2002b.
75. Scaglion 2009b.
76. Boehm 2012.
77. Hoebel 1968/1954,4 , quoting S. P. Simpson and Field 1946, 858.
78. Donovan and Anderson 2003, 10-13; Rosen 2006, 16-17.
79. Fry and Björkqvist 1997.
80. D. Black 1993, 79–83.
81. Ross 1988.
82. Boas 1888, 668.
83. Otterbein 1986, 107.
84. Archer and Gartner 1984, 118–39.
85. Scaglion 2009b; D. Black 1993, 83–86.
86. Ibid.
87. Evans-Pritchard 1940, 291. The discussion of the Nuer follows this source.
88. Hickson 1986.
89. Ibid.; and Koch et al. 1977, 279.
90. J. M. Roberts 1967, 169.
91. Rosen 2006:72.
92. Rosen 2006,72-77.
93. Ibid., 192.
94. Hoebel 1968/1954, Chapter 9.
95. Schwartz 1954, 475; see also discussion in Rosen 2006, 16
96. Textor 1967.
97. Masumura 1977, 388–99.
98. Scaglion 2009b; Black 1993; Newman 1983, 131.
99. C. R. Ember and Ember 1997.
100. Keeley 1996; Gat 2006; Pinker 2011; J. Goldstein 2011.
101. Otterbein and Otterbein 1965 and Fry 2006, 88 do not consider feuding to be warfare.
102. C. R. Ember and Ember 2005; see also Fry 2006.
103. C. R. Ember and Ember 1994.
104. Chacon and Mendoza 2007.
105. Newman 1983, 131; Ericksen and Horton 1992.
106. Gubser 1965, 151.
107. Otterbein and Otterbein 1965, 1476; Otterbein 1994, 131
108. D. R. White 1988.
109. Patterson 1982, 345–52.
110. Gat 1999, 373, as referred to in Wadley 2003.
111. Heider 1970, 105–11; Heider 1979, 88–99.
112. M. Ember and Ember 1992, 188–89; M. Ember and Ember 2004.
113. Burtsev and Korotayev 2004, 35; see also Korotayev 2008, reanalyzing the Embers' (1992a, 1992b) data suggest that the relationship between resource unpredictability (with regard to food) and warfare is reversed in state societies.
114. C. R. Ember and Ember 1992; M. Ember 1982; C. R. Ember et al. 2013. For a discussion of how Dani warfare seems to be motivated mainly by economic considerations, see Shankman 1991. B. W. Kang (2000, 878–79) finds a strong correlation between environmental stress and warfare frequency in Korean history.
115. Otterbein 1970.
116. C. R. Ember and Ember 1992; see also Otterbein 1970 and Loftin 1971.
117. C. R. Ember 1974.
118. Otterbein 1968, 283; Ross 1985.
119. Divale and Harris 1976, 521–38; see also Gibbons 1993.
120. C. R. Ember and Ember 1992, 251–52.
121. Singer 1980.
122. Russett and Oneal 2001, 89.
123. Ibid., 145–48.
124. Younger 2008.
125. Russett 1993, 10–11, 14, 138.

Chapter 23

1. Tylor 2010 [1873]
2. Tylor 1979.
3. Marett 1909.
4. Guthrie 1993.
5. Freud 2010 [1950]; Badcock 1988, 126–27, 133–36.
6. Malinowski 1939, 959; Malinowski 1954, 50–51.
7. W. James 1902.
8. Jung 1938.
9. Fromm 1950.
10. Maslow 1964.
11. Barber 2011.
12. Sosis 2007.
13. Barber 2011.
14. Durkheim 1961/1912; see also S. Davis 2008.
15. Swanson 1969, 1–31.
16. Sosis and Alcorta 2003 and references therein.
17. Henrich 2009.
18. A. Wallace 1966, 60–61.
19. Malefijt 1968, 153.
20. Ray 1954, 172–89.
21. Rosenblatt et al. 1976, 51.
22. Ibid., 55.
23. Swanson 1969, 97–108; see also Sheils 1975; Steadman, Palmer, and Tilley 2010 [1996] suggest that ancestor worship is universal.
24. Middleton 1971, 488.
25. Spiro and D'Andrade 1958.
26. Lambert et al. 1959; Rohner 1975, 108.
27. H. G. Barnett 1960, 79–85.
28. Swanson 1969, 56.
29. Ibid., 55–81; see also W. D. Davis 1971. Peregrine (1996, 84–112) replicated Swanson's finding for North American societies.
30. Textor 1967; R. Underhill 1975; Sanderson and Roberts 2008.
31. Geertz 1966.
32. Swanson 1969, 153–74. In a more recent test, D. Johnson found the presence of money to be related to a high god's concern with morality.
33. Bunzel 1971.
34. Gossen 1979.
35. Dickson et al. 2005.
36. Eller 2007, 111.
37. Ibid., 128.
38. Stark and Finke 2000, 107–08.
39. A. Wallace 1966, 52–67.
40. Winkelman 1986b, 178–83.
41. Bourguignon 1973.
42. Bourguignon and Evascu 1977; Winkelman 1986b, 196–98.
43. Kehoe and Giletti 1981.
44. Raybeck 1998, referring to Raybeck et al. 1989.
45. Bourguignon 2004, 572.
46. Winkleman and Peck 2004; Eller 2007, 75.
47. O. K. Moore 1957.
48. Sheils 1980.
49. Winkelman and Baker 2010, 293–96 and references therein.
50. Evans-Pritchard 1979, 362–66.
51. Swanson 1969, 150; see also H. R. Trevor-Roper 1971, 444–49.
52. Swanson 1969, 150–51.
53. Caporael 1976; Matossian 1982; and Matossian 1989, 70–80. For possible reasons to dismiss the ergot theory, see Spanos 1983.
54. Harner 1972.
55. B. B. Whiting 1950, 36–37; see also Swanson 1969, 137–52, 240–41.
56. Winkelman 2010, 50–58.
57. Ibid.
58. Knecht 2003, 11.
59. Harner and Doore 1987, 3, 8–9; Noll 1987, 49; Krippner 1987, 128.
60. De Laguna 1972, 701C.
61. Noll 1987, 49–50; Krippner 2000.
62. Winkelman 1986a, 27–28; Winkelman 2010, 50–58.
63. Ibid.
64. Ibid.
65. Ibid.
66. M. Harris 1966.
67. Buckser and Glazier 2003; Rambo 2003.
68. Discussion is based on Firth 1970.
69. Ibid., 387.
70. Ibid., 418.
71. Mason 1962.
72. Ensminger 1997, 7.
73. Ibid.
74. Reff 2005; see also McNeill 1998 and Stark 1996.
75. C. R. Ember 1982.
76. A. Wallace 1966, 30.
77. A. Wallace 1970, 239.
78. The Quakers, long-time neighbors and trusted advisers of the Seneca, took pains not to interfere with Seneca religion, principles, and attitudes.
79. Worsley 1957, 12.
80. Ibid., 11, 115.
81. Ibid., 122.
82. Aberle 1971.
83. Knauft 1978.
84. Antoun 2001, 2008.
85. Nagata 2001.
86. Antoun 2008, 18–19.
87. Ibid., 46–47.
88. Stark 1985; Trompf 1990.

Chapter 24

1. Maquet 1986, 9; Perkins 2006
2. R. L. Anderson 1989, 21.
3. R. P. Armstrong 1981, 11.
4. R. L. Anderson 1990, 278; R. L. Anderson 1992.
5. Morphy and Perkins 2006, 15.
6. Davies 2000, 201.
7. Malin 1986, 27.
8. R. L. Anderson 1989, 11.
9. Dutton 2000, 234.
10. Steiner 1990.
11. R. L. Anderson 1990, 225–26.
12. Sweeney 1952, 335.
13. Fischer 1961, 80.
14. Ibid., 81.
15. Peregrine 2007b also finds that the ceramics of complex societies tend toward nonrepetition and complex designs.
16. Ibid., 83.
17. Dressler and Robbins 1975, 427–34.
18. Rohter 2012.
19. Lomax 1968, 117–28; Global Jukebox 2013.
20. Words from "Deck the Halls," printed in the *Franklin Square Song Collection*, 1881.
21. Lomax 1968, 166–67.
22. Ibid., 167–69.
23. Ayres 1973.
24. Ayres 1968.
25. E. Erickson 1968.
26. For a study of variation in music within India that does not support some of Lomax's findings, see E. O. Henry 1976.
27. Dundes 1989, 2005, xxv .
28. Bauman 1992.
29. Brunvand 1993, 14.
30. Ibid., 296.
31. Kluckhohn 1965.
32. As discussed in Robert A. Segal 1987, 1–2.
33. J. Campbell 1949, 30, as quoted in Segal 1987, 4.
34. S. Thompson 1965, 449.
35. Dundes 1965, reported in F. W. Young 1970.
36. Carroll 1979.
37. G. O. Wright 1954.
38. A. Cohen 1990.
39. S. Price 1989 [2001], 82–85.
40. Ibid., 102–103.
41. S. Price 1989, 56–67; S. Price 2006, 168–169.
42. S. Price 1989, 112; S. Price 2006, 169-170.
43. J. A. Warner 1986, 172–75.
44. Layton 1992, 93–94.
45. Ibid., 31, 109.
46. J. C. H. King 1986.
47. S. Price 1989, 77–81.
48. J. A. Warner 1986, 178–86.
49. Myers 2002, 1–3, 17–18; Myers 2006, 182–183, 193.
50. Svašek 2007, 154.
51. Silverman 2006.
52. Merrill 1987.

Chapter 25

1. Nolan 2003, 2.
2. Kushner 1991.
3. Van Willigen 2002, 10.
4. Nolan 2002, 32.
5. American Anthropological Association. Statement on Ethics: Principles of Professional Responsibility 2012. www.aaanet.org/profdev/ethics.
6. Society for Applied Anthropology. Ethical and Professional Responsibilities. http://www.sfaa.net/sfaaethic.html. Accessed May 11, 2013.
7. NAPA Ethical Guidelines for Practitioners. http://practicinganthropology.org/about/ethical-guidelines/. Accessed May 11, 2013.
8. Scudder 1978.
9. Ibid., 204ff.
10. Cernea 2000, 20.
11. A good summary of this extraordinary case was put together by Slayman 1997.
12. Public Law 101–601 (25 U.S.C. 3001–3013).
13. Picchi 1991, 26–38; for a more general description of the Bakairí, see Picchi 2009.
14. Murray 1997, 131.
15. Wulff and Fiste 1987; Murray and Bannister 2004.
16. Ibid.
17. Niehoff 1966, 255–67.
18. Tax 1975; Rylko-Bauer, Singer, and van Willigen 2006.
19. Rylko-Bauer, Singer, and van Willigen. 2006.
20. Fluehr-Lobban 2008; Lassiter 2008.
21. Warry 1990, 61–62.
22. J. Fisher 1996, 57.
23. Ibid., 91; data from Kenya referred to in Oxby 1983.
24. W. H. Fisher 1994.
25. Kedia 2008.
26. Shoreman-Ouimet and Kopnina 2011; McGuire 2005.
27. E. Dean 2011.
28. Moran 2011.
29. J. Hirsch et al. 2011.
30. A. Jordan 2013, 41; Sunderland and Denny 2007, 3337.
31. Ferraro 2002, 57.
32. Ibid., 115.
33. A. Jordan 2013, 25.
34. Kleinberg 1994.
35. Squires 2002 as referred to in A. Jordan 2013, 9192.
36. Ravesloot 1997, 174.
37. Anyon and Ferguson 1995.
38. Anderson, Card, and Feder 2013.
39. Naleimaile, Sean and Lokelani Brandt 2013.
40. Society for American Archaeology 2009.
41. Schlattler 2008; Edson and Dean 1994.
42. Terrell 2011.
43. Komar and Buikstra 2008, 11–12.
44. Manhein 1999.
45. Komar and Buikstra 2008, 126–145.
46. Brace 1995.
47. Komar and Buikstra 2008, 189–200.
48. Joans 1997.
49. "Association Business: Clyde Snow . . ." 2000.

Chapter 26

1. A. H. Goodman and Leatherman 1998; Kleinman et al. 1997.
2. Richard Thomas, personal communication, May 2013.
3. Gaines and Davis-Floyd 2004.
4. Rubel and Haas 1996, 120; Loustaunau and Sobo 1997, 80–81.
5. Loustaunau and Sobo 1997, 82–83, referring to Magner 1992, 93.
6. Loustaunau and Sobo 1997, referring to Gesler 1991, 16.
7. Loustaunau and Sobo 1997, referring to C. Leslie 1976, 4; and G. Foster 1994, 11.
8. Ahern 1975, 92–97, as seen in eHRAF World Cultures, 2000.
9. Murdock 1980, 20.
10. C. C. Moore 1988.
11. T. Gladwin and Sarason 1953, 64–66.
12. Mahony 1971, 34–38, as seen in eHRAF World Cultures, 2000.
13. Gladwin and Sarason 1953, 65.
14. Hallowell 1976.
15. J. E. Levy 1994, 318.
16. Hahn 1995, 133–39; Gaines and Davis-Floyd 2004; Winkelman 2009, 38–50.
17. Loustaunau and Sobo 1997, 115.
18. For an exhaustively documented presentation of the more universalistic approach, see E. A. Berlin and Berlin 1996; see also Browner 1985, 13–32, and Rubel et al. 1984.
19. E. A. Berlin 1996.
20. Browner 1985; Ortiz de Montellano and Browner 1985.
21. Etkin and Ross 1997.
22. Moerman 1997, 240–41.
23. Loustaunau and Sobo 1997, 98–101.
24. Winkelman 1986a.
25. Winkleman 2009, 390.
26. M. Singer 2007, 105.
27. Winkelman 2010, 52.
28. Levi-Strauss 1963a, 169.
29. Boas 1930, 1–41, reported in Lévi-Strauss 1963b, 169–73.
30. Torrey 1972.
31. Womack 2010, 88–89; Winkelman 2009, 340–41.
32. Loustaunau and Sobo 1997, 102.
33. Dow 1986, 6–9, 125.
34. Hahn 1995, 131–72.
35. Winkelman 2009, 181.
36. For a discussion of some of the relevant research, see M. Singer 2007, 152–80.
37. Mascie-Taylor 1990, 118–21.
38. Hahn 1995, 82–87; CDC. Black or African American Populations; MacDorman and Mathews 2011.
39. See references in Hahn 1995, 82–87.
40. A. Cohen 1999.
41. UNAIDS 2007/2012. Global fact sheet, 1. http://www.unaids.org. Accessed May 18 2013.
42. E. C. Green and Ruark 2011, 131.
43. Reported in Carey et al. 2004, 462.
44. Bolton 1989.
45. P. J. Smith et al. 2011.
46. D. McNeill 2011.

47. Carrier and Bolton 1991; Schoepf 1988, 625, cited in Carrier and Bolton 1991.
48. Simmons et al. 1996, 64.
49. E. C. Green and Ruark 2011, 111.
50. Ibid., 136–54.
51. E. C. Green and Ruark, p. 169.
52. Farmer, Connors, and Simmons 2011.
53. L. K. Altman 2008.
54. Schoepf 1988, 637–38.
55. Bolton 1992.
56. Farmer 1997, 414. Married men in Thailand are gradually turning away from commercial sex and having affairs with married women who are believed to be safe; see Lyttleton 2000, 299.
57. Feldman and Johnson 1986, 2.
58. Shen and Siliciano 2000.
59. A. Cohen 2004.
60. Honigmann 1967, 406.
61. Kleinman 1988, 3.
62. Lutz 1985, 63–100.
63. J. Murphy 1981, 813.
64. R. Sullivan et al. 2007.
65. Edgerton 1966.
66. Edgerton 1992, 16–45.
67. J. S. Allen et al. 1996; R. Sullivan et al. 2007.
68. Kleinman 1988, 34–52; Berry et al. 1992, 357–64.
69. Honigmann 1967, 401.
70. Kleinman 1988, 19.
71. A. Wallace 1972.
72. Kleinman 1988, 167–85.
73. Rubel et al. 1984, 8–9; Weller et al. 2008.
74. Ibid., 15–29, 49–69.
75. Ibid., 71–111.
76. A. Cohen 2004.
77. Kleinman 2004.
78. Dressler 1991, 11–16.
79. Ibid., 66–94.
80. Ibid., 165–208.
81. Quandt 1996, 272–89.
82. McElroy and Townsend 2002.
83. See discussion in Leslie Lieberman 2004.
84. Gross and Underwood 1971.
85. Himmelgreen and Romero-Daza 2009.
86. FAO. Hunger.
87. McElroy and Townsend 2002, 187; referring to Harvey and Heywood 1983, 27–35.
88. Quandt 1996, 277.
89. McKee 2009.
90. Messer 2009.

Chapter 27

1. The discussion in this section draws extensively from Aptekar 1994.
2. Kahn 2005.
3. Gaiha et al. 2013.
4. Information collected during Melvin Ember's fieldwork in American Samoa, 1955–1956.
5. Mellor and Gavian 1987.
6. Dirks 1993.
7. Sen 1981; Devereux 2009.
8. Torry 1986.
9. Devereux 2009.
10. UN-HABITAT 2012.
11. Hardoy and Satterthwaite 1987.
12. UN-HABITAT 2012
13. UN-HABITAT 2009.
14. Rodwin and Sanyal 1987.
15. Mangin 1967.
16. Rodwin and Sanyal 1987; for a critique of self-help programs, see Ward 1982.
17. Satterthwaite 2008.
18. Boonyabancha 2009.
19. A. Cohen and Koegel 2009.
20. National Coalition for the Homeless 2009.
21. A. Cohen and Koegel 2009.
22. Baxter and Hopper 1981, 30–33, 50–74; Hopper 2003.
23. Ibid.
24. A. Cohen and Koegel 2009.
25. Herrman 1990.
26. Hopper 2003, 214.
27. Congressional Budget Office 2011.
28. World Bank 2004.
29. Aptekar 1991, 326.
30. UN Works n.d.
31. Aptekar 1991, 326–49; Aptekar 1988.
32. Korbin 1981, 4.
33. Straus 2001, 195–96.
34. Straus 2010.
35. Straus 2001 based on surveys in 1999.
36. U.S. Department of Justice 2005.
37. Office on Child Abuse and Neglect 2006.
38. Levinson 1989, 11–12, 44.
39. Minturn and Stashak 1982. Using a sociobiological orientation, a study by Daly and Wilson (1988, 43–59) also suggests that infanticide is largely due to the difficulty of raising the infant successfully.
40. Straus 2001.
41. Levinson 1989, 26–28.
42. C. R. Ember and Melvin Ember 2005.
43. Lareau 2003, 230.
44. D. Goldstein 1998.
45. Levinson 1989, 31.
46. Ibid., 71.
47. Gelles and Straus 1988, 78–88.
48. WHO 2005.
49. Archer 2006; WHO 2005.
50. Erchak 2009; Levinson 1989, 44–45.
51. Levinson 1989, 104–107.
52. Archer and Gartner 1984, 35.
53. UNODC 2012.
54. Archer and Gartner 1984, 63–97; see other references in J. Warner et al. 2007.
55. Gurr 1989a, 47–48.
56. U.S. Department of Justice n.d.
57. Nivette 2011.
58. Russell 1972; Eckhardt 1975; Sipes 1973.
59. C. R. Ember and Ember 1994.
60. Archer and Gartner 1984, 118–39.
61. Bacon et al. 1963; B. B. Whiting 1965; C. Ember and M. Ember 2001; Barry 2007.
62. Barber 2000, 2007.
63. C. R. Ember and Ember 1994, 625.
64. C. R. Ember and Ember 1993, 227; C. Ember and M. Ember 2001.
65. C. A. Anderson and Bushman 2002, 2377; J. G. Johnson et al. 2002.
66. Thornhill and Fincher 2011.
67. McCall, Parker, and MacDonald 2007; Bond 2004.
68. In preindustrial societies, homicide and assault are similarly predicted by the presence of indigenous money, almost always associated with wealth concentration—see Barry 2007.
69. Loftin et al. 1989; Krahn et al. 1986, as referred to in Daly and Wilson 1988, 287–88; Gartner 2009.
70. C. R. Ember and Ember 1997.
71. J. S. Goldstein 2011; Pinker 2011.
72. M. Ember and Ember 1992, 204–206.
73. Meggitt 1977, 201; Gat 1999, 563–83.
74. C. R. Ember and Ember 1992a. Data from Korea is consistent with this explanation of war: More environmental stress strongly predicts higher frequencies of warfare in Korea between the 1st century b.c. and the 8th century a.d. See B. W. Kang 2000, 878.
75. C. R. Ember and Ember 1992a.
76. Zhang et al. 2007; B. W. Kang 2000.
77. For the cross-cultural results suggesting the theory of war described here, see C. R. Ember and M. Ember 1992a
78. J. S. Goldstein, 292; see research referred to therein.
79. For the results on political participation and peace in the ethnographic record, see C. R. Ember, Ember, and Russett 1992. For the results on political participation and peace in the modern world, see the references in that essay.
80. Russett and Oneal 2001, 49.
81. Mansfield and Snyder 2007.
82. Ibid., 125ff.
83. Some of these examples are from Henderson 2001.
84. See the discussions in Ibid., 3–9, and S. K. Anderson and Sloan 2002, 1–5.
85. S. K. Anderson and Sloan 2002, 465.
86. This definition is adapted from Chomsky, who is quoted in Henderson 2001, 5.
87. Pinker 2011, 347; S. K. Anderson and Sloan 2002, 6–7.
88. S. K. Anderson and Sloan 2002, 6–8.
89. Suárez-Orozco 1992.
90. R. J. Rummel 2002a.
91. R. J. Rummel 2002c.
92. R. J. Rummel 2002d.
93. S. K. Anderson and Sloan 2002, 422; E. Newman 2006.
94. E. Newman 2006.
95. Crossroads for Planet Earth 2005.

Bibliography

'Abd Allah, Mahmud M. 1917. Siwan customs. *Harvard African Studies* 1:1–28.

Abel, Thomas and John Richard Stepp. 2003. A new ecosystems ecology for anthropology. *Conservation Ecology* 7, no. 3:12.

Aberle, David. 1971. A note on relative deprivation theory as applied to millenarian and other cult movements. In *Reader in comparative religion*, 3rd ed., eds. W. A. Lessa and E. Z. Vogt. New York: Harper & Row.

Abi-Rached, L., et al. 2011. The shaping of modern human immune systems by multiregional admixture with archaic humans. *Science* 334 (October 7):89–94.

Abler, Thomas S. 2009. Iroquois: The tree of peace and the war kettle. In MyAnthroLibrary, eds. C. R. Ember, M. Ember, and P. N. Peregrine. MyAnthroLibrary.com. Pearson.

Academic American encyclopedia. 1980. Princeton, NJ: Areté.

Acheson, James M. 2006. Lobster and groundfish management in the Gulf of Maine: A rational choice perspective. *Human Organization* 65:240–52.

Adams, David B. 1983. Why there are so few women warriors. *Behavior Science Research* 18:196–212.

Adams, Robert McCormick. 1960. The origin of cities. *Scientific American* (September):153–68.

Adams, Robert McCormick. 1981. *Heartland of cities: Surveys of ancient settlement and land use on the central floodplain of the Euphrates*. Chicago: University of Chicago Press.

Ahern, Emily M. 1975. Sacred and secular medicine in a Taiwan village: A study of cosmological disorders. In *Medicine in Chinese cultures: Comparative studies of health care in Chinese and other societies*, eds. A. Kleinman, P. Kunstadter, E. R. Alexander and J. L. Gale. Washington, DC: U.S. Department of Health, Education, and Welfare, National Institutes of Health.

Aiello, Leslie C. 1992. Body size and energy requirements. In *The Cambridge encyclopedia of human evolution*, eds. S. Jones, R. Martin, and D. Pilbeam. New York: Cambridge University Press.

Aiello, Leslie C. 1993. The origin of the New World monkeys. In *The Africa-South America connection*, ed. W. George and R. Lavocat, 100–118. Oxford: Clarendon Press.

Aiello, Leslie C., and Mark Collard. 2001. Our newest oldest ancestor? *Nature* 410 (November 29):526–27.

Aiello, Leslie C., and Christopher Dean. 1990. *An introduction to human evolutionary anatomy*. London: Academic Press.

Akmajian, Adrian, Richard A. Demers, Ann K. Farmer, and Robert M. Harnish. 2001. *Linguistics: An introduction to language and communication*. Cambridge, MA: The MIT Press.

Akmajian, Adrian, Richard A. Demers, and Robert M. Harnish. 1984. *Linguistics: An introduction to language and communication*. 2nd ed. Cambridge, MA: MIT Press.

Albert, Steven M., and Maria G. Cattell. 1994. *Old age in global perspective: Cross-cultural and cross-national views*. New York: G. K. Hall/Macmillan.

Alberts, Bruce, president of the National Academy of Sciences. 2000. Setting the record straight regarding *Darkness in El Dorado*, November 9. http://www4.nationalacademies.org/nas/nashome.nsf.

Alexander, John P. 1992. Alas, poor *Notharctus*. *Natural History* (August):55–59.

Algaze, Guillermo. 1993. *The Uruk world system: The dynamics of expansion of early Mesopotamian civilization*. Chicago: University of Chicago Press.

Allen, John S., and Susan M. Cheer. 1996. The nonthrifty genotype. *Current Anthropology* 37:831–42.

Allen, John S., A. J. Lambert, F. Y. Attah Johnson, K. Schmidt, and K. L. Nero. 1996. Antisaccadic eye movements and attentional asymmetry in schizophrenia in three Pacific populations. *Acta Psychiatrica Scandinavia* 94:258–65.

Alperson-Afil, N., et al. 2009. Spatial organization of hominin activities at Gesher Benot Ya'aqov, Israel. *Science* 326 (December 18):1677–83.

Alroy, John. 2001. A multispecies overkill simulation of the End-Pleistocene megafaunal mass extinction. *Science* 292 (June 8):1893–96.

Altman, Lawrence K. 2008. Protective effects of circumcision are shown to continue after trials' end. *New York Times*, August 12. http://www.nytimes.com.

Alvarez, Lizette. 2003. Arranged marriages get a little rearranging. *New York Times*, June 22, p. 1.3.

Ambient Corporation. 2000. Energy: Investing for a new century. *New York Times*, October 30, pp. EN1–EN8. A special advertisement produced by energy companies.

American Anthropological Association. 1991. Revised principles of professional responsibility, 1990. In *Ethics and the profession of anthropology: Dialogue for a new era*, ed. Carolyn Fluehr-Lobban, 274–79. Philadelphia: University of Pennsylvania Press. http://www.aaanet.org/coe/Code_of_Ethics.pdf.

American Anthropological Association. 2012. Statement on ethics: Principles of professional responsibility 2012. http://www.aaanet.org/coe/Code_of_Ethics.pdf (accessed May 5, 2013).

Anbarci, Nejat, Monica Escaleras, and Charles A. Register. 2005. Earthquake fatalities: The interaction of nature and political economy. *Journal of Public Economics* 89, no.9:1907–33.

Anderson, Connie M. 2000. The persistence of polygyny as an adaptive response to poverty and oppression in apartheid South Africa. *Cross-Cultural Research* 34:99–112.

Anderson, Craig A., and Brad J. Bushman. 2002. The effects of media violence on society. *Science* 295 (March 29):2377–79.

Anderson, David G. 2012. Pleistocene settlement in the East. In *Oxford handbook of North American archaeology*, ed. T. Pauketat. Oxford: Oxford University Press.

Anderson, David G., Jeb J. Card, and Kenneth Feder. 2013. Speaking up and speaking out: Collective efforts in the fight to reclaim the public perception of archaeology. *SAA Archaeological Record* 13, no.2:24–27.

Anderson, J. L., C. B. Crawford, J. Nadeau, and T. Lindberg. 1992. Was the Duchess of Windsor right? A cross-cultural review of the socioecology of ideal female body shape. *Ethnology and Sociobiology* 13:197–227.

Anderson, Richard L. 1989. *Art in small-scale societies*. 2nd ed. Englewood Cliffs, NJ: Prentice Hall.

Anderson, Richard L. 1990. *Calliope's sisters: A comparative study of philosophies of art*. Upper Saddle River, NJ: Prentice Hall.

Anderson, Richard L. 1992. Do other cultures have "art"? *American Anthropologist* 94:926–29.

Anderson, Sean K., and Stephen Sloan. 2002. *Historical dictionary of terrorism*. 2nd ed. Lanham, MD: Scarecrow Press.

Andrefsky, William. 1998. *Lithics: Macroscopic approaches to analysis*. New York: Cambridge University Press.

Andrews, Elizabeth. 1994. Territoriality and land use among the Akulmiut of Western Alaska. In *Key issues in hunter-gatherer research*, eds. E. S. Burch Jr., and L. J. Ellanna. Oxford: Berg.

Andrews, Peter. 2000a. Propliopithecidae. In *Encyclopedia of human evolution and prehistory*, eds. I. Tattersall, E. Delson, and J. van Couvering. New York: Garland.

Andrews, Peter. 2000b. Proconsul. In *Encyclopedia of human evolution and prehistory*, eds. I. Tattersall, E. Delson, and J. van Couvering. New York: Garland.

Angier, Natalie. 2002. Why we're so nice: We're wired to cooperate. *New York Times*, Science Times, July 23, pp. F1, F8.

Ankel-Simons, Friederun. 2007. *Primate anatomy*, 3rd ed. San Diego: Academic Press.

Anthony, David, Dimitri Y. Telegin, and Dorcas Brown. 1991. The origin of horseback riding. *Scientific American* (December):94–100.

Antoun, Richard T. 2001. *Understanding fundamentalism: Christian, Islamic, and Jewish movements*. Walnut Creek, CA: AltaMira Press.

Antoun, Richard T. 2008. *Understanding fundamentalism*. 2nd ed. Lanham, MD: Rowman & Littlefield.

Anyon, Roger, and T. J. Ferguson. 1995. Cultural resources management at the Pueblo of Zuni, New Mexico, USA. *Antiquity* 69:913–30.

Aporta, Claudio, and Eric Higgs. 2005. Satellite culture: Global positioning systems, Inuit wayfinding, and the need for a new account of technology. *Current Anthropology* 46:729–46.

Apostolou, Menelaos. 2010. Parental choice: What parents want in a son-in-law and a daughter-in-law across 67 pre-industrial societies. *British Journal of Psychology* 101:695–704.

Appadurai, Arjun. 2000. The grounds of the nation-state: Identity, violence and territory. In *Nationalism and internationalism in the post-cold war era*, eds. U. H. Goldman and C. Westin. London: Routledge.

Appendix A: Report of the Committee on Ethics, Society for Applied Anthropology. 2002. In *Ethics and the profession of anthropology*, ed. C. Fluehr-Lobban. Philadelphia: University of Pennsylvania Press.

Appendix C: Statements on Ethics: Principles of Professional Responsibility, Adopted by the Council of the American Anthropological Association, May 1971. 1991. In *Ethics and the profession of anthropology*, ed. C. Fluehr-Lobban. Philadelphia: University of Pennsylvania Press.

Appendix F: Professional and Ethical Responsibilities, SfAA. 2002. In *Ethics and the profession of anthropology*, ed. C. Fluehr-Lobban. Philadelphia: University of Pennsylvania Press.

Appendix H: National Association of Practicing Anthropologists' Ethical Guidelines for Practitioners, 1988. 1991. In *Ethics and the profession of anthropology*, ed. C. Fluehr-Lobban. Philadelphia: University of Pennsylvania Press.

Appendix I: Revised Principles of Professional Responsibility, 1990. 1991. In *Ethics and the profession of anthropology*, ed. C. Fluehr-Lobban. Philadelphia: University of Pennsylvania Press.

Aptekar, Lewis. 1988. *Street children of Cali*. Durham, NC: Duke University Press.

Aptekar, Lewis. 1991. Are Colombian street children neglected? The contributions of ethnographic and ethnohistorical approaches to the study of children. *Anthropology and Education Quarterly* 22:326–49.

Aptekar, Lewis. 1994. *Environmental disasters in global perspective*. New York: G. K. Hall/Macmillan.

Archer, Dane, and Rosemary Gartner. 1984. *Violence and crime in cross-national perspective*. New Haven, CT: Yale University Press.

Archer, John. 2006. Cross-cultural differences in physical aggression between partners: A social-role analysis. *Personality and Social Psychology Review* 10:133–53.

Ardener, Shirley. 1995a/1964. The comparative study of rotating credit associations. In *Money-go-rounds*, eds. S. Ardener and S. Burman. Oxford: Berg.

Ardener, Shirley. 1995b/1964. Women making money go round: ROSCAs revisited. In *Money-go-rounds*, eds. S. Ardener and S. Burman. Oxford: Berg.

Ardener, Shirley, and Sandra Burman, eds. 1995/1964. *Money-go-rounds: The importance of rotating savings and credit associations for women*. Oxford: Berg.

Argyle, Michael. 1994. *The psychology of social class*. New York: Routledge.

Armelagos, George J., and Alan H. Goodman. 1998. Race, racism, and anthropology. In *Building a new biocultural synthesis: Political-economic perspectives on human biology*, eds. A. H. Goodman and T. L. Leatherman. Ann Arbor: University of Michigan Press.

Armelagos, George J., and Kirstin H. Harper. 2005. Genomics at the origins of agriculture, Part Two. *Evolutionary Anthropology* 14:109–21.

Armstrong, Robert P. 1981. *The powers of presence*. Philadelphia: University of Pennsylvania Press.

Aronoff, Joel, Andrew M. Barclay, and Linda A. Stevenson. 1988. The recognition of threatening facial stimuli. *Journal of Personality and Social Psychology* 54:647–55.

Aronoff, Joel, Barbara A. Woike, and Lester M. Hyman. 1992. Which are the stimuli in facial displays of anger and happiness? Configurational bases of emotion recognition. *Journal of Personality and Social Psychology* 62:1050–66.

Aronson, Joshua. 2002. Stereotype threat: Contending and coping with unnerving expectations. In *Improving academic performance*, ed. J. Aronson. San Francisco: Academic Press.

Aronson, Joshua, Carrie B. Fried, and Catherine Good. 2002. Reducing the effects of stereotype threat on African American college students by shaping theories of intelligence. *Journal of Experimental Social Psychology* 38:113–25.

Asch, Nancy B., and David L. Asch. 1978. The economic potential of *Iva annua* and its prehistoric importance in the Lower Illinois Valley. In *The nature and status of ethnobotany*, ed. R. Ford. Anthropological Papers No 67, Museum of Anthropology. Ann Arbor: University of Michigan.

Asch, Solomon. 1956. Studies of independence and conformity: A minority of one against a unanimous majority. *Psychological Monographs* 70:1–70.

Ascher, Robert. 1961. Analogy in archaeological interpretation. *Southwestern Journal of Anthropology* 17:317–25.

Asfaw, Berhane, Tim White, Owen Lovejoy, Bruce Latimer, Scott Simpson, and Glen Suwa. 1999. *Australopithecus garhi*: A new species of early hominid from Ethiopia. *Science* 284 (April 23):629–36.

Association business: Clyde Snow, forensic anthropologist, works for justice. 2000. *Anthropology News* (October):12.

Association for Cultural Equity. 2013. Global jukebox. http://www.culturalequity.org/rc/ce_rc_psr_global_jukebox.php (accessed April 28, 2013).

Atkinshon, Quentin D., and Patrick Bourrat. 2011. Beliefs about god, the afterlife and morality support the role of supernatural policing in human cooperation. *Evolution and Human Behavior* 32:41–49.

Austin, Peter K., and Julia Sallabank. 2011. Introduction. In *Cambridge handbook of endangered languages*, eds. Peter K. Austin and Julia Sallabank. Cambridge University Press.

Ayala, Francisco J. 1995. The myth of Eve: Molecular biology and human origins. *Science* 270 (December 22):1930–36.

Ayala, Francisco J. 1996. Communication. *Science* 274 (November 29):1354.

Ayres, Barbara C. 1968. Effects of infantile stimulation on musical behavior. In *Folk song style and culture*, ed. A. Lomax. Washington, DC: Transaction Publishers.

Ayres, Barbara C. 1973. Effects of infant carrying practices on rhythm in music. *Ethos* 1:387–404.

Baba, Marietta L., and Carole E. Hill. 2006. What's in the name "Applied Anthropology"? An encounter with global practice. *NAPA Bulletin* 25: 176–207. Washington, DC: American Anthropological Association.

Bachnik, Jane M. 1992. The two "faces" of self and society in Japan. *Ethos* 20:3–32.

Bacon, Margaret, Irvin L. Child, and Herbert Barry, III. 1963. A cross-cultural study of correlates of crime. *Journal of Abnormal and Social Psychology* 66:291–300.

Badcock, Christopher. 1988. *Essential Freud.* Oxford: Blackwell.

Badcock, Christopher. 2000. *Evolutionary psychology: A critical introduction.* Cambridge: Blackwell.

Baer, Hans A., and Merrill Singer. 2009. *Global warming and the political ecology of health: Emerging crises and systemic solutions.* Walnut Creek, CA: Left Coast Press.

Baer, Hans A., Merrill Singer, and Ida Susser. 1997. *Medical anthropology and the world system: A critical perspective.* Westport, CT: Bergin & Garvey.

Bahn, Paul. 1998. Neanderthals emancipated. *Nature* 394 (August 20):719–20.

Bailey, Robert C., Genevieve Head, Mark Jenike, Bruce Owen, Robert Rectman, and Elzbieta Zechenter. 1989. Hunting and gathering in tropical rain forest: Is it possible? *American Anthropologist* 91:59–82.

Baldi, Philip. 1983. *An introduction to the Indo-European languages.* Carbondale: Southern Illinois University Press.

Balikci, Asen. 1970. *The Netsilik Eskimo.* Garden City, NY: Natural History Press.

Balter, Michael. 2001. In search of the first Europeans. *Science* 291 (March 2):1722–25.

Balter, Michael. 2007. Seeking agriculture's ancient roots. *Science* 316 (June 29):1830–35.

Balter, Michael. 2009. Better homes and hearths, Neandertal-style. *Science* 326 (November 20):1056–57.

Balter, Michael. 2010. Neandertal jewelry shows their symbolic smarts. *Science* 327 (January 15):255–56.

Balter, Michael, and Ann Gibbons. 2000. A glimpse of humans' first journey out of Africa. *Science* 288 (May 12):948–50.

Bandy, Michael. 2005. Energetic efficiency and political expediency in Titicaca Basin raised field agriculture. *Journal of Anthropological Archaeology* 24, no. 3:271–296.

Barak, Gregg. 1991. *Gimme shelter: A social history of homelessness in contemporary America.* New York: Praeger.

Barash, David P. 1977. *Sociobiology and behavior.* New York: Elsevier.

Barber, Nigel. 2000. The sex ratio as a predictor of cross-national variation in violent crime. *Cross-Cultural Research* 34:264–82.

Barber, Nigel. 2003. Paternal investment prospects and cross-national differences in single parenthood. *Cross-Cultural Research* 37:163–77.

Barber, Nigel. 2007. Evolutionary explanations for societal differences and historical change in violent crime and single parenthood. *Cross-Cultural Research* 41:123–48.

Barber, Nigel. 2008. Explaining cross-national differences in polygyny intensity: Resource-defense, sex-ratio, and infectious diseases. *Cross-Cultural Research* 42:103–17.

Barber, Nigel. 2011. A cross-national test of the uncertainty hypothesis of religious belief. *Cross-Cultural Research* 45:318–33.

Bard, Kathryn A. 2008. *An introduction to the archaeology of ancient Egypt.* Malden, MA: Blackwell.

Barinaga, Maria. 1992. Priming the brain's language pump. *Science* 255 (January 31):535.

Barlett, Peggy F. 1989. Industrial agriculture. In *Economic Anthropology*, ed. S. Plattner. Stanford, CA: Stanford University Press.

Barnes, Jessica, et al. 2013. Contribution of anthropology to the study of climate change. *Nature Climate Change* 3:541–4.

Barnett, H. G. 1960. *Being a Palauan.* New York: Holt, Rinehart & Winston.

Barnosky, Anthony, Paul Koch, Robert Feranec, Scott Wing, and Alan Shabel. 2004. Assessing the causes of Late Pleistocene extinctions on the continents. *Science* 306 (October 1):70–75.

Barrett, D. E. 1984. Malnutrition and child behavior: Conceptualization, assessment and an empirical study of social-emotional functioning. In *Malnutrition and behavior: Critical assessment of key issues*, eds. J. Brozek and B. Schürch. Lausanne, Switzerland: Nestlé Foundation.

Barrett, Stanley R. 1994. *Paradise: Class, commuters, and ethnicity in rural Ontario.* Toronto: University of Toronto Press.

Barry, Herbert, III. 2007. Wealth concentration associated with frequent violent crime in diverse communities. *Social Evolution & History* 6:29–38.

Barry, Herbert, III, Irvin L. Child, and Margaret K. Bacon. 1959. Relation of child training to subsistence economy. *American Anthropologist* 61:51–63.

Barth, Fredrik. 1965. *Nomads of South Persia.* New York: Humanities Press.

Barth, Fredrik. 1994. Enduring and emerging issues in the analysis of ethnicity. In *The anthropology of ethnicity*, eds. H. Vermeulen and C. Govers. Amsterdam: Het Spinhuis.

Bates, Daniel G., and Susan H. Lees, eds. 1996. *Case studies in human ecology.* New York: Plenum Press.

Bates, E., and V. A. Marchman. 1988. What is and is not universal in language acquisition. In *Language, communication, and the brain*, ed. F. Plum. New York: Raven Press.

Bauman, Richard. 1992. Folklore. In *Folklore, cultural performances, and popular entertainments*, ed. R. Bauman. New York: Oxford University Press.

Baxter, Ellen, and Kim Hopper. 1981. *Private lives/public spaces: Homeless adults on the streets of New York City.* New York: Community Service Society of New York.

Beadle, George, and Muriel Beadle. 1966. *The language of life.* Garden City, NY: Doubleday.

Beard, K. Christopher. 2002. Basal anthropoids. In *The primate fossil record*, ed. W. C. Hartwig. Cambridge: Cambridge University Press.

Bearder, Simon K. 1987. Lorises, bushbabies, and tarsiers: Diverse societies in solitary foragers. In *Primate societies*, eds. Barbara B. Smuts, Dorothy L. Cheney, Robert M. Seyfarth, and Richard W. Wrangham. Chicago: University of Chicago Press.

Beattie, John. 1960. *Bunyoro: An African kingdom.* New York: Holt, Rinehart & Winston.

Beaumont, P. B. 2011. The edge: More on fire-making by about 1.7 million years ago at Wonderwerk Cave in South Africa. *Current Anthropology* 52:585–95

Begler, Elsie B. 1978. Sex, status, and authority in egalitarian society. *American Anthropologist* 80:571–88.

Begun, David. 2002a. European hominoids. In *The primate fossil record*, ed. W. C. Hartwig. Cambridge: Cambridge University Press.

Begun, David. 2002b. Miocene apes. In *Physical anthropology: Original readings in method and practice*, eds. P. N. Peregrine, C. R. Ember, and M. Ember. Upper Saddle River, NJ: Prentice Hall.

Behar, Ruth, and Deborah Gordon, eds. 1995. *Women writing culture.* Berkeley: University of California Press.

Behrman, Jere R., Alejandro Gaviria, and Miguel Székely. 2001. Intergenerational mobility in Latin America. Inter-American Development Bank, Working Paper #45. http://www.iadb.org/res/publications/pubfiles/pubWP-452.pdf (accessed June 2009).

Bellman, Beryl L. 1984. *The language of secrecy: Symbols and metaphors in Poro ritual.* New Brunswick, NJ: Rutgers University Press.

Bellwood, Peter. 2005. *First farmers.* Malden, MA: Blackwell.

Benjamin, Lois. 1991. *The Black elite: Facing the color line in the twilight of the twentieth century.* Chicago: Nelson-Hall.

Bentley, R. Alexander, Carl P. Lipo, Harold A. Herzog, and Matthew W. Hahn. 2007. Regular rates of popular culture change reflect random copying. *Evolution and Human Behavior* 28:151–58.

Berger, L. R., et al. 2010. *Australopithecus sediba*: A new species of *Homo*-like australopith from South Africa. *Science* 328 (April 9):195–204.

Berggren, William A., Dennis V. Kent, John D. Obradovich, and Carl C. Swisher, III. 1992. Toward a revised paleogene geochronology. In *Eocene-Oliocene climatic and biotic evolution*, eds. D. R. Prothero and W. A. Berggren. Princeton, NJ: Princeton University Press.

Berlin, Brent. 1992. *Ethnobiological classification: Principles of categorization of plants and animals in traditional societies.* Princeton, NJ: Princeton University Press.

Berlin, Brent, and Paul Kay. 1969. *Basic color terms: Their universality and evolution.* Berkeley: University of California Press.

Berlin, Elois Ann. 1996. General overview of Maya ethnomedicine. In *Medical ethnobiology of the highland Maya of Chiapas, Mexico*, eds. E. A. Berlin and B. Berlin. Princeton, NJ: Princeton University Press.

Berlin, Elois Ann, and Brent Berlin. 1996. *Medical ethnobiology of the highland Maya of Chiapas, Mexico: The gastrointestinal diseases.* Princeton, NJ: Princeton University Press.

Bernard, H. Russell. 2001. *Research methods in cultural anthropology: Qualitative and quantitative approaches.* 3rd ed. Walnut Creek, CA: AltaMira Press.

Bernard, H. Russell. 2011. *Research methods in anthropology*, 5th ed. Lanham, MD: AltaMira.

Bernardi, B. 1952. The age-system of the Nilo-Hamitic peoples. *Africa* 22:316–332.

Berns, G., J. Chappelow, C. Zink, G. Pagnoni, M. Martin-Skurski, and J. Richards. 2005. Neurobiological correlates of social conformity and independence during mental rotation. *Biological Psychiatry* 58:245–253.

Berreman, Gerald D. 1960. Caste in India and the United States. *American Journal of Sociology* 66:120–27.

Berreman, Gerald D. 1972. Race, caste and other invidious distinctions in social stratification. *Race* 13:403–14.

Berreman, Gerald D. 1973. *Caste in the modern world.* Morristown, NJ: General Learning Press.

Berry, John W. 1971. Ecological and cultural factors in spatial perceptual development. *Canadian Journal of Behavioural Science* 3:324–36.

Berry, John W. 1976. *Human ecology and cognitive style.* New York: Wiley.

Berry, John W., and J. Bennett. 1989. Syllabic literacy and cognitive performance among the Cree. *International Journal of Psychology* 24:429–50.

Berry, John W., Ype H. Poortinga, Marshall H. Segall, and Pierre R. Dasen. 1992. *Cross-cultural psychology: Research and applications.* New York: Cambridge University Press.

Bertrand, Marianne, and Sendhil Mullainathan. 2011. Are Emily and Greg more employable than Lakisha and Jamal? In *Race in an era of change: A reader*, eds. H. Dalmage and B. Katz Rothman. New York: Oxford University Press.

Bestor, Theodore C. 2001. Supply-side sushi: Commodity, market, and the global city. *American Anthropologist* 103:76–95.

Betts, Richard A., Yadvinder Malhi, and J. Timmons Roberts. 2008. The future of the Amazon: New perspectives from climate, ecosystem, and social sciences. *Philosophical Transactions of the Royal Society B* 363:1729–35.

Betzig, Laura. 1988. Redistribution: Equity or exploitation? In *Human reproductive behavior*, eds. L. Betzig, M. B. Mulder, and P. Turke. Cambridge: Cambridge University Press.

Betzig, Laura. 1989. Causes of conjugal dissolution: A cross-cultural study. *Current Anthropology* 30:654–76.

Bickerton, Derek. 1983. Creole languages. *Scientific American* (July):116–22.

Biermann, Frank, and Ingrid Boas. 2010. Preparing for a warmer world: Towards a global governance system to protect climate refugees. *Global Environmental Politics* 10:60–88.

Bilby, Kenneth. 1996. Ethnogenesis in the Guianas and Jamaica: Two Maroon cases. In *Ethnogenesis in the Americas*, ed. J. D. Hill. Iowa City: University of Iowa Press.

Bilsborough, Alan. 1992. *Human evolution.* New York: Blackie Academic & Professional.

Bindon, James R., and Douglas E. Crews. 1993. Changes in some health status characteristics of American Samoan men: Preliminary observations from a 12-year follow-up study. *American Journal of Human Biology* 5:31–37.

Bindon, James R., Amy Knight, William W. Dressler, and Douglas E. Crews. 1997. Social context and psychosocial influences on blood pressure among American Samoans. *American Journal of Physical Anthropology* 103:7–18.

Binford, Lewis R. 1971. Post-Pleistocene adaptations. In *Prehistoric agriculture*, ed. S. Struever. Garden City, NY: Natural History Press.

Binford, Lewis R. 1973. Interassemblage variability: The Mousterian and the "functional" argument. In *The explanation of culture change*, ed. C. Renfrew. Pittsburgh: University of Pittsburgh Press.

Binford, Lewis R. 1984. *Faunal remains from Klasies River mouth.* Orlando, FL: Academic Press.

Binford, Lewis R. 1987. Were there elephant hunters at Torralba? In *The evolution of human hunting*, eds. M. Nitecki and D. Nitecki. New York: Plenum.

Binford, Lewis R. 1990. Mobility, housing, and environment: A comparative study. *Journal of Anthropological Research* 46:119–52.

Binford, Lewis R., and Chuan Kun Ho. 1985. Taphonomy at a distance: Zhoukoudian, 'The cave home of Beijing Man'? *Current Anthropology* 26:413–42.

Binford, Sally R., and Lewis R. Binford. 1969. Stone tools and human behavior. *Scientific American* (April):70–84.

Bishop, Ryan. 1996. Postmodernism. In *Encyclopedia of cultural anthropology*, vol. 3, eds. D. Levinson and M. Ember. New York: Henry Holt.

Black, Donald. 1993. *The social structure of right and wrong.* San Diego: Academic Press.

Black, Francis L. 1992. Why did they die? *Science* 258 (December 11):1739–40.

Blackwood, Evelyn. 1984a. *Cross-cultural dimensions of lesbian relations.* Master's Thesis. San Francisco State University. As referred to in Blackwood and Wieringa 1999.

Blackwood, Evelyn. 1984b. Sexuality and gender in certain Native American tribes: The case of cross-gender females. *Signs* 10:27–42.

Blackwood, Evelyn, and Saskia E. Wieringa. 1999. Sapphic shadows: Challenging the silence in the study of sexuality. In *Female desires: Same-sex relations and transgender practices across cultures*, eds. E. Blackwood and S. E. Weiringa. New York: Columbia University Press.

Blalock, Hubert M. 1972. *Social statistics.* 2nd ed. New York: McGraw-Hill.

Bland, Alastair. 2013. From pets to plates: Why more people are eating guinea pigs. *The Salt: What's on Your Plate.* npr.org, April 2.

Blanton, Richard E. 1976. The origins of Monte Albán. In *Cultural continuity and change*, ed. C. E. Cleland. New York: Academic Press.

Blanton, Richard E. 1978. *Monte Albán: Settlement patterns at the ancient Zapotec capital.* New York: Academic Press.

Blanton, Richard E. 1981. The rise of cities. In *Supplement to the handbook of Middle American Indians*, vol. 1, ed. J. Sabloff. Austin: University of Texas Press.

Blanton, Richard E. 2009. Variation in economy. In MyAnthroLibrary, eds. C. R. Ember, M. Ember, and P. N. Peregrine. MyAnthroLibrary.com. Pearson.

Blanton, Richard E., and Lane Fargher. 2008. *Collective action in the formation of pre-modern states.* New York: Springer.

Blanton, Richard E., Stephen A. Kowalewski, Gary Feinman, and Jill Appel. 1981. *Ancient Mesoamerica: A comparison of change in three regions.* New York: Cambridge University Press.

Bledsoe, Caroline H. 1980. *Women and marriage in Kpelle society.* Stanford, CA: Stanford University Press.

Blight, Garry, Sheila Pulham, and Paul Torpey. 2012. Arab spring: An interactive timeline of the Middle East protests. *The Guardian.* www.guardian.co.uk.

Block, Jean L. 1983. Help! They've all moved back home! *Woman's Day* (April 26):72–76.

Block, Jonathan I., and Doug M. Boyer. 2002. Grasping primate origins. *Science* 298 (November 22):1606–10.

Blount, Ben G. 1981. The development of language in children. In *Handbook of cross-cultural human development*, eds. R. H. Munroe, R. L. Munroe, and B. B. Whiting. New York: Garland.

Bluebond-Langner, Myra. 2007. Challenges and opportunities in the anthropology of childhoods: An introduction to "children, childhoods, and childhood studies." *American Anthropologist* 109:241–46.

Blumenschine, Robert J., et al. 2003. Late Pliocene *Homo* and hominid land use from Western Olduvai Gorge, Tanzania. *Science* 299 (February 21):1217–21.

Blumler, Mark A., and Roger Byrne. 1991. The ecological genetics of domestication and the origins of agriculture. *Current Anthropology* 32:23–35.

Boas, Franz. 1888. *Central Eskimos.* Bureau of American Ethnology Annual Report No. 6. Washington, DC: Smithsonian Institution.

Boas, Franz. 1930. *The religion of the Kwakiutl.* Columbia University Contributions to Anthropology, pt. 2. vol. 10. New York: Columbia University.

Boas, Franz. 1940. *Race, language, and culture.* New York: Macmillan.

Boas, Franz. 1964/1911. On grammatical categories. In *Language in culture and society*, ed. D. Hymes. New York: Harper & Row.

Boaz, Noel T., and Alan J. Almquist. 1997. *Biological anthropology: A synthetic approach to human evolution.* Upper Saddle River, NJ: Prentice Hall.

Boaz, Noel T., and Alan J. Almquist. 1999. *Essentials of biological anthropology.* Upper Saddle River, NJ: Prentice Hall.

Boaz, Noel T., and Alan J. Almquist. 2002. *Biological anthropology: A synthetic approach to human evolution.* 2nd ed. Upper Saddle River, NJ: Prentice Hall.

Bock, Philip K. 1980. *Continuities in psychological anthropology: A historical introduction.* San Francisco: W. H. Freeman and Company.

Bock, Philip K. 1996. Psychological anthropology. In *Encyclopedia of cultural anthropology*, vol. 3, eds. D. Levinson and M. Ember. New York: Henry Holt.

Bodley, John H. 2008. *Victims of progress.* 5th ed. Lanham, MD: AltaMira Press.

Boehm, Christopher. 1993. Egalitarian behavior and reverse dominance hierarchy. *Current Anthropology* 34:230–31.

Boehm, Christopher. 1999. *Hierarchy in the forest: The evolution of egalitarian behavior.* Cambridge, MA: Harvard University Press.

Boehm, Christopher. 2008. Purposive social selection and the evolution of human altruism. *Cross-Cultural Research* 42, no.4:319–52.

Boehm, Christopher. 2012. Ancestral hierarchy and conflict. *Science* 336 (May 18): 844–7.

Boesche, Christophe, P. Marchesi, N. Marchesi, B. Fruth, and F. Joulian. 1994. Is nut cracking in wild chimpanzees a cultural behavior? *Journal of Human Evolution* 26:325–38.

Bogin, Barry. 1988. *Patterns of human growth.* Cambridge: Cambridge University Press.

Bogin, Barry. 1997. Evolutionary hypotheses for human childhood. *Yearbook of Physical Anthropology* 40:63–89.

Bogoras, Waldemar. 1909. The Chukchee. Part 3. *Memoirs of the American Museum of Natural History*, 2.

Bohannan, Laura, and Paul Bohannan. 1953. *The Tiv of central Nigeria.* London: International African Institute.

Bohannan, Paul. 1954. The migration and expansion of the Tiv. *Africa* 24:2–16.

Bollen, Kenneth A. 1993. Liberal democracy: Validity and method factors in cross-national measures. *American Journal of Political Science* 37:1207–30.

Bolton, Ralph. 1973. Aggression and hypoglycemia among the Qolla: A study in psychobiological anthropology. *Ethnology* 12:227–57.

Bolton, Ralph. 1989. Introduction: The AIDS pandemic, a global emergency. *Medical Anthropology* 10:93–104.

Bolton, Ralph. 1992. AIDS and promiscuity: Muddled in the models of HIV prevention. *Medical Anthropology* 14:145–223.

Bond, Michael Harris. 2004. Culture and aggression—From context to coercion. *Personality and Social Psychology Review* 8, no.1:62–78.

Bond, Rod, and Peter B. Smith. 1996. Culture and conformity: A meta-analysis of studies using Asch's (1952b, 1956) line judgment task. *Psychological Bulletin* 11:111–37.

Bondarenko, Dmitri, and Andrey Korotayev. 2000. Family size and community organization: A cross-cultural comparison. *Cross-Cultural Research* 34:152–89.

Boonyabancha, Somsook. 2009. Land for housing the poor—by the poor: Experiences from the Baan Mankong Nationwide Slum Upgrading Programme in Thailand. *Environment and Urbanization* 21:309–29.

Bordaz, Jacques. 1970. *Tools of the Old and New Stone Age.* Garden City, NY: Natural History Press.

Bordes, François. 1961. Mousterian cultures in France. *Science* 134 (September 22): 803–10.

Bordes, François. 1968. *The Old Stone Age.* New York: McGraw-Hill.

Borgerhoff Mulder, Monique, Margaret George-Cramer, Jason Eshleman, and Alessia Ortolani. 2001. A study of East African kinship and marriage using a phylogenetically based comparative method. *American Anthropologist* 103:1059–82.

Borgerhoff Mulder, Monique, et al. 2010. Pastoralism and wealth inequality: Revisiting an old question. *Current Anthropology* 51:35–48.

Bornstein, Marc H. 1973. The psychophysiological component of cultural difference in color naming and illusion susceptibility. *Behavior Science Notes* 8:41–101.

Bortei-Doku, Ellen, and Ernest Aryeetey. 1995/1964. Mobilizing cash for business: Women in rotating *Susu* clubs in Ghana. In *Money-go-rounds*, eds. S. Ardener and S. Burman. Oxford: Berg.

Boserup, Ester. 1970. *Woman's role in economic development.* New York: St. Martin's Press.

Boserup, Ester. 1993/1965. *The conditions of agricultural growth: The economics of agrarian change under population pressure.* Toronto: Earthscan Publishers.

Bossen, Laurel. 2000. Women farmers, small plots, and changing markets in China. In *Women farmers and commercial ventures: Increasing food security in developing countries*, ed. A. Spring. Boulder, CO: Lynne Rienner Press.

Bourguignon, Erika. 1973. Introduction: A framework for the comparative study of altered states of consciousness. In *Religion, altered states of consciousness, and social change*, ed. E. Bourguignon. Columbus: Ohio State University Press.

Bourguignon, Erika. 2004. Suffering and healing, subordination and power: Women and possession trance. *Ethos* 32:557–74.

Bourguignon, Erika, and Thomas L. Evascu. 1977. Altered states of consciousness within a general evolutionary perspective: A holocultural analysis. *Behavior Science Research* 12:197–216.

Bowen, Gabriel J., et al. 2002. Mammalian dispersal at the Paleocene/Eocene boundary. *Science* 295 (March 15):2062–64.

Bowie, Katherine A. 2006. Of corvée and slavery: Historical intricacies of the division of labor and state power in Northern Thailand. In *Labor in cross-cultural perspective*, eds. E. Paul Durrenberger and Judith E. Martí. Lanham: Roman & Littlefield.

Bowler, Peter J. 2009. *Evolution: The history of an idea*. Berkeley: University of California Press.

Bowles, Samuel, H. Gintis, and M. Osborne. 2001. The determinants of earnings: A behavioral approach. *Journal of Economic Literature* 39:1137–76, as referred to in Godoy et al. 2004.

Bowles, Samuel, Eric Alden Smith, and Monique Borgerhoff Mulder. 2010. The emergence and persistence of inequality in premodern societies: Introduction to the special section. *Current Anthropology* 51:7–17.

Boyd, Robert, and Peter J. Richerson. 1996/1985. *Culture and the evolutionary process*. Chicago: University of Chicago Press.

Boyd, Robert, and Peter J. Richerson. 2005. *The origin and evolution of cultures*. New York: Oxford University Press.

Boyd, Robert, and Joan Silk. 2000. *How humans evolved*. 2nd ed. New York: Norton.

Brace, C. Loring. 1995. Region does not mean 'race'—Reality versus convention in forensic anthropology. *Journal of Forensic Sciences* 40:171–75.

Brace, C. Loring. 1996. A four-letter word called race. In *Race and other misadventures: Essays in honor of Ashley Montague in his ninetieth year*, eds. L. T. Reynolds and L. Leiberman. New York: General Hall.

Brace, C. Loring. 2005. *"Race" is a four-letter word*. New York: Oxford University Press.

Brace, C. Loring, David P. Tracer, Lucia Allen Yaroch, John Robb, Kari Brandt, and A. Russell Nelson. 1993. Clines and clusters versus 'race': A test in ancient Egypt and the case of a death on the Nile. *Yearbook of Physical Anthropology* 36:1–31.

Bradley, Candice. 1984–1985. The sexual division of labor and the value of children. *Behavior Science Research* 19:159–85.

Bradley, Candice. 1995. Keeping the soil in good heart: Weeding, women and ecofeminism. In *Ecofeminism*, ed. K. Warren. Bloomington: Indiana University Press.

Bradsher, Keith. 2002. Pakistanis fume as clothing sales to U.S. tumble. *New York Times*, June 23, p. 3.

Braidwood, Robert J. 1960. The agricultural revolution. *Scientific American* (September):130–48.

Braidwood, Robert J., and Gordon R. Willey. 1962. Conclusions and afterthoughts. In *Courses toward urban life*, eds. R. Braidwood and G. Willey. Chicago: Aldine.

Brain, C. K., and A. Sillen. 1988. Evidence from the Swartkrans Cave for the earliest use of fire. *Nature* 336 (December 1):464–66.

Branda, Richard F., and John W. Eaton. 1978. Skin color and nutrient photolysis: An evolutionary hypothesis. *Science* 201 (August 18):625–26.

Brandewie, Ernest. 1991. The place of the big man in traditional Hagen society in the central highlands of New Guinea. In *Anthropological approaches to political behavior*, eds. F. McGlynn and A. Tuden. Pittsburgh, PA: University of Pittsburgh Press.

Brandon, Robert N. 1990. *Adaptation and environment*. Princeton, NJ: Princeton University Press.

Bräuer, Günter. 1984. A craniological approach to the origin of anatomically modern *Homo sapiens* in Africa and implications for the appearance of modern Europeans. In *The origins of modern humans*, eds. F. Smith and F. Spencer. New York: Alan R. Liss.

Braun, David P., and Stephen Plog. 1982. Evolution of "tribal" social networks: Theory and prehistoric North American evidence. *American Antiquity* 47:504–25.

Brettell, Caroline B. 1996. Migration. In *Encyclopedia of cultural anthropology*, vol. 3, 4 vols., eds. D. Levinson and M. Ember. New York: Henry Holt.

Brettell, Caroline B., and Robert V. Kemper. 2002. Migration and cities. In *Encyclopedia of urban cultures: Cities and cultures around the world*, vol. 1, 4 vols., eds. M. Ember and C. R. Ember. Danbury, CT: Grolier/Scholastic.

Briggs, Jean L. 1974. Eskimo women: Makers of men. In *Many sisters: Women in cross-cultural perspective*, ed. C. J. Matthiasson. New York: Free Press.

Bringa, Tone. 1995. *Being Muslim the Bosnian way: Identity and community in a central Bosnian village*. Princeton, NJ: Princeton University Press, as seen in eHRAF World Cultures. ehrafworldcultures.yale.edu. Accessed May 2000.

Brinton, Crane. 1938. *The anatomy of revolution*. Upper Saddle River, NJ: Prentice Hall.

Briody, Elizabeth K., Robert T. Trotter, II, and Tracy L. Meerwarth. 2010. *Transforming culture: Creating and sustaining a better manufacturing organization*. New York: Palgrave Macmillan.

Britannica Online. 1995. Book of the year (1995): World affairs: Rwanda; and Book of the year (1995): Race and ethnic relations: Rwanda's complex ethnic history. *Britannica Online*, December.

Britannica Online. 1998. Printing, typography, and photoengraving; History of prints: Origins in China: Transmission of paper to Europe (12th century). *Britannica Online*, February.

Brittain, John A. 1978. *Inheritance and the inequality of material wealth*. Washington, DC: Brookings Institution.

Brodey, Jane E. 1971. Effects of milk on Blacks noted. *New York Times*, October 15, p. 15.

Brodwin, Paul E. 1996. Disease and culture. In *Encyclopedia of cultural anthropology*, vol. 1, eds. D. Levinson and M. Ember. New York: Henry Holt.

Bromage, Timothy G. 2002. Paleoanthropology and life history, and life history of a paleoanthropologist. In MyAnthroLibrary, eds. Carol R Ember, Melvin Ember, and Peter N. Peregrine. MyAnthroLibrary.com. Pearson.

Bromage, Timothy G., and M. Christopher Dean. 1985. Reevaluation of the age at death of immature fossil hominids. *Nature* 317 (October 10):525–27.

Brooks, Alison S., Fatimah Linda Collier Jackson, and R. Richard Grinker. 1993. Race and ethnicity in America. *Anthro Notes (National Museum of Natural History Bulletin for Teachers)* 15, no. 3(Fall):1–3, 11–15.

Broom, Robert. 1950. *Finding the missing link*. London: Watts.

Broude, Gwen J. 1976. Cross-cultural patterning of some sexual attitudes and practices. *Behavior Science Research* 11:227–62.

Broude, Gwen J. 1980. Extramarital sex norms in cross-cultural perspective. *Behavior Science Research* 15:181–218.

Broude, Gwen J. 2004. Sexual attitudes and practices. In *Encyclopedia of sex and gender: Men and women in the world's cultures*, vol. 1, eds. C. Ember and M. Ember. New York: Kluwer Academic/Plenum Publishers.

Broude, Gwen J. 2009. Variations in sexual attitudes, norms, and practices. In MyAnthroLibrary, eds. C. R. Ember, M. Ember, and P. N. Peregrine. MyAnthroLibrary.com. Pearson.

Broude, Gwen J., and Sarah J. Greene. 1976. Cross-cultural codes on twenty sexual attitudes and practices. *Ethnology* 15:409–29.

Browman, David, Gayle Fritz, and Patty Jo Watson. 2009. Origins of food-producing economies in the Americas. In *The human past*, ed. C. Scarre. New York: Thames and Hudson.

Brown, Cecil H. 1977. Folk botanical life-forms: Their universality and growth. *American Anthropologist* 79:317–42.

Brown, Cecil H. 1979. Folk zoological life-forms: Their universality and growth. *American Anthropologist* 81:791–817.

Brown, Cecil H. 1984. World view and lexical uniformities. *Reviews in Anthropology* 11:99–112.

Brown, Cecil H., and Stanley R. Witkowski. 1980. Language universals. In *Toward explaining human culture*, eds. D. Levinson and M. J. Malone. New Haven, CT: HRAF Press.

Brown, Donald E. 1991. *Human universals*. Philadelphia: Temple University Press.

Brown, Donald E. 2000. Human universals and their implications. In *Being humans: Anthropological universality and particularity in transdisciplinary perspectives*, ed. N. Roughley. Berlin: Walter de Gruyter.

Brown, Frank H. 1992. Methods of dating. In *The Cambridge encyclopedia of human evolution*, eds. S. Jones, R. Martin, and D. Pilbeam. New York: Cambridge University Press.

Brown, Frank H. 2000. Geochronometry. In *Encyclopedia of human evolution and prehistory*, eds. I. Tattersall, G. Delson, and J. van Couvering. New York: Garland.

Brown, James A. 1983. Summary. In *Archaic hunters and gatherers in the American Midwest*, eds. J. L. Phillips and J. A. Brown. New York: Academic Press.

Brown, James A. 1985. Long-term trends to sedentism and the emergence of complexity in the American Midwest. In *Prehistoric hunter-gatherers*, eds. T. Price and J. Brown. Orlando, FL: Academic Press.

Brown, James A., and T. Douglas Price. 1985. Complex hunter-gatherers: Retrospect and prospect. In *Prehistoric hunter-gatherers*, eds. T. Price and J. Brown. Orlando, FL: Academic Press.

Brown, Judith K. 1970a. Economic organization and the position of women among the Iroquois. *Ethnohistory* 17:151–67.

Brown, Judith K. 1970b. A note on the division of labor by sex. *American Anthropologist* 72:1073–78.

Brown, Michael F. 2008. Cultural relativism 2.0. *Current Anthropology* 49:363–83.

Brown, Peter J. 1997. Culture and the evolution of obesity. In *Applying cultural anthropology*, eds. A. Podolefsky and P. J. Brown. Mountain View, CA: Mayfield.

Brown, Peter J., and Jennifer Sweeney. 2009. The anthropology of overweight, obesity, and the body. *AnthroNotes* 30, no.1:6–12.

Brown, Roger. 1965. *Social psychology*. New York: Free Press.

Brown, Roger. 1980. The first sentence of child and chimpanzee. In *Speaking of apes*, eds. T. A. Sebeok and J. Umiker-Sebeok. New York: Plenum Press.

Brown, Roger, and Marguerite Ford. 1961. Address in American English. *Journal of Abnormal and Social Psychology* 62:375–85.

Browner, C. H. 1985. Criteria for selecting herbal remedies. *Ethnology* 24:13–32.

Brues, Alice. 1992. Forensic diagnosis of race—General race versus specific populations. *Social Science and Medicine* 34:125–28.

Brumbach, Hetty Jo, and Robert Jarvenpa. 2006a. Chipewyan society and gender relations. In *Circumpolar lives and livelihood: A comparative ethnoarchaeology of gender and subsistence*, eds. R. Jarvenpa and H. J. Brumbach. Lincoln, Nebraska: University of Nebraska Press.

Brumbach, Hetty Jo, and Robert Jarvenpa. 2006b. Conclusion: Toward a comparative ethnoarchaeology of gender. In *Circumpolar lives and livelihood: A comparative ethnoarchaeology of gender and subsistence*, eds. R. Jarvenpa and H. J. Brumbach. Lincoln, Nebraska: University of Nebraska Press.

Brumfiel, Elizabeth M. 1976. Regional growth in the eastern Valley of Mexico: A test of the "population pressure" hypothesis. In *The early Mesoamerican village*, ed. K. Flannery. New York: Academic Press.

Brumfiel, Elizabeth M. 1983. Aztec state making: Ecology, structure, and the origin of the state. *American Anthropologist* 85:261–84.

Brumfiel, Elizabeth M. 1992. Distinguished lecture in archeology: Breaking and entering the ecosystem—Gender, class, and faction steal the show. *American Anthropologist* 94:551–67.

Brumfiel, Elizabeth M. 2009. Origins of social inequality. In MyAnthroLibrary, eds. C. R. Ember, M. Ember, and P. N. Peregrine. MyAnthroLibrary.com. Pearson.

Brunet, Michel, Alain Beauvilain, Yves Coppens, Elile Heintz, Aladji H. E. Moutaye, and David Pilbeam. 1995. The first australopithecine 2,500 kilometers west of the Rift Valley (Chad). *Nature* 378:273–75.

Brunet, Michel, et al. 2002. A new hominid from the upper Miocene of Chad, Central Africa. *Nature* 418 (July 11):145–51.

Brunvand, Jan Harold. 1993. *The baby train: And other lusty urban legends*. New York: Norton.

Brusco, Elizabeth E. 1996. Religious conversion. In *Encyclopedia of cultural anthropology*, vol. 3, eds. D. Levinson and M. Ember. New York: Henry Holt.

Brutsaert, Tom. 2010. Human adaptation to high altitude. In *Human evolutionary biology*, ed. M. Muehlenbein. Cambridge: Cambridge University Press.

Bryant, Carol A., and Doraine F. C. Bailey. 1990. The use of focus group research in program development. *NAPA Bulletin* 10:24–39.

Buckser, Andrew, and Stephen D. Glazier, eds. 2003. Preface. In *The anthropology of religious conversion*, eds. A. Buckser and S. D. Glazier. Lanham, MD: Roman & Littlefield.

Budiansky, Stephen. 1992. *The covenant of the wild: Why animals chose domestication*. New York: Morrow.

Buettner-Janusch, John. 1973. *Physical anthropology: A perspective*. New York: Wiley.

Bumpass, Larry, and Hsien-Hen Lu. 2000. Trends in cohabitation and implications for children's family contexts in the united states. *Population Studies* 54, no.1:29–41.

Bunzel, Ruth. 1971. The nature of Katcinas. In *Reader in comparative religion*, 3rd ed., eds. W. A. Lessa and E. Z. Vogt. New York: Harper & Row.

Burbank, Victoria K. 1994. *Fighting women: Anger and aggression in aboriginal Australia*. Berkeley: University of California Press.

Burbank, Victoria K. 2009a. Adolescent socialization and initiation ceremonies. In MyAnthroLibrary, eds. C. R. Ember, M. Ember, and P. N. Peregrine. MyAnthroLibrary.com. Pearson.

Burbank, Victoria K. 2009b. Australian Aborigines: An adolescent mother and her family. In MyAnthroLibrary, eds. C. R. Ember, M. Ember, and P. N. Peregrine. MyAnthroLibrary.com. Pearson.

Burbano, H., et al. 2010. Targeted investigation of the Neandertal genome by array-based sequence capture. *Science* 328 (May 7):723–26.

Burch, Ernest S., Jr. 1988. *The Eskimos*. Norman: University of Oklahoma Press.

Burch, Ernest S., Jr. 2009. North Alaskan Eskimos: A changing way of life. In MyAnthroLibrary, eds. C. R. Ember, M. Ember, and P. N. Peregrine. MyAnthroLibrary.com. Pearson.

Burkhalter, S. Brian, and Robert F. Murphy. 1989. Tappers and sappers: Rubber, gold and money among the Mundurucú. *American Ethnologist* 16:100–16.

Burns, Alisa, and Cath Scott. 1994. *Mother-headed families and why they have increased*. Hillsdale, NJ: Lawrence Erlbaum Associates.

Burton, Roger V., and John W. M. Whiting. 1961. The absent father and cross-sex identity. *Merrill-Palmer Quarterly of Behavior and Development* 7, no. 2:85–95.

Burtsev, Mikhail S., and A. Korotayev. 2004. An evolutionary agent-based model of pre-state warfare patterns: Cross-cultural tests. *World Cultures* 15, no. 1:28–36.

Busby, Annette. 2009. Kurds: A culture straddling national borders. In MyAnthroLibrary, eds. C. R. Ember, M. Ember, and P. N. Peregrine. MyAnthroLibrary.com. Pearson.

Butzer, Karl W. 1982. Geomorphology and sediment stratigraphy. In *The Middle Stone Age at Klasies River mouth in South Africa*, eds. R. Singer and J. Wymer. Chicago: University of Chicago Press.

Byrne, Bryan. 1994. Access to subsistence resources and the sexual division of labor among potters. *Cross-Cultural Research* 28:225–50.

Byrne, Roger. 1987. Climatic change and the origins of agriculture. In *Studies in the Neolithic and urban revolutions*, ed. L. Manzanilla. Oxford: British Archaeological Reports, International Series 349.

Calvin, William H. 1983. *The throwing Madonna: Essays on the brain*. New York: McGraw-Hill.

Campbell, Donald T. 1965. Variation and selective retention in socio-cultural evolution. In *Social change in developing areas*, eds. H. Barringer, G. Blankstein, and R. Mack. Cambridge, MA: Schenkman.

Campbell, Joseph. 1949. *The hero with a thousand faces*. New York: Pantheon.

Cancian, Frank. 1980. Risk and uncertainty in agricultural decision making. In *Agricultural decision making*, ed. P. F. Barlett. New York: Academic Press.

Cann, Rebecca, M. 1988. DNA and human origins. *Annual Review of Anthropology* 17:127–43.

Cann, Rebecca, M. Stoneking, and A. C. Wilson. 1987. Mitochondrial DNA and human evolution. *Nature* 325 (January 1):31–36.

Caporael, Linnda R. 1976. Ergotism: The Satan loosed in Salem? *Science* (April 2):21–26.

Carbonell, Eudald, et al. 2008. The first hominin of Europe. *Nature* 452 (March 27):465–69.

Carcopino, Jerome. 1940. *Daily life in ancient Rome: The people and the city at the height of the empire*. Edited with bibliography and notes by Henry T. Rowell. Translated from the French by E. O. Lorimer. New Haven, CT: Yale University Press.

Cardoso, Fernando Luis, and Dennis Werner. 2004. Homosexuality. In *Encyclopedia of sex and gender: Men and women in the world's cultures*, vol. 1, eds. C. Ember and M. Ember. New York: Kluwer Academic/Plenum Publishers.

Carey, James W., Erin Picone-DeCaro, Mary Spink Neumann, Devorah Schwartz, Delia Easton, and Daphne Cobb St. John. 2004. HIV/AIDS research and prevention. In *Encyclopedia of medical anthropology: Health and illness in the world's cultures*, vol. 1, eds. C. R. Ember and M. Ember. New York: Kluwer Academic/Plenum.

Carlson, K. J., et al. 2011. The endocast of MH1, *Australopithecus sediba*. *Science* 333 (September 9):1402–1407.

Carneiro, Robert L. 1968. Slash-and-burn cultivation among the Kuikuru and its implications for settlement patterns. In *Man in adaptation*, ed. Y. Cohen. Chicago, Aldine.

Carneiro, Robert L. 1970. A theory of the origin of the state. *Science* 169 (August 21):733–38.

Carneiro, Robert L. 1978. Political expansion as an expression of the principle of competitive exclusion. In *Origins of the state*, eds. R. Cohen and E. R. Service. Philadelphia: Institute for the Study of Human Issues.

Carneiro, Robert L. 1988. The circumscription theory: Challenge and response. *American Behavioral Scientist* 31:497–511.

Carneiro, Robert L. 1990. Chiefdom-level warfare as exemplified in Fiji and the Cauca Valley. In *The anthropology of war*, ed. J. Haas. New York: Cambridge University Press.

Carneiro, Robert L. 2000. Process vs. Stages: A false dichotomy in tracing the rise of the state. In *Alternatives of social evolution*, eds. N. N. Kradin, A. V. Korotayev, D. M. Bondarenko, V. De Munck, and P. K. Wason. Vladivostok: FEB RAS.

Carneiro, Robert L. 2012. The circumscription theory: A clarification, amplification, and reformulation. *Social Evolution & History* 11, no. 2: 5–30.

Carpenter, C. R. 1940. A field study in Siam of the behavior and social relations of the gibbon (*Hylobates lar*). *Comparative Psychology Monographs* 16, no. 5:1–212.

Carpenter, Sandra. 2000. Effects of cultural tightness and collectivism on self-concept and causal attributions. *Cross-Cultural Research* 34:38–56.

Carrasco, Pedro. 1961. The civil-religious hierarchy in Mesoamerican communities: Pre-Spanish background and colonial development. *American Anthropologist* 63:483–97.

Carrier, Joseph, and Ralph Bolton. 1991. Anthropological perspectives on sexuality and HIV prevention. *Annual Review of Sex Research* 2:49–75.

Carroll, John B., ed. 1956. *Language, thought, and reality: Selected writings of Benjamin Lee Whorf*. New York: Wiley.

Carroll, Michael. 1979. A new look at Freud on myth. *Ethos* 7:189–205.

Cartmill, Matt. 1974. Rethinking primate origins. *Science* (April 26):436–37.

Cartmill, Matt. 1992a. New views on primate origins. *Evolutionary Anthropology* 1:105–11.

Cartmill, Matt. 1992b. Non-human primates. In *The Cambridge encyclopedia of human evolution*, eds. S. Jones, R. Martin, and D. Pilbeam. New York: Cambridge University Press.

Cartmill, Matt. 2009. Explaining primate origins. In MyAnthroLibrary, eds. C. R. Ember, M. Ember, and P. N. Peregrine. MyAnthroLibrary.com. Pearson.

Cartmill, Matt. 2010. Primate classification and diversity. In *Primate neuroethology*, eds. M. Platt and A. Ghazanfar. Oxford: Oxford University Press.

Cashdan, Elizabeth A. 1980. Egalitarianism among hunters and gatherers. *American Anthropologist* 82:116–20.

Cashdan, Elizabeth A. 2001. Ethnic diversity and its environmental determinants: Effects of climate, pathogens, and habitat diversity. *American Anthropologist* 103:968–91.

Castle, Stephen. 2013. Horse meat in food stirs a furor in the British Isles. *New York Times*, February 8. www.nytimes.com.

Caulkins, D. Douglas. 1997. Welsh. In *American immigrant cultures: Builders of a nation*, vol. 2, eds. D. Levinson and M. Ember. New York: Macmillan Reference.

Caulkins, D. Douglas. 2009. Norwegians: Cooperative individualists. In MyAnthroLibrary, eds. C. R. Ember, M. Ember, and P. N. Peregrine. MyAnthroLibrary.com. Pearson.

Cavalli-Sforza, L. Luca, and Marcus W. Feldman. 1981. *Cultural transmission and evolution: A quantitative approach*. Princeton, NJ: Princeton University Press.

Cavalli-Sforza, L. Luca, and Marcus W. Feldman. 2003. The application of molecular genetic approaches to the study of human evolution. *Nature Genetics Supplement* 33:266–75.

Caws, Peter. 1969. The structure of discovery. *Science* 166 (December 12):1375–80.

CDC. n.d. Black or African American populations. http://www.cdc.gov/minorityhealth/populations/REMP/black.html (accessed May 18, 2013).

Ceci, Stephen, and Wendy M. Williams. 2009. YES: The scientific truth must be pursued. *Nature* 457 (February 12):788–789.

Center for Renewal of Science and Culture. 2001. The wedge strategy, cited in Barbara Forrest, "The wedge at work." In *Intelligent design creationism and its critics*, ed. R. Pennock, 16. Boston: IT Press.

Cernea, Michael M., ed. 1991. *Putting people first: Sociological variables in development*, 2nd ed. New York: Oxford University Press.

Cernea, Michael M. 2000. *Risk, safeguards, and reconstruction: A model for population displacement and resettlement*, eds. M. M. Cernea and C. McDowell. Washington, DC: World Bank.

Chacon, Richard J., and Rubén G. Mendoza. 2007. Ethical considerations and conclusions regarding indigenous warfare and ritual violence in Latin America. In *Latin American indigenous warfare and ritual violence*, eds. R. J. Chacon and R. G. Mendoza. Tucson: University of Arizona Press.

Chafetz, Janet Saltzman. 1990. *Gender equity: An integrated theory of stability and change*. Sage Library of Social Research No. 176. Newbury Park, CA: Sage.

Chagnon, Napoleon. 1983. *Yanomamö: The fierce people*. 3rd ed. New York: Holt, Rinehardt, and Winston.

Chambers, J. K. 2002. Patterns of variation including change. In *The handbook of language variation and change*, eds. J. K. Chambers, Peter Trudgill, and Natalie Schilling-Estes. Malden, MA: Blackwell Publishers.

Chang, Kwang-Chih. 1968. *The archaeology of ancient China*. New Haven, CT: Yale University Press.

Chang, Kwang-Chih. 1970. The beginnings of agriculture in the Far East. *Antiquity* 44:175–85.

Chang, Kwang-Chih. 1981. In search of China's beginnings: New light on an old civilization. *American Scientist* 69:148–60.

Chang, Kwang-Chih. 1986. *Archaeology of ancient China*, 4th ed. New Haven, CT: Yale University Press.

Chapais, Bernard. 2008. *Primeval kinship: How pair-bonding gave birth to human society*. Cambridge, MA: Harvard University Press.

Chaplin, William F., J. B. Phillips, J. D. Brown, N. R. Clanton, and J. L. Stein. 2000. Handshaking, gender, personality, and first impressions. *Journal of Personality and Social Psychology* 79, no.1:110–17.

Chapman, Chris, and Alexander Kagaha. 2009. *Resolving conflicts using traditional mechanisms in the Karamoja and Teso regions of Uganda*. London, UK: Minority Rights Group International. http://www.unhcr.org/refworld/pdfid/4a97dc232.pdf (accessed April 13, 2013).

Charanis, Peter. 1953. Economic factors in the decline of the Roman Empire. *Journal of Economic History* 13:412–24.

Chard, Chester S. 1969. *Man in prehistory*. New York: McGraw-Hill.

Charles-Dominique, Pierre. 1977. *Ecology and behaviour of nocturnal primates* trans. R. D. Martin. New York: Columbia University Press.

Chase, Philip, and Harold Dibble. 1987. Middle Paleolithic symbolism: A review of current evidence and interpretations. *Journal of Anthropological Archaeology* 6:263–69.

Chatterjee, Sankar. 1997. *The rise of birds: 225 million years of evolution*. Baltimore: Johns Hopkins.

Chatty, Dawn. 1996. *Mobile pastoralists: Development planning and social change in Oman*. New York: Columbia University Press.

Chatty, Dawn. 2006. Adapting to biodiversity conservation: The mobile pastoralist Harasiis tribe of Oman. In *Modern pastoralism and conservation: Old problems, new challenges*, eds. D. Chatty and T. Sternberg. Beijing: Intellectual Property Publishing House.

Chaucer, Geoffrey. 1926. *The prologue to the Canterbury Tales, the Knights Tale, the Nonnes Prestes Tale*, ed. M. H. Liddell. New York: Macmillan.

Chayanov, Alexander V. 1966. *The theory of peasant economy*, eds. D. Thorner, B. Kerblay, and R. E. F. Smith. Homewood, IL: Richard D. Irwin.

Chen, Denise, Ammeta Katdare, and Nadia Lucas. 2006. Chemosignals of fear enhance cognitive performance in humans. *Chemical Senses* 31:415–23.

Cheney, Dorothy, L., and Richard W. Wrangham. 1987. Predation. In *Primate societies*, eds. B. B. Smuts, D. L. Cheney, R. M. Seyfarth, and R. W. Wrangham. Chicago: University of Chicago Press.

Chessa, Bernardo, et al. 2009. Revealing the history of sheep domestication using retrovirus integrations. *Science* 324 (April 24):532–36.

Chibnik, Michael. 1980. The statistical behavior approach: The choice between wage labor and cash cropping in rural Belize. In *Agricultural decision making*, ed. P. F. Barlett. New York: Academic Press.

Chibnik, Michael. 1981. The evolution of cultural rules. *Journal of Anthropological Research* 37:256–68.

Chibnik, Michael. 1987. The economic effects of household demography: A cross-cultural assessment of Chayanov's theory. In *Household economies and their transformations*, ed. M. D. MacLachlan. Monographs in Economic Anthropology, No 3. Lanham, MD: University Press of America.

Chick, Garry. 1998. Games in culture revisited: A replication and extension of Roberts, Arth, and Bush [1959]. *Cross-Cultural Research* 32:185–206.

Childe, Vere Gordon. 1950. The urban revolution. *Town Planning Review* 21:3–17.

Childe, Vere Gordon. 1956. *Man makes himself*. London: Watts.

Chimpanzee Sequencing and Analysis Consortium. 2005. Initial sequence of the chimpanzee genome and comparison with the human genome. *Nature* 437 (September 1):69–87.

Chivers, David J. 1974. *The siamang in Malaya*. Basel, Switzerland: Karger.

Chomsky, Noam. 1975. *Reflections on language*. New York: Pantheon.

Christensen, Pia, Jenny Hockey, and Allison James. 2001. Talk, silence and the material world: Patterns of indirect communication among agricultural farmers in Northern England. In *An anthropology of indirect communication*, eds. J. Hendry and C. W. Watson. London: Routledge.

Ciochon, Russell L., and Dennis A. Etler. 1994. Reinterpreting past primate diversity. In *Integrative paths to the past*, eds. R. Corruccini and R. Ciochon. Upper Saddle River, NJ: Prentice Hall.

Ciochon, Russell L., and John G. Fleagle, eds. 1993. *The human evolution source book*. Upper Saddle River, NJ: Prentice Hall.

Ciochon, Russell L., John Olsen, and Jamie James. 1990. *Other origins: The search for the giant ape in human prehistory*. New York: Bantam.

Claassen, Cheryl. 1991. Gender, shellfishing, and the Sell Mound Archaic. In *Engendering archaeology*, eds. J. Gero and M. Conkey. Oxford: Blackwell.

Claassen, Cheryl. 2009. Gender and archaeology. In MyAnthroLibrary, eds. C. R. Ember, M. Ember, and P. N. Peregrine. MyAnthroLibrary.com. Pearson.

Clark, J. Desmond. 1970. *The prehistory of Africa*. New York: Praeger.

Clark, J. Desmond. 1977. Interpretations of prehistoric technology from ancient Egyptian and other sources. Part II: Prehistoric arrow forms in Africa as shown by surviving examples of the traditional arrows of the San Bushmen. *Paleorient* 3:127–50.

Clark, Gracia. 2000. Small-scale traders' key role in stabilizing and diversifying Ghana's rural communities and livelihoods. In *Women farmers and commercial ventures: Increasing food security in developing countries*, ed. A. Spring. Boulder, CO: Lynne Rienner Publishers, Inc.

Clark, Grahame. 1975. *The earlier Stone Age settlement of Scandinavia*. Cambridge: Cambridge University Press.

Clark, Grahame, and Stuart Piggott. 1965. *Prehistoric societies*. New York: Knopf.

Clark, W. E. Le Gros. 1964. *The fossil evidence for human evolution*, 184. Chicago: University of Chicago Press.

Clarke, Ronald J., and P. V. Tobias. 1995. Sterkfontein member 2 foot bones of the oldest South African hominid. *Science* 269 (July 28):521–24.

Clayman, Charles B. 1989. *American Medical Association encyclopedia of medicine*, 857–58. New York: Random house.

Clifford, James. 1986. Introduction: Partial truths. In *Writing culture: The poetics and politics of ethnography*, eds. J. Clifford and G. E. Marcus. Berkeley: University of California Press.

Clottes, Jean. 2008. Rock art: An endangered heritage worldwide. *Journal of Anthropological Research* 64:1–18.

Clutton-Brock, Juliet. 1984. Dog. In *Evolution of domesticated animals*, ed. I. Mason. New York: Longman.

Clutton-Brock, Juliet. 1992. Domestication of animals. In *The Cambridge encyclopedia of human evolution*, eds. S. Jones, R. Martin, and D. Pilbeam. New York: Cambridge University Press.

Clutton-Brock, T. H., and Paul H. Harvey. 1977. Primate ecology and social organization. *Journal of Zoology* 183:1–39.

Clutton-Brock, T. H., and Paul H. Harvey. 1980. Primates, brains and ecology. *Journal of Zoology* 190:309–23.

Coale, Ansley J. 1974. The history of the human population. *Scientific American* (September):41–51.

Coe, Michael D. 1966. *The Maya*. New York: Praeger.

Coe, Michael D. 2011. *The Maya*, 8th ed. New York: Thames and Hudson.

Cohen, Alex. 1990. A cross-cultural study of the effects of environmental unpredictability on aggression in folktales. *American Anthropologist* 92:474–79.

Cohen, Alex. 1999. *The mental health of indigenous peoples: An international overview*. Geneva: Department of Mental Health, World Health Organization.

Cohen, Alex. 2004. Mental disorders. In *Encyclopedia of medical anthropology: Health and illness in the world's cultures*, vol. 1, eds. C. R. Ember and M. Ember. New York: Kluwer Academic/Plenum.

Cohen, Alex, and Paul Koegel. 2009. Homelessness. In MyAnthroLibrary, eds. C. R. Ember, M. Ember, and P. N. Peregrine. MyAnthroLibrary.com. Pearson.

Cohen, Joel D. 2011. The beginnings of agriculture in China. *Current Anthropology* 52, Supplement 4:S273–93.

Cohen, Mark Nathan. 1977a. *The food crisis in prehistory: Overpopulation and the origins of agriculture*. New Haven, CT: Yale University Press.

Cohen, Mark Nathan. 1977b. Population pressure and the origins of agriculture. In *Origins of agriculture*, ed. C. A. Reed. The Hague: Monton.

Cohen, Mark Nathan. 1987. The significance of long-term changes in human diet and food economy. In *Food and evolution*, eds. M. Harris and E. Ross. Philadelphia: Temple University Press.

Cohen, Mark Nathan. 1989. *Health and the rise of civilization*. New Haven, CT: Yale University Press.

Cohen, Mark Nathan. 2009. Were early agriculturalists less healthy than food-collectors? In MyAnthroLibrary, eds. C. R. Ember, M. Ember, and P. N. Peregrine. MyAnthroLibrary.com. Pearson.

Cohen, Mark Nathan, and George J. Armelagos. 1984. Paleopathology at the origins of agriculture: Editors' summation. In *Paleopathology at the origins of agriculture*, eds. M. N. Cohen and G. J. Armelagos. Orlando, FL: Academic Press.

Cohen, Myron L. 1976. *House united, house divided: The Chinese family in Taiwan*. New York: Columbia University Press.

Cohen, Ronald. 1988. Introduction. In *State formation and political legitimacy, Vol. 6: Political anthropology*, eds. R. Cohen and J. D. Toland. New Brunswick, NJ: Transaction Books.

Cohen, Ronald, and Elman R. Service, eds. 1978. *Origins of the state: The anthropology of political evolution*. Philadelphia: Institute for the Study of Human Issues.

Cohen, Wesley. 1995. Empirical studies of innovative activity. In *Handbook of the economics of innovation and technological change*, ed. P. Stoneman. Oxford: Blackwell.

COHMAP (Cooperative Holocene Mapping Project) Personnel. 1988. Climatic changes of the last 18,000 years. *Science* 241 (August 26):1043–52.

Colby, Benjamin N. 1996. Cognitive anthropology. In *Encyclopedia of cultural anthropology*, vol. 1, eds. David Levinson and Melvin Ember. New York: Henry Holt.

Collier, Stephen, and J. Peter White. 1976. Get them young? Age and sex inferences on animal domestication in archaeology. *American Antiquity* 41:96–102.

Collins, Desmond. 1976. Later hunters in Europe. In *The origins of Europe*, ed. D. Collins. New York: Thomas Y. Crowell.

Collins, James, and Richard Blot. 2003. *Literacy and literacies*. Cambridge: Cambridge University Press.

Congressional Budget Office. 2011. Trends in the distribution of household income. http://www.cbo.gov/publication/42729 (accessed June 1, 2013).

Conklin, Beth A. 2002. Shamans versus pirates in the Amazonian treasure chest. *American Anthropologist* 104:1050–61.

Connah, Graham. 1987. *African civilizations: Precolonial cities and states in tropical Africa*. Cambridge: Cambridge University Press.

Connah, Graham. 2009. Holocene Africa. In *The human past*, ed. C. Scarre. New York: Thames and Hudson.

Conroy, Glenn C. 1990. *Primate evolution*. New York: Norton.

Coontz, Stephanie. 2005. *Marriage, a history: How love conquered marriage*. New York: Penguin Group.

Cooper, Richard S., Charles N. Rotimi, and Ryk Ward. 1999. The puzzle of hypertension in African Americans. *Scientific American* (February):56–63.

Cordain, Loren, Janette Brand Miller, S. Boyd Eaton, Neil Mann, Susanne H. A. Holt, and John D. Speth. 2000. Plant-animal subsistence ratios and macronutrient energy estimations in worldwide hunter-gatherer diets. *The American Journal of Clinical Nutrition* 71, no.3:682–92.

Coreil, Jeannine. 1989. Lessons from a community study of oral rehydration therapy in Haiti. In *Making our research useful*, eds. J. Van Willigen, B. Rylko-Bauer, and A. McElroy. Boulder, CO: Westview.

Coreil, Jeannine. 2004. Malaria and other major insect vector diseases. In *Encyclopedia of medical anthropology: Health and illness in the world's cultures*, vol. 1, eds. C. R. Ember and M. Ember. New York: Kluwer Academic/Plenum.

Costin, Cathy Lynne. 2009. Cloth production and gender relations in the Inka Empire. In MyAnthroLibrary, eds. C. R. Ember, M. Ember, and P. N. Peregrine. MyAnthroLibrary.com. Pearson.

Coult, Allan D., and Robert W. Habenstein. 1965. *Cross tabulations of Murdock's "World Ethnographic Sample."* Columbia: University of Missouri Press.

Crate, Susan A. 2008. Gone the bull of winter? Grappling with the cultural implications of and anthropology's role(s) in global climate change. *Current Anthropology* 49:569–95.

Crate, Susan A., and Mark Nuttall. 2009. Introduction: Anthropology and climate change. In *Anthropology and climate change: From encounters to actions*, eds. S. A. Crate and M. Nuttall. Walnut Creek, CA: Left Coast Press.

Crawford, Gary W. 1992. Prehistoric plant domestication in East Asia. In *The origins of agriculture*, eds. C. Cowan and P. Watson. Washington, DC: Smithsonian Institution Press.

Crawford, Harriet. 2004. *Sumer and the Sumerians*. Cambridge: Cambridge University Press.

Crawford, R. D. 1984. Turkey. In *Evolution of domesticated animals*, ed. I. Mason. New York: Longman.

Creed, Gerald W. 2009. Bulgaria: Anthropological corrections to Cold War stereotypes. In MyAnthroLibrary, eds. C. R. Ember, M. Ember, and P. N. Peregrine. MyAnthroLibrary.com. Pearson.

Crittenden, Alyssa. 2013. Juvenile foraging among the Hadza: Implications for human life history. *Evolution & Human Behavior* 34:299–304.

Crockett, Carolyn, and John F. Eisenberg. 1987. Howlers: Variations in group size and demography. In *Primate societies*, eds. B. B. Smuts, D. L. Cheney, R. M. Seyfarth, and R. W. Wrangham. Chicago: University of Chicago Press.

Crossroads for Planet Earth. 2005. *Scientific American*, Special issue, September.

Crystal, David. 1971. *Linguistics*. Middlesex, UK: Penguin.

Crystal, David. 2000. *Language death*. Cambridge: Cambridge University Press.

Culotta, Elizabeth. 1995. New hominid crowds the field. *Science* 269 (August 18):918.

Culotta, Elizabeth. 2005. Calorie count reveals Neandertals out-ate hardiest modern humans. *Science* 307 (February 11):840.

Curtin, Philip D. 1984. *Cross-cultural trade in world history*. Cambridge: Cambridge University Press.

Cutright, Phillips. 1967. Inequality: A cross-national analysis. *American Sociological Review* 32:562–78.

Dagosto, Marian. 2002. The origin and diversification of anthropoid primates: Introduction. In *The primate fossil record*, ed. W. C. Hartwig. Cambridge: Cambridge University Press.

Daiger, Stephen. 2005. Was the human genome project worth the effort? *Science* 308 (April 15):362–64.

Daly, Martin, and Margo Wilson. 1988. *Homicide*. New York: Aldine.

Damas, David. 1983. Demography and kinship as variables of adoption in the Carolines. *American Ethnologist* 10:328–44.

Daniel, I. Randolph. 2001. Early Eastern Archaic. In *Encyclopedia of prehistory, Vol. 6: North America*, eds. P. N. Peregrine and M. Ember. Kluwer: Academic/Plenum.

Darnell, Regna. 1989. Correlates of Cree narrative performance. In *Explorations in the ethnography of speaking*, eds. R. Bauman and Joel Sherzer. New York: Cambridge University Press.

Dart, Raymond. 1925. *Australopithecus africanus*: The man-ape of South Africa. *Nature* 115:195.

Darwin, Charles. 1970/1859. The origin of species. In *Evolution of man*, eds. L. B. Young. New York: Oxford University Press.

Dasen, Pierre R., and Alastair Heron. 1981. Cross-cultural tests of Piaget's theory. In *Handbook of cross-cultural psychology, Vol. 4: Developmental psychology*, eds. H. C. Triandis and A. Heron. Boston: Allyn & Bacon.

Dasen, Pierre R., John W. Berry, and N. Sartorius, eds. 1988. *Health and cross-cultural psychology: Toward applications*. Newbury Park, CA: Sage.

Davenport, William. 1959. Nonunilinear descent and descent groups. *American Anthropologist* 61:557–72.

Davies, Stephen. 2000. Non-Western art and art's definition. In *Theories of art today*, ed. N. Carroll. Madison: University of Wisconsin Press.

Davis, Deborah, and Stevan Harrell, eds. 1993. *Chinese families in the post-Mao era*. Berkeley: University of California Press.

Davis, Sarah Henning. 2008. What's not to know? A Durkheimian critique of Boyer's theory of religion. *Ethos* 36:268–81.

Davis, Susan Schaefer. 1993. Rebellious teens? A Moroccan instance. Paper presented at the annual meeting of the Middle East Studies Association, Tucson, AZ, November.

Davis, Susan Schaefer. 2009. Morocco: Adolescents in a small town. In MyAnthroLibrary, eds. C. R. Ember, M. Ember, and P. N. Peregrine. MyAnthroLibrary.com. Pearson.

Davis, William D. 1971. Societal complexity and the nature of primitive man's conception of the supernatural. Ph.D. dissertation. University of North Carolina, Chapel Hill.

Dawson, Alistair. 1992. *Ice age earth*. London: Routledge.

Dawson, J. L. M. 1967. Cultural and physiological influences upon spatial-perceptual processes in West Africa. *International Journal of Psychology* 2:115–28, 171–85.

Day, Michael. 1986. *Guide to fossil man*. 4th ed. Chicago: University of Chicago Press.

DeGreef, S., and G. Willems. 2005. Three-dimensional cranio-facial reconstruction in forensic identification: Latest progress and new tendencies in the 21st century. *Journal of Forensic Sciences* 50:12–17.

De la Puente, Manuel, et al. 2013. *Social security programs throughout the world*. Washington, DC: Social Security Administration.

De Laguna, Frederica. 1972. *Under Mount Saint Elias: The history and culture of the Yakutat Tlingit*. Washington, DC: Smithsonian Institution Press, as seen in eHRAF World Cultures. ehrafworldcultures.yale.edu. Accessed May 2000.

De Lumley, Henry. 1969. A Paleolithic camp at Nice. *Scientific American* (May):42–50.

de Menocal, Peter B. 2001. Cultural responses to climate change during the late Holocene. *Science* 292 (April 27):667–73.

de Menocal, Peter B. 2011. Climate and human evolution. *Science* 331 (February 4):540–42.

de Munck, Victor C. 2000. *Culture, self, and meaning*. Prospect Heights, IL: Waveland Press.

de Munck, Victor C., and Andrey Korotayev. 1999. Sexual equality and romantic love: A reanalysis of Rosenblatt's study on the function of romantic love. *Cross-Cultural Research* 33:265–273.

DeParle, Jason. 2012. Harder for Americans to rise from economy's lower rungs. *New York Times National*, January 5, p. A17.

De Villiers, Peter A., and Jill G. De Villiers. 1979. *Early language*. Cambridge, MA: Harvard University Press.

DeVore, Irven, and Melvin J. Konner. 1974. Infancy in hunter-gatherer life: An ethological perspective. In *Ethology and psychiatry*, ed. N. F. White. Toronto: Ontario Mental Health Foundation and University of Toronto Press.

De Waal, Frans. 2001. *The ape and the sushi master: Cultural reflections of a primatologist*. New York: Basic Books.

De Waal, Frans, and Frans Lanting. 1997. *Bonobo: The forgotten ape*. Berkeley: University of California Press.

Deacon, Terrence. 1992. Primate brains and senses. In *The Cambridge encyclopedia of human evolution*, eds. S. Jones, R. Martin, and D. Pilbeam. New York: Cambridge University Press.

Dean, Erin. 2011. Birds of one tree: Participatory forestry and land claims in Tanzania. *Human Organization* 70:300–309.

Denham, T. P., et al. 2003. Origins of agriculture at Kuk Swamp in the highlands of New Guinea. *Science* 301 (July 11):189–93.

Denny, J. Peter. 1979. The "extendedness" variable in classifier semantics: Universal features and cultural variation. In *Ethnolinguistics*, ed. M. Mathiot. The Hague: Mouton.

Dentan, Robert K. 1968. *The Semai: A nonviolent people of Malaya*. New York: Holt, Rinehart & Winston.

Devereux, Stephen. 2009. Why does famine persist in Africa? *Food security* 1:25–35.

Devillers, Charles, and Jean Chaline. 1993. *Evolution: An evolving theory*. New York: Springer Verlag.

Diament, Michelle. 2005. Diversifying their crops: Agriculture schools, focusing on job prospects, reach out to potential students from cities and suburbs. *The Chronicle of Higher Education*, May 6, pp. A32–34.

Diamond, Jared. 1989. The accidental conqueror. *Discover* (December):71–76.

Diamond, Jared. 1991. The saltshaker's curse—Physiological adaptations that helped American Blacks survive slavery may now be predisposing their descendants to hypertension. *Natural History* (October):20–27.

Diamond, Jared. 1993. Who are the Jews? *Natural History* (November):12–19.

Diamond, Jared. 1997a. *Guns, germs, and steel*, 205–207. New York: Norton.

Diamond, Jared. 1997b. Location, location, location: The first farmers. *Science* 278 (November 14):1243–44.

Diamond, Jared. 2004. The astonishing micropygmies. *Science* 306 (December 17):2047–48.

Diamond, Norma. 1975. Collectivization, kinship, and the status of women in rural China. In *Toward an anthropology of women*, ed. R. R. Reiter. New York: Monthly Review Press.

Diamond, Stanley. 1974. *In search of the primitive: A critique of civilization*. New Brunswick, NJ: Transaction Books.

Dickson, D. Bruce. 1990. *The dawn of belief*. Tucson: University of Arizona Press.

Dickson, D. Bruce, Jeffrey Olsen, P. Fred Dahm, and Mitchell S. Wachtel. 2005. Where do you go when you die? A cross-cultural test of the hypothesis that infrastructure predicts individual eschatology. *Journal of Anthropological Research* 1:53–79.

Dillehay, Thomas. 2000. *The settlement of the Americas*. New York: Basic Books.

Dincauze, Dina. 2000. *Environmental archaeology: Principles and practice*. Cambridge: Cambridge University Press.

Dirks, Robert. 1993. Starvation and famine. *Cross-Cultural Research* 27:28–69.

Dirks, Robert. 2009. Hunger and famine. In MyAnthroLibrary, eds. C. R. Ember, M. Ember, and P. N. Peregrine. MyAnthroLibrary.com. Pearson.

Divale, William T. 1974. Migration, external warfare, and matrilocal residence. *Behavior Science Research* 9:75–133.

Divale, William T. 1977. Living floor area and marital residence: A replication. *Behavior Science Research* 2:109–15.

Divale, William T., and Marvin Harris. 1976. Population, warfare, and the male supremacist complex. *American Anthropologist* 78:521–38.

Dobres, Marcia-Anne. 1998. Venus figurines. In *Oxford companion to archaeology*, ed. B. Fagan. Oxford: Oxford University Press.

Dobzhansky, Theodosius. 1962. *Mankind evolving: The evolution of the human species*. New Haven, CT: Yale University Press.

Dobzhansky, Theodosius. 1973. *Genetic diversity and human equality*. New York: Basic Books.

Donovan, James M., and H. Edwin Anderson, III. 2003. *Anthropology and law*. New York: Berghahn Books.

Dohlinow, Phyllis Jay, and Naomi Bishop. 1972. The development of motor skills and social relationships among primates through play. In *Primate patterns*, ed. Phyllis Jay Dohlinow. New York: Holt, Rinehart & Winston.

Douglas, Mary. 1975. *Implicit meanings: Essays in anthropology*. London: Routledge and Kegan Paul.

Dow, James. 1986. *The shaman's touch: Otomi Indian symbolic healing*. Salt Lake City: University of Utah Press.

Dowling, John H. 1975. Property relations and productive strategies in pastoral societies. *American Ethnologist* 2:419–26.

Doyle, G. A., and R. D. Martin, eds. 1979. *The study of prosimian behavior*. New York: Academic Press.

Doyle, Rodger. 2004. Living together: In the U.S. cohabitation is here to stay. *Scientific American* (January):28.

Doyle, Rodger. 2005. Leveling the playing field: Economic development helps women pull even with men. *Scientific American* (June):32.

Draper, Patricia. 1975. !Kung women: Contrasts in sexual egalitarianism in foraging and sedentary contexts. In *Toward an anthropology of women*, ed. R. R. Reiter. New York: Monthly Review Press.

Draper, Patricia, and Elizabeth Cashdan. 1988. Technological change and child behavior among the !Kung. *Ethnology* 27:339–65.

Dressler, William W. 1991. *Stress and adaptation in the context of culture*. Albany: State University of New York Press.

Dressler, William W. 1993. Health in the African American community: Accounting for health inequalities. *Medical Anthropology Quarterly* 7:325–45.

Dressler, William W., and Michael C. Robbins. 1975. Art styles, social stratification, and cognition: An analysis of Greek vase painting. *American Ethnologist* 2:427–34.

Dressler, William W., Kathryn S. Oths, and Clarence C. Gravlee. 2005. Race and ethnicity in public health research: models to explain health disparities. *Annual Review of Anthropology* 34:231–52.

Driscoll, Carlos A., Juliet Clutton-Brock, Andrew Kitchener, and Stephen O'Brien. 2009. The taming of the cat. *Scientific American* (June):68–75.

Driscoll, Carlos A., et al. 2007. The Near Eastern origin of cat domestication. *Science* (July 27):519–23.

Drucker, Philip. 1965. *Cultures of the north Pacific coast*. San Francisco: Chandler.

Drucker, Philip. 1967. The potlatch. In *Tribal and peasant economies*, ed. G. Dalton. Garden City, NY: Natural History Press.

Du, Shanshan. 2003. Is Buddha a couple: Gender-unitary perspectives from the Lahu of Southwest China. *Ethnology* 42:253–71.

Duane, Daniel. 2003. Turning garbage into oil. *New York Times Magazine*, December 14, p. 100.

Duarte, Cidalia, et al. 1999. The early Upper Paleolithic human skeleton from the Abrigo do Lagar Velho (Portugal) and modern human emergence in Iberia. *Proceedings of the National Academy of Sciences of the United States* 96:7604–7609.

Duhard, Jean-Pierre. 1993. Upper Paleolithic figures as a reflection of human morphology and social organization. *Antiquity* 67:83–91.

Dunbar, Robin, and Susanne Shultz. 2007. Evolution of the social brain. *Science* 317(September 7): 1344–47.

Dundes, Alan. 1965. Structural typology in North American Indian folktales. In *The study of folklore*, ed. A. Dundes. Upper Saddle River, NJ: Prentice Hall.

Dundes, Alan. 1989. *Folklore matters*. Knoxville: University of Tennessee Press.

Dundes, Alan. 2005. *Folklore: Critical concepts in literary and cultural studies*, vol. 1. London: Routledge.

Dupré, John. 2008. What genes are and why there are no genes for race. In *Revisiting race in a genomic age*, eds. B. A. Koening, S. S. J. Lee, and S. S. Richardson. New Brunswick, NJ: Rutgers University Press.

Durham, William H. 1991. *Coevolution: Genes, culture and human diversity*. Stanford, CA: Stanford University Press.

Durkheim, Émile. 1938/1895. *The rules of sociological method*. 8th ed. Trans. Sarah A. Soloway and John H. Mueller. Ed. G. E. Catlin. New York: Free Press.

Durkheim, Émile. 1961/1912. *The elementary forms of the religious life*. Trans. Joseph W. Swain. New York: Collier Books.

Durrenberger, E. Paul. 1980. Chayanov's economic analysis in anthropology. *Journal of Anthropological Research* 36:133–48.

Durrenberger, E. Paul. 2001a. Anthropology and globalization. *American Anthropologist* 103:531–35.

Durrenberger, E. Paul. 2001b. Explorations of class and consciousness in the U.S. *Journal of Anthropological Research* 57:41–60.

Durrenberger, E. Paul, and Nicola Tannenbaum. 2002. Chayanov and theory in economic anthropology. In *Theory in economic anthropology*, ed. J. Ensminger. Walnut Creek, CA: AltaMira Press.

Dutton, Denis. 2000. "But they don't have our concept of art." In *Theories of art today*, ed. N. Carroll. Madison: University of Wisconsin Press.

Dyson-Hudson, Neville. 1966. *Karimojong politics*. Oxford: Clarendon Press.

Dyson-Hudson, Rada, and Eric Alden Smith. 1978. Human territoriality: An ecological reassessment. *American Anthropologist* 80:21–41.

Ebrey, Patricia B. 2010. *The Cambridge illustrated history of China*. Cambridge: Cambridge University Press.

Eckhardt, William. 1975. Primitive militarism. *Journal of Peace Research* 12:55–62.

Eddy, Elizabeth M., and William L. Partridge, eds. 1987. *Applied anthropology in America*, 2nd ed. New York: Columbia University Press.

Edgerton, Robert B. 1966. Conceptions of psychosis in four East African societies. *American Anthropologist* 68:408–25.

Edgerton, Robert B. 1971. *The individual in cultural adaptation: A study of four East African peoples*. Berkeley: University of California Press.

Edgerton, Robert B. 1992. *Sick societies: Challenging the myth of primitive harmony*. New York: Free Press.

Edson, Gary, and David Dean. 1994. *The handbook for museums*. New York: Routledge.

Eiseley, Loren C. 1958. The dawn of evolutionary theory. In *Darwin's century: Evolution and the men who discovered it*, ed. L. C. Eiseley. Garden City, NY: Doubleday.

Eisenberg, John F. 1977. Comparative ecology and reproduction of new world monkeys. In *The biology and conservation of the Callitrichidae*, ed. Devra Kleinman. Washington, DC: Smithsonian Institution.

Eisenstadt, S. N. 1954. African age groups. *Africa* 24:100–111.

Eisner, Manuel. 2012. What causes large-scale variation in homicide rates? In *Aggression in humans and other primates: Biology, psychology, sociology*, eds. Hans-Henning Kortüm and Jürgen Heinze. Berlin; New York: Walter de Guyter.

Ekman, Paul. 1994. Strong evidence for universals in facial expressions: A reply to Russell's mistaken critique. *Psychological Bulletin* 115, no.2:268–87.

Ekman, Paul, and Dachner Keltner. 1997. Universal facial expressions of emotion: An old controversy and new findings. In *Nonverbal communication: Where nature meets culture*, eds. U. Segerstrale and P. Molnar. Mahwah, NJ: Lawrence Erlbaum.

Eldredge, Niles, and Ian Tattersall. 1982. *The myths of human evolution*. New York: Columbia University Press.

Eliot, T. S. 1963. The love song of J. Alfred Prufrock. In *Collected poems, 1909–1962*. New York: Harcourt, Brace & World.

Eller, Jack David. 2007. *Introducing anthropology of religion: Culture to the ultimate*. New York: Routledge.

Ellis, Lee. 1986. Evidence of neuroandrogenic etiology of sex roles from a combined analysis of human, nonhuman primate and nonprimate mammalian studies. *Personality and Individual Differences* 7:519–52.

Ember, Carol R. 1973. Feminine task assignment and the social behavior of boys. *Ethos* 1:424–39.

Ember, Carol R. 1974. An evaluation of alternative theories of matrilocal versus patrilocal residence. *Behavior Science Research* 9:135–49.

Ember, Carol R. 1975. Residential variation among hunter-gatherers. *Behavior Science Research* 9:135–49.

Ember, Carol R. 1977. Cross-cultural cognitive studies. *Annual Review of Anthropology* 6:33–56.

Ember, Carol R. 1978a. Men's fear of sex with women: A cross-cultural study. *Sex Roles* 4:657–78.

Ember, Carol R. 1978b. Myths about Hunter-Gatherers. *Ethnology* 17:439–48.

Ember, Carol R. 1981. A cross-cultural perspective on sex differences. In *Handbook of cross-cultural human development*, eds. R. H. Munroe, R. L. Munroe, and B. B. Whiting. New York: Garland.

Ember, Carol R. 1982. The conditions favoring religious conversion. Paper presented at the annual meeting of the Society for Cross-Cultural Research. Minneapolis, Minnesota, February.

Ember, Carol R. 1983. The relative decline in women's contribution to agriculture with intensification. *American Anthropologist* 85:285–304.

Ember, Carol R. 2007. Using the HRAF Collection of Ethnography in Conjunction with the Standard Cross-cultural Sample and the Ethnographic Atlas. *Cross-Cultural Research* 41, no. 4:396–427.

Ember, Carol R. 2009. Universal and variable patterns of gender difference. In MyAnthroLibrary, eds. C. R. Ember, M. Ember, and P. N. Peregrine. MyAnthroLibrary.com. Pearson.

Ember, Carol R., and Melvin Ember. 1972. The conditions favoring multilocal residence. *Southwestern Journal of Anthropology* 28:382–400.

Ember, Carol R., and Melvin Ember. 1984. The evolution of human female sexuality: A cross-species perspective. *Journal of Anthropological Research* 40:202–10.

Ember, Carol R., and Melvin Ember. 1992a. Resource unpredictability, mistrust, and war: A cross-cultural study. *Journal of Conflict Resolution* 36:242–62.

Ember, Carol R., and Melvin Ember. 1992b. Warfare, aggression, and resource problems: Cross-cultural codes. *Cross-Cultural Research* 26, no. 1–4: 169–226.

Ember, Carol R., and Melvin Ember. 1993. Issues in cross-cultural studies of interpersonal violence. *Violence and Victims* 8:217–33.

Ember, Carol R., and Melvin Ember. 1994. War, socialization, and interpersonal violence: A cross-cultural study. *Journal of Conflict Resolution* 38:620–46.

Ember, Carol R., and Melvin Ember. 1997. Violence in the ethnographic record: Results of cross-cultural research on war and aggression. In *Troubled times*, eds. D. Martin and D. Frayer. Langhorn, PA: Gordon and Breach.

Ember, Carol R., and Melvin Ember. 2001. Father absence and male aggression: A re-examination of the comparative evidence. *Ethos* 29:296–314.

Ember, Carol R., and Melvin Ember. 2005. Explaining corporal punishment of children: A cross-cultural study. *American Anthropologist* 107:609–19.

Ember, Carol R., and Melvin Ember. 2009. *Cross-cultural research methods*. 2nd ed. Lanham, AltaMira Press.

Ember, Carol R., and Melvin Ember. 2010. Explaining male initiation ceremonies: New cross-cultural tests and a catalytic model. *Journal of Cross-Cultural Psychology* 41:605–16.

Ember, Carol R., and David Levinson. 1991. The substantive contributions of worldwide cross-cultural studies using secondary data. *Behavior Science Research* (Special issue, Cross-cultural and comparative research: Theory and method), 25:79–140.

Ember, Carol R., Teferi Abate Adem, and Ian Skoggard. 2013. Risk, uncertainty, and violence in eastern Africa: A cross-regional comparison. *Human Nature* 24:33–58.

Ember, Carol R., Melvin Ember, and Burton Pasternak. 1974. On the development of unilineal descent. *Journal of Anthropological Research* 30:69–94.

Ember, Carol R., Melvin Ember, and Bruce Russett. 1992. Peace between participatory polities: A cross-cultural test of the "democracies rarely fight each other" hypothesis. *World Politics* 44:573–99.

Ember, Carol R., Melvin Ember, Andrey Korotayev, and Victor de Munck. 2005. Valuing thinness or fatness in women: Reevaluating the effect of resource scarcity. *Evolution and Human Behavior* 26:257–70.

Ember, Carol R., Teferi Abate Adem, and Ian Skoggard. 2013. Risk, uncertainty, and violence in Eastern Africa: A regional comparison. *Human Nature* 24:33–58.

Ember, Melvin. 1959. The nonunilinear descent groups of Samoa. *American Anthropologist* 61:573–77.

Ember, Melvin. 1963. The relationship between economic and political development in nonindustrialized societies. *Ethnology* 2:228–48.

Ember, Melvin. 1967. The emergence of neolocal residence. *Transactions of the New York Academy of Sciences* 30:291–302.

Ember, Melvin. 1970. Taxonomy in comparative studies. In *A handbook of method in cultural anthropology*, eds. R. Naroll and R. Cohen. Garden City, NY: Natural History Press.

Ember, Melvin. 1973. An archaelogical indicator of matrilocal versus patrilocal residence. *American Antiquity* 38:177–82.

Ember, Melvin. 1974a. The conditions that may favor avunculocal residence. *Behavior Science Research* 9:203–209.

Ember, Melvin. 1974b. Warfare, sex ratio, and polygyny. *Ethnology* 13:197–206.

Ember, Melvin. 1975. On the origin and extension of the incest taboo. *Behavior Science Research* 10:249–81.

Ember, Melvin. 1978. Size of color lexicon: Interaction of cultural and biological factors. *American Anthropologist* 80:364–67.

Ember, Melvin. 1982. Statistical evidence for an ecological explanation of warfare. *American Anthropologist* 84:645–49.

Ember, Melvin. 1983. The emergence of neolocal residence. In *Marriage, family, and kinship: Comparative studies of social organization*, eds. Melvin Ember and Carol R. Ember. New Haven, CT: HRAF Press.

Ember, Melvin. 1984–1985. Alternative predictors of polygyny. *Behavior Science Research* 19:1–23.

Ember, Melvin. 1985. Evidence and science in ethnography: Reflections on the Freeman-Mead controversy. *American Anthropologist* 87:906–909.

Ember, Melvin, and Carol R. Ember. 1971. The conditions favoring matrilocal versus patrilocal residence. *American Anthropologist* 73:571–94.

Ember, Melvin, and Carol R. Ember. 1979. Male-female bonding: A cross-species study of mammals and birds. *Behavior Science Research* 14:37–56.

Ember, Melvin, and Carol R. Ember. 1983. *Marriage, family, and kinship: Comparative studies of social organization*. New Haven, CT: HRAF Press.

Ember, Melvin, and Carol R. Ember. 1992. Cross-cultural studies of war and peace: Recent achievements and future possibilities. In *Studying war*, eds. S. P. Reyna and R. E. Downs. New York: Gordon and Breach.

Ember, Melvin, and Carol R. Ember. 1999. Cross-language predictors of consonant-vowel syllables. *American Anthropologist* 101:730–42.

Ember, Melvin, and Carol R. Ember, eds. 2002. *Encyclopedia of urban cultures: Cities and cultures around the world*, 4 vols. Danbury, CT: Grolier/Scholastic.

Ember, Melvin, and Carol R. Ember. 2004. Toward the evolution of a more civil world. *Social Evolution & History* 3:137–61.

Ember, Melvin, Carol R. Ember, and Bobbi S. Low. 2007. Comparing explanations of polygyny. *Cross-Cultural Research* 41:428–40.

Ember, Melvin, Carol R. Ember, and Bruce Russett. 1997. Inequality and democracy in the anthropological record. In *Inequality, democracy, and economic development*, ed. M. I. Midlarsky. Cambridge: Cambridge University Press.

Ember, Melvin, Carol R. Ember, and Ian Skoggard, eds. 2005. In *Encyclopedia of diasporas: Immigrant and refugee cultures around the world*, 2 vols. New York: Kluwer Academic/Plenum.

Ensminger, Jean. 1997. Transaction costs and Islam: Explaining conversion in Africa. *Journal of Institutional and Theoretical Economics* 153:4–29.

Ensminger, Jean. 2002. Experimental economics: A powerful new method for theory testing in anthropology. In *Theory in economic anthropology*, ed. J. Ensminger. Walnut Creek, CA: Altamira Press.

Ensor, Bradley E. 2003. Kinship and marriage among the Omaha, 1886–1902. *Ethnology* 42:1–14.

Epple, Suzanne. 2006. Women's life in a society with age organizations: The Bashad of Southern Ethiopia. In *Proceedings of the XVth International Conference on Ethiopian Studies*, 66–74. Wiesbaden: Otto Harrassowitz Verlag.

Epstein, Cynthia Fuchs. 1988. *Deceptive distinctions: Sex, gender, and the social order*. New York: Russell Sage Foundation.

Erchak, Gerald M. 2009. Family violence. In MyAnthroLibrary, eds. C. R. Ember, M. Ember, and P. N. Peregrine. MyAnthroLibrary.com. Pearson.

Ericksen, Karen Paige. 1989. Male and female age organizations and secret societies in Africa. *Behavior Science Research* 23:234–64.

Ericksen, Karen Paige, and Heather Horton. 1992. "Blood feuds": Cross-cultural variations in kin group vengeance. *Behavior Science Research* 26:57–85.

Erickson, Clark. 1988. Raised field agriculture in the Lake Titicaca basin. *Expedition* 30, no. 1:8–16.

Erickson, Clark. 1989. Raised fields and sustainable agriculture in the Lake Titicaca basin of Peru. In *Fragile lands of Latin America*, ed. J. Browder. Boulder: Westview.

Erickson, Clark. 1998. Applied archaeology and rural development. In *Crossing currents: Continuity and change in Latin America*, eds. M. Whiteford and S. Whiteford. Upper Saddle River, NJ: Prentice Hall.

Erickson, Edwin. 1968. Self-assertion, sex role, and vocal rasp. In *Folk song style and culture*, ed. A. Lomax. Washington, DC: Transaction Publishers.

Erlandson, Jon and Todd Braje. 2012. Foundations for the Far West: Paleoindian cultures on the western fringe of North America. In *Oxford handbook of North American archaeology*, ed. T. Pauketat. Oxford: Oxford University Press.

Errington, J. Joseph. 1985. On the nature of the sociolinguistic sign: Describing the Javanese speech levels. In *Semiotic mediation*, eds. E. Mertz and R. J. Parmentier. Orlando, FL: Academic Press.

Ervin, Alexander M. 1987. Styles and strategies of leadership during the Alaskan Native land claims movement: 1959–71. *Anthropologica* 29:21–38.

Eswaran, Vinayak. 2002. A diffusion wave out of Africa. *Current Anthropology* 43:749–74.

Etienne, Mona, and Eleanor Leacock, eds. 1980. *Women and colonization: Anthropological perspectives.* New York: Praeger.

Etienne, Robert. 1992. *Pompeii: The day a city died.* New York: Abrams.

Etkin, Nina L., and Paul J. Ross. 1997. Malaria, medicine, and meals: A biobehavioral perspective. In *The anthropology of medicine*, eds. L. Romanucci-Ross, D. E. Moerman, and L. R. Tancredi. Westport, CT: Bergin & Garvey.

Euripides. 1937. The Trojan women. In *Three Greek plays*, Trans. E. Hamilton, 52. New York: Norton.

Evans-Pritchard, E. E. 1940. The Nuer of the southern Sudan. In *African political systems*, eds. M. Fortes and E. E. Evans-Pritchard. New York: Oxford University Press.

Evans-Pritchard, E. E. 1970. Sexual inversion among the Azande. *American Anthropologist* 72:1428–34.

Evans-Pritchard, E. E. 1979. Witchcraft explains unfortunate events. In *Reader in comparative religion*, 3rd ed., eds. W. A. Lessa and E. Z. Vogt. New York: Harper & Row.

Eveleth, Phyllis B., and James M. Tanner. 1990. *Worldwide variation in human growth.* 2nd ed. Cambridge: Cambridge University Press.

Everett, Margaret. 2007. The "I" in gene: Divided property, fragmented personhood, and the making of a genetic privacy law. *American Ethnologist* 34, no. 2:375–86.

Eversole, Robyn. 2005. "Direct to the poor" revisited: Migrant remittances and development assistance. In *Migration and economy: Global and local dynamics*, ed. L. Trager. Walnut Creek, CA: Altamira Press.

Fagan, Brian M. 1972. *In the beginning.* Boston: Little, Brown.

Fagan, Brian M. 1989. *People of the earth: An introduction to world prehistory.* 6th ed. Glenview, IL: Scott, Foresman.

Fagan, Brian M. 1991. *Ancient North America: The archaeology of a continent.* London: Thames and Hudson.

Falk, Dean. 1987. Hominid paleoneurology. *Annual Review of Anthropology* 16:13–30.

Falk, Dean. 1988. Enlarged occipital/marginal sinuses and emissary foramina: Their significance in hominid evolution. In *Evolutionary history of the "robust" australopithecines*, ed. F. E. Grine. New York: Aldine.

Falk, Dean, et al. 2005. The brain of LBI, *Homo floresiensis. Science* 308 (April 8):242–45.

FAO. n.d. Hunger. http://www.fao.org (accessed May 20, 2013).

Farley, Reynolds. 1996. *The new American reality: Who we are, how we got here, where we are going.* New York: Russell Sage Foundation.

Farmer, Paul. 1997. Ethnography, social analysis, and the prevention of sexually transmitted HIV infection among poor women in Haiti. In *The anthropology of infectious disease*, eds. M. C. Inhorn and P. J. Brown. Amsterdam: Gordon and Breach.

Farmer, Paul, Margaret Connors, and Janie Simmons. 2011. *Women, poverty and AIDS: Sex, drugs and structural violence.* 2nded. Monroe, ME: Common Courage Press.

Featherman, David L., and Robert M. Hauser. 1978. *Opportunity and change.* New York: Academic Press.

Feder, Kenneth. 2000. *Past in perspective.* 2nd ed. Mountain View, CA: Mayfield Publishing Company.

Fedigan, Linda Marie. 1982. *Primate paradigms: Sex roles and social bonds.* Montreal: Eden Press.

Fedoroff, Nina. 2003. Prehistoric GM corn. *Science* 302 (November 14):1158–59.

Fehr, Ernst, and Urs Fischbacher. 2003. The nature of human altruism. *Nature* (October 23):785–91.

Feibel, Craig S., and Francis H. Brown. 1993. Microstratigraphy and paleoenvironments. In *The Nariokotome* Homo erectus *skeleton*, eds. A. Walker and R. Leakey. Cambridge, MA: Harvard University Press.

Feinman, Gary M. 2011. Size, complexity, and organizational variation: A comparative approach. *Cross-Cultural Research* 45:37–58. (Special issue in honor of Melvin Ember. Part I, ed. Peter N. Peregrine).

Feinman, Gary M., and Jill Neitzel. 1984. Too many types: An overview of sedentary prestate societies in the Americas. In *Advances in archaeological method and theory*, vol. 7, ed. M. B. Schiffer. Orlando, FL: Academic Press.

Feinman, Gary M., Stephen A. Kowalewski, Laura Finsten, Richard E. Blanton, and Linda Nicholas. 1985. Long-term demographic change: A perspective from the Valley of Oaxaca, Mexico. *Journal of Field Archaeology* 12:333–62.

Feldman, Douglas A., and Thomas M. Johnson. 1986. Introduction. In *The social dimensions of AIDS*, eds. D. A. Feldman and T. M. Johnson. New York: Praeger.

Ferguson, R. Brian, and Neil L. Whitehead. 1992. Violent edge of empire. In *War in the tribal zone*, eds. R. B. Ferguson and N. Whitehead. Santa Fe, NM: School of American Research Press.

Ferguson, Niall. 2004. *Colossus: The price of America's empire.* New York: Penguin Press.

Fernea, Elizabeth, and Robert Fernea, as reported in M. Kay Martin and Barbara Voorhies, 1975. *Female of the species.* New York: Columbia University Press.

Ferraro, Gary P. 2002. *The cultural dimension of international business.* 4th ed. Upper Saddle River, NJ: Prentice Hall.

Fessler, Daniel M. T. 2002. Windfall and socially distributed willpower: The psychocultural dynamics of rotating savings and credit associations in a Bengkulu village. *Ethos* 30:25–48.

Finley, M. I. 1983. *Politics in the ancient world.* Cambridge: Cambridge University Press.

Finnis, Elizabeth. 2006. Why grow cash crops? Subsistence farming and crop commercialization in the Kolli Hills, South India. *American Anthropologist* 108:363–69.

Firth, Raymond. 1957. *We, the Tikopia.* Boston: Beacon Press.

Firth, Raymond. 1959. *Social change in Tikopia.* New York: Macmillan.

Firth, Raymond. 1970. *Rank and religion in Tikopia.* Boston: Beacon Press.

Fischer, John L. 1958. Social influences on the choice of a linguistic variant. *Word* 14:47–56.

Fischer, John L. 1961. Art styles as cultural cognitive maps. *American Anthropologist* 63:80–83.

Fish, Paul R. 1981. Beyond tools: Middle Paleolithic debitage analysis and cultural inference. *Journal of Anthropological Research* 37:374–86.

Fisher, Julie. 1996. Grassroots organizations and grassroots support organizations: Patterns of interaction. In *Transforming societies, transforming anthropology*, ed. E. F. Moran. Ann Arbor: University of Michigan Press.

Fisher, William F. 1997. Doing good? The politics and antipolitics of NGO practices. *Annual Review of Anthropology* 26:439–64.

Fisher, William H. 1994. Megadevelopment, environmentalism, and resistance: The institutional context of Kayapo indigenous politics in central Brazil. *Human Organization* 53:220–32.

Flannery, Kent V. 1965. The ecology of early food production in Mesopotamia. *Science* 147 (March 12):1247–56.

Flannery, Kent V. 1971. The origins and ecological effects of early domestication in Iran and the Near East. In *Prehistoric agriculture*, ed. S. Struever. Garden City, NY: Natural History Press.

Flannery, Kent V. 1972. The cultural evolution of civilizations. *Annual Review of Ecology and Systematics* 3:399–426.

Flannery, Kent V. 1973a. The origins of agriculture. *Annual Review of Anthropology* 2:271–310.

Flannery, Kent V. 1973b. The origins of the village as a settlement type in Mesoamerica and the Near East: A comparative study. In *Territoriality and proxemics*, ed. R. Tringham. Andover, MA: Warner.

Flannery, Kent V., ed. 1986. *Guila Naquitz: Archaic foraging and early agriculture in Oaxaca, Mexico.* Orlando, FL: Academic Press.

Fleagle, John G. 1994. Anthropoid origins. In *Integrative paths to the past*, eds. R. Corruccini and R. Ciochon. Upper Saddle River, NJ: Prentice Hall.

Fleagle, John G. 1999. *Primate adaptation and evolution.* 2nd ed. San Diego: Academic Press.

Fleagle, John G., and Richard F. Kay. 1983. New interpretations of the phyletic position of Oligocene hominoids. In *New interpretations of ape and human ancestry*, eds. R. Ciochon and R. Corruccini. New York: Plenum.

Fleagle, John G., and Richard F. Kay. 1985. The paleobiology of catarrhines. In *Ancestors*, ed. E. Delson. New York: Alan R. Liss.

Fleagle, John G., and Richard F. Kay. 1987. The phyletic position of the *Parapithecidae. Journal of Human Evolution* 16:483–531.

Fluehr-Lobban, Carolyn. 2006. *Race and racism: An introduction.* Lanham: AltaMira Press.

Fluehr-Lobban, Carolyn. 2008. Collaborative anthropology as twenty-first century ethical anthropology. *Collaborative Anthropologies* 1:175–82.

Foner, Nancy. 2011. The social construction of race in two immigrant eras. In *Race in an era of change: A reader*, eds. H. Dalmage and B. Katz Rothman. New York: Oxford University Press.

Ford, Clellan S. 1941. *Smoke from their fires.* New Haven, CT: Yale University Press.

Ford, Clellan S., and Frank A. Beach. 1951. *Patterns of sexual behavior.* New York: Harper.

Forrest, Barbara. 2001. The wedge at work. In *Intelligent design creationism and its critics*, ed. R. Pennock. Boston: MIT Press.

Fortes, Meyer. 1949. *The web of kinship among the Tallensi.* New York: Oxford University Press.

Fossey, Dian. 1983. *Gorillas in the mist.* Boston: Houghton Mifflin.

Foster, Brian L. 1974. Ethnicity and commerce. *American Ethnologist* 1:437–47.

Foster, George M. 1962. *Traditional cultures and the impact of technological change.* New York: Harper & Row.

Foster, George M. 1969. *Applied anthropology.* Boston: Little, Brown.

Foster, George M. 1994. *Hippocrates' Latin American legacy: Humoral medicine in the New World.* Amsterdam: Gordon and Breach.

Foucault, Michel. 1970. *The order of things: An archaeology of the human sciences.* New York: Random House.

Fowler, Melvin L. 1975. A pre-Columbian urban center on the Mississippi. *Scientific American* (August):92–101.

Frake, Charles O. 1960. The Eastern Subanun of Mindanao. In *Social structure in Southeast Asia*, ed. G. P. Murdock. Chicago: Quadrangle.

Franciscus, Robert G., and Erik Trinkaus. 1988. Nasal morphology and the emergence of *Homo erectus. American Journal of Physical Anthropology* 75:517–27.

Frank, André Gunder. 1967. *Capitalism and underdevelopment in Latin America: Historical studies of Chile and Brazil.* New York: Monthly Review Press.

Fratkin, Elliot. 2008. Pastures lost: The decline of mobile pastoralism among Maasai and Rendille in Kenya, East Africa. In *Economies and the transformation of landscape*, eds. Lisa Cliggett and Christopher A. Pool. Lanham: Altamira Press.

Frayer, David W. 1981. Body size, weapon use, and natural selection in the European Upper Paleolithic and Mesolithic. *American Anthropologist* 83:57–73.

Frayer, David W., and Milford H. Wolpoff. 1985. Sexual dimorphism. *Annual Review of Anthropology* 14:429–73.

Frayer, David W., M. Wolpoff, A. Thorne, F. Smith, and G. Pope. 1993. Theories of modern human origins: The paleontological test. *American Anthropologist* 95:24–27.

Frayser, Suzanne G. 1985. *Varieties of sexual experience.* New Haven, CT: HRAF Press.

Freedman, Daniel G. 1979. Ethnic differences in babies. *Human Nature* (January):36–43.

Freeman, Derek. 1983. *Margaret Mead and Samoa: The making and unmaking of an anthropological myth.* Cambridge, MA: Harvard University Press.

Freeman, J. D. 1961. On the concept of the kindred. *Journal of the Royal Anthropological Institute* 91:192–220.

Freeman, Leslie G. 1994. Torralba and Ambrona: A review of discoveries. In *Integrative paths to the past*, eds. R. Corruccini and R. Ciochon. Upper Saddle River, NJ: Prentice Hall.

Freud, Sigmund. 1943/1917. *A general introduction to psychoanalysis.* Garden City, NY: Garden City Publishing. (Originally published in German)

Freud, Sigmund. 1967/1939. *Moses and monotheism.* Trans. Katherine Jones. New York: Vintage Books.

Freud, Sigmund. 2007/1950. The return of totemism in childhood. In *Ritual and belief: Readings in the anthropology of religion*, 3rd ed., ed. David Hicks, 7–12. Lanham, MD: AltaMira Press.

Freyman, R. 1987. The first technology. *Scientific American* (April):112.

Fried, Morton H. 1967. *The evolution of political society: An essay in political anthropology.* New York: Random House.

Friedl, Ernestine. 1962. *Vasilika: A village in modern Greece.* New York: Holt, Rinehart & Winston.

Friedman, Jeffrey M. 2003. A war on obesity, not the obese. *Science* 299 (February 7):856–58.

Friedman, Saul S. 1980. Holocaust. In *Academic American [now Grolier] encyclopedia*, vol. 10. Princeton, NJ: Areté.

Friedrich, Paul. 1970. *Proto-Indo-European trees: The arboreal system of a prehistoric people.* Chicago: University of Chicago Press.

Friedrich, Paul. 1986. *The language parallax.* Austin: University of Texas Press.

Frisancho, A. Roberto, and Lawrence P. Greksa. 1989. Development responses in the acquisition of functional adaptation to high altitude. In *Human population biology*, eds. M. Little and J. Haas. New York: Oxford University Press.

Frisch, Rose E. 1980. Fatness, puberty, and fertility. *Natural History* (October):16–27.

Fromm, Erich. 1950. *Psychoanalysis and religion.* New Haven, CT: Yale University Press.

Frost, Robert. 1915. The death of the hired hand. In *North of Boston.* New York: Henry Holt.

Fry, Douglas P. 2006. *The human potential for peace: An anthropological challenge to assumptions about war and violence.* New York: Oxford University Press.

Fry, Douglas P., and Kaj Björkqvist, eds. 1997. *Cultural variation in conflict resolution: Alternatives to violence.* Mahwah, NJ: Lawrence Erlbaum Associates.

Fuentes, A., M. A. Wyczalkowski, and K. MacKinnon. 2010. Nich construction through cooperation: A nonlinear dynamics contribution to modeling facets of the evolutionary history of the genus *Homo. Current Anthropology* 51:435–44.

Futuyma, Douglas. 1982. *Science on trial.* New York: Pantheon.

Gabunia, Leo, et al. 2000. Earliest Pleistocene hominid cranial remains from Dmanisi, Republic of Georgia: Taxonomy, geological setting, and age. *Science* 288 (May 12):1019–25.

Gaiha, Raghav, Kenneth Hill, Ganesh Thapa, and Varsha Kulkarni. 2013. Have natural disasters become deadlier? Brooks World Poverty Institute Working Paper No. 181. Available through the Social Science Research Network: http://ssrn.com/abstract=2209714 or http://dx.doi.org/10.2139/ssrn.2209714(accessed May 31, 2013).

Gaines, Atwood D., and Robbie David-Floyd. 2004. Biomedicine. In *Encyclopedia of medical anthropology: Health and illness in the world's cultures*, eds. Carol R. Ember and Melvin Ember. New York: Kluwer Academic/Plenum Publishers.

Gal, Susan. 1988. The political economy of code choice. In *Codeswitching*, ed. M. Heller. Berlin: Mouton de Gruyter.

Galdikas, Biruté M. F. 1979. Orangutan adaptation at Tanjung Puting Reserve: Mating and ecology. In *The great apes*, eds. D. Hamburg and E. McCown. Menlo Park, CA: Benjamin/Cummings.

Gardner, Beatrice T., and R. Allen Gardner. 1980. Two comparative psychologists look at language acquisition. In *Children's language*, vol. 2, ed. K. Nelson. New York: Halsted Press.

Gardner, R. Allen, and Beatrice T. Gardner. 1969. Teaching sign language to a chimpanzee. *Science* 165 (August 15):664–72.

Garn, Stanley M. 1971. *Human races.* 3rd ed. Springfield, IL: Charles C Thomas.

Gartner, Rosemary. 2009. Crime: Variations across cultures and nations. In MyAnthroLibrary, eds. C. R. Ember, M. Ember, and P. N. Peregrine. MyAnthroLibrary.com. Pearson.

Gat, Azar. 1999. The pattern of fighting in simple, small-scale, prestate societies. *Journal of Anthropological Research* 55:563–83.

Gat, Azar. 2006. *War in human civilization.* Oxford: Oxford University Press.

Gaulin, Steven J. C., and James S. Boster. 1990. Dowry as female competition. *American Anthropologist* 92:994–1005.

Gay, Kathlyn. 1986. *Ergonomics: Making products and places fit people.* Hillside, New Jersey: Enslow.

Gebo, Daniel. 2002. Apidiformes: Phylogeny and adaptation. In *The primate fossil record*, ed. W. C. Hartwig, 21–44. Cambridge: Cambridge University Press.

Geertz, Clifford. 1960. *The religion of Java.* New York: Free Press.

Geertz, Clifford. 1966. Religion as a cultural system. In *Anthropological approaches to the study of religion*, ed. M. Banton. New York: Praeger.

Geertz, Clifford. 1973a. Deep play: Notes on the Balinese cockfight. In *The interpretation of cultures*, ed. C. Geertz. New York: Basic Books.

Geertz, Clifford. 1973b. Thick description: Toward an interpretative theory of culture. In *The interpretation of cultures*, ed. C. Geertz. New York: Basic Books.

Geertz, Clifford. 1984. "From the native's point of view": On the nature of anthropological understanding. In *Culture theory*, eds. R. A. Shweder and R. A. LeVine. New York: Cambridge University Press.

Geiger, H. Jack. 2003. Racial and ethnic disparities in diagnosis and treatment: A review of the evidence and a consideration of causes. In *Unequal treatment: Confronting racial and ethnic disparities in health care*, eds. B. D. Smedley, A. Y. Stith, and A. R. Nelson. Washington, DC: National Academy Press.

Gelfand, Michele J., et al. 2011. Differences between tight and loose cultures: A 33-nation study. *Science* 123 (May 27):1100–1104.

Gelles, Richard J., and Murray A. Straus. 1988. *Intimate violence.* New York: Simon & Schuster.

Gentner, W., and H. J. Lippolt. 1963. The potassium-argon dating of upper tertiary and Pleistocene deposits. In *Science in archaeology*, eds. D. Brothwell and E. Higgs. New York: Basic Books.

Gero, Joan M., and Margaret W. Conkey, eds. 1991. *Engendering archaeology: An introduction to women and prehistory.* Oxford: Blackwell.

Gesler, W. 1991. *The cultural geography of health care.* Pittsburgh, PA: University of Pittsburgh Press.

Gibbons, Ann. 1993. Warring over women. *Science* 261 (August 20):987–88.

Gibbons, Ann. 1995. First Americans: Not mammoth hunters, but forest dwellers? *Science* 268 (April 19):346–47.

Gibbons, Ann. 2001. The riddle of co-existence. *Science* 291 (March 2):1725–29.

Gibbons, Ann. 2002. One scientist's quest for the origin of our species. *Science* 298 (November 29):1708–11.

Gibbons, Ann. 2003. Oldest members of *Homo sapiens* discovered in Africa. *Science* 300 (June 13):1641.

Gibbons, Ann. 2008. The birth of childhood. *Science* 322 (November 14):1040–43.

Gibbons, Ann. 2011. A new view of the birth of *Homo sapiens. Science* 311 (January 28):392–94.

Gibbons, Ann. 2012. A crystal-clear view of an extinct girl's genome. *Science* 337 (August 31):1028–29.

Gibbs, James L., Jr. 1965. The Kpelle of Liberia. In *Peoples of Africa*, ed. J. L. Gibbs, Jr. New York: Holt, Rinehart & Winston.

Gibson, Kathleen R., and Stephen Jessee. 1999. Language evolution and expansions of multiple neurological processing areas. In *The origins of language*, ed. B. J. King, 189–227. Santa Fe, NM: School of American Research Press.

Gibson, Kyle. 2009. Differential parental investment in families with both adopted and genetic children. *Evolution and Human Behavior* 30:184–89.

Gilbert, M. Thomas P., et al. 2008. DNA from pre-Clovis human coprolites in Oregon, North America. *Science* 320 (May 9):786–89.

Gill, J. L., J. W. Williams, S. T. Jackson, K. B. Lininger, and G. S. Swanson. 2009. Pleistocene megafaunal collapse, novel plant communities, and enhanced fire regimes in North America. *Science* 326 (November 20): 1100–1103.

Gilligan, Carol. 1982. *In a different voice: Psychological theory and women's development.* Cambridge, MA: Harvard University Press.

Gilligan, Carol, and Jane Attanucci. 1988. Two moral orientations. In *Mapping the moral domain*, eds. C. Gilligan, J. V. Ward, and J. M. Taylor. Cambridge, MA: Harvard University Press.

Gilliland, Mary Kay. 1995. Nationalism and ethnogenesis in the former Yugoslavia. In *Ethnic identity: Creation, conflict, and accommodation*, 3rd ed., eds. L. Romanucci-Ross and G. A. De Vos. Walnut Creek, CA: Alta Mira Press.

Gilman, Antonio. 1990. The development of social stratification in Bronze Age Europe. *Current Anthropology* 22:1–23.

Gimbutas, Marija. 1974. An archaeologist's view of PIE* in 1975. *Journal of Indo-European Studies* 2:289–307.

Gingerich, P. D. 1986. *Pleisiadipis* and the delineation of the order primates. In *Major topics in primate evolution*, eds. B. Wood, L. Martin, and P. Andrews. Cambridge: Cambridge University Press.

Gladwin, Christina H. 1980. A theory of real-life choice: Applications to agricultural decisions. In *Agricultural decision making*, ed. P. F. Barlett. New York: Academic Press.

Gladwin, Thomas, and Seymour B. Sarason. 1953. *Truk: Man in paradise.* New York: Wenner-Gren Foundation for Anthropological Research.

Gleitman, Lila R., and Eric Wanner. 1982. Language acquisition: The state of the state of the art. In *Language acquisition*, eds. E. Wanner and L. R. Gleitman. Cambridge: Cambridge University Press.

Glick Schiller, Nina. 2004. Long-distance nationalism. In *Encyclopedia of diasporas: Immigrant and refugee cultures around the world*, vol. 1, eds. M. Ember, C. R. Ember, and I. Skoggard. New York: Springer.

Goddard, Michael B. 2004. Women in Papua New Guinea village courts. State, society and governance discussion paper. Research School of Pacific and Asian Studies, Australian National University, Acton, Australia.

Godoy, Ricardo, et al. 2004. Patience in a foraging-horticultural society: A test of competing hypotheses. *Journal of Anthropological Research* 60:179–202.

Goebel, Ted, Michael Waters, and Dennis O'Rourke. 2008. The Late Pleistocene dispersal of modern humans in the Americas. *Science* 319 (March 14):1479–1502.

Golden, Frederic, Michael Lemonick, and Dick Thompson. 2000. The race is over. *Time* (July 3):18–23.

Goldizen, Anne Wilson. 1987. Tamarins and marmosets: Communal care of offspring. In *Primate societies*, eds. B. B. Smuts, D. L. Cheney, R. M. Seyfarth, and Richard W. Wrangham. Chicago: University of Chicago Press.

Goldmann, Kjell, Ulf Hannerz, and Charles Westin. 2000. Introduction: Nationalism and internationalism in the post-cold war era. In *Nationalism and internationalism in the post-cold war era*, eds. G. U. Hannerz and C. Westin. London: Routledge.

Goldschmidt, Walter. 1999. Dynamics and status in America. *Anthropology Newsletter* 40, no. 5:62, 64.

Goldstein, Donna. 1998. Nothing bad intended: Child discipline, punishment, and survival in a shantytown in Rio de Janeiro. In *Small wars: The cultural politics of childhood*, eds. N. Scheper-Hughes and C. Sargeant. Berkeley: University of California-Berkeley Press.

Goldstein, Joshua S. 2001. *War and gender: How gender shapes the war system and vice versa.* New York: Cambridge University Press.

Goldstein, Joshua S. 2004. War and gender. In *Encyclopedia of sex and gender: Men and women in the world's cultures*, vol. 1, eds. C. R. Ember and M. Ember. New York: Kluwer Academic/Plenum Publishers.

Goldstein, Joshua S. 2011. *Winning the war on war: The decline of armed conflict worldwide.* New York: Dutton.

Goldstein, Melvyn C. 1971. Stratification, polyandry, and family structure in central Tibet. *Southwestern Journal of Anthropology* 27:65–74.

Goldstein, Melvyn C. 1987. When brothers share a wife. *Natural History* (March): 39–48.

Goodall, Jane. 1963. My life among wild chimpanzees. *National Geographic* (August):272–308.

Goode, William J. 1970. *World revolution and family patterns.* New York: Free Press.

Goode, William J. 1982. *The family.* 2nd ed. Upper Saddle River, NJ: Prentice Hall.

Goodenough, Ward H. 1951. *Property, kin, and community on Truk.* New Haven, CT: Yale University Press.

Goodman, Alan H., and George J. Armelagos. 1985. Disease and death at Dr. Dickson's Mounds. *Natural History* (September):12–19.

Goodman, Alan H., and Thomas L. Leatherman, eds. 1998. *Building a new biocultural synthesis: Political-economic perspectives on human biology.* Ann Arbor: University of Michigan Press.

Goodman, Alan H., John Lallo, George J. Armelagos, and Jerome C. Rose. 1984. Health changes at Dickson Mounds, Illinois (A.D. 950–1300). In *Paleopathology at the origins of agriculture*, eds. M. N. Cohen and G. J. Armelagos. Orlando, FL: Academic Press.

Goodman, Madeleine J., P. Bion Griffin, Agnes A. Estioko-Griffin, and John S. Grove. 1985. The compatibility of hunting and mothering among the Agta hunter-gatherers of the Philippines. *Sex Roles* 12:1199–209.

Goodman, Morris. 1992. Reconstructing human evolution from proteins. In *The Cambridge encyclopedia of human evolution*, eds. S. Jones, R. Martin, and D. Pilbeam. New York: Cambridge University Press.

Goodrich, L. Carrington. 1959. *A short history of the Chinese people.* 3rd ed. New York: Harper & Row.

Goody, Jack. 1970. Cousin terms. *Southwestern Journal of Anthropology* 26:125–42.

Goody, Jack. 1973. Bridewealth and dowry in Africa and Eurasia. In *Bridewealth and dowry*, eds. J. Goody and S. H. Tambiah. Cambridge: Cambridge University Press.

Gordon, C. G., and K. E. Friedl. 1994. Anthropometry in the U.S. armed forces. In *Anthropometry: The individual and the population*, eds. S. J. Ulijaszek and C. G. N. Mascie-Taylor. Cambridge: Cambridge University Press.

Gore, Rick. 2002. The first pioneer? *National Geographic* 202 (August).

Goren-Inbar, Naama, et al. 2004. Evidence of hominid control of fire at Gesher Benot Ya'aqov, Israel. *Science* 304 (April 30):725–27.

Gorman, Chester. 1970. The Hoabinhian and after: Subsistence patterns in Southeast Asia during the Late Pleistocene and early recent periods. *World Archaeology* 2:315–19.

Gossen, Gary H. 1979. Temporal and spatial equivalents in Chamula ritual symbolism. In *Reader in comparative religion*, 4th ed., eds. W. A. Lessa and E. Z. Vogt. New York: Harper & Row.

Gough, Kathleen. 1959. The Nayars and the definition of marriage. *Journal of the Royal Anthropological Institute* 89:23–34.

Gould, Richard A. 1969. *Yiwara: Foragers of the Australian desert.* New York: Scribner's.

Gowlett, John A. J. 2008. Deep roots of kin: Developing the evolutionary perspective from prehistory. In *Early human kinship: From sex to social reproduction*, eds. N. Allen, H. Callan, R. Dunbar, and W. James. Oxford: Blackwell.

Graber, Robert, eds. 2004. Special issue. The future state of the world: An anthropological symposium. *Cross-Cultural Research* 38:95–207

Graburn, Nelson H. 1969. *Eskimos without igloos.* Boston: Little, Brown.

Graham, Susan Brandt. 1979. Biology and human social behavior: A response to van den Berghe and Barash. *American Anthropologist* 81:357–60.

Grant, Bruce S. 2002. Sour grapes of wrath. *Science* 297 (August 9):940–41.

Grant, Peter R. 1991. Natural selection and Darwin's finches. *Scientific American* (October):82–87.

Grant, Peter R., and Rosemary Grant. 2002. Unpredictable evolution in a 30-year study of Darwin's finches. *Science* 296 (April 26):707–11.

Gravlee, Clarence C., H. R. Bernard, and W. R. Leonard. 2003. Heredity, environment, and cranial form: A reanalysis of Boas's immigrant data. *American Anthropologist* 105:125–38.

Gray, J. Patrick. 1985. *Primate sociobiology.* New Haven, CT: HRAF Press.

Gray, J. Patrick. 1996. Sociobiology. In *Encyclopedia of cultural anthropology*, vol. 4, eds. D. Levinson and M. Ember. New York: Henry Holt.

Gray, J. Patrick, and Linda D. Wolfe. 1980. Height and sexual dimorphism of stature among human societies. *American Journal of Physical Anthropology* 53:446–52.

Gray, J. Patrick, and Linda D. Wolfe. 2009. What accounts for population variation in height? In MyAnthroLibrary, eds. C. R. Ember, M. Ember, and P. N. Peregrine. MyAnthroLibrary.com. Pearson.

Grayson, Donald K. 1977. Pleistocene avifaunas and the overkill hypothesis. *Science* 195 (February 18):691–92.

Grayson, Donald K. 1984. Explaining Pleistocene extinctions: Thoughts on the structure of a debate. In *Quaternary extinctions*, eds. P. S. Martin and R. Klein. Tucson: University of Arizona Press.

Green, Edward C., and Allison Herling Ruark. 2011. *Aids, behavior, and culture: Understanding evidence-based prevention.* Walnut Creek, CA: Left Coast Press.

Green, Richard E., et al. 2008. A complete Neandertal mitochondrial genome sequence determined by high-throughput sequencing. *Cell* 134:416–26.

Green, Richard E., et al. 2010. A draft sequence of the Neandertal genome. *Science* 328 (May 7):710–22.

Greenberg, Joseph H. 1972. Linguistic evidence regarding Bantu origins. *Journal of African History* 13:189–216.

Greenberg, Joseph H., and Merritt Ruhlen. 1992. Linguistic origins of Native Americans. *Scientific American* (November):94–99.

Greenfield, Patricia Marks, and E. Sue Savage-Rumbaugh. 1990. Grammatical combination in *Pan paniscus*: Processes of learning and invention in the evolution and development of language. In *"Language" and intelligence in monkeys and apes*, eds. S. Parker and K. Gibson. New York: Cambridge University Press.

Greenfield, Patricia Marks, Ashley E. Maynard, and Carla P. Childs. 2000. History, culture, learning, and development. *Cross-Cultural Research* 34:351–74.

Gregor, Thomas A., and Daniel R. Gross. 2004. Guilt by association: The culture of accusation and the American Anthropological Association' investigation of *Darkness in El Dorado. American Anthropologist* 106:687–98.

Gregory, C. A. 1982. *Gifts and commodities.* New York: Academic Press.

Greksa, Lawrence P., and Cynthia M. Beall. 1989. Development of chest size and lung function at high altitude. In *Human population biology*, eds. M. Little and J. Haas. New York: Oxford University Press.

Grenoble, Lenore A., and Lindsay J. Whaley. 2006. *Saving languages: An introduction to language revitalization.* Cambridge: Cambridge University Press.

Grine, Frederick E. 1988a. Evolutionary history of the "robust" australopithecines: A summary and historical perspective. In *Evolutionary history of the "robust" australopithecines*, ed. F. E. Grine. New York: Aldine.

Grine, Frederick E., eds. 1988b. *Evolutionary history of the "robust" australopithecines.* New York: Aldine.

Grine, Frederick E. 1993. Australopithecine taxonomy and phylogeny: Historical background and recent interpretation. In *The human evolution source book*, eds. R. Ciochon and J. Fleagle. Upper Saddle River, NJ: Prentice Hall.

Gröger, B. Lisa. 1981. Of men and machines: Cooperation among French family farmers. *Ethnology* 20:163–75.

Gross, Daniel R., and Barbara A. Underwood. 1971. Technological change and caloric costs: Sisal agriculture in northeastern Brazil. *American Anthropologist* 73:725–40.

Gross, Daniel R., George Eiten, Nancy M. Flowers, Francisca M. Leoi, Madeline Lattman Ritter, and Dennis W. Werner. 1979. Ecology and acculturation among native peoples of central Brazil. *Science* 206 (November 30):1043–50.

Grossman, Daniel. 2002. Parched turf battle. *Scientific American* (December): 32–33.

Grubb, Henry J. 1987. Intelligence at the low end of the curve: Where are the racial differences? *Journal of Black Psychology* 14:25–34.

Gubser, Nicholas J. 1965. *The Nunamiut Eskimos: Hunters of caribou.* New Haven, CT: Yale University Press.

Guest, Greg, and Eric C. Jones. 2005. Globalization, health, and the environment: An introduction. In *Globalization, health, and the environment: An integrated perspective*, ed. G. Guest. Lanham, MD: Roman & Littlefield.

Guiora, Alexander Z., Benjamin Beit-Hallahmi, Risto Fried, and Cecelia Yoder. 1982. Language environment and gender identity attainment. *Language Learning* 32:289–304.

Gumperz, John J. 1961. Speech variation and the study of Indian civilization. *American Anthropologist* 63:976–88.

Gumperz, John J. 1971. Dialect differences and social stratification in a North Indian village. In *Language in social groups: Essays by John J. Gumperz*, selected and introduced by Anwar S. Dil. Stanford, CA: Stanford University Press.

Gumperz, John J., and Jenny Cook Gumperz. 2008. Studying language, culture, and society: Sociolinguistics or linguistic anthropology? *Journal of Sociolinguistics* 12, no.4:532–45.

Gunders, S., and J. W. M. Whiting. 1968. Mother-infant separation and physical growth. *Ethnology* 7:196–206.

Gunnell, Gregg F., and Kenneth D. Rose. 2002. *Tarsiiformes*: Evolutionary history and adaptation. In *The primate fossil record*, ed. W. C. Hartwig. Cambridge: Cambridge University Press.

Gurr, Ted Robert. 1989a. Historical trends in violent crime: Europe and the United States. In *Violence in America, Vol. 1: The history of crime*, ed. T. R. Gurr. Newbury Park, CA: Sage.

Gurr, Ted Robert. 1989b. The history of violent crime in America: An overview. In *Violence in America, Vol. 1: The history of crime*, ed. T. R. Gurr. Newbury Park, CA: Sage.

Gurven, Michael, Kim Hill, and Hillard Kaplan. 2002. From forest to reservation: Transitions in food-sharing behavior among the Ache of Paraguay. *Journal of Anthropological Research* 58:93–120.

Guthrie, Dale R. 1984. Mosaics, allelochemics, and nutrients: An ecological theory of Late Pleistocene megafaunal extinctions. In *Quaternary extinctions*, eds. P. S. Martin and R. Klein. Tucson: University of Arizona Press.

Guthrie, Stewart Elliott. 1993. *Faces in the clouds: A new theory of religion.* New York: Oxford University Press.

Guttman-Bond, Erica. 2010. Sustainability out of the past: How archaeology can save the planet. *World Archaeology* 42:355–366.

Haas, Jonathan. 1990. Warfare and the evolution of tribal polities in the prehistoric Southwest. In *The anthropology of war*, ed. J. Haas. New York: Cambridge University Press.

Haas, Jonathan. 2007. Warfare and the evolution of culture. In *Archaeology at the millennium: A sourcebook*, eds. G. M. Feinman and T. D. Price, 329–50. New York: Springer.

Haas, Jonathan, Winifred Creamer, and Alvaro Ruiz. 2004. Dating the Late Archaic occupation of the Norte Chico region in Peru. *Nature* 432 (December 23):1020–23.

Haas, Mary R. 1944. Men's and women's speech in Koasati. *Language* 20:142–49.

Habicht, J. K. A. 1979. *Paleoclimate, paleomagnetism, and continental drift.* Tulsa, OK: American Association of Petroleum Geologists.

Haddix, Kimber A. 2001. Leaving your wife and your brothers: When polyandrous marriages fall apart. *Evolution and Human Behavior* 22:47–60.

Hage, Jerald, and Charles H. Powers. 1992. *Post-industrial lives: Roles and relationships in the 21st century.* Newbury Park, CA: Sage.

Hahn, Robert A. 1995. *Sickness and healing: An anthropological perspective.* New Haven, CT: Yale University Press.

Hailie-Selassie, Yohannes. 2001. Late Miocene hominids from the Middle Awash, Ethiopia. *Nature* 412 (July 12):178–81.

Haldane, J. B. S. 1963. Human evolution: Past and future. In *Genetics, paleontology, and evolution*, eds. G. Jepsen, E. Mayr, and G. Simpson. New York: Atheneum.

Hall, Edward T. 1966. *The hidden dimension.* Garden City, NY: Doubleday.

Hall, Edward T., and Mildred Reed Hall. 1990. *Understanding cultural differences.* Nicholas Brealey Publishing.

Hallowell, A. Irving. 1976. Ojibwa world view and disease. In *Contributions to anthropology: Selected papers of A. Irving Hallowell*, 410–13. Chicago: University of Chicago Press.

Halpern, Diane F. 2000. *Sex differences in cognitive abilities.* 3rd ed. Mahwah, NJ: Lawrence Erlbaum Associates.

Hames, Raymond B. 1990. Sharing among the Yanomamö. Part I. The effects of risk. In *Risk and uncertainty in tribal and peasant economies*, ed. E. Cashdan. Boulder, CO: Westview.

Hames, Raymond B. 2009. Yanomamö: Varying adaptations of foraging horticulturalists. In MyAnthroLibrary, eds. C. R. Ember, M. Ember, and P. N. Peregrine. MyAnthroLibrary.com. Pearson.

Hammer, Michael F., and Stephen L. Zegura. 1996. The role of the Y chromosome in human evolutionary studies. *Evolutionary Anthropology* 5:116–34.

Hammer, Michael F., and Stephen L. Zegura. 2002. The human Y chromosome haplogroup tree. *Annual Review of Anthropology* 31:303–21.

Handler, Richard. 2005. Vigorous male and aspiring female: Poetry, personality and culture in Edward Sapir and Ruth Benedict. In *Critics against culture: Anthropological observers of mass society*, 96–122. Madison: University of Wisconsin Press.

Handwerker, W. Penn, and Paul V. Crosbie. 1982. Sex and dominance. *American Anthropologist* 84:97–104.

Hanna, Joel M., Michael A. Little, and Donald M. Austin. 1989. Climatic physiology. In *Human population biology*, eds. M. Little and J. Haas. New York: Oxford University Press.

Hannah, Alison C., and W. C. McGrew. 1987. Chimpanzees using stones to crack open oil palm nuts in Liberia. *Primates* 28:31–46.

Hannerz, Ulf. 1996. *Transnational connections: Culture, people, places.* London: Routledge.

Hanotte, Olivier, D. G. Bradley, J. W. Ochieng, Y. Verjee, E. W. Hill, and J. E. Rege. 2002. African pastoralism: Genetic imprints of origins and migrations. *Science* 296 (April 12):336–43.

Hanson, Jeffery R. 1988. Age-set theory and Plains Indian age-grading: A critical review and revision. *American Ethnologist* 15:349–64.

Harcourt, A. H. 1979. The social relations and group structure of wild mountain gorillas. In *The great apes*, eds. D. Hamburg and E. McCown. Menlo Park, CA: Benjamin/Cummings.

Hardin, Garrett. 1968. The tragedy of the commons. *Science* 162 (December 13):1243–48.

Hardoy, Jorge, and David Satterthwaite. 1987. The legal and the illegal city. In *Shelter, settlement, and development*, ed. L. Rodwin. Boston: Allen & Unwin.

Hare, Brian, Michelle Brown, Christina Williamson, and Michael Tomasello. 2002. The domestication of social cognition in dogs. *Science* 298 (November 22):1634–36.

Harkness, Sara, and Charles M. Super. 1997. "An infant's three Rs." A box in M. Small, "Our babies, ourselves." *Natural History* (October):45.

Harkness, Sara, and Charles M. Super. 2006. Themes and variations: Parental ethnotheories in Western cultures. In *Parenting beliefs, behaviors, and parent-child relations: A cross-cultural perspective*, eds. Kenneth H. Rubin and Ock Boon Chung. New York: Psychology Press.

Harkness, Sara, and C. Jason Throop. 2008. Bruner's search for meaning: A conversation between psychology and anthropology. *Ethos* 36:5.

Harlan, Jack R. 1967. A wild wheat harvest in Turkey. *Archaeology* 20:197–201.

Harlow, Harry F., M. K. Harlow, R. O. Dodsworth, and G. L. Arling 1966. Maternal behavior of rhesus monkeys deprived of mothering and peer association in infancy. *Proceedings of the American Philosophical Society* 110:58–66.

Harner, Michael J. 1972. The role of hallucinogenic plants in European witchcraft. In *Hallucinogens and shamanism.* New York: Oxford University Press.

Harner, Michael J. 1975. Scarcity, the factors of production, and social evolution. In *Population, ecology, and social evolution*, ed. S. Polgar. The Hague: Mouton.

Harner, Michael J., and Gary Doore. 1987. The ancient wisdom in shamanic cultures. In *Shamanism*, ed. S. Nicholson. Wheaton, IL: Theosophical Publishing House.

Harper, Douglas. 2003. Slavery in the North. http://www.slavenorth.com/ (accessed June, 2009).

Harrell-Bond, Barbara. 1996. Refugees. In *Encyclopedia of cultural anthropology*, vol. 3, eds. D. Levinson and M. Ember. New York: Henry Holt.

Harris, David R. 1977. Settling down: An evolutionary model for the transformation of mobile bands into sedentary communities. In *The evolution of social systems*, eds. J. Friedman and M. Rowlands. London: Duckworth.

Harris, Eugene. 2008. Searching the genome for our adaptations. *Evolutionary Anthropology* 17:146–157.

Harris, Marvin. 1964. *Patterns of race in the Americas.* New York: Walker.

Harris, Marvin. 1966. The cultural ecology of India's sacred cattle. *Current Anthropology* 7:51–63.

Harris, Marvin. 1968. *The rise of anthropological theory: A history of theories of culture.* New York: Thomas Y. Crowell.

Harris, Marvin. 1975. *Cows, pigs, wars and witches: The riddles of culture.* New York: Random House, Vintage.

Harris, Marvin. 1979. *Cultural materialism: The struggle for a science of culture.* New York: Random House.

Harrison, G. A., James M. Tanner, David R. Pilbeam, and P. T. Baker. 1988. *Human biology: An introduction to human evolution, variation, growth, and adaptability.* 3rd ed. Oxford: Oxford University Press.

Harrison, Gail G. 1975. Primary adult lactase deficiency: A problem in anthropological genetics. *American Anthropologist* 77:812–35.

Harrison, Peter D., and B. L. Turner, II, eds. 1978. *Pre-Hispanic Maya agriculture.* Albuquerque: University of New Mexico Press.

Harrison, Terry 1986. A reassessment of the phylogenetic relationships of *Oreopithecus bamboli. Journal of Human Evolution* 15:541–84.

Harrison, Terry. 2002. Late Oligocene to Middle Miocene catarrhines from Afro-Arabia. In *The primate fossil record*, ed. W. C. Hartwig. Cambridge: Cambridge University Press.

Harrison, T., and L. Rook. 1997. Enigmatic anthropoid or misunderstood ape? The phylogenetic status of *Oreopithecus bamboli* reconsidered. In *Function, phylogeny and fossils: Miocene hominoid evolution and adaptation*, eds. D. R. Begun, C. V. Ward, and M. D. Rose. New York: Plenum.

Hart, Hornell. 1948. The logistic growth of political areas. *Social Forces* 26:396–408.

Hartwig, W. C. 1994. Pattern, puzzles and perspectives on platyrrhine origins. In *Integrative paths to the past*, eds. R. Corruccini and R. Ciochon. Upper Saddle River, NJ: Prentice Hall.

Harvey, Philip W., and Peter F. Heywood. 1983. Twenty-five years of dietary change in Simbu Province, Papua New Guinea. *Ecology of Food and Nutrition* 13:27–35.

Hassan, Fekri A. 1981. *Demographic archaeology.* New York: Academic Press.

Hassanpour, Amir, and Shahrzad Mojab. 2004. Kurdish diaspora. In *Encyclopedia of diasporas: Immigrant and refugee cultures around the world*, vol. 1, eds. M. Ember, C. R. Ember, and I. Skoggard. New York: Springer.

Hatch, Elvin. 1997. The good side of relativism. *Journal of Anthropological Research* 53:371–81.

Haug, Gerald, Detlef Günther, Larry C. Peterson, Daniel M. Sigman, Konrad A. Hughen, and Beat Aeschlimann. 2003. Climate and the collapse of Maya civilization. *Science* 299 (March 14):1731–35.

Hauser, Marc D., Noam Chomsky, and W. Tecumseh Fitch. 2002. The faculty of language: What is it, who has it, and how did it evolve? *Science* 298 (November 22):1569–79.

Hausfater, Glenn, Jeanne Altmann, and Stuart Altmann. 1982. Long-term consistency of dominance relations among female baboons. *Science* 217 (August 20):752–54.

Hawkins, Alicia, and M. Kleindienst. 2001. Aterian. In *Encyclopedia of prehistory, Vol. 1: Africa*, eds. P. N. Peregrine and M. Ember. New York: Kluwer Academic/Plenum.

Hayashi, Akiko, and Joseph Tobin. 2011. The Japanese preschool's pedagogy of peripheral participation. *Ethos* 39:139–64.

Hayden, Thomas. 2000. A genome milestone. *Newsweek* (July 3):51–52.

Haynes, Vance. 1973. The Calico site: Artifacts or geofacts? *Science* 181 (July 27):305–10.

Hays, Terence E. 1994. Sound symbolism, onomatopoeia, and New Guinea frog names. *Journal of Linguistic Anthropology* 4:153–74.

Hays, Terence E. 2009. From ethnographer to comparativist and back again. In MyAnthroLibrary, eds. C. R. Ember, M. Ember, and P. N. Peregrine. MyAnthroLibrary.com. Pearson.

Heider, Karl. 1970. *The Dugum Dani.* Chicago: Aldine.

Heider, Karl. 1979. *Grand Valley Dani: Peaceful warriors.* New York: Holt, Rinehart & Winston.

Heinrich, Joseph, and Robert Boyd. 2008. Division of labor, economic specialization, and the evolution of social stratification. *Current Anthropology* 49, no.4:715–24.

Heise, David R. 1967. Cultural patterning of sexual socialization. *American Sociological Review* 32:726–39.

Higham, Charles. 2009. East Asian agriculture and its impact. In *The human past*, ed. C. Scarre. New York: Thames and Hudson.

Heller, Monica, eds. 1988. *Codeswitching: Anthropological and sociolinguistic perspectives.* Berlin: Mouton de Gruyter.

Helms, Mary W. 1975. *Middle America.* Upper Saddle River, NJ: Prentice Hall.

Helms, Mary W. 2009. Miskito: Adaptations to colonial empires, past and present. In MyAnthroLibrary, eds. C. R. Ember, M. Ember, and P. N. Peregrine. MyAnthroLibrary.com. Pearson.

Henderson, Harry. 2001. *Global terrorism: The complete reference guide.* New York: Checkmark Books.

Henderson, Stephen. 2002. Weddings: Vows; Rakhi Dhanoa and Ranjeet Purewal. *New York Times*, August 18, p. 9.2.

Hendrix, Lewellyn. 1985. Economy and child training reexamined. *Ethos* 13:246–61.

Hendrix, Lewellyn. 2009. Varieties of marital relationships. In MyAnthroLibrary, eds. C. R. Ember, M. Ember, and P. N. Peregrine. MyAnthroLibrary.com. Pearson.

Henrich, Joseph. 2009. The evolution of costly displays, cooperation and religion: Credibility enhancing displays and their implications for cultural evolution. *Evolution and Human Behavior* 30:244–60.

Henrich, Joseph, Robert Boyd, Samuel Bowles, Colin Camerer, Ernst Fehr, and Herbert Gintis, eds. 2004. *Foundations of human sociality: Economic experiments and ethnographic evidence from fifteen small-scale societies.* Oxford: Oxford University Press.

Henrich, Joseph, et al. 2005. "Economic man" in cross-cultural perspective: Behavioral experiments in 15 small-scale societies. *Behavioral and Brain Sciences* 28:795–814.

Henry, Donald O. 1989. *From foraging to agriculture: The Levant at the end of the Ice Age.* Philadelphia: University of Pennsylvania Press.

Henry, Donald O. 1991. Foraging, sedentism, and adaptive vigor in the Natufian: Rethinking the linkages. In *Perspectives on the past*, eds. G. A. Clark. Philadelphia: University of Pennsylvania Press.

Henry, Edward O. 1976. The variety of music in a North Indian village: Reassessing cantometrics. *Ethnomusicology* 20:49–66.

Henshilwood, Christopher, et al. 2002. Emergence of modern human behavior: Middle Stone Age engravings from South Africa. *Science* 295 (February 15):1278–80.

Herlihy, Laura Hobson. 2007. Matrifocality and women's power on the Miskito Coast. *Ethnology* 46:133–49.

Herrman, Helen. 1990. A survey of homeless mentally ill people in Melbourne, Australia. *Hospital and Community Psychiatry* 41:1291–92.

Herrmann, Esther, Joseph Call, Maria Victoria Herandez-Lloreda, Brain Hare, and Michael Tomasello. 2007. Humans have evolved specialized skills in social cognition: The cultural intelligence hypothesis. *Science* 317 (September 7):1360–65.

Herrnstein, Richard J., and Charles Murray. 1994. *The bell curve: Intelligence and class structure in American life.* New York: Free Press.

Hewes, Gordon W. 1961. Food transport and the origin of hominid bipedalism. *American Anthropologist* 63:687–710.

Hewlett, Barry S. 2004. Diverse contexts of human infancy. In MyAnthroLibrary, eds. C. R. Ember, M. Ember, and P. N. Peregrine. MyAnthroLibrary.com. Pearson.

Hewlett, Barry S., and L. L. Cavalli-Sforza. 1986. Cultural transmission among Aka Pygmies. *American Anthropologist* 88:922–34.

Hiatt, L. R. 1980. Polyandry in Sri Lanka: A test case for parental investment theory. *Man* 15:583–98.

Hickey, Gerald Cannon. 1964. *Village in Vietnam.* New Haven, CT: Yale University Press.

Hickson, Letitia. 1986. The social contexts of apology in dispute settlement: A cross-cultural study. *Ethnology* 25:283–94.

Higley, Stephen Richard. 1995. *Privilege, power, and place: The geography of the American upper class.* Lanham, MD: Rowman & Littlefield.

Hill, Carole. 2000. Strategic issues for rebuilding a theory and practice synthesis. *NAPA Bulletin* 18:1–16.

Hill, Carole E., and Marietta L. Baba. 2006. Global connections and practicing anthropology in the 21st century. *NAPA Bulletin* 25, no.1:1–13.

Hill, Donald R. 2005. Music of the African diaspora in the Americas. In *Encyclopedia of diasporas: Immigrant and refugee cultures around the world*, eds. M. Ember, C. R. Ember, and I. Skoggard. New York: Kluwer Academic/Plenum.

Hill, James N. 1970. *Broken K Pueblo: Prehistoric social organization in the American Southwest.* Anthropological Papers of the University of Arizona, Number 18. Tucson: University of Arizona Press.

Hill, Jane H. 1978. Apes and language. *Annual Review of Anthropology*7:89–112.

Hill, Jane H. 2009. Do apes have language? In MyAnthroLibrary, eds. C. R. Ember, M. Ember, and P. N. Peregrine. MyAnthroLibrary.com. Pearson.

Hill, Jonathan D. 1996. Introduction: Ethnogenesis in the Americas. 1492-1992. In *Ethnogenesis in the Americas*, ed. J. D. Hill, 1–19. Iowa City: University of Iowa Press.

Hill, Kim, and A. Magdalena Hurtado. 2004. The ethics of anthropological research with remote tribal populations. In *Lost paradises and the ethics of research and publication*, eds. F. M. Salzano and A. M. Hurtado. Oxford: Oxford University Press.

Hill, Kim, Hillard Kaplan, Kristen Hawkes, and A. Magdalena Hurtado. 1987. Foraging decisions among Aché hunter-gatherers: New data and implications for optimal foraging models. *Ethology and Sociobiology* 8:1–36.

Hill, Susan T. 2001. *Science and engineering doctorate awards: 2000*, NSF 02-305. National Science Foundation, Division of Science Resources Statistics. VA: Arlington.

Hillel, Daniel. 2000. *Salinity management for sustainable irrigation: Integrating science, environment, and economics.* Washington, DC: The World Bank.

Himmelgreen, David A., and Deborah L. Crooks. 2005. Nutritional anthropology and its application to nutritional issues and problems. In *Applied anthropology: Domains of application*, eds. S. Kedia and J. van Willigen, 149–88. Westport, CT: Praeger.

Himmelgreen, David, and Nancy Romero-Daza. 2009. Anthropological approaches to the global food crisis: Understanding and addressing the "silent tsunami." *NAPA Bulletin* 32:1-11.

Hinkes, Madeleine. 1993. Race, ethnicity, and forensic anthropology. *NAPA Bulletin* 13:48–54.

Hirsch, Jennifer, Sarah Van Deusen Phillips, Edward Labenski, Christine Dunford, and Troy Peters. 2011. Linking climate action to local knowledge and practice. In *Environmental anthropology today*, eds. H. Kopnina and E. Shoreman-Ouimet. New York: Routledge.

Hitchcock, Robert K., and Megan Beisele. 2000. Introduction. In *Hunters and gatherers in the modern world: Conflict, resistance, and self-determinations*, eds. P. P. Schweitzer, M. Biesele, and R. K. Hitchcock. New York: Berghahn Books.

Hoberman, John. 2012. *Black and blue: The origins and consequences of medical racism.* Berkeley: University of California Press.

Hobsbawm, E. J. 1970. *Age of revolution.* New York: Praeger.

Hockett, C. F., and R. Ascher. 1964. The human revolution. *Current Anthropology* 5:135–68.

Hodgson, Jason, and Todd Driscoll. 2008. No evidence of a Neandertal contribution to modern human diversity. *Genome Biology* 9:206.1–206.7.

Hoebel, E. Adamson. 1960. *The Cheyennes: Indians of the Great Plains.* New York: Holt, Rinehart & Winston.

Hoebel, E. Adamson. 1968/1954. *The law of primitive man.* New York: Atheneum.

Hoffecker, John F., W. Roger Powers, and Ted Goebel. 1993. The colonization of Beringia and the peopling of the New World. *Science* 259 (January 1):46–53.

Hoffman, Lois Wladis. 1988. Cross-cultural differences in child-rearing goals. In *Parental behavior in diverse societies*, eds. R. A. LeVine, P. M. Miller, and M. M. West. San Francisco: Jossey-Bass.

Hoijer, Harry. 1964. Cultural implications of some Navaho linguistic categories. In *Language in culture and society*, ed. D. Hymes. New York: Harper & Row.

Holdaway, R. N., and C. Jacomb. 2000. Rapid extinction of the Moas (*Aves: Dinornithiformes*): Model, test, and implications. *Science* 287 (March 24):2250–57.

Holden, Constance. 2000. Selective power of UV. *Science* 289 (September 1):1461.

Hole, Frank. 1992. Origins of agriculture. In *The Cambridge encyclopedia of human evolution*, eds. S. Jones, R. Martin, and D. Pilbeam. New York: Cambridge University Press.

Hole, Frank. 1994. Environmental shock and urban origins. In *Chiefdoms and early states in the Near East*, eds. G. Stein and M. Rothman. Madison, WI: Prehistory Press.

Hole, Frank, Kent V. Flannery, and James A. Neely. 1969. *Prehistory and human ecology of the Deh Luran Plain.* Memoirs of the Museum of Anthropology, No. 1. Ann Arbor: University of Michigan.

Hollan, Douglas. 1992. Cross-cultural differences in the self. *Journal of Anthropological Research* 48:289–90.

Holloway, Marguerite. 1993. Sustaining the Amazon. *Scientific American* (July):91–99.

Holloway, Ralph L. 1974. The casts of fossil hominid brains. *Scientific American* (July):106–15.

Holmes, Janet. 2001. *An introduction to sociolinguistics.* 2nd ed. London: Longman.

Honigmann, John J. 1967. *Personality in culture.* New York: Harper & Row.

Hoogbergen, Wim. 1990. *The Boni Maroon Wars in Suriname.* Leiden: E. J. Brill.

Hooper, Judith. 2002. *Of moths and men: The untold story of science and the peppered moth.* New York: W. W. Norton.

Hopkins, K. 1980. Brother-sister marriage in Roman Egypt. *Comparative Studies in Society & History* 22:303–54.

Hopper, Kim. 2003. *Reckoning with homelessness.* Ithaca, NY: Cornell University Press.

Houston, Stephen D. 1988. The phonetic decipherment of Mayan Glyphs. *Antiquity* 62:126–35.

Howard, Alan, and Jan Rensel. 2009. Rotuma: Interpreting a Wedding. In MyAnthroLibrary, eds. C. R. Ember, M. Ember, and P. N. Peregrine. MyAnthroLibrary.com. Pearson.

Howard, Philip N., Aiden Duffy, Deen Freelon, M. Hussain, W. Mari, and M. Mazaid. 2011. Opening closed regimes: what was the role of social media during the Arab spring? Project on Information Technology & Political Islam. Working paper.

Howell, F. Clark. 1966. Observations on the earlier phases of the European Lower Paleolithic. In *Recent studies in paleoanthropology. American Anthropologist.* Special publication, eds. J. Desmond Clark and F. Clark Howell. April.

Howell, Nancy. 1979. *Demography of the Dobe !Kung.* New York: Academic Press.

Howrigan, Gail A. 1988. Fertility, infant feeding, and change in Yucatan. *New directions for child development* 40:37–50.

Hrdy, Sarah Blaffer. 1977. *The Langurs of Abu: Female and male strategies of reproduction.* Cambridge, MA: Harvard University Press.

Hua, Cai. 2001. *A society without fathers or husbands: The Na of China.* Trans. Asti Hustvedt. New York: Zone Books.

Huang, H. T. 2002. Hypolactasia and the Chinese diet. *Current Anthropology* 43:809–19.

Huber, Evelyne, François Nielsen, Jenny Pribble, and John D. Stephens. 2006. Politics and inequality in Latin America and the Caribbean. *American Sociological Review* 71:943–63.

Human Development Report 1993. 1993. Published for the United Nations Development Programme. New York: Oxford University Press.

Human Development Report 2001. 2001. Published for the United Nations Development Programme. New York: Oxford University Press.

Humphrey, Caroline, and Stephen Hugh-Jones. 1992. Introduction: Barter, exchange and value. In *Barter, exchange and value*, eds. C. Humphrey and S. Hugh-Jones. New York: Cambridge University Press.

Hunt, Morton. 1974. *Sexual behavior in the 1970s.* Chicago: Playboy Press.

Hunt, Robert C. 2000. Labor productivity and agricultural development: Boserup revisited. *Human Ecology* 28:251–77.

Hurtado, Ana M., Kristen Hawkes, Kim Hill, and Hillard Kaplan. 1985. Female subsistence strategies among the Aché hunter-gatherers of eastern Paraguay. *Human Ecology* 13:1–28.

Huss-Ashmore, Rebecca, and Francis E. Johnston. 1985. Bioanthropological research in developing countries. *Annual Review of Anthropology* 14:475–527.

Huxley, Thomas H. 1970. Man's place in nature. In *Evolution of man*, ed. L. Young. New York: Oxford University Press.

Hymes, Dell. 1974. *Foundations in sociolinguistics: An ethnographic approach.* Philadelphia: University of Pennsylvania Press.

Ingram, Catherine J. E., Charlotte A. Mulcare, Yuval Itan, Mark G. Thomas, and Dallas M. Swallow. 2009. Lactose digestion and the evolutionary genetics of lactase persistence. *Human Genetics* 124, no. 6:579–91.

IPPC. 2007. Climate change 2007: Synthesis report. http://www.ipcc.ch/pdf/assessment-report/ar4/syr/ar4_syr_spm.pdf.

Irons, William. 1979. Natural selection, adaptation, and human social behavior. In *Evolutionary biology and human social behavior*, eds. N. Chagnon and W. Irons. North Scituate, MA: Duxbury.

Irwin, Marc H., Gary N. Schafer, and Cynthia P. Feiden. 1974. Emic and unfamiliar category sorting of Mano farmers and U.S. undergraduates. *Journal of Cross-Cultural Psychology* 5:407–23.

Isaac, Glynn. 1971. The diet of early man: Aspects of archaeological evidence from Lower and Middle Pleistocene sites in Africa. *World Archaeology* 2:277–99.

Isaac, Glynn. 1984. The archaeology of human origins: Studies of the Lower Pleistocene in East Africa, 1971-1981. In *Advances in world archaeology*, eds. F. Wendorf and A. Close. Orlando, FL: Academic Press.

Isaac, Glynn, ed., assisted by Barbara Isaac. 1997. *Plio-Pleistocene archaeology.* Oxford: Clarendon Press.

Itkonen, T. I. 1951. The Lapps of Finland. *Southwestern Journal of Anthropology* 7:32–68.

Jablonski, Nina G. 2010. Skin coloration. In *Human evolutionary biology*, ed. M. Muehlenbein. Cambridge: Cambridge University Press.

Jablonski, Nina G., and George Chaplin. 2000. The evolution of human skin color. *Journal of Human Evolution* 39:57–106.

Jacobs, Sue-Ellen, and Christine Roberts. 1989. Sex, sexuality, gender and gender variance. In *Gender and anthropology*, ed. S. Morgen. Washington, DC: American Anthropological Association.

Jaeger, J., et al. 1999. A new primate from the Middle Eocene of Myanmar and the Asian early origins of anthropoids. *Science* 286 (October 15):528–30.

James, Allison. 2007. Giving voice to children's voices: Practices and problems, pitfalls and potentials. *American Anthropologist* 109:261–72.

James, William. 1902. *The varieties of religious experience: A study in human nature.* New York: Modern Library.

Jankowiak, William R. 2009. Urban Mongols: Ethnicity in communist China. In MyAnthroLibrary, eds. C. R. Ember, M. Ember, and P. N. Peregrine. MyAnthroLibrary.com. Pearson.

Jankowiak, William R., and Edward F. Fischer. 1992. A cross-cultural perspective on romantic love. *Ethnology* 31:149–55.

Jankowiak, William, M. Diane Nell, and Ann Buckmaster. 2002. Managing infidelity: A cross-cultural perspective. *Ethnology* 41:85–101.

Jankowiak, William, Monica Sudakov, and Benjamin C. Wilreker. 2005. Co-wife conflict and co-operation. *Ethnology* 44:81–98.

Janzen, Daniel H. 1973. Tropical agroecosystems. *Science* 182 (December 21):1212–19.

Jarvenpa, Robert. 2004. *Silot'ine*: An insurance perspective on Northern Dene kinship networks in recent history. *Journal of Anthropological Research* 60:153–78.

Jarvenpa, Robert, and Hetty Jo Brumbach. 2006. Chipewyan hunters: A task differentiation analysis. In *Circumpolar lives and livelihood: A comparative ethnoarchaeology of gender and subsistence*, eds. R. Jarvenpa and H. J. Brumbach. Lincoln, Nebraska: University of Nebraska Press.

Jayaswal, Vidula. 2002. South Asian Upper Paleolithic. In *Encyclopedia of prehistory, Vol. 8: South and Southwest*

Asia, eds. P. N. Peregrine and M. Ember. New York: Kluwer Academic/Plenum.

Jenkins, D. L., et al. 2012. Clovis age western stemmed projectile points and human coprolites at the Paisley Caves. *Science* 337 (July 13):223–28.

Jelliffe, Derrick B., and E. F. Patrice Jelliffe. 1975. Human milk, nutrition, and the world resource crisis. *Science* 188 (May 9):557–61.

Jennings, J. D. 1968. *Prehistory of North America.* New York: McGraw-Hill.

Jensen, Arthur. 1969. How much can we boost IQ and scholastic achievement? *Harvard Educational Review* 29:1–123.

Joans, Barbara. 1997. Problems in Pocatello: A study in linguistic misunderstanding. In *Applying cultural anthropology: An introductory reader*, 3rd ed., eds. A. Podolefsky and P. J. Brown. Mountain View, CA: Mayfield.

Jobling, Mark A., Matthew E. Hurles, and Chris Tylor-Smith. 2004. *Human evolutionary genetics.* New York: Garland.

Johannes, R. E. 1981. *Words of the lagoon: Fishing and marine lore in the Palau District of Micronesia.* Berkeley: University of California Press.

Johanson, Donald C., and Maitland Edey. 1981. *Lucy: The beginnings of humankind.* New York: Simon & Schuster.

Johanson, Donald C., and Tim D. White. 1979. A systematic assessment of early African hominids. *Science* 203 (January 26):321–30.

Johnson, Allen W., and Timothy Earle. 1987. *The evolution of human societies: From foraging group to agrarian state.* Stanford, CA: Stanford University Press.

Johnson, Allen W., and Timothy Earle. 2000. *The evolution of human societies: From foraging group to agrarian state.* 2nd ed. Stanford, CA: Stanford University Press.

Johnson, Amber Lynn. 2002. Cross-cultural analysis of pastoral adaptations and organizational states: A preliminary study. *Cross-Cultural Research* 36:151–80.

Johnson, Dominic D. P. 2005. God's punishment and public goods: A test of the supernatural punishment hypothesis in 186 world cultures. *Human Nature* 16:410–46.

Johnson, Eric Michael. 2011. I've got your back. *Scientific American* 305 (October):22.

Johnson, Gregory A. 1977. Aspects of regional analysis in archaeology. *Annual Review of Anthropology* 6:479–508.

Johnson, Gregory A. 1987. The changing organization of Uruk administration on the Susiana plain. In *Archaeology of western Iran*, ed. F. Hole. Washington, DC: Smithsonian Institution Press.

Johnson, Jeffrey G., Cohen Patricia, Elizabeth M. Smailies, Stephanie Kasen, and Judith S. Brook. 2002. Television viewing and aggressive behavior during adolescence and adulthood. *Science* 295 (March 29):2468–70.

Johnson-Hanks, Jennifer. 2006. *Uncertain honor: Modern motherhood in an African crisis.* Chicago: University of Chicago Press.

Johnston, David Cay. 1999. Gap between rich and poor found substantially wider. *New York Times*, National, September 5, p. 16

Jolly, Alison. 1985. *The evolution of primate behavior.* 2nd ed. New York: Macmillan.

Jolly, Clifford. 1970. The seed-eaters: A new model of hominid differentiation based on a baboon analogy. *Man* 5:5–28.

Jones, Martin, and Xinyi Liu. 2009. Origins of agriculture in East Asia. *Science* 324 (May 8):730–31.

Jones, Nicholas Blurton, Kristen Hawkes, and James F. O'Connell. 1996. The global process and local ecology: How should we explain differences between the Hadza and the !Kung? In *Cultural diversity among twentieth-century foragers*, ed. S. Kent. Cambridge: Cambridge University Press.

Jones, Steve, Robert Martin, and David Pilbeam, eds. 1992. *The Cambridge encyclopedia of human evolution.* New York: Cambridge University Press.

Jordan, Ann. 2013. *Business anthropology.* 2nd ed. Long Grove, IL: Waveland Press.

Judge, W. James, and Jerry Dawson. 1972. Paleo-Indian settlement technology in New Mexico. *Science* 176 (June 16):1210–16.

Julian, Tiffany A., and Robert A. Kominski. 2011. *Education and synthetic work-life earnings estimates.* American Community Survey Reports, ACS-14. Washington, DC: U.S. Census Bureau.

Jung, Carl G. 1938. *Psychology and religion.* New Haven, CT: Yale University Press.

Jungers, William L. 1988a. New estimates of body size in australopithecines. In *Evolutionary history of the "robust" australopithecines*, ed. F. Grine. New York: Aldine.

Jungers, William L. 1988b. Relative joint size and hominoid locomotor adaptations with implications for the evolution of hominid bipedalism. *Journal of Human Evolution* 17:247–65.

Jungers, William L., et al. 2009. The foot of *Homo floresiensis. Nature* 459 (May 7):81–84.

Kahn, Matthew E. 2005. The death toll from natural disasters: The role of income, geography, and institutions. *The Review of Economics and Statistics* 87:271–84.

Kamin, Leon J. 1995. Behind the curve. *Scientific American* (February):99–103.

Kang, Bong W. 2000. A reconsideration of population pressure and warfare: A protohistoric Korean case. *Current Anthropology* 41:873–81.

Kang, Gay Elizabeth. 1979. Exogamy and peace relations of social units: A cross-cultural test. *Ethnology* 18:85–99.

Kaplan, Hillard, and Kim Hill. 1985. Food sharing among Achéforagers: Tests of explanatory hypotheses. *Current Anthropology* 26:223–46.

Kaplan, Hillard, Kim Hill, and A. Magdalena Hurtado. 1990. Risk, foraging and food sharing among the Aché. In *Risk and uncertainty in tribal and peasant economies*, ed. E. Cashdan. Boulder, CO: Westview.

Kaplan, Hillard, Kim Hill, Jane Lancaster, and A. Magdalena Hurtado. 2000. A theory of human life history evolution, diet, intelligence, and longevity. *Evolutionary Anthropology* 9:156–84.

Kardiner, Abram, with Ralph Linton. 1946/1939. *The individual and his society.* New York: Golden Press.

Kasarda, John D. 1971. Economic structure and fertility: A comparative analysis. *Demography* 8, no.3:307–18.

Katzner, Kenneth. 2002. *Languages of the world.* London: Routledge.

Kay, Paul, Brent Berlin, Luisa Maffi, William R. Merrifield, and Richard Cook. 2009. *The world color survey.* Stanford, California: Center for the Study of Languages and Information.

Kay, Richard F. 2000a. *Parapithecidae.* In *Encyclopedia of human evolution and prehistory*, eds. I. Tattersall, E. Delson, and J. Van Couvering. New York: Garland.

Kay, Richard F. 2000b. Teeth. In *Encyclopedia of human evolution and prehistory*, eds. I. Tattersall, E. Delson, and J. Van Couvering. New York: Garland.

Kay, Richard F., C. Ross, and B. A. Williams. 1997. Anthropoid origins. *Science* 275 (February 7):797–804.

Kedia, Satish. 2008. Recent changes and trends in the practice of anthropology. *NAPA Bulletin* 29:14–28.

Kedia, Satish, and John van Willigen. 2005. Applied anthropology: Context for domains of application. In *Applied anthropology: Domains of application*, eds. S. Kedia and J. van Willigen. Westport, CT: Praeger.

Keeley, Lawrence H. 1980. *Experimental determination of stone tool uses: A microwear analysis.* Chicago: University of Chicago Press.

Keeley, Lawrence H. 1991. Ethnographic models for late glacial hunter-gatherers. In *The late glacial in North-West Europe: Human adaptation and environmental change at the end of the Pleistocene*, eds. N. Barton, A. J. Roberts, and D. A. Roe. London: Council for British Archaeology (CBA Research Report 77).

Keeley, Lawrence H. 1996. *War before civilization: The myth of the peaceful savage.* Oxford: Oxford University Press.

Keenan, Elinor. 1989. Norm-makers, norm-breakers: Uses of speech by men and women in a Malagasy community. In *Explorations in the ethnography of speaking*, 2nd ed., eds. R. Bauman and J. Sherzer. New York: Cambridge University Press.

Kehoe, Alice B., and Dody H. Giletti. 1981. Women's preponderance in possession cults: The calcium-deficiency hypothesis extended. *American Anthropologist* 83:549–61.

Keller, Helen. 1974/1902. *The story of my life.* New York: Dell.

Kelley, Jay. 1992. The evolution of apes. In *The Cambridge encyclopedia of human evolution*, eds. S. Jones, R. Martin, and D. Pilbeam. New York: Cambridge University Press.

Kelley, Jay. 2002. The hominoid radiation in Asia. In *The primate fossil record*, ed. W. C. Hartwig. Cambridge: Cambridge University Press.

Kelly, Raymond C. 1974. Witchcraft and sexual relations: An exploration in the social and semantic implications of the structure of belief. Paper presented at the annual meeting of the American Anthropological Association, Mexico City.

Kelly, Raymond C. 1985. *The Nuer conquest: The structure and development of an expansionist system.* Ann Arbor: University of Michigan Press.

Kelly, Robert L. 1995. *The foraging spectrum: Diversity in hunter-gatherer lifeways.* Washington, DC: Smithsonian Institution Press.

Kent, Susan, ed. 1996. *Cultural diversity among twentieth-century foragers: An African perspective.* Cambridge: Cambridge University Press.

Kerr, Richard A. 1998. Sea-floor dust shows drought felled Akkadian empire. *Science* 299 (January 16):325–26.

Khosroshashi, Fatemeh. 1989. Penguins don't care, but women do: A social identity analysis of a Whorfian problem. *Language in Society* 18:505–25.

Kilbride, Philip L., and Janet C. Kilbride. 1990. Polygyny: A modern contradiction? In *Changing family life in East Africa: Women and children at risk*, eds. P. L. Kilbride and J. C. Kilbride. University Park: Pennsylvania State University Press.

Kimbel, William H., T. D. White, and D. C. Johansen. 1984. Cranial morphology of *Australopithecus afarensis*: A comparative study based on composite reconstruction of the adult skull. *American Journal of Physical Anthropology* 64:337–88.

King, Barbara J. 1999a. Introduction. In *The origins of language*, ed. B. J. King. Santa Fe, NM: School of American Research Press.

King, Barbara J. 1999b. *The origins of language: What nonhuman primates can tell us.* Santa Fe: School of American Research Press.

King, J. C. H. 1986. Tradition in Native American art. In *The arts of the North American Indian*, ed. E. L. Wade. New York: Hudson Hills Press.

King, Marie-Claire, and Arno Motulsky. 2002. Mapping human history. *Science* 298 (December 20):2, 342–43.

King, Seth S. 1979. Some farm machinery seems less than human. *New York Times*, April 8, p. E9.

Kingston, John D., Bruno D. Marino, and Andrew Hill. 1994. Isotopic evidence for Neogene hominid paleoenvironments in the Kenya Rift Valley. *Science* 264 (May 13):955–59.

Kitchen, Andrew, Michael Miyamoto, and Connie Mulligan. 2008. A three-stage colonization model for the peopling of the Americas. *PLoS ONE* 3, no. 2:e1596.

Klass, Morton. 2009. Is there "caste" outside of India? In MyAnthroLibrary, eds. C. R. Ember, M. Ember, and P. N. Peregrine. MyAnthroLibrary.com. Pearson.

Klein, Richard G. 1974. Ice-age hunters of the Ukraine. *Scientific American* (June):96–105.

Klein, Richard G. 1977. The ecology of early man in Southern Africa. *Science* 197 (July 8):115–26.

Klein, Richard G. 1983. The Stone Age prehistory of Southern Africa. *Annual Review of Anthropology* 12:25–48.

Klein, Richard G. 1987. Reconstructing how early people exploited animals: Problems and prospects. In *The evolution of human hunting*, eds. M. Nitecki and D. Nitecki. New York: Plenum.

Klein, Richard G. 1989. *The human career: Human biological and cultural origins.* Chicago: University of Chicago Press.

Klein, Richard G. 1994. Southern Africa before the Ice Age. In *Integrative paths to the past*, eds. R. Corruccini and R. Ciochon. Upper Saddle River, NJ: Prentice Hall.

Klein, Richard G. 2003. Whither the Neanderthals? *Science* 299 (March 7):1525–28.

Klein, Richard G. 2009. *The human career: Human biological and cultural origins*, 3rd ed. Chicago: University of Chicago Press.

Klein, Richard G., and Blake Edgar. 2002. *The dawn of human culture.* New York: John Wiley and Sons.

Kleinberg, Jill. 1994. Practical implications of organizational culture where Americans and Japanese work together. In *Practicing anthropology in corporate America*, ed. A. T. Jordan. Arlington, VA: American Anthropological Association.

Kleinman, Arthur. 1988. *Rethinking psychiatry: From cultural category to personal experience.* New York: Macmillan.

Kleinman, Arthur. 2004. Culture and depression. *New England Journal of Medicine* 351:951–2.

Kleinman, Arthur, Veena Das, and Margaret Lock, eds. 1997. *Social suffering.* Berkeley: University of California Press.

Klima, Bohuslav. 1962. The first ground-plan of an Upper Paleolithic loess settlement in Middle Europe and its meaning. In *Courses toward urban life*, eds. R. Braidwood and G. Willey. Chicago: Aldine.

Klineberg, Otto. 1935. *Negro intelligence and selective migration.* New York: Columbia University Press.

Klineberg, Otto, ed. 1944. *Characteristics of the American Negro.* New York: Harper & Brothers.

Klineberg, Otto. 1979. Foreword. In *Cross-cultural psychology*, ed. M. H. Segall. Monterey, CA: Brooks/Cole.

Kluckhohn, Clyde. 1948. As an anthropologist views it. In *Sex habits of American men*, ed. A. Deutsch. Upper Saddle River, NJ: Prentice Hall.

Kluckhohn, Clyde. 1965. Recurrent themes in myths and mythmaking. In *The study of folklore*, ed. A. Dundes. Upper Saddle River, NJ: Prentice Hall.

Knauft, Bruce M. 1978. Cargo cults and relational separation. *Behavior Science Research* 13:185–240.

Knecht, Peter. 2003. Aspects of shamanism: An introduction. In *Shamans in Asia*, eds. C. Chilson and P. Knecht. London: Routledge Curzon.

Knight, Chris and Camilla Power. 2006. Words are not costly displays: Shortcomings of a testosterone-fuelled model of language evolution. *Behavioral and Brain Sciences* 29:290–291.

Koch, Klaus-Friedrich, Soraya Altorki, Andrew Arno, and Letitia Hickson. 1977. Ritual reconciliation and the obviation of grievances: A comparative study in the ethnography of law. *Ethnology* 16:269–84.

Kolbert, Elizabeth. 2005. Last words. *The New Yorker*, June 6, 46–59.

Komar, Debra A., and Jane E. Buikstra. 2008. *Forensic anthropology: Contemporary theory and practice.* New York: Oxford University Press.

Konner, Melvin. 2010. *The evolution of childhood: Relationships, emotion, mind.* Cambridge, MA: Belknap Press.

Konner, Melvin, and Carol Worthman. 1980. Nursing frequency, gonadal function, and birth spacing among !Kung hunter-gatherers. *Science* 267 (February 15):788–91.

Kopytoff, Igor. 1996. Slavery. In *Encyclopedia of cultural anthropology*, vol. 4, eds. D. Levinson and M. Ember. New York: Henry Holt.

Korbin, Jill E. 1981. Introduction. In *Child abuse and neglect*, ed. J. E. Korbin. Berkeley: University of California Press.

Korotayev, Andrey. 2008. Trade and warfare in cross-cultural perspective. *Social Evolution and History* 7:40–55.

Korotayev, Andrey, and Dmitri Bondarenko. 2000. Polygyny and democracy: A cross-cultural comparison. *Cross-Cultural Research* 34:190–208.

Kottak, Conrad Phillip. 1996. The media, development, and social change. In *Transforming societies, transforming anthropology*, ed. E. F. Moran. Ann Arbor: University of Michigan Press.

Kottak, Conrad Phillip. 1999. The new ecological anthropology. *Current Anthropology* 101:23–35.

Kracke, Waud H. 1979. *Force and persuasion: Leadership in an Amazonian society.* Chicago: University of Chicago Press.

Krahn, H., T. F. Hartnagel, and J. W. Gartrell. 1986. Income inequality and homicide rates: Cross-national data and criminological theories. *Criminology* 24:269–95.

Kramer, Andrew. 2009. The natural history and evolutionary fate of *Homo erectus.* In MyAnthroLibrary, eds. C. R. Ember, M. Ember, and P. N. Peregrine. MyAnthroLibrary.com. Pearson.

Kramer, Samuel Noel. 1963. *The Sumerians: Their history, culture, and character.* Chicago: University of Chicago Press.

Krause, Johannes, et al. 2007. The derived FOXP2 variant of modern humans was shared with Neandertals. *Current Biology* 17, no.21:1908–12.

Krause, Johannes, et al. 2010. The complete mitochondrial DNA genome of an unknown hominin from southern Siberia. *Nature* 464 (April 8):894–97.

Krebs, J. R., and N. B. Davies, eds. 1984. *Behavioural ecology: An evolutionary approach.* 2nd ed. Sunderland, MA: Sinauer.

Krebs, J. R., and N. B. Davies. 1987. *An introduction to behavioural ecology.* 2nd ed. Sunderland, MA: Sinauer.

Kremer-Sadlik, Tamar, Marilena Fatigante, and Alessandra Fasulo. 2008. Discourses on family time: The cultural interpretation of family togetherness in Los Angeles and Rome. *Ethos* 36:283–309.

Krings, Matthias, A. Stone, R. W. Schmitz, H. Krainitzki, M. Stoneking, and S. Paabo. 1997. Neandertal DNA sequences and the origin of modern humans. *Cell* 90:19–30.

Krippner, Stanley. 1987. Dreams and shamanism. In *Shamanism*, comp. S. Nicholson, 125–32. Wheaton, IL: Theosophical Publishing House.

Krippner, Stanley. 2000. The epistemology and technologies of shamanic states of consciousness. *Journal of Consciousness Studies* 7:11–12.

Kristof, Nicholas D. 1995. Japan's invisible minority: Better off than in past, but still outcasts. *New York Times*, International, November 30, p. A18.

Kristof, Nicholas D. 1997. Japan's invisible minority: Burakumin. *Britannica Online*, December.

Kroeber, Theodora. 1967. *Ishi in two worlds.* Berkeley: University of California Press.

Kuehn, Steven. 1998. New evidence for Late Paleoindian—Early Archaic subsistence behavior in the western Great Lakes. *American Antiquity* 63:457–76.

Kulick, Don. 1992. *Language shift and cultural reproduction.* Cambridge: Cambridge University Press.

Kushner, Gilbert. 1991. Applied anthropology. In *Career explorations in human services*, eds. W. G. Emener and M. Darrow. Springfield, IL: Charles C Thomas.

Lacruz, Rodrigo S., Fernando Ramirez Rozzi, and Timothy G. Bromage. 2005. Dental enamel hypoplasia, age at death, and weaning in the Taung child. *South African Journal of Science* 101:567–69.

Lacruz, Rodrigo S., Fernando Ramirez Rozzi, and Timothy G. Bromage. 2006. Variation in enamel development of South African fossil hominids. *Journal of Human Evolution* 51, no. 6:580–90.

Lakoff, Robin. 1973. Language and woman's place. *Language in Society* 2:45–80.

Lakoff, Robin. 1990. Why can't a woman be less like a man? In *Talking power*, ed. R. Lakoff. New York: Basic Books.

Lalueza-Fox, Carles, et al. 2007. A melanocortin 1 receptor allele suggests varying pigmentation among Neanderthals. *Science* 318 (November 30):1453–55.

Lambert, Helen. 2001. Not talking about sex in India: Indirection and the communication of bodily intention. In *An anthropology of indirect communication*, eds. J. Hendry and C. W. Watson. London: Routledge.

Lambert, Patricia M., Banks L. Leonard, Brian R. Billman, Richard A. Marlar, Margaret E. Newman, and Karl J. Reinhard. 2000. Response to critique of the claim of cannibalism at Cowboy Wash. *American Antiquity* 65, no.2:397–406.

Lambert, William W., Leigh Minturn Triandis, and Margery Wolf. 1959. Some correlates of beliefs in the malevolence and benevolence of supernatural beings: A cross-societal study. *Journal of Abnormal and Social Psychology* 58:162–69.

Lamphere, Louise. 2006. Foreward: Taking stock—The transformation of feminist theorizing in anthropology. In *Feminist anthropology: Past, present, and future*, eds. P. L. Geller and M. K. Stockett, ix–xvi. Philadelphia: University of Pennsylvania Press.

Lancy, David F. 2007. Accounting for variability in mother-child play. *American Anthropologist* 109:273–84.

Lancy, David F. 2008. *The anthropology of childhood: Cherubs, chattel, changelings.* Cambridge: Cambridge University Press.

Landauer, Thomas K. 1973. Infantile vaccination and the secular trend in stature. *Ethos* 1:499–503.

Landauer, Thomas K., and John W. M. Whiting. 1964. Infantile stimulation and adult stature of human males. *American Anthropologist* 66:1007–28.

Landauer, Thomas K., and John W. M. Whiting. 1981. Correlates and consequences of stress in infancy. In *Handbook of cross-cultural human development*, eds. R. H. Munroe, R. Munroe, and B. Whiting. New York: Garland.

Landecker, Hannah. 2000. Immortality, in vitro: A history of the HeLa cell line. In *Biotechnology and culture: Bodies, anxieties, ethics*, ed. P. Brodwin. Bloomington: Indiana University Press.

Lang, Sabine. 1999. Lesbians, men-women and two-spirits: Homosexuality and gender in Native American cultures. In *Female desires: Same-sex relations and transgender practices across cultures*, eds. E. Blackwood and S. E. Weiringa. New York: Columbia University Press.

Langdon, John. 2005. *The human strategy.* New York: Oxford University Press.

Langness, Lewis L. 1974. *The study of culture.* San Francisco: Chandler and Sharp.

Lareau, Annette. 2003. *Unequal childhoods: Class, race, and family life.* Berkeley, CA: University of California Press.

Larsen, Clark Spencer. 1997. *Bioarchaeology: Interpreting behavior from the human skeleton.* Cambridge: Cambridge University Press.

Larsen, Clark Spencer. 2009. Bare bones anthropology: The bioarchaeology of human remains. In MyAnthroLibrary, eds. C. R. Ember, M. Ember, and P. N. Peregrine. MyAnthroLibrary.com. Pearson.

Larson, Christine L., J. Aronoff, I. C. Sarinopoulos, and D. C. Zhu. 2009. Recognizing threat: A simple geometric shape activates neural circuitry for threat detection. *Journal of Cognitive Neuroscience* 21:1523–35.

Larson, Christine L., J. Aronoff, and J. Stearns. 2007. The shape of threat: Simple geometric forms evoke rapid and sustained capture of attention. *Emotion* 7:526–34.

Larson, Christine L., Joel Aronoff, Issidoros C. Sarinopoulos, and David C. Zhu. 2009. Recognizing threat: A simple geometric shape activates neural circuitry for threat detection. *Journal of Cognitive Neuroscience* 21:1523–35.

Lassiter, Luke Eric. 2008. Moving past public anthropology and doing collaborative research. *NAPA Bulletin* 29:70–86.

Lassiter, Luke Eric, Hurley Goodall, Elizabeth Campbell, and Michelle Natasya Johnson, eds. 2004. *The other side of Middletown: Exploring Muncie's African American community.* Walnut Creek, CA: AltaMira Press.

Lawless, Robert, Vinson H. Sutlive, Jr., and Mario D. Zamora, eds. 1983. *Fieldwork: The human experience.* New York: Gordon and Breach.

Lawrence, Felicity. 2011. Kenya's flower industry shows budding improvement. *The Guardian*, April 1.

Layton, Robert. 1992. *Australian rock art: A new synthesis.* Cambridge: Cambridge University Press.

Le, Huynh-Nhu. 2000. Never leave your little one alone: Raising an Ifaluk child. In *A world of babies: Imagined child care guides for seven societies*, eds. J. DeLoache and A. Gottlieb. Cambridge: Cambridge University Press.

Leach, Jerry W. 1983. Introduction. In *The Kula*, eds. J. W. Leach and E. Leach. Cambridge: Cambridge University Press.

Leacock, Eleanor. 1954. The Montagnais 'hunting territory' and the fur trade. *American Anthropological Association Memoir* 78:1–59.

Leacock, Eleanor, and Richard Lee. 1982. Introduction. In *Politics and history in band societies*, eds. E. Leacock and R. Lee. Cambridge: Cambridge University Press.

Leakey, Louis S. B. 1960. Finding the world's earliest man. *National Geographic* (September): 420–35.

Leakey, Louis S. B. 1965. *Olduvai Gorge, 1951–1961, Vol. I: A preliminary report on the geology and fauna.* Cambridge: Cambridge University Press.

Leakey, Maeve, C. S. Feibel, I. McDougall, and A. Walker. 1995. New four-million-year-old hominid species from Kanapoi and Allia Bay, Kenya. *Nature* 376 (August 17): 565–71.

Leakey, Maeve, et al. 2001. New hominin genus from eastern Africa shows diverse Middle Pliocene lineages. *Nature* 410 (March 22):433–51.

Leakey, Mary. 1971. *Olduvai Gorge: Excavations in Beds I and II.* Cambridge: Cambridge University Press.

Leakey, Mary. 1979. *Olduvai Gorge: My search for early man.* London: Collins.

Lederman, Rena. 1990. Big men, large and small? Towards a comparative perspective. *Ethnology* 29:3–15.

Lee, Kristen Schultz. 2010. Gender, care work, and the complexity of family membership in Japan. *Gender & Society* 24, no. 5:647–71.

Lee, Phyllis C. 1983. Home range, territory and intergroup encounters. In *Primate social relationship: An integrated approach*, ed. R. A. Hinde. Sunderland, MA: Sinauer.

Lee, Richard B. 1968. What hunters do for a living, or, how to make out on scarce resources. In *Man the hunter*, eds. R. B. Lee and I. DeVore. Chicago: Aldine.

Lee, Richard B. 1972. Population growth and the beginnings of sedentary life among the !Kung bushmen. In *Population growth*, ed. B. Spooner. Cambridge, MA: MIT Press.

Lee, Richard B. 1979. *The !Kung San: Men, women, and work in a foraging society.* Cambridge: Cambridge University Press.

Lees, Susan H., and Daniel G. Bates. 1974. The origins of specialized nomadic pastoralism: A systemic model. *American Antiquity* 39:187–93.

Leibowitz, Lila. 1978. *Females, males, families: A biosocial approach.* North Scituate, MA: Duxbury.

Leis, Nancy B. 1974. Women in groups: Ijaw women's associations. In *Woman, culture, and society*, eds. M. Z. Rosaldo and L. Lamphere. Stanford, CA: Stanford University Press.

Lenski, Gerhard. 1984/1966. *Power and privilege: A theory of social stratification.* Chapel Hill: University of North Carolina Press.

Leonard, William R. 2002. Food for thought: Dietary change was a driving force in human evolution. *Scientific American* (December):108–15.

Leonard, William R., and Peter T. Katzmarzyk. 2010. Body size and shape: Climatic and nutritional influences on human body morphology. In *Human evolutionary biology*, ed. M. Muehlenbein. Cambridge: Cambridge University Press.

Leonhardt, David, and Geraldine Fabrikant. 2009. Rise of the super-rich hits a sobering wall. *New York Times*, New York, August 20, p. A1.

Lepowsky, Maria. 1990. Big men, big women and cultural autonomy. *Ethnology* 29:35–50.

Leslie, C. 1976. Introduction. In *Asian medical systems: A comparative study*, ed. C. Leslie. Los Angeles: University of California Press.

Lev-Yadun, Simcha, Avi Gopher, and Shahal Abbo, 2000. The cradle of agriculture. *Science* 288 (June 2):1602–1603.

Levine, James A., Robert Weisell, Simon Chevassus, Claudio D. Martinez, and Barbara Burlingame. 2002. The distribution of work tasks for male and female children and adults separated by gender. *Science* 296 (May 10):1025.

Levine, Nancy E. 1988. Women's work and infant feeding: A case from rural Nepal. *Ethnology* 27:231–51.

LeVine, Robert A. 1966. *Dreams and deeds: Achievement motivation in Nigeria.* Chicago: University of Chicago Press.

LeVine, Robert A. 1988. Human parental care: Universal goals, cultural strategies, individual behavior. In *Parental behavior in diverse societies*, eds. R. A. LeVine, P. M. Miller, and M. M. West. San Francisco: Jossey-Bass.

LeVine, Robert A. 2007. Ethnographic studies of childhood: A historical overview. *American Anthropologist* 109:247–60.

LeVine, Robert A. 2011. Traditions in transition: Adolescents remaking culture. *Ethos* 39:426–31.

LeVine, Robert A., and Barbara B. LeVine. 1963. Nyansongo: A Gusii Community in Kenya. In *Six cultures*, ed. B. B. Whiting. New York: Wiley.

LeVine, Robert A., and Karin Norman. 2001. The infant's acquisition of culture: Early attachment reexamined in anthropological perspective. In *The psychology of cultural experience*, eds. H. F. Mathews and C. C. Moore. Cambridge: Cambridge University Press.

Levinson, David. 1989. *Family violence in cross-cultural perspective.* Newbury Park, CA: Sage.

Levinson, David, and Melvin Ember, eds. 1997. *American immigrant cultures: Builders of a nation*, 2 vols. New York: Macmillan Reference.

Lévi-Strauss, Claude. 1963a. The sorcerer and his magic. In *Structural anthropology*, ed. C. Lévi-Strauss. New York: Basic Books.

Lévi-Strauss, Claude. 1963b. *Structural anthropology.* Trans. Claire Jacobson and Brooke Grundfest Schoepf. New York: Basic Books.

Lévi-Strauss, Claude. 1966. *The savage mind.* Trans. George Weidenfeld and Nicolson, Ltd. Chicago: University of Chicago Press.

Lévi-Strauss, Claude. 1969a. *The elementary structures of kinship*, rev. ed. Trans. James H. Bell and J. R. Von Sturmer. Boston: Beacon Press.

Lévi-Strauss, Claude. 1969b. *The raw and the cooked.* Trans. John Weightman and Doreen Weightman. New York: Harper & Row.

Levy, Jerrold E. 1994. Hopi shamanism: A reappraisal. In *North American Indian anthropology: Essays on society and culture*, eds. R. J. DeMallie and A. Ortiz. Norman: University of Oklahoma Press.

Lewellen, Ted C. 2003. *Political anthropology: An introduction.* 3rd ed. Westport, CT: Praeger.

Lewin, Roger. 1983a. Fossil Lucy grows younger, again. *Science* 219 (January 7):43–44.

Lewin, Roger. 1983b. Is the orangutan a living fossil? *Science* 222 (December 16):1222–23.

Lewin, Tamar. 1994. Sex in America: Faithfulness in marriage is overwhelming. *New York Times*, National, October 7, pp. A1, A18.

Lewis, Oscar. 1951. *Life in a Mexican village: Tepoztlan revisited.* Urbana: University of Illinois Press.

Lewis, Oscar (with the assistance of Victor Barnouw). 1958. *Village life in Northern India.* Urbana: University of Illinois Press.

Lewontin, Richard. 1972. The apportionment of human diversity. *Evolutionary Biology* 6, no. 1:381–98.

Lichter, Daniel T., Diane K. McLaughlin, George Kephart, and David J. Landry. 1992. Race and the retreat from marriage: A shortage of marriageable men? *American Sociological Review* 57:781–99.

Lieberman, Daniel E. 1995. Testing hypotheses about recent human evolution from skulls: integrating morphology, function, development, and phylogeny. *Current Anthropology* 36:159–97.

Lieberman, Leonard. 1999. Scientific insignificance. *Anthropology Newsletter* 40:11–12.

Lieberman, Leonard, Rodney Kirk, and Alice Littlefield. 2003. Perishing paradigm: Race 1931–99. *American Anthropologist* 105:110–13.

Lieberman, Leslie Sue. 2004. Diabetes mellitus and medical anthropology. In *Encyclopedia of medical anthropology: Health and illness in the world's cultures*, vol. I, eds. C. R. Ember and M. Ember. New York: Kluwer Academic Press/Plenum Publishers.

Light, Ivan, and Zhong Deng. 1995/1964. Gender differences in ROSCA participation within Korean business households in Los Angeles. In *Money-go-rounds: The importance of rotating savings and credit associations for women*, eds. S. Ardener and S. Burman. Oxford: Berg.

Lightfoot, Kent G. 2005. The archaeology of colonialism: California in cross-cultural perspective. In *The archaeology of colonial encounters: Comparative perspectives*, ed. G. J. Stein. Santa Fe, NM: School of American Research.

Lingenfelter, Sherwood G. 2009. Yap: Changing roles of men and women. In MyAnthroLibrary, eds. C. R. Ember, M. Ember, and P. N. Peregrine. MyAnthroLibrary.com. Pearson.

Linton, Ralph. 1936. *The study of man.* New York: Appleton-Century-Crofts.

Linton, Ralph. 1945. *The cultural background of personality.* New York: Appleton-Century-Crofts.

Little, A. C., Robert P. Burriss, Benedict C. Jones, and S. Craig Roberts. 2007. Facial appearance affects voting decisions. *Evolution and Human Behavior* 28: 18–27.

Little, Kenneth. 1957. The role of voluntary associations in West African urbanization. *American Anthropologist* 59:582–93.

Little, Kenneth. 1965. *West African urbanization.* New York: Cambridge University Press.

Little, Kenneth. 1965/1966. The political function of the *Poro. Africa* 35:349–65; 36: 62–71.

Lock, Margaret. 2009. Japan: Glimpses of everyday life. In MyAnthroLibrary, eds. C. R. Ember, M. Ember, and P. N. Peregrine. MyAnthroLibrary.com. Pearson.

Lockett, Hattie Green. 1933. *The unwritten literature of the Hopi.* Social Science Bulletin No. 2, 6, 9–12. Tucson, Arizona: University of Arizona Press.

Loftin, Colin K. 1971. Warfare and societal complexity: A cross-cultural study of organized fighting in preindustrial societies. PhD dissertation, University of North Carolina at Chapel Hill.

Loftin, Colin K., David McDowall, and James Boudouris. 1989. Economic change and homicide in Detroit, 1926-1979. In *Violence in America, Vol. 1: The history of crime*, ed. T. R. Gurr. Newbury Park, CA: Sage.

Lomax, Alan, ed. 1968. *Folk song style and culture.* American Association for the Advancement of Science Publication No. 88. Washington, DC.

Long, Susan Orpett. 2000. Introduction. In *Caring for the elderly in Japan and the U.S.*, ed. S. Orpett Long. London: Routledge.

Long, Susan Orpett, Ruth Campbell, and Chie Nishimura. 2009. Does it matter who cares? A comparison of daughters versus daughters-in-law in Japanese elder care. *Social Science Japan Journal* 12, no. 1:1–21.

Longacre, William. 1970. *Archaeology as anthropology: A case study.* Anthropological papers of the University of Arizona, Number 17. Tucson: University of Arizona Press.

Loomis, W. Farnsworth. 1967. Skin-pigment regulation of vitamin-D biosynthesis in man. *Science* 157 (August 4):501–506.

Los Angeles Times. 1994. Plundering earth is nothing new. Reported in the *New Haven Register*, June 12, pp. A18–A19.

Loustaunau, Martha O., and Elisa J. Sobo. 1997. *The cultural context of health, illness, and medicine.* Westport, CT: Bergin & Garvey.

Lovejoy, Arthur O. 1964. *The great chain of being: A study of the history of an idea.* Cambridge, MA: Harvard University Press.

Lovejoy, C. Owen. 1981. The origin of man. *Science* 211 (January 23):341–50.

Lovejoy, C. Owen. 1988. Evolution of human walking. *Scientific American* (November):118–25.

Lovejoy, C. Owen. 2009. Reexamining human origins in light of *Ardipithecus ramidus. Science* 326 (October 2):74, 74e1–74e8.

Low, Bobbi. 1990a. Human responses to environmental extremeness and uncertainty. In *Risk and uncertainty in tribal and peasant economies*, ed. E. Cashdan. Boulder, CO: Westview.

Low, Bobbi. 1990b. Marriage systems and pathogen stress in human societies. *American Zoologist* 30:325–39.

Low, Bobbi S. 2009. Behavioral ecology, "sociobiology," and human behavior. In MyAnthroLibrary, eds. C. R. Ember, M. Ember, and P. N. Peregrine. MyAnthroLibrary.com. Pearson.

Lowe, Edward D. 2002. A widow, a child, and two lineages: Exploring kinship and attachment in Chuuk. *American Anthropologist* 104:123–37.

Lucy, John A. 1992. *Grammatical categories and cognition: A case study of the linguistic relativity hypothesis.* Cambridge: Cambridge University Press.

Lumbreras, Luis. 1974. *The peoples and cultures of ancient Peru.* Washington, DC: Smithsonian Institution Press.

Luria, A. R. 1976. *Cognitive development: Its cultural and social foundations.* Cambridge, MA: Harvard University Press.

Lutz, Catherine. 1985. Depression and the translations of emotional worlds. In *Culture and depression*, eds. A. Kleinman and B. Good. Berkeley: University of California Press.

Lynd, Robert S., and Helen Merrell Lynd. 1929. *Middletown.* New York: Harcourt, Brace.

Lynd, Robert S., and Helen Merrell Lynd. 1937. *Middletown in transition.* New York: Harcourt, Brace.

Lyons, Nona Plessner. 1988. Two perspectives: On self, relationships, and morality. In *Mapping the moral domain*, eds. C. Gilligan, J. V. Ward, and J. M. Taylor. Cambridge, MA: Harvard University Press.

Lyttleton, Chris. 2000. *Endangered relations: Negotiating sex and AIDS in Thailand.* Bangkok: White Lotus Press.

MacArthur, R. H., and E. O. Wilson. 1967. *Theory of island biogeography.* Princeton, NJ: Princeton University Press.

Maccoby, Eleanor E., and Carol N. Jacklin. 1974. *The psychology of sex differences.* Stanford, CA: Stanford University Press.

Macdonald, Douglas H., and Barry S. Hewlett. 1999. Reproductive interests and forager mobility. *Current Anthropology* 40:501–23.

MacDorman, Marian F., and T. J. Mathews. 2011. *Understanding racial and ethnic disparities in U.S. infant mortality rates.* NCHS Data Brief. No. 74. Hyattsville, MD: National Center for Health Statistics.

MacKinnon, John, and Kathy MacKinnon. 1980. The behavior of wild spectral tarsiers. *International Journal of Primatology* 1:361–79.

MacNeish, Richard S. 1991. *The origins of agriculture and settled life.* Norman: University of Oklahoma Press.

Madrigal, Lorena. 1989. Hemoglobin genotype, fertility, and the malaria hypothesis. *Human Biology* 61:311–25.

Magner, L. 1992. *A history of medicine.* New York: Marcel Dekker.

Mahony, Frank Joseph. 1971. *A Trukese theory of medicine*. Ann Arbor, MI: University Microfilms.

Malefijt, Annemarie De Waal. 1968. *Religion and culture: An introduction to anthropology of religion*. New York: Macmillan.

Malin, Edward. 1986. *Totem poles of the Pacific Northwest Coast*. Portland, OR: Timber Press.

Malinowski, Bronislaw. 1920. Kula: The circulating exchange of valuables in the archipelagoes of eastern New Guinea. *Man* 51, no. 2:97–105.

Malinowski, Bronislaw. 1927. *Sex and repression in savage society*. London: Kegan Paul, Trench, Trubner.

Malinowski, Bronislaw. 1932. *The sexual life of savages in northwestern Melanesia*. New York: Halcyon House.

Malinowski, Bronislaw. 1939. The group and the individual in functional analysis. *American Journal of Sociology* 44:938–64.

Malinowski, Bronislaw. 1954. Magic, science, and religion. In *Magic, science, and religion and other essays*, ed. B. Malinowski. Garden City, NY: Doubleday.

Mangin, William P. 1965. The role of regional associations in the adaptation of rural migrants to cities in Peru. In *Contemporary cultures and societies of Latin America*, eds. D. B. Heath and R. N. Adams. New York: Random House.

Mangin, William P. 1967. Latin American squatter settlements: A problem and a solution. *Latin American Research Review* 2:65–98.

Manhein, Mary H. 1999. *The bone lady: Life as a forensic anthropologist*. Baton Rouge: Louisiana State University Press.

Mansfield, Edward D., and Jack Snyder. 2007. *Electing to fight: Why emerging democracies go to war*. Cambridge, MA: MIT Press.

Maquet, Jacques. 1986. *The aesthetic experience: An anthropologist looks at the visual arts*. New Haven, CT: Yale University Press.

Marano, Louis A. 1973. A macrohistoric trend toward world government. *Behavior Science Notes* 8:35–40.

Marcus, George E., and Michael M. J. Fischer. 1986. *Anthropology as cultural critique: An experimental moment in the human sciences*. Chicago: University of Chicago Press.

Marcus, Joyce. 1983. On the nature of the Mesoamerican city. In *Prehistoric settlement patterns*, eds. E. Vogt and R. Leventhal. Albuquerque: University of New Mexico Press.

Marcus, Joyce. 2009. Maya hieroglyphs: History or propaganda? In MyAnthroLibrary, eds. C. R. Ember, M. Ember, and P. N. Peregrine. MyAnthroLibrary.com. Pearson.

Marcus, Joyce, and Kent V. Flannery. 1996. *Zapotec civilization*. London: Thames and Hudson.

Marett, R. R. 1909. *The thresholds of religion*. London: Methuen.

Marks, Jonathan. 1994. Black, white, other: Racial categories are cultural constructs masquerading as biology. *Natural History* (December):32–35.

Marks, Jonathan. 2002. Genes, bodies, and species. In *Physical anthropology: Original readings in method and practice*, eds. P. N. Peregrine, C. R. Ember, and M. Ember. Upper Saddle River, NJ: Prentice Hall.

Marks, Jonathan. 2008. Race: Past, present, future. In *Revisiting race in a genomic age*, eds. B. A. Koening, S. S. J. Lee, and S. S. Richardson. New Brunswick, NJ: Rutgers University Press.

Marks, Jonathan. 2009. Genes, bodies, and species. In MyAnthroLibrary, eds. C. R. Ember, M. Ember, and P. N. Peregrine. MyAnthroLibrary.com. Pearson.

Marlowe, Frank W. 2003. A critical period for provisioning by Hadza men: Implications for pair bonding. *Evolution and Human Behavior* 24:217–29.

Marshack, Alexander. 1972. *The roots of civilization*. New York: McGraw-Hill.

Marshall, Eliot. 2000. Rival genome sequencers celebrate a milestone together. *Science* 288 (June 30):2294–95.

Marshall, Larry G. 1984. Who killed Cock Robin? An investigation of the extinction controversy. In *Quaternary extinctions*, eds. P. Martin and R. Klein. Tucson: University of Arizona Press.

Marshall, Lorna. 1961. Sharing, talking and giving: Relief of social tensions among !Kung Bushmen. *Africa* 31:239–42.

Martin, M. Kay, and Barbara Voorhies. 1975. *Female of the species*. New York: Columbia University Press.

Martin, Paul S. 1973. The discovery of America. *Science* 179 (March 9):969–74.

Martin, Paul S., and H. E. Wright, eds. 1967. *Pleistocene extinctions: The search for a cause*. New Haven, CT: Yale University Press.

Martin, Robert D. 1975. Strategies of reproduction. *Natural History* (November):48–57.

Martin, Robert D. 1990. *Primate origins and evolution: A phylogenetic reconstruction*. Princeton, NJ: Princeton University Press.

Martin, Robert D. 1992. Classification and evolutionary relationships. In *The Cambridge encyclopedia of human evolution*, eds. S. Jones, R. Martin, and D. Pilbeam. New York: Cambridge University Press.

Martin, Robert D., and K. Bearder Simon. 1979. Radio bush baby. *Natural History* (October):77–81.

Martorell, Reynaldo. 1980. Interrelationships between diet, infectious disease and nutritional status. In *Social and biological predictors of nutritional status, physical growth and neurological development*, eds. L. Greene and F. Johnston. New York: Academic Press.

Martorell, Reynaldo, Juan Rivera, Haley Kaplowitz, and Ernesto Pollitt. 1991. Long-term consequences of growth retardation during early childhood. Paper presented at the Sixth International Congress of Auxology, Madrid, September 15–19.

Marx, David M., Sei Jin Ki, and Ray A. Friedman. 2009. The "Obama effect": How a salient role model reduces race-based performance differences. *Journal of Experimental Social Psychology* 45:953–56.

Mascie-Taylor, C. G. Nicholas. 1990. The biology of social class. In *Biosocial aspects of social class*, ed. C. G. N. Mascie-Taylor. Oxford: Oxford University Press.

Maslow, Abraham H. 1964. *Religions, values, and peak-experiences*. Columbus: Ohio State University Press.

Mason, Philip. 1962. *Prospero's magic*. London: Oxford University Press.

Masumura, Wilfred T. 1977. Law and violence: A cross-cultural study. *Journal of Anthropological Research* 33:388–99.

Mathiassen, Therkel. 1928. *Material culture of Iglulik Ekimos*. Copenhagen: Glydendalske.

Matossian, Mary K. 1982. Ergot and the Salem witchcraft affair. *American Scientist* 70:355–57.

Matossian, Mary K. 1989. *Poisons of the past: Molds, epidemics, and history*. New Haven, CT: Yale University Press.

Matt, Siegel. 2011. Australia says it will open combat roles to women. *New York Times*, September 27.

Matthews, Roger. 2009. Peoples and complex societies of Southwest Asia. In *The human past*, ed. C. Scarre. New York: Thames and Hudson.

Mattingly, Cheryl, Nancy C. Lukehaus, and C. Jason Throop. 2008. Bruner's search for meaning: A conversation between psychology and anthropology. *Ethos* 36:1–28.

Maybury-Lewis, David. 1967. *Akwe-Shavante society*. Oxford: Clarendon Press.

Mayer, Philip, and Iona Mayer. 1970. Socialization by peers: The youth organization of the Red Xhosa. In *Socialization: The approach from social anthropology*, ed. P. Mayer. London: Tavistock.

Mayr, Ernst. 1982. *The growth of biological thought: Diversity, evolution, and inheritance*. Cambridge, MA: Belknap Press of Harvard University Press.

Mazess, Richard B. 1975. Human adaptation to high altitude. In *Physiological anthropology*, ed. A. Damon. New York: Oxford University Press.

McCain, Garvin, and Erwin M. Segal. 1988. *The game of science*. 5th ed. Monterey, CA: Brooks/Cole.

McCall, Patricia L., Karen F. Parker, and John M. MacDonald. 2008. The dynamic relationship between homicide rates and social, economic, and political factors from 1970 to 2000. *Social Science Research* 37:721–35.

McCarthy, Frederick D., and Margaret McArthur. 1960. The food quest and the time factor in Aboriginal economic life. In *Records of the Australian-American scientific expedition to Arnhem Land, Vol. 2: Anthropology and nutrition*, ed. C. P. Mountford. Melbourne: Melbourne University Press.

McCaskey, J. P. 1881. *Franklin Square song collection*. Vol. 1. New York Harper& Brothers.

McClelland, David C. 1961. *The achieving society*. New York: Van Nostrand.

McCorriston, Joy, and Frank Hole. 1991. The ecology of seasonal stress and the origins of agriculture in the Near East. *American Anthropologist* 93:46–69.

McCracken, Robert D. 1971. Lactase deficiency: An example of dietary evolution. *Current Anthropology* 12:479–500.

McDermott, LeRoy. 1996. Self-representation in female figurines. *Current Anthropology* 37:227–75.

McDonald, Kim A. 1998. New evidence challenges traditional model of how the New World was settled. *Chronicle of Higher Education*, March 13, p. A22.

McElrath, Dale and Thomas Emerson. 2012. Reenvisioning Eastern Woodlands archaic origins. In *Oxford handbook of North American archaeology*, ed. T. Pauketat. Oxford: Oxford University Press.

McElreath, Richard, and Pontus Strimling. 2008. When natural selection favors imitation of parents. *Current Anthropology* 49:307–16.

McElroy, Ann, and Patricia Townsend. 2002. *Medical anthropology in ecological perspective*. 3rd ed. Boulder, CO: Westview.

McGuire, Thomas R. 2005. The domain of the environment. In *Applied anthropology: Domains of application*, eds. S. Kedia and J. van Willigen. Westport, CT: Praeger.

McHenry, Henry M. 1982. The pattern of human evolution: Studies on bipedalism, mastication, and encephalization. *Annual Review of Anthropology* 11:151–73.

McHenry, Henry M. 1988. New estimates of body weight in early hominids and their significance to encephalization and megadontia in "robust" australopithecines. In *Evolutionary history of the "robust" australopithecines*, ed. F. E. Grine. New York: Aldine.

McHenry, Henry M. 2009."Robust" australopithecines, our family tree, and homoplasy. In MyAnthroLibrary, eds. C. R. Ember, M. Ember, and P. N. Peregrine. MyAnthroLibrary.com. Pearson.

McKee, Lauris. 1984. Sex differentials in survivorship and the customary treatment of infants and children. *Medical Anthropology* 8:91–108.

McKee, Lauris. 2009. Andean Mestizos: Growing up female and male. In *MyAnthroLibrary*, eds. C. R. Ember, M. Ember, and P. N. Peregrine. MyAnthroLibrary.com. Pearson

McKeown, Adam. 2005. Chinese diaspora. In *Encyclopedia of diasporas: Immigrant and refugee cultures around the world*, vol. 1, eds. M. Ember, C. R. Ember, and I. Skoggard. New York: Kluwer Academic/ Plenum.

McMullin, Ernan. 2001. Plantinga's defense of special creation. In *Intelligent design creationism and its critics*, ed. R. Pennock. Boston: MIT Press.

McNamee, Stephen, and Robert K. Miller. 2009. *The meritocracy myth*. 2nd ed. Lanham: Roman & Littlefield.

McNeil, Donald G., Jr. 2011. AIDS: A price break for antiretroviral drugs in 70 of the world's poorest countries. *New York Times*, May 23. http://www.nytimes.com/2011/05/24/health/24global.html (accessed May 19, 2013).

McNeill, William H. 1967. *A world history*. New York: Oxford University Press.

McNeill, William H. 1976. *Plagues and peoples*. Garden City, NY: Doubleday/Anchor.

McNeill, William H. 1998. *Plagues and peoples*. New York: Anchor Books/Doubleday.

Mead, Margaret. 1931. *Growing up in New Guinea*. London: Routledge & Kegan Paul.

Mead, Margaret. 1950/1935. *Sex and temperament in three primitive societies*. New York: Mentor.

Mead, Margaret. 1961/1928. *Coming of age in Samoa*. 3rd ed. New York: Morrow.

Meek, C. K. 1940. *Land law and custom in the colonies*. London: Oxford University Press.

Meggitt, Mervyn J. 1964. Male-female relationships in the highlands of Australian New Guinea. *American Anthropologist* 66:204–24.

Meggitt, Mervyn J. 1977. *Blood is their argument: Warfare among the Mae Enga tribesmen of the New Guinea highlands*. Palo Alto, CA: Mayfield.

Mehu, Marc, Karl Grammer, and Robin I. M. Dunbar. 2007. Smiles when sharing. *Evolution and Human Behavior* 28, no. 6:415–22.

Meillassoux, Claude. 1968. *Urbanization of an African community*. Seattle: University of Washington Press.

Mellaart, James. 1961. Roots in the soil. In *The dawn of civilization*, ed. S. Piggott. London: Thomas & Hudson.

Mellaart, James. 1964. A Neolithic city in Turkey. *Scientific American* (April):94–104.

Mellars, Paul. 1994. The Upper Paleolithic revolution. In *The Oxford illustrated prehistory of Europe*, ed. B. Cunliffe. Oxford: Oxford University Press.

Mellars, Paul. 1996. *The Neanderthal legacy*, 405–19. Princeton, NJ: Princeton University Press.

Mellars, Paul. 1998. The fate of the Neaderthals. *Nature* 395 (October 8):539–40.

Mellars, Paul, and J. French. 2011. Tenfold population increase in Western Europe at the Neadertal-to-modern human transition. *Science* 333 (July 29):623–27.

Mellor, John W., and Sarah Gavian. 1987. Famine: Causes, prevention, and relief. *Science* 235 (January 30):539–44.

Meltzer, David J. 1993. Pleistocene peopling of the Americas. *Evolutionary Anthropology* 1, no. 1:157–69.

Meltzer, David J. 2009. *First peoples in a new world: Colonizing Ice Age America.* Berkeley: University of California Press.

Mendoza-Denton, Norma. 2008. *Homegirls: Language and cultural practice among Latina youth gangs.* Oxford: Blackwell Publishing.

Merbs, Charles F. 1992. A new world of infectious disease. *Yearbook of Physical Anthropology* 35:3–42.

Merrill, Elizabeth Bryant. 1987. Art styles as reflections of sociopolitical complexity. *Ethnology* 26:221–30.

Mesoudi, Alex, and Stephen J. Lycett. 2009. Random copying, frequency-dependent copying and culture change. *Evolution and Human Behavior* 30:41–48.

Messer, Ellen. 1996. Hunger vulnerability from an anthropologist's food system perspective. In *Transforming societies, transforming anthropology*, ed. E. F. Moran. Ann Arbor: University of Michigan Press.

Messer, Ellen. 2009. Rising food prices, social mobilizations, and violence: Conceptual issues in understanding and responding to the connections linking hunger and conflict. *NAPA Bulletin* 32:12–22.

Middleton, John. 1971. The cult of the dead: Ancestors and ghosts. In *Reader in comparative religion*, 3rd ed., eds. W. A. Lessa and E. Z. Vogt. New York: Harper & Row.

Middleton, Russell. 1962. Brother-sister and father-daughter marriage in ancient Egypt. *American Sociological Review* 27:603–11.

Milanovic, Branko. 2005. *World's apart: Measuring international and global inequality.* Princeton: Princeton University Press.

Milanovic, Branko. 2011. *The haves and the have-nots: A brief and idiosyncratic history of global inequality.* New York: Basic Books.

Miller, Bruce G. 1992. Women and politics: Comparative evidence from the Northwest Coast. *Ethnology* 31:367–82.

Miller, Greg. 2004. Listen, baby. *Science* 306 (November 12):1127.

Miller, Joan G. 1994. Cultural diversity in the morality of caring: Individually oriented versus duty-based interpersonal moral codes. *Cross-Cultural Research* 28:3–39.

Millon, René. 1967. Teotihuacán. *Scientific American* (June):38–48.

Millon, René. 1976. Social relations in ancient Teotihuacán. In *The Valley of Mexico*, ed. E. Wolf. Albuquerque: University of New Mexico Press.

Milner, George. 1998. *The Cahokia chiefdom: The archaeology of a Mississippian society.* Washington, DC: Smithsonian Institution Press.

Milton, Katharine. 1981. Distribution patterns of tropical plant foods as an evolutionary stimulus to primate mental development. *American Anthropologist* 83:534–48.

Milton, Katharine. 1988. Foraging behaviour and the evolution of primate intelligence. In *Machiavellian intelligence: Social expertise and the evolution of intellect in monkeys, apes, and humans*, eds. R. W. Bryne and A. Whiten. Oxford: Clarendon Press.

Milton, Katharine. 2009. The evolution of a biological anthropologist. In MyAnthroLibrary, eds. C. R. Ember, M. Ember, and P. N. Peregrine. MyAnthroLibrary.com. Pearson.

Miner, Horace. 1956. Body rituals among the Nacirema. *American Anthropologist* 58:504–505.

Minturn, Leigh. 1993. *Sita's daughters: Coming out of Purdah: The Rajput women of Khalapur revisited.* New York: Oxford University Press.

Minturn, Leigh, and Jerry Stashak. 1982. Infanticide as a terminal abortion procedure. *Behavior Science Research* 17:70–85.

Mintz, Sidney W. 1956. Canamelar: The subculture of a rural sugar plantation proletariat. In *The people of Puerto Rico*, eds. J. H. Steward, R. A. Manners, E. R. Wolf, E. Padilla Seda, S. W. Mintz, and R. L. Scheele. Urbana: University of Illinois Press.

Minugh-Purvis, Nancy. 2009. Neandertal growth: Examining developmental adaptations in earlier *Homo sapiens.* In MyAnthroLibrary, eds. C. R. Ember, M. Ember, and P. N. Peregrine. MyAnthroLibrary.com. Pearson.

Miracle, Andrew W. 2009. A shaman to organizations. In MyAnthroLibrary, eds. C. R. Ember, M. Ember, and P. N. Peregrine. MyAnthroLibrary.com. Pearson.

Mitchell, Donald. 2009. Nimpkish: Complex foragers on the Northwest Coast of North America. In MyAnthroLibrary, eds. C. R. Ember, M. Ember, and P. N. Peregrine. MyAnthroLibrary.com. Pearson.

Mittermeier, Russell A., and Eleanor J. Sterling. 1992. Conservation of primates. In *The Cambridge encyclopedia of human evolution*, eds. S. Jones, R. Martin, and D. Pilbeam. New York: Cambridge University Press.

Mittermeier, Russell A., et al. 2009. Primates in Peril: The World's 25 Most Endangered Primates, 2008-2010. *Primate Conservation* 24:1–57.

Moerman, Daniel E. 1997. Physiology and symbols: The anthropological implications of the placebo effect. In *The anthropology of medicine*, 3rd ed., eds. L. Romanucci-Ross, D. E. Moerman, and L. R. Tancredi. Westport, CT: Bergin & Garvey.

Molnar, Stephen. 1998. *Human variation: Races, types, and ethnic groups.* 4th ed. Upper Saddle River, NJ: Prentice Hall.

Monot, Marc, et al. 2005. On the origin of leprosy. *Science* 308 (May 13):1040–42.

Monsutti, Alessandro. 2004. Cooperation, remittances, and kinship among the Hazaras. *Iranian Studies* 37:219–40.

Montagu, Ashley. 1997. *Man's most dangerous myth.* Walnut Creek, CA: AltaMira.

Mooney, Kathleen A. 1978. The effects of rank and wealth on exchange among the coast Salish. *Ethnology* 17:391–406.

Moore, Carmella C. 1988. An optimal scaling of Murdock's theories of illness data—An approach to the problem of interdependence. *Behavior Science Research* 22:161–79.

Moore, Carmella C. 1997. Is love always love? *Anthropology Newsletter* (November):8–9.

Moore, Carmella C., A. Kimball Romney, Ti-Lien Hsia, and Craig D. Rusch. 1999. The universality of the semantic structure of emotion terms: Methods for the study of inter- and intra-cultural variability. *American Anthropologist* 101:529–46.

Moore, John H., and Janis E. Campbell. 2002. Confirming unilocal residence in Native North America. *Ethnology* 41:175–88.

Moore, Omar Khayyam. 1957. Divination: A new perspective. *American Anthropologist* 59:69–74.

Moran, Emilio F. 1993. *Through Amazon eyes: The human ecology of Amazonian populations.* Iowa City: University of Iowa Press.

Moran, Emilio F., ed. 1996. *Transforming societies, transforming anthropology.* Ann Arbor: University of Michigan Press.

Moran, Emilio F. 2000. *Human adaptability: An introduction to ecological anthropology.* 2nd ed. Boulder, CO: Westview.

Moran, Emilio. 2011. Environmental anthropology as one of the spatial sciences. In *Environmental anthropology today*, eds. H. Kopnina and E. Shoreman-Ouimet. New York: Routledge.

Moran, Robert T., Philip R. Harris, and Sarah V. Moran. 2007. *Managing cultural differences: Global leadership strategies for the 21st century.* Burlington, MA: Butterworth Heinemann.

Morell, Virginia. 1995. The earliest art becomes older—And more common. *Science* 267 (March 31):1908–1909.

Morgan, Christopher and Robert Bettinger. 2012. Great Basin foraging strategies. In *Oxford handbook of North American archaeology*, ed. Timothy Pauketat, 185–98. Oxford: Oxford University Press.

Morgan, Lewis H. 1964/1877. *Ancient society.* Cambridge, MA: Harvard University Press.

Morphy, Howard, and Morgan Perkins. 2006. The anthropology of art: A reflection on its history and contemporary practice. In *The anthropology of art: A reader*, eds. H. Morphy and M. Perkins. Malden, MA: Blackwell.

Morris, Arthur. 2004. *Raised field technology: The raised field projects around Lake Titicaca.* Burlington, VT: Ashgate.

Morris, John. 1938. *Living with Lepchas: A book about the Sikkim Himalayas.* London: Heinemann.

Morrison, Kathleen D., and Laura L. Junker. 2002. *Forager-traders in South and Southeast Asia: Long-term histories.* Cambridge: Cambridge University Press.

Morwood, M. J., et al. 2004. Archaeology and age of a new hominin from Flores in Eastern Indonesia. *Nature* 431 (October 28):1087–91.

Moser, Stephanie. 1998. *Ancestral images: The iconography of human origins.* Ithaca, NY: Cornell University Press.

Motulsky, Arno. 1971. Metabolic polymorphisms and the role of infectious diseases in human evolution. In *Human populations, genetic variation, and evolution*, ed. L. N. Morris. San Francisco: Chandler.

Moyá-solá, Salvador, Meike Köhler, David M. Alba, Isaac Casanovas-Vilar, and Jordi Galindo. 2004. *Pierolapithecus catalaunicus.* A new Middle Miocene great ape from Spain. *Science* 306 (November 19):1339–44.

Mukerjee, Madhusree. 1996. Field notes: Interview with a parrot. *Scientific American* (April):28.

Mukherjee, Joia. 2007. Preface to the second edition. In *Women, poverty, and AIDS: Sex, drugs, and structural violence*, 2nd ed., eds. P. Farmer, M. Connors, and J. Simmons. Monroe, Maine: Common Courage Press.

Mukhopadhyay, Carol C., and Patricia J. Higgins. 1988. Anthropological studies of women's status revisited: 1977–1987. *Annual Review of Anthropology* 17:461–95.

Muller, Edward N. 1997. Economic determinants of democracy. In *Inequality, democracy, and economic development*, ed. M. Midlarsky. Cambridge: Cambridge University Press.

Müller-Haye, B. 1984. Guinea pig or cuy. In *Evolution of domesticated animals*, ed. I. Mason. New York: Longman.

Munroe, Robert L., Robert Hulefeld, James M. Rodgers, Damon L. Tomeo, and Steven K. Yamazaki. 2000. Aggression among children in four cultures. *Cross-Cultural Research* 34:3–25.

Munroe, Robert L., and Ruth H. Munroe. 1969. A cross-cultural study of sex, gender, and social structure. *Ethnology* 8:206–11.

Munroe, Robert L., Ruth H. Munroe, and John W. M. Whiting. 1981. Male sex-role resolutions. In *Handbook of cross-cultural human development*, eds. R. H. Munroe, R. L. Munroe, and B. B. Whiting. New York: Garland.

Munroe, Robert L., Ruth H. Munroe, and Stephen Winters. 1996. Cross-cultural correlates of the consonant-vowel (cv) syllable. *Cross-Cultural Research* 30:60–83.

Munroe, Ruth H., and Robert L. Munroe. 1980. Infant experience and childhood affect among the Logoli: A longitudinal study. *Ethos* 8:295–315.

Munroe, Ruth H., Robert L. Munroe, and Harold S. Shimmin. 1984. Children's work in four cultures: Determinants and consequences. *American Anthropologist* 86:369–79.

Murdock, George P. 1949. *Social structure.* New York: Macmillan.

Murdock, George P. 1957. World ethnographic sample. *American Anthropologist* 59:664–87.

Murdock, George P. 1967. Ethnographic atlas: A summary. *Ethnology* 6:109–236.

Murdock, George P. 1980. *Theories of illness: A world survey.* Pittsburgh: University of Pittsburgh Press.

Murdock, George P., and Caterina Provost. 1973. Factors in the division of labor by sex: A cross-cultural analysis. *Ethnology* 12:203–25.

Murdock, George P., and Douglas R. White. 1969. Standard cross-cultural sample. *Ethnology* 8:329–69.

Murphy, Jane. 1981. Abnormal behavior in traditional societies: Labels, explanations, and social reactions. In *Handbook of cross-cultural human development*, eds. R. H. Munroe, R. L. Munroe, and B. B. Whiting. New York: Garland.

Murphy, Robert F. 1960. *Headhunter's heritage: Social and economic change among the Mundurucú.* Berkeley: University of California Press.

Murphy, Robert F., and Julian H. Steward. 1956. Tappers and trappers: Parallel process in acculturation. *Economic development and cultural change* 4 (July):335–55.

Murray, G. F. 1997. The domestication of wood in Haiti: A case study in applied evolution. In *Applying cultural anthropology: An introductory reader*, eds. A. Podolefsky and P. J. Brown. Mountain View, CA: Mayfield.

Murray, G. F., and M. E. Bannister. 2004. Peasants, agroforesters, and anthropologists: A 20-year venture in income-generating trees and hedgerows in Haiti. *Agroforestry Systems* 61:383–97.

Musgrave, Jonathan H., R. A. H. Neave, and A. J. N. W. Prag. 1984. The skull from Tomb II at Vergina: King Philip II of Macedon. *Journal of Hellenistic Studies* 104:60–78.

Mutrine, Ann. 2013. Eight other nations that send women to combat. *National Geographic News*. http://news.nationalgeographic.com/news/2013/13/130125-women-combat-world-Australia-Israel-Canada-Norway/ (accessed June 21, 2013).

Myers, Fred R. 1988. Critical trends in the study of hunter-gatherers. *Annual Review of Anthropology* 17:261–82.

Myers, Fred R. 2002. *Painting culture*. Durham, North Carolina: Duke University Press.

Myers, Fred R. 2006. The unsettled business of tradition, indigenous being, and acrylic painting. In *Exploring world art*, eds. E. Venbrux, P. S. Rosi, and R. L. Welsch. Los Angeles: J. Paul Getty Museum.

Nadel, S. F. 1935. Nupe state and community. *Africa* 8:257–303.

Nadel, S. F. 1942. *A black Byzantium: The kingdom of Nupe in Nigeria*. London: Oxford University Press.

Nag, Moni, Benjamin N. F. White, and R. Creighton Peet. 1978. An anthropological approach to the study of the economic value of children in Java and Nepal. *Current Anthropology* 19:293–301.

Nagata, Judith. 2001. Beyond theology: Toward an anthropology of "fundamentalism." *American Anthropologist* 103:481–98.

Nagel, Ernest. 1961. *The structure of science: Problems in the logic of scientific explanation*. New York: Harcourt, Brace & World.

Nāleimaile, Sean, and Lokelani Brandt. 2013. Is Hawaiian archaeology really Hawaiian? A Native Hawaiian perspective. *SAA Archaeological Record* 13, no. 1:31–32.

Napier, J. R. 1970. Paleoecology and catarrhine evolution. In *Old World monkeys: Evolution, systematics, and behavior*, eds. J. R. Napier and P. H. Napier. New York: Academic Press.

Napier, J. R., and P. H. Napier. 1967. *A handbook of living primates*. New York: Academic Press.

Naroll, Raoul. 1961. Two solutions for Galton's problem. In *Readings in cross-cultural methodology*, ed. F. Moore. New Haven, CT: HRAF Press.

Naroll, Raoul. 1967. Imperial cycles and world order. *Peace Research Society: Papers* 7:83–101.

Naroll, Raoul. 1983. *The moral order: An introduction to the human situation*. Beverly Hills, CA: Sage.

Nash, Manning. 1989. *The cauldron of ethnicity in the modern world*. Chicago: University of Chicago Press.

National Association for the Practice of Anthropology. 1988. NAPA ethical guidelines for practitioners. http://practicinganthropology.org/about/ethical-guidelines/ (accessed May 11, 2013).

National Coalition for the Homeless. 2008. How many people experience homelessness? NCH Fact Sheet #2, June. http://www.nationalhomeless.org/factsheets/How_Many.html (accessed September 3, 2009).

National Coalition for the Homeless. 2009. How many people experience homelessness? http://www.nationalhomeless.org/factsheets/How_Many.html (accessed June 1, 2013).

National Science Foundation, Division of Science Resources Statistics. 2008. *Science and engineering doctorate awards: 2006*. Detailed Statistical Tables NSF 09-311. Arlington, VA: National Science Foundation. http://www.nsf.gov/statistics/nsf09311/ (accessed August 14, 2009).

Neel, James V., Willard R. Centerwall, Napoleon A. Chagnon, and Helen L. Casey. 1970. Notes on the effect of measles and measles vaccine in a virgin-soil population of South American Indians. *American Journal of Epidemiology* 91:418–29.

Neihardt, John G. 1951. *When the tree flowered*, 772–83. New York: Macmillan.

Nelson, Nici. 1995/1964. The Kiambu group: A successful women's ROSCA in Mathare Valley, Nairobi (1971 to 1990). In *Money-go-rounds: The importance of rotating savings and credit associations for women*, eds. S. Ardener and S. Burman. Oxford: Berg.

Nepstad, Daniel C., Claudia M. Stickler, Britaldo Soares-Filho, and Frank Merry. 2008. Interactions among Amazon land use, forests, and climate: Prospects for a near-term forest tipping point. *Philosophical Transactions of the Royal Society* B, 363:1737–46.

Nerlove, Sara B. 1974. Women's workload and infant feeding practices: A relationship with demographic implications. *Ethnology* 13:207–14.

Neumann, Katharina. 2003. New Guinea: A cradle of agriculture. *Science* 301 (July 11):180–81.

Nevins, Allan. 1927. *The American states during and after the revolution*. New York: Macmillan.

Newbury, Catherine. 1988. *The cohesion of oppression: Clientship and ethnicity in Rwanda, 1860–1960*. New York: Columbia University.

Newman, Edward. 2006. Exploring the "root causes" of terrorism. *Studies in Conflict and Terrorism* 29:749–72.

Newman, K. S. 1983. *Law and economic organization: A Comparative study of preindustrial societies*. Cambridge, MA: Cambridge University Press.

Newman, K. S. 1988. *Falling from grace: The experience of downward mobility in the American middle class*. New York: The Free Press.

Newman, K. S. 1993. *Declining fortunes: The withering of the American dream*. New York: Basic Books.

Newsweek. 1973. The first dentist, March 5, p. 73.

Nicholls, David, ed. 1998. *The Cambridge history of American music*. Cambridge. Cambridge University Press.

Nicolson, Nancy A. 1987. Infants, mothers, and other females. In *Primate societies*, eds. B. B. Smuts, D. L. Cheney, R. M. Seyfarth, and R. W. Wrangham. Chicago: University of Chicago Press.

Niehoff, Arthur H. 1966. *A casebook of social change*. Chicago: Aldine.

Nielsen, François. 2004. The ecological-evolutionary typology of human societies and the evolution of social inequality. *Sociological Theory* 22:292–314.

Nimkoff, M. F., and Russell Middleton. 1960. Types of family and types of economy. *American Journal of Sociology* 66:215–25.

Nisbett, Richard E. 2009. Education is all in your mind. *New York Times*, Sunday Opinion, February 8, p. 12.

Nishida, Toshisada. 1992. Introduction to the conservation symposium. In *Topics in primatology*, vol. 2, eds. N. Itoigawa, Y. Sugiyama, G. P. Sackett, and R. K. R. Thompson. Tokyo: University of Tokyo Press.

Nissen, Henry W. 1958. Axes of behavioral comparison. In *Behavior and evolution*, eds. A. Roe and G. G. Simpson. New Haven, CT: Yale University Press.

Nivette, Amy E. 2011. Violence in non-state societies. *British Journal of Criminology* 51:578–98.

Nolan, Riall W. 2002. *Development anthropology: Encounters in the real world*. Boulder, CO: Westview Press.

Nolan, Riall W. 2003. *Anthropology in practice: Building a career outside the academy*. Boulder, CA: Lynne Rienner Publishers.

Nolan, Riall W. 2013. *A handbook for practicing anthropology*, 2. Malden, MA: Blackwell Publishing.

Noll, Richard. 1987. The presence of spirits in magic and madness. In *Shamanism*, comp. S. Nicholson, 47–61. Wheaton, IL: Theosophical Publishing House.

Nolte, Christoph, Arun Agrawal, Kirsten M. Silvius, and Britaldo S. Soares-Filho. 2013. Governance regime and location influence avoided deforestation success of protected areas in the Brazilian Amazon. *Proceedings of the National Academy of Sciences* 110, no. 3: 4956–61.

Norenzayan, Ara, and Azim F. Shariff. 2008. The origin and evolution of religious prosociality. *Science* 322 (October 3):58–62.

Normile, Dennis. 1998. Habitat seen playing larger role in shaping behavior. *Science* 279 (March 6):1454–55.

Noss, Andrew J., and Barry S. Hewlett. 2001. The contexts of female hunting in central Africa. *American Anthropologist* 103:1024–40.

Nussbaum, Martha C. 1995. Introduction. In *Women, culture, and development: A study of human capabilities*, eds. M. C. Nussbaum and J. Glover. Oxford: Clarendon Press.

Oakley, Kenneth. 1964. On man's use of fire, with comments on tool-making and hunting. In *Social life of early man*, ed. S. L. Washburn. Chicago: Aldine.

Oboler, Regina Smith. 1980. Is the female husband a man? Woman/woman marriage among the Nandi of Kenya. *Ethnology* 19:69–88.

Oboler, Regina Smith. 2009. Nandi: From cattle-keepers to cash-crop farmers. In MyAnthroLibrary, eds. C. R. Ember, M. Ember, and P. N. Peregrine. MyAnthroLibrary.com. Pearson.

O'Brian, Robin. 1999. Who weaves and why? Weaving, loom complexity, and trade. *Cross-Cultural Research* 33:30–42.

O'Brien, Denise. 1977. Female husbands in southern Bantu societies. In *Sexual stratification*, ed. A. Schlegel. New York: Columbia University Press.

O'Brien, Patricia. 1989. Cahokia: The political capital of the "Ramey" state? *North American Archaeologist* 10, no. 4:275–92.

O'Connor, S., R. Ono, and C. Clarkson. 2011. Pelagic fishing at 42,000 years before the present and the maritime skills of modern humans. *Science* 334 (November 25):1117–21.

Oerlemans, J. 2005. Extracting a climate signal from 169 glacial records. *Science* 38 (April 28):675–77.

Office on Child Abuse and Neglect, U.S. Children's Bureau, Jeffrey Rosenberg, and Bradley W. Wilcox. 2006. The importance of fathers in the healthy development of children. https://www.childwelfare.gov/pubs/usermanuals/fatherhood/chapterthree.cfm.

Ogburn, William F. 1922. *Social change*. New York: Huebsch.

Ogden, Cynthia, Margaret D. Carroll, Brian K. Kit, and Katherine M. Flegal. 2012. *Prevalence of obesity in the United States 2009-2010*. NCHS Data Brief, no. 82 (January). Hyattsville, MD: National Center for Health Statistics.

O'Gorman, Rick, David Sloan Wilson, and Ralph R. Miller. 2008. An evolved cognitive bias for social norms. *Evolution and Human Behavior* 29:71–78.

Okamura, Jonathan Y. 1983. Filipino hometown associations in Hawaii. *Ethnology* 22:341–53.

Oliver, Douglas L. 1955. *A Solomon Island society*. Cambridge, MA: Harvard University Press.

Oliver, Douglas L. 1974. *Ancient Tahitian society: Ethnography*, vol. 1. Honolulu: University of Hawaii Press.

Oliver-Smith, Anthony. 2005. Applied anthropology and development-induced displacement and resettlement. In *Applied anthropology: Domains of application*, eds. S. Kedia and J. van Willigen. Westport, CT: Praeger.

Olsen, Steve. 2002. Seeking the signs of selection. *Science* 298 (November 15):1324–25.

Olszewski, Deborah I. 1991. Social complexity in the Natufian? Assessing the relationship of ideas and data. In *Perspectives on the past*, ed. G. Clark. Philadelphia: University of Pennsylvania Press.

Orlove, Benjamin, and Stephen Brush. 1996. Anthropology and the conservation of biodiversity. *Annual Review of Anthropology* 25:329–52.

Ortiz de Montellano, B. R., and C. H. Browner. 1985. Chemical bases for medicinal plant use in Oaxaca, Mexico. *Journal of Ethnopharmacology* 13:57–88.

Ortner, Sherry B. 1984. Theory in anthropology since the sixties. *Comparative Studies in Society & History* 26:126–66.

Osti, Roberto. 1994. The eloquent bones of Abu Hureyra. *Scientific American* (August):1.

Otterbein, Keith. 1968. Internal war: A cross-cultural study. *American Anthropologist* 70:277–89.

Otterbein, Keith. 1970. *The evolution of war*. New Haven, CT: HRAF Press.

Otterbein, Keith. 1986. *The ultimate coercive sanction: A cross-cultural study of capital punishment*. New Haven, CT: HRAF Press.

Otterbein, Keith. 1994. *Feuding and warfare: Selected works of Keith F. Otterbein*. Langhorne, PA: Gordon and Breach.

Otterbein, Keith, and Charlotte Swanson Otterbein. 1965. An eye for an eye, a tooth for a tooth: A cross-cultural study of feuding. *American Anthropologist* 67:1470–82.

Ovchinnikov, Igor V., Anders Götherström, Galina P. Romanova, Vitaliy M. Kharitonov, Kerstin Lidén, and William Goodwin. 2000. Molecular analysis of Neanderthal DNA from the northern Caucasus. *Nature* 404 (March 30):490–94.

Oxby, Clare. 1983. Farmer groups in rural areas of the third world. *Community Development Journal* 18:50–59.

Paige, Jeffery M. 1975. *Agrarian revolution: Social movements and export agriculture in the underdeveloped world*. New York: Free Press.

Paine, Robert. 1994. *Herds of the tundra*. Washington, DC: Smithsonian Institution Press.

Paley, William. 1810. *Natural theology*. Boston: Joshua Belcher.

Palsson, Gisli. 1988. Hunters and gatherers of the sea. In *Hunters and gatherers. Vol. 1. History, evolution and social change*, eds. T. Ingold, D. Riches, and J. Woodburn. New York: St. Martin's Press.

Paradise, Ruth, and Barbara Rogoff. 2009. Side by side: Learning by observing and pitching in. *Ethos* 37:102–38.

Parfit, Michael. 2000. Who were the first Americans? *National Geographic* (December):41–67.

Parker, Hilda, and Seymour Parker. 1986. Father-daughter sexual abuse: An emerging perspective. *American Journal of Orthopsychiatry* 56:531–49.

Parker, Seymour. 1976. The precultural basis of the incest taboo: Toward a biosocial theory. *American Anthropologist* 78:285–305.

Parker, Seymour. 1984. Cultural rules, rituals, and behavior regulation. *American Anthropologist* 86:584–600.

Parker, Sue Taylor. 1990. Why big brains are so rare. In *"Language" and intelligence in monkeys and apes*, eds. S. Parker and K. Gibson. New York: Cambridge University Press.

Pasternak, Burton. 1976. *Introduction to kinship and social organization*. Upper Saddle River, NJ: Prentice Hall.

Pasternak, Burton. 2009. Han: Pastoralists and farmers on a Chinese frontier. In MyAnthroLibrary, eds. C. R. Ember, M. Ember, and P. N. Peregrine. MyAnthroLibrary.com. Pearson.

Pasternak, Burton, Carol R. Ember, and Melvin Ember. 1976. On the conditions favoring extended family households. *Journal of Anthropological Research* 32:109–23.

Patterson, Leland. 1983. Criteria for determining the attributes of man-made lithics. *Journal of Field Archaeology* 10:297–307.

Patterson, Orlando. 1982. *Slavery and social death: A comparative study*. Cambridge, MA: Harvard University Press.

Patterson, Orlando. 2000. Review of *One drop of blood: The American misadventure of race*, by Scott L. Malcomson. *New York Times Book Review*, October 22, pp. 15–16.

Patterson, Thomas C. 1971. Central Peru: Its population and economy. *Archaeology* 24:316–21.

Patterson, Thomas C. 1981. *The evolution of ancient societies: A world archaeology*. Upper Saddle River, NJ: Prentice Hall.

Pauketat, Timothy. 2004. *Ancient Cahokia and the Mississippians*. Cambridge: Cambridge University Press.

Peacock, James L. 1986. *The anthropological lens: Harsh light, soft focus*. Cambridge: Cambridge University Press.

Peacock, Nadine R., and Robert C. Bailey. 2009. Efe: Investigating food and fertility in the Ituri Forest. In MyAnthroLibrary, eds. C. R. Ember, M. Ember, and P. N. Peregrine. MyAnthroLibrary.com. Pearson.

Peak, Lois. 1991. *Learning to go to school in Japan: The transition from home to preschool*. Berkeley: University of California Press.

Pearsall, Deborah. 1992. The origins of plant cultivation in South America. In *The origins of agriculture*, eds. C. Cowan and P. Watson. Washington, DC: Smithsonian Institution Press.

Pelto, Gretel H., Alan H. Goodman, and Darna L. Dufour. 2000. The biocultural perspective in nutritional anthropology. In *Nutritional anthropology: Biocultural perspectives on food and nutrition*, eds. Alan H. Goodman, Darna L. Dufour, and Gretel H. Pelto. Mountain View, CA: Mayfield Publishing.

Pelto, Pertti J. 1968. The difference between "tight" and "loose" societies. *Transaction* 5:37–40.

Pelto, Pertti J., and Ludger Müller-Wille. 1987. Snowmobiles: Technological revolution in the Arctic. In *Technology and social change*, 2nd ed., eds. H. R. Bernard and P. J. Pelto. Prospect Heights, IL: Waveland Press.

Pelto, Pertti J., and Gretel H. Pelto. 1975. Intra-cultural diversity: Some theoretical issues. *American Ethnologist* 2:1–18.

Pennisi, Elizabeth. 2000. Finally, the book of life and instructions for navigating it. *Science* 288 (June 30):2304–07.

Pennisi, Elizabeth. 2001a. Malaria's beginnings: On the heels of hoes? *Science* 293 (July 20):416–17.

Pennisi, Elizabeth. 2001b. Genetic change wards off malaria. *Science* 294 (November 16):1439.

Pennisi, Elizabeth. 2007. Genomicists tackle the primate tree. *Science* 316 (April 13):218–21.

Pennisi, Elizabeth. 2009. Tales of a prehistoric human genome. *Science* 323 (February 13):866–71.

Pepperberg, Irene Maxine. 1999. *The Alex studies: Cognitive and communicative abilities of grey parrots*. Cambridge, MA: Harvard University Press.

Peregrine, Peter N. 1996. The birth of the gods revisited: A partial replication of Guy Swanson's (1960) cross-cultural study of religion. *Cross-Cultural Research* 30:84–112.

Peregrine, Peter N. 2001a. Cross-cultural approaches in archaeology. *Annual Review of Anthropology* 30:1–18.

Peregrine, Peter N. 2001b. Southern and Eastern Africa Later Stone Age. In *Encyclopedia of prehistory Africa*, vol. 1, eds. P. N. Peregrine and M. Ember. New York: Kluwer Academic/Plenum.

Peregrine, Peter N. 2007a. Cultural correlates of ceramic styles. *Cross-Cultural Research* 41:223–35.

Peregrine, Peter N. 2007b. Racial hierarchy: I. Overview. In *Encyclopedia of race and racism*, ed. John H. Moore, 461–62. New York: Macmillan.

Peregrine, Peter N., and Peter Bellwood. 2001. Southeast Asia Upper Paleolithic. In *Encyclopedia of prehistory: East Asia and Oceania*, eds. P. N. Peregrine and M. Ember, vol. 3. New York: Kluwer Academic/Plenum.

Peregrine, Peter N., Carol R. Ember, and Melvin Ember. 2000. Teaching critical evaluation of Rushton. *Anthropology Newsletter* 41 (February):29–30.

Peregrine, Peter N., Carol R. Ember, and Melvin Ember. 2003. Cross-cultural evaluation of predicted associations between race and behavior. *Evolution and Human Behavior* 24:357–64.

Peregrine, Peter N., Melvin Ember, and Carol R. Ember. 2004. Predicting the future state of the world using archaeological data: An exercise in archaeomancy. *Cross-Cultural Research* 38:133–46.

Perkins, Morgan. 2006. "Do we still have no word for art?" A contemporary Mohawk question. In *Exploring world art*, eds. E. Venbrux, P. S. Rosi, and R. L. Welsch. Los Angeles: J. Paul Getty Museum.

Perry, Donna L. 2005. Wolof women, economic liberalization, and the crisis of masculinity in rural Senegal. *Ethnology* 44:207–26.

Petersen, Erik B. 1973. A survey of the Late Paleolithic and the Mesolithic of Denmark. In *The Mesolithic in Europe*, ed. S. K. Kozlowski. Warsaw: Warsaw University Press.

Petersen, L. R., G. R. Lee, and G. J. Ellis. 1982. Social structure, socialization values, and disciplinary techniques: A cross-cultural analysis. *Journal of Marriage and the Family* 44:131–42.

Pfaff, C. 1979. Constraints on language mixing. *Language* 55:291–318, as cited in *An introduction to sociolinguistics*, 2nd ed., ed. R. Wardhaugh. Oxford: Blackwell.

Pfeiffer, John E. 1978. *The emergence of man*. 3rd ed. New York: Harper & Row.

Phillips, Erica M., and Alan Walker. 2002. Fossil lorisoids. In *The primate fossil record*, ed. W. C. Hartwig. Cambridge: Cambridge University Press.

Phillips, Kevin. 1990. *The politics of rich and poor: Wealth and the American electorate in the Reagan aftermath*. New York: Random House.

Phillipson, David W. 1976. Archaeology and Bantu linguistics. *World Archaeology* 8:65–82.

Phillipson, David W. 1993. *African archaeology*. 2nd ed. New York: Cambridge University Press.

Phillipson, David W. 2005. *African archaeology*, 3rd ed. Cambridge: Cambridge University Press.

Piaget, Jean. 1970. Piaget's theory. In *Carmichael's manual of child psychology*, vol. 1, 3rd ed., ed. P. Mussen. New York: Wiley.

Piaget, Jean, and Bärbel Inhelder. 2000. *The psychology of the child*. New York: Basic Books.

Picchi, Debra. 1991. The impact of an industrial agricultural project on the Bakairí Indians of central Brazil. *Human Organization* 50:26–38.

Picchi, Debra. 2009. Bakairí: The death of an Indian. In MyAnthroLibrary, eds. C. R. Ember, M. Ember, and P. N. Peregrine. MyAnthroLibrary.com. Pearson.

Pickering, R., et al. 2011. *Australopithecus sediba* at 1.977 Ma and Implications for the origins of the genus homo. *Science* 333 (September 9):1421–23.

Pickford, Martin, Brigette Senut, Dominique Gommercy, and Jacques Treil. 2002. Bipedalism in *Orrorin tugenensis* revealed by its femora. *Comptes Rendu de l'Académie des Science des Paris*, Palevol 1, 1–13.

Pilbeam, David. 1972. *The ascent of man*. New York: Macmillan.

Pilbeam, David, and Stephen Jay Gould. 1974. Size and scaling in human evolution. *Science* 186 (December 6):892–900.

Pinker, Steven. 2011. *The better angels of our nature: Why violence has declined*. New York: Viking.

Piperno, Dolores, and Karen Stothert. 2003. Phytolith evidence for early Holocene cucurbita domestication in southwest Ecuador. *Science* 299 (February 14):1054–57.

Plattner, Stuart, ed. 1985. *Markets and marketing*. Monographs in economic anthropology, No. 4. Lanham, MD: University Press of America.

Plattner, Stuart. 1989. Marxism. In *Economic anthropology*, ed. S. Plattner. Stanford, CA: Stanford University Press.

Poggie, John J., Jr., and Richard B. Pollnac. 1988. Danger and rituals of avoidance among New England fishermen. *MAST: Maritime Anthropological Studies* 1:66–78.

Poggie, John J., Jr., Richard B. Pollnac, and Carl Gersuny. 1976. Risk as a basis for taboos among fishermen in Southern New England. *Journal for the Scientific Study of Religion* 15:257–62.

Polanyi, Karl. 1957. The economy as instituted process. In *Trade and market in the early empires*, eds. K. Polanyi, C. M. Arensberg, and H. W. Pearson. New York: Free Press.

Polanyi, Karl, Conrad M. Arensberg, and Harry W. Pearson, eds. 1957. *Trade and market in the early empires*. New York: Free Press.

Polednak, Anthony P. 1974. Connective tissue responses in Negroes in relation to disease. *American Journal of Physical Anthropology* 41:49–57.

Pollier, Nicole. 2000. Commoditization, cash, and kinship in postcolonial Papua New Guinea. In *Commodities and globalization: Anthropological perspectives*, eds. A. Haugerud, M. P. Stone, and P. D. Little. Lanham, MD: Rowman & Littlefield.

Pope, Geoffrey G. 1989. Bamboo and human evolution. *Natural History* (October):49–57.

Popenoe, Rebecca. 2004. *Feeding desire: Fatness, beauty, and sexuality among a Saharan people*. London: Routledge.

Pospisil, Leopold. 1963. *The Kapauku Papuans of West New Guinea*. New York: Holt, Rinehart & Winston.

Post, Peter W., Farrington Daniels, Jr., and Robert T. Binford, Jr. 1975. Cold injury and the evolution of "white" skin. *Human Biology* 47:65–80.

Potts, Richard. 1984. Home bases and early hominids. *American Scientist* 72:338–47.

Potts, Richard. 1988. *Early hominid activities at Olduvai*. New York: Aldine.

Powell, Joseph. 2005. *The first Americans*. New York: Cambridge University Press.

Powers, William K., and Marla N. Powers. 2009. Lakota: A study in cultural continuity. In MyAnthroLibrary, eds. C. R. Ember, M. Ember, and P. N. Peregrine. MyAnthroLibrary.com. Pearson.

Poyatos, Fernando. 2002. *Nonverbal communication across disciplines*, vol. 1. Philadelphia: John Benjamins Publishing Company.

Prag, A. J. N. W. 1990. Reconstructing Phillip II of Macedon: The "nice" version. *American Journal of Archaeology* 94:237–47.

Prag, John, and Richard Neave. 1997. *Making faces: Using forensic and archaeological evidence*. College Station: Texas A&M University Press.

Preuschoft, Holger, David J. Chivers, Warren Y. Brockelman, and Norman Creel, eds. 1984. *The lesser apes: Evolutionary and behavioural biology*. Edinburgh: Edinburgh University Press.

Price, Sally. 1989. *Primitive art in civilized places*. Chicago: University of Chicago Press.

Price, Sally. 2001. *Primitive art in civilized places*. 2nd ed. Chicago: University of Chicago Press.

Price, Sally. 2006. A case in point and afterwords to *Primitive art in civilized places*. In *The anthropology of art: A reader*, eds. H. Morphy and M. Perkins. Malden, MA: Blackwell.

Price-Williams, Douglass. 1961. A study concerning concepts of conservation of quantities among primitive children. *Acta Psychologica* 18:297–305.

Pringle, Heather. 1998. The slow birth of agriculture. *Science* 282 (November 20):1446–50.

Pringle, Heather. 2011. The First Americans. *Scientific American* 305 (November):36–42.

Pryor, Frederic L. 1977. *The origins of the economy: A comparative study of distribution in primitive and peasant economies.* New York: Academic Press.

Pryor, Frederic L. 2005. *Economic systems of foraging, agricultural, and industrial societies.* Cambridge: Cambridge University Press.

Public Law 101-601 25 U.S.C. 3001–3013.

Putnam, Robert D. 1995. Bowling alone: America's declining social capital. *Journal of Democracy* (January):65–78.

Quandt, Sara A. 1996. Nutrition in anthropology. In *Handbook of medical anthropology*, Rev. ed., eds. C. F. Sargent and T. M. Johnson. Westport, CT: Greenwood Press.

Quinn, Naomi. 1977. Anthropological studies on women's status. *Annual Review of Anthropology* 6:181–225.

Radcliffe-Brown, A. R. 1922. *The Andaman Islanders: A study in social anthropology.* Cambridge: Cambridge University Press.

Radcliffe-Brown, A. R. 1952. *Structure and function in primitive society.* London: Cohen & West.

Radin, Paul. 1923. *The Winnebago tribe*, 138. Washington, DC: Smithsonian institute.

Radinsky, Leonard. 1967. The oldest primate endocast. *American Journal of Physical Anthropology* 27:358–88.

Rambo, Lewis R. 2003. Anthropology and the study of conversion. In *The anthropology of religious conversion*, eds. A. Buckser and S. D. Glazier. Lanham, MD: Roman & Littlefield.

Rapp, George and Christopher Hill. 2006. *Geoarchaeology: The earth-science approach to archaeological interpretation.* New Haven, CT: Yale University Press.

Rappaport, Roy A. 1967. Ritual regulation of environmental relations among a New Guinea people. *Ethnology* 6:17–30.

Rasmussen, David Tab. 1990. Primate origins: Lessons from a neotropical marsupial. *American Journal of Primatology* 22:263–77.

Rasmussen, David Tab. 2002. Early catarrhines of the African Eocene and Oligocene. In *The primate fossil record*, ed. W. C. Hartwig. Cambridge: Cambridge University Press.

Rathje, William L. 1971. The origin and development of Lowland Classic Maya civilization. *American Antiquity* 36:275–85.

Ravesloot, John. 1997. Changing Native American perceptions of archaeology and archaeologists. In *Native Americans and archaeologists*, eds. N. Swidler, K. Dongoske, R. Anyon, and A. Downer. Walnut Creek, CA: AltaMira Press.

Ray, Verne F. 1954. *The Sanpoil and Nespelem: Salishan peoples of northeastern Washington.* New Haven, CT: Human Relations Area Files.

Raybeck, Douglas. 1998. Toward more holistic explanations: Cross-cultural research and cross-level analysis. *Cross-Cultural Research* 32:123–42.

Raybeck, Douglas, J. Shoobe, and J. Grauberger. 1989. Women, stress and participation in possession cults: A reexamination of the calcium deficiency hypothesis. *Medical Anthropology Quarterly* 3:139–61.

Redman, Charles L. 1978. *The rise of civilization: From early farmers to urban society in the ancient Near East.* San Francisco: W. H. Freeman.

Redman, Charles L. 1999. *Human impact on ancient environments.* Tucson: University of Arizona Press.

Reed, David, V. Smith, S. Hammond, A. Rogers, and D. Clayton. 2004. Genetic analysis of lice supports direct contact between modern and archaic humans. *PLoS Biology* 2 (November):1972–83.

Reff, Daniel T. 2005. *Plagues, priests, and demons: Sacred narratives and the rise of Christianity in the Old World and the New.* Cambridge: Cambridge University Press.

Reich, D, et al. 2010. Genetic history of an archaic hominin group from Denisovia Cave in Siberia. *Nature* 468 (December 23/30):1053–60.

Reich, David, et al. 2012. Reconstructing native American population history. *Nature* 488 (July 11):370–4.

Reisner, Marc. 1993. *Cadillac desert: The American West and its disappearing water.* Rev. ed. New York: Penguin.

Reitz, Elizabeth and Myra Shackley. 2012. *Environmental archaeology.* New York: Springer.

Relethford, John. 1990. *The human species: An introduction to biological anthropology.* Mountain View, CA: Mayfield.

Renfrew, Colin. 1969. Trade and culture process in European history. *Current Anthropology* 10:156–69.

Renfrew, Colin. 1987. *Archaeology and language: The puzzle of Indo-European origins.* London: Jonathan Cape.

Rennie, John. 2002. Fifteen answers to creationist nonsense. *Scientific American* (July):78–85.

Revkin, Andrew C. 2005. Tracking the imperiled bluefin from ocean to sushi platter. *New York Times*, May 3, pp. F1, F4.

Rhine, Stanley. 1993. Skeletal criteria for racial attribution. *NAPA Bulletin* 13:54–67.

Rice, Patricia C. 1981. Prehistoric Venuses: Symbols of motherhood or womanhood? *Journal of Anthropological Research* 37:402–14.

Rice, Patricia C., and Ann L. Paterson. 1985. Cave art and bones: Exploring the interrelationships. *American Anthropologist* 87:94–100.

Rice, Patricia C., and Ann L. Paterson. 1986. Validating the cave art—Archeofaunal relationship in Cantabrian Spain. *American Anthropologist* 88:658–67.

Richard, Alison F. 1985. *Primates in nature.* New York: W. H. Freeman.

Richard, Alison F. 1987. Malagasy prosimians: Female dominance. In *Primate societies*, eds. B. B. Smuts, D. L. Cheney, R. M. Seyfarth, and R. W. Wrangham. Chicago: University of Chicago Press.

Richardson, Curtis J., Peter Reiss, Najah A. Hussain, Azzam J. Alwash, and Douglas J. Pool. 2005. The restoration potential of the Mesopotamian marshes of Iraq. *Science* 307 (February 25):1307–11.

Richerson, Peter J., and Robert Boyd. 2005. *Not by genes alone: How culture transformed human evolution.* Chicago: University of Chicago Press.

Richmond, Brian G., and William L. Jungers. 2008. *Orrorin tugenensis* femoral morphology and the evolution of human bipedalism. *Science* 319 (March 21):1662–65.

Riesenfeld, Alphonse. 1973. The effect of extreme temperatures and starvation on the body proportions of the rat. *American Journal of Physical Anthropology* 39:427–59.

Rightmire, G. Philip. 1984. *Homo sapiens* in sub-Saharan Africa. In *The origins of modern humans*, eds. F. H. Smith and F. Spencer. New York: Alan R. Liss.

Rightmire, G. Philip. 1990. *The evolution of* Homo erectus: *Comparative anatomical studies of an extinct human species.* Cambridge: Cambridge University Press.

Rightmire, G. Philip. 1997. Human evolution in the Middle Pleistocene: The role of *Homo heidelbergensis. Evolutionary Anthropology* 6:218–27.

Rightmire, G. Philip. 2000. *Homo erectus.* In *Encyclopedia of human evolution and prehistory*, eds. I. Tattersall, E. Delson, and J. van Couvering. New York: Garland.

Rijksen, H. D. 1978. *A field study on Sumatran Orang utans* (Pongo pygmaeus abelii Lesson 1827): *Ecology, behaviour and conservation.* Wageningen, Netherlands: H. Veenman and Zonen.

Ritter, Madeline Lattman. 1980. The conditions favoring age-set organization. *Journal of Anthropological Research* 36:87–104.

Rivers, W. H. R. 1967/1906. *The Todas.* Oosterhout, Netherlands: Anthropological Publications.

Roberts, D. F. 1953. Body weight, race, and climate. *American Journal of Physical Anthropology* 11:533–58.

Roberts, D. F. 1978. *Climate and human variability.* 2nd ed. Menlo Park, CA: Cummings.

Roberts, John M. 1967. Oaths, autonomic ordeals, and power. In *Cross-cultural approaches*, ed. C. S. Ford. New Haven, CT: HRAF Press.

Roberts, John M., and Brian Sutton-Smith. 1962. Child training and game involvement. *Ethnology* 1:166–85.

Roberts, John M., Malcolm J. Arth, and Robert R. Bush. 1959. Games in culture. *American Anthropologist* 61:597–605.

Robins, Ashley H. 1991. *Biological perspectives on human pigmentation.* New York: Cambridge University Press.

Robinson, John G., and Charles H. Janson. 1987. Capuchins, squirrel monkeys, and atelines: Socioecological convergence with Old World primates. In *Primate societies*, eds. B. B. Smuts, D. L. Cheney, R. M. Seyfarth, and R. W. Wrangham. Chicago: University of Chicago Press.

Robinson, John G., Patricia C. Wright, and Warren G. Kinzey. 1987. Monogamous cebids and their relatives: Intergroup calls and spacing. In *Primate societies*, eds. Barbara B. Smuts, Dorothy L. Cheney, Robert M. Seyfarth, and Richard W. Wrangham. Chicago: University of Chicago Press.

Robinson, Roy. 1984. Cat. In *Evolution of domesticated animals*, ed. I. Mason. New York: Longman.

Rodwin, Lloyd, and Bishwapriya Sanyal. 1987. Shelter, settlement, and development: An overview. In *Shelter, settlement, and development*, ed. L. Rodwin. Boston: Allen & Unwin.

Roes, Frans L., and Michel Raymond. 2003. Belief in moralizing gods. *Evolution and Human Behavior* 24:126–35.

Rogers, Alan, D. Iltis, and S. Wooding. 2004. Genetic variation at the MCIR locus and the time since loss of human body hair. *Current Anthropology* 45:105–08.

Rogers, Everett M. 1983. *Diffusion of innovations.* 3rd ed. New York: Free Press.

Rogoff, Barbara. 1981. Schooling and the development of cognitive skills. In *Handbook of cross-cultural psychology: Developmental psychology*, vol. 4, eds. H. C. Triandis and A. Heron. Boston: Allyn & Bacon.

Rogoff, Barbara. 1990. *Apprenticeship in thinking: Cognitive development in social context.* New York: Oxford University Press.

Rogoff, Barbara. 2003. *The cultural nature of human development.* New York: Oxford University Press.

Rohner, Ronald P. 1975. *They love me, they love me not: A worldwide study of the effects of parental acceptance and rejection.* New Haven, CT: HRAF Press.

Rohner, Ronald P. 1976. Sex differences in aggression: Phylogenetic and enculturation perspectives. *Ethos* 4:57–72.

Rohner, Ronald P., and Preston A. Britner. 2002. Worldwide mental health correlates of parental acceptance-rejection: Review of cross-cultural research and intracultural evidence. *Cross-Cultural Research* 36:16–47.

Rohter, Larry. 2012. Folklorist's global jukebox goes digital. *New York Time*, January 30. http://www.nytimes.com.

Romaine, Suzanne. 1994. *Language in society: An introduction to sociolinguistics.* Oxford: Oxford University Press.

Romanucci-Ross, Lola, and George A. De Vos, eds. 1995. *Ethnic identity: Creation, conflict, and accommodation.* 3rd ed. Walnut Creek, CA: AltaMira Press.

Romanucci-Ross, Lola, Daniel E. Moerman, and Laurence R. Tancredi, eds. 1997. *The anthropology of medicine: From culture to method.* 3rd ed. Westport, CT: Bergin & Garvey.

Romney, A. Kimball, Carmella C. Moore, and Craig D. Rusch. 1997. Cultural universals: Measuring the semantic structure of emotion terms in English and Japanese. *Proceedings of the National Academy of Sciences, U.S.A.*, 94:5489–94.

Romney, A. Kimball, Susan C. Weller, and William H. Batchelder. 1986. Culture as consensus: A theory of culture and informant accuracy. *American Anthropologist* 88:313–38.

Roncoli, Carla, Todd Crane, and Ben Orlove. 2009. Fielding climate change in cultural anthropology. In *Anthropology and climate change: From encounters to actions*, eds. S. A. Crate and M. Nuttall. Walnut Creek, CA: Left Coast Press.

Roosens, Eugeen E. 1989. *Creating ethnicity: The process of ethnogenesis.* Newbury Park, CA: Sage Publications.

Roosevelt, Anna Curtenius. 1984. Population, health, and the evolution of subsistence: Conclusions from the conference. In *Paleopathology at the origins of agriculture*, eds. M. Cohen and G. Armelagos. Orlando, FL: Academic Press.

Roosevelt, Anna Curtenius. 1992. Secrets of the forest. *The Sciences* (November/December):22–28.

Roosevelt, Anna Curtenius, et al. 1996. Paleoindian cave dwellers in the Amazon: The peopling of the Americas. *Science* 272 (April 19):373–84.

Roscoe, Paul. 2002. The hunters and gatherers of New Guinea. *Current Anthropology* 43:153–62.

Rose, M. D. 1984. Food acquisition and the evolution of positional behaviour: The case of bipedalism. In *Food acquisition and processing in primates*, eds. D. Chivers, B. Wood, and A. Bilsborough. New York: Plenum.

Roseberry, William. 1988. Political economy. *Annual Review of Anthropology* 17:161–259.

Rosen, Lawrence. 2006. *Law as culture: An invitation.* Princeton: Princeton University Press.

Rosenberger, A. L. 1979. Cranial anatomy and implications of *Dolichocebus*, a Late Oligocene ceboid primate. *Nature* 279 (May 31):416–18.

Rosenblatt, Paul C. 2009. Human rights violations. In MyAnthroLibrary, eds. C. R. Ember, M. Ember, and P. N. Peregrine. MyAnthroLibrary.com. Pearson.

Rosenblatt, Paul C., R. Patricia Walsh, and Douglas A. Jackson. 1976. *Grief and mourning in cross-cultural perspective.* New Haven, CT: HRAF Press.

Ross, Marc Howard. 1981. Socioeconomic complexity, socialization, and political differentiation: A cross-cultural study. *Ethos* 9:217–47.

Ross, Marc Howard. 1985. Internal and external conflict and violence. *Journal of Conflict Resolution* 29:547–79.

Ross, Marc Howard. 1986. Female political participation: A cross-cultural explanation. *American Anthropologist* 88:843–58.

Ross, Marc Howard. 1988. Political organization and political participation: Exit, voice, and loyalty in preindustrial societies. *Comparative Politics* 21:73–89.

Ross, Marc Howard. 2009a. Ethnocentrism and ethnic conflict. In MyAnthroLibrary, eds. C. R. Ember, M. Ember, and P. N. Peregrine. MyAnthroLibrary.com. Pearson.

Ross, Marc Howard. 2009b. Political participation. In MyAnthroLibrary, eds. C. R. Ember, M. Ember, and P. N. Peregrine. MyAnthroLibrary.com. Pearson.

Roth, Eric Abella. 2001. Demise of the *sepaade* tradition: Cultural and biological explanations. *American Anthropologist* 103:1014–23.

Rothman, Barbara Katz. 2011. From the book of life: A personal guide to race, normality, and the implications of the genome project. In *Race in an era of change: A reader*, eds. H. Dalmage and B. Katz Rothman. New York: Oxford University Press.

Rubel, Arthur J., and Michael R. Hass. 1996. Ethnomedicine. In *Medical anthropology*, Rev. ed., eds. C. F. Sargent and T. M. Johnson. Westport, CT: Praeger.

Rubel, Arthur J., Carl O'Nell, and Rolando Collado-Ardón (with the assistance of John Krejci and Jean Krejci). 1984. *Susto: A folk illness.* Berkeley: University of California Press.

Rubel, Paula, and Abraham Rosman. 1996. Structuralism and poststructuralism. In *Encyclopedia of cultural anthropology*, eds. D. Levinson and M. Ember, vol. 4. New York: Henry Holt.

Rubin, J. Z., F. J. Provenzano, and R. F. Haskett. 1974. The eye of the beholder: Parents' views on the sex of new borns. *American Journal of Orthopsychiatry* 44:512–19.

Rudan, Igor, and Harry Campbell. 2004. Five reasons why inbreeding may have considerable effect on post-reproductive human health. *Collegium Antropologicum* 28:943–50.

Rudmin, Floyd Webster. 1988. Dominance, social control, and ownership: A history and a cross-cultural study of motivations for private property. *Behavior Science Research* 22:130–60.

Ruff, Christopher B., and Alan Walker. 1993. Body size and body shape. In *The Nariokotome* Homo erectus *skeleton*, eds. A. Walker and R. Leakey. Cambridge, MA: Harvard University Press.

Rumbaugh, Duane M. 1970. Learning skills of anthropoids. In *Primate behavior*, vol. 1, ed. L. Rosenblum. New York: Academic Press.

Rummel, R. J. 2002a. Death by Government, Chapter 1. http://www.hawaii.edu/powerkills/DBG.CHAP1.HTM.

Rummel, R. J. 2002b. Democracies are less warlike than other regimes. http://www.hawaii.edu/powerkills/DP95.htm.

Rummel, R. J. 2002c. Statistics of democide, Chapter 17. http://www.hawaii.edu/powerkills/SOD.CHAP17.HTM.

Rummel, R. J. 2002d. Statistics of democide, Chapter 21. http://www.hawaii.edu/powerkills/SOD.CHAP21.HTM.

Rummel, R. J. 2009. 20th century democide. http://www.hawaii.edu/powerkills/20th.htm (accessed September 5, 2009).

Ruskin, John. 1963. Of king's treasures. In *The genius of John Ruskin*, ed. J. D. Rosenberg. New York: Braziller.

Russell, Elbert W. 1972. Factors of human aggression. *Behavior Science Notes* 7:275–312.

Russell, James A. 1994. Is there universal recognition of emotion from facial expressions? A review of the cross-cultural studies. *Psychological Bulletin* 115, no. 1:102–41.

Russett, Bruce (with the collaboration of William Antholis, Carol R. Ember, Melvin Ember, and Zeev Maoz). 1993. *Grasping the democratic peace: Principles for a post–cold war world.* Princeton, NJ: Princeton University Press.

Russett, Bruce, and John R. Oneal. 2001. *Triangulating peace: Democracy, interdependence, and international organizations.* New York: Norton.

Russon, Anne E. 1990. The development of peer social interaction in infant chimpanzees: Comparative social, Piagetian, and brain perspectives. In *"Language" and intelligence in monkeys and apes*, eds. S. Parker and K. Gibson. New York: Cambridge University Press.

Ruvolo, Maryellen. 1997. Genetic diversity in hominoid primates. *Annual Review of Anthropology* 26:515–40.

Rylko-Bauer, Barbara, Merrill Singer, and John van Willigen. 2006. Reclaiming applied anthropology: Its past, present, and future. *American Anthropologist* 108:178–90.

Sade, D. S. 1965. Some aspects of parent-offspring and sibling relationships in a group of rhesus monkeys, with a discussion of grooming. *American Journal of Physical Anthropology* 23:1–17.

Saez, Emmanuel. 2012. Striking it richer: The evolution of top incomes in the United States (Updated with 2009 and 2010 Estimates). http://saez-UStopincomes-2010-1.pdf.

Sagan, Carl. 1975. A cosmic calendar. *Natural History* (December):70–73.

Sahlins, Marshall D. 1958. *Social stratification in Polynesia.* Seattle: University of Washington Press.

Sahlins, Marshall D. 1961. The segmentary lineage: An organization of predatory expansion. *American Anthropologist* 63:332–45.

Sahlins, Marshall D. 1962. *Moala: Culture and nature on a Fijian island.* Ann Arbor: University of Michigan Press.

Sahlins, Marshall D. 1963. Poor man, rich man, big-man, chief: Political types in Melanesia and Polynesia. *Comparative Studies in Society and History* 5:285–303.

Sahlins, Marshall D. 1972. *Stone Age economics.* Chicago: Aldine.

Sahlins, Marshall D. 1983. Other times, other customs: The anthropology of history. *American Anthropologist* 85:517–44.

Sahlins, Marshall D., and Elman Service. 1960. *Evolution and culture.* Ann Arbor: University of Michigan Press.

Saito, Osamu. 1998. Two kinds of stem family system? Traditional Japan and Europe compared. *Continuity and Change* 13, no. 1:17–45.

Salzman, Philip Carl. 1996. Pastoralism. In *Encyclopedia of cultural anthropology*, vol. 3, eds. D. Levinson and M. Ember. New York: Henry Holt.

Salzman, Philip Carl. 1999. Is inequality universal? *Current Anthropology* 40:31–61.

Salzman, Philip Carl. 2001. *Understanding culture: An introduction to anthropological theory.* Long Grove, IL: Waveland, 135.

Salzman, Philip Carl. 2002. Pastoral nomads: Some general observations based on research in Iran. *Journal of Anthropological Research* 58:245–64.

Salzman, Philip Carl. 2008. *Culture and conflict in the Middle East.* Amherst, NY: Humanity Books.

Samy, Alim, H., Ibrahim Awad, and Alastair Pennycook, eds. 2009. *Global linguistic flows: Hip Hop cultures, youth identities, and the politics of language.* New York: Routledge.

Sanday, Peggy R. 1973. Toward a theory of the status of women. *American Anthropologist* 75:1682–700.

Sanday, Peggy R. 1974. Female status in the public domain. In *Woman, culture, and society*, eds. M. Z. Rosaldo and L. Lamphere. Stanford, CA: Stanford University Press.

Sanders, William T. 1968. Hydraulic agriculture, economic symbiosis, and the evolution of states in central Mexico. In *Anthropological archaeology in the Americas*, ed. B. Meggers. Washington, DC: Anthropological Society of Washington.

Sanders, William T., and Barbara J. Price. 1968. *Mesoamerica.* New York: Random House.

Sanders, William T., Jeffrey R. Parsons, and Robert S. Santley. 1979. *The Basin of Mexico: Ecological processes in the evolution of a civilization.* New York: Academic Press.

Sanderson, Stephen K. 1995. Expanding world commercialization: The link between world-systems and civilizations. In *Civilizations and world systems: Studying world-historical change*, ed. S. K. Sanderson. Walnut Creek, CA: AltaMira Press.

Sanderson, Stephen K., and Wesley W. Roberts. 2008. The evolutionary forms of the religious life: A cross-cultural, quantitative analysis. *American Anthropologist* 110, no. 4: 454–66.

Sapir, Edward. 1931. Conceptual categories in primitive languages. Paper presented at the autumn meeting of the National Academy of Sciences, New Haven, CT. Published in *Science* 74.

Sapir, Edward. 1938. Why cultural anthropology needs the psychiatrist. *Psychiatry* 1:7–12.

Sapir, Edward, and M. Swadesh. 1964. American Indian grammatical categories. In *Language in culture and society*, ed. D. Hymes. New York: Harper & Row.

Sapolsky, Robert M. 1997. Testosterone rules. *Discover* (March 1997). Reprinted in *The gendered society reader*, eds. M. Kimmel and A. Aronson. New York: Oxford University Press.

Sarich, Vincent M. 1968. The origin of hominids: An immunological approach. In *Perspectives on human evolution*, vol. 1, eds. S. L. Washburn and P. C. Jay. New York: Holt, Rinehart & Winston.

Sarich, Vincent M., and Allan C. Wilson. 1966. Quantitative immunochemistry and the evolution of primate albumins: Micro-component fixations. *Science* 154 (December 23):1563–66.

Sassaman, Kenneth. 1996. Early Archaic settlement in the South Carolina coastal plain. In *The Paleoindian and Early Archaic Southeast*, eds. D. G. Anderson and K. E. Sassaman. Tuscaloosa: University of Alabama Press.

Satterthwaite, David. 2008. Editorial: The social and political basis for citizen action on urban poverty reduction. *Environment and Urbanization* 20:307–18.

Sattler, Richard A. 1996. Remnants, renegades, and runaways: Seminole ethnogenesis reconsidered. In *Ethnogenesis in the Americas*, ed. J. D. Hill. Iowa City: University of Iowa Press.

Savage-Rumbaugh, E. S. 1992. Language training of apes. In *The Cambridge encyclopedia of human evolution*, eds. S. Jones, R. Martin, and D. Pilbeam. New York: Cambridge University Press.

Savage-Rumbaugh, E. S. 1994. Hominid evolution: Looking to modern apes for clues. In *Hominid culture in primate perspective*, eds. D. Quiatt and J. Itani. Niwot: University Press of Colorado.

Savolainen, Peter, J. Luo, J. Lunderberg, and T. Leitner. 2002. Genetic evidence for an East Asian origin of domestic dogs. *Science* 296 (November 22):1610–14.

Scaglion, Richard. 1990. Legal adaptation in a Papua New Guinea village court. *Ethnology* 29:17–33.

Scaglion, Richard. 2009a. Abelam: Giant yams and cycles of sex, warfare, and ritual. In MyAnthroLibrary, eds. C. R. Ember, M. Ember, and P. N. Peregrine. MyAnthroLibrary.com. Pearson.

Scaglion, Richard. 2009b. Law and society. In MyAnthroLibrary, eds. C. R. Ember, M. Ember, and P. N. Peregrine. MyAnthroLibrary.com. Pearson.

Scaglion, Richard, and Rose Whittingham. 1985. Female plaintiffs and sex-related disputes in rural Papua New Guinea. In *Domestic violence in Papua New Guinea*, ed. S. Toft. New Guinea: Law Reform Commission.

Scarr, Sandra, and Kathleen McCartney. 1983. How people make their own environments: A theory of genotype–environment effects. *Child Development*, 54:424–35.

Scarre, Christopher. 2009. The world transformed: From foragers and farmers to states and empires. In *The human past*, ed. C. Scarre. New York: Thames and Hudson.

Schaller, George. 1963. *The mountain gorilla: Ecology and behavior.* Chicago: University of Chicago Press.

Schaller, George. 1964. *The year of the gorilla.* Chicago: University of Chicago Press.

Schaller, George. 1972. *The Serengeti lion: A study of predator-prey relations.* Chicago: University of Chicago Press.

Schick, Kathy D., and Nicholas Toth. 1993. *Making silent stones speak.* New York: Simon & Schuster.

Schlatter, N. Elizabeth. 2008. *Museum careers: A practical guide for students and novices.* Walnut Creek, CA: Left Coast Press.

Schlegel, Alice. 1989. Gender issues and cross-cultural research. *Behavior Science Research* 23:265–80.

Schlegel, Alice. 1991. Status, property, and the value on virginity. *American Ethnologist* 18:719–34.

Schlegel, Alice. 2009. The status of women. In MyAnthroLibrary, eds. C. R. Ember, M. Ember, and P. N. Peregrine. MyAnthroLibrary.com. Pearson.

Schlegel, Alice, and Herbert Barry, III. 1986. The cultural consequences of female contribution to subsistence. *American Anthropologist* 88:142–50.

Schlegel, Alice, and Herbert Barry, III. 1991. *Adolescence: An anthropological inquiry.* New York: Free Press.

Schlegel, Alice, and Rohn Eloul. 1987. A new coding of marriage transactions. *Behavior Science Research* 21:118–40.

Schlegel, Alice, and Rohn Eloul. 1988. Marriage transactions: Labor, property, and status. *American Anthropologist* 90:291–309.

Schmid, Petra, Marianne Schmid Mast, Dario Bombari, and Fred Mast. 2011. Gender effects in information processing on a nonverbal decoding task. *Sex Roles* 65:102–7.

Schneider, David M. 1961a. Introduction: The distinctive features of matrilineal descent groups. In *Matrilineal kinship*, eds. D. M. Schneider and K. Gough. Berkeley: University of California Press.

Schneider, David M. 1961b. Truk. In *Matrilineal kinship*, eds. D. M. Schneider and K. Gough. Berkeley: University of California Press.

Schoepf, B. 1988. Women, AIDS and economic crisis in central Africa. *Canadian Journal of African Studies* 22:625–44.

Schrauf, Robert W. 1999. Mother tongue maintenance among North American ethnic groups. *Cross-Cultural Research* 33:175–92.

Schrire, Carmel, ed. 1984a. *Past and present in hunter-gatherer studies.* Orlando, FL: Academic Press.

Schrire, Carmel. 1984b. Wild surmises on savage thoughts. In *Past and present in hunter-gatherer studies*, ed. C. Schrire. Orlando, FL: Academic Press.

Scheper-Hughes, Nancy. 2008. A talent for life: Reflections on human vulnerability and resilence. *Ethnos* 73:25–56.

Scheper-Hughes, Nancy. 2013. No more angel babies on the Alto do Cruzeiro. *Natural History* (June):28–38.

Schwartz, Richard D. 1954. Social factors in the development of legal control: A case study of two Israeli settlements. *Yale Law Journal* 63 (February):471–91.

Scott, Janny, and David Leonhardt. 2005. Class in America: Shadowy lines that still divide. *New York Times*, National, May 15, pp. 1, 26.

Scribner, Sylvia, and Michael Cole. 1981. *The psychology of literacy.* Cambridge, MA: Harvard University Press.

Scudder, Thayer. 1978. Opportunities, issues and achievements in development anthropology since the mid-1960s: A personal view. In *Applied anthropology in America*, 2nd ed., eds. E. M. Eddy and W. L. Partridge. New York: Columbia University Press.

Seemanová, Eva. 1971. A study of children of incestuous matings. *Human Heredity* 21:108–28.

Segal, Edwin S. 2004. Cultural constructions of gender. In *Encyclopedia of sex and gender: Men and women in the world's cultures*, vol. 1, eds. C. Ember and M. Ember. New York: Kluwer Academic/Plenum Publishers.

Segal, Robert A. 1987. *Joseph Campbell: An introduction.* New York: Garland.

Segall, Marshall H. 1979. *Cross-cultural psychology: Human behavior in global perspective.* Monterey, CA: Brooks/Cole.

Segall, Marshall H., Pierre R. Dasen, John W. Berry, and Ype H. Poortinga. 1990. *Human behavior in global perspective: An introduction to cross-cultural psychology.* New York: Pergamon.

Sellen, Daniel W., and Daniel J. Hruschka. 2004. Extracted-food resource-defense polygyny in Native Western North American societies at contact. *Current Anthropology* 45:707–14.

Semenov, S. A. 1970. *Prehistoric technology.* Trans. M. W. Thompson. Bath, England: Adams & Dart.

Sen, Amartya. 1981. Ingredients of famine analysis: Availability and entitlements. *The Quarterly Journal of Economics* 96, no. 3:433–64.

Sengupta, Somini. 2002. Money from kin abroad helps Bengalis get by. *New York Times*, June 24, p. A3.

Senner, Wayne M. 1989. Theories and myths on the origins of writing: A historical overview. In *The origins of writing*, ed. W. M. Senner. Lincoln: University of Nebraska Press.

Serre, David, et al. 2004. No evidence of Neandertal mtDNA contribution to early modern humans. *PLoS Biology* 2:313–17.

Service, Elman R. 1962. *Primitive social organization: An evolutionary perspective.* New York: Random House.

Service, Elman R. 1975. *Origins of the state and civilization: The process of cultural evolution.* New York: Norton.

Service, Elman R. 1978. *Profiles in ethnology.* 3rd ed. New York: Harper & Row.

Service, Elman R. 1979. *The hunters.* 2nd ed. Upper Saddle River, NJ: Prentice Hall.

Seyfarth, Robert M., and Dorothy L. Cheney. 1982. How monkeys see the world: A review of recent research on East African vervet monkeys. In *Primate communication*, eds. C. T. Snowdon, C. H. Brown, and M. R. Petersen. New York: Cambridge University Press.

Seyfarth, Robert M., Dorothy L. Cheney, and Peter Marler. 1980. Monkey response to three different alarm calls: Evidence of predator classification and semantic communication. *Science* 210 (November 14):801–803.

Shanklin, Eugenia. 1993. *Anthropology and race.* Belmont, CA: Wadsworth.

Shankman, Paul. 1991. Culture contact, cultural ecology, and Dani warfare. *Man* 26:299–321.

Shankman, Paul. 2009a. Sex, lies, and anthropologists: Margaret Mead, Derek Freeman, and Samoa. In MyAnthroLibrary, eds. C. R. Ember, M. Ember, and P. N. Peregrine. MyAnthroLibrary.com. Pearson.

Shankman, Paul. 2009b. *The trashing of Margaret Mead: Anatomy of an anthropological controversy.* Madison: University of Wisconsin Press.

Sheils, Dean. 1975. Toward a unified theory of ancestor worship: A cross-cultural study. *Social Forces* 54:427–40.

Sheils, Dean. 1980. A comparative study of human sacrifice. *Behavior Science Research* 15:245–62.

Shen, Xuefei, and Robert F. Siliciano. 2000. Preventing AIDS but not HIV-1 infection with a DNA vaccine. *Science* 290 (October 20):463–65.

Shibamoto, Janet S. 1987. The womanly woman: Japanese female speech. In *Language, gender, and sex in comparative perspective*, eds. S. U. Philips, S. Steele, and C. Tanz. Cambridge: Cambridge University Press.

Shipman, Pat. 1986. Scavenging or hunting in early hominids: Theoretical framework and tests. *American Anthropologist* 88:27–43.

Shoreman-Ouimet, Eleanor, and Helen Kopnina. 2011. Introduction: Environmental anthropology of yesterday and today. In *Environmental anthropology today*, eds. H. Kopnina and E. Shoreman-Ouimet. New York: Routledge.

Shulman, Seth. 1993. Nurturing native tongues. *Technology Review* (May/June):16.

Shuy, Roger. 1960. Sociolinguistic research at the Center for Applied Linguistics: The correlation of language and sex. *Giornata Internazionale di Sociolinguistica*, Rome: Palazzo Baldassini: 849–57.

Siegel, Jeff. 2009. Pidgins/creoles and second language acquisition. In *The handbook of pidgin and creole studies*, eds. S. Kouwenberg and J. V. Singler. Wiley-Blackwell.

Sih, Andrew, and Katharine A. Milton. 1985. Optimal diet theory: Should the !Kung eat mongongos? *American Anthropologist* 87:395–401.

Silk, Joan. 1980. Adoption and kinship in Oceania. *American Anthropologist* 82:799–820.

Silk, Joan. 2007. Social components of fitness in primate groups. *Science* 317 (September 7):1347–51.

Silver, Harry R. 1981. Calculating risks: The socioeconomic foundations of aesthetic innovation in an Ashanti carving community. *Ethnology* 20:101–14.

Silverman, Eric K. 2006. High art as tourist art, tourist art as high art: Comparing the New Guinea sculpture garden at Stanford University and Sepik River tourist art. In *Exploring world art*, eds. E. Venbrux, P. S. Rosi, and R. L. Welsch. Los Angeles: J. Paul Getty Museum.

Simmons, Alan H., Ilse Köhler-Rollefson, Gary O. Rollefson, Rolfe Mandel, and Zeidan Kafafi. 1988. Ain Ghazal: A major Neolithic settlement in central Jordan. *Science* 240 (April 1):35–39.

Simmons, Janie, Paul Farmer, and Brooke G. Schoepf. 1996. A global perspective. In *Women, poverty, and AIDS: Sex, drugs, and structural violence*, eds. P. Farmer, M. Connors, and J. Simmons. Monroe, ME: Common Courage Press.

Simons, Elwyn L. 1992. The primate fossil record. In *The Cambridge encyclopedia of human evolution*, eds. S. Jones, R. Martin, and D. Pilbeam. New York: Cambridge University Press.

Simons, Elwyn L. 1995. Skulls and anterior teeth of *Catopithecus* (Primates: Anthropoidea) from the Eocene shed light on anthropoidean origins. *Science* 268 (June 30):1885–88.

Simons, Elwyn L., and D. T. Rassmussen. 1996. Skull of *Catopithecus browni*, an Early Tertiary catarrhine. *American Journal of Physical* Anthropology 100:261–92.

Simoons, Frederick J. 1994. *Eat not this flesh: Food avoidances from prehistory to the present*, 65–71, 101, 109–111, 261–265. Madison: University of Wisconsin Press.

Simpson, George Gaylord. 1971. *The meaning of evolution.* New York: Bantam.

Simpson, S. P., and Ruth Field. 1946. Law and the social sciences. *Virginia Law Review* 32:858.

Simpson, Scott W. 2009. *Australopithecus afarensis* and human evolution. In MyAnthroLibrary, eds. C. R. Ember, M. Ember, and P. N. Peregrine. MyAnthroLibrary.com. Pearson.

Simpson, Scott W., et al. 2008. A female *Homo erectus* pelvis from Gona, Ethiopia. *Science* 322 (November 14):1089–91.

Singer, J. David. 1980. Accounting for international war: The state of the discipline. *Annual Review of Sociology* 6:349–67.

Singer, Merrill. 2007. *Introducing medical anthropology: A discipline in action.* Lanham, MD: AltaMira.

Singer, Ronald, and John Wymer. 1982. *The Middle Stone Age at Klasies River Mouth in South Africa.* Chicago: University of Chicago Press.

Sipes, Richard G. 1973. War, sports, and aggression: An empirical test of two rival theories. *American Anthropologist* 75:64–86.

Skoggard, Ian, and Teferi Abate Adem. 2010. From raiders to rustlers: The filial disaffection of a Turkana age-set. *Ethnology* 49:249–62.

Skomal, Susan N., and Edgar C. Polomé, eds. 1987. *Proto-Indo-European: The archaeology of a linguistic problem.* Washington, DC: Washington Institute for the Study of Man.

Slayman, Andrew. 1997. A battle over old bones. *Archaeology* 50:16–23.

Slocum, Sally. 1975. Woman the gatherer: Male bias in anthropology. In *Toward an anthropology of women*, ed. R. Reiter. New York: Monthly Review Press.

Small, Meredith. 1997. Our babies, ourselves. *Natural History* (October):42–51.

Smay, Diana, and George Armelagos. 2000. Galileo wept: A critical assessment of the use of race in forensic anthropology. *Transforming Anthropology* 9:19–29.

Smedley, Audrey. 2004. *Women creating patrilyny.* Walnut Creek, CA: AltaMira.

Smedley, Brian D., Adrienne Y. Stith, and Alan R. Nelson, eds. 2003. *Unequal treatment: Confronting racial and ethnic disparities in health care.* Washington, DC: National Academy Press.

Smeeding, Timothy M., Robert Erikson, and Marcus Jäntti. 2011. Introduction. In *Persistence, privilege, and parenting*, eds. T. M. Smeeding, R. Erikson, and M. Jätti. New York: Russell Sage Foundation.

Smith, B. Holly. 1986. Dental development in *Australopithecus* and early *Homo. Nature* 323 (September 25):327–30.

Smith, Bruce D. 1992a. Prehistoric plant husbandry in eastern North America. In *The origins of agriculture*, eds. C. Cowan and P. Watson. Washington, DC: Smithsonian Institution Press.

Smith, Bruce D. 1992b. *Rivers of change.* Washington, DC: Smithsonian Institution Press.

Smith, Eric Alden. 1983. Anthropological applications of optimal foraging theory: A critical review. *Current Anthropology* 24:625–40.

Smith, Eric Alden, Monique Borgerhoff Mulder, Samuel Bowles, Michael Gurven, Tom Hertz, and Mary K. Shenk. 2010. Production systems, inheritance, and inequality in premodern societies: Conclusions. *Current Anthropology* 51:85–94.

Smith, Fred H. 1984. Fossil hominids from the Upper Pleistocene of central Europe and the origin of modern humans. In *The origins of modern humans*, eds. F. H. Smith and F. Spencer. New York: Alan R. Liss.

Smith, Fred H. 2010. Species, populations and assimilation in later human evolution. In *A companion to biological anthropology*, ed. C. S. Larsen. Hoboken, NJ: Wiley-Blackwell.

Smith, Fred H., and Frank Spencer, eds. 1984. *The origins of modern humans: A world survey of the fossil evidence.* New York: Alan R. Liss.

Smith, John Maynard. 1989. *Evolutionary genetics.* New York: Oxford University Press.

Smith, Michael G. 1966. Preindustrial stratification systems. In *Social structure and mobility in economic development*, eds. N. J. Smelser and S. M. Lipset. Chicago: Aldine.

Smith, M. W. 1974. Alfred Binet's remarkable questions: A cross-national and cross-temporal analysis of the cultural biases built into the Stanford-Binet Intelligence Scale and other Binet tests. *Genetic Psychology Monographs* 89:307–34.

Smith, Philip J., et al. 2011. Parental delay or refusal of vaccine doses, childhood vaccination coverage at 24 months of age, and the health belief model. *Public Health Reports* 126, Supplement 2:135–46.

Smith, Waldemar R. 1977. *The fiesta system and economic change.* New York: Columbia University Press.

Smuts, Barbara B., Dorothy L. Cheney, Robert M. Seyfarth, Richard W. Wrangham, and Thomas T. Struhsaker, eds. 1987. *Primate societies.* Chicago: University of Chicago Press.

Snowdon, Charles T. 1999. An empiricist view of language evolution and development. In *The origins of language*, ed. B. J. King. Santa Fe, NM: School of American Research Press.

Society for American Archaeology. 2009. FAQs for students. http://www.saa.org/ForthePublic/FAQs/ForStudents/tabid/101/Default.aspx (accessed August 26, 2009).

Society for Applied Anthropology. Ethical and professional responsibilities. http://www.sfaa.net/about/ethics/ (accessed May 11, 2013).

Soffer, Olga. 1993. Upper Paleolithic adaptations in central and eastern Europe and man-mammoth interactions. In *From Kostenki to Clovis*, eds. O. Soffer and N. D. Praslov. New York: Plenum.

Soffer, Olga, J. M. Adovasio, and D. C. Hyland. 2000. The "Venus" figurines: Textiles, basketry, gender, and status in the Upper Paleolithic. *Current Anthropology* 41:511–37.

Solis, Ruth Shady, Jonathan Haas, and Winifred Creamer. 2001. Dating Caral, a preceramic site in the Supe Valley on the central coast of Peru. *Science* 292 (April 27):723–26.

Solon, Gary. 2002. Cross-country differences in intergenerational earnings mobility. *Journal of Economic Perspectives* 16:59–66.

Sosis, Richard. 2002. Patch choice decisions among Ifaluk fishers. *American Anthropologist* 104:583–98.

Sosis, Richard. 2007. Psalms for safety: Magico-religious responses to threats of terror. *Current Anthropology* 48:903–11.

Sosis, Richard, and Candace Alcorta. 2003. Signaling, solidarity, and the sacred: The evolution of religious behavior. *Evolutionary Anthropology* 12:264–74.

Sosis, Richard, and Eric R. Bressler. 2003. Cooperation and commune longevity: A test of the costly signaling theory of religion. *Cross-Cultural Research* 37:211–39.

Southworth, Franklin C., and Chandler J. Daswani. 1974. *Foundations of linguistics.* New York: Free Press.

Spanos, Nicholas P. 1983. Ergotism and the Salem witch panic: A critical analysis and an alternative conceptualization. *Journal of the History of the Behavioral Sciences* 19:358–69.

Sparks, Corey, and R. L. Jantz. 2003. Changing times, changing faces: Franz Boas's immigrant study in modern perspective. *American Anthropologist* 105:333–37.

Spencer, Frank. 1984. The Neandertals and their evolutionary significance: A brief historical survey. In *The origins of modern humans*, eds. F. H. Smith and F. Spencer. New York: Alan R. Liss.

Spencer, Robert F. 1968. Spouse-exchange among the North Alaskan Eskimo. In *Marriage, family and residence*, eds. P. Bohannan and J. Middleton. Garden City, NY: Natural History Press.

Sperber, Dan. 1985. *On anthropological knowledge: Three essays.* Cambridge: Cambridge University Press.

Speth, John D. 2009. Were our ancestors hunters or scavengers? In MyAnthroLibrary, eds. C. R. Ember, M. Ember, and P. N. Peregrine. MyAnthroLibrary.com. Pearson.

Speth, John D., and Dave D. Davis. 1976. Seasonal variability in early hominid predation. *Science* 192 (April 30):441–45.

Speth, John D., and Katherine A. Spielmann. 1983. Energy source, protein metabolism, and hunter-gatherer subsistence strategies. *Journal of Anthropological Archaeology* 2:1–31.

Spiro, Melford E. 1982. *Oedipus in the Trobriands.* Chicago: University of Chicago Press.

Spiro, Melford E. 1993. Is the Western conception of the self "peculiar" within the context of the world cultures? *Ethos* 21:107–53.

Spiro, Melford E., and Roy G. D'Andrade. 1958. A cross-cultural study of some supernatural beliefs. *American Anthropologist* 60:456–66.

Spring, Anita. 1995. *Agricultural development and gender issues in Malawi.* Lanham, MD: University Press of America.

Spring, Anita. 2000a. Agricultural commercialization and women farmers in Kenya. In *Women farmers and commercial ventures: Increasing food security in developing countries*, ed. A. Spring. Boulder, CO: Lynne Rienner Publishers.

Spring, Anita. 2000b. Commercialization and women farmers: Old paradigms and new themes. In *Women farmers and commercial ventures: Increasing food security in developing countries*, ed. A. Spring. Boulder, CO: Lynne Rienner Publishers.

Spring, Anita, ed. 2000c. *Women farmers and commercial ventures: Increasing food security in developing countries.* Boulder, CO: Lynne Rienner Publishers.

Squires, Susan. 2002. Doing the work: Customer research in the product development and design industry. In *Creating breakthrough ideas: The collaboration of anthropologists and designers in the product development industry*, eds., S. Squires and B. Byrne. Westport, CT: Greenwood Press.

Stairs, Arlene. 1992. Self-image, world-image: Speculations on identity from experiences with Inuit. *Ethos* 20:116–26.

Stanford, Craig B. 2009. Chimpanzee hunting behavior and human evolution. In MyAnthroLibrary, eds. C. R. Ember, M. Ember, and P. N. Peregrine. MyAnthroLibrary.com. Pearson.

Stark, Rodney. 1985. *The future of religion: Secularization, revival and cult formation.* Berkeley: University of California Press.

Stark, Rodney. 1996. *The rise of Christianity: A sociologist reconsiders history.* Princeton, NJ: Princeton University Press.

Stark, Rodney. 2001. Gods, rituals and the moral order. *Journal for the Scientific Study of Religion* 40:619–36.

Stark, Rodney, and Roger Finke. 2000. *Acts of faith: Explaining the human side of religion.* Berkeley: University of California Press.

Starling, Anne, and Jay Stock. 2007. Dental indicators of health and stress in early Egyptian and Nubian agriculturalists: A difficult transition and gradual recovery. *American Journal of Physical Anthropology* 134:520–28.

Steadman, Lyle B., Craig T. Palmer, and Christopher F. Tilley. 2010 [orig. 1996]. In *Ritual and belief: Readings in the anthropology of religion*, 3rd ed., ed. D. Hicks. Lanham, MD: AltaMira Press.

Stedman, Hansell, et al. 2004. Myosin gene mutation correlates with anatomical changes in the human lineage. *Nature* 428 (March 25):415–18.

Steegman, A. T., Jr. 1975. Human adaptation to cold. In *Physiological anthropology*, ed. A. Damon. New York: Oxford University Press.

Stein, P., and B. Rowe. 2000. *Physical anthropology.* 7th ed. Boston: McGraw-Hill.

Steiner, Christopher B. 1990. Body personal and body politic: Adornment and leadership in cross-cultural perspective. *Anthropos* 85:431–45.

Stephens, William N. 1963. *The family in cross-cultural perspective.* New York: Holt, Rinehart & Winston.

Stephens, William N. 1972. A cross-cultural study of modesty. *Behavior Science Research* 7:1–28.

Stern, Curt. 1973. *Principles of human genetics.* 3rd ed. San Francisco: W. H. Freeman.

Stevens, Phillips, Jr. 1996. Religion. In *Encyclopedia of cultural anthropology*, vol. 3, eds. D. Levinson and M. Ember. New York: Henry Holt.

Steward, Julian H. 1955a. The concept and method of cultural ecology. In *Theory of culture change*, eds. J. H. Steward. Urbana: University of Illinois Press.

Steward, Julian H. 1955b. *Theory of culture change.* Urbana: University of Illinois Press.

Steward, Julian H., and Louis C. Faron. 1959. *Native peoples of South America.* New York: McGraw-Hill.

Stewart, T. D. 1950. Deformity, trephanating, and mutilation in South American Indian skeletal remains. In *Handbook of South American Indians, Vol. 6: Physical anthropology, linguistics, and cultural geography*, ed. J. A. Steward. Washington, DC: Smithsonian Institution Bureau of American Ethnology Bulletin 143.

Stimpson, David, Larry Jensen, and Wayne Neff. 1992. Cross-cultural gender differences in preference for a caring morality. *Journal of Social Psychology* 132:317–22.

Stini, William A. 1971. Evolutionary implications of changing nutritional patterns in human populations. *American Anthropologist* 73:1019–30.

Stini, William A. 1975. *Ecology and human adaptation.* Dubuque, IA: Wm. C. Brown.

Stockett, Miranda K., and Pamela L. Geller. 2006. Introduction. In *Feminist anthropology: Past, present, and future*, eds. P. L. Geller and M. K. Stockett. Philadelphia: University of Pennsylvania Press.

Stodder, James. 1995. The evolution of complexity in primitive exchange. *Journal of Comparative Economics* 20:205.

Stogdill, Ralph M. 1974. *Handbook of leadership: A survey of theory and research.* New York: Macmillan.

Stokstad, Erik. 2008. Privatization prevents collapse of fish stocks, global analysis shows. *Science* 321:1619.

Stone, Linda and Paul E. Lurquin. 2007. *Genes, culture, and human evolution.* Malden, MA: Blackwell.

Stoneking, Mark. 1997. Recent African origin of human mitochondrial DNA. In *Progress in population genetics and human evolution*, eds. P. Donnelly and S. Tavaré. New York: Springer.

Strachan, Laura. 2011. Political ecology and identity: A study of the Harasiis of Oman. *Totem: The University of Western Ontario Journal of Anthropology* 11, no. 1:101–13.

Straus, Murray A. 1991. Physical violence in American families: Incidence rates, causes, and trends. In *Abused and battered*, eds. D. D. Knudsen and J. L. Miller. New York: Aldine.

Straus, Murray A. 1995. Trends in cultural norms and rates of partner violence: An update to 1992. In *Understanding partner violence: Prevalence, causes, consequences, and solutions*, eds. S. M. Stith and M. A. Straus. Minneapolis, MN: National Council on Family Relations. http://pubpages.unh.edu/~mas2/v56.pdf/ (accessed August 2002).

Straus, Murray A. 2001. Physical aggression in the family: Prevalence rates, links to non-family violence, and implications for primary prevention of societal violence. In *Prevention and control of aggression and the impact on its victims*, ed. M. Martinez. New York: Kluwer Academic/Plenum.

Straus, Murray A. 2009. Prevalence and social causes of corporal punishment by parents in world perspective. Paper presented at the annual meeting of the Society for Cross-Cultural Research, Las Vegas, Nevada, February 20, 2009.

Straus, Murray. 2010. Thirty years of denying the evidence on gender symmetry in partner violence: Implications for prevention and treatment. *Partner Abuse* 1:332–63.

Straus, Murray A., and Glenda Kaufman Kantor. 1994. Change in Spouse assault rates from 1975 to 1992: A comparison of three national surveys in the United States. Paper presented at the 13th World Congress of Sociology, Bielefeld, Germany, July. http://pubpages.unh.edu/~mas2/v55.pdf/ (accessed August 2002).

Straus, Murray A., and Glenda Kaufman Kantor. 1995. Trends in physical abuse by parents from 1975 to 1992: A comparison of three national surveys. Paper presented at the annual meeting of the American Society of Criminology, Boston, MA, November 18. http://pubpages.unh.edu/~mas2/V57.pdf/ (accessed August 2002).

Straus, Murray A., and Carrie L. Yodanis. 1996. Corporal punishment in adolescence and physical assaults on spouses in later life: What accounts for the link? *Journal of Marriage and the Family* 58:825–41.

Strauss, Lawrence Guy. 1982. Comment on White. *Current Anthropology* 23:185–86.

Strauss, Lawrence Guy. 1989. On early hominid use of fire. *Current Anthropology* 30:488–91.

Stringer, Christopher B. 1985. Evolution of a species. *Geographical Magazine* 57:601–607.

Stringer, Christopher B. 2000. Neandertals. In *Encyclopedia of human evolution and prehistory*, eds. I. Tattersall, E. Delson, and J. van Couvering. New York: Garland.

Stringer, Christopher B. 2003. Out of Ethiopia. *Nature* 423 (June 12):692–95.

Stringer, Christopher B., and Clive Gamble. 1993. *In search of the Neanderthals*. New York: Thames and Hudson.

Stringer, Christopher B., J. J. Hublin, and B. Vandermeersch. 1984. The origin of anatomically modern humans in western Europe. In *The origins of modern humans*, eds. F. H. Smith and F. Spencer. New York: Alan R. Liss.

Suárez-Orozco, Marcelo. 1992. A grammar of terror: Psychocultural responses to state terrorism in dirty war and post-dirty war Argentina. In *The paths to domination, resistance, and terror*, eds. C. Nordstrom and J. Martin. Berkeley, CA: University of California Press.

Sullivan, Roger J., John S. Allen, and Karen L. Nero. 2007. Schizophrenia in Palau: A biocultural analysis. *Current Anthropology* 48:189–213.

Summerhayes, G. R., et al. 2010. Human adaptation and plant use in highland New Guinea 49,000 to 44,000 years ago. *Science* 330 (October 1):78–81.

Sunderland, Patricia L., and Rita M. Denny. 2007. *Doing anthropology in consumer research*. Walnut Creek, CA: Left Coast Press.

Super, Charles M., and Sara Harkness. 1997. The cultural structuring of child development. In *Handbook of cross-cultural psychology*, vol. 2, 2nd ed., eds. J. W. Berry, P. R. Dasen, and T. S. Saraswathi. Boston: Allyn & Bacon.

Susman, Randall L., ed. 1984. *The Pygmy Chimpanzee: Evolutionary biology and behavior*. New York: Plenum.

Susman, Randall L. 1994. Fossil evidence for early hominid tool use. *Science* 265 (September 9):1570–73.

Susman, Randall L., Jack T. Stern, Jr., and William L. Jungers. 1985. Locomotor adaptations in the Hadar hominids. In *Ancestors: The hard evidence*, ed. E. Delson. New York: Alan R. Liss.

Sussman, Robert W. 1972. Child transport, family size, and the increase in human population size during the Neolithic. *Current Anthropology* 13:258–67.

Sussman, Robert W. 1991. Primate origins and the evolution of angiosperms. *American Journal of Primatology* 23:209–23.

Sussman, Robert W., and W. G. Kinzey. 1984. The ecological role of the *Callitrichidae*: A review. *American Journal of Physical Anthropology* 64:419–49.

Sussman, Robert W., and Peter H. Raven. 1978. Pollination by lemurs and marsupials: An archaic coevolutionary system. *Science* 200 (May 19):734–35.

Svašek, Maruška. 2007. *Anthropology, art and cultural production*. London: Pluto Press.

Swanson, Guy E. 1969. *The birth of the gods: The origin of primitive beliefs*. Ann Arbor: University of Michigan Press.

Sweeney, James J. 1952. African Negro culture. In *African folktales and sculpture*, ed. P. Radin. New York: Pantheon.

Swisher, C. C., III, G. H. Curtis, T. Jacob, A. G. Getty, A. Suprijo, and Widiasmoro. 1994. Age of the earliest known hominids in Java, Indonesia. *Science* 263 (February 25):1118–21.

Szalay, Frederick S. 1968. The beginnings of primates. *Evolution* 22:32–33.

Szalay, Frederick S. 1972. Paleobiology of the earliest primates. In *The functional and evolutionary biology of the primates*, ed. R. Tuttle. Chicago: University of Chicago Press.

Szalay, Frederick S. 1975. Hunting-scavenging protohominids: A model for hominid origins. *Man* 10:420–29.

Szalay, Frederick S., and Eric Delson. 1979. *Evolutionary history of the primates*. New York: Academic Press.

Szalay, Frederick S., I. Tattersall, and R. Decker. 1975. Phylogenetic relationships of "*Plesiadipis*"—Postcranial evidence. *Contributions to Primatology* 5:136–66.

Szklut, Jay, and Robert Roy Reed. 1991. Community anonymity in anthropological research: A reassessment. In *Ethics and the profession of anthropology: Dialogue for a new era*, ed. C. Fluehr-Lobban. Philadelphia: University of Pennsylvania Press.

Tainter, Joseph. 1988. *The collapse of complex societies*. Cambridge: Cambridge University Press, 128–52.

Takahata, Naoyuki, and Yoko Satta. 1997. Evolution of the primate lineage leading to modern humans: Phylogenetic and demographic inferences from DNA sequences. *Publications of the National Academy of Sciences* 94 (April 29):4811–15.

Takezawa, Yasuko. 2006. Race should be discussed and understood across the globe. *Anthropology News* (February/March):6–7.

Talmon, Yonina. 1964. Mate selection in collective settlements. *American Sociological Review* 29:491–508.

Tamari, Tal. 1991. The development of caste systems in West Africa. *Journal of African History* 32:221–50.

Tamari, Tal. 2005. Kingship and caste in Africa: History, diffusion and evolution. In *The character of kingship*, ed. D. Quigley. Oxford: Berg Publishers.

Tannen, Deborah. 1990. *You just don't understand: Women and men in conversation*. New York: William Morrow and Company.

Tannenbaum, Nicola. 1984. The misuse of Chayanov: "Chayanov's Rule" and empiricist bias in anthropology. *American Anthropologist* 86:927–42.

Tanter, Raymond, and Manus Midlarsky. 1967. A theory of revolution. *Journal of Conflict Resolution* 11:3, 266.

Tattersall, Ian. 1982. *The primates of Madagascar*. New York: Columbia University Press.

Tattersall, Ian. 1997. Out of Africa again...and again? *Scientific American* 276 (April):60–68.

Tattersall, Ian. 1999. *The last Neanderthal*. Boulder, CO: Westview, 115–16.

Tattersall, Ian. 2002. Paleoanthropology and evolutionary theory. In *Physical anthropology: Original readings in method and practice*, eds. P. N. Peregrine, C. R. Ember, and M. Ember. Upper Saddle River, NJ: Prentice Hall.

Tattersall, Ian. 2009. Paleoanthropology and evolutionary theory. In MyAnthroLibrary, eds. C. R. Ember, M. Ember, and P. N. Peregrine. MyAnthroLibrary.com. Pearson.

Tattersall, Ian, and Jeffrey Schwartz. 2000. *Extinct humans*. Boulder, CO: Westview.

Tattersall, Ian, Eric Delson, and John Van Couvering, eds. 2000. *Encyclopedia of human evolution and prehistory*. New York: Garland.

Tattersall, Ian and Rob DeSalle. 2011. *Race? Debunking a scientific myth*. College Station, TX: Texas A&M University Press.

Tax, Sol. 1975. Action anthropology. *Current Anthropology* 16:514–7.

Taylor, Christopher C. 2005. Mutton, mud, and runny noses: A hierarchy of distaste in early Rwanda. *Social Analysis* 49:213–30.

Taylor, Paul, et al. 2010. *The return of the multigenerational family household*. Pew Research Center Report. Washington, DC: Pew Research Center.

Taylor, R. E. 1998. Radiocarbon dating. In *Chronometric dating in archaeology*, eds. R. E. Taylor and M. J. Aiken. New York: Plenum.

Taylor, R. E., and M. J. Aitken, eds. 1997. *Chronometric dating in archaeology*. New York: Plenum.

Teleki, Geza. 1973. The omnivorous chimpanzee. *Scientific American* (January):32–42.

Templeton, Alan R. 1993. The "Eve" hypotheses: A genetic critique and reanalysis. *American Anthropologist* 95:51–72.

Templeton, Alan R. 1996. Gene lineages and human evolution. *Science* 272 (May 31):1363.

Terborgh, John. 1983. *Five New World primates: A study in comparative ecology*. Princeton, NJ: Princeton University Press.

Terrell, John. 2011. *Building new bridges, not new walls: A handbook for hosting Marae encounters*. Chicago: Field Museum.

Textor, Robert B., comp. 1967. *A cross-cultural summary*. New Haven, CT: HRAF Press.

Thomas, David Hurst. 1986. *Refiguring anthropology: First principles of probability and statistics*. Prospect Heights, IL: Waveland.

Thomas, David Hurst. 2000. *Skull wars*. New York: Basic Books.

Thomas, Elizabeth Marshall. 1959. *The harmless people*. New York: Knopf.

Thomas, Richard. 2013. Personal communication, May.

Thomas, Wesley. 1993. A traditional Navajo's perspectives on the cultural construction of gender in the Navajo world. Paper presented at the University of Frankfurt, Germany. As referred to in Lang 1999.

Thomason, Sarah Grey, and Terrence Kaufman. 1988. *Language contact, creolization, and genetic linguistics*. Berkeley: University of California Press.

Thompson, Elizabeth Bartlett. 1966. *Africa, past and present*. Boston: Houghton Mifflin.

Thompson, Ginger. 2002. Mexico is attracting a better class of factory in its south. *New York Times*, June 29, p. A3.

Thompson, Richard H. 1996. Assimilation. In *Encyclopedia of cultural anthropology*, vol. 1, 4 vols., eds. D. Levinson and M. Ember. New York: Henry Holt.

Thompson, Richard H. 2009. Chinatowns: Immigrant communities in transition. In MyAnthroLibrary, eds. C. R. Ember, M. Ember, and P. N. Peregrine. MyAnthroLibrary.com. Pearson.

Thompson, Stith. 1965. Star Husband Tale. In *The study of folklore*, ed. A. Dundes. Upper Saddle River, NJ: Prentice Hall.

Thompson-Handler, Nancy, Richard K. Malenky, and Noel Badrian. 1984. Sexual behavior of *Pan paniscus* under natural conditions in the Lomako Forest, Equateur, Zaire. In *The Pygmy Chimpanzee*, ed. R. Susman. New York: Plenum.

Thornhill, Randy, and Corey L. Fincher. 2011. Parasite stress promotes homicide and child maltreatment. *Philosophical Transactions of the Royal Society B* 366:3466–77.

Thorpe, S. K. S., R. L. Holder, and R. H. Compton. 2007. Origin of human bipedalism as an adaptation for locomotion on flexible branches. *Science* 316 (June):1328–31.

Thurnwald, R. C. 1934. Pigs and currency in Buin: Observations about primitive standards of value and economics. *Oceania* 5:119–41.

Tierney, Patrick. 2000. *Darkness in El Dorado*. New York: Norton.

Tishkoff, Sarah A., et al. 2009. The genetic structure and history of Africans and African Americans. *Science Express 22* 324, no. 5930 (May):1035–44.

Tobias, Philip V. 1994. The craniocerebral interface in early hominids: Cerebral impressions, cranial thickening, paleoneurobiology, and a new hypothesis on encephalization. In *Integrative paths to the past*, eds. R. Corruccini and R. Ciochon. Upper Saddle River, NJ: Prentice Hall.

Tobin, Joseph J., David Y. H. Wu, and Dana H. Davidson. 1989. *Preschool in three cultures: Japan, China, and the United States*. New Haven, CT: Yale University Press.

Tocheri, Matthew, et al. 2007. The primitive wrist of *Homo floresiensis* and its implications for hominin evolution. *Science* 317 (September 21):1743–45.

Todorov, Alexander, Anesu N. Mandisodza, Amir Goren, and Crystal C. Hall. 2005. Inference of competence from faces predict election outcomes. *Science* 308 (June 10):1623–26.

Tollefson, Kenneth. 2009. Tlingit: Chiefs past and present. In MyAnthroLibrary, eds. C. R. Ember, M. Ember, and P. N. Peregrine. MyAnthroLibrary.com. Pearson.

Tomasello, Michael. 1990. Cultural transmission in the tool use and communicatory signaling of chimpanzees. In *"Language" and intelligence in monkeys and apes*, eds. S. Parker and K. Gibson. New York: Cambridge University Press.

Torrey, E. Fuller. 1972. *The mind game: Witchdoctors and psychiatrists*. New York: Emerson Hall.

Torry, William I. 1986. Morality and harm: Hindu peasant adjustments to famines. *Social Science Information* 25:125–60.

Traphagan, John W. 2006. Power, family, and filial responsibility related to elder care in rural Japan. *Case Management Journals* 7, no. 4:205–12.

Traphagan, John W. 2009. The oddness of things: Morality games and interpretations of social change among elders in rural Japan. *The Asia Pacific Journal of Anthropology* 10, no. 4:329–47.

Traphagan, John W., and L. Keith Brown. 2002. Fast food and intergenerational commensality in Japan: New styles and old patterns. *Ethnology* 41:119–34.

Travis, John. 2000. Human genome work reaches milestone. *Science News* (July 1):4–5.

Treiman, Donald J., and Harry B. G. Ganzeboom. 1990. Cross-national comparative status-attainment research. *Research in Social Stratification and Mobility* 9:117.

Trevor-Roper, H. R. 1971. The European witch-craze of the sixteenth and seventeenth centuries. In *Reader in comparative religion*, 3rd ed., eds. W. A. Lessa and E. Z. Vogt. New York: Harper & Row.

Triandis, Harry C. 1995. *Individualism and collectivism.* Boulder, CO: Westview.

Trigger, Bruce G. 1989. *A history of archaeological thought.* Cambridge: Cambridge University Press.

Trinkaus, Erik. 1984. Western Asia. In *The origins of modern humans*, eds. F. H. Smith and F. Spencer. New York: Alan R. Liss.

Trinkaus, Erik. 1985. Pathology and the posture of the La Chapelle-aux-Saints Neandertal. *American Journal of Physical Anthropology* 67:19–41.

Trinkaus, Erik. 1986. The Neandertals and modern human origins. *Annual Review of Anthropology* 15:193–218.

Trinkaus, Erik. 1987a. Bodies, brawn, brains and noses: Human ancestors and human predation. In *The evolution of human hunting*, eds. M. Nitecki and D. Nitecki. New York: Plenum.

Trinkaus, Erik. 1987b. The Neandertal face: Evolutionary and functional perspectives on a recent hominid face. *Journal of Human Evolution* 16:429–43.

Trinkaus, Erik. 2007. Human evolution: Neandertal gene speaks out. *Current Biology* 17, no. 21:R917–R919.

Trinkaus, Erik, and William W. Howells. 1979. The Neanderthals. *Scientific American* (December):118–33.

Trinkaus, Erik, and Pat Shipman. 1993a. *The Neandertals: Changing the image of mankind.* New York: Knopf.

Trinkaus, Erik, and Pat Shipman. 1993b. Neandertals: Images of ourselves. *Evolutionary Anthropology* 1:194–201.

Trompf, G. W., ed. 1990. *Cargo cults and millenarian movements: Transoceanic comparisons of new religious movements.* Berlin: Mouton de Gruyter.

Trouillot, Michel-Rolph. 2001. The anthropology of the state in the age of globalization: Close encounters of the deceptive kind. *Current Anthropology* 42:125–38.

Trudgill, Peter. 1983. *Sociolinguistics: An introduction to language and society.* Rev. ed. New York: Penguin.

Turner, B. L. 1970. Population density in the Classic Maya lowlands: New evidence for old approaches. *Geographical Review* 66 (January):72–82.

Turner, Christy G. 1987. Telltale teeth. *Natural History* (January):6–9.

Turner, Christy G. 1989. Teeth and prehistory in Asia. *Scientific American* (February):88–95.

Turner, Christy G. 2005. A synoptic history of physical anthropological studies on the peopling of Alaska and the Americas. *Alaska Journal of Anthropology* 3:157–70.

Turner, Terence. 1993. The role of indigenous peoples in the environmental crisis: The example of the Kayapo of the Brazilian Amazon. *Perspectives in Biology and Medicine* 36:526–45.

Turner, Terence. 1995. An indigenous people's struggle for socially equitable and ecologically sustainable production: The Kayapo revolt against extractivism. *Journal of Latin American Anthropology* 1:98–121.

Tuttle, Russell H. 1986. *Apes of the world: Their social behavior, communication, mentality, and ecology.* Park Ridge, NJ: Noyes.

Tylor, Edward B. 1971/1958. *Primitive culture.* New York: Harper Torchbooks.

Tylor, Edward B. 2010 [orig. 1873]. Animism. In *Ritual and belief: Readings in the anthropology of religion*, 3rd ed., ed. D. Hicks. Lanham, MD: AltaMira Press.

Uberoi, J. P. Singh. 1962. *The politics of the Kula Ring: An analysis of the findings of Bronislaw Malinowski.* Manchester, UK: University of Manchester Press.

Ucko, Peter J., and Andrée Rosenfeld. 1967. *Paleolithic cave art.* New York: McGraw-Hill.

Udy, Stanley H., Jr. 1970. *Work in traditional and modern society.* Upper Saddle River, NJ: Prentice Hall.

UNAIDS. 2007. AIDS epidemic update, December. http://data.unaids.org/pub/EPISlides/2007/2007_epiupdate_en.pdf.

UNAIDS. 2012. Global fact sheet. http://www.unaids.org (accessed May 18 2013).

UN-HABITAT. 2009. Planning sustainable cities: Global report on human settlements 2009. http://www.unhabitat.org/content.asp?typeid=19&catid=555&cid=5607 (accessed May 31, 2013).

UN-HABITAT. 2012. State of the world's cities 2012/2013. http://sustainabledevelopment.un.org/content/documents/745habitat.pdf.

UNHCR. 2013. Displacement: The new 21st century challenge. http://www.unhcr.org/51bacb0f9.html.

U.N. Human Development Report. 2011. http://hdr.undp.org/en/media/HDR_2011_EN_Table3.pdf (accessed September 7, 2012).

UN News Centre. 2005. Norway at top, Niger at bottom of UN's 2005 human development index. http://www.un.org/apps/news/story.asp?NewsID=15707&Cr=human&Cr1=development (accessed June 20, 2009).

UNODC. 2012. Homicide statistics. http://www.unodc.org/unodc/en/data-and-analysis/homicide.html.

UN Works. n.d. United Nations, Homeless Kids in Mongolia, with National Standards linked lesson plans http://www.un.org/works/goingon/mongolia/lessonplan_homelessness.html.

Underhill, Ralph. 1975. Economic and political antecedents of monotheism: A cross-cultural study. *American Journal of Sociology* 80:841–61.

Underhill, Ruth M. 1938. *Social organization of the Papago Indians.* New York: Columbia University Press.

Ungar, P. S., and M. Sponheimer. 2011. The diets of early hominins. *Science* 334 (October 14):190–93.

Union of International Associations. 2013. www.uia.be.

United Nations. n.d. We can end poverty. 2015 Millenium Development Goals. http://www.un.org/millenniumgoals/environ.shtml.

United Nations Development Programme (UNDP). 2007. Human development report 2007/2008: Fighting climate change: Human solidarity in a divided world. http://hdr.undp.org/en/media/HDR_20072008_EN_Complete.pdf (accessed June 20, 2009).

United Nations Development Programme (UNDP). 2010. The real wealth of nations: Pathways to human development. In Summary: Human Development Report 2010. http://hdr.undp.org/en/media/HDR10%20EN%20summary_without%20table.pdf.

United Nations Human Settlements Programme. 2003. The challenge of slums: global report on human settlements. http://www.unhabitat.org/pmss/listItemDetails.aspx?publicationID=1156 (accessed January 17, 2014).

Unnithan, N. Prabha. 2009. Nayars: Tradition and change in marriage and family. In MyAnthroLibrary, eds. C. R. Ember, M. Ember, and P. N. Peregrine. MyAnthroLibrary.com. Pearson.

U.S. Census Bureau. 2002. The big payoff: Educational entertainment and synthetic estimates of work-life earnings. In *Statistical abstract of the United States: 1993*, 113th ed. Washington, DC: U.S. Government Printing Office.

U.S. Department of Justice. 1988. *Prevalence, incidence, and consequences of violence against women: Findings from the National Violence against Women Survey*, November. Washington, DC: Bureau of Justice Statistics.

U.S. Department of Justice. 1994. *Violent crime.* NCJ-147486, April. Washington, DC: Bureau of Justice Statistics.

U.S. Department of Justice. 2000. *Children as victims. Juvenile Justice Bulletin 1999.* National Report Series. Washington, DC: Bureau of Justice Statistics.

U.S. Department of Justice. 2005. *Family violence statistics: including statistics on strangers and acquaintances.* Washington, DC: Bureau of Justice Statistics.

U.S. Department of Justice. n.d. Bureau of Justice statistics homicide trends in the U.S: Long-term trends and patterns. http://www.ojp.gov/bjs/homicide/hmrt.htm (accessed September5, 2009).

U. S. Department of State. 2013. Fact sheet: Non-Governmental Organizations (NGOs) in the United States. www.humanrights.gov.

U.S. Environmental Protection Agency. 2009. http://www.epa.gov/oecaagct/ag101/demographics.html (accessed February 2, 2014).

Vadez, Vincent, Victoria Reyes-Garcia, Tomás Huanca, and William R. Leonard. 2008. Cash cropping, farm technologies, and deforestation: What are the connections? A model with empirical data from the Bolivian Amazon. *Human Organization* 67:384–96.

Valente, Thomas W. 1995. *Network models of the diffusion of innovations.* Cresskill, NJ: Hampton Press.

Valla, Jeffrey M., Stephen J. Ceci, and Wendy M. Williams. 2011. The accuracy of inferences about criminality based on facial appearance. *Journal of Social, Evolutionary, and Cultural Psychology* 5, no. 1:66–91.

Valladas, H., J. L. Joron, G. Valladas, O. Bar-Yosef, and B. Vandermeersch. 1988. Thermoluminescence dating of Mousterian "Proto-Cro-Magnon" remains from Israel and the origin of modern man. *Nature* 337 (February 18):614–16.

Van der Leeuw, Sander. 1999. *The Archaeomedes Project: Understanding the natural and anthropogenic causes of desertification and land degradation.* Luxembourg: European Union.

Van der Leeuw, Sander, François Favory, and Jean Jacques Girardot. 2002. The archaeological study of environmental degradation: An example from southeastern France. In *The archaeology of global change*, eds. C. Redman, S. R. James, P. Fish, and J. D. Rogers. Washington, DC: Smithsonian.

Van der Merwe, N. J. 1992. Reconstructing prehistoric diet. In *The Cambridge encyclopedia of human evolution*, eds. S. Jones, R. Martin, and D. Pilbeam. New York: Cambridge University Press.

Van Hear, Nicholas. 2004. Refugee diasporas or refugees in diaspora. In *Encyclopedia of diasporas: Immigrant and refugee cultures around the world*, vol. 1, eds. M. Ember, C. R. Ember, and I. Skoggard. New York: Kluwer Academic/Plenum.

Van Hear, Nicholas. 2006. Refugees in diaspora: From durable solutions to transnational relations. *Refuge: Canada's Journal on Refugees* 23:9–14.

Van Hemert, Dianne A., Ype H. Poortinga, and Fons J. R. van de Vijver. 2007. Emotion and culture: A meta-analysis. *Cognition & Emotion* 21:913–43.

Van Hemert, Dianne A., Fons J. R. Van de Vijver, and Ad J. J. M. Vingerhoets. 2011. Culture and crying: Prevalences and gender differences. *Cross-Cultural Research* 45:399–431.

Van Ijzendoorn, Marinus H., Marian J. Bakermans-Kranenburg, and Abraham Sagi-Schwartz. 2006. Attachment across diverse sociocultural contexts: The limits of universality. In *Parenting beliefs, behaviors, and parent-child relations: A cross-cultural perspective*, eds. K. H. Rubin and O. B. Chung. New York: Psychology Press.

Van Lawick-Goodall, Jane. 1971. *In the shadow of man.* Boston: Houghton Mifflin.

Van Schaik, C. P. M. Ancrenaz, et al. 2003. Orangutan cultures and the evolution of material culture. *Science* 299 (January 3):102–05.

Van Willigen, John. 2002. *Applied anthropology: An introduction.* 3rd ed. Westport, CT: Bergin and Garvey.

Vayda, Andrew P., and Roy A. Rappaport. 1968. Ecology: Cultural and noncultural. In *Introduction to cultural anthropology*, ed. J. H. Clifton. Boston: Houghton Mifflin.

Vayda, Andrew P., Anthony Leeds, and David B. Smith. 1962. The place of pigs in Melanesian subsistence. In *Symposium* on patterns of land utilization, ed. V. E. Garfield. Seattle: University of Washington Press.

Vekua, Abesalom, et al. 2002. A new skull of early *Homo* from Dmanisi, Georgia. *Science* 297 (July 5):85–89.

Vigil, James Diego. 1988. Group processes and street identity: Adolescent Chicano gang members. *Ethos* 16:421–45.

Vigil, James Diego. 2009. Mexican Americans: Growing up on the streets of Los Angeles. In MyAnthroLibrary, eds. C. R. Ember, M. Ember, and P. N. Peregrine. MyAnthroLibrary.com. Pearson.

Vigilant, Linda, Mark Stoneking, Henry Harpending, Kristen Hawkes, and Allan C. Wilson. 1991. African populations and the evolution of human mitochondrial DNA. *Science* 253 (September 27):1503–1507.

Vincent, Joan. 1978. Political anthropology: Manipulative strategies. *Annual Review of Anthropology* 7:175–94.

Visaberghi, Elisabetta, and Dorothy Munkenbeck Fragaszy. 1990. Do monkeys ape? In *"Language" and intelligence in monkeys and apes*, eds. S. Parker and K. Gibson. New York: Cambridge University Press.

Vogel, Joseph O. 2009. De-mystifying the past: The Great Zimbabwe, King Solomon's mines, and other tales of Old Africa. In MyAnthroLibrary, eds. C. R. Ember, M. Ember, and P. N. Peregrine. MyAnthroLibrary.com. Pearson.

Vohs, Kathleen D., Nicole L. Mead, and Miranda R. Goode. 2006. The psychological consequences of money. *Science* 314 (November 17):154–56.

von Frisch, Karl. 1962. Dialects in the language of the bees. *Scientific American* (August):78–87.

Vrba, Elizabeth S. 1995. On the connection between paleoclimate and evolution. In *Paleoclimate and evolution*, eds. E. S. Vrba, G. H. Denton, T. C. Partridge, and L. H. Burckle. New Haven, CT: Yale University Press.

Vrba, Elizabeth S. 1996. Climate, heterochrony, and human evolution. *Journal of Anthropological Research* 52, no. 1:1–28.

Wadley, Reed L. 2003. Lethal treachery and the imbalance of power in warfare and feuding. *Journal of Anthropological Research* 59:531–54.

Wagley, Charles. 1974. Cultural influences on population: A comparison of two Tupi tribes. In *Native South Americans*, ed. P. J. Lyon. Boston: Little, Brown.

Waguespack, Nicole. 2012. Early Paleoindians from colonization to Folsom. In *Oxford handbook of North American archaeology*, ed. T. Pauketat. Oxford: Oxford University Press.

Wald, Matthew L. 2000. Hybrid cars show up in M.I.T.'s crystal ball. *New York Times*, November 3, p. Fl.

Waldbaum, Jane C. 2005. Helping hand for China. *Archaeology* 58:6.

Waldman, Amy. 2005. Sri Lankan maids' high price for foreign jobs. *New York Times*, May 8, pp. 1, 20.

Walker, Alan, and R. Leakey. 1988. The evolution of *Australopithecus boisei*. In *Evolutionary history of the "robust" australopithecines*, ed. F. Grine. New York: Aldine.

Wallace, Alfred Russell. 1970/1858. On the tendency of varieties to depart indefinitely from the original type. In *Evolution of man*, ed. L. B. Young. New York: Oxford University Press. (Originally published in 1858.)

Wallace, Anthony. 1966. *Religion: An anthropological view*. New York: Random House.

Wallace, Anthony. 1970. *The death and rebirth of the Seneca*. New York: Knopf.

Wallace, Anthony. 1972. Mental illness, biology and culture. In *Psychological anthropology*, 2nd ed., ed. F. L. K. Hsu. Cambridge, MA: Schenkman.

Wallerstein, Immanuel. 1974. *The modern world-system*. New York: Academic Press.

Walter, R. C. 1998. Potassium-argon/argon-argon dating methods. In *Chronometric dating in archaeology*, eds. R. E. Taylor and M. J. Aiken. New York: Plenum.

Wanner, Eric, and Lila R. Gleitman, eds. 1982. *Language acquisition: The state of the art*. Cambridge: Cambridge University Press.

Ward, Peter M. 1982. Introduction and purpose. In *Self-help housing*, ed. P. M. Ward. London: Mansell.

Ward, Steve. 1997. The taxonomy and phylogenetic relationships of *Sivapithecus* revisited. In *Function, phylogeny and fossils: Miocene hominoid evolution and adaptation*, eds. D. R. Begun, C. V. Ward, and M. D. Rose. New York: Plenum.

Ward, Steve, B. Brown, A. Hill, J. Kelley, and W. Downs. 1999. *Equatorius*: A new hominoid genus from the Middle Miocene of Kenya. *Science* 285 (August 27):1382–86.

Ward, Steven C., and Dana L. Duren. 2002. Middle and Late Miocene African hominoids. In *The primate fossil record*, ed. W. C. Hartwig. Cambridge: Cambridge University Press.

Wardhaugh, Ronald. 2002. *An introduction to sociolinguistics*. 4th ed. Oxford: Blackwell.

Warneken, Felix, and Michael Tomasello. 2009. The roots of human altruism. *British Journal of Psychology* 100:355–471.

Warner, Jessica, Gerhard Gmel, Kathryn Graham, and Bonnie Erickson. 2007. A time-series analysis of war and levels of interpersonal violence in an English military town 1700–1781. *Social Science History* 31, no. 4:575.

Warner, John Anson. 1986. The individual in Native American art: A sociological view. In *The arts of the North American Indian*, ed. E. L. Wade. New York: Hudson Hills Press.

Warner, W. Lloyd, and Paul S. Lunt. 1941. *The social life of a modern community*. New Haven, CT: Yale University Press.

Warren, Dennis M. 1989. Utilizing indigenous healers in national health delivery systems: The Ghanaian experiment. In *Making our research useful*, eds. J. van Willigen, B. Rylko-Bauer, and A. McElroy. Boulder, CO: Westview.

Warry, Wayne. 1986. Kafaina: Female wealth and power in Chuave, Papua New Guinea. *Oceania* 57:4–21.

Warry, Wayne. 1990. Doing unto others: Applied anthropology, collaborative research and native self-determination. *Culture* 10:61–62.

Washburn, Sherwood. 1960. Tools and human evolution. *Scientific American* (September):62–75.

Waters, M. R., et al. 2011. Pre-Clovis mastodon hunting 13,800 years ago at the Manis site, Washington. *Science* 334 (October 21):351–53.

Watkins, Trevor. 2009. From foragers to complex societies in Southwest Asia. In *The human past*, ed. C. Scarre, 200–33. New York: Thames and Hudson.

Watson, James L. 2004. Presidential address: Virtual kinship, real estate, and diaspora formation—The man lineage revisited. *Journal of Asian Studies* 63:893–910.

Weaver, Muriel Porter. 1993. *The Aztecs, Maya, and their predecessors*. 3rd ed. San Diego: Academic Press.

Webb, Karen E. 1977. An evolutionary aspect of social structure and a verb "have." *American Anthropologist* 79:42–49.

Weber, Max. 1947. *The theory of social and economic organization*, Trans. A. M. Henderson and Talcott Parsons. New York: Oxford University Press.

Weiner, Annette B. 1976. *Women of value, men of renown: New perspectives in Trobriand exchange*. Austin: University of Texas Press.

Weiner, Annette B. 1987. *The Trobrianders of Papua New Guinea*. New York: Holt, Rinehart and Winston.

Weiner, J. S. 1954. Nose shape and climate. *Journal of Physical Anthropology* 4:615–18.

Weiner, Jonathan. 1994. *Beak of the finch*. New York: Vintage.

Weiner, Steve, Q. Xi, P. Goldberg, J. Liu, and O. Bar-Yousef. 1998. Evidence for the use of fire at Zhoukoudian, China. *Science* 281 (July 10):251–53.

Weingarten, Carol Popp, and James S. Chisholm. 2009. Attachment and cooperation in religious groups: An example of a mechanism for cultural group selection. *Current Anthropology* 50:759–85.

Weinreich, Uriel. 1968. *Languages in contact*. The Hague, The Netherlands: Mouton.

Weisner, Thomas S. 2004. The American dependency conflict. *Ethos* 29:271–95.

Weisner, Thomas S., and Ronald Gallimore. 1977. My brother's keeper: Child and sibling caretaking. *Current Anthropology* 18:169–90.

Weisner, Thomas S., Mary Bausano, and Madeleine Kornfein. 1983. Putting family ideals into practice: Pronaturalism in conventional and nonconventional California families. *Ethos* 11:278–304.

Weiss, Harvey, and Raymond S. Bradley. 2001. What drives societal collapse? *Science* 291 (January 26):609–10.

Weiss, Harvey, et al. 1993. The genesis and collapse of third millennium north Mesopotamian civilization. *Science* 261 (August 20):995–1004.

Weller, Susan C. 2009. The research process. In MyAnthroLibrary, eds. C. R. Ember, M. Ember, and P. N. Peregrine. MyAnthroLibrary.com. Pearson.

Weller, Susan C., Roberta D. Baer, Javier Garcia de Alba Garcia, and Ana L. Salcedo Rocha. 2008. Susto and nervios: Expressions for stress and depression. *Culture, Medicine, and Psychiatry* 32, no. 3: 406–20.

Wells, Jonathan C. K. and Jay T. Stock. 2007. The biology of the colonizing ape. *Yearbook of Physical Anthropology* 50:191–222.

Wenke, Robert J. 1984. *Patterns in prehistory: Humankind's first three million years*. 2nd ed. New York: Oxford University Press.

Wenke, Robert J. 1990. *Patterns in prehistory: Humankind's first three million years*. 3rd ed. New York: Oxford University Press.

Wenke, Robert J., and Deborah Olszewski. 2007. *Patterns in prehistory*, 5th ed. New York: Oxford.

Werner, Dennis. 1975. On the societal acceptance or rejection of male homosexuality. Master's thesis, Hunter College of the City University of New York.

Werner, Dennis. 1978. Trekking in the Amazon forest. *Natural History* (November):42–54.

Werner, Dennis. 1979. A cross-cultural perspective on theory and research on male homosexuality. *Journal of Homosexuality* 4:345–62.

Werner, Dennis. 1982. Chiefs and presidents: A comparison of leadership traits in the United States and among the Mekranoti-Kayapo of central Brazil. *Ethos* 10:136–48.

Werner, Dennis. 1984. Child care and influence among the Mekranoti of central Brazil. *Sex Roles* 10:395–404.

Westermarck, Edward. 1894. *The history of human marriage*. London: Macmillan.

Weston, Eleanor, and Adrian Lister. 2009. Insular dwarfism in hippos and a model for brain size reduction in *Homo floresiensis*. *Nature* 459 (May 7):85–88.

Wheat, Joe B. 1967. A Paleo-Indian bison kill. *Scientific American* (January):44–52.

Wheatley, Paul. 1971. *The pivot of the four quarters*. Chicago: Aldine.

Wheeler, Peter. 1984. The evolution of bipedality and loss of functional body hair in hominids. *Journal of Human Evolution* 13:91–98.

Wheeler, Peter. 1991. The influence of bipedalism in the energy and water budgets of early hominids. *Journal of Human Evolution* 23:379–88.

Whitaker, Ian. 1955. *Social relations in a nomadic Lappish community*. Oslo: Utgitt av Norsk Folkemuseum.

White, Benjamin. 1973. Demand for labor and population growth in colonial Java. *Human Ecology* 1, no. 3 (March):217–36.

White, Douglas R. 1988. Rethinking polygyny: Co-wives, codes, and cultural systems. *Current Anthropology* 29:529–88.

White, Douglas R., and Michael L. Burton. 1988. Causes of polygyny: Ecology, economy, kinship, and warfare. *American Anthropologist* 90:871–87.

White, Douglas R., Michael L. Burton, and Lilyan A. Brudner. 1977. Entailment theory and method: A cross-cultural analysis of the sexual division of labor. *Behavior Science Research* 12:1–24.

White, Frances J. 1996. *Pan paniscus* 1973 to 1996: Twenty-three years of field research. *Evolutionary Anthropology* 5:11–17.

White, Leslie A. 1939. A problem in kinship terminology. *American Anthropologist* 41:569–70.

White, Leslie A. 1949. *The science of culture: A study of man and civilization*. New York: Farrar, Straus & Cudahy.

White, Leslie A. 1968. The expansion of the scope of science. In *Readings in anthropology*, vol. 1, 2nd ed., ed. M. H. Fried. New York: Thomas Y. Crowell.

White, Randall. 1982. Rethinking the Middle/Upper Paleolithic transition. *Current Anthropology* 23:169–75.

White, Tim D. 2003. Early hominids—Diversity or distortion? *Science* 299 (March 28):1994–97.

White, Tim D., and Pieter Arend Folkens. 2000. *Human osteology*. 2nd ed. San Diego: Academic Press.

White, Tim D., Donald C. Johanson, and William H. Kimbel. 1981. *Australopithecus africanus*: Its phyletic position reconsidered. *South African Journal of Science* 77:445–70.

White, Tim D., et al. 2009. *Ardipithecus ramidus* and the paleobiology of early hominids. *Science* 326 (October 2):75–86.

White, Timothy D., G. Suwa, and B. Asfaw. 1994. *Australopithecus ramidus*, a new species of early hominid from Aramis, Ethiopia. *Nature* 371 (September 22):306–33.

White, Timothy D., G. Suwa, and B. Asfaw. 1995. Corrigendum: *Australopithecus ramidus*, a new species of early hominid from Aramis, Ethiopia. *Nature* 375 (May 4):88.

Whitehead, Barbara Defoe, and David Popenoe. 2005. *The state of our unions: Marriage and family: What does the Scandinavian experience tell us?* National Marriage Project. Charlottesville: University of Virginia.

Whiten, A., et al. 1999. Cultures in chimpanzees. *Nature* 399 (June 17):682–85.

Whiting, Beatrice B. 1950. *Paiute sorcery*. Viking Fund Publications in Anthropology No. 15. New York: Wenner-Gren Foundation.

Whiting, Beatrice B. 1965. Sex identity conflict and physical violence. *American Anthropologist* 67:123–40.

Whiting, Beatrice B., and Carolyn Pope Edwards. 1973. A cross-cultural analysis of sex differences in the behavior of children aged three through eleven. *Journal of Social Psychology* 91:171–88.

Whiting, Beatrice B., and Carolyn Pope Edwards (in collaboration with Carol R. Ember, Gerald M. Erchak, Sara Harkness, Robert L. Munroe, Ruth H. Munroe, Sara B. Nerlove, Susan Seymour, Charles M. Super, Thomas S. Weisner, and Martha Wenger). 1988. *Children of different worlds: The formation of social behavior*. Cambridge, MA: Harvard University Press.

Whiting, Beatrice B., and John W. M. Whiting (in collaboration with Richard Longabaugh). 1975. *Children of six cultures: A psycho-cultural analysis*. Cambridge, MA: Harvard University Press.

Whiting, John W. M. 1941. *Becoming a Kwoma*. New Haven, CT: Yale University Press.

Whiting, John W. M. 1964. Effects of climate on certain cultural practices. In *Explorations in cultural anthropology*, ed. W. Goodenough. New York: McGraw-Hill.

Whiting, John W. M., and Irvin L. Child. 1953. *Child training and personality: A cross-cultural study.* New Haven, CT: Yale University Press.

Whiting, John W. M., Richard Kluckhohn, and A. Anthony. 1958. The function of male initiation ceremonies at puberty. In *Readings in social psychology*, eds. E. E. Maccoby, T. M. Newcomb, and E. L. Hartley. New York: Holt Rinehardt and Winston.

Whittaker, John C. 1994. *Flintknapping: Making and understanding stone tools.* Austin: University of Texas Press.

WHO. 2005. *WHO multi-country study on women's health and domestic violence against women: Summary report of initial results on prevalence, health outcomes and women's responses.* Geneva: World Health Organization.

Whyte, Martin K. 1978a. Cross-cultural codes dealing with the relative status of women. *Ethnology* 17:211–37.

Whyte, Martin K. 1978b. *The status of women in preindustrial societies.* Princeton, NJ: Princeton University Press.

Wiberg, Hakan. 1983. Self-determination as an international issue. In *Nationalism and self-determination in the Horn of Africa*, ed. I. M. Lewis. London: Ithaca Press.

Wierzbicka, Anna. 2005. Empirical universals of language as a basis for the study of other human universals and as a tool for exploring cross-cultural differences. *Ethos* 33, no. 2:256–91.

Wikan, Unni. 1982. *Beyond the veil in Arabia.* Baltimore: The Johns Hopkins University Press.

Wilden, Anthony. 1987. *The rules are no game: The strategy of communication.* London: Routledge and Kegan Paul.

Wilford, John Noble. 1995. The transforming leap, from 4 legs to 2. *New York Times*, September 5, p. C1ff.

Wilford, John Noble. 1997. Ancient German spears tell of mighty hunters of Stone Age. *New York Times*, March 4, p. C6.

Wilkinson, Robert L. 1995. Yellow fever: Ecology, epidemiology, and role in the collapse of the Classic Lowland Maya civilization. *Medical Anthropology* 16:269–94.

Williams, George C. 1992. *Natural selection: Domains, levels, and challenges.* New York: Oxford University Press.

Williams, Melvin D. 2009. Racism: The production, reproduction, and obsolescence of social inferiority. In MyAnthroLibrary, eds. C. R. Ember, M. Ember, and P. N. Peregrine. MyAnthroLibrary.com. Pearson.

Williams, Walter L. 1992. *The spirit and the flesh.* Boston: Beacon Press.

Wilmsen, Edwin N., ed. 1989. *We are here: Politics of aboriginal land tenure.* Berkeley: University of California Press.

Wilson, Christopher G. 2008. Male genital mutilation: An adaptation to sexual conflict. *Evolution and Human Behavior* 29:149–64.

Wilson, Edward O. 1975. *Sociobiology: The new synthesis.* Cambridge, MA: Belknap Press of Harvard University Press.

Wilson, Monica. 1963/1951. *Good company: A study of Nyakyusa age villages.* Boston: Beacon Press.

Winkelman, Michael. 1986a. Magico-religious practitioner types and socioeconomic conditions. *Behavior Science Research* 20:17–46.

Winkelman, Michael. 1986b. Trance states: A theoretical model and cross-cultural analysis. *Ethos* 14:174–203.

Winkelman, Michael. 2009. *Culture and health: Applying medical anthropology.* San Francisco: Wiley and Sons.

Winkelman, Michael. 2010. *Shamanism: A biopsychosocial paradigm of consciousness and healing.* 2nd ed. Santa Barbara, CA: Praeger/ABC-CLIO.

Winkelman, Michael, and John R. Baker. 2010. *Supernatural as natural: A biocultural approach to religion.* Upper Saddle River, NJ: Pearson Prentice Hall.

Winkleman, Michael, and Philip M. Peck, eds. 2004. *Divination and healing: Potent vision.* Tucson: University of Arizona Press.

Winterbottom, Robert. 1995. The tropical forestry plan: Is it working? *NAPA Bulletin* 15:60–70.

Winterhalder, Bruce. 1990. Open field, common pot: Harvest variability and risk avoidance in agricultural and foraging societies. In *Risk and uncertainty in tribal and peasant economies*, ed. E. Cashdan. Boulder, CO: Westview.

Witkin, Herman A. 1967. A cognitive style approach to cross-cultural research. *International Journal of Psychology* 2:233–50.

Witkowski, Stanley R. 1975. Polygyny, age of marriage, and female status. Paper presented at the annual meeting of the American Anthropological Association, San Francisco.

Witkowski, Stanley R., and Cecil H. Brown. 1978. Lexical universals. *Annual Review of Anthropology* 7:427–51.

Witkowski, Stanley R., and Harold W. Burris. 1981. Societal complexity and lexical growth. *Behavior Science Research* 16:143–59.

Wittfogel, Karl. 1957. *Oriental despotism: A comparative study of total power.* New Haven, CT: Yale University Press.

Wolf, Arthur. 1968. Adopt a daughter-in-law, marry a sister: A Chinese solution to the problem of the incest taboo. *American Anthropologist* 70:864–74.

Wolf, Arthur P., and Chieh-Shan Huang. 1980. *Marriage and adoption in China, 1845–1945.* Stanford, CA: Stanford University Press.

Wolf, Eric R. 1955. Types of Latin American peasantry: A preliminary discussion. *American Anthropologist* 57:452–71.

Wolf, Eric R. 1956. San José: Subcultures of a "traditional" coffee municipality. In *The people of Puerto Rico*, eds. J. H. Steward, R. A. Manners, E. R. Wolf, E. Padilla Seda, S. W. Mintz, and R. L. Scheele. Urbana: University of Illinois Press.

Wolf, Eric R. 1966. *Peasants.* Upper Saddle River, NJ: Prentice Hall.

Wolf, Eric R. 1984. Culture: Panacea or problem. *American Antiquity* 49:393–400.

Wolf, Naomi. 1991. *The beauty myth: How images of beauty are used against women.* New York: Morrow.

Wolff, Ronald G. 1991. *Functional chordate anatomy.* Lexington, MA: D. C. Heath.

Wolpoff, Milford H. 1971. Competitive exclusion among Lower Pleistocene hominids: The single species hypothesis. *Man* 6:601–13.

Wolpoff, Milford H. 1983. *Ramapithecus* and human origins: An anthropologist's perspective of changing interpretations. In *New interpretations of ape and human ancestry*, eds. R. Ciochon and R. Corruccini. New York: Plenum.

Wolpoff, Milford H. 1999. *Paleoanthropology*, 2nd ed. Boston: McGraw-Hill.

Wolpoff, Milford H., and Abel Nkini. 1985. Early and Early Middle Pleistocene hominids from Asia and Africa. In *Ancestors*, ed. E. Delson. New York: Alan R. Liss.

Wolpoff, Milford H., A. G. Thorne, J. Jelinek, and Zhang Yinyun. 1993. The case for sinking *Homo erectus*: 100 years of *Pithecanthropus* is enough! In *100 years of Pithecanthropus: The* Homo erectus *problem*, ed. J. L. Franzen.

Courier Forshungsinstitut Senckenberg 171:341–61.

Womack, Mari. 2010. *The anthropology of health and healing.* Lanham, MD: AltaMira.

Women in Science '93: Gender and the culture of science. 1993. *Science* 260 (April 16):383–430.

Wong, Kate. 2003. An ancestor to call our own. *Scientific American* (January):54–63.

Wong, Kate. 2005. The littlest human. *Scientific American* (February):56–65.

Wood, Bernard A. 1992. Evolution of australopithecines. In *The Cambridge encyclopedia of human evolution*, eds. S. Jones, R. Martin, and D. Pilbeam. New York: Cambridge University Press.

Wood, Bernard A. 1994. Hominid paleobiology: Recent achievements and challenges. In *Integrative paths to the past*, eds. R. Corruccini and R. Ciochon. Upper Saddle River, NJ: Prentice Hall.

Wood, Gordon S. 1992. *The radicalism of the American Revolution.* New York: Knopf.

Wood, James W., George R. Milner, Henry C. Harpending, and Kenneth M. Weiss. 1992. The osteological paradox: Problems of inferring prehistoric health from skeletal samples. *Current Anthropology* 33:343–70.

Wood, Wendy, and Alice H. Eagly. 2002. A cross-cultural analysis of the behavior of women and men: Implications for the origins of sex differences. *Psychological Bulletin* 128:699–727.

Woodburn, James. 1968. An introduction to Hadza ecology. In *Man the hunter*, eds. R. B. Lee and I. DeVore. Chicago: Aldine.

World Bank. 2004. *World development indicators 2004.* Washington, DC: World Bank Publications.

World Bank. 2011. *World bank development report 2012: Gender equality and development.* Washington, DC: World Bank.

Worsley, Peter. 1957. *The trumpet shall sound: A study of "cargo" cults in Melanesia.* London: MacGibbon & Kee.

Wrangham, Richard W. 1980. An ecological model of female-bonded primate groups. *Behaviour* 75:262–300.

Wrangham, Richard W. 2009. *Catching fire: How cooking made us human.* New York: Basic Books.

Wright, Gary A. 1971. Origins of food production in Southwestern Asia: A survey of ideas. *Current Anthropology* 12:447–78.

Wright, George O. 1954. Projection and displacement: A cross-cultural study of folktale aggression. *Journal of Abnormal and Social Psychology* 49:523–28.

Wright, Henry T. 1986. The evolution of civilizations. In *American archaeology past and future*, eds. D. Meltzer, D. Fowler, and J. Sabloff. Washington, DC: Smithsonian Institution Press.

Wright, Henry T., and Gregory A. Johnson. 1975. Population, exchange, and early state formation in southwestern Iran. *American Anthropologist* 77:267–77.

Wulff, Robert, and Shirley Fiste. 1987. The domestication of wood in Haiti. In *Anthropological praxis*, eds. R. M. Wulff and S. J. Fiste. Boulder, CO: Westview.

Yamei, Hou, et al. 2000. Mid-Pleistocene Acheulean-like stone technology of the Bose Basin, South China. *Science* 287 (March 3):622–26.

Yan, Yunxiang. 2006. Girl power: Young women and the waning of patriarchy in rural North China. *Ethnology* 45:105–23.

Yergin, Daniel. 2002. Giving aid to world trade. *New York Times*, June 27, p. A29.

Yinger, J. Milton. 1994. *Ethnicity: Source of strength? Source of conflict?* Albany: State University Press.

Young, Frank W. 1970. A fifth analysis of the Star Husband Tale. *Ethnology* 9:389–413.

Young, T. Cuyler, Jr. 1972. Population densities and early Mesopotamian urbanism. In *Man, settlement and urbanism*, eds. P. J. Ucko, R. Tringham, and G. W. Dimbleby. Cambridge, MA: Scherkmn.

Younger, Stephen M. 2008. Conditions and mechanisms for peace in precontact Polynesia. *Current Anthropology* 49:927–34.

Zebrowitz, Leslie A., and Joann M. Montepare. 2005. Appearance does matter. *Science* 308 (June 10):1565–66.

Zechenter, Elizabeth M. 1997. In the name of culture: Cultural relativism and the abuse of the individual. *Journal of Anthropological Research* 53:319–47.

Zeder, Melinda A. 1991. *Feeding cities: Specialized animal economy in the ancient Near East.* Washington, DC: Smithsonian Institution Press.

Zeder, Melinda A. 1994. After the revolution: Post-Neolithic subsistence in northern Mesopotamia. *American Anthropologist* 96:97–126.

Zeder, Melinda A. 2011. The origins of agriculture in the Near East. *Current Anthropology* 52, Supplement 4:S221–235.

Zhang, David D., Jane Zhang, Harry F. Lee, and Yuan-qing He. 2007. Climate change and war frequency in Eastern China over the last millennium. *Human Ecology* 35:403–14.

Zihlman, Adrienne L. 1992. The emergence of human locomotion: The evolutionary background and environmental context. In *Topics in primatology*, vol. 1, eds. T. Nishida, William McGrew, Peter Marler, Martin Pickford, and Frans de Waal. Tokyo: University of Tokyo.

Zimmer, Carl. 1999. Kenyan skeleton shakes ape family tree. *Science* 285 (August 27):1335–37.

Zimmer, Carl. 2004. Faster than a hyena? Running may make humans special. *Science* 306 (November 19):1283.

Zohary, Daniel. 1969. The progenitors of wheat and barley in relation to domestication and agriculture dispersal in the Old World. In *The domestication and exploitation of plants and animals*, eds. P. J. Ucko and G. W. Dimbleby. Chicago: Aldine.

Credits

Text Credits

Chapter 1. Page 6: Crittenden, Alyssa. 2013. Juvenile Foraging among the Hadza: Implications for Human Life History. *Evolution & Human Behavior* 34: 299–304.

Chapter 2. Page 18: Salzman, Philip Carl. 2001. *Understanding culture: An introduction to anthropological theory,* 135. Long Grove, IL: Waveland; Page 21: Vayda, Andrew P., and Roy A. Rappaport. 1968. Ecology: Cultural and noncultural. In *Introduction to cultural anthropology,* ed. J. H. Clifton. Boston: Houghton Mifflin; Page 23: Caws, Peter. 1969. *The structure of discovery.* Science 166 (December 12): 1375–80; Page 38: Leakey, Louis S. B. 1965. *Olduvai Gorge, 1951–1961, Vol. I: A Preliminary Report on the Geology and Fauna.* Copyright ©1965 Cambridge University Press. Reprinted with the permission of Cambridge University Press; Page 39: ©Pearson Education, Upper Saddle River, New Jersey.

Chapter 12. Page 228: Durkheim, Émile. 1938/1895. *The rules of sociological method.* 8th ed. Trans. Sarah A. Soloway and John H. Mueller. Ed. George E. Catlin. New York: Free Press; Page 229: Horace Miner's Body Rituals Among the Nacirema as published in the *American Anthropologist* 58, Issue 3, pages 503–507, June 1956; Page 231: Based on Rosenblatt, Paul C. 2009. Human rights violations. In MyAnthroLibrary, eds. C. R. Ember, M. Ember, and P. N. Peregrine. MyAnthroLibrary.com. Pearson; Page 234: Courtesy of Carol Ember; Page 242: Linton, Ralph. 1936. *The Study of Man.* New York: Appleton-Century-Crofts; Page 249: Data extracted from http://www.socialsecurity.gov/OACT/babynames/decades/index.html; Page 249: Courtesy of the United States Social Security Administration.

Chapter 16. Page 347: Bowie, Katherine A. 2006. Of corvée and slavery: Historical intricacies of the division of labor and state power in northern Thailand. In *Labor in cross-cultural perspective,* eds. E. Paul Durrenberger and Judith E. Martí, 245–64. Lanham: Roman & Littlefield; Page 348: (c) Pearson Education; Page 352: Mooney, Kathleen A. 1978. The effects of rank and wealth on exchange among the coast Salish. *Ethnology* 17: 391–406.

Chapter 18. Page 393: I. Opie and P. Opie, *The Oxford Dictionary of Nursery Rhymes* (Oxford: Oxford University Press, 1951, 2nd edn., 1997), pp. 100–1; Page 396: Based on Murdock, George P., and Caterina Provost. 1973. Factors in the division of labor by sex: A cross-cultural analysis. *Ethnology* 12: 203–25; Whyte, Martin K. 1978a. Cross-cultural codes dealing with the relative status of women. *Ethnology* 17: 211–37; Weisner, Thomas S., and Ronald Gallimore. 1977. My brother's keeper: Child and sibling caretaking. *Current Anthropology* 18:169–90.

Chapter 19. Page 417: Murdock, George P. 1949. *Social structure.* New York: Macmillan; Page 418: Radin, Paul. 1923. *The Winnebago Tribe.* Washington, DC: Smithsonian Institute. p. 138; Page 422: LeVine, Robert A., and Barbara B. LeVine. 1963. Nyansongo: A Gusii Community in Kenya. In *Six cultures,* ed. B. B. Whiting. New York: Wiley; Page 426: Wolf, Arthur. 1968. Adopt a daughter-in-law, marry a sister: A Chinese solution to the problem of the incest taboo. *American Anthropologist* 70: 864–74; Page 429: Firth, Raymond. 1957. *We, the Tikopia.* Boston: Beacon Press; Page 433: Stephens, William N. 1963. *The family in cross-cultural perspective.* New York: Holt, Rinehart & Winston; Page 434: Whiting, John W. M. 1964. Effects of climate on certain cultural practices. In *Explorations in cultural anthropology,* ed. W. Goodenough. New York: McGraw-Hill.

Chapter 20. Page 447: Calculated from Coult, Allan D., and Robert W. Habenstein. 1965. *Cross tabulations of Murdock's "World ethnographic sample."* Columbia: University of Missouri Press; Page 461: Adapted from Ember, Melvin, and Carol R. Ember. 1983. *Marriage, family, and kinship: Comparative studies of social organization.* New Haven, CT: HRAF Press.

Chapter 22. Page 493: Salzman, Philip Carl. 2008. Culture and Conflict in the Middle East. *Humanities Press;* Page 493: Adapted from Bohannan, Laura, and Paul Bohannan. 1953. *The Tiv of central Nigeria.* London: International African Institute; Page 495: Carneiro, Robert L. 1970. A theory of the origin of the state. *Science* 169 (August 21): 733–38; Page 495: Sahlins, Marshall D. 1962. *Moala: Culture and nature on a Fijian island.* Ann Arbor: University of Michigan Press; Page 504: Ross, Marc Howard. 1988. Political organization and political participation: Exit, voice, and loyalty in preindustrial societies. *Comparative Politics* 21: 73–89; Page 505: Hoebel, E. Adamson. 1968/1954. *The law of primitive man.* New York: Atheneum; Page 506: Boas, Franz. 1888. Central Eskimos. *Bureau of American Ethnology Annual Report No. 6.* Washington, DC; Pages 508 and 509: Schwartz, Richard D. 1954. Social factors in the development of legal control: A case study of two Israeli settlements. *Yale Law Journal* 63 (February): 471–91.

Chapter 23. Page 522: Middleton, John. 1971. The cult of the dead: Ancestors and ghosts. In *Reader in comparative religion,* 3rd ed., eds. W. A. Lessa and E. Z. Vogt. New York: Harper & Row.

Chapter 24. Pages 547 and 548: Lomax, Alan, ed. 1968. Folk song style and culture. *American Association for the Advancement of Science Publication* No. 88. Washington, DC; Page 551: Thompson, Stith. 1965. Star Husband Tale. In *The study of folklore,* ed. A. Dundes. Upper Saddle River, NJ: Prentice Hall.

Chapter 25. Page 563: Tax, Sol. 1975. Action anthropology. *Current Anthropology* 16: 514–517; Rylko-Bauer, Barbara, Merrill Singer, and John van Willigen. 2006. Reclaiming applied anthropology: Its past, present, and future. *American Anthropologist* 108: 178–190; Page 568: Ravesloot, John. 1997. Changing Native American perceptions of archaeology and archaeologists. In *Native Americans and archaeologists,* eds. N. Swidler et al. Walnut Creek, CA: AltaMira Press; Page 568: Naleimaile, Sean, and Lokelani Brandt. 2013. Is Hawaiian Archaeology Really Hawaiian? A Native Hawaiian Perspective. *SAA Archaeological Record* 13(1): 31–32.

Chapter 26. Page 579: Lévi-Strauss, Claude. 1963a. The sorcerer and his magic. In *Structural anthropology.* New York: Basic Books; Page 580: Torrey, E. Fuller. 1972. *The mind game: Witchdoctors and psychiatrists.* New York: Emerson Hall; Page 584: Honigmann, John J. 1967. *Personality in culture.* New York: Harper & Row.

Chapter 27. Page 600: Goldstein, Donna. 1998. Nothing bad intended: Child discipline, punishment, and survival in a shantytown in Rio de Janeiro. In *Small wars: The cultural politics of childhood,* eds. Nancy Scheper-Hughes and Carolyn Sargeant, 389–415. Berkeley: University of California-Berkeley Press.

Photo Credits

Chapter 1. Page 1: Bruno Morandi/Robert Harding World Imagery; Page 5: Spooner /Redmond-Callow/Zuma Press; Page 6: Firestick Productions - UNLV; Page 7: Darla Hallmark/Fotolia; Page 8: Mireille Vautier/Alamy; Page 10: Timothy G. Bromage, New York University College of Dentistry, and Friedemann Schrenk, Senckenberg Research Institute, at their camp discussing the jaw fragment, UR 51, the oldest fossil representative of the genus *Homo,* which they recovered from Late Pliocene sediments in northern Malawi. Photo by Thomas Ernsting; Page 12: Mark Peterson/Corbis Saba/Corbis News/Corbis; Pages 15 and 16: Andrey Zyk /Shutterstock; Page 16: Bruno Morandi /Robert Harding World Imagery.

Chapter 2. Page 17: National Geographic Image Collection/Alamy; Page 18: Ron Hilton/Shutterstock; Page 22: Richard Scaglion/University of Pittsburgh; Page 24: Ariana Cubillos/AP Images; Page 25: Doc White/Nature Picture Library; Page 28: Irven DeVore/Anthro-Photo; Page 31: The Trustees of the British Museum /Art Resource, NY; Page 34: Richard Vogel/AP Images; Page 36: World History Archive/AGE Fotostock; Page 40: Lincoln Journal Star/AP Images; Page 43: Martin Plöb/insadco Photography/Alamy.

Chapter 12. Page 224: Scott Stulberg/Ivy/Corbis; Page 229 (bl): Skjold Photographs /The Image Works; Page 229 (br): Bubbles Photolibrary/Alamy; Page 232: John Lund /Blend Images/Getty Images; Page 234 (tl): Jeremy Horner/Corbis; Page 234 (tr): Jonathan Blair/Corbis; Page 238: Reza/Webistan; Page 242: Joseph Van Os/Stone/ Getty Images; Page 244: HG/Magnum Photos; Page 247: Abdeljalil Bounhar/AP Images; Page 250: Robert Huberman/SuperStock/Alamy; Page 252: Smithsonian American Art Museum, Washington, DC/Art Resource, NY; Page 253: Marco Baroncini/Corbis; Page 258: Scott Stulberg/Corbis.

Chapter 15. Page 316: Hoang Dinh Nam/AFP/Getty Images; Page 318: Claire Leimbach/Robert Harding World Imagery; Page 322: Stringer/Reuters/Corbis; Page 325: Bill Bachmann/PhotoEdit; Page 326: PhotoStock-Israel/PhotoEdit; Page 328: Steven Lunetta/PhotoEdit; Page 329: Tiziana and Gianni Baldizzone/Corbis; Page 332: Tom McHugh/Science Source; Page 336: hoang dinh nam/AFP/Getty Images.

Chapter 16. Page 337: Alan Copson/Jon Arnold Images Ltd/Alamy; Page 340: Aurora Photos/Robert Harding World Imagery; Page 341: George Holton/Science Source; Page 345: Benelux Press BV/Science Source; Page 347: Still Pictures/Robert Harding World Imagery; Page 350: Kim Walker/Robert Harding World Imagery; Page 351: Chris Hellier/Alamy; Page 354: Charles & Josette Lenars/Corbis; Page 358: Bill Bachmann/Science Source; Page 360: Russell Gordon/Danita Delimont/Alamy; Page 361: Patrick Olear/PhotoEdit; Page 363: Radharc Images /Alamy; Page 368: Alan Copson/Jon Arnold Images Ltd/Alamy.

Chapter 17. Page 369: David Mdzinarishvili/Reuters/Corbis; Page 371: Wendy Stone/Corbis; Page 374: University of Washington Libraries, Special Collections, PH Coll 130/10.52, NA 3728; Page 376: University of Washington Libraries, Special Collections, PH Coll 130/10.52, NA 3728; Page 377: Mike Goldwater/Alamy; Page 378: AGE Fotostock/Robert Harding World Imagery; Page 380: View Stock /Alamy; Page 383: Syracuse University; Page 386: Michael Runkel/Robert Harding World Imagery; Page 391: David Mdzinarishvili/Reuters/Corbis.

Chapter 18. Page 392: Athit Perawongmetha/Reuters/Landov; Page 397: Tina Manley/Alamy; Page 399: Still Pictures/Robert Harding World Imagery; Page 404: Bruce G. Miller; Page 406: Jake Lyell/Alamy; Page 407: Kevin Cozad/O'Brien Productions/Corbis; Page 407: John Neubauer/PhotoEdit; Page 408: EmmePi Stock Images/Alamy; Page 411: Maciej Dakowicz/Alamy; Page 415: Athit Perawongmetha /Reuters /Landov.

Chapter 19. Page 416: Stock Connection USA/Newscom; Page 418: David McLain /Aurora Photos; Page 420: John Shaw/Science Source; Page 424: Susan Meiselas /Magnum Photos; Page 426: Boaz Rottem/Alamy; Page 431: Jonathan Player/*The New York Times*/Redux; Page 435: Michele Burgess/Alamy; Page 436: GAMMA /Gamma-Keystone /Getty Images; Page 438: Ariadne Van Zandbergen/Alamy; Page 444: Stock Connection USA/Newscom.

Chapter 20. Page 445: Norma Joseph/Alamy; Page 448: Bert Hoferichter/Alamy; Page 455: Tom Allwood/Alamy; Page 457: Shrikrishna Paranjpe/ephotocorp/Alamy; Page 460: George H. H. Huey/Alamy; Page 462: Designpics/Glow Images; Page 466: Stock Montage/Getty Images; Page 470: norma joseph/alamy.

Chapter 22. Page 489: David McNew/Getty Images; Page 492: John Warburton-Lee Photography/Alamy; Page 495: Danita Delimont/Alamy; Page 497: Peter Andrews /Reuters/Corbis; Page 499: Bettmann/Corbis; Page 503: Maria Lepowsky;

Page 506: Bill Aron/PhotoEdit; Page 508: jackie ellis/Alamy; Page 511: Yasuyoshi Chiba/AFP/Getty Images; Page 514: David McNew/Getty Images News/Getty Images.

Chapter 23. Page 515: Images and Stories/Alamy; Page 517: Michele Burgess /Alamy; Page 519: Joshua Roper/Alamy; Page 521: Aurora Photos/Robert Harding World Imagery; Page 524: North Wind Picture Archives/Alamy; Page 529: Catherine Karnow/Terra/Corbis; Page 532: Carles Zamorano Cabello/Alamy; Page 534: The Granger Collection, NYC; Page 538: Images & Stories/Alamy.

Chapter 24. Page 539: Ueslei Marcelino/Reuters/Landov; Page 542: Hemis/Alamy; Page 544 (tl): B.S.P.I./Corbis; Page 544 (tr): Paul Chesley/National Geographic Image Collection/Alamy; Page 545 (bl): The Trustees of the British Museum/Art Resource, NY; Page 545 (br): The Trustees of the British Museum/Art Resource, NY; Page 546: Debby Wong/Shutterstock; Page 549: Travelscape Images/Alamy; Page 550: Wendy Stone/Corbis; Page 551: Susan McCartney/Science Source; Page 554: George H. H. Huey/Alamy; Page 556: Ueslei Marcelino/Reuters/Landov.

Chapter 25. Page 557: Michael Horowitz, Professor; Page 560: Paul Jeffrey /Kairos Photos; Page 563: Ricardo Moraes/Reuters; Page 564: Europics/Newscom; Page 566: Robert T. Trotter, II; Page 567: Yannis Kontos/Sygma/Corbis; Page 569: Bob Elam/Alamy; Page 570: Horacio Villalobos/Corbis; Page 572: Michael Horowitz.

Chapter 26. Page 573: Universal Images Group/Getty Images; Page 575: Jochen Schlenker/Robert Harding World Imagery; Page 579: epa european pressphoto agency b.v./Alamy; Page 582: Jon Hursa/Pool/epa/Corbis; Page 585: Tony Anderson /Corbis; Page 588: Peter Bowater/Science Source; Page 590: Universal Images Group/Getty Images.

Chapter 27. Page 591: Stuart Kelly/Alamy; Page 593: STR/AFP/Getty Images; Page 597: Sucheta Das/Reuters/Corbis Wire/Corbis; Page 598: Gemunu Amarasinghe /AP Images; Page 603: BSIP/UIG/Getty Images; Page 605: Iraq/Reuters/Corbis; Page 607: Honda/AFP/Getty Images; Page 610: Stuart Kelly/Alamy.

The following pages contain maps that have been adapted from the *DK Atlas of World History: Mapping the Human Journey* and *Atlas of Anthropology*, produced by Dorling Kindersley. Each map focuses on a topic that is discussed in more detail within the text itself and is intended to bring the richness of anthropology to life.

maps

Prentice Hall would sincerely like to thank Dorling Kindersley for helping to put this feature together.

THE LIVING PRIMATES

The great apes are the chimpanzees, gorillas, and Asian orangutans, while the lesser, smaller apes are the gibbons and siamangs of South and Southeast Asia. Primates are the mammalian order that includes apes, monkeys, and humans. Prosimians, the most primitive of primates, are mainly small, solitary nocturnal creatures. Anthropoids, including apes, monkeys and ourselves, have larger bodies, and are organized on social groups. All primates have well developed visual sense, forward-directed eyes, and larger brains for their body sizes than other mammals. Most live in the tropics, and move around in a variety of different ways.

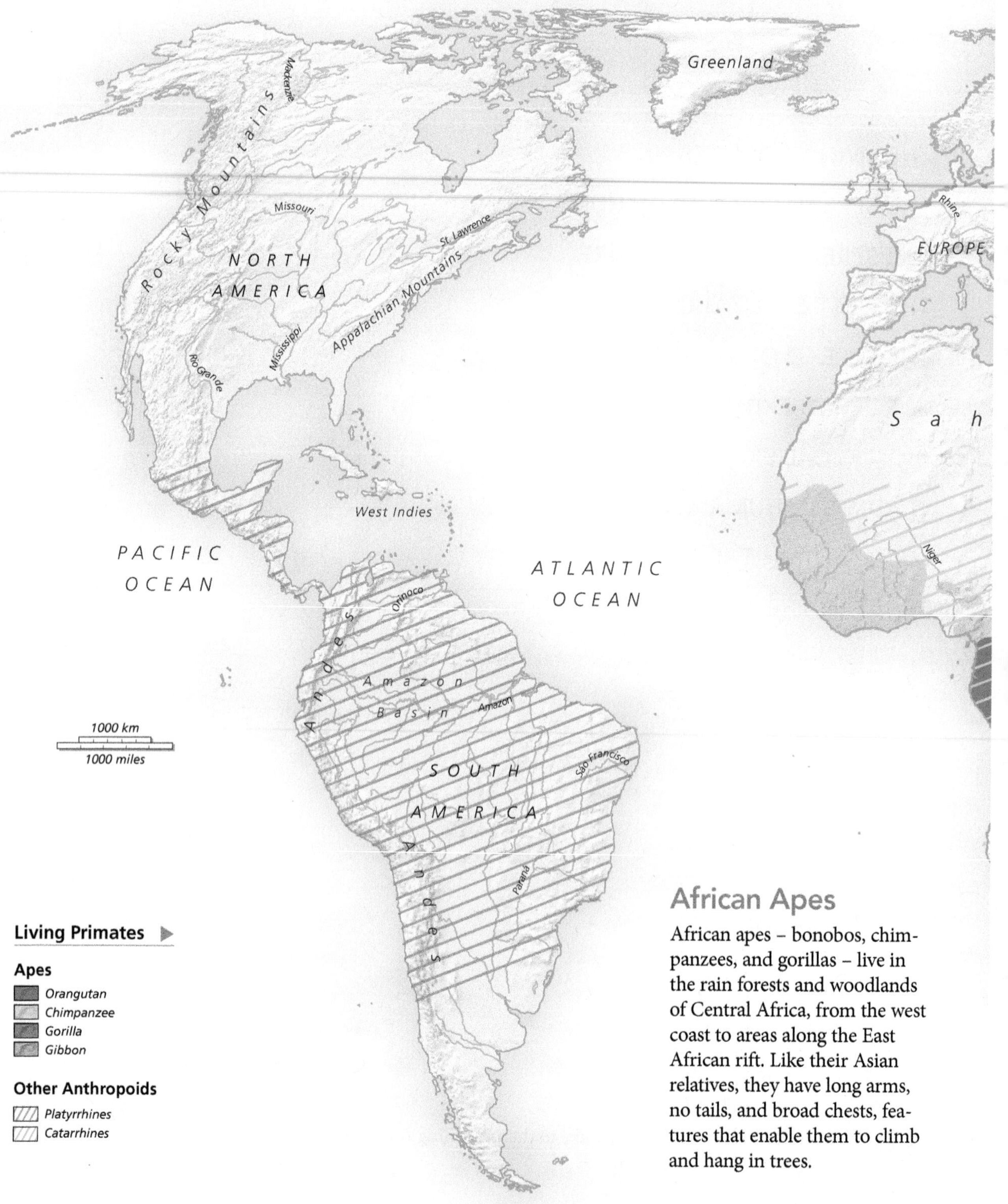

African Apes

African apes – bonobos, chimpanzees, and gorillas – live in the rain forests and woodlands of Central Africa, from the west coast to areas along the East African rift. Like their Asian relatives, they have long arms, no tails, and broad chests, features that enable them to climb and hang in trees.

Asian Apes

Gibbons and their relatives, the siamangs and orangutans, are confined to South and Southeast Asia. Gibbons are the smallest and most anatomically primitive of all apes, retaining many monkeylike traits. Orangutans are the largest arboreal mammals. Once widespread, they are now confined to forested regions of Borneo and Sumatra.

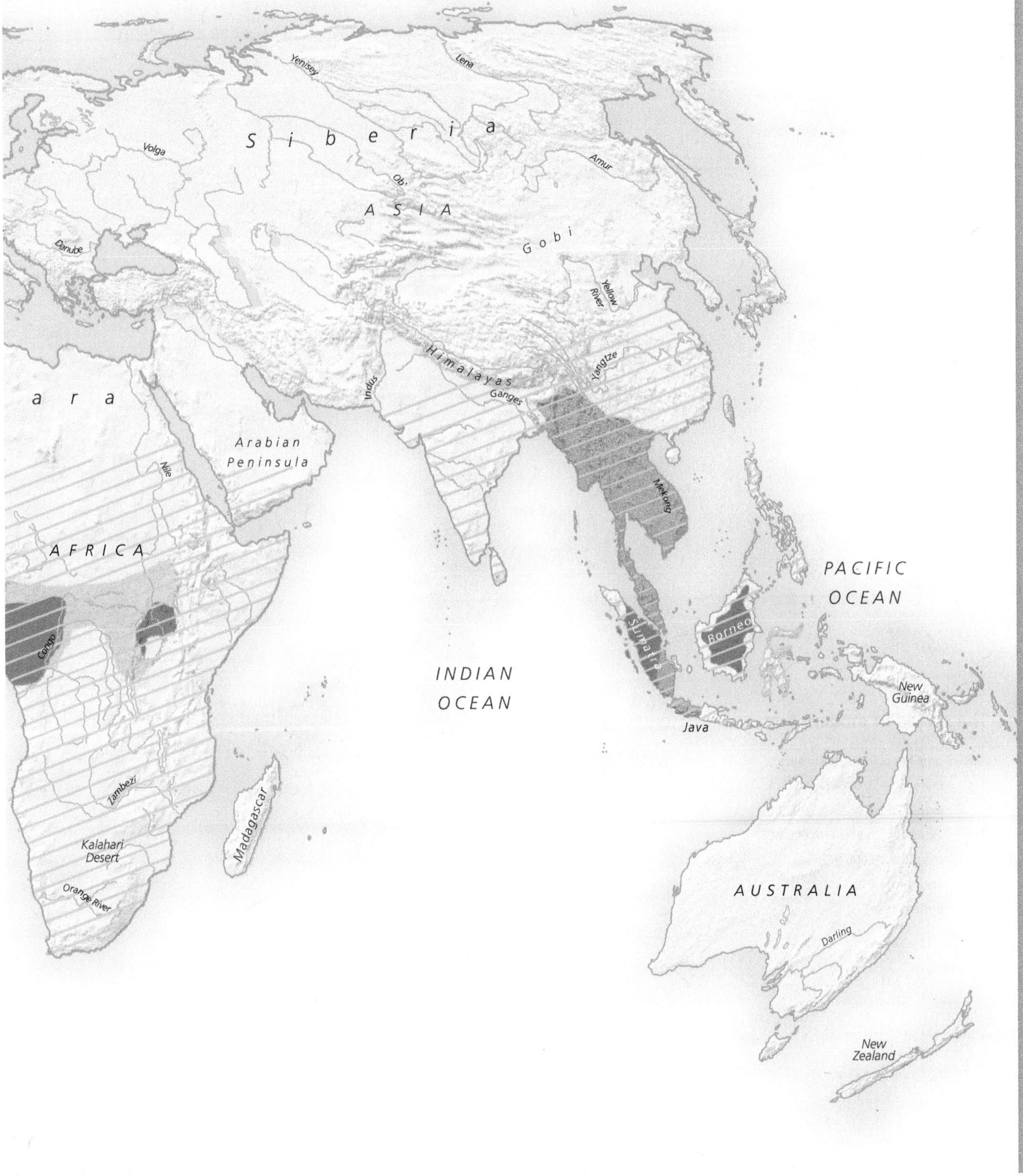

THE SPREAD OF MODERN HUMANS

Fully modern humans evolved in Africa, probably between 200,000 and 100,000 years ago. By 30,000 years ago, they had colonized much of the globe. Rising temperatures at the end of the last Ice Age allowed plants and animals to become more abundant, and new areas were settled. By 8000 B.C., larger populations and intense hunting had contributed to the near extinction of large mammals, such as mastodons and

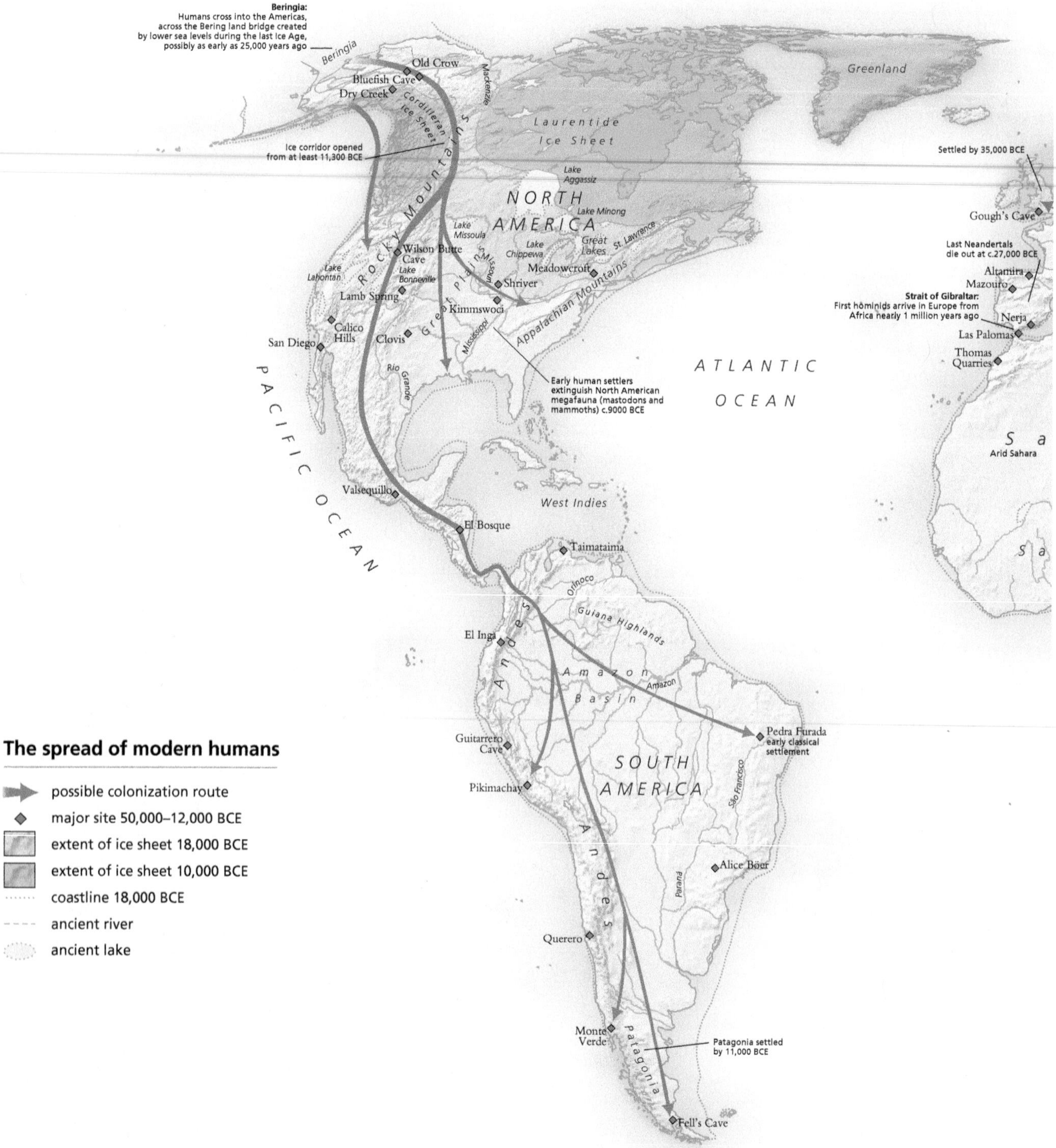

mammoths. In the Near East, groups of hunter gatherers were living in permanent settlements, harvesting wild cereals, and experimenting with the domestication of local animals. The transition to agriculture was under way.

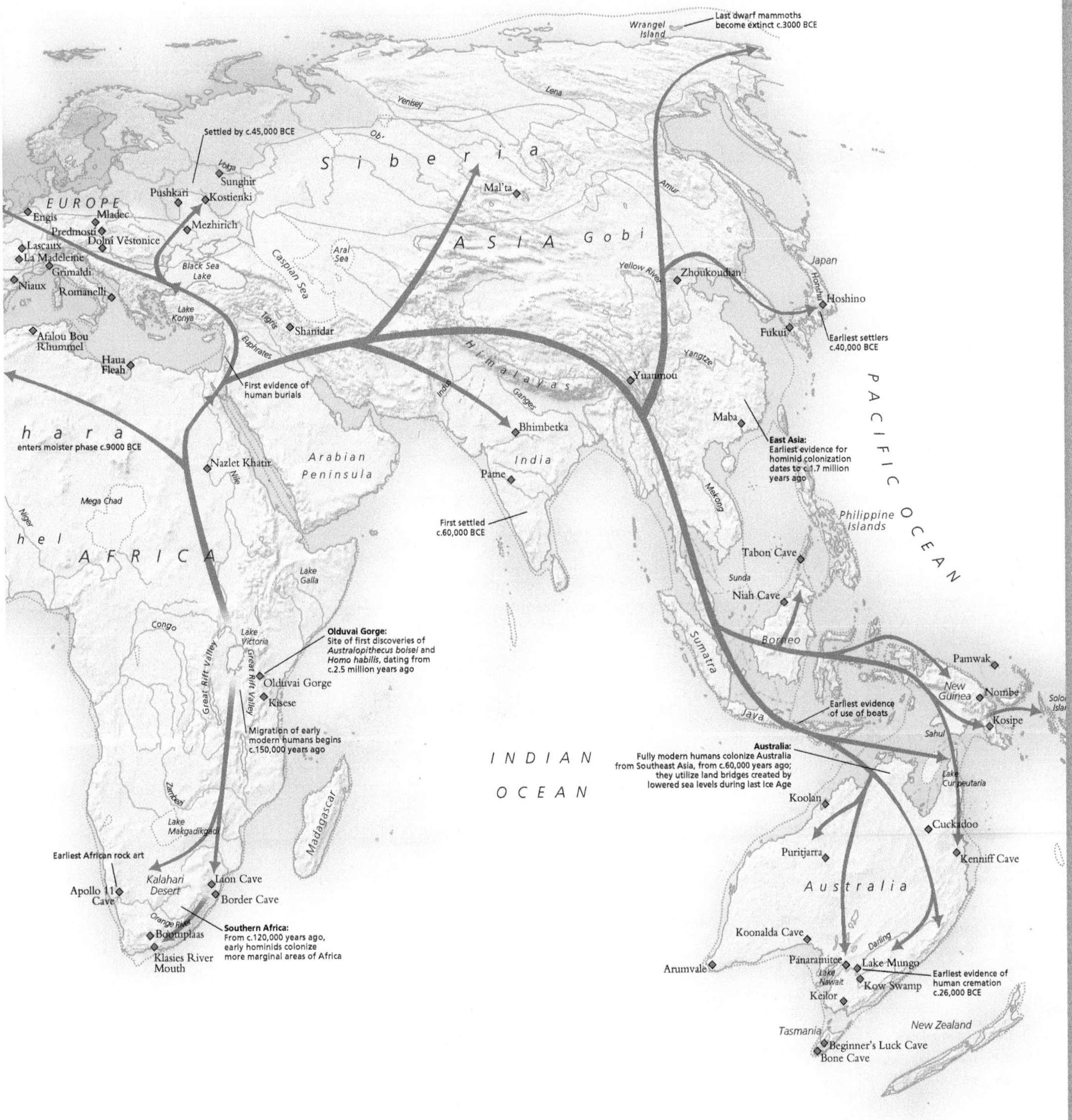

THE SPREAD OF AGRICULTURE

The appearance of farming transformed the face of the Earth. It was not merely a change in subsistence, it also transformed the way in which our ancestors lived. Agriculture, and the vastly greater crop yields it produced, enabled larger groups of people to live together, often in permanent villages. After agriculture emerged, craft, religious, and political specialization became more likely, and the first signs of social

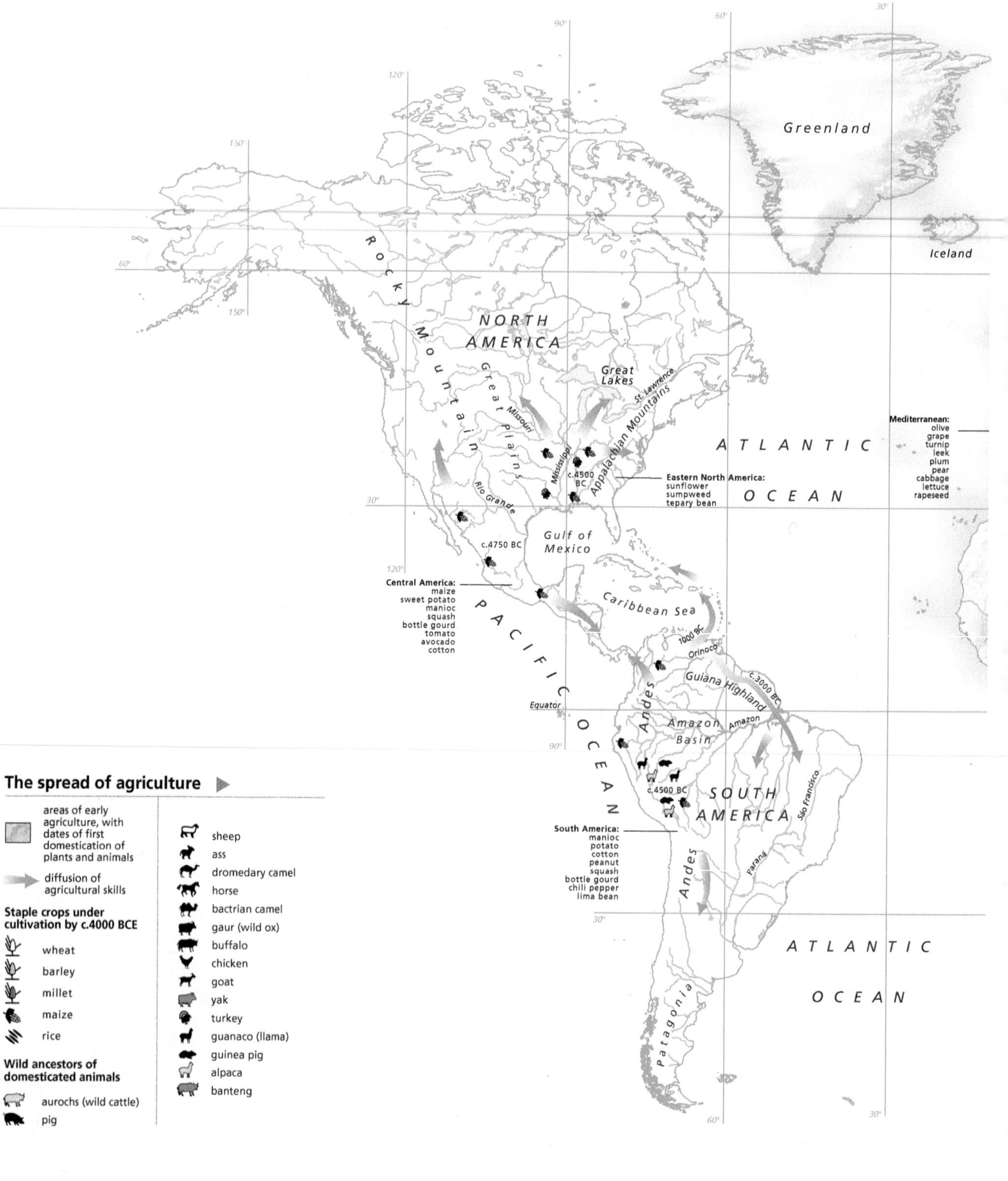

inequality appeared. In 5000 B.C., only a limited number of regions were fully dependent on agriculture. In many parts of the globe, small-scale farming began to supplement hunting and gathering, the first steps in the gradual transition to the sedentary agricultural way of life.

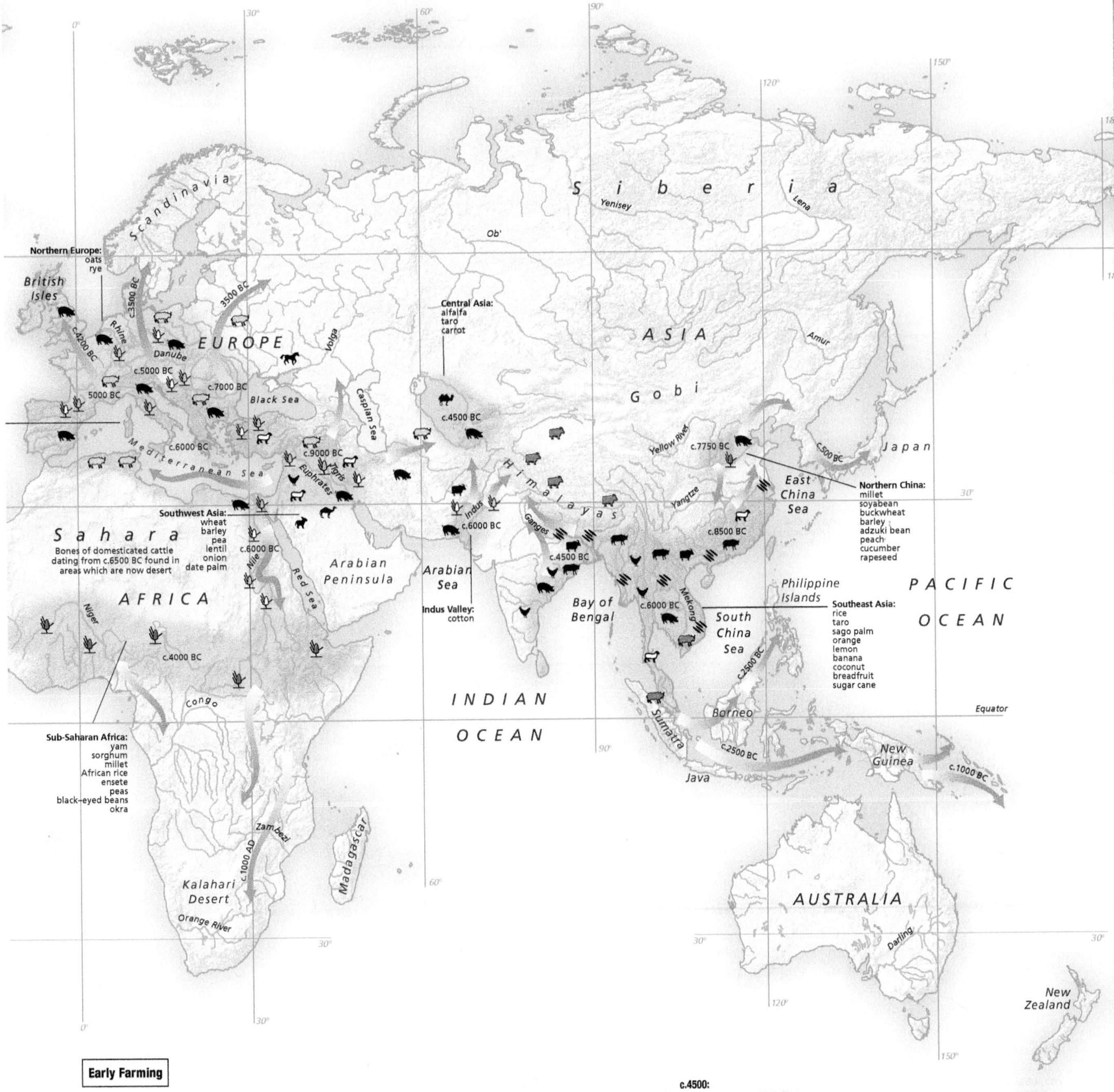

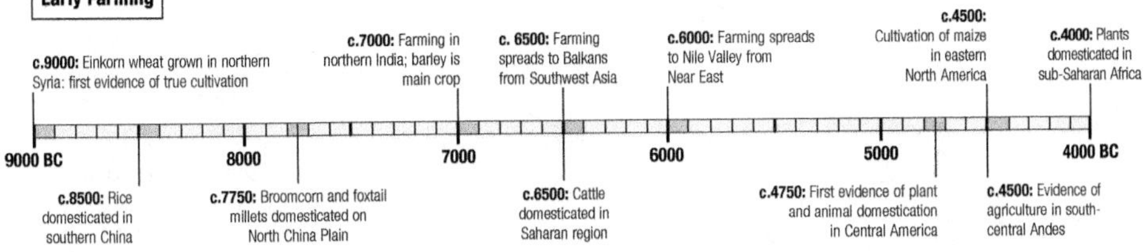

THE FIRST CIVILIZATIONS

The period between 5000 and 2500 B.C. saw the development of complex urban civilizations in the fertile river valleys of the Nile, Tigris, Euphrates, and Indus. Mesopotamian city states formed small kingdoms, which competed with one another. A literate elite ruled over each civilization, and their artisans experimented with new technologies such as bronze and copper metallurgy. Many village societies developed important ritual centers or buried their dead in communal sepulchers.

The Americas

- **c.4750:** First agriculture in Americas: maize grown in Central America's Tehuacan valley
- **4000:** First pottery in the Americas from Amazon Basin
- **3500:** Cotton cultivated in Central America; used to make fishing nets and textiles
- **3400:** Farming villages established in Tehuacan Valley
- **2600:** Large temple complexes built in villages along the Andean coast
- **2500:** Evidence of long distance trade throughout South America, mainly of valuables

5000 BC | 4500 | 4000 | 3500 | 3000 | 2500 BC

Africa

- **3400:** First walled towns appear in Egypt
- **3100:** King Narmer unifies Upper and Lower Egypt, and becomes first pharaoh. City of Memphis is founded
- **3000:** First evidence of hieroglyphic writing system
- **2650:** The step pyramid of Djoser, the first Egyptian pyramid, is built at Saqqara
- **2530:** Construction of Great Pyramid of Khufu, the largest of the Egyptian pyramids, at Giza

5000 BC | 4500 | 4000 | 3500 | 3000 | 2500 BC

Europe

- **c.5000:** Metallurgy discovered in south-eastern Europe
- **4500:** Large cemeteries, for example on the western coast of the Black Sea, contain rich burials with elaborate gold jewelry
- **c.4500:** In western Europe, megalithic (large stone) chamber tombs, built as communal burial places
- **3800:** Ditched enclosures around settlements in central Europe create defended villages
- **3200:** Stone circles and rows of standing stones built throughout northern and western Europe
- **2900:** Earliest burials containing Corded Ware pottery in northern and central Europe

5000 BC | 4500 | 4000 | 3500 | 3000 | 2500 BC

East Asia

- **c.4000:** Planned villages in northern China, with distinct residential, workshop, and burial areas
- **3000:** First evidence of farming (millet cultivation) in Korea
- **c.3000:** Potter's wheel invented during formative phase of Longshan culture of eastern China
- **2750:** First Chinese bronze artifacts
- **2500:** Banshan culture of western China produces boldly painted burial urns

5000 BC | 4500 | 4000 | 3500 | 3000 | 2500 BC

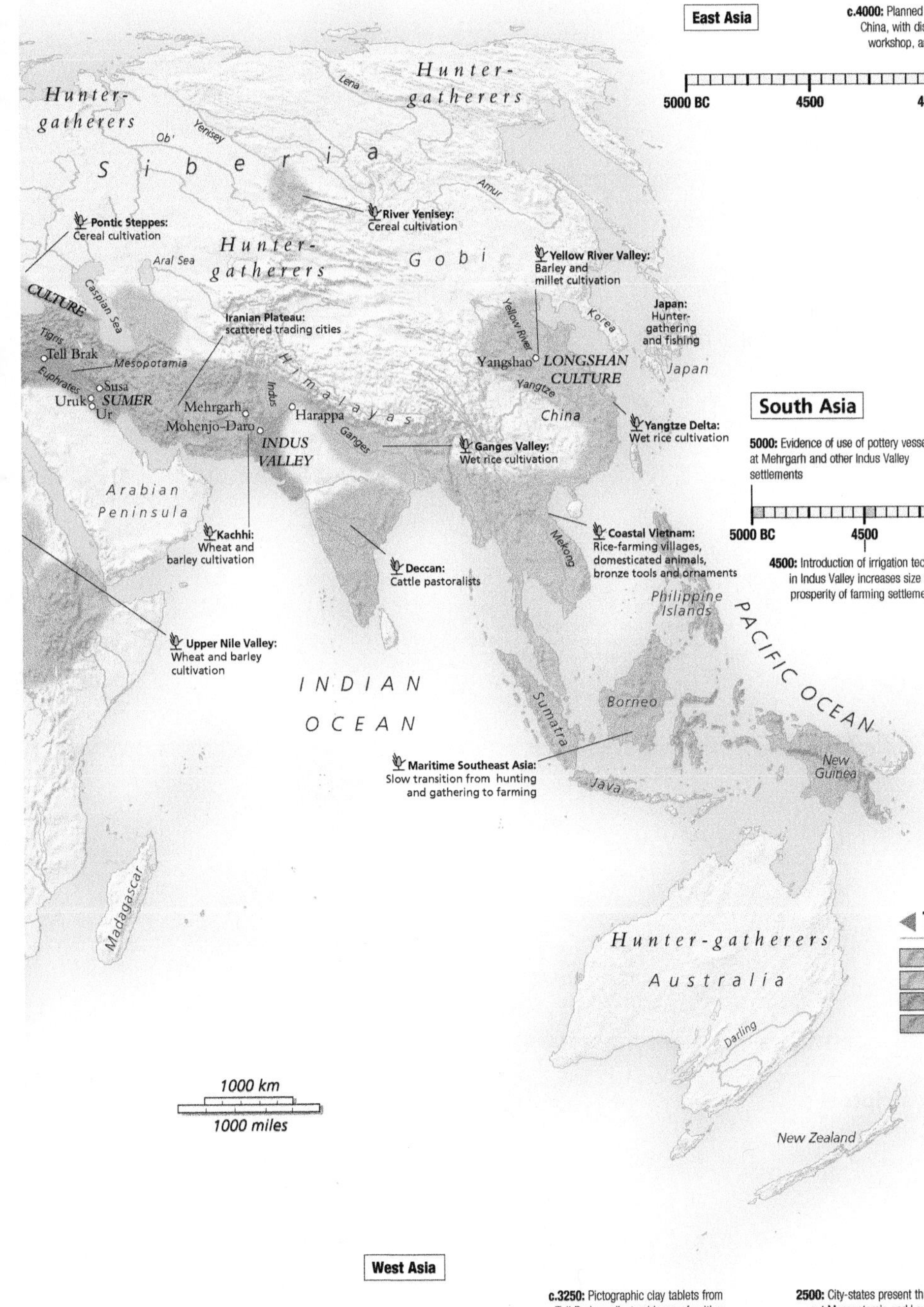

The world in 2500 BC

- transition from hunting and gathering to agriculture
- agricultural areas
- urban areas
- urban hinterland

South Asia

- **5000:** Evidence of use of pottery vessels at Mehrgarh and other Indus Valley settlements
- **4500:** Introduction of irrigation techniques in Indus Valley increases size and prosperity of farming settlements
- **3500:** Indus Valley lowlands settled by farmers; walled towns develop
- **2500:** True cities emerge in Indus Valley. Cultural uniformity throughout Indus plain. Evidence of trade links with Central Asia and Mesopotamia

5000 BC | 4500 | 4000 | 3500 | 3000 | 2500 BC

West Asia

- **3500:** Emergence of Uruk, the first city-state
- **c.3250:** Pictographic clay tablets from Tell Brak: earliest evidence of writing
- **2500:** City-states present throughout Mesopotamia and Levant
- **2500:** Rich array of grave goods at Royal Graves at Ur indicate extensive trade links

5000 BC | 4500 | 4000 | 3500 | 3000 | 2500 BC

THE SPREAD OF WRITING

The precursors of the first known writing and numerical systems were clay counting tokens, used in southwest Asia before c.3400 B.C. to record quantities of stored goods. They were eventually sealed in clay envelopes, and marked on the outside with signs indicating their contents—the first written symbols. Within a thousand years, writing and numerical systems had spread throughout western Asia. Writing became a powerful tool of government, and a means of communicating, codifying laws, and recording history.

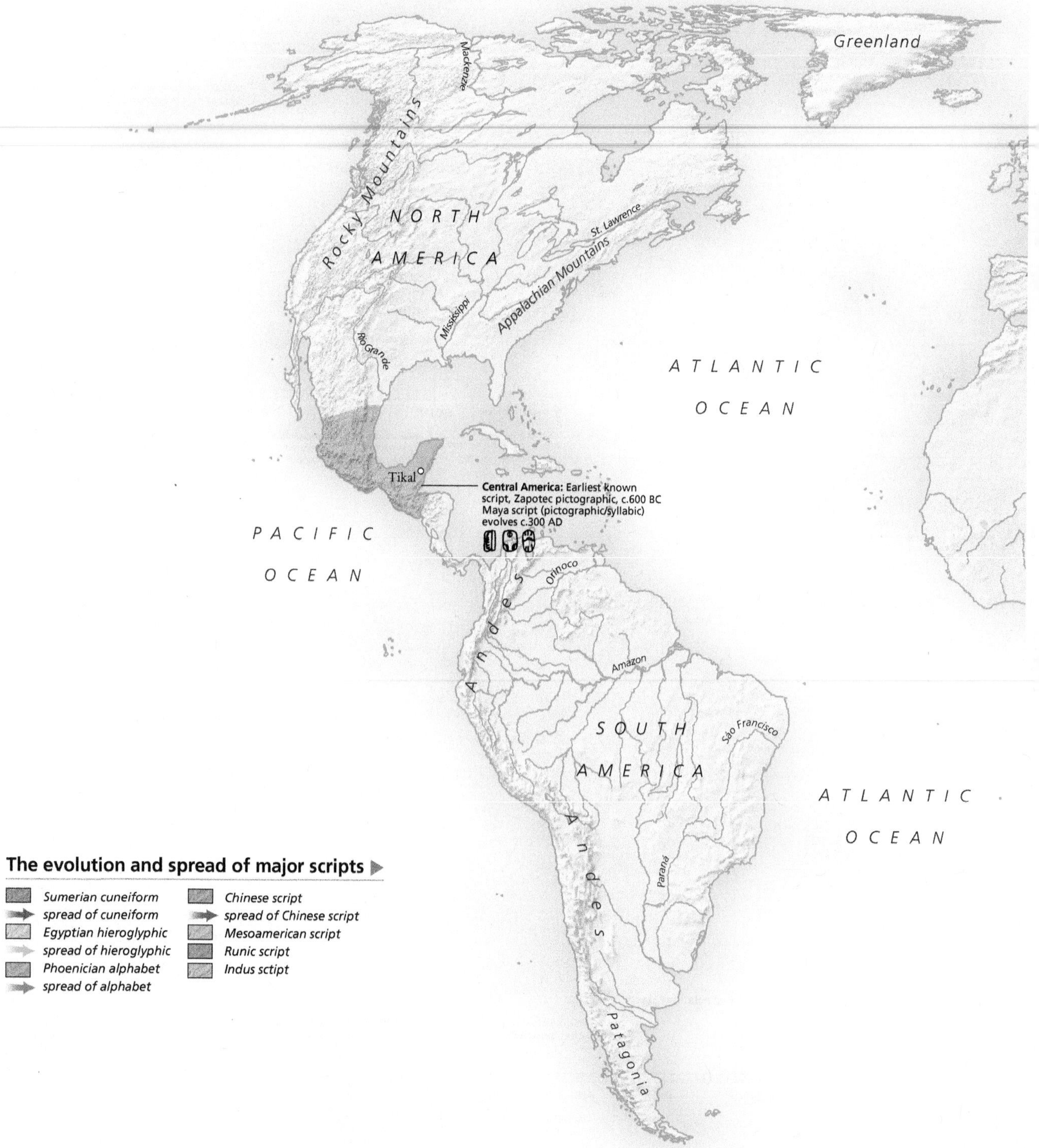

Major developments in writing, counting, and calendrical systems

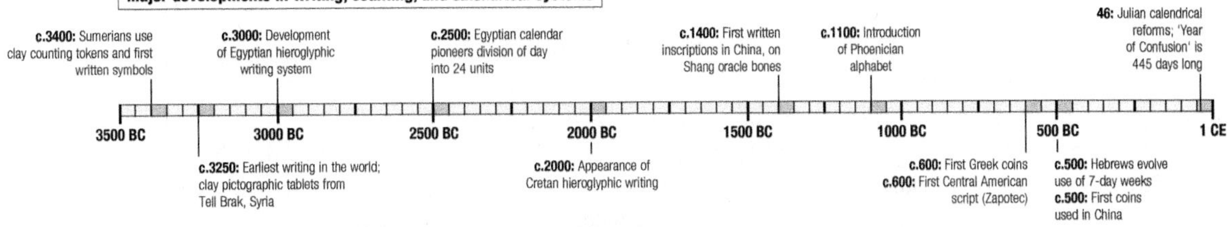

EUROPEAN EXPANSION IN THE 16TH CENTURY

The 16th century saw the expansion of several of the great European nations far beyond their continental limits. Explorers searching for new sources of luxury goods and precious metals began to open up new territories which monarchs such as Philip II of Spain quickly built up into great empires in the "New World." The Spanish and Portuguese, inspired by the voyages of Columbus and da Gama, led the way, closely followed by the Dutch and the English. The explorers were aided by technological advances in shipbuilding, navigational equipment, and cartography. At the start of the 16th century, the Americas were virtually unknown to Europeans; by 1700, outposts of a greater European empire had been established almost everywhere the explorers landed.

Spain and Portugal were the leaders of world exploration in the 16th century. In search of maritime trade routes to Asia, the Portuguese found sea lanes through the Atlantic and Indian oceans to India. By 1512, fortified trading posts were in place at Goa and Malacca, and they had reached the "Spice Islands" of the Moluccas in eastern Indonesia. The Spanish, taking a westward route, found the Caribbean islands and the Americas instead. Magellan's three-year global circumnavigation revealed a western route through the Strait of Magellan and across the Pacific Ocean. English and French mariners sought northern passages to Asian markets and their voyages paved the way for the establishment of European settlements in North America.

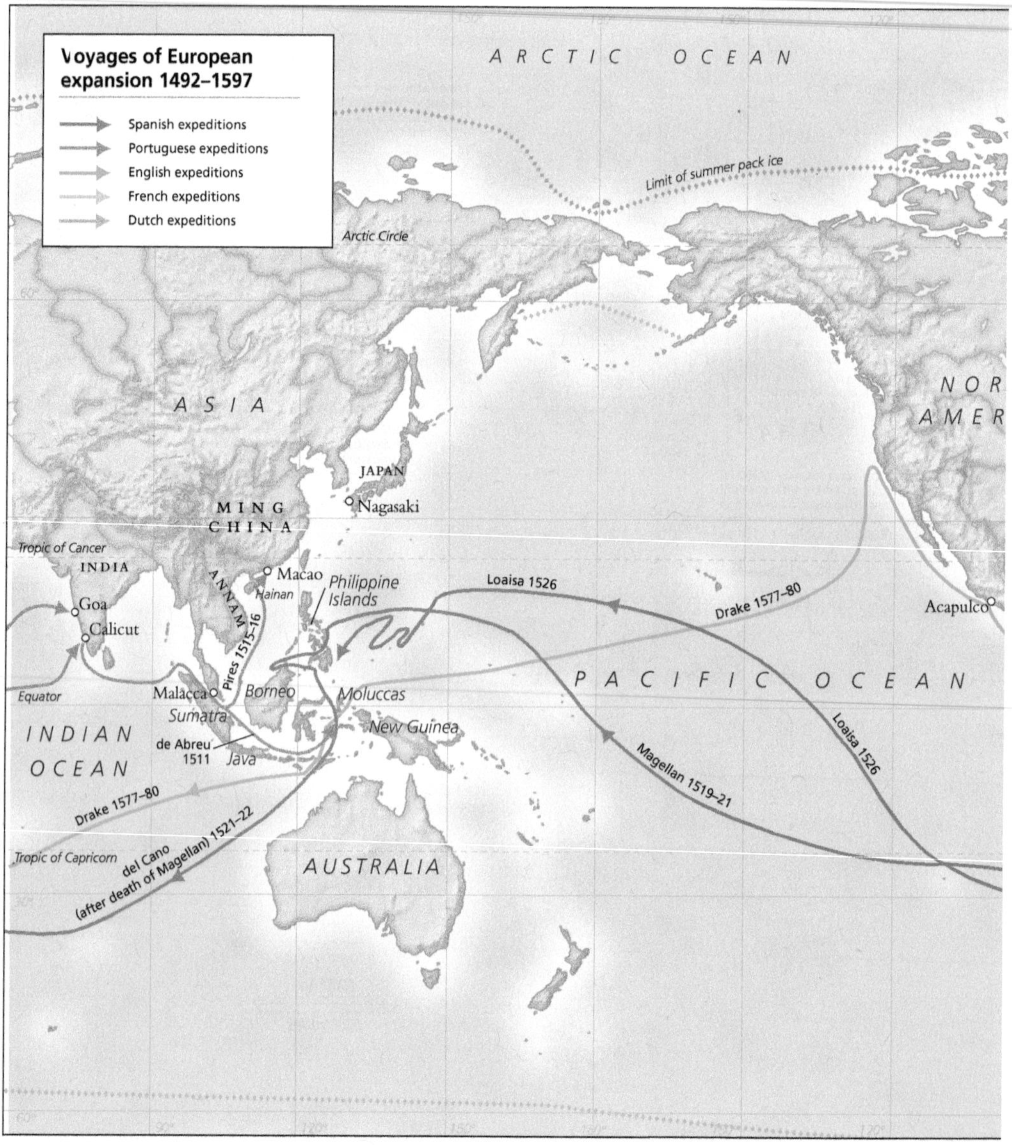

Voyages of expansion 1492–1590

- **1492:** Columbus, in search of Asia, reaches Cuba and the Bahamas
- **1498:** Vasco da Gama rounds Cape of Good Hope and reaches India
- **1500:** Cabral sights Brazilian coast on voyage to India
- **1509–16:** Portuguese voyages to Moluccas, Malacca, and Macao
- **1519–22:** Magellan and del Cano complete first global circumnavigation reaching Moluccas via the Philippine Islands
- **1532:** Cartier explores Strait of Belle Isle and St Lawrence
- **1553:** Willoughby reaches Archangel on Northeast Passage
- **1576:** Frobisher reaches Baffin Island
- **1577–80:** Drake circumnavigates globe

1490 1510 1530 1550 1570 1590

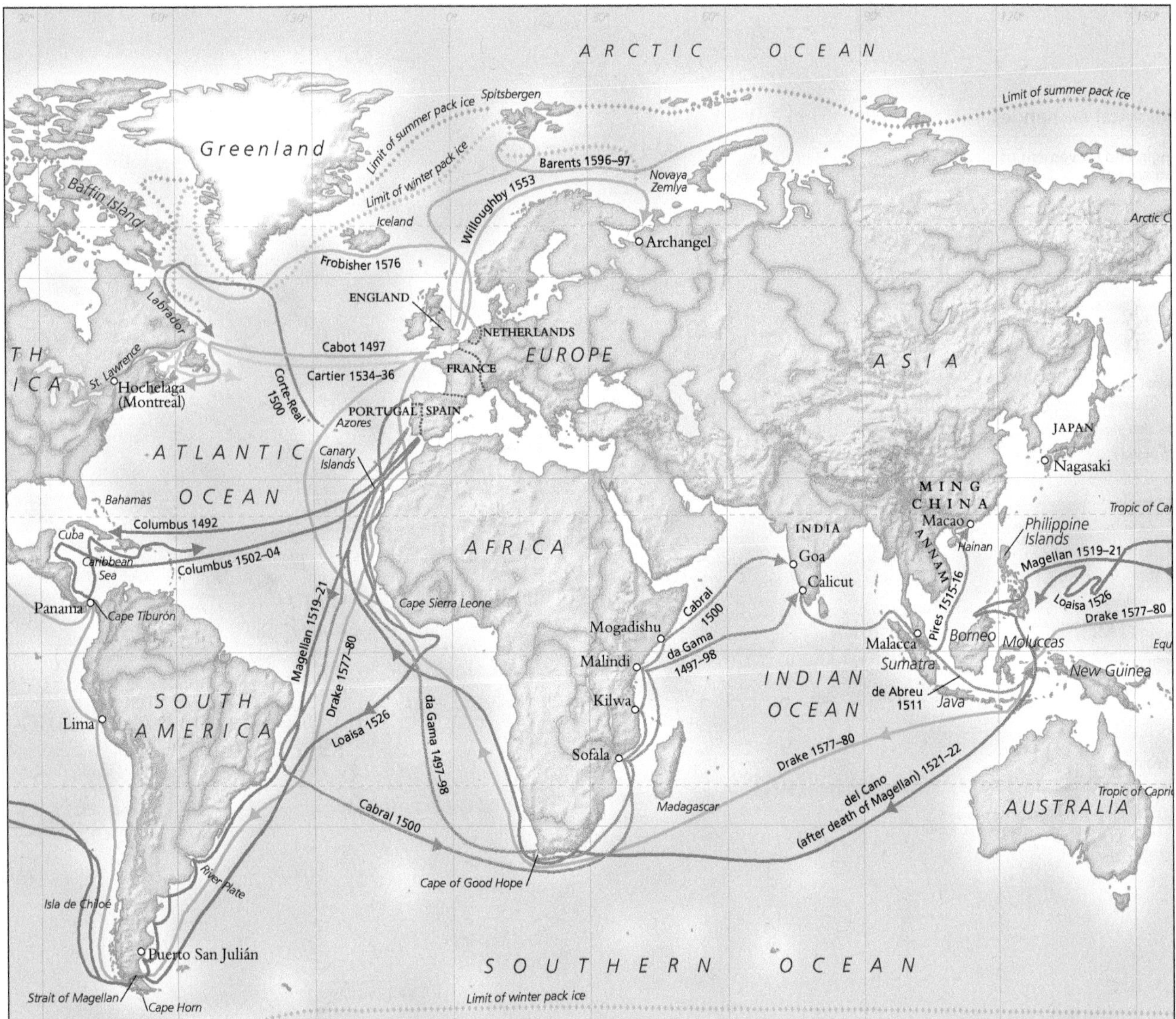

BIOLOGICAL EXCHANGES

European expansion had a profound biological impact. Travelers transported numerous species of fruits, vegetables, and animals from the Americas to Europe. At the same time, settlers introduced European species to the Americas and Oceania. Horses, pigs, and cattle were transported to the western hemisphere where, without natural predators, their numbers increased spectacularly. The settlers consciously introduced food crops, such as wheat, grapes, apples, peaches, and citrus fruits. Some plants, such as nettles, dandelions, and

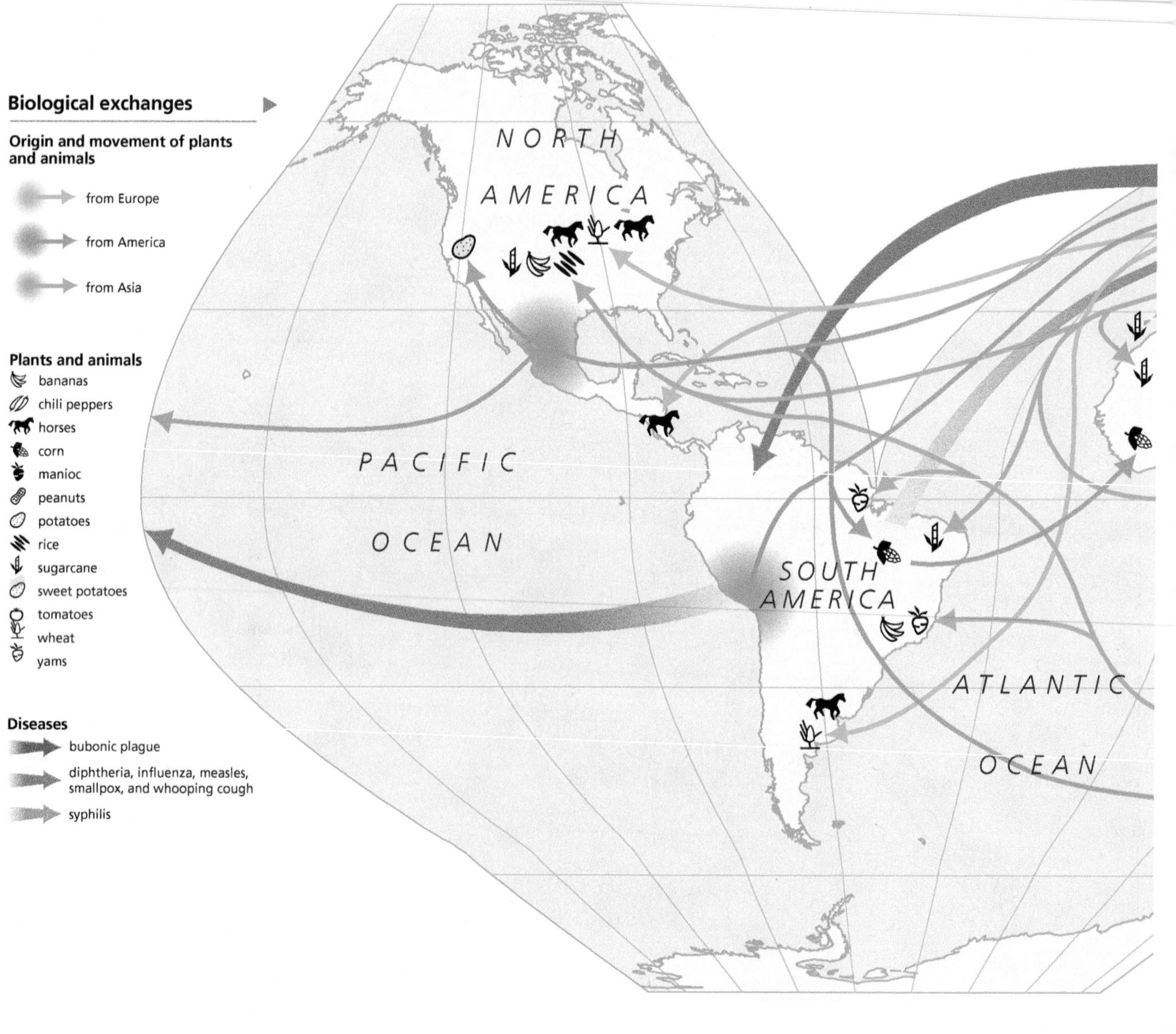

other weeds were inadvertently dispersed by the winds or on the coats of animals. European expansion also led to a spread of European diseases. Vast numbers of indigenous American peoples died from measles and smallpox, which broke out in massive epidemics among populations with no natural or acquired immunity. During the 16th century, syphilis—thought now to be the result of the fusion of two similar diseases from Europe and the New World—killed a million Europeans.

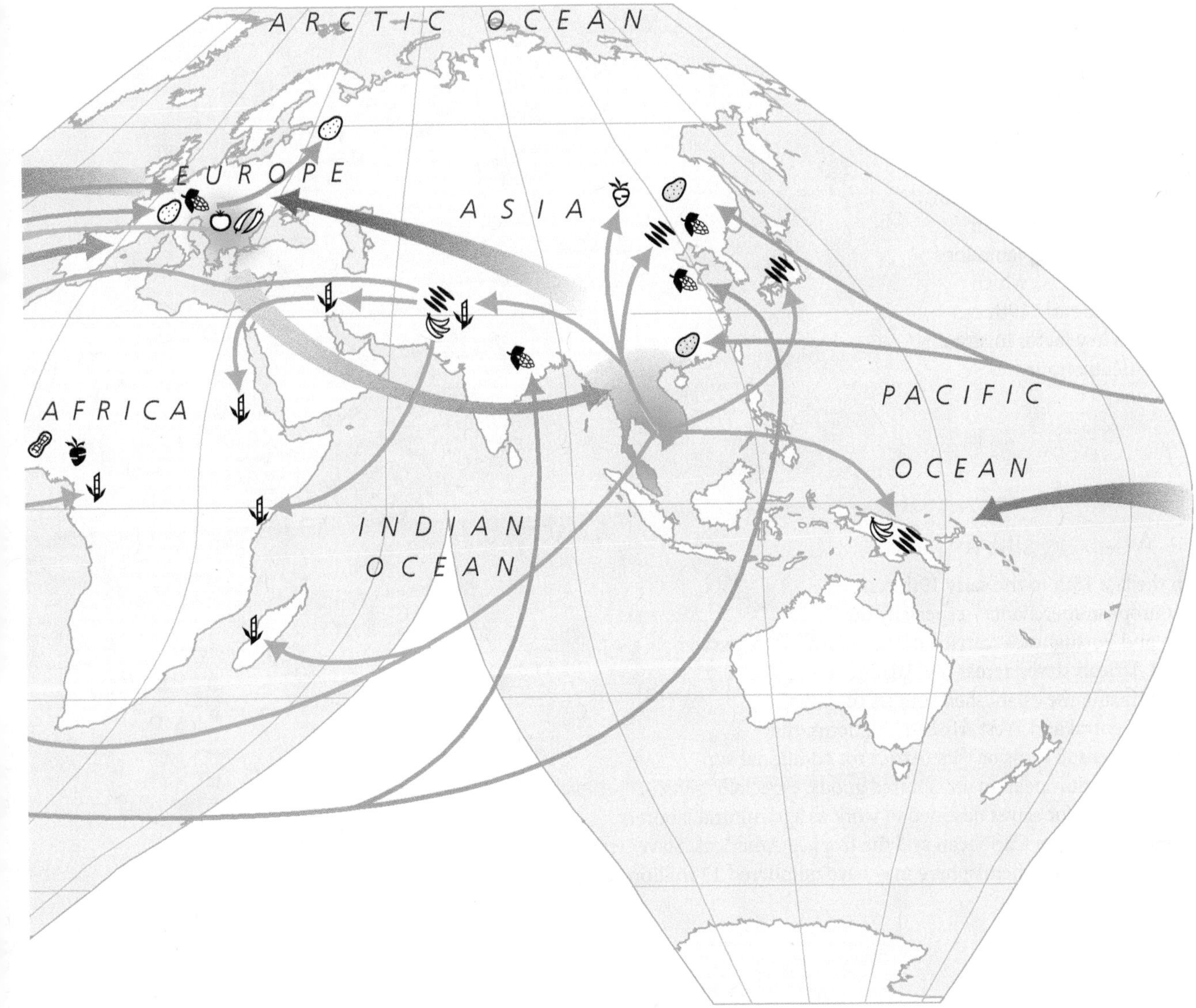

TRADING IN HUMAN LIVES

The use of slaves seems to have been endemic in many human societies. Normally taken as prisoners of war, slaves were also acquired as a form of tribute. The establishment of European colonies and overseas empires between the 16th and 19th centuries saw the creation of a slave trade on an industrial scale, a commerce which laid the foundations for pan-global trading networks. Trading concerns such as the English and Dutch East India companies developed trade on a larger scale than ever before; but it was the need to supply labor for the plantations of the Americas which led to the greatest movement of peoples across the face of the earth.

Slaves in the New World

The great plantation systems and mining concerns that arose in the New World from the 16th century onward demanded large reservoirs of labor. Though the Spanish and Portuguese initially used enslaved indigenous people, they soon required a more reliable source of labor. The Portuguese began bringing African slaves to the Caribbean and Brazil in the early 16th century. The cotton plantations of the southern U.S., which boomed in the early 19th century, were a key factor in sustaining the Atlantic trade.

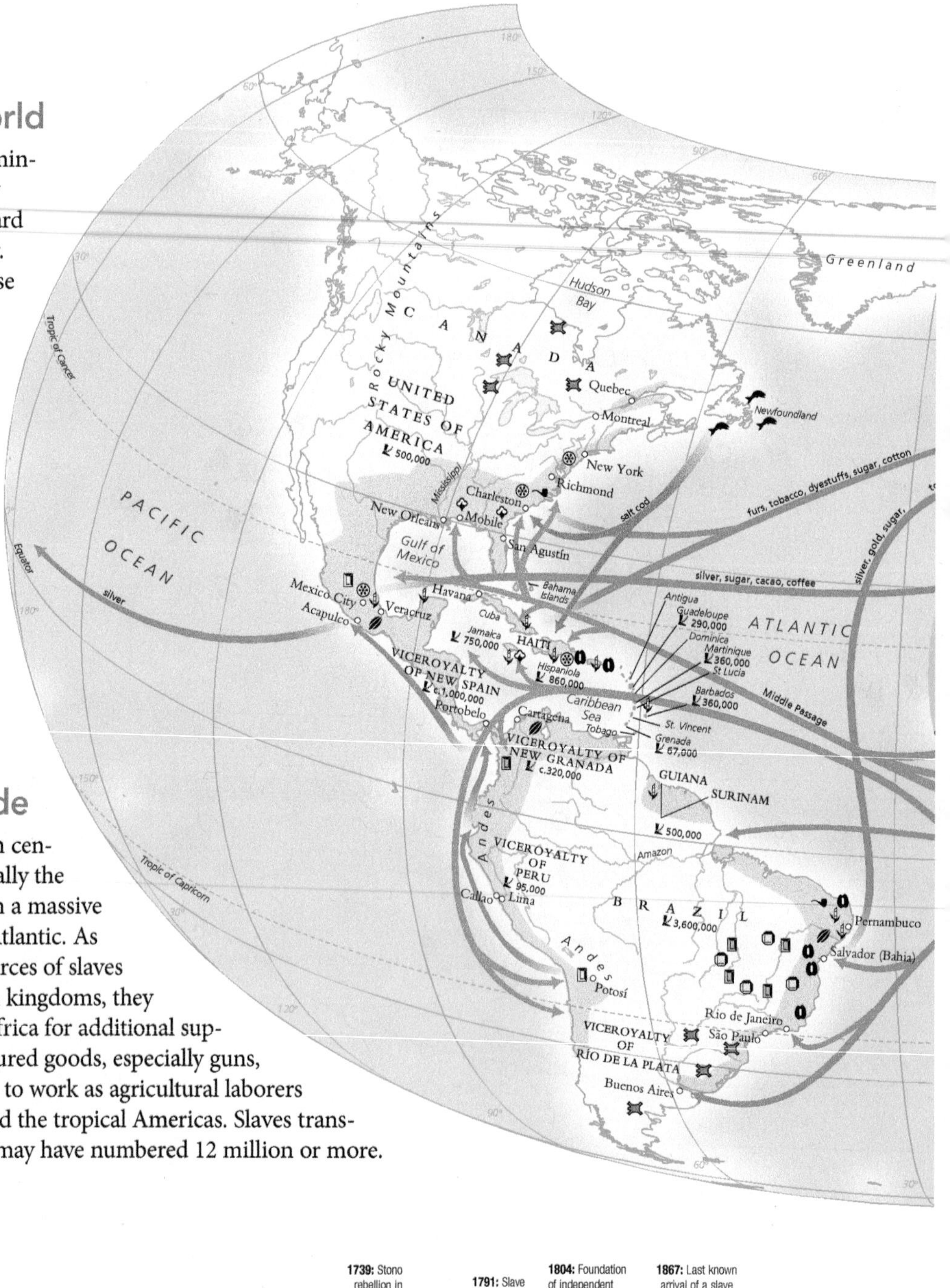

The Atlantic slave trade

From the late 15th to the early 19th century, European merchants—especially the British and Portuguese—carried on a massive trade in African slaves across the Atlantic. As well as utilizing the established sources of slaves from the Central and West African kingdoms, they also raided coastal areas of West Africa for additional supplies of slaves. European manufactured goods, especially guns, were exchanged for slaves destined to work as agricultural laborers on plantations in the Caribbean and the tropical Americas. Slaves transported to the western hemisphere may have numbered 12 million or more.

Slave Trades

- **1479:** Treaty of Alcaçovas permits Portuguese importation of slaves into Spain
- **1502:** Introduction of African slaves to the Caribbean
- **1522:** First American slave revolt in Hispaniola
- **1685:** French *Code Noir* restricts slavery in French Caribbean colonies
- **1739:** Stono rebellion in South Carolina
- **1791:** Slave revolt in Haiti
- **1804:** Foundation of independent Haitian state
- **1807:** Slave trade outlawed in Britain
- **1850:** Effective end of slave trade in Brazil
- **1863:** Emancipation proclamation frees slaves in Confederate states
- **1867:** Last known arrival of a slave ship in Cuba

1450 · 1500 · 1550 · 1600 · 1650 · 1700 · 1750 · 1800 · 1850 · 1900

Other slave trades

By the 9th and 10th centuries, a number of complex slave-trading routes were in existence in Europe and the Near East. Viking and Russian merchants traded in slaves from the Balkans who were often sold to harems in southern Spain and North Africa. The Baghdad Caliphate drew slaves from western Europe via the ports of Venice, Prague, and Marseille, and Slavic and Turkic slaves from eastern Europe and Central Asia. In the 13th century, the Mongols sold slaves at Karakorum and in the Volga region. There was long-standing commerce in African slaves—primarily from East Africa before European mariners entered the slave trade. Between the 9th and 19th centuries Muslim merchants may have transported as many as 14 million across the Sahara by camel caravan and through East African ports, principally to destinations in the Indian Ocean basin.

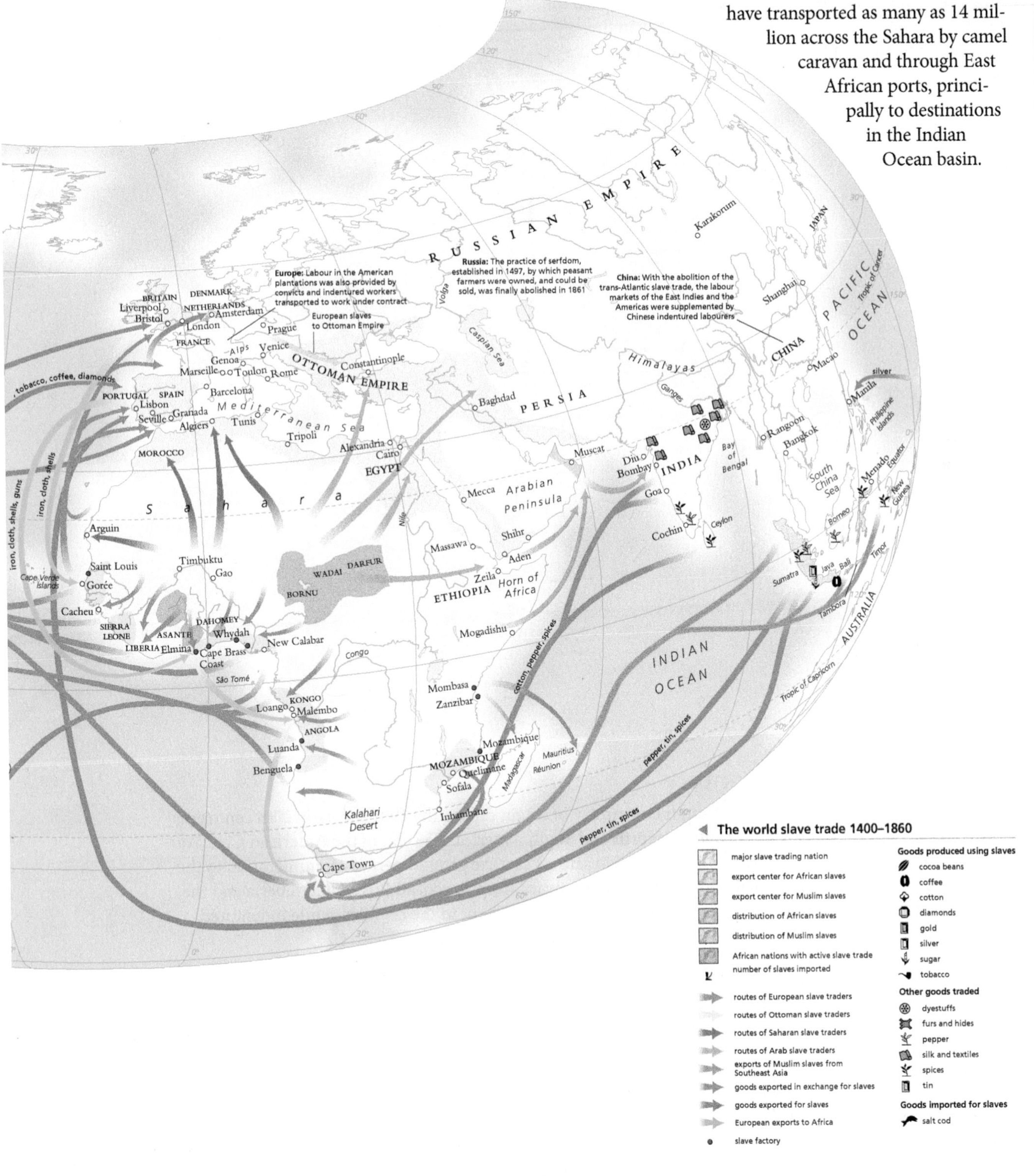

The world slave trade 1400–1860

MIGRATION IN THE 19TH CENTURY

The technical innovations of the Industrial Revolution made the 19th-century world a much smaller place. Railroads could quickly transport large human cargoes across continents, the Suez and Panama canals reduced travel times—sometimes by as much as 50%, and ships became larger, faster, and more seaworthy. The mechanization and centralization of industry required the concentration of labor on a scale never seen before. At the same time, the European imperial powers were exploiting their tropical possessions for economic benefit. Cash crops, grown on large plantations, needed a plentiful supply of labor as well. Political upheaval, wars, and economic hardship provided the most dramatic impetus to emigration—especially in the Russian Empire and Central Europe, and in southeastern China.

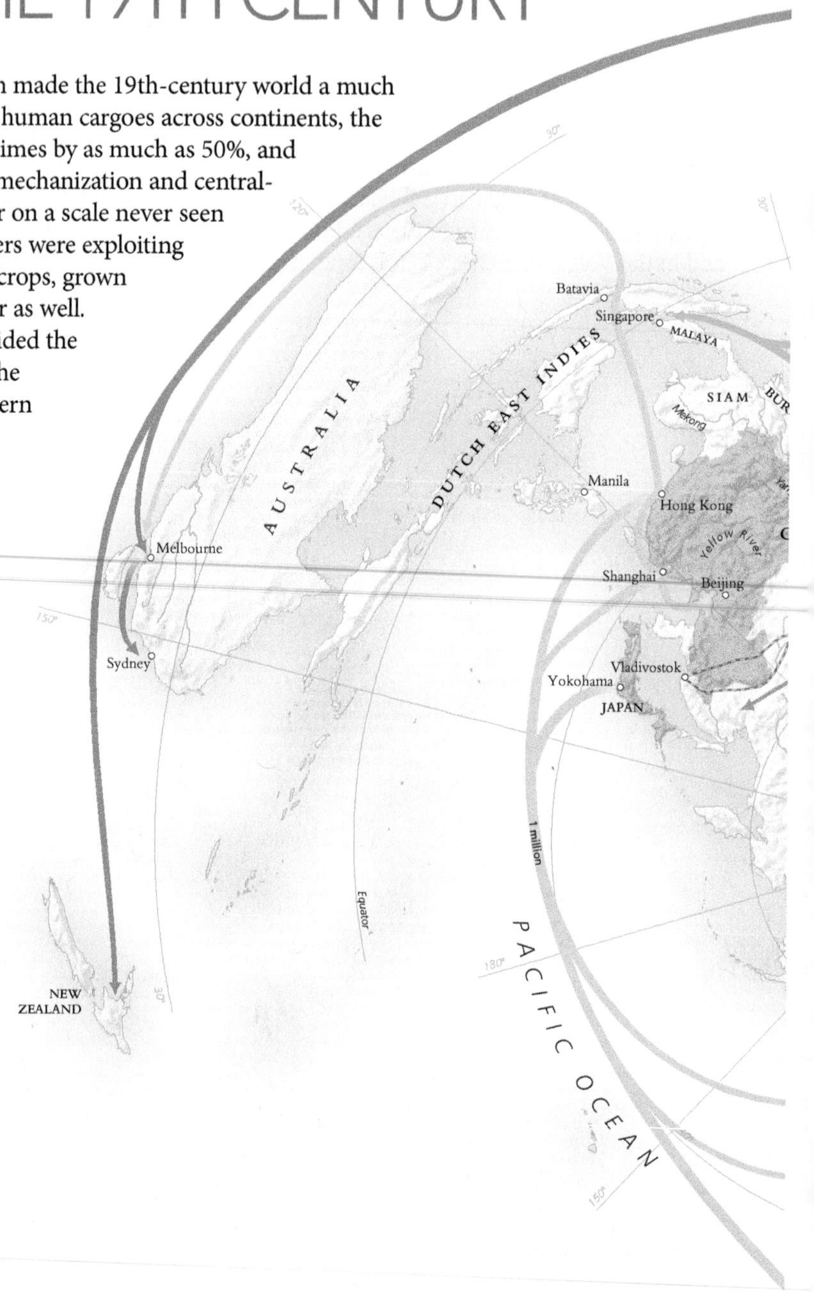

Migration in the 19th century

More than 80 million people emigrated from their country of origin during the 19th and early 20th centuries. Over half of them moved across the Atlantic to North and South America. The end of the American Civil War in 1865, and the opening up of Native American land to settlers saw the greatest period of immigration to the U.S. and Canada. In the Russian Empire, movement was eastward from European Russia into Siberia and the Caspian region. Europeans moved south and east to take up employment in the colonies, while indentured laborers traveled to the Americas, Africa, and Southeast Asia.

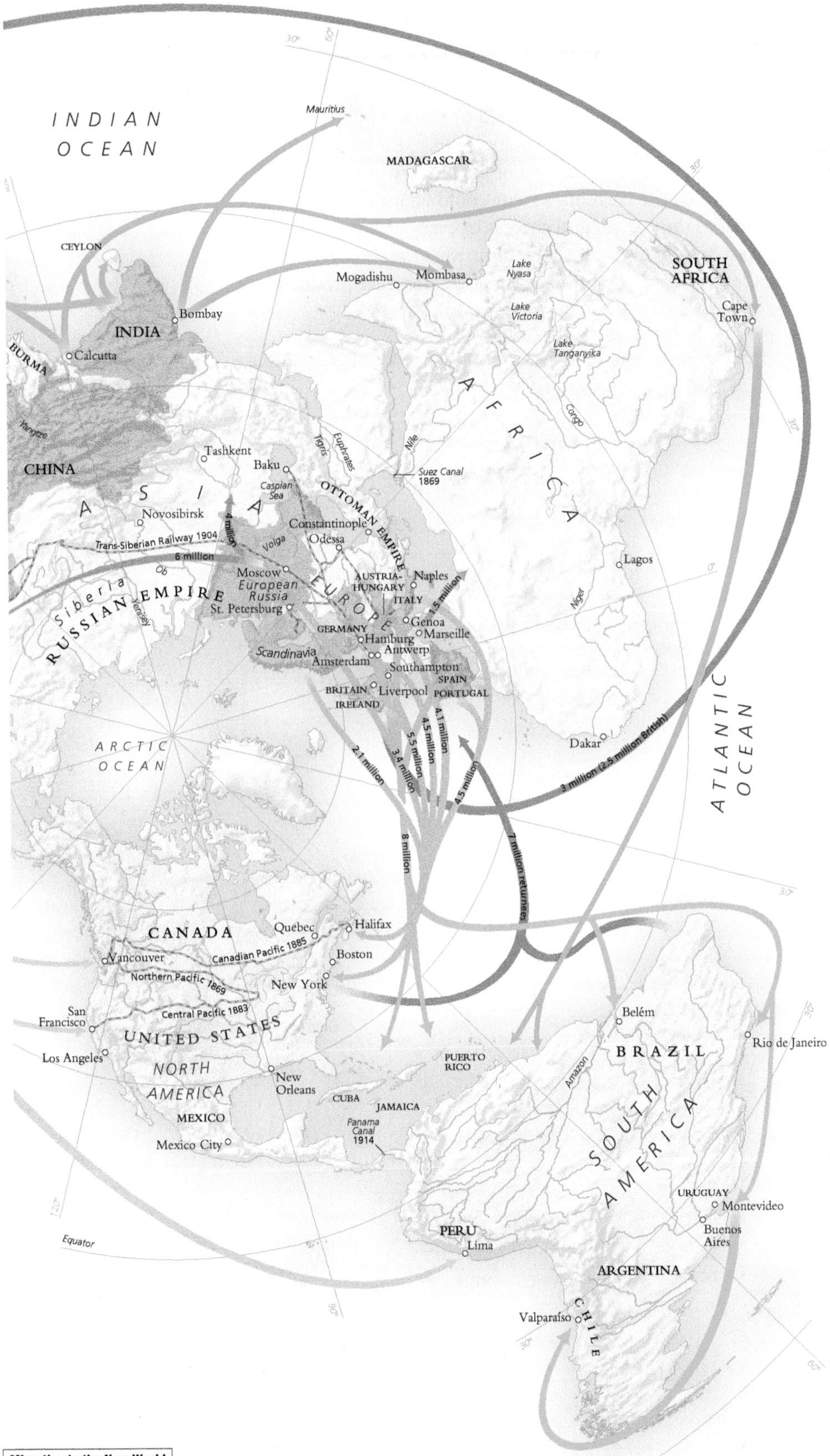

World migration c.1860–1920

Transatlantic migration

- to North America
- to South America and the Caribbean
- to Europe from the Americas

Other European migration

- to Australia and New Zealand
- to North Africa

Asian migration

- to the Americas and Australia
- Russian migration into Siberia
- Indian intercolonial migration

- transcontinental railroad
- major exporters of people
- major importers of people

Migration to the New World

1800 · 1820 · 1840 · 1860 · 1880 · 1900

- **1816–17:** Emigration from southwest Germany following Napoleonic wars
- **1818:** 20,000 Irish emigrate to US as a result of famine
- **1831–41:** 200,000 people leave Ireland for Canada, many traveling on to the US
- **1845–54:** Irish Potato Famine leads 1.6 million to emigrate
- **1848–49:** Revolutions lead to political crackdown and exodus of democrats from Central Europe
- **1849:** California Gold Rush draws large numbers of migrants from Europe, Australia, Chile, and China
- **1850s:** Height of emigration from England and Scotland: more than 50,000 per year
- **1881–90:** Peak years of German emigration to US (1,300,000)
- **1882:** Beginning of major Jewish emigration from Russian Empire
- **1882:** 80,000 Scandinavians emigrate to US
- **1888:** Abolition of slavery in Brazil; next decade sees over a million immigrants
- **1900:** Start of major Italian emigration to US and Argentina; by 1910, more than two million have arrived

TRADE IN THE 19TH CENTURY

In the first half of the 19th century, world trade and industry was dominated by Britain; by the 1870s, the industrial balance was shifting in favor of other nations, especially Germany, France, Russia, and the U.S., with rapid industrialization occurring throughout most of Europe by the end of the century. A stable currency, a standard (for example, the price of gold) against which the currency's value could be measured, and an effective private banking system were seen as essential to the growth and success of every industrializing nation. The major industrial nations also began to invest heavily overseas. Their aims were the discovery and exploitation of cheaper raw materials, balanced by the development of overseas markets for their products.

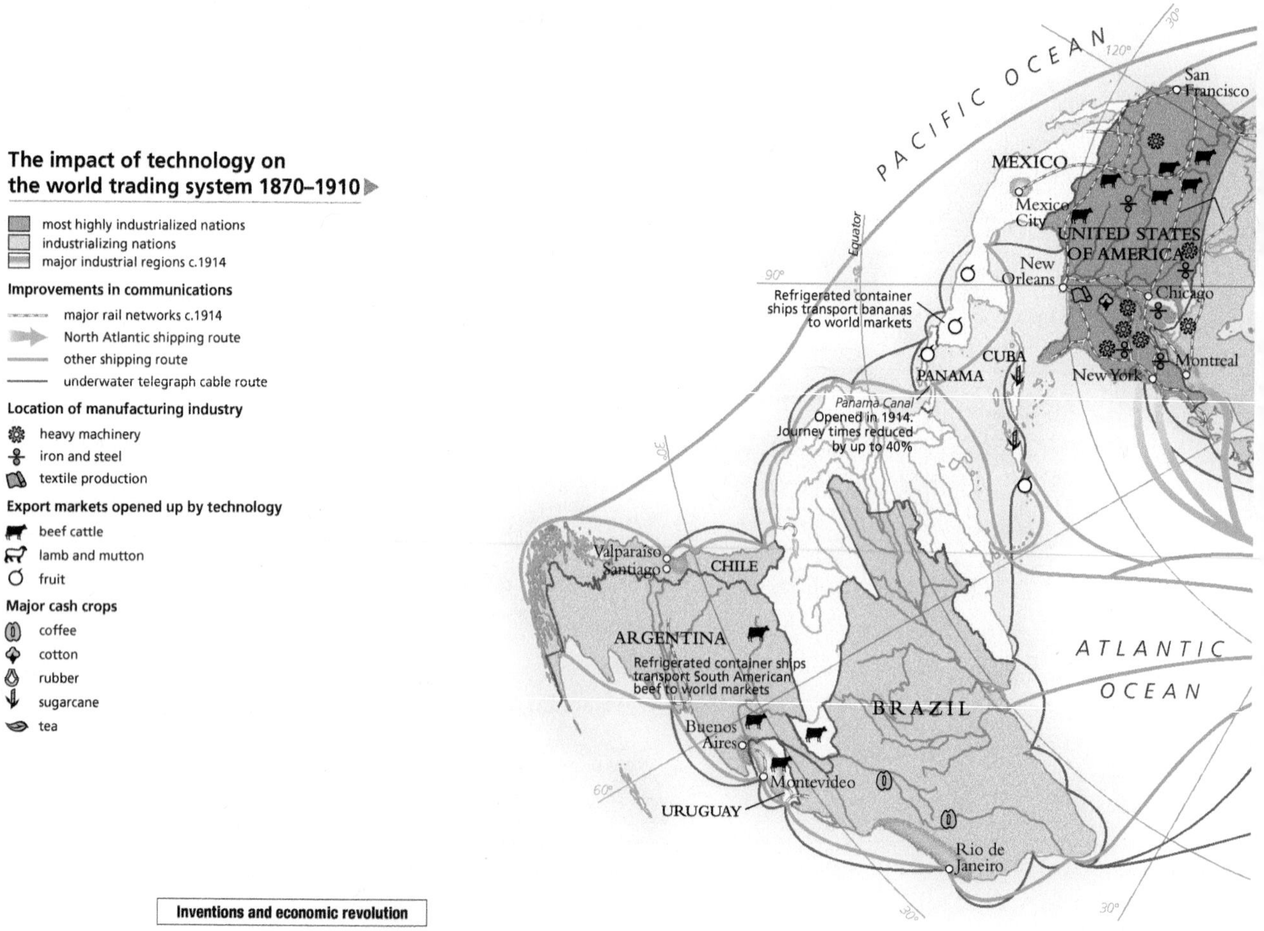

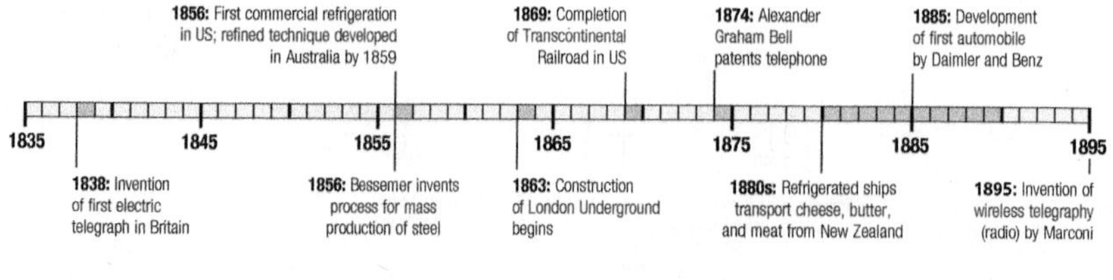

The Impact of the Industrial Revolution

World industrial output from 1870–1914 increased at an extraordinary rate: coal production by as much as 650%; steel by 2500%; steam engine capacity by over 350%. Technology revolutionized the world economy: the invention of refrigerated ships meant that meat, fruit, and other perishables could be shipped to Europe from as far away as New Zealand; sewing machines and power looms allowed the mass production of textiles and clothing; telephones, telegraphs, and railroads made communications faster.

Index

N

Q

R

S

Readings

READING 1

Body Ritual Among the Nacirema

HORACE MINER

The anthropologist has become so familiar with the diversity of ways in which different peoples behave in similar situations that he is not apt to be surprised by even the most exotic customs. In fact, if all of the logically possible combinations of behavior have not been found somewhere in the world, he is apt to suspect that they must be present in some yet undescribed tribe. This point has, in fact, been expressed with respect to clan organization by Murdock (1949:71). In this light, the magical beliefs and practices of the Nacirema present such unusual aspects that it seems desirable to describe them as an example of the extremes to which human behavior can go.

Professor Linton first brought the ritual of the Nacirema to the attention of anthropologists twenty years ago (1936:326), but the culture of this people is still very poorly understood. They are a North American group living in the territory between the Canadian Cree, the Yaqui and Tarahumare of Mexico, and the Carib and Arawak of the Antilles. Little is known of their origin, though tradition states that they came from the east. According to Nacirema mythology, their nation was originated by a culture hero, Notgnishaw, who is otherwise known for two great feats of strength—the throwing of a piece of wampum across the river Pa-To-Mac and the chopping down of a cherry tree in which the Spirit of Truth resided.

Nacirema culture is characterized by a highly developed market economy which as evolved in a rich natural habitat. While much of the people's time is devoted to economic pursuits, a large part of the fruits of these labors and a considerable portion of the day are spent in ritual activity. The focus of this activity is the human body, the appearance and health of which loom as a dominanat concern in the ethos of the people. While such a concern is certainly not unusual, its ceremonial aspects and associated philosophy are unique.

The fundamental belief underlying the whole system appears to be that the human body is ugly and that its natural tendency is to debility and disease. Incarcerated in such a body, man's only hope is to avert these characteristics through the use of the powerful influences of ritual and ceremony. Every household has one or more shrines devoted to this purpose. The more powerful individuals in the society have several shrines in their houses and, in fact, the opulence of a house is often referred to in terms of the number of such ritual centers it possesses. Most houses are of wattle and daub construction, but the shrine rooms of the more wealthy are walled with stone. Poorer families imitate the rich by applying pottery plaques to their shrine walls.

While each family has at least one such shrine, the rituals associated with it are not family ceremonies but are private and secret. The rites are normally only discussed with children, and then only during the period when they are being initiated into these mysteries. I was able, however, to establish sufficient rapport with the natives to examine these shrines and to have the rituals described to me.

The focal point of the shrine is a box or chest which is built into the wall. In this chest are kept the many charms and magical potions without which no native believes he could live. These preparations are secured from a variety of specialized practitioners. The most powerful of these are the medicine men, whose assistance must be rewarded with substantial gifts. However, the medicine men do not provide the curative potions for their clients, but decide what the ingredients should be and then write them down in an ancient and secret language. This writing is understood only by the medicine men and by the herbalists who, for another gift, provide the required charm.

The charm is not disposed of after it has served its purpose, but is placed in the charm-box of the household shrine. As these magical materials are specific for certain ills, and the real or imagined maladies of the people are many, the charm-box is usually full to overflowing. The magical packets are so numerous that people forget what their purposes were and fear to use them again. While the natives are very vague on this point, we can only assume that the idea in retaining all the old magical materials is that their presence in the charm-box, before which the body rituals are conducted, will in some way protect the worshipper.

Beneath the charm-box is a small font. Each day every member of the family, in succession, enters the shrine room, bows his head before the charm-box, mingles different sorts of holy water in the font, and proceeds with a brief rite of ablution. The holy waters are secured from the Water Temple of the community, where the priests

From *American Anthropologist,* June 1956, pp. 503–507.

conduct elaborate ceremonies to make the liquid ritually pure.

In the hierarchy of magical practitioners, and below the medicine men in prestige, are specialists whose designation is best translated "holy-mouth-men." The Nacirema have an almost pathological horror and fascination with the mouth, the condition of which is believed to have a supernatural influence on all social relationships. Were it not for the rituals of the mouth, they believe that their teeth would fall out, their gums bleed, their jaws shrink, their friends desert them, and their lovers reject them. (They also believe that a strong relationship exists between oral and moral characteristics. For example, there is a ritual ablution of the mouth for children which is supposed to improve their moral fiber.)

The daily body ritual performed by everyone includes a mouth-rite. Despite the fact that these people are so punctilious about care of the mouth, this rite involves a practice which strikes the uninitiated stranger as revolting. It was reported to me that the ritual consists of inserting a small bundle of hog hairs into the mouth, along with certain magical powders, and then moving the bundle in a highly formalized series of gestures.

In addition to the private mouth-rite, the people seek out a holy-mouth-man once or twice a year. These practitioners have an impressive set of paraphernalia, consisting of a variety of augers, awls, probes, and prods. The use of these objects in the exorcism of the evils of the mouth involves almost unbelievable ritual torture of the client. The holy-mouth-man opens the client's mouth and, using the above mentioned tools, enlarges any holes which decay may have created in the teeth. Magical materials are put into these holes. If there are no naturally occurring holes in the teeth, large sections of one or more teeth are gouged out so that the supernatural substance can be applied. In the client's view, the purpose of these ministrations is to arrest decay and to draw friends. The extremely sacred and traditional character of the rite is evident in the fact that the natives return to the holy-mouth-men year after year, despite the fact that their teeth continue to decay.

It is to be hoped that, when a thorough study of the Nacirema is made, there will be a careful inquiry into the personality structure of these people. One has but to watch the gleam in the eye of a holy-mouth-man, as he jabs an awl into an exposed nerve, to suspect that a certain amount of sadism is involved. If this can be established, a very interesting pattern emerges, for most of the population shows definite masochistic tendencies. It was to these that Professor Linton referred in discussing a distinctive part of the daily body ritual which is performed only by men. This part of the rite involves scraping and lacerating the surface of the face with a sharp instrument. Special women's rites are performed only four times during each lunar month, but what they lack in frequency is made up in barbarity. As part of this ceremony, women bake their heads in small ovens for about an hour. The theoretically interesting point is that what seems to be a preponderantly masochistic people have developed sadistic specialists.

The medicine men have an imposing temple, or *latipso,* in every community of any size. The more elaborate ceremonies required to treat very sick patients can only be performed at this temple. These ceremonies involve not only the thaumaturge but a permanent group of vestal maidens who move sedately about the temple chambers in distinctive costume and headdress.

The *latipso* ceremonies are so harsh that it is phenomenal that a fair proportion of the really sick natives who enter the temple ever recover. Small children whose indoctrination is still incomplete have been known to resist attempts to take them to the temple because "that is where you go to die." Despite this fact, sick adults are not only willing but eager to undergo the protracted ritual purification, if they can afford to do so. No matter how ill the supplicant or how grave the emergency, the guardians of many temples will not admit a client if he cannot give a rich gift to the custodian. Even after one has gained admission and survived the ceremonies, the guardians will not permit the neophyte to leave until he makes still another gift.

The supplicant entering the temple is first stripped of all his or her clothes. In every-day life the Nacirema avoids exposure of his body and its natural functions. Bathing and excretory acts are performed only in the secrecy of the household shrine, where they are ritualized as part of the body-rites. Psychological shock results from the fact that body secrecy is suddenly lost upon entry into the *latipso.* A man, whose own wife has never seen him in an excretory act, suddenly finds himself naked and assisted by a vestal maiden while he performs his natural functions into a sacred vessel. This sort of ceremonial treatment is necessitated by the fact that the excreta are used by a diviner to ascertain the course and nature of the client's sickness. Female clients, on the other hand, find their naked bodies are subjected to the scrutiny, manipulation, and prodding of the medicine men.

Few supplicants in the temple are well enough to do anything but lie on their hard beds. The daily ceremonies, like the rites of the holy-mouth-men, involve discomfort and torture. With ritual precision, the vestals awaken their miserable charges each dawn and roll them about on their beds of pain while performing ablutions, in the formal movements of which the maidens are highly trained. At other times they insert magic wands in the supplicant's mouth or force him to eat substances which are supposed to be healing. From time to time the medicine men come to their clients and jab magically treated needles into their flesh. The fact that these temple ceremonies may not cure, and may even kill the neophyte, in no way decreases the people's faith in the medicine men.

There remains one other kind of practitioner, known as a "listener." This witch-doctor has the power to exorcise the devils that lodge in the heads of people who have been bewitched. The Nacirema believe that parents bewitch their own children. Mothers are particularly suspected of putting a curse on children while teaching them the secret body rituals. The counter-magic of the witch-doctor is unusual in its lack of ritual. The patient simply tells the "listener" all his troubles and fears, beginning with the earliest difficulties he can remember. The memory displayed by the Nacirema in these exorcism sessions is truly remarkable. It is not uncommon for the patient to bemoan the rejection he felt upon being weaned as a babe, and a few individuals even see their troubles going back to the traumatic effects of their own birth.

In conclusion, mention must be made of certain practices which have their base in native esthetics but which depend upon the pervasive aversion to the natural body and its functions. There are ritual fasts to make fat people thin and ceremonial feasts to make thin people fat. Still other rites are used to make women's breasts large if they are small, and smaller if they are large. General dissatisfaction with breast shape is symbolized in the fact that the ideal form is virtually outside the range of human variation. A few women afflicted with almost inhuman hypermammary development are so idolized that they make a handsome living by simply going from village to village and permitting the natives to stare at them for a fee.

Reference has already been made to the fact that excretory functions are ritualized, routinized, and relegated to secrecy. Natural reproduction functions are similarly distorted. Intercourse is taboo as a topic and scheduled as an act. Efforts are made to avoid pregnancy by the use of magical materials or by limiting intercourse to certain phases of the moon. Conception is actually very infrequent. When pregnant, women dress so as to hide their condition. Parturition takes place in secret, without friends or relatives to assist, and the majority of women do not nurse their infants.

Our review of the ritual life of the Nacirema has certainly shown them to be a magic-ridden people. It is hard to understand how they have managed to exist so long under the burdens which they have imposed upon themselves. But even such exotic customs as these take on real meaning when they are viewed with the insight provided by Malinowski when he wrote (1948:70):

> Looking from far and above, from our high places of safety in the developed civilization, it is easy to see all the crudity and irrelevance of magic. But without its power and guidance early man could not have mastered his practical difficulties as he has done, nor could man have advanced to the higher stages of civilization.

References

Linton, Ralph. 1936. *The Study of Man.* New York, D. Appleton-Century Co.

Malinowski, Bronislaw. 1948. *Magic, Science, and Religion.* Glencoe, The Free Press.

Murdock, George P. 1949. *Social Structure.* New York, The Macmillan Co.

Body Ritual Among the Nacirema

1. In this article, how does Horace Miner create an unfamiliar culture from a familiar one?
2. Why, when describing another culture, is it important to use the language and concepts of that culture and not the language and concepts of your own culture?
3. What information in the text tells us who the Nacirema actually are?

READING 2

Queer Customs

CLYDE KLUCKHOHN

In this selection, written more than half a century ago, Clyde Kluckhohn explains the anthropological concept of culture in a way that is eminently understandable for the beginning student of comparative cultures. Referring to culture as a "design for living," Kluckhohn, who for much of his career was the leading authority on the Navajo, used the anthropological perspective to explain what most nonanthropologists at the time considered to be "queer customs." He examined culture by showing how it is different from biological influences on our behavior, how culture influences biological processes, how it is learned rather than being genetically transmitted, and how it functions to help people adapt to their environment. Even though some of his references are today politically incorrect (for example, the use of such terms as primitive and heathen), Kluckhohn's piece serves as a valuable reminder that the study of other cultures allows us to better understand our own culture.

Why do the Chinese dislike milk and milk products? Why would the Japanese die willingly in a Banzai charge that seemed senseless to Americans? Why do some nations trace descent through the father, others through the mother, still others through both parents? Not because different peoples have different instincts, not because they were destined by God or Fate to different habits, not because the weather is different in China and Japan and the United States. Sometimes shrewd common sense has an answer that is close to that of the anthropologist: "because they were brought up that way." By "culture" anthropology means the total life way of a people, the social legacy the individual acquires from his group. Or culture can be regarded as that part of the environment that is the creation of man.

This technical term has a wider meaning than the "culture" of history and literature. A humble cooking pot is as much a cultural product as is a Beethoven sonata. In ordinary speech a man of culture is a man who can speak languages other than his own, who is familiar with history, literature, philosophy, or the fine arts. In some cliques that definition is still narrower. The cultured person is one who can talk about James Joyce, Scarlatti, and Picasso. To the anthropologist, however, to be human is to be cultured. There is culture in general, and then there are the specific cultures such as Russian, American, British, Hottentot, Inca. The general abstract notion services to remind us that we cannot explain acts solely in terms of the biological properties of the people concerned, their individual past experience, and the immediate situation. The past experience of other men in the form of culture enters into almost every event. Each specific culture constitutes a kind of blueprint for all of life's activities.

One of the interesting things about human beings is that they try to understand themselves and their own behavior. While this has been particularly true of Europeans in recent times, there is no group which has not developed a scheme or schemes to explain man's actions. To the insistent human query "why?" the most exciting illumination anthropology has to offer is that of the concept of culture. Its explanatory importance is comparable to categories such as evolution in biology, gravity in physics, disease in medicine. A good deal of human behavior can be understood, and indeed predicted, if we know a people's design for living. Many acts are neither accidental nor due to personal peculiarities nor caused by supernatural forces nor simply mysterious. Even those of us who pride ourselves on our individualism follow most of the time a pattern not of our own making. We brush our teeth on arising. We put on pants—not a loincloth or a grass skirt. We eat three meals a day—not four or five or two. We sleep in a bed—not in a hammock or on a sheep pelt. I do not have to know the individual and his life history to be able to predict these and countless other regularities, including many in the thinking process, of all Americans who are not incarcerated in jails or hospitals for the insane.

To the American woman a system of plural wives seems "instinctively" abhorrent. She cannot understand how any woman can fail to be jealous and uncomfortable if she must share her husband with other women. She feels it "unnatural" to accept such a situation. On the other hand, a Koryak woman of Siberia, for example, would find it hard to understand how a woman could be so selfish and so undesirous of feminine companionship in the home as to wish to restrict her husband to one mate.

From *Mirror for Man: Anthropology and Modern Life* by Clyde Kluckhohn, pp. 17–27. Used with permission.

Some years ago I met in New York City a young man who did not speak a word of English and was obviously bewildered by American ways. By "blood" he was as American as you or I, for his parents had gone from Indiana to China as missionaries. Orphaned in infancy, he was reared by a Chinese family in a remote village. All who met him found him more Chinese than American. The facts of his blue eyes and light hair were less impressive than a Chinese style of gait, Chinese arm and hand movements, Chinese facial expression, and Chinese modes of thought. The biological heritage was American, but the cultural training has been Chinese. He returned to China.

Another example of another kind: I once knew a trader's wife in Arizona who took a somewhat devilish interest in producing a cultural reaction. Guests who came her way were often served delicious sandwiches filled with a meat that seemed to be neither chicken nor tuna fish yet was reminiscent of both. To queries she gave no reply until each had eaten his fill. She then explained that what they had eaten was not chicken, not tuna fish, but the rich, white flesh of freshly killed rattlesnakes. The response was instantaneous—vomiting, often violent vomiting. A biological process is caught in a cultural web.

A highly intelligent teacher with long and successful experience in the public schools of Chicago was finishing her first year in an Indian school. When asked how her Navaho pupils compared in intelligence with Chicago youngsters, she replied, "Well, I just don't know. Sometimes the Indians seem just as bright. At other times they just act like dumb animals. The other night we had a dance in the high school. I saw a boy who is one of the best students in my English class standing off by himself. So I took him over to a pretty girl and told them to dance. But they just stood there with their heads down. They wouldn't even say anything." I inquired if she knew whether or not they were members of the same clan. "What difference would that make?"

"How would you feel about getting into bed with your brother?" The teacher walked off in a huff, but, actually, the two cases were quite comparable in principle. To the Indian the type of bodily contact involved in our social dancing has a directly sexual connotation. The incest taboos between members of the same clan are as severe as between true brothers and sisters. The shame of the Indians at the suggestion that a clan brother and sister should dance and the indignation of the white teacher at the idea that she should share a bed with an adult brother represent equally nonrational responses, culturally standardized unreason.

All this does not mean there is no such thing as raw human nature. The very fact that certain of the same institutions are found in all known societies indicates that at bottom all human beings are very much alike. The files of the Cross-Cultural Survey at Yale University are organized according to categories such as "marriage ceremonies," "life crisis rites," "incest taboos." At least seventy-five of these categories are represented in every single one of the hundreds of cultures analyzed. This is hardly surprising. The members of all human groups have about the same biological equipment. All men undergo the same poignant life experiences such as birth, helplessness, illness, old age, and death. The biological potentialities of the species are the blocks with which cultures are built. Some patterns of every culture crystallize around focuses provided by the inevitables of biology: the difference between the sexes, the presence of persons of different ages, the varying physical strength and skill of individuals. The facts of nature also limit culture forms. No culture provides patterns for jumping over trees or for eating iron ore.

There is thus no "either-or" between nature and that special form of nurture called culture. Culture determinism is as one-sided as biological determinism. The two factors are interdependent. Culture arises out of human nature, and its forms are restricted both by man's biology and by natural laws. It is equally true that culture channels biological processes—vomiting, weeping, fainting, sneezing, the daily habits of food intake and waste elimination. When a man eats, he is reacting to an internal "drive," namely, hunger contractions consequent upon the lowering of blood sugar, but his precise reaction to these internal stimuli cannot be predicted by physiological knowledge alone. Whether a healthy adult feels hungry twice, three times, or four times a day and the hours at which this feeling recurs is a question of culture. *What* he eats is of course limited by availability, but is also partly regulated by culture. It is a biological fact that some types of berries are poisonous; it is a cultural fact that, a few generations ago, most Americans considered tomatoes to be poisonous and refused to eat them. Such selective, discriminative use of the environment is characteristically cultural. In a still more general sense, too, the process of eating is channeled by culture. Whether a man eats to live, lives to eat, or merely eats and lives is only in part an individual matter, for there are also cultural trends. Emotions are physiological events. Certain situations will evoke fear in people from any culture. But sensations of pleasure, anger, and lust may be stimulated by cultural cues that would leave unmoved someone who has been reared in a different social tradition.

Except in the case of newborn babies and of individuals born with clear-cut structural or functional abnormalities we can observe innate endowments only as modified by cultural training. In a hospital in New Mexico where Zuñi Indian, Navaho Indian, and white American babies are born, it is possible to classify the newly arrived infants as unusually active, average, and quiet. Some babies from each "racial" group will fall into each category, though a higher proportion of the white babies will fall into the unusually active class. But if a Navaho baby, a Zuñi baby, and a white baby—all classified as unusually active at birth—are again observed at the age of two years, the Zuñi baby will no longer seem given to quick and restless activity—*as compared with the white child*—though he may seem so as compared with the other Zuñis of the same age. The Navaho child is likely to fall in between as contrasted with the Zuñi and the white, though he will probably still seem more active than the average Navaho youngster.

It was remarked by many observers in the Japanese relocation centers that Japanese who were born and brought up in this country, especially those who were reared apart from any large colony of Japanese, resemble in behavior their white neighbors much more closely than they do their own parents who were educated in Japan.

I have said "culture channels biological processes." It is more accurate to say "the biological functioning of individuals is modified if they have been trained in certain ways and not in others." Culture is not a disembodied force. It is created and transmitted by people. However, culture, like well-known concepts of the physical sciences, is a convenient abstraction. One never sees gravity. One sees bodies falling in regular ways. One never sees an electromagnetic field. Yet certain happenings that can be seen may be given a neat abstract formulation by assuming that the electromagnetic field exists. Similarly, one never sees culture as such. What is seen are regularities in the behavior or artifacts of a group that has adhered to a common tradition. The regularities in style and technique of ancient Inca tapestries or stone axes from Melanesian islands are due to the existence of mental blueprints for the group.

Culture is a *way* of thinking, feeling, believing. It is the group's knowledge stored up (in memories of men; in books and objects) for future use. We study the products of this "mental" activity: the overt behavior, the speech and gestures and activities of people, and the tangible results of these things such as tools, houses, cornfields, and what not. It has been customary in lists of "culture traits" to include such things as watches or lawbooks. This is a convenient way of thinking about them, but in the solution of any important problem we must remember that they, in themselves, are nothing but metals, paper, and ink. What is important is that some men know how to make them, others set a value on them, are unhappy without them, direct their activities in relation to them, or disregard them.

It is only a helpful shorthand when we say "The cultural patterns of the Zulu were resistant to Christianization." In the directly observable world of course, it was individual Zulus who resisted. Nevertheless, if we do not forget that we are speaking at a high level of abstraction, it is justifiable to speak of culture as a cause. One may compare the practice of saying "syphilis caused the extinction of the native population of the island." Was it "syphilis" or "syphilis germs" or "human beings who were carriers of syphilis?"

"Culture," then, is "a theory." But if a theory is not contradicted by any relevant fact and if it helps us to understand a mass of otherwise chaotic facts, it is useful. Darwin's contribution was much less the accumulation of new knowledge than the creation of a theory which put in order data already known. An accumulation of facts, however large, is no more a science than a pile of bricks is a house. Anthropology's demonstration that the most weird set of customs has a consistency and an order is comparable to modern psychiatry's showing that there is meaning and purpose in the apparently incoherent talk of the insane. In fact, the inability of the older psychologies and philosophies to account for the strange behavior of madmen and heathens was the principal factor that forced psychiatry and anthropology to develop theories of the unconscious and of culture.

Since culture is an abstraction, it is important not to confuse culture with society. A "society" refers to a group of people who interact more with each other than they do with other individuals—who cooperate with each other for the attainment of certain ends. You can see and indeed count the individuals who make up a society. A "culture" refers to the distinctive ways of life of such a group of people. Not all social events are culturally patterned. New types of circumstances arise for which no cultural solutions have as yet been devised.

A culture constitutes a storehouse of the pooled learning of the group. A rabbit starts life with some innate responses. He can learn from his own experience and perhaps from observing other rabbits. A human infant is born with fewer instincts and greater plasticity. His main task is to learn the answers that persons he will never see, persons long dead, have worked out. Once he has learned the formulas supplied by the culture of his group, most of his behavior becomes almost as automatic and unthinking as if it were instinctive. There is a tremendous amount of intelligence behind the making of a radio, but not much is required to learn to turn it on.

The members of all human societies face some of the same unavoidable dilemmas, posed by biology and other facts of the human situation. This is why the basic categories of all cultures are so similar. Human culture without language is unthinkable. No culture fails to provide for aesthetic expression and aesthetic delight. Every culture supplies standardized orientations toward the deeper problems, such as death. Every culture is designed to perpetuate the group and its solidarity, to meet the demands of individuals for an orderly way of life and for satisfaction of biological needs.

However, the variations on these basic themes are numberless. Some languages are built up out of twenty basic sounds, others out of forty. Nose plugs were considered beautiful by the predynastic Egyptians but are not by the modern French. Puberty is a biological fact. But one culture ignores it, another prescribes informal instructions about sex but no ceremony, a third has impressive rites for girls only, a fourth for boys and girls. In this culture, the first menstruation is welcomed as a happy, natural event; in that culture the atmosphere is full of dread and supernatural threat. Each culture dissects nature according to its own system of categories. The Navaho Indians apply the same word to the color of a robin's egg and to that of grass. A psychologist once assumed that this meant a difference in the sense organs, that Navahos didn't have the physiological equipment to distinguish "green" from "blue." However, when he showed them objects of the two colors and asked them if they were exactly the same colors, they looked at him with astonishment. His dream of discovering a new type of color blindness was shattered.

Every culture must deal with the sexual instinct. Some, however, seek to deny all sexual expression before marriage, whereas a Polynesian adolescent who was not promiscuous would be distinctly abnormal. Some cultures enforce lifelong monogamy; others, like our own, tolerate serial monogamy, in still other cultures, two or more women may be joined to one man or several men to a single woman. Homosexuality has been a permitted pattern in the Greco-Roman world, in parts of Islam, and in various primitive tribes. Large portions of the population of Tibet, and of Christendom at some places and periods, have practiced completely celibacy. To us marriage is first and foremost an arrangement between two individuals. In many more societies marriage is merely one facet of a complicated set of reciprocities, economic and otherwise, between two families or two clans.

The essence of the cultural process is selectivity. The selection is only exceptionally conscious and rational. Cultures are like Topsy. They just grew. Once, however, a way of handling a situation becomes institutionalized, there is ordinarily great resistance to change or deviation. When we speak of "our sacred beliefs," we mean of course that they are beyond criticism and that the person who suggests modification or abandonment must be punished. No person is emotionally indifferent to his culture. Certain cultural premises may become totally out of accord with a new factual situation. Leaders may recognize this and reject the old ways in theory. Yet their emotional loyalty continues in the face of reason because of the intimate conditionings of early childhood.

A culture is learned by individuals as the result of belonging to some particular group, and it constitutes that part of learned behavior which is shared with others. It is our social legacy, as contrasted with our organic heredity. It is one of the important factors which permits us to live together in an organized society, giving us ready-made solutions to our problems, helping us to predict the behavior of others, and permitting others to know what to expect of us.

Culture regulates our lives at every turn. From the moment we are born until we die there is, whether we are conscious of it or not, constant pressure upon us to follow certain types of behavior that other men have created for us. Some paths we follow willingly, others we follow because we know no other way, still others we deviate from or go back to most unwillingly. Mothers of small children know how unnaturally most of this comes to us—how little regard we have, until we are "culturalized," for the "proper" place, time, and manner for certain acts such as eating, excreting, sleeping, getting dirty, and making loud noises. But by more or less adhering to a system of related designs for carrying out all the acts of living, a group of men and women feel themselves linked together by a powerful chain of sentiments. Ruth Benedict gave an almost complete definition of the concept when she said, "Culture is that which binds men together."

It is true any culture is a set of techniques for adjusting both to the external environment and to other men. However, cultures create problems as well as solve them. If the lore of a people states that frogs are dangerous creatures, or that it is not safe to go about at night because of witches or ghosts, threats are posed which do not arise out of the inexorable facts of the external world. Cultures produce needs as well as provide a means of fulfilling them. There exists for every group culturally defined, acquired drives that may be more powerful in ordinary daily life than the biologically inborn drives. Many Americans, for example, will work harder for "success" than they will for sexual satisfaction.

Most groups elaborate certain aspects of their culture far beyond maximum utility or survival value. In other words, not all culture promotes physical survival. At times, indeed, it does exactly the opposite. Aspects of culture which once were adaptive may persist long after they have ceased to be useful. An analysis of any culture will disclose many features which cannot possibly be construed as adaptations to the total environment in which the group now finds itself. However, it is altogether likely that these apparently useless features represent survivals, with modifications through time, of cultural forms which were adaptive in one or another previous situation.

Any cultural practice must be functional or it will disappear before long. That is, it must somehow contribute to the survival of the society or to the adjustment of the individual. However, many cultural functions are not manifest but latent. A cowboy will walk three miles to catch a horse which he then rides one mile to the store. From the point of view of manifest function this is positively irrational. But the act has the latent function of maintaining the cowboy's prestige in the terms of his own subculture. One can instance the buttons on the sleeve of a man's coat, our absurd English spelling, the use of capital letters, and a host of other apparently nonfunctional customs. They serve mainly the latent function of assisting individuals to maintain their security by preserving continuity with the past and by making certain sectors of life familiar and predictable.

Every culture is a precipitate of history. In more than one sense history is a sieve. Each culture embraces those aspects of the past which, usually in altered form and with altered meanings, live on in the present. Discoveries and inventions, both material and ideological, are constantly being made available to a group through its historical contacts with other peoples or being created by its own members. However, only those that fit the total immediate situation in meeting the group's needs for survival or in promoting the psychological adjustment of individuals will become part of the culture. The process of culture building may be regarded as an addition to man's innate biological capacities, an addition providing instruments which enlarge, or may even substitute for, biological functions, and to a degree compensating for biological limitations—as in ensuring that death does not always result in the loss to humanity of what the deceased has learned.

Culture is like a map. Just as a map isn't the territory but an abstract representation of a particular area, so also a culture is an abstract description of trends toward uniformity in the words, deeds, and artifacts of a human group. If a map is accurate and you can read it, you won't get lost; if you know a culture, you will know your way around in the life of a society. Many educated people have the notion that culture applies only to exotic ways of life or to societies where relative simplicity and relative homogeneity prevail. Some sophisticated missionaries, for example, will use the anthropological conception in discussing the special modes of living of South Sea Islanders, but seem amazed at the idea that it could be applied equally to inhabitants of New York City. And social workers in Boston will talk about the culture of a colorful and well-knit immigrant group but boggle at applying it to the behavior of staff members in the social-service agency itself.

In the primitive society the correspondence between the habits of individuals and the customs of the community is ordinarily greater. There is probably some truth in what an old Indian once said, "In the old days there was no law; everybody did what was right." The primitive tends to find happiness in the fulfillment of intricately involuted cultural patterns; the modern more often tends to feel the pattern as repressive to his individuality. It is also true that in a complex stratified society there are numerous exceptions to generalizations made about the culture as a whole. It is necessary to study regional, class, and occupational subcultures. Primitive cultures have greater stability than modern cultures; they change—but less rapidly.

However, modern men also are creators and carriers of culture. Only in some respects are they influenced differently from primitives by culture. Moreover, there are such wide variations in primitive cultures that any black-and-white contrast between the primitive and the civilized is altogether fictitious. The distinction which is most generally true lies in the field of conscious philosophy.

The publication of Paul Radin's *Primitive Man as a Philosopher* did much toward destroying the myth that an abstract analysis of experience was a peculiarity of literate societies.

Queer Customs

1. How is *Queer Customs* an example of an ethnology?
2. How do the examples Kluckhohn uses demonstrate the power of culture over biology?
3. How is nature different than the notion of nurture?

READING 3

Lessons from the Field

GEORGE GMELCH

Ethnographic fieldwork is a valued tradition in anthropology. Most anthropologists believe that the experience of living and working in another culture is essential to successful research. They also realize, however, that there is more to the experience than discovering and describing the culture of others. Like a rite of passage, fieldwork is an intense personal experience, one that yields deeper insight into one's own culture and personal life. It is this reflexive power of fieldwork that George Gmelch discusses. He bases his analysis on the experiences of undergraduate students he has sent to do fieldwork in Barbados since 1978. He argues that, after a stressful beginning, students gain valuable new insight into their own views on materialism, gender, race, social class, the United States, and the value of education as well as Barbadian culture.

Sara, Eric, and Kristen heave their backpacks and suitcases—all the gear they'll need for the next ten weeks—into the back of the Institute's battered Toyota pick-up. Sara, a tense grin on her face, gets up front with me; the others climb in the back and make themselves comfortable on the soft luggage.

Leaving Bellairs Research Institute on the west coast of the island of Barbados, we drive north past the posh resort hotels. The scene changes abruptly as we move from tourism to agriculture, from the hustle and noise of the coast to the green and quiet of rolling sugar cane fields. There are no more white faces.

Graceful cabbage palms flank a large plantation house, one of the island's "great houses." On the edge of its cane fields is a tenantry, a cluster of small board houses whose inhabitants are the descendants of the slaves who once worked on the plantation.

Entering the village of Mile and a Quarter, so named because that is the distance from the village to nearby Speighstown, I point out the small orange and blue board house that one of my first students lived in. Sara and the others know of Ellen, as she became a documentary film maker and has made several films about the island which they have seen.

Two monkeys emerge from a cane field and scamper across the road. I mention that monkeys came to Barbados on early slave ships, 300 years ago. But Sara, absorbed in her own thoughts, doesn't seem to hear me. I've taken enough students to the "field" to have an idea of what's on her mind. She is wondering what her village will be like—the one we just passed through looked unusually poor. And will she like the family she is going to live with? Will they like her? Many people are walking along the road; clusters of men sit outside a rum shop shouting loudly while slamming dominoes on a wobbly plywood table. She is wondering how she will ever make friends with these people and gain their acceptance, which as a student anthropologist she must do.

Earlier in the day, Eric told me that many of the ten students on the field program thought they had made a mistake coming to Barbados. If they had chosen to go on the term abroad to Greece or England or even Japan, they mused, they would be together on a campus, among friends, and safe. They wouldn't have to live in a village, they wouldn't have to go out and make friends with all these strange people; and to do it all alone now seemed more of a challenge than many wanted.

We drive toward the northeastern corner of the island to the village of Pie Corner, where I had arranged for Sara to live with a family. This is the unsheltered side of the island. From several miles off we could see huge swells rolling in off the Atlantic and beating against the cliffs. The village only has a few hundred people but six small wooden churches, one of which—Bennett's Temple—has windows painted on the wall instead of real glass. Marcus Hinds and his family all come out to the truck to welcome Sara. Mrs. Hinds gives her a big hug, as though she were a returning relative, and daughter Yvette takes Sara into the backyard to show her the pigs and chickens. I explain to the Hinds, for a second time, the nature of the program, that Sara, like the other students, would be spending most of her time in the village talking to people and as much as possible participating in the life of the community, which meant everything from attending church to cutting sugar cane. Marcus is puzzled as my description doesn't fit his conception of what a university education is all about. The lives of Caribbean villagers are not something he thinks worthy of a university student's attention.

Back in the truck Eric and Kristen commented on the curiosity of the children and the stares from the houses we'd passed. But they also appeared relieved at seeing the warm welcome and friendliness of the family.

Things were different at Eric's village. Chalky Mount sits high on a narrow ridge, on land unsuitable for cultivation. The land drops away so abruptly that most residents have little flat ground so that many activities take place on the road. Most houses are simple wooden affairs with corrugated metal roofs. Eric's homestay "mother" shows him around. I see the disappointment in Eric's face when we are shown his bedroom. It is more cramped than he had ever imagined, barely larger than the bed. His new "mother," mostly out of her nervousness and uncertainty over what to do with a foreigner, much less a white man, seems aloof and uncaring. Later, Eric wrote about his arrival in his field notes:

> It was awful. I expected my homestay mother to welcome me with open arms and be so excited. But she had nothing to say. The only solution was to go to my room and unpack.

Back in the truck, Kristen, who had seemed more relaxed after the first drop off, after meeting Sara's family, began to bite her nails.

For fifteen years I have been taking students to the field, and like most anthropologists I know a good deal about what they learn about the foreign culture in which they live. But it wasn't until serving on a committee that evaluated my college's international study programs that I ever thought much about what it is that they learn about their own culture by living in another. The notion that you have to live in another culture before you can truly understand your own has gained wide acceptance. But what is it that we learn?

I questioned other anthropologists who also took students to the field, and they too were unclear about its lessons. A search through the literature didn't help. All the research on the educational outcomes of foreign study has been on students who study at universities in foreign countries.

As a result, I decided to examine the experiences of my own students in Barbados. Using a variety of techniques—questionnaires, tape recorded interviews, and analysis of their daily field notes and journals—I looked at their adjustment to Bajan village life and what they learned about themselves and their own culture by living in Barbados. It is primarily the latter that I wish to address here.

Typically, my students go to Barbados expecting to learn a great deal about how people in this Caribbean society live and think. What they don't expect is that they will also learn much about themselves and their own culture. Nor do they imagine that they will discover attitudes and perspectives that they will take back home and incorporate into their own lives.

Rural Life

Living in a Barbadian village brings many lessons in the difference between rural and urban. About 90 percent of my students come from suburbs or cities and have never lived in the countryside before. For them a significant part of their experience in Barbados is living among people who are close to the land. The host families, like most villagers, grow crops and raise animals. Each morning, before dawn, the students are awakened by the sounds of animals in the yard. They quickly begin to learn about the behavior of chickens, pigs, sheep, and cows. They witness animals giving birth and being slaughtered. They see the satisfaction families get from consuming food they have produced themselves. One student described the effect an everyday occurrence had on her.

> I was in Mrs. S.'s kitchen and she was making sugar cakes. The recipe calls for a lime, and when she didn't have any in the kitchen she just walked into the yard and pulled a few off the nearest tree. It was nothing to her but I was amazed, and I thought how in that situation I would've had to drive to the supermarket.

In the villages most students live close to nature for a prolonged period of time. They may share their bedrooms with a green lizard or two, mice, cockroaches, and sometimes a whistling frog. They become aware of how different are the sounds of the countryside and are struck by the darkness of the sky and the brightness of the stars with no city lights to diminish their intensity. A student from Long Island described it as "like living in a planetarium."

The social world of the village is unlike anything most students know. In doing a household survey, for example, students discover that not only does everybody seem to know everybody else and that many families are related to one another, but that they know one another in more than one context—that people are tied to one another in multiple ways. Relationships are not single stranded as they often are in the urban America the students come from.

Students have never known a place of such intimacy, where relationships are so embedded with different meanings and a shared history. Some students reflect upon and compare the warmth, friendliness, and frequent sharing of food and other resources with the impersonality, individualism, and detachment of suburban life at home. But they also learn the drawbacks to living in small communities: there is no anonymity. People are nosy and unduly interested in the affairs of their neighbors. As the students become integrated into the community, they soon discover that they too may be the object of local gossip. Several female students learned from village friends that there were stories afoot that they were either mistresses to their host fathers or sleeping with their host brothers. The gossip hurt, for the students had worked hard to gain acceptance, greatly valued the friendships they had made, and naturally were concerned about the damage such rumors might do to their reputations (even though the students spend only ten weeks in their villages and most will never return, they still care greatly that villagers think well of them).

One of the biggest adjustments students must make to village life is to its slow pace, and the absence of the diversions and entertainment that they are accustomed to at home. Early in their stay there seems to be little to do apart from their research. At times they are desperate to escape the village but they are not allowed to leave except on designated days (all students initially hate this restriction, but by the end of the term they recommend that it be continued). The outcome of their forced isolation from other students is that they must satisfy their needs for companionship and recreation within their communities. They must learn to be resourceful in finding ways to entertain themselves. The outcome is that they spend a good deal of time hanging out—socializing—with people in the village, a practice which strengthens friendships and results in a good deal of informal education about culture. By the mid-point in their term most students have adapted so well to village life that they no longer report being bored or desperate to get away. And many no longer leave the village on their day off.

Materialism

Many students arrive at a new awareness of wealth and materialism. One of the strongest initial perceptions the students have of their villages is that the people are poor—that most of their houses are tiny, that their diets are restricted, and that they have few of the amenities and comforts the students are accustomed to. Even little things may remind students of the difference in wealth, as anthropology major Betsy recounted after her first week in the field:

> At home [Vermont] when I go into a convenience store and buy a soda, I don't think twice about handling the clerk a 20 dollar bill. But here when you hand a man in the rum shop a 20 dollar bill [equals $10 U.S.] they often ask if you have something smaller. It makes me self-conscious of how wealthy I appear, and of how little money the rum shop man makes in a day.

The initial response of the students to such incidents and to the poverty they perceive around them is to feel embarrassed and even guilty that they, like many Americans, have so much wealth. However, such feelings are short-lived for as the students get to know the families better they no longer see poverty; even the houses no longer seem so small. They discover that most people not only manage quite well on what they have but that they are reasonably content. In fact, most students eventually come to believe that the villagers are, on the whole, actually more satisfied with their lives than are most Americans. Whether or not this is true, it's an important perception for students whose ideas about happiness have been shaped by an ethos which measures success and satisfaction by material gain. About his host family, Dan said:

> I ate off the same plate and drank from the same cup every night. We only had an old fridge, an old stove, and an old TV, and a few dishes and pots and pans. But that was plenty. Mrs. H. never felt like she needed any more. And after awhile I never felt like I needed any more either.

Many students say that after Barbados they became less materialistic. Many said that when they returned home from Barbados they were surprised at how many possessions they owned; and that when they came back to campus they didn't bring nearly as many things with them as they usually do. A few had gone through their drawers and closets and given away to the Goodwill or Salvation Army the things they didn't really need. Most said they would no longer take for granted the luxuries, such as hot showers, that they are accustomed to at campus and home. Amy said:

> When I came back I saw how out of control the students here are. It's just crazy. They want so much, they talk about how much money they need to make, as if these things are necessities and you'll never be happy without them. Maybe I was like that too, but now I know I don't need those things; sure I'd like a great car, but I don't need it.

When alumni of the program were asked in a survey how they had been changed by their experience in Barbados, most believed they were less materialistic today.

Gender

Female students quickly learn that gender relations are quite different in Barbados. Indeed, the most difficult adjustment for many women students is learning how to deal with the frequent and aggressive advances of Bajan men. At the end of her first week in the field, Jenny described a plight common to the students:

> When I walk through the village, the guys who hang out at the rum shop yell comments. I have never heard men say some of the things they tell me here. My friend Andrew tells me that most of the comments are actually compliments. Yet I still feel weird. . . . I am merely an object that they would like to conquer. I hate that feeling, so I am trying to get to know these guys. I figure that if they know me as a person and a friend, they will stop with the demeaning comments. Maybe it's a cultural thing they do to all women.

Indeed, many Bajan men feel it is their right—as males—to accost women in public with hissing, appreciative remarks, and offers of sexual services. This sexual bantering is tolerated by Bajan women who generally ignore the men's comments. Most women consider it harmless, if annoying; some consider it flattering. Students like Jenny, however, are not sure what to make of it. They do not know whether it is being directed at them because local men think white girls are "loose" or whether Bajan men behave in this fashion toward all women. Anxious to be accepted and not wanting to be rude or culturally insensitive, most female students tolerate the remarks the best they can, while searching for a strategy to politely discourage them. Most find that as people get to know them by name, the verbal harassment subsides.

But they still must get accustomed to other sexual behavior. For example, when invited to their first neighborhood parties most are shocked at the sexually explicit dancing, in which movements—*grinding*—imitate intercourse. One female student wrote, after having been to several *fetes,* or parties:

> I was watching everyone dance when I realized that even the way we dance says a lot about culture. We are so con-

> servative at home. Inhibited. In the U.S. one's body is a personal, private thing, and when it is invaded we get angry. We might give a boyfriend some degree of control over our bodies, but no one else. Bajans aren't nearly as possessive about their bodies. Men and women can freely move from one dance partner to the next without asking, and then grind the other person—it's like having sex with your clothes on.

Students discover that, to an even greater degree than in the United States, women are regarded by men as both subordinates and sexual objects. Masculinity is largely based on men's sexual conquest of women and on their ability to give them pleasure. Being sexually active, a good sex partner, and becoming a father all enhance young men's status among male peers. As time passes, the students discover male dominance in other areas of Barbadian life as well—that women earn less than men, are more likely to be unemployed, and are less likely to attain political office. They conclude that while their own society is sexist Barbados is far more so.

Race

In Barbados my students become members of a racial minority for the first time in their lives. Everyone in the villages in which they live is black, while nearly all of my students have been white. Before going to Barbados, most of my students have had little contact with blacks and as a result they feel awkward and in some cases hold negative stereotypes. The students have never experienced racial prejudice themselves. During their first few weeks in the field, however, they become acutely aware of their own "race," of their being white while everyone around them is dark. Female students are often called "white girl" by people in the village until they get to know them personally. Village children ask if they can touch the students' skin, some want to feel the student's straight hair; they marvel at the blue veins which show through the students' light skin, and sometimes ask those with freckles if they have a skin disease. Characteristically, during the second week one student wrote:

> I have never been in a situation before where I was a minority purely due to the color of my skin, and treated differently because of it. When I approach people I am very conscious of having white skin. Before I never thought of myself as having color.

A few students become hypersensitive to race during the early weeks of their stay. When students leave their villages, they travel by bus. The buses are often crowded, with the students usually being the only white person on board. Often they are stared at (sometimes because as the buses head into the countryside the passengers assume the student has missed her stop or taken the wrong bus). The students notice that as the bus fills up, the seat next to them is often the last to be taken. Here is the extreme reaction of one female student who has gone by bus to a remote area during her first week in Barbados. There she encounters a woman who stares at her:

> The woman glared at me as if she was seeing the evil white woman who has been responsible for the oppression of her people. I felt like I had chained, maimed, and enslaved every black person who had ever lived. The feelings were so strange . . . somehow I felt responsible for the entire history of the relationship between blacks and whites. I carried this woman's face with me for the rest of the day. When I got on the bus to go back to my village I felt very alone and very unwanted, like the mere presence of my color was making a lot of people very uneasy.

But concerns about race, even the very awareness of race, diminish rapidly as the students make friends and become integrated into their villages. In fact, by the end of the term most said they were "rarely" aware of being white. Several students described incidents in which they had become so unaware of skin color that they were shocked when someone made a remark or did something to remind them of their being different. Sara was startled when, after shaking the hand of someone in her village, the person remarked that she had never touched the hand of a white person before. Several students reported being surprised when they walked by a mirror and got a glimpse of their white skin. One student wrote that although she knew she wasn't black, she no longer felt white.

What is the outcome of all this? Do students now have an understanding of what it means to be a minority, and does this translate into their having more empathy at home? I think so. All the students from the previous Barbados programs whom I questioned about the impact of their experiences mentioned a heightened empathy for blacks, and some said other minorities as well. Several said that when they first returned home, they wanted to go up to any black person they saw and have a conversation. "But I kept having to remind myself," said one student, "that most blacks in America are not West Indians and they wouldn't understand where I am coming from." Another said her first, admittedly naive, reaction upon coming home and seeing black people was to want to hug every one of them.

Social Class

American students, particularly compared to their European counterparts, have little understanding of social class. Even after several weeks in Barbados, most students are fairly oblivious to class and status distinctions in their villages. The American suburbs that my students grew up in are fairly homogenous in social composition and housing—most homes fall in the same general price range. In contrast, the Barbadian villages the students now live in exhibit a broad spectrum, ranging from the large two-story masonry homes of return migrants to tiny board houses of small farmers who eke out a living from a few acres. The students are slow to translate such differences in the material conditions of village households into status or class differences. Also, Barbadians' well-developed class consciousness, fostered by three centuries of British rule, is foreign to American students steeped in a culture that stresses, at least on an ideological level, egalitarianism. Hence, the students, who have never given much thought to social class, tend to view the population of the villages as all the same.

It is largely from the comments that their host families make about other people that students gradually become aware of status distinctions. But equally, they learn about class and status from making mistakes, from violating norms concerning relationships between different categories of people. Kristen learned that there are different standards of behavior for the more affluent families after she walked home through the village carrying a bundle on her head: "Mrs. C. told me never to do that again, that only poor people carry things on their heads, and that my doing it reflected badly on her family."

As in most field situations, the first villagers to offer the students friendship are sometimes marginal members of the community and this creates special problems in that the students are usually guests in the homes of "respectable" and often high-status village families. The host parents become upset when they discover their student has been seeing a disreputable man or woman. Most serious were, in the early years of the field program, female students who went out with lower-class local men. The women entered into these relationships oblivious to what the local reaction might be, and equally oblivious to how little privacy there is in a village where everyone knows everyone else's business. One student said she wrongly assumed that people would look favorably upon her going with a local man because it would show she wasn't prejudiced and that she found blacks just as desirable as whites. Another female student was befriended by some Rastafarians—orthodox Rastas who wore no clothes, lived off the land, and slept in caves in the hills above her village. When villagers discovered she had been seeing the Rastas, her homestay mother nearly evicted her and others gave her the cold shoulder. The student wrote:

> I have discovered the power of a societal norm: nice girls don't talk to Rastas. When girls who were formerly nice talk to Rastas, they cease to be known as nice. Exceptions none.

New Perspectives on North America

In learning about Barbadian society, students inevitably make comparisons with their own culture. Especially in the early stages of fieldwork, students think about Barbadian customs in terms of how similar or different they are from customs at home. The students are often assisted in such comparisons by villagers who know a lot about North America from television, tourism, and for some, travel. Students quickly discover, however, that the villagers' perspectives are often at odds with their own. Based on a steady diet of American soap operas, many villagers, for example, believe that all students are wealthy, own late model cars, vacation in exotic places, etc.

Early in the term, many students find themselves defending the United States from criticism and from stereotypes. For example, one student described getting very annoyed when a guest at his host family's dinner table criticized the United States and talked about the chemical adulteration of American chicken. He knew this to be true, but later he said, "I couldn't take it anymore and fought back. I felt like an idiot afterward, defending American chicken."

Over time the students become less eager to defend their own society. Indeed, many become quite critical of the United States, or at least aspects of it. Why? What makes them question their own culture after a few months in Barbados? Part of the answer is found in their growing appreciation for Bajan life and their identification with local people. They come to see many things from the perspective of their village friends. Another factor is the students' exposure to North American tourists. When students go to the beach or town on their free day they encounter tourists and are sometimes embarrassed by what they see and hear—tourists entering shops and walking the street in skimpy beach attire, and their loud and intrusive voices. From a variety of sources, students learn about the social impacts of tourism—drug trafficking, materialism, crime, environmental damage, and American cultural penetration. Viewing tourism as part of a broader Americanization of the region, many students become critical not only of tourists but of America's presence abroad generally.

Fieldwork and Education

Students learn more than about just cultural differences from their experience of living and doing anthropology alone in a Caribbean village. Most returned from Barbados with a more positive attitude toward education. This appears to stem both from their own experiences in doing research and from seeing the high value that villagers place on formal education, which is their chief means of upward mobility. They see that they are accorded respect and adult status largely because they are working toward a university degree. Also, as the weeks pass, most students become deeply involved in their own research. They are surprised at how much satisfaction they get from doing something that they previously regarded as "work." A number of the students from past terms have said they didn't see education as an end in itself, something to be enjoyed, until doing fieldwork in Barbados. One student wrote about her attitude after returning from the field:

> I feel isolated from many of my old friends on campus, and I no longer feel guilty missing social events. . . . I appreciate my education more and I do much more work for my own understanding and enjoyment rather than just for the exam or grades. I find myself on a daily basis growing agitated with those who don't appreciate what is being offered to them here. Several of my classmates blow off class and use other peoples' notes. A lot of what I feel is from seeing how important education was to my Bajan friends in Barbados compared to the lax attitude of my Union friends here.

Students spend much of their time in the field talking to people; a good part of each day is spent in conversations which they must direct onto the topics that they are investigating. To succeed at their studies, they must learn to be inquisitive, to probe sensitively into the villager's knowledge or memory of events and aspects of culture, and to concentrate, to listen to what they are being told, and later to be able to recall it so that they can record it in field notes. The students become proficient at maintaining lengthy conversations with adults and at asking pertinent questions. These are interpersonal skills they bring back with them and make use of in many aspects of their own lives.

While the students spend a semester discovering and making sense of the differences between their own culture and the Barbadians around them, most arrive at the notion that beneath differences in skin color and culture, Barbadians and Americans are basically alike, that beneath the veneer of custom there is something fundamental about "human nature" which is shared by everyone. In the words of one student, who is now an anthropologist:

> If I had to sum up my whole trip in one experience it would be this: It was late at night, a full moon, and I sat in a pasture with a local Rastafarian. After hours of talking, about everything from love to politics, the two of us came to an interesting conclusion. Although we lived a thousand miles away from each other, and that our skin color, hair style, and many personal practices were quite different, at heart we were the same people.

While this may seem like common sense it is surprisingly not a notion that many college students share today.

As the world's economies intertwine and its societies move closer to the "global village" Marshall McLuhan envisioned, it is more imperative than ever that we seek to understand other peoples and cultures. Without understanding there can be neither respect, nor prosperity, nor lasting peace. "The tragedy about Americans," noted Mexican novelist Carlos Fuentes, "is that they understand others so little." Students who study abroad, like those described in these pages, not only enrich themselves but in countless small ways help bridge the gulf between "us" and "them." Getting to know another culture is to look in the proverbial mirror and get glimpse of onself and of what it means to be an "American."

Lessons from the Field

1. How did the students' experiences with the Rastafarians teach them about the issue of social class in Barbadian culture?
2. How does travel help people develop a greater understanding and respect for cultural differences and similarities?
3. How did the students change after their field experience? Do you think the change will last?

READING 4

Eating Christmas in the Kalahari

RICHARD BORSHAY LEE

In this selection, cultural anthropologist Richard Lee recounts his experience while conducting fieldwork among the !Kung (today referred to as the Ju/'hoansi) of southwest Africa. Much to Lee's dismay, his attempt to give the local !Kung the largest and fattest oxen to slaughter and share as a Christmas feast was met with ridicule.

This is a classic example of cross-cultural misunderstanding. Lee's confusion and hurt feelings stemmed from a common mistake made by people (even anthropologists!) operating in a culturally unfamiliar environment—that is, they try to understand other peoples' behavior in terms of the assumptions of their own culture. To Lee, his gift to the community of the fattest oxen he could find was no more than a generous expression of his gratitude for their assistance and hospitality. Yet the group taunted Lee with insults about the inadequacy of the gift. Did the !Kung truly not appreciate the gift, or was there another explanation for their negative reaction?

The !Kung Bushmen's knowledge of Christmas is third-hand. The London Missionary Society brought the holiday to the southern Tswana tribes in the early nineteenth century. Later, native catechists spread the idea far and wide among the Bantu-speaking pastoralists, even in the remotest corners of the Kalahari Desert. The Bushmen's idea of the Christmas story, stripped to its essentials, is "praise the birth of white man's god-chief"; what keeps their interest in the holiday high is the Tswana-Herero custom of slaughtering an ox for his Bushmen neighbors as an annual goodwill gesture. Since the 1930's, part of the Bushmen's annual round of activities has included a December congregation at the cattle posts for trading, marriage brokering, and several days of trance-dance feasting at which the local Tswana headman is host.

As a social anthropologist working with !Kung Bushmen, I found that the Christmas ox custom suited my purposes. I had come to the Kalahari to study the hunting and gathering subsistence economy of the !Kung, and to accomplish this it was essential not to provide them with food, share my own food, or interfere in any way with their food-gathering activities. While liberal handouts of tobacco and medical supplies were appreciated, they were scarcely adequate to erase the glaring disparity in wealth between the anthropologist, who maintained a two-month inventory of canned goods, and the Bushmen, who rarely had a day's supply of food on hand. My approach, while paying off in terms of data, left me open to frequent accusations of stinginess and hard-heartedness. By their lights, I was a miser.

The Christmas ox was to be my way of saying thank you for the cooperation of the past year; and since it was to be our last Christmas in the field, I determined to slaughter the largest, meatiest ox that money could buy, insuring that the feast and trance dance would be a success.

Through December I kept my eyes open at the wells as the cattle were brought down for watering. Several animals were offered, but none had quite the grossness that I had in mind. Then, ten days before the holiday, a Herero friend led an ox of astonishing size and mass up to our camp. It was solid black, stood five feet high at the shoulder, had a five-foot span of horns, and must have weighed 1,200 pounds on the hoof. Food consumption calculations are my specialty, and I quickly figured that bones and viscera aside, there was enough meat—at least four pounds—for every man, woman, and child of the 150 Bushmen in the vicinity of /ai/ai who were expected at the feast.

Having found the right animal at last, I paid the Herero £20 ($56) and asked him to keep the beast with his herd until Christmas day. The next morning word spread among the people that the big solid black one was the ox chosen by/ontah (my bushman name; it means, roughly, "whitey") for the Christmas feast. That afternoon I re-

Editor's note: The !Kung and other Bushmen speak click languages. In the story, three different clicks are used:

1. The dental click (/), as in /ai/ai, /ontah, and /gaugo. The click is somethimes written in English as tsk-tsk.
2. The alveopalatal click (!), as in Ben!a and !King.
3. The lateral click (//), as in //gom. Clicks junction as consonants; a word may have more than one, as in/n!au.

ceived the first delegation. Ben!a, an outspoken sixty-year-old mother of five, came to the point slowly.

"Where were you planning to eat Christmas?"

"Right here at/ai/ai," I replied.

"Alone or with others?"

"I expect to invite all the people to eat Christmas with me."

"Eat what?"

"I have purchased Yehave's black ox, and I am going to slaughter and cook it."

"That's what we were told at the well but refused to believe it until we heard it from yourself."

"Well, it's the black one," I replied expansively, although wondering what she was driving at.

"Oh, no!" Ben!a groaned, turning to her group. "They were right." Turning back to me she asked, "Do you expect us to eat that bag of bones?"

"Bag of bones! It's the biggest ox at /ai/ai."

"Big, yes, but old. And thin. Everybody knows there's no meat on that old ox. What did you expect us to eat off it, the horns?"

Everybody chuckled at Ben!a's one-liner as they walked away, but all I could manage was a weak grin.

That evening it was the turn of the young men. They came to sit at our evening fire. /gaugo, about my age, spoke to me man-to-man.

"/ontah, you have always been square with us," he lied. "What has happened to change your heart? That sack of guts and bones of Yehave's will hardly feed one camp, let alone all the Bushmen around /ai/ai." And he proceeded to enumerate the seven camps in the /ai/ai vicinity, family by family. "Perhaps you have forgotten that we are not few, but many. Or are you too blind to tell the difference between a proper cow and an old wreck? That ox is thin to the point of death."

"Look, you guys," I retorted, "that is a beautiful animal, and I'm sure you will eat it with pleasure at Christmas."

"Of course we will eat it; it's food. But it won't fill us up to the point where we will have enough strength to dance. We will eat and go home to bed with stomachs rumbling."

That night as we turned in, I asked my wife Nancy: "What did you think of the black ox?"

"It looked enormous to me. Why?"

"Well, about eight different people have told me I got gypped; that the ox is nothing but bones."

"What's the angle?" Nancy asked. "Did they have a better one to sell?"

"No, they just said that it was going to be a grim Christmas because there won't be enough meat to go around. Maybe I'll get an independent judge to look at the beast in the morning."

Bright and early, Halingisi, a Tswana cattleowner, appeared at our camp. But before I could ask him to give me his opinion on Yehave's black ox, he gave me the eye signal that indicated a confidential chat. We left the camp and sat down.

"/ontah, I'm surprised at you; you've lived here for three years and still haven't learned anything about cattle."

"But what else can a person do but choose the biggest, strongest animal one can find?" I retorted.

"Look, just because an animal is big doesn't mean that it has plenty of meat on it. The black one was a beauty when it was younger, but now it is thin to the point of death."

"Well, I've already bought it. What can I do at this stage?"

"Bought it already? I thought you were just considering it. Well, you'll have to kill it and serve it, I suppose. But don't expect much of a dance to follow."

My spirits dropped rapidly. I could believe that Ben!a and /gaugo just might be putting me on about the black ox, but Halingisi seemed to be an impartial critic. I went around that day feeling as though I had bought a lemon of a used car.

In the afternoon it was Tomazo's turn. Tomazo is a fine hunter, a top trance performer, and one of the most reliable informants. He approached the subject of the Christmas cow as part of my continuing Bushman education.

"My friend, the way it is with us Bushmen," he began, "is that we love meat. And even more than that, we love fat. When we hunt we always search for the fat ones, the one dripping with layers of white fat: fat that turns into a clear, thick oil in the cooking pot, fat that slides down your gullet, fills your stomach and gives you a roaring diarrhea," he rhapsodized.

"So, feeling as we do," he continued, "it gives us pain to be served such a scrawny thing as Yehave's black ox. It is big, yes, and no doubt its giant bones are good for soup, but fat is what we really crave and so we will eat Christmas this year with a heavy heart."

The prospect of a gloomy Christmas now had me worried, so I asked Tomazo what I could do about it.

"Look for a fat one, a young one . . . smaller, but fat. Fat enough to make us *//gom* ('evacuate the bowels'), then we will be happy."

My suspicions were aroused when Tomazo said that he happened to know of a young, fat, barren cow that the owner was willing to part with. Was Toma working on commission, I wondered? But I dispelled this unworthy thought when we approached the Herero owner of the cow in question and found that he had decided not to sell.

The scrawny wreck of a Christmas ox now became the talk of the /ai/ai water hole and was the first news told to the outlying groups as they began to come in from the bush for the feast. What finally convinced me that real trouble might be brewing was the visit from u!au, an old conservative with a reputation for fierceness. His nickname meant spear and referred to an incident thirty years ago in which he had speared a man to death. He had an intense manner; fixing me with his eyes, he said in clipped tones:

"I have only just heard about the black ox today, or else I would have come here earlier. /ontah, do you honestly think you can serve meat like that to people and avoid a fight?" He paused, letting the implications sink in. "I don't meant fight you, /ontah; you are a white man. I mean a fight between Bushmen. There are many fierce ones here, and with such a small quantity of meat to distribute, how can you give everybody a fair share? Someone is sure to accuse another of taking too much or hogging all the choice pieces. Then you will see what happens when some go hungry while others eat."

The possibility of at least a serious argument struck me as all too real. I had witnessed the tension that surrounds the distribution of meat from a kudu or gemsbok kill, and had documented many arguments that sprang up from a real or imagined slight in meat distribution. The owners of a kill may spend up to two hours arranging and rearranging the piles of meat under the gaze of a circle of recipients before handing them out. And I also knew that the Christmas feast at /ai/ai would be bringing together groups that had feuded in the past.

Convinced now of the gravity of the situation, I went in earnest to search for a second cow; but all my inquiries failed to turn one up.

The Christmas feast was evidently going to be a disaster, and the incessant complaints about the meagerness of the ox had already taken the fun out of it for me. Moreover, I was getting bored with the wisecracks, and after losing my temper a few times, I resolved to serve the beast anyway. If the meat fell short, the hell with it. In the Bushmen idiom, I announced to all who would listen:

"I am a poor man and blind. If I have chosen one that is too old and too thin, we will eat it anyway and see if there is enough meat there to quiet the rumbling of our stomachs."

On hearing this speech, Ben!a offered me a rare word of comfort. "It's thin," she said philosophically, "but the bones will make a good soup."

At dawn on Christmas morning, instinct told me to turn over the butchering and cooking to a friend and take off with Nancy to spend Christmas alone in the bush. But curiosity kept me from retreating. I wanted to see what such a scrawny ox looked like on butchering, and if there *was* going to be a fight, I wanted to catch every word of it. Anthropologists are incurable that way.

The great beast was driven up to our dancing ground, and a shot in the forehead dropped it in its tracks. Then, freshly cut branches were heaped around the fallen carcass to receive the meat. Ten men volunteered to help with the cutting. I asked /gaugo to make the breast bone cut. This cut, which begins the butchering process for most large game, offers easy access for removal of the viscera. But it also allows the hunter to spotcheck the amount of fat on the animal. A fat game animal carries a white layer up to an inch thick on the chest, while in a thin one, the knife will quickly cut to bone. All eyes fixed on his hand as /gaugo, dwarfed by the great carcass, knelt to the breast. The first cut opened a pool of solid white in the black skin. The second and third cut widened and deepened the creamy white. Still no bone. It was pure fat; it must have been two inches thick.

"Hey /gau," I burst out, "that ox is loaded with fat. What's this about the ox being too thin to bother eating? Are you out of your mind?"

"Fat?" /gau shot back, "You call that fat? This wreck is thin, sick, dead!" And he broke out laughing. So did everyone else. They rolled on the ground, paralyzed with laughter. Everybody laughed except me; I was thinking.

I ran back to the tent and burst in just as Nancy was getting up. "Hey, the black ox. It's fat as hell! They were kidding about it being too thin to eat. It was a joke or something. A put-on. Everyone is really delighted with it!"

"Some joke," my wife replied. "It was so funny that you were ready to pack up and leave /ai/ai."

If it had indeed been a joke, it had been an extraordinarily convincing one, and tinged, I thought, with more than a touch of malice as many jokes are. Nevertheless, that it was a joke lifted my spirits considerably, and I returned to the butchering site where the shape of the ox was rapidly disappearing under the axes and knives of the butchers. The atmosphere had become festive. Grinning broadly, their arms covered with blood well past the elbow, men packed chunks of meat into the big cast-iron cooking pots, fifty pounds to the load, and muttered and chuckled all the while about the thinness and worthlessness of the animal and /ontah's poor judgment.

We danced and ate that ox two days and two nights; we cooked and distributed fourteen potfuls of meat and no one went home hungry and no fights broke out.

But the "joke" stayed in my mind. I had a growing feeling that something important had happened in my relationship with the Bushmen and that the clue lay in the meaning of the joke. Several days later, when most of the people had dispersed back to the bush camps, I raised the question with Hakekgose, a Tswana man who had grown up among the !Kung, married a !Kung girl, and who probably knew their culture better than any other non-Bushman.

"With us whites," I began, "Christmas is supposed to be the day of friendship and brotherly love. What I can't figure out is why the Bushmen went to such lengths to criticize and belittle the ox I had bought for the feast. The animal was perfectly good and their jokes and wisecracks practically ruined the holiday for me."

"So it really did bother you," said Hakekgose. "Well, that's the way they always talk. When I take my rifle and go hunting with them, if I miss, they laugh at me for the rest of the day. But even if I hit and bring one down, it's no better. To them, the kill is always too small or too old or too thin; and as we sit down on the kill site to cook and eat the liver, they keep grumbling, even with their mouths full of meat. They say things like, 'Oh this is awful! What a worthless animal! Whatever made me think that this Tswana rascal could hunt!' "

"Is this the way outsiders are treated?" I asked.

"No, it is their custom; they talk that way to each other too. Go and ask them."

/gaugo had been one of the most enthusiastic in making me feel bad about the merit of the Christmas ox. I sought him out first.

"Why did you tell me the black ox was worthless, when you could see that it was loaded with fat and meat?"

"It is our way," he said smiling. "We always like to fool people about that. Say there is a Bushman who has been hunting. He must not come home and announce like a braggard, 'I have killed a big one in the bush!' He must first sit down in silence until I or someone else comes up to his fire and asks, 'What did you see today?' He replies quietly, 'Ah, I'm no good for hunting. I saw nothing at all [pause] just a little tiny one.' Then I smile to myself," /gaugo continued, "because I know he has killed something big.

"In the morning we make up a party of four or five people to cut up and carry the meat back to the camp. When we arrive at the kill we examine it and cry out, 'You mean to say you have dragged us all the way out here in order to make us cart home your pile of bones? Oh, if I had known it was this thin I wouldn't have come.' Another one pipes up, 'People, to think I gave up a nice day in the shade for this. At home we may be hungry but at least we have nice cool water to drink.' If the horns are big, someone says, 'Did you think that somehow you were going to boil down the horns for soup?'

"To all this you must respond in kind. 'I agree,' you say, 'this one is not worth the effort; let's just cook the liver for strength and leave the rest for the hyenas. It is not too late to hunt today and even a duiker or a steenbok would be better than this mess.'

"Then you set to work nevertheless; butcher the animal, carry the meat back to the camp and everyone eats," /gaugo concluded.

Things were beginning to make sense. Next, I went to Tomazo. He corroborated /gaugo's story of the obligatory insults over a kill and added a few details of his own.

"But," I asked, "why insult a man after he has gone to all that trouble to track and kill an animal and when he is going to share the meat with you so that your children will have something to eat?"

"Arrogance." was his cryptic answer.

"Arrogance?"

"Yes, when a young man kills much meat he comes to think of himself as a chief or a big man, and he thinks of the rest of us as his servants or inferiors. We can't accept this. We refuse one who boasts, for someday his pride will make him kill somebody. So we always speak of his meat as worthless. This way we cool his heart and make him gentle."

"But why didn't you tell me this before?" I asked Tomazo with some heat.

"Because you never asked me," said Tomazo, echo-ing the refrain that has come to haunt every field ethnographer.

The pieces now fell into place. I had known for a long time that in situations of social conflict with Bushmen I held all the cards. I was the only source of tobacco in a thousand square miles, and I was not incapable of cutting an individual off for noncooperation. Though my boycott never lasted longer than a few days, it was an indication of my strength. People resented my presence at the water hole, yet simultaneously dreaded my leaving. In short I was a perfect target for the charge of arrogance and for the Bushmen tactic of enforcing humility.

I had been taught an object lesson by the Bushmen; it had come from an unexpected corner and had hurt me in a vulnerable area. For the big black ox was to be the one totally generous, unstinting act of my year at /ai/ai, and I was quite unprepared for the reaction I received.

As I read it, their message was this: There are no totally generous acts. All "acts" have an element of calculation. One black ox slaughtered at Christmas does not wipe out a year of careful manipulation of gifts given to serve your own ends. After all, to kill an animal and share the meat with people is really no more than Bushmen do for each other every day and with far less fanfare.

In the end, I had to admire how the Bushmen had played out the farce—collectively straight-faced to the end. Curiously, the episode reminded me of the *Good Soldier Schweik* and his marvelous encounters with authority. Like Schweik, the Bushmen had retained a thoroughgoing skepticism of good intentions. Was it this independence of spirit, I wondered, that had kept them culturally viable in the face of generations of contact with more powerful societies, both black and white? The thought that the Bushmen were alive and well in the Kalahari was strangely comforting. Perhaps, armed with that independence and with their superb knowledge of their environment, they might yet survive the future.

Eating Christmas in the Kalahari

1. After spending three years in the Kalahari with the !Kung, why did Lee have such a difficult time understanding the !Kung's reaction to his gift of the ox?
2. Why do the !Kung share?
3. Why is sharing less important in our culture than in the !Kung's culture?

READING 5

India's Sacred Cow

MARVIN HARRIS

News photographs that came out of India during the famine of the late 1960s showed starving people stretching out bony hands to beg for food while sacred cattle strolled behind them undisturbed. The Hindu, it seems, would rather starve to death than eat his cow or even deprive it of food. The cattle appear to browse unhindered through urban markets eating an orange here, a mango there, competing with people for meager supplies of food.

By Western standards, spiritual values seem more important to Indians than life itself. Specialists in food habits around the world like Fred Simoons at the University of California at Davis consider Hinduism an irrational ideology that compels people to overlook abundant, nutritious foods for scarcer, less healthful foods.

What seems to be an absurd devotion to the mother cow pervades Indian life. Indian wall calendars portray beautiful young women with bodies of fat white cows, often with milk jetting from their teats into sacred shrines.

Cow worship even carries over into politics. In 1966 a crowd of 120,000 people, led by holy men, demonstrated in front of the Indian House of Parliament in support of the All-Party Cow Protection Campaign Committee. In Nepal, the only contemporary Hindu kingdom, cow slaughter is severely punished. As one story goes, the car driven by an official of a United States agency struck and killed a cow. In order to avoid the international incident that would have occurred when the official was arrested for murder, the Nepalese magistrate concluded that the cow had committed suicide.

Many Indians agree with Western assessments of the Hindu reverence for their cattle, the zebu, or *Bos indicus*, a large-humped species prevalent in Asia and Africa. M. N. Srinivas, an Indian anthropologist, states: "Orthodox Hindu opinion regards the killing of cattle with abhorrence, even though the refusal to kill the vast number of useless cattle which exists in India today is detrimental to the nation." Even the Indian Ministry of Information formerly maintained that "the large animal population is more a liability than an asset in view of our land resources." Accounts from many different sources point to the same conclusion: India, one of the world's great civilizations, is being strangled by its love for the cow.

The easy explanation for India's devotion to the cow, the one most Westerners and Indians would offer, is that cow worship is an integral part of Hinduism. Religion is somehow good for the soul, even if it sometimes fails the body. Religion orders the cosmos and explains our place in the universe. Religious beliefs, many would claim, have existed for thousands of years and have a life of their own. They are not understandable in scientific terms.

But all this ignores history. There is more to be said for cow worship than is immediately apparent. The earliest Vedas, the Hindu sacred texts from the Second Millennium B.C., do not prohibit the slaughter of cattle. Instead, they ordain it as a part of sacrificial rites. The early Hindus did not avoid the flesh of cows and bulls; they ate it at ceremonial feasts presided over by Brahman priests. Cow worship is a relatively recent development in India; it evolved as the Hindu religion developed and changed.

This evolution is recorded in royal edicts and religious texts written during the last 3,000 years of Indian history. The Vedas from the First Millennium B.C. contain contradictory passages, some referring to ritual slaughter and others to a strict taboo on beef consumption. A. N. Bose, in *Social and Rural Economy of Northern India, 600 B.C.–200 A.D.*, concludes that many of the sacred-cow passages were incorporated into the texts by priests of a later period.

By 200 A.D., the status of Indian cattle had undergone a spiritual transformation. The Brahman priesthood exhorted the population to venerate the cow and forbade them to abuse it or to feed on it. Religious feasts involving the ritual slaughter and consumption of livestock were eliminated and meat eating was restricted to the nobility.

By 1000 A.D., all Hindus were forbidden to eat beef. Ahimsa, the Hindu belief in the unity of all life, was the spiritual justification for this restriction. But it is difficult to ascertain exactly when this change occurred. An important event that helped to shape the modern complex was the Islamic invasion, which took place in the Eighth Century A.D. Hindus may have found it politically expedient to set themselves off from the invaders, who were beefeaters, by emphasizing the need to prevent the slaughter of their sacred animals. Thereafter, the cow taboo assumed its modern form and began to function much as it does today.

The place of the cow in modern India is everyplace—on posters, in the movies, in brass figures, in stone and wood carvings, on the streets, in the fields. The cow is a symbol of health and abundance. It provides the milk that Indians consume in the form of yogurt and ghee (clarified butter), which contribute subtle flavors to much spicy Indian food.

This, perhaps, is the practical role of the cow, but cows provide less than half the milk produced in India. Most cows in India are not dairy breeds. In most regions, when an Indian farmer wants a steady, high-quality source of milk he usually invests in a female water buffalo. In India the water buffalo is the specialized dairy breed because its milk has a higher butterfat content than zebu milk. Although the farmer milks his zebu cows, the milk is merely a by-product.

More vital than zebu milk to South Asian farmers are zebu calves. Male calves are especially valued because from bulls come oxen, which are the mainstay of the Indian agricultural system.

Small, fast oxen drag wooden plows through late-spring fields when monsoons have dampened the dry, cracked earth. After harvest, the oxen break the grain from the stalk by stomping through mounds of cut wheat and rice. For rice cultivation in irrigated fields, the male water buffalo is preferred (it pulls better in deep mud), but for most other crops, including rainfall rice, wheat, sorghum, and millet, and for transporting goods and people to and from town, a team of oxen is preferred. The ox is the Indian peasant's tractor, thresher, and family car combined; the cow is the factory that produces the ox.

If draft animals instead of cows are counted, India appears to have too few domesticated ruminants, not too many. Since each of the 70 million farms in India requires a draft team, it follows that Indian peasants should use 140 million animals in the fields. But there are only 83 million oxen and male water buffalo on the subcontinent, a shortage of 30 million draft teams.

In other regions of the world, joint ownership of draft animals might overcome a shortage, but Indian agriculture is closely tied to the monsoon rains of late spring and summer. Field preparation and planting must coincide with the rain, and a farmer must have his animals ready to plow when the weather is right. When the farmer without a draft team needs bullocks most, his neighbors are all using theirs. Any delay in turning the soil drastically lowers production.

Because of this dependence on draft animals, loss of the family oxen is devastating. If a beast dies, the farmer must borrow money to buy or rent an ox at interest rates so high that he ultimately loses his land. Every year foreclosures force thousands of poverty-stricken peasants to abandon the countryside for the overcrowded cities.

If a family is fortunate enough to own a fertile cow, it will be able to rear replacements for a lost team and thus survive until life returns to normal. If, as sometimes happens, famine leads a family to sell its cow and ox team, all ties to agriculture are cut. Even if the family survives, it has no way to farm the land, no oxen to work the land, and no cows to produce oxen.

The prohibition against eating meat applies to the flesh of cows, bulls, and oxen, but the cow is the most sacred because it can produce the other two. The peasant whose cow dies is not only crying over a spiritual loss but over the loss of his farm as well.

Religious laws that forbid the slaughter of cattle promote the recovery of the agricultural system from the dry Indian winter and from periods of drought. The monsoon, on which all agriculture depends, is erratic. Sometimes it arrives early, sometimes late, sometimes not at all. Drought has struck large portions of India time and again in this century, and Indian farmers and the zebus are accustomed to these natural disasters. Zebus can pass weeks on end with little or no food and water. Like camels they store both in their humps and recuperate quickly with only a little nourishment.

During droughts the cows often stop lactating and become barren. In some cases the condition is permanent but often it is only temporary. If barren animals were summarily eliminated, as Western experts in animal husbandry have suggested, cows capable of recovery would be lost along with those entirely debilitated. By keeping alive the cows that can later produce oxen, religious laws against cow slaughter assure the recovery of the agricultural system from the greatest challenge it faces—the failure of the monsoon.

The local Indian governments aid the process of recovery by maintaining homes for barren cows. Farmers reclaim any animal that calves or begins to lactate. One police station in Madras collects strays and pastures them in a field adjacent to the station. After a small fine is paid, a cow is returned to its rightful owner when the owner thinks the cow shows signs of being able to reproduce.

During the hot, dry spring months most of India is like a desert. Indian farmers often complain they cannot feed their livestock during this period. They maintain the cattle by letting them scavenge on the sparse grass along the roads. In the cities cattle are encouraged to scavenge near food stalls to supplement their scant diet. These are the wandering cattle tourists report seeing throughout India.

Westerners expect shopkeepers to respond to these intrusions with the deference due a sacred animal; instead, their response is a string of curses and the crack of a long bamboo pole across the beast's back or a poke at its genitals. Mahatma Gandhi was well aware of the treatment sacred cows (and bulls and oxen) received in India. "How we bleed her to take the last drop of milk from her. How we starve her to emaciation, how we ill-treat the calves, how we deprive them of their portion of milk, how cruelly we treat the oxen, how we castrate them, how we beat them, how we overload them."

Oxen generally receive better treatment than cows. When food is in short supply, thrifty Indian peasants feed their working bullocks and ignore their cows, but rarely do they abandon the cows to die. When cows are sick, farmers worry over them as they would over members of the family and nurse them as if they were children. When the rains return and when the fields are harvested, the farmers again feed their cows regularly and reclaim their abandoned animals. The prohibition against beef consumption is a form of disaster insurance for all India.

Western agronomists and economists are quick to protest that all the functions of the zebu cattle can be improved with organized breeding programs, cultivated pastures, and silage. Because stronger oxen would pull the plow faster, they could work multiple plots of land, allowing farmers to share their animals. Fewer healthy, well-fed cows could provide Indians with more milk. But pastures and silage require land, land needed to produce wheat and rice.

A look at Western cattle farming makes plain the cost of adopting advanced technology in Indian agriculture. In a study of livestock production in the United States, David Pimentel of the College of Agriculture and Life Sciences at Cornell University found that 91 percent of the cereal, legume, and vegetable protein suitable for human consumption is consumed by livestock. Approximately three quarters of the arable land in the United States is devoted to growing food for livestock. In the production of meat and milk, American ranchers use enough fossil fuel to equal more than 82 million barrels of oil annually.

Indian cattle do not drain the system in the same way. In a 1971 study of livestock in West Bengal, Stewart Odend'hal of the University of Missouri found that Bengalese cattle ate only the inedible remains of subsistence crops—rice straw, rice hulls, the tops of sugar cane, and mustard-oil cake. Cattle graze in the fields after harvest and eat the remains of crops left on the ground; they forage for grass and weeds on the roadsides. The food for zebu cattle costs the human population virtually nothing. "Basically," Odend'hal says, "the cattle convert items of little direct human value into products of immediate utility."

In addition to plowing the fields and producing milk, the zebus produce dung, which fires the hearths and fertilizes the fields of India. Much of the estimated 800 million tons of manure produced annually is collected by the farmers' children as they follow the family cows and bullocks from place to place. And when the children see the droppings of another farmer's cattle along the road, they pick those up also. Odend'hal reports that the system operates with such high efficiency that the children of West Bengal recover nearly 100 percent of the dung produced by their livestock.

From 40 to 70 percent of all manure produced by Indian cattle is used as fuel for cooking; the rest is returned to the fields as fertilizer. Dried dung burns slowly, cleanly, and with low-heat—characteristics that satisfy the household needs of Indian women. Staples like curry and rice can simmer for hours. While the meal slowly cooks over an unattended fire, the women of the household can do other chores. Cow chips, unlike firewood, do not scorch as they burn.

It is estimated that the dung used for cooking fuel provides the energy-equivalent of 43 million tons of coal. At current prices, it would cost India an extra 1.5 billion dollars in foreign exchange to replace the dung with coal. And if the 350 million tons of manure that are being used as fertilizer were replaced with commercial fertilizers, the expense would be even greater. Roger Revelle of the University of California at San Diego has calculated that 89 percent of the energy used in Indian agriculture (the equivalent of about 140 million tons of coal) is provided by local sources. Even if foreign loans were to provide the money, the capital outlay necessary to replace the Indian cow with tractors and fertilizers for the fields, coal for the fires, and transportation for the family would probably warp international financial institutions for years.

Instead of asking the Indians to learn from the American model of industrial agriculture, American farmers might learn energy conservation from the Indians. Every step in an energy cycle results in a loss of energy to the system. Like a pendulum that slows a bit with each swing, each transfer of energy from sun to plants, plants to animals, and animals to human beings involves energy losses. Some systems are more efficient than others; they provide a higher percentage of the energy inputs in a final, useful form. Seventeen percent of all energy zebus consume is returned in the form of milk, traction, and dung. American cattle raised on Western range land return only 4 percent of the energy they consume.

But the American system is improving. Based on techniques pioneered by Indian scientists, at least one commercial firm in the United States is reported to be building plants that will turn manure from cattle feedlots into combustible gas. When organic matter is broken down by anaerobic bacteria, methane gas and carbon dioxide are produced. After the methane is cleansed of the carbon dioxide, it is available for the same purposes as natural gas—cooking, heating, electricity generation. The company constructing the biogasification plant plans to sell its product to a gas-supply company, to be piped through the existing distribution system. Schemes similar to this one could make cattle ranches almost independent of utility and gasoline companies, for methane can be used to run trucks, tractors, and cars as well as to supply heat and electricity. The relative energy self-sufficiency that the Indian peasant has achieved is a goal American farmers and industry are now striving for.

Studies like Odend'hal's understate the efficiency of the Indian cow, because dead cows are used for purposes that Hindus prefer not to acknowledge. When a cow dies, an Untouchable, a member of one of the lowest ranking castes in India, is summoned to haul away the carcass. Higher castes consider the body of the dead cow polluting; if they do handle it, they must go through a rite of purification.

Untouchables first skin the dead animal and either tan the skin themselves or sell it to a leather factory. In the privacy of their homes, contrary to the teachings of Hinduism, untouchable castes cook the meat and eat it. Indians of all castes rarely acknowledge the existence of these practices to non-Hindus, but most are aware that beefeating takes place. The prohibition against beefeating restricts consumption by the higher castes and helps distribute animal protein to the poorest sectors of the population that otherwise would have no source of these vital nutrients.

Untouchables are not the only Indians who consume beef. Indian Muslims and Christians are under no restriction that forbids them beef, and its consumption is legal in many places. The Indian ban on cow slaughter is state, not national, law and not all states restrict it. In many cities, such as New Delhi, Calcutta, and Bombay, legal slaughterhouses sell beef to retail customers and to the restaurants that serve steak.

If the caloric value of beef and the energy costs involved in the manufacture of synthetic leather were included in the estimates of energy, the calculated efficiency of Indian livestock would rise considerably.

As well as the system works, experts often claim that its efficiency can be further improved. Alan Heston, an economist at the University of Pennsylvania, believes that Indians suffer from an overabundance of cows simply because they refuse to slaughter the excess cattle. India could produce at least the same number of oxen and the same quantities of milk and manure with 30 million fewer cows. Heston calculates that only 40 cows are necessary to maintain a population of 100 bulls and oxen. Since India averages 70 cows for every 100 bullocks, the difference, 30 million cows, is expendable.

What Heston fails to note is that sex ratios among cattle in different regions of India vary tremendously, indicating that adjustments in the cow population do take place. Along the Ganges River, one of the holiest shrines of Hinduism, the ratio drops to 47 cows for every 100 male animals. This ratio reflects the preference for dairy buffalo in the irrigated sectors of the Gangetic Plains. In nearby Pakistan, in contrast, where cow slaughter is permitted, the sex ratio is 60 cows to 100 oxen.

Since the sex ratios among cattle differ greatly from region to region and do not even approximate the balance that would be expected if no females were killed, we can assume that some culling of herds does take place; Indians do adjust their religious restrictions to accommodate ecological realities.

They cannot kill a cow but they can tether an old or unhealthy animal until it has starved to death. They cannot slaughter a calf but they can yoke it with a large wooden triangle so that when it nurses it irritates the mother's udder and gets kicked to death. The cannot ship their animals to the slaughterhouse but they can sell them to Muslims, closing their eyes to the fact that the Muslims will take the cattle to the slaughterhouse.

These violations of the prohibition against cattle slaughter strengthen the premise that cow worship is a vital part of Indian culture. The practice arose to prevent the population from consuming the animal on which Indian agriculture depends. During the First Millennium B.C., the Ganges Valley became one of the most densely populated regions of the world.

Where previously there had been only scattered villages, many towns and cities arose and peasants farmed every available acre of land. Kingsley Davis, a population expert at the University of California at Berkeley, estimates that by 300 B.C. between 50 million and 100 million people were living in India. The forested Ganges Valley became a windswept semi-desert and signs of ecological collapse appeared; droughts and floods became commonplace, erosion took away the rich topsoil, farms shrank as population increased, and domesticated animals became harder and harder to maintain.

It is probable that the elimination of meat eating came about in a slow, practical manner. The farmers who decided not to eat their cows, who saved them for procreation to produce oxen, were the ones who survived the natural disasters. Those who ate beef lost the tools with which to farm. Over a period of centuries, more and more farmers probably avoided beef until an unwritten taboo came into existence.

Only later was the practice codified by the priesthood. While Indian peasants were probably aware of the role of cattle in their society, strong sanctions were necessary to protect zebus from a population faced with starvation. To remove temptation, the flesh of cattle became taboo and the cow became sacred.

The sacredness of the cow is not just an ignorant belief that stands in the way of progress. Like all concepts of the sacred and the profane, this one affects the physical world; it defines the relationships that are important for the maintenance of Indian society.

Indians have the sacred cow; we have the "sacred" car and the "sacred" dog. It would not occur to us to propose the elimination of automobiles and dogs from our society without carefully considering the consequences, and we should not propose the elimination of zebu cattle without first understanding their place in the social order of India.

Human society is neither random or capricious. The regularities of thought and behavior called culture are the principal mechanisms by which we human beings adapt to the world around us. Practices and beliefs can be rational or irrational, but a society that fails to adapt to its environment is doomed to extinction. Only those societies that draw the necessities of life from their surroundings without destroying those surroundings, inherit the earth. The West has much to learn from the great antiquity of Indian civilization, and the sacred cow is an important part of that lesson.

For Further Information

Gandhi, Mohandas K. *How to Serve the Cow:* Navajivan Publishing House, 1954.

Harris, Marvin, *Cows, Pigs, Wars and Witches: The Riddles of Culture.* Random House, 1974.

Heston, Alan, et al. "An Approach to the Sacred Cow of India." *Current Anthropology,* Vol. 12, 1971, pp. 191–209.

Odend'hal, Stewart. "Gross Energetic Efficiency of Indian Cattle in Their Environment." *Journal of Human Ecology,* Vol. 1, 1972, pp. 1–27.

Raj, K. N. "Investment in Livestock in Agrarian Economies: An Analysis of Some Issues Concerning 'Sacred Cows' and 'Surplus Cattle.'" *Indian Economic Review,* Vol. 4, 1969, pp. 1–33.

India's Sacred Cow

1. How does Marvin Harris explain how the cow became sacred in India?
2. What do cows contribute to Indian life?
3. According to Harris, we do not have a "sacred" cow, but we do have a "sacred" car. How is a car "sacred" in our culture?

READING 6

The Potlatch

MARVIN HARRIS

Franz Boas, the father of anthropology in the United States, was one of the first to study the practice of the potlatch. On the face of it, the potlatch would appear to be a bizarre, if not irrational, cultural practice. As practiced by the Kwakuitl and other Native American groups in British Columbia, the potlatch is a form of competitive feasting which involves giving away or destroying more material wealth (e.g., food, clothing, and blankets) than one's rival. Since the original description of this practice by Boas in the late nineteenth century, the potlatch has been cited often as an excellent example of conspicuous consumption gone berserk, or at least an irrational practice. By taking a materialist interpretation rather than a psychological one, Harris suggests that the potlatch is more than just an insane pursuit of social status. Instead, Harris sees the potlatch as a rational response to economic and social forces. While not denying that the potlatch involves fierce competition for status and prestige, it also serves a number of other important functions which contribute to the overall well-being of the society, not the least of which is as a mechanism of economic distribution.

Some of the most puzzling lifestyles on exhibit in the museum of world ethnography bear the imprint of a strange craving known as the "drive for prestige." Some people seem to hunger for approval as others hunger for meat. The puzzling thing is not that people hunger for approval, but that occasionally their craving seems to become so powerful that they begin to compete with each other for prestige as others compete for land or protein or sex. Sometimes this competition grows so fierce that it appears to become an end in itself. It then takes on the appearance of an obsession wholly divorced from, and even directly opposed to, rational calculations of material costs.

Vance Packard struck a responsive chord when he described the United States as a nation of competitive status seekers. Many Americans seem to spend their entire lives trying to climb further up the social pyramid simply in order to impress each other. We seem to be more interested in working in order to get people to admire us for our wealth than in the actual wealth itself, which often enough consists of chromium baubles and burdensome or useless objects. It is amazing how much effort people are willing to spend to obtain what Thorstein Veblen described as the vicarious thrill of being mistaken for members of a class that doesn't have to work. Veblen's mordant phrases "conspicuous consumption" and "conspicuous waste" aptly convey a sense of the peculiarly intense desire for "keeping up with the Joneses" that lies behind the ceaseless cosmetic alterations in the automotive, appliance, and clothing industries.

Early in the present century, anthropologists were surprised to discover that certain primitive tribes engaged in conspicuous consumption and conspicuous waste to a degree unmatched by even the most wasteful of modern consumer economies. Ambitious, status-hungry men were found competing with each other for approval by giving huge feasts. The rival feast givers judged each other by the amount of food they provided, and a feast was a success only if the guests could eat until they were stupefied, stagger off into the bush, stick their fingers down their throats, vomit, and come back for more.

The most bizarre instance of status seeking was discovered among the American Indians who formerly inhabited the coastal regions of Southern Alaska, British Columbia, and Washington. Here the status seekers practiced what seems like a maniacal form of conspicuous consumption and conspicuous waste known as *potlatch.* The object of potlatch was to give away or destroy more wealth than one's rival. If the potlatch giver was a powerful chief, he might attempt to shame his rivals and gain everlasting admiration from his followers by destroying food, clothing, and money. Sometimes he might even seek prestige by burning down his own house.

Potlatch was made famous by Ruth Benedict in her book *Patterns of Culture,* which describes how potlatch operated among the Kwakiutl, the aboriginal inhabitants of Vancouver Island. Benedict thought that potlatch was part of a megalomaniacal lifestyle characteristic of Kwakiutl culture in general. It was the "cup" God had given them to drink from. Ever since, potlatch has been a monument to the belief that cultures are the creations of inscrutable forces and deranged personalities. As a result of reading *Patterns of Culture,* experts in many fields concluded that the drive for prestige makes a shambles of attempts to explain lifestyles in terms of practical and mundane factors.

I want to show here that the Kwakiutl potlatch was not the result of maniacal whims, but of definite economic and ecological conditions. When these conditions are absent, the need to be admired and the drive for prestige express themselves in completely different lifestyle practices. Inconspicuous consumption replaces conspicuous consumption, conspicuous waste is forbidden, and there are no competitive status seekers.

The Kwakiutl used to live in plank-house villages set close to the shore in the midst of cedar and fir rain forests. They fished and hunted along the island-studded sounds and fiords of Vancouver in huge dugout canoes. Always eager to attract traders, they made their villages conspicuous by erecting on the beach the carved tree trunks we erroneously call "totem poles." The carvings on these poles symbolized the ancestral titles to which the chiefs of the village laid claim.

A Kwakiutl chief was never content with the amount of respect he was getting from his own followers and from neighboring chiefs. He was always insecure about his status. True enough, the family titles to which he laid claim belonged to his ancestors. But there were other people who could trace descent from the same ancestors and who were entitled to vie with him for recognition as a chief. Every chief therefore felt the obligation to justify and validate his chiefly pretensions. The prescribed manner for doing this was to hold potlatches. Each potlatch was given by a host chief and his followers to a guest chief and his followers. The object of the potlatch was to show that the host chief was truly entitled to chiefly status and that he was more exalted than the guest chief. To prove this point, the host chief gave the rival chief and his followers quantities of valuable gifts. The guests would belittle what they received and vow to hold a return potlatch at which their own chief would prove that he was greater than the former host by giving back even larger quantities of more valuable gifts.

Preparations for potlatch required the accumulation of fresh and dried fish, fish oil, berries, animal skins, blankets, and other valuables. On the appointed day, the guests paddled up to the host village and went into the chief's house. There they gorged themselves on salmon and wild berries while dancers masked as beaver gods and thunderbirds entertained them.

The host chief and his followers arranged in neat piles the wealth that was to be given away. The visitors stared at their host sullenly as he pranced up and down, boasting about how much he was about to give them. As he counted out the boxes of fish oil, baskets full of berries, and piles of blankets, he commented derisively on the poverty of his rivals. Laden with gifts, the guests finally were free to paddle back to their own village. Stung to the quick, the guest chief and his followers vowed to get even. This could only be achieved by inviting their rivals to a return potlatch and obliging them to accept even greater amounts of valuables than they had given away. Considering all the Kwakiutl villages as a single unit, potlatch stimulated a ceaseless flow of prestige and valuables moving in opposite directions.

An ambitious chief and his followers had potlatch rivals in several different villages at once. Specialists in counting property kept track of what had to be done in each village in order to even the score. If a chief managed to get the better of his rivals in one place, he still had to confront his adversaries in another.

At the potlatch, the host chief would say things like, "I am the only great tree. Bring your counter of property that he may try in vain to count the property that is to be given away." Then the chief's followers demanded silence from the guests with the warning: "Do not make any noise, tribes. Be quiet or we shall cause a landslide of wealth from our chief, the overhanging mountain." At some potlatches blankets and other valuables were not given away but were destroyed. Sometimes successful potlatch chiefs decided to hold "grease feasts" at which boxes of oil obtained from the candlefish were poured on the fire in the center of the house. As the flames roared up, dark grease smoke filled the room. The guests sat impassively or even complained about the chill in the air while the wealth destroyer ranted, "I am the only one on earth—the only one in the whole world who makes this smoke rise from the beginning of the year to the end for the invited tribes." At some grease feasts the flames ignited the planks in the roof and an entire house would become a potlatch offering, causing the greatest shame to the guests and much rejoicing among the hosts.

According to Ruth Benedict, potlatching was caused by the obsessive status hunger of the Kwakiutl chiefs. "Judged by the standards of other cultures the speeches of their chiefs are unabashed megalomania," she wrote. "The object of all Kwakiutl enterprises was to show oneself superior to one's rivals." In her opinion, the whole aboriginal economic system of the Pacific Northwest was "bent on the service of this obsession."

I think that Benedict was mistaken. The economic system of the Kwakiutl was not bent to the service of status rivalry; rather, status rivalry was bent to the service of the economic system.

All of the basic ingredients of the Kwakiutl giveaways, except for their destructive aspects, are present in primitive societies widely dispersed over different parts of the globe. Stripped down to its elementary core, the potlatch is a competitive feast, a nearly universal mechanism for assuring the production and distribution of wealth among peoples who have not yet fully acquired a ruling class.

Melanesia and New Guinea present the best opportunity to study competitive feasting under relatively pristine conditions. Throughout this region, there are so-called big men who owe their superior status to the large number of feasts that each has sponsored during his lifetime. Each feast has to be preceded by an intensive effort on the part of an aspiring big man to accumulate the necessary wealth.

Among the Kaoka-speaking people of the Solomon Islands, for example, the status-hungry individual begins his career by making his wife and children plant larger yam gardens. As described by the Australian anthropologist Ian Hogbin, the Kaoka who wants to become a big man then gets his kinsmen and his age-mates to help him fish. Later he begs sows from his friends and increases the size of his pig herd. As the litters are born he boards additional animals among his neighbors. Soon his relatives and friends feel that the young man is going to be a success. They see his large gardens and his big pig herd and they redouble their own efforts to make the forthcoming feast a memorable one. When he becomes a big man they want the young candidate to remember that they helped him. Finally, they all get together and build an extra-fine house. The men go off on one last fishing expedition. The women harvest yams and collect firewood, banana leaves, and coconuts. As the guests arrive (as in the case of potlatch), the wealth is stacked in neat piles and put on display for everyone to count and admire.

On the day of the feast given by a young man named Atana, Hogbin counted the following items: 250 pounds of dried fish, 3,000 yam and coconut cakes, 11 large bowls of yam pudding, and 8 pigs. All this was the direct result of the extra work effort organized by Atana. But some of the guests themselves, anticipating an important occasion, brought presents to be added to the giveaway. Their contributions raised the total to 300 pounds of fish, 5,000 cakes, 19 bowls of pudding and 13 pigs. Atana proceeded to divide this wealth into 257 portions, one each for every person who had helped him or who had brought gifts, rewarding some more than others. "Only the remnants were left for Atana himself," notes Hogbin. This is normal for status seekers in Guadalcanal, who always say: "The giver of the feast takes the bones and the stale cakes; the meat and the fat go to the others."

The feast-giving days of the big man, like those of the potlatch chiefs, are never over. On threat of being reduced to commoner status, each big man is obliged to busy himself with plans and preparations for the next feast. Since there are several big men per village and community, these plans and preparations often lead to complex competitive maneuvering for the allegiance of relatives and neighbors. The big men work harder, worry more, and consume less than anybody else. Prestige is their only reward.

The big man can be described as a worker- entrepreneur—the Russians call them "Stakhanovites"—who renders important services to society by raising the level of production. As a result of the big man's craving for status, more people work harder and produce more food and other valuables.

Under conditions where everyone has equal access to the means of subsistence, competitive feasting serves the practical function of preventing the labor force from falling back to levels of productivity that offer no margin of safety in crises such as war and crop failures. Furthermore, since there are no formal political institutions capable of integrating independent villages into a common economic framework competitive feasting creates an extensive network of economic expectations. This has the effect of pooling the productive effort of larger populations than can be mobilized by any given village. Finally, competitive feasting by big men acts as an automatic equalizer of annual fluctuations in productivity among a series of villages that occupy different microenvironments---seacoast, lagoon, or upland habitats. Automatically, the biggest feasts in any given year will be hosted by villages that have enjoyed conditions of rainfall, temperature, and humidity most favorable to production.

All of these points apply to the Kwakiutl. The Kwakiutl chiefs were like Melanesian big men except that they operated with a much more productive technological inventory in a richer environment. Like big men, they competed with each other to attract men and women to their villages. The greatest chiefs were the best providers and gave the biggest potlatches. The chief's followers shared vicariously in his prestige and helped him to achieve more exalted honors. The chiefs commissioned the carving of the "totem poles." These were in fact grandiose advertisements proclaiming by their height and bold designs that here was a village with a mighty chief who could cause great works to be done, and who could protect his followers from famine and disease. In claiming hereditary rights to the animal crests carved on the poles, the chiefs were actually saying that they were great providers of food and comfort. Potlatch was a means of telling their rivals to put up or shut up.

Despite the overt competitive thrust of potlatch, it functioned aboriginally to transfer food and other valuables from centers of high productivity to less fortunate villages. I should put this even more strongly: Because of the competitive thrust, such transfers were assured. Since there were unpredictable fluctuations in fish runs, wild fruit and vegetable harvests, intervillage potlatching was advantageous from the standpoint of the regional population as a whole. When the fish spawned in nearby streams and the berries ripened close at hand, last year's guests became this year's hosts. Aboriginally, potlatch meant that each year the haves gave and the have-nots took. To eat, all a have-not had to do was admit that the rival chief was a great man.

Why did the practical basis of potlatch escape the attention of Ruth Benedict? Anthropologists began to study potlatch only long after the aboriginal peoples of the Pacific Northwest had entered into commercial and wage-labor relations with Russian, English, Canadian, and American merchants and settlers. This contact rapidly gave rise to epidemics of smallpox and other European diseases that killed off a large part of the native population. For example, the population of the Kwakiutl fell from 23,000 in 1836 to 2,000 in 1886. The decline automatically intensified the competition for manpower. At the same time, wages paid by the Europeans pumped unprecedented amounts of wealth into the potlatch network. From the Hudson's Bay Company, the Kwakiutl received thousands of trade blankets in exchange for animal skins. At the great potlatches these blankets replaced food as the most important item to be given away. The dwindling population soon found itself with more blankets and other valuables than it could consume. Yet the need to attract followers was greater than ever due to the labor shortage. So the potlatch chiefs ordered the destruction of property in the vain hope that such spectacular demonstrations of wealth would bring the people back to the empty villages. But these were the practices of a dying culture struggling to adapt to a new set of political and economic conditions; they bore little resemblance to the potlatch of aboriginal times.

Competitive feasting thought about, narrated, and imagined by the participants is very different from competitive feasting viewed as an adaptation to material constraints and opportunities. In the social dreamwork—the lifestyle consciousness of the participants—competitive feasting is a manifestation of the big man's or potlatch chief's insatiable craving for prestige. But from the point of view followed in this book, the insatiable craving for prestige is a manifestation of competitive feasting. Every society makes use of the need for approval, but not every society links prestige to success in competitive feasting.

Competitive feasting as a source of prestige must be seen in evolutionary perspective to be properly understood. Big men like Atana or the Kwakiutl chiefs carry out a form of economic exchange known as redistribution. That is, they gather together the results of the productive effort of many individuals and then redistribute the aggregated wealth in different quantities to a different set of people. As I have said, the Kaoka redistributor-big man works harder, worries more, and consumes less than anybody else in the village. This is not true of the Kwakiutl chief-redistributor. The great potlatch chiefs performed the entrepreneurial and managerial functions that were necessary for a big potlatch, but aside from an occasional fishing or sea-lion expedition, they left the hardest work to their followers. The greatest potlatch chiefs even had a few war captives working for them as slaves. From the point of view of consumption privileges, the Kwakiutl chiefs had begun to reverse the Kaoka formula and were keeping some of the "meat and fat" for themselves, leaving most of the "bones and stale cakes" for their followers.

Continuing along the evolutionary line leading from Atana, the impoverished worker-entrepreneur big man, to the semihereditary Kwakiutl chiefs, we end up with state-level societies ruled over by hereditary kings who perform no basic industrial or agricultural labor and who keep the most and best of everything for themselves. At the imperial level, exalted divine-right rulers maintain their prestige by building conspicuous palaces, temples, and mega-monuments, and validate their right to hereditary privileges against all challengers—not by potlatch, but by force of arms. Reversing direction, we can go from kings to potlatch chiefs to big men, back to egalitarian lifestyles in which all competitive displays and conspicuous consumption by individuals disappear, and anyone foolish enough to boast about how great he is gets accused of witchcraft and is stoned to death.

In the truly egalitarian societies that have survived long enough to be studied by anthropologists, redistribution in the form of competitive feasting does not occur. Instead, the mode of exchange known as reciprocity predominates. Reciprocity is the technical term for an economic exchange that takes place between two individuals in which neither specifies precisely what is expected in return nor when they expect it. Superficially, reciprocal exchanges don't look like exchanges at all. The expectation of one party and obligation of the other remain unstated. One party can continue to take from the other for quite a while with no resistance from the giver and no embarrassment in the taker. Nonetheless, the transaction cannot be considered a pure gift. There is an underlying expectation of return, and if the balance between two individuals gets too far out of line, eventually the giver will start to grumble and gossip. Concern will be shown for the taker's health and sanity, and if the situation does not improve, people begin to suspect that the taker is possessed by malevolent spirits or is practicing witchcraft. In egalitarian societies, individuals who consistently violate the rules of reciprocity are in fact likely to be psychotic and a menace to their community.

We can get some idea of what reciprocal exchanges are like by thinking about the way we exchange goods and services with our close friends or relatives. Brothers, for example, are not supposed to calculate the precise dollar value of everything they do for each other. They should feel free to borrow each other's shirts or phonograph albums and ought not to hesitate to ask for favors. In brotherhood and friendship both parties accept the principle that if one has to give more than he takes, it will not affect the solidary relationship between them. If one friend invites another to dinner, there should be no hesitation in giving or accepting a second or a third invitation even if the first dinner still remains unreciprocated. Yet there is a limit to that sort of thing, because after a while unreciprocated gift-giving begins to feel suspiciously like exploitation. In other words, everybody likes to be thought generous, but nobody wants to be taken for a sucker. This is precisely the quandary we get ourselves into at Christmas when we attempt to revert to the principle of reciprocity in drawing up our shopping lists. The gift can neither be too cheap nor too expensive; and yet our calculations must appear entirely casual, so we remove the price tag.

But to really see reciprocity in action you must live in an egalitarian society that doesn't have money and where nothing can be bought or sold. Everything about reciprocity is opposed to precise counting and reckoning of what one person owes to another. In fact, the whole idea is to deny that anybody really owes anything. One can tell if a lifestyle is based on reciprocity or something else by whether or not people say thank you. In truly egalitarian societies, it is rude to be openly grateful for the receipt of material goods or services. Among the Semai of central Malaya, for example, no one ever expressed gratitude for the meat that a hunter gives away in exactly equal portions of his companions. Robert Dentan, who has lived with the Semai, found that to say thank you was very rude because it suggested either that you were calculating the size of the piece of meat you had been given, or that you were surprised by the success and generosity of the hunter.

In contrast to the conspicuous display put on by the Kaoka big man, and the boastful ranting of potlatch chiefs, and our own flaunting of status symbols, the Semai follow a lifestyle in which those who are most successful must be the least conspicuous. In their egalitarian lifestyle, status seeking through rivalrous redistribution or any form of conspicuous consumption or conspicuous waste is literally unthinkable. Egalitarian peoples are repelled and frightened by the faintest suggestion that they are being treated generously or that one person thinks he's better than another.

Professor Richard Lee of the University of Toronto tells an amusing story about the meaning of reciprocal exchange among egalitarian hunters and gatherers. For the better part of a year, Lee had been following the Bushmen around the Kalahari Desert observing what they ate. The Bushmen were very cooperative and Lee wanted to show his gratitude, but he had nothing to give them that would not disturb their normal diet and pattern of activity. As Christmas approached he learned that the Bushmen were likely to camp at the edge of the desert near villages from which they sometimes obtained meat through trade. With the intention of giving them an ox for a Christmas present, he drove about in his jeep from one village to another, trying to find the biggest ox that he could buy. In a remote village, Lee finally located an animal of monstrous proportions, one covered with a thick layer of fat. Like many primitive peoples, the Bushmen crave fatty meat because the animals they obtain by hunting are usually lean and stringy. Returning to camp, Lee took his Bushmen friends aside and told them one by one that he had bought the largest ox he had ever seen and that he was going to let them slaughter it at Christmas time.

The first man to hear the good news became visibly alarmed. He asked Lee where he had bought the ox, what color it was, and what size its horns were, and then he shook his head. "I know that ox," he said. "Why, it is nothing but skin and bones! You must have been drunk to buy such a worthless animal!" Convinced that his friend didn't really know what ox he was talking about Lee confided in several other Bushmen, but continued to meet with the same astonished reaction: "You bought that worthless animal? Of course we will eat it," each would say, "but it won't fill us up. We will eat and go home to bed with stomachs rumbling." When Christmas came and the ox was finally slaughtered, the beast turned out to be covered with a thick layer of fat, and it was devoured with great gusto. There was more than enough meat and fat for everybody. Lee went over to his friends and insisted upon an explanation. "Yes, of course we knew all along what the ox was really like," one hunter admitted. "But when a young man kills much meat he comes to think of himself as a chief or big man, and he thinks of the rest of us as his servants or inferiors. We cannot accept this," he went on. "We refuse one who boasts, for someday his pride will make him kill somebody. So we always speak of his meat as worthless. This way we cool his heart and make him gentle."

The Eskimos explained their fear of boastful and generous gift-givers with the proverb "Gifts make slaves just as whips make dogs." And that is exactly what happened. In evolutionary perspective, the gift-givers at first gave gifts that came from their own extra work; soon people found themselves working harder to reciprocate and to make it possible for the gift-givers to give them more gifts; eventually the gift-givers became very powerful, and they no longer needed to obey the rules of reciprocity. They could force people to pay taxes and to work for them without actually redistributing what was in their storehouses and palaces. Of course, as assorted modern big men and politicians occasionally recognize, it is still easier to get "slaves" to work for you if you give them an occasional big feast instead of whipping them all the time.

If people like the Eskimo, Bushmen, and Semai understood the dangers of gift-giving, why did others permit the gift-givers to flourish? And why were big men permitted to get so puffed up that they could turn around and enslave the very people whose work made their glow possible? Once again, I suspect that I am on the verge of trying to explain everything at once. But permit me to make a few suggestions.

Reciprocity is a form of economic exchange that is primarily adapted to conditions in which the stimulation of intensive extra productive effort would have an adverse effect upon group survival. These conditions are found among certain hunters and gatherers such as the Eskimo, Semai, and Bushmen, whose survival depends entirely on the vigor of the natural communities of plants and animals in their habitat. If hunters suddenly engage in a concerted effort to capture more animals and uproot more plants, they risk permanently impairing the supply of game in their territory.

Lee found, for example, that his Bushmen worked at subsistence for only ten to fifteen hours a week. This discovery effectively destroys one of the shoddiest myths of industrial society—namely that we have more leisure today than ever before. Primitive hunters and gatherers work less than we do—without benefit of a single labor union—because their ecosystems cannot tolerate weeks and months of intensive extra effort. Among the Bushmen, Stakhanovite personalities who would run about getting friends and relatives to work harder by promising them a big feast would constitute a definite menace to society. If he got his followers to work like the Kaoka for a month, an aspiring Bushman big man would kill or scare off every game animal for miles around and starve his people to death before the end of the year. So reciprocity and not redistribution predominates among the Bushmen, and the highest prestige falls to the quietly dependable hunter who never boasts about his achievements and who avoids any hint that he is giving a gift when he divides up an animal he has killed.

Competitive feasting and other forms of redistribution overwhelmed the primordial reliance upon reciprocity when it became possible to increase the duration and intensity of work without inflicting irreversible damage upon the habitats carrying capacity. Typically this became possible when domesticated plants and animals were substituted for natural food resources. Within broad limits, the more work you put into planting and raising domesticated species, the more food you can produce. The only hitch is that people don't usually work harder than they have to. Redistribution was the answer to this problem. Redistribution began to appear as people worked harder in order to maintain a reciprocal balance with prestige-hungry, overzealous producers. As the reciprocal exchanges became unbalanced, they became gifts; and as the gifts piled up, the gift-givers were rewarded with prestige and counter-gifts. Soon redistribution predominated over reciprocity and highest prestige went to the most boastful, calculating gift-givers, who cajoled, shamed, and ultimately forced everybody to work harder than the Bushman ever dreamed was possible.

As the example of the Kwakiutl indicates, conditions appropriate for the development of competitive feasting and redistribution sometimes also occurred among nonagricultural populations. Among the coastal peoples of the Pacific Northwest, annual runs of salmon, other migratory fish, and sea mammals provided the ecological analogue of agricultural harvests. The salmon or candlefish ran in such vast numbers that if people worked harder they could always catch more fish. Moreover, as long as they fished with the aboriginal dip net, they could never catch enough fish to influence the spawning runs and deplete next year's supply.

Stepping away for the moment from our examination of reciprocal and redistributive prestige systems, we can surmise that every major type of political and economic system uses prestige in a distinctive manner. For example, with the appearance of capitalism in Western Europe, competitive acquisition of wealth once more became the fundamental criterion for big-man status. Only in this case, the big men tried to take away each other's wealth, and highest prestige and power went to the individual who managed to accumulate and hold onto the greatest fortune. During the early years of capitalism, highest prestige went to those who were richest but lived most frugally. After their fortunes had become more secure, the capitalist upper class resorted to grand-scale conspicuous consumption and conspicuous waste in order to impress their rivals. They built great mansions, dressed in exclusive finery, adorned themselves with huge jewels, and spoke contemptuously of the impoverished masses. Meanwhile, the middle and lower classes continued to award highest prestige to those who worked hardest, spent least, and soberly resisted all forms of conspicuous consumption and conspicuous waste. But as the growth of industrial capacity began to saturate the consumer market, the middle and lower classes had to be weaned away from their frugal habits. Advertising and mass media joined forces to induce the middle and lower classes to stop saving and to buy, consume, waste, destroy, or otherwise get rid of ever-larger quantities of goods and services. And so among middle-class status seekers, highest prestige now goes to the biggest and most conspicuous consumer.

But in the meantime, the rich found themselves threatened by new forms of taxation aimed at redistributing their wealth. Conspicuous consumption in the grand manner became dangerous, so highest prestige now once again goes to those who have most but show least. With the most prestigious members of the upper class no longer flaunting their wealth, some of the pressure on the middle class to engage in conspicuous consumption has also been removed. This suggests to me that the wearing of torn jeans and the rejection of overt consumerism among middle-class youth of late has more to do with aping the trends set by the upper class than with any so-called cultural revolution.

One final point. As I have shown, the replacement of reciprocity by competitive status seeking made it possible for larger human populations to survive and prosper in a given region. One might very well wish to question the sanity of the whole process by which mankind was tricked and cajoled into working harder in order to feed more people at substantially the same or even lower levels of material well-being than that enjoyed by people like the Eskimo or Bushmen. The only answer that I see to such a challenge is that many primitive societies refused to expand their productive effort and failed to increase their population in density precisely because they discovered that the new "labor-saving" technologies actually meant that they would have to work harder as well as suffer a loss in living standards. But the fate of these primitive people was sealed as soon as any one of them—no matter how remotely situated—crossed the threshold to redistribution and the full-scale stratification of classes that lay beyond. Virtually all of the reciprocity-type hunters and gatherers were destroyed or forced into remote areas by bigger and more powerful societies that maximized production and population and that were organized by governing classes. At bottom, this replacement was essentially a matter of the ability of larger, denser, and better-organized societies to defeat simple hunters and gatherers in armed conflict. It was work hard or perish.

The Potlatch

1. How does the potlatch redistribute goods?
2. How, in the United States, do we demonstrate social status?
3. Why is a surplus of goods necessary for competitive feasts/gift giving?

READING 7

When Brothers Share a Wife

MELVYN C. GOLDSTEIN

Anthropologists recognize three major types of marriage based on the number of spouses permitted: monogamy (the marriage of one woman to one man at a time); polygyny (the marriage of a man to more than one woman at a time); and polyandry (the marriage of a woman to two or more men at a time.) The rarest of the three forms is polyandry, practiced in fewer than one percent of the cultures in the world. In this selection, Melvyn Goldstein explores fraternal polyandry (two or more brothers married to the same woman) as practiced among Tibetans. Whereas most Americans uncritically dismiss any form of plural marriage as inherently immoral, Goldstein reveals the basic rationale behind polyandry which, for Tibetans, make it a logical form of marriage. He argues that when brothers marry a single wife, they are able to preserve scarce resources by actually keeping their family land in tact.

Eager to reach home, Dorje drives his yaks hard over the 17,000-foot mountain pass, stopping only once to rest. He and his two older brothers, Pema and Sonam, are jointly marrying a woman from the next village in a few weeks, and he has to help with the preparations.

Dorje, Pema, and Sonam are Tibetans living in Limi, a 200-square-mile area in the northwest corner of Nepal, across the border from Tibet. The form of marriage they are about to enter—fraternal polyandry in anthropological parlance—is one of the world's rarest forms of marriage but is not uncommon in Tibetan society, where it has been practiced from time immemorial. For many Tibetan social strata, it traditionally represented the ideal form of marriage and family.

The mechanics of fraternal polyandry are simple. Two, three, four, or more brothers jointly take a wife, who leaves her home to come and live with them. Traditionally, marriage was arranged by parents, with children, particularly females, having little or no say. This is changing somewhat nowadays, but it is still unusual for children to marry without their parents' consent. Marriage ceremonies vary by income and region and range from all the brothers sitting together as grooms to only the eldest one formally doing so. The age of the brothers plays an important role in determining this: very young brothers almost never participate in actual marriage ceremonies, although they typically join the marriage when they reach their midteens.

The eldest brother is normally dominant in terms of authority, that is, in managing the household, but all the brothers share the work and participate as sexual partners. Tibetan males and females do not find the sexual aspect of sharing a spouse the least bit unusual, repulsive, or scandalous, and the norm is for the wife to treat all the brothers the same.

Offspring are treated similarly. There is no attempt to link children biologically to particular brothers, and a brother shows no favoritism toward his child even if he knows he is the real father because, for example, his other brothers were away at the time the wife became pregnant. The children, in turn, consider all of the brothers as their fathers and treat them equally, even if they also know who is their real father. In some regions children use the term "father" for the eldest brother and "father's brother" for the others, while in other areas they call all the brothers by one term, modifying this by the use of "elder" and "younger."

Unlike our own society, where monogamy is the only form of marriage permitted, Tibetan society allows a variety of marriage types, including monogamy, fraternal polyandry, and polygyny. Fraternal polyandry and monogamy are the most common forms of marriage, while polygyny typically occurs in cases where the first wife is barren. The widespread practice of fraternal polyandry, therefore, is not the outcome of a law requiring brothers to marry jointly. There is choice, and in fact, divorce traditionally was relatively simple in Tibetan society. If a brother in a polyandrous marriage became dissatisfied and wanted to separate, he simply left the main house and set up his own household. In such cases, all the children stayed in the main household with the remaining brother(s), even if the departing brother was known to be the real father of one or more of the children.

The Tibetans' own explanation for choosing fraternal polyandry is materialistic. For example, when I asked Dorje why he decided to marry with his two brothers rather than take his own wife, he thought for a moment, then said it prevented the division of his family's farm (and animals) and thus facilitated all of them achieving a higher standard of living. And when I later asked Dorje's bride whether it wasn't difficult for her to cope with three brothers as husbands, she laughed and echoed the rationale of avoiding fragmentation of the family and land, adding that she expected to be better off economically, since she would have three husbands working for her and her children.

Exotic as it may seem to Westerners, Tibetan fraternal polyandry is thus in many ways analogous to the way primogeniture functioned in nineteenth-century England. Primogeniture dictated that the eldest son inherited the family estate, while younger sons had to leave home and seek their own employment—for example, in the military or the clergy. Primogeniture maintained family estates intact over generations by permitting only one heir per generation. Fraternal polyandry also accomplishes this but does so by keeping all the brothers together with just one wife so that there is only one *set* of heirs per generation.

While Tibetans believe that in this way fraternal polyandry reduces the risk of family fission, monogamous marriages among brothers need not necessarily precipitate the division of the family estate: brothers could continue to live together, and the family land could continue to be worked jointly. When I asked Tibetans about this, however, they invariably responded that such joint families are unstable because each wife is primarily oriented to her own children and interested in their success and well-being over that of the children of the other wives. For example, if the youngest brother's wife had three sons while the eldest brother's wife had only one daughter, the wife of the youngest brother might begin to demand more resources for her children since, as males, they represent the future of the family. Thus, the children from different wives in the same generation are competing sets of heirs, and this makes such families inherently unstable. Tibetans perceive that conflict will spread from the wives to their husbands and consider this likely to cause family fission. Consequently, it is almost never done.

Although Tibetans see an economic advantage to fraternal polyandry, they do not value the sharing of a wife as an end in itself. On the contrary, they articulate a number of problems inherent in the practice. For example, because authority is customarily exercised by the eldest brother, his younger male siblings have to subordinate themselves with little hope of changing their status within the family. When these younger brothers are aggressive and individualistic, tensions and difficulties often occur despite there being only one set of heirs.

In addition, tension and conflict may arise in polyandrous families because of sexual favoritism. The bride normally sleeps with the eldest brother, and the two have the responsibility to see to it that the other males have opportunities for sexual access. Since the Tibetan subsistence economy requires males to travel a lot, the temporary absence of one or more brothers facilitates this, but there are also other rotation practices. The cultural ideal unambiguously calls for the wife to show equal affection and sexuality to each of the brothers (and vice versa), but deviations from this ideal occur, especially when there is a sizable difference in age between the partners in the marriage.

Dorje's family represents just such a potential situation. He is fifteen years old and his two older brothers are twenty-five and twenty-two years old. The new bride is twenty-three years old, eight years Dorje's senior. Sometimes such a bride finds the youngest husband immature and adolescent and does not treat him with equal affection; alternatively, she may find his youth attractive and lavish special attention on him. Apart from that consideration, when a younger male like Dorje grows up, he may consider his wife "ancient" and prefer the company of a woman his own age or younger. Consequently, although men and women do not find the idea of sharing a bride or a bridegroom repulsive, individual likes and dislikes can cause familial discord.

Two reasons have commonly been offered for the perpetuation of fraternal polyandry in Tibet: that Tibetans practice female infanticide and therefore have to marry polyandrously, owing to a shortage of females; and that Tibet, lying at extremely high altitudes, is so barren and bleak that Tibetans would starve without resort to this mechanism. A Jesuit who lived in Tibet during the eighteenth century articulated this second view: "One reason for this most odious custom is the sterility of the soil, and the small amount of land that can be cultivated owing to the lack of water. The crops may suffice if the brothers all live together, but if they form separate families they would be reduced to beggary."

Both explanations are wrong, however. Not only has there never been institutionalized female infanticide in Tibet, but Tibetan society gives females considerable rights, including inheriting the family estate in the absence of brothers. In such cases, the woman takes a bridegroom who comes to live in her family and adopts her family's name and identity. Moreover, there is no demographic evidence of a shortage of females. In Limi, for example, there were (in 1974) sixty females and fifty-three males in the fifteen- to thirty-five-year age category, and many adult females were unmarried.

The second reason is also incorrect. The climate in Tibet is extremely harsh, and ecological factors do play a major role perpetuating polyandry, but polyandry is not a means of preventing starvation. It is characteristic, not of the poorest segments of the society, but rather of the peasant landowning families.

In the old society, the landless poor could not realistically aspire to prosperity, but they did not fear starvation. There was a persistent labor shortage throughout Tibet, and very poor families with little or no land and few animals could subsist through agricultural labor, tenant farming, craft occupations such as carpentry, or by working as servants. Although the per person family income could increase somewhat if brothers married polyandrously and pooled their wages, in the absence of inheritable land, the advantage of fraternal polyandry was not generally sufficient to prevent them from setting up their own households. A more skilled or energetic younger brother could do as well or better alone, since he would completely control his income and would not have to share it with his siblings. Consequently, while there was and is some polyandry among the poor, it is much less frequent and more prone to result in divorce and family fission.

An alternative reason for the persistence of fraternal polyandry is that it reduces population growth (and thereby reduces the pressure on resources) by relegating some females to lifetime spinsterhood. Fraternal polyandrous marriages in Limi (in 1974) averaged 2.35 men per woman, and not surprisingly, 31 percent of the females of child-bearing age (twenty to forty-nine) were unmarried. These spinsters either continued to live at home, set up their own households, or worked as servants for other families. They could also become Buddhist nuns. Being unmarried is not synonymous with exclusion from the reproductive pool. Discreet extramarital relationships are tolerated, and actually half of the adult unmarried women in Limi had one or more children. They raised these children as single mothers, working for wages or weaving cloth and blankets for sale. As a group, however, the unmarried woman had far fewer offspring than the married women, averaging only 0.7 children per woman, compared with 3.3 for married women, whether polyandrous, monogamous, or polygynous. While polyandry helps regulate population, this function of polyandry is not consciously perceived by Tibetans and is not the reason they consistently choose it.

If neither a shortage of females nor the fear of starvation perpetuates fraternal polyandry, what motivates brothers, particularly younger brothers, to opt for this system of marriage? From the perspective of the younger brother in a landholding family, the main incentive is the attainment or maintenance of the good life. With polyandry, he can expect a more secure and higher standard of living, with access not only to this family's land and animals but also to its inherited collection of clothes, jewelry, rugs, saddles, and horses. In addition, he will experience less work pressure and much greater security because all responsibility does not fall on one "father." For Tibetan brothers, the question is whether to trade off the greater personal freedom inherent in monogamy for the real or potential economic security, affluence, and social prestige associated with life in a larger, labor-rich polyandrous family.

A brother thinking of separating from his polyandrous marriage and taking his own wife would face various disadvantages. Although in the majority of Tibetan regions all brothers theoretically have rights to their family's estate, in reality Tibetans are reluctant to divide their land into small fragments. Generally, a younger brother who insists on leaving the family will receive only a small plot of land, if that. Because of its power and wealth, the rest of the family usually can block any attempt of the younger brother to increase his share of land through litigation. Moreover, a younger brother may not even get a house and cannot expect to receive much above the minimum in terms of movable possessions, such as furniture, pots, and pans. Thus, a brother contemplating going it on his own must plan on achieving economic security and the good life not through inheritance but through his own work.

The obvious solution for younger brothers—creating new fields from virgin land—is generally not a feasible option. Most Tibetan populations live at high altitudes (above 12,000 feet), where arable land is extremely scarce. For example, in Dorje's village, agriculture ranges only from about 12,900 feet, the lowest point in the area, to 13,300 feet. Above that altitude, early frost and snow destroy the staple barley crop. Furthermore, because of the low rainfall caused by the Himalayan rain shadow, many areas in Tibet and northern Nepal that are within the appropriate altitude range for agriculture have no reliable sources of irrigation. In the end, although there is plenty of unused land in such areas, most of it is either too high or too arid.

Even where unused land capable of being farmed exists, clearing the land and building the substantial terraces necessary for irrigation constitute a great undertaking. Each plot has to be completely dug out to a depth of two to two and a half feet so that the large rocks and boulders can be removed. At best, a man might be able to bring a few new fields under cultivation in the first years after separating from his brothers, but he could not expect to acquire substantial amounts of arable land this way.

In addition, because of the limited farmland, the Tibetan subsistence economy characteristically includes a strong emphasis on animal husbandry. Tibetan farmers regularly maintain cattle, yaks, goats, and sheep, grazing them in the areas too high for agriculture. These herds produce wool, milk, cheese, butter, meat, and skins. To obtain these resources, however, shepherds must accompany the animals on a daily basis. When first setting up a monogamous household, a younger brother like Dorje would find it difficult to both farm and manage animals.

In traditional Tibetan society, there was an even more critical factor that operated to perpetuate fraternal polyandry—a form of hereditary servitude somewhat analogous to serfdom in Europe. Peasants were tied to large estates held by aristocrats, monasteries, and the Lhasa government. They were allowed the use of some farmland to produce their own subsistence but were required to provide taxes in kind and corvée (free labor) to their lords. The corvée was a substantial hardship, since a peasant household was in many cases required to furnish the lord with one laborer daily for most of the year and more on specific occasions such as the harvest. This enforced labor, along with the lack of new land and ecological pressure to pursue both agriculture and ani- mal husbandry, made polyandrous families particularly beneficial. The polyandrous family allowed an internal division of adult labor, maximizing economic advantage. For example, while the wife worked the family fields, one brother could perform the lord's corvée, another could look after the animals, and a third could engage in trade.

Although social scientists often discount other people's explanations of why they do things, in the case of Tibetan fraternal polyandry, such explanations are very close to the truth. The custom, however, is very sensitive to changes in its political and economic mileu and, not surprisingly, is in decline in most Tibetan areas. Made less important by the elimination of the traditional serf-based economy, it is disparaged by the dominant non-Tibetan leaders of India, China, and Nepal. New opportunities for economic and social mobility in these countries, such as the tourist trade and government employment, are also eroding the rationale for poly-andry, and so it may vanish within the next generation.

When Brothers Share a Wife

1. How does fraternal polyandry provide status to the Tibetans?
2. What explanation does Goldstein offer for why fraternal polyandry exists in Tibet?
3. What problems do the Tibetans believe arise from brothers sharing a wife?

READING 8

Death Without Weeping

NANCY SCHEPER-HUGHES

Most anthropologists acknowledge a special emotional bond that exists between mother and child, owing to the physical nature of pregnancy and birth, in whatever culture they may be found. But can these strong psychological bonds undergo significant changes in the face of severe economic and social conditions? In this article about mothers in a Brazilian shantytown, anthropologist Nancy Scheper-Hughes examines how extreme poverty, deprivation, hunger, and economic exploitation can cause mothers not to mourn the death of their children. She found that mothers living under these extreme conditions develop a strategy of delayed attachment to their children, withholding emotional involvement until they are reasonably sure the child will survive. Such a strategy—while appearing cruel and unfeeling to those of us in our comfortable, middle-class surroundings—is really an emotional coping strategy for mothers living with an extraordinarily high infant and child mortality rate. Rather than seeing "mother love" as an absolute cultural universal, Scheper-Hughes suggests that, under these extreme conditions, it is a luxury reserved for those children who survive. This article, and the book on which it is based written in 1992, provide a thoughtful and wrenching analysis of how poverty and injustice can lead to the demise of a mother's basic human right of weeping for her dead children.

Scheper-Hughes reminds us that cultures are not isolated, insulated entities which determine people's behavior. Instead we are compelled to look at the factors from the wider society—such as political, religious, and economic institutions—impinging on people's behavior.

I have seen death without weeping
The destiny of the Northeast is death
Cattle they kill
To the people they do something worse

—ANONYMOUS BRAZILIAN SINGER (1965)

"Why do the church bells ring so often?" I asked Nailza de Arruda soon after I moved into a corner of her tiny mud-walled hut near the top of the shantytown called the Alto do Cruzeiro (Crucifix Hill). I was then a Peace Corps volunteer and a community development/health worker. It was the dry and blazing hot summer of 1965, the months following the military coup in Brazil, and save for the rusty, clanging bells of N. S. das Dores Church, an eerie quiet had settled over the market town that I call Bom Jesus da Mata. Beneath the quiet, however, there was chaos and panic. "It's nothing," replied Nailza, "just another little angel gone to heaven."

Nailza had sent more than her share of little angels to heaven, and sometimes at night I could hear her engaged in a muffled but passionate discourse with one of them, two-year-old Joana. Joana's photograph, taken as she lay propped up in her tiny cardboard coffin, her eyes open, hung on a wall next to one of Nailza and Ze Antonio taken on the day they eloped.

Nailza could barely remember the other infants and babies who came and went in close succession. Most had died unnamed and were hastily baptized in their coffins. Few lived more than a month or two. Only Joana, properly baptized in church at the close of her first year and placed under the protection of a powerful saint, Joan of Arc, had been expected to live. And Nailza had dangerously allowed herself to love the little girl.

In addressing the dead child, Nailza's voice would range from tearful imploring to angry recrimination: "Why did you leave me? Was your patron saint so greedy that she could not allow me one child on this earth?" Ze Antonio advised me to ignore Nailza's odd behavior, which he understood as a kind of madness that, like the birth and death of children, came and went. Indeed, the premature birth of a stillborn son some months later "cured" Nailza of her "inappropriate" grief, and the day came when she removed Joana's photo and carefully packed it away.

More than fifteen years elapsed before I returned to the Alto do Cruzeiro, and it was anthropology that provided the vehicle of my return. Since 1982 I have returned several times in order to pursue a problem that first attracted my attention in the 1960s. My involvement with the people of the Alto do Cruzeiro now spans a quarter of a century and three generations of parenting in a community where mothers and daughters are often simultaneously pregnant.

The Alto do Cruzeiro is one of three shantytowns surrounding the large market town of Bom Jesus in the sugar plantation zone of Pernambuco in Northeast Brazil, one of the many zones of neglect that have emerged in the shadow of the now tarnished economic miracle of Brazil. For the women and children of the Alto do Cruzeiro the only miracle is that some of them have managed to stay alive at all.

The Northeast is a region of vast proportions (approximately twice the size of Texas) and of equally vast social and developmental problems. The nine states that make up the region are the poorest in the country and are representative of the Third World within a dynamic and rapidly industrializing nation. Despite waves of migrations from the interior to the teeming shantytowns of coastal cities, the majority still live in rural areas on farms and ranches, sugar plantations and mills.

Life expectancy in the Northeast is only forty years, largely because of the appallingly high rate of infant and child mortality. Approximately one million children in Brazil under the age of five die each year. The children of the Northeast, especially those born in shantytowns on the periphery of urban life, are at a very high risk of death. In these areas, children are born without the traditional protection of breast-feeding, subsistence gardens, stable marriages, and multiple adult caretakers that exists in the interior. In the hillside shantytowns that spring up around cities or, in this case, interior market towns, marriages are brittle, single parenting is the norm, and women are frequently forced into the shadow economy of domestic work in the homes of the rich or into unprotected and oftentimes "scab" wage labor on the surrounding sugar plantations, where they clear land for planting and weed for a pittance, sometimes less than a dollar a day. The women of the Alto may not bring their babies with them into the homes of the wealthy, where the often-sick infants are considered sources of contamination, and they cannot carry the little ones to the riverbanks where they wash clothes because the river is heavily infested with schistosomes, and other deadly parasites. Nor can they carry their young children to the plantations, which are often several miles away. At wages of a dollar a day, the women of the Alto cannot hire baby sitters. Older children who are not in school will sometimes serve as somewhat indifferent caretakers. But any child not in school is also expected to find wage work. In most cases, babies are simply left at home alone, the door securely fastened. And so many also die alone and unattended.

Bom Jesus da Mata, centrally located in the plantation zone of Pernambuco, is within commuting distance of several sugar plantations and mills. Consequently, Bom Jesus has been a magnet for rural workers forced off their small subsistence plots by large landowners wanting to use every available piece of land for sugar cultivation. Initially, the rural migrants to Bom Jesus were squatters who were given tacit approval by the mayor to put up temporary straw huts on each of the three hills overlooking the town. The Alto do Cruzeiro is the oldest, the largest, and the poorest of the shantytowns. Over the past three decades many of the original migrants have become permanent residents, and the primitive and temporary straw huts have been replaced by small homes (usually of two rooms) made of wattle and daub, sometimes covered with plaster. The more affluent residents use bricks and tiles. In most Alto homes, dangerous kerosene lamps have been replaced by light bulbs. The once tattered rural garb, often fashioned from used sugar sacking, has likewise been replaced by store-bought clothes, often castoffs from a wealthy *patrão* (boss). The trappings are modern, but the hunger, sickness, and death that they conceal are traditional, deeply rooted in a history of feudalism, exploitation, and institutionalized dependency.

My research agenda never wavered. The questions I addressed first crystallized during a veritable "die-off" of Alto babies during a severe drought in 1965. The food and water shortages and the political and economic chaos occasioned by the military coup were reflected in the handwritten entries of births and deaths in the dusty, yellowed pages of the ledger books kept at the public registry office in Bom Jesus. More than 350 babies died in the Alto during 1965 alone—this from a shantytown population of little more than 5,000. But that wasn't what surprised me. There were reasons enough for the deaths in the miserable conditions of shantytown life. What puzzled me was the seeming indifference of Alto women to the death of their infants, and their willingness to attribute to their own tiny offspring an aversion to life that made their death seem wholly natural, indeed all but anticipated.

Although I found that it was possible, and hardly difficult, to rescue infants and toddlers from death by diarrhea and dehydration with a simple sugar, salt, and water solution (even bottled Coca-Cola worked fine), it was more difficult to enlist a mother herself in the rescue of a child she perceived as ill-fated for life or better off dead, or to convince her to take back into her threatened and besieged home a baby she had already come to think of as an angel rather than as a son or daughter.

I learned that the high expectancy of death, and the ability to face child death with stoicism and equanimity, produced patterns of nurturing that differentiated between those infants thought of as thrivers and survivors and those thought of as born already "wanting to die." The survivors were nurtured, while stigmatized, doomed infants were left to die, as mothers say, *a mingua*, "of neglect." Mothers stepped back and allowed nature to take its course. This pattern, which I call mortal selective neglect, is called passive infanticide by anthropologist Marvin Harris. The Alto situation, although culturally specific in the form that it takes, is not unique to Third World shantytown communities and may have its correlates in our own impoverished urban communities in some cases of "failure to thrive" infants.

I use as an example the story of Zezinho, the thirteen-month-old toddler of one of my neighbors, Lourdes. I became involved with Zezinho when I was called in to help Lourdes in the delivery of another child, this one a fair and robust little tyke with a lusty cry. I noted that while Lourdes showed great interest in the newborn, she totally ignored Zezinho who, wasted and severely malnourished, was curled up in a fetal position on a piece of urine- and feces-soaked cardboard placed under his mother's hammock. Eyes open and vacant, mouth slack, the little boy seemed doomed.

When I carried Zezinho up to the community day-care center at the top of the hill, the Alto women who took turns caring for one another's children (in order to free themselves for part-time work in the cane fields or washing clothes) laughed at my efforts to save Ze, agreeing with Lourdes that here was a baby without a ghost of a chance. Leave him alone, they cautioned. It makes no sense to fight with death. But I did do battle with Ze, and after several weeks of force-feeding (malnourished babies lose their interest in food), Ze began to succumb to my ministrations. He acquired some flesh across his taut chest bones, learned to sit up, and even tried to smile. When he seemed well enough, I returned him to Lourdes in her miserable scrap-material lean-to, but not without guilt about what I had done. I wondered whether returning Ze was at all fair to Lourdes and to his little brother. But I was busy and washed my hands of the matter. And Lourdes did seem more interested in Ze now that he was looking more human.

When I returned in 1982, there was Lourdes among the women who formed my sample of Alto mothers—still struggling to put together some semblance of life for a now grown Ze and her five other surviving children. Much was made of my reunion with Ze in 1982, and everyone enjoyed retelling the story of Ze's rescue and of how his mother had given him up for dead. Ze would laugh the loudest when told how I had had to force-feed him like a fiesta turkey. There was no hint of guilt on the part of Lourdes and no resentment on the part of Ze. In fact, when questioned in private as to who was the best friend he ever had in life, Ze took a long drag on his cigarette and answered without a trace of irony. "Why my mother, of course." "But of course," I replied.

Part of learning how to mother in the Alto do Cruzeiro is learning when to let go of a child who shows that it "wants" to die on that it has no "knack" or no "taste" for life. Another part is learning when it is safe to let oneself love a child. Frequent child death remains a powerful shaper of maternal thinking and practice. In the absence of firm expectation that a child will survive, mother love as we conceptualize it (whether in popular terms or in the psychobiological notion of maternal bonding) is attenuated and delayed with consequences for infant survival. In an environment already precarious to young life, the emotional detachment of mothers toward some of their babies contributes even further to the spiral of high mortality—high fertility in a kind of macabre lock-step dance of death.

The average woman of the Alto experiences 9.5 pregnancies, 3.5 child deaths, and 1.5 stillbirths. Seventy percent of all child deaths in the Alto occur in the first six months of life, and 82 percent by the end of the first year. Of all deaths in the community each year, about 45 percent are of children under the age of five.

Women of the Alto distinguish between child deaths understood as natural (caused by diarrhea and communicable diseases) and those resulting from sorcery, the evil eye, or other magical or supernatural afflictions. They also recognize a large category of infant deaths seen as fated and inevitable. These hopeless cases are classified by mothers under the folk terminology "child sickness" or "child attack." Women say that there are at least fourteen different types of hopeless child sickness, but most can be subsumed under two categories—chronic and acute. The chronic cases refer to infants who are born small and wasted. They are deathly pale, mothers say, as well as weak and passive. They demonstrate no vital force, no liveliness. They do not suck vigorously; they hardly cry. Such babies can be this way at birth or they can be born sound but soon show no resistance, no "fight" against the common crises of infancy: diarrhea, respiratory infections, tropical fevers.

The acute cases are those doomed infants who die suddenly and violently. They are taken by stealth overnight, often following convulsions that bring on head banging, shaking, grimacing, and shrieking. Women say it is horrible to look at such a baby. If the infant begins to foam at the mouth or gnash its teeth or go rigid with its eyes turned back inside its head, there is absolutely no hope. The infant is "put aside"—left alone—often on the floor in a back room, and allowed to die. These symptoms (which accompany high fevers, dehydration, third-stage malnutrition, and encephalitis) are equated by Alto women with madness, epilepsy, and worst of all, rabies, which is greatly feared and highly stigmatized.

Most of the infants presented to me as suffering from chronic child sickness were tiny, wasted famine victims, while those labeled as victims of acute child attack seemed to be infants suffering from the deliriums of high fever or the convulsions that can accompany electrolyte imbalance in dehydrated babies.

Local midwives and traditional healers, praying women, as they are called, advise Alto women on when to allow a baby to die. One midwife explained: "If I can see that a baby was born unfortuitously, I tell the mother that she need not wash the infant or give it a cleansing tea. I tell her just to dust the infant with baby powder and wait for it to die." Allowing nature to take its course is not seen as sinful by these often very devout Catholic women. Rather, it is understood as cooperating with God's plan.

Often I have been asked how consciously women of the Alto behave in this regard. I would have to say that consciousness is always shifting between allowed and disallowed levels of awareness. For example, I was awakened early one morning in 1987 by two neighborhood children who had been sent to fetch me to a hastily organized wake for a two-month-old infant whose mother I had unsuccessfully urged to breast-feed. The infant was being sustained on sugar water, which the mother referred to as *soro* (serum), using a medical term for the infant's starvation regime in light of his chronic diarrhea. I had cautioned the mother that an infant could not live on *soro* forever.

The two girls urged me to console the young mother by telling her that it was "too bad" that her infant was so weak that Jesus had to take him. They were coaching me in proper Alto etiquette, I agreed, of course, but asked, "And what do *you* think?" Xoxa, the eleven-year-old, looked down at her dusty flip-flops and blurted out, "Oh, Dona Nanci, that baby never got enough to eat, but you must never say that!" And so the death of hungry babies remains one of the best kept secrets of life in Bom Jesus da Mata.

Most victims are waked quickly and with a minimum of ceremony. No tears are shed, and the neighborhood children form a tiny procession, carrying the baby to the town graveyard where it will join a multitude of others. Although a few fresh flowers may be scattered over the tiny grave, no stone or wooden cross will mark the place, and the same spot will be reused within a few months' time. The mother will never visit the grave, which soon becomes an anonymous one.

What, then, can be said of these women? What emotions, what sentiments motivate them? How are they able to do what, in fact, must be done? What does mother love mean in this inhospitable context? Are grief, mourning, and melancholia present, although deeply repressed? If so, where shall we look for them? And if not, how are we to understand the moral visions and moral sensibilities that guide their actions?

I have been criticized more than once for presenting an unflattering portrait of poor Brazilian women, women who are, after all, themselves the victims of severe social and institutional neglect. I have described these women as allowing some of their children to die, as if this were an unnatural and inhuman act rather than, as I would assert, the way any one of us might act, reasonably and ra- tionally, under similarly desperate conditions. Perhaps I have not emphasized enough the real pathogens in this environment of high risk: poverty, deprivation, sexism, chronic hunger, and economic exploitation. If mother love is, as many psychologists and some feminists believe, a seemingly natural and universal maternal script, what does it mean to women for whom scarcity, loss, sickness, and deprivation have made that love frantic and robbed them of their grief, seeming to turn their hearts to stone?

Throughout much of human history—as in a great deal of the impoverished Third World today—women have had to give birth and to nurture children under ecological conditions and social arrangements hostile to child survival, as well as to their own well-being. Under circumstances of high childhood mortality, patterns of selective neglect and passive infanticide may be seen as active survival strategies.

They also seem to be fairly common practices historically and across cultures. In societies characterized by high childhood mortality and by a correspondingly high (replacement) fertility, cultural practices of infant and child care tend to be organized primarily around survival goals. But what this means is a pragmatic recognition that not all of one's children can be expected to live. The nervousness about child survival in areas of northeast Brazil, northern India, or Bangladesh, where a 30 percent or 40 percent mortality rate in the first years of life is common, can lead to forms of delayed attachment and a casual or benign neglect that serves to weed out the worst bets so as to enhance the life chances of healthier siblings, including those yet to be born. Practices similar to those that I am describing have been recorded for parts of Africa, India, and Central America.

Life in the Alto do Cruzeiro resembles nothing so much as a battlefield or an emergency room in an overcrowded inner-city public hospital. Consequently, morality is guided by a kind of "lifeboat ethics," the morality of triage. The seemingly studied indifference toward the suffering of some of their infants, conveyed in such sayings as "little critters have no feelings," is understandable in light of these women's obligation to carry on with their reproductive and nurturing lives.

In their slowness to anthropomorphize and personalize their infants, everything is mobilized so as to prevent maternal overattachment and, therefore, grief at death. The bereaved mother is told not to cry, that her tears will dampen the wings of her little angel so that she cannot fly up to her heavenly home. Grief at the death of an angel is not only inappropriate, it is a symptom of madness and of a profound lack of faith.

Infant death becomes routine in an environment in which death is anticipated and bets are hedged. While the routinization of death in the context of shantytown life is not hard to understand, and quite possible to empathize with, its routinization in the formal institutions of public life in Bom Jesus is not as easy to accept uncritically. Here the social production of indifference takes on a different, even a malevolent, cast.

In a society where triplicates of every form are required for the most banal events (registering a car, for example), the registration of infant and child death is informal, incomplete, and rapid. It requires no documentation, takes less than five minutes, and demands no witnesses other than office clerks. No questions are asked concerning the circumstances of the death, and the cause of death is left blank, unquestioned and unexamined. A neighbor, grandmother, older sibling, or common-law husband may register the death. Since most infants die at home, there is no question of a medical record.

From the registry office, the parent proceeds to the town hall, where the mayor will give him or her a voucher for a free baby coffin. The full-time municipal coffinmaker cannot tell you exactly how many baby coffins are dispatched each week. It varies, he says, with the seasons. There are more needed during the drought months and during the big festivals of Carnaval and Christmas and São Joao's Day because people are too busy, he supposes, to take their babies to the clinic. Record keeping is sloppy.

Similarly, there is a failure on the part of city- employed doctors working at two free clinics to recognize the malnutrition of babies who are weighed, measured, and immunized without comment and as if they were not, in fact, anemic, stunted, fussy, and irritated starvation babies. At best the mothers are told to pick up free vitamins or a health "tonic" at the municipal chambers. At worst, clinic personnel will give tranquilizers and sleeping pills to quiet the hungry cries of "sick-to-death" Alto babies.

The church, too, contributes to the routinization of, and indifference toward, child death. Traditionally, the local Catholic church taught patience and resignation to domestic tragedies that were said to reveal the imponderable workings of God's will. If an infant died suddenly, it was because a particular saint had claimed the child. The infant would be an angel in the service of his or her heavenly patron. It would be wrong, a sign of a lack of faith, to weep for a child with such good fortune. The infant funeral was, in the past, an event celebrated with joy. Today, however, under the new regime of "liberation theology," the bells of N.S. das Dores parish church no longer peal for the death of Alto babies, and no priest accompanies the procession of angels to the cemetery where their bodies are disposed of casually and without ceremony. Children bury children in Bom Jesus da Mata. In this most Catholic communities, the coffin is handed to the disabled and irritable municipal gravedigger, who often chides the children for one reason or another. It may be that the coffin is larger than expected and the gravedigger can find no appropriate space. The children do not wait for the gravedigger to complete his task. No prayers are recited and no sign of the cross made as the tiny coffin goes into its shallow grave.

When I asked the local priest, Padre Marcos, about the lack of church ceremony surrounding infant and childhood death today in Bom Jesus, he replied: "In the old days, child death was richly celebrated. But those were the baroque customs of a conservative church that wallowed in death and misery. The new church is a church of hope and joy. We no longer celebrate the death of child angels. We try to tell mothers that Jesus doesn't want all the dead babies they send him." Similarly, the new church has changed its baptismal customs, now often refusing to baptize dying babies brought to the back door of a church or rectory. The mothers are scolded by the church attendants and told to go home and take care of their sick babies. Baptism, they are told, is for the living; it is not to be confused with the sacrament of extreme unction, which is the anointing of the dying. And so it appears to the women of the Alto that even the church has turned away from them, denying the traditional comfort of folk Catholicism.

The contemporary Catholic church is caught in the clutches of a double bind. The new theology of liberation imagines a kingdom of God on earth based on justice and equality, a world without hunger, sickness, or childhood mortality. At the same time, the church has not changed its official position on sexuality and reproduction, including its sanctions against birth control, abortion, and sterilization. The padre of Bom Jesus da Mata recognizes this contradiction intuitively, although he shies away from discussions on the topic, saying that he prefers to leave questions of family planning to the discretion and the "good consciences" of his impoverished parishioners. But this, of course, sidesteps the extent to which those good consciences have been shaped by traditional church teachings in Bom Jesus, especially by his recent predecessors. Hence, we can begin to see that the seeming indifference of Alto mothers toward the death of some of their infants is but a pale reflection of the official indifference of church and state to the plight of poor women and children.

Nonetheless, the women of Bom Jesus are survivors. One woman, Biu, told me her life history, returning again and again to the themes of child death, her first husband's suicide, abandonment by her father and later by her second husband, and all the other losses and disappointments she has suffered in her long forty-five years. She concluded with great force, reflecting on the days of Carnaval '88 that were fast approaching:

> No, Dona Nanci, I won't cry, and I won't waste my life thinking about it from morning to night. . . . Can I argue with God for the state that I'm in? No! And so I'll dance and I'll jump and I'll play Carnaval! And yes, I'll laugh and people will wonder at a *pobre* like me who can have such a good time.

And no one did blame Biu for dancing in the streets during the four days of Carnaval—not even on Ash Wednesday, the day following Carnaval '88 when we all assembled hurriedly to assist in the burial of Mercea, Biu's beloved *casula*, her last-born daughter who had died at home of pneumonia during the festivities. The rest of the family barely had time to change out of their costumes. Severino, the child's uncle and godfather, sprinkled holy water over the little angel while he prayed: "Mercea, I don't know whether you were called, taken, or thrown out of this world. But look down at us from your heavenly home with tenderness, with pity, and with mercy." So be it.

Death Without Weeping

1. In Bom Jesus, how have women been desensitized to the death of their babies?
2. What does passive infanticide mean to the women of Bom Jesus?
3. What role did Nancy Scheper- Hughes take in dealing with the ongoing early childhood deaths in Bom Jesus?

"Death Without Weeping"—*Natural History* Article UPDATE June 2008

Epilogue

Many students write to me after reading this article asking whether the situation has changed in the Alto do Cruzeiro. Is life better or worse for mothers and newborn babies? One of the advantages of traditional, long-term ethnographic research is that one gets to see history in the making. I began my engagements with the people of the Alto in 1964 at the start of twenty years of military rule, a ruthless political–economic regime that produced widespread impoverishment among those excluded populations living in deep urban slums (*favelas*) and in peripheral rural communities. The scarcities and insecurities of that era contributed to the death of infants and small babies. By the time I completed my study of mother love and child death in the early 1990s Brazil was well on its way to democratization which ushered in many important changes, most notably a free, public, national health care system (SUS) which guaranteed poor women adequate pre-natal care, hospital delivery and basic maternal-infant care during the first years of life. The decade of the 1990s witnessed in Brazil what population experts call the demographic or epidemiologic transition. Both births and infant deaths declined which radically transformed the way newborns were perceived and received by Alto mothers. The old stance of maternal "watchful waiting" that was accompanied by maternal "de-selections" of those infants viewed as having no 'taste' or 'talent' for life, was replaced by a maternal ethos of 'holding on' and 'holding dear' each infant now seen as potentially capable of survival.

Today, young women of the Alto can expect to give birth to three or fewer infants and to see all of them live to adolescence. Many factors came together in producing this reproductive transition. The new teachings of liberation theology did eventually dislodge a baroque folk Catholicism that saw God and the saints as 'authorizing' infant death by 'calling' the infants to themselves. Women began to think of themselves as capable of deciding how many pregnancies they would have. The availability of over or 'under' the counter drug, Cytoteças a risky "morning after" pill provided an easy means of birth spacing that had not existed before. President Fernando Henrique Cardoso (1995–2003) fortified the national health care system (Serviço Único de Saúde) with a program of local 'health agents' , 'barefoot doctors", who visit poor households door to door, identifying those at risk and rescuing a great many vulnerable infants, toddlers and old people from premature death. The primary cause of the decline in infant mortality on the Alto do Cruzeiro, however, was the result of a 'simple' municipal program, the installation of water pipes reaching almost all the homes in the shantytown with sufficient and clean water. Water = life! It is painful to consider how 'culture', 'belief' and even maternal sentiments and practices follow basic changes in the material conditions—and therefore the possibilities—of everyday life. Motherhood is not only a social and a cultural construction but a constellation of embodied practices responding to the requirements and limitations of the political economy that determines the food people eat or don't eat, the water they drink or don't drink, the shoes they wear or don't wear, the books they read or cannot read, the homes made of mud and sticks or of brick and tiles.

There are other new problems faced by the people of the Alto do Cruzeiro today. Since the publication of "Death wiyhout Weeping" drugs and gangs have made their ugly mark on the community as have new disease epidemics. Death squads and 'extermination groups' have sprung up to minister a kind of vigilante justice. These new features of anti-social life in "Bom Jesus da Mata" take some of the pleasure away, as one now sees the young boys of the Alto do Cruzeiro who survived that dangerous first year of life only to be cut down by bullets and knives at the age of 15 or 17 by local gangs, 'strong men', bandidos, and local police in almost equal measure. But that story awaits another and much longer telling.

Nancy Scheper-Hughes

READING 9

Society and Sex Roles

ERNESTINE FRIEDL

Although it is possible to find societies in which gender inequalities are kept to a minimum, the overwhelming ethnographic and archaeological evidence suggests that females are subordinate to men in terms of exerting economic and political control. This gender asymmetry is so pervasive that some anthropologists over the years have concluded that this gender inequality is the result of biological differences between men and women. That is, men are dominant because of their greater size, physical strength, and innate aggressiveness. In this selection, Ernestine Friedl argues that the answer to this near universal male dominance lies more with economics than with biological predisposition.

A former president of the American Anthropological Association, Friedl argues that men tend to be dominant because they control the distribution of scarce resources in the society, both within and outside of the family. Quite apart from who produces the goods, "the person controlling the distribution of the limited and valued resources possesses the currency needed to create the obligations and alliances that are at the center of all political relations." Using ethnographic examples from foraging societies, Friedl shows how women have relative equality in those societies where they exercise some control over resources. Conversely, men are nearly totally dominant in those societies in which women have no control over scarce resources.

"Women must respond quickly to the demands of their husbands," says anthropologist Napoleon Chagnon describing the horticultural Yanomamo Indians of Venezuela. When a man returns from a hunting trip, "the woman, no matter what she is doing, hurries home and quietly but rapidly prepares a meal for her husband. Should the wife be slow in doing this, the husband is within his rights to beat her. Most reprimands . . . take the form of blows with the hand or with a piece of firewood. . . . Some of them chop their wives with the sharp edge of a machete or axe, or shoot them with a barbed arrow in some nonvital area, such as the buttocks or leg."

Among the Semai agriculturalists of central Malaya, when one person refuses the request of another, the offended party suffers *punan*, a mixture of emotional pain and frustration. "Enduring *punan* is commonest when a girl has refused the victim her sexual favors," reports Robert Dentan. "The jilted man's 'heart becomes sad.' He loses his energy and his appetite. Much of the time he sleeps, dreaming of his lost love. In this state he is in fact very likely to injure himself 'accidentally.'" The Semai are afraid of violence; a man would never strike a women.

The social relationship between men and women has emerged as one of the principal disputes occupying the attention of scholars and the public in recent years. Although the discord is sharpest in the United States, the controversy has spread throughout the world. Numerous national and international conferences, including one in Mexico sponsored by the United Nations, have drawn together delegates from all walks of life to discuss such questions as the social and political rights of each sex, and even the basic nature of males and females.

Whatever their position, partisans often invoke examples from other cultures to support their ideas about the proper role of each sex. Because women are clearly subservient to men in many societies, like the Yano-mamo, some experts conclude that the natural pattern is for men to dominate. But among the Semai no one has the right to command others, and in West Africa women are often chiefs. The place of women in these societies supports the argument of those who believe that sex roles are not fixed, that if there is a natural order, it allows for many different arrangements.

The argument will never be settled as long as the opposing sides toss examples from the world's cultures at each other like intellectual stones. But the effect of biological differences on male and female behavior can be clarified by looking at known examples of the earliest forms of human society and examining the relationship between technology, social organization, environment, and sex roles. The problem is to determine the conditions in which different degrees of male dominance are found, to try to discover the social and cultural arrangements that give rise to equality or inequality between the sexes, and to attempt to apply this knowledge to our understanding of the changes taking place in modern industrial society.

From "Society and Sex Roles" by Ernestine Friedl in *Human Nature*, April 1978, pp. 68–75. Reprinted with permission from the author.

As Western history and the anthropological record have told us, equality between the sexes is rare; in most known societies females are subordinate. Male dominance is so widespread that it is virtually a human universal; societies in which women are consistently dominant do not exist and have never existed.

Evidence of a society in which women control all strategic resources like food and water, and in which women's activities are the most prestigious has never been found. The Iroquois of North America and the Lovedu of Africa came closest. Among the Iroquois, women raised food, controlled its distribution, and helped to choose male political leaders. Lovedu women ruled as queens, exchanged valuable cattle, led ceremonies, and controlled their own sex lives. But among both the Iroquois and the Lovedu, men owned the land and held other positions of power and prestige. Women were equal to men; they did not have ultimate authority over them. Neither culture was a true matriarchy.

Patriarchies are prevalent, and they appear to be strongest in societies in which men control significant goods that are exchanged with people outside the family. Regardless of who produces food, the person who gives it to others creates the obligations and alliances that are at the center of all political relations. The greater the male monopoly on the distribution of scarce items, the stronger their control of women seems to be. This is most obvious in relatively simple hunter-gatherer societies.

Hunter-gatherers, or foragers, subsist on wild plants, small land animals, and small river or sea creatures gathered by hand; large land animals and sea mammals hunted with spears, bows and arrows, and blow guns; and fish caught with hooks and nets. The 300,000 hunter-gatherers alive in the world today include the Eskimos, the Australian aborigines, and the Pygmies of Central Africa.

Foraging has endured for two million years and was replaced by farming and animal husbandry only 10,000 years ago; it covers more than 99 percent of human history. Our foraging ancestry is not far behind us and provides a clue to our understanding of the human condition.

Hunter-gatherers are people whose ways of life are technologically simple and socially and politically egalitarian. They live in small groups of 50 to 200 and have neither kings, nor priests, nor social classes. These conditions permit anthropologists to observe the essential bases for inequalities between the sexes without the distortions induced by the complexities of contemporary industrial society.

The source of male power among hunter-gatherers lies in their control of a scarce, hard to acquire, but necessary nutrient—animal protein. When men in a hunter-gatherer society return to camp with game, they divide the meat in some customary way. Among the !Kung San of Africa, certain parts of the animal are given to the owner of the arrow that killed the beast, to the first hunter to sight the game, to the one who threw the first spear, and to all men in the hunting party. After the meat has been divided, each hunter distributes his share to his blood relatives and his in-laws, who in turn share it with others. If an animal is large enough, every member of the band will receive some meat.

Vegetable foods, in contrast, are not distributed beyond the immediate household. Women give food to their children, to their husbands, to other members of the household, and rarely, to the occasional visitor. No one outside the family regularly eats any of the wild fruits and vegetables that are gathered by the women.

The meat distributed by the men is a public gift. Its source is widely known, and the donor expects a reciprocal gift when other men return from a successful hunt. He gains honor as a supplier of a scarce item and simultaneously obligates others to him.

These obligations constitute a form of power or control over others, both men and women. The opinions of hunters play an important part in decisions to move the village; good hunters attract the most desirable women; people in other groups join camps with good hunters; and hunters, because they already participate in an internal system of exchange, control exchange with other groups for flint, salt, and steel axes. The male monopoly on hunting unites men in a system of exchange and gives them power; gathering vegetable food does not give women equal power even among foragers who live in the tropics, where the food collected by women provides more than half the hunter-gatherer diet.

If dominance arises from a monopoly on big-game hunting, why has the male monopoly remained unchallenged? Some women are strong enough to participate in the hunt and their endurance is certainly equal to that of men. Dobe San women of the Kalahari Desert in Africa walk an average of 10 miles a day carrying from 15 to 33 pounds of food plus a baby.

Women do not hunt, I believe, because of four interrelated factors: variability in the supply of game; the different skills required for hunting and gathering; the incompatibility between carrying burdens and hunting; and the small size of seminomadic foraging populations.

Because the meat supply is unstable, foragers must make frequent expeditions to provide the band with gathered food. Environmental factors such as seasonal and annual variation in rainfall often affect the size of the wildlife population. Hunters cannot always find game, and when they do encounter animals, they are not always successful in killing their prey. In northern latitudes, where meat is the primary food, periods of starvation are known in every generation. The irregularity of the game supply leads hunter-gatherers in areas where plant foods are available to depend on these predictable foods a good part of the time. Someone must gather the fruits, nuts, and roots and carry them back to camp to feed unsuccessful hunters, children, the elderly, and anyone who might not have gone foraging that day.

Foraging falls to the women because hunting and gathering cannot be combined on the same expedition. Although gatherers sometimes notice signs of game as they work, the skills required to track game are not the same as those required to find edible roots or plants. Hunters scan the horizon and the land for traces of large game; gatherers keep their eyes to the ground, studying the distribution of plants and the texture of the soil for hidden roots and animal holes. Even if a woman who was collecting plants came across the track of an antelope, she could not follow it; it is impossible to carry a load and hunt at the same time. Running with a heavy load is difficult, and should the animal be sighted, the hunter would be off balance and could neither shoot an arrow nor throw a spear accurately.

Pregnancy and child care would also present difficulties for a hunter. An unborn child affects a woman's body balance, as does a child in her arms, on her back, or slung at her side. Until they are two years old, many hunter-gatherer children are carried at all times, and until they are four, they are carried some of the time.

An observer might wonder why young women do not hunt until they become pregnant, or why mature women and men do not hunt and gather on alternate days, with some women staying in camp to act as wet nurses for the young. Apart from the effects hunting might have on a mother's milk production, there are two reasons. First, young girls begin to bear children as soon as they are physically mature and strong enough to hunt, and second, hunter-gatherer bands are so small that there are unlikely to be enough lactating women to serve as wet nurses. No hunter-gatherer group could afford to maintain a specialized female hunting force.

Because game is not always available, because hunting and gathering are specialized skills, because women carrying heavy loads cannot hunt, and because women in hunter-gatherer societies are usually either pregnant or caring for young children, for most of the last two million years of human history men have hunted and women have gathered.

If male dominance depends on controlling the supply of meat, then the degree of male dominance in a society should vary with the amount of meat available and the amount supplied by the men. Some regions, like the East African grasslands and the North American woodlands, abounded with species of large mammals; other zones, like tropical forests and semideserts, are thinly populated with prey. Many elements affect the supply of game, but theoretically, the less meat provided exclusively by the men, the more egalitarian the society.

All known hunter-gatherer societies fit into four basic types: those in which men and women work together in communal hunts and as teams gathering edible plants, as did the Washo Indians of North America; those in which men and women each collect their own plant foods although the men supply some meat to the group, as do the Hadza of Tanzania; those in which male hunters and female gatherers work apart but return to camp each evening to share their acquisitions, as do the Tiwi of North Australia; and those in which the men provide all the food by hunting large game, as do the Eskimo. In each case the extent of male dominance increases directly with the proportion of meat supplied by individual men and small hunting parties.

Among the most egalitarian of hunter-gatherer societies are the Washo Indians, who inhabited the valleys of the Sierra Nevada in what is now southern California and Nevada. In the spring they moved north to Lake Tahoe for the large fish runs of sucker and native trout. Everyone—men, women, and children—participated in the fishing. Women spent the summer gathering edible berries and seeds while the men continued to fish. In the fall some men hunted deer but the most important source of animal protein was the jack rabbit, which was captured in communal hunts. Men and women together drove the rabbits into nets tied end to end. To provide food for the winter, husbands and wives worked as teams in the late fall to collect pine nuts.

Since everyone participated in most food-gathering activities, there were no individual distributors of food and relatively little difference in male and female rights. Men and women were not segregated from each other in daily activities; both were free to take lovers after marriage; both had the right to separate whenever they chose; menstruating women were not isolated from the rest of the group; and one of the two major Washo rituals celebrated hunting while the other celebrated gathering. Men were accorded more prestige if they had killed a deer, and men directed decisions about the seasonal movement of the group. But if no male leader stepped forward, women were permitted to lead. The distinctive feature of groups such as the Washo is the relative equality of the sexes.

The sexes are also relatively equal among the Hadza of Tanzania but this near-equality arises because men and women tend to work alone to feed themselves. They exchange little food. The Hadza lead a leisurely life in the seemingly barren environment of the East African Rift Gorge that is, in fact, rich in edible berries, roots, and small game. As a result of this abundance, from the time they are 10 years old, Hadza men and women gather much of their own food. Women take their young children with them into the bush, eating as they forage, and collect only enough food for a light family meal in the evening. The men eat berries and roots as they hunt for small game, and should they bring down a rabbit or a hyrax, they eat the meat on the spot. Meat is carried back to the camp and shared with the rest of the group only on those rare occasions when a poisoned arrow brings down a large animal—an impala, a zebra, an eland, or a giraffe.

Because Hadza men distribute little meat, their status is only slightly higher than that of the women. People flock to the camp of a good hunter and the camp might take on his name because of his popularity, but he is in no sense a leader of the group. A Hadza man and a woman have an equal right to divorce and each can repudiate a marriage simply by living apart for a few weeks. Couples tend to live in the same camp as the wife's mother but they sometimes make long visits to the camp of the husband's mother. Although a man may take more than one wife, most Hadza males cannot afford to indulge in this luxury. In order to maintain a marriage, a man must supply both his wife and his mother-in-law with some meat and trade goods, such as beads and cloth, and the Hadza economy gives few men the wealth to provide for more than one wife and mother-in-law. Washo equality is based on cooperation; Hadza equality is based on independence.

In contrast to both these groups, among the Tiwi of Melville and Bathurst Islands off the northern coast of Australia, male hunters dominate female gatherers. The Tiwi are representative of the most common form of foraging society, in which the men supply large quantities of meat, although less than half the food consumed by the group. Each morning Tiwi women, most with babies on their backs, scatter in different directions in search of vegetables, grubs, worms, and small game such as bandicoots, lizards, and opossums. To track the game, they use hunting dogs. On most days women return to camp with some meat and with baskets full of *korka,* the nut of a native palm, which is soaked and mashed to make a porridge-like dish. The Tiwi men do not hunt small game and do not hunt every day, but when they do they often return with kangaroo, large lizards, fish, and game birds.

The porridge is cooked separately by each household and rarely shared outside the family, but the meat is prepared by a volunteer cook, who can be male or female. After the cook takes one of the parts of the animal traditionally reserved for him or her, the animal's "boss," the one who caught it, distributes the rest to all near kin and then to all others residing with the band. Although the small game supplied by the women is distributed in the same way as the big game supplied by the men, Tiwi men are dominant because the game they kill provides most of the meat.

The power of Tiwi men is clearest in their betrothal practices. Among the Tiwi, a woman must always be married. To ensure this, female infants are betrothed at birth and widows are remarried at the gravesides of their late husbands. Men form alliances by exchanging daughters, sisters, and mothers in marriage and some collect as many as 25 wives. Tiwi men value the quantity and quality of the food many wives can collect and the many children they can produce.

The dominance of the men is offset somewhat by the influence of adult women in selecting their next husbands. Many women are active strategists in the political careers of their male relatives, but to the exasperation of some sons attempting to promote their own futures, widowed mothers sometimes insist on selecting their own partners. Women also influence the marriages of their daughters and granddaughters, especially when the selected husband dies before the bestowed child moves to his camp.

Among the Eskimo, representative of the rarest type of forager society, inequality between the sexes is matched by inequality in supplying the group with food. Inland Eskimo men hunt caribou throughout the year to provision the entire society, and maritime Eskimo men depend on whaling, fishing, and some hunting to feed their extended families. The women process the carcasses, cut and sew skins to make clothing, cook, and care for the young; but they collect no food of their own and depend on the men to supply all the raw materials for their work. Since men provide all the meat, they also control the trade in hides, whale oil, seal oil, and other items that move between the maritime and inland Eskimos.

Eskimo women are treated almost exclusively as objects to be used, abused, and traded by men. After puberty all Eskimo girls are fair game for any interested male. A man shows his intentions by grabbing the belt of a woman and if she protests, he cuts off her trousers and forces himself upon her. These encounters are considered unimportant by the rest of the group. Men offer their wives' sexual services to establish alliances with trading partners and members of hunting and whaling parties.

Despite the consistent pattern of some degree of male dominance among foragers, most of these societies are egalitarian compared with agricultural and industrial societies. No forager has any significant opportunity for political leadership. Foragers, as a rule, do not like to give or take orders, and assume leadership only with reluctance. Shamans (those who are thought to be possessed by spirits) may be either male or female. Public rituals conducted by women in order to celebrate the first menstruation of girls are common, and the symbolism in these rituals is similar to that in the ceremonies that follow a boy's first kill.

In any society, status goes to those who control the distribution of valued goods and services outside the family. Equality arises when both sexes work side by side in food production, as do the Washo, and the products are simply distributed among the workers. In such circumstances, no person or sex has greater access to valued items than do others. But when women make no contribution to the food supply, as in the case of the Eskimo, they are completely subordinate.

When we attempt to apply these generalizations to contemporary industrial society, we can predict that as long as women spend their discretionary income from jobs on domestic needs, they will gain little social recognition and power. To be an effective source of power, money must be exchanged in ways that require returns and create obligations. In other words, it must be invested.

Jobs that do not give women control over valued resources will do little to advance their general status. Only as managers, executives, and professionals are women in a position to trade goods and services, to do others favors, and therefore to obligate others to them. Only as controllers of valued resources can women achieve prestige, power, and equality.

Within the household, women who bring in income from jobs are able to function on a more nearly equal basis with their husbands. Women who contribute services to their husbands and children without pay, as do some middle-class Western housewives, are especially vulnerable to dominance. Like Eskimo women, as long as their services are limited to domestic distribution they have little power relative to their husbands and none with respect to the outside world.

As for the limits imposed on women by their procreative functions in hunter-gatherer societies, childbearing and child care are organized around work as much as work is organized around reproduction. Some foraging groups space their children three to four years apart and have an average of only four to six children, far fewer than many women in other cultures. Hunter-gatherers nurse their infants for extended periods, sometimes for as long as four years. This custom suppresses ovulation and limits the size of their families. Sometimes, although rarely, they practice infanticide. By limiting reproduction, a woman who is gathering food has only one child to carry.

Different societies can and do adjust the frequency of birth and the care of children to accommodate whatever productive activities women customarily engage in. In horticultural societies, where women work long hours in gardens that may be far from home, infants get food to supplement their mothers' milk, older children take care of younger children, and pregnancies are widely spaced. Throughout the world, if a society requires a woman's labor, it finds ways to care for her children.

In the United States, as in some other industrial societies, the accelerated entry of women with preschool children into the labor force has resulted in the development of a variety of childcare arrangements. Individual women have called on friends, relatives, and neighbors. Public and private child-care centers are growing. We should realize that the declining birth rate, the increasing acceptance of childless or single-child families, and a de-emphasis on motherhood are adaptations to a sexual division of labor reminiscent of the system of production found in hunter-gatherer societies.

In many countries where women no longer devote most of their productive years to childbearing, they are beginning to demand a change in the social relationship of the sexes. As women gain access to positions that control the exchange of resources, male dominance may become archaic, and industrial societies may one day become as egalitarian as the Washo.

Society and Sex Roles

1. Why is equality between the sexes so rare?
2. Why is it possible in some societies like the Washo or the Hazda for the sexes to be relatively equal, while in Eskimo society they are not?
3. What evidence do we have to suggest sexual inequality exists in American culture?

READING 10

Baseball Magic

GEORGE GMELCH

On each pitching day for the first three months of a winning season, Dennis Grossini, a pitcher on a Detroit Tiger farm team, arose from bed at exactly 10:00 A.M. At 1:00 P.M. he went to the nearest restaurant for two glasses of iced tea and a tuna fish sandwich. When he got to the ballpark at 3:00 P.M., he put on the sweatshirt and jock he wore during his last winning game; one hour before the game he chewed a wad of Beech-Nut chewing tobacco. After each pitch during the game he touched the letters on his uniform and straightened his cap after each ball. Before the start of each inning he replaced the pitcher's rosin bag next to the spot where it was the inning before. And after every inning in which he gave up a run, he washed his hands.

When I asked which part of his ritual was most important, he said, "You can't really tell what's most important so it all becomes important. I'd be afraid to change anything. As long as I'm winning, I do everything the same."

Trobriand Islanders, according to anthropologist Bronislaw Malinowski, felt the same way about their fishing magic. Trobrianders fished in two different settings: in the *inner lagoon* where fish were plentiful and there was little danger, and on the *open sea* where fishing was dangerous and yields varied widely. Malinowski found that magic was not used in lagoon fishing, where men could rely solely on their knowledge and skill. But when fishing on the open sea, Trobrianders used a great deal of magical ritual to ensure safety and increase their catch.

Baseball, America's national pastime, is an arena in which players behave remarkably like Malinowski's Trobriand fishermen. To professional ballplayers, baseball is more than just a game, it is an occupation. Since their livelihoods depend on how well they perform, many use magic in an attempt to control the chance that is built into baseball. There are three essential activities of the game—pitching, hitting, and fielding. In the first two, chance can play a surprisingly important role. The pitcher is the player least able to control the outcome of his efforts. He may feel great and have good stuff warming up in the bullpen and then get in the game and get clobbered. He may make a bad pitch and see the batter miss it for a strike or see it hit hard but right into the hands of a fielder for an out. Conversely, his best pitch may be blooped for a base hit. He may limit the opposing team to just a few hits yet lose the game, and he may give up many hits and win. And the good and bad luck don't always average out over the course of a season. For instance, this past season (2007) Matt Cain gave up fewer runs per game than his teammate Noah Lowry but only won 7 games while losing 16 while Lowry won 14 games and only lost 8. Both pitched for the same team—the San Francisco Giants—which meant they had the same fielders behind them. By chance, when Cain pitched the Giants scored few runs while his teammate Lowry enjoyed considerable run support. Regardless of how well a pitcher performs, the outcome of the game also depends upon the proficiency of his teammates, the ineptitude of the opposition, and luck.

Hitting, which many observers call the single most difficult task in the world of sports, is also full of uncertainty. Unless it's a home run, no matter how hard the batter hits the ball, fate determines whether it will go into a waiting glove or find a gap between the fielders. The uncertainty is compounded by the low success rate of hitting: the average hitter gets only one hit in every four trips to the plate, while the very best hitters average only one hit in every three trips. Fielding, which we will return to later, is the one part of baseball where chance does not play much of a role.

How does the risk and uncertainty in pitching and hitting affect players? How do they try to control the outcomes of their performance? These are questions that I first became interested in many years ago both as a ballplayer and as an anthropology student. I had devoted much of my youth to baseball, and played professionally as a first baseman in the Detroit Tiger organization in the 1960s. It was shortly after the end of one baseball season that I took an anthropology course called "Magic, Religion, and Witchcraft." As I listened to my professor describe the magical rituals of the Trobriand Islanders, it occurred to me that what these so-called "primitive" people did wasn't all that different from what my teammates and I did for luck and confidence at the ballpark.

Routines and Rituals

The most common way players attempt to reduce chance and their feelings of uncertainty is to develop a routine—a course of action which is regularly followed. Talking about the routines of ballplayers, Pittsburgh Pirates coach Rich Donnelly said:

> They're like trained animals. They come out here [ballpark] and everything has to be the same, they don't like anything that knocks them off their routine. Just look at the dugout and you'll see every guy sitting in the same spot every night. It's amazing, everybody in the same spot. And don't you dare take someone's seat. If a guy comes up from the minors and sits here, they'll say, 'Hey, Jim sits here, find another seat.' You watch the pitcher warm up and he'll do the same thing every time. . . . You got a routine and you adhere to it and you don't want anybody knocking you off it.

Routines are comforting, they bring order into a world in which players have little control. The varied elements in routines can produce the tangible benefit of helping the player concentrate. All ballplayers know that it is difficult to think and hit at the same time, and that following a routine can keep them from thinking too much. But often what players do goes beyond mere routine. These actions become what anthropologists define as *ritual*—prescribed behaviors in which there is no empirical connection between the means (e.g., tapping home plate three times) and the desired end (e.g., getting a base hit). Because there is no real connection between the two, rituals are not rational. Sometimes they are quite irrational. Similar to rituals are the nonrational beliefs that form the basis of taboos and fetishes, which players also use to bring luck to their side. But first let's take a close look at rituals.

Baseball rituals are infinitely varied. Most are personal, and are performed by individuals rather than by a team or group. Most are done in a private and unemotional manner, in much the same way players apply pine tar and rosin to their bats to improve the grip. A ballplayer may ritualize any activity that he considers important or somehow linked to good performance. Recall the variety of things that Dennis Grossini does, from specific times for waking and eating to foods and dress. Many pitchers listen to the same song on their ipods on the day they are scheduled to start. Pitcher Al Holland always played with two dollar bills in his back pocket. The Oriole's Glenn Davis used to chew the same gum every day during hitting streaks, saving it under his cap. Astros infielder Julio Gotay always played with a cheese sandwich in his back pocket (he had a big appetite, so there might also have been a measure of practicality here). Red Sox Wade Boggs ate chicken before every game during his career, and that was just one of many elements in his pre- and post game routine, which also included leaving his house for the ballpark at precisely the same time each day (1:47 for a night game), running wind sprints at 7:17 for a 7:35 start, and drawing a chai—the Hebrew symbol for life—upon entering the batter's box.

Many hitters go through a series of preparatory rituals before stepping into the batter's box. These include tugging on their caps, touching their uniform letters or medallions, crossing themselves, and swinging, tapping, or bouncing the bat on the plate a prescribed number of times. Consider the Dodger's Nomar Garciaparra. After each pitch he steps out of the batters box, kicks the dirt with each toe, adjusts his right batting glove, adjusts his left batting glove, and touches his helmet before getting back into the box. He insists that it is a routine, not superstition. "I'm just doing it to get everything tight. I like everything tight, that's all it is, really." Mike Hargrove, former Cleveland Indian first baseman, had so many time-consuming elements in his batting ritual that he was nicknamed "the human rain delay." Both players believe their batting rituals helped them regain their concentration after each pitch. But others wondered if the two had become prisoners of their elaborate superstitions.

Players who have too many or particularly bizarre rituals risk being labeled as flakes, and not just by teammates but by fans and the media as well. For example, ex-Mets pitcher Turk Wendell's eccentric rituals, which include chewing black licorice while pitching, only to spit it out, brush his teeth and reload the candy between innings, and wearing a necklace of teeth from animals he has killed, made him a cover story subject in the *New York Times Sunday Magazine*.

Baseball fans observe a lot of this ritual behavior, such as pitchers smoothing the dirt on the mound before each new batter and position players tagging a base when leaving and returning to the dugout between innings, never realizing its importance to the player. The one ritual many fans do recognize, largely because it's a favorite of TV cameramen, is the "rally cap"—players in the dugout folding their caps and wearing them bill up in hopes of sparking a rally.

Rituals grow out of exceptionally good performances. When a player does well, he seldom attributes his success to skill alone; he knows that his skills don't change much from day to day. So, then, what was different about today which can explain his three hits? He makes a correlation. That is, he attributes his success, in part, to an object, a food he ate, not having shaved, a new shirt he bought that day, or just about any behavior out of the ordinary. By repeating those behaviors, the player seeks to gain control over his performance, to bring more good luck. Outfielder John White explained how one of his rituals started:

> I was jogging out to centerfield after the national anthem when I picked up a scrap of paper. I got some good hits that night and I guess I decided that the paper had something to do with it. The next night I picked up a gum wrapper and had another good night at the plate. . . . I've been picking up paper every night since.

When outfielder Ron Wright played for the Calgary Cannons he shaved his arms once a week It all began two years before when after an injury he shaved his arm so it could be taped, and then hit three homers. Now he not only has one of the smoothest swings in the minor leagues, but two of the smoothest forearms. Wade Boggs' routine of eating chicken before every game began when he was a rookie in 1982 and noticed a correlation between multiple-hit games and poultry plates (his wife has 40 chicken recipes). One of Montreal Expo farmhand Mike Saccocio's rituals also concerned food: "I got three hits one night after eating at Long John Silver's. After that when we'd pull into town, my first question would be, "Do you have a Long John Silver's?" Unlike Boggs, Saccocio abandoned his ritual and looked for a new one when he stopped hitting well.

During one game New York Yankee manager Joe Torre stood on the dugout steps instead of sitting on the bench when his team was batting. The Yankees scored a few runs, so he decided to keep on doing it. As the Yankees won nine games in a row, Torre kept standing. Torre explained, "I have a little routine going now. . . . As long as we score, I'll be doing the same thing."

When in a slump, most players make a deliberate effort to change their routines and rituals in an attempt to shake off their bad luck. One player tried taking different routes to the ballpark, another tried sitting in a different place in the dugout, another shaved his head, and several reported changing what they ate before the game. I had one manager who would rattle the bat bin when the team was not hitting well, as if the bats were in a stupor and could be aroused by a good shaking. Some of my teammates rubbed their hands along the handles of the bats protruding from the bat bin in hopes of picking up some luck from the bats of others. Diamondbacks left fielder Luis Gonzalez sometimes places his bats in the room where Baseball Chapel—a Sunday church service—is about to get underway. Gonzales hopes his bats will get some benefit, though he doesn't usually attend the service himself.

Taboo

Taboos (the word comes from a Polynesian term meaning prohibition) are the opposite of rituals. These are things you shouldn't do. Breaking a taboo, players believe, leads to undesirable consequences or bad luck. Most players observe at least a few taboos, such as never stepping on the chalk foul lines. A few, like Nomar Gar-ciaparra, leap over the entire base path. One teammate of mine would never watch a movie on a game day, despite our playing virtually every day from April to September. Another teammate refused to read anything before a game because he believed it weakened his batting eye.

Many taboos take place off the field, out of public view. On the day a pitcher is scheduled to start, he is likely to avoid activities he believes will sap his strength and detract from his effectiveness. On the day they are to start, some pitchers avoid shaving, eating certain foods and even having sex (this nostrum is probably based on an 18th century belief about preserving vital body fluids, but experts now agree there is no ill effect and there may actually be a small benefit).

Taboos usually grow out of exceptionally poor performances, which players attribute to a particular behavior. During my first season of pro ball I ate pancakes before a game in which I struck out three times. A few weeks later I had another terrible game, again after eating pancakes. The result was a pancake taboo: I never again ate pancakes during the season. (Conversely, Orioles pitcher Jim Palmer, after some success, insisted on eating pancakes before each of his starts).

While most taboos are idiosyncratic, there are a few that all ballplayers hold and that do not develop out of individual experience or misfortune. These form part of the culture of baseball, and are sometimes learned as early as Little League. Mentioning a no-hitter while one is in progress is a well-known example. The origins of such shared beliefs are lost in time, though some scholars have proposed theories. For example, the taboo against stepping on the chalk foul lines when running onto or off the field between innings, suggests National Baseball Hall of Fame research director Tim Wiles may be rooted in the children's superstition, "step on a crack, break your mother's back."

Fetishes

Fetishes are charms, material objects believed to embody supernatural power that can aid or protect the owner. Good-luck charms are standard equipment for some ballplayers. These include a wide assortment of objects from coins, chains, and crucifixes to a favorite baseball hat. The fetishized object may be a new possession or something a player found that coincided with the start of a streak and which he holds responsible for his good fortune. While playing in the Pacific Coast League, Alan Foster forgot his baseball shoes on a road trip and borrowed a pair from a teammate. That night he pitched a no-hitter, which he attributed to the shoes. Afterwards he bought them from his teammate and they became a fetish. Expo farmhand Mark LaRosa's rock has a different origin and use:

> I found it on the field in Elmira after I had gotten bombed. It's unusual, perfectly round, and it caught my attention. I keep it to remind me of how important it is to concentrate. When I am going well I look at the rock and remember to keep my focus. The rock reminds me of what can happen when I lose my concentration.

For one season Marge Schott, former owner of the Cincinnati Reds, insisted that her field manager rub her St. Bernard "Schotzie" for good luck before each game. When the Reds were on the road, Schott would sometimes send a bag of the dog's hair to the field manager's hotel room. Religious medallions, which many Latino players wear around their necks and sometimes touch before going to the plate or mound, are also fetishes, though tied to their Roman Catholicism. (Also relating to their religion, some players some make the sign of the cross or bless themselves before every at bat (a few like Pudge Rodriguez do so before every pitch), and a few point or blow a kiss to the heavens after hitting a home run.

Some players regard certain uniform numbers as lucky. When Ricky Henderson came to the Blue Jays in 1993, he paid teammate Turner Ward $25,000 for the right to wear number 24. Don Sutton got off cheaper. When he joined the Dodgers he convinced teammate Bruce Boche to give up number 20 in exchange for a new set of golf clubs. Oddly enough, there is no consensus about the effect of wearing number 13. Some players shun it, while a few request it. When Jason Giambi arrived with the Oakland A's his favorite number 7 was already taken, so he settled for 16 (the two numbers add up to 7). When he signed with the Yankees, number 7 (Mickey Mantle's old number) was retired and 16 was taken, so he settled for 25 (again, the numbers add up to 7).

Number preferences emerge in different ways. A young player may request the number of a former star, sometimes hoping that it will bring him the same success. Or he may request a number he associates with good luck. Colorado Rockies' Larry Walker's fixation with the number 3 has become well known to baseball fans. Besides wearing 33, he takes three practice swings before stepping into the box, he showers from the third nozzle, sets his alarm for three minutes past the hour and he was wed on November 3 at 3:33 P.M.[1] Fans in ballparks all across America rise from their seats for the seventh- inning stretch before the home club comes to bat because the number 7 is lucky, although the specific origin of this tradition has been lost.[2]

Clothing, both the choice and the order in which it is put on, combine elements of both ritual and fetish. Some players put on the part of their uniform in a particular order. Expos farmhand Jim Austin always puts on his left sleeve, left pants leg, and left shoe before the right. Most players, however, single out one or two lucky articles or quirks of dress for ritual elaboration. After hitting two home runs in a game, for example, ex-Giant infielder Jim Davenport discovered that he had missed a buttonhole while dressing for the game. For the remainder of his career he left the same button undone. Phillies' Len Dykstra would discard his batting gloves if he failed to get a hit in a single at-bat. In a hitless game, he might go through four pair of gloves. For outfielder Brian Hunter the focus is shoes: "I have a pair of high tops and a pair of low tops. Whichever shoes don't get a hit that game, I switch to the other pair." At the time of our interview, he was struggling at the plate and switching shoes almost every day. For Birmingham Baron pitcher Bo Kennedy the arrangement of the different pairs of baseball shoes in his locker is critical:

> I tell the clubbies [clubhouse boys] when you hang stuff in my locker don't touch my shoes. If you bump them move them back. I want the Ponys in front, the turfs to the right, and I want them nice and neat with each pair touching each other. . . . Everyone on the team knows not to mess with my shoes when I pitch.

During hitting or winning streaks players may wear the same clothes day after day. Once I changed sweatshirts midway through the game for seven consecutive nights to keep a hitting streak going. Clothing rituals, however, can become impractical. Catcher Matt Allen was wearing a long sleeve turtle neck shirt on a cool evening in the New York-Penn League when he had a three-hit game. "I kept wearing the shirt and had a good week," he explained. "Then the weather got hot as hell, 85 degrees and muggy, but I would not take that shirt off. I wore it for another ten days—catching—and people thought I was crazy." Former Phillies, Expos, Twins, and Perhaps taking a ritual to the extreme, Leo Durocher, managing the Brooklyn Dodgers to a pennant in 1941, spent three and a half weeks in the same gray slacks, blue coat, and knitted blue tie. Losing streaks often produce the opposite effect, such as the Oakland A's players who went out and bought new street clothes after losing 14 in a row.

Former Oakland A's manager Art Howe often wouldn't wash his socks after the A's were victorious; and he would also write the line up card with the same pen, and tape the pregame radio show in the same place on the field. In the words of one veteran, "It all comes down to the philosophy of not messing with success—or deliberately messing with failure."

Baseball's superstitions, like most everything else, change over time. Many of the rituals and beliefs of early baseball are no longer observed. In the 1920s-30s sportswriters reported that a player who tripped en route to the field would often retrace his steps and carefully walk over the stumbling block for "insurance." A century ago players spent time on and off the field intently looking for items that would bring them luck. To find a hairpin on the street, for example, assured a batter of hitting safely in that day's game. A few managers were known to strategically place a hairpin on the ground where a slumping player would be sure to find it. Today few women wear hairpins—a good reason the belief has died out. In the same era, Philadelphia Athletics manager Connie Mack hoped to ward off bad luck by employing a hunchback as a mascot. Hall of Famer Ty Cobb took on a young black boy as a good luck charm, even taking him on the road during the 1908 season. It was a not uncommon then for players to rub the head of a black child for good luck.

To catch sight of a white horse or a wagon-load of barrels were also good omens. In 1904 the manager of the New York Giants, John McGraw, hired a driver with a team of white horses to drive past the Polo Grounds around the time his players were arriving at the ballpark. He knew that if his players saw white horses, they would have more confidence and that could only help them during the game. Belief in the power of white horses survived in a few backwaters until the 1960s. A gray-haired manager of a team I played for in Drummondville, Quebec, would drive around the countryside before important games and during the playoffs looking for a white horse. When he was successful, he would announce it to everyone in the clubhouse.

One belief that appears to have died out recently is a taboo about crossed bats. Several of my Latino teammates in the 1960s took it seriously. I can still recall one Dominican player becoming agitated when another player tossed a bat from the batting cage and it landed on top of his bat. He believed that the top bat might steal hits from the lower one. In his view, bats contained a finite number of hits. It was once commonly believed that when the hits in a bat were used up no amount of good hitting would produce any more. Hall of Famer Honus Wagner believed each bat contained only 100 hits. Regardless of the quality of the bat, he would discard it after its 100th hit. This belief would have little relevance today, in the era of light bats with thin handles—so thin that the typical modern bat is lucky to survive a dozen hits without being broken.

Other superstitions about bats do survive, however. Position players on the Class A Asheville Tourists would not let pitchers touch or swing their bats, not even to warm up. Poor-hitting players, as most pitchers are, were said to pollute or weaken the bats.

While the elements in many rituals have changed over time, the reliance of players on them has not. Moreover, that reliance seems fairly impervious to advances in education. Way back in the 1890s, in an article I found in the archives of the National Baseball Hall of Fame, one observer predicted that the current influx of better educated players into the game and the "gradual weeding out of bummers and thugs" would raise the intellectual standard of the game and reduce baseball's rampant superstitions. It didn't. I first researched baseball magic in the late 1960s; when I returned 30 years later to study the culture of baseball, I expected to find less superstition. After all, I reasoned, unlike in my playing days most of today's players have had some college. I did find that today's players are less willing to admit to having superstitions, but when I asked instead about their "routines" they described rituals and fetishes little different from my teammates in the 60s.

Uncertainty and Magic

The best evidence that players turn to rituals, taboos, and fetishes to control chance and uncertainty is found in their uneven application. They are associated mainly with pitching and hitting—the activities with the highest degree of chance—and not fielding. I met only one player who had any ritual in connection with fielding, and he was an error-prone shortstop. Unlike hitting and pitching, a fielder has almost complete control over the outcome of his performance. Once a ball has been hit in his direction, no one can intervene and ruin his chances of catching it for an out (except in the unlikely event of two fielders colliding). Compared with the pitcher or the hitter, the fielder has little to worry about. He knows that in better than 9.7 times out of 10 he will execute his task flawlessly. With odds like that there is little need for ritual.

Clearly, the rituals of American ballplayers are not unlike those of the Trobriand Islanders studied by Malinowski many years ago.[3] In professional baseball, fielding is the equivalent of the inner lagoon while hitting and pitching are like the open sea.

While Malinowski helps us understand how ball- players respond to chance and uncertainty, behavioral psychologist B. F. Skinner sheds light on why personal rituals get established in the first place.[4] With a few grains of seed Skinner could get pigeons to do anything he wanted. He merely waited for the desired behavior (e.g. pecking) and then rewarded it with some food. Skinner then decided to see what would happen if pigeons were rewarded with food pellets regularly, every fifteen seconds, regardless of what they did. He found that the birds associate the arrival of the food with a particular action, such as tucking their head under a wing or walking in clockwise circles. About ten seconds after the arrival of the last pellet, a bird would begin doing whatever it associated with getting the food and keep doing it until the next pellet arrived. In short, the pigeons behaved as if their actions made the food appear. They learned to associate particular behaviors with the reward of being given seed.

Ballplayers also associate a reward—successful performance—with prior behavior. If a player touches his crucifix and then gets a hit, he may decide the gesture was responsible for his good fortune and touch his crucifix the next time he comes to the plate. Unlike pigeons, however, most ballplayers are quicker to change their rituals once they no longer seem to work. Skinner found that once a pigeon associated one of its actions with the arrival of food or water, only sporadic rewards were necessary to keep the ritual going. One pigeon, believing that hopping from side to side brought pellets into its feeding cup, hopped ten thousand times without a pellet before finally giving up. But, then, Wade Boggs ate chicken before every game, through slumps and good times, for seventeen years.

Obviously the rituals and superstitions of baseball do not make a pitch travel faster or a batted ball find the gaps between the fielders, nor do the Trobriand rituals calm the seas or bring fish. What both do, however, is give their practitioners a sense of control, and with that added confidence. And we all know how important that is. If you really believe eating chicken or hopping over the foul lines will make you a better hitter, it probably will.

Bibliography

Gmelch, G. *Inside Pitch: Life in Professional Baseball* (*Smithsonian Institution Press,* 2001)

Malinowski, B. *Magic, Science and Religion and Other Essays* (Glencoe, III., 1948).

Skinner, B. F. *Behavior of Organisms: An Experimental Analysis* (D. Appleton-Century Co., 1938).

Skinner, B. F. *Science and Human Behavior* (New York: Macmillan, 1953).

Torrez, D. *High Inside: Memoirs of a Baseball Wife.* (New York: G. P. Putnam's Sons, 1983.)

Notes

1. Sports Illustrated. . . . , 48
2. Allen, The Superstitions of Baseball Players," 104.
3. Malinowski, B. *Magic, Science and Religion and Other Essays.*
4. Skinner, B. F. B*ehavior of Organisms: An Experimental Analysis.*
   Skinner, B. F. *Science and Human Behavior.*

Question Set

1. Why do certain sports and other activities like deep-sea fishing rely so heavily on magic?
2. Pertaining to your own life, identify what you see as a fetish, taboo, and a ritual.
3. How does George Gmelch demonstrate that American culture is not quite as scientific and rational as Americans would like to think?

READING 11

Tourism and Conservation: Kachikally Sacred Crocodile Pool in the Gambia, West Africa

ABIGAIL MEATYARD, BILL ROBERTS, AND OUSMAN BOJANG

Africa. The word invokes powerful images about a continent that is the ancestral home for us all. Storytelling is an ancient tradition among Africans. Stories entertain, educate and encapsulate part of the African spirit. In that same spirit, three distinct voices and perspectives (two American and one African) collaborate here to tell a story about a sacred place that has slowly transformed into a tourist attraction.

The following story of Kachikally Sacred Crocodile pool is based on St. Mary's College alumnus Abby Meatyard's 2004 Gambia summer field research. Abby spent seven weeks learning about crocodiles and their conservation. Much of her work was with Ousman Bojang, the head of the Bojang family *(kabila)* in Bakau Old Town, and the caretaker of Kachikally. Abby focused her research on Kachikally's history and what the surrounding community members think of this increasingly popular tourist attraction. Her 2004 research became the basis for her senior thesis and a presentation at the 2005 SfAA meetings in Albuquerque.

As her professor, I [Bill] worked with Abby during the field school and advised her as she wrote her thesis. After the SfAA meetings I encouraged her to submit this contribution to *PA*. When I returned to the Gambia in July to teach a summer course at the university, I shared Abby's work with Ousman Bojang. I have included his comments on Abby's paper as well as any additional insights he shared about tourism at Kachikally or in Gambia.

The Place

Bakau Old Town is a fishing village that has been absorbed by the growing urban conglomeration known as the Greater Banjul Area. Bakau lies entirely within the government designated Tourism Development Zone that runs along the coast of the country's south bank, and Kachikally is one of the tourist features in the community. Kachikally is a 12-acre oasis for both Gambian wildlife and culture, nestled among hundreds of compounds, open sewers, and dirt roads. The pool is believed to bring fertility to barren women and heal the sick.

According to Ousman Bojang, the pool is blessed by the spirit Kachikally who, 500 years ago when the Bojang ancestors first settled in the area, appeared to the family as an elderly woman asking for assistance in rescuing her child from the pool. After the family helped her, she revealed to them that she was actually a spirit who lived in the woods surrounding the pool. She had tested the family to see whether they deserved custodianship over the pool and its healing powers. She told them that they had passed her test and that the family would forever be responsible for the care of this sacred area. She also told them to find an animal to live in the pool. During a fishing trip, the Bojangs caught two small crocodiles and Kachikally gave permission to put them in the pool where they would reside.

The sacred pool is widely known for its healing powers and as a place where people pray for blessings. Kachikally is best known as a place of last resort for barren women who wish to conceive, although many others with chronic ailments or misfortunes come to Kachikally. The supplicant brings kola nuts and other small offerings for the Bojang family. The Bojang women then wash the misfortunate person with water from the natural spring. In the case of a barren woman, once she has been washed she is told to keep faithful to her husband and not "shake hands with another man" for a year [this is a Gambian euphemism warning the woman not to commit adultery]. Faithfulness and prayer over the next year will bring forth a child. After giving birth, the woman brings the child to Kachikally where it is washed to ensure its safety.

Ousman Bojang claimed that approximately 40–60 women had come to the pool during the first six months of 2004. When Abby asked about how many women had been successful, Bojang gave her a funny look and said "All of them [will be] successful." Skeptical, she asked other community members if this was true. No one disagreed with Bojang's statement. Many stated that they personally knew someone who had bathed in the pool, and all now had children. Abby was told that women from all over The Gambia and West Africa, and even some Westerners, come to Kachikally with hopes to be healed.

Oral History

Traditionally, the eldest son of the Bojang family gains custodianship over the pool when the father dies. Ousman Bojang, not the oldest in his family, moved away from the Bakau area and the family legacy in the 1950s when he joined the police force. He spent the next 20 years assigned to various Gambian rural villages and towns. By the 1970s, the pool's condition had deteriorated from neglect.

One night in 1978 Ousman awakened from a terrible dream. In his dream he had returned home and discovered that both the pool and the spirit Kachikally were gone. Bojang was so shaken from the dream that he returned home on his next leave and discovered his dream had almost come true. The pool was being used as a watering hole for cattle, and none of the resident crocodiles had been seen for many years. He confronted his brothers and told them that if they did not have the heart to maintain their family's legacy, then he would. He subsequently quit the police force and returned to Bakau.

Bojang began his resurrection of the pool by installing a fence around the property to keep the cattle out. He wrote many letters to then Gambian President Jawara's office asking for support. The President's office finally gave him money and materials to build a wall around the spring-fed pool. Bakau community members assisted him with the work. When they finally removed enough of the sediment that was blocking the flow of the natural spring, two crocodiles emerged. Community members cheered that Kachikally had returned to the pool.

The Bojang family resumed fishing to assure an adequate food supply for the crocodiles. By 1982, the pool contained 6 adult and 12 baby crocodiles. As the crocodiles became habituated to their caretakers, they began to let the family members touch them. One particularly tame crocodile was given the name "Charlie." As word of a tame crocodile spread, tourists began to take notice. The Bojang family, who needed ever more resources for the pool's upkeep, began charging admission. As the popularity of the pool grew and more tourists came, the Bojangs were able to reduce their fishing activities and live on the tourist money they collected. By 2004, the entrance fee was just under $1 U.S. Non-African tourists pay a fee; Gambians and other Africans are free to visit the sacred pool and seek its blessings.

In 2004, with the help of the curator from the Gambia National Museum, the Bojangs invested some tourism earnings to build a modest ethnographic museum. Visitors can view Gambian ethnic exhibits on medicinal plants and healing practices, musical instruments, traditional dress, tools and weapons. When asked about future innovations, Bojang stated that he wants to build a facility where visitors can buy food and drinks while they sit and watch the crocodiles.

Tourism in The Gambia

Scandinavian tourists "discovered" Gambia in 1966. Nearly 40 years later, tourism is one of the most important foreign exchange earners for Gambia, and many jobs in the formal and informal sectors are linked to the annual rhythm of tourist arrivals. The largest numbers of tourists come to Gambia between November and April, when the Gambian climate and beaches are at their best, to enjoy the sun, sand and sea. Over the past decade, the Gambian government, in collaboration with tourism sector actors, has successfully diversified attractions that now include ecotourism, heritage tourism, cultural festival tourism and educational tourism.

An example of heritage and cultural festival tourism is the biennial International Roots Festival. Every other year, Gambia hosts this festival in an attempt to reach out to members of the African diaspora in Europe and the U.S.A. and bring them back where they can reconnect with their ancestral homeland. In the 2004 Roots Festival brochure, Kachikally Sacred Crocodile Pool was recommended as the fifth "MUST SEE" attraction in the country, along with the country's oldest nature reserve at Abuko.

Tourists come to Kachikally to see these special crocodiles. Bojang explains that the crocodiles, like the spirit Kachikally, are peaceful. This peacefulness reflects on everything it touches, the Bojang family, the Bakau Old Town community, and the crocodiles. For example, when it comes time for the annual removal of sediment from the pool, Ousman Bojang wades into the pool and asks the spirit for permission to proceed with the work. He then asks all the crocodiles to leave the pool and rest in the surrounding forest. Skeptical again, Abby asked other community members about this claim. People who have helped the Bojangs with the annual cleaning confirmed this as true. Further, every rainy season when the pool overflows and some of the crocodiles wander into someone's home compound in Bakau, they simply call the Bojangs who come and tie a rope onto the crocodile and walk it back to the pool.

Changing Community Attitudes

Abby spent several weeks conducting participant observation at the pool. One of the most frequent groups of visitors to the pool she encountered during the summer of 2004 was Gambian school children on a fieldtrip. They toured the museum, visited the pool, and then walked through the surrounding forest. There was always a great deal of nervous giggling and excitement when it came time to pet Charlie. Whether the visitor was African or European, Charlie represented a test of "faith" for those brave enough to reach out and touch him.

In order to understand how Bakau community members felt about Kachikally, Abby conducted group and individual interviews of other Bojang family members, and groups of young men and women. She wanted people to be comfortable answering her questions, and so let the groups set their own pace when answering. In each case, she began by asking the group or individual a simple, open-ended question. "Why do you believe Kachikally Sacred Crocodile Pool is important?"

The responses she received to this question were more diverse than any answer to other questions she subsequently asked. Depending on the age of the person interviewed, the two most common answers were either that the pool was important because of its sacredness and its ability to heal people, or because it brought so many people and tourists to the area. This difference was even expressed among Bojang family members. The elderly women and Ousman Bojang responded that the pool's importance is due to its sacred spirituality. The younger Bojangs answered that crocodiles and tourist income were the most important features of the pool.

The surprise of such different responses by Bojang family members was also expressed in their versions of the pool's history. Every Bojang elder knew the details of the pool's history, while the younger women began their version with a description of when the crocodiles were placed in the pool. During individual interviews with people who had set up souvenir shops near the entrance to Kachikally, the importance of the income they earned from tourists was an unmistakable part of their answers. A few people responded that they believed Kachikally was important because it protected Gambian wildlife that was threatened by habitat destruction and development. In addition to the crocodiles, people can see many bird species and sometimes even monkeys in the area.

Another important question Abby asked her informants was whether they had any concerns about the future of the pool. What did the community think about the development that had occurred since Ousman Bojang assumed responsibility for the pool in the 1970s?

Responses were mixed. Among the positive changes, people pointed to the ethnographic museum that provides the community and tourists a window on traditional Gambian culture. Everybody concurred that Kachikally remains an important part of their local culture, and that it is important for people to maintain the pool as a way of preserving cultural traditions and lifeways.

One concern people spoke about was the attention given to tourists and the money they spent at the pool. Some said the pool was losing its sacredness, and they believed that the spirit had already left the pool. As proof of this, they pointed out that the water lilies associated with Kachikally's spirit were only visible during part of the year. During the dry season the pool was covered with a layer of green slime. They said that when you pray these days, prayers are not answered as often. They also mentioned that at one time a white crocodile could be seen at the pool. Whenever somebody saw the white crocodile after offering a prayer, then the prayer would come true. They explained that the white crocodile was actually the spirit of Kachikally. But since no one had seen the white crocodile in many years, some community members think she has left the pool. When asked what could be done to bring back the spirit, they suggested that if tourist money was not such an important issue to the family, the spirit might return.

Final Thoughts

Kachikally Sacred Crocodile Pool offers us a view of the struggle between spirituality and the economics of cultural commodification in the modern world. The Bojang family in essence is sharing part of their family and community's heritage with outsiders for a price. Locals who are left out of the economic gain seem concerned about the diminishing sacredness of the area. Similar struggles are likely taking place around the world, as tourism continues to expand and be associated with both positive and negative changes. Kachikally has become, in effect, something of a small conservatory for part of The Gambia's biological and cultural diversity.

Abby's work with Ousman Bojang prompted his decision to ceremonially "adopt," and incorporate all the St. Mary's students from the 2004 field school, into his family. The naming ceremony symbolized a link to future cohorts from the college and all the resources educational tourism could potentially bring the Bojangs. Ousman's emerging problem with the community is whether, or how, he can share the benefits of his success with his neighbors. This is still being worked out. But now, working with me and others from the college, we are talking about and imagining a Kachikally Crocodile and Culture Conservatory where students interested in biology, culture, ecology, and history can come study the ecosystem of a place filled with stories, crocodiles and spirits.

Ousman Bojang's Response

Ousman Bojang leaned back on the cement bench as I finished reading the paper. "That's important," he said, "that's very important." His eldest son, Doudou, next in line to take care of the sacred pool, turned his attention back to the camera I'd given him so he could take a picture of Ousman and me.

"I want to clarify a couple of things," said Ousman. "First, about that white crocodile. Now, all the crocodiles dig holes, sometimes deep in the ground, where they spend up to 40 days. Some of the crocs have dug holes into this layer of white clay, and after they come out of their hole, the sun dries this white clay on them. So that's how this idea of a white crocodile came about—there's no white crocodile. In fact, there's no real connection between the crocodiles and the spirituality of the pool."

Ousman and Doudou both agreed that there is a growing feeling of jealousy among some people in Bakau about the income the family earns from the pool. "But most of the money from the pool goes back into maintaining the pool and the crocodiles," he said. "I also give donations to the Bakau health center, the Bakau Lower Basic School, the Bakau mosque and the Catholic church in Bakau. Not money, but gifts in kind, depending on what the people who run these facilities for the community tell me they need."

"This is what I do," he said, and then stood up to walk me out. As we walked out, I noticed his limp, and the ankle and foot on his left leg looked swollen. "Oh yes, I couldn't walk for about three months. But then I began to treat myself with the *Never Die* tree. Do you know that tree?" He pointed out a *Never Die* tree in a nearby compound. "Everything is good on that tree; the leaves, the seeds, the root and bark—it's all good medicine."

"Abby did good work, and you've done good work, I hope the people who read this will come for a visit. And I hope they will all realize how important it is to try and understand one another, and work for a peaceful world. Without peace, we can have nothing."

We stopped and clasped one another's left hand. This is the handshake that symbolizes our hopes to see one another again. Then he turned, and headed back towards the pool that he has so carefully tended for so many years.

[Acknowledgements: Many thanks to the members of the Bojang extended family and other Bakau residents who patiently helped Abby and other students with their research. Thanks also to members of the Meatyard family and anthropologist Dan Ingersoll for their support.]

Abigail Meatyard *graduated from St. Mary's College of Maryland in 2005. Her degree is in anthropology with a concentration in environmental studies. She plans to return to The Gambia to continue her research on Kachikally as part of a long term study. She can be reached via email at <ammeatyard@smcm.edu>.*

Bill Roberts *is an applied anthropologist at St. Mary's College of Maryland and co-editor of* Practicing Anthropology. *He began the Gambia Field Study Program in 1996, and will take the next cohort of students into the field in 2006. For the last three summers, he has taught research methods at the University of The Gambia. Students, faculty or practitioners who want to get involved with the Gambia project should contact Bill at <wcroberts@smcm.edu>.*

Ousman Bojang *is the well-recognized and respected head of the Bakau Old Town Bojang family. A retired policeman, he is the caretaker of the crocodile pool, and part-time farmer and fisherman. Ousman prays every day for peace, prosperity, mutual understanding, and cooperation. He can be contacted at <kachimuseum@yahoo.com>.*

Tourism and Conservation: Kachikally Sacred Crocodile Pool in the Gambia, West Africa

1. How is the work described in this article an example of applied anthropology?
2. How does the sacred crocodile pool provide some evidence of the tension that exists between spirituality and economics?
3. What evidence does Abby offer to suggest that the people believe the pool is sacred?
4. What impact does tourism have on traditional communities?

READING 12

Teetering Towards Economic Sustainability: Alternatives for Commercial Fishermen

BARBARA JONES

Sustainable fishing has become a challenging problem for commercial fishermen all over the world. Many efforts to pursue a livelihood based on commercially harvesting fish suffer from catch limits and closings intended to protect diminishing fish resources; rising prices for waterfront real estate that currently houses their home ports; and competition from recreational fishermen. In order to continue a commercial fishing way of life, fishermen are resorting to what they are told represent economic sustainable alternatives to fishing, including aquaculture, retail markets, educational/museum facilities, restaurants, and parks. Yet, can a fisherman remain a fisherman if he is seen as an 'artist in residence' in an educational facility or a farmer tending his tilapia? Are these truly economically sustainable alternatives to fishing or merely ways of maintaining a visceral connection to our maritime heritage and as such offer little to the fishermen in terms of maintaining their way of life? This paper explores a case study with fishermen in Belford, New Jersey, and suggests fisherman can be willing to become part of a new vision for the area and how some are surprisingly comfortable with the creation of an educational/museum facility as a way to keep fishing in Belford.

This article is about how natural resource users, in this case fishermen, might address changing economic and ecological conditions with their culture and dignity still intact. As a way to protect and promote their culturally and environmentally meaningful spaces before these unique settings disappear, communities throughout the world are creating cultural tourism (Brassiuer 2005; Duggan 1990), agrotourism (Busby and Rendle 2000) and ethical ecotourism (Wearing, Archer, and Jackson 2003) partnerships. These experience-driven tourism partnerships tend to encourage a sense of environmental and social responsibility because they place the visitor's experiences in a socio-cultural context, thus potentially promoting the preservation and protection of unique cultural, as well as ecological landscapes. Natural resource-dependent communities that rely on resource extraction like forestry, commercial fishing or agriculture are faced with the need to consider such alternative strategies for resource management as they struggle to redefine themselves for the 21st century.

Commercial fishing is a resource-dependent industry that operates within an ecosystem with tremendous sociocultural appeal because the industry is water dependent. For many people living in these water-dependent communities near working fish ports, there is the feeling, exemplified by one fisherman, that "it is important to protect the cultural heritage of the waterfronts *and* [at the same time] to make a living doing it." Recognizing the multiplier effect that commercial fishing has on local economies, it becomes clear that communities feel great pressures to develop alternative sources of income for commercial fishermen.

These alternative livelihoods should not be confused with a "complete switch from one livelihood activity to another, but the ability to adopt multiple alternatives and options" (Howard 2003:22). This notion of economic alternatives has always existed for inshore commercial fishermen who make their living following a seasonal rotation. This seasonal rotation has been called a variety of things, but is commonly understood as following the cycle or following the bay (Harris and Reyes 1991; McCay 1984). Following the bay is an economic strategy that allows fishermen the flexibility to participate in a wide variety of economic activities that include estuarine, agricultural and even non-fishing occupations, often on a seasonal basis. As part of this seasonal pattern of work, fishermen might drive an oil truck or build fences for a construction company in the winter and then return in the spring to catch eels or harvest clams. This seasonal pattern of work has the potential to work well with a cultural tourism model and could become part of what some have proposed as a new paradigm for commercial fishing. This new paradigm mirrors the notion of multiple alternatives in that, while commercial fishing must remain an integral part of any new plan, additional opportunities need to be considered to improve the overall baseline economy of the port (Kavanaugh and Flimlin nd.).

According to Betty Duggan (2005) in her work on cultural heritage tourism, more than half of all US states have cultural or heritage tourism programs and internationally even the most remote places are reconnecting to their cultural heritage and environment to generate dollars from tourism. Brassiuer's (2005) work with public boat building in Louisiana demonstrates the cultural appeal of what he describes as waterborne cultural and eco-tourism, while Roberts' work in the Gambia (Meatyard et al. 2005) indicated that tourism is the top earner of foreign currency for Gambia, and jobs in formal and informal sectors are tied to the tourism's annual rhythm. In an example involving an overt partnership after closure of the cod fishery, the Canadian government encouraged the development of a tourism industry to help provide an alternative livelihood for cod fishermen. As a result, from 1992 to 2002, after spending money on product development, training and advertising to highlight the cultural, historical, and environmental features of Newfoundland and Labrador, the number of tourists to the region increased 40 percent (Howard 2003).

Belford, New Jersey

Belford, a traditional inshore commercial fish port that sits along the Raritan Bay across from New York City in New Jersey, is one of the oldest commercial fish ports on the East coast and is currently facing tremendous pressure to redefine itself. For almost one-hundred years, Belford was the home of a large menhaden fish processing plant and a fleet of purse seiners, as well as the 300 men who worked the 125 pound nets that covered Raritan Bay. Th is way of life ended in the 1980s with the closing of the fish plant and, since then, Belford fishermen have struggled in various ways to continue as commercial fishermen.

As part of an economic feasibility study and conceptual development plan for the Port of Belford, tremendous eff ort has been expended to suggest ways to remake the port following its downward spiral away from the hey day of commercial fishing to the plight of commercial fishermen there today (Louis Berger Group et al. 2008). Not only are fishermen being driven out of fishing because of catch limits and closings, but they can no longer, in many cases, afford to maintain the highly prized waterfront property that supports their way of life. This situation is evidenced in the proliferation of alternatives to the maritime way of life around the US coasts, in the form of museums, aquaculture facilities, retail markets, and open space. These soutions are offered as sustainable alternatives for many fishermen in an effort to help them morph into "artists in residence" in museums and farmers in aquaculture facilities.

Although it might be unusual to imagine commercial fishermen as docents or educators, the possible changes to the Port of Belford include capitalizing on the port's 100-year old commercial fishing tradition through the development of an educational/interactive museum facility that highlights the region's maritime heritage. Its lack of a recreational (head/party boat) fishing presence and because so much of the waterfront in Belford was owned by J. Howard Smith's fish factory, Belford became what Shelly Drummond of the Tuckerton Baymen's Museum in South Jersey; called a "truly preserved area" (Louis Berger Group et al. 2008:26), and as such is well positioned to generate dollars from its unique cultural heritage.

Alternatives to Commercial Fishing: An Education or Museum Facility

Belford fishermen seem particularly fond of the educational/museum alternative because they see themselves growing into an 'artist in residence' position as they move through their life cycle as fishermen. This willingness to accept an alternative to fishing, particularly one that requires fishermen to interact with outsiders and to share their fishing space is, to many who know fishers, truly amazing. The feeling among Belford fishermen, stated by one of their own as "fishermen are an endangered species along the Bayshore" because they are a "cultural icon that is not cherished by the community" displays their wariness about partnering with others.

Commercial fishermen, particularly those operating out of Belford, tend to be very reticent about exposing themselves and their lives to outsiders. These men historically cherished their anonymity and antisocial ways, such that being called a bootlegger or a pirate were considered compliments. One fisherman proudly described how in the old days they had what he called pirate season, in that the men would power dredge for clams with a "rocking chair" instead of hand dredging them as the law required. They also were known to use illegal otter-trawls to drag the bay for fluke and to sell short lobsters. These piratical behaviors were a response to a decline in the number of porgies and menhaden Belford men had relied on in the 1960s and 1970s to make a living (McCay 1984), and an increase in regulations and enforcement agents that the fishermen saw as tools outsiders used to limit their right to fish. Both the decrease in available fish and the increase in regulatory oversight encouraged a tough and edgy reputation to take root.

But, by the late 1990s and early into the 21st century, many Belford fishermen were beginning to realize they needed to be more political, or as one warden put it, "more aware of the need to play the game." A new way of thinking took root in Belford, one that now includes a greater willingness to participate in the political process and to accept some change. This new way of thinking has the potential to integrate the older fishermen, who have more time and are less driven to actually fish, to participate in a process that can protect their interests. To them, an educational/museum tourist driven facility could educate people about the value of fishing to the region and with that the opportunity, as one fisherman said, to stay "in fishing until I can't walk no more".

This need to stay close to fishing and its ability to complement their existing seasonal rotation makes the development of an educational/museum facility an appealing solution to the changes that are going on within commercial fishing. One fisherman, who historically fished out of Belford and now works for a maritime museum in South Jersey, sees his role as an artist in residence and teacher in a very positive way. According to him, "I can relate to people and tell them what fishing is all about". He also sees the potential for educating children to be very valuable because by teaching children about the value of commercial fishing, attitudes in the community might change.

Other waterfront communities are capitalizing on their heritage to create similar museum facilities. In North Carolina, the goal of the Core Sound Waterfowl Museum is to not only provide the local craftsmen with an outlet for their traditional crafts, but to remind the community of the importance and the need to protect the region's natural resources and traditions that make up their coastal way of life. Shelly Drummond believes using Belford fishermen as local experts would be helpful for succession planning, in that the men who mend the fishnets now and still fish could become part of the educational process, such that "their knowledge could provide visitors with a window into the days of factory boats, the railroad, tar pots, and even piracy" (Louis Berger Group et al. 2008:26).

One problem some see with this succession planning is the authenticity of the participants. Chanty singers, men from Virginia and North Carolina who traveled up to New Jersey during the peak years of the factory fishing era and sang as they hauled in the nets for the fish factory boats, are an example of the importance of authenticity. These men who still sing the chanty songs are now between 66 and 84 years old, yet they believe in order to sing the songs you have to be someone who has pulled the nets. William Hudnall, a retired net hauler from the 1930s, says, "there is only one way to keep it genuine. People have asked if we would pass the songs on, and we say no, because if you hadn't actually worked pulling those nets by hand, you couldn't really appreciate what the songs meant and the chanting wouldn't be genuine" (Sherrod 2000). Some admit that in time though, there will have to be a mix-and-match approach in that some singers might learn the songs without ever having experienced life on the water. Will this mix-and-match approach jeopardize their sense of history and how the stories they convey through song are understood and interpreted?

In 2002, the Columbia River Maritime Museum in Astoria, Oregon expanded their forty year old facility to incorporate interactive exhibits into their museum space. Visitors use cutting edge technology, touchable exhibits and interviews to experience what it was like to live and work on the river. They can pilot a tugboat, participate in a Coast Guard rescue or live in Astoria as a salmon fisherman. For museums today, these types of interactive tourist experiences (see MacCannell 1999; Norkura 1993) are essential. Not only do they provide the visitor with the experience, but they engage them in a way of life. Just as farmers incorporate harvest tours and hay wagon rides to their fields, fishermen can encourage people to experience life on the ocean. In Tuckerton, one local clammer, when he is not out clamming, offers boat trips out on the bay. These trips work well with his clamming schedule and they provide him with both an additional source of income and a way to share his intimate knowledge of the bay to visitors.

In addition to a museum, other experience-driven tourist ideas include building an outdoor band shell or auditorium for summer concerts and movies, holding maritime flavored festivals, and encouraging water-based activities like canoeing, kayaking and recreational fishing. For Belford, encouraging an outdoor water sport culture that is associated with canoeing or kayaking has not met with tremendous success. The tendency of these fishermen to distrust outsiders has made the channels and waterways around Belford unattractive to any visitor intent on kayaking or canoeing. One avid kayaker and biker conveyed that a kayak rental on Compton's Creek would be a good way to share the property with the whole community. Currently, he kayaks on Compton's Creek, but he senses that "visitors are not welcome here." Right now there are only a handful of recreational users, but he believes if there "wasn't a feeling that you were trespassing on a fishing enterprise, you would feel more welcome and more recreational paddlers would come." Whether the fishermen want to share the property with the whole community is another challenge when considering alternatives for men who typically operate in a closed and somewhat suspicious fishing environment.

While aquaculture is too much like farming and as such has little appeal to commercial fishermen who like their freedom, the connection between an educational facility and an aquaculture facility should not be overlooked. Watching and learning about fish as they grow through their life cycle in tanks could provide visitors with a connection to both the biology of certain marine species and the need for sustainable alternatives to wild caught fish. There is even the possibility that commercial fishermen could provide some of the live fish that would be grown and maintained in an aquaculture facility. This connection might help make aquaculture seem less like farming and more like something they can incorporate into their cycle of working the bay.

Based on conversations with members of the Belford community and other maritime museums, some combination of a museum/educational facility has the potential to provide, by complementing an existing seasonal rotation, a legitimate alternative to commercial fishing. To the fishermen in Belford a museum/educational facility would not only celebrate the bay, but would also provide "a sense of continuity for those men and women who have worked at Belford and continue to rely on the commercial fish port for their livelihood" (Louis Berger Group et al. 2008:27).

Barbara Jones, Department of Anthropology, Brookdale Community College, docjones920@msn.com

References Cited

Brassiuer, C.R. 2005 Bateau fait a la main: Public boat building and waterborne tourism in Louisiana. *Practicing Anthropology* 27(4):22–26.

Busby, G., and S. Rendle. 2000 The transition from tourism on farms to farm tourism. *Tourist Management* 21(6):635–642.

Duggan, B.J. 1990 "New ways for old: Assessing contributions of the Tennessee Heritage Project," in *Cultural heritage Conservation in the American South.* Edited by B. J. Howell, pp. 54–65. Athens, GA: University of Georgia Press.

Duggan, B.J. 2005 Introduction: The practice of collaboration and partnership. *Practicing Anthropology* 27(4):2–4.

Harris, W., and E. Reyes. 1991 Cultural resources investigation, Compton Creek and Shoal Harbor, Belford, Monmouth County, New Jersey. New York, NY: U.S. Army Corps of Engineers, Environmental Analysis Branch.

Howard, M. 2003 When fishing grounds are closed: Developing alternative livelihoods for fishing communities. *SPC Women in Fisheries Information Bulletin* 13:19–22.

Kavanaugh, D., and G. Flimlin. Nd. A proposal for a new paradigm for commercial fishing in the Raritan and Sandy Hook estuaries. Unpublished manuscript.

Lours Berger Group, Inc., B. McCay and B. Jones. 2008 *Economic feasibility study and conceptual development plan for the Port of Belford November* 2008. Unpublished report. Township of Middletown, NJ.

MacCannell, D. 1999 *The tourist: A new theory of the leisure class.* Berkeley, CA: University of California Press.

McCAY, B. 1984 The pirates of Piscary: Ethnohistory of illegal fishing in New Jersey. *Ethnohistory* 31(1):17–37.

Meatyard, A., B. Roberts, and O. Bojang. 2005 Tourism and conservation: Kachikally sacred crocodile pool in the Gambia, West Africa. *Practicing Anthropology* 27(4):35–38.

Norkura, M.K. 1993 *The politics of public memory: Tourism, history, and ethnicity in Monterey, California.* Albany, NY: State University of New York Press.

Sherrod, B. 2000 The soul of generations. *Cooperative Living* May.

Wearing, S., D. Archer, and M. Jackson. 2003 Nature for sale: The rise of decommodifying interpretation and ecotourism. *Journal of Hospitality and Tourism Management* 10(2): 157–170.

Teetering Towards Economic Sustainability: Alternatives for Commercial Fishermen

1. How has it been to the baymen's advantage to follow the cycle of the bay?
2. How can tourism provide a way to preserve Belford's cultural heritage and the baymen's way of life?
3. How is a "mix-and-match" approach a possible solution to the changes occurring for commercial fishermen?